RETAILING MANAGEMENT

FOURTH CANADIAN EDITION

Michael Levy, Ph.D.

Babson College

Barton A. Weitz, Ph.D.

University of Florida

Dea Watson, MBA

Conestoga College

McGraw-Hill Education | McGraw-Hill Ryerson

McGraw-Hill
Ryerson

RETAILING MANAGEMENT

Fourth Canadian Edition

ISBN-13: 978-0-07-089320-7
ISBN-10: 0-07-089320-9

2 3 4 5 6 7 8 9 WEB 1 9 8 7 6 5 4

Printed and bound in Canada.

Care has been taken to trace ownership of copyright material contained in this text; however, the publisher will welcome any information that enables them to rectify any reference or credit for subsequent editions.

Director Product Management: *Rhondda McNabb*
Group Product Manager: *Leanna MacLean*
Senior Product Manager: *Karen Fozard*
Executive Marketing Manager: *Joy Armitage Taylor*
Product Developer: *Sarah Fulton*
Product Team Associate: *Amelia Chester/Stephanie Giles*
Supervising Editor: *Stephanie Gay*
Copy Editor: *Mike Kelly*
Photo/Permissions Researcher: *Tracy Leonard*
Plant Production Coordinator: *Sheryl MacAdam*
Manufacturing Production Coordinator: *Emily Hickey*
Cover and Interior Design: *Dave Murphy/Valid Design*
Page Layout: *ArtPlus Limited*
Printer: *Webcom*

Library and Archives Canada Cataloguing in Publication

Levy, Michael, 1950–, author Retailing management / Michael Levy, Ph.D., Babson College, Barton A. Weitz, Ph.D., University of Florida, Dea Watson, MBA, Conestoga College.—Fourth Canadian edition.

Includes bibliographical references and index.

ISBN 978-0-07-089320-7 (pbk.)

1. Retail trade—Management—Textbooks. 2. Retail trade—Canada—Textbooks. I. Weitz, Barton A., author II. Watson, Dea, author III. Title.

HF5429.L47 2014   658.8'7   C2014-900438-9

Michael Levy, Ph.D., is the Charles Clarke Reynolds Professor of Marketing and Director of the Retail Supply Chain Institute at Babson College (www.babson.edu/retail). He received his Ph.D. in business administration from The Ohio State University and his undergraduate and MS degrees in business administration from the University of Colorado at Boulder. He taught at Southern Methodist University before joining the faculty as professor and chair of the marketing department at the University of Miami.

Professor Levy received the 2009 Lifetime Achievement Award by the American Marketing Association Retailing Special Interest Group. He has developed a strong stream of research in retailing, business logistics, financial retailing strategy, pricing, and sales management. He has published over 50 articles in leading marketing and logistics journals, including the *Journal of Retailing, Journal of Marketing, Journal of the Academy of Marketing Science,* and *Journal of Marketing Research.* He currently serves on the editorial review boards of the *Journal of Retailing, International Journal of Logistics Management, International Journal of Logistics and Materials Management,* and *European Business Review.* He is co-author of *Marketing* (3e, 2012) and *M-Marketing* (2e, 2011), both with McGraw-Hill/Irwin. Professor Levy was co-editor of *Journal of Retailing* from 2001 to 2007. He co-chaired the 1993 Academy of Marketing Science conference and the 2006 Summer AMA conference.

Professor Levy has worked in retailing and related disciplines throughout his professional life. Prior to his academic career, he worked for several retailers and a housewares distributor in Colorado. He has performed research projects with many retailers and retail technology firms, including Accenture, Federated Department Stores, Khimetrics (SAP), Mervyn's, Neiman Marcus, ProfitLogic (Oracle), Zale Corporation, and numerous law firms.

Barton A. Weitz, Ph.D., received an undergraduate degree in electrical engineering from MIT and an MBA and a Ph.D. in business administration from Stanford University. He has been a member of the faculty at the UCLA Graduate School of Business and the Wharton School at the University of Pennsylvania and is presently the JCPenney Eminent Scholar Chair in Retail Management in the Warrington College of Business Administration at the University of Florida.

Professor Weitz is the founder of the David F. Miller Center for Retailing Education and Research at the University of Florida (www.cba.ufl.edu/mkt/retailcenter). The activities of the centre are supported by contributions from 35 retailers and firms supporting the retail industry, including JCPenney, Macy's, Walmart, Office Depot, Walgreens, Target, Build-A-Bear, Brown Shoe, NPD, and the International Council of Shopping Centers. Each year, the centre places more than 250 undergraduates in paid summer internships and management trainee positions with retail firms and funds research on retailing issues and problems.

Professor Weitz has won awards for teaching excellence and made numerous presentations to industry and academic groups. He has published over 50 articles in leading academic journals on channel relationships, electronic retailing, store design, salesperson effectiveness, and salesforce and human resource management. His research has been recognized with two Louis Stern Awards for his contributions to channel management research and a Paul Root Award for the *Journal of Marketing* article that makes the greatest contribution to marketing practice. He serves on the editorial review boards of the *Journal of Retailing, Journal of Marketing, International Journal of Research in Marketing, Marketing Science,* and *Journal of Marketing Research.* He is a former editor of the *Journal of Marketing Research.*

Professor Weitz has been the chair of the American Marketing Association and a member of the board of directors of the National Retail Federation, the National Retail Foundation, and the American Marketing Association. In 1989, he was honoured as the AMA/Irwin Distinguished Educator in recognition of his contributions to the marketing discipline. He was selected by the National Retail Federation as Retail Educator of the Year in 2005 and been recognized for lifetime achievements by American Marketing Association Retailing, Sales, and Inter-Organizational Special Interests Groups.

Dea Watson, MBA, has been a faculty member at Conestoga College Institute of Technology & Advanced Learning in Kitchener, Ontario, for 11 years. Dea holds an undergraduate degree in sociology from Wilfrid Laurier University and an MBA in retailing from the Retail Institute at the University of Stirling, Scotland.

Prior to her academic career, she had a variety of opportunities in Canadian retail over a 15-year span. She spent a significant amount of time delivering a national customer service training program and managed a variety of multi-million dollar soft goods departments for several major Canadian department stores.

As a professor and program coordinator for business marketing programs at Conestoga College, she possesses a passion for the Retail Industry and a wealth of knowledge and practical experience. Dea coaches the college's Retail Case team for the Ontario Colleges Marketing Competition, which consists of industry judges who determine the most viable, realistic business solutions to pre-determined real-world cases. The competition consists of a minimum of 16 competing Ontario colleges marketing student teams. A founding member of the charity Jessica's Footprint, Dea has used her knowledge of marketing and sponsorship to raise money to fund paediatric brain cancer research at the Hospital for Sick Children in Toronto. With Dea's help, the charity has achieved an impressive $1.4 million in donations since its inception in 2005.

brief contents

contents

New Ways to Communicate with Customers

Retailers communicate with customers using a mix of methods, such as advertising, sales, promotion, publicity, e-mail, and social media using Twitter, Facebook, YouTube, and blogs. Although many of these traditional methods, such as advertising, have been used for decades, Internet-enabling technology has changed the way retailers utilize their promotional budgets and communicate with customers. For example,

- The impact of social networks on buying behaviour
- The increased use of smartphones to allow customers to make price comparisons, locate merchandise, receive coupons, and buy merchandise
- The use of blogs, Twitter, Facebook, and YouTube to promote retailers and specific merchandise, as well as to collect customer attitudes about retailers and reviews of their product
- The use of the technology to customize and deliver coupons and other targeted promotions to customers, who also utilize Internet sites to find coupons to redeem at their favourite retailers

Social Responsibility of Retailers

Retail institutions are pervasive in our society and thus have a major impact on the welfare of their customers, suppliers, and employees. Given the importance of their societal role, both consumers and retailers are becoming more concerned about societal issues facing the world, such as global warming, immigration, health care, and working conditions in less developed economies. Some of these social responsibility issues are discussed in the Fourth Canadian Edition. For example,

- Consumer interest in green products
- Issues in sourcing merchandise globally
- Considering sustainability issues in store operations

Expanded Treatment of Brand Development Issues

To differentiate their offerings and build a competitive advantage, retailers are devoting more resources to the development of exclusive products—whether products that the retailer designs (private label) or exclusive brands produced by national brand manufacturers. For example, Club Monaco founder Joseph Mimran personally oversees the design and development of the extensive Joe Fresh clothing range for the Loblaws group.

Retailers are placing more emphasis on developing their brand image, building a strong image for their private-label merchandise, and extending their image to new retail formats. These exclusive brands, as the term implies, are available only from the retailer, and thus customers loyal to these brands can find them only in one store. Some examples of our extended treatment of exclusive brands in this edition are:

- Strategic importance of private labels
- Private-label approaches and types
- Process for developing and sourcing private labels
- Building a strong brand image

Emphasis on International Retailing

Retailing is a global industry and it is imperative that students understand how firms adapt their business practices to the cultural and infrastructural differences in international markets. With a greater emphasis being placed on private-label merchandise, retailers are working with manufacturers located throughout the world to acquire merchandise. In addition, retailers are increasingly looking to international markets for growth opportunities. We examine international retailing strategies, ranging from those used to enter new international markets to the global sourcing of merchandise.

Active Learning and Application

Concept Checks can be found in the chapters that deal with financial analysis, pricing, and HR management. These stopping points allow students to reflect on the mathematical components of various types of analysis and test their knowledge. Solutions are provided to students on Connect so that they can self-assess as they study.

The Get Out & Do It! exercises suggest projects that students can undertake by either visiting local retail stores or using the Internet. The exercises are designed to provide a hands-on learning experience for students. The Discussion Questions and Problems allow the student to critically analyze the chapter material in a particular scenario or context.

End-of-text cases and video cases provide discussion questions for a comprehensive examination of a scenario or case covering multiple topics and chapters. These use current and exciting examples of retailers students see every day. New cases in this edition include companies such as Target, MEC, and Stitch It.

New Features in the Fourth Canadian Edition

Up-to-Date and Cutting Edge!

Many of the Spotlight on Retailing vignettes have been replaced with new examples and photos to help put the text material into a real-world context. The Did You Know? boxes throughout and the cases at the end of the text have been updated for currency.

Chapter-by-Chapter Updates

In addition to reorganization within some chapters to improve flow and structure, the following changes have been made for the Fourth Canadian Edition.

Chapter 1

- New chapter opener on Aritzia: "People: The Winning Retail Ingredient"
- Updated listing of Canada's leading retail corporations (Exhibit 1–6)
- Updated Canadian industry statistics
- Updated Retailing Views

Chapter 2

- New chapter opener on Sobeys: "Commitment to Customer Key to Grocer's Success"
- New Retailing Views
  - 2.1: "Rent Some Luxury"
  - 2.2: "Helping Couples Get Ready for the Big Day"
  - 2.3: "The Build-a-Bear Workshop Uses Multiple Channels to Enhance Its Image"
- Updated exhibit of Canadian franchises
- Expanded content includes online retail in Canada, m-commerce and the rise of omni-channel retailing

Chapter 3

- New chapter opener: "Making the Connection Is Key for Today's Students"
- Updated Retailing Views
- New Retailing View 3.3: "Retailing to Tweens"
- New Appendix (available on Connect): "Consumer Behaviour toward Fashion"

Chapter 4

- New chapter opener: "Mobile Delivering Magic Results for Retailers"
- New Retailing Views
  - 4.1: "The IKEA Way"
  - 4.4: "London Drugs: Prescription to Lead"
- Updated Exhibit 4–1: Retail Strategy

Chapter 5

- New chapter opener: "Cloverdale Mall: The Scrappy Survivor"
- Addition of QR code to take readers directly to discussed content
  - QR code to www.utahbluemedia.com, which demonstrates Pitney Bowes Cluster Index
- New Retailing View 5.1: "Who Needs a Kitchen When You Have Sobeys Urban Fresh Downstairs?"
- New content-supporting exhibits
  - Exhibit 5–3: Site Characteristics
  - Exhibit 5–12: Canada's Ten Largest Malls
- Updated exhibits
  - Exhibit 5–4: Vancouver Canadian Demographics 2012
  - Exhibit 5–5: Neighbourhood Lifestyle Clusters for Five-Kilometre Ring Surrounding European Optical
  - Exhibit 5–6: Descriptions of Largest Clusters Surrounding European Optical
  - Exhibit 5–7: Descriptions of European Optical and Four Potential Locations' Trade Areas
  - Exhibit 5–10: Competitive Analysis of Potential Locations

Chapter 6

- New chapter opener: "Canadian Tire: Rethinking Product Presentation"
- New Retailing Views
  - 6.1: "Sony: Making Lasting Impressions"
  - 6.4: "Suggestions for Merchandising a Pet Food Category"
  - 6.5: "Home Depot Truckload Event"
  - 6.6: "Metro: Rethinking Product Presentation—Appealing to Customer Needs"
- Updated Retailing View 6.2: "Walmart Canada Opening High-Efficiency Superstores"
- Addition of QR codes to take readers directly to discussed content
  - QR code to Walmart website for additional information on how Walmart Canada is contributing to the environment
  - QR code to Bass Pro Shops
- New content added discussing legal considerations when designing or redesigning a store

Chapter 7

- New Retailing Views
  - 7.1: "Can Joe Fresh Save JCPenney ... and Retail?"
  - 7.2: "Mega-Malls in Asia"
  - 7.3: "The Fashion Mavens Are Men in India"
  - 7.4: "Direct Selling in China"
- New exhibits
  - Exhibit 7–2: Global Retail Opportunity Rankings
  - Exhibit 7–3: The Largest Mega-Malls
  - Exhibit 7–4: Top 250 Quick Stats, 2011

- Updated Exhibit 7–5: Ten Largest Global Retailers and the Ten Canadian Companies That Fall in the Top 250 Global Retailers: 2011

Chapter 8

- New chapter opener: "*easyhome* Ltd."
- New Retailing Views
  - 8.1: "Private Equity Firms Invest in Retailers"
  - 8.2: "Dollarama and Nordstrom: Retailers Targeting Customers at the Opposite Ends of the Income Distribution Spectrum"
  - 8.3: "Cutting Costs at Costco Wholesale"
- Updated exhibits
  - Exhibit 8–12: Strategic Profit Models for Selected Retailers
  - Exhibit 8–15: Costco Wholesale Corporation
  - Exhibit 8–16: Performance Compared to Competitors

Chapter 9

- This new chapter includes a new chapter opener: "Lifting Spirits: Cloud-Based Software Smooths LCBO's Purchase Order and Delivery Operations"
- New Retailing Views
  - 9.1: "Zara Delivers Fast Fashion"
  - 9.2: "How Netflix Makes Sure You Enjoy Your Movie"
  - 9.3: "Quick Response and Efficient Consumer Response"
  - 9.4: "West Marine Uses CPFR to Build a Competitive Advantage"
  - 9.5: "RFID at American Apparel"

Chapter 10

- Reorganized chapter content (was Chapters 9 and 10 in third edition)
- New chapter opener: "ALDO Group Inc.: Canadian Global Success Story"
- Revised Retailing View 10.5: "Retailers Utilize State-of-the-Art Merchandise Management Systems"

Chapter 11

- New chapter opener: "Partnering for Positive Impact"
- New Retailing View 11.2: "Only at Hudson's Bay"

Chapter 12

- New chapter opener: "Pricing without Borders"
- New Retailing View 12.4: "Group Buying Sites"

Chapter 13

- New chapter opener on Shoppers Drug Mart: "Developing and Retaining Talent to Improve Operations and Save Costs"

- New Retailing Views
  - 13.1: "Recruiting Top Talent for Your Small Business"
  - 13.5: "Ensuring Accessibility in Ontario's Retail Environment"
- New Retail Roundtables spotlighting human resource discussions among key retailers
  - 13.3: "Corporate Culture"
  - 13.6: "Retention"
  - 13.8: "Nuts and Bolts of Store Management"
  - 13.10: "Recruitment"
- New exhibits
  - Exhibit 13–8: The Top Merchandise Categories That Contribute Most to Shrinkage
  - Exhibit 13–10: Activities Used to Manage Loss Prevention Efforts, 2008 and 2012
- Enhanced discussion about store security management including a shrinkage incidents chart from PwC Canada and the Retail Council of Canada, "Securing the Bottom Line"

Chapter 14

- New chapter opener: "Loyalty Programs: Big Information Business"
- New Exhibit 14–1: Loyalty Census Snapshot: Canada, 2008–2012
- New Retailing Views
  - 14.1: "Tesco Uses Data Collection from Its Frequent-Shopper Program"
  - 14.2: "Retailers Increase Focus on Applications to Enhance Customer Loyalty, Reveals IOC Retail Insights"
  - 14.3: "Air Miles for Social Change—Rewards Motivate Canadians to Be Healthy"
  - 14.6: "Adoption Problems Plague Digital Wallets"
- New discussion about mobile applications and their impact on CRM programs

Chapter 15

- New chapter opener: "Hudson's Bay Adds a Bit of Shazam to Its Radio Ads"
- New exhibits
  - Exhibit 15–2: Interest in Mobile Advertising
  - Exhibit 15–3: Use of Short Code Texting
  - Exhibit 15–4: Interest in Mobile Payments
  - Exhibit 15–5: Smartphone Shopping Adoption by Store Category
  - Exhibit 15–6: Facebook
  - Exhibit 15–7: Twitter
  - Exhibit 15–8: Pinterest

- New Retailing Views
  - Retailing View 15.3: "Sportsgirl"
  - Retailing View 15.4: "KFC: The Power of a Single Tweet"
- New discussion on mobile marketing and online marketing
- Addition of QR codes to take readers directly to discussed content
  - Lululemon's blog
  - Home Depot YouTube channel: "How to Make a Flower Tower"
  - Southwest Air: "Not So Silent Bob!"
  - Checkout 51: "Buy groceries, get cash back"
  - Staples: "Easyrebates"
  - Coolspotters

Cases

- New cases
  - Case 1: The Arrival of Target
  - Case 4: Attracting Generation Y to a Retail Career
  - Case 5: Supplementing for Success in the Canadian Market
  - Case 11: Innovating the In-Store Experience
  - Case 14: Mountain Equipment Co-op: Revitalizing a Brand
  - Case 15: Tiffany & Co. and TJX: Comparing Financial Performance
  - Case 16: The Chocolate Shop
  - Case 17: Creating Loss Prevention Programs That Fit the Culture
  - Case 19: Merchandise Strategy: Process for Success
  - Case 26: HR Technology Is All about Connections
  - Case 27: Preparing for Succession, Stitch by Stitch
  - Case 28: Customer Service and Relationship Management at Nordstrom
  - Case 29: Active Endeavors Analyzes Its Customer Database
  - Case 31: Diamond in the Rough
  - Case 32: Target Marketing with Google AdWords
  - Case 33: Generating Advertising Revenue from a Digital Screen Network at Harrods of London

about *retailing* management: guided tour

Spotlight on Retailing: Each chapter opens with a brief vignette, highlighting a retailer or retailing trend that is related to the material in the chapter. These spotlights illustrate how successful organizations view the industry and provide students with first-hand information about what people in retailing do and their successes and challenges. Thirteen of the 15 Spotlight on Retailers boxes are new to the Fourth Canadian Edition.

Did You Know? Boxes: Highlighted boxes in the margin of each chapter contain interesting facts about retailing. For instance, did you know that expensive toilet paper sells better during the holiday season between Thanksgiving and New Year's, since people have guests in their homes?

DID YOU KNOW?

One plastic bag can take up to 500 years to decay in a landfill.

Key Terms: Found in the margins of the chapter content—key terms are defined as students encounter them, making for easy, on-the-spot referencing.

kiosk A small selling space offering a limited merchandise assortment.

mixed-use development (MXD) Development that combines several uses in one complex—for example, shopping centre, office tower, hotel, residential complex, civic centre, and convention centre.

Retailing Views: The textbook contains vignettes called Retailing Views to relate concepts to activities and decisions made by retailers. The vignettes, over 30 of which are new to this edition, look at major retailers such as Walmart, Costco, and IKEA. They also discuss innovative retailers including Netflix, Sobeys Urban Fresh, and AirMiles.

1.2 RETAILING VIEW

Retail Council of Canada

Since 1963, the Retail Council of Canada (RCC) has been the voice of retail in Canada. RCC is an industry-funded, not-for-profit association that represents more than 40 000 members across the country. The association provides support to merchants, vendors, and suppliers so that they in turn are able to meet the challenges of offering goods and services to consumers in a competitive marketplace.

As members, they have the opportunity to become a part of a national network of retailers, participate in money-saving benefit programs, access industry research and information, and make their collective voices heard through the RCC in terms of government lobbying. They also provide their members with a full range of services and programs including education and training

and labour relations, international trade, environmental protection, and market practices.

Retailers recognize the growing importance of employing skilled people at every level of their organizations. In response to this growing importance, the Retail Council of Canada has a team that oversees training and certification programs through the Canadian Retail Institute. As a division of the Retail Council of Canada, the Canadian Retail Institute promotes retail as a rewarding career through educational programs, scholarships, and partnerships with post-secondary institutions offering retail programs across the country. They focus their efforts on strengthening the industry by encouraging retail education, increasing career awareness, and advancing professional designation

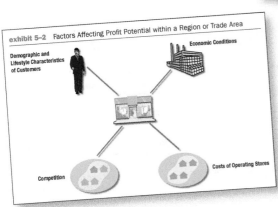

exhibit 5–2 Factors Affecting Profit Potential within a Region or Trade Area

Exhibits: Charts, illustrations, and tables give visual meaning to complex subject matter and provide easy reference for students.

QR Codes: Embedded in relevant chapter content to enable students a fast, flexible, and user-friendly way to access additional content and to allow them to connect the virtual to the physical.

1. Set up a skeletal income statement, given the following information:

   Net sales
   Gross margin $525 000
   Expenses   44.6%
                                   45.0%

2. Set up a skeletal income statement, given the following information:

   Gross margin $118 500

Concept Checks: These boxes allow students to take a look at some of the more challenging math-related concepts they have been introduced to, test their knowledge, and then check the solutions on Connect.

Summary: Chapter summaries recap the chapter content—a great tool for studying!

SUMMARY

A retailer's long-term performance is largely determined by its strategy. A strategy coordinates employees' activities and communicates the direction the retailer plans to take. Thus, retail market strategy describes both the strategic direction and the process by which the strategy is to be developed.

The retail strategy statement includes an identification of the target market and the retail format (its offering) to be directed toward that target market. The statement also needs to indicate the retailer's methods to build a sustain-

(2) conducting a situation audit, (3) identifying strategic opportunities, (4) evaluating the alternatives, (5) establishing specific objectives and allocating resources, (6) developing a retail mix to implement strategy, and (7) evaluating performance and making adjustments.

Strategic planning is an ongoing process. Every day, retailers audit their situations, examine customer trends, study new technologies, and monitor competitive activities. But the retail strategy statement does not change every year

Get Out and Do It!: At the end of each chapter, these exercises suggest hands-on projects that students can complete either by visiting a local retailer or using the Internet.

Get Out & Do It!

1. **INTERNET EXERCISE** Visit the website for Restoration Hardware (**www.restorationhardware.com**). Does this Internet site reflect the retail strategies for the company as discussed here?

2. **GO SHOPPING** Visit two stores that sell similar merchandise categories and cater to the same target segment(s). How are their retail formats similar? Dissimilar? On what bases do they have a

3. **GO SHOPPING** Develop a strategic plan for your favourite retailer. Go to the store. Observe and interview the store manager. Supplement your visit with information available online through Hoovers, the store's website (which should include its annual report), and other published sources.

4. Visit the websites for IKEA (**www.ikea.com**) and Starbucks (**www.starbucks.com**). Is the look/feel of these Internet sites consistent with the

DISCUSSION QUESTIONS AND PROBLEMS

1. What approaches can a retailer use to develop a competitive advantage? Choose a retailer and describe how it has developed a competitive strategic advantage.

2. Give an example of a market penetration, a retail format development, a market expansion, and a diversification growth strategy that Future Shop might use.

3. Draw and explain a positioning map such as that shown

7. Do a situation analysis for McDonald's. What is its mission? What are its strengths and weaknesses? What environmental threats might it face over the next ten years? How could it prepare for these threats?

8. Assume you are interested in opening a restaurant in your town. Go through the steps in the strategic retail planning process shown in Exhibit 4–6. Focus on doing

Discussion Questions and Problems: These questions propose thoughtful questions and encourage analysis and application of the text material.

End-of-Text Cases: Following the chapters there are 33 comprehensive cases and accompanying questions, including 16 brand new cases. The inclusion of some longer cases will allow students to explore the important text concepts in greater depth.

CASE 2 Retailing in India—Impact of Hypermarkets

The history of India contains a wealth of change and alteration, and the modern era is no different as the country blossoms into a major player in the global economy. Sizable economic growth during the past decade, particularly in the retail sector, has changed the way consumers behave. Although the size of the current Indian retail sector is impressive, its potential really speaks to what retailing will mean in the future. The retail market in India was approximately $353 billion in 2010, and by 2014 it will reach $543 billion in total sales, of which modern retailing accounts for 27 percent.

International retailers are slowly making their way into India. India's government allows foreign compa-

draw customers from 20 to 25 *kiranas* and fruit and vegetable stands, affecting over 100 000 vendors.

Most *kiranas* cannot compete with hypermarkets, because these larger retail outlets create more efficiency within the supply chain. Much local produce in India currently gets wasted, because the country lacks sufficient infrastructure. Even as it progresses through rapid development, India still lacks some amenities that Westerners take for granted, such as refrigeration in retail operations. If a large retailer wants to open a hypermarket in India, it will have to invest capital to ensure freshness throughout the supply chain and help reduce waste. The Indian government is expected to spend US$500 billion over the

Connect

McGraw-Hill Connect™ is a web-based assignment and assessment platform that gives students the means to better connect with their coursework, with their instructors, and with the important concepts that they will need to know for success now and in the future. With Connect, instructors can deliver assignments, quizzes, and tests easily online. Students can practise important skills at their own pace and on their own schedule. With Connect, students also get 24/7 online access to an eBook—an online edition of the text—to aid them in successfully completing their work, wherever and whenever they choose.

Supplements for Instructors

The following instructor supplements are available on Connect.

Instructor's Manual and Video Notes, containing an annotated outline and notes, answers to Discussion Questions and Problems, ancillary lectures and exercises, and notes to the end-of-text and video cases.

Videos A wealth of video segments are available to illustrate issues addressed in the text.

Computerized Test Bank, multiple-choice, essay, fill-in-the-blank, and short answer questions. Professors may use this software to create, edit, and print a variety of tests.

Microsoft PowerPoint® Lecture Slides to support and organize lectures.

Superior Learning Solutions and Support

The McGraw-Hill Ryerson team is ready to help you assess and integrate any of our products, technology, and services into your course for optimal teaching and learning performance. Whether it's helping your students improve their grades, or putting your entire course online, the McGraw-Hill Ryerson team is here to help you do it. Contact your Learning Solutions Consultant today to learn how to maximize all of McGraw-Hill Ryerson's resources!

For more information on the latest technology and Learning Solutions offered by McGraw-Hill Ryerson and its partners, please visit us online: **www.mcgrawhill.ca/he/solutions**.

acknowledgements

The support, expertise, and occasional coercion from the team at McGraw-Hill Ryerson—Leanna MacLean, Group Product Manager; Stephanie Gay, Supervising Editor; Tracy Leonard, Permissions Editor; Sarah Fulton, Product Developer; and Michael Kelly, Copy Editor—are greatly appreciated. Thanks for your patience, thanks for your dedication to this project, and most of all thanks for pushing me to be and do the best.

Thank you to the Retail Council of Canada for generously allowing the use of several excerpts and articles in this Fourth Canadian Edition.

Providing support and recommendations throughout the development process were reviewers from across Canada, and I'd like to thank them for their invaluable feedback and guidance:

Oye Abioye, *Humber College*
Patricia Browne, *Kwantlen Polytechnic*
Terri Champion, *Niagara College*
Cuiping Chen, *University of Ontario Institute of Technology*
Jocelyn Choy, *University of the Fraser Valley*
Mary Ann Cipriano, *Concordia University*
Vic de Witt, *Red River College*
Tanya Drollinger, *University of Lethbridge*
Kate Ellis, *York University*
Chuck Hendriks, *York University*
Charles Ireland, *Centennial College*
Pat Kolodziejski, *Mohawk College*
Helen Mallette, *Mount Saint Vincent University*
David Moscovitz, *Concordia University*
Mario Pascucci, *George Brown College*
Wei Song, *Thompson Rivers University*
Ken Kwong-Kay Wong, *Ryerson University and University of Toronto*

introduction to the world of retailing

LEARNING OBJECTIVES

Lo1 Define retailing.

Lo2 Understand the role retailers play in the distribution channel and the functions they perform.

Lo3 Know the economic significance of retailing in Canada.

Lo4 Examine the various career and entrepreneurial opportunities retail offers.

Lo5 Discuss different types of decisions retail managers make.

Lo6 Understand the meaning of ethics and social responsibility and how they relate to the individual, retailer, and society.

SPOTLIGHT ON RETAILING

People: The Winning Retail Ingredient

"Retail just seemed to be what I knew."

This is how Brian Hill explains why he built a career in retail. No big story. No light that went off. No moment of revelation. For the CEO of Aritzia, growing up in a retail family made retail come naturally to him.

"It just seemed like a natural progression for me that when I finished university that's what I would do. I never really considered doing anything else. That's how I ended up getting in the retail business."

Smart decision. When he speaks about his career, Hill is plain-spoken and factual. His modesty belies the enormous successes he's had in retail. Aritzia, the women's fashion boutique he co-founded, is one of the highest-performing retail brands in Canada. Hill opened the store in Vancouver in 1984 and has gathered up some of the best sales numbers in the retail industry. Under his leadership, the company has spread across Canada and streamed south into New York, Chicago, San Francisco, Portland, and Seattle. The company now has 52 stores across North America.

It's this business success, along with his contributions to arts, health care, and community programs, that earned Hill the 2012 Distinguished Retailer of the Year Award.

Hill credits part of his success as a retailer to a single decision: to turn Aritzia from a single retailer to a vertical retailer with a design and manufacturing business.

"I don't think we'd be here today if we hadn't designed and manufactured our own products," says Hill. In hindsight, the decision seems like a stroke of genius. Hill downplays his decision. "The industry went vertical," he says.

"We didn't all of a sudden (jump into fashion design) because I had this crystal ball, thinking that specialty retail would all be vertical in 10 or 15 years. It was more happenstance. We just couldn't find what we were looking for. After spending hours and days and weeks and months looking for product, we thought, okay, this is going to be easier just to make it ourselves."

Today, Aritzia sells a variety of products and styles under a number of house brands, including Talula, T. Babaton, TNA, Wilfred, Wilfred Free, Le Fou, and Community.

Leading people. Hill says Aritzia's success stems from the company's ability to develop a team of intelligent, focused people, and in keeping these people in the company for the long term. He likens building a company to "creating an environment."

"The people who work for you are so important. I've always felt that you have to create an environment such that they are challenged and there is opportunity to grow, where there are educational opportunities as well for your people, and that they are compensated and remunerated fairly."

In a way, the reliability of the business speaks to the reliability of the people. "You need to be able to rely on your team of people and be able to grow your team of people. You don't have time to be retraining and rebuilding teams if you're trying to grow your business. Keeping the people who are really contributing to our business in our business has probably been our greatest success. And probably some of our greatest regrets have been losing the odd person, and I think that's probably because retail is about the people."

Entering e-commerce. Hill conquered Canada with a national expansion, proved Aritzia as a fashion innovator with its in-house fashions and Soho roots, made it a member of retail royalty with its palace on Fifth Avenue, and stretched its reach with locations in major cities in the U.S.

For any retailer, that's a lot. For Hill, it's not enough. Next, he says, Aritzia has to take its strategy to the digital retail world with an e-commerce site.

Building an online store, however, hasn't been easy. "Going into it, we probably underestimated how many different departments would be affected and how many different business units we'd have to create," says Hill. "When we look at the team we've had to assemble here, we've almost had to go out and create a brand new business."

As he lists the changes e-commerce has forced on the company, Hill says it's been like building the store from scratch. The company had to redevelop its distribution centre, set up a call centre, develop a store design that works for the web, re-educate its IT department on a whole new set of technologies, set up photo studios, and assemble an e-commerce team of 60 people—a task that has taken two years since the company's first attempts at a digital strategy.

With all this change, all this risk, how does Hill keep his cool? He says it's the excitement of the job—and the necessity for survival. "You don't really have a choice in our business to (avoid e-commerce). It's not like it's optional," he says.

As a retailer who has distinguished himself, however, Hill still comes back to his team when he speaks about the future of his business and the challenges that lie ahead.

"Anytime you're learning new things and working with different types of partners and teams, it can be very exciting. Even though it's a big job and a big task, our team has been up to it."

Source: Robert Price, "People: The Winning Retail Ingredient," *Canadian Retailer,* store 2012, Volume 22, Issue 4, pp. 24–25.

Retailing is a global high-tech industry. Walmart is the world's largest corporation, with retail sales of $447 billion for the fiscal year 2012 and has over 10 000 stores in 27 countries worldwide. French-based Carrefour, the world's second-largest retailer, operates 12 000 hypermarkets in 30 countries (but not in Canada or the United States). The largest retailer in Canada, Loblaws, with annual sales of $31.6 billion, has over 1400 corporate, franchised, and associated banner stores; offers over 8000 private label products; and is also Canada's largest wholesale food distributor. In July 2013, Loblaws agreed to buy Shoppers Drug Mart for $12.4 billion, merging the largest grocery retailer with the largest pharmacy chain in the country. The merger grows Loblaws by 1200 stores.

Retailing in Canada is a vibrant industry, with total retail sales in 2012 of $469.9 billion. The retail sector is the largest employer nationally, employing almost 13 percent of Canadians. Success in retailing is about understanding and engaging your customer. Retailers use sophisticated technologies and information systems to improve their customers' shopping experience, reduce costs, and provide better value. Small local retailers such as Grassroots Environmental Products, a retailer of eco-friendly products with two stores in Toronto and a full-service

e-commerce site, offers customers the opportunity to shop in their store as well as online, thus expanding their market share. Customers today want to interact with retailers as they seek information and buy merchandise ranging from concert tickets to a new iPod, shopping through multiple channels, such as smartphones, tablets, computers, web-enabled kiosks, telephone lines to call centres, and retail stores. In addition to selling merchandise, retailers use the Internet to build brand images, provide customer service, and manage their employees. Retailers such as Amazon.com use advanced analytical techniques and data warehousing to customize approaches to online customers, suggesting books and products that might be of interest based on previous sales.

To compete against nonstore retailers, stores are becoming more than just places to buy products. They are offering entertaining and educational experiences to their customers. For example, Running Room operates 114 stores across Canada and the U.S. and connects to its customers with a Learn to Run program that offers advice to the novice runner. As well, Running Room produces a free magazine to advise 130 000 customers of new products and community runs.[1] These features enhance customers' visual experiences, provide them with educational information, and enhance sales potential by enabling them to "try before they buy."

Retailing is such a part of our everyday lives that it's often taken for granted. Customers often aren't aware of the sophisticated business decisions retail managers make and the technologies they use to provide goods and services. Retail managers must make complex decisions in selecting target markets and retail locations, determining what merchandise and services to offer, negotiating with suppliers and distributing merchandise to stores, training and motivating sales associates, and deciding how to price, promote, and present merchandise. Considerable skill and knowledge are required to make these decisions effectively. Working in this highly competitive, rapidly changing environment is challenging and exciting and offers significant financial rewards.

This book describes the world of retailing and provides principles for effectively managing businesses in this challenging environment. Knowledge of retailing principles and practices will help you develop management skills you can apply in many business contexts. For example, Procter & Gamble and Hewlett-Packard brand managers need to have a thorough understanding of how retailers operate and make money so that they can get their products on retail shelves and work with retailers to sell them to consumers. Financial and health care institutions use retail principles to develop assortments of services, improve customer service, and make their offerings available at convenient locations for their customers. Thus, any student interested in professional business-to-consumer (B-to-C) selling, marketing management, or finance will find this book useful.

Lo 1 What Is Retailing?

Retailing is the set of business activities that add value to the products and services sold to consumers for their personal or family use. Often, people think of retailing only as the sale of products in stores, but retailing also involves the sale of services: overnight lodging in a motel, a doctor's exam, a haircut, a movie rental, or a home-delivered pizza. Not all retailing is done in stores. Examples of nonstore retailing are Internet sales of books and music, direct sales of cosmetics by Avon, catalogue sales by Canadian Tire, and DVD rentals through Redbox kiosks.

A Retailer's Role in a Distribution Channel

A **retailer** is a business that sells products or services, or both, to consumers for their personal or family use. Retailers attempt to satisfy consumer needs by having the *right merchandise,* at the *right price,* at the *right place,* in the *right quantities,* at the *right time* when the consumer wants it. Retailers also provide markets for producers to sell their merchandise. Retailers are the final business in a distribution channel that links manufacturers to consumers. A **distribution channel** is a set of firms that facilitate the movement of products from the point of production to the point of sale to the ultimate consumer. Exhibit 1–1 shows the retailer's position within a distribution channel.[2]

Manufacturers typically make products and sell them to retailers or wholesalers. When manufacturers such as Roots and Dell Computers sell directly to consumers, they are performing both the production and retailing business activities. Wholesalers, in contrast, engage in buying, taking title to, often storing, and physically handling goods in large quantities, then reselling the goods (usually in smaller quantities) to retailers or industrial or business users. Wholesalers and retailers may perform many of the same functions, but wholesalers uniquely satisfy retailers' needs, whereas retailers direct their efforts to satisfying the needs of ultimate consumers. Some retail chains, such as Rona, Loblaws, and Costco, function as both retailers and wholesalers. They're performing retailing activities when they sell to consumers and wholesaling activities when they sell to other businesses such as building contractors, independent grocers, or restaurant owners.

retailing A set of business activities that adds value to the products and services sold to consumers for their personal or family use.

retailer A business that sells products and services to consumers for their personal or family use.

distribution channel A set of firms that facilitate the movement of products from the point of production to the point of sale to the ultimate consumer.

exhibit 1–1 Example of a Distribution Channel

In some distribution channels, the manufacturing, wholesaling, and retailing activities are performed by independent firms, but most distribution channels feature some vertical integration.

Vertical integration means that a firm performs more than one set of activities in the channel, such as investments by retailers in wholesaling or manufacturing. *Backward integration* arises when a retailer performs some distribution and manufacturing activities, such as operating warehouses or designing private-label merchandise. *Forward integration* occurs when a manufacturer undertakes retailing activities, such as Roots operating its own retail stores.

Most large retailers—such as Walmart and Staples Business Depot—engage in both wholesaling and retailing activities. They buy directly from manufacturers, have merchandise shipped to their warehouses for storage, and then distribute the merchandise to their stores. Other retailers, such as The Gap, Aritzia, Aldo, and Joe Fresh, are even more vertically integrated. They also design the merchandise they sell and then contract with manufacturers to produce it exclusively for them.

Functions Performed by Retailers

Why are retailers necessary? After all, wouldn't it be easier and cheaper to buy directly from those who produce the products? The answer is, generally no. Although there are situations where it is easier and cheaper to buy directly from manufacturers, such as at a farmers' market or from Dell Computer, retailers provide important functions that increase the value of the products and services they sell to consumers and facilitate the distribution of those products and services for those who produce them. These value-creating functions are:

- Providing an assortment of products and services
- Breaking bulk
- Holding inventory
- Providing service and services

Providing Assortments Supermarkets typically carry 20 000 to 30 000 different items made by over 500 companies. Offering an assortment enables customers to choose from a wide selection of brands, designs, sizes, colours, and prices in one location. Manufacturers specialize in producing specific types of products. For example, Campbell makes soup, Kraft makes dairy products, Kellogg makes breakfast cereals, and McCormick makes spices. If each of these manufacturers had its own stores that sold only its

own products, consumers would have to go to many different stores to buy groceries to prepare a single meal.

All retailers offer assortments of products, but they specialize in the assortments they offer. Supermarkets provide assortments of food, health and beauty care, and household products; whereas Club Monaco provides assortments of clothing and accessories. Most consumers are well aware of the product assortments retailers offer; even small children tend to know where to buy different types of products. But new types of retailers offering unique assortments appear each year. WineStyles is a wine store that arranges wine by taste category instead of region or type of wine and provides extensive information to reduce the complexity of buying wines. Riva's: The Eco Store sells a wide assortment of environmentally healthy products such as apparel, housewares, skin care products, and building supplies.

Breaking Bulk To reduce transportation costs, manufacturers and wholesalers typically ship cases of frozen dinners or cartons of shirts to retailers. Retailers then offer the products in smaller quantities tailored to the individual consumer's and household's consumption patterns. This is called breaking bulk. Breaking bulk is important to both manufacturers and consumers. It is cost-effective for manufacturers to package and ship merchandise in larger rather than smaller quantities. It is also easier for consumers to purchase merchandise in the smaller, more manageable quantities they prefer.

Holding Inventory A major function of retailers is to keep inventory that is already broken into user-friendly sizes so that products will be available when consumers want them. By maintaining an inventory, retailers provide a benefit to consumers—they reduce the consumer's cost of storing products. This function is particularly important to consumers with limited storage space and when purchasing perishable merchandise such as meat and produce.

Providing Service and Services Retailers provide services that make it easier for customers to buy and use products. They offer various methods of payment, including debit, direct, and credit payment, as well as various payment plans so that customers can have a product now and pay for it later, thus encouraging sales. Retailers display products so that consumers can see and test them before buying. Increasingly, retailers must have knowledgeable sales staff on hand to answer questions and provide information about products. Multichannel retailers offer flexibility to the customer by answering questions online and enabling buying any time, day or night.

By providing assortments, breaking bulk, holding inventory, and providing services, retailers increase the value consumers receive from their products and services. To illustrate, consider a closet door in a shipping crate in a manufacturer's warehouse. The door won't satisfy the needs of a do-it-yourselfer who wants to replace a closet door today. For the customer, a conveniently located home improvement centre such as Rona sells one door that is available when the customer wants it. The home improvement centre helps the customer select the door by displaying doors so that they can be examined before they're purchased. An employee is available to explain which door is best for closets and how the door should be hung. The centre has an assortment of hardware, paint, and tools that the customer will need for the job. Thus, retailers can increase the value of products and services bought by their customers.

Social and Economic Significance of Retailing

Social Responsibility

Most retailers try to be socially responsible. Corporate social responsibility (CSR) describes the voluntary actions taken by a company to address the ethical, social, and environmental impacts of its business operations and the concerns of its stakeholders.[4] As corporate social responsibility continues to grow in popularity within the Canadian retail industry, more significance is being placed on the need for retailers to explain the impact of their business practices and to implement suitable strategies to seize the related opportunities.[5] Firms typically go through several stages before they fully integrate corporate social responsibility into their strategy. Companies in the first stage engage only in CSR activities required by law. In this stage, companies are not actually convinced of the importance of CSR actions. In the second stage, companies go beyond activities required by law to engage in CSR activities that provide a short-term financial benefit to the company. For example, a retailer might reduce the energy consumption of its stores just because doing so costs less. In the third stage, companies operate responsibly because they believe this is the "right thing" to do. Companies in the fourth and final stage engage in socially and environmentally responsible actions because they believe these activities must be done for the "well being" of everyone. These companies have truly incorporated the concept of CSR into their business strategy.[6] Retailing View 1.1 illustrates how retailers provide value to their communities and society, as well as to their customers.

Retail Sales in Canada

Retail is a driving force of Canada's economy and affects every facet of life. Just think of how much contact you have with retailers when you eat meals, furnish your apartment, have your car fixed, or buy clothing for a party or a job interview. In 2012, total retail sales in Canada amounted to $469.9 billion, up 2.5 percent from

DID YOU KNOW?

6%. The percentage of sales during the holiday season that retailers can expect through e-commerce if they are present with a product offering on the web.[7]

Lo 3

exhibit 1–2   Retail Sales by Trade Group, Canada: 2012 (unadjusted*)

Retail Trade Group	Sales 2011 ($ millions)	Sales 2012 ($ millions)	Annual Growth (%)	2012 Share of Sales
Motor Vehicle and Parts Dealers	100 248.2	105 332.0	5.1	22.4
Gasoline Stations	58 074.8	59 716.5	2.8	12.7
Furniture and Home Furnishings Stores	15 021.5	15 206.0	1.2	3.2
Electronics and Appliance Stores	15 949.9	15 171.1	(5.1)	3.2
Building Material and Garden Equipment and Supplies Dealers	26 993.7	27 036.1	0.2	5.8
Food and Beverage Stores	105 337.9	107 050.9	1.6	22.8
Health and Personal Care Stores	33 054.1	33 609.3	1.7	7.2
Clothing and Clothing Accessories Stores	25 540.7	26 160.4	2.4	5.6
General Merchandise Stores	58 593.2	58 794.7	0.4	12.5
Sporting Goods, Hobby, Book and Music Stores	10 681.3	10 696.2	0.1	2.3
Miscellaneous Store Retailers	10 976.2	11 151.0	1.6	2.4
Total Retail Sales (Unadjusted)	458 471.5	469 924.2	2.5	100.0

*Chart contains raw unadjusted data accessed May 26, 2013.

Source: Statistics Canada, CANSIM, table 080-0020 and catalogue no. 63-005-x, http://www.statcan.gc.ca/tables-tableaux/sum-som/101/sct01/trad15a-eng.htm.

For the Greater Good

Canadian retailers are increasingly going above and beyond for their customers and the communities they serve with innovative corporate social responsibility initiatives.

A few years ago, when big-screen TV sales started gaining momentum, a London Drugs customer suggested to one of the retailer's employees on the floor that maybe the store could look at doing something about all that cardboard, Styrofoam, and plastic. Because London Drugs, the 2012 winner of the Retail Council of Canada's Excellence in Retailing Award for Corporate & Social Responsibility, Large Size Retailer, has gone out of its way to ensure employee feedback reaches its leadership, the suggestion was quickly considered by its executives.

"We said we already have diversion programs in place for our packaging and Styrofoam, so it's no big deal to open that up to our customers," says Maury McCausland, the company's retail operations administrator. "Allowing our customers to return all the packaging is also the right thing to do because we have a recycling stream for it."

So London Drugs introduced its "Bring Back the Pack" program, which allows customers to return the packaging for all the products sold in its stores.

"The community, our staff, and customers love that we're recycling the Styrofoam," says McCausland, whose company has set a goal of diverting 95 percent of all the waste it produces by 2015. "Is there a return on investment? Not really. Is it a way to get the customer to come back? Not really. It's just a convenience for our customer. Also, we're selling these products. It's one of our goals that whatever we sell, we are able to recycle. And we

think all retailers should be heading in that direction. We want to be responsible for what we sell to people."

Looking for opportunities. That proactive approach to seizing the opportunities to make improvements in the communities they sell in is something shared by all of 2012's Corporate & Social Responsibility Award nominees. They have their eyes and ears open at all times. They are constantly looking around, searching for gaps and needs, and then jumping in. West 49 Inc., the winner of the 2012 Excellence in Retailing Award for Corporate & Social Responsibility, Mid Size Retailer, "wanted to go beyond selling skate gear to kids by creating an environment where they can get physically active and experience skateboarding in a safe environment," says Cindy Mielke, the company's director of marketing. So last year, West 49 partnered with DisneyXD for 31 stops in mall parking lots and community centres across the country to provide free skateboarding lessons to children and youth.

Using their strength to help those who help others. There is a long tradition in CSR of businesses supporting and empowering others within the community who are doing good work by forming long-term partnerships with them. Take The Source, for example, which has long-term partnerships with Habitat for Humanity, Kids Help Phone, and United Way. "It is in collaboration with each of these valued partners that we create and execute specific campaigns to

---

2011 and 10.4 percent over a four-year period. Ontario (35.1 percent) and Quebec (22 percent) contributed the largest share of retail sales, followed by Alberta (14.7 percent) and British Columbia (13.2 percent). Canada's leading retailers tend to concentrate their operations in these four provinces as they include the country's largest cities. For example, within a one-day drive from Toronto, there is a multinational market of 22 million people with an economic value of $550 billion, making it the 5th largest market in North America and the 12th largest in the world. To take advantage of these markets, some of the biggest and best retailers are expanding into North America by opening stores in cities such as Toronto and Calgary (for example, Zara and Zara Home).[8]

Sales in the retail sector were dominated by the motor vehicle and parts sub-sector, which totalled $105 billion in

sales in 2012, or 22.4 percent of market share, and the food and beverage stores sub-sector, which totaled $107.1 billion, or 22.8 percent of market share. Exhibit 1–2 shows a list of total sales by retail sub-sectors in Canada for 2012. According to *The Consumer Trends Update* issued by the Office of Consumer Affairs, Industry Canada, retail sales in Canada were equivalent to retail sales in the U.S. on a per capita basis for the first time,[9] reaching US$13 000 per person.[10] This reveals that while sales growth in the U.S. has slowed, growth in Canada has continued to accelerate. Canadians, in general, have remained more positive about the Canadian economic climate when compared to American consumers respecting their marketplace following the 2008–2009 global recession.[11]

Retail establishments retain major presence in the Canadian marketplace, representing an 8.96 percent share assist with funding and development needs," says Kelly Reid, the retailer's supervisor of communications, community relations, and recognition. "Simply put, we utilize our resources. With our national reach and over 3000 knowledgeable and friendly associates, The Source has the opportunity to make a big impact in our communities, which allows our associates to get involved in some way—big or small. Working with Habitat for Humanity ensures that more Canadian families have a safe and comfortable home. Our partnership with Kids Help Phone ensures that counselling for children and youth across the country is being provided, and with United Way, we directly support and give back to other local charities."

Thinking bigger and leading the way. CSR is increasingly not just about doing the right thing and helping people and communities today. It's often also about looking for opportunities to help society and the world grow and develop into a better planet for all tomorrow. Sobeys took a look at the *Accessibility for Ontarians with Disabilities Act* and decided it wanted to be part of changing society's and businesses' attitudes toward persons with disabilities. "We approached the province's compliance requirement as an opportunity to re-educate and inform our employees about the needs of customers with disabilities and how employees can enhance the customer service experience for this particular group," says Gerard Betsch, director of occupational health safety and wellness of Sobeys in Ontario, who led the initiative. In 2011, the retailer created a video, entitled "How may I help you?" that was launched at a province-wide Health and Safety Conference with the attendance and endorsement of the lieutenant governor of Ontario, His Honour David C. Onley. It has since gone on to become part of the company's staff and training and, based on the feedback Sobeys has received from staff and customers, it has made a positive difference in how people perceive and treat others with disabilities.

Loblaw Companies Limited looked at the state of the world's oceans and lakes and the seafood they provide to feed humanity. "Some scientists predict that at this rate we won't have any wild fish by 2050," says Paul Uys, vice president of sustainable seafood for Loblaw Brands Limited. The company decided to lead in turning away from this disastrous direction. It committed to sourcing only sustainable seafood by 2013. Now to understand the extent of the company's commitment to having a profound impact, it's important to note that Loblaw wasn't just talking about the fresh and frozen seafood it sells. It was talking about any seafood ingredient in any of the products on its shelves. That's some 2500 products to date that contain sustainable seafood ingredients.

Its successful sustainable seafood program, which seemed a daunting venture in its early days, has now become a template for other projects that the company is contemplating. "If Loblaw can set the new benchmark, others will follow. Nothing begets success like success," says Uys.

Source: Alexandra Lopez-Pacheco, "For the greater good," *Canadian Retailer*, Store 2012, Volume 22, Issue 4, pp. 54–55.

of all business in Canada, with 196 606 retail establishments, making it the nation's third-largest industry by number of businesses. A dominant characteristic of the retail sector in Canada is the small size of many of the establishments—72 percent of all retail businesses employ fewer than five persons. The retail industry represents the largest segment of small business in this country with more than 146 000 firms employing more than 795 000 individuals. Although several trade groups (such as car dealerships and grocery stores) measure their annual sales per store in the millions of dollars, for most trade groups, the average annual revenue per store in Canada is less than $800 000. The majority of small retail business operating in Canada is concentrated within the "grocery and convenience stores, car dealerships, pharmacies, gasoline stations, clothing stores and appliance retailers."[12]

While there are a large number of small retail businesses operating in Canada, large retail chains dominate many segments. The top 124 retail organizations still control 75 percent of the non-automotive retail sales.[13] In 2011, 30 retailers that operated in Canada controlled a combined 20 565 store locations and approximately 66 percent of total non-automotive retail sales in Canada, or 43.1 percent of total retail sales in the Canadian market (see Exhibits 1–3, 1–4, and 1–5). In most countries, when the market concentration percentage for a particular industry or industry sub-sector reaches 40 percent, oligopolistic behaviour becomes likely in the marketplace.[14] Exhibit 1–5 demonstrates that five of the nine retail sub-sectors have concentration ratio levels higher than 55 percent amongst the top four retailers in each sub-sector. This group of large retailers, identified by their relative

exhibit 1-3 Distribution of Retail Sales (in $ millions) (NAICS): 2010 and 2011

2010				
Sector		**Sales**		
Automotive		144 245		
All Others		294 278		
	Top 126 retailers		218 869	74.4%
	Other retailers		75 409	25.6%
Total		**438 523**		
2011				
Sector		**Sales**		
Automotive		157 689		
All Others		298 701		
	Top 124 retailers		224 361	75.1%
	Other retailers		74 340	24.9%
Total		**456 390**		

Source: Centre for the Study of Commercial Activity, Ryerson University.

exhibit 1-4 Retail Sales Distribution (in $ millions) (NAICS): 2011

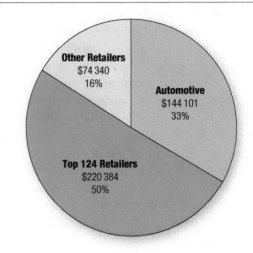

Other Retailers $74 340 16%

Automotive $144 101 33%

Top 124 Retailers $220 384 50%

Source: Centre for the Study of Commercial Activity, Ryerson University.

dominance of Canadian retail market segments, includes Loblaws (30 percent), Shoppers Drug Mart (31.8 percent), Rona (23.9 percent), Walmart (41.5 percent), and Best Buy/Future Shop (40.2 percent).

The list of the top 50 leading retailers (Exhibit 1-6) shows that the top three retailers in Canada (Weston Group, Walmart, and the Empire Company [Sobeys]) control 23.9 percent of the non-automotive retail market and have more than 3100 retail locations between them. Acquisitions by the Weston Group (of Shoppers Drug Mart, the sixth-largest retailer in Canada with more than 1300 locations) and the Empire Company (of Safeway Inc., the ninth-largest retailer in Canada with more than 200 locations, and Shell gas stations in Quebec and Atlantic Canada, with 250 locations) position these two top-performing Canadian retailers to compete more effectively within an increasingly competitive retail landscape.

The Canadian retail market continues to evolve and change as foreign-owned retailers continue to increase their presence within the Canadian marketplace. In 2011, 53 percent (or 67) of the top 124 leading retail organizations in Canada were foreign owned and operated,[15] and accounted for approximately 40.4 percent of total leading retail corporations' sales in Canada. American retailers account for 95 percent of retail sales by foreign retailers in Canada (see Exhibit 1-7).[16] The American presence is significant, as Exhibit 1-6 demonstrates. Ten out of the top 20 retailers (by sales) in Canada are American, with four of these companies being among the top ten retailers operating in the country. Notable U.S. retailers that have expanded operations into Canada include the Apple Store, J. Crew, Lowe's, Marshall's, Nordstrom, and Target, among others.[17] The increased presence of foreign, especially U.S.-based, retailers is expected to benefit Canadian consumers,

providing important advantages, such as wider variety of products, more convenient locations and formats, and the potential for a more competitive pricing environment.[18] Exhibit 1-5 illustrates the profound impact U.S. retailers have had on the Canadian retail landscape as many of these retailers have captured significant market share of retail sales across many sub-sectors. Walmart and Costco cumulatively own approximately 67 percent of the general merchandise sector, and Best Buy, with its Best Buy and Future Shop stores, accounts for 40.2 percent of the electronics and appliances sector. However, as mentioned above, Canadian-based retailers still dominate the grocery (with 55.5 percent among Loblaw, Empire Company, and Metro) and pharmaceutical sectors (with 60.7 percent among Shoppers Drug Mart, Katz Group, and Jean Coutu) of the Canadian retail industry.

Canadian retailers have yet to experience the same level of success with expansion into the United States and abroad. With that being said, there are some great Canadian success stories, such as Couche Tard, Fruits & Passion, Aldo, Lululemon, Joe Fresh, and Aritzia, that have successfully expanded globally through a mix of corporate and franchise stores. Joe Fresh is a stand-out as in 2012 they signed a deal with JCPenney to open 700 shops within 1100 of its locations in the United States.[19]

Global Retailers

Retailing is becoming a global industry, as more and more retailers pursue growth by expanding their operations to other countries. The large retail firms are becoming increasingly international in the geographical scope of their operations. Amway, Avon, Ace Hardware, and Inditex (Zara) operate in more than 20 countries. The share of the global retail market accounted for by retailers operating in more than one country also is increasing, because these global retailers are growing at an even faster rate than are global retail sales. International operations account for a larger proportion of sales by these large firms, as is particularly apparent in European firms with their longer internationalization experience. The percentage of retail revenue generated from foreign operations for the top ten global retailers is approximately 33 percent of their total revenue. As a group, the top ten have a much larger geographic footprint than the top 250 overall. Exhibit 7–5 (in Chapter 7) lists the ten largest global retailers along with Canada's top entries of the top 250 as published by Deloitte. (To see the entire list, go to http://www.deloitte.com/view/en_CH/ch/industries/consumer_business/retailers_wholesalers_and_distributors/a21917cfaa74c310VgnVCM2000003356f70aRCRD.htm.) These big retailers operate in 16.7 countries, on average, nearly twice as many as the average for the entire group (nine countries).[20] In 2011, for the first time, the share of North American top 250 retailers that remained single-country operators fell to less than half.

With worldwide retail revenue estimated at $4.27 trillion, the ten largest global retailers represent a 29 percent share of the world market.[21] The average size of the top 250 global retailers in 2011, as measured by retail revenue, topped $17 billion. The threshold to join the top 250 in 2011 was $3.7 billion. Canada has ten retailers that broke that threshold: Loblaw ($31 billion), Alimentation Couche-Tard ($23 billion), Empire Company ($16.1 billion), Metro Inc. ($11.6 billion), Shoppers Drug Mart ($10.6 billion), Canadian Tire Corporation ($9.5 billion), Katz Group Canada Ltd. ($8.7 billion), Rona ($4.9 billion), Hudson's Bay Company ($3.9 billion), and LCBO ($3.8 billion).

> **DID YOU KNOW?**
>
> The acronym IKEA is made up of the initials of the founder's name (Ingvar Kamprad) plus those of Elmtaryd, his family farm, and the nearby village of Agunnard.[22]

exhibit 1–5 Market Concentration (CR4) by NAICS: 2010, 2011

NAICS	Sector	2011 Sales (millions)	%	First	%	Second	%	Third	%	Fourth	CR4 2011 %	CR4 2010 %
442	Furniture and Home Furnishings	$15 028	10.7	Sears Holdings Corp.	10.2	The Brick Ltd.	8.5	IKEA AB	5.9	Leon's Furniture Ltd.	35.2	35.6
443	Electronics and Appliance	$14 982	40.2	Best Buy Co.	4.7	Apple Inc.	3.7	BCE Inc.	3.6	GameStop Corp.	52.2	52.5
444	Home Improvement	$27 037	23.9	Rona Inc.	23.8	The Home Depot Inc.	17.6	Home Hardware Stores Ltd.	9.4	Tim-Br Marts Ltd.	74.6	73.2
445	Grocery	$104 134	30.0	Weston Group	15.1	Empire Company Ltd.	10.4	Metro Inc.	6.4	Safeway Inc.	61.9	61.4
446	Pharmacy and Personal Care	$32 848	31.8	Shoppers Drug Mart Inc.	16.7	The Katz Group Inc.	12.2	Le Groupe De La Famille Jean Coutu	7.9	McKesson Corp.	68.6	67.9
448	Clothing and Accessory	$26 049	7.7	TJX Companies Inc.	3.9	The Reitman Group	3.8	Canadian Tire Corp. Ltd.	3.5	GAP Inc.	18.9	20.1
451	Hobby Stores	$11 155	15.1	Canadian Tire Corp. Ltd.	8.3	Indigo Books & Music Inc.	7.2	Toys "R" Us Inc.	4.4	Golf Town	35.0	35.4
452	General Merchandise	$56 770	41.5	Walmart Stores Inc.	24.4	Costco Co. Inc.	10.2	Canadian Tire Corp. Ltd.	9.6	NRDC Equity Partners	85.7	82.6
453	Miscellaneous	$10 696	28.4	Staples Inc.	2.9	Petsmart Inc.	2.3	Roark Capital Group	1.2	Hallmark Cards	34.8	33.8

Source: Centre for the Study of Commercial Activity, Ryerson University.

exhibit 1-6 Profile of Canada's Leading Retail Corporations: 2010–2011

Rank 2011	Corporate Ownership	Selected Banners	Capital Control	Retail Sales ($ Millions)	Cum % Sales	No of Chains	Sq Ft (000s)	Employees Total No	No of Stores	Activity (NAICS)
1	Weston Group	The Real Canadian Superstore/Whle Club, No Frills, Loblaws	CAN	31 705	10.61%	20	51 938	137 163	1 429	445, 452, 448
2	Walmart Stores Inc.	Walmart Supercentres, Walmart	USA	23 551	18.50%	2	48 062	90 000	334	452
3	Empire Company Ltd.	Sobeys, IGA, Foodland	CAN	16 055	23.87%	17	30 435	97 997	1 385	445, 446
4	Costco Co. Inc.	Costco	USA	13 867	28.52%	1	11 200	21 764	82	452
5	Metro Inc	Metro, Food Basics, Super C	CAN	11 431	32.34%	11	21 154	65 000	914	445, 446
6	Shoppers Drug Mart	Shoppers Drug Mart/Pharmaprix, Home Health Care	CAN	10 459	35.84%	4	13 200	52 714	1 328	446
7	Canadian Tire Corp. Ltd	Canadian Tire, Mark's Work Wearhouse, Sport Chek	CAN	8 437	38.67%	16	29 867	73 199	1 423	452, 451, 448
8	Rona Inc.	Rona, Rona Home & Garden, Rona Warehouse/L'Entrepot	CAN	6 800	40.95%	16	18 311	30 221	968	444, 452, 453
9	Safeway Inc.	Safeway/Safeway Superstore	USA	6 707	43.19%	1	9 994	22 684	214	445
10	The Home Depot Inc.	The Home Depot	USA	6 426	45.34%	1	18 900	26 621	180	444
11	Best Buy Co.	Future Shop, Best Buy, Best Buy Mobile	USA	6 023	47.36%	3	6 407	17 941	256	443
12	NRDC Equity Partners	Zellers, The Bay, Home Outfitters	USA	5 763	49.29%	5	46 189	50 699	618	452, 442
13	Sears Holdings Corp.	Sears Store, Cantrex, Sears Whole Home Furniture	USA	5 717	51.20%	7	31 005	47 412	1 750	452, 442, 443
14	The Katz Group Inc.	Rexall Pharma Plus, IDA Pharmacy, Rexall Drug Store	CAN	5 498	53.04%	5	5 722	12 834	1 243	446
15	Home Hardware Stores Ltd.	Home Hardware, Home Building Centre, Home Furniture	CAN	4 977	54.71%	3	10 493	31 518	1 443	444, 442
16	Le Groupe De La Famille Jean Coutu	Jean Coutu Pharmacy, PJC Clinic/Clinique, PJC Sante Beaute	CAN	4 002	56.05%	3	3 253	19 811	391	446
17	The Jim Pattison Group	Save on Foods & Drugs, Price$mart, AG Foods	CAN	3 420	57.19%	11	6 233	17 024	201	445
18	Staples Inc.	Business Depot/Staples	USA	3 040	58.21%	1	8 851	15 000	334	453
19	TJX Companies Inc.	Winners, HomeSense, Marshalls	USA	2 651	59.10%	4	8 556	17 111	311	448, 442
20	McKesson Corp.	HealthCare Pharmacy, Proxim, Clinique Sante	USA	2 585	59.96%	4	2 774	6 877	586	446
21	Tim-Br Marts Ltd.	Tim-Br Mart, BMR, IRLY Building Centres	CAN	2 530	60.81%	3	4 910	11 293	491	444
22	H.Y. Louie Company	London Drigs, MarketPlace IGA	CAN	2 490	61.64%	2	3 578	9 440	116	446, 445
23	Pharmasave Drugs Ltd.	Pharmasave	CAN	2 474	62.47%	1	2 866	5 316	443	446
24	Developments Orano Inc.	Mac's, Couche-Tard, Daisy Mart	CAN	2 167	63%	8	4 327	18 211	1 958	445
25	Dollarama Inc.	Dollarama	CAN	1 603	63.73%	1	6 977	14 507	704	452
26	Uniprix Inc	Uniprix, Unipharm, Uniclinique	CAN	1 537	64.25%	3	1 490	3 279	244	446
27	The Brick Ltd.	The Brick, United Furniture Warehouse	CAN	1 535	64.76%	6	7 755	8 062	235	442
28	IKEA AB	Ikea	SWE	1 270	65.19%	1	2 970	3 552	11	442
29	Lowe's Companies	Lowe's	USA	1 127	65.57%	1	4 379	4 402	31	444
30	The Reitman Group	Reitman's, Penningtons, Smart Set	CAN	1 019	65.91%	10	4 411	10 601	942	448
31	Indigo Books & Music Inc.	Chapters, Indigo Books & Music, Coles The Book People	CAN	934	66.22%	7	2 759	6 601	246	451, 453
32	GAP Inc.	Old Navy, Banana Republic, Gap	USA	908	66.52%	5	2 802	9 944	254	448
33	YM Inc.	Urban Planet, Suzy Shier, Bluenotes	CAN	896	66.82%	14	2 771	6 875	589	448
34	Leon's Furniture Ltd.	Leon's Furniture	CAN	880	67.12%	1	6 000	2 864	75	442
35	Familiprix Inc.	Familiprix Extra, Familiprix Pharmacy, Familiprix Clinique	CAN	861	67.41%	3	1 395	4 267	301	446
36	International Clothiers Inc.	Fairweather, Stockhomme, International Clothiers	CAN	837	67.69%	17	1 680	2 788	288	448, 452
37	Toys 'R' Us	Toys 'R' Us, Toys 'R' Us Express	USA	802	68%	2	2 634	3 629	89	451
38	Seven-Eleven Japan Co. Ltd.	7-Eleven Food Stores	JPN	759	68.21%	1	1 013	5 423	471	445
39	BMTC Group Inc.	BMTC Brault & Martineau, Tanguay Ameublements Inc	CAN	749	68.46%	5	1 544	2 263	33	442
40	Apple Inc.	Apple Store	USA	709	68.70%	1	174	1 839	22	443
41	North West Co. Fund	Northern Stores, Northmart	CAN	662	68.92%	2	839	2 621	130	445
42	Longo Brothers Fruit Markets Inc.	Longo's	CAN	629	69.13%	1	921	3 120	24	445
43	Davaldou Holdings Inc.	Globo Shoes, Aldo, Spring	CAN	614	69.33%	13	1 174	4 871	457	448
44	Calgary Co-operative Association Ltd.	Calgary Co-op	CAN	594	69.53%	1	1 495	4 914	27	445
45	Giant Tiger Stores Ltd.	Giant Tiger/Tigre Geant	CAN	582	69.73%	1	5 418	6 732	204	452
46	BCE Inc	The Source	CAN	555	69.91%	1	920	2 645	708	443
47	M & M Meats Shops Ltd	M & M Meats Shops	CAN	541	70.10%	1	644	2 760	460	445
48	GameStop Corp.	EB Games, GameStop	USA	538	70.28%	2	551	2 779	344	443
49	Limited Brands Inc.	La Senza, Bath & Body Works, Victoria's Secret	USA	517	70.45%	5	1 187	10 531	320	448, 446
50	Golf Town	Golf Town	CAN	494	70.61%	1	982	2 322	54	451

Source: Centre for the Study of Commercial Activity, Ryerson University.

exhibit 1–7 Market Control by Origin of Capital, 2011 (in $ millions)

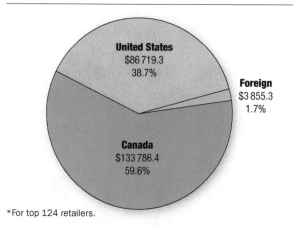

United States
$86 719.3
38.7%

Foreign
$3 855.3
1.7%

Canada
$133 786.4
59.6%

*For top 124 retailers.

Source: Centre for the Study of Commercial Activity, Ryerson University.

Of the top global retailers, 30.4 percent are headquartered in the United States, 35.3 percent in Europe, 5.2 percent in Japan, and 4 percent in Canada.[23] Walmart remains the undisputed leader in the retail world, with sales more than three times as great as those of Carrefour, the second-largest retailer, and accounting for more than 10 percent of the total top 250 retailers' worldwide revenue. Eight of the ten largest retailers sell food, and more than 50 percent of the 250 largest retailers have supermarket, warehouse, hypermarket/supercentre, or convenience store formats, or some combination thereof. The dominance of food retailing would be even more pronounced if drugstore chains and other stores that carry food were included as food retailers. Exhibit 1–8 lists the top 50 grocery retailers and wholesalers in North America. Canada fares well, with three major players falling within the top 25. Will Canada break into the top ten in 2014 with Loblaw's recent acquisition of Shoppers Drug Mart?

Opportunities in Retailing

Management Opportunities

To cope with a highly competitive and challenging environment, retailers are hiring and promoting people with a wide range of skills and interests. Students often view retailing as a part of marketing because management of distribution channels is part of a manufacturer's marketing function. Retailers undertake most of the traditional business activities. Retailers raise capital from financial institutions; purchase goods and services; develop accounting and management information systems to control operations; manage warehouses and distribution systems; and design and develop new products as well as undertake marketing activities such as advertising, promotions, sales force management, and market research. Thus, retailers employ people with expertise and interest in finance, accounting, human resources management, logistics, and computer systems as well as marketing.

Retail managers often are given considerable responsibility early in their careers. Retail management is also financially rewarding. After completing a management training program in retailing, managers can increase their starting salary in three to five years if they perform well. Aspects of retail careers are discussed in Appendix 1A, available on Connect.

Entrepreneurial Opportunities

Retailing also provides opportunities for people wishing to start their own businesses. Some of the most successful people are retail entrepreneurs, such as Canada's John Forzani. Some are household names because their names appear over the stores' doors; these include Tim Horton (Tim Hortons), Eddie Black (Black's Cameras), and John Holt and G.R. Renfrew (Holt Renfrew). Some other innovative retail entrepreneurs include John Stanton, John Forzani, Jeff Bezos, and Ingvar Kamprad. Retailing View 1.2 examines the importance of the Retail Council of Canada and its impact on career opportunities in retailing.

The Retail Management Decision Process

Understanding the World of Retailing

The first step in the retail management decision process is understanding the world of retailing. Retail managers need to understand their environment, especially their customers and competition, before they can develop and implement effective strategies. The first section of this book provides a general overview of the retailing industry and its customers.

The critical environmental factors in the world of retailing are the macro-environment and the micro-environment. The impacts of the macro-environment—including technological, social, and ethical/legal/political factors on retailing—are discussed throughout the book. The successful retailer will react to changes in the macro-environment. Huge technological changes in the macro-environment are having significant impact on retailers, enabling database marketing to provide information about consumers, the Internet to connect to customers, and RFID technology to increase retail efficiencies. The retailer's micro-environment focuses specifically on its competitors and customers.

exhibit 1-8 Top 50 Grocery Retailers and Wholesalers in North America

"Elite 50"—2011 top U.S. and Canadian supermarkets, convenience stores, drug chains, dollar stores, warehouse clubs, mass merchants, wholesalers, and buying cooperatives. All sales figures expressed in U.S. dollars.

Retail Sales Rank (FY11)	Name of Company	Country of Origin	2011 Total Sales (US$ million)	% Change vs. Previous Year	Store Count	Fiscal Year Ending	Private Label Examples
1	Walmart Stores, Inc.	U.S.	443 854	+5.9	10 130	1/31/12	Great Value, Equate, Our Finest
2	McKesson Corp.	U.S.	122 734	+10.0	40 000+	3/31/12	Medicine Shoppe Canada, Health Mart
3	Cardinal Health	U.S.	107 552	+5.0	60 000+	6/30/12	Medicine Shoppe, Medicap
4	CVS Caremark	U.S.	107 100	+11.8	7327+	12/31/11	CVS, Just the Basics
5	Costco Wholesale Corp.	U.S.	97 062	+12.0	598	9/02/12	Kirkland Signature
6	The Kroger Co.	U.S.	90 374	+10.2	3213	1/28/12	Big K, Simple Truth, Mirra Beauty
7	AmeriSource Bergen	U.S.	80 218	-2.9	3600+	9/30/11	Good Neighbor Pharmacy, Brite-Life
8	Walgreen Co.	U.S.	71 633	-0.8	7944	8/31/11	Walgreens, Café W, Good & Delish
9	Target Corp.	U.S.	68 466	+4.1	1772	1/28/12	Boots & Barkley, Mossimo, Threshold
10	Safeway	U.S.	43 630	+6.3	1666	1/01/12	Safeway Select, Signature Café
11	Supervalu	U.S.	36 100	-3.8	4400	2/25/12	Shoppers Value, Essential Everyday
12	Independent Grocery Alliance (IGA)	U.S.	31 000+	n/a	5000		IGA, IGA Tablerite
13	Loblaw Companies Ltd.	Canada	30 703	+1.3	1046	12/31/11	President's Choice, Joe Fresh, Exact
14	Publix Super Markets	U.S.	26 967	+7.3	1061	12/31/11	Publix, Quick Takes
15	Rite Aid	U.S.	26 121	+3.6	4639	3/03/12	Rite Aid, Pure Spring, Simplify
16	Ahold USA	U.S.	25 072	+6.6	754	1/01/12	Stop & Shop, Nature's Promise
17	Wakefern Foods	U.S.	22 300	+8.5	260	10/01/10	Ave Bean, Gourmet Club, Price Rite
18	7-Eleven	U.S.	20 789	+2.8	7149	12/31/11	Big Gulp, Slurpee, 7-Select
19	C&S Wholesale Grocers	U.S.	20 400	+0.0	3900	9/01/11	Best Yet, Piggly Wiggly,
20	Alimentation Couche-Tard	Canada	18 966	+15.4	5803	4/28/12	Sunshine Joe Coffee Co., Thirst Buster
21	H-E-B	U.S.	18 000	n/a	340+	10/30/11	Central Market, EconoMax
22	Sobeys	Canada	16 361	+1.8	1575	5/05/12	Compliments, Gourmet Minute
23	BP Products North America	U.S.	15 627	n/a	4691	12/31/11	Good Stuff, El Mero
24	Kmart	U.S.	15 285	-2.0	1305	1/28/12	Jaclyn Smith, Joe Boxer
25	Dollar General Stores	U.S.	14 807	+13.6	10 000+	2/03/12	DG Everyday, Rexall
26	Meijer	U.S.	14 630	+2.6	~200	1/27/12	Meijer
27	Delhaize America	U.S.	13 815	+1.3	1650	12/31/11	Healthy Accents, Home 360
28	Military Exchanges	U.S.	13 100	+4.35	5300	1/28/11	American Mercantile, Basic Concepts
29	Metro Inc.	Canada	11 639	+0.8	1509	9/24/11	Irresistibles, Selection
30	Topco Associates	U.S.	11 600	+2.7	(co-op)	12/31/11	Clear Value, Top Care
31	BJ's Wholesale Club	U.S.	10 880	+6.8	190	01/31/12	Berkley & Jensen, Earth's Pride
32	Shoppers Drug Mart Corp.	Canada	10 645	+2.6	1328	12/31/11	Life Brand, Quo, Simply Food, Everyday Market
33	Whole Foods Market	U.S.	10 108	+12.0	335	9/25/11	365 Everyday Value, Whole Catch
34	Trader Joe's	U.S.	9500	+11.8	375	12/31/11	Trader Jacques', Trader Jose's
35	Giant Eagle	U.S.	9300	+7.4	397	6/30/11	Farmers Market, Giant Eagle
36	Family Dollar Stores	U.S.	9331	+9.2	7442	8/25/12	Family Dollar, Family Gourmet
37	ALDI Inc.	U.S.	9200	+6.9	1200+	12/31/11	Baker's Corner, Friendly Farms
38	BI-LO Holding	U.S.	9100	n/a	687	n/a	Chef's Catch, Southern Home
39	Federated Co-operatives	Canada	8223	+16.3	265	10/31/11	Co-op
40	The Great Atlantic & Pacific Tea Co.	U.S.	8080	-8.3	320	2/28/12	The Food Emporium Trading Co., America's Choice
41	Cumberland Farms	U.S.	8020	+22.0	~600	9/30/12	Cumberland Farms, Farmhouse Blend
42	Associated Wholesale Grocers	U.S.	7766	+7.1	2500+	12/31/11	Best Choice, Superior Selections
43	Hy-Vee Food Stores	U.S.	7270	n/a	235+	10/02/11	Hy-Vee, Midwest Country Fare
44	Wawa	U.S.	6990	+18.6	570+	12/31/11	Wawa
45	Dollar Tree	U.S.	6630	+12.7	4523	1/28/12	Breckenridge Farms, Naturally Select
46	Wegmans Food Markets	U.S.	6340	n/a	80	12/31/11	Wegmans, Wegmans Foods
47	Sheetz	U.S.	5230	+30.5	429	9/30/11	Sheetz Bros. Coffee, Shweetz Bakery
48	Nash Finch	U.S.	4807	-3.7	1,979	12/31/11	Nash Bros. Trading Co., Value Choice
49	Save Mart Supermarkets	U.S.	4800	+2.0	225	12/31/11	Sunny Select, Master Select
50	WinCo Foods	U.S.	4730	+2.3	86	3/31/11	WinCo Foods

+ = includes retail locations to which retailer distributes private label products

Source: Kathie Canning, Randy Hofbauer, and David Litwak, "Top 50 retailers and wholesalers," *Private Label Store Brands*, November 2012, www.plstorebrands.com/article-top_50_retailers_and_wholesalers-5170.html (accessed October 11, 2013).

Retail Council of Canada

Since 1963, the Retail Council of Canada (RCC) has been the voice of retail in Canada. RCC is an industry-funded, not-for-profit association that represents more than 40 000 members across the country. The association provides support to merchants, vendors, and suppliers so that they in turn are able to meet the challenges of offering goods and services to consumers in a competitive marketplace.

As members, they have the opportunity to become a part of a national network of retailers, participate in money-saving benefit programs, access industry research and information, and make their collective voices heard through the RCC in terms of government lobbying. They also provide their members with a full range of services and programs including education and training, benchmarking, best practices, and networking.

RCC works with all levels of government and other stakeholders as a strong advocate for retailing in Canada to support career opportunities and employment growth in retail, to improve consumer choice and industry competitiveness, and to support and sustain retail investments in Canadian communities from coast to coast.

The retail agenda is put on the radar screens of Canada's policy-makers at the federal and provincial levels by RCC's Government Relations Team. They have been a united voice for retail in Canada since the RCC was called upon to represent retailers' interests in the 1960s, when credit cards were first introduced into retail operations. That early success led to other policy challenges, including the introduction of UPC codes and bilingual packaging requirements in the 1970s; negotiations of the General Agreement on Tariffs and Trade and the North American Free Trade Agreement in the 1980s; the introduction of the goods and services tax, debit cards, and e-commerce in the 1990s; and gift card, environmental, and consumer privacy legislation in the 2000s. The agenda going forward includes a variety of topics including, but not limited to, issues relating to taxation, human resources training, employment and labour relations, international trade, environmental protection, and market practices.

Retailers recognize the growing importance of employing skilled people at every level of their organizations. In response to this growing importance, the Retail Council of Canada has a team that oversees training and certification programs through the Canadian Retail Institute. As a division of the Retail Council of Canada, the Canadian Retail Institute promotes retail as a rewarding career through educational programs, scholarships, and partnerships with post-secondary institutions offering retail programs across the country. They focus their efforts on strengthening the industry by encouraging retail education, increasing career awareness, and advancing professional designation programs such as "First Level Manager" Certification and "Retail Sales Associate" Certification.

In partnership with industry sponsors, RCC awards more than $80 000 in scholarships and benefits to students entering or currently enrolled in a business, marketing, or retail-related program at a Canadian post-secondary institution. Students who receive the scholarships not only benefit from the financial assistance for their post-secondary education, but also are invited to attend the annual STORE conference in Toronto. This gives the winners the opportunity to network with the brightest retail professionals in the Canadian retail industry. For more information about these retail scholarships, go to www.retaileducation.ca.

In today's competitive environment, it is fundamental that retailers are able to tap into key trends and developments and access information in a variety of formats. Retail Council of Canada's Communications team publishes the country's retail magazine, *Canadian Retailer*, as well as industry newsletters in electronic format. Additionally, RCC's website is a gateway to Canada's retail world, offering white papers, current events, retail statistics, and a plethora of other relevant retail information.

Source: Retail Council of Canada.

Competitors At first glance, identifying competitors appears easy. A retailer's primary competitors are those with the same format. Thus, department stores compete against other department stores and supermarkets against other supermarkets. This competition between retailers of the same type is called intratype competition.

To appeal to a broader group of consumers and provide one-stop shopping, many retailers are increasing their variety of merchandise. Variety is the number of different merchandise categories within a store or department. By offering greater variety in one store, retailers can offer one-stop shopping to satisfy more of the needs of their target market. For example, clothing and food are now available in grocery, department, and discount stores and drugstores. Fast food is available at McDonald's and

intratype competition Competition between retailers of the same type (e.g., Loblaws versus Sobeys).

variety The number of different merchandise categories within a store or department.

convenience stores. The offering of merchandise not typically associated with the store type, such as clothing in a drugstore, is called scrambled merchandising. Scrambled merchandising increases intertype competition—competition between retailers that sell similar merchandise using different formats, such as discount and department stores.

Increasingly, intertype competition has made it harder for retailers to identify and monitor their competition. In one sense, all retailers compete against each other for the dollars consumers spend on goods and services. But the intensity of competition is greatest among retailers located close together with retail offerings that are viewed as very similar, such as in a shopping mall.

Management's view of competition may differ depending on the manager's position within the retail firm. For example, the manager of Hudson's Bay's women's sportswear department in Toronto views the other women's sportswear specialty stores in the Yorkdale Mall as her major mall competitors. But Hudson's Bay's store manager views the Holt Renfrew store in the mall as her strongest competitor. These differences in perspective arise because the department sales manager is primarily concerned with customers for a specific category of merchandise, whereas the store manager is concerned with customers seeking the entire selection of all merchandise and services offered by a depart-

ment store. The CEO of a retail chain, in contrast, views competition from a much broader geographic perspective. For example, Shoppers Drug Mart might identify its strongest competitor as London Drugs in the west, the Katz Group (Rexall, Pharma Plus) in central Canada, and Jean Coutu in Quebec. The CEO may also take a broader strategic perspective and recognize that other activities compete for consumers' disposable income. For example, Loblaw's CEO adopts the consumer's perspective and recognizes that grocery stores are competing with drugstores, convenience stores, and restaurants for customers' food dollars.

Retailing is intensely competitive. Understanding the different types of retailers and how they compete with each other is critical to developing and implementing a retail strategy.

Customers The second factor in the micro-environment is customers. Customer needs are changing at an ever-increasing rate. Retailers are responding to broad demographic and lifestyle trends in our society, such as the growth in the elderly and minority segments of the Canadian population and the increasing importance of shopping convenience to the rising number of two-income families. To develop and implement an effective strategy, retailers need to understand why customers shop, how they select a store, and how they select among that store's merchandise.

Developing a Retail Strategy

The next stages in the retail management decision making process, formulating and implementing a retail strategy, are based on an understanding of the macro- and micro-environments. Section 2 in this book focuses on decisions related to developing a retail strategy.

The retail strategy indicates how the firm plans to focus its resources to accomplish its objectives. It identifies:

- The target market, or markets, toward which the retailer will direct its efforts
- The nature of the merchandise and/or services the retailer will offer to satisfy needs of the target market
- How the retailer will build a long-term advantage over competitors

The nature of a retail strategy can be illustrated by comparing strategies of Walmart and Toys "R" Us. Walmart offers name-brand merchandise at low prices in a broad array of categories, ranging from laundry detergent to girls' dresses. Although Walmart stores have many different categories of merchandise, selection in each category is limited. A store might have only three brands of detergents in two sizes, while a supermarket carries eight brands in five sizes.

In contrast, Toys "R" Us identified its target as consumers living in suburban areas of large cities. Rather than carrying a broad array of merchandise categories, Toys "R" Us stores specialize in toys, games, bicycles, and furniture for children. Although Toys "R" Us has limited categories of merchandise, it has almost all the different types and brands of toys and games currently available in the market.

Both Walmart and Toys "R" Us emphasize self-service. Customers select their merchandise, bring it to the checkout line, and then carry it to their cars. Customers may even assemble the merchandise at home.

Since Walmart and Toys "R" Us emphasize competitive prices, they've made strategic decisions to develop a cost advantage over competitors. Both firms have sophisticated distribution and management information systems to manage inventory. Their strong relationships with suppliers enable them to buy merchandise at low prices.

Strategic Decision Areas   The key strategic decision areas for a retailer involve determining a market strategy, a financial strategy, a location strategy, organizational structure and human resources strategies, information systems and supply chain strategies, and customer relationship management strategies.

The selection of a retail *market strategy* is based on analyzing the environment and the firm's strengths and weaknesses. When major environmental changes occur, the current strategy and the reasoning behind it are re-examined. The retailer then decides what, if any, strategy changes are needed to take advantage of new opportunities or avoid new threats in the environment.

The retailer's market strategy must be consistent with the firm's *financial objectives*. Financial variables such as sales, costs, expenses, profits, assets, liabilities, and owner's equity are used to evaluate the market strategy and its implementation.

Decisions regarding *location strategy* are important for both consumer and competitive reasons. First, location is typically consumers' top consideration when selecting a store. Generally, consumers buy gas at the closest service station and patronize the shopping mall that's most convenient to their home or office. Second, location offers an opportunity to gain long-term advantage over competition. When a retailer has the b est location, a competing retailer has to settle for the second-best location.

A retailer's *organization design and human resources management strategies* are intimately related to its market strategy. For example, retailers that attempt to serve national or regional markets must make trade-offs between the efficiency of centralized buying and the need to tailor merchandise and services to local needs. Retailers that focus on customer segments seeking high-quality customer service must motivate and enable sales associates to provide the expected levels of service. The organization structure and human resources policies coordinate the implementation of the retailing strategy by buyers, store managers, and sales associates.

Retail information and supply chain management systems will offer a significant opportunity for retailers to gain strategic advantage in the coming decade. Retailers are developing sophisticated computer and distribution systems to monitor flows of information and merchandise from vendors to retail distribution centres to retail stores. Point-of-sale (POS) terminals read price and product information that's coded into Universal Product Codes (UPCs) affixed to the merchandise. This information is then transmitted to distribution centres or directly to vendors electronically, computer to computer. These technologies are part of an overall inventory management system that enables retailers:

- To give customers a more complete selection of merchandise
- To increase awareness of inventory levels
- To decrease inventory investment

Basic to any strategy is understanding the customers in order to provide them with the goods and services they want. And even more important is to understand and cater to the wants of the retailer's most-valued customers. After all, these customers account for the major share of a retailer's sales and profits. Customer relationship management (CRM) is a business philosophy and set of strategies, programs, and systems that focus on identifying and building loyalty with a firm's most-valued customers.

customer relationship management (CRM)   A business philosophy and set of strategies, programs, and systems that focuses on identifying and building loyalty with a retailer's most-valued customers.

DID YOU KNOW?

One plastic bag can take up to 500 years to decay in a landfill.[25]

ethics A system or code of conduct based on universal moral duties and obligations that indicate how one should behave.

Data analysis is used by retailers to identify their most-valued customers. Once these customers are identified, special programs are designed to build their loyalty.

Implementing the Retail Strategy

To implement a retail strategy, management develops a retail mix that satisfies the needs of its target market better than that of its competitors. The retail mix includes the decision variables retailers use to satisfy customer needs and influence their purchase decisions. Elements in the retail mix (Exhibit 1–9) include the types of merchandise and services offered, merchandise pricing, the communication program, convenience of the store's location and its layout and design, people (assistance to customers provided by salespeople), HR training programs, and logistical processes.

Managers in the buying organization must decide how much and what types of merchandise to buy, the vendors to use and the purchase terms, the retail prices to set, and how to advertise and promote merchandise.

Store managers must determine how to recruit, select, and motivate sales associates; where and how merchandise will be displayed; and the nature of services to provide customers (see Exhibit 1–10).

LO 6 Ethical and Legal Considerations

When making the strategic and tactical decisions discussed previously, managers need to consider the ethical and legal implications of their decisions, in addition to the effects those decisions have on the profitability of their firms and the satisfaction of their customers. Ethics are the principles governing the behaviour of individuals and companies to establish appropriate behaviour and indicate what is right and wrong. Defining the term is easy, but determining what the principles are is difficult. What one person thinks is right, another may consider wrong.

What is ethical can vary from country to country and from industry to industry. For example, offering bribes to overcome bureaucratic roadblocks is an accepted practice in some countries, but is considered unethical, and even illegal, in

Canada. An ethical principle also can change over time. For example, some years ago, doctors and lawyers who advertised their services were considered unethical. Today, such advertising is accepted.

Some examples of difficult situations that retail managers face are:

- Should a retailer sell merchandise it suspects was made using child labour?
- Should a retailer advertise that its prices are the lowest available in the market even though some items are not?
- Should a retail buyer accept an expensive gift from a vendor?
- Should retail salespeople use a high-pressure sales approach when they know the product is not the best for the customer's needs?
- Should a retailer give preference to minorities when making promotion decisions?
- Should a retailer treat some customers better than others?

Laws dictate which activities society has deemed to be clearly wrong, those activities for which retailers and their employees will be punished through the federal or provincial legal systems. However, most business decisions are not regulated by laws. Often, retail managers have to rely on their firms' and industries' codes of ethics and/or their own codes of ethics to determine the right thing to do.

Many companies have codes of ethics to provide guidelines for their employees in making their ethical decisions. These ethical policies provide a clear sense of right and wrong so that companies and their customers can depend on their employees when questionable situations arise. However, in many situations, retail managers need to rely on their personal code of ethics—their personal sense of what is right or wrong.

Exhibit 1–11 lists some questions you can ask yourself to determine whether a behaviour or activity is

exhibit 1–9 Elements in the Retail Mix

Element	Description	Detail
Product	Intensity, assortment	Types of merchandise/services offered
Place	Size, layout and design, location	Store design, merchandise display, and convenience of the store's location
Process	Logistics	Distribution, economies of scale
Price	Quality, value, price	Value perception
People	Climate, knowledge, service	Climate is the measure of what it is like to shop in the store. Knowledge refers to product knowledge and policies. Service includes getting customers in and out efficiently.
Promotion	Promotional communication mix	Public relations, sales promotion, advertising, direct marketing, personal selling

unethical. The questions emphasize that ethical behaviour is determined by widely accepted views of what is right and wrong. Thus, you should engage only in activities about which you would be proud to tell your family, friends, employer, and customers.

If the answer to any of these questions is yes, the behaviour or activity is probably unethical, and you should not do it.

Your firm can strongly affect the ethical choices you will have to make. When you view your firm's policies or requests as improper, you have three choices:

1. Ignore your personal values and do what your company asks you to do. Self-respect suffers when you have to compromise your principles to please an employer. If you take this path, you will probably feel guilty and be dissatisfied with your job in the long run.
2. Take a stand and tell your employer what you think. Try to influence the decisions and policies of your company and supervisors.
3. Refuse to compromise your principles. Taking this path may mean you will get fired or be forced to quit.

You should not take a job with a company whose products, policies, and conduct conflict with your standards.

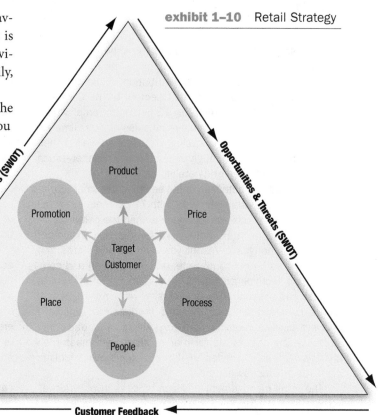

exhibit 1–10   Retail Strategy

Before taking a job, investigate the company's procedures and selling approach to see if they conflict with your personal ethical standards. In this text, we will highlight the legal and ethical issues associated with the retail decisions made by managers.

exhibit 1–11   The Six Tests of Ethical Action

The Publicity Test
· Would I want to see this action that I'm about to take described on the front page of the local paper or in a national magazine?
· How would I feel about having done this if everyone were to find out all about it, including the people I love and care about the most?

The Moral Mentor Test
· What would the person I admire the most do in this situation?

The Admired Observer Test
· Would I want the person I admire most to see me doing this?
· Would I be proud of this action in the presence of a person whose life and character I really admire?
· What would make the person I admire most proud of me in this situation?

The Transparency Test
· Could I give a clear explanation for the action I'm contemplating, including an honest and transparent account of all my motives, that would satisfy a fair and dispassionate moral judge?

The Person in the Mirror Test
· Will I be able to look at myself in the mirror and respect the person I see there?

The Golden Rule Test
· Would I like to be on the receiving end of this action and all its potential consequences?
· Am I treating others the way I'd want to be treated?

Source: Tom Morris, *The Art of Achievement: Success in Business and in Life*, Fine Communications, 2003.

SUMMARY

This chapter provides an overview of the importance of the retailing sector to the Canadian economy. The retailing process is the final stage in the distribution of merchandise and is one of the most important sectors of the Canadian economy, providing approximately 13 percent of employment in Canada and producing annual retail sales of approximately $469.9 billion in 2012. Increasingly, retailers are selling their products and services through more than one channel—such as stores, the Internet, and catalogues.

A dominant characteristic of the sector is the small size of many of the retail establishments, with 72 percent of all retail businesses in Canada employing fewer than five persons.

The Canadian retail industry has witnessed a number of dramatic changes in recent years as big-box stores and power centres hit our landscape, and information and communication technology grow in sophistication. Retailing in Canada has responded with diversity, with many types of stores competing in this dynamic marketplace; specialty retailers compete against category killers, and traditional department stores battle for market share with mass merchandisers. The examples in this chapter provide real-life glimpses of what is happening.

The retail management decision process involves developing a strategy for creating a competitive advantage in the marketplace and then developing a retail mix to implement that strategy. The strategic decisions involve selecting a target market, defining the nature of the retailer's offering, and building a competitive advantage through locations, human resources management, information and supply chain management systems, and customer relationship management programs. The tactical decisions for implementing the strategy involve selecting a merchandise assortment, buying merchandise, setting prices, communicating with customers, managing the store, presenting merchandise in stores, and providing customer service. There is no doubt that the nature of retailing has changed, as sophisticated technologies create efficiency of product distribution and improve daily operations to satisfy customer needs.

The key to successful retailing is offering the right product, at the right price, in the right place, in the right quantities, at the right time, and making a profit. To accomplish all this, retailers must understand what customers want and what competitors are offering now and in the future. Retailers' wide range of decisions extends from setting a sweater's price to determining whether a new multi-million dollar store should be built in a mall.

Retailing offers opportunities for exciting, challenging careers, either by working for a retail firm or starting your own business. Aspects of retail careers are discussed in Appendix 1A, available on Connect.

KEY TERMS

breaking bulk
corporate social responsibility (CSR)
customer relationship management (CRM)
distribution channel

ethics
intertype competition
intratype competition
retailer
retailing

retail strategy
scrambled merchandising
variety
vertical integration

1. **GO SHOPPING** Visit your favourite multichannel retailer by going to a store and going to its Internet site. Evaluate how well the company has integrated these channels into one seamless strategy.

2. **GO SHOPPING** Visit a local retail store and describe each of the elements in its retail mix.

3. **GO TO CAREER WEBSITES** Visit the career sites for Best Buy (www.recruitingsite.com/CSBsites/best-buycareers/Careers.asp), Hudson's Bay (www.hbc.monstermediaworks.ca), and the Canadian Retail Institute (www.retaileducation.ca). Find information about retail careers with these companies and within your area. In which positions would you be interested? Which positions are not of interest to you? Which company would interest you? Why?

DISCUSSION QUESTIONS AND PROBLEMS

1. Read the profile of Brian Hill, founder & CEO, Artizia.
   a) Describe Hill's entrepreneurial traits.
   b) What factors contributed to the success of Artizia?

2. Choose one clearly identifiable item (e.g., a pair of jeans, a white shirt). Visit one big-box retailer (e.g., Costco, Walmart) or a department store, one specialty chain retailer, and one online retailer.
   a) Conduct a price comparison and determine which is the better buy.
   b) Observe customers in the store.
   Take notes. Be prepared to discuss your research.

3. Does Walmart contribute to or detract from the communities in which it operates stores? Check out www.walmart-csr.ca.

4. How might managers at different levels of a retail organization define their competition?

5. Explain the strategy used by your favourite retailer.

6. Choose one of the top 20 retailers. Go to the company's website and find out how the company started and how it has changed over time.

7. You are familiar with The Gap as a retailer currently undergoing changes to attract more customers. You have been given $150 to go shopping. Go to The Gap online (www.gapcanada.ca) and go through the process of picking your product. Describe your experience.

8. Retailing View 1.1 describes how some retailers are acting socially responsibly. Take the perspective of a stockholder in the company. What effect will these activities have on the value of its stock? Why might they have a positive or negative effect?

McGraw Hill Education **connect**®   Practise and learn online with Connect.

chapter 1: introduction to the world of retailing   **21**

types of retailers

LEARNING OBJECTIVES

LO1 Explore various trends that are shaping today's retailers.

LO2 Compare and contrast the different types of retailers.

LO3 Examine how retailers differ in terms of how they meet the needs of their customers.

LO4 Review how services retailers differ from merchandise retailers.

LO5 Explore how multichannel retailers provide more value to their customers.

LO6 Recognize the key success factors in multichannel retailing.

LO7 Identify the types of ownership for retail firms.

SPOTLIGHT ON RETAILING

Commitment to Customer Key to Grocer's Success

Bill McEwan started in the grocery business as a 15-year-old high school student in his hometown of Trail, British Columbia He worked evenings and weekends—stocking shelves, sweeping floors, cleaning washrooms, bagging groceries, and carrying them to the car for the customer. In short, he did everything that needed to be done, and then some.

Four full and rewarding decades later, the 55-year-old McEwan took his leave of a business he loved, having done just about everything there was to do in grocery. By then, he was president and CEO of Sobeys Inc., the Stellarton, Nova Scotia–based retail giant that boasts annual revenues of $16 billion and either owns or oversees 1350 stores that operate under five different banners from coast to coast.

"I was fascinated with the business as a teenager and I still have the same fascination with how it all comes together," says McEwan, who is stepping aside for health reasons. "I'm going to miss the industry terribly and I'm going to miss the company."

McEwan received a number of accolades and honours upon his retirement, including the Retail Council of Canada's (RCC) Lifetime Achievement Award. The award recognizes senior executives who have a minimum of 25 years of continuous service in retail and who have demonstrated outstanding business success and community service.

"RCC is proud to honour Bill McEwan," says Diane J. Brisebois, president and CEO of RCC. "Over his 40 years in the industry, Bill's visionary leadership, driven by his passion for the grocery business, has inspired all those who have had the opportunity to work with him. His business success is exceeded only by the inspiration and influence he has had on the countless individuals he has worked with throughout his career."

Bill McEwan spent the early years of his career with the family-owned business Ferraro Foods, where he had worked as a high school student. In 1989, he began working for Coca-Cola, where he stayed until 1993, gaining invaluable experience and insights from a world leader in marketing, branding, manufacturing, and consumer research. And then the grocery industry came knocking again in 1994 when he joined A&P Canada as senior vice-president of marketing.

When McEwan took over Sobeys, the entire retail industry was going through a fundamental change. Retailers began moving beyond traditional boundaries and introduced entirely new lines of merchandise.

Some of the national drugstore chains, for example, added substantial grocery departments. Grocers beefed up their pharmacy departments, added outdoor garden centres in the spring and summer, and, in some cases, built warehouse-sized stores in order to introduce a broad assortment of general merchandise.

Under McEwan's stewardship, however, Sobeys went against the prevailing winds. The company made a strategic decision to stick to a pure grocery offering in smaller format stores. Even in large urban and suburban centres, Sobeys stores top out at 45 000 to 50 000 square feet, whereas some competitors have built 100 000-square-foot grocery and general merchandise outlets.

"We're all about food," he said. "We decided we were going to stick with what we know and love. We don't sell pipe wrenches and dishwashers and hammocks. That wasn't considered the right strategy at the time. A lot of people questioned why we weren't doing what others were doing. But it proved to be the right approach."

Sobeys decided to follow the customer, rather than join the rush to create a new market for consumers. The company also recognized the fact that there is no single shopper, and Sobeys has positioned its various banners—Sobeys, IGA, Foodland, FreshCo, and Urban Fresh—to address the demands of various markets.

"We identified a food consumer who didn't want to walk around a 100 000-square-foot store to buy milk and fresh peppers," he says. "We always said we want the right size stores, not the biggest."

As he departed the industry, McEwan had some simple, straightforward advice for anyone considering a career in retail: go for it. "There's so much to choose from, so much diversity," he says. "There's real estate, finance, purchasing, and merchandising, among other things. I think it's unrivalled as a career."

And he has a special affection for the grocery business. "I love the rhythm and seasonality of it," he says. "There's summer merchandise and fall merchandise and all the holidays and special events—Hallowe'en, Christmas, Easter. You become a big part of the lives of your customers."

Indeed, listening to McEwan talk about the business, it's easy to understand why he's going to miss it.

Source: D'Arcy Jennish, "Commitment to Customer—Key to Grocer's Success," *Canadian Retailer,* store 2012, Volume 22, Issue 4, pp. 30–31.

To develop and implement a retail strategy, retailers need to understand the nature of competition in the retail marketplace. This chapter describes the different types of retailers—both store- and nonstore-based retailers. Retailers differ in terms of the types of merchandise and services they offer to customers, the nature of the retail mix used to satisfy customer needs, the degree to which their offerings emphasize services versus merchandise, the prices charged, and the ownership of the firm.

Growing Diversity of Retail Formats

LO 1

As discussed in Boston Consulting Group's *Retail 2020* report, the following ten trends are profoundly changing the retail industry.

1. *Empowered, discriminating consumers.* Consumers can make informed decisions with the increased access to product information, price comparisons, and user reviews, and then widely share their experiences with others. These empowered, discriminating consumers are putting pressure on retailers to add meaningful value to what they can find for themselves, both online and in stores.
2. *Ubiquitous connectivity.* It has never been more critical for retailers to integrate digital opportunities into the shopping experience, with the Internet available at work, at home, and on the go (mobile). Digital and physical experiences are converging, with shoppers expecting interactive, value-added experiences anytime, anywhere, and through any channel.
3. *Buying local, going green.* Consumers want to consume in a responsible, sustainable way. Retailers are responding by embracing the issues and helping customers and suppliers do the same.
4. *Explosion of consumer data.* The enormous amount of data generated by points of sale, social media, corporate websites, and tracking URLs is greater than the ability of many retailers to exploit the potential value of this input.
5. *New age of marketing.* With increasing amounts of data available on customers, their online activities, and their purchasing patterns, retailers will be able to create more targeted marketing campaigns.
6. *Scientific retailing.* By applying smart algorithms and deep, data-driven analytics to the massive amounts of data, retailers will be able to maximize all aspects of their business, including pricing, assortments, shelf displays, staffing, and warehouse space.
7. *Growing retailer power.* The top five grocery stores in Canada now have 67 percent share of the market, with Loblaw Companies Ltd. dominating with 29.9 percent. Canadian Tire's recent acquisition of the Forzani Group is a critical component of its strategy to maintain leading market share in sporting goods in Canada, with the entry of mass merchant Target into the Canadian market in spring 2013.
8. *Maturing retail technologies.* A wide range of maturing technologies is allowing companies to streamline backroom functions and increase efficiency, helping to offset higher labour costs.
9. *Blurring boundaries among channels, formats, and brands.* Shoppers Drug Mart is selling food; Loblaws

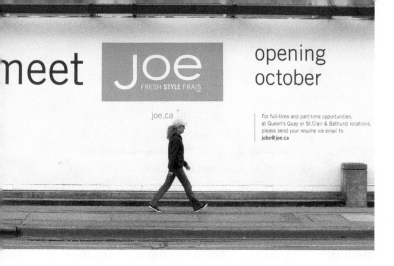

has in-house bank branches; and Indigo has Starbucks cafés in store. Retailers are evolving into a more integrated business model where all channels share a common strategy for profitable growth.

10. *Challenged store economics.* Physical stores turning into showrooms in the minds of consumers and the rise of online buying are forcing retailers to rethink their costly real-estate assets and merchandising formats.[1]

As consumer needs and competition have changed, new retail formats have been created and continue to evolve. Consider the theory of natural selection and its relevance for explaining change in retailing. It follows Charles Darwin's view that organisms evolve and grow on the basis of the *survival of the fittest*. In retailing, those businesses best able to adapt to change in customer demands, technological advances, and increased competition have the greatest chance of success.

Expanding Retail Breadth

Over the past 20 years, many new retail formats have been developed. Consumers now can purchase the same merchandise from a wide variety of retailers. The initial category specialists in toys, consumer electronics, and home improvement supplies have been joined by a host of specialists including Sport Chek (sportswear), Bed Bath & Beyond (home decor), and PETsMART (pet supplies). Grocery stores such as Loblaws have added pharmacies, clothing (Joe Fresh), and home decor products to expand their retail mix; Shoppers Drug Mart has added shelves full of grocery products to the traditional health and beauty options. Rental companies represent an interesting retail format that has evolved from simple car or equipment rental to Netflix (movie rentals) and *easyhome* (sales and lease ownership firm). The Internet has spawned a new set of retailers offering consumers the opportunity to buy merchandise and services (www.alibaba.com), participate in auctions (www.ebay.com), or submit "take-it-or-leave-it" bids (www.priceline.com).

Many new types of retailers coexist with traditional retailers. Each type of retailer offers a different set of benefits. Thus, consumers patronize different retailers for different purchase occasions. For example, a consumer might purchase a pair of pants from a catalogue as a gift for a friend in another city and then visit a local store to try on and buy the same pants for himself. The greater diversity of retail formats increases competition in the industry and also enables consumers to buy merchandise and services from a retailer that better satisfies their needs for the specific purchase.

Increasing Industry Concentration

Although the number of different types of retailers has grown, the number of competitors within each format is decreasing. The Canadian marketplace is powered by a small number of large retailers who dominate in their specific retail category. For example, Walmart (which entered the Canadian market in 1994) and Canadian Tire are the major mass merchandisers (with Target entering the market in April 2013), and Shoppers Drug Mart is the largest drugstore chain. In Canada, the consumer electronics specialists are Future Shop and Best Buy (both owned by Best Buy parent company in the U.S.). The dominant warehouse club Costco has little direct competition since Sam's Club closed its Canadian locations in winter 2009. Three major department stores dominate the Canadian retail landscape: Holt Renfrew, Hudson's Bay, and Sears (a subsidiary of Sears Roebuck and Co. in the U.S.). Loblaw Companies Ltd. (including Loblaws, Fortinos, No Frills, and Provigo chains) is Canada's largest grocery chain, with $31.3 billion in sales and a 29.9 percent grocery market share in Canada. Its nearest national competitor is the Empire Company and its Sobeys chain with sales of $15.8 billion and a 14.4 percent market share. Metro is the third-largest grocery player in Canada with sales of $11.4 billion and a 10.9 percent market share.[2] Dominant in home improvement retailing are American giant Home Depot and Quebec retailer Rona. Both have had rapid growth across Canada.

The trend toward a blurring of retail channels will continue: Drugstores have moved into high-end cosmetics, traditionally the territory of the department stores; grocery stores have invaded the pharmacy business. Meanwhile, banks have a problem—more and more customers are not coming into their branches. Banking online or by phone is now the norm. In addition, there is competition from retailers (including Loblaws and Canadian Tire) offering banking services that include mortgages and loans that extend the customer relationship. In response, progressive banks are luring customers with plasma TVs, iPods, and comfy chairs to attract more profitable clients to invest in financial advisory services. Ultimately, it will be the customer who makes the retail decisions.

North American Industry Classification System (NAICS) Classification of retail firms into a hierarchical set of six-digit codes based on the types of products and services they produce and sell.

Retailer Characteristics

Store-based retailers range from street vendors selling hot dogs to large corporations such as Staples that offer products in their stores and through catalogue and Internet channels. Each retailer survives and prospers by satisfying a group of consumers' needs more effectively than its competitors. Over time, different types of retailers have emerged and prospered because they have attracted and maintained a significant customer base.

The most basic characteristic of a retailer is its retail mix—the elements used by a retailer to satisfy its customers' needs (see Exhibits 1–9 and 1–10). Four elements of the retail mix are particularly useful for classifying retailers:

- Type of merchandise/services offered
- Breadth and depth of merchandise offered
- Level of customer service
- Price of the merchandise

Type of Merchandise

The United States, Canada, and Mexico have developed a classification scheme, called the North American Industry Classification System (NAICS), to collect data on business activity in each country. Every business is assigned a hierarchical, six-digit code based on the type of products and services it produces and sells. The first two digits identify the firm's business sector, and the remaining four digits identify various subsectors.

The classifications for retail firms selling merchandise, based largely on the type of merchandise sold, are illustrated in Exhibit 2–1. Merchandise retailers constitute sectors 44 and 45, and the third digit breaks down these retailers further. For example, retailers selling clothing and clothing accessories are in classification 448, whereas general merchandise retailers are in classification 452. The fourth and fifth digits provide a finer classification. As shown in Exhibit 2–1, the fourth digit subdivides clothing and accessories retailers (448) into clothing stores (4481), shoe stores (4482), and jewellery, luggage, and leather goods stores (4483). The fifth digit provides a further breakdown into men's clothing stores (44811) and women's clothing stores (44812). The sixth digit, not illustrated in Exhibit 2–1, captures differences in the three North American countries using the classification scheme.

Most services retailers appear in sectors 71 (arts, entertainment, and recreation) and 72 (accommodation and food services). For example, food services and drinking places are in category 722, which gets subdivided into full-service restaurants (7221) and limited-service eating places like fast-food restaurants (7222).

Breadth and Depth

Even if retailers sell the same type of merchandise, they might not compete directly. For example, the primary classification for retailers selling clothing and clothing accessories is 448. But clothing can be purchased in sporting goods stores (45111),

exhibit 2–1 NAICS Codes for Retailers

441	Motor vehicle and parts dealers
442	Furniture and home furnishings stores
443	Electronics and appliance stores
444	Building material and garden equipment and supplies dealers
445	Food and beverage stores
446	Health and personal care stores
447	Gasoline stations
448	Clothing and clothing accessories stores
451	Sporting goods, hobby, book, and music stores
452	General merchandise stores
453	Miscellaneous store retailers
454	Nonstore retailers

4481	Clothing stores
4482	Shoe stores
4483	Jewellery, luggage, and leather goods stores

44811	Men's clothing stores
44812	Women's clothing stores
44813	Children's and infants' clothing stores
44814	Family clothing stores
44815	Clothing accessories stores
44819	Other clothing stores
44821	Shoe stores
44831	Jewellery stores
44832	Luggage and leather goods stores

department stores (4521), warehouse clubs and supercentres (45291), and electronic shopping and mail-order houses (4541). These different types of retailers do not compete directly because they appeal to different customer needs and thus offer different assortments and varieties of merchandise and services. Variety (breadth of merchandise) is the number of merchandise categories a retailer offers. Depth of merchandise is the number of different items in a merchandise category. Breadth of merchandise means that the retailer carries a number of different product lines. For example, large department stores carry a wide range of different types of products (shoes, appliances, apparel, and cosmetics). Depth of merchandise is the number of *items* within each product line. For example, the shoe department in the department store will offer a large assortment of shoes (running shoes, dress shoes, children's shoes, walking shoes). Retailers can have product/service assortment strategies that range from wide and deep (many merchandise categories and a large assortment in each category) like Hudson's Bay; wide and shallow (many merchandise categories and a limited assortment in each category) like Walmart; narrow and deep (limited number of merchandise categories and a large assortment in each category) like House of Knives; or a narrow and shallow strategy (few merchandise categories and a limited assortment in each category) like M&M Meat Shops (see Exhibit 2–2).

Each different *item* of merchandise is called a SKU (stock keeping unit). For example, a 3.7 kg box of Tide laundry detergent and a white, button-down-collar Tommy Hilfiger shirt, size 16–33, are both SKUs.

Warehouse club stores (Costco), discount stores (Walmart, Giant Tiger), and toy stores all sell toys. However, warehouse clubs and discount stores sell many other categories of merchandise in addition to toys. (They have greater variety or breadth of merchandise.) Stores specializing in toys stock more types of toys (more SKUs). For each type of toy, such as dolls, the specialty toy retailer offers more assortment or depth of merchandise (more models, sizes, and brands, and deeper assortment) than general merchants such as warehouse clubs or discount stores.

Exhibit 2–3 shows the breadth and depth of kayaks carried by EMS (Eastern Mountain Sports), an outdoor gear and equipment specialist; Outdoorplay.com, an Internet kayak specialty retailer; and Walmart, a full-line discount store. Although EMS carries many of the same brands as Outdoorplay.com, EMS offers a narrower assortment—only four of the five categories—than Outdoorplay.com. Outdoorplay.com carries a deeper assortment of kayaks. Walmart has the least variety (only two categories) and the shallowest assortment, offering only 5 SKUs compared with 24 at EMS and 82 at Outdoorplay.com.

Customer Services

Retailers differ in the services they offer customers. For example, EMS offers assistance in selecting the appropriate kayak as well as repairing kayaks. Outdoorplay.com and Walmart

variety (breadth of merchandise) The number of different merchandise categories within a store or department.

depth of merchandise The number of SKUs within a merchandise category; also called *assortment* and *depth of stock*.

SKU (stock keeping unit) The smallest unit available for keeping inventory control. In soft goods merchandise, a SKU usually means size, colour, and style.

exhibit 2–2 Breadth versus Depth of Merchandise Lines

	Breadth: Number of different product lines			
	Shoes	Appliances	CDs	Men's clothing
Depth: Number of items within each product line	Nike running shoes Florsheim dress shoes Top Sider boat shoes Adidas tennis shoes	Sony TV sets Sanyo DVD players General Electric dishwashers Sharp microwave ovens	Classical Rock Jazz Country Rap Christian	Suits Ties Jackets Overcoats Socks Shirts

exhibit 2–3 Breadth and Depth of Kayaks in Different Retail Outlets

Retailer	Brand	White-Water	Recreational	Sea Touring	Fishing
EMS (Eastern Mountain Sports)	Necky		X	X	
	Wilderness Systems		X	X	X
	Hurricane			X	
	Perception		X		
	Old Town		X		
	Airis				X
			7 SKUs $489–$1209	14 SKUs $1259–$1695	3 SKUs $975–$1365
Outdoorplay.com	Axiom	X			
	Axis	X			
	WaveSport	X			
	Dagger	X	X	X	
	Airis	X	X		
	NRS	X			
	Wilderness Systems		X	X	X
	Perception		X	X	
	Necky		X	X	
	Advanced Elements		X		
	Ocean Kayak				X
	Freedom Hawk				X
		27 SKUs $649–$1538	23 SKUs $449–$1299	20 SKUs $794–$1699	12 SKUs $849–$1999
Walmart	K2			X	
	Waterquest		X		
	Airhead		X		
	Coleman		X		
			4 SKUs $299.98–$377.99	1 SKU $349.99	

do not provide these services. Customers expect retailers to provide some services: accepting credit and debit payment, providing parking, and being open at convenient hours. Some retailers charge customers for additional services, such as home delivery and gift wrapping. Retailers that cater to service-oriented consumers offer most of these services at no charge.

Cost of Offering Breadth and Depth of Merchandise and Services

Stocking a deep assortment like the EMS offering in kayaks is appealing to customers but costly for retailers. When a retailer offers customers many SKUs, inventory investment increases because the retailer must have backup stock for each SKU.

Similarly, services attract customers to the retailer, but they're also costly. More salespeople are needed to provide information and assist customers, to alter merchandise to meet customers' needs, and to demonstrate merchandise. Child care facilities, washrooms, dressing rooms, and check rooms take up valuable store space that could be used to stock and display merchandise. Offering delayed billing, credit, and instalment payments requires a financial investment that could be used to buy more merchandise.

To make a profit, retailers that offer broader variety, deeper assortments, and/or additional services need to

charge higher prices. For example, department stores have higher prices because of their higher costs, which result from stocking a lot of fashionable and seasonal merchandise, discounting merchandise when they make errors in forecasting consumer tastes, providing some personal sales service, and having expensive mall locations. In contrast, discount stores appeal to customers who are looking for lower prices and are less interested in services but want to see a broad range of merchandise brands and models. Thus, a critical retail decision involves the trade-off between the costs and benefits of maintaining additional inventory or providing additional services.

To compare their offering with competitive offerings, retailers often shop their competitors' stores. In the next section, we discuss the different types of general merchandise, then food retailers and nonstore retailers. Exhibit 2–4 contains information about the size and growth rates for each of these retail sectors.

General Merchandise Retailers

Types of general merchandise retailers include discount stores, specialty stores, category specialists, department stores, home improvement centres, off-price retailers, and value retailers. Exhibit 2–5 summarizes

exhibit 2–4 Sales and Growth Rate for Retail Sectors

	Estimated Sales, 2013 ($ millions)	Estimated Sales Growth 2008–2013 (%)
Food Retailers		
Conventional supermarkets	622 896	3.3
Supercentres	354 905	7.1
Warehouse clubs	159 075	6.7
Convenience stores	748 186	3.0
General Merchandise Retailers		
Department stores	73 291	20.9
Apparel and accessory specialty stores	210 236	4.5
Jewellery stores	36 848	3.4
Shoe stores	29 606	1.8
Furniture stores	66 262	2.2
Home furnishing stores	59 465	2.8
Office supply stores	26 404	2.2
Sporting goods stores	49 717	5.3
Bookstores	19 101	2.1
Building material, hardware, and garden supply stores	393 254	3.6
Consumer electronics and appliance stores	141 800	4.4
Drugstores	250 172	4.2
Full-line discount stores	126 385	0.0
Extreme-value stores	52 454	3.1
Nonstore Retailers		
Nonstore retailing	340 421	9.0
E-commerce	282 055	15.0

Sources: *Economic Forecast: Outlook to 2013 Food, Drug, Mass* (Columbus, OH: Retail Forward, November 2008); *Economic Forecast: Outlook to 2013 Homegoods* (Columbus, OH.: Retail Forward, November 2008); *Economic Forecast: Outlook to 2013 Softgoods* (Columbus, OH: Retail Forward, November 2008).

characteristics of general merchandise retailers that sell through stores. Many of these general merchandise retailers sell through multichannels, such as stores, online, catalogues, call centres, social networking, digital displays, and mobile.

Discount Stores

A discount store is a retailer that offers a broad variety of merchandise, limited service, and low prices. Discount stores offer both private labels and national brands. Discount stores can also be referred to as *mass merchandisers* or *full-line discount stores*. Examples include Target, Giant Tiger, and Walmart.

Walmart alone accounts for almost 67 percent of full-line discount store retail sales, so the most significant trend in this sector is Walmart's conversion of discount stores to supercentres. This change in emphasis is the result of the increased competition faced by full-line discount stores and the operating efficiencies of supercentres. Full-line discount stores confront intense competition from discount specialty stores that focus on a single category of merchandise, such as Golf Town, Staples Business Depot, Future Shop, HomeSense, Sport Chek, and Rona.

They also compete with Old Navy and Hudson's Bay for apparel, Sears for home furnishings, and Shoppers Drug Mart for health and beauty products. To respond to this competitive environment, discount stores have created more attractive shopping environments, placed

exhibit 2–5 Characteristics of General Merchandise Retailers

Type	Variety	Assortment	Service	Prices	Size (000 sq. ft.)	SKUs (000)	Location
Department stores	Broad	Deep to average	Average to high	Average to high	100–200	100	Regional malls
Discount stores	Broad	Average to shallow	Low	Low	60–80	30	Stand-alone, power strip centres
Specialty stores	Narrow	Deep	High	High	4–12	5	Regional malls
Category specialists	Narrow	Very deep	Low to high	Low	50–100	20–40	Stand-alone, power strip centres
Home improvement centres	Narrow	Very deep	Low to high	Low	80–120	20–40	Stand-alone, power strip centres
Drugstores	Narrow	Very deep	Average	Average to high	3–15	10–20	Stand-alone, strip centres
Off-price stores	Average	Deep but varying	Low	Low	20–30	50	Outlet malls
Extreme-value retailers	Average	Average and varying	Low	Low	7–15	3–4	Urban, strip

more emphasis on apparel, and developed strong private-label merchandise programs.

Walmart pioneered the everyday low price concept. And its efficient operations have allowed it to offer the lowest-priced basket of merchandise in every market in which it competes. This doesn't mean that Walmart has the lowest price on every item in every market. But it tries to be the lowest across a wide variety of things. Many scholars of business believe Walmart has the best and most sophisticated supply chain and information systems in the industry, allowing for retail efficiency and lower prices.

There is no doubt that Walmart's global success has been a matter of efficiency and timing. Target, on the other hand, wins with merchandising. Opting for quality and style, Target has even developed a certain cult quality among fashion hipsters with its private labels. Target has also successfully read several important broad consumer trends: Consumers are looking for good value, but that doesn't mean the same thing as cheap. Target has also realized that consumers who are further up the economic ladder than typical discount shoppers will become customers if the merchandise is well designed and of high quality.

In January 2011, Target announced its plans to acquire the leasehold interests in up to 220 sites operated by Zellers Inc., a subsidiary of the Hudson's Bay Company (HBC), and open stores in Canada. Beginning in spring 2013, Target began opening 125 to 135 stores across every province of the country. Approximately $10 to $11 million will be invested to remodel each facility in order to bring the full Target brand experience to consumers in Canada.[4]

Specialty Stores

A specialty store concentrates on a limited number of complementary merchandise categories and provides a high level of service in an area typically under 8000 square feet. For example, Pro Hockey Life, owned by Sports Gilbert Rousseau Inc. of Montreal, and Hockey Experts, owned by Calgary-based Forzani Group Ltd., are examples of new specialty hockey chains that specialize in hockey gear ranging from relatively inexpensive to higher end.

Issues in Specialty Store Retailing Specialty stores tailor their retail strategy toward a very specific market segment by offering deep but narrow assortments along with knowledgeable sales staff. For example,

West 49 retails action sports clothing that had its origins with young skateboard enthusiasts. West 49 has very specific strategies to make sure that it appeals to the under-16 demographic. For example, the mall is a perfect location for this retailer because the target age group does not drive and usually relies on a parent to drop them off at the shopping centre.

Sephora, France's leading cosmetic chain and a division of the luxury goods conglomerate LVMH (Louis Vuitton–Moet Hennessy), is an example of an innovative specialty store concept. In Canada, prestige cosmetics were historically sold in department stores. Sephora is a cosmetic and perfume specialty store offering a deep assortment of merchandise in a 6000- to 9000-square-foot self-serve retail environment. Each cosmetic brand has a separate counter with testers and sales staff available to answer questions. The concept is extremely popular with customers, who are encouraged to browse and experiment in a friendly environment.

Its stores offer over 15 000 SKUs and more than 200 brands, including its own private-label brand. Merchandise is grouped by product category, with the brands displayed alphabetically so that customers can locate them easily. Customers are free to shop and experiment on their own. Sampling is encouraged. Knowledgeable salespeople are available to assist customers. The low-key, open-sell environment results in customers spending more time shopping.

Because specialty retailers focus on specific market segments, they are vulnerable to shifts in consumer tastes and preferences. For example, mall-based specialty retailers are affected by consumers who prefer the convenience of shopping in retail locations outside the mall. Ease of parking and time saving are two factors that influence the

Sephora offers a unique shopping experience, differentiating it from other specialty stores selling beauty products.

Interior of a Bass Pro Shops sporting goods store.

consumer. Apparel and footwear specialty retailers are capturing fewer consumers' dollars because consumers are spending more on necessities such as rent or mortgage, school expenses, and transportation costs and are enjoying eating out, a concert, or club.

Europe-based apparel specialty stores Zara (Spain) and H&M (short for Hennes & Mauritz, in Sweden) are very successful in Europe, and are expanding into Canada. Zara's philosophy is "fashion on demand." At the end of every day in each of the chain's more than 1000 shops around the world, the manager goes online to company headquarters in Spain and describes which items were moving and which weren't. Using this simple method as a guide, designers can get a newly created item on the racks within little more than a week, compared to as long as six months for The Gap. In the fickle and fast-changing world of fashion, agility means success. Zara produces more than half of its own clothes and makes 40 percent of its own fabric. H&M also responds quickly to fashion trends. In contrast, however, H&M has 800 suppliers and does not own factories.[5] H&M also competes at lower price points than both Zara and The Gap. Its philosophy is "disposable chic," and its merchandise is so inexpensive that it doesn't matter if it goes out of style quickly.[6]

Fast-fashion companies like H&M introduce new products two to three times per week, compared with 10 to 12 times per year at traditional specialty stores, to ensure that they offer the most trendy and up-to-date fashions. Because of the constantly fresh atmosphere, customers develop "buy it now" shopping behaviour; next week, the store will have different merchandise. As a result, fast-fashion retailers actually sell 85 percent of their merchandise at full price compared with only 60 percent at traditional stores.

Many manufacturers have opened their own specialty stores in recent years. Tired of being at the mercy of retailers to purchase and merchandise their products, these manufacturers and specialty retailers can control their own destiny by operating their own stores. Consider, for instance, Apple (computers and phones) and Lucky Brand (jeans and apparel).

Category Specialist/Category Killer

Bass Pro Shops' Outdoor World is a **category specialist** offering merchandise for outdoor recreational activities. The stores offer everything a person needs for hunting and fishing—from 27-cent plastic bait to boats and recreational vehicles costing $45 000. Sales associates are knowledgeable outdoors people. Each is hired for a particular department that matches that person's expertise. All private-branded products are field tested by Bass Pro Shops' professional teams: Redhead Pro Hunting Team and Tracker Pro Fishing Team.

By offering a complete assortment in a category at low prices, category specialists can "kill" a category of merchandise for other retailers and thus are frequently called *category killers*. Because category specialists dominate a category of merchandise, they can use their buying power to negotiate low prices and are assured of supply when items are scarce. Department stores and full-line discount stores located near category specialists often have to reduce their offerings in the category because consumers are drawn to the deep assortment and low prices at the category killer.

Many of these category killers are operating in a big-box format. These large format stores typically range in size from approximately 40 000 to 200 000 square feet. But it must be realized that it is the size of the store in comparison to its competitors that would qualify it as a big-box category killer, as shown in Exhibit 2–6.

category specialist A discount retailer that offers a narrow but deep assortment of merchandise in a category and thus dominates the category from the customers' perspective. Also called *category killer*.

DID YOU KNOW?

Although 42 percent of Canadians surveyed said they use social media at least once a day—with an additional 17 percent using them once a week—only 4 percent of those polled said they use social platforms to shop, according to PwC Canada's *2013 Global Multi-channel Retail Survey*.[7]

exhibit 2–6 Big-Box Comparative Size Advantage

- Superstores—three times the traditional supermarket
- Home Depot—18 times the traditional hardware store
- Chapters—12 times the traditional book store
- Winners—six times the traditional fashion store
- Staples Business Depot—five times the traditional office supply store
- Michaels Craft Stores—nine times the traditional arts and crafts store
- Sport Chek—six times the traditional sporting goods store

department store A retailer that carries a wide variety and deep assortment, offers considerable customer services, and is organized into separate departments for displaying merchandise.

Issues for Category Specialists

Most category specialist chains started in one region of the country and saturated that region before expanding to other regions. During this period of expansion, competition between specialists in a category was limited.

Competition between specialists in each category becomes intense as firms expand into regions originally dominated by another firm. In many merchandise categories, the major firms are now in direct competition across the country. This direct competition focuses on price, resulting in reduced profits because the competitors have difficulty differentiating themselves on other elements of the retail mix. All the competitors in a category provide similar assortments since they have similar access to national brands. These sophisticated big-box, category killer venues are often grouped together in power centres, dominating the industry with their low prices, extensive product offerings, and ample customer parking.[8]

In response to this increasing competitive intensity, the category killers continue to concentrate on reducing costs by increasing operating efficiency and acquiring smaller chains to gain scale economies. Where appropriate, category specialists have attempted to differentiate themselves with service. For example, Home Depot, Rona, and Lowe's hire licensed contractors as sales associates to help customers with electrical and plumbing repairs. They also provide classes to train home owners in tiling, painting, and other tasks to give shoppers the confidence to tackle their do-it-yourself (DIY) projects on their own.

As retailers try to satisfy today's ever-changing consumer, many are realizing that big is not always better. More and more North American retailers are turning to the smaller format concepts that have been trending in Europe, Asia, and Latin America. Real estate is not always available for big-box players; populations are shifting; and the web is having a significant impact on consumer in-store expectations and shopping processes. Rona is moving to reduce the number of its big-box locations from 80 to 57 and is focusing its expansion efforts on smaller-format neighbourhood stores. Best Buy is responding to the shift by reducing the footprint of new store builds by 10 000 square feet and launching new mobile device stores that are less than 3000 square feet. The days of the big-box experience are not over, says Nick Jones, executive vice-president and retail practice lead for Leo Burnett/Arc Worldwide in Chicago, "The big box will survive. But only by virtue of how it addresses the competitive advantage of physical retail over e-tail. But, in either channel, the most successful retailers will deliver real shopper experiences that entertain and inspire shoppers and give them ideas and solutions, not just product."[9]

Department Stores

A **department store** is a retailer that carries a broad variety and deep assortment of stock, offers some customer services, and is organized into separate departments for displaying merchandise. The largest department store chains in Canada are Sears Canada and Hudson's Bay, bought in 2006 by Jerry Zucker, U.S. billionaire investor,[10] and then sold again in 2008 to the owners of U.S.-based Lord and Taylor, NRDC Equity partners. Department store chains are very diverse and can be categorized into three tiers. The first tier includes upscale, high-fashion chains with exclusive designer merchandise and excellent customer service, such as Holt Renfrew in Canada and Nordstrom in the United States. Hudson's Bay represents the second tier of upscale department stores, in which retailers sell more modestly priced merchandise with less customer service. The value-oriented third tier—Sears Canada—caters to more price-conscious consumers. Holt Renfrew in the first tier has had an established, clearly defined, differentiated position for years, whereas the value-oriented tier has been facing significant competitive challenges from discount stores.

The entire category, including the first tier, is about to get a big shake-up with American luxury retailer Nordstrom announcing plans in September 2012 to open its first Canadian stores in four cities as early as 2014 (Pacific Centre Vancouver, the Chinook Centre Calgary, the Rideau Centre Ottawa, and Sherway Gardens Toronto). Further, it is rumoured that department store Bloomingdale's is in talks with Hudson's Bay Company to expand into Canada, citing Toronto, Vancouver, and Calgary

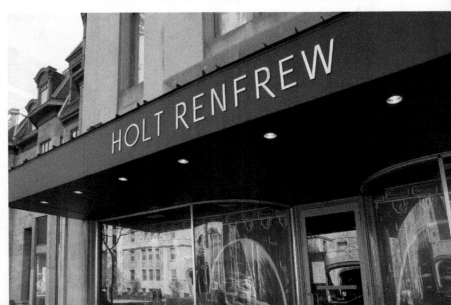

as prime locations. Only time will tell how significantly these stores will affect department store retailing in Canada and the Canadian luxury market.[11]

Traditionally, department stores attracted customers by offering a pleasing ambience, attentive service, and a wide variety of merchandise under one roof. They sold both soft goods (apparel and bedding) and hard goods (appliances, furniture, and consumer electronics). Each department within the store has a specific selling space allocated to it, a POS terminal to transact and record sales, and salespeople to assist customers. The department store often resembles a collection of specialty shops. The major departments are women's, men's, and children's clothing and accessories; home furnishings and furniture; kitchenware and small appliances; and cosmetics and fragrances.

In some situations, departments in a department store or discount store are leased and operated by an independent company. A leased department is an area in a retail store that is leased or rented to an independent firm. The lease holder is typically responsible for all retail mix decisions involved in operating the department and pays the store a percentage of its sales as rent. Retailers lease departments when they feel they lack expertise to operate the department efficiently. Commonly leased departments in Canadian stores are beauty salons, pharmacies, shoes, jewellery, furs, photography studios, and repair services.

Department stores are unique in terms of the shopping experience they offer, the services they provide, and the atmosphere of the store. They offer a full range of services from altering clothing to home delivery. To create excitement, apparel is displayed on mannequins, attention is drawn to displays with theatrical lighting, and sales associates are frequently stationed throughout the store demonstrating products. Department stores also emphasize special promotions such as elaborate displays during the Christmas season.

Issues in Department Store Retailing Department stores' overall sales have stagnated and market share has fallen in recent years due to increased competition from discount stores and specialty stores, as well as a decline in perceived value for merchandise and services. Department stores, which started in the nineteenth century, attracted consumers by offering them ambience, attentive service, and a wide variety of merchandise under one roof. They still account for some of retailing's romance—its parades, its Santa Claus lands, and its holiday windows. Department stores also offer designer brands that are not available at other retailers.

Unfortunately, many consumers believe that department stores are no longer romantic or convenient. Many

believe that they are difficult to get to because they are located in large malls, that it is difficult to find specific merchandise because the same category is often located in several designer departments, and that it is difficult to get professional sales assistance because of labour cutbacks. At the same time, department stores typically charge higher prices than their discount and specialty store competitors.

To deal with eroding market share, department stores are (1) attempting to increase the amount of exclusive merchandise they sell, (2) undertaking marketing campaigns to develop strong images for their stores and brands, and (3) expanding their online presence.

Drugstores

A drugstore is a specialty store that concentrates on health and personal grooming merchandise. Pharmaceuticals often represent over 50 percent of drugstore sales and an even greater percentage of their profits. The largest drugstore chain in Canada is Shoppers Drug Mart with a market share of 30.1 percent.[12] In July 2013, Shoppers Drug Mart was acquired by Loblaw Companies Ltd. for approximately $12.4 billion.

Issues in Drugstore Retailing Drugstores, particularly the national chains, are experiencing sustained sales growth because the aging population requires more prescription drugs and the profit margins for prescription pharmaceuticals are higher than for other drugstore merchandise. The nonprescription side of drugstores is also being squeezed by considerable competition from pharmacies in discount stores and supermarkets, as well as from prescription mail-order retailers.

In response, the major drugstore chains are building larger stand-alone stores offering a wider assortment of merchandise, more frequently purchased food items, and drive-through windows for picking up prescriptions.[13] To build customer loyalty, the chains are also changing the role of their pharmacists from dispensing pills (referred

DID YOU KNOW?

97% The percentage of Pinterest users who are women. The biggest demographic are women aged 25 to 34.[14]

DID YOU KNOW?

Although not considered a drugstore per se, Walmart is the third-largest pharmacy operator in the United States.

DID YOU KNOW?

North Americans rate pharmacists as the most trusted profession.

Pharmaprix retail pharmacy chain in Quebec, which is part of Shoppers Drug Mart, Canada's largest pharmacy chain.

off-price retailer A retailer that offers an inconsistent assortment of brand-name, fashion-oriented soft goods at low prices.

closeout retailers Off-price retailers that sell a broad but inconsistent assortment of general merchandise as well as apparel and soft home goods, obtained through retail liquidations and bankruptcy proceedings.

outlet stores Off-price retailers owned by a manufacturer or a department or specialty store chain.

factory outlets Outlet stores owned by a manufacturer.

to as count, pour, lick, and stick) to providing health care assistance.

Shoppers Drug Mart, Canada's largest pharmacy, operates 1811 Shoppers Drug Mart/Pharmaprix drugstores, 58 medical clinic pharmacies called Shoppers Simply Pharmacy, 63 Shoppers Health Care stores, and 8 luxury beauty destinations operating as Murale, with 2011 sales in excess of $10.5 billion.[15] Shoppers has launched beauty boutiques by adding prestige cosmetics and fragrance brands. Following suit, London Drugs and Jean Coutu are also giving their cosmetics sections a major makeover, borrowing ideas from the department stores to chase new revenue opportunities.

Off-Price Retailers

An off-price retailer offers an inconsistent assortment of brand-name, fashion-oriented soft goods at low prices. Winners—launched in Canada in 1982—had grown to over 200 stores across the country by 2011. The company, which is owned by U.S.-based TJX Companies (which owns T.J. Maxx, Marshalls, and other off-price retailers), has 70 buyers worldwide in Canada, Hong Kong, New York, Los Angeles, and London searching for the best buys in fashion. The flagship store, which opened in 2003 at the College Park location in Toronto, receives about 10 000 new items a week and is a shopper's dream.[16,17] In 2005, Winners arrived on fashionable Bloor Street in Toronto, not far from Tiffany, Chanel, and Holt Renfrew. The off-price concept appeals to the Canadian shopper and the company is cashing in with its Winners (apparel), Home-Sense (home), and StyleSense (accessories) formats. As

announced in 2010, TJX Companies brought the Marshall's banner to Canada in 2011 to operate alongside sister chains Winners and HomeSense. Similar to the Winners chain, Marshall's offers current fashions at discount prices, with a stronger focus on clothing selections for the entire family, compared to the Winners selection that is more oriented toward women. TJX opened six Marshall's stores in the Greater Toronto Area in 2011 and sees the chain as the next growth vehicle for its Canadian operations, with plans to expand the format up to 100 locations.

Off-price retailers can sell brand-name and even designer-label merchandise at low prices due to their unique buying and merchandising practices. Most merchandise is bought opportunistically from manufacturers or other retailers with excess inventory at the end of the season. This merchandise might be in odd sizes or unpopular colours and styles, or it might be irregular (having minor mistakes in construction). Typically, merchandise is purchased at one-fifth to one-fourth of the original wholesale price. Off-price retailers can buy at low prices because they don't ask suppliers for advertising allowances, return privileges, markdown adjustments, or delayed payments. (For a different take on off-price retailing, Retailing View 2.1 describes Bag Borrow or Steal, which rents luxury products.)

Due to this pattern of opportunistic buying, customers can't be confident that the same type of merchandise will be in stock each time they visit the store. Different bargains will be available on each visit. To improve their offerings' consistency, some off-price retailers complement opportunistically bought merchandise with merchandise purchased at regular wholesale prices. Two special types of off-price retailers are closeout and outlet stores.

- Closeout retailers are off-price retailers that sell a broad but inconsistent assortment of merchandise usually obtained from a store closing or bankruptcy, consisting of general merchandise, apparel, and home furnishings. Examples are XSCargo and Liquidation World.

- Outlet stores are off-price retailers owned by manufacturers or retailers. Outlet stores owned by manufacturers are referred to as factory outlets. Outlet stores can be found clustered together in a geographic area, such as the Southworks Outlet Mall in Cambridge, Ontario; maps are distributed to shoppers indicating outlet locations. The outlet mall provides a shopping location that includes added services such as food and beverages, parking, and a climate-controlled environment, along with the bargains of off-price merchandise.

Manufacturers view outlet stores as an opportunity to sell irregulars, production overruns, and merchandise

Rent Some Luxury

DETAILS

Designers : Chloe : Chloe Paddington Satchel

CHLOE

Chloe Paddington Satchel
SKU# BBOS5828

A chic little bag with a funky edge. The Chloe Paddington has a whiskey colored pebbled leather exterior with a large padlock closure, and its thick round straps are easy on the shoulders. Soft, tan fabric interior has a secure zip pocket. Dimensions: 13"L x 7"W x 8"H; 7" drop handle.

This item is not available at this time. Click below to add it to your Wait List and it will be shipped to you as soon as it becomes available.

WAIT LIST

Can't afford this purse? Just rent it from Bag Borrow or Steal.

Bag Borrow or Steal, founded in 2004 (www.BagBorrow OrSteal.com) rents luxury products such as handbags, jewellery, watches, and sunglasses to more than 1 million members. Customers have the option of becoming members by paying a monthly subscription fee that allows them to rent items for 20 percent off the listed prices and provides additional perks such as priority access to certain merchandise and reward points. For example, a BCBG clutch is available for about $9 a week or $25 a month for nonmembers, but members get 20 percent off. On the higher end, a Chloe Small Paddington Satchel bag that retails for about $1300 rents for about $100 a week or $250 a month for nonmembers and about $65 a week and $200 a month for members. If a customer "falls in love" with an item, she has the option of paying a reduced price for it, based on its condition and age. The website also offers an outlet store that sells items at 40 to 85 percent off the suggested retail price, depending on their condition.

When it was just getting started, 70 percent of Bag Borrow or Steal's sales were from its opening price point bags, those under $500, and included many well-known brands such as Kate Spade and Coach. Now about 80 percent of its sales are from the bags that retail for $1500 and up from well-known designers like Gucci and Prada. The business has grown considerably; a typical wholesale buy from a vendor is from $500 000 to $750 000, an amount rare for even the biggest luxury retailers like Bergdorf Goodman.

Many of their customers already have designer bags or other high-end accessories but cannot afford to buy the selection that is available to them through Bag Borrow or Steal. A bag, for instance, is an accessory item for which many consumers are willing to spend up to their limit, or above, because of its "noticeability" compared with other articles of clothing. "Fashionistas" especially value the ability to carry many designer bags throughout the year rather than just one or two.

Sources: http://fora.tv/2009/02/13/Weathering_the_Storm_Retail_Solutions_for_All_Seasons#Bag_Borrow_or_Steal_Fashion_Meets_On-line_Innovation (accessed October 6, 2009); Paul Demery, "New Capital Wave," InternetRetailer.com, September 2008; Sarah Lacy, "The Tech Beat," *BusinessWeek*, March 7, 2006; Kate M. Jackson, "Renting a Handful of Luxury," Boston Globe, October 13, 2005; www.bagborrow-orsteal.com (accessed October 6, 2009).

returned by retailers. Outlet stores also allow manufacturers some control over where their branded merchandise is sold at discount prices.

Retailers with strong brand names such as Holt Renfrew (Last-Call) operate outlet stores. By selling excess merchandise in outlet stores rather than selling it at markdown prices in their primary stores, these department and specialty store chains can maintain an image of offering desirable merchandise at full price.

Canadian retailers operating outlet stores include Roots outdoor apparel, Club Monaco trendy urban apparel, and Danier Leather. Problems occur as traditional mall landlords dispute with tenants who are opening branches in power centres located close to their shopping centres. Fashion retailers are selling identical merchandise and price points of clothes at their power centre stores and their mall locations. The end result: The consumer is confused, assumes there are higher prices at the mall, and thus avoids shopping at the traditional shopping centre.

Value Retailers

Value retailers are general merchandise discount stores that are found in either lower-income urban, or middle-income suburbs, or in rural areas and are much smaller than traditional discount stores. Value retailers are the fastest-growing segment in Canadian retailing.[19] Many value retailers target low-income consumers, whose shopping behaviour differs from typical discount store or warehouse club customers. For instance, although these consumers demand well-known national brands, they often can't afford to buy large-size packages. Since this segment of the retail industry is growing rapidly and is known to pay its bills on time, vendors are creating special smaller packages for these people.

Value retailers follow a variety of business models. Although most cater to low-income groups, some draw from multiple-income groups and are generally located in suburban strip malls. They specialize in giftware, party, and craft items rather than consumables. Despite some of these chains' names, few just sell merchandise for a dollar. The $1 price is the focus, but the chains carry many different price points, all rounded off in even dollars. Your Dollar Store With More, a Kelowna, B.C., franchise chain, has grown to 150 stores in five years and incorporates a similar pricing strategy. Dollar stores are attracting the "tween" market with low-cost, trendy cosmetics

and jewellery for girls ages 8 to 13. The names imply a *good value*, while not limiting the customer to the arbitrary dollar price point.

Pop-Up Stores

So-called pop-up stores—temporary stores—are creating retail buzz as they respond to customers by reaching out in nontraditional ways and locations such as unfinished space. These stores pop up unexpectedly for hours, days, or months, draw word-of-mouth crowds, then vanish and may resurface someplace else. Subscribers are usually given notice via e-mail as to time and place of the event. Smart retailers must be prepared to cater aggressively to their customers anywhere and anytime.

It is not enough for retailers to build a store and expect customers will find them. Strong retailers are reaching customers through touch points. Pop-up stores can also act as an effective promotional medium. These stores most often exist for a defined period of time in a place where the target customer will be focused. For example, a garden centre may open a temporary site to attract customers during the spring months to capture additional sales. Mobile wireless technology allows retailers to provide a full range of POS services to their nonpermanent locations.

Pop-up stores are the perfect embodiment of a here today, replaced tomorrow retail ethic, which has built-in obsolescence at the core of the consumer dynamic. Brands and retailers love them because they create buzz, provide an incubator for new ideas, and permit targeted market research. Pop-ups can also provide benefits to a community, turning a forgotten neighbourhood into a destination or, like old-fashioned craft shows, allowing market exposure for those who can't afford the retail infrastructure.

In February 2012, Target opened a one-day pop-up shop featuring a limited edition collection from Canadian designer Jason Wu in downtown Toronto to create hype ahead of its opening of 135 stores across Canada in 2013. More than 1500 shoppers snapped up high fashion at bargain prices with approximately $60 000 in sales going to the United Way of Toronto.

Food Retailers

Ten years ago, people purchased food primarily at conventional supermarkets. Today, however, discount stores and warehouse clubs are significantly changing consumers' food purchasing patterns because they also sell food (see Exhibit 2–7). At the same time, traditional food retailers carry many nonfood items, plus many have pharmacies, photo processing centres, banks, and cafés.

The world's largest food retailer is Walmart, with supermarket-type sales of US$165 billion in 2009, followed by Carrefour (France), Tesco (United Kingdom), Metro Group (Germany), Schwartz Group (Germany), and Kroger (United States). The largest supermarket chains in Canada are Loblaws, Sobeys, and Metro.

Loblaws continues to achieve success with the President's Choice brand and build convenience convergence by forming strategic alliances with coffee shops, fitness studios, photo marts, wine shops, dry cleaners, and other companies to provide its customers with the convenience of one-stop shopping. The addition of a "community room" that is available to local groups and charities, and which can be used for cooking classes by local chefs, is a popular community connection in Loblaws' new stores. The experiences are all designed to build loyalty and stimulate sales.[20]

It is now easy to see that one can't easily answer the question, When is a food retailer really not a food retailer? Nonetheless, our discussion of food and combination stores will include conventional supermarkets, big-box food retailers, and convenience stores. Exhibit 2–8 shows the sales revenues and retail mixes for different types of food retailers.

Supermarkets

A conventional supermarket is a large, self-service retail food store offering groceries, meat, and produce, as well as nonfood items, such as health and beauty aids and general merchandise.[21] Perishables, including meat, produce, baked goods, and dairy products, account for 44 percent of supermarket sales and typically have higher margins than packaged goods.[22]

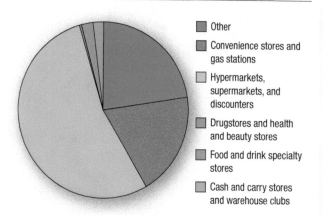

exhibit 2–7 Canadian Food Retail Market Share, 2009

- Other
- Convenience stores and gas stations
- Hypermarkets, supermarkets, and discounters
- Drugstores and health and beauty stores
- Food and drink specialty stores
- Cash and carry stores and warehouse clubs

combination stores Retailers that sell both food and nonfood items.

conventional supermarket A self-service food store that offers groceries, meat, and produce with limited sales of nonfood items, such as health and beauty aids and general merchandise.

limited-assortment supermarkets Supermarkets offering a limited number of SKUs; also called *extreme-value food retailers*.

superstore A large supermarket between 35 000 and 45 000 square feet in size.

Whereas conventional supermarkets carry about 30 000 SKUs, limited-assortment supermarkets (also called *extreme-value food retailers*) stock only about 2000 SKUs.[23] Canadian retailer M&M Meat Shops is a good example of a successful limited-assortment supermarket. Each store is set up with one convenient aisle and large, glass-door freezers to display the entire selection. Certified product consultants serve the counter, answer questions, and provide helpful preparation tips and meal suggestions. M&M Meat Shops offer approximately 375 products, the majority of which are flash-frozen.[24] Dollar Tree Canada is an example of an extreme-value food retailer, with almost half of its product mix being food and drink, including perishable items such as milk and ice cream. A superstore is a larger conventional supermarket with

Market Shares of the Canadian Food Market

Loblaws	29.9%
Sobeys	14.4%
Metro	10.9%
Safeway (Canada)	6.2%
Costco	5.6%
Walmart	4.3%
Co-ops	3.3%
Overwaitea Foods	3.0%
Couche-Tard	1.2%
Shoppers Drug Mart	0.7%
The North West Company	0.7%

Sources: Kenric S. Tyghe and Sara Kohbodi, "Loblaw Companies Ltd.," Canada Research, Raymond James, January 16, 2012, p. 6, www.raymondjames.ca/en_ca//equity_capital_markets/equity_research/sample_research/docs/Loblaw%20Companies%20Ltd.%20011612.pdf (accessed February 2, 2013).

exhibit 2–8 Characteristics of Food Retailers

	Conventional Supermarket	Limited-Assortment Supermarket	Supercentre	Warehouse Club	Convenience Store
Percentage food	70–80	80–90	30–40	60	90
Size (000 sq. ft.)	35–40	7–10	160–200	100–150	3–5
SKUs (000)	30–40	1–1.5	100–150	20	2–3
Variety	Average	Narrow	Broad	Broad	Narrow
Assortment	Average	Shallow	Deep	Shallow	Shallow
Ambience	Pleasant	Minimal	Average	Minimal	Average
Service	Modest	Limited	Limited	Limited	Limited
Prices	Average	Lowest	Low	Low	High
Gross margin (%)	20–22	10–12	15–18	12–15	25–30

power perimeter
The area around the outside walls of a supermarket that has fresh-merchandise categories.

fair trade
Purchasing practices that require producers to pay workers a living wage, well more than the prevailing minimum wage, and offer other benefits, such as on-site medical treatment.

locavore movement
A movement whose adherents' primary source of food originates within a specified radius of where they live.

expanded-service deli, bakery, seafood, and nonfood sections.[25]

To compete successfully against intrusions by other food retailing formats, conventional supermarkets are differentiating their offerings by (1) emphasizing fresh perishables, (2) targeting health-conscious and ethnic consumers, (3) providing a better in-store experience, and (4) offering more private-label brands.

Fresh Merchandise Fresh-merchandise categories are the areas around the outer walls of a supermarket, known as the power perimeter, that include dairy, bakery, meat, florist, produce, deli, and coffee bar. These departments attract consumers and are very profitable. The dairy and produce sections in particular are high-need items that, if of high quality and priced competitively, can increase store loyalty among customers. Conventional supermarkets are building on this strength by devoting more space to fresh merchandise with cooking exhibitions and "action" stations, such as store-made sushi and freshly grilled meat.

Another example of emphasis on "fresh" is the offering of meal solutions for time-pressured consumers. Canadian retailers such as Sobeys have introduced fresh formats like Sobeys Urban Fresh in an effort to boost their presence in urban markets. The largest store is 10 000 square feet, but the average is only about 3900 square feet, offering a broad assortment of grocery items in a much smaller footprint.

Health/Organic Merchandise Conventional supermarkets are also offering more natural, organic, and fair-trade foods for the growing segment of consumers who

are health and environmentally conscious.[26] Fair trade means purchasing from factories that pay workers a living wage, considerably more than the prevailing minimum wage, and offer other benefits such as on-site medical treatment. Although Whole Foods continues to be the world's largest retailer of natural and organic foods with stores throughout North America, other supermarket chains such as Loblaws and Metro are devoting significant space to natural and organic foods.

A related food retailing trend is offering locally grown products, a trend brought about in response to environmental concerns and the increasing financial costs (e.g., fuel) of transporting food long distances. The locavore movement focuses on reducing the carbon footprint caused by the transportation of food throughout the world. Food miles are calculated using the distance that food travels from the farm to the plate. Many Canadians appreciate the idea of supporting local businesses, but they also want the variety of products they can find in their grocery store. It is difficult to maintain a balance between buying locally and maintaining such variety. Leading the growing movement toward buying local and satisfying consumer demand when it comes to sourcing food, Loblaws launched the "Ontario Grown—Picked at Its Peak" produce program in 2007 across all Ontario Loblaws, Fortinos, Zehrs, Valu-Mart, and Your Independent Grocer stores.

Private-Label Merchandise Conventional supermarket chains are leveraging their quality reputation to offer more private-label merchandise. Private-label brands benefit both customers and retailers. The benefits to customers include having more choices and finding the same ingredients and quality as in national brands at a lower price. The benefits of private-label brands to retailers include increased store loyalty, the ability to differentiate themselves from the competition, lower promotional costs, and higher gross margins compared with national brands. In Canada, just over 40 percent of consumers think that private-label brands are a good alternative to national brands, versus 37 percent of Americans.[27] According to a March 2011 report by Nielsen, titled *The Rise of the Value-Conscious Shopper*, 60 percent of Canadians indicated that their purchase of private-label products increased during the recession, while 95 percent indicated that they will continue purchasing private-label products post-recession.[28] Loblaw's private-label products (with more than 8000 products marketed under private-label brands such as President's Choice, no name, Blue Menu, Mini Chefs, and more) have traditionally performed well, accounting for 26.9 percent of the company's sales in 2010. Loblaw continues in its strategy to leverage its private-label capabilities and scale with the launch of its Black Label line.[29] Premium private label (as evidenced by Tesco's success in the U.K. with Tesco Finest) is the fastest-growing segment within the private-label category. PC Black Label represents affordable indulgence and targets the so-called cross-shopping between Loblaw stores, which range in price point and selection from hard discount (No Frills) to superstore (Real Canadian Superstores) and supermarket (Loblaws), and specialty grocers like Whole Foods Market, Pusateri's, and Urban Fare.[30]

Improving the Shopping Experience Creating enjoyable experience through better store ambience and customer service is another approach that supermarket chains use to differentiate themselves from low-cost, low-price competitors. Supermarkets are increasingly incorporating "food as theatre" concepts, such as open-air market designs, cooking and nutrition classes, demonstrations, babysitting services, and food tasting.

Big-Box Food Retailers

Over the past 25 years, supermarkets have increased in size and have begun to sell a broader variety of merchandise.

Supercentres are 160 000 to 200 000 square feet in size and offer a wide variety of food (30–40 percent) and nonfood merchandise (60–70 percent).[31] They are the fastest-growing retail category. Supercentres stock between 100 000 and 150 000 individual items (SKUs). With the popularity of the superstore concept in Canada in the 1990s, Loblaws expanded its product offering by including clothing, pharmaceuticals, and other nonfood items. By maintaining its quality and position through a three-part strategy of innovation, market domination, and reduction of costs, Loblaws remains relatively unchallenged in the Canadian grocery retail marketplace.[32]

By offering broad assortments of grocery and general merchandise under one roof, supercentres provide a one-stop shopping experience. Customers will typically drive farther to shop at these stores than to visit conventional supermarkets (which offer a smaller selection). General merchandise items (nonfood items) are often purchased on impulse when customers' primary reason for coming to the store is to buy groceries. The general merchandise has higher margins, enabling the supercentres to price food items more aggressively. However, since supercentres are very large, some customers find them frustrating because it can take a long time to find the items they want.

Hypermarkets are also large (greater than 200 000 square feet) combination food (60–70 percent) and general merchandise (30–40 percent) retailers. Hypermarkets typically stock less than supercentres, between 40 000 and 60 000 items ranging from groceries, hardware, and sports equipment, to furniture and appliances, computers, and electronics.[33]

Hypermarkets were created in France after the Second World War. By building large stores on the outskirts of metropolitan areas, French retailers could attract customers and not violate strict land-use laws. They have spread throughout Europe and are popular in some South American countries such as Argentina and Brazil.

Consider, for instance, France-based Auchan. It is a hypermarket chain with a workforce of 145 000 operating in 14 countries, including Taiwan, China, Argentina, the United States, Mexico, and most European countries. A typical store is 250 000 square feet and has 60 checkout counters, more than 100 000 food and nonfood items, and 2000 shopping carts. Auchan offers everything from fresh produce to groceries to housewares to electronics.

Supercentres versus Hypermarkets Hypermarkets, per se, are not prevalent in North America,[34] although the differences between a French hypermarket and a Walmart or Target supercentre are sometimes difficult to distinguish. Both hypermarkets and

supercentres Large stores (160 000 to 200 000 square feet) combining a discount store with a supermarket.

hypermarkets Large combination food (60–70 percent) and general merchandise (30–40 percent) retailers.

DID YOU KNOW?

Loblaw Groceterias in Toronto was the first self-serve and cash and carry grocery retailer in Canada, opening in 1919.[35]

supercentres are large, carry grocery and general merchandise categories, are self-service, and are located in warehouse-type structures with large parking facilities. However, hypermarkets carry a larger proportion of food items than supercentres, with a greater emphasis on perishables—produce, meat, fish, and bakery items. Supercentres, in contrast, have a larger percentage of nonfood items and focus more on dry groceries, such as breakfast cereal and canned goods, instead of fresh items.

Although supercentres and hypermarkets are the fastest-growing segments in food retailing, they face challenges in finding locations for new, large, limited-service big-box stores. In Europe and Japan, land for building large stores is limited and expensive. New supercentres and hypermarkets in these areas often have to be multi-storey, which increases operating costs and reduces shopper convenience. Furthermore, some countries place restrictions on the size of new retail outlets. In both Canada and the United States, there has been a backlash against large retail stores, particularly Walmart outlets. These opposing sentiments are based on local views that big-box stores drive local retailers out of business.

Warehouse Club A warehouse club is a retailer that offers a limited assortment of food and general merchandise with little service at low prices to ultimate consumers and small businesses. Stores are large (100 000 to 150 000 square feet)[37] and located in low-rent districts. They have simple interiors and concrete floors. Aisles are wide so that forklifts can pick up pallets of merchandise and arrange them on the selling floor. Little service is offered. Customers pick merchandise off shipping pallets, take it to checkout lines in the front of the store, and pay with cash, credit, or debit. The largest warehouse club chains are Costco and Sam's Club, a division of Walmart. Costco is the fifth-largest food retailer in Canada, with estimated food sales of $6.7 billion in 2010.[38]

Merchandise in warehouse clubs is about half food and half general merchandise. Specific brands and items may differ from time to time because the stores buy merchandise available on special promotions from manufacturers. Warehouse clubs reduce prices by using low-cost locations and store designs. They reduce inventory holding costs by carrying a limited assortment of fast-selling items. Merchandise usually is sold before the clubs need to pay for it.

Most warehouse clubs have two types of members: wholesale members who own small businesses, and individual members who purchase for their own use. For example, many small restaurants are wholesale customers who buy their supplies, food ingredients, and desserts from a warehouse club rather than from food distributors.

Typically, members must pay an annual fee of $55 to $110. In some stores, individual members pay no fee but pay 5 percent over an item's ticketed price. Wholesale members typically represent less than 30 percent of the customer base but account for over 70 percent of sales. The membership fee–driven warehouse club is a U.S.-based phenomenon.

Convenience Stores

Convenience stores provide a limited variety and assortment of merchandise at a convenient location in a 3000- to 5000-square-foot store with speedy checkout. They are the modern version of the neighbourhood mom-and-pop grocery/general store.

Convenience stores enable consumers to make purchases quickly, without having to search through a large store and wait in a long checkout line. Over half the items bought are consumed within 30 minutes of purchase. Due to their small size and high sales, convenience stores typically receive deliveries every day.

Convenience stores offer a limited breadth and depth, and they charge higher prices than supermarkets. Milk, eggs, and bread once represented the majority of their sales. Now almost all convenience stores in nonurban areas sell gasoline, which accounts for over 55 percent of annual sales.

Although the convenience store concept has stagnated a bit in Canada and Europe, it has been growing throughout Japan, the rest of Asia, and in parts of Latin America. The reason is that the stores are so convenient. In many Asian countries, consumers face space constraints at home, so they prefer buying in smaller quantities at neighbourhood locations. Additionally, many e-tailers in Asia use convenience stores as distribution points. Customers buy online and pick up at the store.[39] The largest convenience store retailer in Canada is Alimentation Couche-Tard with $15.8 billion in revenue in 2011.[40] The company operates a network of over 5800 stores, over 4200 of which sell motor fuel. Grouped under three main brands—Couche-Tard, Mac's, and Circle

Traditional food retailers are competing with convenience stores for customers who want prepared meals.

K—its neighbourhood stores feature a friendly, modern setting, and most of them are open 24 hours a day, seven days a week.[41]

Convenience stores also face increased competition from other formats. Sales tend to increase during periods of rising gasoline prices, but their dependency on gasoline sales is a problem because gasoline sales have low margins. In addition, supercentre and supermarket chains are attempting to increase customer store visits by offering gasoline and tying gasoline sales to their frequent shopper programs (Walmart, Canadian Tire, Real Canadian Superstore). Drugstores and full-line discount stores also are setting up easily accessed areas of their stores with convenience store merchandise (Shoppers Drug Mart, Walmart, and Target).

Issues in Food Retailing

The primary issue facing food retailers in general, and supermarket and convenience store retailers in particular, is the increasing level of competition from other types of retailers. As mentioned earlier, supercentres in North America and hypermarkets in the rest of the world are growing at a rapid pace. In Canada, this growth has been spurred by Walmart's aggressive supercentre strategy. Competition is coming from other sources as well. Other retailers such as department stores, drugstores, convenience stores, gas stations, and even dollar stores are increasingly displaying food items on their shelves. Fast-food restaurants such as Subway sandwich shops have positioned themselves as a healthy food alternative.

In response to these competitive pressures, convenience stores are taking steps to decrease their dependency on gasoline sales, tailoring assortments to local markets, and making their stores even more convenient to shop. To get gasoline customers to spend more on other merchandise and services, convenience stores are offering more fresh food and healthy fast food that appeals to today's on-the-go consumers, especially women and young adults. For example, Mac's combines a convenience store and takeout restaurant. Mac's has ready-to-heat meals, a sandwich bar, salads, and a ready-to-eat section. It also offers fresh produce, beverages, snacks, and other food. Customers can park, walk in, pick up tonight's dinner and tomorrow's breakfast, and be back in their cars in 10 minutes.[42]

The U.K. supermarket giant Tesco's Fresh & Easy stores sell fresh produce, meats, and ready-to-eat meals targeted at customers who do not want to visit a regular grocery store or spend too much time cooking.[43] Finally, convenience stores are adding new services, such as financial service kiosks that give customers the opportunity to cash cheques, pay bills, and buy prepaid telephone minutes, theatre tickets, and gift cards.

Traditional grocery chains are fighting back by making significant investments in providing meal solutions, either hot food or partially cooked entrées. The market for prepared foods can be quite profitable. Profit margins on prepared foods are higher than most other grocery categories. Also, although shoppers rarely visit a supermarket in search of prepared foods alone, those who do spend almost 40 percent more than those who seldom or never purchase prepared foods.[44] Imagine being greeted by chefs in white hats tossing fresh pasta, with a dining area in the grocery store. The store could offer an extensive variety of prepared meals ranging from Caesar salads to Chinese food made by chefs in full view of its customers, and a satisfied customer saying, "They have the drama. I ask for a fresh salmon sautéed with a little lemon, browse ten minutes in the store, and take it home for dinner."[45]

DID YOU KNOW?

According to Mintel, 73 percent of Canadian consumers shop at least once per week, and Statistics Canada reports that food purchases directly from retail stores comprise 77 percent of all food expenditures in Canada.[46]

Nonstore Retail Formats

In the preceding sections, we have examined retailers whose *primary* modes of operation are bricks-and-mortar stores. In this section, we will discuss types of retailers that operate primarily in nonstore environments. The major types of nonstore retailers are electronic retailers, catalogue and direct-mail retailers, direct selling, television home shopping, and vending machines.

Electronic Retailing

Electronic retailing (also called *e-tailing, online retailing,* and *Internet retailing*) is a retail format in which the retailers communicate with customers and offer products and services for sale over the Internet. Shopping over the Internet provides the safety and convenience of catalogues and other nonstore formats. However, the Internet, compared with store and catalogue channels, also has the potential to offer a greater selection of products and more personalized information about products and services.

Broader and Deeper Assortments   One benefit of the Internet channel, compared with other channels, is the vast number of alternatives that consumers can consider. The number of SKUs available in a store is limited by the store's size. The number of pages in a catalogue limits that channel.

More Timely Information for Evaluating Merchandise   An important service offered to customers is providing information that helps them make better buying decisions. The retail channels differ in terms of how much information customers can access. The amount of information available through the store channel is limited by the number of sales associates and the space for signage. Similarly, the information available through a catalogue channel is limited by the number of pages in the catalogue. In contrast, the information provided through the Internet channel is unlimited. The vast amount of information available through the Internet channel enables customers using this channel to solve problems rather than just get information about specific products.

In addition to providing more information, the Internet channel offers customers more current information whenever they want it. Retailing View 2.2 describes an Internet site that offers products plus information, some of which is generated by customers, which can help couples solve the problems associated with planning a wedding.

Finally, consumers can access information from other consumers through the Internet channel—information that may be viewed as less biased than information provided by a retailer or manufacturer. Many retailers provide an opportunity for customers to post reviews of products or services they have bought.

Personalization   Due to the web's interactive nature, the most significant potential benefit of the Internet channel is its ability to personalize merchandise offerings and information for each customer electronically. Customers control some of this personalization. Customers shopping on an Internet channel can drill down through web pages until they have enough information to make a purchase decision. In addition, when using the Internet channel, customers can format the information so that it can be effectively used when they are comparing alternatives.

The retailer can play a more proactive role in personalizing merchandise and information through the Internet channel. For example, many retailers offer live chats: Customers can click a button at any time and have an instant messaging, e-mail, or voice conversation with a customer service representative. This technology also enables retailers to send a proactive chat invitation automatically to customers on the site. The timing of these invitations can be based on the time the visitor has spent on the site, the specific page the customer is viewing, or a product on which the customer has clicked. At Bluefly.com, for example, if a visitor searches for more than three items in five minutes, thereby demonstrating more than a passing interest, Bluefly will display a pop-up window with a friendly face offering help.

The interactive nature of the Internet also provides an opportunity for retailers to personalize their offerings for each of their customers. For example, Amazon.com serves customers a personalized landing page with information about books and other products of interest based on the customer's past purchases and search behaviour on the website. Amazon also sends interested customers customized e-mail messages that notify them that their favourite author or recording artist has published a new book or released a new CD. Another personalization opportunity is presenting customers with recommendations of complementary merchandise. Just as a well-trained salesperson would make recommendations to customers before checkout, an interactive web page can make suggestions to shoppers about additional items that they might like to consider.

Online Retail in Canada   Despite Canada's reputation as one of the world's most wired and digitally social people, Canadians spent only $18 billion online in 2010, or 3.4 percent of total retail sales, according to Boston

Helping Couples Get Ready for the Big Day

The typical engagement and wedding planning process lasts 14 months, costs almost $25 000, and involves many emotionally charged decisions, such as how many and which people to invite, what print style to use on the invitations, where to hold the reception, what music to play during the ceremony, and what gifts to list in the bridal registry. Traditionally, the bride's family managed the wedding planning process. With more couples getting married when they are older, both working, and living farther from their parents, planning a wedding has become much more challenging.

Internet wedding sites, such as The Knot (www.theknot.com) and the WeddingChannel (www.weddingchannel.com), offer couples and their families planning guides and

TheKnot.com offers information and merchandise to help couples prepare for their weddings.

advice. A budgeting tool allows the couple to enter a dollar amount (say, $9000) and the number of guests (30), and it calculates, on the basis of national averages, how much they can spend on elements such as the bride's dress ($540) and bouquet ($68). With the tool, couples can also enter what they have actually spent, and it recalculates the sums that can be spent elsewhere. A planning tool is available to make sure arrangements are made, and reminders are e-mailed to the couple when key dates loom.

Couples can chat with experts and other couples on issues such as dealing with a micromanaging mother-

in-law or divorced parents. Gift registries can be created at different retailers and broadcast to guests through e-mail. Couples can collect information from home rather than having to make visits to different suppliers. They can narrow the list of potential places for the reception by looking at photos on the web, and they can download bands' audio clips from the web instead of going to hear different bands play. Hotel reservations for out-of-town guests can be made over the Internet, and maps can be created to show those guests how to get to the hotel and reception. Finally, couples can have their own personal site on which they post their wedding pictures.

Sources: www.weddingchannel.com; www.theknot.com (accessed January 10, 2010).

Consulting Group—well behind other developed countries such as the United States at 5 percent and the United Kingdom at 13.5 percent, as well as behind the G20 average of 6 percent.[47] Even though Canadians spend more time online compared with all other countries, with the average being 24 hours per week, online sales in Canada have some catching up to do. The online market is not as mature as the U.S. (less than 1/10 the size of the U.S.; see Exhibit 2–9), where a long history of catalogue sales, better shipping infrastructure, and other factors have made online buying a fast friend to many consumers.[48]

Large Canadian retailers have struggled to serve their customers on the web: Canadian Tire abandoned online selling three years ago, and while it now has plans to return, the only thing customers can buy through its website are tires. Hudson's Bay Company is straggling back after shutting down its online efforts in 2009. And Holt Renfrew and Shoppers Drug Mart offer only e-flyers and directions to their nearest stores online. Their U.S. peers, meanwhile, operate full e-stores.[49]

Some blame the lack of a catalogue-buying tradition in Canada; others blame our sprawling geography that

exhibit 2–9 Canada Grabs Greater Share of E-commerce Sales in North America

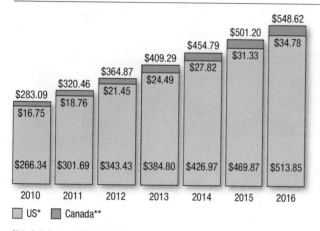

	2010	2011	2012	2013	2014	2015	2016
Total	$283.09	$320.46	$364.87	$409.29	$454.79	$501.20	$548.62
Canada**	$16.75	$18.76	$21.45	$24.49	$27.82	$31.33	$34.78
US*	$266.34	$301.69	$343.43	$384.80	$426.97	$469.87	$513.85

☐ US*   ☐ Canada**

Note: includes travel, digital downloads and event tickets; excludes online gaming; *excludes event tickets, **converted at the exchange rate of US$1=CA$0.99; numbers may not add up to total due to rounding

Source: "Canada Grabs Greater Share of Ecommerce Sales in North America," eMarketer.com, September 7, 2012, http://www.emarketer.com/Article/Canada-Grabs-Greater-Share-of-Ecommerce-Sales-North-America/1009328 (accessed November 25, 2013).

catalogue channel
A nonstore retail format in which the retailer communicates directly with customers using catalogues sent through the mail.

can make shipping slow and expensive. Four in ten dollars spent online in Canada goes abroad, meaning a large portion of spending isn't going back into the Canadian economy.[51] Getting e-commerce right needs to be part of making the Canadian retail sector more productive and competitive (see Exhibit 2–10).

Catalogue Channel

The **catalogue channel** is a nonstore retail channel in which the retail offering is communicated to customers through a catalogue, whereas direct-mail retailers communicate with their customers using letters and brochures. Historically, catalogue and direct-mail retailing were most successful with rural consumers, who lacked ready access to retail stores. Today's consumers enjoy the convenience of shopping by catalogue. The major catalogue retailers have embraced a multichannel strategy by integrating the Internet into their catalogue operations. Customers often get a catalogue in the mail, look it over, and go to the Internet for more information and to place an order. The merchandise categories with the greatest catalogue sales are drugs and beauty aids, computers and software, clothing and accessories, furniture and housewares, and books, music, and magazines.[52]

In recent years, a new breed of catalogue has sprung up to give this old form of retailing a new look—niche

catalogue retailing. These retailers are focused on niche markets, such as retired middle-class women or young mothers. Artigiano, for example, sells high-end Italian fashion from catalogues and the web, while the U.S.-based Lollipop Moon sells hard-to-find, trendy baby clothing. The success of these retailers comes down to a number of factors: People are increasingly prepared to pay more for quality products; they prefer niche to mass-market brands; and they like the convenience of being able to shop and order from home.

As indicated in Exhibit 2–11, catalogue retailers are best positioned to exploit an electronic retail channel. They have very efficient systems for taking orders from individual customers, packaging the merchandise ordered for shipping, delivering it to homes, and handling returned merchandise. They also have extensive information about their customers and database management strategies to effectively personalize service. Finally, the visual merchandising skills necessary for preparing catalogues are similar to those needed in setting up an effective website.

The IKEA catalogue, considered to be the main marketing tool of the company, first published in Sweden in 1951 and is distributed both by mail and in store for no charge to its customers. The Swedish home furnishing retailer printed and distributed its IKEA catalogue to over 200 million consumers worldwide in 62 versions and 42 countries in 2012 and inspired people around the world to create homes that they love.[53] IKEA customers have also been able to access the catalogue online since 2011 and can now also use the IKEA Catalogue App on their smartphone and tablet to scan select pages to unlock films, interactive experiences, photo galleries, and more home furnishing inspiration.[54]

exhibit 2–10 Online Shoppers Are Spending More When They Use Multiple Channels

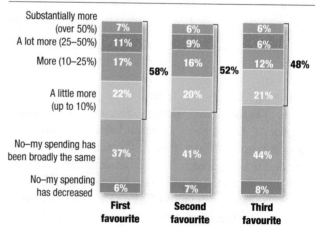

Source: *2013 Global Multi-channel Retail Survey*, PwC, Figure 17, p. 34; http://www.pwc.com/ca/en/retail-consumer/multi-channel-customer-survey-canadian-perspective.jhtml.

exhibit 2–11 Capabilities Needed to Successfully Sell Merchandise Online

Capabilities	Electronic-only Retailers	Catalogue Retailers	Store-based Retailers	Merchandise Manufacturers
Strong brand name and image to build traffic and reduce customers' perceived risk	Low	Medium to high	High	Medium to high
Availability of customer information to tailor presentations	Medium to high	High	Medium to high	Low
Providing and managing complementary merchandise and services	High	High	High	Medium
Offering unique merchandise	Low	Medium to high	Medium to high	High
Presenting merchandise and information in electronic format	High	High	Medium to high	Medium
Efficient distribution system to deliver merchandise to homes and accept returns	Low	Medium to high	High	Low

The Internet has become a natural extension to most cataloguers' selling strategy; 95 percent of catalogues describe themselves as multichannel retailers, with 53 percent defining their companies as catalogue/Internet/retail and 42 percent as catalogue/Internet.[55] Although firms spend millions of dollars mailing catalogues, only about 1.3 percent of the catalogues mailed generate a direct sale.[56] The use of catalogues is coming under attack from consumer groups that believe that catalogues are an unnecessary waste of natural resources. In the U.S., catalogues account for 3 percent of the roughly 80 million tonnes of paper products used annually. That is more than either magazines or books.[57] Further, catalogues' share of sales is declining relative to the Internet. But catalogues are not going away. Analysts believe that their role is shifting from primarily generating sales to driving traffic to the Internet and physical stores.

Direct-mail retailers typically mail brochures and pamphlets to sell a specific product or service to customers at one point in time. For example, American Express sells a broad array of financial services targeted to the consumer. In addition to the focus on a specific product or service, most direct-mail retailers are primarily interested in making a single sale from a specific mailing, whereas catalogue retailers typically maintain relationships with customers over time.

The catalogue channel provides some benefits to customers, such as safety and convenience, that are associated with all nonstore channels. However, catalogues also have some unique convenience advantages over other nonstore formats.

Safety Security in malls and shopping areas is becoming an important concern for many shoppers, particularly the elderly. Nonstore retail channels enable customers to review merchandise and place orders from a safe environment—their home.[58]

Convenience Catalogues offer the convenience of looking at merchandise and placing an order from almost anywhere 24/7. However, catalogues are easier to browse through than websites. Consumers can refer to the information in a catalogue anytime by simply picking it up from the coffee table. They can take a catalogue to the beach and browse through it without an Internet connection. Finally, the information in a catalogue is easily accessible for a long period of time. However, it is important to note that the use of smartphones and tablets has changed how consumers can access and view information.

Direct Selling

Direct selling is a retail channel in which salespeople interact with customers face-to-face in a convenient location, either at the customer's home or at work. Direct salespeople demonstrate merchandise benefits and/or explain a service, take an order, and deliver the merchandise. Direct selling is a highly interactive retail channel in which considerable information is conveyed to customers through face-to-face discussions. However, providing this high level of information, including extensive demonstrations, is costly. Home parties organized by associates of the Pampered Chef are a method used to sell kitchenware.

The Canadian Direct Sellers Association (DSA) represents 50 companies with sales revenue of over $2 billion annually and accounts for over 16 percent of nonstore retail sales in Canada.[59] According to the Canadian DSA, over 900 000 Canadians are associated with the direct selling industry, and 91 percent of direct sellers in this country are women.[60] Annual U.S. sales through direct selling are over $30 billion; worldwide, they are more than $100 billion.[61] The largest categories of merchandise sold through direct selling are personal care (e.g., cosmetics, fragrances), home and family care (e.g., cooking, kitchenware), wellness (e.g., weight loss products, vitamins), and leisure and educational items (e.g., books, videos, toys). Similar

direct selling A retail format in which a salesperson, frequently an independent distributor, contacts a customer directly in a convenient location (either at a customer's home or at work), demonstrates merchandise benefits, takes an order, and delivers the merchandise to the customer.

to catalogue retailers and television shopping networks, direct sellers are using the Internet to complement their face-to-face selling. Approximately 73 percent of all direct sales are made face-to-face, mostly in homes.[62] Salespeople who work in direct sales are independent agents who are not employed by the direct sales firms but, rather, act as independent distributors, buying merchandise from the firms and then reselling it to customers. In addition, 87 percent of direct salespeople work part-time (fewer than 30 hours per week). In most cases, direct salespeople may sell their merchandise to anyone, but some companies, such as Avon, assign territories to salespeople who regularly contact households in their territory.

Two special types of direct selling are the party plan and multilevel systems. About one-quarter of all direct sales are made using a party plan system. Salespeople encourage customers to act as hosts and invite friends or co-workers to a "party" at which the merchandise is demonstrated.[63] Sales made at the party are influenced by the social relationship of the people attending with the host or hostess, who receives a gift or commission for arranging the party. At the party, the merchandise is demonstrated and attendees place orders. A party system can be, but does not have to be, used in a multilevel network.

Almost three-quarters of all direct sales are made through multilevel sales networks. In a multilevel system, independent businesspeople serve as master distributors, recruiting other people to become distributors in their network. The master distributors either buy merchandise from the firm and resell it to their distributors or receive a commission on all merchandise purchased by the distributors in their network. In addition to selling merchandise themselves, the master distributors are involved in recruiting and training other distributors.

Some multilevel direct selling firms are illegal pyramid schemes. A pyramid scheme develops when the firm and its program are designed to sell merchandise and services to other distributors rather than to end users. The founders and initial distributors in pyramid schemes profit from the inventory bought by later participants, but little merchandise is sold to consumers who use it.

Television Home Shopping

Television home shopping, also known as *T-commerce* or *teleshopping*, is a retail format in which customers watch a TV program demonstrating merchandise and

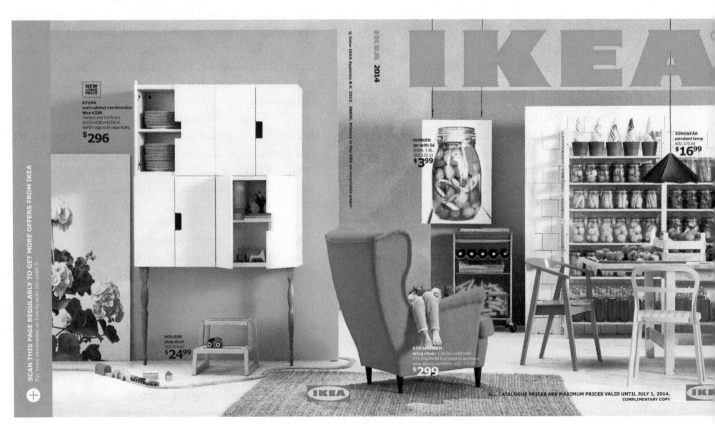

then place orders for the merchandise by telephone. Recent technology advances even allow viewers to purchase products using their TV's remote control.[64] The three forms of electronic home shopping retailing are:

- Cable channels dedicated to television shopping
- Infomercials
- Direct-response advertising

Infomercials are TV programs, typically 30 minutes long, that mix entertainment with product demonstrations and then solicit orders placed by telephone. Direct-response advertising includes advertisements on TV and radio that describe products and provide an opportunity for consumers to order them.

The Shopping Channel Facts

364: The number of days the channel broadcasts live (every day but Christmas).

18: The number of hours the channel broadcasts live each day.

10 000: The number of phone calls/e-mails/chats received in a day.

2 802 262: The number of phone calls/e-mails/chats received in 2012.

8 500 000: The number of homes The Shopping Channel programming reaches in Canada.

3 966 103: The number of items shipped in 2012.

16 000: The average number of packages the distribution centre ships a day.

208 727: The number of videos viewed on TheShoppingChannel.com on average per month.

3500: The number of BlackBerry PlayBooks sold in one day.

800: The number of products presented each week.

26 115: The number of videos the channel currently holds as resource material.

200: The number of operators in the channel's customer care centre.

24: The number of hours those operators staff the customer care centre.

6552: The hours of live TV produced by the channel each year.

Source: Paul Irish, "The Shopping Channel can be an alternative to crowded mall at Christmas," *Toronto Star*, December 6, 2012, http://www.thestar.com/life/2012/12/06/the_shopping_channel_can_be_an_alternative_to_crowded_mall_at_christmas.html.

The Shopping Channel is located in Mississauga, Ontario, and on any given day the business can move thousands of units of a single item, such as a necklace. The potential sales volume of the daily show stopper—the station's version of a door crasher—is staggering. For example, the company moved $4 million in Dell computers in one day. The Shopping Channel broadcasts 18 hours of live broadcasting a day. This is a multichannel retailer offering up bargains through TV cable/satellite households, The Shopping Channel website, catalogue, and soon via interactive television that combines television with a computer.

The logistical issues connected with television retailing are apparent when you consider 10 000 products in stock and between 200 to 1000 new items arriving each week. Every item must be photographed, videotaped, catalogued, and made ready for television and to accommodate online sales through www.theshoppingchannel.com.

Competitors to the Canadian Shopping Channel are home shopping networks out of the U.S. that broadcast through infomercials and online, Amazon and eBay, and Sears Canada, which offers a department store selection.

The major advantage of TV home shopping compared to catalogue retailing is that customers can see the merchandise demonstrated on the TV screen. However, customers can't examine a particular type of merchandise or a specific item when they want to, as they can with catalogues. They have to wait for the time when the merchandise shows up on the screen. To address this limitation, home shopping networks schedule categories of merchandise for specific times so that customers looking for specific merchandise can plan their viewing time.

Vending Machine Retailing

Vending machine retailing is a nonstore format in which merchandise or services are stored in a machine and dispensed to customers when they deposit cash or use a credit card. Vending machines are placed at convenient, high-traffic locations such as in the workplace, at the airport, or on university campuses, and primarily contain snacks or drinks.

Although $25.6 billion in goods is sold annually through vending machines in North America, vending machine sales growth is relatively slow, less than 5 percent, and closely mirrors the growth in the economy.[67] Vending machine sales growth has been declining during the past few years. The vast majority of vending machine sales are cold beverages, candy, and snacks, but sales in these categories are being adversely affected by growing concerns among consumers about healthy eating habits.

Technological developments in vending machine design may result in long-term sales growth. New video kiosk vending machines enable consumers to see the merchandise in use, get information about it, and use their credit cards to make a purchase.

The new vending machine designs also enable the retailers to increase the productivity of the machines. Electronic systems in the machine keep track of inventory, cash, and other operating conditions. Then radio devices transmit data back to a host computer. These data are analyzed, and communications are sent to route drivers telling them when stockouts and malfunctions occur.[68]

Svetlana Uduslivaia, senior research analyst with Euromonitor International, says vending operators are branching out from the traditional vending offerings of snacks and beverages in order to stay relevant to today's consumers. "Products that have not traditionally been a stronghold of the vending industry, for instance, consumer electronics (Apple and Best Buy) and skin care products (Sephora and Pro Active), are now starting to be sold through vending machines in the U.S. and Canada. Consumers are seeing them in airports, shopping malls, grocery stores, and department stores."[69]

Canadian retailer Mark's Work Wearhouse is experimenting with vending machines at two Ontario Go Transit bus terminals. "The theory is to be in more places, and places consumers may not have expected to see us," says Robin Lynas, vice-president of corporate development.[70]

"DVD rentals [through vending machines], which have been fairly successful in the U.S., are now coming into Canada as well. With the closure of Blockbuster locations and the general lack of extensive DVD rentals, industries are trying to see if they can fill the void and benefit from that," Uduslivaia says.

One new retail concept, Get & Go Express, combines a convenience store with vending machines.[71] No one works at these stores, nothing gets stolen, and they are open 24 hours a day, 7 days a week. The "store" consists of 16 vending machines that accept credit or debit cards and cash. They supply up to 500 different varieties of snacks, packaged beverages, fresh sandwiches, and DVD rentals but none of the traditional convenience store merchandise, like tobacco, gasoline, lottery tickets, or alcoholic beverages.

Services Retailing   LO 4

The retail firms discussed in the previous sections sell products to consumers. However, **services retailers**, firms selling primarily services rather than merchandise, are a large and growing part of the retail industry. Consider a typical Saturday. After a bagel and cup of coffee at a nearby Tim Hortons, you go to the laundromat to wash and dry your clothes, drop a suit off at a dry cleaner, leave film to be developed at a Shoppers Drug Mart, and make your way to the Jiffy Lube to have your car's oil changed. Since you are in a hurry, you drive through a Taco Bell so that you can eat lunch quickly and not be late for your haircut at 1 P.M. By midafternoon, you're ready for a swim at your health club. After stopping at home for a change of clothes, you're off to dinner, a movie, and dancing with a friend. Finally, you end your day with a caffe latte at Starbucks, having interacted with ten different services retailers during the day.

There are several trends that suggest considerable future growth in services retailing. For example, the

These are retailers, too. You start the day with a bagel, go to the bank, and then burn off the calories at the fitness centre.

aging of the population will increase demand for health services. Younger people too are spending increasing amounts of time and money on health and fitness. Parents in two-income families are willing to pay to have their homes cleaned, lawns maintained, clothes washed and pressed, and meals prepared so that they can spend more time with their families.

There is a wide variety of services retailers. These companies are retailers because they sell goods and services to consumers. However, some of these companies are not just retailers. For example, airlines, banks, hotels, and insurance and express mail companies sell their services to businesses as well as consumers. Also, a large number of services retailers, such as lawyers, doctors, and dry cleaners, focus on local markets and do not have a Canada-wide presence.

Many organizations—such as banks, hospitals, health spas, legal clinics, entertainment firms, and universities—that offer services to consumers traditionally haven't considered themselves as retailers. Due to increased competition, these organizations are adopting retailing principles to attract customers and satisfy their needs.

All retailers provide goods and services for their customers. However, the emphasis placed on the merchandise versus the services differs across retail formats, as Exhibit 2–12 shows. On the left side of the exhibit are supermarkets and warehouse clubs. These retail formats consist of self-service stores that offer very few services. However, these formats do offer a few services, such as cheque cashing and some assistance from store employees. Moving along the continuum from left to right, we find category specialists, which also emphasize self-service but have employees who can answer questions, demonstrate merchandise, and make recommendations. Next, department and specialty stores provide even higher levels of service. In addition to assistance from sales associates, these stores offer services such as gift wrapping, bridal registries, and alterations.

Optical centres and restaurants lie somewhere in the middle of the merchandise/service continuum. In addition to selling frames, eyeglasses, and contact lenses, optical centres also provide important services such as eye examinations and eyeglass fittings. Similarly, restaurants offer food plus a place to eat, music in the background, a pleasant ambience, and table service. As we move to the right end of the continuum, we encounter retailers whose offering is primarily services. However, even these retailers have some products associated with the services offered, such as a meal on the airplane or a chequebook at a bank. Services retailers are defined as retailers for which the major aspect of their offerings is services versus merchandise.

Differences between Services and Merchandise Retailers

As a retailer falls more to the right on the merchandise/service continuum, services become a more important aspect of the retailer's offering. Four important differences in the nature of the offering provided by services and merchandise retailers are as follows:

- Intangibility
- Simultaneous production and consumption
- Perishability
- Inconsistency of the offering to customers[72]

Intangibility Services are generally intangible—customers cannot see, touch, or feel them. They are performances or actions rather than objects. For example, health care services cannot be seen or touched by a patient. Even after diagnosis and treatment, the patient may not realize the full extent of the service that has been performed.

Services retailers also have difficulty in evaluating the quality of services they are providing. To evaluate

exhibit 2–12 Merchandise/Service Continuum

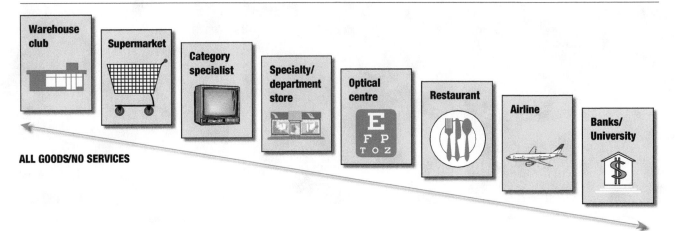

the quality of their offering, services retailers emphasize soliciting customer evaluations and complaints.

Simultaneous Production and Consumption

Products are typically made in a factory, stored and sold by a retailer, and then used by consumers in their homes. Service providers, on the other hand, create and deliver the service as the customer is consuming it. For example, when you eat at a restaurant, the meal is prepared and consumed almost at the same time.

Because services are produced and consumed at the same time, it is difficult to reduce costs through mass production. For this reason, most services retailers are small, local firms. Large national retailers are able to reduce costs by "industrializing" the services they offer. They make substantial investments in equipment and training to provide a uniform service. For example, McDonald's has a detailed procedure for cooking french fries and hamburgers to make sure they come out the same whether cooked in Paris, France; Paris, Ontario; or Paris, Illinois.

Perishability

Because the creation and consumption of services are inseparable, services are perishable. They can't be saved, stored, or resold. This is in contrast to merchandise that can be held in inventory until a customer is ready to buy it.

Due to the perishability of services, an important aspect of services retailing is matching supply and demand. Most services retailers have a capacity constraint, and the capacity cannot be changed easily. There is a fixed number of tables in a restaurant, seats in a classroom, and beds in a hospital, as well as a finite amount of electricity that can be generated by a power plant. To increase capacity, services retailers need to make major investments such as buying more airplanes.

In addition, demand for service varies considerably over time. Consumers are most likely to fly on airplanes during holidays and the summer, and eat in restaurants at lunch and dinner time. Thus, services retailers often have times when their services are underutilized and other times when they have to turn customers away because they can't accommodate them.

Services retailers use a variety of programs to match demand and supply. For example, airlines and hotels set lower prices on weekends when they have excess capacity because businesspeople aren't travelling.

Inconsistency

Merchandise is often produced by machines with very tight quality control so that customers are reasonably assured that, for example, all boxes of a cereal will be identical. Because services are performances produced by people (employees and customers), no two services will be identical. The waiter at a restaurant can be in a bad mood and make your dining experience a disaster.

Thus, an important challenge for services retailers is to provide consistently high-quality services. Services retailers expend considerable time and effort selecting, training, managing, and motivating their service providers.

Multichannel Retailing

Retailers were classified either as store-based or nonstore (electronic, catalogue/direct mail, direct selling, TV home shopping, and vending machine) retailers. However, many retail firms use more than one channel to reach their customers. For example, Gateway started as an electronic retailer and has opened up stores; Amazon.com now distributes a catalogue; and Eddie Bauer and Sears interface with customers through their stores, catalogues, and websites.

A **multichannel retailer** is a retailer that sells merchandise or services through more than one channel. Single-channel retailers are evolving into multichannel retailers to attract and satisfy more customers. By using a combination of channels, retailers can exploit the unique benefits provided by each channel.

Exhibit 2-13 lists the unique benefits of stores, catalogues, and the Internet. These benefits illustrate how the channels can be used to complement each other.[73]

exhibit 2-13   Channel Benefits

Stores	Catalogue	Internet
• Browsing • Touching and feeling products • Personal service • Cash payment • Immediate gratification • Entertainment and social interaction	• Convenience • Portability; easily accessible • Safety • Visual presentation	• Convenience • Safety • Broad and deep selection • Extensive and timely information • Personalization • Products and services available anytime/anywhere

Store Channel

Stores offer a number of benefits to customers that they cannot get when shopping through catalogues and the Internet.

The climbing wall in a Mountain Equipment Co-op store provides an exciting, entertaining experience for customers that cannot be matched by the retailer's catalogue and Internet offerings.

Browsing Although many consumers surf the Internet and look through catalogues for ideas, most consumers still prefer browsing in stores.

Touching and Feeling Products Perhaps the greatest benefit offered by stores is the opportunity for customers to use all of their senses when examining products—touching, smelling, tasting, seeing, and hearing.

Personal Service Although shoppers can be critical of the personal service they get in stores, sales associates still have the capability of providing meaningful, personalized information.

Cash Payment Stores are the only channel that accepts cash payments.

Immediate Gratification Stores have the advantage of allowing customers to get the merchandise immediately after they buy it.

Entertainment and Social Experience In-store shopping can be a stimulating experience for some people, providing a break in their daily routine and enabling them to interact with friends. Paco Underhill, author of *How We Shop*, points out, "Stores are a social experience. I don't care how many chat rooms there are on a site, they will never provide what the experience of bricks-and-mortar shopping provides for all five senses, if not six or seven."[74]

multichannel retailer Retailer that sells merchandise or services through more than one channel.

DID YOU KNOW?

Forty percent of consumers said they rely more on online recommendations from others when considering a purchase than on marketing messages from retailers, and 25 percent said they use smartphones to read or view consumer-written reviews.[75]

Convenience All nonstore formats offer the convenience of looking at merchandise and placing an order any day at any time from almost anywhere.

Safety Nonstore retail formats have an advantage over store-based retailers by enabling customers to review merchandise and place orders from a safe environment—their homes.[78]

Quality of Visual Presentation The photographs of merchandise in catalogues, although not as useful as in-store presentations, are superior to the visual information that can be displayed on a CRT screen.

LO 6 Tuning into the Multichannel Universe

Consumers desire a seamless experience when interacting with multichannel retailers. They want to be recognized, whether they interact with a sales associate or kiosk in-store; log on to the retailer's website through a PC, smartphone, or tablet; or contact the retailer's call centre by telephone. Customers may want to buy a product through the retailer's Internet or catalogue channel, and pick it up or return it to a local store; find out if a product offered on the Internet channel is available at a local store; and, when unable to find a product in a store, determine whether it is available for home delivery through the retailer's Internet channel.

Retailers also benefit by using multiple channels synergistically. Multichannel retailers can use one channel to promote the services offered by other channels. For example, the URL of a store's website can be advertised on in-store signs, shopping bags, credit card billing statements, point-of-sale (POS) receipts, and the print or broadcast advertising used to promote the store. The physical stores and catalogues are also advertisements for a retailer's other channels. The retailer's electronic channel can be used to stimulate store visits by announcing special store events and promotions. Multichannel retailers can leverage their stores to lower the cost of fulfilling orders and processing returned merchandise. They can use their stores as "warehouses" for gathering merchandise for delivery to customers. Customers also can be offered the opportunity to pick up and return merchandise at the retailer's stores rather than pay shipping charges. Many retailers will waive shipping charges when orders are

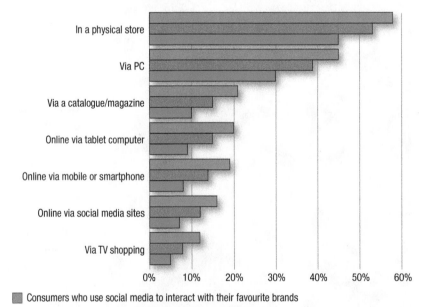

Social Brand Lovers Shop More Often in Every Channel

- In a physical store
- Via PC
- Via a catalogue/magazine
- Online via tablet computer
- Online via mobile or smartphone
- Online via social media sites
- Via TV shopping

0%   10%   20%   30%   40%   50%   60%

- Consumers who use social media to interact with their favourite brands
- Consumers who use social media to follow their favourite brands or retailers
- Total sample

Source: "Demystifying the Online Shopper: 10 Myths of Multi-Channel Retailing," PwC, p. 7, http://www.pwc.com/ca/en/retail-consumer/multi-channel-customer-survey-canadian-perspective.jhtml (accessed October 1, 2013).

placed online or through the catalogue if the customer physically comes into the store.

The retail store is not dead and it's not going away. But it will evolve as the lines between the physical and virtual worlds continue to blur and customers demand an integrated experience across channels.[79] However, providing this seamless experience for customers and exploiting the synergies between channels is challenging. Retailers need to consider how to connect with customers across channels to provide them with an immersive and meaningful brand experience. After all, consumers think of "shopping"—whether it is online, in-store, with a catalogue, or on mobile device—as one shopping experience, and therefore, so must retailers.[80]

M-Commerce

Customers can access a retailer's Internet channel using a variety of devices, ranging from a desktop computer to a mobile phone or tablet. Due to the rapid growth of domestic and international broadband access through mobile devices, retailers are very interested in developing m-commerce—the purchase of products and services through mobile devices. In addition, retailers have developed apps—small computer programs—that enable mobile device users to engage in an activity such as shopping. For example, The Brick, working with the development company Imagiu Software Ltd., has an app that allows consumers to scan QR codes on furniture tags and size the furniture against a photo of a room in their home.

The adoption of mobile devices by consumers is growing at a rapid rate. According to research conducted by Deloitte Consulting LLP, mobile (defined as smartphones) influences 5.1 percent of all retail store sales in the United States.[81] Mobile is a natural fit for the Canadian consumer, as Canadians are adopting mobile technology at a similar pace to the U.S. Many retailers are currently focusing on optimizing their websites for mobile devices. Strategies vary from having a mobile site with the same functionality as their websites, to developing sites that focus on what consumers would mainly need to access when they are out and about doing their shopping (for example, store locations, store hours, store contact information, etc.). According to Deloitte's research and analysis, the biggest impact of smartphones isn't direct sales generated through the mobile channel, but rather the influence they exert over traditional in-store sales to drive in-store conversion and in-store average order size.[82]

- Seventy percent of Canadians have mobile phones, and 30 percent of these are smartphones, and that number is rising fast.

m-commerce The purchase of products and services through mobile devices.

- Roughly 58 percent of consumers who own a smartphone have used it for store-related shopping.

- Twenty-three percent of smartphone users who mobile-shop will research on the smartphone, visit the store to check out the product, and then purchase online (using a computer or Internet-enabled device).[83]

- Among smartphone shoppers, the percentage who use their smartphones for shopping varies by store category, from 49 percent in electronics and appliances stores to 19 percent in convenience stores and gas stations.

- Once consumers start using their smartphones for shopping, they tend to use them a lot—typically for 50 to 60 percent of their store shopping trips, depending on the store category.

Mobile's influence is expected to grow exponentially over the next few years, driven by a perfect storm of rising smartphone penetration, increased adoption by shoppers, decreasing barriers to use, and improved mobile functionality for retail applications.[84] With 17 to 21 percent of store sales potentially being mobile-influenced by 2016,[85] store-based retailers should consider mobile as a strategic imperative because it can impact the entire business, not just online or m-commerce. Retailers need to understand how their consumers may use their mobile devices, whether it is as simple as store locations or as complex as understanding what subset of their inventory consumers would be likely to buy through a mobile device.

Consumer needs vary by product and shopping trip, and retailers need to customize mobile app capabilities accordingly. Smartphones are most likely to be used for store-related shopping when the customer is close to or at the point of making a purchase, rather than as a passive shopping device. Deloitte's Mobile Influence Survey 2012 indicated that over 60 percent of mobile shoppers use their smartphones while in a store, and another 50 percent while on the way to a store. Retail analysts suggest that today's consumers merely use retail stores as a showroom before buying elsewhere. Deloitte's survey results echoed this threat, finding that 37 percent of shoppers surveyed who used a smartphone on their last trip used an external app or website (such as a price comparison tool or deal finder).[86]

The mobile landscape is changing at a rapid rate, and retailers need to consider the ways in which they can leverage the mobile capabilities in ways to best serve their customers. Mobile offers retailers a means to influence sales revenue and potentially improve conversion rates

omni-channel retailing
Seamless integration between all channels so that shoppers can shop any way they want with the exact same results.

in-store kiosks
Spaces located within stores containing a computer connected to the store's central offices or to the Internet.

by engaging with customers and thereby significantly improving the customer experience.

The Rise of Omni-Channel Retailing

This new phrase has surfaced recently in retail and is being hyped as "the next big trend." Omni-channel is definitely an iteration of multichannel as it is still a marketing strategy in which the retailer offers multiple ways for shoppers to buy its products, but with a stronger focus on a seamless approach to the customer experience through all available shopping channels. Multichannel means that the retailer and its branded products are on a variety of the key channels (store, online, mobile, TV, catalogue, or whichever medium the customer is interested in buying). Omni-channel retailing requires *seamless integration* between all channels so that shoppers can shop any way they want with the *exact same results*. In a blog post on Econsultancy, Darren Hitchcock defines omni-channel retailing as "an integrated sales experience that melds the advantages of physical stores with the information-rich

experience of online shopping."[87] With an omni-channel strategy, retailers allow customers to experience the brand, not a channel within the brand. Merchandise, promotions, pricing, customer service, and communications are not channel specific, but rather are consistent across all of the retail channels, not just one or two. That means that whatever channel the customers touch, they will see the same stock at the same price with the same promotions merchandised in the same way and that connection is made and updated in real time.[88] The physical stores and e-commerce sites become an extension of the supply chain in which consumers can make purchases, but they are researched through other "channels" of communication.[89]

With an omni-channel strategy, each channel needs to be *aware* of the other if the experience is to be seamless. The retail industry is already dominated by performance marketing (site optimization, monetization modelling, search engine optimization, and paid search); an omni-channel strategy requires retailers to pay more attention to tagging and reporting, and then pulling all of the data collected together to build a sophisticated consumer profile. Awareness and seamlessness are possible only if retailers are integrating that customer and shopping data with behavioural profiling and preferences and being rigorous about adding to it at every opportunity. Consumers move from channel to channel on a regular basis, often to perform the same task, and they have expectations that what they do in one place will influence the experience in another. The challenge for retailers is to tell a continuous story that plays out whenever or wherever the consumer interacts with their brand.[90]

In-Store Electronic Kiosks

Another multichannel approach to retailing is the addition of the electronic kiosk. In-store kiosks are spaces located within stores containing a computer connected to the store's central offices or to the Internet. In-store kiosks can be used by customers or salespeople to order merchandise through a retailer's electronic channel, check on product availability at distribution centres or other stores, get more information about the merchandise, and scan bar codes to check the prices. Retailers are interested in installing these kiosks because they create a synergy between the store and the Internet site. Kiosks provide additional assortment choices that aren't available in stores. For instance, The Source makes slower-moving electronic accessories available at its kiosks so that it doesn't have to carry them in its stores.[91] The typical Staples store has 9000 SKUs, compared to 100 000 offered via in-store kiosks.[92]

Starbucks Monetizing Its Multichannel Strategy

- Starbucks uses over 11 online channels to engage (Facebook and Twitter to reach, engage, and solicit feedback) and collaborate with customers (improve offerings).
- Starbucks uses location-based services (Foursquare and Placecast) to offer rewards (mobile coupons) to customers.
- Starbucks has launched a mobile loyalty and commerce platform to further monetize mobility (3.6 million customers in My Starbucks Rewards program).
- Starbucks launched e-gift cards, which integrate with Facebook, and m-gift cards via mobile app. In 2011, customers loaded $2.4 billion in credits on prepaid loyalty cards.
- Starbucks has monetized its social media by creating a journey for its customers.
- Starbucks processed more than 26 million mobile payments in 2011.

Source: Deloitte, *Retail's changing landscape: Evolving from a multichannel to an omni-channel customer experience,* May 24, 2012, p. 27.

Smartphones Are a Multi-Activity Portal

83% Communication

E-mailed (sent or read)	75%
Accessed a social network (e.g., updated a status message checked messages or friends' pages)	64%

53% Stay Informed

Read news on newspaper or magazine portals	38%
Reviewed websites blogs or message boards	37%

88% Entertainment

Browsed the Internet	73%
Played games	63%
Listened to music	61%
Watched videos on a video-sharing website (e.g., YouTube.com)	54%

Source: Our Mobile Planet: United States, Google/Ipsos OTX MediaCT, US, May 2012
Base: Private smartphone users who use the internet in general, Smartphone n= 1,000
Q23: Which of the following activities do you do with your smartphone? Please indicate whether you ever do this at all.

Smartphones Allow Users to Research Products Anytime, Anywhere

Place of Search

58% At home

43% On the go

31% In a store

Home	58%
On the go	43%
In a store	31%
Work	29%
Restaurant	19%
At a social gathering	13%
Café or coffee shop	12%

Source: Our Mobile Planet: United States, Google/Ipsos OTX MediaCT, US, May 2012
Base: Private smartphone users who use the internet in general, Smartphone n= 1,000
Q51a: And where were you when you researched for products or services with your smartphone?

will use them. Gap Inc. abandoned its program because shoppers didn't use them enough.[96] Finally, there are significant costs in maintaining the kiosks—making sure they are working properly.

Customer Service Using Technology Many retailers are installing kiosks with broadband Internet access in the stores. In addition to offering customers the opportunity to order merchandise not available in the store, kiosks can provide routine customer service, freeing employees to deal with more demanding customer requests and problems. For example, customers can use kiosks to locate merchandise in the store and to inquire whether specific products, brands, and sizes are available in the store. Kiosks can also be used to automate existing store services such as gift registry management, rain checks, film drop-off, and credit applications, and to preorder service for bakeries and delicatessens.

Customers can use a kiosk to find out more information about products and how they are used. A Best Buy customer can use a kiosk to provide side-by-side comparisons of two DVD players and to find more detailed information than is available from the shelf tag or from a sales associate. The customer can also access evaluations of the models as reported by *Consumer Reports*. The information provided by the kiosk could be tailored to specific customers by accessing the retailer's customer database. For example, a customer who is considering a new set of speakers might not remember the preamplifier purchased previously from Best Buy. This customer might not know whether the speakers are compatible with the preamplifier or what cables are needed to connect the new speakers. These concerns could be addressed by accessing the retailer's customer database through the kiosk.

Kiosks can also be used to provide customized solutions. For example, a customer, perhaps with the assistance of a salesperson, wants to design a home entertainment system.

Do kiosks cannibalize store sales? Yes, but only initially. Shoppers who purchase in stores and online from an in-store kiosk tend to buy more. When REI installed in-store kiosks, it found that customers who shop both online and in the store spend 22 percent more than those who buy only from traditional stores.[93] Staples provided an incentive to store managers to push the use of kiosks. Online sales are credited to the stores from which they're placed.[94]

There are downsides to making investments in these kiosks, however. First, they can be expensive—anywhere from $3000 to $25 000 per kiosk.[95] Second, once the investment is made, there is no guarantee that customers

DID YOU KNOW?

In January 2013, Sport Chek opened a concept store in Toronto with more than 140 digital screens to experiment with a mixed digital and retail experience.[97]

A kiosk could allow the customer to see what the system would look like after setup. Music store customers could use a kiosk to review and select tracks and make a custom compact disc. Finally, customers could use a kiosk to see how different colour cosmetics would look on them without having to apply the cosmetics. These types of applications could complement the efforts of salespeople and improve the service they can offer to customers.[99]

Integrated Concept   In summary, to provide this same face to a customer across multiple channels, retailers need to integrate their customer databases and systems used to support each channel.[100] In addition to the information technology issues, other critical issues facing retailers that desire to provide an integrated, customer-centric offering involve:

- Centralized customer database
- Brand image
- Merchandise assortment
- Pricing[101]

Centralized Customer Database   While there are differences in opinion about whether to integrate or separately manage many key multichannel activities, there is a general consensus on the need to establish a centralized customer data warehouse with a complete history of each customer's interaction with the retailer.[102] The centralized customer data warehouse is crucial for exploiting the ability to collect detailed customer data through the Internet channel and providing a seamless experience for customers when they interact with the retailer through multiple channels.

Brand Image   Multichannel retailers need to project the same image to their customers through all channels. For example, Talbots reinforces its image of classic-style apparel and excellent customer service in its stores, catalogues, and website. Customers enter the website through an image of the red doors used in its stores and are greeted by "Always classic, never closed." At the website, customers can consult an online style guide offering seasonal fashion tips and articles about how to buy the right size swimsuit, the art of layering, and petite sizing. Talbots' commitment to "friendly" service is reinforced by the availability of 24/7 personal service.

Mountain Equipment Co-op (MEC) reinforces its image of selling high-quality, environmentally friendly sports equipment, not fashion, in the descriptions of MEC products. MEC's concerns about the environment are communicated by carefully engineered stores and using recycled polyester in many of its clothes, as well as only organic, rather than pesticide-intensive, cotton. Its web blog, **blog.mec.ca**, is dedicated to essays and other features on sports, innovative design, and environmental activism. Retailing View 2.3 describes how Build-A-Bear Workshop uses multiple channels to build and reinforce its brand image.

Merchandise Assortment   Typically, customers expect that everything they see in a retailer's store will also be available on its website. A significant product overlap across channels reinforces the one-brand image in the customer's mind. The trend now is to integrate the merchandise offerings across channels.

Multichannel retailers often offer a broader and deeper merchandise assortment through their Internet channel than through their store channel. The Internet channel is more efficient for selling merchandise that does not have broad appeal.

The channels also differ in terms of their effectiveness in generating sales for types of merchandise. For example, the store channel is better suited for selling products with important "touch-and-feel" attributes such as the fit of a shirt, the taste of an ice cream flavour, or the smell of a perfume. On the other hand, an Internet channel might be just as effective as a store channel for selling products with important "look-and-see" attributes such as price, colour, and grams of fat. Evaluating these products does not require senses beyond sight. Because of the problems of providing touch-and-feel information, apparel retailers experience return rates of more than 20 percent on purchases made through an electronic channel but only 10 percent on purchases made in-store.

Pricing   Pricing is another difficult decision for a multichannel retailer. Customers expect pricing consistency across channels (excluding shipping charges and sales tax). However, in some cases, retailers need to adjust their pricing strategy because of the competition they face in different channels. For example, chapters.indigo.ca offers lower prices over its electronic channel to compete effectively against Amazon.com.

Retailers with stores in multiple markets often set different prices for the same merchandise to deal with differences in local competition. Typical customers do not notice these price differences because they are exposed

The Build-A-Bear Workshop Uses Multiple Channels to Enhance Its Image

The Build-A-Bear Workshop creates a memorable experience for children that contributes to its strong brand image. Children enter the store, choose the type of animal, stuff and dress the animal, and then bring the stuffed animal to life by inserting a heart, giving it a name, and registering it. The child leaves the store with a new furry friend and its birth certificate. "Kids today move seamlessly between online and real-world play," says Dave Finnegan, Build-A-Bear Workshop's chief information and logistics bear. "We're already an interactive brand and a place where kids use their imagination, creativity, and self-expression to have fun. All of this interactive customization makes things come to life in a new way."

The Build-A-Bear Internet channel (www.buildabearville.com) reinforces and extends its brand image. At the website, children can create an avatar for themselves and choose a gender, hair style, eye colour, skin tone, and clothing style. When the code on the birth certificate of the animal bought in the store is entered, the animal springs to life on the website, appearing in a backpack carried by the avatar. Together, the child and the animal can play games, learn, and interact with other avatars and their furry friends.

Each Build-A-Bear animal has a unique virtual item that comes with it. Children can trade or collect the items in Bearville. Bearville residents receive a Cub Condo, which they can paint and decorate, and to which they can invite guests. They also can purchase virtual items for their Cub Condo or outfits for themselves or their animal. The virtual avatar earns points when a "real" child makes a purchase in a Build-A-Bear store. The receipt from the purchase has a code that the child redeems online for Bear Bucks.

Build-A-Bear also tries to make sure the site is safe. When a child signs up, parents receive an e-mail inviting them to select and control communication options based on age and comfort level. Build-A-Bear also monitors the site for safe socialization. Thus, Build-A-Bear uses its Internet channel to enhance its image and encourage children to continue their interaction with the retailer and visit its stores multiple times.

The Build-A-Bearville website (left) reinforces its brand image generated by its stores (right).

Sources: Sandy Smith, "Beary Interactive: Build-A-Bear Is Hands-On in Kids' Real and Virtual Worlds," *Stores*, June 2009; Samantha Murphy, "New to the Neighborhood," *Chain Store Age*, February 2008, p. 51.

only to the prices in their local markets. Multichannel retailers may have difficulties sustaining these regional price differences when customers can easily check prices on the Internet.

Multichannel retailers are beginning to offer new types of pricing, such as auctions, that take advantage of the unique properties of the Internet.

Reduction of Channel Migration The availability of an Internet channel enables customers to easily search for information about products and their prices. Browsing on the Internet channel and purchasing the merchandise at a store is the most common use of multiple channels during a shopping episode. Many consumers are now simply accessing the Internet on smartphones or tablets to browse social networks or shopping applications to find product information, read customer reviews, compare prices, or buy items.[103] In a recent Deloitte study, 42 percent of shoppers used smartphones for shopping-related activities at least once in the past year for apparel, while 48 percent used devices to shop for consumer electronics.[104]

wholesale-sponsored voluntary coopera- tive group An orga- nization operated by a wholesaler offering a merchandising pro- gram to small, inde- pendent retailers on a voluntary basis.

retail chain A firm that consists of mul- tiple retail units under common ownership and usually has some centralization of deci- sion making in defining and implementing its strategy.

DID YOU KNOW?

With 79 percent of Canadian smartphone users unable to leave their homes without their device, and 60 percent having used their smartphone to access a web page every day over the past seven days, smartphones and tablets can officially be considered to be Canadian consumers' companions.[105]

However, multichannel retailers want to prevent channel migration— consumers' collecting information about products and pricing on their channels and then buying the prod- uct from a competitor.[106] Retail- ers want customers to both search for information and complete the transaction through their channels, but the low cost of searching on the Internet increases the opportunity for channel migration. Thus, cus- tomer retention during shopping episodes is a challenge for multi- channel retailers. Note that before the Internet and mobile technol- ogy, customers typically researched and purchased products during a trip to one store because it was too "costly" to visit multiple stores. Two approaches that multichannel retail- ers can use to reduce channel migra- tion are (1) to offer uniquely relevant information based on proprietary data the retailer has collected about the customers, and (2) promote pri- vate-label or exclusive merchandise that can be purchased only from the retailer.

Types of Ownership

Previous sections of this chapter discussed how retailers are classified in terms of their retail mix (the variety and depth of merchandise and services offered to customers) and the merchandise and services they sell (food, gen- eral merchandise, and services). Another way to classify retailers is by their ownership. The major classifications of retail ownership are:

- Independent, single-store establishments
- Corporate retail chains
- Franchises

Independent, Single-Store Establishments

Retailing is one of the few sectors in our economy where entrepreneurial activity is extensive. Over 60 000 new retail businesses are started in North America each year.[107]

Many such stores are owner-managed. Thus, manage- ment has direct contact with customers and can respond quickly to their needs. Small retailers are also very flex- ible and can therefore react quickly to market changes and customer needs. They aren't bound by bureaucracies inherent in large retail organizations.

Although single-store retailers can tailor their offerings to their customers' needs, corporate chains can more effectively negotiate lower prices for merchan- dise and advertising due to their larger size. In addition, corporate chains have a broader management base, with people who specialize in specific retail activities. Single- store retailers typically have to rely on owner–managers' capabilities to make the broad range of necessary retail decisions.

To better compete against corporate chains, some independent retailers join a wholesale-sponsored vol- untary cooperative group, which is an organization operated by a wholesaler offering a merchandising program to small, independent retailers on a volun- tary basis. Independent Grocers Alliance (IGA) is an example of a wholesale-sponsored voluntary cooper- ative group. In addition to buying, warehousing, and distribution, these groups offer members services such as store design and layout, site selection, bookkeep- ing and inventory management systems, and employee training programs.

Corporate Retail Chains

A retail chain is a company operating multiple retail units under common ownership and usually has centralized decision making for defining and implementing its strat- egy. There were about 2688 chains operating in Canada in 2012 with approximately 85 826 chain-store locations across the country.[108] Retail chains can range in size from a drugstore with two stores to retailers with many stores such as Loblaws, No Frills, Zehrs, Fortinos, and Real Canadian Superstore. Some retail chains are divisions of larger corporations or holding companies. For example, Venator owns Foot Locker, Lady Foot Locker, Kids Foot Locker, Foot Locker International, Champs Sports, and Footlocker.com/Eastbay.Champs; Intimate Brands owns Victoria's Secret, La Senza, Bath & Body Works, and The White Barn Candle Co.

There has been considerable concern that corporate retail chains drive independent retailers out of business. For example, Walmart has pursued a strategy of opening full-line discount stores and supercentres on the outskirts of small towns.[109] These stores offer a broader selection of merchandise at much lower prices than previously avail- able from local retailers. Due to scale economies and an efficient distribution system, corporate chains can sell at low prices. This forces some directly competing local retailers out of business and alters the community fabric.

On the other hand, local retailers offering complementary merchandise and services can prosper. When large chain stores open, more consumers are attracted to the community from surrounding areas. Thus, the market for the local stores expands. Although chain stores may have cost advantages over local retailers, large retail chains can be very bureaucratic, stifling managers' creativity with excessive rules and procedures. Often, all stores in the chain have the same merchandise and services, whereas local retailers can provide merchandise compatible with local market needs.

Franchises

Franchising is a contractual agreement between a franchisor and a franchisee that allows the franchisee to operate a retail outlet using a name and format developed and supported by the franchisor. Approximately one-third of all North American retail sales are made by franchisees.

In a franchise contract, the franchisee pays a lump sum plus a royalty on all sales for the right to operate a store in a specific location. The franchisee also agrees to operate the outlet in accordance with procedures prescribed by the franchisor. The franchisor provides assistance in locating and building the store, developing the products or services sold, management training, and advertising. To maintain the franchisee's reputation, the franchisor also makes sure that all outlets provide the same quality of services and products.

The franchise ownership format attempts to combine advantages of owner-managed businesses with efficiencies of centralized decision making in chain-store operations. Franchisees are motivated to make their store successful because they receive the profits (after the royalty is paid). The franchisor is motivated to develop new products and systems and to promote the franchise because it receives a royalty on all sales. Advertising, product development, and system development are efficiently done by the franchisor, with costs shared by all franchisees (see Exhibit 2–14).

franchising A contractual agreement between a franchisor and a franchisee that allows the franchisee to operate a retail outlet using a name and format developed and supported by the franchisor.

exhibit 2–14 Sampling of Selected Canadian Franchises (2009)

Franchisor	Number of Units Owned in Canada	Number of Franchisees/ Dealers in Canada	Initial Fee	Royalty	Advertising Program	Approximate Investment Required	Website
Boston Pizza	3	330	$69 000	7%	2.5%	$500 000–$800 000	www.bostonpizza.com
Dairy Queen Canada	-	574	$30 000–$45 000	4%	5–6%	$300 000+	www.dairyqueen.com
McDonald's Restaurants of Canada	338	1083	$45 000	17%, including rent, services fee, and advertising		$400 000+	www.mcdonalds.com
Midas Muffler Shop	8	186	$30 000	5%	5%	$300 000–$400 000	www.midas.com
1-800-Got-Junk	1	31	$12 000	-	-	$70 000–$110 000	www.1800gotjunk.com
Tim Hortons	102	2800	$50 000	4.5%	4%	$430 000–$480 000	www.timhortons.com

Source: Adapted from the *Franchise Canada Directory 2010*, Canadian Franchise Association (www.cfa.ca).

SUMMARY

This chapter reviews the types of retailers and ownership classifications. This is an excellent resource for students and highlights strategies for success in a competitive retail marketplace. Definitions of the retail formats and the examples explain the diversity and innovation within the retail sector.

Many different types of retailers now offer multichannel approaches to their retail customers in an attempt to gain loyalty. Multichannel is not a format in itself but rather an additional way of reaching the customer and increasing revenue.

This chapter explained different types of retailers and how they compete with different retail mixes to sell merchandise and services to customers. To collect statistics about retailing, the federal government classifies retailers by type of merchandise and services sold. But this classification method may not be useful in determining a retailer's major competitors. A more useful approach for understanding the retail marketplace is classifying retailers on the basis of their retail mix, the merchandise variety and assortment, services, location, pricing, and promotion decisions made to attract customers.

Over the past 30 years, North American retail markets have been characterized by the emergence of many new retail institutions. Traditional institutions (supermarkets, convenience, department, discount, and specialty stores) have been joined by category specialists, superstores, hypermarkets, convenience stores, warehouse clubs, off-price retailers, catalogue showrooms, and hypermarkets. In addition, there has been substantial growth in services retailing. The inherent differences between services and merchandise result in services retailers emphasizing store management while merchandise retailers emphasize inventory control issues.

Traditional retail institutions have changed in response to these new retailers. For example, department stores have increased their emphasis on fashion-oriented apparel and improved the services they offer. Supermarkets are focusing more attention on meal solutions and perishables.

Although the bubble burst for most pure electronic retailers, traditional store-based and catalogue retailers are adding an electronic channel and evolving into being integrated, customer-centric, multichannel retailers. This evolution toward multichannel retailing is driven by the increasing desire of customers to communicate with retailers anytime, anywhere, anyplace.

Each of the channels (stores, catalogues, and websites) offers unique benefits to customers. The store channel enables customers to touch and feel merchandise and use the products shortly after they are purchased. Catalogues enable customers to browse through a retailer's offering anytime and anyplace. A unique benefit offered by the electronic channel is the opportunity for consumers to search across a broad range of alternatives, develop a smaller set of alternatives based on their needs, and get specific information about the alternatives they want.

By offering multiple channels, retailers overcome the limitations of each channel. Websites can be used to extend the geographical presence and assortment offered by the store channel. Websites also can be used to update the information provided in catalogues. Stores can be used to provide a multisensory experience and an economical distribution capability supporting the electronic channel.

Providing a seamless interface across channels is very challenging for multiple retailers. Meeting customer expectations will require the development and use of common customer databases and integrated systems. In addition, omni-channel retailers will have to make decisions about how to use the different channels to support the retailer's brand image and how to present consistent merchandise assortments and pricing across channels.

KEY TERMS

big-box stores
catalogue channel
category specialist
closeout retailers
combination stores
convenience stores
conventional supermarket
department store
depth of merchandise
direct-response advertising
direct selling
discount store
drugstore
electronic retailing
factory outlets
fair trade

franchising
hypermarkets
infomercials
in-store kiosks
leased department
limited-assortment supermarkets
locavore movement
m-commerce
multichannel retailer
multilevel system
North American Industry Classification System (NAICS)
off-price retailer
omni-channel retailing
outlet stores
party plan system

power perimeter
pyramid scheme
retail chain
services retailers
SKU (stock keeping unit)
specialty store
supercentres
superstore
television home shopping
value retailers
variety (breadth of merchandise)
vending machine retailing
warehouse club
wholesale-sponsored voluntary cooperative group

Get Out & Do It!

1. **GO SHOPPING** Go to an athletic footwear specialty store such as Foot Locker, a department store, and a discount store. Analyze their variety and assortment of athletic footwear by creating a table similar to Exhibit 2–3.

2. **GO SHOPPING** Keep a diary of where you shop, what you buy, and how much you spend for two weeks. Tabulate your results by type of retailer. Are your shopping habits significantly different from your parents'? Do your and your parents' shopping habits coincide with the trends discussed in this chapter? Explain why or why not.

3. **INTERNET EXERCISE** Two large associations of retailers are the National Retail Federation (**www.nrf.com**) and the Retail Council of Canada (**www.retailcouncil.org**). Visit these sites and report the latest retail developments and issues confronting the industry.

4. **INTERNET EXERCISE** Go to **corporate.walmart. com**. Click on "Our Story," then "Our Business," and then "Walmart U.S." Scroll down to read "Walmart Supercenter." Now go to **www.groupe-auchan.com** and click on "Our Businesses." See if you can determine the differences between a Walmart supercentre and an Auchan hypermarket.

5. **INTERNET EXERCISE** Check out Mark's Work Wearhouse at **www.marks.com**. Explain why Mark's retail product is a successful addition to Canadian Tire's assortments, broadening the product mix for consumers.

6. **INTERNET EXERCISE** Do an online search for "Craigslist." Explain the popularity of this unique site.

7. **GO SHOPPING AND INTERNET EXERCISE** Compare the merchandise assortment offered and the prices in your favourite store and on the store's website. If there are differences, what is the reason for these differences?

8. **INTERNET EXERCISE** Go to The Gap (**www.gap.com**), Sears (**www.sears.ca**), and Lands' End (**www. landsend.com**) and shop for a pair of pants. Evaluate your shopping experience at each site. Compare the sites and experience on characteristics you think are important to consumers.

9. **INTERNET EXERCISE** Examine a variety of online stores. Explain what works for you and what doesn't work for you.

10. **INTERNET EXERCISE** Visit **www.bombay.ca** and take a virtual tour of the store. Describe the experience.

DISCUSSION QUESTIONS AND PROBLEMS

1. Distinguish between variety and assortment. Why are these important elements of retail market structure?

2. How can small independent retailers compete against the large national chains?

3. What do off-price retailers need to do to compete against other formats in the future?

4. Compare and contrast the retail mixes of convenience stores, traditional supermarkets, supercentres, hypermarkets, and warehouse stores. Can all of these food retail institutions survive over the long run? Explain why or why not.

5. Why haven't hypermarkets been successful in North America? Do you believe they will be successful in the future?

6. The same brand and model personal computer is sold in specialty computer stores, discount stores, category specialists, and warehouse stores. Why would a customer choose one store over the others?

7. Choose a product category that both you and your parents purchase (e.g., clothing, DVDs, electronic equipment). In which type of store do you typically purchase this merchandise? What about your parents? Explain why there is, or is not, a difference in your store choices.

8. At many optical stores, you can get your eyes checked and purchase glasses or contact lenses. How is the shopping experience different for the service as compared to the product? Design a strategy to get customers to purchase both the service and the product. In so doing, delineate specific actions that should be taken to acquire and retain optical customers.

9. Many experts believe that customer service is one of retailing's most important issues in the coming years. How can retailers that emphasize price (such as discount stores, category specialists, and off-price retailers) improve customer service without increasing costs and, thus, prices?

10. Should a multichannel retailer offer the same assortment of merchandise for sale on its website at the same price as it sells in its stores? Explain why or why not.

Practise and learn online with Connect.

customer buying behaviour

SPOTLIGHT ON RETAILING

Making the Connection Is Key for Today's Students

It's no surprise that mobile use among the student population is gaining rapid momentum. Venture onto any college or university campus, and you'll find students using laptops, tablets, and even smartphones to take notes and do research. They're also using mobile technology to access social media sites such as Facebook or Twitter so that they can update their posts frequently and keep on top of what their friends are posting about. In fact, these days, most universities in Canada have social media links right on their admission pages or home pages.

"I can look at e-mails, my calendar, a PDF, any links—all in the palm of my hand," says University of Alberta student David Myszkiewicz, who says he can't remember the last time he used a pen and paper to take notes. "It's an excellent way to stay connected wherever you are," he says. "Technology has revolutionized our world, there's no doubt about it."

And sure enough, mobile use is extending far beyond the classroom and campus into other facets of student life. According to results from the 2012 study, *The Pulse of the Canadian Student Shopper*, 56 percent of Canadian student shoppers use or own a smartphone. More than one-third of them follow a brand online via social media, and 57 percent have downloaded at least one retailer application. Yet, a recent survey of retail executives by Deloitte, called *The Next Evolution: Store 3.0*, shows that while many retailers believe IT strategy and investment should be a top priority, only 18 percent feel they're "ahead of the curve." In fact, more than half of the leading retailers surveyed did not have WiFi-enabled stores to allow for customer service options, such as real-time loyalty program signup, SKU availability checks, or product reviews. More than a third had no plans to implement such technology either, despite experiences by early adopters that suggest "connected" shoppers often end up spending more.

Myszkiewicz says that retailers would benefit from continually engaging their customers to keep this generation of frequent web users interested—and the ones that do it right stand to gain tremendously. "You need to create that connection and that doesn't mean posting once a week on Twitter," he says. "If you as a company can reach me and I have 1000 friends on Facebook, and even if one reposts, and he has 1000 friends, that's 2000 people you've potentially reached with one posting."

Source: Rosalind Stefanac, "The Future of Retail: Students and Educators Weigh In on What the Next Generation of Employees Really Want," *Canadian Retailer*, summer 2012, Volume 22, Issue 3, pp. 48–50.

An effective retail strategy satisfies customer needs better than competitors' strategies. Thus, understanding customer needs and buying behaviour is critical for effective retail decision making. We're not all the same. This is a mistake many marketers make when going after a demographic group, particularly the Boomer segment, a population segment that has over half of the country's discretionary spending potential. Consider the teen population: Not all teens are the same. Some are jocks, others are geeks; some like rap music, others are part of the hipster culture. Retailers are beginning to realize the importance of understanding the subgroups in the marketplace in order to connect with the customer. You cannot be all things to all customers.

This chapter focuses on the needs and buying behaviour of customers and market segments. It describes the stages customers go through to purchase merchandise and the factors that influence the buying process. We then use the information about the buying process to discuss how consumers can be grouped into market segments.[1]

New Consumer Mindset

According to a recent study by PricewaterhouseCoopers (PwC) and TNS Retail Forward, *Retailing 2015: New Frontiers,* a new set of underlying drivers will permeate our society and our shopping behaviour. They predict four mindset mega-trends that will have far-reaching implications for the retail marketplace of 2015:

- **Interconnected.** Consumer expectations will be to connect to anyone, at any time, about anything, from anywhere. Interconnectivity will be a way of life—the way people get and share information, communicate, transact business, and even socialize. Social networking sites designed to expand the individual's reach will likely explode and social status may become more about whom you connect to and who wants to connect to you.

- **In control.** As consumers become interconnected, they will become more adept at controlling the ways in which they interact. The study suggests that control will take three forms:
  - **Clout control.** This is where consumers will find strength by association to drive change. Groups of consumers working together will be able to demand products they want, via the shopping experience they want, from retailers that will do business the way that they want.

  - **Context control.** The tools and technology available to consumers will allow them to capture information, communicate, and conduct transactions regardless of the time or the place.

  - **Contacts control.** As consumers become more interconnected, they are gaining more control over whom they let into their "interconnected" world. Unlike many of the mega-networks that are currently designed to extend reach, the goal of newer micro-networks is to narrow reach to specific niches of similar interests. With filtering mechanisms today, such as spam filters, permission-based marketing, cellphone as primary phone, caller ID, and sites where consumers can "reject" unwanted contacts, consumers are creating *closed loop societies,* where connectivity is limited to the contacts they allow in. As a result, we are likely to see in the near future more social networks that are finely focused and, in some cases, more exclusive in the ways people find and join them.

- **Indulgent.** Consumer indulgence will be fuelled by the interconnected shopper's ability to easily discover, find, filter, and try the next new thing. According to the study, given virtually unlimited accessibility to the next new thing, consumer indulgence will shift to the next best thing—niche products, experiences, and services uniquely suited to their tastes, interests, and aspirations.

- **Individualized.** As consumers become more interconnected and controlling, they will gravitate toward products and experiences that offer individual focus, interaction, and involvement. They will seek out products and experiences that they perceive as meeting their unique needs. According to the study, taken to the extreme, consumers will seek out opportunities for involvement in the entire chain of activities that brings a product to market—from conception, design, and creation, to marketing and retailing, and even to funding and rewarding.[2]

The Buying Process

Consider your most recent shopping trip as we describe the customer buying process. The buying process, the steps consumers go through when buying a product or service, begins when customers recognize an unsatisfied need. They seek information about how to satisfy the need, such as what products might be useful and how they can be bought. Customers evaluate the alternative retailers and channels available for purchasing the merchandise, such as stores, catalogues, and the Internet, and then choose a store or Internet site to visit or a catalogue to review. This encounter with a retailer provides more information and may alert customers to additional needs. After evaluating the retailer's merchandise offering by weighing both objective and subjective criteria, customers may make a purchase or go to another retailer to collect more information. Eventually, customers make a purchase, use the product, and then decide whether the product satisfies their needs during the post-purchase evaluation stage of the customer buying process.

Exhibit 3–1 outlines the buying process—the stages in selecting a retailer and buying merchandise. Retailers attempt to influence consumers as they go through the buying process to encourage them to buy their merchandise and services. Each stage in the buying process is addressed in the following sections.

Need Recognition

The buying process is triggered when consumers recognize they have an unsatisfied need. An unsatisfied need arises when a customer's desired level of satisfaction differs from his or her present level of satisfaction. Need recognition can be triggered by realizing you need a haircut, by feeling the need for an uplifting experience after a final exam, or by a message from a Facebook group member about an addition to his or her profile.

Types of Needs The needs that motivate customers to go shopping and purchase merchandise can be classified as utilitarian or hedonic. When consumers go shopping

to accomplish a specific task, such as buying a suit for job interviews, they are seeking to satisfy utilitarian needs. When consumers go shopping for pleasure, they are seeking to satisfy their hedonic needs—their needs for an entertaining, emotional, and recreational experience. Thus, from the consumer's perspective, utilitarian needs are associated with work, whereas hedonic needs are associated with fun.[3]

Successful retailers attempt to satisfy both the utilitarian and hedonic needs of their customers. Consumers motivated by utilitarian needs typically shop in a more deliberate and efficient manner; thus, retailers need to make the shopping experience easy and effortless for them by providing the desired merchandise in a way that can be easily located and purchased. Some hedonic needs that retailers can satisfy include stimulation, social experience, learning new trends, status and power, self-reward, and adventure.[4]

1. *Stimulation.* Retailers and mall managers use background music, visual displays, scents, and demonstrations in stores and malls to create a carnival-like, stimulating experience for their customers. These environments encourage consumers to take a break from their everyday lives and visit stores.[5] Retailers also attempt to stimulate customers with exciting graphics and photography in their catalogues and on their websites.[6]

2. *Social experience.* Marketplaces traditionally have been centres of social activity, places where people could meet friends and develop new relationships. Regional shopping malls in many communities have replaced open markets as social meeting places, especially for teenagers. Mall developers are focusing on mixed-use developments to satisfy consumers' need for social experiences. Lifestyle centres are allocating significant space to restaurants, movie theatres, outdoor entertainment, and even condominium living. Chapters bookstores host cafés in which customers can discuss novels while sipping lattes. Online retailers provide similar social experiences by enabling customers to e-mail products to

utilitarian needs
Needs motivating consumers to go shopping to accomplish a specific task.

hedonic needs
Needs motivating consumers to go shopping for pleasure.

exhibit 3–1 The Buying Process

STAGES	SELECTING A RETAILER AND CHANNEL	SELECTING MERCHANDISE
Need recognition	Recognize needs	Recognize needs
Information search	Search for information about retailers	Search for information about merchandise
Evaluation	Evaluate retailers and channels	Evaluate merchandise
Choice	Select a retailer and channel	Select merchandise
Visit	Visit store or Internet site, or read catalogue	Purchase merchandise
Loyalty	Repeat patronage of retailer	Post-purchase evaluation

their friends, create personal blogs with their shopping lists to be shared with other people, or participate in a particular interest-driven forum. For example, visitors to Amazon.com can write reviews and opinions about books they have read and make them available to all potential customers on the website.

3. *Learning new trends.* By visiting retailers, people learn about new trends and ideas. These visits satisfy customers' needs to be informed about their environment. For example, teens might go to The Body Shop to learn about new products, as well as ways they can live an environmentally friendly lifestyle. Customers also learn about trends through normal social encounters and surfing the web.

4. *Status and power.* For some people, a store or a service provider is one of the few places where they get attention and respect. Canyon Ranch offers upscale health resorts in Tucson, Arizona, and Lenox, Massachusetts, as well as spa clubs in Las Vegas, Nevada, and Kissimmee, Florida. All Canyon Ranch resorts and spas make the customer the centre of attention, offering spa services, medical and nutritional consultations and workshops, spiritual pursuits, and healthy gourmet cuisine.

5. *Self-reward.* Customers frequently purchase merchandise to reward themselves when they have accomplished something or want to dispel depression. Perfume, cosmetics, apparel, and jewellery are common self-gifts. Retailers satisfy these needs by, for example, "treating" customers to personalized makeovers while they are in the store.

6. *Adventure.* Often consumers go shopping because they enjoy finding bargains, looking for sales, and finding discounts or low prices. They treat shopping as a game to be "won." Off-price retailers like Winners, warehouse clubs like Costco, discount stores like Target, and fast-fashion retailers like Zara and H&M cater to this need by constantly changing their assortment so that customers never know what kind of treasure they will find.

Some people view shopping as a leisure-time activity, just like any other sport. Frequent leisure-time shoppers spend an average of $113.33 per shopping trip, making this segment of consumers one of the most profitable and informed. They buy primarily apparel, health and beauty aids, entertainment and leisure items, and electronics.[8]

Conflicting Needs Most customers have multiple needs. Moreover, these needs often conflict. For example, a graduating student would like to wear a DKNY suit, which would enhance her self-image, earn her the admiration of her university friends, and be appropriate for her upcoming job interviews. But this hedonic need conflicts with her budget and her utilitarian need to get a job. Employers might feel that she's not responsible if she wears a suit that is too expensive for an interview for an entry-level position. Typically, customers make trade-offs between their conflicting needs. Later in this chapter, we will discuss a model of how customers make such trade-offs.

Because needs often cannot be satisfied in one store or by one product, consumers may appear to be inconsistent in their shopping behaviour. For example, a skier may purchase expensive Spyder goggles but wear an inexpensive snow suit from Sport Chek. A grocery shopper might buy an inexpensive store brand of paper towels and a premium national brand of orange juice like Tropicana. The pattern of buying both premium and low-priced merchandise or patronizing both expensive, status-oriented retailers and price-oriented retailers is called cross-shopping.

Although all cross-shoppers seek value, their perception of value varies across product classes. Thus, a cross-shopper might feel it is worth the money to dine at an expensive restaurant but believe there is little quality difference between kitchen utensils at Walmart and designer brands at a specialty store. Similarly, consumers may cut back on their vacations at costly resorts but still want to treat themselves to expensive, high-quality jams, mustards, and olive oils from the supermarket. Retailers might not be able to discern how the buying patterns of cross-shoppers make sense, but they certainly make sense to their customers.

Stimulating Need Recognition As we have noted, customers must recognize unsatisfied needs before they are motivated to visit a store or go online to buy merchandise. Sometimes these needs are stimulated by an event in a person's life. For example, a consumer's department store visit to buy a suit was stimulated by an impending interview, an examination of her current wardrobe, and a visit to BrandHabit.com. Retailers use a variety of approaches to stimulate problem recognition and motivate customers to visit their stores and buy merchandise. Advertising, Internet promotions, direct mail, publicity, and special events communicate the availability of merchandise or special prices. SeenOn.com stimulates need recognition by showing products that celebrities or television actors have worn. Within the store, visual merchandising and salespeople can stimulate need recognition, such as when a salesperson shows a customer a scarf or tie to stimulate the need for an accessory to complement a new suit.

Information Search

Once customers identify a need, they may seek information about retailers or products to help them satisfy that need. More extended buying processes may involve collecting a lot of information, visiting several retailers, spending more time on the Internet, or deliberating a long time before making a purchase.[9]

Amount of Information Searched In general, the amount of information search depends on the value customers feel they can gain from searching versus the cost of searching. Consumers will often spend more time searching for information when they have little prior experience with the merchandise category. The value of the search stems from how it improves the customer's purchase decision. Will the search help the customer find a lower-priced product or one that will give superior performance? The costs of search include both time and money. Travelling from store to store can cost money for gas and parking, but the major cost incurred is the customer's time.

Technology can dramatically reduce the cost of information search. For example, NearbyNow.com sends promotions to customers' cellphones via a text message and enables them to search their local malls for products and brands via text messages. This way, customers can save time in the search process by going directly to the retailer that sells the desired product.[10] Vast information about merchandise sold across the world is just a mouse click away. Retailing View 3.1 describes how readily available information on the web is affecting the automobile buying process.

Factors influencing the amount of information search include (1) the nature and use of the product being purchased, (2) characteristics of the individual customer, and (3) aspects of the market and buying situation in which the purchase is made. Some people search more than others. For example, social shoppers spend more time shopping than other customers, and do so for the sheer enjoyment of the process and interacting with other potential customers and retailer customer service and sales representatives.[11] Also, customers who are self-confident or have prior experience purchasing and using the product or service tend to search less.

Marketplace and situational factors affecting information search include (1) the number of competing brands and retail outlets and (2) the time pressure under which the purchase must be made. When competition is greater and there are more alternatives to consider, the amount of information search increases. However, the amount decreases as time pressure increases.

Sources of Information Customers have two sources of information: internal and external. Internal sources of information are in a customer's memory, such as names, images, and past experiences with different stores. The major source of internal information is the customer's past shopping experience. Even if they remember only a small fraction of the information to which they are exposed, customers have an extensive internal information bank to draw upon when deciding where to shop and what to buy.

DID YOU KNOW?

Three-quarters of new-vehicle buyers use the Internet during the shopping process.[12]

The Internet Has Changed the Car-Buying Process

The Internet has dramatically reduced the time and effort needed to collect information—and increased the quality of information acquired—to make a decision when buying an automobile.

Ten years ago, if consumers wanted to buy a car, they would visit several dealers, look at different models, test drive the cars sold by each dealer, and then negotiate price and financing with a dealer. Many consumers viewed this traditional process of buying a car as about as pleasurable as a visit to the dentist. But now the Internet is changing this experience, as well as the nature of automobile retailing.

The Internet is giving consumers more control over the car-buying process. Consumers can go to websites such as www.autobytel.com, www.cars.com, or www.edmunds.com; access a wealth of information, including the dealer's costs for cars and options; compare vehicles in a side-by-side chart that lists their price, features, horsepower, mileage, legroom, and options; read multiple reviews for most models; and even take a 360-degree photo tour of car interiors that gives them an idea of what the view looks like from the driver's seat.

Through the sites' relationships with car dealers, consumers can request prices from dealers in their area. A handy calculator tells customers how much the monthly payment would be if they were to buy a car on credit. The sites also have calculators to help car buyers figure out how much they can afford to spend on a car, whether they should buy a new or used car, and whether they should lease or buy. This information enables consumers to walk into a dealership knowing as much as or more than the dealer's salespeople.

The Build Your Own Honda site offers a simple four-step process that customers can use to select a model, a trim level (including exterior colour), and an accessory package. Then, a summary of selections with front and back views of the customer-designed vehicle is generated. Another tool lets users compare Honda products to vehicles from other manufacturers.

CarFax (www.carfax.com) enables customers to access a vehicle's history report by typing in its vehicle identification number (VIN). This history describes any accidents the vehicle was in, its past ownership, odometer fraud, and any other events that might be related to the vehicle. Services such as CarFax make it much easier for customers to purchase used cars with confidence.

Sources: Geoffrey A. Fowler, John D. Stoll, Scott Morrison, "GM, eBay Will Let Car Buyers Dicker Online," *Wall Street Journal*, August 11, 2009, p. B1; Thomas Pack, "Kicking the Virtual Tires: Car Research on the Web," *Information Today*, January 2009, pp. 44–45; www.cars.com (accessed January 21, 2010); www.carfax.com (accessed January 21, 2010).

External sources of information refer to information provided by ads and other people. When customers feel that their internal information is inadequate, they turn to external information sources. External sources of information play a major role in the acceptance of fashions, as discussed in Appendix 2A, available on Connect.

The Internet has had a profound impact on consumers' ability to gather external information. If consumers want to search for something specific, they can try specialized search engines such as Google Shopping (www.google.com/shopping).[13] The site relies on artificial intelligence technology to search images on the web and then serves up goods for sale that visually match items on a shopper's wish list. Visitors to the site can search for products in one of two ways. First, they may type in, say, "silver earrings" and receive pages filled with images that match the description, along with prices and links to the product pages of the websites on which the items are sold. Second, users may browse through selected items in the wardrobes of about a dozen celebrities, including Scarlett Johansson and Jessica Simpson, and choose, perhaps, the dress that Johansson wore on the cover of *Esquire* magazine. The site then searches for similar dresses, returning more than 5000 ranging in price from $40 to $8000.

Two other sites, NearbyNow.com and GPShopper.com, have introduced mobile Internet applications that allow shoppers to use their cellphones and tablets to search inventory and prices while at a particular mall, saving them wasted time and sometimes turning up last-minute bargains and promotions.[14]

However, retailers are concerned that the ease of collecting price information through the Internet will increase price competition. Traditionally, price competition between store-based retailers offering the same merchandise was reduced by geographic constraints. Through the Internet and mobile technology, the number of stores that consumers can visit to compare prices is no longer limited by physical distance.

Increasingly, retailers are encouraging their customers to post information on their websites too, such as product reviews, ratings, and, in some cases, photos and videos.[15] Consumers can also get product reviews from other consumers on retailer sites like Amazon and Golfsmith (www.golfsmith.com). The result is that customer reviews are emerging as a prime source for online shoppers as they collect information during the buying process.

Reducing Information Search

The retailer's objective at the information search stage of the buying process is to limit the customer's search to its store or website. One measure of a retailer's performance on this objective is the conversion rate, that is, the percentage of customers who enter a store or access a website and then buy a product at the store or website. Each element of the retailing mix can be used to achieve this objective. Category specialists such as Best Buy and Rona provide a very deep assortment of merchandise, everything a customer might want in the category, so that the customer can collect all of the information and make the necessary comparisons in their stores or on their websites.

Services provided by retailers can also limit search to the retailer's location. The availability of credit and delivery may be important for consumers who want to purchase large durable goods, such as furniture and appliances. Salespeople can provide enough information to customers that they don't feel the need to collect additional information by visiting other stores. For example, most men have no idea how to buy lingerie for their girlfriends or wives and are embarrassed to ask female sales associates. So London's Marks & Spencer department store used several "Stocking Fellas" as a one-time holiday promotion to help them shop for these items.[16] Thanks to the Stocking Fellas, lingerie sales are up, and merchandise returns are down.

Everyday low pricing is another way retailers increase the chance that customers will buy in their store and not search for a better price elsewhere. An **everyday low pricing strategy (ELDP)** maintains the continuity of retail prices at a level somewhere between the regular nonsale price and the deep discount sale price of the retailer's competitors. Walmart and The Source have everyday low pricing policies, which make customers confident that they won't find that merchandise at a lower price at another retailer. Many stores with everyday low pricing offer price-matching guarantees if a competitor offers the same merchandise at a lower price.

Increasingly, consumers are embracing digital technologies and devices in all stages of their buying journey. They are moving from channel to channel on a regular basis, searching for information, and they have expectations that their behaviour in one place will influence the experience in another. In a *2012 Shopping Outlook Survey* published by PriceGrabber, the methods that online shoppers plan to use to shop are as follows: 45 percent plan to combine online, bricks-and-mortar, and mobile shopping; 42 percent plan to shop mostly online; 1 percent plan to use primarily a mobile device; and 12 percent plan to shop mostly in bricks-and-mortar stores. As a result, retailers are looking at embracing omni-channel strategies that will require them to build bridges between their online and offline environments for a single customer view. Retailers

external sources of information Information provided by the media and other people.

everyday low pricing strategy (EDLP) A pricing strategy that stresses continuity of retail prices at a level somewhere between the regular nonsale price and the deep-discount sale price of the retailer's competitors.

need to make use of social media and social communities to entice peer-to-peer communication and help build their brand through consumer discussions and recommendations. Like social media, reviews are powerful advertising tools that retailers can use to help disseminate information to consumers. Reviews and product guides can be available in-store and online, allowing consumers to access information while they shop and use it to help make purchasing decisions. Finally, location-based social media like Foursquare and Facebook Places will allow retailers to link mobile users to their friends via "check-ins," showing who has stopped where and any comments they had about the experience. Retailers can offer coupons, sales alerts, messages about important events, and more, delivering advertising and information to consumers as they go about their daily routines.[17]

Although retailers hope to confine their customers' information search to their stores and websites, they also want to encourage customers to spend as much time shopping in their channels as possible. The more time customers spend shopping, the more they will buy. Stores use food and personal service to create a comfortable environment that encourages customers to keep shopping.[18] For instance, Talbots offers the personal attention of a sales associate, by appointment, along with a light snack. American Eagle Outfitter's Martin + Osa Division, which targets a slightly older audience, serves bottled water and apples. Gymboree provides a television playing videos at the back of its stores to keep its youngest customers occupied while their parents shop.

Evaluation of Alternatives: The Multiattribute Attitude Model

The multiattribute attitude model provides a useful way to summarize how customers use the information they have and collect about alternative products,

evaluate the alternatives, and select the one that best satisfies their needs. We discuss it in detail because it offers a framework for developing a retailing strategy.[19]

The multiattribute attitude model is based on the notion that customers see a retailer, a product, or a service as a collection of attributes or characteristics. The model is designed to predict a customer's evaluation of a product, service, or retailer based on (1) its performance on relevant attributes and (2) the importance of those attributes to the customer.

Beliefs about Performance To illustrate this model, consider the store choice decision confronting a young, single, professional woman from Mississauga who needs groceries. She considers three alternatives: a supercentre in the next suburb, her local supermarket, or an Internet grocery retailer such as Grocery Gateway (www.grocerygateway.com), as compared in Exhibit 3–2.

The customer mentally processes the "objective" information about each grocery retailer in Exhibit 3–2A and forms an impression of the benefits each one provides. Exhibit 3–2B shows her beliefs about these benefits. Notice that some benefits can combine several objective characteristics. For example, the convenience benefit combines travel time, checkout time, and ease of finding products. Grocery prices and delivery cost affect her beliefs about the economy of shopping at the various retail outlets.

The degree to which each retailer provides each benefit is represented on a 10-point scale: 10 means the

exhibit 3–2 Characteristics of Food Retailers

A. Information about Stores Selling Groceries			
Store Characteristics	**Supercentre**	**Supermarket**	**Internet Grocer**
Grocery prices	20% below average	average	10% above average
Delivery cost ($)	0	0	10
Total travel time (minutes)	30	15	0
Typical checkout time (minutes)	10	5	2
Number of products, brands, and sizes	40 000	30 000	40 000
Fresh produce	Yes	Yes	Yes
Fresh fish	Yes	Yes	No
Ease of finding products	Difficult	Easy	Easy
Ease of collecting nutritional information about products	Difficult	Difficult	Easy

B. Beliefs about Stores' Performance Benefits*			
Performance Benefits	**Supercentre**	**Supermarket**	**Internet Grocer**
Economy	10	8	6
Convenience	3	5	10
Assortment	9	7	5
Availability of product information	4	4	8

*10 = excellent, 1 = poor.

retailer performs well in providing the benefit; 1 means it performs poorly. Here, no retailer has superior performance on all benefits. The supercentre performs well on economy and assortment but is low on convenience. The Internet grocer offers the best convenience but is weak on economy and assortment.

Importance Weights The young woman in the preceding example forms an overall evaluation of each alternative on the basis of the importance she places on each benefit the stores provide. The importance she places on a benefit can also be represented using a 10-point rating scale, with 10 indicating the benefit is very important and 1 indicating it's very unimportant. Using this rating scale, the importance of the retailer benefits for the young woman and for a parent with four children are shown in Exhibit 3–3, along with the performance beliefs previously discussed. Notice that the single woman may value convenience and the availability of product information much more than economy and assortment. But the parent may place a lot of importance on economy, assortment is moderately important, and convenience and product information aren't very important.

The importance of a retailer's benefits differs for each customer and also may differ for each shopping trip. For example, the parent with four children may stress economy for major shopping trips but place more importance on convenience for a fill-in trip.

In Exhibit 3–3, the single woman and parent may have the same beliefs about each retailer's performance, but they differ in the importance they place on the benefits the retailers offer. In general, customers can differ in their beliefs about the retailers' performance as well as in their importance weights.

Evaluating Stores Research has shown that a customer's overall evaluation of an alternative (in this situation, two stores and the Internet channel) relates closely to the sum of the performance beliefs multiplied by the importance weights.[20] Thus, we calculate the young, single woman's overall evaluation or score for the supercentre as follows:

$$
\begin{aligned}
4 \times 10 &= 40 \\
10 \times 3 &= 30 \\
5 \times 9 &= 45 \\
9 \times 4 &= 36 \\
\hline
& 151
\end{aligned}
$$

Exhibit 3–3 shows the overall evaluation of the three retailers using the importance weights of the single woman and the parent. For the single woman, the Internet grocer has the highest score, 221, and thus the most favourable evaluation. Therefore, on the one hand, she would probably select this retailer for most of her grocery shopping. On the other hand, the supercentre has the highest score, 192, for the parent, who'd probably buy the family's weekly groceries there.

When customers are about to select a retailer, they don't actually go through the process of listing store characteristics, evaluating retailers' performances on these characteristics, determining each characteristic's importance, calculating each store's overall score, and then patronizing the retailer with the highest score! The multiattribute attitude model does not reflect customers' actual decision process, but it does predict their evaluation of alternatives and their choice.[21] In addition, the model provides useful information for designing a retail offering. For example, if the supermarket could increase its performance rating on assortment from 7 to 10 (perhaps by adding a bakery and a wide selection of prepared meals), customers like the parent might shop at the supermarket more often than at the supercentre.

Customers don't thoroughly evaluate all alternatives, as is suggested by the multiattribute attitude model. Instead, they simply buy merchandise that's good enough or very good on one particular attribute. In general, customers don't spend the time necessary to find the very best product. Once they've found a product that satisfies their need, they stop searching.[22]

exhibit 3–3 Evaluation of Retailers

Characteristic	Importance Weights*		Performance Beliefs		
	Young Single Woman	**Parent with Four Children**	**Supercentre**	**Supermarket**	**Internet Grocer**
Economy	4	10	10	8	6
Convenience	10	4	3	5	10
Assortment	5	8	9	7	5
Availability of product information	9	2	4	4	8
OVERALL EVALUATION					
Young single woman			151	153	221
Parent with four children			192	164	156

*10 = very important, 1 = very unimportant.

Implications for Retailers How can a retailer use the multiattribute attitude model to encourage customers to shop at it more frequently? First, the model indicates what information customers use to decide which retailer to patronize and which channel to use. Second, it suggests tactics that retailers can undertake to influence customer store choices and merchandise selection.

Thus, to develop a program for attracting customers, the retailer must do market research to collect the following information:

1. Alternative retailers that customers consider
2. Characteristics or benefits that customers consider when evaluating and choosing a retailer
3. Customers' ratings of each retailer's performance on the characteristics
4. The importance weights that customers attach to the characteristics

Armed with this information, the retailer can use several approaches to influence customers to patronize its store or Internet site.

Getting into the Consideration Set The retailer needs to make sure that it is included in the customer's consideration set, or the set of alternatives the customer evaluates when making a selection. To be included in the consideration set, retailers develop programs to increase the likelihood that customers will remember them when they're about to go shopping. Retailers influence this top-of-the-mind awareness through Internet, advertising, and location strategies. They get exposure on search engines like Google or Yahoo! by placing ads that are shown on pages related to the search items. Advertising expenditures that stress the retailer's name can increase top-of-the-mind awareness. When a retailer such as Starbucks locates several stores in the same area, customers are exposed more frequently to the store name as they drive through the area.[23]

After ensuring that it is in consumers' consideration set, a retailer can use four methods to increase the chances that customers will select its store for a visit:

1. Increase beliefs about the store's performance
2. Decrease the performance beliefs for competing stores in the consideration set
3. Increase customers' importance weights
4. Add a new benefit

Changing Performance Beliefs The first approach involves altering customers' beliefs about the retailer's performance by increasing the retailer's performance rating on a characteristic.

For example, the supermarket in Exhibit 3–3 would want to increase its overall rating by improving its rating on all four benefits. The supermarket could improve its rating on economy by lowering prices and its assortment rating by stocking more gourmet and ethnic foods. Retailing View 3.2 illustrates how Lowe's altered the performance beliefs of women for its stores.

Because it can get costly for a retailer to improve its performance on all benefits, retailers must focus on improving their performance on those benefits that are important to customers in their target markets. For example, Best Buy knows that its customers don't want to be without their computers for lengthy amounts of time when they are in need of repair.[24] So it has a 165 000-square-foot "Geek Squad City" warehouse designed to cut the time it takes to repair and return a PC to one to three days. Inside the facility's sprawling repair room, PC parts and precision tools are spread over the rows and rows of desks where hundreds of computer techs—Geek Squad's "agents"—fix more than 2000 laptops a day. Best Buy recognizes the sizable investment this warehouse requires, but it also believes it is worth it to achieve high ratings on a service attribute that is very important to its customers.

A change in a performance belief about an important benefit results in a large change in customers' overall evaluations. In Exhibit 3–3, the supermarket should attempt to improve its convenience ratings if it wants to attract more young, single women who presently shop on the Internet. If its convenience rating rose from 5 to 8, its overall evaluation among young, single women would increase from 153 to 183 and thus be much higher

Do It Herself at Lowe's

You might think that home improvement centres are a retail recreation destination mostly for men. Men visit the stores on the weekends to check out the new tools and buy material for do-it-yourself (DIY) projects. But more than 50 percent of the purchases at home improvement centres actually are made to women. Women not only make the decisions about what materials to use for home improvement projects but also end up doing much of the work themselves.

Lowe's was early to recognize the importance of female customers. It redesigned its stores to be brighter, lose the warehouse look, and feature departments more appealing to women. Aisles were widened to help eliminate "butt brush," the uncomfortable contact that can occur as customers navigate narrow, crowded aisles—and something that women particularly dislike.

To make the store feel less intimidating, Lowe's made the shelves shorter and used aisle markers like those in grocery stores, with maps to help customers find products. However, Lowe's needed to balance the performance beliefs and importance weights that women have about their store with those of men. Its male customers might shun stores if they find them too feminine. Yet Lowe's also found that women held the

What has Lowe's done to make its stores and services more appealing to women?

same negative view of overly feminine home improvement stores, so it decided to teach women about tools rather than carrying tools specifically designed for women. One section of its website, www.lowes.com/howto, provides online clinics and videos to help all customers successfully implement their own DIY projects at home.

Sources: John Birger, "Second Mover Advantage," *Fortune*, April 20, 2006, pp. 10–11; and Patricia Anstett, "Hammer Time: Women Who Want To Tackle Repairs Around The House Can Get Help From Home Improvement Stores," *Knight Ridder Tribune Business News*, November 4, 2006 (accessed December 24, 2007).

than their evaluation of supercentres. Note that an increase in the rating from 8 to 10 for a less important benefit, such as economy, would have less effect on the store's overall evaluation. The supermarket might try to improve its rating on convenience by increasing the number of checkout stations, using customer scanning to reduce checkout time, or providing more in-store information so that customers could locate merchandise more easily.

Research further suggests that consumers in Germany, France, and the United Kingdom place different weights on three important attributes—price/value, service/quality, and relationships—when selecting a retailer to patronize. German consumers tend to place more weight on price/value, whereas customer service and product quality are more important for French consumers, and affinity benefits such as loyalty cards and preferred customer programs are more important for English consumers. Thus, in general, retailers that

emphasize price and good value will be more successful in Germany than in France or the United Kingdom.[25]

Another approach tries to decrease customers' performance ratings of a competing store. This approach may be illegal and usually isn't very effective, because bad-mouthing competitors generally backfires and customers typically don't believe a firm's negative comments about its competitors anyway.

Changing Importance Weights Altering customers' importance weights is another approach to influencing store choice. A retailer wants to increase the importance customers place on benefits for which its performance is superior and decrease the importance of benefits for which it has inferior performance. For example, if the supermarket in Exhibit 3–3 tried to attract families who shop at supercentres, it could increase the importance of convenience for them. Typically, changing importance weights is harder than changing performance beliefs, because importance weights reflect customers' personal values.[26]

Adding a New Benefit Finally, retailers might try to add a new benefit to the set of benefits customers consider when selecting a store. For example, Fair Indigo (www.fairindigo.com), along with other retailers, is adding a new benefit that is important to many consumers: the degree to which the retailer is socially responsible. Fair Indigo emphasizes that the apparel sold through its multiple channels is made by workers who are paid a fair wage, not just a minimum wage. A fair wage means that workers are able to live relatively comfortably within the context of their local area, with enough money for housing, food, health care, education for their children, and some disposable income. To get a high evaluation on this new benefit, Fair Indigo handpicked the most ethical factories around the globe to make its apparel.[27] The approach of adding a new benefit is often effective, because it's easier to change customer evaluations of new than of old benefits.

Purchasing the Merchandise or Service

Customers don't always purchase a brand or item of merchandise with the highest overall evaluation. The product or service offering the greatest benefits (having the highest evaluation) may not be available in the store, or the customer may feel that its risks outweigh the potential benefits. One measure of retailers' success at converting positive evaluations to purchases is the number of real or virtual abandoned carts in the retailer's store and website.

Retailers use various tactics to increase the chances that customers will convert their positive merchandise or service evaluations into purchases. Retailers can reduce the number of abandoned carts by making it easier to purchase merchandise. They reduce the actual wait time to buy merchandise by having more checkout lanes open and placing them conveniently inside the store. To reduce perceived wait times, they install digital displays to entertain customers waiting in line. On a website, the ease of navigation is critical for decreasing the number of abandoned virtual carts.

Customers' perceived risk in making a purchase decision can be reduced by providing sufficient information that reinforces the customer's positive evaluation. For those customers browsing the Internet, retailers offer online reviews.[28] Finally, risks are reduced when retailers offer liberal return policies, money-back guarantees, price-matching policies, and refunds if customers find the same merchandise available at lower prices from another retailer.

Conversion rates are particularly low for consumers using an Internet channel because consumers are able to easily keep track of things they like. They can look at products, throw them in their cart, and delay a purchase decision. Retailers do a few things to encourage customers to make a purchase decision. For example, Zappos.com and Overstock.com create urgency by alerting customers when an item they have put in their shopping car is almost sold out. Other sites, such as Gilt Groupe, offer items for a specified 36-hour period, and Future Shop runs time-based, online-only sales. While the Internet channel makes it easier for shoppers to delay purchase decisions, it also makes it easier to identify potential customers and encourage them to buy. Petco.com devotes entire sections within each pet category to "top rated" products. Shoppers who browse these products purchase 35 percent more than those who browse assortments arranged in a traditional manner. Those who buy from "top rated" sections spend 40 percent more than those who do not.[29] Many retailers send reminder e-mails to visitors about times in carts they have abandoned.[30]

Post-purchase Evaluation

The buying process doesn't end when a customer purchases a product. After making a purchase, the customer uses the product and then evaluates the experience to determine whether it was satisfactory or unsatisfactory. Satisfaction is a post-consumption evaluation of how well a store or product meets or exceeds customer expectations. This post-purchase evaluation then becomes part of the customer's internal information and affects future store and product decisions. Unsatisfactory experiences can motivate customers to complain to the retailer, patronize other stores, and select different brands in the future.[32] Consistently high levels of satisfaction build store and brand loyalty, important sources of competitive advantage for retailers.

Types of Buying Decisions

In some situations, customers spend considerable time and effort selecting a retailer and evaluating alternative products—going through all the steps in the buying process described in the preceding section. In other situations, buying decisions are made automatically with little thought. Three types of customer decision-making processes are extended problem solving, limited problem solving, and habitual decision making.

Extended Problem Solving

Extended problem solving is a purchase-decision process in which customers devote considerable time and effort to analyzing their alternatives. Customers typically engage in extended problem solving when the purchase decision involves a lot of risk and uncertainty. Financial risks arise when customers purchase an expensive product or service. Physical risks are important when customers feel that a product or service may affect their health or safety. Social risks arise when customers believe a product will affect how others view them. Lasik eye surgery, for instance, involves all three types of risks: It can be expensive, potentially damage the eyes, and change a person's appearance.

Consumers engage in extended problem solving when they are making a buying decision to satisfy an important need or when they have little knowledge about the product or service. Due to the high risk in such situations, customers go beyond their internal knowledge to consult with friends, family members, or experts. They may visit several retailers before making a purchase decision.

Retailers stimulate sales from customers engaged in extended problem solving by providing the necessary information in a readily available and easily understood manner and by offering money-back guarantees. For example, retailers that sell merchandise involving extended problem solving provide information on their websites describing the merchandise and its specifications, have informational displays in their stores (such as a sofa cut in half to show its construction), and use salespeople to demonstrate features and answer questions.

Limited Problem Solving

Limited problem solving is a purchase-decision process involving a moderate amount of effort and time. Customers engage in this type of buying process when they have had some prior experience with the product or service and their risk is moderate. In such situations, customers tend to rely more on personal knowledge than on external information. They usually choose a retailer they have shopped at before and select merchandise they have bought in the past. The majority of customer purchase decisions involve limited problem solving.

Retailers attempt to reinforce this buying pattern and make it habitual when customers are buying merchandise from them. If customers are shopping elsewhere,

however, retailers need to break this buying pattern by introducing new information or offering different merchandise or services.

One type of limited problem solving is impulse buying, or unplanned purchasing, which is a buying decision made by customers on the spot after seeing the merchandise.[33] Retailers encourage impulse-buying behaviour by using prominent point-of-purchase (POP) or point-of-sale (POS) displays to attract customers' attention. Retailers have long recognized that the most valuable real estate in the store is at the point of purchase. An increasing number of nonfood retailers are looking to increase impulse buys from customers by offering gum, candy, and mints at their cash registers. Electronic shoppers are also stimulated to purchase impulsively when Internet retailers put special merchandise on their home pages and suggest complementary merchandise just before checkout.

Habitual Decision Making

Habitual decision making is a purchase-decision process involving little or no conscious effort. Today's customers have many demands on their time. One way they cope with these time pressures is by simplifying their decision-making process. When a need arises, customers automatically respond with, "I'll buy the same thing I bought last time from the same store." Typically, this habitual decision-making process occurs when decisions aren't very important to customers and involve familiar merchandise they have bought in the past. When customers are loyal to a brand or a store, they engage in habitual decision making.

Brand loyalty means that customers like and consistently buy a specific brand in a product category. They are reluctant to switch to other brands if their favourite brand isn't available. For example, loyal Coca-Cola drinkers won't buy Pepsi, no matter what. Thus, retailers can satisfy these customers' needs only if they offer the specific brands desired.

Brand loyalty creates both opportunities and problems for retailers. Customers are attracted to stores that carry popular brands, but because retailers must carry these high-loyalty brands, they may not be able

extended problem solving A buying process in which customers spend considerable time at each stage of the decision-making process because the decision is important and they have limited knowledge of alternatives.

limited problem solving A purchase-decision process involving a moderate amount of effort and time. Customers engage in this type of buying process when they have some prior experience with the product or service and their risk is moderate.

habitual decision making A purchase decision involving little or no conscious effort.

brand loyalty Indicates customers like and consistently buy a specific brand in a product category. They are reluctant to switch to other brands if their favourite brand isn't available.

to negotiate favourable terms with the suppliers of the popular national brands. If, however, the high-loyalty brands are private-label brands (i.e., brands owned by the retailer), retailer loyalty is heightened.

Retailer loyalty means that customers like and habitually visit the same retailer to purchase a type of merchandise. All retailers would like to increase their customers' loyalty, and they can do so by selecting a convenient location, offering complete assortments of national and private-label brands, reducing the number of stockouts, rewarding customers for frequent purchases, or providing good customer service.

Many purchase decisions consider the needs of family members other than the shopper.

Social Factors Influencing Buying Decisions

Exhibit 3–4 illustrates that a customer's buying decisions are influenced by both the customer's beliefs, attitudes, and values *and* factors in the customer's social environment. In this section, we discuss how buying decisions are affected by the customer's social environment—the customer's family, reference groups, and culture.

Family

Many purchase decisions are made for products that the entire family will consume or use. Thus, retailers must understand how families make purchase decisions and how various family members influence these decisions.

Family Decision Making When families make purchase decisions, they often consider the needs of all family members.[34] In a situation such as choosing a vacation site, all family

members may participate in the decision making. In other situations, one member of the family may assume the role of making the purchase decision. For example, the husband might buy the groceries, the wife uses them to prepare their child's lunch, and the child consumes the lunch in school. In this situation, the store choice decision might be made by the husband, but the brand choice decision might be made by the wife, though greatly influenced by the child.

Children play an important role in family buying decisions.[35] Satisfying the needs of children is particularly important for many Baby Boomers who decide to have children late in life. They often have high disposable income and want to stay in luxury resorts, but they still want to take their children on vacations. Resort hotels now realize they must satisfy children's needs as well as adults'. For example, Hyatt hotels greet families by offering books and games tailored to the children's ages. Parents checking in with infants receive a first-day supply of baby food or formula and diapers at no charge. Baby-sitting and escort services to attractions for children are offered.[36]

exhibit 3–4   Factors Affecting Buying Decisions

Beliefs About performance of retailers and products		Customer Buying Decision		Family
Values Importance weights				Reference Group
Attitudes Evaluations of retailers and products				Culture

Retailers can attract consumers who shop with other family members by satisfying the needs of all family members. For example, IKEA, a Swedish furniture store chain, has a "ball pit" in which children can play while their parents shop. By accommodating the needs of children who might not be interested in shopping, the family stays in the stores longer and buys more merchandise.[37]

Reference Groups

A reference group is composed of two or more people whom a person uses as a basis of comparison for his or her beliefs, feelings, and behaviours. A consumer might have a number of different reference groups, although the most important reference group is the family. These reference groups affect buying decisions by:

- Offering information
- Providing rewards for specific purchasing behaviours
- Enhancing a consumer's self-image

Reference groups provide information to consumers directly through conversation or indirectly through observation. Celebrity sports people can capture the hearts and wallets of consumers through product endorsements and retailer relationships. For example, Canadian professional golfer Mike Weir has a business relationship with Sears. Female golfers might look to Lori Kane or Michelle Wei to guide their purchase decisions. Canadian hockey hero Wayne Gretzky has added his face to Ford's advertising campaign.

By identifying and affiliating with reference groups, consumers create, enhance, and maintain self-image. Customers who want to be seen as members of an elite social class may shop at Holt Renfrew, whereas others who want to create an image of an athletic enthusiast might buy merchandise from Lululemon.

Retailers are particularly interested in identifying and reaching out to those in a reference group who act as store advocates and actively influence others in the group. Store advocates are customers who like a store so much that they actively share their positive experiences with family and friends. Consumers see so much advertising that they have become suspicious of the claims being made. So they are relying more on their own social networks for information about stores to patronize and merchandise to buy. Research has found that advocacy for a particular supermarket is not built on low prices. It is stimulated by a store design that enables advocates to find items easily, by courteous and helpful employees, and by having a wide selection of fresh vegetables and fruits.[38]

Alpha moms are good example of store advocates. Educated, tech-savvy, Type A moms have a common goal: mommy excellence.[39] An alpha mom is a multitasker, kidcentric, and hands-on. She may or may not work outside the home, but at home, she views motherhood as a job that can be mastered with diligent research. As the label implies, she is a leader of the pack who influences how other moms spend. She's also wired—online 87 minutes a day, she spends a hefty 7 percent more than the typical Internet user. The impact of her purchases or what she touts can spread on the Internet, far beyond her personal e-mail list or blog.

Canada's Multicultural Market

Visible minorities in Canada have grown threefold over the last two decades and now make up 13 percent of the population. It is predicted that visible minorities will make up 20 percent of Canada's population and 18 percent of the labour force by 2016. Today more than eight out of ten visible minorities are first-generation immigrants. More than 48 percent of Toronto's population is now foreign-born, making Toronto the most ethnically diverse city in the world, and Vancouver is more ethnically diverse than any city in the United States. According to Statistics Canada, in another few years Toronto's population will be more than half foreign-born. Almost a quarter of southern Ontario residents, 37 percent of Vancouver citizens, and approximately 20 percent of people living in Calgary and Montreal are first-generation immigrants. Across Canada, 5.4 million people are first-generation immigrant Canadians. According to Statistics Canada, immigrants from India, Pakistan, south China, the Philippines, and other South Asian countries will represent the largest proportion of new Canadians by 2017.

Canada has evolving societal issues; no one comes here and discards his culture (values shared by most members of a society). These people bring unique culture and world views to Canada, and they also bring unique shopping preferences: They like to shop around and haggle with shop owners, and if they don't feel like they can negotiate a better price, they will shop somewhere else. Haggling is about building a relationship. It is all about learning about the product, talking to a shop owner, and negotiating a special price; think of it as a shopping ritual. For South Asians, it is a way of gaining respect. This aspect of Canada's new

reference group One or more people whom a person uses as a basis of comparison for his or her beliefs, feelings, and behaviours.

store advocates Customers who like a store so much that they actively share their positive experiences with friends and family.

culture The meaning and values shared by most members of a society.

cultural influx is going to be a challenge for many retailers.

For Canada's large retailers with centralized pricing and buying, it will be difficult to adjust prices and product to meet the needs of individual markets. It may be important to connect to community leaders who can talk to people from their population and find out about retail preferences of the ethnic market. Show the market that you are talking to them by acknowledging special times, for example, Chinese New Year.

The one thing that ethnic consumers and aging Boomers have in common is their desire for quality service. They know the value of a dollar and they will not trade away quality.

Marketers must understand how new immigrants think before they can market to them, because the solution is not simply to take a commercial and add a voiceover in another language. The way to optimize the multicultural market is to build relationships. It is not just about selling to the market, but rather about serving the market. For example, General Motors Canada capitalizes on the fact that the Chinese culture considers 2, 8, and 9 to be lucky numbers by trying to help customers obtain licence plates reflecting this preference.

In this changing marketplace, you cannot afford not to invest in research. Retailers need to keep their research up to date and look at their product mix, fashion sizes, and service and match them to the market preferences. Hiring an ethnically diverse staff will also assist retailers to understand the market. The reality is, if you don't keep up with the market someone else will. Two important points to remember:

- Immigrants often arrive in Canada with only money and a suitcase. They will need to buy necessary supplies and household items to set up a home.
- Immigrants are often used to sophisticated marketing from their home country and will look to advertising for information, store product, price, and location.

Walmart began airing ethnic ads in 1998 in Toronto, featuring customers of different ethnicities speaking in their own language.

In addition, not only does retailing have to differ for Canadian- and foreign-born market segments, but differences can arise among groups of native Canadians as well. What appeals to the rest of Canada may not work in Quebec. The needs and tastes of the Quebec market are particular to its culture and its self-contained nature. Quebecers differ in their shopping behaviour; retailers who are not of Quebec origin generally have a tough time becoming successful in this marketplace. Many non-Quebec retailers who have entered the market have had limited success and subsequently have left the market. Quebecers are loyal to Quebec-based retailers whether they are francophone or not. Quebec represents its own media universe that is unique in Canada; the province has more beauty and fashion publications than the rest of Canada combined. Tween girls have a strong cultural background where pop icons and cultural references are different; for example, when Nicki Minaj is hot, she's hot in Quebec too, but most of the Quebec pop icons are francophones. It is good to tie your product to a spokesperson, but make sure that you know the market to find the best match for your product. Young Quebecers watch French-language movies and reality shows, and are not fond of clothes displaying big logos and brand names that may be popular in the rest of Canada. Language is responsible for fundamental cultural distinctions.[41]

A **subculture** is a distinctive group of people within a culture. Members of a subculture share some customs and norms with the overall society but also have some unique perspectives.[42] Subcultures can be based on geography (southerners), age (Baby Boomers), ethnicity (Asian Canadians), or lifestyle (hipster).

Lo 4 Market Segmentation

The preceding discussion focused on how individual customers evaluate and select stores and merchandise and factors affecting their decision making. To increase their efficiency, retailers identify groups of customers (market segments) and target their offerings to meet the needs of typical customers in that segment rather than the needs of a specific customer. A **retail market segment** is a group of customers whose needs are satisfied by the same retail mix because they have similar needs. For example, families travelling on a vacation have different needs than do executives on business trips. Thus, Marriott offers hotels with different retail mixes for each of these segments.

The Internet enables retailers to efficiently target individual customers and market products to them on a one-to-one basis.

Criteria for Evaluating Market Segments

Customers are grouped into segments in many different ways. For example, customers can be grouped on the basis that they live in the same city, have similar incomes and education, or barbecue at their homes twice a week or more. Exhibit 3–5 shows different methods for segmenting retail markets. There's no simple way to determine which method is best. Four criteria for evaluating whether a retail segment is a viable target market are actionability, identifiability, accessibility, and size.

Actionability The fundamental criteria for evaluating a retail market segment are as follows:

- Customers in the segment must have similar needs, seek similar benefits, and be satisfied by a similar retail offering.
- Those customers' needs must be different from the needs of customers in other segments.

Actionability means that the definition of a segment must clearly indicate what the retailer should do to satisfy its needs. According to this criterion, it makes sense for Addition Elle (which caters to full-figured women) to segment the apparel market on the basis of the demographic characteristic, physical size of women. Customers who wear large sizes have different needs than those who wear small sizes, so they are attracted to a store offering a unique merchandise mix. Plus-size retailers have been striving to offer fashion to this consumer group that wants more than just clothing that fits—they insist on style. The plus-size market has been a growing segment of the women's apparel market over the last few years.

On the other hand, it wouldn't make sense for a supermarket to segment its market on the basis of the customer size. Large and small men and women probably have the same needs, seek the same benefits, and go through the same buying process for groceries. This segmentation approach wouldn't be actionable for a supermarket retailer because the retailer couldn't develop unique mixes for large and small customers. Thus, supermarkets usually segment markets using demographics such as income or ethnic origin to develop their retail mix.

Identifiability Retailers must be able to identify the customers in a target segment. Identifiability is important because it permits the retailer to determine the following:

- The segment's size
- With whom the retailer should communicate when promoting its retail offering

Accessibility Accessibility is the ability of the retailer to deliver the appropriate retail mix to the customers in the segment. Customers for Marriott convention hotels and resort hotels are accessed in different ways because they use different sources to collect information about products and services. Convention hotel customers are best reached through newspapers such as the *National Post* and the *Globe and Mail*, whereas resort hotel customers are best reached through ads on TV and in travel and leisure magazines.

Size A target segment must be large enough to support a unique retailing mix. For example, in the past, health food and vitamins were found primarily in small, owner-operated stores that catered to a relatively small market. In the wake of higher consciousness about exercise and nutrition, health food stores such as Whole Foods have gained customer loyalty. Supermarkets have also expanded their offering of health foods, vitamins, and organic produce to meet this substantial market segment's needs.

retail market segment A group of customers whose needs will be satisfied by the same retail offering because they have similar needs and go through similar buying processes.

actionability Means that the definition of a market segment must clearly indicate what the retailer should do to satisfy its needs.

identifiability Permits a retailer to determine a market segment's size and with whom the retailer should communicate when promoting its retail offering.

accessibility (1) The degree to which customers can easily get into and out of a shopping centre; (2) ability of the retailer to deliver the appropriate retail mix to the customers in the segment.

DID YOU KNOW?

In 1994, the Swedish furniture retailer IKEA aired the first mainstream TV ad targeted toward the gay subculture by featuring a gay relationship.[43]

geographic segmentation Segmentation of potential customers by where they live. A retail market can be segmented by countries, provinces, cities, and neighbourhoods.

On the other hand, the number of consumers in a target segment may not be a good indicator of potential sales. For example, international retailers are very interested in China because it has 1.2 billion consumers. Although many consumers in China's coastal cities have considerable disposable income, 70 percent of all Chinese live in rural areas with minimal incomes. Even in the urban areas, many Chinese consumers are in their twenties and live with their parents in an apartment.[44]

Approaches for Segmenting Markets

Exhibit 3–5 illustrates the wide variety of approaches for segmenting retail markets. No single approach is best for all retailers. They must explore various factors that affect customer buying behaviour and determine which factors are most important. Now we'll discuss methods for segmenting retail markets.

Geographic Segmentation   Geographic segmentation groups customers by where they live. A retail market can be segmented by countries (Japan, Mexico) and by areas within a country such as provinces, cities, and neighbourhoods. Since customers typically shop at stores convenient to where they live and work, individual retail outlets usually focus on the customer segment reasonably close to the outlet.

In the United States, many food retailers concentrate on regions of the country. For example, HEB concentrates on Texas; Wegmans concentrates on Western New York. However, in the U.K., supermarket retailing is dominated

exhibit 3–5   Methods for Segmenting Retail Markets

Segmentation Descriptor	Example of Categories
Geographic	
Region	Pacific, Prairies, Central, Maritimes
Population density	Rural, suburban, urban
Climate	Cold, warm
Demographic	
Age	Under 6, 6–12, 13–19, 20–29, 30–49, 50–65, over 65
Gender	Male, female
Family life cycle	Single; married with no children; married with youngest child under 6; married with youngest child over 6; married with children no longer living at home; widowed
Family income	Under $19 999; $20 000–29 999; $30 000–49 999; $50 000–$74 999; over $75 000
Occupation	Professional, clerical sales, craftsperson, retired, student, homemaker
Education	Some high school, high school graduate, some university, university graduate, graduate degree
Religion	Catholic, Protestant, Jewish, Muslim
Race	Caucasian, African American, Hispanic, Asian
Nationality	American, Japanese, British, French, German, Italian, Chinese
Psychosocial	
Social class	Lower, middle, upper
Lifestyle	Striver, driver, devotee, intimate, altruist, fun seeker, creative
Personality	Aggressive, shy, emotional
Feelings and Behaviours	
Attitudes	Positive, neutral, negative
Benefit sought	Convenience, economy, prestige
Stage in decision process	Unaware, aware, informed, interested, intend to buy, bought previously
Perceived risk	High, medium, low
Innovativeness	Innovator, early adopter, early majority, late majority, laggard
Loyalty	None, some, complete
Usage rate	None, light, medium, heavy
Usage situation	Home, work, vacation, leisure
User status	Non-user, ex-user, potential user, current user

by national firms such as Sainsbury and Tesco. The Canadian grocery industry is dominated by George Weston Ltd., the country's largest food processor and distributor and owner of Loblaws, the country's biggest grocery chain.

Even though national retailers such as The Gap and Sears have no geographic focus, they do tailor their merchandise selections to different regions of North America. Snow sleds don't sell well in Florida, and surfboards don't sell well in Alberta. Even within a metropolitan area, stores in a chain must adjust to the unique needs of customers in different neighbourhoods. For example, supermarkets in affluent neighbourhoods typically have more gourmet foods than stores in less affluent neighbourhoods.

Segments based on geography are identifiable, accessible, and substantial. It's easy to determine who lives in a geographic segment such as the Paris metropolitan area and to target communications and locate retail outlets for customers in Paris. When customers in different geographic segments have similar needs, it would be inappropriate to develop unique retail offerings by geographic markets. For example, a fast-food customer in Toronto probably seeks the same benefits as a fast-food customer in Vancouver. Thus, it wouldn't be useful to segment the fast-food market geographically. Even though Hudson's Bay and The Gap vary some merchandise assortments geographically, the majority of their merchandise is identical in all of their stores because customers who buy basic clothing (underwear, slacks, shirts, and blouses) have many of the same needs in all regions of North America. On the other hand, Home Depot and many supermarket chains have significantly different assortments in stores located in the same city.

Demographic Segmentation Demographics are numbers about people, and this information on the population is collected through a census of the population in Canada by Statistics Canada and in the United States by the U.S. Census Bureau. The law requires that all people living in the country complete the questionnaire accurately. The general demographic information collected is available to all researchers, businesspeople, and students to assist in decision making. Demographic segmentation groups consumers on the basis of easily measured, objective characteristics such as age, gender,

income, and education. Demographic variables are the most common means to define segments because consumers in these segments can be easily identified and accessed. The media used by retailers to communicate with customers are defined in terms of demographic profiles. Demographics such as gender are related to differences in shopping behaviour.

Who Is the Male Shopper? It does appear that men are from Mars and women are from Venus when the sexes go shopping. Men show little ability or interest in honing their shopping skills, whereas women view the supermarket as a place where they can demonstrate their expertise in getting the most value for their money. Rather than looking for items on sale or making price comparisons, men tend to select well-known brands. They also tend not to pay attention at the checkout register, whereas women watch the cashier to be sure they're charged the right price. Men and women even buy different merchandise. Women buy more health-oriented foods (such as cottage cheese and refrigerated yogourt) and household essentials (such as cleaning and personal health products). Men's shopping baskets contain more beer, cupcakes, ice cream, and hot dogs. Men also do less planning and make numerous last-minute grocery trips. Single men visit supermarkets 99 times a year; single women make 80 trips a year. These eleventh-hour trips make men more susceptible to impulse purchases such as potato chips and cookies.[45]

demographic segmentation
A method of segmenting a retail market that groups consumers on the basis of easily measured, objective characteristics such as age, sex, income, and education.

The Power of Women Women comprise 52 percent of the North American population and have significant buying power, making 85 percent of all retail and service purchases ($3.7 trillion), and buying 51 percent of consumer electronics, 51 percent of all cars (and influencing 85 percent of all auto purchases), 50 percent of computers, and 51 percent of all travel.[46] Women bring in half or more of the income in most North American households. Unlike their male counterparts, who rely on promotions to make a purchasing decision, women will seek out a product's credibility or discuss the product's attributes with a friend. Well-known retailers such as Home Depot are aware of the importance of understanding gender difference in marketing to both sexes. The big-box stores are recognizing that women are wearing the overalls and thus are designing stores with wider aisles, detailed signage, samples of finished projects, and lots of helpful staff to assist with decisions. Even men's clothier Harry Rosen understands the influence of women in closing a sale; you talk to the men but sell to their wives. Women are rapidly surpassing men in starting to use online services, and nearly half of first-time web buyers are women (WiredNews.com). According to GenderMark International, up to 70 percent of women ignore marketing campaigns that don't speak to them, and if they have a bad experience with a product or service, on average, women will tell 28 people. The bottom line is that women want a more intelligent, more honest approach to retailing. Women make up 80 percent of The Shopping Channel's paying customers, and 50 percent of online shoppers are women ages 35 to 54. Even in time spent on social media, (PC, mobile, web, and apps), women are more deeply engaged than men, spending an average of 8 hours and 37 minutes of social networking time versus 6 hours and 13 minutes for men.[47] It seems that women want it all—make them feel special please online and offline, but when it comes right down to it, they show no loyalty because price matters more than brand.

Knowledge of Demographics Is Critical Demographics is critical to understanding product demand and defining a retailer's strategy. Demographics can explain the growth of specialty beers and skin care creams, the demand for healthy food, the trends in real estate, and golf memberships. A study by AOL and Bovitz Research Group took a look at how women are spending their time online and what they want from the web. The study broadly categorized web-savvy women into three distinct behavioural groups. First, social expressionistas are women who are community creators who are passionate about spreading the word online and are highly active on social networking sites. Second, alpha trendsetters are women who take their social lives and careers seriously and are very brand conscious; these women are the perfect market for retailers of luxury brands that aim their products at women. Finally, shopsessives are women who believe they are experts in all areas ranging from fashion to health and are shopping online across all product categories; this group of women highly influences the shopping decisions of her friends and family.[48]

David Foot—demographer, professor at the University of Toronto, and author of *Boom, Bust & Echo* (followed by *Boom, Bust & Echo 2000*)—has discussed the impact of demographics on Canadian life. For example, he explains that one-third of the North American population was born after the Second World War. Known as the Boomers (born from 1946 to 1960), by sheer numbers this large group has had immense impact on every aspect of social and economic life. By 2015, leading-edge Baby Boomers will be staring 70 head-on; trailing-edge Boomers will be looking at 50 in the rearview mirror. If 50 was the new 30, will 70 be the new 50? Retailers need to recognize that Baby Boomers will not go conventionally into maturity but will in fact continue to redefine older age and retirement, remaining active and involved.[49]

The Digital Generation

This new youth culture is smart, savvy, and the first generation to grow up surrounded by digital media: the Internet, smartphones, tablets, computer games, DVDs, MP3, mobile technology, social media, and digital cameras. This digital generation will epitomize the new mindset of the decade as they have grown up in a world where there are very few physical or psychological barriers to try new ways of doing things. Everything is interconnected, anything goes, everything is available, and nothing is private. Retailers and suppliers will need to respond by providing this generation with the tools they need to create, co-create, or re-create to suit themselves.[50]

Retailing to Tweens

Tweens, those between the ages of 8 and 13 years, are the fastest-growing segment in Canada. The 2.5 million tweens spend $4.9 million annually on candy, clothing, shoes, games, and toys, using money from allowances and birthday and holiday gifts, and also influence the $20 billion their parents spend (see Retailing View 3.3). This phenomenon is known as *kidfluence,* the influence that kids have over the family's purchase decisions.

The tweens of today are very sophisticated for their young years, primarily because they have been exposed to so much knowledge and information through various media.

Female tweens spend $700 million a year on retail items, more than double that of boys at the same age. This group has tremendous retail power and is a huge influence on parents' purchases of consumer electronics, computers, home entertainment systems, restaurant meals, and holidays. According to *YTV Kid & Tween Report,* Canada's 2.5 million tweens are given on average $74 of birthday money each year, and a regular allowance of $7.70 a week. Research by YTV also revealed that one in six has a part-time job, such as babysitting, walking a dog, or shovelling snow, for which they are paid on average $5.60 an hour. It is estimated that Canadian parents spend $800 million each fall on back-to-school clothing and books for tween children. This young consumer is often catered to as working parents compensate for their absence at home by buying whatever their kids want. Shopkeepers often ignore kids, but it is wise to remember that they are the consumers of tomorrow and will long remember poor shopping experiences.[51]

However, demographics may not be useful for defining segments for some retailers. For example, demographics are poor predictors of users of active wear such as jogging suits and running shoes. At one time, retailers assumed that active wear would be purchased exclusively by young people, but the health and fitness lifestyle trend has led people of all ages to buy this merchandise. Relatively inactive consumers find active wear to be comfortable. Initially, retailers felt that DVDs would be a luxury product purchased mainly by wealthy customers. But retailers found that low-income customers and families with young children were strongly attracted to DVDs because they offered low-cost, convenient entertainment.

Geodemographic Segmentation

Geodemographic segmentation uses both geographic and demographic characteristics to classify consumers. This segmentation scheme is based on the principle that "birds of a feather flock together."[52] Consumers in the same neighbourhoods tend to buy the same types of cars, appliances, and apparel and shop at the same types of retailers.

Geodemographers are busy tracking consumer habits across Canada, postal code by postal code. This is the business of data mining. They tabulate and map information from surveys and census data and then fit together a picture of Canadians. Based on information gathered, they are able to formulate a statistical prediction of the likely behaviour the next time someone picks a movie or a restaurant, or hands over a credit card at the shopping mall.

Geodemographers do not know you by name, but from juggling postal codes and probabilities they have a good idea of your lifestyle and spending habits.

Environics Analytics specializes in data mining. They break the country down into recognizable clusters of consumer habits, by region, city, and even neighbourhood. They have clients who pay to know what consumers want, how to track them down, and how to get their attention. Environics can advise on retail locations, best products to succeed in specific markets, and appropriate advertising strategies.

With each retail transaction, consumers give valuable data that will provide insight into buying behaviour. Retail stores want to track where their customers live and what they purchase, in order to target the biggest-spending potential buyers. Privacy laws in Canada prevent companies from trading customers' names, so they collect information based on customers' postal codes. The idea is based on the premise that people live and act more or less like their neighbours.

geodemographic segmentation A market segmentation system that uses both geographic and demographic characteristics to classify consumers.

DID YOU KNOW?

In a recent survey of tweens, responses showed that, during the last week, 42 percent of the girls surveyed shopped at the mall, 39 percent played a video game, and 29 percent gave product advice to parents. Only 24 percent of the boys shopped at the mall, but 83 percent played a video game, and 31 percent gave product advice to parents.[53]

Retailing to Tweens

Tween shoppers, between the ages of 5 and 12, are a large and growing market for retailers. Today's tweens want to express themselves and make their own decisions. They have a fairly developed sense of style, which makes them a hot market for clothes, music, and entertainment. But retailing to tweens can be complicated as they are still forming their personalities, are torn between family and BFFs (best friends forever), and are torn between fitting in and learning how to be an individual. Friends and status are important for tweens. For boys, friendships revolve around technology and sports. Girls like to talk, either about other girls or about boys, but the boys are not really into girls yet.

Tween girls may want to emulate their older sister, but they are still girls at heart. They like fun, frilly, glittery, sensory environments that tap into the kid in them. They want to be treated as young, but not babyish. Tween girls might want to look like their 16-year-old sister, but the apparel assortments need to be fine-tuned to their younger body type and be more modest and sensible. Retailers need to create a mood of power and excitement for tween girls—colourful storefront windows and websites, light displays, photographic sticker booths, ear-piercing stations, and gumball machines. Special fixtures should be placed at eye level for younger girls, even though the girls will be visiting the store with mom, because the tweens choose and the parents pay.

Some of the best tween shopping destinations (a.k.a. totally cool or hip) include retailers like the following:

- **Justice for Girls** (www.shopjustice.com) is right on top of tween trends and offers a large selection of school clothes, dresses, underwear, pyjamas, and seasonal wear, as well as locker and room accessories.

The purchase decisions of tweens are influenced by family members and friends.

- **Aéropostale** (www.aeropostale.com) offers clothing for both boys and girls, and was originally intended for the tween market. You get the style of American Eagle and Abercrombie with the price tags of Old Navy.

- **Hollister** (www.hollisterco.com) transcends from later tween to junior sizes. Styles are pretty basic, laid-back southern California, hip and super comfy—a brand that grabs the target audience at an early age and transcends all the way into adulthood.

- **West 49** (www.west49.com) has very specific strategies to sell to tweens and young teens. The tween-friendly environment is a media-soaked retail space devoted to "the brotherhood of the board."

Sources: Sharon Jayson, "It's Cooler Than Ever to Be a Tween," *USA Today*, September 2, 2009; Jane O'Donnell, "Marketers Keep Pace with 'Tweens,'" *USA Today*, April 11, 2007; Jennifer O'Donnell, "Where Tween Girls Shop for Clothing," About.com Guide, http://tweenparenting.about.come/od/tweenculture/qt/Stores-For-Girls.htm.

Geodemographers group people into clusters, using census data to determine factors such as age, income, education, and ethnicity, and overlay the findings with consumer purchasing and attitudinal data. In Canada, 66 consumer clusters were identified; for example, the wealthiest—the *Cosmopolitan Elite*—represents those earning in excess of $330 000 annually, and accounts for only 0.21 percent of the population. They can be found in Toronto's Forest Hill and Montreal's Westmount. The *Young Digerati* segment consists of tech-savvy singles and couples living in fashionable urban neighbourhoods in a handful of large cities. But by adding social values data, retailers learn that the values of *Young Digerati* are as cutting-edge as their laptops. These young Canadians see themselves as belonging to the global village and show their recognition of the shrinking world in their global ecological consciousness. While they are eager to succeed, they don't want to climb an outdated corporate hierarchy to do so; any marketing campaign should highlight their independent spirit, working on their own outside the cubicles of a large corporation.[54] The cluster profiles also make a strong case for cultural influences. Environics was able to determine that there were 15 clusters that were unique to Quebec. Quebecers shop differently than other Canadians, and Quebec cities appear as almost uniform groupings, enjoying good wine, fine restaurants, and high-fashion conscious than the rest of the country. Only 16 Canadian clusters were similar to clusters found in the United States, leaving 50 clusters unique to Canada.

Some interesting tidbits: There are more coffee addicts per capita in Medicine Hat than anywhere else in Canada; more wine connoisseurs in Quebec; more bottle blondes in Oshawa, Ontario; more dieters in Barrie, Ontario; and more gadget-mad consumers in Vancouver.

Geodemographic segmentation is particularly appealing to store-based retailers, because customers typically patronize stores close to their neighbourhood. Thus, retailers can use geodemographic segmentation to select locations for their stores and tailor assortment in the stores to the preferences of the local community.

Lifestyle Segmentation

Lifestyle segmentation is a method of segmenting a retail market based on consumers' lifestyle. This method of segmentation is achieved through the study of consumer psychographics, which refers to how consumers live, how they spend their time and money, what activities they pursue, and their attitudes and opinions about the world they live in. When you are conducting market research, you want more information than basic market size and growth. You need to understand your market's attitudes, interests, and opinions. The aim is to narrowly define your target market so that you can effectively sell to the customers with the most potential for sales (see Exhibit 3–6). Retailers today are placing more emphasis on lifestyles than on demographics to define a target segment.

Although psychographics can provide revealing information about your market, they can also be the most difficult to access. In Canada, the most readily available psychographics information is in the publication *FP Markets—Canadian Demographics* by the *Financial Post*. This annual publication has two sets of consumer "PSYTE" categories. The first examines lifestyle patterns and segments the population into 60 different categories.

lifestyle segmentation
A method of segmenting a retail market based on consumers' lifestyles.

psychographics
Refers to how consumers live, how they spend their time and money, what activities they pursue, and their attitudes and opinions about the world they live in.

exhibit 3–6 Canada Post's Snapshot Segmentation System

Canada is an extremely diverse multicultural society of more than 32 million people. Canada Post's Snapshot Segmentation System segments Canada's population into five major spending categories: Big Spenders, Beyond Basics, Wannabe Shoppers, Smart Shoppers, and Penny Pinchers. This system is designed to provide information to:

- Build direct mail circulation based on target market
- Increase relevance of product offerings
- Customize marketing according to target market's lifestyle and preferences

BIG SPENDERS
Income: $80 000 plus
High-maintenance lifestyle
Purchase goods to enhance their status
Respond to direct mail
Use Internet for purchases
Hot Spends: home decor, clothing, garden supplies, sporting goods, toys/games/ novelties

SMART SHOPPERS
Income: $50 000 to $75 000
Work–life balance important
Respond to direct mail
Shop by catalogue
Look for quality, family-oriented products
Shop around for the best deal
Shop online
Hot Spends: household tools, appliances, home decor, digital camera, garden supplies

BEYOND BASICS
Income: $40 000 to $65 000
Empty nesters
Own their home
Enjoy dining and theatre
More disposable income than other segments
Respond to direct mail
Shop by catalogue
Hot Spends: garden supplies, jewellery, flowers

PENNY PINCHERS
Income: $30 000 to $50 000
Low income/high aspirations
Like to buy for their children
Respond to direct mail
Spend conservatively
Hot Spends: electronics, kids stuff, household tools, computer, sporting goods

WANNABE SHOPPERS
Income: $35 000 to $50 000
"It's all about me"
Impulsive, want to lead glamorous life
Early adopters of technology and new trends
Shop online
Hot Spends: clothing, DVD equipment and home electronics, computer, music/CDs

Lifestyle segmentation is useful because it identifies what motivates buying behaviour. However, it is difficult to identify and access consumers in specific lifestyle segments.

For example, The Affluents are educated middle-aged executive and professional families with older children and teenagers who live in expensive lightly mortgaged houses in stable, older, executive sections of larger cities. The second set of PSYTE categories provides segmentation based on financial psychographics; for example, the Mortgages and Minivans category is a large family with young children. The average household income is above average, but dwelling values are significantly below average. Dual incomes predominate in this group, and jobs are a mix of the white- and grey-collar categories. The tendency toward larger families results in significant expenditures on child care, toys, and sports equipment.

Michael Adams is a social scientist, the president of Environics Research Group, and a bestselling author. In his second book, *Better Happy Than Rich* (2000), Adams looks at money and its changing meaning in the lives of Canadians. He makes the point that today money has achieved an unprecedented primacy as a lens through which we see ourselves and others. Instead of eroding our values, money is becoming the primary manifestation of our values. The way Canadians earn, spend, invest, and give away their money expresses how they think the world works—and how they would like to see it work.[55] His bestseller *Fire and Ice* (2003) definitively laid to rest the notion that Canadians are simply Americans with snow shovels at the ready. In *Stayin' Alive* (2010), Adams divides the Boomers into four "values" tribes, reasoning that people's beliefs shape our opinions to external forces at least as powerfully as more traditional categories (e.g., age, region, party affiliation). He slots himself into the *Autonomous Rebel* tribe, which most closely resembles the prevailing stereotype of the Boomer as a countercultural hippie.

Looking ahead to the Boomers' dotage, Adams doesn't expect the much-studied generation born between 1946 and 1964 to make a sharp right turn into reactionary old age. The Boomers, his findings further indicate, are not morphing into their parents, and the progressive values of their youth remain intact.[56]

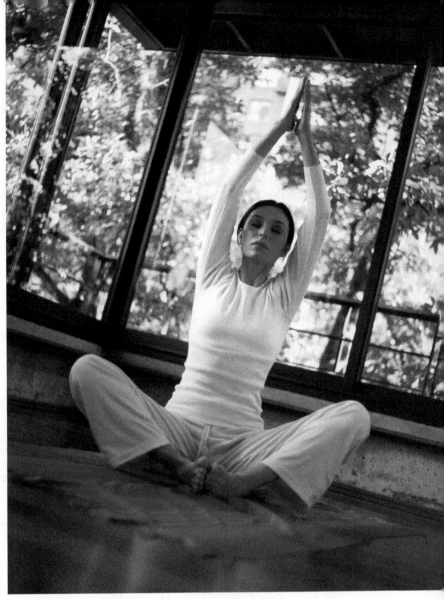

PSYTE HD (www.utahbluemedia.com/pbbi/psyte/psyteCanada.html), developed by Pitney Bowes Business Insight, is geodemographic data solution software that pulls Canadian information together (household-level data by postal code). Go to the above website and click on "PSYTE HD Cluster Index." The Cluster Index presents 59 different clusters and a text box in which to enter a Canadian postal code to find out which cluster most represents that postal code. Conducting larger scale research can be very expensive, but a suggested affordable option for collecting secondary data is GDSourcing (www.gdsourcing.com). Sometimes it is possible to uncover detailed data free of charge. Check the following: Ipsos (www.ipsos.ca), Leger Marketing (www.legermarketing.com), Pollara (www.pollara.ca), Decima Research (www.decima.ca), and Environics (www.environics.ca).

Buying Situation Segmentation   Buying behaviour of customers with the same demographics or lifestyle can differ depending on their buying situation. Thus, retailers may use buying situation segmentation, such as fill-in versus weekly shopping to segment a market. For example, a parent with four children prefers the supercentre to the Internet grocer or supermarket for weekly grocery purchases. But if the parent ran out of milk during the week, he or she would probably go to the convenience store rather than the warehouse club for this fill-in shopping. Convenience would be more important than assortment in the fill-in shopping situation. Similarly, an executive will stay at a convention hotel on a business trip and a resort on a family vacation.

Benefit Segmentation   Another approach to defining a target segment is to group customers seeking similar benefits; this is called benefit segmentation. In the multi-attribute attitude model, customers in the same benefit segment would attach a similar set of importance weights to the attributes of a store or a product. For example, customers who place high importance on fashion and style and low importance on price would form a fashion segment, whereas customers who place more importance on price would form a price segment.

Benefit segments are very actionable. Benefits sought by customers in the target segment clearly indicate how retailers should design their offerings to appeal to the segment. But customers in benefit segments aren't easily identified or accessed. It's hard to look at a person and determine what benefits he or she is seeking. Typically, the audience for media used by retailers is described by demographics rather than by the benefits sought.

Composite Segmentation Approaches

As we've seen, no one approach meets all the criteria for useful customer segmentation. For example, segmenting by demographics and geography is ideal for identifying and accessing customers, but these characteristics often are unrelated to customers' needs. Thus, these approaches may not indicate the actions necessary to attract customers in these segments. On the other hand, knowing what benefits customers are seeking is useful for designing an effective retail offering; the problem is identifying which customers are seeking these benefits. For these reasons, composite segmentation plans use multiple variables to identify customers in the target segment. They define target customers by benefits sought, lifestyles, and demographics.

Best Buy has introduced its "Customer Centricity" program to target five composite segments.[57] Each of these segments, referred by a first name, has a manager responsible for developing a retail strategy for the market segment. "Barrys" are the best customers. They are affluent professional men, 30 to 60 years of age, who make a minimum of $150 000 a year, and drive luxury cars. Barry is the kind of guy who walks in to Best Buy, sees a $30 000 home theatre system, and says, "I'll take it." In contrast, "Jills" are the busy suburban moms; "Buzzes" are focused, active younger men; and "Rays" are family men who like their technology practical. The fifth segment consists of small businesses buying their consumer electronics at Best Buy.

A group of stores has been redesigned to focus on a specific segment or two with significant representation in the local area. For example, Jill stores have personal shoppers and areas for children to play while mom shops. The soundtrack playing in the background is often children's music. Stores catering to Barrys have special areas to display high-end entertainment systems and experts in mobile technology; stores for Jills dedicate more inventory to things like learning software and feature softer colours and a children's technology department. The Buzz-oriented stores, by contrast, feature the very latest technologies and video games. They have comfortable places in which customers can sample technologies, complete with sofas and flat-screen televisions for testing video games and consoles. Ray stores focus more on low price.

buying situation segmentation A method of segmenting a retail market based on customer needs in a specific buying situation, such as a fill-in shopping trip versus a weekly shopping trip.

benefit segmentation A method of segmenting a retail market on the basis of similar benefits sought in merchandise or services.

composite segmentation A method of segmenting a retail market using multiple variables, including benefits sought, lifestyles, and demographics.

SUMMARY

This chapter takes a look at trends that are impacting consumer buying decisions. Based on life stage and lifestyle influences, dominant market segments—for example, the influential tween market and the time-starved working woman—are emerging to reshape the retail environment. The very nature of our multitasking lifestyles will influence how and where we choose to shop in the future.

Understanding consumer buying behaviour is essential to describing a retailer's target market. Awareness of the consumer's needs will assist the retailer in developing a strategic plan that includes the right product, at the right price, and available at a desired retailer.

To satisfy customer needs, retailers must thoroughly understand how customers make store choice and purchase decisions and the factors they consider when deciding. This chapter describes the six stages in the buying process (need recognition, information search, evaluation of alternatives, choice of alternatives, purchase, and post-purchase evaluation) and how retailers can influence their customers at each stage. The importance of the stages depends on the nature of the customer's decision. When decisions are important and risky, the buying process is longer; customers spend more time and effort on information search and evaluating alternatives. When buying decisions are less important to customers, they spend little time in the buying process and their buying behaviour may become habitual. The buying process of consumers is influenced by their personal beliefs, attitudes, and values and by their social environment. The primary social influences are provided by the consumers' families, reference groups, and culture.

To develop cost-effective retail programs, retailers group customers into segments. Some approaches for segmenting markets are based on geography, demographics, geodemographics, lifestyles, usage situations, and benefits sought. Since each approach has its advantages and disadvantages, retailers typically define their target segment by several characteristics.

KEY TERMS

accessibility
actionability
benefit segmentation
brand loyalty
buying process
buying situation segmentation
composite segmentation
consideration set
cross-shopping
culture
demographic segmentation
everyday low pricing strategy (EDLP)

extended problem solving
external sources of information
geodemographic segmentation
geographic segmentation
habitual decision making
hedonic needs
hype
identifiability
information search
internal sources of information
lifestyle segmentation

limited problem solving
multiattribute attitude model
post-purchase evaluation
psychographics
reference group
retail market segment
retailer loyalty
satisfaction
store advocates
subculture
utilitarian needs

Get Out & Do It!

1. **CONNECT EXERCISE** Access Connect to develop a multiattribute attitude model describing your evaluation and decision concerning some relatively expensive product you bought recently, such as a car or consumer electronics. Open the multiattribute attitude model exercise. List the attributes you considered in the left-hand column. List the alternatives you considered in the top row. Now fill in the importance weight for each attribute in the second column on the left (10—very important, 1—very unimportant). Now fill in your evaluation of each product on each attribute (10—excellent performance, 1—poor performance). Based on your weight and beliefs, the evaluation of each product is shown in the bottom row. Did you buy the product with the highest evaluation?

2. **INTERNET EXERCISE** Visit SRI's website at **www.strategic businessinsights.com/vals/presurvey.shtml**. Click on the "Take the survey" button near the bottom of the page and answer the questions used to classify people into different VALS segments. When you have completed the survey and click on "submit," you should get a form that states your primary and secondary types. You can read descriptions of the types at **www.strategicbusinessinsights.com/vals/ustypes.shtml**. Type up a two-page, double-spaced report on what the survey said about you and whether you agree with it. How can retailers effectively use the results of this survey when planning and implementing their business strategies?

3. INTERNET EXERCISE Check out **www.ytv.com** and learn more about tweens.

4. INTERNET EXERCISE What are the consumer trends at **www.trendwatching.com**?

DISCUSSION QUESTIONS AND PROBLEMS

1. Does the customer buying process end when a customer buys some merchandise? Explain your answer.

2. What would get a consumer to switch from making a habitual choice decision to eat at Wendy's to making a limited or extended choice decision?

3. Reflect on your decision process in selecting a university or college. (Universities are non-profit service retailers.) Was your decision-making process extensive, limited, or habitual?

4. Considering the steps in the consumer buying process (Exhibit 3–1), describe how you (and your family) used this process to select your college/university. How many schools did you consider? How much time did you invest in this purchase decision? When you were deciding on which school to attend, what objective and subjective criteria did you use in the alternative evaluation portion of the consumer buying process?

5. Why is geodemographic segmentation used by retailers to locate stores?

6. Any retailer's goal is to get a customer in its store to stop searching and buy a product at its outlet. How can a sporting goods retailer ensure that the customer buys athletic equipment at its outlet?

7. A family-owned used CD store across the street from a major university campus wants to identify the various segments in its market. What approaches might the store owner use to segment its market? List two potential target market segments based on this segmentation approach. Then contrast the retail mix that would be most appropriate for two potential target segments.

8. Develop a demographic profile for two different target market segments for a hardware store. Outline the difference in the retail mixes that would be most appealing to each of these target markets.

9. How would you expect the buying decision process to differ when shopping on the Internet compared to shopping in a store?

10. Using the multiattribute attitude model, identify the probable choice of a local car dealer for a young single woman and for a retired couple with limited income (see the table below). What can the national retail chain do to increase the chances of the retired couple patronizing its dealership? You can use the multiattribute attitude model template at Connect.

	Importance Weights			Performance Beliefs	
Performance Attributes	**Young Single Woman**	**Retired Couple**	**Local Gas Station**	**National Service Chain**	**Local Car Dealer**
Price	2	10	9	10	3
Time to complete repair	8	5	5	9	7
Reliability	2	9	2	7	10
Convenience	8	3	3	6	5

Practise and learn online with Connect.

retail market strategy

Lo 1 Review the basic principles of retail strategy.

Lo 2 Examine how a retailer can build a sustainable competitive advantage.

Lo 3 Identify different strategic opportunities retailers can pursue.

Lo 4 Explore the steps retailers go through to develop a strategy.

SPOTLIGHT ON RETAILING

Mobile Delivering Magic Results for Retailers

Retailers are barely scratching the surface of mobile device usage when it comes to customer service. Even though wireless devices have been used in retail operations for such functions as inventory and checkout, the latest iterations of tablets and smartphones promise to be significant game-changers in defining the retail experience for both e-commerce and bricks-and-mortar players.

That's in part because service excellence and customer service are emerging as the key focus for retailers, according to a recent survey by American Express Canada. That focus, says Colin D. Temple, vice president of merchant services, is playing into the role of mobile as a means to enrich the customer experience.

"Competition is intensifying and a lot of retailers are learning to understand how to differentiate themselves," he says. "Part of that is leveraging new and emerging channels. Mobile enables retailers to extend their reach and connect to a broader base of potential customers."

Retailers are definitely becoming mesmerized by the thought of leveraging mobile to enhance the consumer experience, notes Robert Passikoff, founder and president of Brand Keys Inc. in New York. "Retail looks to anything it can get its hands on to create a different type of retail experience. In some cases, it's less about inventory control as much as it is a way to present options in a way that's cool."

A mobile groundswell. It doesn't hurt that penetration of smartphones and tablets has been accelerating at breakneck speed. According to Social Media Today, an independent, online community for professionals in PR, marketing, and advertising, Apple sold more iOS devices in 2011 (156 million) than the total number of Macs sold in all 28 years of its existence (122 million). Google recently announced that 850 000 new Android devices are activated daily, and activations are experiencing a year-on-year growth rate of more than 250 percent.

Retailers can't afford to overlook the burgeoning population of smartphone users, says Robert Levy, president of Brand-Spark International, a market research firm specializing in consumer shopping behaviour. "Our latest survey shows that 37 percent of Canadian shoppers have smartphones. That's a big group looking to buy things."

The implications of this are extremely important for retailers seeking new service-related opportunities, notes Mike Dover, research group director for J.C. Williams Group. "Mobile opens the doors to all sorts of applications to improve the in-store experience. For one, it allows retailers to offer deals and make suggestions based on profiles or collaborative filtering consumers."

Dover says the mobile move is taking hold everywhere. "In grocery, Tesco does a great job, for example. Customers can scan an item in-store, the purchase is done electronically, and the items are delivered to the customer's home. In clothing, Wet Seal is doing some interesting things, including social shopping. Target is good for finding a location/search for inventory, etc. The thing is you can do so many innovative things with these devices."

The power of rapid response. The advent of QR (quick response) codes and NFC (near field communications) features in the latest smartphone models is also stretching the possibilities of what retailers can do, from couponing to transaction processing.

BrandSpark reports that QR usage is growing strong, with 88 percent awareness and 40 percent usage rates on the part of Canadian consumers. While still in its infancy, NFC shows even more promise since it doesn't require an application download, and it's simpler to use, Levy says.

With NFC, retailers can communicate with smartphones to advertise, hold contests, or deliver coupons and special offers that are meaningful to customers, he explains. "That's significant when you realize that 96 percent of Canadian shoppers still browse flyers at grocery stores. They like to use those coupons and NFC would make that easier."

E-commerce retailer Well.ca is breaking new ground with its QR code–based shopping trials. The online provider of drug-store sundries wrapped up its virtual store pilot at Union Station in Toronto, which was based on similar retail concepts in Asia targeted at the consumer on the move. Life-size photographs of 120 products included QR codes that commuters could simply scan and enter their delivery information for next-day shipping.

"This was about letting Canadians imagine what shopping can become," says J. Paige Malling, vice president of marketing for Well.ca.

The response was dramatic, she notes. "Sales of featured products skyrocketed. For example, single-day sales for Tide alone were higher than the entire previous month."

Reaching a moving target. Harry Rosen has added its mobile technology repertoire to improve customer service. Stephen Jackson, the clothier's chief information officer, says that wireless devices were first used in-store to help sales associates connect with a customer's information, including sizing, preferences, and preferred brands.

Now the plan is to extend reach even further by using mobile to connect with customers outside of the store or online. A new E-PICS program, for example, lets associates use their smartphones to take and send pictures of laid-out merchandise to their clients. New initiatives are also in the works to loop store associates with online customers via their mobile devices.

When it comes to choosing apps, "It's a matter of finding what adds value and gives them what they really want," Jackson says.

In March 2012, Mac's Convenience and Couche-Tard stores began the first broadcasts of an in-store mobile advertising network from iSIGN Media Solutions Inc. An in-store intelligent antenna detects mobile devices within range of the store and pings them with opt-ins for special offers or loyalty points.

"Mobile is the greatest revolution for retail in the last couple of years and creates the perfect advertising point," says Alex Romanoff, iSIGN founder and CEO in Vancouver. He estimates that the program will reach 1.5 million devices a day. In a test site in Japan, he reports that in the space of two years, an electronics store increased sales by 6 percent, loyalty card adoption by 20 percent, and extended warranty sales by 20 percent.

As mobile continues to generate sales numbers, retailers have a veritable ocean of opportunities to explore the mobile front. As Malling says, "The sky's the limit in terms of execution and what this can become."

Source: Denise Deveau, "Mobile Delivering Magic Results for Retailers," *Canadian Retailer*, Summer 2012, Volume 22, Issue 3, pp. 44–45.

The growing intensity of retail competition due to the emergence of new competitors, formats, and technologies, as well as shifts in consumer preferences, is forcing retailers to devote more attention to long-term strategic planning. This chapter on retailing strategy is the bridge between understanding the world of retailing, that is, the analysis of the retail environment and the more tactical merchandise management decisions and store operations activities undertaken to implement the retail strategy. The retail strategy provides the direction retailers need to take to deal effectively with their environment, their customers, and competitors.[2]

Canadian retailers must be innovative and differentiate themselves from their competitors if they are to survive in a marketplace that is characterized by a blurring of retail channels, increasing competition, and changing consumer preferences.

Retailers need to examine every aspect of their business, assessing the "easy-to-navigate" factor of their store layout, merchandise offerings, efficiency of distribution systems, service attributes, loyalty programs, and their position in the retail marketplace.

DID YOU KNOW?

The word *strategy* comes from the Greek word meaning the "art of the general."[1]

What Is a Retail Strategy?

Lo 1

The term *strategy* is frequently used in retailing. For example, retailers talk about their merchandise strategy, promotion strategy, location strategy, and private-brand strategy. In fact, the term is used so commonly it appears that all retailing decisions are now strategic decisions. But retail strategy isn't just another expression for retail management (see Exhibit 4–1).

Definition of Retail Market Strategy

A retail strategy is a statement identifying the following:

- The retailer's target market
- The format the retailer plans to use to satisfy the target market's needs
- The bases upon which the retailer plans to build a sustainable competitive advantage[3]

The target market is the market segment(s) toward which the retailer plans to focus its resources and retail mix. A retail format describes the nature of the retailer's operations—that is, the retailer's mix (product, price [value], promotion [communication], place, people, and processes)—that is designed to satisfy the needs of its target market. A sustainable competitive advantage is an advantage over competition that cannot be easily copied and can be maintained over a long period of time. Here are two examples of retailing strategies:

- Curves has grown to more than 10 000 franchises in over 70 countries, making it by far the world's top fitness centre in terms of number of clubs. Curves is the market leader in Canada and 23 other countries around the world, including the United States. Over the past 15 years, Curves has been recognized as the fastest-growing franchise in history. Other clubs go after the prized 18-to-34-year-old demographic segment; Curves' customers are aging Baby Boomers, typically living in small towns. This retailer's fitness centres don't have treadmills, saunas, locker rooms, mirrors, aerobics classes, or free weights. Members work out on 8 to 12 hydraulic resistance machines, stopping between stations to walk or jog in place. The clubs' standard routine is finished in 30 minutes and designed to burn 500 calories. Club members usually pay $29 a month, far less than conventional fitness clubs. Rather than attract customers from other clubs, Curves generates customers who haven't considered joining a fitness club before.[4]

- Magazine Luiza is one of Brazil's largest nonfood retailers.

Magazine Luiza targets low-income consumers by selling consumer electronics and appliances on instalment payment plans and offering affordable credit in a country with a significant number of people living in poverty. Customers buying merchandise on credit return to the store each month to make payments in person. Frequently, they are enticed to purchase more merchandise during these visits. In a country where almost half the population does not have a chequing account, the retailer also provides services—including personal loans and insurance policies—that would otherwise be out of reach to most customers. Even though 80 percent of its loans are paid for in instalments, its default rate is 50 percent lower than that of other Brazilian retailers.[5]

Every retail strategy involves the following:

- Selecting target market segment(s)
- Selecting a retail format
- Selecting the elements in the retail mix
- Developing a sustainable competitive advantage that enables the retailer to reduce the level of competition it faces

Now let's examine these central concepts in a retail strategy, as shown in Exhibit 4–1.

target market The market segment(s) toward which the retailer plans to focus its resources and retail mix.

retail format The retailers' type of retail mix (product, price [value], promotion [communication], place, people, and processes).

sustainable competitive advantage A distinct competency of a retailer relative to its competitors that can be maintained over a considerable time period.

exhibit 4–1 Retail Strategy

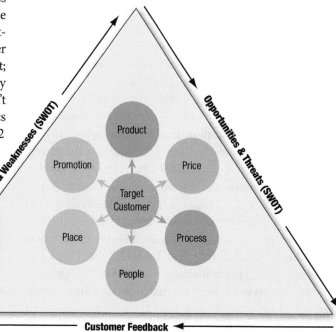

Target Market and the Retail Mix

The **retailing concept** is a management orientation that focuses a retailer on determining the needs of its target market and satisfying those needs more effectively and efficiently than its competitors. Successful retailers satisfy the needs of customers in their target segment better than the competition does. The selection of a target market focuses the retailer on a group of consumers whose needs it will attempt to satisfy. The selection of a retail format outlines the retail mix to be used to satisfy needs of those customers. The retail strategy determines the markets in which a retailer will compete. Traditional markets, such as a farmers' market, are places where buyers and sellers meet and make transactions—say, a consumer buys six ears of corn from a farmer. But in modern markets, potential buyers and sellers aren't necessarily located in one place. Transactions can occur without face-to-face interactions. For example, many customers contact retailers and place orders with a smartphone or tablet.

A **retail market** is a group of consumers with similar needs (a market segment) and a group of retailers using a similar retail format to satisfy those consumer needs.[6] Exhibit 4–2 illustrates a set of retail markets for women's clothing, with a number of retail formats listed down the left-hand column. Each format offers a different retail mix to its customers. Customer market segments are listed in the exhibit's top row. These segments can be defined in terms of the customers' geographic location, demographics, lifestyle, buying situation, or benefits sought. In this illustration, we divide the market into three fashion-related segments: conservative, those who place little importance on fashion and are price-sensitive; traditional, those who want classic styles that are moderately priced; and fashion-forward, those who want the most fashionable merchandise. Each square of the matrix shown in Exhibit 4–2 describes a potential retail market where two or more retailers compete with each other. For example, Sears and Hudson's Bay compete against each other with a department store format targeting the traditional segment looking for moderately priced fashions.

The women's clothing market in Exhibit 4–2 is just one of several representations that could have been used. Retail formats could be expanded to include outlet stores and electronic retailing. Rather than being segmented by fashion orientation, the market could have been segmented using other approaches. Although Exhibit 4–2 isn't the only way to describe the women's retail clothing market, it does illustrate how retail markets are defined in terms of retail format and customer market segment. Each fashion segment—conservative, traditional, and fashion-forward—is likely to shop multiple retail formats. For example, a fashion-forward customer might shop H&M for casual wear, Holt Renfrew for shoes, and Marshalls for a sweater. Each of these retailers then uses a variation of the retail mix to help build and sustain a competitive advantage.

Basically, the matrix in Exhibit 4–2 describes the battlefield on which women's clothing retailers compete. The position in this battlefield indicates the first two elements of a retailer's strategy: its target market segment and retail format. Consider the situation confronting The Gap as it develops a retail strategy for the women's clothing market. Should The Gap compete in multiple retail markets, or should it focus on a limited set of retail markets? If The Gap decides to focus on a limited set of markets, which should it pursue? The Gap's answers to these questions define its retail strategy and indicate how it plans to focus its resources.

The retailer controls the six elements of the retailing mix (outlined below), but the strategies for all of the components must be blended for optimum results. Variations in retailing mixes do not occur by chance. By manipulating the components of the mix and focusing on one or two of the elements in particular, retailers can fine-tune

Most fitness centres target the 18-to-34-year-old segment; Curves' retail offering appeals to aging Baby Boomers.

exhibit 4–2 Retail Market for Women's Apparel

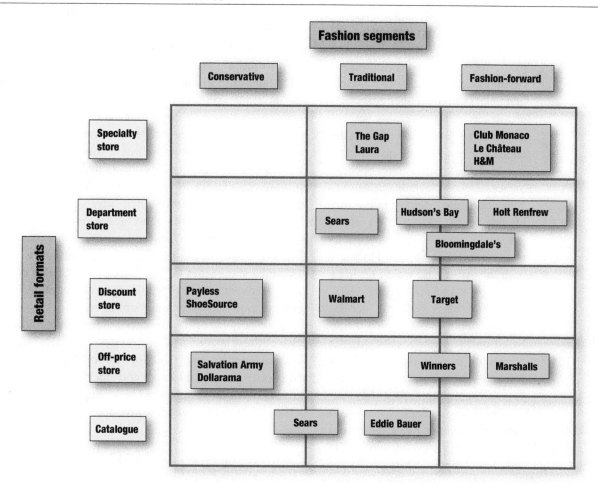

their customer offerings to gain advantages over competitors and best serve the wants and needs of their particular target market segment.

- **Product.** Product and/or service, package, warranty, after-sales service, brand name, company image, and other factors

- **Price (value).** Prestige pricing, competitive (at-the-market) pricing, discount pricing, everyday low pricing (EDLP)

- **Place.** Use of a store or nonstore format, placement in a geographic area, the kind of site, the physical facilities

- **Promotion.** Communication mix: advertising, direct marketing, personal selling, sales promotion, and public relations

- **People.** Human resource management (recruiting, selecting, training, recognition, retaining, and supervising), customer service (personal attention provided)

- **Process.** Database management, retail information system (RIS), data mining and micromarketing, IT, return policies, physical distribution (collaborative planning, forecasting, and replenishment [CPFR], QR)

Building a Sustainable Competitive Advantage

LO 2

Any business that retailers engage in can be the basis for a competitive advantage, but some advantages are more sustainable over a long period of time.

When developing a retail strategy, two sets of variables that will impact your retail business must be assessed:

- The micro-environment
- The macro-environment

Consider the **micro-environment** to be all of the things that are within your control and can be changed; this would include the retail product that will be sold, the price at which you will sell the product, the location of your store, the promotion (including the visual image of your store and promotion activities), the processes, and human resource management decisions. Remember that a retailer can change these factors as needed. But it

micro-environment
All of the things within the retailer's control, including the retail product that will be sold, the price for the product, the store location, the promotion and visual image of the store, the processes, and human resource management decisions.

must be understood that these decisions are never made in a vacuum.

The external environment that the retailer cannot control is called the macro-environment. The macro-environment consists of five subsections: competition; economic stability of a trade area; the technology that will make retailing more efficient; the regulatory and ethical environment in which the business operates; and the social trends, including consumer behaviour and demographic and lifestyle trends. A SWOT analysis (strengths, weaknesses, opportunities, and threats) is designed to assess both the micro- and macro-environments and the retailer's position relative to these issues.

Developing a proactive position based on the knowledge of what is happening in your retail trade area will help establish a sustainable competitive advantage. Any business activity that a retailer engages in can be a basis for a competitive advantage, but some advantages are sustainable over a long period of time, while others can be duplicated by competitors almost immediately.[7] For example, it would be hard for Starbucks to get a long-term advantage over Tim Hortons by simply offering the same coffee specialties at lower prices. If Starbucks' lower prices were successful in attracting customers, Tim Hortons would know what Starbucks had done and would match the price reduction. Similarly, it's hard for retailers to develop a long-term advantage by offering broader or deeper merchandise assortments. If broader and deeper assortments attract a lot of customers, competitors will simply go out and buy the same merchandise for their stores (see Exhibit 4–3).

Establishing a retailer's competitive advantage is similar to building a strong wall around its position in a retail market. If the wall is strong, it will be hard for competitors outside the wall to contact customers in the retailer's target market. If the retailer has built a wall around an attractive market, competitors will attempt to break down the wall. Over time, advantages may be eroded due to these competitive forces; but by building high, thick walls, retailers can sustain their advantage, minimize competitive pressure, and boost profits for a longer time. Thus, establishing a sustainable competitive advantage is the key to positive long-term financial performance.

Three approaches for developing a sustainable competitive advantage are (1) building strong relationships with customers, (2) building strong relationships with suppliers, and (3) achieving efficient internal operations. Each of these approaches involves developing an asset—loyal customers, strong vendor relationships, committed effective human resources and efficient systems, and attractive locations—that is not easily duplicated by competitors.[8] Let's look at each of these approaches.

Relationships with Customers

Customer Loyalty

Customer loyalty means that customers are committed to shopping at a particular retailer. For instance, having dedicated employees, unique merchandise, and superior

exhibit 4–3 Methods for Developing Competitive Advantage

Sources of Advantage	Sustainability of Advantage	
	Less Sustainable	**More Sustainable**
Customer loyalty	Habitual repeat purchasing; repeat purchases because of limited competition in the local area	Building a brand image with an emotional connection with customers; using databases to develop and utilize a deeper understanding of customers
Location		Convenient locations
Human resource management	More employees	Committed, knowledgeable employees
Distribution and information systems	Bigger warehouses; automated warehouses	Shared systems with vendors
Unique merchandise	More merchandise; greater assortment; lower price; higher advertising budgets; more sales promotions	Exclusive merchandise
Vendor relations	Repeat purchases from vendor due to limited alternatives	Coordination of procurement efforts; ability to get scarce merchandise
Customer service	Hours of operation	Knowledgeable and helpful salespeople

customer service all help solidify a loyal customer base. But having loyal customers is, in and of itself, an important method of sustaining an advantage over competitors.

Loyalty is more than simply preferring one retailer over another.[9] Loyalty means that customers will be reluctant to patronize competitive retailers. For example, loyal customers will continue to shop at Canadian Tire even if Home Depot opens a store nearby and provides a slightly superior assortment or slightly lower prices. Some ways that retailers build loyalty include the following:

- Developing clear and precise positioning strategies
- Developing a strong brand for the store or store brands
- Providing outstanding customer service
- Creating an emotional attachment with customers through loyalty programs[10]

In addition, other activities discussed in this section also contribute to developing customer loyalty. For example, providing convenient locations encourages patronage, which can develop into loyalty. Engaging in human resource management practices develops competent, committed sales associates, leading to better customer and subsequent customer loyalty.

Brand Image

Retailers build customer loyalty by developing a well-known attractive image of their brand—their name. For example, when most consumers think about fast food or hamburgers or french fries, they immediately think of McDonald's. Their image of McDonald's includes many favourable impressions, such as fast service, consistent quality, and clean washrooms.

Strong brand images facilitate customer loyalty because they reduce the risks associated with purchases. They assure customers that they will receive a consistent level of quality and satisfaction from the retailer. The retailer's image can also create an emotional tie with a customer that leads the customer to trust the retailer. Consumers know, for instance, that when they purchase products from L.L. Bean, the retailer guarantees that its customers will be pleased with their purchases. L.L. Bean guarantees "to give 100% satisfaction in every way. Return anything purchased from us at any time if it proves otherwise. We do not want you to have anything from L.L. Bean that is not completely satisfactory. [We] do not consider a sale complete until goods are worn out and [the] customer [is] still satisfied."[11]

A retail brand, whether it is the name of the retailer or a private label, can create an emotional tie with customers that builds their trust and loyalty. Retail brands also facilitate loyalty because they stand for a predictable level of quality that customers feel comfortable with and often seek. A strong retail brand also becomes part of a retailer's positioning strategy, the topic discussed next.

Positioning

A retailer builds customer loyalty by developing a clear, distinctive image of its retail offering and consistently reinforcing that image through its merchandise and service. Positioning is the design and implementation of a retail mix to create an image of the retailer in the customer's mind relative to its competitors.[12]

Positioning emphasizes that the image in the customer's mind (not the retail manager's mind) is critical. Thus, the retailer needs to research what its image is and make sure that it is consistent with what customers in its target market want. A perceptual map is frequently used to represent the customer's image and preference for retailers.

Exhibit 4–4 is a hypothetical perceptual map of retailers selling women's clothing. The two dimensions in this map, fashion/style and service, represent the two primary characteristics that consumers in this example use in forming their impression of retail stores. Perceptual maps are developed so that the distance between two retailers' positions on the map indicates how similar the stores appear to consumers. For example, Sears and Hudson's Bay are somewhat close to each other on the map because consumers in this illustration see them as offering similar service and fashion. On the other hand, Holt Renfrew and Target are far apart, indicating that consumers think they're quite different. Note that stores close to each other compete vigorously with each other because consumers feel they provide similar benefits.

According to Exhibit 4–4, The Gap has an image of offering moderately priced fashionable women's clothing with good service. Winners offers more fashionable clothing with less service. Sears is viewed as a retailer offering women's clothing that's less fashionable and has relatively limited service.

The ideal points (marked by green dots on the map) indicate characteristics of an ideal retailer for consumers in different market segments. For example, consumers in Segment 3 prefer a retailer that offers high-fashion merchandise with low service, whereas consumers in Segment 1 want less expensive/more traditional apparel and aren't concerned about service. The ideal points are located so that the distance between the retailer's position

brand images Sets of associations consumers have about a brand that are usually organized around some meaningful themes.

positioning The design and implementation of a retail mix to create in the customer's mind an image of the retailer relative to its competitors; also called *brand building*.

(marked with a blue "x") and the ideal point indicates how consumers in the segment evaluate the retailer. Retailers that are closer to an ideal point are evaluated more favourably by the consumers in the segment than retailers located farther away. Thus, consumers in Segment 6 prefer Le Château to Holt Renfrew because their target customers do not require such high service levels.

Customers of The Gap have complained that they can't get the same assortment of high-quality basics—button-down shirts and khaki pants—that made The Gap famous. Probably the biggest problem is that The Gap's success spawned lower-priced imitators, including its own lower-priced chain, Old Navy, which is closer to Segment 2 than The Gap. At the same time, Winners has become more fashion-forward. So both Winners and Old Navy are vying for customers in the huge Segment 2 in Exhibit 4–4. Additionally, The Gap is positioned too far away from Segment 5 to compete successfully with Holt Renfrew on service. In fact, its sister chain, Banana Republic, is closer to Segment 5 and is therefore also siphoning sales from The Gap.[13] Finally, The Gap has two strong competitors for Segment 2 with Tristan and American Eagle Outfitters.

and consequently generates considerable loyalty toward the Loblaw group of stores. The quality image of its private-label products makes a significant contribution to the image of Loblaw. Retailing View 4.1 describes how IKEA builds customer loyalty through its unique merchandise. Store brands now account for one of every five items sold and are achieving new levels of growth every year. The low search associated with electronic shopping increases the importance of unique merchandise as a source of competitive advantage.

Customer Service

Retailers also build a sustainable competitive advantage by offering excellent customer service.[14] Offering good service consistently is difficult because customer service is provided by retail employees—and humans are less consistent than machines. Have you ever received less than perfect service from a salesperson or customer service representative? It is possible that the employee wasn't trained properly, that she didn't like her job, or that he was either inept or just plain rude. It is also possible that you were the 497th customer the salesperson interacted with that day, and she was at the end of her shift. Retailers that offer good customer service instill its importance in their employees over a long

Unique Merchandise

It is difficult for retailers to develop a competitive advantage through merchandise because most competitors can purchase and sell the same popular national brands. But many retailers realize a sustainable competitive advantage by developing private-label brands (also called *store brands*), which are products developed and marketed by a retailer and available only from that retailer. For example, if you want to buy a Kenmore washer or dryer, you have to buy it from Sears. Loblaw's powerful private-label brand, President's Choice, engenders strong brand loyalty among a significant group of consumers

exhibit 4–4 Hypothetical Perceptual Map of Women's Apparel Market

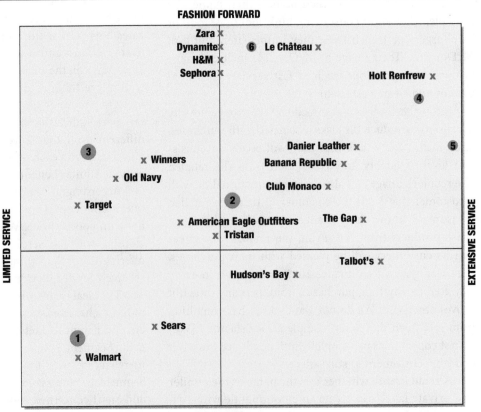

The IKEA Way

IKEA, a global retailer headquartered in Sweden, offers a wide range of well-designed and functional home-furnishing products at low prices. It's easy to make high-quality products and sell them at a high price or make low-quality products to sell at a low price. But IKEA has to be cost-effective and innovative to sell quality products at low prices.

Creating IKEA's unique merchandise starts on the factory floor. IKEA product developers and designers work closely with suppliers to efficiently use production equipment and raw materials and keep waste to a minimum. For example, an IKEA product developer learned about board-on-frame construction touring a door factory. This technique is cost-effective and environmentally friendly because sheets of wood are layered over a honeycomb core to provide a strong, lightweight structure with minimal wood content. This type of construction is used in many IKEA products, such as its LACK tables.

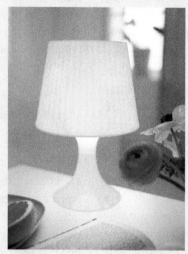

IKEA considers all costs when designing its unique, low-cost, fashionable merchandise. The LACK table and LAMPAN lamp are classic IKEA designs.

IKEA's designers go beyond the factory floor to consider transportation costs. Many items IKEA sells are shipped and sold disassembled in flat packs to reduce transportation costs and make it easier for customers to take them home. However, some products, like lamps, take up a lot of space even when disassembled. The LAMPAN illustrates the IKEA way of offering extremely low price with beautiful design and high quality. This was achieved by developing a new packing method in which the lamp shade could be used as a bucket for the lamp base.

IKEA reduces labour costs in its stores by providing signage with extensive information about its products and their quality, presenting its products in room settings, and prominently displaying price tags. These features enable customers to serve themselves and reduce IKEA's labour costs.

Sources: www.IKEA.com (accessed March 30, 2010); "The Man Who Named the Furniture," *Financial Times*, January 16, 2010, p. 30; Yongquan Hu and Huifang Jiang, "Innovation Strategy of Retailers: From the View of Global Value Chains," *6th International Conference on Service Systems and Service Management*, 2009, pp. 340–345.

---

period of time. Customer service must become part of the retailer's organizational culture through coaching and training.

It takes considerable time and effort to build a tradition and reputation for customer service, but good service is a valuable strategic asset. Once a retailer has earned a service reputation, it can sustain this advantage for a long time because it's hard for a competitor to develop a comparable reputation.

Loyalty Programs

Loyalty programs are part of an overall customer relationship management (CRM) program. These programs are prevalent in retailing, from airlines and department stores to the corner pizza shop. Popular examples include Canadian Tire Money, Shoppers Optimum Card, HBC Rewards, Air Miles, and Aeroplan.

Customer loyalty programs work hand-in-hand with CRM. Members of loyalty programs are identified when they buy because they use some type of loyalty card. The purchase information is stored in a huge database known as a **data warehouse**. From this data warehouse, analysts determine what types of merchandise and services certain groups of customers are buying. Data and information gathered can be used to build store loyalty by targeting promotional activities to specific market segments, to provide a more focused merchandise mix, and to produce higher profits by efficiently targeting advertising efforts.

Customers may join loyalty programs of competing retailers and continue to patronize multiple retailers.

data warehouse
The coordinated and periodic copying of data from various sources, both inside and outside the enterprise, into an environment ready for analytical and informational processing. It contains all of the data the firm has collected about its customers and is the foundation for subsequent CRM activities.

However, the data collected about customer shopping behaviour by these programs can provide insights that enable retailers to build and maintain loyalty. For instance, Harry Rosen, a Canadian specialty retailer selling designer menswear (see Retailing View 4.2), has a system for collecting and saving customer data. Every Harry Rosen salesperson can access the firm's customer database from any point-of-sale (POS) terminal in any store. The database indicates what the customer has bought in the past and also provides personal information. All sales associates are urged to contribute to the database. If a wife buys a birthday gift for her husband, salespeople are encouraged to find out when his birthday is and how old he is and include this information in the system rather than in their personal notebooks.

The information system improves Harry Rosen's customer service and the targeting of retail promotions. For example, when garments are left in the store for alterations, the system tracks their progress and electronically notifies the salesperson of any delay so that the salesperson can relay this information to the customer. Heavy spenders are identified and invited to special promotional events. When new merchandise arrives, the salesperson can identify customers who have bought that type of merchandise in the past and inform them of the new merchandise.[15] Thus, the data developed through the loyalty program enables a retailer to develop a personal relationship with customers that builds loyalty.

Finding a prime location is a competitive advantage that is not easily duplicated.

Relationships with Suppliers

A second approach for developing competitive advantage is developing strong relationships with companies that provide merchandise and services to the retailer, such as real estate developers, advertising agencies, and transportation companies. Of these relationships with suppliers, the most important are relationships with vendors.

Vendor Relations

By strengthening relationships with each other, both retailers and vendors can develop mutually beneficial assets and programs that will give the retailer–vendor pair an advantage over competing pairs. These collaborations are win-win situations. By working together, both parties develop a sustainable competitive advantage and increase their sales and profits.

The relationship between Proctor & Gamble (P&G) and Walmart initially focused on improving supply chain efficiencies. Today, the partners in this relationship share sensitive information with each other so that Walmart is better able to plan for the introduction of new P&G products and even develop some unique packaging for P&G's national brands exclusively available at Walmart. Walmart shares its sales data with P&G so that P&G can better plan its production and use a just-in-time inventory management system to reduce the level of inventory in the system. From their initial focus on improving supply chain efficiency, P&G and Walmart now work together on other initiatives, such as Family Moments to produce family-friendly TV programming.

By developing strong relations with vendors, retailers may gain the following exclusive rights:

- Selling merchandise in a specific region
- Obtaining special terms of purchase that are not available to competitors who lack such relations
- Receiving popular merchandise in short supply

Relationships with vendors, like relationships with customers, are developed over a long time and may not be easily offset by a competitor.[16] For example, Ahold, the Holland-based food retailer, works very closely with Swiss food giant Nestlé to provide products tailored to meet the local tastes of customers in specific markets.[17]

Efficiency of Internal Operations

In addition to strong relationships with external parties—customers and suppliers—retailers can develop competitive advantages by having more efficient internal operations. Efficient internal operations enable retailers to have a cost advantage over competitors or offer customers more benefits than do competitors at the same cost.

A larger company size typically produces more efficient internal operations. Larger retailers have more bargaining power with vendors and thus can buy merchandise at lower costs. Larger retailers can also invest in developing sophisticated systems and spread the fixed cost of these systems over more sales. In addition to size, other approaches for improving internal operating efficiencies are human resource management and information and supply chain management systems.

Human Resource Management

Retailing is a labour-intensive business. Employees play a major role in providing services for customers and building customer loyalty. Knowledgeable and skilled employees committed to the retailer's objectives are critical assets that support the success of companies such as Harry Rosen, Whole Foods, Canadian Tire, and Black's Photo.

Recruiting and retaining great employees is not easy. Retailers gain a sustainable competitive advantage by developing programs to motivate and coordinate employee efforts, by providing appropriate incentives, by fostering a strong and positive organizational culture and environment, and by managing diversity.

Distribution and Information Systems

All retailers strive to reduce operating costs—the costs associated with running the business—and make sure that the right merchandise is available at the right time and place. The use of sophisticated distribution and information systems offers an opportunity for retailers to achieve these efficiencies.[18] Through its data sharing about merchandise sales, information flows seamlessly from Walmart to its vendors to facilitate quick and efficient merchandise replenishment that avoids costly stockouts. Walmart's distribution and information systems have enabled it to have a cost advantage that its competitors cannot overcome.

In addition to using information systems to improve supply chain efficiency, the customer purchase data collected by information systems provide an opportunity for retailers to tailor store merchandise assortments to the market served by each of its stores and to tailor promotion to the specific needs of individual customers. These data about its customer buying behaviour are a valuable asset offering an advantage not easily duplicated by competitors.

Location

The classic response to the question, "What are the three most important things in retailing?" is "Location, location, and location." Location is the critical factor in consumer selection of a store. It is also a competitive advantage that is not easily duplicated. For instance, once Shoppers Drug Mart has put a store at the best location of an intersection, other drugstores are relegated to the second-best location. Finding great locations is particularly challenging in older urban locations, where space is limited and tenant turnover is relatively low.

Starbucks has developed a national presence and a strong competitive advantage with its location strategy. It conquers one area of the city at a time and then expands in the region, saturating a major market before entering a new market. Starbucks will frequently open several stores close to one another. It has two stores on two corners of the intersection of Robson and Thurlow in Vancouver. Starbucks has such a high density of stores that it lets the storefront promote the company and does very little media advertising. In heavily trafficked downtown districts, Starbucks often operates kiosks in commercial buildings. Neighbourhood locations that attract customers in the evenings and on weekends are important because they become part of the path of people's weekly shopping experience or their route to work.

By concentrating its locations, Starbucks creates a market presence that is difficult for competition to match. In addition, multiple locations facilitate scale economies that enable frequent deliveries, thereby ensuring fresh merchandise.

In contrast to Starbucks' urban locations, Tim Hortons chooses suburban locations with easy drive-through access in smaller cities, communities, and neighbourhoods across Canada.

Multiple Sources of Advantage

To build a sustainable advantage, retailers typically don't rely on a single approach such as low cost or excellent service.[19] They need multiple approaches to build as high a wall around their position as possible. In addition to its exclusive product and associated customer loyalty, IKEA has a large group of loyal customers due to its strong brand

Harry Rosen, President, Harry Rosen Menswear

Harry Rosen has been in the business of selling high-priced menswear for 50 years and has become a Canadian icon. The business has evolved from a tiny tailor shop in Toronto to 15 stores from Montreal to Vancouver. This retailer, with annual sales of $150 million, accounting for 30 percent of all sales of high-end menswear in Canada, has a celebrity clientele and a long list of honours. Not only is Rosen a dynamic retailer, he's a great corporate citizen, initiating major fundraising events in support of prostate cancer research. In 2004, Harry Rosen was named to the prestigious Order of Canada.

Harry Rosen at 82 is a psychoanalyst, social anthropologist, businessman, and brilliant marketer.

Harry Rosen builds loyalty and competitive advantage by using its customer database to tailor its promotional offerings.

His prize-winning advertisements have become recognized for innovation, such as the series, "What So and So Is Wearing Today" featuring well-known Canadians, from former NHL star Frank Mahovlich to musician Oscar Peterson. Always enthusiastic, Rosen once posed nude, except for a strategically placed necktie—all part of a very creative advertising campaign.

Each Harry Rosen salesperson has a commitment to their customers and can access the firm's data warehouse with customer information from any POS terminal in the store. The database tells what the customer has bought in the past and also provides personal information, such as preferences in style and colour. All sales associates are urged to contribute to the database. Harry Rosen believes that men are in need of help; they are not like women who like to shop and will make an enlightened choice. Rosen thinks most men are lazy and lack the knowledge critical to choosing quality menswear. The customer database is designed to enable sales associates to advise customers on promotions and develop valuable one-to-one relationships.

Even though only 3 percent of Canadian men actually shop in his stores, the first name that comes to mind when most men dream of buying a special wardrobe is Harry Rosen's. Rosen attributes his success to two things: his commitment to quality clothing and his insistence that staff make sure their clients understand why quality matters.

image and the unique shopping experience it provides its customers. Walmart complements its size advantage with strong vendor relationships and its clear positioning as a retailer that offers superior value. Starbucks combines its location advantage with unique products, committed employees, a strong brand name, and strong relationships with coffee growers to build an overall advantage that is very difficult for competitors to erode.

The success of McDonald's is based on providing customers with a good value that meets their expectations, having good customer service, maintaining good vendor relations, and having great locations. By doing all of these things right, McDonald's has developed a huge cadre of loyal customers.

McDonald's has always positioned itself as providing fast food at a good value—customers get a lot for not much money. Its customers don't have extraordinary expectations. They don't expect a meal prepared to their specific tastes. But customers do expect and get hot, fresh food that is reasonably priced.

McDonald's customers also don't expect friendly table service with linen tablecloths and sterling cutlery.

Their service expectations, which are typically met, are simple. By developing a system for producing its food and using extensive training for store managers, McDonald's reduces customers' waiting time. This training also means that customers will be handled quickly and courteously.

McDonald's vendor relationships ensure that it will always have quality ingredients. Its distribution and inventory control systems enable it to make sure that the ingredients are available at each location.

Furthermore, McDonald's has a strong brand name with very high levels of awareness around the world. When most people think of fast food, they think of McDonald's. The brand also has a number of favourable brand associations, such as Ronald McDonald, fast, clean, and french fries.

Finally, McDonald's has a large number of great locations. It is important for convenience products, such as fast food, to have lots of locations. Given its market power, it has been successful in finding and opening stores in prime retail locations. In every city in which it operates around the world, McDonald's has outstanding locations.

By developing unique capabilities in a number of areas, McDonald's has maintained its position as a service retailer, using a fast-food format directed toward families with young children.

Each of the retail strategies outlined in the chapter involves multiple sources of advantage. For example, Tim Hortons has developed a strong competitive position through its excellent product line with a strong Canadian brand name, high-quality service provided by committed employees, and excellent and plentiful locations. Tim Hortons' donuts are a tradition in all communities across Canada.

Lo3 Growth Strategies

Four types of growth opportunities that retailers may pursue (market penetration, market expansion, retail format development, and diversification) are shown in Exhibit 4–5.[20] The vertical axis indicates the synergies between the retailer's present markets and growth-opportunity markets—whether the opportunity involves markets the retailer is presently pursuing or new markets. The horizontal axis indicates the synergies between the retailer's present retail mix and the growth-opportunity retail mix—whether the opportunity exploits the retailer's present format or requires a new format.

Market Penetration

A **market penetration opportunity** involves directing efforts toward existing customers by using the present retailing format. The retailer can achieve this growth strategy either by attracting consumers in its current target market who don't shop at its outlets or by devising strategies that induce current customers to visit a store more often or to buy more merchandise on each visit.

Approaches for increasing market penetration include attracting new customers by opening more stores in the target market and keeping existing stores open for longer hours. Other approaches are displaying merchandise to increase impulse purchases and training salespeople to cross-sell. Cross-selling means that sales associates in one department attempt to sell complementary merchandise from other departments to their customers. For example, a sales associate who has just sold a dress to a customer will take the customer to the accessories department to sell her a handbag or scarf that will go with the dress. More cross-selling increases sales from existing customers.

For example, The North West Company a leading community retailer to underserved rural communities and urban neighbourhood markets in northern Canada, western Canada, rural Alaska, the South Pacific, and the Caribbean, is driven by a strategy aimed at growing "with and within" each market that they serve.

market penetration opportunity An investment opportunity strategy that focuses on increasing sales to present customers using the present retailing format.

cross-selling When sales associates in one department attempt to sell complementary merchandise from other departments to their customers.

exhibit 4–5 Growth Opportunities

TARGET MARKETS

	Existing	New
Existing	Market Penetration	Market Expansion
New	Format Development	Diversification (unrelated/related)

RETAIL FORMAT

Market Expansion

A market expansion opportunity employs the existing retail format in new market segments. For example, Abercrombie & Fitch (A&F) Co.'s primary target market is university students, not high-schoolers. Since university-aged people don't particularly like to hang out with teens, A&F rolled out a lower-priced chain called Hollister Co. to appeal to teens. Although the merchandise and ambience are slightly different than A&F, the retail format is essentially the same.[21] When the French hypermarket chain Carrefour expanded into other European and South American countries, it was also employing a market expansion growth strategy because it was entering a new geographic market segment with essentially the same retail format.[22]

Retail Format Development

A retail format development opportunity involves offering a new retail format—a format with a different retail mix—to the same target market. For example, Chapters exploited a format development opportunity when it began selling books to its present target market over the Internet (www.chapters.indigo.ca).

Another example of a retail format development opportunity occurs when a retailer adds merchandise categories, such as when Amazon.com began selling DVDs and electronics in addition to books. Adjusting the type of merchandise or services offered typically involves a small investment; whereas providing an entirely different format, such as a store-based retailer going into electronic retailing, requires a much larger and riskier investment.

Another example of a retail format development opportunity is Best Buy offering professional services to install new high-tech electronic equipment for consumers. Best Buy offers a Geek Squad to customers with 24-hour computer support and service. Although this growth opportunity is directed toward the same customers who buy merchandise in the stores, it involves running a service rather than a merchandise-based retail business.

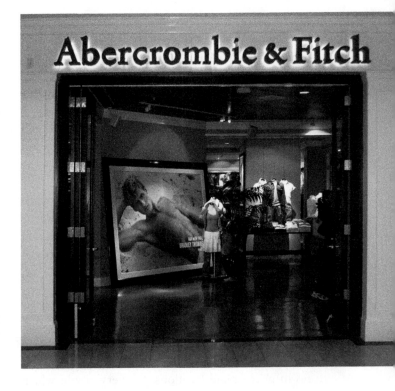

The U.K.-based retailer Tesco has employed a retail format development growth strategy by operating several different food store formats that all cater to essentially the same target markets. The smallest Tesco Express is no larger than 3000 square feet. These stores are located close to where customers work and live. Tesco Metro stores are 7000 to 15 000 square feet, bring convenience to city centre locations, and specialize in offering a wide range of ready-to-eat meals. Tesco Superstores (up to 50 000 square feet) are the oldest format. In recent years, the company has added nonfood products, such as DVDs and books, to improve customer satisfaction. Finally, Tesco Extra stores (more than 60 000 square feet) are designed to be a one-stop destination, with the widest range of food and nonfood products, from housewares and clothing to garden furniture.[23]

Diversification

A diversification opportunity occurs when a retailer introduces a new retail format directed toward a market segment that's not currently served, such as when La Senza opened La Senza Girl to attract the lucrative tween market. Today's tweens will be La Senza women in the future. Diversification opportunities are either related or unrelated.

Related versus Unrelated Diversification In a related diversification opportunity, the present target market or retail format shares something in common with the new opportunity. This commonality might entail purchasing from the same vendors, using the same distribution or management information system, or advertising in the same newspapers to similar target markets. In contrast, an **unrelated diversification** lacks any commonality between the present business and the new business.

Through acquisition, Canadian Tire Corporation purchased the Forzani Group, acquiring younger shoppers in the 18-to-35-year-old demographic who prefer Forzani's banners to Canadian Tire. Many of this new demographic head to enclosed malls, where Forzani chains tend to be located, rather than open-air power centres, where Canadian Tire stores are more commonly based.

Through acquisition, Home Depot built a wholesale building-supply business called HD Supply, which generated over $3 billion annual sales. Management felt that this growth opportunity would be synergistic with the firm's retail business, because its stores were already selling similar merchandise to contractors. Thus, Home Depot viewed this growth opportunity as a related diversification, because the targeted customers (i.e., contractors) would be similar, and the new large contractor market could be served using warehouses similar to Home Depot's present retail stores. In addition, Home Depot would realize cost savings by placing larger orders with vendors because it would be selling to both retail and wholesale customers. However, HD Supply actually was an unrelated diversification. The large contractor market served by HD Supply sold primarily pipes, lumber, and concrete—products with limited sales in Home Depot's retail stores. Selling these supplies to large contractors involved competitive bidding and transporting large bulky orders to job sites—skills that Home Depot lacked. So Home Depot sold this unrelated diversification to concentrate on its core retail small-contractor business.

Unrelated diversifications are considered to be very risky and often don't work, as was the case with Home Depot. As a result, most retailers apply the old adage "stick to your knitting" and seek growth opportunities that are closer in nature to their current operations.

Vertical Integration Vertical integration is diversification by retailers into wholesaling or manufacturing.[24] Examples of vertical integration are The Limited's

> **unrelated diversification** Diversification in which there is no commonality between the present business and the new business.

Canadian Tire's purchase of Forzani Group retailers such as Sport Chek represents an unrelated diversification opportunity.

acquisition of Mast Industries (a trading company that contracts for private-label manufacturing) and Zale Corporation's manufacturing of jewellery. When retailers integrate by manufacturing products, they are making risky investments because the skills required to make products are different from those associated with retailing. Additionally, retailers and manufacturers have different customers; the immediate customers for a manufacturer's merchandise are retailers, whereas a retailer's customers are consumers. Thus, a manufacturer's marketing activities are very different from those of a retailer. Designing private-label merchandise is a related diversification because it builds on the retailer's knowledge of its customers, but actually making the merchandise is considered an unrelated diversification. Some manufacturers and designers such as Nike, Prada, and Ralph Lauren forward-integrate into retailing. In this case, the designer/manufacturer has control of both the manufacturing and distribution processes and makes the strategic decision to move forward and control the retailing process by opening its own stores.

Strategic Opportunities and Competitive Advantage

Typically, retailers have the greatest competitive advantage in opportunities that are similar to their present retail strategy. Thus, retailers would be most successful engaging in market penetration opportunities that don't involve entering new, unfamiliar markets or operating new, unfamiliar retail formats (see Retailing View 4.3).

When retailers pursue market expansion opportunities, they build on their strengths in operating a retail format and apply this competitive advantage to a new market. Those retailers that successfully expand globally

---

4.3 | RETAILING VIEW

Rona

Rona was established in 1939 as a buying group for independent Quebec hardware retailers. Rona has evolved from a dealer-owned chain into a publicly traded company. The largest Canadian distributor and retailer of hardware, home renovation, and gardening products, the corporation operates a network of close to 800 corporate, franchise, and affiliate stores under several banners and a network of 14 hardware and construction materials distribution centres. With stores in every province, Rona currently owns a 19 percent share in the $36 billion Canadian industry.

In 2000, Rona purchased the 66-store chain Cashway Building Centres; in 2001, Western-based Revelstoke and Revy and Ontario's Lansing were added to the Rona banner. Rona has also purchased the Chester Dawe Ltd. chain of stores in Newfoundland. More recently, the company is benefiting from economic growth in Western Canada.

Rona is a mixed toolbox with a variety of retail formats, including big boxes, franchise stores, and independents. Rona's business plan is focused on three complementary sectors of activity in the hardware, renovation, and construction marketplace: distribution, retail and commercial, and professional.

Rona recognizes that consumers, like dealer-owners, have varying needs and goals, which is why

Rona has developed a unique business model designed to satisfy different types of customers and as well as different types of dealer-owners. This unique model comprises various store formats that address specific markets or consumer sectors and three ownership formulas. So even dealer-owners who prefer to remain independent can still enjoy all the advantages, energy, and solid foundation that make Rona what it is today.

The battle for the home hardware man, or more often today, woman, continues across Canada with the three major competitors Rona, Home Depot, and Home Hardware all doing over $4 billion a year in Canadian sales. The home hardware retail market is extremely competitive, and the entrance of the U.S. hardware giant Lowes has pressured all players in the battle for the home hardware consumer.

For years, Rona has been supporting Canadian sports and athletes from both professional and amateur levels, acting as a proud national partner of the Canadian Olympic and Paralympic teams since 2006 and remaining so for the 2012 London Summer Games.

Rona's aggressive bid to secure a spot as a leader in home improvement retailing in Canada will no doubt continue to keep the company in the headlines.

---

are able to translate what they do best—their core competencies—to a new culture and market.

A retail format development opportunity builds on the retailer's reputation and success with present customers. Even if a retailer doesn't have experience and skills in operating the new format, it hopes to attract its loyal customers to it. For example, retailers that have successfully developed multichannel strategies by seamlessly integrating stores, the Internet, and catalogues provide extra convenience and multiple opportunities for their current customers to shop.

Retailers have the least competitive advantage when they pursue diversification opportunities. Thus, these opportunities are generally risky and often don't work, as was the case with Home Depot. Vertical integration, however, albeit risky, often has overwhelming benefits for those large and sophisticated retailers that can invest heavily for the long term. By making direct investments in distribution or manufacturing facilities, these retailers have total control over the entire marketing channel.

Global Growth Opportunities

International expansion is a market growth opportunity that successful retailers find attractive. The most commonly targeted regions are Mexico, Latin America, Europe, China, and Japan. International expansion can be risky because retailers must deal with differences in government regulations, cultural traditions, supply chain considerations, and language.

The issues connected to global expansion are discussed in Chapter 7, International Retailing Strategy.

The Strategic Retail Planning Process

Lo 4

The strategic retail planning process is the set of steps a retailer goes through to develop a strategic retail plan[27] (see Exhibit 4–6). It describes how retailers select target market segments, determine the appropriate retail format, and build sustainable competitive advantages. It is not always necessary to go through the entire process each time an evaluation is performed. For instance, a retailer could evaluate its performance and go directly to Step 2, conduct a situation audit.

The planning process can be used to formulate strategic plans at different levels within a retail business. For example, the corporate strategic plan of American Express indicates how resources are to be allocated across the corporation's various businesses such as credit cards and travel services. Each business within American Express has its own strategic plan, and then strategies

are developed for products within a business such as for the American Express Gold card.

As we discuss the steps in the retail planning process, we will apply each step to the planning process Kelly Bradford is undertaking. Kelly owns Gifts To Go, a small, two-store chain in the Vancouver area. One of her 1000-square-foot stores is located in the downtown area; the other is in an upscale suburban mall. The target market for Gifts To Go is upper-income men and women looking for gifts in the $50 to $500 price range. The stores have an eclectic selection of merchandise, including handmade jewellery and crafts, fine china and glassware, perfume, watches, writing instruments, and a variety of one-of-a-kind items. Gifts To Go also has developed a number of loyal customers who are contacted by sales associates when family anniversaries and birthdays come up. In many cases, customers have a close relationship with a sales associate and enough confidence in the associate's judgment that they tell the associate to pick out an appropriate gift. The turnover of Gifts To Go sales associates is low for the industry, because Kelly

strategic retail planning process The steps a retailer goes through to develop a strategic retail plan. It describes how retailers select target market segments, determine the appropriate retail format, and build sustainable competitive advantages.

exhibit 4–6   Steps in Strategic Retail Planning Process

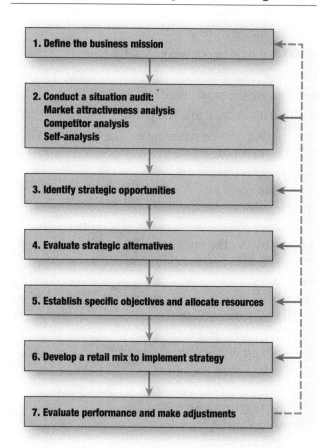

mission statement
A broad description of the scope of activities a business plans to undertake.

situation audit An analysis of the opportunities and threats in the retail environment and the strengths and weaknesses of the retail business relative to its competitors.

treats associates as part of the family. The company offers employee benefits for all associates, and they share in the profits of the firm.

Step 1: Define the Business Mission

The first step in the strategic retail planning process is to define the business mission. The mission statement is a broad description of a retailer's objectives and the scope of activities it plans to undertake.[28] The objective of a publicly held firm is to maximize its stockholders' wealth by increasing the value of its stock and paying dividends.[29] Owners of small, privately held firms frequently have other objectives, such as achieving a specific level of income and avoiding risks rather than maximizing income.

The mission statement should define the general nature of the target segments and retail formats that the firm will consider. For example, the mission statement of an office supply category specialist, "Serve the customer, build value for shareholders, and create opportunities for associates," is too broad. It does not provide a sense of strategic direction. (See Retailing View 4.4 to read about how one CEO provides leadership and direction in an evolving retail segment.)

In developing the mission statement, managers must answer five questions:

- What business are we in?
- What should be our business in the future?
- Who are our customers?
- What are our capabilities?
- What do we want to accomplish?

Gifts To Go's mission statement is "The mission of Gifts To Go is to be the leading retailer of higher-priced gifts in the Vancouver area and provide a stable income of $100 000 per year for the owner."

Because the mission statement defines the retailer's objectives and the scope of activities it plans to undertake, Gifts To Go's mission statement clarifies that its management won't consider retail opportunities outside the Vancouver area, for selling low-priced gifts, or that would jeopardize its ability to generate $100 000 in annual income.[30]

Step 2: Conduct a Situation Audit

After developing a mission statement and setting objectives, the next step in the strategic planning process is to do a situation audit. A situation audit or SWOT analysis is an analysis of the strengths and weaknesses of the retail business relative to its competitors and the opportunities and threats in the retail environment. The elements in the situation analysis are shown in Exhibit 4–7.[31]

Market Factors Some critical factors related to consumers and their buying patterns are market size and growth, sales cyclicality, and seasonality. Market size, typically measured in retail sales dollars, is important because it indicates a retailer's opportunity for generating revenues to cover its investment. Large markets are attractive to large retail firms. But they are also attractive to small entrepreneurs because they offer more opportunities to focus on a market segment. Some retailers, however, prefer to concentrate on smaller markets.

Growing markets are typically more attractive than mature or declining markets. For example, retail markets for specialty stores are growing faster than those for department stores. Typically, margins and prices are higher in growing markets because competition is less intense than in mature markets. Since new customers are just beginning to patronize stores in growing markets, they may not have developed strong store loyalties and thus might be easier to attract to a new store. Some retailers, however, prefer to locate in mature markets. These locations are attractive when the customer base is stable and competition is weak.

Firms are often interested in minimizing the business cycle's impact on their sales. Thus, retail markets for merchandise affected by economic conditions (such as cars and major appliances) are less attractive than retail markets unaffected by economic conditions (such as food). In general, markets with highly seasonal sales are unattractive because

exhibit 4–7 Elements in Market Analysis/SWOT (Strengths, Weaknesses, Opportunities, and Threats)

MARKET FACTORS	**COMPETITIVE FACTORS**	**ENVIRONMENTAL FACTORS**	**ANALYSIS OF STRENGTHS AND WEAKNESSES**
Size	Barriers to entry	Technology	Management capabilities
Growth	Bargaining power of vendors	Economic	Financial resources
Seasonality	Competitive rivalry	Regulatory	Locations
Business cycles		Social	Operations
			Merchandise
			Store management
			Customer loyalty

London Drugs: Prescription to Lead

As the retail industry continues to go through change and transformation, it could be argued that no sector has been expected to rethink their business model more so than pharmacies. Provincial legislations passed across the country require pharmacists to include more responsibilities within their practice, such as administering immunizations and providing patient education. The sector has also been faced with technological challenges as they are now required to purchase and maintain new software to allow them to better track customer care information. Considering that these challenges are combined with the challenges faced by all retailers, one might assume that overseeing a chain of pharmacies would require a leader with not only natural ability and know-how, but one with steel and determination as well.

Wynne Powell, CEO and president of London Drugs—the 100 percent Canadian-owned pharmacy that operates 75 locations across Alberta, Saskatchewan, Manitoba, and British Columbia—is one such leader.

How important is the culture that's created within an organization? "The DNA of a company is extremely important. In our particular case, we have a family company—the HY Louie Group—that's been in business for 108 years. London Drugs has been in business for 66 years. The culture here has been built over a layering of time with management actions and management consistencies. The Louie family instilled a culture of respect, fairness, and trust; those are the principles that are absolutely fundamental to our DNA."

What are some of the challenges facing pharmacies today? "The pharmacy industry is being impacted strongly by the government need to cut their costs. Retail pharmacy is being closely monitored by governments. That will continue as pressure placed on health care costs in Canada increases—governments will continue to become extremely active in trying to describe what they feel the retail experience should be. Pharmacists in particular have a profession that can be used in far greater boundaries than they're currently being used. They are a cost-effective way of reaching a mass population. It's up to all of us within the industry to educate governments about the power of pharmacy and about the cost efficiency of pharmacy because it's too easy for any government to make an incorrect decision not understanding that their policy decisions can greatly impact pharmacies."

Where can some of the opportunities for pharmacies be found? "With aging demographics, longer lives, and the choice of average Canadians to live healthier lifestyles, the pharmacy sector is very well positioned to assist clients in understanding that their policy decisions can greatly impact pharmacies."

How do you define a satisfied customer? "At London Drugs, we look at a customer for life. If we can't keep a customer for life, we haven't done our job. We're in a variety of industries and we're broadly based, so we look at that share of the basket for life. We know that there will be certain points in a customer's lifecycle when they will not favour our store, and then they'll suddenly come in favouring our store. We know what those lifecycles are, and when the time is right, we want to earn our customer's business for life. We do this by caring about our customers and being sincere about their needs. People can instantly tell if your message is just a slogan. Slogans don't work; substance does."

What makes a great retail organization? "Great people. Obviously, you have to have the financial wherewithal to buy well. You have to have the capital. You have to have the ability to survive . . . but at the end of the day this is a people business."

Source: Sean C. Tarry, "Prescription to Lead," *Canadian Retailer*, Winter 2012, Volume 22, Issue 1, pp. 22–23.

barriers to entry
Conditions in a retail market that make it difficult for firms to enter the market.

scale economies
Cost advantages due to the size of a retailer.

bargaining power of vendors A competitive factor that makes a market unattractive when a few vendors control the merchandise sold in it. In these situations, vendors have an opportunity to dictate prices and other terms, reducing retailer's profits.

competitive rivalry
The frequency and intensity of reactions to actions undertaken by competitors.

a lot of resources are needed to accommodate the peak season, but then resources are underutilized the rest of the year. For example, to minimize these problems due to seasonality, ski resorts promote summer vacations to generate sales during all four seasons.

To conduct an analysis of the market factors for Gifts To Go, Kelly Bradford went on the Internet to get information about the size, growth, and cyclical and seasonal nature of the gift market in general and, more specifically, in Vancouver. On the basis of her analysis, she concluded that the market factors were attractive; the market for more-expensive gifts was large, growing, and not vulnerable to business cycles. The only negative aspect was the high seasonality of gifts, with peaks at Valentine's Day, June (due to weddings), Christmas, and other holidays.

Competitive Factors The nature of the competition in retail markets is affected by barriers to entry, bargaining power of vendors, and competitive rivalry.[32] Retail markets are more attractive when competitive entry is costly. Barriers to entry are conditions in a retail market that make it difficult for firms to enter the market. These conditions include scale economies, customer loyalty, and availability of great locations.

Scale economies are cost advantages due to a retailer's size. Markets dominated by large competitors with scale economies are typically unattractive. For example, a small entrepreneur would avoid becoming an office supply category specialist because the market is dominated by Staples Business Depot. This firm has a considerable cost advantage over the entrepreneur because it can buy merchandise more cheaply and operate more efficiently by investing in the latest technology and spreading its overhead across more stores.

Retail markets dominated by a well-established retailer that has developed a loyal group of customers offer limited profit potential. For example, Home Depot's high customer loyalty makes it hard for a competing home improvement centre to enter the same market.

Finally, the availability of locations may impede competitive entry. A retail market with high entry barriers is very attractive to retailers presently competing in that market because those barriers limit competition. However, markets with high entry barriers are unattractive to retailers not already in the market. For example, the lack

of good retail locations in Hong Kong makes this market attractive to retailers already in the region, but less attractive to retailers desiring to enter the market.

Another competitive factor is the bargaining power of vendors. Markets are less attractive when a few vendors control the merchandise sold in them. In these situations, vendors have an opportunity to dictate prices and other terms (such as delivery dates), reducing the retailer's profits. For example, the market for retailing fashionable cosmetics is less attractive because two suppliers, Estée Lauder (Estée Lauder, Clinique, Prescriptives, Aramis, Tommy Hilfiger, M.A.C., and Origins)[33] and L'Oréal (Maybelline, Giorgio Armani, Helena Rubinstein, Lancôme, Lanvin, and Ralph Lauren brands),[34] provide the most desired premium brands. Since department stores need these brands to support a fashionable image, these suppliers have the power to sell their products to retailers at high prices.

The final industry factor is the level of competitive rivalry in the retail market. Competitive rivalry is the frequency and intensity of reactions to actions undertaken by competitors. When rivalry is high, price wars erupt, advertising and promotion expenses increase, and profit potential falls. Conditions that may lead to intense rivalry include the following:

- A large number of competitors that are all about the same size
- Slow growth
- High fixed costs
- The lack of perceived differences between competing retailers

Tim Hortons and Starbucks have an intense rivalry in some markets. Starbucks has extended its food/lunch menu, while Tim's is encroaching on Starbucks' gourmet coffee turf. Pricing for similar items is close, though Starbucks is still more expensive. To provide easier accessibility, Starbucks is offering Tim-style drive-through windows in some locations.

When Kelly Bradford started to analyze the competitive factors for Gifts To Go, she realized that identifying her competitors wasn't easy. Although there were no gift stores carrying similar merchandise at the same price points in the Vancouver area, there were various other retailers from which a customer could buy gifts. She identified her primary competitors as department stores, craft galleries, catalogues, and Internet retailers. Kelly felt there were some scale economies in developing customer databases to support gift retailing. The lack of large suppliers meant that vendors' bargaining power wasn't a problem, and competitive rivalry was minimal because the gift business was not a critical part of the department store's overall business. In addition, merchandise carried by the various retailers offered considerable differentiation opportunities.

Macro-environment The macro-environment factors that affect market attractiveness span technological, economic, regulatory, and social changes.[35] When a retail market is going through significant changes in technology, present competitors are vulnerable to new entrants that are skilled at using the new technology. For example, in the late 1990s, many traditional retailers were nervously scrambling to define their space in e-tailing. Thousands of pure-play e-tailers with technological sophistication flooded the Internet. Many of the bricks-and-mortar retailers invested heavily in Internet technology and were able to integrate the Internet with their other selling channels.

Some retailers may be more affected by economic conditions than others. During tough economic times, retailers that offer a perceived high value offering, such as discount, off-price, warehouse clubs, and extreme value retailers, are in a much better position than retailers specializing in luxury goods, such as jewellery stores, designer apparel specialty stores, and gourmet and organic grocers. Harry Rosen employs many well-paid salespeople to provide high-quality customer service. When unemployment is low, costs may increase significantly, as salespeople's wages rise due to the difficulty in hiring qualified people. But retailers such as Walmart that provide little service and have much lower labour costs as a percentage of sales may be less affected by low unemployment.

Government regulations can reduce the attractiveness of a retail market. For example, it is difficult for large retailers to open new stores in France due to size restrictions placed on new stores. Also, many local governments within Canada have tried to stop Walmart from entering their market in an attempt to protect locally owned retailers.[36]

Finally, trends in demographics, lifestyles, attitudes, and personal values affect retail markets' attractiveness. Harry Rosen, for example, has been struggling with several trends simultaneously. Known for traditional suits and dress shirts, the company had to learn how to appeal to younger customers and businesspeople who prefer to dress casually without alienating its traditional customer base.[37]

Retailers need to answer three questions about the macro-environment:

- What new developments or changes might occur, such as new technologies and regulations or different social factors and economic conditions?
- What is the likelihood that these environmental changes will occur? What key factors affect whether these changes will occur?
- How will these changes impact each retail market, the firm, and its competitors?

Kelly Bradford's primary concern when she did an environmental analysis was the potential growth of Internet gift retailers such as RedEnvelope. Gifts seem ideal for an electronic channel, because customers can order the item over the Internet and have it shipped directly to the gift recipient. Kelly also recognized that the electronic channel could effectively collect information about customers and then target promotions and suggestions to them when future gift-giving occasions arose.

Strengths and Weaknesses Analysis The most critical aspect of the situation audit is for a retailer to determine its unique capabilities in terms of its strengths and weaknesses relative to the competition.[38] A strengths and weaknesses analysis indicates how well the business can seize opportunities and avoid harm from threats in the environment. Exhibit 4–8 outlines issues to consider in performing a self-analysis.

Below is Kelly Bradford's analysis of Gifts To Go's strengths and weaknesses:

strengths and weaknesses analysis A critical aspect of the situation audit in which a retailer determines its unique capabilities—its strengths and weaknesses relative to its competition.

Management capability	Limited—Two excellent store managers and a relatively inexperienced person helped Kelly buy merchandise. An accounting firm kept the financial records for the business but had no skills in developing and utilizing customer databases.
Financial resources	Good—Gifts To Go had no debt and a good relationship with a bank. Kelly had saved $255 000 that she had in liquid securities.
Operations	Poor—While Kelly felt Gifts To Go had relatively low overhead, the company did not have a computer-based inventory control system or management and customer information systems. Her competitors (local department stores, catalogue, and Internet retailers) certainly had superior systems.
Merchandising capabilities	Good—Kelly had a flair for selecting unique gifts, and she had excellent relationships with vendors providing one-of-a-kind merchandise.
Store management capabilities	Excellent—The store managers and sales associates were excellent. They were very attentive to customers and loyal to the firm. Employee and customer theft were kept to a minimum.
Locations	Excellent—Both of Gifts To Go's locations were excellent. The downtown location was convenient for office workers. The suburban mall location was at a heavily trafficked juncture.
Customers	Good—While Gifts To Go did not achieve the sales volume in gifts done in department stores, the company had a loyal base of customers.

Step 3: Identify Strategic Opportunities

After completing the situation audit, the next step is to identify opportunities for increasing retail sales. Some growth opportunities could involve a redefinition of the retailer's mission statement. The strategic opportunities could involve market preparation, market expansion, retail format development, or diversification. Kelly Bradford presently competes in gift retailing using a specialty store format. The strategic alternatives she is considering are defined in terms of the growth opportunities in Exhibit 4–5. Note that some of these growth strategies involve a redefinition of her mission.

Step 4: Evaluate Strategic Opportunities

The fourth step in the strategic planning progress is to evaluate opportunities that have been identified in the situation audit. The evaluation determines the retailer's potential to establish a sustainable competitive advantage and reap long-term profits from the opportunities under evaluation. Thus, a retailer must focus on opportunities that utilize its strengths and its area of competitive advantage. For example, expertise in developing private-label apparel is one of Club Monaco's sources of competitive advantage. Thus, Club Monaco would positively evaluate opportunities that involve development of private-label merchandise. Some of the areas retailers should consider when evaluating new opportunities are shown in Exhibit 4–8.

Both the market attractiveness and the strengths and weaknesses of the retailer need to be considered in evaluating strategic opportunities. The greatest investments should be made in market opportunities where the retailer has a strong competitive position. The table below represents Kelly's informal analysis:

Step 5: Establish Specific Objectives and Allocate Resources

After evaluating the strategic investment opportunities, the next step in the strategic planning process is to establish a specific objective for each opportunity. The retailer's overall objective is included in the mission statement. The specific objectives are goals against which progress toward the overall objective can be measured. Thus, these specific objectives have three components:

- The performance sought, including a numerical index against which progress may be measured
- A time frame within which the goal is to be achieved
- The level of investment needed to achieve the objective

Typically, the performance levels are financial criteria such as return on investment, sales, or profits. Kelly's objective is to increase profits by 20 percent in each of the next five years. She expects she will need to invest an additional $25 000 in her apparel and other nongift merchandise inventory.

Step 6: Develop a Retail Mix to Implement Strategy

The sixth step in the planning process is to develop a retail mix for each opportunity in which investment will be made and to control and evaluate performance.

Step 7: Evaluate Performance and Make Adjustments

The final step in the planning process is evaluating the results of the strategy and implementation program. If the retailer is meeting or exceeding its objectives, changes aren't needed. But if the retailer fails to meet its objectives, re-analysis is needed. Typically, this re-analysis starts with reviewing the implementation programs; but it may indicate that the strategy (or even the mission statement) needs to be reconsidered. This conclusion would result

Growth Opportunity	Market Attractiveness	Competitive Position
Increase size of present stores and amount of merchandise in stores	Low	High
Open additional gift stores in Vancouver area	Medium	Medium
Open gift stores outside the Vancouver area (new geographic segment)	Medium	Low
Sell lower-priced gifts in present stores or open new stores selling low-priced gifts (new benefit segment)	Medium	Low
Sell apparel and other nongift merchandise to same customers in same or new stores	High	Medium
Sell similar gift merchandise to same market segment using the Internet	High	Low
Open apparel stores targeted at teenagers	High	Low
Open a category specialist selling low-priced gifts	High	Low

in starting a new planning process, including a new situation audit. Changes in the macro-environment can force retailers to re-evaluate their strategy. For example, the strategy could involve targeting a new market segment, and tailoring their offering to meet the needs of this new segment.

Strategic Planning in the Real World

The planning process in Exhibit 4–6 indicates that strategic decisions are made in a sequential manner. After the business mission is defined, the situation audit is performed, strategic opportunities are identified, alternatives are evaluated, objectives are set, resources are allocated, the implementation plan is developed, and, finally, performance is evaluated and adjustments are made. But actual planning processes have interactions among the steps. For example, the situation audit may uncover a logical alternative for the firm to consider, even though this alternative isn't included in the mission statement. Thus, the mission statement may need to be reformulated. Development of the implementation plan might reveal that resource allocation to the opportunity is insufficient to achieve the objective. In that case, the objective would need to be changed or the resources would need to be increased, or the retailer might consider not investing in the opportunity at all.

Remember that a situation analysis is an essential part of developing a sustainable retail strategy. The analysis will reveal the retailer's potential for success by analyzing both the macro-environment and the micro-environment to highlight the retailer's unique capabilities. It is a competitive business world and smart retailers are always on alert for a competitive edge. Retail is a game of survival of the fittest!

exhibit 4–8   Strengths and Weaknesses Analysis

In performing a self-analysis, the retailer considers the potential areas for developing a competitive advantage listed below and answers the following questions:

- At what is our company good?
- In which of these areas is our company better than our competitors?
- In which of these areas does our company's unique capabilities provide a sustainable competitive advantage or a basis for developing one?

 MANAGEMENT CAPABILITY

Capabilities and experience of top management

Depth of management—capabilities of middle management

Management's commitment to firm

 FINANCIAL RESOURCES

Cash flow from existing business

Ability to raise debt or equity financing

 OPERATIONS

Overhead cost structure

Quality of operating systems

Distribution capabilities

Management information systems

Loss prevention systems

Inventory control systems

 MERCHANDISING CAPABILITIES

Knowledge and skills of buyers

Relationships with vendors

Capabilities in developing private brands

Advertising and promotion capabilities

 STORE MANAGEMENT CAPABILITIES

Management capabilities

Quality of sales associates

Commitment of sales associates to firm

 LOCATIONS

 CUSTOMERS

Loyalty of customers

SUMMARY

A retailer's long-term performance is largely determined by its strategy. A strategy coordinates employees' activities and communicates the direction the retailer plans to take. Thus, retail market strategy describes both the strategic direction and the process by which the strategy is to be developed.

The retail strategy statement includes an identification of the target market and the retail format (its offering) to be directed toward that target market. The statement also needs to indicate the retailer's methods to build a sustainable competitive advantage. Three approaches for developing competitive advantage are (1) building strong relationships with customers, (2) building strong relationships with suppliers, and (3) achieving efficient internal operations. Each of these approaches involves developing an asset—loyal customers, strong vendor relationships, committed effective human resources and efficient systems, and attractive locations—that is not easily duplicated by competitors.

The strategic planning process consists of a sequence of steps, including (1) defining the business mission, (2) conducting a situation audit, (3) identifying strategic opportunities, (4) evaluating the alternatives, (5) establishing specific objectives and allocating resources, (6) developing a retail mix to implement strategy, and (7) evaluating performance and making adjustments.

Strategic planning is an ongoing process. Every day, retailers audit their situations, examine customer trends, study new technologies, and monitor competitive activities. But the retail strategy statement does not change every year or every six months; the strategy statement is reviewed and altered only when major changes in the retailer's environment or capabilities occur.

When a retailer undertakes a major re-examination of its strategy, the process for developing a new strategy statement may take a year or two. Potential strategic directions are generated by people at all levels of the organization, then evaluated by senior executives and operating personnel to ensure that the eventual strategic direction is profitable in the long run and can be implemented.

KEY TERMS

bargaining power of vendors
barriers to entry
brand images
competitive rivalry
cross-selling
customer loyalty
data warehouse
diversification opportunity
macro-environment
market expansion opportunity

market penetration opportunity
micro-environment
mission statement
positioning
private-label brands
related diversification opportunity
retail format development opportunity
retail format
retail market
retailing concept

scale economies
situation audit
strategic retail planning process
strengths and weaknesses analysis
sustainable competitive advantage
SWOT analysis
target market
unrelated diversification

Get Out & Do It!

1. **INTERNET EXERCISE** Visit the website for Restoration Hardware (**www.restorationhardware.com**). Does this Internet site reflect the retail strategies for the company as discussed here?

2. **GO SHOPPING** Visit two stores that sell similar merchandise categories and cater to the same target segment(s). How are their retail formats similar? Dissimilar? On what bases do they have a sustainable competitive advantage? Explain which you believe has a stronger position.

3. **GO SHOPPING** Develop a strategic plan for your favourite retailer. Go to the store. Observe and interview the store manager. Supplement your visit with information available online through Hoovers, the store's website (which should include its annual report), and other published sources.

4. Visit the websites for IKEA (**www.ikea.com**) and Starbucks (**www.starbucks.com**). Is the look/feel of these Internet sites consistent with the in-store experience of these stores?

DISCUSSION QUESTIONS AND PROBLEMS

1. What approaches can a retailer use to develop a competitive advantage? Choose a retailer and describe how it has developed a competitive strategic advantage.

2. Give an example of a market penetration, a retail format development, a market expansion, and a diversification growth strategy that Future Shop might use.

3. Draw and explain a positioning map such as that shown in Exhibit 4–4 for the retailers and customer segments (ideal points) for your favourite retailer.

4. View the video "Build-A-Bear Workshop" on Connect and complete a situation analysis identifying the retailer's strategy (see Exhibit 4–1). Detail the micro-environment and the macro-environment in the analysis. What are the strengths and weaknesses? Explain what threats and opportunities exist for this unique retailer.

5. Go to www.harryrosen.com and read the profile of Harry Rosen. Identify why Harry has been so successful in marketing to the high-end menswear market segment.

6. Read the Rona profile in Retailing View 4.3. What is Rona's sustainable competitive advantage?

7. Do a situation analysis for McDonald's. What is its mission? What are its strengths and weaknesses? What environmental threats might it face over the next ten years? How could it prepare for these threats?

8. Assume you are interested in opening a restaurant in your town. Go through the steps in the strategic retail planning process shown in Exhibit 4–6. Focus on doing a situation audit of the local restaurant market, identifying alternatives, evaluating alternatives, and selecting a target market and a retail mix for the restaurant.

9. The Gap owns several chains, including Old Navy and Banana Republic. What type of growth opportunity was The Gap pursuing when it opened each of these retail concepts? Which is most synergistic with the original The Gap chain?

10. Identify a store or service provider that you believe has an effective loyalty program. Explain why it is effective.

retail locations strategy— trade area decisions and site assessment

Lo 1 Examine the four major factors retailers consider when evaluating an area.

Lo 2 Consider the three factors retailers consider when evaluating and selecting a specific site.

Lo 3 Define what a trade area is for a store and how retailers determine the trade area, and develop an understanding of the nature of consumers in the site's trade area.

Lo 4 Review the three approaches for estimating potential sales for a store site.

Lo 5 Explore the types of locations that are available to retailers and the relative advantages of each location type.

Lo 6 Discuss why some locations are particularly well-suited to specific retail strategies.

SPOTLIGHT ON RETAILING

Cloverdale Mall: The Scrappy Survivor

A shopping centre, shopping mall, or shopping plaza is the modern version of the historical marketplace where people would go to buy goods from local artisans, farmers, and craftspeople. The first shopping centre, a marketplace with retail stores, was the Agora at the foot of the Parthenon in Athens in 600 B.C. It was the centre of all commerce, politics, and entertainment in ancient Greece.

In Canada, Norgate Shopping Centre was the first shopping mall (strip mall). Norgate was built in 1949 in the then-suburb of Saint-Laurent, Quebec, now the Saint-Laurent borough of Montreal, and continues to be owned and operated by the Lupovich family.

The first covered or enclosed mall in Canada, the Park Royal Shopping Centre, was built a year later in 1950 in West Vancouver. Park Royal currently markets itself as a five-star shopping facility and has undergone significant changes in its 63 years.

West Edmonton Mall in Alberta was built years later in 1981 and was considered to be the largest mall in the world from 1986 until 2004, when the Mall of Arabia opened in Dubai. Currently, the West Edmonton Mall is the tenth-largest mall in the world and the largest mall in North America.

Cloverdale Mall cannot boast any of the above accolades as the first or the biggest; in fact, Cloverdale Mall is a small-ish, somewhat remarkable, yet unremarkable community shopping centre located in the Etobicoke area of Toronto, squished between the East Mall, Highway 427, and an unattractive stretch of Dundas West. Built in the 1950s on farmland that had originally been known as Eatonville (land used by the Eaton family to provide milk and cream for their department stores), the mall currently houses 90 retailers, four anchors, and approximately 500 000 square feet of retail floor space.

The mall opened in 1956 as an open-air plaza—a mall with no roof, just rows of side-by-side shops simulating a city streetscape with canopies that provided cover for shoppers. The two major anchor stores, Dominion and Morgan's (a Montreal-based department store chain purchased in 1960 by the Hudson's Bay Company), had no difficulties drawing local families to the mall. However, after the opening of Sherway Gardens in 1971 less than a couple of kilometres away, the popularity of Cloverdale began to decline.

By the 1980s, a major revamping and enclosing of the mall was completed, along with an addition of new retail space that would later be occupied by retailers such as Dollarama, Zellers, and others. The mall seemed to have been given a new lease on life.

Possessing a valuable mix of the ordinary, and a strong understanding of the local community, Cloverdale Mall's claim to fame is its ability to survive despite its existence in the shadow of not just one major shopping centre (Sherway) but three.

Square One in Mississauga is one of the largest malls in North America and is less than 10 kilometres away to the west. Sherway Gardens, one of the Toronto area's largest and most upscale malls, is less than a couple of kilometres away to the south. The Dixie Outlet Mall is one of Canada's largest value-oriented malls and is located just 5 kilometres away. It seems to defy logic that Cloverdale Mall would be able to survive in the shadow of these other malls.

True, Cloverdale lacks the sparkly fashion-forward splendour of nearby Sherway Gardens. But for its "estimated 90 000 weekly shoppers trying to squeeze ten errands into one outing between soccer practice and *Big Bang Theory*," it is very convenient. After all, not one of the three major centres that surround Cloverdale Mall can boast that within its walls it is possible to renew your health card at Service Canada; grab a bottle of Chardonnay at the LCBO, some bulk candy at Bulk 'n' Bits, and a pair of flip-flops at Ardene; get your watch battery changed at Peoples Jewellers; and stock up on rubber gloves at Dollarama.

The mall also includes an amazing assortment of marquee retailers such as Winners, Metro (formally Dominion), Kitchen Stuff Plus, and most recently, Target. Many independents are also located in this community gem, including menswear store Taylor Somers (since 1956), quaint regional indies such as Hampton Row ladies wear, sundry dental and medical providers, and Hot Oven Bakery, a popular west-end bakery.

While Sherway Gardens, Square One, and Dixie Outlet Mall draw from a larger area, Cloverdale's offerings mainly serve the local convenience of those in west Toronto and east Mississauga. Cloverdale prides itself in being in touch with its demographics. According to Jennifer Bolton, mall marketing director, Cloverdale was "one of the first centres to have a play structure for kids to play on."

Running a "community-type centre" is part of what makes this community shopping centre unique. Under its Community Kiosk program, for instance, Cloverdale Mall offers free space to local non-profit and charitable organizations raising awareness and funds, such as Scouts Canada, Etobicoke EMS Services, and the Kiwanis Club of Islington.

The Cloverdale Heartwalkers gather each morning before opening to walk the mall aisles to stay fit, not necessarily unique as many malls boast such walking groups. However, Cloverdale organizes activities and social events for these 200-plus walkers such as tai chi, square dancing, guest speakers, and an annual holiday party. It is difficult to imagine this sense of community and involvement in the halls of Sherway, Yorkdale, or Square One.

Justin Deknatel, general manager of Cloverdale Mall, offers this: "Cloverdale has always been a part of the local community. It established itself as a community shopping centre and that keeps drawing people back to their roots. You can count on one hand the number of malls like this one that are left. It's a testament to the community and to the mall itself. It has stood a long time."

Sources: Shawn Micallef, "A Tale of Two Malls," *Toronto Star*, March 7, 2013, www.thestar.com/life/2013/03/07/a_tale_of_two_malls_micallef.html (accessed November 13, 2013); "Cloverdale Mall/Then and Now" Lost Toronto blog, November 9, 2010, http://lost-toronto.blogspot.ca/2010/11/cloverdale-mallthen-and-now.html (accessed November 13, 2013); Prange Way, "Cloverdale Mall; Toronto, Ontario," Labelscar: The Retail History Blog, December 20, 2006, www.labelscar.com/canada/cloverdale-mall (accessed November 13, 2013); Derek Flack, "What malls used to look like in Toronto," blogTO, May 19, 2011, www.blogto.com/city/2011/05/what_malls_used_to_look_like_in_toronto (accessed November 13, 2013); Kim Hughes, "How the hell is Cloverdale Mall still around?" The gridTO, April 29, 2013, www.thegridto.com/city/places/how-the-hell-is-cloverdale-mall-still-around (accessed November 13, 2013).

For several reasons, store location is often the most important decision made by a retailer. First, location is typically the prime consideration in a customer's store choice. For instance, when choosing where you're going to have your car washed, you usually pick the location closest to your home or work. Second, location decisions have strategic importance because they can be used to develop a sustainable competitive advantage. Retailers can change their pricing, service, and merchandise assortments in a relatively short time. However, location decisions are harder to change because retailers frequently have to either make substantial investments to buy and develop real estate or commit to long-term leases with developers. It's not unusual, for instance, for a national chain store to sign a lease for seven to ten years. If that location is the best in a particular mall or central business district, the retailer then has a strategic advantage competitors can't easily copy, because they are precluded from locating there.

Location decisions have become even more important in recent years. First, there are more retailers opening new locations, making the better locations harder to obtain. This problem is made more complex by a slowdown in both population growth and new shopping centre construction. A retailer may find a suitable location, but high rent, complicated leases, and expensive fixturing and remodelling can make it very costly. Many experts believe that there is too much retail space in Canada and that the best retail locations are already taken. Retailers must consider issues of suitability or compatibility, availability, affordability, accessibility, and visibility.

This chapter describes the types of locations available to retailers and the relative advantages of each. We then examine factors that retailers should consider when choosing a particular location type.

Evaluating Specific Areas for Locations

Many types of locations are available for retail stores—each with its own strengths and weaknesses. Choosing a particular location type involves evaluating a series of trade-offs. These trade-offs generally concern the cost of the location versus its value to customers.

Exhibit 5–1 breaks the location decision into four levels: country, region, trade area, and specific site. The country is a decision of international expansion that will be discussed in Chapter 7. The region refers to a part of the country, a particular city, or a CMA (census metropolitan area). A trade area is the geographic area encompassing most of the customers who would patronize a specific retail site, and that accounts for the majority of the store's sales and customers. A trade area may be part of a city, or it can extend beyond the city's boundaries, depending on the type of store and the density of potential customers surrounding it. For example, the best locations for a 7-Eleven convenience store are not the best locations for a category specialist such as a Best Buy.

In making store location decisions, retailers must examine all four levels simultaneously. For instance, suppose Pizza Pizza is expanding operations in the Atlantic provinces and has plans to open several stores simultaneously. Its research indicates that competition in the Halifax market is relatively weak, making it an attractive region. But maybe it can't find enough suitable sites, so it must temporarily postpone locating there.

In examining a site, we look at the factors that affect the attractiveness of a particular region and trade area. Then we examine what retailers look for in choosing a particular site.

The best areas for locating stores are those that generate the highest long-term profits for a retailer. Some factors affecting the long-term profit generated by stores that should be considered when evaluating an area include (1) the economic conditions, (2) competition, (3) the strategic fit of the area's population with the retailer's target market, and (4) the costs of operating stores (see Exhibit 5–2). Note that these factors are similar to those that retailers consider when evaluating an investment in a new business opportunity or entry into a foreign market.

Economic Conditions

Because locations involve a commitment of resources over a long time horizon, it is important to examine an area's level and growth of population and employment.

In most cases, areas where the general population is growing are preferable to those with declining populations. Some retailers, such as Subway, often go into new strip shopping centres in anticipation that the surrounding suburban area will eventually be built up enough to support demand. Yet population growth alone doesn't tell the whole story.

It's important to examine a market's employment trends because a high level of employment usually means high purchasing power and high levels of retail sales. For

region In retail location analysis, refers to a part of the country, a particular city, or a census metropolitan area (CMA).

trade area A geographic sector that contains potential customers for a particular retailer or shopping centre.

exhibit 5–1 Location Decisions Based on Four Levels

Country → Regional analysis → Trade area analysis → Site analysis

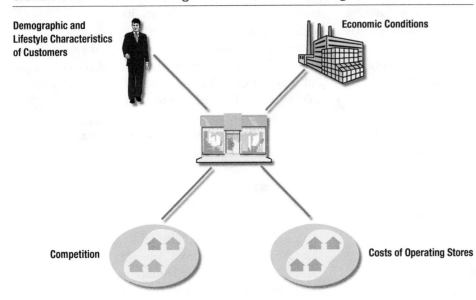

Demographic and Lifestyle Characteristics of Customers

Economic Conditions

Competition

Costs of Operating Stores

instance, Ottawa has become a desirable retail location because of its proximity to government and corporate headquarters. Retail location analysts must determine how long such growth will continue and how it will affect demand for their merchandise. For instance, the economies of some cities such as Oshawa and Windsor experience greater peaks and valleys due to their dependence on specific industries such as automobiles (General Motors and Ford).

Employment growth in and of itself isn't enough to ensure a strong retail environment in the future. If growth isn't diversified in a number of industries, the area may suffer from adverse cyclical trends. For instance, many areas that have been traditionally dependent on agriculture have attempted to bring in new industries, either manufacturing or high-tech, to help diversify their economies.

Competition

The level of competition in an area also affects demand for a retailer's merchandise. The level of competition can be defined as saturated, understored, or overstored. A **saturated trade area** offers customers a good selection of goods and services, while allowing competing retailers to make good profits. Since customers are drawn to these areas because of the

great selections, retailers who believe they can offer customers a superior retail format in terms of merchandise, pricing, or service may find these areas attractive. Some restaurants such as Burger King seek locations where their major competition—McDonald's—has a strong presence. They believe that it's important to go head-to-head with their strongest competitors so that they can develop methods and systems that will allow them to compete successfully with them. They contend that locating in areas with weak competition allows them to become complacent. The strongest competitor will eventually enter the trade area. By then, however, it will have lost its competitive edge.[2]

Another strategy is to locate in an **understored trade area**—an area that has too few stores selling a specific good or service to satisfy the needs of the population. Walmart's early success was based on a location strategy of opening stores in small towns that were relatively understored. Now these stores experience high market share in their towns and draw from surrounding communities.

In effect, these areas have gone from being understored before Walmart arrived to being an **overstored trade area**—having so many stores selling a specific good or service that some stores will fail. Unable to compete head-to-head with Walmart on price or breadth of selection, many family-owned retailers in those cities have had to either reposition their merchandising or service strategies or else go out of business.

saturated trade area   A trade area that offers customers a good selection of goods and services, while allowing competing retailers to make good profits.

understored trade area   An area that has too few stores selling a specific good or service to satisfy the needs of the population.

overstored trade area   An area having so many stores selling a specific good or service that some stores will fail.

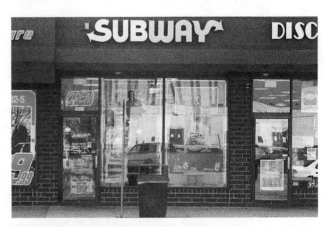

Some retailers, such as Subway, often go into new strip shopping centres in anticipation that the surrounding suburban area will eventually be built up enough to support demand.

Retailing View 5.1 describes how Sobeys Urban Fresh caters to an urban market segment, another area that tends to experience little competition in certain retail segments.

Strategic Fit

Population level, growth, and competition alone don't tell the whole story. The area needs to have consumers who are in the retailer's target market—who are attracted to the retailer's offerings and interested in patronizing its stores. Thus, the area must have the right demographic and lifestyle profile. The size and composition of households in an area can be an important determinant of success. For instance, Laura, Laura Petites, and Laura II (a chain of stores specializing in traditional and business apparel for women) generally locate in areas with high-income, dual-career families; household size, however, isn't a particularly critical issue. Toys "R" Us, on the other hand, is interested in locations with heavy concentrations of families with young children.

Finally, lifestyle characteristics of the population may be relevant, depending on the target market(s) that a particular retailer is pursuing. Many college and university students, for instance, have relatively low incomes. However, they may come from well-to-do families, and by the fact that they are in university or college, they're relatively educated. Their lifestyles more closely resemble those of recent graduates in professional jobs making a good income than they do people with similar incomes working odd jobs in a rural area. Thus, the way people spend their money is often as important as how much money people make.

Operating Costs

The cost of operating stores can vary across areas. Operating costs are also affected by the proximity of the area being considered to other areas in which the retailer operates stores. For example, if a store is located near other stores and the retailer's distribution centres, the cost of shipping merchandise to the store is lower, as is the cost and travel time spent by the district manager supervising the stores' operations.

The local and provincial legal and regulatory environment can have a significant effect on operating costs. For example, according to Section 63 of Quebec's French Language Charter, the name of a business must be in French. Some companies have changed their name to comply with the Charter; for example, Kentucky Fried Chicken is known as "Poulet Frit Kentucky" in Quebec.

Others are being taken to task by the Office Québécois de la Langue Française to change their signs to either give themselves a French name or add a slogan or explanation that reflects what it is they're selling. Changing signing to comply can be a costly venture for retailers.

Number of Stores in an Area

Having selected an area in which to locate its stores, a retailer's next decision is how many stores to operate in the area. At first glance, you might think that a retailer should choose the one best location in each CMA, but clearly, larger CMAs can support more stores than smaller CMAs. It may therefore be more advantageous to locate several stores in one CMA and none in others. But there is a limit to how many stores can be operated in even the largest of CMAs. When making the decision about how many stores to open in an area, retailers must consider the trade-offs between lower operating costs and potential sales cannibalization from having multiple stores in an area.

Economies of Scale versus Cannibalization

At first glance, you would expect that a retailer should choose the one best location in a given trade area. But most chains plan to go into an area with a network of stores. After all, promotion and distribution economies of scale can be achieved with multiple locations. The total cost is the same to run a newspaper ad for a retailer with 20 stores in an area as it is if the retailer has only one store. Likewise, chains such as Canadian Tire expand into areas only where they have distribution capabilities designed to support the stores.

The question is: What is the best number of stores to have in an area? The answer depends on who owns the stores. For company-owned stores, the objective is to maximize profits for the entire chain. In this case, the retailer would continue to open stores as long as the marginal revenues achieved by opening a new store are greater than the marginal costs. Home Depot subscribes to this fundamental axiom of site selection: It is better to have two stores producing $75 million each than one store producing $100 million. The company believes that a store can do too much business. The store might

Home Depot believes that if a store is underperforming, then it may be overcrowded. So the company builds another store in the same trade area.

Retail Site Selection LO 2

Retail site selection is a very strategic decision. Opening a store at a site often involves committing to a lease of five years or more, purchasing land and building a store, or buying an existing building, each of which requires a considerable investment. Consider the tragic results if the store's performance is below expectations: The retailer may not be able to find another business to assume the lease, damage to the business credibility can be disastrous, and the investment capital may be very difficult to recover. The difference between moving into a superior trade area and an inferior one can mean the difference between success and failure. Furthermore, even if a retailer finds the "right" neighbourhood, the wrong site can spell disaster. Consider, for instance, the location of a new doughnut shop. The retailer has the option to locate in two sites, one across the street from the other. One might think that it should simply choose the cheaper site. But one site has easier access and its signs are highly visible to motorists passing by. More important, that same site is on the way into the central business district, whereas the other is on the way to the suburbs. People who enjoy a morning doughnut know that it tastes best on the way to work with a big cup of coffee. Without careful analysis of trade areas and specific sites, multi-million dollar mistakes can be easily made. Fortunately, sophisticated statistical models are available through firms that provide geographic and demographic data and consulting services critical to evaluating specific sites, including MapInfo/Location Intelligence at www.mapinfo.com and ACNielsen Canada at www.acnielsen.ca.

The following questions will be discussed in assessing the retail site:

- What issues should be considered when determining in which region or trade area to locate a store?
- What is a trade area, and why should a retailer choose one over another?
- What factors should retailers consider when deciding on a particular site?
- How can retailers forecast sales for new store locations?

franchisors The owners of a franchise in a franchise agreement.

franchisees The owners of an individual store in a franchise agreement.

be overcrowded, offer poor service, have a hard time staying in stock, and actually be underperforming. Home Depot believes that the solution to an underperforming store is to build another store in the same trade area. Although this strategy may seem illogical at first glance, it works for Home Depot. Best Buy and Future Shop, owned by the same company, use a similar location strategy to control the electronics retail market.

For franchise operations, however, each individual franchise owner wants to maximize his or her profits. Some franchisors (owners of the franchise) grant their franchisees (owners of the individual stores) an exclusive geographic territory so that other stores under the same franchise do not compete directly with them. In other franchise operations, the franchisees have not been afforded this protection and often have been involved in very antagonistic negotiations with the franchisors in an attempt to protect their investment.

Evaluating a Site for Locating a Retail Store

Having decided to locate stores in an area, the retailer's next step is to evaluate and select a specific site. In making this decision, retailers consider three factors: (1) the characteristics of the site, (2) the characteristics of the trading area for a store at the site, and (3) the estimated potential sales that can be generated by a store at the site.

Who Needs a Kitchen When You Have Sobeys Urban Fresh Downstairs?

If you have ever lived in an urban location, you'd know that going grocery shopping is not a trivial experience. You have to get to your car, drive to the store and back, and then negotiate a temporary space while you unload and take the goods upstairs. Grocery stores in urban locations are often cramped for space and therefore lack adequate assortment. Given the lack of competition, they are also often overpriced.

Sobeys is slowly seizing the opportunity to enter traditionally low-competition areas to cater to their well-heeled customers by introducing a new grocery store concept they call Urban Fresh. These stores cater specifically to the lifestyles of those living in downtown areas. Each store is built to suit the particular neighbourhood it is located in, which helps to ensure sustainability of both the store and the community in which it resides. These stores tend to be significantly smaller than traditional grocery stores, but

smaller space does not translate into lack of variety and selection. The Urban Fresh stores carry specialty products and feature an extensive salad bar, a sushi section, a made-to-order pizza and pasta component, numerous meals to go, and a café offering gourmet coffees. Urban Fresh is a destination store for many consumers looking for gourmet food products and those customers walking home from work or school, giving them quick, easy access to fresh, quality food on a daily basis.

While the prices of Urban Fresh products tend to be higher than those of competitors such as Loblaw's Real Canadian Superstore or Walmart, customers are finding value through other benefits provided. These very urban locations give a competitive advantage to the apartment buildings in which the stores reside, as well as much needed high-quality groceries in markets that are typically underserved.

Source: Kelly McCabe, "Trader Joe's Opening First Brooklyn Store Next Week," *Real Deal*, September 16, 2008; Michael Stoler, "Luxury Seems to Be Set for the Lower East Side," *New York Sun*, May 17, 2007; Mark Hamstra, "Slow Start for Newest Whole Foods," *Supermarket News*, April 9, 2007; www.avalonchrystieplace.com (accessed November 31, 2009); www.wholefoods.com (accessed November 31, 2009); Rosalind Stefanac for Retail Council of Canada, "Sobeys Finds Its Fit with the Urban Crowd," *Canadian Retailer*, January/February 2010, pp. 11–12.; http://www2.canada.com/edmontonjournal/news/business/story.html?id=20007a77-0b12-4r68-bidb-0af5e7ee37c5; Terrence Belford, "Urban builders forge new alliance with retail," *The Globe and Mail*, February 20, 2009, p. G3.

The first two sets of factors are typically considered in an initial screening of potential sites. The methods used to forecast sales, the third factor, can involve a more complex analytical approach. Each of these factors is discussed in the following sections (see Retailing View 5.1).

Factors Affecting the Attractiveness of a Site

Some characteristics of a site that affect store sales and thus are considered in selecting a site are traffic flow past the site and accessibility to the site, as well as its advantages within the location (Exhibit 5–3).

Traffic Flow and Accessibility

The accessibility of a site is the ease with which a customer may get into and out of it. The accessibility analysis has two stages: a macro analysis and then a micro analysis.

Macro Analysis The macro analysis considers the primary trade area, such as the area five to ten kilometres around the site in the case of a supermarket or drugstore. To assess a site's accessibility on a macro level, the retailer simultaneously evaluates several factors, such as road patterns, road conditions, and barriers.

In the macro analysis, the analyst should consider the road pattern. The primary trade area needs major arteries or highways so that customers can travel easily to the site. A related factor is the road condition, including the age, number of lanes, number of stoplights, congestion, and general state of repair of roads in the primary trade area. For instance, a location on an old, narrow, congested secondary road in disrepair with too many stoplights wouldn't be a particularly good site for a retail store.

road pattern A consideration used in measuring the accessibility of a retail location via major arteries, highways, or roads.

road condition Includes the age, number of lanes, number of stoplights, congestion, and general state of repair of roads in a trade area.

exhibit 5–3 Site Characteristics

Traffic Flow and Accessibility	Restrictions
Vehicular traffic	Zoning
Ease of vehicular access	Signage
Access to major highways	Restrictions on tenant mix
Street congestion	Safety code restrictions
Pedestrian traffic	
Availability of mass transit	
Location Characteristics	**Costs**
Parking spaces	Rental fee
Access to store entrance and exit	Common area maintenance cost
Visibility of store from street	Local taxes
Access for deliveries	Advertising and promotion fees
Size and shape of store	Length of lease
Condition of building	
Adjacent retailers	

The success of a site with a good traffic flow is a question of balance. The site should have a substantial number of cars per day, but not so many that congestion impedes access to the store. To assess the level of vehicular traffic, the analyst can usually obtain data from the regional planning commission or highway department. But the data may have to be adjusted for special situations. As a result, it's sometimes easier and more accurate to do the analysis in-house. For instance, the analyst must consider that the presence of large places of employment, schools, or big trucks may lessen a site's desirability. Also, areas congested during rush hours may have a good traffic flow during the rest of the day when most shopping takes place. Finally, some retailers might wish to adjust the raw traffic counts by excluding out-of-province licence plates or counting only homeward-bound traffic.

The amount and quality of parking facilities are critical to a shopping centre's overall accessibility. If there aren't enough spaces or if they're too far from the stores, customers will be discouraged from entering the area. On the other hand, if there are too many open spaces, the shopping centre may be seen as a failure or as having unpopular stores. It's hard to assess how many parking spaces are enough, although location analysts use parking ratios as a starting point. A standard rule of thumb is 5.9:100 (5.9 spaces per 1000 square feet of retail store space).[4] Nevertheless, there's no good substitute for observing the shopping centre at various times of the day, week, and season. The analyst must also assess the availability of employee parking, the proportion of shoppers using cars, parking by nonshoppers, and the typical length of a shopping trip.

An issue that's closely related to the amount of available parking facilities, but extends into the shopping centre itself, is the relative congestion of the area. Congestion can refer to the amount of crowding of either cars or people. There's some optimal range of comfortable congestion for customers. Too much congestion can make shopping slow, irritate customers, and generally discourage sales. On the other hand, a relatively high level of activity in a shopping centre creates excitement and can stimulate sales.[5]

The last factor to consider in the accessibility analysis is ingress/egress—the ease of entering and exiting the site's parking lot. Often, medians or one-way streets make entering or exiting difficult from one or more directions, limiting accessibility.

Adjacent Tenants Locations with complementary, as well as competing, adjacent retailers have the potential to build traffic. Complementary retailers target the same market segment but have a different, noncompeting

natural barriers Barriers, such as rivers or mountains, that affect accessibility to a site.

artificial barriers In site evaluations for accessibility, barriers such as railroad tracks, major highways, or parks.

visibility The customers' ability to see the store and enter the parking lot safely.

amount and quality of parking facilities A store's having enough parking spaces, close enough to the building, that the store is ideally accessible to customers, but not so many open spaces that the store is viewed as being unpopular. A standard rule of thumb is 5.9 spaces per 1000 square feet of retail store space.

congestion The amount of crowding of either cars or people.

ingress/egress The means of entering/ exiting the parking lot of a retail site.

Natural barriers, such as rivers or mountains, and **artificial barriers**, such as railroad tracks, major highways, or parks, may also affect accessibility. These barriers' impact on a particular site primarily depends on whether the merchandise or services are available on both sides of the barrier. If, for instance, only one supermarket serves both sides of a highway, people on the opposite side must cross to shop.

Micro Analysis The micro analysis concentrates on issues in the immediate vicinity of the site, such as visibility, traffic flow, parking, congestion, and ingress/egress.

Visibility refers to customers' ability to see the store and enter the parking lot safely. Good visibility is less important for stores with established and loyal customers and for stores with limited market areas because customers know where the store is. Nonetheless, large national retailers such as Canadian Tire insist that there be no impediments to a direct, undisturbed view of their store. In an area with a highly transient population, such as a tourist centre or large city, good visibility from the road is particularly important.

merchandise offering. For example, Price Chopper, a limited assortment supermarket targeting price-sensitive consumers, prefers to be co-located with other retailers targeting price-sensitive consumers, such as Dollarama or even Walmart.

Have you ever noticed that competing fast-food restaurants, automobile dealerships, antiques dealers, and even shoe and apparel stores in a mall are located next to one another? Consumers looking for these types of merchandise are involved in convenience or comparison shopping situations. They want to be able to make their choice easily in the case of convenience shopping or to have a good assortment so that they can "shop around."

This location approach is based on the principle of cumulative attraction, in which a cluster of similar and complementary retailing activities will generally have greater drawing power than isolated stores that engage in the same retailing activities.

Locational Advantages within a Centre

Once the centre's accessibility is evaluated, the analyst must evaluate the locations within it. Since the better sites cost more, retailers must consider their importance. For instance, in a strip shopping centre, the more expensive locations are closest to the grocery store. A liquor store or a flower shop that may attract impulse buyers should thus be close to the grocery store. But a shoe repair store, which shouldn't expect impulse customers, could be in an inferior location because customers in need of this service will seek out the store.

The same issues apply when evaluating regional multilevel shopping centres. It's advantageous for apparel stores such as Club Monaco to be clustered in the more expensive locations near a department store in a mall. People shopping for clothing may start at the department store and naturally gravitate to stores near it. Yet a store such as Sport Chek, another destination store, needn't be in the most expensive location, since many of its customers know they're in the market for this type of product before they even get to the centre.

Another consideration is to locate stores that appeal to similar target markets close together. In essence, customers want to shop where they'll find a good assortment of merchandise. This is based on the principle of cumulative attraction, in which a cluster of similar and complementary retailing activities will generally have greater drawing power than isolated stores that engage in the same retailing activities. This is why antiques shops, car dealers, and shoe and clothing stores all seem to do better if they're close to one another. Of course, an area can become overstored when it has too many competing stores to profitably satisfy demand.

The principle of cumulative attraction applies both to stores that sell complementary merchandise and those that compete directly with one another. Thus a good location is one whose tenant mix provides:

- A good selection of merchandise that competes with itself
- Complementary merchandise

Trade Area Characteristics

Lo 3

After identifying several sites that have acceptable traffic flow, accessibility, and other location characteristics, the next step is to collect information about the trade area that can be used to forecast sales for a store located at the site. Once the trade area is defined, the retailer can use several different information sources to develop a detailed understanding of the nature of consumers in the site's trade area.

Trade Area

A trade area is a contiguous geographic area that accounts for the majority of a store's sales and customers. Trade areas can be divided into two or three zones. Such trade areas are called polygons because their boundaries conform to streets and other map features. The zones' exact definitions should be flexible to account for particular areas' nuances.

The primary zone is the geographic area from which the store or shopping centre derives 60 to 65 percent of its customers. The secondary zone is the geographic area of secondary importance in terms of customer sales, generating about 20 percent of a store's sales. The tertiary zone (the outermost ring) includes customers who occasionally shop at the store or shopping centre. There are several reasons for the tertiary zone. First, these customers may lack adequate retail facilities closer to home. Second, there are excellent highway systems to the store or centre so that customers can get there easily. Third, customers may drive near the store or centre on the way to or from work.

cumulative attraction The principle that a cluster of similar and complementary retailing activities will generally have greater drawing power than isolated stores that engage in the same retailing activities.

polygons Trade areas whose boundaries conform to streets and other map features rather than being concentric circles.

primary zone The geographic area from which the store or shopping centre derives 60 to 65 percent of its customers; also called *primary trade area*.

secondary zone The geographic area of secondary importance in terms of customer sales, generating about 20 percent of a store's sales; also called *secondary trade area*.

tertiary zone The outermost ring of a trade area that includes customers who occasionally shop at the store or shopping centre; also called *tertiary trade area*.

A 7-Eleven convenience store's trade area is small, possibly only a kilometre or two, compared to a Sears store that may draw customers from 50 kilometres away.

symbiotic store A store that does not create its own traffic and whose trade area is determined by the dominant retailer in the shopping centre or retail area; also called a *parasite store*.

Finally, customers are drawn to the store or centre because it is in or near a tourist area.

Factors Defining Trade Areas

The actual boundaries of a trade area are determined by the store's accessibility, natural and physical barriers, type of shopping area, type of store, and competition. Driving time is a useful criterion for defining trade areas because the time it takes to get to a particular shopping area is more important to the potential customer than distance. For example, driving to the retailer's location might take 5 minutes for those in the primary trade area, 10 minutes for those in the secondary trade area, and 20 minutes for those in the tertiary trade area.

Trade area size is also influenced by the type of store or shopping area. A 7-Eleven convenience store's trade area, for example, may extend less than a kilometre, whereas a category specialist such as Toys "R" Us may draw customers from 50 kilometres away. The difference is due to the nature of the merchandise sold and the total size of the assortment offered. Convenience stores succeed because customers can buy products such as milk and bread quickly and easily. If customers must drive great distances, the store is no longer convenient. Category specialists offer a large choice of shopping and specialty products for which customers are willing to put forth additional effort to shop. Thus, customers will generally drive some distance to shop at a category specialist.

Another way of looking at how the type of store influences the size of a trade area is whether it's a destination or a symbiotic store. A destination store is one in which the merchandise, selection, presentation, pricing, or other unique features act as a magnet for customers. A symbiotic store is one that does not create its own traffic and whose trade area is determined by the dominant retailer in the shopping centre or retail area. In general,

destination stores have larger trade areas than symbiotic stores—people are willing to drive farther to shop there. Hakim Optical would qualify as a destination store due to the exclusive nature of its merchandise. Other examples of destination stores are anchor stores in shopping centres, such as grocery stores or department stores; certain specialty stores, such as RadioShack and Polo/Ralph Lauren; category killers, such as Staples Business Depot; and some service providers, such as movie theatres.

The level of competition also affects the size and shape of a trade area for a particular store. If two convenience food stores are too close together, their respective trade areas will shrink since they offer the same merchandise. On the other hand, Hakim Optical is one of several optical shops in this business district. Having similar shopping goods stores in the same vicinity generally expands the trade area boundaries; more people are drawn to the area to shop because of its expanded selection. Additionally, a retailer's trade area is limited by a large regional shopping centre that has several stores carrying similar merchandise.

Sources of Information

Three types of information are required to define a trade area:

- Retailers must determine how many people are in the trade area and where they live. For this, retailers use a technique known as *customer spotting*.

- Retailers use the demographic and GIS (geographic information systems) data to describe their potential customers in an attempt to assess how much they will buy in the proposed trade area.

- Retailers use the Internet and other published sources to assess their competition. In strongly competitive trade areas, a retailer can expect to achieve a smaller piece of the total market potential for a particular type of merchandise or store.

Customer Spotting The purpose of the customer spotting technique is to spot, or locate, the residences of customers for a store or shopping centre.[6] Data specific to a retailer's customers are usually obtained from information from credit card or cheque purchases or from customer loyalty programs. Retailers can also collect this information manually as part of the checkout process.

Another method is to note automobile licence plates in the parking lot and trace them to the owner by purchasing the information from governments or private research companies. A word of caution, however: This method is thought to be inaccurate and is illegal in some areas. Experts believe that at least 500 plates are necessary to provide a good sample. The plates can be matched against a national vehicle registration database and summarize where the vehicles originate. This approach may, however, be the easiest way to understand the trade area of competitors.

The data collected from customer spotting can be processed in two ways: by manually plotting the location of each customer on a map, or by using a GIS system.

Once the customers are spotted, the retailer can delineate a trade area. This process involves a lot of subjectivity, so the guidelines presented earlier in this chapter are helpful.

Statistics Canada A census is taken every five years in Canada. The population of each census tract area can range from 2500 to 8000 people, but the preferred average is 4000 people; city cores will have a higher population density. In Canada, there are 25 CMAs (census metropolitan areas) across the country.

In the census, each household in the country is counted to determine the number of persons per household, household relationships, sex, race, age, and marital status. The information is detailed under the following themes: population, education, earnings, work, income, families, dwellings, and religion. Detailed census information is also available through *GeoPost Plus,* which can be purchased from Canada Post. A report on each building identifies the number of housing units at the address, whether the dwelling is owned or rented, whether the dwelling is owner-occupied, the housing value, the rent, and the vacancy status. Additional information is obtained from *Financial Post Markets Canadian Demographics. FP Markets* is a valuable tool when trying to determine the profile of consumers living in a specific area. The book provides percentage increases in population over the past five years and projects population growth for the next six years. Consumer spending patterns are broadly defined, and the psychographic profiles of people living in the area are identified as well. *FP Markets* divides Canadians into 60 predefined psychographic clusters and 19 financial clusters; explanations of the clusters are included (see Exhibit 5–4).

FP Markets features tables that identify buying indices by province, economic region, census division, urban market, metropolitan area, city, and town. Retail sales estimates by class of business, economic region, and census division are identified and income projections are included.

geographic information systems (GIS) Computerized systems that enable analysts to visualize information about their customers' demographics, buying behaviour, and other data in a map format.

Demographic Data and GIS Vendors There are hundreds of private companies specializing in providing retailers with information that will help them make better store-location decisions. Some, known as *demographic data vendors,* such as Environics Analytics, specialize in repackaging and updating census-type data in a format that's easy to understand, easy and quick to obtain, and relatively inexpensive. Since the data from the census can be dated, these firms construct computer models to generate estimates of current and future population and demographic characteristics.

Other firms, such as Pitney Bowes Business Insight PSYTE HD Canada, specialize in geographic information systems (GIS), computerized systems that enable analysts to illustrate their customers' demographics, buying behaviour, and other data in a map format.[7] In many ways, a GIS resembles a database program because it analyzes and relates information stored as records. Additionally, however, each record contains information used to draw a geometric shape—usually a point, a line, or a polygon—and represents a unique place on Earth to which the data corresponds. As such, GIS is a spatial database, a database that stores the location and shape of information. Using GIS, analysts can identify the boundaries of a trade area and isolate target customer groups. Data for GIS are collected at the point of sale and stored in data warehouses and combined with the type of information that is available from the demographic data vendors.

GIS firms offer a wide range of tools useful for assessing consumer demand in an area. They utilize data from consumer surveys from private marketing research companies.

Check out this demographic resource to see how this is done by clicking on the Cluster Index at www.utahbluemedia.com/pbbi/psyte/psyteCanada.html.

Measuring Competition Estimating the demand for a retailer's products is a critical success factor, but it tells only half the story. It's equally important to determine the level of competition in the trade area. Earlier in this chapter, we concluded that either a saturated or an understored trade area offers a potentially good location opportunity, but that retailers should avoid trade areas that are overstored. How can a retailer such as Hakim exhibit 5-4 Vancouver Canadian Demographics 2012

VANCOUVER
(City)
Vancouver CMA
In Greater Vancouver Regional District

Population

July 1, 2012, Estimate	668,726
% Cdn. Total	1.91
'06–'12 % Population Change	11.82
Avg annual % rate of pop change '06–'12	1.88
2014 Projected Population	689,677
2017 Projected Population	721,180
2012 Households Estimate	302,573
2014 Projected Households	317,060
2017 Projected Households	338,847

Income

% Above/Below Ntl. Avg. (per Capita)	+10
2012 Total Income Estimate $	25,260,881,979
% Cdn. Total	2.11
2012 Average Hhld. Income $	83,487
2012 per Capita	$37,775
% 2012 Hhlds., Income $100,000+	21.15
2014 Projected Total Income $	28,574,426,653
2017 Projected Total Income $	33,907,299,550

Retail Sales

% Above/Below Ntl. Avg. (per Capita)	–12
2012 Retail Sales Estimate $	8,095,451,902
% Cdn. Total	1.69
2012 per Household	26,755
2012 per Capita $	12,106
2012 No. of Establishments	5,133
2014 Projected Retail Sales $	9,202,692,346
2017 Projected Retail Sales $	10,730,321,133

Population
2012 Estimates:

Age groups	Total	Male	Female
All	668,726	332,393	336,333
0–4	27,735	14,679	13,056
5–9	24,446	12,541	11,905
10–14	24,042	12,468	11,574
15–19	29,886	15,505	14,381
20–24	53,440	26,329	27,111
25–29	72,218	36,620	35,598
30–34	64,564	32,366	32,198
35–39	53,277	26,992	26,285
40–44	52,325	26,589	25,736
45–49	50,300	25,367	24,933
50–54	47,911	23,648	24,263
55–59	43,298	21,565	21,733
60–64	34,170	16,637	17,533
65–69	27,541	13,465	14,076
70+	63,573	27,622	35,951

Daytime Population
2012 Estimates:

Working Population	444,601
At Home Population	281,730
Total	726,331

Income
2012 Estimates:

Avg. Household Income $	83,487
Avg. Family Income $	102,383
Avg. per Capita Income $	37,775
Avg. Employment Income Male $	55,487
Avg. Employment Income Male (Full-Time) $	74,682
Avg. Employment Income Female $	37,981
Avg. Employment Income Female (Full-Time) $	55,988

Disposable & Discretionary Income
2012 Estimates:

Disposable Income per Hhld. $	63,941
Discretionary Income per Hhld. $	23,649

Liquid Assets
2010 Estimates:

Equity Investments per Hhld. $	42,822
Interest Bearing Investments per Hhld. $	64,584
Total Liquid Assets per Hhld. $	107,406
Total Liabilities per Hhld. $	122,240

Labour Force

2012 Estimates	Male	Female
In the Labour Force	201,450	185,546
Participation Rate	70.1	62.9
Employed	185,030	173,539
Unemployed	16.420	12,007
Unemployment Rate	8.2	6.5
Not in Labour Force	86,021	109,235

Occupations by Major Groups

2012 Estimates:	Male	Female
Management	26,840	16,705
Business, Finance & Admin.	24,527	43,451
Natural & Applied Sci. & Rel'd	26,551	7,773
Health	6,442	16,239
Social Sci., Gov't Serv's & Relig'n	7,961	13,709
Education	7,947	11,248
Arts, Culture, Recr'n & Sport	13,252	12,041
Sales & Service	44,686	50,612
Trades, Transp. & Equip. Ops.	28,746	2,667
Primary Industries	3,375	1,242
Processing, Mfg. & Utilities	7,498	6,431

Level of Schooling
2012 Estimates:

Population 25+ years	498,926
No certificate, diploma or degree	70,997
Certificate, diploma or degree	427,929
High school certif. or equivalent	101,523
Apprenticeship or trades certif. or diploma	33,110
College, CEGEP or non-univ. certif. or dip.	76,716
Univ. certif. diploma or degree	216,580
Univ. certif. or dip. below bach. level	31,965
Univ. certif. or degree	184,615
Bachelor's degree	115,154
Univ. certif. or dip. above bach. level	15,142
Degree in med., dent., vet. med. or optom	6,667
Master's degree	38,919
Earned doctorate	8,733

Average Household Expenditures
2012 Estimates:

Food $	8,378
Shelter $	16,578
Clothing $	3,572
Transportation $	8,738
Health & Personal Care$	3,198
Recr'n, Read'g & Education $	5,778
Taxes & Securities $	21,568
Other $	10,721
Total Expenditures $	78,530

Private Households
2012 Estimates:

Private Households, Total	302,573
Pop. in Private Households	658,475
Avg. No. per Household	2.2

Families
2012 Estimates:

Families in Private Households	166,990
Couple Families	140,321
Lone-Parent Families	26,669
Avg. No. Persons per Family	2.8
Avg. No. Children at Home	1.0

Housing
2012 Estimates:

Occupied Private Dwellings	302,573
Owned	145,609
Rented	156,964
Band Housing	0
Single-Detached House	53,646
Semi-Detached House	4,196
Row Houses	9,163
Apartment, 5+ Storeys	89,179
Owned Apartment, 5+ Storeys	29,969
Apartment, Fewer than 5 Storeys	97,894
Apartment, Detached Duplex	47,833
Other Single-Attached	524
Movable Dwelling	138

Vehicles

2010 NVR ('10 Year End)	20,265
'09–'11 Model Yrs VIO (Dec. '10)	42,580
% '09–'11 MY of Total VIO (Dec. '10)	13.71
'81–'08 Model Yrs VIO (Dec. '10)	267,919
% '81–'08 MY of Total VIO (Dec. '10)	86.29
Total VIO ('81–'11) (Dec. '10)	310,499

NVR = New Vehicle Registrations
VIO = Vehicles in Operation

Marital Status
2012 Estimates (Age 15+):

Single (never married)	212,523
Married (legal & common-law)	298,782
Separated (legally married)	14,545
Widowed	29,283
Divorced	37,370

PSYTE HD Canada Clusters

2012 Estimates:	No. of Hhlds.	% Total	Index
Canadian Elite	4,571	1.51	307
Flourishing Families	206	0.07	12
Professional Duets	748	0.25	55
Castles & Condos	4,394	1.45	306
Empty Nest Bliss	7,603	2.51	205
Asian Heights	427	0.14	32
New-New Families	5,949	1.97	165
Trucks & Tradesmen	243	0.08	3
Young Technocrats	14,334	4.74	366
Euro Adapters	913	0.30	9
Next Gen Rising	1,263	0.42	15
Euro Traditionals	191	0.06	2
Cozy Rows	3,036	1.00	26
Metro Singles	55,914	18.48	1,405
Families on the Go	705	0.23	25
Asian Fusion	83,381	27.56	2,303
Europa Blend	4,249	1.40	108
High-Rise Sunsets	2,484	0.82	92
Family Crossroads	2,395	0.79	35
Workers' Landing	2,783	0.92	119
Rural Blues	136	0.04	3
Tenants & Twenties	623	0.21	10
Rods & Rifles	4,160	1.37	68
Cross-Town Hustle	859	0.28	13
Mussels & Malbec	56,990	18.84	733
Swing Shift	797	0.26	9
Nouveaux Depart	387	0.13	14
High-Rise High Hopes	22,915	7.57	473
Urban Verve	4,106	1.36	98
Tea & Good Books	9,326	3.08	108
Nouveaux Quebecois	3,178	1.05	32
Metro Medley	2,625	0.87	62
Urban Struggle	682	0.23	40

Vancouver (continued)
(City)
Vancouver CMA

PSYTE HD Financial

2012 Estimates:	No. of Hhlds.	% Total	Index
Platinum Domain	10,816	3.57	490
Blue Chip Investors	7,746	2.56	119
Upper Middle Amenities	6,940	2.29	35
Monster Mortgage	983	0.32	4
Cautious Consumer	64,710	21.39	475
Kids & Credit	86,566	28.61	718
Baby Bills	670	0.22	4
Frugal Families	4,021	1.33	45
Rent-to-Own	12,949	4.28	29
Just Checking	1,471	0.49	5
New Beginnings	31,662	10.46	96
Next in Line	64,187	21.21	240
Looking Back	9,852	3.26	108

Home Language

2012 Estimates:		%Total
English	425,225	64.58
French	4,547	0.69
Cantonese	57,898	8.79
Chinese, n.i.e	47,771	7.25
Mandarin	22,189	3.37
Panjabi (Punjabi)	12,564	1.91
Vietnamese	9,058	1.38
Tagalog (Pilipino, Filipino)	9,016	1.37
Korean	7,852	1.19
Spanish	6,224	0.95
Japanese	4,486	0.68
Persian (Farsi)	3,894	0.59
Italian	2,282	0.35
Russian	2,232	0.34
Hindi	2,200	0.33
Serbian	1,670	0.25
Greek	1,428	0.22
Portuguese	1 398	0.21
Arabic	1,106	0.17
Polish	1,085	0.16
Tamil	1,047	0.16
Malay	932	0.14
German	805	0.12
Bengali	643	0.10
Croatian	602	0.09
Romanian	565	0.09
Hungarian	562	0.09
Gujarati	552	0.08
Hebrew	535	0.08
Ilocano	427	0.06
Serbo-Croatian	353	0.05
Urdu	345	0.05
Other languages	5,889	0.89
Multiple responses	21,093	3.20
Total	658,475	100.00

Building Permits

	2010	2009	2008
Value $000	1,475,485	1,270,073	1,432,822

Media Information

see Vancouver, CMA

Optical determine the level of saturation of the trade area for a potential new location? In other words, what's the level of trade area competition?

One of the most powerful methods of measuring competition is over the Internet.[8] Most websites list not only all current locations but future sites as well. Demographic information for prospective sales in other countries might eliminate the need for an in-person visit. A more traditional method of accessing competitive information is through the Yellow Pages of the telephone book. This information is also available on CD-ROM. Other sources of competitive information are directories published by trade associations, chambers of commerce, the International Council of Shopping Centres (shopping centres), the Urban Land Institute (shopping centres), local newspaper advertising departments, municipal and provincial governments, specialized trade magazines, and list brokers.

A relatively easy way to determine level of competition is to calculate the total square footage of retail space devoted to a type of store per household. For example, published sources can estimate the total square feet devoted to optical retailers in their trade area and divide it by the number of households. The higher the ratio, the higher the level of competition will be. Of course, there's no substitute for personal visits, as observation will lend valuable insight to gathering competitive intelligence.

Methods of Estimating Demand

A number of complementary analytical methods are used to estimate the demand for a new store. One of the most widely used techniques, the analogue approach, was first developed by William Applebaum for the Kroger Company in the 1930s. A more formalized statistical version of the analogue approach uses regression analysis. A third approach, known as Huff's gravity model, is based on Newton's law of gravity. We discuss these location analysis methods below.

> **DID YOU KNOW?**
>
> The worldwide market for GIS software, hardware, and services is greater than US$6 billion.[9]

The Analogue Approach The analogue approach could just as easily be called the *similar store approach*. Suppose European Optical wants to open a new location. Since its present location in Vancouver has been very successful, it would like to find a location whose trade area has similar characteristics. It would estimate the size and customer demographic characteristics of its current trade area and then attempt to match those characteristics to new potential locations. Thus, knowledge of customer demographics, the competition, and sales of currently operating stores can be used to predict the size and sales potential of a new location.

Using the analogue approach, European Optical would undertake the following steps:

- Complete a competitive analysis of the optional sites to estimate potential sales for the store sites.
- Define the current trade area, based on density of customers to the store, drive zones, major roads, and natural or manmade barriers.
- Determine the trade area characteristics based on demographic research and psychographic profiles.
- Match the characteristics of the current trade area with the potential new store locations to determine the best site.

Step 1: Conduct Competitive Analysis to Estimate Potential Sales
Unlike other optical stores, European Optical carries a very exclusive merchandise selection. In general, the higher the trade area potential, the lower the relative competition will be (see Exhibits 5–5 and 5–6).

Step 2: Define the Current Trade Area
On the basis of customer spotting data gathered from a data warehouse of current customers, a trade area map can be generated. The trade area map can also be defined based on drive times: 5 minutes for the primary trade area, 10 minutes for the secondary trade area, and 20 minutes for the tertiary trade area. Major highways and heavily travelled roads will bring traffic to the area but can also divide a trade area, as can a river or bridge, and may limit trade area potential.

Because European Optical is in a business district, the trade area will be smaller than it would be if located in a regional shopping centre. The regional shopping centre has complementary stores that attract more people to the area to shop because of the expanded selection of retailers and restaurants.

Step 3: Determine Trade Area Characteristics
Financial Post Markets charts demographic trends (see Exhibit 5–4), including data on population, on households by number of persons, race, ethnic origin, and on age by sex. An interesting characteristic of the area surrounding European Optical is that an estimated 27.7 percent of the population was of Chinese descent (2011).

As we said earlier in this chapter, it is just as important to look at consumer lifestyles or psychographics as it is to examine their demographics. We know that European Optical's trade area is generally affluent, but are the residents the kind of people who would purchase its upscale fashion eyewear?

Exhibit 5–5 summarizes the most prominent lifestyle report for the five-kilometre ring surrounding European Optical. These clusters, described in Exhibit 5–6, indicate an

exhibit 5–5 Neighbourhood Lifestyle Clusters for Five-Kilometre Ring Surrounding European Optical

Cluster Classification	Population Count in Five-Kilometre Ring	Percentage of Population in Each Classification
Metro Singles	14 538	26.00%
Asian Fusion	12 424	14.90
Mussels & Malbec	7010	12.30
Young Technocrats	2773	12.10

exhibit 5–6 Descriptions of Largest Clusters Surrounding European Optical

Metro Singles
Urban neighbourhoods share a diversity of spirit as well as a diversity of culture. As they cater to the needs of the Metro Singles youthful cluster, these areas epitomize an urban lifestyle that takes advantage of each 24-hour day. Their average income of $85 000 may fall in the middle of the bi-polar income distribution of students and professors, but it nevertheless provides a spending cushion for basics as well as extras. They ride bicycles or walk to work or school, and live in older apartments and newer condo rentals. Most either have or are working on a university or college degree. If they drive at all, their preference is for an older luxury vehicle.

Asian Fusion
Immigrants from the Asia-Pacific Rim have come to Canada and to all her major metropolitan areas, but Vancouver may have attracted a disproportionate share. The result is a set of neighbourhoods with distinctive Asian origins as well as others with an impressive "fusion" of several Asian cultures. Average household incomes of $83 000 often support more than one or two generations. Living in apartments and attached duplex housing, Asian Fusion residents index high on service industry jobs, including many in the information and cultural employment sectors. They also enjoy their luxury imported vehicles.

Mussels & Malbec
A young, urban cluster, Mussels & Malbec residents are interested in living independently, experimenting with exotic foods—perhaps a mussels mariniere appetizer with a bottle of Argentine Malbec red or Torrontes white, if you're fussy—and generally living life to the fullest while there's still time. What matters is maintaining the relatively fast pace of work and leisure in an urban core setting. On incomes of $58 000 and no children to feed (they don't go for the mussels anyway), these neighbourhoods have the discretionary income needed for their diverse pursuits. Information industry careers plus cultural, artistic, and entertainment industry jobs predominate. Mussels & Malbec index high for household maintainers under age 25 with a university degree. If they do have a car, look for the pre-owned sporty imports.

Young Technocrats
Fresh out of university and with a few years of work in technical jobs, Young Technocrats know the new and next new technologies. Still single or coupling "informally," they live in rental housing and have some money to burn travelling abroad or frequenting local entertainment venues. Having postponed starting a family, this cluster can live a lot on $94 000 a year. With the third-highest index for work in professional and technical jobs, this cluster also indexes high on work in artistic and cultural activities. Many drive a sporty imported vehicle when they're not out jogging or biking.

exhibit 5-7 Descriptions of European Optical and Four Potential Locations' Trade Areas

Store Location	Average Household Income	White-Collar Occupations	Percentage Residents Age 45 and Over	Predominant Profile	Level of Competition
European Optical	$94 279	High	23%	Young Technocrats	Low
Site A	83 000	High	22	Asian Fusion	Medium
Site B	60 000	Low	31	High-Rise Sunsets	Low
Site C	85 000	High	24	Metro Singles	High
Site D	124 000	High	28	Empty Nest Bliss	Medium

Average household income is taken from the year 2011 projections in Exhibit 5-4. Level of white-collar occupations is estimated from data in Exhibit 5-5. Percentage of residents 45 years old and over is estimated from Exhibit 5-4. Level of competition was subjectively determined.

interesting mix of potential customers. The Metro Singles, Mussels & Malbec, Young Technocrats, and Asian Fusion clusters should be drawn to European Optical's high-fashion product lines. Generally, the reports show that the area is affluent and is therefore ideal for selling exclusive and expensive eyewear.

Step 4: Match Characteristics of Current Store with Potential New Store's Location to Determine the Best Site
Now that the trade area for European Optical's existing store is defined, the information can be used to choose a new store location. The trick is to find a location whose market area is similar or analogous to its existing store.

On the basis of the factors affecting demand described earlier in the chapter, it can be concluded that the five factors that contribute most to the success of European Optical's current location are high income, predominantly white-collar occupations, relatively large percentage of older residents, upscale profile, and relatively low competition for expensive, high-fashion eyewear. Exhibit 5-7 compares European Optical's current location with four potential locations on these five factors. These locations are pictured in Exhibit 5-8.

The potential customers of Site A typically have white-collar occupations; they have relatively good incomes and tend to support more than one generation, so expensive eyewear may not be a priority purchase. Finally, there's a medium level of competition in the area.

The older residents surrounding Site B have moderate incomes and are mostly retired. Even though competition would be low and most residents need glasses, these customers are more interested in value than in fashion.

Site C has strong potential since the twenty-something residents in the area are young and have a strong interest in fashion. Although working, they are busy furnishing their first homes and apartments and paying off university loans. Although they would appreciate European Optical's fashionable assortment, they won't appreciate the high prices. Also, other high-end optical stores are entrenched in the area.

Site D is the best location for European Optical. These "prime of life" couples are primarily "empty nesters" and are sophisticated consumers of adult luxuries such as high-fashion eyewear. Importantly, this area's shopping preferences are similar to Metro Singles, Young Technocrats, and Mussels & Malbec.

Unfortunately, finding analogous situations isn't always as easy as in this example. The weaker the analogy, the more difficult the location decision will be. When a retailer has a relatively small number of outlets (say, 20 or fewer), the analogue approach is often best. Even retailers with just one outlet can use the analogue approach. As the number of stores increases, it becomes more difficult for the analyst to organize the data in a meaningful way. More analytical approaches are necessary.

exhibit 5-8 Potential Locations for a European Optical Store

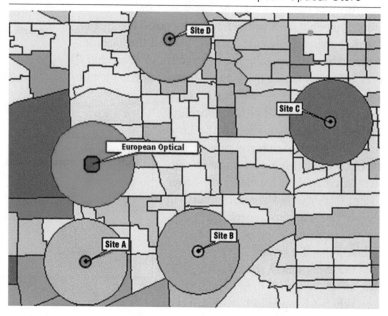

Estimating Potential Sales for a Store

Huff gravity model
A trade area analysis model used to determine the probability that a customer residing in a particular area will shop at a particular store or shopping centre.

Three approaches for using the information about the trade area to estimate the potential sales for a store at the location are (1) gravitational theory, (2) regression analysis, and (3) the analogue method.

Gravitational Theory

The Huff gravity model[10] for estimating the sales of a retail store is based on the concept of gravity: Consumers are attracted to a store location just like Newton's falling apple was attracted to the Earth. In this model, the force of the attraction is based on two factors: the size of the store (larger stores have more pulling power) and the time it takes to travel to the store (stores that take more time to get to have less pulling power). The mathematical formula to predict the probability of a customer going to a specific store location is as follows:

$$P_{ij} = \frac{S_j \div T_{ij}^b}{\sum_{j=1}^{n} S_j \div T_{ij}^b}$$

where

P_{ij} = probability that customer i shops at location j,

S_j = size of the store at location j, and

T_{ij} = travel time for customer i to get to location j.

λ = parameter used to estimate the effect of travel time on different kinds of shopping trips.

n = number of different shopping locations

The formula indicates that the larger the size (S_j) of the store compared with competing stores' sizes, the greater the probability that a customer will shop at the location. A larger size is generally more attractive in consumers" eyes because it means more merchandise assortment and variety. Travel time or distance (T_{ij}) has the opposite effect on the probability that a consumer will shop at the location. The greater the travel time or distance to the consumer, compared with that of competing locations, the lower the probability that the consumer will shop at the location. Generally, customers would rather shop at a close store rather than a distant one.

The exponent λ reflects the relative effect of travel time versus store size. When λ is equal to 1, store size and travel time have an equal but opposite effect on the probability of a consumer shopping at a store location. When λ is greater than 1, travel time has a greater effect, and when λ is less than 1, store size has a greater effect. The value of λ is affected by the nature of the shopping trips consumers generally take when visiting the specific type of store. For instance, travel time or distance is generally more important for convenience goods than for shopping goods because people are less willing to travel a great distance for a litre of milk than they are for a new pair of shoes. Thus, a larger value for λ is assigned if the store being studied specializes in convenience shopping trips rather than comparison shopping trips. The value of λ is usually estimated statistically using data that describe shopping patterns at existing stores.

To illustrate the use of the Huff model, consider the situations shown in Exhibit 5–9. A small town has two communities: Rock Creek and Oak Hammock. The town currently has one 5000 square-foot drugstore with annual sales of $8 million, $3 million of which come from Oak Hammock residents and $5 million from Rock Creek residents. A competitive chain is considering opening a 10 000 square-foot store. As the exhibit illustrates, the driving time for the average Rock Creek resident to the existing store is 10 minutes but would be only 5 minutes to the new store. In contrast, the driving time for the typical Oak Hammock resident to the existing drugstore is 5 minutes and would be 15 minutes to the new store. Based on its past experience, the drugstore chain has found that λ equals 2 for its store locations. Using the Huff formula, the probability of a Rock Creek resident shopping at the new location, PRC, is

$$P_{RC} = \frac{10\,000/5^2}{10\,000/5^2 + 5000/10^2} = .889$$

The probability of Oak Hammock residents shopping at the new location, P_{OH}, is

$$P_{OH} = \frac{10\,000/15^2}{10\,000/15^2 + 5000/5^2} = .182$$

exhibit 5–9 Application of Huff Gravity Models for Estimating Store Sales

Rock Creek
Market size = $5 million annual sales

Existing Store

Oak Hammock
Market size = $3 million annual sales

10 minutes

5 minutes

5 minutes

15 minutes

New Store

The expected sales (probability of patronage times market size) for the new location thus would be

.889 × $3 million + .182 × $5 million = $4 910 000

This simple application assumes that the market size for drugstores in the community will remain the same at $8 million with the addition of the new store. We also could have considered that two drugstores would increase the total size of the market. In addition, rather than do the calculations for the average customer located in the middle of each community, we could have calculated the probabilities that each customer in the two communities would go to the new location.

Even though the Huff gravity model considers only two factors affecting store sales—travel time and store size—its predictions are quite accurate because these two factors typically have the greatest effect on store choice.[11] The regression approach discussed in the next section provides a way to incorporate additional factors into the sales forecast for a store under consideration.

Reilly's law of retail gravitation[12] is the traditional means of trading area delineation. The trading area of two cities or communities can be determined by establishing a point of indifference between the two. This point is often referred to as point of indifference and is defined as the point up to which one city or community dominates and beyond which the other city or community is dominant. The mathematical formula to predict the probability of a customer[13] going to a specific store location is as follows:

$$BP = \frac{\text{distance between city a and b}}{1 + \sqrt{\dfrac{\text{pop. b}}{\text{pop. a}}}}$$

BP is distance from city a to breaking point.

BP = boundary between the two areas is called the breaking point

D = distance in kilometres along a major roadway between cities (communities) A and B

P_a = population of city (community) A

P_b = population of city (community)[a]

The following is an example showing how a catchment area boundary is drawn using Reilly's law.

A city (A) has a population of 250 000, and a city (B) has a population of 100 000. City A is 75 kilometres from city B. One would think that the point of indifference between the two cities would be halfway between the two cities (35 km). However, the point of indifference is 45.9 km away from city A and 29.1 km away from city B.

This method of analysis can provide an idea of the sphere of influence. Breaking points for other surrounding cities or communities can be calculated. This sphere of influence can be quantified by drawing a series of these breaking points from the other nearby cities (C and D) or communities to form a catchment area boundary.

Regression Analysis

The regression analysis approach is based on the assumption that factors that affect the sales of existing stores in a chain will have the same impact on stores located at new sites being considered. When using this approach, the retailer employs a technique called multiple regression to estimate a statistical model that predicts sales at existing store locations. The technique can consider the effects of the wide range of factors discussed in this chapter, including site characteristics, such as visibility and access, and characteristics of the trade area, such as demographics and lifestyle segments.

Consider the following example: A chain of sporting goods stores has analyzed the factors affecting sales in its existing stores and found that the following model is the best predictor of store sales (the weights for the factors, such as 275 for the number of households, are estimated using multiple regression):

Store sales = 275 × number of households in trade area (15-minute drive time)

+ 1 800 000 × percentage of households in trade area in children under 15 years of age

+ 2 000 000 × percentage of households in trade area in Tapestry segment "aspiring young"

+ 8 × shopping centre square feet

+ 250 000 if visible from the street

+ 300 000 if Walmart in centre

The sporting goods chain is considering the following two locations:

Variable	Location A	Location B
Households within 15-minute drive time	11 000	15 000
% of households with children under 15 years old	70%	20%
% of households in aspiring young geodemographic segment	60%	10%
Sq ft of shopping centre	200 000	250 000
Visible from street	yes	no
Walmart in shopping centre	yes	no

Reilly's law of retail gravitation A model used in trade area analysis to define the relative ability of two cities to attract customers from the area between them.

regression analysis A statistical approach based on the assumption that factors that affect the sales of existing stores in a chain will have the same impact on stores located at new sites.

Using the statistical model, the forecasted sales for location A are:

Store sales at location A
$$= \$7\,635\,000 + 275 \times 11\,000$$
$$+ 1\,800\,000 \times .7$$
$$+ 2\,000\,000 \times .6$$
$$+ 8 \times 200\,000$$
$$+ 250\,000$$
$$+ 300\,000$$

And forecasted sales for location B are:

Store sales at location B
$$= \$6\,685\,000 + 275 \times 15\,000$$
$$+ 1\,800\,000 \times .2$$
$$+ 2\,000\,000 \times .1$$
$$+ 8 \times 250\,000$$

Note that location A has greater forecasted sales, even though it has a smaller trading area population and shopping centre size, because the profile of its target market fits the profile of the trade area better.

Analogue Approach

As discussed, to develop a regression model, a retailer needs data about the trade area and site characteristics from a large number of stores. Because small chains cannot use the regression approach, they use the similar but more subjective analogue approach. When using the analogue approach, the retailer simply describes the site and trade area characteristics for its most successful stores and attempts to find a site with similar characteristics.

Suppose European Optical was deciding to open another location and had four potential sites as identified in Column 1 of Exhibit 5–10. Using the analogue approach, the retailer undertakes the following steps to estimate potential sales for a store site.

First, estimate the number of eyeglasses sold per person per year in Column 2. The area population is identified in Column 3 (this includes the number of your targeted customers living in the area); these numbers can be taken from Statistics Canada or *Financial Post Markets*. Next, estimate the trade area potential by multiplying Column 2 by Column 3. This will identify the total eyeglasses potential for the area in Column 4.

Column 5 is the rough estimates of the number of eyeglasses sold in the trade areas, based on visits to the competitive stores. Column 6 represents the unit sales potential for eyeglasses in the trade areas (Column 4 minus Column 5). The trade area potential penetration is calculated by dividing Column 6 by Column 4. For instance, because the total eyeglasses potential for the current Vancouver store trade area is 17 196 pairs and an additional 9646 pairs could be sold in that trade area, 56.09 percent of the eyeglasses market in the area remains untapped.

In general, the higher the trade area potential, the lower the relative competition will be. Column 8, the relative level of competition, is subjectively estimated on the basis of Column 7. According to the information in Exhibit 5–10, the best location for the new optical store would be Site B. The trade area potential is high and the competition is low.

Choosing the Best Method(s)   In any decision, the more information that's available, the better the outcome is likely to be. This is true for research in general and location analysis in particular. Therefore, if a combination of the techniques is applied and the same conclusion is reached, the retailer should have more confidence in the decision.

Some methods used for analyzing trade areas are better in certain situations, however. The analogue and gravitational approaches are best when the number of stores with obtainable data is small, usually fewer than 30. These approaches can also be used by small retailers. The regression approach, on the other hand, is best when there are multiple variables expected to explain sales, since it's hard to keep track of multiple predictor

exhibit 5–10   Competitive Analysis of Potential Locations

Trade Area (1)	Eyeglasses/ Year/ Person (2)	Trade Area Population (3)	Total Eyeglasses Potential (4)	Estimated Eyeglasses Sold (5)	Trade Area Potential Units (6)	Trade Area Potential Percentage (7)	Relative Level of Competition (8)
Vancouver	0.2	85 979	17 196	7 550	9 646	56.09%	Low
Site A	0.2	91 683	18 338	15 800	2 537	13.83	Medium
Site B	0.2	101 972	20 394	12 580	7 814	38.32	Low
Site C	0.2	60 200	12 040	11 300	740	6.15	High
Site D	0.2	81 390	16 278	13 300	2 978	18.29	Medium

variables when using a manual system such as the analogue approach. Also, the Huff gravity model and Reilly's law of retail gravitation explicitly consider the attractiveness of competition and customers' distance or travel time to the store or shopping centre in question. Finally, since Huff's gravity model and Reilly's law usually do not utilize demographic variables, it's particularly important to use them in conjunction with the analogue or regression methods.

There are three trends that will shape site selection research in the next few decades.[15] First, it will be easier to collect and store data on customers in data warehouses. Second, advanced statistical modelling techniques, such as CHAID (chi square automatic interaction detection) and spatial allocation models, will become more popular. Finally, geographic information systems will become more sophisticated and at the same time more accessible to users.

LO5 Types of Locations

Retailers have three basic types of locations to choose from: a shopping centre, a city or town location, or a freestanding location. Retailers can also locate in a nontraditional location such as an airport or within another store. The following sections describe each type of location and present criteria for choosing a particular location type.

Shopping Centres

From the 1950s through the 1980s, suburban shopping centres grew as populations shifted to the suburbs. Large shopping centres provide huge assortments for consumers. Combining many stores under one roof creates a synergy that attracts more customers than if the stores had separate locations. It's not uncommon, for instance, for a store's sales to increase after a competing store enters a shopping centre.

The term *shopping centre* has been evolving since the early 1950s. A shopping centre is a group of retail and other commercial establishments that is planned, developed, owned, and managed as a single property. The two main configurations of shopping centres are strip centres and enclosed malls. A strip centre is a shopping centre that usually has parking directly in front of the stores. A mall, on the other hand, is a shopping centre where customers park in outlying areas and walk to the stores. Traditional malls are enclosed, with a climate-controlled walkway between two facing strips of stores. The main shopping centre types are defined in Exhibit 5–11.

shopping centre
A group of retail and other commercial establishments that is planned, developed, owned, and managed as a single property.

strip centre A shopping centre that usually has parking directly in front of the stores and does not have enclosed walkways linking the stores.

mall A shopping centre with a pedestrian focus where customers park in outlying areas and walk to the stores.

exhibit 5–11 Shopping Centre Definitions

Type	Concept	Square Feet	Number of Anchors	Types of Anchors	Trade Area*
Strip Centres					
Traditional	General merchandise; convenience	30 000–350 000	One or more	Discount; supermarket; drug; home improvement; large specialty discount apparel	3–7 square miles
Power	Category-dominant anchors; few small tenants	250 000–600 000	Three or more	Category specialist; home improvement; discount; warehouse club; off-price	5–10 square miles
Shopping Malls					
Regional	General merchandise; fashion (typically enclosed)	400 000–800 000	Two or more	Department; discount; fashion apparel; other specialty stores	5–15 square miles
Superregional	Similar to regional but has more variety and assortment	800 000+	Three or more	Department; discount; fashion apparel; other specialty stores	5–25 square miles
Lifestyle	Higher-end, fashion-oriented	Variable	N/A	Higher-end specialty stores and restaurants	5–15 square miles
Fashion/specialty	Higher-end, fashion-oriented	80 000–250 000	N/A	Higher-end fashion and other specialty stores	5–15 square miles
Outlet	Manufacturers' outlet stores	50 000–400 000	N/A	Manufacturer's outlet stores	25–75 square miles
Theme/festival	Leisure; tourist-oriented	80 000–250 000	N/A	Restaurants; entertainment; fashion; other specialty stores	N/A

*The area from which 60 to 80 percent of the centre's sales originate.

The developer and shopping centre management carefully select a set of retailers that are complementary; this tenant mix is planned to attract a specific market segment to the shopping centre. The goal of a successful tenant mix is to provide customers with a one-stop shopping experience by providing a well-balanced assortment of product offerings including retailers, services, and entertainment.

The shopping centre management maintains the common facilities (referred to as common area maintenance [CAM]), such as the parking area, and is responsible for activities such as providing security, parking lot lighting, outdoor signage for the centre, and advertising and special events to attract consumers. The stores in the centre typically pay a negotiated annual fee based on their size to cover the CAM costs. The shopping centre management can also place restrictions on the operating hours, signage, and even the type of merchandise sold in the stores.

Most shopping centres have at least one or two major retailers, referred to as anchors. These retailers are courted by the centre developer because they attract a significant number of consumers and consequently make the centre more appealing to other retailers. To get these anchor retailers to locate in a centre, developers frequently make special deals, such as reduced lease costs, for the anchor tenants. For example, the median rental cost is less than $35 per square metre for anchors in an enclosed mall but $350 for nonanchor retailers.[17]

In strip centres, supermarkets are typically anchors, whereas department stores traditionally anchor shopping malls. However, a lifestyle centre may not have anchors, whereas power centres are composed primarily of multiple "anchor" stores. The different types of shopping centres are discussed next.

A traditional strip centre is a shopping centre that is designed to provide convenient shopping for the day-to-day needs of consumers in their immediate neighbourhood. Smaller strip centres are typically anchored by a supermarket or a drugstore; the larger strips are anchored by discount stores, off-price stores, or category killers selling such items as apparel, home improvement/furnishings, toys, shoes, pet supplies, electronics, and sporting goods. These anchors are supported by stores offering sundries, food, and a variety of personal services such as barber shops and dry cleaners.

Strip Shopping Centres The primary advantages of strip centres or community shopping centres are that they offer customers convenient locations and easy parking, and they entail relatively low rents for retailers. The primary disadvantages are that there is no protection from the weather, and they offer less assortment and entertainment options for customers than malls. As a result, strip centres do not attract as many customers as larger shopping centres that rely on community participation.

The strip centres of today have a mix of mom-and-pop stores and national tenants such as A Buck or Two and Shoppers Drug Mart. National chains like these are able to compete effectively in strip centres against their rival stores in malls. They can offer lower prices, partly because of the lower rents, plus their customers can drive right up to the door. New spinoff grocery franchises such as No Frills and Price Chopper are popular with value-conscious consumers and are often located in strip centres.

Power Centres A power centre is a shopping centre that is dominated by several big-box retailers, including discount stores (Walmart), off-price stores (Winners), warehouse clubs (Costco), or category specialists such as Home Depot, Staples Business Depot, Best Buy, and Toys "R" Us. Unlike traditional strip centres, power centres often include several freestanding (unconnected) anchors and only a minimum number of small specialty tenants. They are typically unenclosed in a strip centre configuration. Many power centres are located near an enclosed shopping mall and are becoming major competition for the shopping centres.

Power centres were virtually unknown before the 1990s, but they have steadily grown in number. Many are

The first shopping centre, a marketplace with retail stores, was the Agora at the foot of the Parthenon in Athens in 600 B.C. It was the centre of all commerce, politics, and entertainment in ancient Greece.

now larger than some regional malls and attract customers from a large trade area. Why have they become so popular? First and foremost, their tenants have experienced tremendous growth and prosperity. A power centre is a natural location for these large tenants. They don't want to pay the high rents of regional shopping malls, and they benefit from the synergy of being with other big-box stores. Also, shoppers are seeking value alternatives to the stores found in shopping malls.

Shopping Malls

Shopping malls have several advantages over alternative locations. First, because of the many different types of stores, the merchandise assortments available within those stores, and the opportunity to combine shopping with entertainment, shopping malls have become the Main Street for today's shoppers. Teenagers hang out and meet friends, older citizens in Nikes get their exercise by walking the malls, and families make trips to the mall a form of entertainment. To enhance the total shopping experience, many malls incorporate food and entertainment such as movies and amusement parks.

The second major advantage of locating in a shopping mall is that the tenant mix can be planned. Shopping mall owners control the number of different types of retailers so that customers can have a one-stop shopping experience with a well-balanced assortment of merchandise. For instance, it's important to have several women's clothing stores in a major mall to draw in customers. Mall managers also attempt to create a complementary tenant mix. They like to have all stores that appeal to certain target markets (such as all upscale specialty clothing stores) located together. Thus, customers know what types of merchandise they can expect to find in a particular mall or location within a mall. Managers also strive for a good mix between shopping and specialty goods stores. A strong core of shopping goods stores, such as shoe stores, brings people to the mall. Specialty stores, such as computer software stores, also bring shoppers to the mall. While specialty store customers are in the mall, they'll likely be attracted to other stores.

The third advantage of shopping malls is that the retailers and their customers don't have to worry about their external environment. The mall's management takes care of maintenance of common areas. Mall tenants can look forward to a strong level of homogeneity with the other stores. For instance, most major malls enforce uniform hours of operation. Most malls control the external signage used for window displays and sales. Since most shopping malls are enclosed, customers are protected from the Canadian weather.

Although shopping centres are an excellent site option for many retailers, they have some disadvantages. Mall rents are higher than those of some strip centres, freestanding sites, and most central business districts. As a result, retailers that require large stores, such as home improvement centres, typically seek other options. Some tenants may not like mall managers' control of their operations. Mall managers can, for instance, dictate store hours and have strict rules regarding window displays and signage. Finally, competition within shopping centres can be intense. It may be hard for small specialty stores to compete directly with large department stores.

In addition, shopping malls are facing several challenges. First, shopping malls appeal to consumers who have the time to enjoy wandering through stores, punctuated by a leisurely lunch or an afternoon movie. The increasing number of two-income families and families with a single household head is creating more time pressures for consumers, limiting the time they can devote to shopping. Freestanding locations, strip centres, and power centres are more convenient because customers can park in front of a store, go in and buy what they want, and go about their other errands. There is increasing competition from other types of retail location alternatives, such as power and lifestyle centres, catalogues, and the Internet. Many of today's shoppers are looking for value alternatives to stores found in shopping malls. Also, the apparel business, which makes up a large percentage of mall tenants (Exhibit 5–12), has continued to be weak,

exhibit 5–12 Canada's Ten Largest Malls (by ownership of apparel specialty chains, February 1, 2013)

Mall	Apparel Specialty Chains	% Domestic Ownership	% Foreign Ownership
West Edmonton Mall, AB	73	44%	56%
Metropolis, BC	56	61%	39%
Square One, ON	72	56%	44%
Eaton Centre, ON	63	37%	63%
Yorkdale, ON	57	37%	63%
Galeries de la Capitale, QC	61	84%	16%
Bramalea City Centre, ON	60	58%	42%
Pacific Centre, BC	20	30%	70%
Chinook Centre, AB	78	53%	47%
Carrefour Level, QC	87	71%	29%

According to Trendex research, foreign retailers account for 41 percent of the apparel specialty chains in Canada's ten largest malls.

Source: *Canadian Retailer*, "Canada's Ten Largest Malls," Spring 2013, Volume 23, Issue 2, p. 8.

DID YOU KNOW?

Known around the world for its unrivalled combination of shopping, dining, and entertainment, West Edmonton Mall stands 5.3 million square feet and spans the equivalent of 48 city blocks, generating 28.4 million annual visits.[19]

causing some specialty store chains to close. Finally, many malls are getting old and are in need of major renovation to appeal to consumers.

What are they doing about their problems? Some mall owners are turning their centres into traditional town squares with lots of entertainment opportunities.[18] They believe if they can encourage people to spend more time in the mall, they will spend more money there. The owners are renting to nontraditional mall tenants such as dry cleaners, doctors' offices, and even chapels—everything that you would have found in a town square in the 1950s. Others are forging links to their communities by opening wellness centres, libraries, city halls, and children's play areas. In this environment, people can ride the midway, go to a movie, visit the petting zoo, or eat at a theme restaurant.

A more extreme approach to revitalizing a mall is known as demalling.[20] Demalling usually involves demolishing a mall's small shops, scrapping its common space and food courts, enlarging the sites once occupied by department stores, and adding more entrances to the parking lot.

Regional Centres A regional centre is a shopping mall that provides general merchandise (a large

According to the Guinness Book of World Records, *the world's largest shopping, amusement, and recreation centre is the West Edmonton Mall in Alberta, with 5.3 million square feet of covered space.*

percentage of which is apparel) and services in full depth and variety. Its main attractions are its anchors, department and discount stores, or fashion specialty stores. A typical regional centre is usually enclosed with an inward orientation of the stores connected by a common walkway, with parking surrounding the outside perimeter.

Superregional Centres A superregional centre is a shopping centre that is similar to a regional centre, but because of its larger size, it has more anchors and a deeper selection of merchandise, and it draws from a larger population base. As with regional centres, the typical configuration is an enclosed mall, frequently with multilevels.

According to the *Guinness Book of Records*, the world's largest shopping, amusement, and recreation centre is the West Edmonton Mall in Alberta. It has 5.3 million square feet of covered space, 3.8 million square feet of selling space, more than 800 stores and services, and 110 restaurants. But the mall has more than shopping to attract millions of people a year. It also sports the Galaxyland Amusement park, a 7.5-acre waterpark, an NHL-size ice arena, submarines, an exact replica of the *Santa Maria* ship, a lagoon, Fantasyland Hotel, a miniature golf course, 26 movie theatres and IMAX, and a casino. Don't worry about parking. It also has the largest parking capacity in the world, enough for 20 000 vehicles.

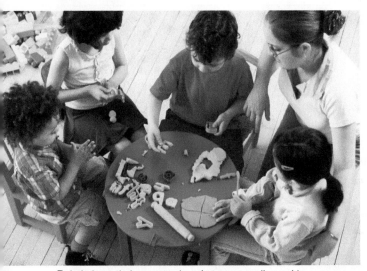

To help keep their parents shopping, some malls provide entertainment for their kids.

Located on just under 200 acres north of Toronto, Vaughan Mills features 14 anchor tenants and more than 200 specialty stores, theme restaurants, cinemas, and recreation activities in a 1.1 million square-foot complex. Many of the tenants were the first of their kind in Canada, including Bass Pro Shops Outdoor World, NASCAR SpeedPark, Lucky Strike Lanes, and Hudson's Bay Company's Designer Depot. The centre also features the world's largest Tommy Hilfiger Outlet and the only Holt Renfrew Last Call in Canada. Located at the southeast corner of Highway 400 and Rutherford Road in Vaughan, Ontario, the mall is located in an area that is home to 60 percent of Ontario's population (and almost 25 percent of Canada's population), and there are 10 million people within 160 kilometres of the mall (including Buffalo and Niagara Falls, New York). Vaughan Mills is a joint venture between Ivanhoe Cambridge, Canada, and Mills Corp of the U.S., and opened in the fall of 2004. It was the first enclosed regional shopping centre build in Canada in more than 16 years.

The design of the mall is innovative and fresh and is based on the design concept "Discover Ontario." The mall is divided into six neighbourhoods based on the themes of lakes, nature, rural living, small towns, city, and fashion. It is estimated that Vaughan Mills and its retailers employ more than 3500 workers on a full- or part-time basis and add approximately $12.5 million in taxes to the local economy annually.[21]

Lifestyle Centres A lifestyle centre is an outdoor traditional streetscape layout with sit-down restaurants and a conglomeration of retailers such as Williams-Sonoma, Pottery Barn, and Eddie Bauer.

The centres offer shoppers convenience, safety, an optimum tenant mix, and a pleasant atmosphere. Like "Main Street" locations, shoppers go because it's an attractive, energetic place to meet their friends and have fun. Some lifestyle centres consist only of stores and restaurants; some have cinemas and entertainment; and still others mingle retail with homes and offices. Nearly all are located in high-income areas. They have gone into posh neighbourhoods where they depend on a market radius far smaller, but a lot richer, than malls.

Many of the projects are designed to look as though they've been there for decades. As a result, they are expensive to build. Park Place is a 1.5 million square-foot lifestyle centre planned for Barrie, Ontario, that will combine office space, retail outlets, entertainment centres, restaurants, and bars, plus four hotels and a hockey rink. High-end retailers are slated to be placed alongside big-box discount stores, and green space will allow customers to walk between stores on the outside of the centre. Park Place is designed to bring back the fun of shopping.[22]

lifestyle centre A shopping centre with an outdoor, traditional streetscape layout with sit-down restaurants and a conglomeration of specialty retailers.

DID YOU KNOW?

The average income of lifestyle centre customers is about double that of mall shoppers: They visit 2.5 times more often and spend 50 percent more per visit.[23]

Vaughan Mills is where fashion and outlets, plus dining and entertainment, equal something consumers have to experience to believe.

Fashion/Specialty Centres

A fashion/specialty centre is a shopping centre that is composed mainly of upscale apparel shops, boutiques, and gift shops carrying selected fashions or unique merchandise of high quality and price. These centres need not be anchored, although sometimes gourmet restaurants and theatres can function as anchors. The physical design of these centres is very sophisticated, emphasizing a rich decor and high-quality landscaping.

Fashion/specialty centres are similar to lifestyle centres in terms of the clientele and the types of stores they attract. The difference is that these centres are typically enclosed and are larger than most lifestyle centres.

Fashion/specialty centres usually are found in trade areas having high income levels, in tourist areas, or in some central business districts. These centres' trade areas may be large because of the specialty nature of the tenants and their products. Customers are more likely to travel great distances to shop for specialty products sold at nationally known shops such as Holt Renfrew and Ralph Lauren/Polo than for other types of goods.

Outlet Centres

Outlet centres are shopping centres that consist mostly of manufacturers' outlet stores selling their own brands, supposedly at a discount.[24] These centres also sometimes include off-price retailers such as Winners or HomeSense. As a result of the shifting tenant mix in some of these centres, various industry experts now refer to outlet centres as *value centres* or *value megamalls*. Similar to power centres, a strip configuration is most common, although some are enclosed malls, such as Dixie Outlet Mall in Mississauga, Ontario.

Outlet centre tenants view this location option as an opportunity to get rid of excess or distressed merchandise, sell more merchandise, and, to a lesser extent, test new merchandise ideas.

Consumer demand for stores in outlet centres is declining. Although customers can shop for an extensive assortment within individual brands and buy below full retail prices every day, they have to deal with broken assortments, distressed or damaged goods, and less convenient locations. Additionally, traditional retailing has become more price-competitive.

Outlet centres have progressed from no-frills warehouses to well-designed buildings with landscaping and food options that make them hard to distinguish from more traditional shopping centres. The newest outlet centres have a strong entertainment component, including movie theatres and theme restaurants, comprising about 15 to 20 percent of the leasable area.[25] Mall developers believe that these entertainment concepts help keep people on the premises longer. Outlet centre tenants have also upgraded their offerings by adding credit, dressing rooms, high-quality fixtures and lighting, and a merchandise return policy.

Outlet centres are often located some distance from regional shopping centres so that outlet tenants don't compete directly for department and specialty store customers, although most manufacturer outlets have learned to peacefully coexist with their department and specialty store customers by editing assortments in their outlet stores to minimize overlap. Outlet centres can be located in strong tourist areas. For instance, since shopping is a favourite vacation pastime, and Niagara Falls attracts 15 million tourists per year, the 1.2 million square-foot Factory Outlet megamall in Niagara Falls, New York, is a natural location for an outlet centre. Some centre developers actually organize bus tours to bring people hundreds of kilometres to their malls. As a result, the primary trade area for some outlet centres is 100 kilometres or more.

In August 2013, Premium Outlets, the first of its kind in Canada, opened a 500 000 square-foot mall in Halton Hills west of Toronto. The project is a 50/50 venture of Simon Property Group Inc. and one of the world's largest real estate companies, Ontario-based Calloway Real Estate. When complete, the outlet centre will house more than 100 high-quality outlet stores and is expected to be the Canadian entry point for selected U.S. retailers and designer brands.[26]

Freestanding Sites

Although most retailers locate in strip centres or planned shopping malls, a frequent option for large retailers is a freestanding site. A freestanding site is a retail location that's not connected to other retailers, although many are located adjacent to malls. Retailers with large space requirements, such as warehouse clubs and hypermarkets, are often freestanding. Category specialists such as Toys "R" Us also utilize freestanding sites. Advantages of freestanding locations are greater visibility, lower rents, ample parking, no direct competition, greater convenience for customers, fewer restrictions on signs, hours, or merchandise (which might be imposed in a shopping centre), and ease of expansion. The most serious disadvantage is the lack of synergy with other stores. A retailer in a freestanding location must be a primary destination point for customers. It must offer customers something special in merchandise, price, promotion, or services to get them into the store.

Many retailers report that freestanding stores perform better than stores in malls. Shoppers Drug Mart shifted to freestanding locations because it wanted more space for the front-end merchandise.

Other Retail Location Opportunities

Merchandise kiosks, mixed-use developments, airports, resorts, hospitals, and stores within a store are interesting, if not unusual, location alternatives for many retailers.

Merchandise Kiosks   Although not a type of shopping mall, merchandise kiosks are found in shopping malls of all types and are a popular location alternative for retailers with small space needs. A merchandise kiosk is a small selling space offering a limited merchandise assortment. These selling spaces are typically between 40 and 500 square feet and can be in prime mall locations. Surprisingly, kiosks may be small in size but the rental costs are not—kiosks, because of their central locations can cost more than a traditional storefront location. It is important to note that rental costs for kiosks vary depending on the province, the mall's location, and customer traffic. They usually have short-term leases, shielding tenants from the liability of having to pay long-term rent in case the business fails. Some merchandise kiosks operate seasonally, for instance, selling polar fleece in winter and baseball hats in summer. Of course, vendors also can be evicted on short notice. These alternatives to regular stores are often a great way for small retailers to begin or expand. Kiosks have been the venue of choice for Vivah Jewellery, a retail concept that focuses specifically on fashion jewellery.

Mall operators see these alternative selling spaces as an opportunity to generate rental income in otherwise vacant space. Some of the nation's biggest mall developers are installing merchandise kiosks in every available space. These kiosks sell everything from concert tickets to gift certificates. They also can generate excitement, leading to additional sales for the entire mall. Mall operators must be sensitive to their regular mall tenants' needs, however. These kiosks can block a store, be incompatible with its image, or actually compete with similar merchandise.

Mixed-Use Developments   A mixed-use development (MXD) combines several different uses in one complex, including shopping centres, office towers, hotels, residential complexes, civic centres, and convention centres. MXDs are popular with retailers because they bring additional shoppers to their stores. Developers like MXDs because they use space productively. For instance, land costs the same whether a developer builds a shopping mall by itself or builds an office tower over the mall or parking structure.

Airports   One important high-pedestrian-traffic area that has become popular with national retail chains is airports. After all, what better way to spend waiting time than to have a Second Cup coffee or stop into Victoria's Secret? Sales per square metre at airport malls are often three to four times as high as at regular mall stores.[27] However, rents are at least 20 percent higher than at malls. Also, costs can be higher—hours are longer, and since the location is often inconvenient for workers, the businesses have to pay higher wages. The best airport locations tend to be ones where there are many layovers and international flights. The best-selling products are those that make good gifts, necessities, and easy-to-pack items such as books and magazines.

Resorts   Who needs anchor stores to bring in customers when there are mountains or a beach to attract people? Retailers view resorts as prime location opportunities for

kiosk A small selling space offering a limited merchandise assortment.

mixed-use development (MXD) Development that combines several uses in one complex—for example, shopping centre, office tower, hotel, residential complex, civic centre, and convention centre.

Merchandise kiosks are found in shopping malls of all types and are a popular location alternative for retailers with small space needs.

A smaller-format Fox Sports Sky Box sportsbar and restaurant was created for several airports and features a video control centre that resembles Fox's NFL anchor desk.

Pop-Up Stores and Other Temporary Locations

Retailers and manufacturers sometimes open pop-up stores, which are stores in temporary locations that focus on new products or a limited group of products. A few years ago, pop-up stores were a major investment for retailers because of high start-up costs amortized over a very short lease and relatively high lease costs. Now with retail space more plentiful and less expensive, these stores have become more popular. Retailers and manufacturers are using these spaces to create buzz, test new concepts, or even evaluate a new neighbourhood or city. Target used a pop-up store in Toronto to create buzz and hype about its entry into the Canadian marketplace.

Other retailers, often one-person operations, open temporary stores to take advantage of the holiday season in December or to get visibility and additional sales at festivals or concerts. Local retailers, who pay high rents, aren't necessarily so enthusiastic, because some of the temporary retailers use the same suppliers.

City or Town Locations

Although shopping centres are also located in cities or towns, the locations that are discussed in this section are typically unplanned, have multiple owners, and have access from the street. In particular, we will examine central business districts, downtown locations (or "Main Streets"), and the redevelopment efforts being undertaken in these locations.

Central Business Districts

The central business district (CBD) is the traditional downtown business area in a city or town. Due to its business activity, it draws many people into the area during business hours. Also, people must go to the area for work. The CBD is also the hub for public transportation, and there is a high level of pedestrian traffic. Finally, the most successful CBDs for retail trade are those with a large number of residents living in the area.

But many central business district locations in Canada have been declining in popularity with retailers and their customers for years. Retailers can be concerned about CBDs because high security may be required and parking is often limited. Urban decay and no control over the weather can discourage shoppers. Shopping in the evening and on weekends can be particularly slow in many CBDs. Also, unlike modern shopping centres, CBDs tend to suffer from a lack of planning. One block may contain upscale boutiques, and the next may be populated with low-income housing, so consumers may not have enough interesting retailers that they can visit on a shopping trip.

pop-up stores Stores in temporary locations that focus on new products or a limited group of products.

central business district (CBD) The traditional downtown business area of a city or town.

golf courses, entertainment spas, and complementary retailers. There is a captive audience of well-to-do customers with lots of time on their hands. As noted earlier, outlet malls are popular in tourist areas. Resort retailing also attracts small, unique local retailers, premium national brands such as Tim Hortons or Roots, and can support dozens of art galleries and fashion retailers. Popular resort areas such as Whistler or Big White (near Kelowna) in British Columbia have developed town centres that attract tourists worldwide.

Hospitals Hospitals are an increasingly popular location alternative. Both patients and their guests often have time to shop. Necessities are important for patients since they can't readily leave. Gift-giving opportunities abound. Chapters has opened retail locations in large hospitals.

Store within a Store Another nontraditional location for retailers is within other, larger stores. Retailers, particularly department stores, have traditionally leased space to other retailers such as sellers of cosmetics and fine jewellery or furs. Grocery stores have been experimenting with the store-within-a-store concept for years with service providers such as banks, photo processors, and video outlets. Chapters has Starbucks Coffee outlets in many of its stores. A variation on the store-within-a-store concept is the kiosk within a store that OfficeMax is partnering with Hewlett-Packard, through which customers can configure computers to order.

Downtown Locations

A downtown location is the CBD located in the traditional shopping area of smaller towns, or a secondary business district in a suburb or within a larger city. Downtown locations share most of the characteristics of the primary CBD. But their occupancy costs are generally lower than that of the primary CBD. They do not draw as many people as the primary CBD because fewer people work in the area, and fewer stores generally mean a smaller overall selection. Finally, downtown locations typically don't offer the entertainment and recreational activities available in the more successful primary CBDs.

Redevelopment Efforts in City and Town Locations

Some city and town locations have become very attractive location alternatives to shopping centres. Why is this happening?

- Some of these locations have undergone a process of gentrification, which is the renewal and rebuilding of offices, housing, and retailers in deteriorating areas, coupled with the influx of more affluent people that often displaces earlier, usually poorer residents. Retailers are simply locating where their customers are.

- Developers aren't building as many malls as before, and it's often hard to find a good location in a successful mall.

- These same chains are finding that occupancy costs in city and town locations compare favourably to malls.

- City and town locations often offer retailers incredible expansion opportunities because of a stable and mature customer base and relatively low competition.

- Cities often provide significant incentives to locate in urban centres. Not only do these retailers bring needed goods and services to the area, but they also bring jobs. If, for instance, a major retailer hires 500 people, there would be more than 100 additional new jobs created to satisfy the retailing needs of that retailer's employees.

- Young professionals and retired empty-nesters are moving to urban centres to enjoy the convenience of shopping, restaurants, and entertainment.

Successful national chain stores such as Staples Business Depot, Mountain Equipment Co-op, and Tim Hortons need these locations to fuel their expansion. Even big-box stores such as Home Depot and Walmart are opening up city and town locations. Walmart solved the space problem associated with urban locations by opening a three-level store in Los Angeles.[28]

Location and Retail Strategy

The selection of a location type must reinforce the retailer's strategy. Thus, the location type decision needs to be consistent with the shopping behaviour and size of its target market and the retailer's positioning in its target market. Each of these factors is discussed next.

Shopping Behaviour of Consumers in Retailer's Target Market

A critical factor affecting the location consumers select to visit is the shopping situation in which they are involved. Three types of shopping situations are convenience shopping, comparison shopping, and specialty shopping.

Convenience Shopping When consumers are engaged in convenience shopping situations, they are primarily concerned with minimizing their effort to get the product or service they want. They are indifferent about which brands to buy or the retailer's image and are somewhat insensitive to price. Thus, they don't spend much time evaluating different brands or retailers; they simply want to make the purchase as quickly and as easily as possible. Examples of convenience shopping situations are getting a cup of coffee during a work break or buying milk for breakfast in the morning.

Retailers targeting customers involved in convenience shopping, such as convenience stores, usually locate their stores close to where their customers are and make it easy for them to park, find what they want, and go about their other business. Thus, convenience stores should and generally do locate in neighbourhood strip centres, freestanding spots, and city and town locations. Drugstores and fast-food restaurants also cater to convenience shoppers and thus select locations with easy access, parking, and locations that enable them to offer the additional convenience of a drive-through window. Convenience also plays an important role for supermarkets and full-line discount stores. Generally, shoppers

downtown location The central business district located in the traditional shopping area of smaller towns, or a secondary business district in a suburb or within a larger city, generally featuring lower occupancy costs, fewer people, fewer stores, smaller overall selection of goods or services, and fewer entertainment and recreational activities than more successful primary central business districts.

gentrification A process in which old buildings are torn down or are restored to create new offices, housing developments, and retailers.

DID YOU KNOW?

Baby boomers and echo boomers are moving to downtown areas to have easy access to everything and to save on transportation costs.[29]

destination stores
Retail stores in which the merchandise, selection, presentation, pricing, or other unique feature acts as a magnet for customers.

at these stores are not particularly brand or store loyal and do not find shopping in these stores enjoyable. Thus, these stores typically are also located in neighbourhood strip centres and freestanding locations.

Comparison Shopping Consumers involved in comparison shopping situations have a general idea about the type of product or service they want, but do not have a strong preference for a brand, model, or specific retailer to patronize. Similar to many convenience shopping situations, consumers are not particularly brand or store loyal. However, the purchase decisions are more important to them, so they seek information and are willing to expend considerable effort planning and making their purchase decisions. Consumers typically engage in this type of shopping behaviour when buying furniture, appliances, apparel, consumer electronics, hand tools, and cameras.

Furniture retailers, for instance, often locate next to each other to create a "furniture row." In Toronto, a number of retailers selling furniture are all located on Dundas Street West. These competing retailers locate near one another because doing so facilitates comparison shopping and thus attracts customers to the locations to compare different types of furniture and prices. The advantage of attracting a large number of shoppers to this area of Dundas Street outweighs the disadvantage of sharing these customers with other retailers.

Enclosed malls offer the same benefits to consumers interested in comparison shopping for fashionable apparel. For example, a customer who is looking for a business suit for job interviews could easily compare the suits offered at Hudson's Bay and Club Monaco with the suits at Sears by simply walking to these other stores located in the same mall. Thus, department stores and specialty apparel retailers locate in enclosed malls for the same reason that houseplant retailers locate together on 6th Avenue in New York City. By co-locating in the same mall, they attract more potential customers interested in comparison shopping for fashionable apparel. Even though the enclosed mall might be inconvenient compared with a freestanding location, comparison shopping is easier after the customers have arrived.

Category specialists offer the same benefit of comparison shopping as a collection of co-located specialty stores such as those described previously. Rather than going to a set of specialty stores when comparison shopping for consumer electronics, consumers know they can see almost all of the brands and models they would want to buy in either Best Buy or Future Shop. Thus, category specialists are **destination stores**, places where

As a destination store, Best Buy offers many brands of merchandise to give consumers the opportunity to comparison shop for consumer electronics.

consumers will go even if it is inconvenient, just as enclosed malls are destination locations for fashionable apparel comparison shopping. Category specialists locate in power centres primarily to reduce their costs and create awareness of their location and secondarily to benefit from the multiple retailers attracting more consumers and the potential for cross-shopping. Basically, power centres are a collection of destination stores.

Specialty Shopping When consumers are going specialty shopping, they know what they want and will not accept a substitute. They are brand and/or retailer loyal and will pay a premium or spend extra effort, if necessary, to get exactly what they want. Examples of these shopping occasions include buying an expensive designer-brand perfume, adopting a dog from the animal shelter, or buying a dress made by a specific designer. The retailer they patronize when specialty shopping also becomes a destination store. Thus, consumers are willing to travel to an inconvenient location to patronize a unique gourmet restaurant or a health food store that specializes in organic vegetables. Having a convenient location is not as important for retailers selling unique merchandise or services. Hudson's Bay's relaunch of the iconic in-store boutique The Room at its Toronto flagship store, in October 2009, hoped to woo back its specialty shoppers. The Room, formerly called the St. Regis Room, used to be the shopping destination for the who's who of Toronto society.[30]

Density of Target Market

A second, but closely related factor that affects the choice of location type is the density of the retailer's target market in relation to the location. A good location has many people in the target market that are drawn to it. So, a convenience store located in a CBD (central business district) can be sustained by customers living or working in fairly close proximity to the store. Similarly, a comparison shopping store located next to Hudson's Bay is a potentially good location because Hudson's Bay draws lots of customers from a very large area. It is not as important to have high customer density near a store that sells specialty merchandise because people are willing to search out this type of merchandise. A Porsche dealer, for instance, need not be near other car dealers or in close proximity to its target market because those seeking this luxury car will drive to wherever the dealer may be.

Uniqueness of Retail Offering

Finally, the convenience of their locations is less important for retailers with unique, differentiated offerings than for retailers with an offering similar to other retailers. For example, Bass Pro Shops provides a unique merchandise assortment and store atmosphere. Customers will travel to wherever the store is located, and its location will become a destination.

Each Bass Pro Shops store is unique and offers a truly unforgettable shopping experience—as close to the Great Outdoors as you can get indoors!

SUMMARY

Location decisions are probably the most important decisions that a retailer will make. Compensation for a poor location may mean lowering prices and spending extra money on advertising to draw customers to the store. Remember that the most important factors in store location are the traffic flow and the demographics of people living in the area. If either attribute is inappropriate for the store location, then the site should be avoided.

Decisions about where to locate a store are critical to any retailer's success. A clear, coherent strategy should specify location goals. A location decision is particularly important because of its high cost and long-term commitment. A location mistake is clearly more devastating to a retailer than a buying mistake, for instance.

Retailers have a plethora of types of sites from which to choose. Many central business districts and downtown locations have become a more viable option than in the past due to gentrification of the areas and lack of suburban mall opportunities. Retailers also have many types of shopping centres from which to choose. They can locate in a strip or power centre, or they can go into a mall. We examined the relative advantages of several types of malls, including regional and superregional centres, lifestyle, fashion/specialty centres, and outlet centres. We also examined the viability of kiosks, freestanding sites, mixed-use developments, and other nontraditional locations.

Retailers have a hard time finding a perfect site. Each site has its own set of advantages and disadvantages. In assessing the viability of a particular site, a retailer must make sure the store's target markets will patronize that location. The location analyst's job isn't finished until terms of occupancy and other legal issues are considered.

Retailers consider several issues when assessing the attractiveness of a particular region, market, or trade area. They want to know about the people living in the area. What are their lifestyles? How wealthy and large are the households? Is the area growing or declining? Does it have a favourable business climate? Importantly, what is the level of competition?

Retailers should only locate in areas with heavy competition if they believe their retailing format is superior to that of their competitors. A safer strategy is to locate in an area with little competition. Of course, in today's overbuilt retail environment, such areas are nearly impossible to find. Does a retailer have the ability to manage multiple stores in an area or in multiple areas? What is the most profitable number of stores to operate in a particular area?

In assessing the viability of a particular site, a retailer must consider the location's accessibility as well as locational advantages within the centre.

Trade areas are typically divided into primary, secondary, and tertiary zones. The boundaries of a trade area are determined by how accessible it is to customers, the natural and physical barriers that exist in the area, the type of shopping area in which the store is located, the type of store, and the level of competition.

Retailers have three types of information at their disposal to help them define a trade area. First, they use a customer spotting technique to determine how many people are in their trade area and where they live. Second, they use demographic data and GIS firms and Statistics Canada. Finally, to assess their competition they use the Internet, other sources of secondary information, and a good old-fashioned walk through the neighbourhood.

Once retailers have the data that describes their trade areas, they use several analytical techniques to estimate demand. The analogue approach—one of the easiest to use—can be particularly useful for smaller retailers. Using this method, the retailer makes predictions about the sales of a new store based on sales in stores in similar areas. Regression analysis uses the same logic as the analogue approach but is statistically based and requires more objective data. Finally, we showed how the Huff gravity model and Reilly's law of retail gravitation are used to predict the probability that a customer will frequent a particular store in a trade area. It is based on the premise that customers are more likely to shop at a given store or shopping centre if it's conveniently located and offers a large selection.

KEY TERMS

amount and quality of parking facilities
analogue approach
anchors
artificial barriers
central business district (CBD)
congestion
cumulative attraction
demalling
destination stores
downtown location
fashion/specialty centre
franchisees
franchisors
freestanding site
gentrification
geographic information systems (GIS)

Huff gravity model
ingress/egress
kiosk
lifestyle centre
mall
mixed-use development (MXD)
natural barriers
outlet centres
overstored trade area
polygons
pop-up stores
power centre
primary zone
region
regional centre
regression analysis

Reilly's law of retail gravitation
road condition
road pattern
saturated trade area
secondary zone
shopping centre
strip centre
superregional centre
symbiotic store
tertiary zone
trade area
traditional strip centre
understored trade area
visibility

1. **INTERNET EXERCISE** The largest mall in the world is the West Edmonton Mall in Alberta. Go to **wem.ca**. Do you think the attractions overshadow the shopping?

2. **GO SHOPPING** Go to your favourite shopping centre and analyze the tenant mix. Do the tenants appear to complement each other? What changes would you make in the tenant mix to increase the overall health of the centre?

3. **INTERNET EXERCISE** Go to **www.esri.com/what-is-gis** (the site for Esri Geographical Information Systems) and click on Overview. After reading the overview, explain how retailers can make better decisions with GIS.

4. **INTERNET EXERCISE** Do a competitive trade area analysis for a store of your choice by going to competitors' corporate websites and determining the probability that they will be entering a particular trade area.

5. **GO SHOPPING** Go to two stores owned by the same chain. Define and evaluate their trade area. Which store do you think is more successful?

6. **GO SHOPPING** Go to a shopping mall. Get or draw a map of the stores. Analyze whether the stores are clustered appropriately. For instance, are all the high-end stores together? Is there a good mix of shopping goods stores adjacent to each other?

DISCUSSION QUESTIONS AND PROBLEMS

1. Why have location decisions become more important in recent years?

2. Pick your favourite store. Explain why you believe it is (or isn't) in the best location, given its target market.

3. Read the profile of the Cloverdale Mall. What are the strengths and weaknesses of its location strategy?

4. As a consultant to 7-Eleven convenience stores, American Eagle Outfitters, and BMW car dealerships, what would you say is the single most important factor in choosing a site for these three very different types of stores?

5. Retailers have a tradition of developing shopping centres and freestanding locations in neighbourhoods or central business districts that have suffered decay. Some people have questioned the ethical and social ramifications of this process, which is known as gentrification. What are the benefits and problems associated with gentrification?

6. Staples Business Depot has a strong multichannel strategy. How does the Internet affect its strategies for locating stores?

7. In many malls, fast-food retailers are located together in an area known as a food court. What are this arrangement's advantages and disadvantages to the fast-food retailer?

8. Why would a Payless ShoeSource store locate in a neighbourhood shopping centre instead of a regional shopping mall?

9. Why would a company such as Coach, a manufacturer of high-quality leather goods, open outlet stores? What are the disadvantages to such a strategy?

10. What are the shape and size of the trade area zones of a shopping centre near your school?

11. When measuring trade areas, why is the analogue approach not a good choice for a retailer with several hundred outlets?

12. True Value Hardware plans to open a new store. Two sites are available, both in middle-income neighbourhood centres. One neighbourhood is 20 years old and has been well maintained. The other was recently built in a newly planned community. Which site is preferable for True Value? Why?

13. Trade areas are often described as concentric circles emanating from the store or shopping centre. Why is this practice used? Suggest an alternative method. Which would you use if you owned a store in need of a trade area analysis?

14. Under what circumstances would a retailer use the analogue approach for estimating demand for a new store? What about regression?

15. Some specialty stores prefer to locate next to or close to an anchor store. But Little Caesars, a takeout pizza retailer typically found in strip centres, wants to be at the end of the centre away from the supermarket anchor. Why?

16. Retailers have a choice of locating on a mall's main floor or second or third level. Typically, the main floor offers the best, but most expensive, locations. Why would specialty stores such as RadioShack and Foot Locker choose the second or third floor?

17. A drugstore is considering opening a new location at shopping centre A, with hopes of capturing sales from a new neighbourhood under construction. Two nearby shopping centres, C and E, will provide competition. Using the following information and Huff's gravity model, determine the probability that residents of the new neighbourhood will shop at shopping centre A:

Shopping Centre	Size (sq. ft.)	Distance from New Neighbourhood (kilometres)
A	3 500 000	4
C	1 500 000	5
E	300 000	3

Assume that $b = 2$

18. Identify the location strategies for each of the following types of retailers:
   - Department stores
   - Specialty apparel stores
   - Category killers/specialists
   - Grocery stores

store design, layout, and visual merchandising strategy

Lo1 Discuss the potential objectives retailers consider when designing or redesigning a store.

Lo2 Understand the power of the retail environment to influence customers and that retailers need to balance store design elements and generate traffic through feature areas.

Lo3 Examine the factors that retailers consider when deciding how much floor or shelf space to allocate to merchandise categories and brands.

Lo4 Review how stores can increase customer appeal and sales through various merchandise presentation techniques.

Lo5 Describe the atmospheric elements that enhance store environment and strengthen store brand or image.

Lo6 Explore the good design principles that can apply to both physical store and web/mobile sites and the importance of reflecting the retailer's target market.

SPOTLIGHT ON RETAILING

Canadian Tire: Rethinking Product Presentation

Canadian Tire, the winner of Excellence in Retailing In-Store Merchandising Award 2012, was facing ongoing competition from mass retailers and car dealerships when it came to its mainstay product—tires. So last fall, the company decided it was time to better showcase its vast selection of car-related products and knowledgeable in-house staff.

"We wanted to make sure we delivered a best-in-class experience and asserted our position as an authority on all things automotive," says Micheline Davies, vice-president of store design and customer experience. The team looked at how to make an impactful tire department that was simple enough for customers to use yet sophisticated enough to fulfill all of their automotive needs.

Enhanced and renewed customer service. Using its own design team, the company created an Automotive Renewal Concept, complete with a portal into the department that incorporated high-gloss red colours and finishes to mimic the feeling of a sports car. The whole tire-shopping process was simplified by implementing a brand new tire wall to prominently showcase product. Point-of-purchase signage was improved so that customers could easily understand features and benefits. Products were also grouped together to provide several "solution centres." For example, one area could feature everything needed to do an oil change, from drip pans and funnels to the oil itself.

The concept also integrated technology with assisted self-serve areas where customers could use interactive tools to help them select the ideal products to meet their specific needs. Davies says there was also a big emphasis on training so that customers who needed help could always deal with knowledgeable staff who could highlight product features and provide expert advice.

The results so far have been telling. The majority of customers surveyed (91 percent) said the department had an improved product assortment and exceeded their expectations. Customers noted spending almost a third more of their time in the new department than previously. Browsing and impulse shopping increased, and customers anticipated spending more money in the department than they had previously. They also said they would recommend the department to their friends.

Creating an inspiring environment. Interestingly, while the intent was to target men primarily, research showed a 13 percent increase in female shoppers browsing the automotive aisles, which the company credits to a new section showcasing car safety elements.

"The intent was to create a more inspirational environment and we did that," says Davies. "And it was mostly with products we previously had but just packaged in a way that made for a simpler shopping experience."

In the spring of 2013, the company revamped the automotive experience in some 30 other Canadian Tire stores. "We're testing all the elements of the department and rolling out the best of it as we move forward," says Davies.

Source: Rosalind Stefanac, "Rethinking product presentation," *Canadian Retailer,* Store 2012, Volume 22, Issue 4, pp. 64–65.

Retail revenue accounts for about 12 percent of Canada's gross domestic product.[2] Retail also represents nearly 50 percent of total household spending in this country. Retailers should ask: "How do I get consumers to stop, shop, and keep coming back to my store?" To solve these challenges, retailers must link store design to their strategic plan.

The environment in a store, the design of the store, and the presentation and location of merchandise in the store have a significant impact on shopping behaviour. The store image that a retailer creates is strategically planned to attract a specific target market's demographic and psychographic profile and to enhance the appeal of merchandise to that customer. The design of a store, website, or mobile site can attract customers to visit the location, increase the time they spend in the store or at the site(s), and increase the amount of merchandise they purchase. Store design can also have long-term effects on building customer loyalty toward the retailer by enhancing the retailer's brand image and providing rewarding shopping experiences that encourage repeat visits.

> **DID YOU KNOW?**
>
> Retailers remodel their stores every eight years on average.[1]

Store managers are responsible for implementing the design and visual merchandising developed by specialists at the retailer's corporate headquarters. They adapt the prototype plans to the unique characteristics of their stores and then make sure the image and experience provided by the design are consistent over time. As discussed in this chapter, store design and visual merchandising are also elements of a retailer's communication mix (Chapter 15) and play an important role in creating and reinforcing a retailer's brand image.

A good store design should be like a good story.[3] Every story has a beginning, middle, and end, usually in that order. The entrance sets up the story. It creates expectations and contains promises. As for the first impression, the storefront says, "I'm cheap" or "I'm sophisticated" or "I'm cool." Too often, stores launch right into "Here's what we've got to sell. Don't you love it?" A good entrance should entice, hint, and tease. There should be mystery.

The cost of making an eye-catching window display doesn't have to be great, but the price of not making the effort could be.

Inside the store comes the middle of the story. It should start off slowly. Customers need a few seconds to orient themselves after the entrance. A single message has a far greater chance of sticking than do a dozen products cluttering the way.

Seventy percent of purchase decisions are made in the store. This statistic is driving in-store marketing trends. Shopping today is less about utility and more about experience. Consumers want and now usually expect more from stores than products lined up neatly on a shelf. Customers need to be led on a journey throughout the store. Using visuals, light, and motion, take customers down a path of discovery.

There should, for instance, be visual destinations at the end of a long aisle. Exciting stores should be like Paris. Sighting down the Champs-Elysées, you are enticed by the Arc de Triomphe as a powerful destination. Finally, the cash wrap or checkout counter is the story's climactic finale. It's where retailers can convey subtle messaging without hard selling.

Store Design Objectives   LO 1

Retail giants such as Holt Renfrew, Mountain Equipment Co-op, and Home Depot increase store traffic by creating experiences that go beyond attractive sales prices and product samples, from store events and interactive displays to in-store emotional and memorable experiences for shoppers. A growing trend in experiential marketing known as "retailtainment" is a concept in retail marketing that engages shoppers in various interactive events such as contests, shows, giveaways, and activities. The results are sales increases and long-term customer loyalty. When designing or redesigning a store, some objectives are to (1) implement the retailer's strategy, (2) build loyalty, (3) increase sales on visits, (4) control costs, and (5) meet legal requirements.

The Apple Store in New York City reinforces the company's image of developing products with innovative features.

Implement Retail Strategy

To meet the first objective, retail managers must define the target customer and then design a store that complements customers' needs.[4] For instance, warehouse clubs, such as Costco, have high ceilings with metal grids and concrete floors instead of tile—all of those things are perceived to indicate low prices. Actually, they are more expensive than some alternatives, but they are used to maintain an image.[5] ACNielsen Canada, the world's leading marketing information provider, offers services to help its customers create tailored retail experiences and ultimately increase sales. Customers would find it hard to accurately judge value if the physical environment were inconsistent with the merchandise or prices.

To appeal better to European customers, McDonald's remodelled its stores with lime-green designer chairs and

This McDonald's restaurant in Europe features an innovative design that creates an appealing brand image.

dark leather upholstery to create a more relaxed experience in a sophisticated atmosphere.[6] It also implemented nine different designs for different location types and target markets, ranging from "purely simple," with minimalist decor in neutral colours, to "Qualite," featuring large pictures of lettuces and tomatoes and gleaming stainless kitchen utensils, such as meat grinders. In developing these redesigns, McDonald's had to make sure that the new designs projected a more appealing image but still enabled customers to recognize the store as a McDonald's and continue to have favourable associations with the McDonald's brand.

The Apple Store on Fifth Avenue in Manhattan reinforces the company's image of developing products with innovative design features. Its most striking feature is a transparent glass cube, 32 feet on each side, marking the entrance to the store. The cube houses a cylindrical glass elevator and a spiral glass staircase leading to a 10 000 square-foot subterranean retail space.[7] Another example is Sony, a master of matching its target customer with store design (see Retailing View 6.1).

Build Loyalty

To meet the second design objective of building loyalty and influencing customer buying decisions, retailers concentrate on store layout and space-planning issues. When customers consistently have rewarding experiences when patronizing a retailer's store, website, or mobile app, they are motivated to visit the store or web repeatedly and develop loyalty toward the retailer. Store design plays an important role in making shopping experiences rewarding. Specifically, retailers want the store design to attract customers to the store; enable them to locate merchandise of interest easily; motivate them to make unplanned, impulse purchases; and provide them with a satisfying shopping experience.

Customers seek two types of benefits when shopping—utilitarian and hedonic benefits.[8] Store design provides a utilitarian benefit when it enables customers to locate and purchase products in an efficient and timely manner with minimum hassle.

Utilitarian benefits are becoming increasingly important with the rise of two-income and single head-of-household families. Due to the limited time these families have, they are spending less time shopping. They want to get their shopping done as quickly as possible.

To accommodate these utilitarian-oriented shoppers, Walmart Supercentre stores in Canada have redesigned a section of their checkout areas so that customers with fewer than eight to ten items form a serpentine single line that feeds into multiple cash registers. Although banks and amusement parks have used a similar checkout system for decades, supermarkets and general merchandise retailers have generally favoured the one-line-per-register system, because they are concerned that a long line will scare off shoppers. However, when customers stand in one line that feeds multiple checkout stations, there are no "slow" lines, delayed by a coupon-counting customer or slow cashier. Using this system, the wait can be reduced 50 to 75 percent compared with using a traditional system.

Store design provides a hedonic benefit by offering customers an entertaining and enjoyable shopping experience. This shopping experience encourages customers to spend more time in a store because the visit

---

6.1 | RETAILING VIEW

Sony: Making Lasting Impressions

Given that the Sony store in the Upper Canada Mall had already been around for a decade, the company saw an opportunity to really shake things up with a complete redesign last fall that earned the company [2012's] Excellence in Retailing Mid-Size Retailer Store Design Award.

Starting from the outside in, the store was designed with an exterior that aimed to be open and welcoming. A façade of brushed aluminum panels with a wide-open storefront was intended to act as a portal into not just the store, but the entire Sony entertainment experience.

An enhanced in-store experience. "We have a long history of Sony stores and this was an opportunity to try something completely different," says Robin Powell, vice-president of the company's retail division. "I've stood and watched people who are passing by, and the storefront really catches their eye—they make a detour inside." He notes that traffic has increased by more than 25 percent with the new design, and company research indicates that younger customers and more women are now venturing in as well.

Everything within the 3100 square-foot space is about integrating products. Sony music plays throughout

and Sony artists appear on the in-store display screens. Products are powered and running so that customers can actually test them. "We really tried to make the whole store interactive," says Powell. "Instead of telling you our PlayStation is 3D, we set up a fully functional PlayStation 3D game section you can play with." Even the TVs feature "try it" prompts to encourage customers to engage.

To ensure the construction of the space was straightforward enough for a global rollout, the shell of the store is simple but accented with colour and relocatable elements to make it fun and interesting. Colourful side panels are used to discreetly cover wiring. Held together by magnetic strips, they can also be reconfigured and adjusted to reflect changing markets or seasons.

Rather than using fixed signage, the space is divided with three fixed frames and one moveable one that display video monitors with easily updatable digital signage. The back of the frames contain accessories to reduce clutter while providing shoppers with easy access to products.

"This has really proved that the three-dimensional look can engage people to invest with the brand," says Powell, adding that design has been replicated in Sony stores in Quebec and British Columbia as well as overseas.

Source: Rosalind Stefanac, "Making Lasting Impressions," *Canadian Retailer*, Store 2012, Volume 22, Issue 4, pp. 66–67.

itself is rewarding. For example, Bass Pro Shops, a chain of stores catering to outdoor enthusiasts, provides an educational and entertaining experience with a mix of museum-quality animal displays in colourful dioramas, huge aquariums stocked with native fish, and a shooting gallery providing fun along with the opportunity to learn basic shooting skills in a safe environment. Its stores are known as shopping and tourism destinations, drawing customers not only from the local area but also from hundreds of kilometres away. Mrs. Fields stores and Cinnabon stores attract customers because of the smell of fresh-baked cookies and cinnamon buns.

Increase Sales on Visits

A third design objective is to increase sales made to customers on a visit. Store design has a substantial impact on which products customers buy, how long they stay in the store, and how much they spend during a visit. Grocery stores are organized to facilitate the shopping trip and to display as much merchandise as possible to encourage impulse sales. Yet boutiques are laid out in a free-form design that allows customers to browse.

Due to the limited time consumers have, they are spending less time planning shopping trips and making more purchase decisions in stores. So retailers are making adjustments to their stores to get people in and out more quickly. The purchase decisions are greatly influenced by what products customers see during their visit, and what they see is affected by the store layout and how the merchandise is presented.

Customers' purchasing behaviour is also influenced, both positively and negatively, by the store's atmosphere. Signs are designed to attract attention. On a more subtle level, Mrs. Fields stores attract customers because of the smell of cookies. This chapter explores the methods retailers use to positively influence consumers' purchase behaviour and in-store experience.

Control Costs

Consistent with any retail decision, the fourth design objective is to consider the costs associated with each store design element versus the value received in terms of higher sales and profits. For instance, the free-form design found in many boutiques is much more costly than rows of gondolas in a discount store. (A *gondola* is an island type of self-service counter with tiers of shelves, bins, or pegs.) Also, the best locations within a store are "worth" the most, so they're reserved for certain types of merchandise. For instance, many grocery stores place their produce near the store's entrance because it has a higher margin than other merchandise categories and it creates a nice atmosphere. Retailers develop maps called *planograms* that prescribe the location of merchandise based on profitability and other factors.

The store design can also affect labour costs and inventory shrinkage. Traditional department stores typically are organized into departments that are isolated from one another. This design provides an intimate and comfortable shopping experience that can result in more sales. However, the design prevents sales associates from observing and covering adjacent departments, which makes it necessary to have at least one sales associate permanently stationed in each department to provide customer service and prevent shoplifting. When considering atmospheric issues of store design, retailers must weigh the costs along with the strategy and customer attraction issues. For instance, certain types of lighting used to highlight expensive jewellery and crystal cost more than rows of bare fluorescent bulbs. Retailing View 6.2 describes how Walmart is building environmentally sensitive stores that reduce energy costs and help build Walmart's image as a socially responsible retailer.

Retailing is a very dynamic business. Competitors might enter a market and cause existing retailers to change the mix of merchandise offered. As the merchandise mix changes, so must the space allocated to merchandise categories and the layout of the store change. Thus, store planners attempt to design stores with maximum flexibility. Flexibility can take two forms: the ability to physically move store components, and the ease with which components can be modified.

For instance, a sporting goods store must be prepared to accommodate seasonal merchandise demands, expanding or contracting space to accommodate the seasonal flux inherent in the sporting goods business. Stores with built-in design flexibility can respond to seasonal changes and renew themselves from an image

Walmart Canada Opening High-Efficiency Superstores

Walmart Canada opened its first high-efficiency (HE) prototype Wednesday, September 23, 2009, in the community of Waterdown, Ontario. The supercentre uses 30 percent less energy and integrates industry-leading heating, cooling, and refrigeration systems to conserve energy and reduce greenhouse gas emissions. The high-efficiency prototype will become the norm for all future Walmart stores nationwide.

The Waterdown Supercentre is also Walmart Canada's first high-waste-diversion store, incorporating a vast number of waste programs including, but not limited to, paper, plastic, organics, polystyrene, wood, and metal recycling and diversion. Ultimately, the company intends to operate the entire facility waste-free.

"As we design and build new stores, our goal is to be the greenest business on the block," said David Cheesewright, president and CEO for Walmart Canada. "We continue to pilot new technologies, drive innovation, and experiment with new prototypes to create some of the most sustainable stores in retail. With our new sustainable prototypes, we are on track to achieve our environmental goals, which include using less energy, and producing less waste."

The HE store includes the following energy-efficient operations and features:

- Waste heat from refrigeration captured and reused to heat store.

- Environmentally preferable glycol refrigeration system.

- Energy-saving, motion-activated LED lights in refrigerators and freezers that reduce energy use.

- LED lights in various applications, like storefront signs, that use 90 percent less energy.

- Low-wattage parking lot lights.

- Cutting energy used to light sales floors by 20 percent.

- Low-flow water fixtures such as toilets, urinals, and sinks.

- Energy recovery ventilation systems and CO_2 sensor controls.

- White roof membrane to deflect sunlight by an estimated 85 percent to reduce both heat gain in the summer and demand on the electrical grid.

- Increased roof insulation to reduce heat and cooling loss.

Other sustainable features of the store include concrete floors for chemical-free cleanup and hundreds of environmentally preferable products ranging from organic produce, dry groceries, and dairy to cleaning products and paper products.

Walmart Canada opened its first environmental demonstration store in Burlington, Ontario. The Burlington Walmart Supercentre features geothermal technology and energy-conserving lighting innovations, among other sustainable features.

For more information on how Walmart Canada is contributing to the environment, visit www.walmartcsr.ca.

Sources: Walmart Goes Green: Marianne Wilson "Lighting The Way," *Chain Store Age*, October 2007, pp. 112; Marianne Wilson, "Supercenter Is Super Efficient," *Chain Store Age*, October 2007, p. 112; Marianne Wilson, "The Machine Goes Green," *Chain Store Age*, October 2007, pp. 110–112. Copyright Lebhar-Friedman Inc., 425 Park Avenue, New York, NY. Reprinted by permission.

perspective without the need for large-scale renovations. For example, as much as 30 percent more retail space can be provided for in-season sports equipment or apparel through the use of flexible fixturing systems that are movable and accommodate additional tie-in units and shelves.

Legal Considerations

In the United States, store design or redesign decisions must comply with the 1990 *Americans with Disabilities Act (ADA)*.[9] This law protects people with disabilities from discrimination in employment, transportation, public accommodations, telecommunications, and activities of state and local governments. It affects store design because the act calls for "reasonable access" to merchandise and services in retail stores that were built before 1993. Stores built after 1993 must be fully accessible.

The act also states that retailers should not have to incur "undue burdens" to comply with ADA requirements. Although retailers are concerned about the needs of their disabled customers, they are also worried that making merchandise completely accessible to people in a wheelchair or a motorized cart will result in less space available to display merchandise and thus reduce sales. However, providing for wider aisles and more space around fixtures can result in a more pleasant shopping experience for able-bodied as well as disabled customers.

The ADA does not clearly define critical terms such as "reasonable access," "fully accessible," or "undue burden." So the actual ADA requirements are being defined through a series of court cases in which disabled plaintiffs have filed class action suits against retailers.[10] On the basis of these court cases, retailers are typically required to (1) provide 32-inch-wide pathways in the main aisle; to bathrooms, fitting rooms, and elevators; and around most fixtures; (2) lower most cash wraps (checkout stations) and fixtures so that they can be reached by a person in a wheelchair; and (3) make bathrooms and fitting rooms fully accessible. These accessibility requirements are somewhat relaxed for retailers in very small spaces and during peak sales periods such as the Christmas holidays.[11]

It has been 25 years since the Canadian federal government spearheaded a National Strategy for the Integration of Persons with Disabilities, and 15 years since the federal, territorial, and provincial First Ministers identified disability issues as a priority.[12] While many smaller pieces of legislation related to the well-being of people with disabilities exist at the federal level in Canada, the possibility of overarching federal disability legislation has been a matter of public debate to a greater or lesser degree for three decades.[13]

In 2005, the Ontario government took a step toward building a more accessible province when it passed the *Accessibility for Ontarians with Disabilities Act (AODA)*, calling for the development of standards for accessibility in five key areas of daily living: customer service, information and communications, employment, transportation, and built environment. As of January 1, 2012, the AODA legally requires all organizations, both public and private, that provide goods and services either directly to the public or to other organizations in Ontario (third parties) and that have one or more employees to provide accessible customer service to persons of all ability levels.[14]

Retailers were encouraged to review the customer service standards and develop compliance strategies in advance of January 1, 2012. The review should have included things such as consumer-facing material and customer communication methods to ensure that they took into account potential customer disabilities (e.g., written materials available in Braille or by audio) and websites that could be accessible by the visually impaired.[15]

People with disabilities dine out, work, travel, shop, and do business. People with disabilities have spending power! A Royal Bank study released in the year 2000 estimated the spending power of people with disabilities to be $25 billion a year in Canada. Businesses that are accessible attract more customers and improve services for everyone.[16]

Design Trade-Offs

Typically, a store design cannot achieve all of these objectives, so managers need to make trade-offs among them. Home Depot's traditional warehouse design can efficiently store and display a lot of merchandise with long rows of floor-to-ceiling racks, but this design is not conducive for a pleasant shopping experience, particularly for the female customers who account for more than half of the sales in home improvement centres. Women preferred to shop in Lowes' stores. So Home Depot lowered the ceilings, increased the lighting, widened the aisles, and provided better signage—design aspects that tend to appeal to women.[17]

Retailers often make trade-offs between stimulating impulse purchases and making it easy to buy products. For example, supermarkets place milk, a commonly purchased item, at the back of the store to make customers walk through the entire store and thus stimulate more impulse purchases. Realizing that some customers may want to buy only milk, Walgreen's places its milk at the front of the store, enabling it to compete more effectively with convenience stores.

The trade-off between the ease of finding merchandise and providing an interesting shopping experience is determined by the customer's shopping needs. For example, supermarket shoppers typically want to minimize the time they spend shopping, so supermarkets emphasize the ease of locating merchandise. In contrast, customers shopping for specialty goods like a computer, a home entertainment centre, or furniture are more likely to spend time in the store browsing, comparing products, and talking with the salesperson. Thus, specialty store retailers that offer this type of merchandise place more emphasis on encouraging exploration rather than the ease of finding merchandise.

Another trade-off is the balance between giving customers adequate space in which to shop and productively using this scarce resource for displaying merchandise. For example, customers are attracted to stores with wide aisles and fixtures whose primary purpose is to display rather than hold the merchandise. However, this type of design reduces the amount of merchandise that can be available to buy, which may also reduce impulse purchases and the customers' chances of finding what they are looking for. But too many racks and displays in a store can cause customers to feel uncomfortable and even confused. The issue of overcrowded display fixtures and merchandise is particularly important when retailers consider the special needs of persons with disabilities.

Store Design Elements

grid layout A store design, typically used by grocery stores, in which merchandise is displayed on long gondolas in aisles with a repetitive pattern.

Three elements in the design of stores are (1) layout, (2) signage, and (3) feature areas. Each of these elements is discussed in this section. Research shows that 70 percent of final retail purchase decisions are made in the store. Increasingly, retailers must understand the power of the retail environment to influence customers at that critical moment when awareness, brand loyalty, and impulse converge.

To develop a good store layout, store designers must balance many objectives—objectives that often conflict. For example, the store layout should entice customers to move around the store to purchase more merchandise than they may have originally planned. However, if the layout is too complex, customers may find it difficult to locate the merchandise they are looking for and decide not to patronize the store. A well-thought-out store layout will increase store traffic, drive sales, and build store loyalty.

The study of customer movement is a science. Research indicates that about 80 to 90 percent of consumers will turn to the right when entering a store unless they have a specific destination. According to Joseph Weisher, international store designer and president of New Vision Studios, it does not seem to matter whether you are right- or left-handed, read from left to right, drive on the left side of the road, or are male or female: Consumers are predisposed to turn right. The reason for this is that we receive and compute information from the left to the right side of our brains.

This right-entry pattern seems to be consistent as consumers enter, scan the space from left to right, and proceed right. At the same time, the head moves in a natural 45-degree turn and the right foot leads into the retail space. Having this knowledge can be an asset when designing a store and positioning high-margin merchandise. Placing fixtures at a 45-degree angle to the entrance of the store will encourage customers to move along a fixed path exposing maximum merchandise and stimulating impulse sales. The Gap places its new and high-margin merchandise at key points along a path, leading the eyes and the body to the wall.

Traffic patterns are meant to lead the customer from the entrance in and around merchandise, creating various points of interest along the way. The proper distance for visualizing a presentation is up to 26 feet from the point of entry. Larger stores (over 5000 square feet) will need to map traffic patterns and place multiple merchandise presentations along the customer's path. The goal is to move the customer from the aisles to the wall, the most important fixture in the store. There is a saying in retail that, "The longer a customer stays in a store, the more he or she will buy."

If customers enter to the right, then they will naturally exit on the left. Placing the cash/transaction area at the end of the shopping trip near the front left—in other words, putting it on the customers' right when they exit—will encourage impulse sales at the point of purchase.[18]

Customers can be enticed to follow what amounts to a yellow brick road, as in *The Wizard of Oz*. For instance, Toys "R" Us uses a layout that almost forces customers to move through sections of inexpensive impulse-purchase products to get to larger, more expensive goods. It takes a strong-willed parent to navigate through the balloons and party favours without making a purchase.

Another method of helping customers move through the store is to provide interesting design elements. For example, antiques stores have little nooks and crannies that entice shoppers to wander around. Off-price retailers intentionally create some degree of messiness so that people will be encouraged to look through the racks for bargains. Another objective of a good layout is to provide a balance between giving customers adequate space in which to shop and productively using this space for merchandise.

To meet their objectives, retailers must decide which design type to use and how to generate traffic through feature areas.

Types of Design

Today's modern retailers use three general types of store layout design: grid, racetrack, and free-form.

Grid The **grid layout** is best illustrated by most grocery and drugstore operations. It contains long gondolas of merchandise and aisles in a repetitive pattern.

Sixty percent of sales come from impulse purchases.

This Home Depot store plan is an example of a grid layout.

The grid isn't the most aesthetically pleasing arrangement, but it's very good for shopping trips in which customers need to move throughout the entire store and easily locate and access products they want to buy. For instance, when customers do their weekly grocery shopping, they weave in and out of the specific aisles picking up similar products every week. Since they know where everything is, they can minimize the time spent on a task that many don't especially enjoy. The grid layout is also cost-efficient in terms of space and that it allows orderly stocking.

There's less wasted space with the grid design than with others because the aisles are all the same width and are designed to be just wide enough to accommodate shoppers and their carts. Since the grid design is used with long gondolas that have multiple shelf levels, the amount of merchandise on the floor can be significantly more than with other layouts. Thus, space productivity is enhanced. (Space productivity is discussed later in this chapter.) The grid layout creates natural sightlines, which lead to focal points at the end of aisles. Finally, since the fixtures are generally standardized and repetitive, the fixturing cost is reduced.

Many of the massive superstores opened in the past few years run aisles horizontally. The layout allows a wider central aisle for promotions and breaks up the large expanse with effective endcaps facing the main aisle. Loblaws' addition of the Joe Fresh apparel line to the traditional grocery mix breaks the repetitive grid pattern with a fashion image boutique layout.

Racetrack

One problem with the grid design is that customers aren't exposed to all of the merchandise in the store. This isn't an issue in grocery stores, where most customers have a good notion of what they're going to purchase before they enter the store. But how can design pull customers through stores to encourage them to explore and seek out new and interesting merchandise?

The racetrack layout facilitates the goal of getting customers to visit multiple departments. The racetrack layout, also known as a *loop*, is a type of store design that provides a major aisle to facilitate customer traffic, with access to the store's multiple entrances. This aisle loops through the store, providing access to all the departments. The racetrack design encourages impulse purchasing. As customers go around the racetrack, their eyes are forced to take different viewing angles rather than looking down one aisle as in the grid design.

Exhibit 6–1 shows the layout of a department store. Since the store has multiple entrances, the loop design tends to place all departments on the main aisle by drawing customers through the store in a series of major and minor loops. To entice customers through the various departments, the design has placed some of the more important departments, such as juniors, toward the rear of the store. The newest items are featured on the aisles to draw customers into departments and around the loop. IKEA's racetrack layout leads the customer in a particular direction using arrows on the floor to move customers throughout the lifestyle vignettes and merchandise groups. To direct customers through the store, the aisles must be defined by a change in surface or colour. For

racetrack layout
A type of store layout that provides a major aisle to facilitate customer traffic that has access to the store's multiple entrances. Also known as a *loop*.

This racetrack layout draws customers through the store and encourages impulse purchasing.

exhibit 6-1   Racetrack Layout

Mall entry

free-form layout
A store design, used primarily in small specialty stores or within the boutiques of large stores, that arranges fixtures and aisles asymmetrically. Also called *boutique layout*.

instance, the aisle flooring is of marble-like tile, and the departments vary in material, texture, and colour, depending on the desired ambiance.

Free-Form   A free-form layout, also known as *boutique layout*, arranges fixtures and aisles asymmetrically (Exhibit 6–2). It's successfully used primarily in small specialty stores or within the departments of large stores. In this relaxed environment, customers feel like they're at someone's home, which facilitates shopping and browsing. A pleasant atmosphere isn't inexpensive, however. For one thing, the fixtures are likely to be expensive custom units. Since the customers aren't naturally drawn around the store as they are in the grid and racetrack layouts, personal selling becomes more important. Also, since sales associates can't easily watch adjacent departments, theft is higher than with the grid design. Finally, the store sacrifices some storage and display space to create the more spacious environment. If the free-form layout is

carefully designed, however, the increased costs can be easily offset by increased sales and profit margins because the customer feels at home.

To illustrate a free-form boutique within a racetrack layout, consider the picture above. The designers' objective was to create a simple, clear space that draws customers into the area. Fixtures with the latest garments are placed along the perimeter of the boutique. Yet the flooring and lighting clearly delineate the area from adjacent departments and the walkway.[19]

Signage and Graphics

Signage and graphics help customers locate specific products and departments, provide product information, and suggest items or special purchases. Graphics, such as photo panels, can reinforce a store's image.

Signage is used to identify the location of merchandise categories within a store and the types of products offered in the category. The signs are typically hung from the ceiling to enhance their visibility. Frequently, icons rather than words are used to facilitate communication

Digital Signage Traditional print signage is typically developed and produced at corporate headquarters, distributed to stores, and installed by store employees or contractors.[20] Many retailers are beginning to replace traditional signage with digital signage systems. Digital signage includes signs with visual content that is delivered digitally through a centrally managed and controlled network, distributed to servers in stores, and displayed on a flat-panel screen. The content delivered can range from entertaining video clips to simple displays of the price of merchandise.

Digital signage provides a number of benefits over traditional static-print signage. Due to their dynamic nature, digital signs are more effective in attracting the attention of customers and helping them recall the messages displayed. Digital signage also offers the opportunity to enhance a store's environment by displaying graphics and videos to provide an atmosphere that customers find appealing.[21]

Digital signage overcomes the time-to-message hurdle associated with traditional print signage. Changing market developments or events can immediately be incorporated into the digital sign. The ease and speed (flexibility) of content development and deployment of digital signage enables the content to be varied within and across stores at different times of the day or days of the week. For example, the weather could lead to automatic adjustments to digital in-store signage such as automatically advertising cold drinks when the temperature rises above 30 degrees Celsius or advertising sunscreen three days before a weekend that's forecast to be sunny and warm.

Because the content is delivered digitally, it can easily be tailored to a store's market and changed during the week or even the day and hour. For instance, one retailer experimented with changing the content of its storefront digital signage. In the morning, the signage emphasized

category signage
Signage within a particular department or sector of the store; category signs are usually smaller than directional signs. Their purpose is to identify types of products offered; they are usually located near the goods to which they refer.

promotional signage
Describes special offers and may be displayed in windows to entice the customer into the store.

point-of-sale signage
Signs placed near the merchandise; they refer to so that customers know the price and other detailed information.

digital signage
Signs whose visual content is delivered digitally through a centrally managed and controlled network and displayed on a television monitor or flat-panel screen.

with customers speaking different languages. Smaller signs are used to identify sale items and provide more information about specific products. Finally, retailers may use images, such as pictures of people and places, to create moods that encourage customers to buy products. Some different types of signs follow:

- **Category signage.** Used within a particular department or sector of the store, category signs are usually smaller than directional signs. Their purpose is to identify types of products offered; they are usually located near the goods to which they refer.

- **Promotional signage.** This signage describes special offers and may be displayed in windows to entice the customer into the store. For instance, value apparel stores for young women often display large posters in their windows of models wearing the items on special offer.

- **Point-of-sale signage.** Point-of-sale signs are placed near the merchandise they refer to so that customers know its price and other detailed information. Some of this information may already be on product labels or packaging. However, point-of-sale signage can quickly identify for the customer those aspects likely to be of greater interest, such as whether the product is on special offer.

Digital signs are more effective at attracting the attention of shoppers than are traditional statics signs.

H&M effectively uses graphic photo panels to enhance its store image.

merchandise with lower price points and sale items. The merchandise at higher price points and more consistent with the retailer's brand image was displayed later in the day.

The ability to control digital signage content centrally ensures that the retailer's strategy for communicating with its customers is properly executed system-wide. Digital signage thus eliminates the challenge facing retailers that send out static signage to stores announcing a special promotion or a new marketing initiative and then find the signage stacked in the storage area, never put out on the selling floor during the promotion. Digital signage ensures that the signage is installed in the right place at the right time.

Finally, digital signage eliminates the costs associated with printing, distributing, and installing static signage. In addition, it may decrease store labour costs while improving labour productivity. However, the drawback to using digital signage is the initial cost of the display devices and the system that supports the delivery of the signage.

Visual Communications

Visual communications—composed of graphics, signs, and theatrical effects, both in the store and in windows—help boost sales by providing information on products, special purchases, and value propositions. Signs and graphics also help customers find a department or merchandise. Graphics, such as photo panels, can add personality, beauty, and romance to the store's image.

Retailers should consider the following seven issues when designing visual communications strategies for their stores.

Coordinate Signs and Graphics with the Store's Image Signs and graphics should act as a bridge between the merchandise and the target markets. The colours and tone of the signs and graphics should complement the merchandise. For example, a pastel pink sign in a store selling nautical supplies would not be as appropriate as bold red, white, and blue. Also, a formally worded black-and-white rectangular sign doesn't relate to a children's display as well as a red-and-yellow circus tent design does. Colour combinations should appeal to specific target customers or highlight specific merchandise—primary colours for kids, hot vivid colours for teens, pastels for lingerie, brights for sportswear, and so forth. At Athlete's Foot, for instance, sliding graphic panels highlight the lifestyles of the target market while at the same time displaying product and concealing inventory.

Inform the Customer   Informative signs and graphics make merchandise more desirable. For instance, Athlete's Foot uses a series of freestanding prints to explain its five-step fitting process.[22] The process begins with a foot scanner, which ensures a perfect fit for each customer. Then, after analyzing customers' activity levels, in-store personnel help them choose the right shoes and determine the best way to tie shoes to fit their feet.

Use Signs and Graphics as Props   Using signs or graphics that masquerade as props, or vice versa, is a great way to unify a theme and merchandise for an appealing overall presentation. For instance, a store selling educational toys uses lively graphics and props in a unifying theme that is consistent with the store's image.

Keep Signs and Graphics Fresh
Signs shouldn't be left in the store or in windows after displays are removed. Forgotten, faded, and fraught with water spots, such signs do more to disparage a store's image than sell merchandise. Also, new signs imply new merchandise.

Limit the Copy on Signs   As a general rule, signs with too much text won't be read. Customers must be able to quickly grasp the information on the sign as they walk through the store.

Use Appropriate Typefaces on Signs   Different typefaces impart different messages and moods. For instance, carefully done calligraphy in an Old English script provides a very different message than a hastily written price-reduction sign.

Create Theatrical Effects   To heighten store excitement and enhance store image, retailers have borrowed from the theatre. Bold graphic posters, photographs, or fabrics can be hung from ceilings and walls to decorate, provide information, or camouflage less aesthetic areas, such as the ceiling structure.

Feature Areas

Besides the area where most of the merchandise is displayed and stored, there are feature areas—areas within a store designed to get the customer's attention. They include end caps, promotional aisles or areas, freestanding fixtures and mannequins that introduce a soft goods department, windows, point-of-sale or cash-wrap areas, and walls.

Entrances   The first impression caused by the entry area affects the customer's image of the store. Department stores typically have cosmetics and fragrance categories at the main entrance because these categories are visually appealing and create a sense of excitement. While the entry area plays a prominent role in creating an image, the first ten feet of the store is often referred to as the "decompression zone," because customers are making an adjustment to the

exhibit 6–2   Free-Form Store Layout

end caps Display fixtures located at the end of an aisle.

promotional aisle or area Aisle or area of a store designed to get the customer's attention. An example might be a special "trim-the-tree" department that seems magically to appear right after Halloween every year for the Christmas holidays.

freestanding fixtures Fixtures and mannequins located on aisles that are designed primarily to get customers' attention and bring them into a department.

point-of-sale (POS) areas Areas where the customer waits at checkout. This area can be the most valuable piece of real estate in the store, because the customer is almost held captive in that spot; also called *point-of-purchase (POP) areas*.

checkout areas The places in a store where customers can purchase merchandise and have it "wrapped"—placed in a bag; also called *cash-wrap areas*.

new environment: escaping from the noisy street or mall, taking off their sunglasses, closing umbrellas, and developing a visual impression of the entire store. Customers are not prepared to evaluate merchandise or make purchase decisions in the decompression zone, so retailers try to keep this area free of merchandise, displays, and signage.[23]

End Caps End caps are displays located at the end of an aisle. For instance, a food store's large end-cap display of Coca-Cola is designed to catch consumers' attention. The Coca-Cola is located near the rest of the soft drinks, but is on sale. It's not always necessary to use end caps for sales, however. Due to their high visibility, end caps can also be used to feature special promotional items.

Promotional Aisle or Area A promotional aisle or area is an aisle or area used to display merchandise that is being promoted. Canadian Tire, for instance, uses a promotional aisle to sell seasonal merchandise, such as lawn and garden in the summer and Christmas decorations in the fall. Apparel stores, such as The Gap, often place their sale merchandise in the back of the store so that customers must wander through the full-price merchandise to get to the sale merchandise.

Freestanding Fixtures and Mannequins Freestanding fixtures and mannequins located on aisles are designed primarily to get customers' attention and bring them into a department. These fixtures often display and store the newest, most exciting merchandise in the department.

Windows Although windows are clearly external to the store, they can be an important component of the store layout. Properly used, window displays can help draw customers into the store. They provide a visual message about the type of merchandise for sale in the store and the type of image the store wishes to portray. Window displays should be tied to the merchandise and other displays in the store window. For instance, if beach towels are displayed in a Hudson's Bay store, they should also

be prominently displayed inside. Otherwise, the drawing power of the window display is lost. Finally, windows can be used to set the shopping mood for a season or holiday such as Christmas or Valentine's Day.

Point-of-Sale (POS) Areas Point-of-sale (POS) areas, also known as *point-of-purchase (POP) areas*, are places in the store where customers can purchase merchandise. Also called checkout areas (or *cash-wrap areas*), these areas can be the most valuable piece of real estate in the store, because the customers often wait there for the transactions to be completed. While waiting in a long checkout line at a grocery store, notice how people pick up things such as batteries, candy, razors, and magazines. Did they need these items? Not really, but the wait bored them, so they spent the extra time shopping.

Several department store chains are experimenting with centralized checkout stations.[24] Discount and value-priced retailers, such as Dollarama, have long used centralized checkouts at the front of their stores. But department stores have traditionally placed cash registers deep within each department. By centralizing the checkout areas, these department stores hope to reduce staff as well as customer complaints arising from slow or poor checkout service. Hudson's Bay and Sears have moved to centralized checkout stations located in the centre of the store.

Walls Since retail space is often scarce and expensive, many retailers have successfully increased their ability to store extra stock, display merchandise, and creatively present a message by utilizing wall space. Merchandise can be stored on shelving and racks. The merchandise can be coordinated with displays, photographs, or graphics featuring the merchandise.

The goal of good store design is to get customers to approach the wall. The distance from the main aisle to the wall (or column) should be no more than 20 to 30 feet— beyond this, a customer's visual perception diminishes.

The wall is the most important fixture, according to visual merchandiser John Weishar. The wall:

- holds more merchandise
- can present coordinated face-outs with a multiple fashion story in a small space
- can facilitate a variety of fixturing methods, such as shelving and hanging
- is the focal point for seasonal merchandise
- can present a feature display to attract the customer
- effectively sells more high-margin merchandise than floor fixtures
- is visible from a distance

The power wall is usually considered to be the wall space to the right as the customer enters the store or department. Most often associated with the free-form layout, this wall space is capable of generating the highest sales. Skilled visual merchandisers will plan the wall presentation first and then group the floor fixtures. The most successful retailers are those that understand the power of the wall to sell.[25]

Dressing Rooms Dressing rooms are critical spaces in which customers decide whether to purchase an item. Large, clean, and comfortable dressing rooms put customers in the mood to buy merchandise. Retailers are using technologies in their dressing rooms to enhance the buying experience. Interactive mirrors, 3-D scanners, and holographic sales assistants may sound like they belong in a sci-fi movie, but they'll likely be part of the shopping experience in the near future. Currently, customers bring five or six items into the dressing room and try to narrow down their selection. Often they cannot remember how they looked in each outfit as they try the items on. By putting an interactive mirror in a dressing room, customers can simultaneously see pictures of themselves in all the items they try on.[26]

By using interactive mirrors and webcams, customers can include friends or parents in their shopping experience. Through RFID tagging, the dressing room registers the items shoppers take in to try on and produces video and images of the merchandise. A touch screen gives shoppers the option to invite friends to participate in the buying process. Through their personal cellphones, they can send an e-mail or text message to

In this store, mannequins with the latest garments are placed in the front window to draw customers in.

friends. By clicking on a URL and logging on to a website, the friends can see the items being tried on and make comments. The website could also suggest other, complementary merchandise available from the retailer. Customers can then click on one of the recommendations, and it will appear in the mirror superimposed over their image, as though they were trying on the garment.[27]

Although technology and decor can enhance the experience of trying on clothing, some retailers are cautious about the extent to which they will use technology. The personal attention by sales associates remains the most effective agent for providing customer service.

Space Management LO 3

Allocation of store space to merchandise categories and brands, the location of the departments in the store, and where to place items to attract attention are a few of store planners' and buyers' most complicated and difficult decisions. They must answer four questions:

1. What items, brands, categories, and departments should be carried?
2. How much of each item should be carried?
3. How much space should the merchandise take?
4. Where should the merchandise be located to create maximum exposure?

Space management thus involves two resource decisions: (1) the allocation of store space to merchandise categories and brands and (2) the location of departments or merchandise categories in the store.

Space Allocated to Merchandise Categories

Some factors that retailers consider when deciding on how much floor or shelf space to allocate to merchandise categories and brands are (1) the productivity of the allocated space, (2) the merchandise's inventory turnover, (3) impact on store sales, and (4) the display needs for the merchandise.

Space Productivity Store planners in conjunction with buyers typically start by allocating space based on sales productivity. For instance, if knit shirts represent 15 percent of the total expected sales for the men's furnishings department, they will initially get 15 percent of the space. Store planners must then adjust the initial estimate on the basis of the following five factors:

- How profitable is the merchandise?
- How will the planned inventory turnover and the resulting stock-to-sales ratio affect how many SKUs will normally be carried in stock? Buyers and store planners must allocate space on the basis of seasonal fluctuations that recognize space demands during peak times, such as Christmas and back-to-school.
- How will the merchandise be displayed?
- Will the location of certain merchandise draw the customer through the store, thus encouraging sales?
- What items does the retailer wish to emphasize?

Exhibit 6–3 shows typical floor space allocation based on sales potential. The front of the store is a much stronger selling space, with the potential to produce 48 percent of sales, whereas the back of the store generates only 16 percent of store sales. Thus, the newest merchandise should be placed at the front of the store to encourage customer response.

But as the discussion of marginal analysis for advertising allocations in Chapter 15 indicates, retailers should allocate space to a merchandise category on the basis of its effect on the profitability of the entire store. In practice, this recommendation means that the men's furnishings department should add more space to the knit shirts section as long as the profitability of the additional space is greater than the profitability of the category from which space was taken away. In this condition, the additional space for knit shirts will increase the profitability of the entire store. However, at some point, it will be more profitable to not take away space from other categories.

Two commonly used measures of space productivity are sales per square foot and sales per linear foot. Apparel retailers that display most of their merchandise on freestanding fixtures typically measure space productivity as sales per square foot. In supermarkets, most merchandise is displayed on shelves. Because the shelves have approximately the same width, only the length, or the linear dimensions sales per linear foot, is used to assess space productivity.

A more appropriate productivity measure, such as gross margin per square foot, would consider the contribution generated by the merchandise, not just the sales. Thus, if salty snacks generate $400 in gross margin per linear foot and canned soup generates only $300 per linear foot, more space should be allocated to salty snacks. However, factors other than marginal productivity need to be considered when making space allocation decisions. These factors will be discussed in the next section.

In addition, retailers need to allocate space to maximize the profitability of the store, not just a particular

exhibit 6–3   Floor Space Allocation Based on Sales Potential

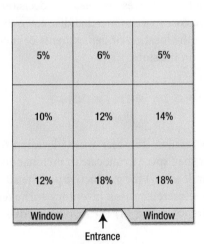

Rent allocation by areas based on consumer traffic patterns and sales potential

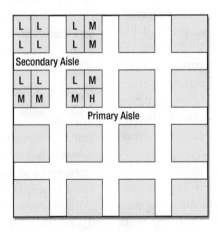

Rent allocation based on traffic aisles

H = High-rent area/high sales
M = Medium-rent area/medium sales
L = Low-rent area/low sales

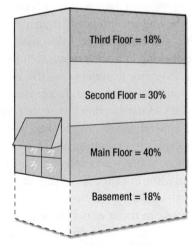

Rent allocation by floors based on consumer traffic patterns and sales potential

merchandise category or department. For instance, supermarkets "over-allocate" space to some low-profitability categories such as milk because an extensive assortment in these categories attracts customers to the store and positively affects the sales of other categories. Retailers might also over-allocate space to categories purchased by their platinum customers, the customers with the highest lifetime value.

Inventory Turnover　Inventory turnover affects space allocations in two ways. First, as will be discussed in Chapter 8, both inventory turnover and gross margin contribute to gross margin return on investment (GMROI)—a measure of the retailer's return on its merchandise inventory investment. Thus, merchandise categories with higher inventory turnover merit more space than merchandise categories with lower inventory turnover.

Display Considerations　The physical limitations of the store and its fixtures affect space allocation. For example, the store planner needs to provide enough merchandise to fill an entire fixture dedicated to a particular item.

A retailer might decide that it wants to use a merchandise display to build its image. For example, Target has a very appealing offering of its private-label bath towels. To emphasize this offering, it might over-allocate space for bath towels and present a wide range of colours.

Location of Merchandise Categories and Design Elements

As discussed previously, the store layout, signage, and feature areas can guide customers through the store. The location of merchandise categories also plays a role in how customers navigate through the store.[28] By strategically placing impulse and demand/destination merchandise throughout the store, retailers increase the chances that customers will shop the entire store and that their attention will be focused on the merchandise that the retailer is most interested in selling—merchandise with a high GMROI. Demand/destination merchandise is products that customers have decided to buy before entering the store.

As customers enter the store and pass through the decompression zone, they are welcomed with introductory displays, including graphics. Once through the decompression zone, they often turn right (Western cultures) and observe the prices and quality of the first items they encounter. This area, referred to as the "strike zone," is critical because it creates the customer's first impression of the store's offering. Thus, retailers display some of their most compelling merchandise in the strike zone.

After passing through the strike zone, the most heavily trafficked and viewed area is the right-hand side of the store. By this point in their journey through the store, customers have become accustomed to the environment, have developed a first impression, and are ready to make purchase decisions. Thus, the right-hand side is a prime area for displaying high GMROI merchandise. For example, supermarkets typically locate the produce section in this area because produce appeals to shoppers' senses. The smell of fresh fruits and vegetables gets a shopper's mouth watering, and the best grocery store customer is a hungry one.

Impulse Merchandise　The prime store locations for selling merchandise are heavily trafficked areas such as 10 feet beyond the entrance on the right side of the store, the right-hand side of the store, and areas near escalators and cash wraps. In multilevel stores, a space's value decreases the farther it is from the entry-level floor. Thus, impulse products—products that are purchased without planning, such as fragrances and cosmetics in department stores and magazines in supermarkets—are almost always located near the front of the store, where they're seen by everyone and may actually draw people into the store.

inventory turnover Net sales divided by average retail inventory; used to evaluate how effectively managers utilize their investment in inventory.

gross margin The difference between the price the customer pays for merchandise and the cost of the merchandise (the price the retailer paid the supplier of the merchandise). More specifically, gross margin is net sales minus cost of goods sold.

gross margin return on investment (GMROI) Gross margin dollars divided by average (cost) inventory.

impulse products Products that are purchased by customers without prior plans. These products are almost always located near the front of the store, where they're seen by everyone and may actually draw people into the store.

Why are cosmetics counters typically located near the front of the store?

Demand Merchandise Some merchandise categories involve a buying process that is best accomplished in a lightly trafficked area. For example, women's lingerie is typically located in a remote area to offer a more private shopping experience.

Categories that require large amounts of floor space, like furniture, are often located in less desirable locations. Some categories, like curtains, need significant wall space, whereas others, like shoes, require easily accessible storage rooms.

Category Adjacencies Retailers often put complementary categories next to each other to encourage unplanned purchases. For example, men's dress shirts and ties are located next to each other between men's and boy's apparel. Some stores are now combining traditionally separate departments or categories to facilitate multiple purchases using market-basket analysis. Stores are laid out according to the way customers purchase merchandise (by brand, for example, or by lifestyle image), rather than by traditional categories or departments (see Retailing View 6.3).

Seasonal Needs Some departments need to be more flexible than others. For instance, it's helpful to locate winter coats near sportswear. Extra space in the coat department can be absorbed by sportswear or swimwear in the spring when most of the winter coats have been sold.

Location of Merchandise within a Category

Retailers use a variety of rules to locate specific SKUs within a category.[29] For instance, supermarkets and drugstores typically place private-label brands to the right of national brands. Because Western consumers read from left to right, they will see the higher-priced national brand first and then see and possibly purchase the lower-priced, higher-margin private-label item on the right that looks similar to the national brand. Produce departments in grocery stores are arranged so that apples are the first item most customers see, because apples are a very popular produce item and thus can best initiate a buying pattern.

Supermarkets typically display merchandise on four shelves, with the most profitable merchandise on the third shelf from the floor. The third shelf attracts the most attention because it is at eye level for most adults. Merchandise that appeals to a smaller group of customers is often displayed on the top shelf because reaching for items requires significant effort. Heavy, bulky items are stocked on the bottom shelf for safety reasons.

However, when purchase decisions are influenced by shorter consumers, positioning merchandise on the lower shelves might be more effective. For example, children may influence breakfast cereal purchases when accompanying their parents to the supermarket. Thus, the second shelf from the floor might be a prime location for the most profitable cereal brands. The most appealing and profitable placement for pet treats might be on the bottom shelf to appeal to pets accompanying their pet parents on visits to a pet supply supercentre.

Some tools, discussed in the following section, that retailers use to make decisions on the positioning of items in a category are planograms, videotapes of consumers as they move through the store, and virtual-store software. Retailing View 6.4 outlines suggestions that a vendor, Nestlé Purina, has for merchandising the pet food category.

Planograms A planogram is a diagram that shows how and where specific SKUs should be placed on retail shelves or displays to increase customer purchases. The locations can be illustrated using photographs, computer output, or artists' renderings. In developing the planogram, retailers need to make the category visually appealing, consider the manner in which customers shop (or the manner in which the retailer would like customers to shop), and achieve the retailer's strategic and financial objectives. The technology for computer-generated planograms is quite sophisticated.

Planograms are also useful for merchandise that doesn't fit nicely on shelves in supermarkets or discount stores. Most specialty retailers provide their managers with photographs and diagrams of how merchandise should be displayed. Retailing View 6.5 provides an example from the Home Depot planogram playbook.

Videotaping Consumers Another research method used to assess customer reactions to planograms involves tracking customers in actual store environments. GPS tracking devices are placed in customer shopping carts and on shoppers to determine where customers and carts go in a store. Small video cameras are strapped on the shoppers' foreheads to provide information on their eye movements. These videos can be used to improve layouts and planograms by identifying the causes of slow-moving merchandise, such as poor shelf placement. By studying customers' movements, retailers can also learn where customers pause or move quickly or where there is congestion. This information can help retailers decide, for instance, if the layout and merchandise placement is operating as expected or if new or promoted merchandise is getting the attention it deserves.

Shopping Behaviour and Store Design

Envirosell, a consulting firm in New York, has made a science out of determining the best ways to lay out a department or a store. Although the firm utilizes lots of hidden video cameras and other high-tech equipment, its most important research tool is a piece of paper called a track sheet in the hands of people called trackers. Trackers follow shoppers and note everything they do. They also make inferences about consumer behaviour on the basis of what they've observed. Examples of their quantitative research findings appear in Exhibits 6–4 and 6–5. Here are just a few of the things that they have learned:

- **Avoid the butt-brush effect.** The "butt-brush effect" was discovered at a New York City Bloomingdale's. The researchers taped shoppers attempting to reach the tie rack while negotiating an entrance during busy times. They noticed that after being bumped once or twice, most shoppers abandoned their search for neckwear. The conclusion: Shoppers don't like to shop when their personal space is invaded.

- **Place merchandise where customers can readily access it.** Toy store designers are, for the most part, still designing stores as if the customer were taller than 5 feet. Designers should be made to get down on their hands and knees (sitting on a skateboard also works quite well) and tour the store from a child's point of view.

- **Make information accessible.** Older shoppers often have a hard time reading the small print on the boxes and the prices. Thus, selective displays should take some of the information off the boxes and enlarge it with a simple 6 foot × 6 foot sign.

exhibit 6–4 Percentage of Shoppers Visiting Different Areas of the Store

exhibit 6–5 Number of Shoppers Entering the Store at Different Times of the Day

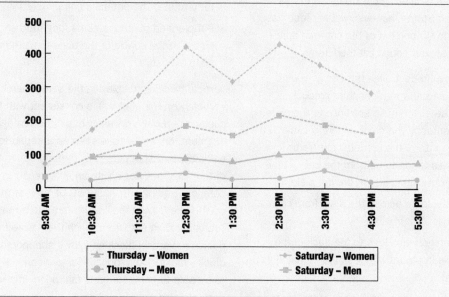

Source: www.envirosell.com (accessed November 19, 2007); "Customer Behavior Insights of Paco Underhill," *Inside Retailing*, November 2, 2007; Paco Underhill, *Call of the Mall: The Geography of Shopping* (New York: Simon & Schuster, 2004); Paco Underhill, *Why We Buy: The Science of Shopping* (New York: Simon & Schuster, 2000).

Suggestions for Merchandising a Pet Food Category

On the basis of an audit of many major retailers across multiple retail formats, Nestlé Purina offers the following suggestions on how to best allocate space within the pet category.

Space allocation. The typical supermarket dedicates about 100 feet of gondola run to the pet category. The allocation varies widely, however, from a low of about 60 feet to a high of nearly 150 feet. Supermarkets with larger sets (space devoted to the pet category) have roughly a 60–40 split between foods (traffic drivers) and nonfoods (higher margin). Supercentres and pet category specialists have about one-third of the space for foods and two-thirds for higher-margin supplies. Supermarkets with smaller sets have about three-quarters of the space dedicated to foods and one-quarter to supplies. Retailers tend to dedicate about 60 percent of available food space to dog items and about 40 percent to cat items. Space allocated across food types (wet, dry, treats) differs widely between species and also by region of the country. The typical retailer across all formats allocates about half or more of total dog food space to dry foods. The remaining space is nearly evenly split between dog treats and wet dog foods. On the cat side, however, the dry-wet division is much more evenly split. Dry cat foods represent half of the cat category space, while the other half is occupied mostly by wet foods, except for about 5 to 10 percent that is filled by cat treats. In the eastern region of the United States, however, wet cat food has approximately 50 to 60 percent of the cat food space dedicated to canned and pouch cat food items.

Merchandising tips. To best align the category with the in-store traffic flow, the most popular product segments should be at the main entrance to the aisle. Since customers entering the store generally circle in a counter-clockwise pattern, the predominant traffic flow in centre-store aisles tends to be from the back of the store toward the front checkouts. In the pet aisle:

- Dog products should be across the aisle from cat products.
- Place the pet category as close to the back of the store as possible in stores with less than a full aisle for pet products.
- Face in-aisle shippers toward the back of the store.

This is a pet food category set consistent with recommendations developed by Nestlé Purina, a leading manufacturer of pet foods, using category and consumer research.

- Establish back-of-store dedicated end caps—this is the gateway to the aisle.
- Place shippers and clip strips on the left side of the aisle, since shoppers with carts buy two-to-one from items on their left in centre-store aisles.
- Place treats, supplies, premium products, and signature items in the hot zone (the first eight feet that can be seen as customers circle the core) to attract the "aisle skippers," those shoppers who tend to skip the pet aisle completely.
- Put planned purchase items, dog food and cat food, closer to the centre of the aisle to increase total aisle exposure.

Vertical blocking (displaying the same merchandise vertically on the shelves) is consistent with the way customers buy the dry and wet pet food categories. Each segment, dry and wet, is seen as a separate purchase decision, and shoppers view these product categories differently. They begin with an initial scan of a product category, seeing only about 50 percent of the brands on the shelf. Then they return to a more manageable "consideration set" from which they make their final decision. Vertical blocking allows shoppers to easily and quickly make "like-product" comparisons. Shoppers need to be able to compare products, price, ingredients, and package size on similar items.

Source: Nestlé Purina PetCare, "Creating Your Most Effective Pet Aisle," www.retailwire.com/objects/objects.ctm.851.

Virtual-Store Simulation Virtual-store simulations are another tool used to determine the effects of placing merchandise in different areas of a store and evaluating the potential for the new items.[30] In these simulations, customers stand in front of computer screens that depict a store aisle. Retina-tracking devices record the eye movements of the customers. When the customers push forward on a handle, similar to the handle on a shopping cart, they progress down the simulated aisle. Customers can virtually reach forward, pick an item off the shelf, look at the packaging, and then place the item in the virtual cart. These virtual shopping trips allow retailers and their suppliers to develop a better understanding of how customers will respond to different planograms.

LO4 Visual Merchandising

Visual merchandising is the presentation of a store and its merchandise in ways that will attract the attention of potential customers.

Many methods are available to retailers for effectively presenting merchandise to the customer. To decide which is best for a particular situation, store planners must consider the following four issues:

- Merchandise should be displayed in a manner consistent with the store's image. For instance, some traditional men's stores display dress shirts by size, so all size 16–34 shirts are together. Thus, the customer can easily determine what's available in his size. This is consistent with a no-nonsense image of the store.

  Other stores keep all colour/style combinations together. This presentation evokes a more fashion-forward image and is more aesthetically pleasing.

- Store planners must consider the nature of the product. Basic jeans can easily be displayed in stacks, but skirts must be hung so that the customer can more easily examine the design and style.

- Packaging often dictates how the product is displayed. Discount stores sell small packages of nuts and bolts, for example, but some hardware stores still sell individual nuts and bolts. Although the per-unit cost is significantly higher for the packages, self-service operations don't have adequate personnel to weigh and bag these small items.

- Products' profit potential influences display decisions. For example, low-profit, high-turnover items such as back-to-school supplies don't require the same elaborate, expensive displays as Mont Blanc fountain pens.

In this section, we'll examine some specific presentation techniques. Then we'll describe the fixtures used in these merchandise presentations.

Presentation Techniques

Idea-Oriented Presentation

Some retailers successfully use an idea-oriented presentation—a method of presenting merchandise based on a specific idea or the image of the store. Women's fashions, for instance, are often displayed to present an overall image or idea. Also, furniture is combined in room settings to give customers an idea of how it would look in their homes. Individual items are grouped to show customers how the items could be used and combined. This approach encourages the customer to make multiple complementary purchases.

Style/Item Presentation

Probably the most common technique of organizing stock is by style or item. Discount stores, grocery stores, hardware stores, and drugstores employ this method for nearly every category of merchandise. Also, many apparel retailers use this technique. When customers look for a particular type of merchandise, such as sweaters, they expect to find all items in the same location.

Arranging items by size is a common method of organizing many types of merchandise, from nuts and bolts to apparel. Since the customer usually knows the desired size, it's easy to locate items organized in this manner.

visual merchandising The presentation of a store and its merchandise in ways that will attract the attention of potential customers.

idea-oriented presentation A method of presenting merchandise based on a specific idea or the image of the store.

Kimberly-Clark uses virtual-store software that employs a retina-tracking device to record a customer's glances. The information obtained from the software enables the retailer to get a fast read on new product designs and displays without having to conduct real-life tests in the early stages of product development.

Home Depot Truckload Event

FLOORING TRUCKLOAD

We will be featuring great deals on flooring in March to drive traffic in stores and to offer our customers great flooring solutions at great prices. The details are as follows:

Dates:
Thursday, March 21, 2013, to Sunday, March 31, 2013

Applicable Markets:
National

Marketing Support:
Messaging in the flyer (fiscal week seven), call outs on homedepot.ca, direct mail pieces to customers and much more.

Signage:
All stores will receive signage for this event prior to the start date. It should be placed around the store **(after closing)** on March 20 in an effort to generate excitement.

Merchandising Requirements:
The items listed below are incremental product buys (this means that new inventory will be arriving in your store).
Please ensure these articles are placed in the flooring laydown area and merchandised with signage.

Article Number	Description
1000741618	12MM SOHO OAK 12.06 SQFT
1000749920	3/4″ × 1/4″ Oak Gunstock 22SF/CA
1000687267	7MM PLYMOUTH OAK 28.67 SQFT
1000753511	HB 10MM Lisbon Maple 13.78 SQFT
1000724818	12×12 Dakota Sand
1000764940	18×30 Korhani Coco mats
1000719641	5×7 Bound Remnant
1000533897	8×10 Assorted Bound Remnant Rug
1000755979	5×8 Assorted woven polypropolene rugs
1000776826	28×40 assorted shag mats
1000772687	3×4 Lexington Assorted 20RIB

vertical merchandising
A method whereby merchandise is organized to follow the eye's natural up-and-down movement.

Colour Presentation A powerful merchandising technique is referred to as colour blocking. Fashion apparel and home fashion retailers realize that by grouping merchandise by colour not only does the store look more attractive but also the technique encourages multiple sales. Women are particularly attracted to colour presentation, and most will have strong colour preferences according to personal favourites or fashion dominance. Red is the most noticeable colour and has the ability to grab the customer's attention when used in visual presentation and signage. Home Outfitters uses colour blocking to increase buyer appeal in everything from kitchenware to home fashions.

Price Lining Organizing merchandise in price categories, or *price lining* (when retailers offer a limited number of predetermined price points within a classification), is a strategy that helps customers easily find merchandise at the price they wish to pay. For instance, men's dress shirts may be organized into three groups selling for $30, $45, and $60. Moore's Clothing has an effective program of price lining: good–better–best.

Vertical Merchandising Another common way of organizing merchandise is vertical merchandising. Here, merchandise is presented vertically using walls and high gondolas. Customers shop much as they read a newspaper—from left to right, going down each column, and top to bottom. Stores can effectively organize merchandise to follow the eye's natural movement. Good vertical merchandising techniques will maximize product visibility as the customer scans from left to right. A poor presentation would be horizontal merchandising, where the customer only sees a small assortment of products for sale. See Exhibit 6–6 for a comparison of vertical and horizontal merchandising.

Retailers take advantage of this tendency in several ways. Many grocery stores put national brands at eye level and store brands on lower shelves because customers scan from eye level down. Finally, retailers often display merchandise in bold vertical bands of an item. For instance, you'll see vertical columns of towels of the same colour displayed in a department store or a vertical band of yellow-and-orange boxes of Tide detergent followed by a band of blue Cheer boxes in a supermarket.

By presenting the merchandise vertically, stores show more merchandise per square foot—making better use of floor space by increasing its selling capacity and getting a better return for their money (floor space is expensive). The customer has a category or style of merchandise right in front of her—at eye and hand level—and does not have to run back and forth along the fixture to find what the store has in a given category or style. Customer access to merchandise on the sales floor has positive implications for payroll.

Tonnage Merchandising As the name implies, tonnage merchandising is a display technique in which large quantities of merchandise are displayed together. Customers have come to equate tonnage with low price, following the retail adage "stock it high and let it fly." Tonnage merchandising is therefore used to enhance and reinforce a store's price image. Using this display concept, the merchandise itself is the display. The retailer hopes customers will notice the merchandise and be drawn to it. For instance, before many holidays, grocery stores use an entire end of a gondola (i.e., an end cap) to display six-packs of pop.

Frontal Presentation It is important to show as much of the merchandise as possible. The frontal presentation is a method of displaying merchandise in which the retailer exposes as much of the product as possible to catch the customer's eye. Book manufacturers, for instance, make great efforts to create eye-catching covers. But bookstores usually display books exposing only the spine. To create an effective display and break the monotony, book

retailers often face the cover out like a billboard to catch the customer's attention. A similar frontal presentation is achieved on a rack of apparel by simply turning one item out to show the merchandise. The goal is to face the merchandise out to the customer's viewpoint whenever possible. For example, clothing on a straight rack may show only the sleeve; using the face-out technique for the garment will show its collar and unique details. Employing merchandise face-outs will encourage sales.

Fixtures

The primary purposes of fixtures are to efficiently hold and display merchandise. At the same time, they must help define areas of a store and encourage traffic flow. Fixtures must be in concert with the other physical aspects of the store, such as floor coverings and lighting, as well as the overall image of the store. For instance, in stores designed to convey a sense of tradition or history, customers automatically expect to see lots of wood rather than plastic or metal fixtures. Wood mixed with metal, acrylic, or stone changes the traditional orientation. The rule of thumb is that the more unexpected the combination of textures, the more contemporary the image.

Fixtures come in an infinite variety of styles, colours, sizes, and textures, but only a few basic types are commonly used. For apparel, retailers utilize the straight rack, rounder, and four-way. The mainstay fixture for most other merchandise is the gondola.

The straight rack consists of a long pipe suspended with supports going to the floor or attached to a wall (Exhibit 6–7A). Although the straight rack can hold a lot of apparel, it's hard to feature specific styles or colours. All the customer can see is a sleeve or a pant leg. As a result, straight racks are often found in discount and off-price apparel stores.

A rounder, also known as a *bulk fixture* or *capacity fixture*, is a round fixture that sits on a pedestal (Exhibit 6–7B). Although smaller than the straight rack, it's designed

tonnage merchandising A display technique in which large quantities of merchandise are displayed together.

frontal presentation A method of displaying merchandise in which the retailer exposes as much of the product as possible to catch the customer's eye.

straight rack A type of fixture that consists of a long pipe suspended with supports going to the floor or attached to a wall.

rounder A round fixture that sits on a pedestal. Smaller than the straight rack, it is designed to hold a maximum amount of merchandise. Also known as a *bulk fixture* or *capacity fixture*.

exhibit 6–6 Vertical versus Horizontal Presentation

exhibit 6–7 Four Fixture Types

four-way fixture A fixture with two cross-bars that sit perpendicular to each other on a pedestal. Also known as a *feature fixture*.

gondola An island type of self-service counter with tiers of shelves, bins, or pegs.

atmospherics The design of an environment via visual communications, lighting, colours, music, and scent to stimulate customers' perceptual and emotional responses and ultimately to affect their purchase behaviour.

to hold a maximum amount of merchandise. Since they're easy to move and they efficiently store apparel, rounders are found in most types of apparel stores. But as with the straight rack, customers can't get a frontal view of the merchandise.

A **four-way fixture**, also known as a *feature fixture*, has two cross-bars that sit perpendicular to each other on a pedestal (Exhibit 6–7C). This fixture holds a large amount of merchandise and allows the customer to view the entire garment. The four-way is harder to properly maintain than the rounder or straight rack, however. All merchandise on an arm must be of a similar style and colour, or the customer may become confused. Due to their superior display properties, four-way fixtures are commonly utilized by fashion-oriented apparel retailers.

A **gondola**, an island type of self-service counter with tiers of shelves, bins, or pegs, is extremely versatile (Exhibit 6–7D). They're used extensively, but not exclusively, in grocery and discount stores to display everything from canned foods to baseball gloves. Gondolas are also found displaying towels, sheets, and housewares in department stores. Folded apparel too can be efficiently displayed on gondolas, but because the items are folded, it's even harder for customers to view apparel on gondolas than on straight racks.

(A) Straight rack

(B) Rounder

(C) Four-way

(D) Gondola

Creating an Appealing Store Atmosphere

To provide a rewarding shopping experience, retailers go beyond presenting appealing merchandise. For example, Disney plans to spend about $1 million per store to create a highly entertaining and rewarding experience for its customers using interactive technology. The chain's traditional approach for displaying row after row of toys and apparel geared to Disney franchises will be given a high-tech makeover. Children will be able to watch film clips of their own selections in a theatre, participate in karaoke contests, or chat live with Disney stars via satellite. Computer chips embedded in packaging will activate hidden features. When children walk by a "magic mirror" while holding a Princess tiara, Cinderella will appear and say something to them.

Disney will adopt Apple touches like mobile checkout (employees will carry miniature receipt printers in their aprons) and emphasis on community (Disney's theatre idea is an extension of Apple's lecture spaces). The focus will be on interactivity—parents will be able to book a Disney Cruise on touch-screen kiosks while their children play.[33]

Employees also play a major role in creating an appealing store environment. For example, the atmosphere at Pike Place Market in Seattle is unusual. Employees, known as fishmongers, throw fish over the counters to co-workers for wrapping. The fishmongers also invite customers to get in on the action and try to catch fish. What could be a dull retail space is transformed into a place where customers and employees are smiling, laughing, and connecting with one another, while keeping an eye out for flying fish.[34]

In addition to these interactive technologies, retailers are using lighting, colours, music, and scent. **Atmospherics** refers to the design of an environment via visual communications, colours, lighting, music, and scent to stimulate customers' perceptual and emotional responses and ultimately to affect their purchase behaviour.[35] Many retailers have discovered the subtle benefits of developing atmospherics that complement other aspects of the store design and the merchandise. Research has shown that it is important for these atmospheric elements to work together, for example, the right music with the right scent.[36] Now let's explore some basic principles of good atmospheric design and examine a few new, exciting, and somewhat controversial trends.

Lighting

Good lighting in a store involves more than simply illuminating space. Lighting is used to highlight merchandise, sculpt space, and capture a mood or feeling that enhances the store's image. Lighting can also be used to downplay less attractive features that can't be changed. Having the appropriate lighting has been shown to positively influence customer shopping behaviour.[37]

Highlight Merchandise A good lighting system helps create a sense of excitement in the store. At the same time, lighting must provide an accurate colour rendition of the merchandise. A green silk tie should look the same colour in the store as outside. Similarly, lighting should complement the customer. A department store's cosmetics area, for instance, requires more expensive lighting than the fluorescent lighting found in many grocery stores because it has to complement the customer and make her skin look natural.

Another key use of lighting is called popping the merchandise—focusing spotlights on special feature areas and items. Using lighting to focus on merchandise moves shoppers' eyes to the merchandise and draws customers strategically through the store. For example, limited and one-of-a-kind glass sculptures are highlighted with special lighting.

Capture a Mood and Maintain an Image Traditionally, North American specialty and department stores have employed incandescent lighting sources to promote a warm and cozy ambience.[38] Overall lighting sources are reduced and accent lighting is added to call attention to merchandise and displays.

European stores have long favoured high light levels, cool colours, and little contrast or accent lighting. European lighting design has been bolder, starker, and more minimal than in North America, creating a very different mood and image than the softer incandescent lighting. Lighting can hide errors and outmoded store designs. A popular technique is to focus product lighting very high compared to the rest of the store and paint the ceiling dark to downplay unsightly concrete and ventilation ducts.

Energy-Efficient Lighting As the price of energy soars and retailers and their customers become more energy-conscious, retailers are looking for ways to cut their energy costs and be more ecologically friendly. One obvious source of energy consumption is the lighting in a store. Stores are switching from incandescent lighting to more energy-efficient fluorescent lights, installing display lights that turn off and on based on customer motion detectors, cutting energy used to light sales floors by as much as 20 percent and installing LED lights in storefront signs as they can use 90 percent less energy than traditional lighting applications.

popping the merchandise Focusing spotlights on special feature areas and items.

Colour

The creative use of colour can enhance a retailer's image and help create a mood. Research has shown that warm colours (red and yellow) produce opposite physiological and psychological effects from cool colours (blue and green), which are opposite on the colour spectrum.[39] For example, red and other warm colours have been found to increase blood pressure, respiratory rate, and other physiological responses. As we translate these findings to a retail store environment, warm colours are thought to attract customers and gain attention, yet they can be distracting and even unpleasant if too strong a hue. Fast-food restaurants often use warm colours to facilitate rapid turnover.

In contrast, research has shown that cool colours, such as blue or green, are relaxing, peaceful, calm, and pleasant. Thus, cool colours may be most effective for retailers selling anxiety-causing products, such as expensive shopping goods, or services such as those provided at a dentist's office.

Music

Like colour and lighting, music can either add to or detract from a retailer's total atmospheric package. Unlike other atmospheric elements, however, music can be easily changed. Although research in grocery stores indicates that music's tempo and volume don't significantly influence patrons' shopping time or purchase amount,[40] other research has shown that the presence of music positively affects customers' attitudes toward the store.[41]

Retailers can also use music to affect customers' behaviour. Music can control the pace of store traffic, create an image, and attract or direct consumers' attention. For instance, the Disney Stores pipe in soundtracks from famous Disney movies that are tied directly to the merchandise.

Scent

Researchers say smell can affect a shopper's behaviour, but it's mainly about trying to make sure that shoppers are having a pleasant experience; for example, the smell of baby powder in an infant clothing department or the aroma of freshly baked cookies in a model home. Consider the ice cream chain that introduced the smell of waffle cones and saw sales rise by more than a third.

Vancouver-based Enhance Air Technologies believes that tapping customers' noses will also open their wallets to beat slow retail sales.

Many buying decisions are based on emotions, and smell has a large impact on our emotions. "Smell, more than any other sense, is a straight line to feelings of happiness, hunger, disgust, and nostalgia—the same feelings marketers want to tap."[42] Research has shown that scent, in conjunction with music, has a positive impact on impulse buying behaviour and customer satisfaction.[43] Scents that are neutral were found to produce better perceptions of the store than no scent. The research found that customers in the scented store perceived that they had spent less time in the store than subjects in the no-scent store. This study suggests that stores using scents may improve customers' subjective shopping experience by making them feel that they are spending less time examining merchandise or waiting for sales help or to check out.

Retailers must carefully plan the scents that they use, depending on their target market. Gender of the target customer should be taken into account in deciding on the intensity of the fragrance in a store. Research has shown that women have a better ability to smell than men. Age and ethnic background are also factors. As people get older, their sense of smell decreases. Half of all people over 65 and three-quarters over 80 have almost

no sense of smell at all.[44] Nevertheless, many retailers are trying to cash in on what the nose knows. Retailing View 6.6 describes Metro Ontario's "fresh" approach to merchandising.

How Exciting Should a Store Be?

Retailers such as REI, Build-A-Bear Workshop, Bass Pro Shops, and Indigo attempt to create an entertaining shopping environment by viewing their stores as theatrical scenes: The floor and walls constitute the stage and scenery; the lighting, fixtures, and displays are the props; and the merchandise represents the performance. This creation of a theatrical experience in stores has resulted in the combination of retailing and entertainment. In contrast, retail chains such as Costco and Home Depot successfully use minimalist, warehouse-style shopping environments.

Does providing an exciting, entertaining store environment lead customers to patronize a store more frequently and spend more time and money during each visit? The answer to this question: It depends.[45]

The impact of the store's environment depends on the customer's shopping goals. The two basic shopping goals are task completion, such as buying a new suit for a job interview, and recreation, such as spending a Saturday afternoon with a friend wandering through a mall.

When customers are shopping to complete a task that they view as inherently unrewarding, they prefer to be in a soothing, calming environment—a simple atmosphere with slow music, dimmer lighting, and blue/green colours. However, when customers go shopping for fun, an inherently rewarding activity, they want to be in an exciting atmosphere—a complex environment with fast music, bright lighting, and red/yellow colours.

What does this mean for retailers? They must consider the typical shopping goals for their customers when designing their store environments. For example, grocery shopping is typically viewed as an unpleasant task, and thus supermarkets should be designed in soothing colours and use slow background music. In contrast, shopping for fashion apparel is typically viewed as fun, so an arousing environment in apparel retail outlets will have a positive impact on the shopping behaviour of their customers.

The level of excitement caused by the environment might vary across the store. For example, a consumer electronics retailer might create a low-arousal environment in the accessories area to accommodate customers who typically are task-oriented when shopping for print cartridges and batteries, but then create a high-arousal environment in the home-entertainment centres that are typically visited by more pleasure-seeking shopping customers.

Finally, retailers might vary the nature of their websites for customers depending on their shopping goals. For example, research suggests that Amazon should serve up complex, high-arousal websites with rich media to customers who indicate they are browsing but simpler, low-arousal sites to customers looking for a specific book.[46] Some similar parallels between store and website designs are drawn in the following section.

Website Design

LO 6

In many, but not all, cases, good design principles that apply to a physical store can also be applied to a website and/or mobile app.[47] Consider the following examples.

Simplicity Matters

A good store design allows shoppers to move freely, unencumbered by clutter. There is a fine line between providing customers with a good assortment and confusing them with too much merchandise.[48]

6.6 | **RETAILING VIEW**

Metro: Rethinking Product Presentation—Appealing to Customer Needs

Metro Ontario, finalist in the 2012 ERA In-Store Merchandising category, also proved that you can make things exciting using exciting product. Through its own market research, the company discovered that fresh, quality produce was extremely important to customers and a key factor in determining where they choose to shop. Project Produce Freshness, which was introduced in April 2011 but was nearly two years in the making, provided the ticket to deliver on these customer demands.

"We wanted to show our customers our commitment to the quality and variety of our produce offer," says Andre Gagne, vice-president fresh merchandising, adding that the project was truly a national initiative for Metro. Prior to the execution of the in-store element, the merchandising team set out on a major initiative to improve the overall quality of produce by setting strict specification standards for each and every produce SKU and then communicating those standards to all produce suppliers.

"Given the breadth and importance of this project, gaining and sustaining company-wide buy-in was important, but not difficult," says Gagne. "This was managed through structured weekly meetings, cross-functional action planning, and disciplined goal setting."

The project made good on two key goals, which were to organize produce displays to allow adequate space for a variety of unique produce and easier customer movement, and to increase produce sales. In fact, total produce sales have seen a 1.9 percent increase year over year, and Gagne says customer feedback has been favourable due to "uncompromising quality, increased variety, improved and consistent merchandising, and a pleasant overall shopping experience."

Furthermore, these enhancements to the produce department are now in place in more than 90 percent of Metro stores.

Source: Rosalind Stefanac, "Rethinking Product Presentation," *Canadian Retailer,* Store 2012, Volume 22, Issue 4, pp. 64–65.

Similarly in a website, it is not necessary to mention all the merchandise available at a site on each page. It is better to present a limited selection tailored to the customer's needs and then provide links to related merchandise and alternative assortments. It is also important to include navigation headings and a search engine feature on each page in case a customer gets lost. The search feature in the virtual world is similar to having sales associates readily available in the physical world. Also, less is more. Having a small number of standard links on every page makes it more likely that users can learn the navigation scheme for the site.

Getting Around

When a store is properly designed, customers should be able to find what they are looking for easily. The products that customers frequently purchase together are often displayed together. For example, umbrellas are displayed with raincoats, soft drinks with snack foods, and tomato sauce with pasta. One way to help customers get around a website is by using links to other sections of the site. When establishing local links, websites should connect:

- Products that are similar in price.

- Complementary products.

- Products that differ from the product shown on some important dimension (e.g., a link to organic produce if the user is looking at natural breakfast cereals).

- Different versions of the shown product (e.g., the same blouse in yellow if the customer is viewing a red blouse).

Chapters/Indigo has a comfy and creative setting for grown-ups and kids alike.

Let Them See It

Stores are designed so that customers can easily view the merchandise and read the signs. But in a store, if the lighting isn't good or a sign is too small to read, the customer can always move around to get a better view. Customers don't have this flexibility on the Internet. Web designers should assume that all potential viewers lack perfect vision. They should strive for realistic colours and sharpness. Some retailers that use the Internet channel have developed interesting ways of viewing merchandise in multiple dimensions (see, for instance, www.landsend.com).

Blend the Website with the Store

It is important to visually reassure customers that they're going to have the same satisfactory experience on the website that they have in stores. Even if the electronic store is designed for navigation efficiency, there should still be some design elements that are common to both channels. For instance, though very different store types, www.tiffany.com and www.officedepot.com each have similar looks and feels to those of their stores.

Prioritize

Stores become annoying if everything jumps out at you as if to say, "Buy me! No, buy me!" Other stores are so bland that the merchandise appears boring. Setting priorities for merchandise displays and locations is just as important on the website as it is in a physical store. A common mistake on many Internet sites is that everything is too prominent, resulting from an overuse of colours, animation, blinking, and graphics. If everything is equally prominent, then *nothing* is prominent. Being too bland is equally troublesome. The site should be designed to advise the customers and guide them to the most important or most promising choices, while also ensuring their freedom to go anywhere they please. Like a newspaper, the most important items or categories should be given the bigger headlines and more prominent placement.

Type of Layout

Some stores are laid out to be functional, like supermarkets and discount stores. They use a grid design to make it easy to locate merchandise. Other stores, like department stores or bookstores, use a more relaxed layout to encourage browsing. The trick is to pick the appropriate layout that matches the typical motives of the shopper.

Here is where store layout and website layout differ. Although many higher-end multichannel retailers experimented with fancy and complex designs in their early years on the Internet, most have become much more simple and utilitarian than their bricks-and-mortar counterparts (see, for instance, www.polo.com, www.harryrosen.com, and www.marks.com). When shopping on the web, customers are interested in speed, convenience, and ease of navigation, not necessarily fancy graphics.[49]

Store designers also strive to make their stores seem different, to stand out in the crowd. A website, however, must strike a balance between keeping customers' interest and providing them with a basic comfort level based on convention. Users spend most of their time on *other* sites, so that's where they form their expectations about how most sites work.

When trying to make a decision about website design, good designers look at the most visited sites on the Internet to see how they organize their information. If 90 percent or more of the big sites do things in a single way, then it is the de facto standard.

Checkout

Physical stores recognize the perils of long lines at checkout, and some have taken steps to alleviate the problem, as we discussed earlier in this chapter. The problem of abandoned carts at checkout is even more acute with Internet sites. Approximately half of all online customers abandon their purchases during the checkout process—one of the greatest causes of lost revenue for online retailers.[50] Some tips for lessening the abandoned online cart problem are as follows:[51]

- **Make the process seem clear and simple.** Make sure the customer knows what to expect from the checkout process, how long it will take, and what details he or she must provide. Because customers hate hidden charges and delivery costs, make this information clear at the beginning of the process. Giving some visible signs of progress through the checkout stages also helps.

- **Close off the checkout process.** Remove links to any parts of the site other than the specific stages of the checkout process to focus the customer's mind. Once in the checkout area, there should be only one place customers can go: purchase confirmation.

- **Make the process navigable without threatening the loss of information.** Customers may need to make changes at different stages, so making it possible for them to go back and forth through the process without losing any of the details they have already entered is vital to minimize frustration. Back buttons on the form, which save data when clicked, are a good way to achieve this functionality and offer an alternative to hitting the back button on a browser, which causes customers to lose information. Enabling them to use the browser to navigate through checkout and still not lose their data would be even better.

- **Reinforce trust in the checkout process.** Display clear signs of server security and third-party verification logos. The company's full address and phone number should also be provided, as well as links to information about the terms and conditions, delivery, and payment rules.

SUMMARY

This chapter explains how retailers can set up a series of stimuli through merchandise presentation that will encourage customers to move from point to point in the store until they reach, touch, and make a purchase. Retailers have the ability to control the eye and body movements of their customers. Ultimately, store design shapes the shopping experience and has a tremendous impact on retail sales potential.

Amid the competitive marketplace, retailers are increasingly realizing that the key to success is identity. Now more than ever, it is important to stand out from the retail crowd and be noticed. Most customers will pass by the front of a retail store in 10 seconds or less. Therefore, understanding and controlling the retail image become essential parts of the retailer's strategic plan.

This chapter examined issues facing store designers, buyers, and merchandise planners. A good store layout helps customers find and purchase merchandise. Several types of layouts are commonly used by retailers. The grid design is best for stores in which customers are expected to explore the entire store, such as grocery stores and drugstores. Racetrack designs are more common in large upscale stores such as department stores. Free-form designs are usually found in small specialty stores and within large stores' departments. Store planners also must carefully delineate different areas of the store. Feature areas, bulk of stock, and walls each have their own unique purpose but must also be coordinated to create a unifying theme.

There's more to assigning space to merchandise and departments than just determining where they'll fit.

Departments' locations should be determined by the overall profitability and inventory turnover goals of the assortment, type of product, consumer buying behaviour, the relationship with merchandise in other departments, and the physical characteristics of the merchandise. Planograms, both manual and computer generated, are used to experiment with various space allocation configurations to determine the most productive use of space. When evaluating the productivity of retail space, retailers generally use sales per square foot.

Several tricks of the trade can help retailers present merchandise to facilitate sales. Retailers must attempt to empathize with the shopping experience and answer the following questions: How does the customer expect to find the merchandise? Is it easier to view, understand, and ultimately purchase merchandise when it's presented as a total concept or presented by manufacturer, colour, style, size, or price? Ultimately, retailers must decide on the appropriate type of fixture to use for a particular purpose.

Retailers utilize various forms of atmospherics—graphics, signs, and theatrical effects—to facilitate sales. Strategies involve lighting, colours, music, and scent. The use of atmospherics can create a calming environment for task-oriented shoppers or an exciting environment for recreational shoppers.

Although a retailer's website is different than its physical store, in many cases, good design principles that apply to a physical store space can also be applied to a website.

KEY TERMS

atmospherics
category signage
checkout areas
digital signage
end caps
feature areas
four-way fixture
free-form layout
freestanding fixtures
frontal presentation
gondola

grid layout
gross margin
gross margin return on investment (GMROI)
hedonic benefit
idea-oriented presentation
impulse products
inventory turnover
planogram
point-of-sale (POS) areas
point-of-sale signage
popping the merchandise

promotional aisle or area
promotional signage
racetrack layout
rounder
sales per linear foot
sales per square foot
straight rack
tonnage merchandising
utilitarian benefit
vertical merchandising
visual merchandising

Get Out & Do It!

1. **GO SHOPPING:** Go into a store of your choice and evaluate its layout, design, and visual merchandising.
   - In general, are the techniques consistent with the exterior image of the store and location?
   - Is the store's ambience consistent with the merchandise presented and the target customer?
   - Does the store need to be redesigned? Do you think it needs a facelift, update, remodel, or renovation?
   - To what extent are the store's layout, design, and merchandising techniques flexible?

   - Notice the lighting. Does it do a good job in highlighting merchandise, structuring space, capturing a mood, and downplaying unwanted features?
   - Does the layout maximize sales potential?
   - Are the fixtures consistent with the merchandise and the overall ambience of the store? Are they flexible?
   - Evaluate the store's signage. Does it do an effective job in selling merchandise?
   - Has the retailer used any theatrical effects to help sell merchandise?

- Does the layout draw people through the store?
- Evaluate the retailer's use of empty space.
- Has the retailer taken advantage of the opportunity to sell merchandise in feature areas?
- Does the store make creative use of wall space?
- What type of layout does the store use? Is it appropriate for the type of store? Would another type of layout be better?
- Ask the store manager how the profitability of space is evaluated. Is there a better approach?
- Ask the store manager how space is assigned to merchandise. Critically evaluate the answer.
- Ask the store manager if planograms are used. If so, try to determine what factors are considered when putting together a planogram.
- Has the retailer employed any techniques for achieving greater space productivity, such as using the cube, downsizing gondolas and racks, and minimizing nonselling space?
- Are departments in the most appropriate locations? Would you move any departments?
- What method(s) has the retailer used for organizing merchandise? Suggest appropriate changes.

2. **INTERNET EXERCISE** Envirosell (**www. envirosell.com**) is a New York–based research company specializing in studying retail and service environments. Envirosell has worked in 26 countries around the world studying spaces—stores, banks, restaurants, and service facilities. Visit the website and answer the following questions:
   a) Describe the three proprietary research tools used by Envirosell to document and analyze consumer behaviour.
   b) In its research, Envirosell collects data to measure shopping behaviour in a retail environment. Identify the specific data that are collected.
   c) View the videos on the Envirosell website. Observe and discuss consumer behaviour.

3. **INTERNET EXERCISE** Go to the following websites and review the white papers by Retail Shelf Planner: http://www.planograms.eu/Documents/White_Paper_-_Planogram_Data_Requirements.pdf and http://www.planograms.eu/Documents/White_Paper_-_Analyzing_your_first_planogram.pdf. What are the five levels at which planograms can be used? How can retailers use planograms to evaluate the best shelf placement for new products in terms of visual impact, consumers' shopping patterns, and financial earnings potential?

DISCUSSION QUESTIONS AND PROBLEMS

1. Name your favourite retail store.
   a) Describe in detail the aspects of store design and merchandise that appeal to you.
   b) Describe how this image attracts the target customer.

2. Assume you have been hired to assess a local discount store's space productivity. What analytical tools would you use to assess the situation? What suggestions would you make to improve the store's space productivity?

3. What are the different types of design that can be used in a store layout? Why are some stores more suited for a particular type of layout than others?

4. Generally speaking, departments located near entrances, on major aisles, and on the main level of multilevel stores have the best profit-generating potential. What additional factors help to determine the location of departments? Give examples of each factor.

5. A department store is building an addition. The merchandise manager for furniture is trying to convince the vice-president to allot this new space to the furniture department. The merchandise manager for men's clothing is also trying to gain the space. What points should each manager use when presenting his or her rationale?

6. Which retailers are particularly good at presenting their store as theatre? Why?

7. Lighting in a store has been said to be similar to makeup on a model. Why?

8. Why do supermarkets put candy at the front of the store, and milk and eggs at the back of the store?

9. One of the fastest-growing sectors of the population is aged 60 and over, who may have limitations in their vision, hearing, and movement. How can retailers develop store designs with the older population's needs in mind?

10. Name your favourite store. Analyze the merchandise layout with reference to Exhibit 6–3 sales potential.

11. Consider the following types of retail formats that you likely have visited in the past: discount store, department store, office superstore, food store, clothing specialty store, and a card and gift store. Describe which retail formats have implemented the best practices for coordinating signs and graphics with each store's image and which formats should improve this aspect of their store layout, design, and visual merchandising. What was appealing to you as a shopper in the stores with a coordinated strategy for store signage and retail brand image?

Practise and learn online with Connect.

international retailing strategy

LEARNING OBJECTIVES

Lo1 Examine Canada's changing retail marketspace.

Lo2 Review the factors in the marketplace that would encourage a move to international retail expansion.

Lo3 Review the four characteristics of retailers that have successfully exploited international growth opportunities.

Lo4 Identify strategic decisions that must be considered when entering the international marketplace.

Lo5 Discuss the differences between a global retailer and a multinational retailer.

Lo6 Explore the top 250 global retailers.

SPOTLIGHT ON RETAILING

IKEA: Bringing Its Philosophy to a World Market

As it expands globally, IKEA is not just selling products, it's also selling its philosophy: This is how things are done in Sweden. The IKEA concept is based on offering unique, well-designed, functional furniture at low prices. Home furnishing solutions and products are displayed in realistic room settings. Customers are encouraged to get actively involved in the shopping experience by sitting on the sofas and opening and closing drawers. Price and product information is clearly marked on large, easy-to-read tags, making it easier for customers to serve themselves. Merchandise is purchased in unassembled flat packs. The guiding philosophy is: "You do your part. We do our part. Together, we save money."

Store openings generate tremendous excitement and large crowds. In September 2004, two men were trampled to death and 16 shoppers were injured in a rush by 20 000 people to claim vouchers at the first IKEA in Saudi Arabia. In February 2005, a riot at the opening of a new IKEA in North London forced the store to close just 30 minutes after opening. IKEA currently operates 130 stores in 29 countries.

> **DID YOU KNOW?**
>
> The name IKEA was derived from the founder's initials plus the first letters of the farm and village where he grew up.

Other global retailers such as McDonald's make changes to adapt to local preferences; IKEA is less willing to make concessions. For example, there is only one set of instructions to assemble a piece of IKEA furniture, wherever you are in the world. Every store opening begins in the same way: a Swedish breakfast and a traditional log sawing ceremony, which founder Ingvar Kamprad often attends. Every store is decorated in blue and yellow, the colours of Sweden's flag, with a complex layout. One of the most frequently asked questions is how to get out of the store.

When IKEA entered North America in 1987, it discovered that consumers were not buying into its "one size fits all" philosophy, and it had to make some changes. For example, IKEA initially tried to sell its Scandinavian beds in Canada before discovering they were the wrong size for North American bed linens. Its Scandinavian-styled bookshelves were too small to hold a TV for Canadians who wanted shelving for an entertainment system. Even IKEA's European-style bath towels were too small and thin, and its glasses were deemed too small for the super-sized thirsts of North Americans. The European-style sofas were too hard for Canadian bottoms, and the IKEA dining room tables weren't big enough to fit a turkey in the centre on Thanksgiving.

IKEA's system of self-service, self-assembly, and consumer involvement in the whole retail process also was a new concept to many Canadians. However, rather than deviate from its philosophy and sell assembled merchandise, IKEA decided to improve its instructions and offer an assembly service.

Sources: Elen Lewis, "Is IKEA for Everyone?" *Brandchannel.com*, March 28, 2005; James Scully, "IKEA," *Time*, Summer 2004, pp. 16–19, www.IKEA.com.

International Retailing: Canadian Issues

American Retailers Come to Canada

Faced with an overcrowded domestic market, a growing number of American retailers looked northward to augment their brands. In 1952, the multimillion-dollar merger of two of the world's largest mail-order companies—Simpsons Ltd. of Toronto and Sears, Roebuck and Co. of Chicago—transpired to create Simpsons-Sears. The Canadian consumer became attracted to Sears and so it was that the Simpsons name was dropped in 1971 to avoid confusion. In 1994, Walmart acquired 120 Canadian Woolco stores and wisely kept the former president of the Woolco chain (who had 28 years of Canadian retail experience and could provide cultural guidance). Sears and Walmart account for approximately two-thirds of all department store sales in Canada. Walmart continues to catch the public's attention by adding organics to the grocery mix, developing energy-efficient lighting systems for its stores, and setting reduced packaging requirements for its vendors.

In January 2011, Target announced its plans to acquire the leasehold interests in sites operated by Zellers Inc., a subsidiary of the Hudson's Bay Company (HBC), and open stores in Canada. Beginning in spring 2013, Target began opening stores in every province across the country. Plans are in place to open 100 stores in 2013 and up to 150 stores by 2017, all of which are forecasted to generate 10 percent of system-wide earnings for the company. Approximately $10 to $11 million was invested to remodel each facility in order to bring the full Target brand experience to guests in Canada.[1]

The Hudson's Bay Company, Canada's oldest retailer, was acquired in 2006 by American billionaire businessman, Jerry Zucker and was sold and acquired by NRDC Equity Partners in July of 2008. The Hudson Bay Trading Company (HBTC) was formed, which is a leading North American retailer with four divisions: Lord & Taylor, an upscale specialty retailer with 47 stores in nine states; Fortunoff, a 23-store retail chain specializing in fine jewellery and home furnishings in the New York tri-state area; Creative Design Studios, the fashion design and manufacturing division that creates branded collections for customers throughout North America and internationally, and the Hudson's Bay Company. Hudson's Bay, has more than 160 retail outlets across Canada, including Hudson's Bay (90), Home Outfitters (69), and Designer Depot (9).

Free trade also encouraged American retailers to venture north as many retailers regarded Canada as "The Promised Land." The North American Free Trade Agreement (NAFTA, 1994) prompted a surge of big-box retailers and category killers across the border. As a result, by 1995 the Canadian retail industry was in crisis, experiencing a record number of bankruptcies and the descent into receivership of five major Canadian retailers: Eaton's, Woolco, Kmart, Woolworth Inc., and Consumer's Distributing. According to retail analyst John Winter, by the fall of 1997, 15 percent of the Canadian retail sales market was made up of warehouse outlets. The fallout also forced many Canadian retailers who had moved into the American market to withdraw, bringing the failure rate of Canadian retailers expanding into the U.S. to 90 percent, according to the Centre for the Study of Commercial Activity at Ryerson University.

Then there were the buyouts, and many popular Canadian retailers were acquired by American giants. Examples include Shoppers Drug Mart (acquired in 1999 by Manhattan-based buyout experts Kohlberg Kravis Roberts and Co.), Club Monaco Inc. (purchased in 1999 for $80 million by Polo Ralph Lauren, U.S.), Canadian icon Tim Hortons (merged with American fast-food giant Wendy's), the successful Future Shop electronics chain (purchased in 2002 by Best Buy), and Winners (now owned by TJ Maxx).

Success in Canada came quickly, and U.S. retail banners now control approximately 38 percent of all retail sales in Canada. San Francisco's Gap Inc. expanded quickly to include Gap stores, urban chic Banana Republic stores, and the trendy youth-oriented, big-box store, Old Navy.

What is the trouble with Canadian retailing and why is the sector becoming Americanized so quickly? Retail experts are quick to judge, pointing toward the lack of attention to customer service, lacklustre Canadian stores that need an image update, and sales staff who lack initiative and product knowledge. According to experts at the Retail Council of Canada, this is a bad rap as many Canadian retailers at all levels strive to exceed customer expectations and remain very competitive in an increasingly complex marketplace. Still, Nordstrom in the U.S., scheduled to begin opening stores in Canada in 2014, remains the gold standard globally and a tough act to follow, excelling in visual merchandising, knowledgeable staff, and unbeatable customer service.

Perhaps the reality is that Canadian retailers do not have the deep pockets of their southern neighbour. Consider this: When the 127-year-old T. Eaton Co. Ltd. was going through its bankruptcy problems in 1998 and trying desperately to attract customers, a $60 million renovation took place across its 64-store chain. In stark contrast, Marshall Fields in Chicago spent twice that amount on a single store.[2]

Canadian Retailers in the United States

Retailers who have made unsuccessful ventures into the United States include Canadian Tire (twice), Future Shop, Mark's Work Wearhouse, Shoppers Drug Mart, Coles Books, Colour Your World, Second Cup, and La Senza. Cheap-chic fashion retailer Le Chateau and Danier Leather both managed through several difficult years operating a handful of stores in New York. Canadian companies such as Jean Coutu and Alimentation Couche-Tard have had better luck buying existing U.S. stores and turning them around. Canadian retailers often choose to penetrate the United States market because of the close proximity, but are poorly prepared to conquer the market. Some of the problems have been identified as:

- Inability to secure good real estate
- Underfunded advertising budgets. U.S. retailers spend about 6 percent of overall sales on advertising compared to 3 percent in Canada.
- Underestimating the competitiveness of the U.S. market
- Failing to do adequate research
- Not devoting enough money and resources to the project

Montreal's Aldo Shoes has 100 shoe stores in several states, and Roots, which has drawn on its popularity resulting from outfitting the U.S. Olympic team, operates six stores in major cities. Unfortunately, Roots' inability to secure the 2010 Canadian Olympic clothing deal has had a negative impact on the Roots image globally.

The copycat approach to retail strategy provides no strong basis for being a competitor in the American marketplace and is a formula for disaster. A more successful route for Canadian retailers has been to expand cautiously through:

- Acquisition of existing U.S. retailers
- Developing a unique product that people want

The Quebec-based, 50-year-old Pharm-Escomptes Jean Coutu pharmacy practically owns the Quebec market, with 269 stores. Looking to expand further into the U.S. market, the company announced in 2004 the purchase of Eckerd drugstores in the eastern United States for $3.1 billion.

This strategic move was based on Coutu's long track record of successfully operating in the U.S., extending back to 1987 and its takeover of 333 Brooks Pharmacies in seven northeastern states. Coutu's success was built on retaining the old management at Brooks and learning the business before making any major moves.

The Canadian brand Aldo has been successful internationally since 2001; it now has over 1000 Aldo stores operating in 65 countries and more than 160 Aldo Accessories stores in 19 countries with plans to expand into Italy, Norway, France, and Korea. Aldo sells shoes in the mid-market price range ($59 to $89); the private-label fashion-oriented shoes are designed by and made for the company through a well-established distribution network and licensee agreements. Aldo, Joe Fresh, Aritzia, and Lululemon are examples of Canadian retailers that not only are succeeding internationally but have been able to build global consumer brands (see Retailing View 7.1).

Global Growth Opportunities

As retailers saturate their domestic markets, many find international expansion to be an attractive growth opportunity. Of the 50 largest retailers in the world, only two operate in one country.[3] By expanding internationally, retailers can increase their sales, leverage their knowledge and systems across a greater sales base, and gain more bargaining power with vendors. But international expansion is risky because retailers must deal with different government regulations, cultural traditions, consumer preferences, supply chains, and languages. Retailing View 7.3 describes the substantial differences in apparel preferences for men and women in India compared to those in Western countries.

Attractiveness of International Markets

Two factors that are often used to determine the attractiveness of different international opportunities are (1) the potential size of the retail market in the country and (2) the degree to which the country does and can support the entry of foreign retailers.[4] Some indicators of these factors are shown in Exhibit 7–1. The (+) or (−) indicates whether the indicator is positively or negatively related to the factor.

The most attractive countries are those with large and growing potential sales as indicated by the level and growth rate of present retail sales and the amount of money people have in the country to spend on services and merchandise as indicated by gross domestic product (GDP), GDP growth rate, and GDP per capita. Income and age distribution can be either positively or negatively related to market attractiveness, depending on the type of retailer evaluating the country for entry. For example, a retailer of video games, such as EB Games (GameStop), would find a country with a large percentage of people under 19 to be more attractive than a country with a large percentage of people over 65. High fashion retailers that sell expensive merchandise, such as Nordstrom and Cartier, would find a country that has a significant percentage of the population with high incomes to be more attractive than a country that has a large percentage of people in poverty.

Can Joe Fresh Save JCPenney ... and Retail?

If observers of Canada's fashion industry have learned anything over the last 30 years, it's this: don't bet against Joe Mimran.

The brains behind Joe Fresh, which in spring 2013 celebrated its first anniversary of bringing contemporary styles and affordable prices to the U.S. with an exclusive fashion show at its flagship store on Fifth Avenue in New York, continues to be a fashion force and is showing no signs of getting stale.

The 61-year-old is currently overseeing a major countrywide expansion south of the 49th parallel. Joe Fresh's "store-within-a-store" concept opened in spring 2013 to rave reviews in nearly 700 of JCPenney's 1100 locations. Amidst JCPenney's ongoing retail debacle, much of the media attention had centred on now-ousted JCPenney CEO Ron Johnson hitching perhaps his last cart to Mimran. It's obvious that if Joe Fresh and the sampling of other top designers can't pull through with improved sales figures for the chain, JCPenney's days will surely be numbered.

"If Joe Fresh doesn't work, this could be the worst ides of March since Brutus greeted Caesar on the floor of the Senate," analyst Rick Snyder told *BusinessWeek*. "(Joe Fresh) is kind of a microcosm of what they're trying to do, and if it doesn't work, I think it's going to get really ugly."

Never mind Martha Stewart—if Joe Fresh can't boost JCPenney—whose shares jumped 5 percent on Joe's debut weekend—then nobody can. All it takes is one quick look at Mimran's resumé and it's plain to see—the Moroccan-born fashionista knows his stuff and he's got the market share, revenue, and real estate to back it up.

He started Club Monaco in the mid-1980s with a 5000 square-foot store on Queen Street West in Toronto. By 1999, it had 125 stores worldwide, in countries including the U.S., Japan, Turkey, and Sweden. Later that year, Club Monaco was bought by a little clothing company called Polo Ralph Lauren for millions; however, the retail chain still operates under its own name.

Mimran dabbled in a few other fashion-related businesses before launching Joe Fresh Style for the Loblaws grocery chain in 2006. Loblaws' stores had long sold children's clothing but had never branched out into the adult market until the Joe Fresh store-within-a-store concept was unveiled in 40 of its grocery outlets. Within its first 18 months, Joe Fresh had reportedly racked up $400 million in sales. (The "Style" was eventually dropped from the brand.)

Four years later, it unveiled its first stand-alone Joe Fresh store in Vancouver. Today, Joe Fresh apparel is available in more than 300 supermarkets and stand-alone locations in Canada and is widely credited for boosting Loblaws' market share. After all, what's more convenient for on-the-go moms than picking up groceries and some overalls, socks, and hoodies all under the same roof?

Joe Fresh has also branched out into sleepwear, lingerie, kids' clothing, swimwear, sunglasses, and even cosmetics. But the long-term success of Joe Fresh in the U.S. isn't purely tied to earnings, according to Wharton marketing professor David Bell. "There will need to be some boost in traffic and sales," he said. "But the arrangement might also be considered successful if it helps to reinvigorate the JCPenney brand as well."

The positive vibrations from Joe Fresh's U.S. splash could signal further changes at JCPenney if a report by research firm International Strategy & Investment is to be believed. The report advises that the smartest move JCPenney could make is to cut its own brand out altogether and sublet its space out to other retailers.

Bell is a fan of the idea, pointing out that many e-commerce retailers are finding it helps boost sales if they have physical stores, too. "[Men's clothing] e-commerce retailer Bonobos has guide shops and a deal with Nordstrom, and [eyeglass company] Warby Parker has 13 showroom partnerships and will soon open flagship stores. My sense is that there are a large number of e-tailers that would love to have a physical presence."

That may be the case but considering Mimran's track record, JCPenney would be wise to give him a chance to work Joe's magic one more time.

Source: Renee Alexander, "Can Joe Fresh Save JC Penney ... And Retail?" Brand Channel, April 18, 2013, http://www.brandchannel.com/home/post/2013/04/18/Joe-Fresh-Save-Retail-041813.aspx (accessed July 27, 2013).

With respect to company support, most retailers considering entry into foreign markets are successful retailers that use sophisticated management practices. Thus they would find countries that support modern retailing, have more advanced infrastructures, and have significant urban populations to be more attractive (see Retailing View 7.2). In addition, countries lacking strong domestic retailers but having a stable economy and political environment would be more attractive.

The factors outlined in Exhibit 7–1 are weighted to develop an attractiveness index. One index ranking the 20 most attractive international retail markets, along with some demographic information about the countries, is shown in Exhibit 7–2. Of the top 20 countries in this ranking, 10 are emerging countries. The emerging international markets that receive the most attention from global retailers are India, China, Russia, and Brazil, collectively referred to as "the BRIC" (Brazil, Russia, India, China) countries.

China and India are by far the largest retail markets in emerging economies. However, these two countries offer different opportunities and challenges for retailers contemplating entry.

India In India, the retail industry is divided into organized and unorganized sectors. The unorganized retailing includes the small independent retailers—the local *kirana* shops, owner-operated general stores; *paan/beedi* shops, convenience stores; and

exhibit 7–1 Indicators of the Attractiveness of International Markets

Country Potential	Country Support
· Population (+)	· Market share of modern retailing (+)
· Population growth rate (+)	· Quality of infrastructure, transportation, and communications (+)
· Gross domestic product (GDP) (+)	· Urban population (+)
· GDP per capita (+)	· Market share of leading domestic retailers (−)
· Retail sales (+)	· Ease of doing business (+)
· Growth rate in retail sales (+)	· Business-friendly laws and regulations (+)
· Retail sales per capita (+)	· Political stability (+)
· Income distribution (+) or (−)	
· Age distribution (+) or (−)	

exhibit 7–2 Global Retail Opportunity Rankings

Rank	Country	Index	Retail Sales* (2008)	Retail Sales Growth Rate** (2008–2013)	GDP per Capita (2008)	% of Population under 20 (2008)	% of Income Made by Highest Quintile
1	China	83	$1004	7.0%	3315	28.7	51.9
2	Russia	71	478	6.6	11 807	21.5	46.6
3	United States	69	3686	2.8	45 859	27.5	45.6
4	India	62	435	5.7	1016	40.9	45.3
5	Malaysia	58	59	4.6	8141	41.5	54.3
6	South Africa	54	95	5.0	5693	40.5	62.2
7	United Kingdom	52	851	1.6	43 785	23.5	44.0
8	Australia	51	229	2.9	47 400	25.5	41.3
9	Canada	50	384	2.1	45 426	23.1	39.9
10	Brazil	50	467	4.2	8197	35.4	61.1
11	France	49	828	1.0	46 016	24.8	40.2
12	Vietnam	49	43	5.5	1040	36.0	44.3
13	Philippines	48	79	5.2	1866	45.7	50.6
14	Sweden	47	109	2.0	52 790	23.1	36.6
15	Argentina	46	102	5.0	8214	34.2	55.4
16	Japan	45	1278	0.0	38 559	18.5	35.7
17	Spain	45	484	2.0	35 331	19.4	42.0
18	Nigeria	44	94	4.0	1451	52.4	49.2
19	Turkey	43	341	3.3	10 472	36.6	49.7
20	Thailand	42	120	3.0	4115	28.9	49.0

*Billions of U.S. dollars.
**Estimated compound annual growth rate.

Source: Frank Badillo, "Global Retail Outlook," *Retail Forward*, May 2009.

Mega-Malls in Asia

Eight of the ten largest malls in the world are located in Asia, and of these, seven were built since 2004 (see Exhibit 7–3). The West Edmonton Mall is the largest mega-mall in North America; the King of Prussia Mall is the largest mega-mall in the United States, but the 11th-largest in the world. The largest mall in the world, the New South China Mall in Dongguan, China, was built in 2005 and has 7.1 million gross leasable square feet. Unfortunately, its poor location was unable to attract retail tenants, and it is currently 99 percent vacant. The Dubai Mall is currently the seventh-largest mega mall in the world, but when completed, it will be the largest in the world.

Mall development is rapidly growing to keep up with the lifestyle and income changes in Asia. Mega-malls are mixed-use centres with

retail, dining, entertainment, and residential living. They house many familiar global, luxury brands, including Gucci, Hermes, Versace, and Cartier. The malls, located in places like Singapore, Hong Kong, and Kuala Lumpur, are impressive because of their large size and the entertainment choices they offer (cinemas, bowling alleys, windmills, children's theme parks, skating rinks, and an abundance of restaurants).

When customers get tired of shopping at the Dubai Mall in the United Arab Emirates, they can go skiing inside!

Sources: Stan Sesser, "The New Spot for Giant Malls: Asia," *Wall Street Journal*, September, 16, 2006; Tom Van Riper, "World's Largest Malls," *Forbes*, January 9, 2007; http://www.easternct.edu/depts/amerst/MallsWorld.htm (accessed July 25, 2007).

handcart and street vendors. Most Indians shop in open markets and millions of independent grocery shops called *kirana*. However, India's growing, well-educated, aspirational middle class wants a more sophisticated retail environment and global brands.

While the demand for modern (organized) retailing exists in India, entering the Indian market is challenging. As the world's largest pluralistic democracy, with diverse cultures and 22 official languages, India actually is a conglomeration of discrete markets. In addition, government regulations impede foreign investment in retailing. Non-Indian firms cannot have a controlling interest in retail firms and thus must partner with an Indian firm. Retailers must comply with a myriad of regulations before opening stores and shipping merchandise. For example, there are taxes for moving goods to different states and even within states. Walmart's entry into India is a partnership with Bharti Enterprises to open wholesale

outlets called Best Price Modern Wholesale. The outlets are allowed to sell only to firms that register by showing tax documents that prove they own retail outlets. The development of organized retailing is being undertaken by industrial conglomerates that have limited expertise in running retail chains.[5]

China Government regulations of retailing are much less onerous in China than in India and direct foreign investment is encouraged. Since the lifting of most operational restrictions on international retailers, six global food retailers (Auchan, Carrefour, Ito-Yokado, Metro, Tesco, and Walmart) have entered China. Although much of this retail development has been in the large eastern cities of Shanghai, Beijing, Guangzhou, and Shenzhen, these tier 1 markets are approaching saturation for hypermarkets; the interior tier 2 and tier 3 markets are very attractive. (However, see Retailing View 7.5, later in this chapter, for

exhibit 7-3 The Largest Mega-Malls

Shopping Mall	Year Opened	GLA* (million sq. ft.)	Total Area (million sq. ft.)	Stores	Comments
1 Jin Yuan (Golden Resources Shopping Mall), Beijing, China	2004	6.0	7.3	1000+	Also known as the "Great Mall of China," this mega-mall has six floors and is located near the Fourth Ring Road, west of Beijing.
2 SM City North EDSA, Philippines	1985	5.0		1100+	
3 Central World Plaza, Bangkok, Thailand	2006	4.6	11	500+	21-screen cinemas, bowling lanes, and restaurants; also a convention centre (not included in the GLA).
4 SM Mall of Asia, Philippines	2006	4.2	4.4	600	
5 West Edmonton Mall, Edmonton, Alberta, Canada	1981	3.8	6.0	800	Largest shopping mall in North America; includes indoor wave pool, amusement areas, hotel, restaurants, and 20 000 parking spaces.
6 Cevahir Istanbul, Istanbul, Turkey	2005	3.8	4.5	280	The largest shopping mall in Europe; has six floors, cinemas, a roller coaster, and a theatre.
7 The Dubai Mall, Dubai, United Arab Emirates	2008	3.77	5.9	600	
8 Berjaya Times Square, Kuala Lumpur, Malaysia	2003	3.5	7.5	1000+	Includes 45 restaurants, a theme park, and a 3D Digi-IMAX theatre.
9 Beijing Mall, Beijing, China	2005	3.4	4.7	600	Four levels of shopping with interior residences; located near Fifth Ring Road, southeast of Beijing.
10 Zhengjia Plaza (Grandview Mall), Guangzhou, China	2005	3.0	4.5		Enclosed in a complex that includes a 48-story hotel and 30-story office building.
11 King of Prussia Mall, Philadelphia, Pennsylvania, USA	1962	2.8		327	Created by connecting together three adjacent malls, managed by a single company.
12 South Coast Plaza, Costa Mesa, California, USA	1967	2.7		280	The highest revenue volume mall in the United States. It also is home to the Orange Lounge, a branch of the Orange County Museum of Art.

*Gross leasable area—the total useable, rental space in a building.

a discussion of one area in which supermarkets and hypermarkets in China struggle to compete.)

China is rapidly developing the infrastructure to support modern retailing. Highway density in China is already approaching that in the United States. China has a number of high-quality airports and a rapidly developing sophisticated railroad network.[6]

However, doing business in China is still challenging. Operating costs are increasing, managerial talent is becoming more difficult to find and retain, and an underdeveloped and inefficient supply chain predominates.

Russia In Russia, the impediments to market entry are less visible but more problematic. Corruption is rampant, with various administrative authorities capable of impeding operations if payments are not made. Retailers encounter severe logistical challenges in supporting operations in Russia. There are long delays at borders and ports and a scarcity of containers. Over 70 percent of international container shipments come through the Saint Petersburg port, which is very congested. Retailers often cannot rely on domestic products because the quality of products made in Russia is poor. Finally, much of the purchasing power is concentrated in Moscow, where salaries are about double those in other regions. But Moscow is already saturated with shopping centres.

Brazil Brazil has the largest population and strongest economy in Latin America. It is a country of many poor people and few very wealthy families. Brazilian retailers have developed some very innovative practices for retailing to low-income families, including offering credit and instalment purchases. Many low-income customers go from week to week paying their credit card commitments. Most major retailers own their own credit card facility, with "signing up" booths at entrances to their stores.

The very wealthy Brazilians provide a significant market for luxury goods and retailers. Even though they are approximately 1 percent of the population, this equates to approximately 19 million people, a market just a little smaller than all of Australia.

Global Consumer Attitudes and Retail Trends

Following changing consumer attitudes and retail trends around the world has provided a unique career for Canadians Anthony Stoken and Russell Connolly. In their book, *Naked Consumption*, they highlight ten global retail trends:

1. *It's a Wally, Wally World*—Walmart will increase its retail power across all income levels.
2. *The Death of Inspiration*—Price emphasis focuses on utilitarian store environments.
3. *Experience Shopping*—Go beyond entertainment to attract niche markets.
4. *Empowered Consumers*—Consumers use the Internet to comparison shop.
5. *Kidopoly*—Kids are a big market opportunity; $25 billion in direct sales and $500 billion worth influencing parents' spending in North America.
6. *Dollar Store Euphoria*—Consumers like the value-low priced merchandise.
7. *Luxury for All*—Affordable luxury elements in product for all shoppers.
8. *E-Commerce: Action/Transaction*—Sales online will remain a minor share of overall retail sales.
9. *The Loyalty Myth*—Value in keeping and growing existing customer base.
10. *The New Brand Management*—Successful retailers will build their own brands.

Retailers engage in international ventures for many reasons. When the home marketplace is not producing desired sales and profits diminish over time, some of the problems may be attributed to:

- Saturated home marketplace with no room to grow
- Highly competitive marketplace
- Aging population that spends less and saves more
- Economic recession, which limits consumer spending
- High operating costs including staff wages, rental costs, and taxes
- Restrictive policies on retail development
- Shareholder pressure

The age factor is a dominant issue in Canada and the U.S., where aging populations have put their spending years behind them; the prediction for the future is that the North American economy will be much slower growing. North American retailers who want to maintain growth rates have no alternative but to sell their products in an international arena. The reality is that if you want 8 percent growth in sales you are forced to go to new growing economies, probably in South America, Mexico, or Chile, where a dominant young population between the ages of 15 and 25 (the desirable demographic) is entering the workplace, producing and spending.

It should be noted that countries such as Taiwan, South Korea, and Singapore are also now aging quite rapidly. Although younger than Canada, these countries over the next ten years will experience a dramatic slowdown in consumption. China has an immense population of 1.2 billion, and even if you get a small portion of the market, success can be huge. China appears to have stronger retail market potential than India, with a population of 1 billion. China has a one-child-per-family policy, whereas Indians still have three children per family. If a population includes many children, then much of its resources are used for the health care and education of its young people, inevitably putting a taxation burden on those of working age and limiting disposable income for retail purchases.

To succeed as an international retailer, the company must have a thorough understanding of the macro-environment, including cultural differences, government policies, and the economic stability in the international trade area. Other important factors include the sources of product production and the distribution capabilities within the international market. Some of the factors that would encourage a retailer to enter into the international marketplace include:[7]

- Limited competition in the international marketplace
- Rising numbers of middle-class consumers with improved standard of living
- Younger population with purchasing power
- Trade agreements and organizations, including North American Free Trade Agreement (NAFTA), World Trade Organization (WTO), European Union (EU)
- Relaxed regulatory framework
- Favourable operating costs, including lower wages and taxes
- Opportunity to diversify
- Opportunity to try innovative concepts

Both the micro- and macro-environments must be wisely managed for a retailer to be successful.

Italian designer Giorgio Armani made his first venture into Beijing, China, in 1998. According to Armani, "The Chinese market is growing full steam ahead. We are seeing very good results from Chinese tourists buying in our Hong Kong flagship store and the future possibilities are endless." The designer was well aware of the growing Chinese market for luxury goods; the decision to open a new flagship store in Shanghai in 2004 was part of an ambitious strategy to have 30 stores in China by 2008.[8] By 2013, he had 289 stores in that country.[9]

The World's Largest Shopping District

Launched in May 2006, Bawadi, the multibillion-dollar leisure and tourism destination in Dubailand, will have the world's largest shopping experience, with over 400 million square feet of gross leasable area. Dubai is one of the United Arab Emirates in the eastern Arabian Peninsula, and Dubai City is the main city.

As part of Dubai's Strategic Plan 2015, the world's largest shopping area will provide support to the tourism and hospitality industry, which in turn will play a major role in the diversification and development of Dubai's economy. Bawadi includes a 10 kilometre–long hotel and shopping strip, entertainment, convention centres, and residential complexes. The 31 hotels, ranging from three to five star, will focus Dubai as one of the world's premier family destinations.

The centrepiece of Bawadi will be the world's largest hotel, Asia-Asia, with 6500 rooms. The first phase of the development was scheduled to be completed in 2012.

Dubai's fantastic, even bizarre previous developments include The Mall of the Emirates, featuring a ski slope in the desert and man-made islands shaped like palm fronds. It helped draw six million tourists in 2006 to this tiny desert land that is fast running out of oil.

Who Is Successful and Who Isn't

Retailers—particularly specialty store retailers with strong brand names such as The Gap and Zara, and food and discount retailers such as Walmart, Carrefour, Royal Ahold, and Metro AG—may have a strong competitive advantage when competing globally.

Some retailers such as Roots and The Gap have a competitive advantage in global markets because the North American culture is emulated in many countries, particularly by young people. Due to rising prosperity and rapidly increasing access to cable TV with North American programming, fashion trends are spreading to young people in emerging countries. The global MTV generation prefers Coke to tea, athletic shoes to sandals, Chicken McNuggets to rice, and credit cards to cash.[10] In the last few years, China's major cities have sprouted American stores and restaurants, including KFC, Pizza Hut, and McDonald's. Shanghai and Beijing each have more than two dozen Starbucks. Coffee was not the drink of choice until Starbucks came to town. But these Chinese urban dwellers go there to impress a friend or because it's a symbol of a new kind of lifestyle. Although Western products and stores have gained a reputation for high quality and good service in China, in some ways it is the American culture that many Chinese want.[11]

On the other hand, some large European and Japanese retailers have considerably more experience operating retail stores in non-domestic markets. For example, France's Carrefour has been operating stores in non-domestic markets for almost 30 years. It is very good at adapting its hypermarket format to local tastes. The company buys many products locally and hires and trains local managers, passing the power and authority to them quickly. Even though Walmart has a more efficient distribution system, Carrefour has competed effectively against Walmart in Brazil and Argentina.[12]

Category killers and hypermarket retailers may be particularly suited to succeed internationally because of the expertise they've already developed at home. First, these retailers are leaders in the use of technology to manage inventories, control global logistical systems, and tailor merchandise assortments to local needs. For instance, firms such as Home Depot provide consumers with an assortment of brand-name merchandise procured from sources around the world. This advantage is particularly valuable if brand-name merchandise is important to consumers. Second, retailers such as Walmart and Carrefour have become the low-price provider in every market they enter because of their

globally sustainable competitive advantage One of the characteristics of retailers that have successfully exploited international growth opportunities.

adaptability A company's recognition of cultural differences and adaptation of its core strategy to the needs of local markets.

global culture A company's embracing a multicultural perspective and developing an infrastructure that makes maximal use of local management.

financial resources Resources that enable companies to make strategic decisions, such as expansion into international markets, requiring significant and ongoing financial commitment, often at the expense of short-term profit.

DID YOU KNOW?

The world's largest retailers are likely to be global players. Thirty-eight out of the top 50 global retailers operate in more than one country. The implication: Eventually one must go global to keep growing.[15]

buying scale economies and efficient distribution systems. Third, despite idiosyncrasies in the international environment, category killers and hypermarket retailers have developed unique systems and standardized formats that facilitate control over multiple stores. These systems and procedures should work well regardless of the country of operation. Fourth, because of the category killer's narrow assortment and focused strategy, communications across national boundaries and cultures are specifically focused, which improves management coordination. Finally, at one time, people felt that consumers outside North America were used to high levels of personalized service and would not accept the self-service concept employed by category killers and hypermarket retailers. However, consumers around the globe are willing to forgo the service for lower prices.[16]

Global expansion is often difficult and full of pitfalls. For instance, The Gap is pulling back on some of its European store base. U.K.-based Marks & Spencer (M&S) has sold off its Canadian operations, Brooks Brothers, as part of an overall withdrawal from markets outside Britain. Its plan to close its 18 stores in France demonstrates the difficulty of operating in foreign markets. M&S found it was in violation of French labour laws when it announced the closures. The laws require prior consultation with the employees. U.K.-based J. Sainsbury, on the other hand, got caught up in a geopolitical conflict. It has abandoned expansion plans into Egypt because of a consumer boycott and heavy losses. The Egyptians believe that the company is pro-Israel, despite Sainsbury's denials.[17]

Keys to Success

Four characteristics of retailers that have successfully exploited international growth opportunities are:

- Globally sustainable competitive advantage
- Adaptability
- Global culture
- Financial resources[18]

Globally Sustainable Competitive Advantage

Entry into nondomestic markets is most successful when the expansion opportunity is consistent with the retailer's core bases of competitive advantage. Some core competitive advantages for global retailers are shown next:

Core Advantage	Global Retailer
Low cost; efficient operations	Walmart, Carrefour
Strong private brands	Royal Ahold, IKEA, Starbucks
Fashion reputation	The Gap, Zara, H&M (Hennes & Mauritz)
Category dominance	Office Depot, Home Depot
Image	Disney, Warner Brothers

Thus, Walmart and Carrefour are successful in international markets where price plays an important role in consumer decision making and distribution infrastructure is available to enable these firms to exploit their logistical capabilities. On the other hand, The Gap and Zara are successful in international markets that value fashionable merchandise.

Adaptability Successful global retailers build on their core competencies. They also recognize cultural differences and adapt their core strategy to the needs of local markets.[19] Colour preferences, the preferred cut of apparel, and sizes differ between cultures. For example, in China, white is the colour of mourning and brides wear red dresses. Food probably has the greatest diversity of tastes. Ahold operates under nearly 20 brand names around the globe, including Superdiplo in Spain, ICA in Sweden, Albert Heijn in the Netherlands, and Stop & Shop and Giant in the United States. Ahold firmly believes that, like politics, all retailing is local, as customers develop loyalty toward a store brand they've known for decades. Ahold's mantra: "Everything the customer sees, we localize. Everything they don't see, we globalize."[20]

Selling seasons also vary across countries. The Gap's major Canadian selling season is back-to-school in August; however, this is one of the slowest sales periods in Europe because most people are on vacation. Back-to-school in Japan is in April.

Store designs need to be adjusted. In some cultures, social norms dictate that men's and women's clothing cannot be displayed next to each other. In North America, the standard practice is to place low-priced, private-label merchandise on the shelf to the right of national brands, assuming that customers' natural eye movement is from left to right. This merchandising approach does not work in cultures where people read from right to left or up and down. IKEA initially tried to sell its Scandinavian beds in Canada before discovering they were the wrong size for North American bed linens.

Government regulations and cultural values also affect store operations. Some differences such as holidays, hours of operation, and regulations governing part-time employees and terminations are easy to identify. Other factors require a deeper understanding. For example, the Latin American culture is very family oriented. Thus, North American work schedules need to be adjusted so that employees can have more time with their families. Boots, a U.K. drugstore chain, has the checkout clerks in its Japanese stores standing up because it discovered that Japanese shoppers found it offensive to pay money to a seated clerk. Retailers in Germany must recycle packaging materials sold in their stores.[21] Also in Germany, seasonal sales can be held only during specific weeks and apply to only specific product categories, and discounts are limited. Unlimited guarantees are generally forbidden, which is why Lands' End may not describe such a guarantee on its goods in an ad and may only talk about it if customers ask for it first.[22]

Global Culture   To be global, one has to think globally. It is not sufficient to transplant a home-country culture and infrastructure into another country. In this regard, Carrefour is truly global. In the early years of its international expansion, it started in each country slowly, which reduced the company's ethnocentrism. Further enriching its global perspective, Carrefour has always encouraged rapid development of local management and retains few expatriates in its overseas operations. Carrefour's management ranks are truly international. One is just as likely to run across a Portuguese regional manager in Hong Kong as a French or Chinese one. Finally, Carrefour discourages the

---

7.3   RETAILING VIEW

The Fashion Mavens Are Men in India

The steady growth of the Indian economy has provided an increased propensity to spend among a growing middle class of 25- to 35-year-olds. This has stimulated growth of the Indian retail industry. For a number of years, India has been among the two or three most attractive nations for international retail market expansion. However, there are significant cultural challenges for Western apparel retailers contemplating entry into the Indian market.

In India, men's ready-made apparel generates about two to three times more sales than women's apparel—just the opposites of the sales pattern in Western countries. For the affluent male consumer, clothing is reflective of lifestyle and social status. Awareness of preference for luxury brands is very high. International luxury brands carry symbolic meanings and enhance emotional rewards for male consumers.

While brands play an important role in Indian male consumers' apparel selection, international brands are not important to Indian females in general. Indian ethnic garments and garments mixing ethnic and Western styling are desired by Indian women. International retail firms in this sector face competition from numerous local designers because most Indian women patronize designer

boutiques. They have confidence in their personal assessments of product quality and are willing to buy from small and less well-known brands. In addition, body shapes differ significantly between Western and Indian women. To be successful, retailers entering the women's apparel market need to offer culturally relevant products that are connected with Indian tradition.

Most Indian women prefer to wear traditional garments at work and in social contexts.

Sources: V. Chattaraman, "The Indian Consumer," *Journal of the International Fashion and Apparel Industry* 4 (July 2009); Dale Anne Reiss and Ranjan Biswas, "The Evolving Retail Market in India," *ICSC Research Review* 14, no. 1 (2007), pp. 26–37.

DID YOU KNOW?

American firms accounted for approximately 38 percent of all retail sales in Canada in 2007 and controlled nearly 9500 stores.[24]

classic overseas "tour of duty" mentality often found in North American firms. International assignments are important in themselves, not just as stepping stones to ultimate career advancement back in France. The globalization of Carrefour's culture is perhaps most evident in the speed with which ideas flow throughout the organization. A global management structure of regional "committees," which meet regularly, advances the awareness and implementation of global best practices.

The proof of Carrefour's global commitment is in the numbers. It has had almost 30 years of international experience in 21 countries—both developed and developing.[25]

Financial Resources Expansion into international markets requires a long-term commitment and considerable upfront planning. Retailers find it very difficult to generate short-term profit when they make the transition to global retailing. Although firms such as Walmart, Carrefour, Office Depot, and Costco often initially have difficulty achieving success in new global markets, these large firms generally are in a strong financial position and therefore have the ability to keep investing in projects long enough to become successful. Walmart's US$8.2 billion cash flow and 48 percent share of the US$225 billion discount store industry in the United States provides the financial ability to maintain this type of staying power.[26] Walmart is the world's largest retailer, the 2nd largest retailer in Canada, and the 22nd largest organization in Canada.

Lo 4 Entry Strategies

Four approaches that retailers take when entering non-domestic markets are:

- Direct investment
- Joint venture
- Strategic alliance
- Franchising[27]

Direct Investment Direct investment involves a retail firm investing in and owning a division or subsidiary that builds and operates stores in a foreign country. This entry strategy requires the highest level of investment and exposes the retailer to significant risks, but it has the highest potential returns. One advantage of direct investment is that the retailer has complete control of the operations. For example, McDonald's chose this entry strategy for the U.K. market, building a plant to produce buns when local suppliers could not meet its specifications.

Joint Venture A joint venture is formed when the entering retailer pools its resources with a local retailer to form a new company in which ownership, control, and profits are shared. Examples of successful joint ventures are Royal Ahold (the Netherlands) and Velox Holdings (Argentina); Metro AG (Germany) and Koc Group's Migros (Turkey); Carrefour and Sabanci Holding (Turkey); Metro AG (Germany) and Marubeni (Japan); and Monsoon (United Kingdom) and Charming Shoppes (United States).[28]

A joint venture reduces the entrant's risks. Besides sharing the financial burden, the local partner understands the market and has access to resources—vendors and real estate. Many foreign countries, such as China, require joint ownership, although these restrictions may loosen as a result of World Trade Organization (WTO) negotiations.[29] Problems with this entry approach can arise if the partners disagree or the government places restrictions on the repatriation of profits.

Strategic Alliance A strategic alliance is a collaborative relationship between independent firms. For example, a foreign retailer might enter an international market through direct investment but develop an alliance with a local firm to perform logistical and warehousing activities.

Franchising Franchising offers the lowest risk and requires the least investment. However, the entrant has limited control over the retail operations in the foreign country, potential profit is reduced, and the risk of assisting in the creation of a local domestic competitor is increased. U.K.-based Marks & Spencer, for example, has 136 franchised stores in 27 countries, including Cyprus (8), Greece (28), Indonesia (10), and Thailand (10).[30]

Costs Associated with Global Sourcing Decisions Retailers use production facilities located in developing economies for much of their private-label merchandise because of the very low labour costs in these countries. To counterbalance the lower acquisition costs, however, there are other more subtle expenses that increase the costs of sourcing private-label merchandise from other countries. These costs include foreign currency fluctuations, tariffs, longer lead times, and increased transportation costs.

Direct Selling in China

While sales growth through the direct selling channel is limited in the United States, companies like Avon and Mary Kay have effectively used this channel to sell products in less developed countries. Using the direct selling channel is particularly effective in less developed countries because an extensive infrastructure to supply stores is not required. Products are sent to hundreds of thousands of sales representatives in small villages. They pay for the products when they sell them.

The direct selling channel also is part of a movement around the world for women to have more economic independence. For example, Zhang Xiaoying, a 19-year-old woman from Guizhou, one of China's poorest regions, says, "I love the corporate culture of Mary Kay. This company teaches you to aspire to a higher level."

The direct selling channel is particularly effective in less developed areas that lack the infrastructure to support retail stores.

Before joining the company, many Mary Kay sales agents in China held low-paying jobs as secretaries, cashiers, and rural schoolteachers. Many were looking for a new focus in their lives. "Because my husband is a businessman, and he is busy, we talked less and less," says Lu Laidi, a Mary Kay sales director. "I felt my life was boring. I stayed home and barely dressed up."

The use of a direct selling channel has been controversial in China. Many direct sellers have been accused of operating sophisticated pyramid schemes and other sales swindles. In response to these concerns, China banned direct selling in 1998, saying that it was often a cover for "evil cults, secret societies and lawless and superstitious activities." In 2006, after heavy lobbying from American companies, China lifted its ban, and since then direct selling has grown into an $8 billion industry.

Sources: David Barboza, "Direct Selling Flourishes in China," *New York Times*, December 26, 2009; J. Alex Tarquinio, "Selling Beauty on a Global Scale," *New York Times*, November 1, 2008, p. B2.

Fluctuations in currency exchange rates can increase costs. For example, if the Indian rupee increases relative to the Canadian dollar, the cost of private-label merchandise produced in India and imported for sale into Canada will increase. If this increase occurs between the time the order is placed and when it is delivered, Canadian retailers will have to pay more for the merchandise than planned. Most retailers use financial instruments such as options and futures contracts to minimize the effects of currency fluctuations.

Tariffs, also known as *duties*, are taxes placed by a government on imports that increase the cost of merchandise imported from international sources. Import tariffs have been used to shield domestic manufacturers from foreign competition. Because tariffs raise the cost of imported merchandise, retailers have a strong incentive to use their political clout to reduce them.

Inventory turnover is likely to be lower when purchasing from suppliers outside the United States than from domestic suppliers, which will result in higher inventory carrying costs. Consider The Spoke bicycle store in Aspen, Colorado, which is buying Moots bicycles manufactured in Steamboat Springs, Colorado. The Spoke buyer knows that the lead time—the amount of time between the recognition that an order needs to be placed and the point at which the merchandise arrives in the store and is ready for sale—is usually two weeks, plus or minus three days. But if The Spoke ordered bikes from Italy, the lead time might be three months, plus or minus three weeks. Since lead times are longer, retailers using foreign sources must maintain larger inventories to ensure that merchandise is available when the customer wants it. Larger inventories mean larger inventory carrying costs.

tariffs Taxes placed by a government upon imports; also called *duties*.

DID YOU KNOW?

Twelve percent of China's exports to the United States are sent to Walmart. Walmart's purchases account for 1 percent of China's gross domestic product.[31]

International Human Resources Issues The legal-political system in countries often dictates the human resource management practices that retailers can use. For example, Canada has led the world in eliminating workplace discrimination. However, in Singapore it is perfectly legal to place an employment ad specifying that candidates must be male, between the ages of 25 and 40, and ethnic Chinese. In the Netherlands, a retailer can make a substantial reduction in its workforce only if it demonstrates to the government that the cutback is absolutely necessary. In addition, a Dutch retailer must develop a plan for the cutback, which must then be approved by unions and other involved parties.

In countries with a collectivist culture such as China and Japan, employees downplay individual desires and focus on the needs of the group. Thus, group-based evaluations and incentives are more effective in those countries.

Finally, the staffing of management positions in foreign countries raises a wide set of issues. Should management be local or should expatriates be used? How should the local managers or expatriates be selected, trained, and compensated? Cole Peterson, during his tenure as vice-president of the People Division of Walmart, said its biggest problem with international expansion was its lack of "human capital." Walmart makes every effort to replace expatriates with locals, and in every overseas country except China, its operations are now led by a non-American. Yet it is expanding faster than it can train people internally and has lost high-quality local managers to rivals.[33]

Global versus Multinational Retailers

A McDonald's in China looks the same as a McDonald's in Calgary or in Chicago: It has the same visual concept with the golden arches and the always popular Big Mac and fries. But worldwide, there may be some differences: In Germany, the restaurant looks the same but beer is added to the menu; and in Japan, the same predictable Big Mac and fries is accompanied by an unusual blue drink. The same holds true with The Gap and The Body Shop throughout the world. These retailers use a global strategy, which means that they replicate their standard retail format and centralized management throughout the world in each new market. Often the global retailer will develop franchising initiatives based on its standardized form of doing business in return for a substantial franchise fee. The global retailer can expand rapidly but it is learning little from its internationalization.[34]

Retailers who change their products and image to reflect the international marketplace use a multinational strategy. These retailers use a decentralized format, learning about the country's culture and changing their retail concept to adapt to cultural differences and cater to local market demands. Each country they enter enhances their knowledge portfolio. The greater the cultural diversity, the more likely is the multinational retailer to enter a joint venture with a company from the host country. The Spanish retailer Zara has opened at the Eaton Centre in Toronto. The trendy fashions are ordered daily with the newest fabrics and styles to appeal to the trend-conscious Canadian consumer. Zara's just-in-time small production facilities are able to cater to specific market demands with quick turnaround time.[35]

Global Location Issues

Many of the issues and procedures used for making global location decisions are the same as we have discussed in the previous chapter.[36] The retailer needs to decide on a region, a trade area within that region, and a specific site. The retailer still needs to examine competition, the population characteristics, traffic patterns, and the like. What makes global location decisions more difficult and potentially interesting is that those in charge of making these decisions are typically not as familiar with the nuances of the foreign location issues as they are with the same issues in their home country. Furthermore, national chains in Canada typically have close working relationships with a handful of major developers. Developers work with retailers on a strategic level while the malls are still on the drawing board.

Although similar developer–retailer relationships are growing worldwide, often retailers must deal with landlords directly—and cope with a confusing world of site requirements, red tape, and restrictions. For example, a retailer may be surprised to learn that the local government requires a $1-million key payment upfront. A landlord may demand a 25-year lease. And if there's to be construction, it's likely to be a slow, politically charged process.

Real estate selection is where many grand global designs ultimately succeed or fail. A retailer may devote

Wet Markets in Shanghai

Shanghai, with more than 23 million inhabitants, is the largest city by population in the world. It is a sophisticated international city, like New York, London, and Tokyo, with substantial influence in global commerce, culture, finance, media, fashion, technology, and transportation. It is a major financial centre and the busiest container port in the world. The major international food retailers (Walmart, Carrefour, Metro, and Tesco) have now opened more than 200 Western-style hypermarkets in Shanghai. In addition, there are more than 2000 modern supermarkets operated mostly by Chinese firms. But the majority of perishable goods (fish, meat, chicken, pork, vegetables, and fruit) are still sold in traditional wet markets.

Even though there are many modern supermarkets and hypermarkets in Shanghai, the majority of perishable groceries are still bought at traditional wet markets.

Wet markets are buildings divided into small stalls lined along narrow corridors with small, independent retailers selling perishables in the stalls. The retailers lease the stalls from market operators. They buy the perishables from various sources, including wholesale markets, rural merchants, and farmers' cooperatives, and then sort, clean, and package the perishables for sale to their customers. These markets are called "wet markets" because the concrete floor is constantly wet from the spraying of perishables and cleaning of live meat and fish. There are more than 900 wet markets in Shanghai.

The Chinese government would like to close all wet markets because they do not reflect the modern China and because they pose health risks due to poor hygiene. But Chinese urban consumers cross-format shop for groceries: They buy manufactured goods in supermarkets and hypermarkets but perishables in wet markets. Two factors contribute to this preference for wet markets.

First, Chinese consumers place great importance on freshness. Perishables sold at supermarkets and hypermarkets usually get to the store around 8 P.M. the night before and have been shelved for at least half a day before reaching consumers. At wet markets, vendors buy their perishables around 4 A.M. and constantly trim, spray, clean, and sort the perishables to keep them fresh. Also, wet-market vendors do not have or use refrigerators for storage; thus, they have to replenish their inventory with fresh supplies every day. The modern-format retailers simply cannot win the freshness contest.

Second, for logistical reasons, most Chinese consumers shop for groceries every day and buy just enough to prepare for that day's meals. In their small homes, the average kitchen size is about 60 square feet, leaving little room to store any items for extended periods, especially perishable foods that require refrigeration. Furthermore, though the automotive market is growing in China, many families still travel by other means. In Shanghai for example, bicycles (20 percent), buses (30 percent), and walking (40 percent) are more common means of transport for shopping trips. In these locations, the small wet markets provide far more convenient locations than larger supermarkets or hypermarkets.

Sources: "Buying the Store," *China Economic Review*, June 14, 2012; Louise Herring, Daniel Hui, Paul Morgan, and Caroline Tufft, *Inside China's Hypermarkets: Past and Prospects* (Hong Kong: McKinsey By McKinsey, 2012); and Qian Forrest Zhang and Zi Pan, *The Transformation of Urban Vegetable Retail in China: Wet Markets, Supermarkets, and Informal Markets in Shanghai*, Research Collection School of Social Sciences, 2012.

months to targeting a region—Latin America, for instance—before choosing a country to enter. From that point, a city must be chosen. But when it comes to picking an exact site within that city—a decision that often demands knowing local traffic flow, the most desirable side of a street, or urban development patterns—the decision is sometimes rushed and made without the right knowledge. As with many locations in Canada, particularly congested urban areas, if the retailer chooses the wrong side of the street, it may fail.

Costs can also be troublesome. Compared to North American locations, occupancy costs in cities such as

traffic flow The balance between a substantial number of cars and not so many that congestion impedes access to the store.

London, Paris, or Tokyo are extremely high. Retailers have to be extremely high-volume to survive. Real estate rental costs are 30 percent more in the U.K. than they are in Germany, which are 30 percent more than they are in the United States, which are 30 percent more than they are in Canada.

Real estate restrictions also complicate international location decisions. For instance, tough European laws make it difficult for big-box retailers to open large stores that have historically required a large piece of property. Solutions occasionally demand a little ingenuity and flexibility. Costco Wholesale's solution, for example, has been to modify store formats in some overseas markets—most notably, the adoption of two-level operations in Korea and Taiwan. Some retailers prefer to open locations within a mall setting, and for some, the bigger the mall, the better. See Exhibit 7–3 for a list of the world's largest shopping malls.

Although there may be a downturn in outlet centres in North America, their popularity is beginning to take off in other areas such as Japan and Europe. Japan is particularly attractive given its large population, love for American brands, and growing consumer enthusiasm for value retailing concepts. European growth is more problematic, however, given Western Europe's more restrictive planning environment, strong opposition by High Street (downtown) retailers,[39] and overall lower levels of enthusiasm for American brands. Compared to American outlet centres, the existing European centres are smaller, have fewer entertainment options, and have fewer well-known manufacturer outlets of European brands due to concern about channel conflict.

The Top 250 Global Retailers

Deloitte, in conjunction with *STORES* magazine, publishes an annual report on the Global Powers of Retailing. This report identifies the 250 largest retailers around the world based on publicly available data for the companies' fiscal year 2011 (see, for example, Exhibit 7–4). Exhibit 7–5 lists the ten largest global retailers in 2011 from this report. With worldwide retail sales estimated at US$4.271 trillion, an increase of 5.1 percent from 2011's top 250, with the top ten garnering 29 percent of the total top 250 sales.[40]

As a group, the ten largest global retailers have a much larger geographic footprint than the top 250 global retailers overall. These large retailers (see Exhibit 7–5 for list) operate on average in 16.7 countries, which is nearly two times as many as the average for the entire group of 250 retailers. The revenue from foreign operations, according to the Deloitte report, account for nearly one-third of the total top ten global retailers' retail revenue.[41]

Composition of the top ten remained the same as in the previous year with little to no movement. With a 6 percent revenue growth, retail giant Walmart is still the undisputed leader. The French retailer Carrefour maintained its number-two position despite a sales decline resulting from the spinoff of its Dia hard discount chain in July 2011. Although its revenue fell slightly, Metro was able to hang onto fourth place. Robust growth boosted Costco ahead of Schwarz, while Aldi overtook both Walgreen and The Home Depot on the back of a stronger euro against the U.S. dollar in 2011.

Walmart, which accounted for more than 10 percent of total top 250 revenue, acquired South Africa's Massmart in June 2011, its biggest deal in more than a decade. This will allow Walmart to widen its lead over its top ten rivals in the future.[42]

According to the study by Deloitte, the top 250 retailers continued to extend their global reach in 2011. Sixty-two percent (155) of the top 250 retailers operated in more than one country in 2011, and 82 percent of those retailers (127) operated in more than one sub-region. Forty of the top 250 retailers began operations in a new

exhibit 7–4 Top 250 Quick Stats, 2011

Quick Facts about the Top 250 Retailers in 2011

- $4.271 trillion: aggregate retail revenue of the top 250 retailers
- $17.085 billion: average size of the top 250 retailers
- $3.721 billion: minimum retail revenue required to be among the top 250 retailers
- 5.1%: composite year-over-year retail revenue growth
- 5.4%: composite compound annual growth rate in retail revenue from 2006 to 2011
- 3.8%: composite net profit margin
- 5.9%: composite return on assets
- 23.8%: percent of top 250 retail revenue from foreign operations
- 9.0: average number of countries in which top 250 companies have retail operations

Source: *Global Powers of Retailing 2013: Retail Beyond*, Deloitte, January 2013, p. G12, http://www.deloitte.com/assets/Dcom-Australia/Local%20Assets/Documents/Industries/Consumer%20business/Deloitte_Global_Powers_of_Retail_2013.pdf (accessed November 18, 2013).

exhibit 7–5 Ten Largest Global Retailers and the Ten Canadian Companies That Fall in the Top 250 Global Retailers: 2011

Retail Revenue Rank (FY11)	Name of Company	Country of Origin	2011 Retail Revenue (US$M)	2011 Group Revenue[1] (US$M)	2011 Group Net Income (US$M)	Dominant Operational Format	# Countries of Operation 2011
1	Walmart Stores, Inc.	U.S.	446 950	446 950	16 387	Hypermarket/Supercentre/Superstore	28
2	Carrefour S.A.	France	113 197	115 277	563	Hypermarket/Supercentre/Superstore	33
3	Tesco PLC	U.K.	101 574	103 244	4502	Hypermarket/Supercentre/Superstore	13
4	Metro AG	Germany	92 905	92 905	1032	Cash & Carry/Warehouse Club	33
5	The Kroger Co.	U.S.	90 374	90 374	596	Supermarket	1
6	Costco Wholesale Corp.	U.S.	88 915	88 915	1542	Cash & Carry/Warehouse Club	9
7	Schwarz Unternehmens Treuhand KG	Germany	87 841	87 841	n/a	Discount Store	26
8	Aldi Einkauf GmbH & Co. oHG	Germany	73 375 (est.)	73 375 (est.)	n/a	Discount Store	17
9	Walgreen Co.	U.S.	72 184	72 184	2714	Drugstore/Pharmacy	2
10	Home Depot, Inc.	U.S.	70 395	70 395	3883	Home Improvement	5
31	Loblaw Companies Ltd.	Canada	31 070*	31 624*	778	Hypermarket/Supercentre/Superstore	1
43	Alimentation Couche-Tard Inc.	Canada	22 998	22 998	458	Convenience/Forecourt Store	10
58	Empire Co. Ltd. / Sobeys	Canada	16 135	16 330	354	Supermarket	1
86	Metro Inc.	Canada	11 595*	11 595*	392	Supermarket	1
94	Shoppers Drug Mart Corp.	Canada	10 584	10 584	621	Drugstore/Pharmacy	1
107	Canadian Tire Corp., Ltd.	Canada	9475*	10 511*	473	Other Specialty	1
122	Katz Group Canada Ltd.	Canada	8710 (est.)	8710 (est.)	n/a	Drugstore/Pharmacy	1
188	RONA Inc.	Canada	4862*	4862*	–76	Home Improvement	1
236	Hudson's Bay Co.	Canada	3889	3889	1464	Department Store	2
242	Liquor Control Board of Ontario	Canada	3808 (est.)	4748*	1671	Other Specialty	1

[1] Revenue and net income for the parent company or group may include results from non-retail operations
* Revenue includes wholesale and retail sales

country in 2011 (the same number as in 2010), with a combined total of 107 new market entries (up from 88 in 2010) involving 72 different countries (57 in 2010). It is important to point out that these numbers are based on the information available to Deloitte at the time of the study and may not capture all activity. The numbers also reflect new bricks-and-mortar retail activity only, except for companies that are primarily non-store retailers.

Of the four methods of market entry Deloitte tracked for this analysis, franchising was the predominant method employed in 2011, as was also the case in 2010. Franchising accounted for 40 percent of the activity (43 new market entries). All of the retailers that entered a Middle Eastern country for the first time in 2011 used a franchising model. Organic growth was the next most frequent

market entry method (38 times). Retailers that entered Western European countries for the first time in 2011 did so mostly through organic growth (11 of 15 times). Acquisitions accounted for 23 new market entries. Joint ventures were established as the market entry method on only three occasions.

Perhaps not surprisingly, the study indicated that 80 percent of the retailers that entered a new market in 2011 (32 of 40 companies) were from mature, saturated markets: the United States (15), Japan (5), or one of the big three European economies (12). Almost half of the new market entries involved fashion retailers looking to extend their brands around the globe. Most pursued a franchise strategy, viewing it as a fast, low-capital, lower-risk way to expand internationally.[43]

The majority of the largest global retailers remain involved in the food sector and other fast-moving consumer goods. More than half of the top 250 companies (134) are fast-moving consumer good retailers accounting for more than two-thirds of top 250 sales. In addition to being the most numerous these retailers are also the biggest with average 2011 retail sales of US$21 billion. Supermarkets are the most common store format operated by 103 of the top 250 retailers.

The number of U.S companies in the top 250 and their share of sales dropped down from 87 retailers in 2007 to 84 in 2008, and to 76 in 2011. Walmart alone represents 10 percent of the top 250 sales. As in the past, six of the top ten retailers are from the U.S., three are from Germany, and one from France.

Canada represents 4 percent share of top 250 retailers by region/country, and 2.9 percent share of top 250 sales by region/country, 2011. Canadian-controlled retail remains relatively strong in the Canadian retail sector as a whole with about 60 percent of Canada's total retail sales coming from domestic retailers, 38 percent of sales from American firms, and the remaining 2 percent coming from other foreign firms such as Zara and H&M.[47]

Historically, a large consumer market and relatively abundant land have kept many Canadian retailers from seeking global expansion. But with domestic markets reaching saturation, companies are seeking opportunities abroad. Still, the North American companies have not caught up to the largest European firms, which operate in an average of seven countries.

Structure of Retailing and Distribution Channels Around the World

The nature of retailing and distribution channels in North America is unique. Some critical differences between Canadian, U.S., European, and Japanese retailing and distribution systems are summarized in Exhibit 7–6.

The U.S. distribution system has the greatest retail density and the greatest concentration of large retail firms. Some people think that North America is over-stored. Many retail firms are large enough to operate their own warehouses, eliminating the need for wholesalers. The fastest-growing types of retailers sell through large stores with over 20 000 square feet. The combination of large stores and large firms results in a very efficient distribution system.

In contrast, the Japanese distribution system is characterized by small stores operated by relatively small firms and a large independent wholesale industry. To make daily deliveries efficiently to these small retailers, merchandise often moves through three distributors between the manufacturer and retailer. This difference in efficiency results in a much larger percentage of the Japanese labour force being employed in distribution and retailing than in Canada.

The European distribution system falls between North American and Japanese systems on this continuum of efficiency and scale, but the northern, southern, and central parts of Europe have to be distinguished, with northern European retailing being the most similar to the North American system. In northern Europe, concentration levels are high—in some national markets, 80 percent or more of sales in a sector such as food or home improvements are accounted for by five or fewer firms. Southern European retailing is more fragmented across all sectors. For example, traditional farmers' market retailing is still important in some sectors, operating alongside large "big-box" formats. In central Europe, the privatization of retail trade has resulted in a change from a previously highly concentrated government controlled structure to one of extreme fragmentation characterized by many small family-owned retailers.

Some factors that have created these differences in distribution systems in the major markets are:

- **Social and political objectives.** A top priority of the Japanese economic policy is to reduce unemployment by protecting small businesses such as neighbourhood retailers. Japan's *Large Scale Retail Stores Law* regulates the locations and openings of stores of over 5000 square feet. Several European countries have also passed laws protecting small retailers. For example, in 1996, France tightened its existing laws to constrain the opening of stores of over 3000 square feet. European governments have also passed strict zoning laws to preserve green spaces, protect town centres, and inhibit the development of large-scale retailing in the suburbs.

- **Geography.** The population density in Canada is much lower than in Europe and Japan. Thus, Europe and Japan have less low-cost real estate available for building large stores.

- **Market size.** The North American retail market is larger than Japan or any single European country. In Europe, distribution centres and retail chains typically operate within a single country and are therefore not able to achieve the scale economies of North American retailers serving a broader customer base. Even with the euro and other initiatives designed to make trade within European countries easier and more efficient, barriers to trade still exist that are not found in the Canadian and American marketplaces.

Counterfeiting Is a Global Threat

Counterfeit merchandise is imitation or fake, usually made with the intent to deceptively represent its contents or origins. Counterfeiting usually involves forged currency or documents, but can also describe clothing, software, electronic stock shares or certificates, pharmaceuticals, watches, or more recently, auto parts, cars, and motorcycles. Often this results in patent infringement and trademark infringement. Widespread use of counterfeit products undermines the North American system of standards, testing, and certification that is designed to protect consumers, retailers, manufacturers, and regulators.

The term bootleg is more often used when there is little or no attempt at hiding the fact that this is a counterfeit product, as in CDs, DVDs, computer software, and toys. The user is fully aware of its illegal status. By contrast, a knockoff item may imitate a well-known brand, may be sold for a lower price, and may be of inferior quality, but there is usually no attempt to deceive the buyer or infringe upon the original product.

The appearance of counterfeit products in North America has increased dramatically in recent years. According to Manny Gratz, manager of Anti-Counterfeiting & Intellectual Property Enforcement, the manufacture and distribution of counterfeit products have been linked to organized crime. He feels that people who deliberately choose to buy counterfeit products are not victims; instead they support the criminally deceptive practices of counterfeiters by creating a built-in market for their goods.

counterfeit merchandise Goods that are made and sold without permission of the owner of a trademark, a copyright, or a patented invention that is legally protected in the country where it is marketed.

bootleg The sale of imitation goods where there is little or no attempt at hiding the fact that the product is counterfeit.

knockoff A copy of the latest styles displayed at designer fashion shows and sold in exclusive specialty stores. These copies are sold at lower prices through retailers targeting a broader market.

DID YOU KNOW?

Mountain Equipment Co-op has more than 2 million members in 192 countries.[48]

exhibit 7–6 Comparison of Retailing and Distribution Channels across the World

| | | | EUROPE | | | | | | | | |
| | | | NORTHWEST | | | | SOUTHERN | | CENTRAL | | |
Characteristic	Canada	U.S.	U.K.	Belgium	France	Germany	Spain	Italy	Hungary	Czech	Japan
Concentration (% of retail sales in category by top three firms)	High	High	High				Low		Very Low		Medium
Number of outlets per 1000 people	Medium	Medium	Medium				High		Low		High
Retail density (sq. ft. of retail space per person)	High	High	Medium				Low		Low		Medium
Store size (% of retail sales made in stores over 10 000 square feet)	High	High	Medium				Low		Low		Low
Role of wholesaling (wholesale sales as a % of retail sales)	Low	Low	Medium				Medium		High		High
Distribution Inefficiency (average maintained markup–distribution costs as a % of retail price)	Low	Low	Medium				High		High		High

SUMMARY

This chapter provides an overview for understanding international retailing. Understanding the macro-environment becomes increasingly critical in making strategic decisions to expand internationally. Questions about the local economy, legal environment, technological capabilities, consumer behaviour, and the retail competition must be answered. Business laws and regulations will not only impact the ability to conduct business but will also dictate how to function operationally in a global marketplace. The macro-environment is different for each country and must be constantly monitored.

Issues of global location strategy will impact retailing success or failure on a day-to-day basis. International retailers must be intimately aware of the cultural climate in domestic markets and respond to the market demands of the micro-environment. Understanding the importance of place, including the retail location and store environment, product mix, price, and management decisions is critical. Retailing is geographically tied and must therefore gain insight into the direct-to-customer link.

Global retailers will develop strength through centralized management and a standardized image, whereas multinational retailers gain success by adapting to the local environment through decentralized management and a more flexible approach to retail store design.

KEY TERMS

adaptability

bootleg

counterfeit merchandise

direct investment

financial resources

global culture

global strategy

globally sustainable competitive advantage

joint venture

knockoff

multinational strategy

strategic alliance

tariffs

traffic flow

1. INTERNET EXERCISE Go to the websites for Walmart (**www.walmartstores.com**), Carrefour (**www.carrefour.com**), Royal Ahold (**www.ahold.com**), and Metro AG (**www.metro.de**). Which chain has the most global strategy? Justify your answer.

2. INTERNET EXERCISE Choose your favourite national retail chain. Pick a country for it to enter. Using information found on the Internet, collect information on that country and the retailer. Develop a report that analyzes whether the retailer should enter the country, and if so, how it should do so.

3. INTERNET EXERCISE

a) Go to **www.counterfeitchic.com**. Review recent blogs.

b) Read the paper by Renee Richardson Gosline, "The Real Value of Fakes," at http://gradworks.umi.com/3371273.pdf, the article by Meg Tirrell, "Fake Louis Vuitton Bags Look Fake Without a Tony Aura (Update1)," at http://www.bloomberg.com/apps/news?pid=newsarchive&sid=a2goSFXqnqiw, and the blog entry by Felix Salmon, "Those weirdly persistent counterfeiting statistics," at http://blogs.reuters.com/felix-salmon/2009/12/06/those-weirdly-persistent-counterfeiting-statistics. Discuss the economic impact of counterfeiting, taking the unique perspective and research findings of Gosline into consideration.

Explain the economic impact of counterfeiting.

DISCUSSION QUESTIONS AND PROBLEMS

1. Read "IKEA: Bringing its Philosophy to a World Market" at the beginning of the chapter and visit www.ikea.com.

   a) Explain why IKEA has had such strong appeal in the global marketplace.

   b) Why does the philosophy "one size fits all" not work in global markets? Suggest situations where this policy is problematic.

2. Explain how global culture can impact the success or failure of a global retailer such as Toys "R" Us.

3. What advantages does a multinational retailer such as Avon have over a global retailer?

4. Why are global companies such as McDonald's Restaurants gaining worldwide customer appeal?

5. Explain the strengths and weaknesses of global companies versus multinational retailers.

6. Why is a joint venture alliance often a favourable approach to facilitating an international retail venture?

7. Why is it important to understand the macro-environment when making decisions about an international retail venture?

8. Explain the importance of understanding the micro-environment when planning to open a retail store in an international location.

9. Complete a research study to determine what laws and regulations exist for opening a retail store in the following countries:
- China
- India
- Russia
- Mexico

10. Choose a retailer that you believe would be, but is not yet, successful in other countries. Explain why you think it would be successful.

Practise and learn online with Connect.

financial strategy

LEARNING OBJECTIVES

Lo1 Explore why retailers need to evaluate their performance.

Lo2 Identify the measures retailers use to assess their performance.

Lo3 Explore the strategic profit model and examine how it is used.

Lo4 Examine how retail strategy is reflected in retailers' financial objectives.

SPOTLIGHT ON RETAILING

easyhome Ltd.

easyhome Ltd. offers Canadian customers alternatives that may not be available from other retailers or financial institutions. *easyhome* operates through three business units: *easyhome* Leasing, *easyhome* Franchising, and *easyfinancial* Services.

easyhome Leasing is Canada's largest merchandise leasing retailer and provides its customers with access to brand-name household goods (furnishings, appliances, and electronic products) under weekly or monthly leasing agreements. They provide lease programs for those customers who wish to lease merchandise on a short-term basis, to try a product before making a purchase decision, or to obtain a product they may not otherwise be able to have as a result of being either cash or credit constrained. The retailer began operations in 1990 and currently operates 195 corporate *easyhome* Leasing stores and nine consolidated franchise locations. *easyhome* Leasing is the company's largest business unit, generating $160 million in revenues, or 80 percent of total revenues, in 2012.

easyhome Franchising was launched in 2007 with the goal of helping the company grow faster and capitalize on the potential for *easyhome* Leasing in the United States. The franchising business was built around the same operational strategy as the company's core leasing business. The company believes that the U.S. marketplace provides an attractive opportunity for growth as it is estimated to be a $6 billion market that is highly fragmented, with approximately half the market served by small, independent operators and a population of consumers that have a good understanding of merchandise leasing. Franchise revenue increased 37 percent in 2012, contributing $1.6 million to the total *easyhome* revenue.

easyfinancial Services is a lending alternative that fills a gap in the consumer finance market by offering products that are more affordable than payday loans and more accessible than traditional bank loans. *easyfinancial* began operations in 2006 and initially developed using a kiosk that was physically located within an existing *easyhome* Leasing location. By 2011, the company determined that the *easyfinancial* business would scale more successfully by operating out of stand-alone locations that were physically separated from the *easyhome* Leasing stores. As of December 2012, the company operated 82 kiosk locations and 17 stand-alone locations as well as one national loan office. *easyfinancial* grew its loan portfolio by 49 percent during 2012, increased revenues 54 percent, and contributed 19 percent of total *easyhome* revenues.

David Ingram took over as chief operating officer of RTO Enterprises (now *easyhome* Ltd.) in late 2000. The then 100-store rent-to-own company had grown rapidly through acquisitions, but was relying on extremely expensive debt for funding and simply wasn't generating enough revenue to keep it in business. He saved the company from imminent bankruptcy by initiating a rights issue that allowed existing shareholders to reinvest at a very low share price. The proceeds—some $10 million—went to pay down high-interest debt and positioned the company for growth.

Ingram and his management team isolated three key factors that had led to RTO's financial situation. First, they determined that, due to growth through acquisition, the company did not have a cohesive brand identity as it had six different brands across 100 stores. The six different brands had nothing particularly unique about them as the product offered was the same, the pricing was the same, and the service(s) offered was the same. They determined that it was an inefficient strategy as they could not market a single brand message with six different brands in the marketplace.

The team worked on building the single, unified brand we see today by looking at the products sold; the name, organization, and location of stores; and consumer insights through focus groups. The team developed the company's new name, *easyhome*, by writing down the key words used by focus group participants. According to Ingram, two words kept recurring: "easy," because customers wanted something that would make life easier for them, and "home," the cherished place where they could be with family. "We put those two words together and we came up with *easyhome*," says Ingram.

Second, the management team determined that customers did not want access to second-tier merchandise simply because they were looking for alternative payment opportunities. To grow the business, the team seriously addressed consumers' desire to access premium-brand goods, particularly electronics. The team worked with brand leaders to become suppliers. Today, the company offers brands such as Ashley, Dynasty, Eztia, and Serta mattresses; Samsung and Whirlpool appliances; Sony, Samsung, LG, and Toshiba home electronics; and Dell, HP, Acer, and Toshiba computers. In order to keep the higher-priced merchandise manageable, *easyhome* offers customers the flexibility to pay for products weekly, bi-weekly, or monthly over 18 to 36 months.

Finally, Ingram and his team in the beginning of 2002 considered the look and feel of the stores, from window presentation to signage, lighting, and even location. They determined that stores required a facelift to bring them up to date and connect with *easyhome*'s average customer. In order to appeal to young to middle-aged women with kids, they incorporated wide aisles that could accommodate strollers and revamped stores to make them brightly lit, secure, and inviting with a modern appeal. "Our customers wanted to have the same shopping experience as they'd expect from a decent furniture retail or electronics store," says Ingram. "They wanted a place they could feel proud of, where they wouldn't worry about bringing young children."

The new *easyhome* brand (name, in-store look, and pricing structure) was tested in ten stores and was rolled out to all (110) stores in April 2003. The rebranding effort took three months as Ingram believed that a drawn-out rollout would not allow the company to get the momentum and traction they required from the rebrand.

Since Ingram took over the top spot, the company has almost doubled in size, the addition of the highly profitable *easyfinancial* loan-issuing business unit is expecting revenue growth of between 8 and 12 percent for 2013, and the *easyhome* leasing franchise concept has proven to be a robust business opportunity to increase North American market presence. Overall, the company has achieved 11 consecutive years of revenue growth.

Sources: *Annual Report 2011, easyhome* Ltd., March 6, 2012; Camilla Cornell, "Easyhome: A Forward Regression," *Canadian Retailer*, Spring 2012, Volume 22, Issue 2, pp. 52–54.

Financial decisions are an integral component in every aspect of a retailer's strategy. In this chapter, we look at financial tools retailers use to measure and evaluate their performance.

Retail store owners need to know how well they are doing because they want to be successful and stay in business. Retailers are aware of how many customers enter their stores and count up the receipts at the end of the day to see how much has been sold. Unfortunately, these simple measures aren't enough. For instance, sometimes a retailer finds that sales are good, but still can't afford to buy new merchandise. When things are good, they often don't think about their retail strategy. But when things go bad, the retailer thinks about nothing else.

Based on strategies the retailer set, it is important to establish quantifiable performance objectives. If the retailer is achieving objectives, changes in strategy or implementation programs aren't needed. But if the performance information indicates that objectives aren't being met, the retailer needs to reanalyze plans and programs. For example, after reviewing the accountant's financial report, the retailer might conclude that she is not earning a fair return on the time and money invested in the stores. Based on this evaluation, she might consider changing the strategy by appealing to a different target market and lowering the average price point of the merchandise in order to improve the turnover rate.

Objectives and Goals

As we discussed in Chapter 4, the first step in the strategic planning process involves articulating the retailer's strategy and the scope of activities it plans to undertake to be successful. Three types of objectives that a retailer might have are (1) financial, (2) societal, and (3) personal.[1]

Financial Objectives

When assessing financial performance, most people focus on profits: What were the retailer's profits or profit margin (profit as a percentage of sales) last year, and what will they be this year and into the future? But the appropriate financial performance measure is not profits but rather return on investment (ROI). For example, Kelly Bradford, the owner of Gifts To Go, whom we introduced in Chapter 4, set a financial objective of making a profit of at least $100 000 a year, but she really needs to consider how much she needs to invest to make the $100 000, the profit she desires from her investment.

Think of the decisions you might make when planning how to invest some money you might have. In making this investment, you want to determine the highest percentage return you can—the highest interest rate or greatest percentage increase in stock price—not the absolute amount of the return. You can always get a greater absolute return by investing more money. For example, Kelly Bradford would be delighted if she made $100 000 and only needed to invest $500 000 (a 20 percent ROI) in the business but disappointed if she had to invest $2 000 000 to make $100 000 profit (a 5 percent ROI). A commonly used measure of the return on investment is return on assets (ROA), or the profit return on all the assets possessed by the firm.

Societal Objectives

Societal objectives are related to broader issues about providing benefits to society—making the world a better place to live. For example, retailers might be concerned about providing employment opportunities for people in a particular area or more specifically for minorities or persons with disabilities. Other societal objectives might include offering people unique merchandise, such as environmentally sensitive products, providing an innovative service to improve personal health, such as weight reduction programs, or sponsoring community events.

For example, McDonald's values diversity among its employees and suppliers. The company ensures diversity among its corporate employees by including it in the business planning process. "As business units and corporate departments put together their business plans, diversity is included in them. We have diversity business planning guidelines that we provide to the McDonald's leadership so that they're incorporated in the strategic planning process," explains chief diversity officer Pat Harris. McDonald's also values diversity in its supply chain and has been recognized by *Fortune* magazine as the "top purchaser from minority suppliers, spending more than $3 billion a year, or 27 percent of its total, at minority-owned firms."[2]

return on assets (ROA) Net profit after taxes divided by total assets.

Performance with respect to societal objectives is more difficult to measure than financial objectives. But explicit societal goals can be set, such as the percentage of executives or store managers that are women or minorities or the percentage of profits donated to worthy charities.

Personal Objectives

Many retailers, particularly owners of small, independent businesses, have important personal objectives, including self-gratification, status, and respect. For example, Lululemon Athletica believes that its core values and distinctive corporate culture allow it to attract passionate and motivated employees who are driven to succeed and share its vision. Lululemon provides its employees with a supportive, goal-oriented environment and encourages them to reach their full professional, health, and personal potential. The company offers programs such as personal development workshops and goal-coaching to assist its employees in realizing their long-term personal objectives.[3]

Whereas societal and personal objectives are important to some retailers, financial objectives should be the primary focus of managers of publicly held retailers—retailers whose stocks are listed on and bought through a stock market. Investors in publicly held companies, namely, the people who buy stock in a company, are primarily interested in getting a return on their investment, and the managers of these companies must have the same objectives as the investors. Therefore, the remaining sections of this chapter focus on financial objectives and the factors affecting a retailer's ability to achieve financial goals. (Retailing View 8.1 discusses the impact of private equity investment in retailers.)

Ratio Analysis

In order to fully appreciate the concepts of finance, it is necessary to understand material from the accounting area. The analysis of a retailer's financial statements—income statement and balance sheet—is based on the knowledge and use of ratios. The income statement measures the profitability of a retailer over a time period (quarter or year) while the balance sheet indicates the retailer's holdings and obligations at a point in time (usually fiscal year end).[4]

A ratio is a numerator divided by a denominator. The resulting calculation could be a ratio of one of three types: (1) a percent (e.g., ROA, net profit or expense), (2) a multiplier (e.g., asset turnover, inventory turnover), and (3) a number of days. It is important to understand the ratio

Private Equity Firms Invest in Retailers

Private equity firms have been making significant investments in retail firms. For example, Blackstone Group and Bain Capital teamed up to buy the craft store chain Michaels for $6 billion; KKR and several other firms bought Toys "R" Us for $6.6 billion; Texas Pacific, with its partners, bought Neiman Marcus for $5.1 billion; and Leonard Green & Partners bought The Container Store.

Private equity firms are firms that invest their money and the money of others, such as union pension funds and university endowments. Rather than buying stock in companies, private equity investors buy the entire company from its stockholders, improve the efficiency of the firm (often by hiring new senior managers), and then sell the acquired company after the acquisition. Because the companies are not traded on any stock exchange, the company can take a long-term perspective toward improving the firm's operations since it does not have to issue the quarterly reports required by government securities overseers. The managers of the acquired firms thus can reengineer a business away from Wall Street's ceaseless scrutiny of monthly comparable store sales and quarterly growth in earnings.

Private equity firms find retailers attractive investments because many of them have strong cash flows and undervalued assets and respond quickly to efficiency improvements and changes in strategic direction. Whereas the typical small investor focuses on profits and return on assets, private equity firms are interested in cash flow—the money that the retailer generates from its operations. A company with a higher cash flow reduces the risk of bankruptcy and provides money to invest in improving efficiencies, such as installing information systems or remodelling stores.

Retailers frequently have undervalued assets, such as well-known private-label brands, leases for space in attractive locations, or the land on which their stores are located. A private equity firm can sell these assets after it acquires a retailer or use the assets as collateral to get loans. For example, a private equity firm might sell the rights to use a well-known private-label brand to a company that would license the brand to other firms. Thus, the whole of the retailer is often less than the sum of its parts.

The recession and the accompanying credit crisis have dampened private equity firms' interest in retail acquisitions. The decline in consumer spending has made it difficult to make money on core operating businesses. In the past, many of these acquisitions were financed with short-term acquisition loans, which were meant to be eventually replaced with permanent financing. But private equity firms have had trouble getting permanent loans since late 2007. Finally, the dramatic drop in real estate values and increasing vacancies in the retail sector have taken away the safety net created by the undervalued real estate.

Sources: Elaine Misonzhnik, "Private Equity Racks Up Checkered Record in Retail Buyouts," *Retail Traffic*, June 29, 2009; Marcus Leroux, "Private Equity Shrugs Off Its Big Image as a Big Bad Wolf Stalking the High Street," *The Times*, November 2, 2009; Dan Freed, "Stocking Up: Why Buyout Firms Love Retail," *Investment Dealers' Digest*, July 23, 2007, pp. 16–20.

---

cross-sectional ratio analysis The analysis of a financial ratio of a company with the same ratio of different companies in the same industry.

time-series analysis A comparison of a variable to itself over time.

to know the unit of the answer. For example, you do not want to calculate a ratio of .59 and convert it to a percent when it is supposed to be a multiplier (asset turnover).

Ratio analysis is more than just the application of a formula to financial data, it is "the measure of the inter-relationship between different sections of the financial statements, which then is compared with the budgeted or forecasted results, prior year results"[5] and or industry results. In other words, it is the interpretation of the ratio value that is important.

There are three types of ratio comparisons that can be made: cross-sectional, time-series, or a combination of the two. A cross-sectional ratio analysis is where a retailer compares its company's ratios to another company's or to the industry ratios. It is important to note that cross-sectional ratios must be calculated for the same time period—the same year or quarter—to be relevant. Time-series analysis evaluates performance over time. Retailers would compare ratios for the most recent fiscal year or quarter with previous ratios to determine whether they are meeting financial objectives. By using time-series comparisons, retailers can identify developing trends and use the knowledge of these trends to assist in future planning. The third type of ratio comparison is one that combines cross-sectional and time-series analyses. By combining these two analyses, the retailer can evaluate its performance over time as well as assess its performance against the industry average.[6]

Overview: Strategic Profit Model

_{LO2}

The **strategic profit model**, illustrated in Exhibit 8–1, is a method for summarizing the factors found in the income statement and balance sheet that affect a firm's financial performance as measured by return on assets. Return on assets (ROA) determines how much profit can be generated from the retailer's investment in assets. The model decomposes ROA into two components: (1) net profit margin and (2) asset turnover. The **net profit margin** is simply how much profit (after tax) a firm makes divided by its net sales. Thus, it reflects the profits generated from each dollar of sales. If a retailer's net profit margin is 5 percent, it makes $.05 for every dollar of merchandise or services it sells.

Asset turnover is the retailer's net sales divided by its assets. This financial measure assesses the productivity of a firm's investment in its assets and indicates how many sales dollars are generated by each dollar of assets. Thus, if a retailer's asset turnover is 3.0, it generates $3 in sales for each dollar invested in the firm's assets.

The retailer's ROA is determined by multiplying the two components together:

$$\frac{\text{Net profit}}{\text{Net sales}} \times \frac{\text{Net sales}}{\text{Total assets}} = \frac{\text{Net profit}}{\text{Total assets}}$$

Net profit margin × Asset turnover = Return on assets (ROA)

exhibit 8–1 Components of the Strategic Profit Model

These two components of the strategic profit model illustrate that return on assets (ROA) is determined by two sets of activities, profit margin management and asset management, and that a high ROA can be achieved by various combinations of net profit margin and asset turnover.

Specifically, retailers have two paths available to achieve a high level of performance: the profit path and the turnover path. Different retailers, however, pursue different strategies, resulting in different types of financial performance (see Retailing View 8.2). The two paths are combined into the strategic profit model to illustrate that retailers using very different strategies and financial performance characteristics can both be financially successful. As a vehicle for discussion, we'll compare the financial performance of two very different retailers: Birks (a national jewellery store chain) and Walmart (the world's largest retailer).

Then we will discuss how retailers set performance objectives and how different performance measures are used throughout the organization. For a description of activity-based costing and how it is used to make retailing decisions, see Appendix 8A on Connect.

We begin our examination of corporate-level performance measures by looking at the strategic profit model.

		PROFIT PATH		**TURNOVER PATH**
Return on assets (ROA)	=	Net profit margin	×	Asset turnover
	=	$\dfrac{\text{Net profit}}{\text{Net sales}}$	×	$\dfrac{\text{Net sales}}{\text{Total assets}}$
	=	$\dfrac{\text{Net profit}}{\text{Total assets}}$		

To illustrate how the strategic profit model works, consider the two very different hypothetical retailers in Exhibit 8–3. La Madeline Bakery has a net profit margin of 1 percent and asset turnover of ten times, resulting in a return on assets of 10 percent. The profit margin is low due to the competitive nature of this commodity-type business. Asset turnover is relatively high, because the firm doesn't have its own credit card system (no accounts receivable). Also, it rents its store, so fixed assets are relatively low, and it has a very fast inventory turnover—in fact, its inventory turns every day!

On the other hand, Kalame Jewellery Store has a net profit margin of 10 percent and an asset turnover of one time, again resulting in a return on assets of

strategic profit model (SPM)
A tool used for planning a retailer's financial strategy based on both margin management (net profit margin), asset management (asset turnover), and financial leverage management (financial leverage ratio). Using the SPM, a retailer's objective is to achieve a target return on owners' equity.

net profit margin
The profit (after tax) a firm makes divided by its net sales.

asset turnover
Net sales divided by total assets.

Dollarama and Nordstrom: Retailers Targeting Customers at the Opposite Ends of the Income Distribution Spectrum

Dollarama and Nordstrom both have a high ROA but they achieve this high level of financial performance (see Exhibit 8–2) with significantly different retail strategies. Canadian-owned and -operated since the first Dollarama store opened in 1992 in Matane, Quebec, Dollarama is a value retailer with over 700 stores across the country, employing nearly 15 000 people. The firm has differentiated itself from other value retailers by offering a more consistent product selection, which includes everyday household needs and a selection of nationally branded products, as well as an assortment of unique and seasonal items. Merchandise is sold in individual or multiple units at select fixed price points up to $3. Stores are all corporately managed, providing a consistent shopping experience, and nearly all are located in high-traffic areas, such as strip malls and shopping centres in various locations including metropolitan areas, mid-sized cities, and small towns. Dollarama continues to pursue its original vision of operating relatively convenient-sized (average

9905 square feet), self-service, no-frills store environments to offer a compelling value proposition on a wide variety of everyday merchandise to a broad base of customers.

Nordstrom is an upscale department store chain in the United States. It operates over 115 Nordstrom department stores, its online store at www.nordstrom.com, and more than 100 Nordstrom Rack off-price stores in 30 states. Its other retail channels include its online private-sale subsidiary HauteLook, its two Jeffrey boutiques, one philanthropic treasure and bond store, and one clearance store that operates under the name Last Chance. The company also owns a credit segment that includes its wholly owned federal savings bank, Nordstrom fsb, through which it provides a private-label credit card, two Nordstrom VISA credit cards, and a debit card.

Nordstrom is now set to move across the U.S. border to establish its presence in Canada. In September 2012, the company announced that it had identified four ideal locations for Nordstrom stores, which include premier

exhibit 8–2 Retail Strategy Comparison: Dollarama versus Nordstrom

Dollarama (2011)			Nordstrom (2011)		
Income Statement	**Balance Sheet**	**Key Stats and Ratios**	**Income Statement**	**Balance Sheet**	**Key Stats and Ratios**
Revenue: $1602	Inventory: $315	Net profit margin: 10.82%	Revenue: $10 877	Inventory: $1148	Net profit margin: 6.28%
Cost of goods: $1002	Total assets: $1407	Operating margin: 16.34%	Cost of goods: $6592	Total assets: $8491	Operating margin: 11.48%
Gross profit: $600	Total liabilities: $512	Return on assets: 12.76%	Gross profit: $4285	Total liabilities: $6535	Return on assets: 8.56%
SG&A: $305	Total equity: $894	Return on equity: 21.34%	SG&A: $3036	Total equity: $1956	Return on equity: 34.35%
Income before tax: $245		Employees: 14 824	Income before tax: $1119		Employees: 56 500
Income after tax: $173			Income after tax: $683		

Note: SG&A refers to selling, general, and administrative expenses. All figures are in $ millions, except for margins and employee numbers.

shopping malls in Calgary, Ottawa, Toronto, and Vancouver. Three of the holdings, Pacific Centre in Vancouver, Calgary's Chinook Centre, and Rideau Centre in Ottawa, were at the time of the announcement occupied by Sears Holdings Corporation. The fourth location at Toronto's Sherway Gardens is a new construction.

These Nordstrom stores are scheduled to be open to the Canadian public starting in fall 2014, with the first opening scheduled to take place at the Chinook Centre in Calgary. This two-level store will be spread over a space of about 140 000 square feet. Following this, the company will open another two-level 157 000 square-foot store at the Rideau Centre in Ottawa in spring 2015. The company's third Canadian two-level store is slated to open in fall 2016 at the Sherway Gardens in Toronto, encompassing an area of 138 000 square feet. Nordstrom has not yet scheduled the opening date for its fourth and largest Canadian store at the Pacific Centre in Vancouver. This three-level store will be spread across an area of 230 000 square feet.

John W. Nordstrom opened the first Nordstrom store in 1887 in Seattle, which continues to be Nordstrom's headquarters and the site of its flagship store. While the initial store was a shoe retailer, today the stores also sell clothing, accessories, handbags, jewellery, cosmetics, fragrances, and, in some locations, home furnishings. However, Nordstrom continues to carry an extraordinarily deep and broad assortment of shoes, about 15 000 SKUs in a typical department store.

Nordstrom is known for its outstanding customer service. Its customer-centric organizational culture is epitomized by its "handbook" that is given to new employees. The original handbook was a single 5- by 8-inch grey card containing 75 words:

WELCOME TO NORDSTROM

We're glad to have you with our Company. Our number one goal is to provide outstanding customer service. Set both your personal and professional goals high. We have great confidence in your ability to achieve them.

Nordstrom Rules: Rule #1: Use good judgment in all situations. There will be no additional rules. Please feel free to ask your department manager, store manager, or division general manager any questions at any time.

Now, in addition to this card, a full handbook of other more specific rules and legal regulations is given to new employees.

Sources: www.nordstrom.com (accessed April 1, 2010); Robert Spector and Patrick McCarthy, *The Nordstrom Way to Customer Service Excellence* (Hoboken, NJ: Wiley, 2005); "Nordstrom to Foray into Canada – Analyst Blog," Nasdaq.com, September 14, 2012, http://community.nasdaq.com/News/2012-09/nordstrom-to-foray-into-canada-analyst-blog.aspx?storyid=173455#ixzz27UpSmVAO (accessed November 21, 2013); Nordstrom Inc. Annual Report 2011, https://materials.proxyvote.com/Approved/655664/20120309/AR_121724/INDEX.HTML (accessed November 21, 2013); "Our History," Dollarama.com, http://www.dollarama.com/about_us/our_history (accessed November 21, 2013); "Dollarama Inc. Annual Information Form," April 27, 2012, http://www.dollarama.com/wp-content/uploads/2012/04/2012-Annual-Information-Form-English-SEDAR.pdf (accessed November 21, 2013).

DID YOU KNOW?

Lululemon believes its culture and community-based business approach provides the retailer with competitive advantages that are responsible for its strong financial performance. Net revenue has increased from $40.7 million in fiscal 2004 to $1000.8 million in fiscal 2011, representing a 58 percent compound annual growth rate. Corporate-owned stores averaged sales of approximately $2004 per square foot, compared to sales per square foot of approximately $1726 for fiscal 2010. These results are among the best in the apparel retail sector.[7]

10 percent. The difference is that even though the jewellery store has higher operating expenses than the bakery, its gross margin is much more—it may double the cost of jewellery to arrive at a retail price. Kalame's asset turnover is so low compared to the bakery's because Kalame has very expensive fixtures and precision jewellery-manufacturing equipment (fixed assets), offers liberal credit to customers (accounts receivable), and has very slow inventory turnover—possibly only one-half to one turn per year. In sum, these two very different types of retailers could have exactly the same return on assets.

Thus, La Madeline is achieving its 10 percent return on assets by having a relatively high asset turnover—the *turnover path*. Kalame Jewellery, on the other hand, achieves its return on assets with a relatively high net profit margin—the *profit path*.

We will examine the relationship between these ratios and retailing strategy and describe where the information can be found in traditional accounting records.

One way to define financial success is to provide the owners of the firm with a good return on their investment. Although retailers pursue similar financial goals, they employ different strategies. For instance, Birks has broad assortments of jewellery and gifts, exceptionally high levels of service, and a beautiful store image. Birks concentrates on the profit path. Walmart takes the opposite approach.

exhibit 8-3 Return on Assets Model for a Bakery and a Jewellery Store

	Net profit margin	× Asset turnover	= Return on assets
La Madeline Bakery	1%	10 times	10%
Kalame Jewellery	10%	1 time	10%

It concentrates on the turnover path. Walmart has narrow assortments, relatively little service, and functional decor. Based on this description, why would anyone shop at Walmart? The answer is that Walmart strives for and maintains everyday low prices. The strategic profit model is used to evaluate the performance of different retailers that, like Birks and Walmart, may employ very different strategies.

The Profit Path

The information used to analyze a firm's profit path comes from the income statement. The income statement summarizes a firm's financial performance over a period of time, typically a quarter or a year. To capture all the sales, gift card purchases, and returns from the holiday season, many retailers set their fiscal year as beginning on February 1 and ending on January 31 of the following year. Exhibit 8–4 shows income statements in a hypothetical situation for Walmart and Birks. The profit path portion of the strategic profit model that utilizes such income statement data appears in Exhibit 8–5. Let's look at each item in the income statement. (Throughout this chapter, dollar figures are expressed in millions.)

Net Sales

The four main components in the profit margin management path are net sales, cost of goods sold (COGS), gross margin, and operating profit margin. The term net sales refers to the total number of dollars received by a retailer after all refunds have been paid to customers for returned merchandise:

$$\text{Net sales} = \text{Gross amount of sales} + \text{Promotional allowance} - \text{Customer returns}$$

Customer returns represent the value of merchandise that customers return and for which they receive a refund of cash or a credit. To calculate customer returns percentage, divide the dollar sum of customer returns by gross sales. (This is the only time that a retail ratio is calculated on gross sales.) Promotional allowances are payments made by vendors to retailers in exchange for the retailer promoting the vendor's merchandise. For example, consumer packaged-goods manufacturers will frequently pay supermarket chains to stock a new product (called slotting fees) or advertise a product. Retailing View 8.2 describes the impact of these promotional allowances on a retailer's reported net sales. For warehouse clubs such as Costco, membership fees are an additional source of revenue. About 4 percent of Costco's $48 billion in sales are from membership fees.

Sales are an important measure of performance because they indicate the activity level of the merchandising function. Retailers are particularly interested in sales growth due to its direct link to the firm's overall profitability.

Cost of Goods Sold

Cost of goods sold is a major component in determining a retailer's operating profit. Cash discounts, alteration/workroom costs, billed costs of merchandise, and transportation costs all influence total cost of merchandise sold. In order to maintain or improve profit, retailers must figure ways to control these factors.

Gross Margin

$$\text{Gross margin} = \text{Net sales} - \text{Cost of goods sold}$$

Gross margin, also called *gross profit*, is an important measure in retailing. It gives the retailer a measure of

exhibit 8-4 Hypothetical Income Statements for Walmart Stores, Inc., and Birks, 2013 ($ in millions)

	Walmart	Birks
Net sales	219 812	1 607
Less: Cost of goods sold	171 562	663
Gross margin	48 250	944
Less: Operating expense	36 173	634
Less: Interest expense	1 326	20
Total expense	37 499	653
Net profit, pretax	10 751	291
Less: Taxes*	3 897	116
Tax rate	36.25%	39.79%
Net profit after tax	6 854	175

*Effective tax rates often differ among corporations due to different tax breaks and advantages.

how much profit it's making on merchandise sales without considering the expenses associated with operating the store. Gross margin is the amount that retailers use to cover expenses and provide profit for the organization.

Gross margin, like other performance measures, is also expressed as a percentage of net sales so that retailers can compare performances of various types of merchandise and their own performance with other retailers with higher or lower levels of sales.

$$\frac{\text{Gross margin}}{\text{Net sales}} = \text{Gross margin \%}$$

Walmart: $\dfrac{\$48\ 250}{\$219\ 812} = 21.95\%$

Birks: $\dfrac{\$944}{\$1607} = 58.75\%$

Superficially, Birks appears to outperform Walmart on gross margin. However, further analysis will show that other factors interact with gross margin to determine overall performance. But first, let's consider the factors that contribute to differences in gross margin performance.

Discount stores such as Walmart generally have lower gross margins than jewellery stores because discount stores pursue a deliberate strategy of offering merchandise at everyday low prices with minimal service to several cost-oriented market segments. Discount stores have tried to increase their average gross margin by adding specialty products and departments such as gourmet foods and jewellery. Discount stores grow profit based on volume of sales.

Expenses

Expenses are costs incurred in the normal course of doing business to generate revenues. Types of retail operating expenses are broken down in Exhibit 8–6 and are further defined in the hypothetical balance sheet in Exhibit 8–7. Operating expenses are the selling, general, and administrative expenses (SG&A), plus the depreciation and amortization of assets. The SG&A includes costs, other than the cost of merchandise, incurred in the normal course of doing business, such as salaries for sales associates and managers, advertising, utilities, office supplies, information technology, and rent. Retailing View 8.3 reviews the creative ways that Costco reduces its SG&A costs.

$$\frac{\text{Operating expenses}}{\text{Net sales}} = \text{Operating expenses \%}$$

Walmart: $\dfrac{\$36\ 173}{\$219\ 812} = 16.56\%$

Birks: $\dfrac{\$634}{\$1607} = 39.45\%$

expenses Costs incurred in the normal course of doing business to generate revenues.

operating expenses Costs, other than the cost of merchandise, incurred in the normal course of doing business, such as salaries for sales associates and managers, advertising, utilities, office supplies, and rent.

selling, general, and administrative expenses (SG&A) Operating expenses, plus the depreciation and amortization of assets.

exhibit 8–5 Profit Margin Models for Walmart Stores, Inc., and Birks, 2013 ($ in millions)

Top number = Walmart
Bottom number = Birks

Boxes:
- Net sales: $219 812 / $1 607
- Cost of goods sold: $171 562 / $663
- Gross margin: $48 250 / $944
- Operating expenses: $36 173 / $634
- Interest expense: $1 326 / $20
- Total expenses: $37 499 / $653
- Net profit before tax: $10 751 / $291
- Taxes: $3 897 / $116
- Net profit after taxes: $6 854 / $175
- Net sales: $219 812 / $1 607
- Net profit margin: 3.12% / 10.89%

exhibit 8–6 Types of Retail Operating Expenses

Selling expenses	= Sales staff salaries + Commissions + Benefits
General expenses	= Rent + Utilities + Miscellaneous expenses
Administrative expenses	= Salaries of all employees other than salespeople + Operations of buying offices + Other administrative expenses

Another major expense category, interest, is the cost of financing everything from inventory to the purchase of a new store location. For instance, if a bank charges Birks 10 percent interest, Birks pays $49 million in interest to borrow $490 million. Offsetting the interest expense is the interest income a retailer can generate through proprietary credit cards, bank deposits, bonds, fixed income investments, and other investments.

Most retailers incur expenses for interest and taxes. However, these costs of doing business may not reflect the retailer's performance in its primary business activity, which is selling its merchandise and services. That is, the interest expense is a financial, not an operating, decision, based on the evaluation of the relative cost of borrowing money or raising funds by selling more stock in the company. Taxes can be affected by the retailer's losses in the previous year and/or changes in government regulations and laws.

Birks has significantly higher total expenses as a percentage of net sales than Walmart. Like gross margin, total expenses are also expressed as a percentage of net sales to facilitate comparisons across items and departments within firms.

$$\frac{\text{Total expenses}}{\text{Net sales}} = \text{Total expenses/Net sales ratio}$$

Walmart: $\dfrac{\$37\,499}{\$219\,812} = 17.06\%$

Birks: $\dfrac{\$634}{\$1607} = 40.65\%$

The total expenses to net sales ratio is only approximately 17 percent for Walmart; at Birks, it's over 40 percent. This difference is to be expected. Discount stores have relatively low selling expenses. They're also typically located on comparatively inexpensive real estate, so rent is relatively low. Finally, discount stores operate with a smaller administrative staff than a store like Birks. For instance, buying expenses are much lower for discount stores. Their buyers don't have to travel very far, and much of the purchasing consists of re-buying staple merchandise that's already in the stores. On the other hand, a jewellery store's total expenses are much higher because its large,

experienced sales staff requires a modest salary plus commission and benefits. Unlike Walmart stores' locations that are usually suburban or in rural areas, Birks stores are in some of the most expensive areas in the country. Birks locations therefore command high rent and incur other expenses.

Net Operating Income

Due to the lack of control over taxes, interest, and extraordinary expenses, a commonly used profit measure is the net profit percentage before interest expenses/income, taxes, and extraordinary expenses. Like the gross margin and operating expenses, net operating income is often expressed as a percentage of net sales to facilitate comparisons across items, merchandise categories, and departments with different sales levels.

$$\frac{\text{Gross margin} - \text{Operating expenses}}{\text{Net sales}} = \frac{\text{Net operating}}{\text{income \%}}$$

Walmart: $\dfrac{\$48\,250 - \$36\,173}{\$219\,812} = 5.49\%$

Birks: $\dfrac{\$944 - \$634}{\$1607} = 19.29\%$

Net Profit

Net profit is a measure of the firm's overall performance:

$$\text{Net profit} = \text{Gross margin} - \text{Expenses}$$

Net profit can be expressed either before or after taxes. Generally, it's more useful to express net profit after taxes, since this is the amount of money left over to reinvest in the business, disburse as dividends to stockholders or owners, or repay debt.

Net profit margin, like gross margin, is often expressed as a percentage of net sales:

$$\text{Net profit percentage} = \frac{\text{Net profit}}{\text{Net sales}}$$

However, net profit measures the profitability of the entire firm, whereas gross margin measures the profitability of merchandising activities. In Exhibit 8–5, the after-tax net profit margin is 3.12 percent for Walmart and 10.89 percent for Birks. From a profit perspective alone, Birks, with 70 stores in Canada, is outperforming Walmart. Even though Birks has a higher total expenses/net sales ratio, its

Cutting Costs at Costco Wholesale

Costco Wholesale Corporation is the largest warehouse club chain in the world, with more than $74 billion in sales from its 567 stores. It positions itself as having low prices on a wide assortment ranging from wheels of Parmesan cheese to 55-inch flat-screen TVs. Keeping prices low is challenging in light of increasing commodity prices, so Costco works with its vendors to control costs.

For example, Costco typically buys 70 percent of the large, premium macadamia nuts produced by Mauna Loa, a division of Hershey, leaving Mauna Loa with an inventory of small nuts. Costco buyers have worked with Mauna Loa to use smaller nuts in a new chocolate-nut cluster that will be sold exclusively at Costco. Because Mauna Loa won't have to face the uncertainty of selling those smaller nuts at a steep discount, it can afford to offer Costco better prices for its premium nuts.

Simple packaging changes can have impressive results. For example, packaging cashews into square containers instead of traditional round ones enables Costco to increase the number of units it can stack on a pallet from 280 to 426. This relatively minor change to a product selling $100 million a year decreases the number of pallets shipped annually by 24 000, decreases the number of truck trips by 600, and reduces the number of pallets Costco needs by 200 000.

Changing this jar of nuts from a round shape to a square shape made a significant reduction in Costco's SG&A.

However, Costco does not scrimp on its employees. Eighty-six percent of its employees get health care and other benefits, even though half of its employees are part-timers. The average compensation of store employees is $20 an hour, more than 50 percent higher than the industry average. No Costco employees were laid off during the recession. Costco believes that treating its employees well actually reduces labour costs in the long run. Its employee turnover is only 13 percent, among the lowest in the retail industry.

Sources: Amanda Ruggeri, "Building an Empire from the Employees Up," *U.S. News & World Report*, November 2009, p. 51; Jenna McGregor, "Costco's Artful Discounts," *BusinessWeek*, October 20, 2008, p. 58.

---

gross margin percentage is so large compared to Walmart's that it still surpasses the discount store's profit performance in this scenario.

Skeletal Income Statement Using the profit path information discussed above and incorporating it into a series of skeletal statements will help provide a better understanding of the relationship between sales volume, cost of merchandise sold, and expenses, the basic merchandising factors found in an income statement. A skeletal statement demonstrates these three basic merchandising factors, plus gross margin and profit results. In working with basic income statement numbers in a skeletal format, the results of these three relationships can be demonstrated. The two columns can be checked for accuracy by adding up from the bottom and the

correlation between the numbers becomes more evident, in both dollars and percents.

Example of a skeletal statement	$	%
Net sales	48 000	100.00
(*minus*) Cost of goods sold	24 280	50.58
Gross margin	23 720	49.42
(*minus*) Expenses	12 360	25.75
Operating profit/loss	11 360	23.67

Even if some of the data were missing from the above skeletal statement it could still be completed by setting up the relationships among the basic merchandising factors (net sales, cost of goods sold, and expenses). To find the percent

skeletal statement
An analysis of the five key categories found in all operating statements.

of any one factor, divide the dollar amount of that factor by net sales. (Remember that net profit percent always equals 100 percent unless working with customer returns when gross sales represent 100 percent.)

Example of a skeletal statement	$	%
Net sales		100.00
(*minus*) Cost of goods sold		
Gross margin	23 720	
(*minus*) Expenses	12 360	
Operating profit/loss		23.67

Profit = $23 720 − $12 360 = $11 360

Net sales = $11 360 ÷ 23.67% = $48 000

Cost of goods sold = $48 000 − $23 720 = $24 280

Cost of goods sold % = $24 280 ÷ $48 000 = 50.58%

Gross margin % = $23 720 ÷ $48 000 = 49.42%

Expense % = $12 360 ÷ $48 000 = 25.75%

The Turnover Path

assets Economic resources, such as inventory or store fixtures, owned or controlled by an enterprise as a result of past transactions or events.

liabilities Obligations of a retail enterprise to pay cash or other economic resources in return for past, present, or future benefits.

owners' equity The amount of assets belonging to the owners of the retail firm after all obligations (liabilities) have been met; also known as *net worth* and *shareholders' equity*.

current assets Cash or any assets that can normally be converted into cash within one year.

accounts receivable The amount of money due to the retailer from selling merchandise on credit.

The information used to analyze a firm's turnover path primarily comes from the balance sheet. Whereas, the income statement summarizes the financial performance over a period of time (usually a year or quarter), the balance sheet summarizes a retailer's financial position at a given point in time, typically the end of its fiscal year. The balance sheet shows the following relationship:

Assets = Liabilities + Owners' equity

Assets are economic resources (such as inventory, buildings, or store fixtures) owned or controlled by an enterprise as a result of past transactions or events. There are two types of assets: current and fixed. Liabilities are an enterprise's obligations (such as accounts or notes payable) to pay cash or other economic resources in return for past, current, or future benefits. Owners' equity (owners' investment in the business) is the difference between assets and liabilities. It represents the amount of assets belonging to the owners of the retail firm after all obligations (liabilities) have been met.

1. Set up a skeletal income statement, given the following information:

Net sales	$525 000
Gross margin	44.6%
Expenses	45.0%

2. Set up a skeletal income statement, given the following information:

Gross margin	$118 500
Expenses	$52 930
Profit	26.44%

3. Determine the percent of gross margin necessary for Staples to achieve a net profit of 4.89 percent. Estimated net sales are $319 607; estimated operating expenses are $54 333.

4. Set up a skeletal income statement, given the following information:

Gross sales	$385 620
Customer returns	6.85%
Cost of goods sold	35.84%
Expenses	$152 078

Exhibit 8–7 shows a hypothetical balance sheet for Birks and Walmart Stores, Inc. ($ millions). The turnover path portion of the strategic profit model is shown in Exhibit 8–8's asset turnover model.

Current Assets

By accounting definition, current assets are those that can normally be converted to cash within one year. In retailing, current assets are primarily cash, accounts receivable, and merchandise inventory.

$$\text{Accounts receivable} + \text{Merchandise inventory} + \text{Cash} + \text{Other current assets} = \text{Current assets}$$

Accounts Receivable

Accounts receivable are monies due to the retailer from selling merchandise on credit. This current asset is substantial for some retailers. For example, Walmart's investment in accounts receivable is proportionally much smaller than Birks' due to Walmart customers' high propensity to pay cash or use third-party credit cards such as Visa or MasterCard. Here are their accounts receivable:

Walmart: $2000, or 0.9 percent of sales

Birks: $99, or 6.1 percent of sales

exhibit 8–7 Hypothetical Balance Sheets for Walmart Stores, Inc., and Birks ($ in millions)

	Walmart (as of 1/31/13)	Birks (as of 1/31/13)
ASSETS		
Current assets		
Accounts receivable	$ 2 000	$ 99
Merchandise inventory	22 614	612
Cash	2 161	174
Other current assets	1 471	71
Total current assets	28 246	955
Fixed assets		
Building, equipment, and other fixed assets, less depreciation	55 205	675
Total assets	$83 451	$1 630
LIABILITIES		
Current liabilities	$27 282	$ 341
Long-term liabilities	18 732	221
Other liabilities	2 335	30
Total liabilities	$48 349	$ 593
OWNERS' EQUITY		
Common shares	$ 1 929	$ 332
Retained earnings	33 173	705
Total owners' equity	$35 102	$1 037
Total liabilities and owners' equity	$83 451	$1 630

proprietary store credit card system
A system in which credit cards have the store's name on them and the accounts receivable are administered by the retailer; also known as an *in-house credit system*.

exhibit 8–8 Asset Turnover Model for Walmart Stores, Inc., and Birks ($ in millions)

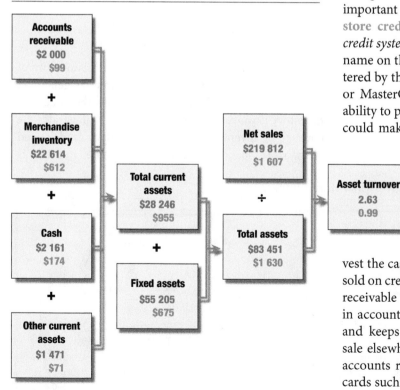

Top number = Walmart
Bottom number = Birks

From a marketing perspective, the accounts receivable generated from credit sales may be the result of an important service provided to customers. A proprietary store credit card system, also known as an *in-house credit system*, is one in which credit cards have the store's name on them, and the accounts receivable are administered by the retailer, not a credit card company like Visa or MasterCard or a financial institution.[10] The retailer's ability to provide credit, particularly at low interest rates, could make the difference between making or losing a sale. Paying cash for a sizable purchase such as a diamond engagement ring or car may be difficult for many people.

Unfortunately, having a large amount of accounts receivable is expensive for retailers, who of course would like to sell a product for cash and immediately reinvest the cash in new merchandise. When merchandise is sold on credit, proceeds of the sale are tied up as accounts receivable until collection is made. The money invested in accounts receivable costs the retailer interest expense and keeps the retailer from investing proceeds of the sale elsewhere. To ease the financial burden of carrying accounts receivable, retailers can use third-party credit cards such as Visa or MasterCard, give discounts to customers who pay with cash, discourage credit sales, and control delinquent accounts.

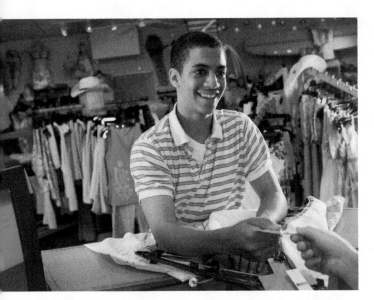

Since credit card sales can be expensive for retailers, why do they take them?

Think of inventory as "merchandise in motion." The faster it moves through the store, the greater the inventory turnover.

Merchandise Inventory

inventory turnover
Net sales divided by average retail inventory; used to evaluate how effectively managers utilize their investment in inventory.

Merchandise inventory is a retailer's lifeblood, representing 27.10 percent of total assets for Walmart and 37.53 percent of total assets for Birks. An exception to this generalization is service retailers such as Sears Pest Control Service, Marriott Hotels, and your local barber shop/beauty salon, which carry little or no merchandise inventory.

$$\frac{\text{Inventory}}{\text{Total assets}}$$

Walmart: $\dfrac{\$22\,614}{\$83\,451}$ = 27.10%

Birks: $\dfrac{\$612}{\$1630}$ = 37.53%

Inventory turnover is used to evaluate how effectively managers utilize their investment in inventory and can be figured on the basis of retail, cost, or units of merchandise. Turnover measures stock purchase, sale, and repurchase as demonstrated in Exhibit 8–9. The cost method of calculating inventory turnover is not often used because most retailers keep their merchandise records at retail. To calculate inventory at cost, both stock and sales figures (cost of goods sold) must be cost values. (Cost of goods sold divided by average inventory at cost equals inventory turnover at cost.) Inventory turnover by unit is impractical with categories of merchandise consisting of many small items, but becomes practical with large or high-priced items like furniture, fine jewellery, and major electronics. Calculating inventory turnover at retail is the most common method, and if not otherwise stated, most inventory turnover ratios are at retail. Inventory turnover is defined as follows:

$$\text{Inventory turnover} = \frac{\text{Net profit}}{\text{Average inventory}}$$

Think of inventory as a measure of the productivity of inventory—how many sales dollars can be generated from $1 invested in inventory. Generally, the larger the inventory turnover, the better. Exhibit 8–9 illustrates the concept of inventory turnover. Inventory is delivered to the store, spends some time in the store, and then is

exhibit 8–9 Inventory Turnover

sold. We can think of inventory turnover as how many times, on average, the inventory cycles through the store during a specific period of time (usually a year). Inventory turnover can vary from less than 2 to over 20 turns depending upon the type of merchandise. Merchandise that is purchased frequently like gasoline or perishable grocery items tend to have a high turnover while more specialized goods like furniture or fine jewellery will have a much lower inventory turn. Not only is it important to determine how many sales dollars can be generated from one dollar invested in inventory, but keep in mind the gross margin generated on each sales dollar.

Walmart's inventory turnover is about seven times Birks': 7.59 compared to 1.08.[11]

$$\frac{\text{Net sales}}{\text{Average inventory}} = \text{Inventory turnover}$$

Walmart: $\dfrac{\$219\,812}{\$28\,974} = 7.59$

Birks: $\dfrac{\$1607}{\$1484} = 1.08$

	Margin	Turnover
Birks	High	Low
Walmart	Low	High

Walmart's faster inventory turnover is expected due to the nature of discount and grocery stores. First, most items in Walmart are commodities and staples such as batteries, housewares, and basic apparel items. Its new superstores carry grocery products such as baked goods, frozen meat, and produce. Birks, on the other hand, specializes in unique luxury items. Second, since Walmart–type merchandise is available at other discount and grocery stores, it competes by offering lower prices, which results in rapid turnover. Third, discount stores carry a simpler stock selection than jewellery stores do. In a Walmart store, for example, there may be only two brands of ketchup, each in two sizes, which represents four inventory items. Jewellery stores, on the other hand, may stock 100 distinctly different types of necklaces. Finally, due to Birks' unique positioning strategy, much of its inventory, particularly the jewellery, is made especially for it in other countries, requiring buyers to place orders several months in advance of delivery. Discount stores, on the other hand, order items daily or weekly. These factors, when taken together, explain why Walmart has a faster inventory turnover than Birks.

Measuring Inventory Turnover

The notion of inventory turnover was introduced as "merchandise in motion." Jeans are delivered to the store through the loading dock in the back, spend some time in the store on the racks, and then are sold and go out the front door. The faster this process takes place, the higher the inventory turnover will be. We thus can think of inventory turnover as how many times, on average, the jeans cycle through the store during a specific period of time, usually one year. It's a measure of the productivity of inventory—that is, how many sales dollars can be generated from a dollar invested in jeans.

Again, inventory turnover can be defined as follows:

A. $\text{Inventory turnover} = \dfrac{\text{Net sales}}{\text{Average inventory at retail}}$

or

B. $\text{Inventory turnover} = \dfrac{\text{Cost of goods sold}}{\text{Average inventory at cost}}$

Since most retailers tend to think of their inventory at retail, the first definition is preferable. Arithmetically there's no difference between these two definitions; they yield the same result.[12] Be careful, however; since both the numerator and denominator must be at retail or at cost, it is different than the sales-to-stock ratio where the inventory is always expressed at cost. To illustrate:

$\text{Sales-to-stock ratio} = \dfrac{\text{Net sales}}{\text{Average cost inventory}}$

So if

Sales = $100 000

and

Average cost inventory = $33 333

then

$\text{Sales-to-stock ratio} = \dfrac{\$100\,000}{\$33\,333} = 3$

Thus,

$\text{Inventory turnover} = \text{Sales-to-stock ratio} \times (100\% - \text{Gross margin \%})$[13]

Continuing the example, if

Gross margin = 40 percent

then

$\text{Inventory turnover} = 3 \times (100\% - 40\%) = 1.8$

Retailers normally express inventory turnover rates on an annual basis rather than for parts of a year. Suppose the net sales used in an inventory turnover calculation are for a three-month season. If turnover for a quarter is calculated as 2.3 turns, then annual turnover will be four times that number (9.2). Thus, to convert an inventory turnover calculation based on part of a year to an annual figure, multiply it by the number of such time periods in the year. Exhibit 8–10 shows inventory turnover ratios for selected departments from discount stores. The range

exhibit 8–10 Gross Margin Percentage, Inventory Turnover, and GMROI for Selected Departments in Discount Stores

Category	Gross Margin (%)	Inventory Turnover	GMROI
Apparel	37	4	235
Housewares	35	3	162
Food	20	7	175
Jewellery	38	2	123
Furniture	31	2	90
Health and beauty	22	4	113
Consumer electronics	21	4	106

is from 7 (food) to 2 (jewellery and furniture). There are no real surprises in these data. One would expect food to have the highest turnover. Food is either sold quickly or it spoils. It is perishable. By the same token, being a luxury item, jewellery turns relatively slowly. Furniture achieves a low turnover because a relatively large assortment of expensive items is needed to support the sales level.

Calculating Average Inventory Average inventory is calculated by dividing the inventory at the beginning of the month (BOM) for each of several months, plus the inventory at the end of the month (EOM), divided by the total number of months plus 1.

Average inventory (1 month)

$$= \frac{\text{BOM inventory} + \text{EOM inventory}}{2}$$

Average inventory (6 months)

$$= \frac{\text{BOM inventory for each of the 6 months} + \text{EOM inventory for last month}}{7}$$

Average inventory (1 year)

$$= \frac{\text{BOM inventory for each of the 12 months} + \text{Last month's EOM}}{13}$$

For example, if a variety store had $330 000 of inventory at the beginning of January and $370 000 of inventory at the beginning of February, what was the store owner's average inventory for the month of January?

Average inventory

$$= \frac{\text{BOM inventory} + \text{EOM inventory for last month}}{\text{Number of months} + 1}$$

$$= \frac{330\,000 + 370\,000}{2}$$

$$= \$350\,000$$

If the variety store owner had sales of $156 000 for the month of January, what would the variety store's inventory turnover be for the month?

Inventory turnover

$$= \text{Net sales} \div \text{Average inventory}$$
$$= \$156\,000 \div \$350\,000$$
$$= 0.45 \text{ for the month}$$

What if the owner of the same variety store wanted to find out what his inventory turnover for the four-month period from January through April was with reported net sales for the period being $545 000?

Month	BOM Inventory
January	$330 000
February	$370 000
March	$350 000
April	$345 000
May	$320 000

Average inventory =

$$\frac{\text{BOM inventory for each month} + \text{EOM inventory for last month}}{\text{Number of months} + 1}$$

$$= \frac{\$330\,000 + \$370\,000 + \$350\,000 + \$345\,000 + \$320\,000}{5}$$

$$= \$343\,000$$

Inventory turnover $= \text{Net sales} \div \text{Average inventory}$
$$= \$545\,000 \div \$343\,000$$
$$= 1.59 \text{ times in the four-month time frame}$$

Given the above information it can be determined that if inventory turnover equals net sales divided by average inventory, then average inventory can also be calculated by taking net sales and dividing by inventory turnover.

Average inventory $= \text{Net sales} \div \text{Inventory turnover}$

Most retailers no longer need to use physical counts to determine average inventory. Point-of-sale (POS) terminals capture daily sales and automatically subtract them from on-hand inventory. Retailers with POS systems can get accurate average inventory estimates by averaging the inventory on hand for each day in the year. Retailers do typically take occasional physical inventories, usually twice a year, to determine the amount of inventory shrinkage due to theft or paperwork/entry mistakes.

Advantages of High Inventory Turnover Retailers want rapid inventory turnover—but not too rapid, as we'll soon see. Advantages of rapid inventory turnover include increased sales volume, less risk of obsolescence and markdowns, improved salesperson morale, more money for market opportunities, decreased operating expenses, and increased asset turnover.[15]

Increased Sales Volume   A rapid inventory turnover increases sales volume since fresh merchandise is available to customers, and fresh merchandise sells better and faster than old, shopworn merchandise. Fresh merchandise encourages customers to visit the store more frequently because they see new things. Also, notice the produce next time you're in a less-than-successful supermarket... brown bananas! Since turnover is slow, the produce is old, which makes it even harder to sell.

Quick response delivery systems are inventory management systems designed to reduce retailers' lead time for receiving merchandise. Retailers order less merchandise, more often, so merchandise supply is more closely aligned with demand. As a result, inventory turnover rises since inventory investment falls, and sales climb since the retailer is out of stock less often.

Less Risk of Obsolescence and Markdowns   The value of fashion and other perishable merchandise is said to start declining as soon as it's placed on display. When inventory is selling quickly, merchandise isn't in the store long enough to become obsolete. As a result, markdowns are reduced and gross margins increase.

Improved Salesperson Morale   With rapid inventory turnover and the fresh merchandise that results, salesperson morale stays high. No one likes to sell yesterday's merchandise. Salespeople are excited over new merchandise, the assortment of sizes is still complete, and the merchandise isn't shopworn. When salespeople's morale is high, they try harder so sales increase—increasing inventory turnover even further.

More Money for Market Opportunities   When inventory turnover is high, money previously tied up in inventory is freed to buy more merchandise. Having money available to buy merchandise late in a fashion season can open tremendous profit opportunities. Suppose Levi Strauss overestimates demand for its seasonal products. It has two choices:

- Hold the inventory until next season
- Sell it to retailers at a lower-than-normal price

If retailers have money available because of rapid turnover, they can take advantage of this special price. Retailers can pocket the additional markup or choose to maintain their high-turnover strategy by offering the special merchandise at a reduced cost to the consumer. In either case, sales and gross margin increase.

Decreased Operating Expenses   An increase in turnover may mean that a lower level of inventory is supporting the same level of sales. And lower inventory means lower inventory carrying costs, which is an operating expense. For instance, if a retailer has $1 million in inventory and the cost to carry the inventory—including money borrowed from a bank, insurance, and taxes—is 20 percent a year, the inventory carrying cost is $200 000. Lowering inventory can therefore represent a significant savings.

Increased Asset Turnover   Finally, since inventory is a current asset, and if assets decrease and sales stay the same or increase, then asset turnover increases. This directly affects return on assets, the key performance measure for top management.

Disadvantages of Too High an Inventory Turnover
Retailers should strike a balance in their rate of inventory turnover. An excessively rapid inventory turnover can hurt the firm due to a lower sales volume, an increase in the cost of goods sold, and an increase in operating expenses.

Lowered Sales Volume   One way to increase turnover is to limit the number of merchandise categories or the number of SKUs within a category. But if customers can't find the size or colour they seek—or even worse, if they can't find the product line at all—a sale is lost. Customers

---

8.2   CONCEPT CHECK

1. What is the inventory turnover if a store has $48 000 of BOM inventory for June and $38 000 for July. Net sales for June were $18 275.

2. Figure the average inventory for a store with annual sales of $550 000 and an annual inventory turnover of 3.8.

3. Determine the average inventory of a store for its third quarter (August to October) given the following inventory information:

Month	Sales	BOM inventory
February	$ 12 000	$ 22 000
March	$ 10 000	$ 16 000
April	$ 7 000	$ 15 500
May	$ 16 000	$ 25 000
June	$ 14 425	$ 26 250
July	$ 18 000	$ 36 000
August	$ 17 000	$ 22 250
September	$ 13 000	$ 20 000
October	$ 21 575	$ 28 800
November	$ 25 250	$ 29 400
December	$ 30 370	$ 36 000
January	$ 15 000	$ 24 000

4. Using the information from the previous question, figure the inventory turnover for the following time frames:
   a. Month of June
   b. Six-month spring-summer season (February to July)

who are disappointed on a regular basis will shop elsewhere and will possibly urge their friends to do the same. In this case, not only is a sale lost, but so are the customers and their friends.

Increased Cost of Goods Sold   To achieve rapid turnover, merchandise must be bought more often and in smaller quantities, which reduces average inventory without reducing sales. But by buying smaller quantities, the buyer can't take advantage of quantity discounts and transportation economies of scale. It may be possible, for instance, to buy a year's supply of Levi's at a quantity discount that offsets the high costs of carrying a large inventory.

Retailers who pay transportation costs must consider that the more merchandise shipped and the slower the mode of transportation, the smaller the per-unit transportation expense. For instance, to ship a 10-kilogram package of jeans from Toronto to Halifax, overnight delivery, would cost about $50 ($5 per kilogram). If the retailer could order 50 kilograms of jeans at the same time and could wait 5 to 10 days for delivery, the cost would be only about $30 (60 cents per kilogram). In this example, it costs over eight times more to ship small packages quickly.

Increased Operating Expenses   Economies of scale can also be gained when a retailer purchases large quantities. A buyer spends about the same amount of time meeting with vendors and writing orders whether the order is large or small. It also takes about the same amount of time, for both large and small orders, to print invoices, receive merchandise, and pay invoices—all factors that increase merchandise's cost.

In summary, rapid inventory turnover is generally preferred to slow turnover. But the turnover rate can be pushed to the point of diminishing returns, a key concern for merchandise managers in all retail sectors.

Cash and Other Current Assets

Cash = Monies on hand
   + Demand and savings accounts in banks to which a retailer has immediate access
   + Marketable securities such as treasury bills

Other current assets = Prepaid expenses + Supplies

Walmart reports cash of about 0.98 percent of sales, whereas Birks' cash percentage is 10.81 percent.

Fixed Assets

Fixed assets are assets that require more than a year to convert to cash. In retailing,

Fixed assets = Buildings (if store property is owned rather than leased)
   + Fixtures (such as display racks)
   + Equipment (such as computers or delivery trucks)
   + Long-term investments such as real estate or stock in other firms

In retailing, the principal fixed assets are buildings (if store property is owned rather than leased), fixtures (e.g., display racks), equipment (e.g., computers, delivery trucks), and other long-term investments such as stock in other forms.

Typically, large retailers such as Walmart and Home Depot own their store locations.[16] Other retailers rent their retail space and use the money they would have used to buy the land to remodel stores or buy merchandise. Yet ownership appeals to many retailers, because it enables them to secure their costs and avoid the possibility of increasing rents. When a retailer owns though, the area around the location may change and become unattractive, which would force the retailer to sell the location at a loss.

Fixed assets represent 66.15 percent and 41.44 percent of total assets for Walmart and Birks, respectively. Walmart's fixed assets are relatively higher than Birks' because they have vast real estate holdings in stores and distribution centres, whereas Birks typically rents space in malls and has direct store delivery.

$$\text{Asset cost} - \text{Depreciation} = \text{Fixed assets}$$

Since most fixed assets have a limited useful life, those assets' value should be less over time—in other words, they're depreciated. For instance, Birks stores require refurbishing every few years due to general wear-and-tear. So, carpet and some fixtures are depreciated over three to five years, whereas a building may be depreciated over 25 years.

Asset Turnover

Asset turnover is an overall performance measure from the asset side of the balance sheet.

$$\frac{\text{Net sales}}{\text{Total assets}} = \text{Asset turnover}$$

Although fixed assets don't turn over as quickly as inventory, asset turnover can be used to evaluate and compare how effectively managers use their assets. When a retailer redecorates a store, for example, old fixtures, carpeting, and lights are removed and replaced with new ones. Thus, like inventory, these assets cycle through the store. The difference is that the process is a lot slower. The life of a fixture in a Birks store may be five years (instead of five months, as it might be for a diamond ring in the store's inventory), yet the concept of turnover is the same. When a retailer decides to invest in a fixed asset, it should determine how many sales dollars can be generated from that asset.

Suppose that Birks needs to purchase a new fixture for displaying dinnerwear. It has a choice of buying an expensive antique display cabinet for $5000 or having a simple plywood display constructed for $500. Using the expensive antique, it forecasts sales of $50 000 in the first year, whereas the plywood display is expected to generate only $40 000. Ignoring all other assets for a moment,

$$\frac{\text{Net sales}}{\text{Total assets}} = \text{Asset turnover}$$

Antique cabinet: $\dfrac{\$50\ 000}{\$5000} = 10$

Plywood cabinet: $\dfrac{\$40\ 000}{\$500} = 80$

The antique cabinet will certainly help create an atmosphere conducive to selling expensive dinnerwear. Exclusively from a marketing perspective, the antique would

thus appear appropriate. But it costs much more than the plywood shelves. From a strictly financial perspective, Birks should examine how much additional sales can be expected to be generated from the added expenditure in assets. Clearly, by considering only asset turnover, the plywood shelves are the way to go. In the end, a combination of marketing and financial factors should be considered when making the asset purchase decision.[17]

In this case, Walmart's asset turnover is 2.7 times Birks'. The asset turnover is 2.63 for Walmart and 0.99 for Birks. This finding is consistent with the different strategies each firm is implementing. We saw earlier that Walmart has a higher inventory turnover. Its other assets are relatively lower than Birks' as well. For instance, the fixed assets involved in outfitting a store (such as fixtures, lighting, and mannequins) would be relatively lower for a discount store than a jewellery store.

The other side of the balance sheet equation from assets involves liabilities and owners' equity. Now let's look at the major liabilities and components of owners' equity.

Liabilities and Owners' Equity

Current Liabilities Like current assets, **current liabilities** are debts that are expected to be paid in less than one year. The most important current liabilities are accounts payable, notes payable, and accrued liabilities. Current liabilities as a percentage of net sales are 12.41 percent for Walmart and 21.24 percent for Birks.

Accounts Payable **Accounts payable** refers to the amount of money owed to vendors, primarily for merchandise inventory. Accounts payable is an important source of short-term financing. Retailers buy merchandise on credit from vendors. The longer the period of time they have to pay for that merchandise, the larger their accounts payable—and the less they need to borrow from financial institutions (notes payable), issue bonds or shares, or finance internally through retained earnings. Since retailers normally don't have to pay interest to vendors on their accounts payable, they have strong incentive to negotiate for a long time period before payment for merchandise is due.

Accounts payable management can play an important role in a retailer's profit strategy. This is the case for many European hypermarkets such as Carrefour. Hypermarkets are similar to Canadian-style supercentres but have some key differences. Hypermarkets are primarily food-based and emphasize fresh products to drive customer traffic, whereas supercentres are primarily

> **current liabilities**
> Debts that are expected to be paid in less than one year.
>
> **accounts payable**
> The amount of money owed to vendors, primarily for merchandise inventory.

To provide a more attractive store environment, department store retailers (top) have higher fixed assets than warehouse club retailers (bottom).

notes payable
Current liabilities representing principal and interest the retailer owes to financial institutions (banks) that are due and payable in less than a year.

accrued liabilities
Liabilities that accumulate daily but are paid only at the end of a period.

long-term liabilities
Debts that will be paid after one year.

shareholders' equity
The amount of assets belonging to the owners of the retail firm after all obligations (liabilities) have been met.

retained earnings
The portion of owners' equity that has accumulated over time through profits but has not been paid out in dividends to owners.

nonfood retailers that focus on dry goods. Carrefour is able to negotiate extended supplier terms because, like most European food retailers, it has national scope and is able to exert significant influence over its suppliers. As a result, Carrefour manages its accounts payable as a profit centre. For example, Carrefour typically has about 42 days of inventory on hand and roughly 90 days in payables. That 48-day float generates income that contributes as much as 25 to 35 percent to Carrefour's operating profit.[18]

Notes Payable Notes payable under the current liabilities section of the balance sheet are the principal and interest the retailer owes to financial institutions (banks) that are due and payable in less than a year. Retailers borrow money from financial institutions to pay for current assets, such as inventory.

Accrued Liabilities Accrued liabilities include taxes, salaries, rent, utilities, and other incurred obligations that haven't yet been paid. These are called accrued liabilities because they usually accumulate daily but are only paid at the end of a time period, such as a month.

Long-Term Liabilities Long-term liabilities are debts that will be paid after one year. The notes payable entry in the long-term liability section of the balance sheet is similar to the one in the current liability section except that it's due to be paid in more than one year. Other long-term liabilities include bonds and mortgages on real estate.

Owners' Equity Owners' equity, also known as shareholders' equity, represents the amount of assets belonging to the owners of the retail firm after all obligations (liabilities) have been met. In accounting terms, the relationship can be expressed as

$$\text{Owners' equity} = \text{Total assets} - \text{Total liabilities}$$

Although there are several entries in the owners' equity category, two of the most common are common shares and retained earnings.

Common shares are the type of shares most frequently issued by corporations.[19] Owners of common shares usually have voting rights in the retail corporation.

They also have the right to share in distributed corporate earnings. If the firm is liquidated, common share owners have the right to share in the sale of its assets. Finally, they have the right to purchase additional shares to maintain the same percentage ownership if new shares are issued.

Retained earnings refers to the portion of owners' equity that has accumulated over time through profits but hasn't been paid out in dividends to owners. The decision of how much of the retailer's earnings should be retained in the firm and how much should be returned to the owners in the form of dividends is related to the firm's growth potential. Specifically, retailers with a propensity toward and opportunities for growth will retain and reinvest their profits to fund growth opportunities. For example, a high-growth retailer such as Walmart retains most of its earnings to pay for the new stores, inventory, and expenses associated with its growth.

In the case discussed, total owners' equity is over $35 102 million for Walmart and over $1037 million for Birks.

Examining the Strategic Profit Model

The previous sections defined the most important balance sheet and income statement entries as well as the most useful performance ratios. Yet many of these items are interrelated, and when examined alone they can be confusing. More important, it's hard to compare the performance of retailers with different operating characteristics, such as Birks and Walmart. The strategic profit model (Exhibit 8–11) combines the two performance ratios from the income statement and balance sheets: net profit margin and asset turnover. By multiplying these ratios together, you get return on assets.

Return on Assets

Overall performance, as measured by return on assets (ROA), is determined by considering the effects of both paths by multiplying the net profit margin by asset turnover. Return on assets determines how much profit can be generated from the retailer's investment in assets.

$$\text{Return on assets} = \text{Net profit margin} \times \text{Asset turnover}$$
$$= \frac{\text{Net profit}}{\text{Net sales}} \times \frac{\text{Net sales}}{\text{Total assets}}$$
$$= \frac{\text{Net profit}}{\text{Total assets}}$$

(Note that when we multiply net profit margin by asset turnover, net sales drops out of the equation.)

exhibit 8–11   The Strategic Profit Model

The most important issue associated with return on assets is that the money that would be invested in retailing could also be invested in any other asset, such as a CD or Canada Savings Bond. For instance, if a retailer can achieve 9 percent return on assets by opening a new store and 10 percent by investing in a nearly risk-free savings bond, the retailer should take the higher-yield, lower-risk investment. In fact, should the return on assets of another investment with similar risk be greater, it would be the manager's fiduciary duty to invest in the other asset. In general, return on assets is effective in evaluating the profitability of individual investments in assets because it can easily be compared with yields of other investments with similar risk. It has also been shown to be an effective predictor of business failures.[20]

$$\frac{\text{Net profit}}{\text{Total assets}} = \text{Return on assets}$$

Walmart: $\dfrac{\$6854}{\$83\,451} = 8.21\%$

Birks: $\dfrac{\$175}{\$1630} = 10.74\%$

Return on assets for Birks and Walmart are very similar! Birks generated a larger net profit margin, 10.89 percent, compared to 3.12 for Walmart (Exhibit 8–5). But Walmart outperformed Birks on asset turnover, 2.63 compared to 0.99, respectively (Exhibit 8–8).

The strategic profit model illustrates two important issues. First, retailers and investors need to consider both net profit margin and asset turnover when evaluating their financial performance. Firms can achieve high performance (high ROA) by effectively managing both net profit margins and asset turnover. Second, retailers need to consider the implications of their strategic decisions on both components of the strategic profit model. For example, simply increasing prices will increase the gross margin and net profit margins (profit margin management path). However, increasing prices will result in fewer sales, and assuming the level of assets stays the same, asset turnover will decrease. Thus, profit margin increases, asset turnover decreases, and the effect on ROA depends on how much the profit margin increases compared with the decrease in asset turnover.

Exhibit 8–12 shows strategic profit model (SPM) ratios for a variety of retailers. The exhibit illustrates that supermarket and discount chains typically have higher asset turnovers and lower net profit margin percentages. The apparel specialty stores have lower asset turnovers and higher net profit margin percentages; however, the drugstore chains are just the opposite. The next section examines the performance measure on which the merchandise plan is evaluated. This measure, GMROI (gross margin/return on investment), is composed of two ratios: inventory turnover and gross margin percentage. The section concludes with a discussion of how retailers forecast sales.

Putting Margin, Sales, and Turnover Together: GMROI

At the corporate level, return on assets is used to plan and evaluate performance of overall retail operations.

$$\text{Return on assets} = \text{Net profit margin} \times \text{Asset turnover}$$
$$= \frac{\text{Net profit}}{\text{Net sales}} \times \frac{\text{Net sales}}{\text{Total assets}}$$
$$= \frac{\text{Net profit}}{\text{Total assets}}$$

With the strategic profit model, one can use return on assets to plan and compare the performance of executives since they are responsible for managing all of the retailer's assets and realizing a return based on these assets.

But merchandise managers have control over only the merchandise they buy and manage. Buyers generally have control over gross margin but not expenses involved with the operation of the stores and the management of exhibit 8–12 Strategic Profit Models for Selected Retailers

	Net Profit Margin (%)	Asset Turnover	Return on Assets (%)
	Net profit / Net sales	Net sales / Total assets	Net profit margin × asset turnover
Discount Stores			
Best Buy Co., Inc.	−2.4%	3.17	−7.6%
Costco Wholesale Corp.	1.7%	3.65	6.2%
Walmart Stores, Inc.	3.5%	2.31	8.1%
Grocery			
Empire Co. Ltd. / Sobeys	2.1%	2.36	4.9%
Loblaw Companies Ltd.	2.1%	1.76	3.7%
Metro Inc.	4.0%	2.33	9.3%
Drugstore			
Jean Coutu Group Inc.	8.4%	2.55	21.4%
Shoppers Drug Mart Corp.	5.6%	1.44	8.1%
Specialty			
Cineplex Inc. / Galaxy	11.0%	0.82	9.0%
Indigo Inc. / Chapters	9.9%	1.58	15.6%
Leon's Furniture	6.9%	1.16	8.0%
Lululemon Athletica Inc.	19.7%	1.30	25.6%
Reitmans Canada Ltd.	4.7%	1.61	7.6%
Home Improvement			
Canadian Tire Corp., Ltd.	4.4%	0.87	3.8%
Home Depot, Inc.	6.1%	1.82	11.1%
Rona Inc.	0.4%	1.74	0.7%

Source: Company filings for fiscal 2012; Google.ca/Finance.

the retailer's human resources, locations, and systems. As a result, the financial ratio that is useful for planning and measuring merchandising performance is a return on investment measure called gross margin return on inventory investment, or GMROI.[21] It measures how many gross margin dollars are earned on every dollar of inventory investment.

GMROI is a similar concept to return on assets, only its components are under the control of the buyer rather than other managers. Instead of combining net profit margin and asset turnover, GMROI uses gross margin percentage and the sales-to-stock ratio, which is similar to inventory turnover.

$$\text{GMROI} = \text{Gross margin percentage} \times \text{Sales-to-stock ratio}$$

$$= \frac{\text{Gross margin}}{\text{Net sales}} \times \frac{\text{Net sales}}{\text{Average inventory}}$$

$$= \frac{\text{Gross margin}}{\text{Average inventory}}$$

Average inventory in GMROI is measured at cost, because a retailer's investment in inventory is the cost of the inventory, not its retail value.

Like return on assets, GMROI combines the effects of both profits and turnover. It's important to use a measure that considers both of these factors so that departments with different margin/turnover profiles can be compared and evaluated. For instance, within a grocery store, some departments (such as wine) are high margin/low turnover, whereas other departments (such as dairy products) are low margin/high turnover. If the wine department's performance is compared to that of dairy products using inventory turnover alone, the contribution of wine to the grocery store's performance will be undervalued. On the other hand, if only gross margin is used, wine's contribution will be overvalued.

Consider the situation in Exhibit 8–13. Here a grocery store manager wants to evaluate performance of two classifications: bread and ready-to-eat prepared foods. If evaluated on gross margin percentage or sales alone, prepared foods is certainly the winner with a 50 percent gross margin and sales of $300 000 compared to bread's gross margin of 1.333 percent and sales of $150 000. Yet prepared foods turns (sales-to-stock ratio) only four times a year, whereas bread turns 150 times a year.

exhibit 8–13 Illustration of GMROI

			Bread		Prepared Foods		
		Gross margin	$2000		$150000		
		Sales	$150000		$300000		
		Average inventory	$1000		$75000		
Bread	GMROI = $\dfrac{\text{Gross margin}}{\text{Net sales}}$		×	$\dfrac{\text{Net sales}}{\text{Average inventory}}$		=	$\dfrac{\text{Gross margin}}{\text{Average inventory}}$
	GMROI = $\dfrac{\$2000}{\$150\,000}$		×	$\dfrac{\$150\,000}{\$1000}$		=	$\dfrac{\$2000}{\$1000}$
	= 1.333%		×	150 times		=	200%
Prepared Foods	GMROI = $\dfrac{\$150\,000}{\$300\,000}$		×	$\dfrac{\$300\,000}{\$75\,000}$		=	$\dfrac{\$150\,000}{\$75\,000}$
	= 50%		×	4		=	200%

Using GMROI, both classifications achieve a GMROI of 200 percent and so are equal performers from a return on investment perspective.

GMROI is used as a return on investment profitability measure to evaluate departments, merchandise classifications, vendor lines, and items. It's also useful for management in evaluating buyers' performance since it can be related to the retailer's overall return on investment. As we just demonstrated, merchandise with different margin/turnover characteristics can be compared. Exhibit 8–10 shows GMROI percentages for selected departments from discount stores. The range is from 235 (for apparel) to 90 (for furniture). It's no wonder that many discount stores are placing so much emphasis on apparel and that some have discontinued furniture. They continue to carry consumer electronics and health and beauty products—both with low GMROIs—because they have traditionally brought customers into the store. The retailers hope that while there, customers will purchase higher-GMROI items.

The gross margin component of GMROI is affected by pricing decisions. GMROI answers the question: For each dollar at cost, how many dollars of gross profit will I generate in one year? GMROI is traditionally calculated by using one year's gross profit against the average of 12 or 13 units of inventory at cost. A rule of thumb is that a GMROI of at least 3.2 is the break-even point for a business.

8.3 CONCEPT CHECK

1. Figure GMROI if average inventory at cost is $84 250 and gross margin is $240 500.

2. Determine GMROI, given net sales of $280 000, average inventory at cost of $80 000, and gross margin of 42 percent.

3. If net sales for July are $162 000, beginning of the month inventory at cost is $36 000, closing inventory at cost is $38 000, and gross margin is 46 percent, what is the GMROI?

4. Calculate asset turnover for a retailer who has total current assets of $46 282, fixed assets of $51 438, gross sales of $812 912, and customer returns of $89 426.

5. Figure the ROA for an organization with a net profit of $89 345 and $12 260 in total assets.

6. Determine the ROA for a retailer with the following information:

Gross margin	$800 811
Expenses	$180 925
Profit	44%
Current assets	$64 270
Total assets	$98 694

Recap of the Strategic Profit Model

The strategic profit model is useful to retailers because it combines two decision-making areas—margin management and asset management—so managers can examine interrelationships between them. The strategic profit model uses return on assets as the primary criterion for planning and evaluating a firm's financial performance.

The strategic profit model can also be used to evaluate financial implications of new strategies before they're implemented. For instance, suppose a retailer wishes to increase sales by 10 percent. Using the strategic profit model, he/she can estimate this action's impact on other

top-down planning
One side of the process of developing an overall retail strategy where goals are set at the top of the organization and filter down through the operating levels.

bottom-up planning
When goals are set at the bottom of the organization and filter up through the operating levels.

parts of the strategic profit model. For instance, to increase sales, the retailer may choose to have a sale. Lowering prices will reduce gross margin. In addition, the retailer would have to advertise the sale and hire additional sales help, thus increasing operating expenses. So, although the retailer may be able to achieve the 10 percent sales increase, net profit margin might go down.

Looking at the turnover path, increasing sales without an appreciable change in inventory will increase inventory turnover. Assuming other assets aren't affected, asset turnover will also increase. When they multiply the lower net profit margin by the higher asset turnover, the resulting return on assets may remain unchanged.

Setting Performance Objectives

Setting performance objectives is a necessary component of any firm's strategic planning process. How would a retailer know how it has performed if it doesn't have specific objectives in mind to compare actual performance against? Performance objectives should include:

- The performance sought, including a numerical index against which progress may be measured
- A time frame within which the goal is to be achieved
- The resources needed to achieve the objective

For example, "earning reasonable profits" isn't a good objective. It doesn't provide specific goals that can be used to evaluate performance. What's reasonable? When do you want to realize the profits? A better objective would be "earning $100 000 in profit during calendar year 2014 on $500 000 investment in inventory and building."

Top-Down versus Bottom-Up Processes

Setting objectives in large retail organizations entails a combination of the top-down and bottom-up approaches to planning.

Top-down planning means that goals get set at the top of the organization and are passed down to the lower operating levels. In a retailing organization, top-down planning involves corporate officers developing an overall retail strategy and assessing broad economic, competitive, and consumer trends. With this information, they develop performance objectives for the corporation. These overall objectives are then broken down into specific objectives for each buyer and merchandise category and for each region, store, and even each department within stores and the sales associates working in those departments.

The overall strategy determines the merchandise variety, assortment, and product availability, plus the store size, location, and level of customer service. Then the merchandise vice presidents decide which types of merchandise are expected to grow, stay the same, or shrink. Next, performance goals are established for each buyer and merchandise manager.

Similarly, regional store vice presidents translate the company's performance objectives into objectives for each district manager, who then develop objectives with their store managers. The process then trickles down to department managers in the stores and individual sales associates.

This top-down planning is complemented by a bottom-up planning approach. Bottom-up planning involves lower levels in the company developing performance objectives that are aggregated up to develop overall company objectives. Buyers and store managers estimate what they can achieve, and their estimates are transmitted up the organization to the corporate executives.

Frequently there are disagreements between the goals that have trickled down from the top and those set by lower-level employees of the organization. For example, a store manager may not be able to achieve the 10 percent sales growth set for his or her region because a major employer in the area has announced plans to lay off 2000 employees. These differences between bottom-up and top-down plans are resolved through a negotiation process involving corporate executives and operating managers. If the operating managers aren't involved in the objective setting process, they won't accept the objectives and thus will be less motivated to achieve them.

Accountable for Performance

At each level of the retail organization, the business unit and its manager should be held accountable only for the revenues, expenses, and contribution to ROA that they can control. Thus, expenses that affect several levels of the organization (e.g., labour and capital expenses associated with operating a corporate headquarters) shouldn't be arbitrarily assigned to lower levels. In the case of a store, for example, it may be appropriate to set performance objectives based on sales, sales associate productivity, store inventory shrinkage due to employee theft and shoplifting, and energy costs. If the buyer lowers prices to get rid of merchandise and therefore profits suffer, it is not fair to assess a store manager's performance on the basis of the resulting decline in store profit.

Performance objectives and measures can be used to pinpoint problem areas. The reasons that performance may be above or below planned levels must be examined. Perhaps the managers involved in setting the objectives aren't very good at making estimates. If so, they may need to be trained in forecasting. Also, buyers may misrepresent their business unit's ability to contribute to the firm's financial goals to get a larger inventory budget than is warranted and consequently earn a higher bonus. In either case, investment funds would be misallocated.

Actual performance may be different than the plan predicts due to circumstances beyond the manager's control. For example, there may have been a recession. Assuming the recession wasn't predicted, or was more severe or lasted longer than anticipated, there are several relevant questions: How quickly were plans adjusted? How rapidly and appropriately were pricing and promotional policies modified? In short, did the manager react to salvage an adverse situation, or did those reactions worsen the situation?

Performance Objectives and Measures

Many factors contribute to a retailer's overall performance, which makes it hard to find a single measure to evaluate performance. For instance, sales is a global measure of a retail store's activity level. However, a store manager could easily increase sales by lowering prices, but the profit realized on that merchandise (gross margin) would suffer as a result. Clearly, an attempt to maximize one measure may lower another. Managers must therefore understand how their actions affect multiple performance measures. It's usually unwise to use only one measure, because it rarely tells the whole story.

The measures used to evaluate retail operations vary depending on (1) the level of the organization at which the decision is made and (2) the resources the manager controls. For example, the principal resources controlled by store managers are space and money for operating expenses (such as wages for sales associates and utility payments to light and heat the store). Thus, store managers focus on performance measures like sales per square foot and employee cost as a percent of sales.

Types of Measures

Exhibit 8–14 breaks down a variety of retailers' performance measures into three types: input measures, output measures, and productivity measures. An input measure represents the resources or money allocated by a retailer to achieve outputs, or results. For example, the amount and selection of merchandise inventory, the number of stores, the size of the stores, the employees, advertising, markdowns, store hours, and promotions are managerial decisions involving resource allocations.

An output measure assesses the results of a retailer's investment decisions. For example, sales revenue, gross margin, and net profit margin are all output measures and ways to evaluate a retailer's input or resource allocations decisions. A productivity measure (the ratio of an output to an input) determines how effectively retailers use their resources—what return they get on their investments.

In general, since productivity measures are a ratio of outputs to inputs, they can be used to compare different business units. Suppose a retail chain's two stores are different sizes: One has 5000 square feet and the other has 10 000 square feet. It's hard to compare stores' performances using just output or input measures. The larger store will probably generate more sales and have higher expenses. But if the larger store generates $180 net sales per square foot and the smaller store generates $300 per square foot, the retailer knows that the smaller store is operating more efficiently even though it's generating lower sales.

Corporate Performance   At a corporate level, retail executives have three critical resources (inputs)—merchandise inventory, store space, and employees—that they can manage to generate sales and profits (outputs). Thus, effective productivity measures of the utilization of these assets include asset and inventory turnover, sales per square foot of selling space, and sales per employee.

As we have discussed, ROA is an overall productivity measure combining the profit margin percentage and asset turnover management. Comparable store sales growth (also called *same-store sales growth*) is a commonly used measure of a retailer's performance. There are two sources of annual sales growth, sales from new stores opened during the year and sales growth from stores that were open during the previous year. Comparable store sales growth is the sales growth in stores that have been open for at least a year—the second source of sales growth. Thus, growth in comparable store sales assesses how well the retailer is doing with its core business strategy and execution. Comparable store sales growth is a preferable measure to overall sales growth because the inclusion of new store sales clouds the long-term performance assessment. For example, overall sales might be increasing because the retailer

input measure   A performance measure used to assess the amount of resources or money used by the retailer to achieve outputs.

output measure   Measure that assesses the results of retailers' investment decisions.

productivity measure   The ratio of an output to an input determining how effectively a firm uses a resource.

comparable store sales growth   The sales growth in stores that have been open for over one year; also known as *same-store sales growth*.

exhibit 8–14   Performance Objectives and Measures Used by Retailers

Level of Organization	Output	Input	Productivity (output/input)
Corporate (measures for entire corporation)	Net sales Net profits Growth in sales, profits, comparable store sales	Square footage of store space Number of employees Inventory Advertising expenditures	Return on assets Asset turnover Sales per employee Sales per square foot
Merchandise management (measures for a merchandise category)	Net sales Gross margin Growth in sales	Inventory level Markdowns Advertising expenses Cost of merchandise	Gross margin return on investment (GMROI) Inventory turnover Advertising as a percentage of sales* Markdown as a percentage of sales*
Store operations (measures for a store or department within a store)	Net sales Gross margin Growth in sales	Square footage of selling areas Expenses for utilities Number of sales associates	Net sales per square foot Net sales per sales associate or per selling hour Utility expenses as a percentage of sales* Inventory shrinkage*

*These productivity measures are commonly expressed as an input/output ratio.

is opening new stores, but over time, the sales in the retailer's stores, new and existing, is decreasing. Thus, when the new store openings slow down, the retailer will experience negative sales growth. By excluding the sales from new stores, retailers and investors can better assess how the overall strategy and implantation are working. Comparable store sales growth assesses how well the retailer's fundamental business approach is not being well received by its customers.

Merchandise Management Measures   The critical resource (input) controlled by merchandise managers is merchandise inventory. Merchandise managers also have the authority to set initial prices and lower prices when merchandise is not selling (i.e., take a markdown). Finally, they negotiate with vendors over the paid price for merchandise.

Inventory turnover is a productivity measure of the management of inventory; higher turnover means greater inventory management productivity. Gross margin percentage indicates the performance of merchandise managers in negotiating with vendors and buying merchandise that can generate a profit. Discounts (markdowns) as a percentage of sales are also a measure of the quality of the merchandise buying decisions. If merchandise managers have a high percentage of markdowns, they may not be buying the right merchandise or the right quantities, because they weren't able to sell some of it at its original retail price. Note that gross margin and discount percentages are productivity measures, but they are typically expressed as an input divided by an output

as opposed to the typical productivity measures that are outputs divided by inputs.

Store Operations Measures   The critical assets controlled by store managers are the use of the store space and the management of the store's employees. Thus, measures of store operations productivity include sales per square foot of selling space and sales per employee (or sales per employee working hour, to take into account that some employees work part-time). Store management is also responsible for controlling theft by employees and customers (referred to as inventory shrinkage), store maintenance, and energy costs (lighting, heating, and air conditioning). Thus, some other productivity measures used to assess the performance of store managers are inventory shrinkage and energy costs as a percentage of sales.

Assessing Performance: The Role of Benchmarks

As we have discussed, the financial measures used to assess performance reflect the retailer's market strategy. For example, because Costco has a different business strategy than Hudson's Bay, it has a lower profit margin (see Exhibit 8–15). It earns an acceptable ROA because it increases its inventory and asset turnovers by stocking a more limited merchandise assortment of less fashionable, staple items. In contrast, Hudson's Bay specializes in apparel and accessories, which requires a broad and deep merchandise assortment. Thus, it has lower

exhibit 8–15   Costco Wholesale Corporation

METRICS	2010	2011	2012
Revenue	$77 946	$88 915	$99 137
Net Income	$1303	$1462	$1709
Net Profit Margin	1.7%	1.6%	1.7%
Total Assets	$23 815	$26 761	$27 140
Asset Turnover	3.27	3.32	3.65
ROA	5.6%	5.3%	6.2%
Employees	147 000	164 000	174 000

Note: All amounts expressed in USD millions, except for margins and employee numbers.

Source: Company filings for fiscal 2012; Google.ca/Finance.

inventory and asset turnover but achieves an acceptable ROA through its higher profit margins. In other words, the performance of a retailer cannot be assessed accurately simply by looking at isolated measures, because they are affected by the retailer's strategy. To get a better assessment of a retailer's performance, we need to compare it to a benchmark. Two commonly used benchmarks are (1) the performance of the retailer over time and (2) the performance of the retailer compared with that of its competitors.

Performance over Time (Time-Series Analysis)

One useful approach for assessing a retailer's performance compares its recent performance in the preceding months, quarters, or years. Exhibit 8–15 shows the performance measures for Costco over a three-year period.

Costco experiences greater inventory turnover and sales per square foot, due to the type of merchandise sold (food and staples versus fashion apparel), as well as lower sales per employees due to its self-service offering compared with the customer service provided by the sales associates at a retailer such as Hudson's Bay. In terms of the strategic profit model components, Costco's ROA shows a general upward trend.

Performance Compared to Competitors (Cross-Sectional Ratio Analysis)

A second approach for assessing a retailer's performance involves comparing it with that of its competitors. Exhibit 8–16 compares the performance of Best Buy Co., Inc., and Walmart Stores, Inc. How does this data then compare to the Costco Wholesale Corporation data in Exhibit 8–15?

exhibit 8–16   Performance Compared to Competitors

METRICS	BEST BUY CO., INC.			WALMART STORES, INC.		
	2010	2011	2012	2010	2011	2012
Revenue	$49 243	$49 747	$50 705	$408 085	$421 849	$446 950
Net Income	$1317	$1277	($1231)	$14 370	$16 389	$15 699
Net Profit Margin	2.7%	2.6%	−2.4%	3.5%	3.9%	3.5%
Total Assets	$18 302	$17 849	$16 005	$170 407	$180 782	$193 406
Asset Turnover	2.69	2.79	3.17	2.39	2.33	2.31
ROA	7.3%	7.3%	−7.6%	8.4%	9.1%	8.1%

Note: All $ expressed in USD millions, except for margins and employee numbers.

Source: Company filings for fiscal 2012; Google.ca/Finance.

SUMMARY

Financial management involves a thorough understanding of the importance of return on investment and how this relates to the retailer's image. It must also be understood that clearly defined quantifiable performance objectives are essential to evaluating business strategies and making changes to correct problems.

This chapter explains some basic elements of retailing financial strategy and examines how retailing strategy affects the financial performance of a firm. We used the strategic profit model as a vehicle for understanding the complex interrelations between financial ratios and retailing strategy. We found that different types of retailers have different financial operating characteristics. Specifically, jewellery store chains such as

Birks generally have higher profit margins and lower turnover than discount stores such as Walmart. Yet, when margin and turnover are combined into return on assets, we showed that it's possible to achieve similar financial performance.

We also described some financial performance measures used to evaluate different aspects of a retailing organization. Although the return on assets ratio in the strategic profit model is appropriate for evaluating the performance of retail operating managers, other measures are more appropriate for more specific activities. For instance, gross margin return on investment (GMROI) is appropriate for buyers, whereas store managers should be concerned with sales or gross margin per square foot.

KEY TERMS

accounts payable
accounts receivable
accrued liabilities
asset turnover
assets
bottom-up planning
comparable store sales growth
cost of goods sold
cross-sectional ratio analysis
current assets
current liabilities
customer returns
expenses
fixed assets

gross margin
input measure
interest
interest income
inventory turnover
liabilities
long-term liabilities
net profit
net profit margin
net sales
notes payable
operating expenses
output measure

owners' equity
productivity measure
promotional allowances
proprietary store credit card system
retained earnings
return on assets (ROA)
selling, general, and administrative expenses (SG&A)
shareholders' equity
skeletal statement
strategic profit model (SPM)
time-series analysis
top-down planning

Get Out & Do It!

1. **INTERNET EXERCISE** Go to **www.hoovers.com**, **www.google.com/finance**, or the company's latest annual reports and use the financial information to update the numbers in the profit margin model in Exhibit 8–5 and the asset turnover model in Exhibit 8–8. Use these two models to develop the strategic profit model in Exhibit 8–11 for Walmart and Birks. Then repeat the process for Amazon and Bally Total Fitness. Have there been any significant changes in their financial performance? Why are the key financial ratios for these four retailers so different?

2. **GO SHOPPING** Go to your favourite store and interview the manager. Determine how the retailer sets its performance objectives. Evaluate its procedures relative to the procedures presented in the text.

3. **INTERNET EXERCISE/GO SHOPPING** Get balance sheet and income statement information for your favourite publicly traded retailer by going to **www.hoovers.com**, **www.google.com/finance**, or the retailer's annual report, or by visiting the store and interviewing the owner/manager. Construct a strategic profit model and evaluate its financial performance.

Explain why you believe its ratios are or are not consistent with its strategy.

4. **CONNECT EXERCISE** Access Connect and go to the Strategic Profit Model (SPM) under additional resources for this chapter. The SPM tutorial was designed to provide a refresher for the basic financial ratios leading to return on assets. The tutorial walks you through it step-by-step. A "calculation page" is also included that will calculate all the ratios. You can type in the numbers from a firm's balance sheet and income statement to see the financial results that are produced with the current financial figures. You can also access an Excel spreadsheet for doing SPM calculations. The calculation page or the Excel spreadsheet can be used for the case on Blue Nile and Tiffany's.

5. **INTERNET EXERCISE** Go to **www.retailowner.com**. Under the Benchmarks menu, click on each of the following and then compare GMROI:
   a) General Merchandiser Stores – Department Stores
   b) Bldg. Materials, Garden Supplies Dealers – Building Materials Dealers

c) Apparel, Accessories Stores – Jewelry Stores

d) Motor Vehicles, Parts Dealers – Motorcycle Dealers

6. **INTERNET EXERCISE** Go to **www.bizstats.com**. Compare industry benchmarks with the retailer results found in Exhibit 8–12 by clicking on Industry Financials/Corporations/Retail Trade and then the applicable NAICS category (i.e., food and beverage). What are your findings?

DISCUSSION QUESTIONS AND PROBLEMS

1. Why must a retailer use multiple performance measures to evaluate its performance?

2. Describe how a multiple-store retailer would set its annual performance objectives.

3. Buyers' performance is often measured by their gross margin. Why is this figure more appropriate than net profit or loss?

4. How does the strategic profit model (SPM) assist retailers in planning and evaluating marketing and financial strategies?

5. Holt Renfrew (a high-service department store) and Costco (a chain of warehouse clubs) target different groups of customers. Which should have the higher asset turnover, net profit margin, and return on assets? Why?

6. Given the following information, construct an income statement and determine if there was a profit or loss. (Figures are in $000.)

Sales	$3 015 534
Cost of goods sold	2 020 954
Operating expenses	193 628
Interest expense	15 188
Taxes	67 807

7. Using the following information taken from Sharper Image Corporation's balance sheet, determine the asset turnover. (Figures are in US$ millions.)

Net sales	$383 222
Total assets	162 338
Total liabilities	67 595

8. Using the following information taken from the 2011 balance sheet and income statement for Lululemon, develop a strategic profit model.

Sales	$1 000 839
Cost of goods	431 569
Gross profit	569 270
Operating expense	282 312
Interest expenses	0
Income	286 958
Net income	184 964
Inventory	104 100
Accounts receivable	5200
Total assets	734 630
Total liabilities	133 260

9. Assume Sears is planning a special promotion for the upcoming holiday season. It has purchased 2.5 million Santa Bears, stuffed teddy bears dressed like Santa Claus, from a vendor in Taiwan. The GMROI for the bears is expected to be 144 percent (gross margin = 24 percent and sales-to-stock ratio = 6), about average for a seasonal promotion. Besides the invoice cost of the bears, Sears will incur import fees, transportation costs from Taiwan to distribution centres and then to stores, and distribution centre and store costs such as marking and handling. Since the bears arrived early in April, additional storage facilities are needed until they are shipped to the stores the first week of October. Is GMROI an adequate measure for evaluating the performance of Santa Bears? Explain your answer.

10. Increasing inventory turnover is an important goal for a retail manager. What are the consequences of turnover that is too slow?

11. The fine jewellery department in a department store has the same GMROI as the small appliances department even though characteristics of the merchandise are quite different. Explain this situation.

12. Calculate GMROI and inventory turnover given:

Annual sales	$20 000
Average inventory (at cost)	$75 000
Gross margin	45%

13. Calculate GMROI and inventory turnover given:

Annual sales	$12 000
Average inventory (at cost)	$4000
Gross margin	35%

14. Using the following information taken from the 2011 balance sheet and 2011 income statement for Loblaw Companies Ltd., develop a strategic profit model. (Figures are in $000.) You can access an Excel spreadsheet for SPM calculations on the student side of the book's website.

Net sales	$31 250
Cost of goods sold	23 894
Operating expenses	5 972
Interest expenses	0
Inventory	2 025
Accounts receivable	2 568
Current assets	6 462
Total assets	17 428
Total liabilities	11 421

information systems and supply chain management

SPOTLIGHT ON RETAILING

Lifting Spirits: Cloud-Based Software Smooths LCBO's Purchase Order and Delivery Operations

Step-by-step, the Liquor Control Board of Ontario (LCBO) is making business flow better by moving some core supply chain procedures into the cloud.

The Ontario government agency, responsible for purchasing and retailing wine and spirits in the province, has steadily been looking for ways to streamline procedures, reduce errors, and free up staff from clerical duties so that they can perform more complex, higher-value work. To that end, the LCBO has completely reworked both its purchase order and inbound delivery scheduling systems, and turned them from labourious, inefficient, paper-, fax- and telephone-based processes into web-based, automated, self-serve systems.

The LCBO buys alcoholic beverages from roughly 2700 suppliers in 75 countries. Some suppliers are major, multinational organizations. Others are small artisanal producers who sell only a few cases of wine to the LCBO every year. In total, the agency issues about 40 000 purchase orders (PO) annually. Implementing a system that was both robust enough to handle the number of purchase orders the LCBO issues and simple enough that it could be used by its entire supplier base made choosing the type of platform a pretty easy decision.

"We knew it needed to be web-based. We knew it needed to be accessible from anywhere in the world, around the clock. It had to provide that PO visibility. It had to be secure and have a secure protocol for access, and it had to provide online training for problem issues and support problem resolution 24/7. We also needed it to provide good audit-trail tracking, exception reporting, and real-time visibility," says Lisa MacGregor, director of supply chain for the LCBO.

The LCBO was already using a few applications, including its new submission system (NISS), developed and hosted by the Mississauga, Ontario–based QLogitek division of Logitek Data Sciences Ltd., so it returned to that company to create a web-based purchase-order management system, referred to inside the LCBO as WEB PO. WEB PO, however, was much larger in scope and was to be the first step in a more integrated supply chain management solution.

Because of the vast changes this system would bring, the LCBO knew it had to invest a great deal in supplier training and preparation before the system could go live, says project manager David Collins.

"With 2700 suppliers around the world, getting them registered was a big task before rollout. That was the main hurdle for the WEB PO rollout. We developed our own in-house application for them to register. We had them sign up as an administrator. They would provide an e-mail address and background information. We would verify that. We held back all the passwords and user IDs until the weekend before we actually rolled out, so they didn't lose them ahead of time. After they became an administrator, they could sign up additional people from their own office."

One of the challenges facing the LCBO was the multilingual nature of its supplier base. The software itself is available only in English, but suppliers who had problems due to language were able to call the QLogitek-run support line and receive assistance delivered in their native languages.

WEB PO has all but eliminated phone calls and faxes for regular transactions. Now, only exception-based incidents need to be dealt with manually. The software handles the rest of the normal, everyday transactions.

"If we issue a purchase order to a supplier for 1000 cases to be delivered by September 1, the supplier can request a change and say, 'I only have 800 cases and I can't make September 1, but I can make September 15.' That then comes back to us for us to approve or reject, and it's all automated. We don't have to deal with that manually. An alert goes to our LCBO staff. It's up to them to accept or reject, but it's still in the system," says MacGregor.

"They'll actually re-issue the PO, and then it goes back through the normal channels, and the supplier will see a revised PO come through," adds Collins.

Beyond its automated order-handling capabilities, MacGregor says one of WEB PO's biggest advantages is it now gives the LCBO the ability to track supplier performance.

"We have the audit trail, so we know if suppliers aren't meeting demands or time frames. That was a key point for us in terms of being able to have good data to track a supplier's performance. It's done by data extraction to a vendor scorecard. That process is a little more manual in terms of data extraction, but at least now we have the data in terms of being able to identify problem vendors."

Sources: Carolyn Gruske, "Lifting spirits," *Materials Management & Distribution*, October 30, 2012.

Joe Jackson wakes up in the morning, takes a shower, dresses, and goes to his kitchen to make a cup of coffee and toast a bagel. He slices the bagel and puts it in his toaster oven, but, to his dismay, the toaster oven is not working. As he reads the newspaper and eats his untoasted bagel with his coffee, he notices that Target is having a sale on Sunbeam toaster ovens. The toaster ovens look great. So, on his way home from work, he stops at a Target store to buy one. He finds the advertised Sunbeam model on the shelf and buys it.

Joe expected to find the Sunbeam toaster oven, as well as other models, available at Target, but he probably didn't realize that a lot of behind-the-scene activities were going on to get those toaster ovens to the store. Target uses sophisticated information and supply chain management systems to make sure that the Sunbeam toaster ovens and other brands are available in its stores whenever Joe and other customers want them. When Joe bought the toaster oven, the information about his transaction was automatically forwarded by the information systems to Target's regional distribution centre, the home appliance planner at Target Canada's corporate headquarters in Mississauga, and the toaster oven manufacturer in China. A computer information system monitors all toaster oven sales and inventory levels in every Target store and indicates when to have toaster ovens shipped from the manufacturer in China to the regional distribution centres and then from the centres to the stores.

Shipments to the distribution centres and stores are monitored using a satellite tracking system that locates the ships and trucks transporting the toaster ovens.

Of course, Target could ensure the availability of toaster ovens and other merchandise by simply keeping a large number of units in the stores at all times. But stocking a large number of each SKU would require much more space to store the items and a significant investment in additional inventory. So the challenge for Target is to limit its inventory and space investment but still make sure products are always available when customers want them.

This chapter begins by outlining how retailers can gain a strategic advantage through supply chain management and information systems. Then the chapter describes information and product flows in the supply chain and the activities undertaken in distribution centres. Next, it examines a set of decisions that retailers make to determine the structure of the supply chain, such as whether to use distribution centres or direct store deliveries and whether to outsource some supply chain functions. The chapter continues with a discussion of how vendors and retailers work together to efficiently manage the movement of merchandise from the vendor through the retailer's distribution centres to its stores and customers. The chapter concludes with a discussion of a new technology, radio frequency identification (RFID), being used to improve supply chain efficiency.

Creating Strategic Advantage Through Supply Management and Information Systems

As discussed in Chapter 1, retailers are the connection between customers and product manufacturers. It is the retailers' responsibility to gauge customers' wants and needs and work with the other members of the supply chain—distributors, vendors, and transportation companies—to make sure the merchandise that customers want is available when they want it. A simplified supply chain is illustrated in Exhibit 9–1. Vendors ship merchandise either to a distribution centre (as is the case for vendors V_1 and V_3) or directly to stores (as is the case for vendor V_2). The factors considered in deciding to ship directly to stores versus to distribution centres are discussed later in this chapter.

Supply chain management is a set of activities and techniques firms employ to efficiently and effectively manage the flow of merchandise from the vendors to the retailer's customers. These activities ensure that the customers are able to purchase merchandise in the desired quantities at a preferred location and appropriate time.[1]

Retailers are increasingly taking a leadership role in managing their supply chains. When retailers were predominantly small businesses, larger manufacturers and distributors dictated when, where, and how merchandise was delivered. But with the consolidation and emergence of large, international retail chains, retailers now play an active role in coordinating supply chain management activities. The size of these international retailers typically makes them more knowledgeable and powerful than their vendors and thus better able to control their supply chains. Retailers are in a unique position to collect information about customer shopping behaviour and purchases. As we will discuss later in the chapter, this information is being shared with suppliers to plan production, promotions, deliveries, assortments, and inventory levels. Efficient supply chain management is important to retailers because it can provide a strategic advantage that increases product availability and an inventory turnover that produces a higher return on assets.

distribution centre A warehouse that receives merchandise from multiple vendors and distributes it to multiple stores.

supply chain management The set of approaches and techniques firms employ to efficiently and effectively integrate their suppliers, manufacturers, warehouses, stores, and transportation intermediaries to efficiently have the right quantities at the right locations, and at the right time.

exhibit 9–1 Illustration of a Supply Chain

stockout A situation occurring when an SKU that a customer wants is not available.

Strategic Advantage

As we discussed in Chapter 4, strategic advantage is the unique and sustainable advantage that enables retailers to realize a higher-than-average return on their assets. Of course, all retailers strive to develop a competitive advantage, but not all retailers can develop a competitive advantage from their information and supply chain systems. However, if they do develop such an advantage, the advantage is sustainable because it is difficult for competitors to duplicate it.

For example, a critical factor in Walmart's success is its information and supply chain management systems. Even though competitors recognize this advantage, they have difficulty achieving the same level of performance as Walmart's systems for four reasons. First, Walmart has made substantial initial and continuing investments in developing its systems over a long time period. Second, it has the scale economies to justify these investments. Third, the supply chain activities take place within the firm and are not easily known or copied by competitors. Its systems are not simply software packages that any firm can buy from a software supplier. Through its continuous learning process, Walmart is always refining its systems to improve its performance. Fourth, the effective use of these systems requires top management support and the coordinated effort of employees and functional areas throughout the company.

Walmart's systems are so well regarded that retailers in emerging economies are anxious to partner with Walmart in hopes of acquiring some of these skills. For example, Bharti Enterprises in India has a joint venture with Walmart to wholesale food and other products to small Indian retailers. With Walmart's supply chain management systems in place, farmers and small manufacturers are directly linked to retailers, thus streamlining the supply chain.[4]

To understand the complexity of the tasks performed by these systems and the need for coordinated efforts, consider the various activities that retailers undertake to keep merchandise in stock:

- Accurately forecast sales and needed inventory levels for each category and SKU.
- Monitor sales to detect derivations from the forecast.
- Transport the right amount of merchandise from the distribution centres to each store.
- Make sure that accurate information is available that indicates where the merchandise is—either in the vendor's warehouse, the distribution centre, the store, sold to customer, or in transit.
- Place accurate, timely orders with vendors and distribution centres.
- Replenish merchandise from distribution centres with the right quantities when the stores need it.
- Ensure that buyers and marketing managers coordinate merchandise delivery with special sales and promotional materials.
- Collect and process returned merchandise.

Improved Product Availability

Efficient supply chain management provides two benefits to retailers and their customers: (1) fewer stockouts and (2) tailored assortments. These benefits translate into greater sales, lower costs, higher inventory turnover, and lower markdowns for retailers.

Fewer Stockouts A stockout occurs when an SKU that a customer wants is not available. What would happen if Joe went to the Target store and the store did not have Sunbeam toaster ovens because the distribution centre did not ship enough to the store? The store would give Joe a rain check so that he could come back and still pay the sale price when the store receives a new shipment. But Joe would not be pleased because he would have made a wasted trip to the store. As a result of the stockout, Joe might decide to buy another model, or he might go to a nearby Walmart to buy a toaster oven. While at Walmart, he could buy other items in addition to the toaster oven. He also might be reluctant to shop at Target in the future and might tell all of his friends about the negative experience he had. This bad experience could have been avoided if Target had done a better job of managing its supply chain.

In general, stockouts have significant short- and long-term effects on sales and profits. Data show that the first time customers experience a stockout, they will purchase a substitute item 70 percent of the time. With a second out-of-stock occurrence, that rate drops to 50 percent, with customers going to a competitor the other 50 percent of the time. By the third instance, there is a 70 percent chance that the retailer has lost the sale entirely and, most likely, the customers' loyalty as well. Customers may never come back.[5]

Tailored Assortments Another benefit provided by information systems that support supply chain systems is making sure that the right merchandise is available at the right store. Most national retail chains adjust assortments in their stores on the basis of climate—stocking more wool sweaters during the winter and cotton sweaters in fall. Some retailers are now using sophisticated statistical methods to analyze sales transaction data and adjust store assortments for a wide range of merchandise on the basis of the characteristics of customers in each store's local market.

Higher Return on Assets

From the retailer's perspective, an efficient supply chain and information system can improve its return on assets (ROA) because the system increases sales and net profit margins, without increasing inventory. Net sales increase because customers are offered more attractive, tailored assortments that are in stock. Consider Joe Jackson's toaster oven purchase. Target, with its information systems, could accurately estimate how many Sunbeam toaster ovens each store would sell during the special promotion. Using its supply chain management system, it would make sure sufficient stock was available at Joe's store so that all customers who wanted to buy one could.

Net profit margin is improved by increasing the gross margin and lowering expenses. An information system that coordinates buyers and vendors allows retailers to take advantage of special buying opportunities and obtain the merchandise at a lower cost, thus improving their gross margins. Retailers also can lower their operating expenses by coordinating deliveries, thus reducing transportation expenses. With more efficient distribution centres, merchandise can be received, prepared for sale, and shipped to stores with minimum handling, further reducing expenses.

By efficiently managing their supply chains, retailers can carry less backup inventory yet still avoid stockouts. Thus, inventory levels are lower, and with a lower inventory investment, total assets are also lower, so the asset and inventory turnovers are both higher. Retailing View 9.1 describes how supply chain management is changing the way fashion comes to market.

Lo 2

The Flow of Information and Products in a Supply Chain

The complexities of the merchandise and information flows in a typical multistore chain are illustrated in Exhibit 9–2. Although information and merchandise flows are intertwined, in the following

sections we describe first how information about customer demand is captured at the store, which triggers a series of responses from buyers and planners, distribution centres, and vendors. This information is used to make sure that merchandise is available at the store when the customer wants it. Then we discuss the physical movement of merchandise from vendors through distribution centres to the stores.

Information Flows

When Joe Jackson bought his toaster oven at Target, he initiated the information flows illustrated in Exhibit 9–3 (the numbers in circles refer to the path in the exhibit).

The Target cashier scans the Universal Product Code (UPC) tag on the toaster oven box (1), and a sales receipt is generated for Joe. The UPC tag is a black-and-white bar code containing a 13-digit code that indicates the manufacturer of the item, a description of the item, information about special packaging, and special promotions. The codes for all products are issued by GS1 US (gs1us.org), formerly the Uniform Code Council. In the future, RFID tags, discussed later in this chapter, may replace UPC tags.

Universal Product Code (UPC) The black-and-white bar code found on most merchandise that is used to collect sales information at the point of sale using computer terminals that read the code. This information is transmitted computer to computer to buyers, distribution centres, and then to vendors, who in turn quickly ship replenishment merchandise.

DID YOU KNOW?

Shortly after 8 A.M. on June 26, 1974, the first UPC tag was scanned in Troy, Ohio, when Clyde Dawson bought a 10-pack of Wrigley's Juicy Fruit gum for 67 cents in a Marsh supermarket. Now, over 10 billion items are scanned each day.[6]

exhibit 9–2   Information and Merchandise Flows

----- **Merchandise flow**   ——— **Information flow**

Zara Delivers Fast Fashion

Fast fashion is a retail business strategy that involves using the supply chain management process to introduce fashionable merchandise rapidly and respond to customer demand for the merchandise quickly. This business strategy was pioneered by Zara, a global specialty apparel chain located in La Coruna, Spain, and adopted by other retailers such as H&M (headquartered in Sweden), TopShop (United Kingdom), and Forever 21 (United States).

The fast-fashion process starts with receiving timely information from store managers. At Zara, store managers are equipped with handheld devices linked directly to the company's corporate office in Spain. They report daily on what customers are buying and not buying and what they are asking for but not finding. For instance, when buyers find that customers are requesting a purple shirt that is similar to one they are selling in pink, they pass this information on to the designers in Spain, who initiate a process that results in making and shipping purple shirts to its stores in a very short period of time.

Zara successfully reduces lead time by communicating electronically with the factory, and using automated equipment, assemblers who are in close proximity to the factory, and premium transportation.

Zara's competitive advantage in specialty apparel retailing is based on its efficient supply chain that delivers fashionable merchandise to its stores frequently.

Zara buys undyed fabric from Asia, but the bulk of its apparel manufacturing occurs in Spain and Portugal. On the basis of its new design concepts and the customer response in stores, fabric gets cut and dyed by robots in the company's 23 highly automated factories in Spain. The final construction is entrusted to a network of 300 or so small assemblers located near its factories in

---

exhibit 9-3   Information Flows

The information about the transaction is captured at the point-of-sale (POS) terminal and sent to Target's information system, where it can be accessed by the planner for the toaster oven product category (2). The planner uses this information to monitor and analyze sales and decide when to reorder more toaster ovens or reduce their prices if sales are below expectations.

The sales transaction data also are sent to Target's distribution centre (6). When the store inventory drops to a specified level, more toaster ovens are shipped to the store, and the shipment information is sent to the Target computer system (5) so that the planner knows the inventory level that remains in the distribution centre.

Galicia, Spain, and northern Portugal. To ensure that the apparel is delivered in a timely manner, merchandise is shipped by truck to stores in Europe and by air express to stores in the rest of the world.

Instead of shipping new products a few times a season (as many fashion retailers do), Zara makes deliveries to each of its stores every few days. The purple shirts would be in stores in two weeks—compared with the several months it would take for most department stores and other specialty apparel stores to accomplish the same feat. For instance, if a Zara store is running low on a medium kelly green sweater, its fast-fashion system will ensure a shorter lead time than that of more traditional retailers. As a result, it's less likely that the Zara store will be out of stock before the next sweater shipment arrives. Limiting the stock in stores also creates a sense of scarcity among its customers. If they don't buy now, the item might not be available next time they visit the store. Finally, by producing and shipping small quantities, Zara can quickly recover from a fashion faux pas.

Due to the efficiency of its supply chain, Zara does not have to discount nonselling merchandise as much as do other specialty store apparel retailers. At Zara,

the number of items that end up marked down is about half the industry average. Zara is able to achieve these results and still have 10 000 new designs and 40 000 new SKUs each year.

H&M and Forever 21 use a slightly different strategy. About one-quarter of their assortments are made up of fast-fashion items that are designed in-house and produced by independent, local factories. As at Zara, these items move quickly through the stores and are replaced frequently with fresh designs. But H&M also keeps a significant inventory of basic, everyday items sourced from low-cost Asian factories.

The fast-fashion approach is particularly effective for specialty apparel retailers targeting customers who are very fashion-conscious and always want to have a new look, not the same things their friends are wearing. And these customers want to achieve this fashion ability on a limited budget. Because more shoppers are loading up on fast fashion every few weeks instead of purchasing a few higher-priced basics once every few months, they are less sentimental about quickly unloading them to help finance the next round. Thus, sales of fast-fashion merchandise in second-hand stores are growing dramatically.

Sources: Vertica Bhardwaj and Ann Fairhurst, "Fast Fashion: Response to Changes in the Fashion Industry," *International Review of Retail, Distribution and Consumer Research 20* (February 2010), pp.165–173; Carmen Lopez and Ying Fan, "Case Study: Internationalisation of the Spanish Fashion Brand Zara," *Journal of Fashion Marketing and Management* 13, no. 2 (2009), pp. 279–296; Mark Mulligan, "Spanish Professor Who Uncovers the Detail in Retail: Constant Contact with Corporate Life Is a Valuable Teaching Tool," *Financial Times*, August 18, 2008, p. 12; Brian Dunn, "Inside the Zara Business Model," *DNR*, March 20, 2006, p. 11.

When the inventory drops to a specified level in the distribution centre (4), the planner negotiates terms and shipping dates and places an order with the manufacturer of the toaster ovens. The planner then informs the distribution centre about the new order and when the store can expect delivery (5).

When the manufacturer ships the toaster ovens to the Target distribution centre, it sends an advanced shipping notice to the distribution centre (7). An advance shipping notice (ASN) is a document that tells the distribution centre what specifically is being shipped and when it will be delivered. The distribution centre then makes appointments for trucks to make the delivery at a specific time, date, and loading dock. When the shipment is received at the distribution centre, the planner is notified (5) and then authorizes payment to the vendor.

In some situations, discussed later in this chapter, the sales transaction data are sent directly from the store to the vendor (3), and the vendor decides when to ship more merchandise to the distribution centre and stores. The fulfillment of sales from nonstore channels may involve the vendor shipping merchandise directly to the customer. In other situations, especially when merchandise is reordered frequently, the ordering process is done automatically, bypassing the planners.

advance shipping notice (ASN) An electronic document received by a retailer's computer from a supplier in advance of a shipment.

Data Warehouse Purchase data collected at the point of sale goes into a database known as a *data warehouse*. The information stored in the data warehouse is accessible on various dimensions and levels, as depicted in the data cube in Exhibit 9–4.

electronic data interchange (EDI) The computer-to-computer exchange of business documents from retailer to vendor and back.

security policy The set of rules that applies to activities in the computer and communications resources that belong to an organization.

DID YOU KNOW?

By analyzing its customer database, Walmart knows that sales of strawberry Pop Tarts increase by 700 percent in areas facing the arrival of a hurricane.[8]

As shown on the horizontal axis, data can be accessed according to the level of merchandise aggregation—SKU (item), vendor, category (dresses), department (women's apparel), or all merchandise. Along the vertical axis, data can be accessed by level of the company—store, division, or total company. Finally, along the third dimension, data can be accessed by point in time—day, season, or year.

The CEO might be interested in how the corporation is generally doing and could look at the data aggregated by quarter for a merchandise division, a region of the country, or the total corporation. A buyer may be more interested in a particular vendor in a specific store on a particular day. Analysts from various levels of the retail operation extract information from the data warehouse to make a plethora of retailing decisions about developing and replenishing merchandise assortments.

Data warehouses also contain detailed information about customers, which is used to target promotions and group products together in stores. These applications are discussed in Chapter 14. To economically collect this information, most of the communication between vendors and retailers and within the retailer is done via electronic data interchange (EDI).

exhibit 9–4   Retail Data Warehouse

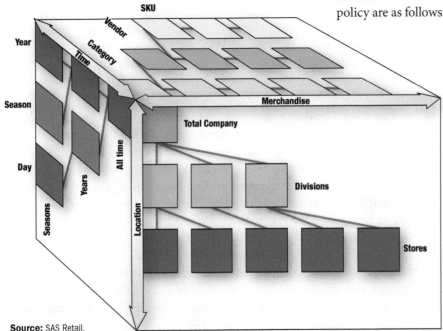

Source: SAS Retail.

Electronic Data Interchange   In the past, retailer–vendor information flows were accomplished by sending handwritten or typed documents through the mail or by fax. Now, most communications between vendors and retailers occur via electronic data interchange. Electronic data interchange (EDI) is the computer-to-computer exchange of business documents in a standardized format. To facilitate the adoption of EDI, the retail industry agreed to use specific symbols to delineate the purchase order number, the vendor's name, the address the merchandise is being shipped to, and so forth.

Retailers also have developed standards for exchanging information about purchase order changes, order status, transportation routings, advance shipping notices, on-hand inventory status, and vendor promotions, as well as information that enables vendors to put price tags on merchandise. The development and use of these standards is critical to the use of EDI because they enable all retailers to use the same format when transmitting data to their vendors.

EDI transmissions between retailers and vendors occur over the Internet. Because the Internet is a publicly accessible network, its use to communicate internally and externally with vendors and customers raises security issues. Some potential implications of security failures are the loss of business data essential to conducting business, disputes with vendors and customers, loss of public confidence and its effect on brand image, bad publicity, and loss of revenue from customers using an electronic channel.

To help secure information, retailers have incorporated security policies. A security policy is the set of rules that applies to activities involving computer and communication resources that belong to an organization. Retailers also train employees and add the necessary software and hardware to enforce the rules. The objectives of a security policy are as follows:

- **Authentication.** The system ensures or verifies that the person or computer at the other end of the communication really is who or what it claims to be.

- **Authorization.** The system ensures that the person or computer at the other end of the comunication has permission to carry out the request.

- **Integrity.** The system ensures that the arriving information is the same as that sent, which means that the data have been protected from unauthorized changes or tampering through a data encryption process.

The Physical Flow of Merchandise— Logistics

Exhibit 9–5 illustrates the physical flow of merchandise within the supply chain.

1. Merchandise flows from vendor to distribution centre.

2. Merchandise goes from distribution centre to stores.

3. Alternatively, merchandise can go from vendor directly to stores or even the customer.

Logistics is the aspect of supply chain management that refers to the planning, implementation, and control of the efficient flow and storage of goods, services, and related information from the point of origin to the point of consumption to meet customers' needs.[9] In addition to managing inbound and outbound transportation, logistics involves the activities undertaken in the retailer's distribution centre. For example, sometimes merchandise is temporarily stored at the distribution centre; other times it just passes through the centre from an inbound to an outbound truck. Merchandise shipments might be prepared for stores in the centre. For example, the centre might break down received shipping cartons into smaller quantities that can be more readily utilized by the individual stores and/or apply price tags and the retailer's labels. The following section describes activities undertaken in a distribution centre.

◨ The Distribution Centre

The distribution centre performs the following activities: coordinating inbound transportation; receiving, checking, storing, and cross-docking; getting merchandise

exhibit 9–5 Merchandise Flow

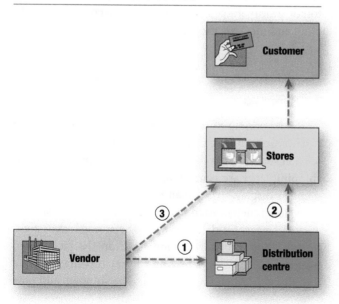

"floor-ready"; and coordinating outbound transportation. To illustrate these activities, we shall follow a shipment of Sony PlayStation systems that is arriving at a Sears distribution centre.

Management of Inbound Transportation

Traditionally, buyers focused their efforts, when working with vendors, on developing merchandise assortments, negotiating prices, and arranging joint promotions. Now, buyers and planners are much more involved in coordinating the physical flow of merchandise to the stores. The Sears game buyer has arranged for a truckload of systems to be delivered to its St. Laurent, Quebec, distribution centre on Monday between 1 and 3 P.M. The buyer has also specified the particular way that the merchandise should be placed on pallets for easy unloading.

The truck must arrive within the specified time because the distribution centre has all of its 100 receiving docks allocated throughout the day and much of the merchandise on this particular truck is going to be shipped to stores that evening. Unfortunately, the truck was delayed in a snowstorm. The dispatcher—the person who coordinates deliveries to the distribution centre—reassigns the truck delivering the Sony game stations to a Wednesday morning delivery slot, notifies the planner, and charges the firm several hundred dollars for missing its delivery time. Although many manufacturers pay transportation expenses, some retailers negotiate with their vendors to absorb this expense.

Receiving and Checking

Receiving is the process of recording the receipt of merchandise as it arrives at a distribution centre. Checking is the process of going through the goods on receipt to make sure that they arrived undamaged and that the merchandise ordered was the merchandise received.

Checking merchandise is a very labour-intensive and time-consuming task. When retailers have developed good relationships with vendors, they often do not check the number of items received compared to the number sent as indicated on the vendor's ASN for all merchandise received. They randomly check a sample of

logistics Part of the supply chain process that plans, implements, and controls the efficient, effective flow and storage of goods, services, and related information from the point of origin to the point of consumption to meet customers' requirements.

dispatcher A person who coordinates deliveries from the vendor to the distribution centre or stores, or from the distribution centre to stores.

receiving The process of filling out paperwork to record the receipt of merchandise that arrives at a store or distribution centre.

checking The process of going through goods upon receipt to make sure that they arrived undamaged and that the merchandise received matches the merchandise ordered.

cross-docked Items that are unloaded from the shippers' truck and within a few hours reloaded onto trucks going to stores. These items are prepackaged by the vendor for a specific store, such that the UPC labels on a carton indicate the store to which it is to be sent.

floor-ready merchandise Merchandise received at the store ready to be sold, without the need for any additional preparation by retail employees.

ticketing and marking Procedures for making price labels and placing them on the merchandise.

pick ticket A document that tells the order filler how much of each item to get from the storage area.

shipments to monitor the accuracy of the vendor's ASNs. In the future, retailers may be able to automatically check the contents of each carton by detecting signals sent from RFID chips placed on each item of merchandise in a carton.

Storing and Cross-Docking

After the PlayStations are received and checked, they are either stored or cross-docked. When PlayStations are stored, the cartons are transported by a conveyor system and forklift trucks to racks that go from the distribution centre's floor to its ceiling. Then, when the PlayStations are needed in the stores, a forklift driver goes to the rack, picks up the carton, and places it on a conveyor system that routes the carton to the loading dock of a truck going to the stores.

Cross-Docking PlayStation cartons that are cross-docked are prepackaged by Sony for a specific store. The UPC label on each carton indicates the store to which it is to be sent. Sony may also affix a price tag to each item in the carton. The PlayStation cartons are placed on a conveyor system that routes them from the unloading dock at which they were received to the loading dock for the truck going to the specific store—thus, the term *cross-docked*. The cartons are routed on the conveyor system automatically by sensors that read the UPC labels on the cartons. These cross-docked cartons are only in the distribution centre for a few hours before they are shipped to the stores.

The size, sales rate, and vendor performance typically determine whether cartons are cross-docked or stored. Merchandise is cross-docked only if an entire carton can be shipped to a store. For example, it would be inefficient to cross-dock toothbrush cartons if a received carton contained 500 units but a store only sold 50 units a day. In this situation, the received toothbrush carton would be opened and a smaller number of units along with other merchandise would be put in a carton going to a store. Finally, when cross-docking cartons, retailers are assuming that the number and type of merchandise, as well as the store designation, are correctly encoded in the vendor's UPC labels. Thus, retailers are reluctant to cross-dock merchandise from unreliable vendors because it is very costly to correct errors that are not discovered until the cartons are first opened in stores.

Important activities undertaken in distribution centres are ticketing and marking merchandise so that it is floor-ready.

Getting Merchandise Floor-Ready

For some merchandise, additional tasks are undertaken in the distribution centre to make the merchandise floor-ready. **Floor-ready merchandise** is merchandise that is ready to be placed on the selling floor. Getting merchandise floor-ready entails ticketing, marking, and, in the case of some apparel, placing garments on hangers.

Ticketing and marking refer to affixing price and identification labels to the merchandise. It is more efficient for a retailer to perform these activities at a distribution centre than in its stores. In a distribution centre, an area can be set aside and a process implemented to efficiently add labels and put apparel on hangers. Conversely, getting merchandise floor-ready in stores can block aisles and divert salespeople's attention from their customers. An even better approach from the retailer's perspective is to get vendors to ship floor-ready merchandise, thus totally eliminating the expensive, time-consuming ticketing and marking process.

Preparing to Ship Merchandise to a Store

At the beginning of the day, the computer system in the distribution centre generates a list of items to be shipped to each store on that day. For each item, a pick ticket and shipping label are generated. The **pick ticket** is a document or display on a screen in a forklift truck that indicates how much of each item to get from specific storage areas. The forklift driver goes to the storage area, picks up the number of cartons indicated on the pick ticket, places UPC shipping labels on the cartons that indicate the stores to which the items are to be shipped, and puts the cartons on the conveyor system, where they are automatically routed to the loading dock for the truck going to the stores.

Pick tickets and labels are also generated for the break pack area. In the break pack area, cartons with too many items to be shipped to a single store (like the toothbrushes discussed above) are packaged for the store. Employees, using the pick ticket, select items from open cartons and put them into a new carton. When all the items have been picked, a shipping label indicating the store's destination is attached to the carton, which is then placed on the conveyor system and routed to the appropriate loading dock.

So the conveyor system feeds cartons from three sources to the loading dock for a truck going to a specific store: (1) cross-docked cartons directly from the vendor's delivery trucks, (2) cartons stored in the distribution centre, and (3) cartons from the break pack area. These cartons are then loaded onto the trucks by employees.

Management of Outbound Transportation

The management of outbound transportation from distribution centre to stores is quite complex. Most distribution centres run 50 to 100 outbound truck routes each day. To handle this complex transportation problem, the centres use sophisticated routing and scheduling computer systems that consider the locations of the stores, road conditions, and transportation operating constraints to develop the most efficient routes possible. As a result, stores are provided with an accurate estimated time of arrival, and vehicle utilization is maximized.

Retailers also need to determine the mode of transportation—planes, ships, or trucks. Some retailers mix modes of transportation to reduce overall costs and time

An automated conveyor system moves most cartons to outbound trucks for delivery to stores.

delays. For example, many Chinese vendors send Europe-bound cargo by ship to the U.S. West Coast. From there, the cargo is flown to its final destination in Europe. By combining the two modes of transport, sea and air, the entire trip takes about two weeks, as opposed to four or five weeks with an all-water route, and the cost is about half that of an all-air route.

Dollar General, an extreme-value, full-line discount store, developed an interesting, low-tech approach for dealing with a challenge it faced with outbound transportation to its stores. Controlling cost and distributing merchandise efficiently to its 8000 stores is key to maintaining its low prices and still making a profit. Each week, more than 2000 cartons are delivered to a typical store, and 12 person-hours are required to unload a delivery truck—time the employees could have spent helping customers. Labour scheduling is a real problem because store managers have to schedule additional staff on truck days and then, in some cases, the drivers cannot make deliveries at the preplanned time. In addition, many of the stores are located in urban areas that make it difficult to park delivery trucks at a convenient location for an extended time period.

To address these challenges, Dollar General invested $100 million in a delivery system called *EZ store*. The EZ store system involves packing merchandise for shipment to stores in easy-to-move containers called *roll-tainers*. Instead of having store staff unload the truck when it arrives, the truck drivers alone can unload the 25 roll-tainers for the typical store in about 90 minutes. Store employees no longer need to wait for the truck to arrive and then walk 3 to 8 miles, lifting 6000 pounds of merchandise, on truck days. Instead, they can unpack merchandise from the roll-tainers and stock it on shelves during slow times in the day. The roll-tainers are also designed to protect the merchandise. When drivers make their next delivery, they offload the filled roll-tainers and pick up the empty ones. The system has led to significant reductions in employee injuries and turnover, reduced labour hours, and greater customer satisfaction.[10]

Retailing View 9.2 describes how Netflix automates many of these activities so that it can efficiently process and ship over 2 million DVDs a day and make sure the customers get the right ones.

System Design Issues   LO 4

This section reviews the factors affecting the decisions made by retailers concerning their supply chains. These decisions involve determining what activities, if any, should be outsourced to independent firms; what merchandise, if any, should be delivered directly to the store, bypassing the distribution centre; and how shipments directly to customers should be made.

How Netflix Makes Sure You Enjoy Your Movie

Imagine the disappointment of inserting the DVD of *The Blind Side* and sitting back on your couch to enjoy the movie only to suddenly realize that the DVD is actually *Shrek 2*. Netflix, the California-based online movie subscription rental service, has a sophisticated system to ensure that customers get exactly what they want and don't have to wait more than a day or two to receive it.

In order to support its disc rental services, the company operates 58 distribution centres in the United States. The fulfillment process starts at 3 A.M., when employees seated at rows of desks start tearing open thousands of red envelopes. To get the envelopes to the facility that early, Netflix sends trucks to postal facilities at night to pick up the DVDs that have been returned by customers and bring them back to the hub.

For the next five hours, each employee repeats the same few steps over and over: Rip red envelope. Remove disc from white sleeve. Inspect disc for scratches and cracks. Make sure it's the correct disc. Clean disc. Return to sleeve. Place the disc in appropriate bin. An average employee can go through 650 discs in an hour, after receiving a month-long training.

Next, the envelopes are fed twice through a sorting machine—once to register the DVDs Netflix has received, a process which automatically e-mails the customer who sent it and asks him or her to rate the movie, and a second time to determine if that DVD has been promised to another customer. If it has, the machine automatically places it in a bin marked with its destination.

Continuing on its journey, the bin with the envelope is brought over to "The Stuffer," a machine Netflix created to speed up the process of stuffing and sealing the red envelopes. At a rate of 3200 an hour, the

Netflix's semi-automated system for processing rented DVDs gives it a competitive advantage.

machine opens an envelope, stuffs the sleeve inside, removes the adhesive strip, seals the envelope, and places another seal on it.

The final stop is another trip to the mail sorter, where the sealed envelope gets scanned to determine its destination, has the address printed on it, and then gets sorted by zip code into a bin attached to the machine. Starting about 4 P.M., white trucks drive the bins to mail-processing and distribution centres. All the postal service has to do is load them on its trucks to send that little red envelope on its way to someone else's mailbox.

Sources: Etan Horowitz, "Netflix Distribution Centres: A Portrait of Speed and Efficiency," *Orlando Sentinel*, August 2009; Christopher Borrelli, "How Netflix Gets Your Movies to Your Mailbox So Fast," *Chicago Tribune*, August 4, 2009.

Outsourcing Logistics

outsource Obtain a service from outside the company that had previously been done by the firm itself.

To streamline their operations and make more productive use of their assets and personnel, some retailers **outsource** supply chain functions.

Many independent companies are very efficient at performing individual activities or all the supply chain activities. There are a large number of companies that can transport merchandise from the vendor to distribution centres or from the centres to the retailer's stores.

Rather than owning warehouses to store merchandise, retailers can use public warehouses that are owned and operated by an independent company. Rather than outsource specific activities, retailers can use freight forwarders to arrange for the storage and shipping of their merchandise. Freight forwarders usually provide a full range of services including tracking inland transportation, preparing shipping and export documents, warehousing, booking cargo space, negotiating freight charges, consolidating freight, insuring cargo, and filing insurance claims.[11]

Advantages and Disadvantages of Outsourcing Supply Chain Activities

The primary benefit of outsourcing is that the independent firms can perform the activity at a lower cost or more efficiently than the retailer. Independent firms typically have a lower cost because they perform the activity for many retailers and thus realize scale economies. For example, independent trucking firms have more opportunities to fill their trucks on the return trip (backhaul) with merchandise for other retailers after delivering merchandise to one retailer's stores. In addition, when there are many independent firms available to undertake the activity, retailers can have the firms bid against each other to undertake the activity and thus drive down the costs.

However, when retailers outsource a supply chain activity, they can no longer develop a competitive advantage based on the performance of this activity. If the retailer's competitor discovers that the retailer is significantly reducing its costs or improving its efficiency by using an independent firm, the competitor can match the performance improvement by contracting with the same provider.[12]

Pull and Push Supply Chains

Another supply chain decision retailers make is determining whether merchandise will be pushed from the distribution centres to the stores or pulled from the distribution centres to the stores. Information and merchandise flows such as those described in Exhibit 9–2 illustrate a pull supply chain—a supply chain in which requests for merchandise are generated at the store level on the basis of sales data captured by POS terminals. Basically, in this type of supply chain, the demand for an item pulls it through the supply chain. An alternate and less sophisticated approach is a push supply chain, in which merchandise is allocated to stores on the basis of forecasted demand. Once a forecast is developed, specified quantities of merchandise are shipped (pushed) to distribution centres and stores at predetermined time intervals.

In a pull supply chain, there is less likelihood of being overstocked or out of stock because the store requests for merchandise are based on customer demand. A pull approach increases inventory turnover and is more responsive to changes in customer demand, and it becomes even more efficient than a push approach when demand is uncertain and difficult to forecast.[13]

Although generally more desirable, a pull approach is not the most effective in all situations. First, a pull approach requires a more costly and sophisticated information system to support it. Second, for some merchandise, retailers do not have the flexibility to adjust inventory levels on the basis of demand. For example, commitments must be made months in advance for fashion and private-label apparel. Because these commitments cannot be easily changed, the merchandise has to be allocated to the stores at the time the orders are formulated. Third, push supply chains are efficient for merchandise that has steady, predictable demand, such as milk and eggs, basic men's underwear, and bath towels. Because both pull and push supply chains have their advantages, most retailers use a combination of these approaches.

Distribution Centres versus Direct Store Delivery

As indicated in Exhibit 9–5, retailers can have merchandise shipped directly to their stores—direct store delivery (path 3)—or to their distribution centres (paths 1 and 2). Direct store delivery (DSD) is a method of delivering merchandise to stores in which vendors distribute merchandise directly to the stores.[14]

The vendors offering DSD also undertake additional services such as merchandising (arranging merchandise on racks or shelves) and information gathering about inventory levels. As part of the DSD process, vendor employees visit the retailer's store several times a week. In those store visits, trained personnel assess stock levels and backroom inventory to determine the right order amount, replenish the order, and display products based on local preferences.

public warehouses
Warehouses that are owned and operated by a third party.

freight forwarders
Companies that purchase transport services. They then consolidate small shipments from a number of shippers into large shipments that move at a lower freight rate.

pull supply chain
Strategy in which orders for merchandise are generated at store level on the basis of demand data captured by point-of-sale terminals.

push supply chain
Strategy in which merchandise is allocated to stores on the basis of historical demand, the inventory position at the distribution centre, and the stores' needs.

direct store delivery (DSD)
A method of delivering merchandise to stores in which vendors distribute merchandise directly to the stores rather than going through distribution centres.

Having Dolly Madison's products delivered directly to stores, bypassing the supermarkets' distribution centres, enables customers to get fresher baked goods.

store delivery when retailers need to prepare merchandise for sale, such as affixing price labels. When preparation is done in a centre, several employees can be trained to perform the activity efficiently rather than having 50 people (one in each store) do the preparation along with other duties.

Distribution centres, however, aren't appropriate for all retailers. If retailers have only a few outlets, the expense of a distribution centre is probably unwarranted. Also, direct store delivery gets merchandise to the stores faster and thus is used for perishable goods (meat and produce), items that help create the retailer's image of being the first to sell the latest product (e.g., video games), or fad items. DSD also is most efficient for fragile products for which freshness is important, such as salty snacks, bread, milk, and ice cream. For example, by developing a supply chain that bypasses the distribution centre, ProFlowers reduced the time from flower cutting to store delivery from twelve to three days. Finally, some vendors provide direct store delivery for retailers to ensure that their products are on the store's shelves, properly displayed, and fresh. For example, employees delivering Frito-Lay snacks directly to supermarkets replace products that have been on the shelf too long and are stale, replenish products that have been sold, and arrange products so that they are neatly displayed.

reverse logistics
The process of capturing value from and/or properly disposing of merchandise returned by customers and/or stores.

The decision to use DSD or distribution centres depends on the characteristics of the merchandise and the nature of demand. To determine which distribution system is more efficient, retailers balance the total cost of each alternative and the impact of the alternatives on customer satisfaction.

Distribution centres lower inventory levels because the amount of backup stock needed in a centralized distribution centre is less than the amount of backup stock needed in all the stores served by the centre. For example, to achieve the desired product availability with direct delivery, each store might need to stock 10 Sunbeam toaster ovens for a total of 500 units in the 50 stores served by a distribution centre. By delivering products to a distribution centre and feeding the 50 stores from the centre, the retailer could achieve the same level of product availability with only 350 toaster ovens (5 in each store and 100 in the distribution centre). Since the stores get frequent deliveries from the distribution centre, they need to carry relatively less extra merchandise as backup stock. Thus, distribution centres enable the retailer to carry less merchandise in the individual stores, and this results in lower inventory investments systemwide. In addition, retail store space is typically much more expensive than space at a distribution centre. Distribution centres are typically located in remote areas near highways, while stores are located in more expensive areas near customers' homes. In addition, distribution centres are more efficient than direct

Reverse Logistics

Reverse logistics is the process of capturing value from and/or properly disposing of merchandise returned by customers and/or stores. The reverse-logistics system processes merchandise that is returned because it is damaged, has been recalled, is no longer sold to customers because its selling season has ended or the product has been discontinued, or has excessive inventory. Packaging and shipping materials are also processed through the reverse-logistics system. The returned merchandise might involve returns from a customer to a retail store, from a retail store to a distribution centre, or from a distribution centre to a vendor.[16]

Reverse-logistics systems are challenging. The returned items may be damaged or lack the original shipping carton and thus require special handling. Transportation costs are high because items are shipped back in small quantities. Of the 48 million units shipped by L.L. Bean each year, 6 million are returned. About 85 percent of these returns are refunds and 15 percent are exchanges. For whatever reason, the products have disappointed the customer. L.L. Bean is committed to getting it right the second time. Although the returned merchandise moves through its system on a conveyor belt, one person handles each returned item from the time it is picked up off the conveyor to be scanned, processed, and prepped to the time it is sorted and placed back on the conveyor for reintroduction into the inventory system. This process has streamlined the return process and reduced errors.

Supply Chain for Fulfilling Catalogue and Internet Orders

The distribution centres and supply chains for supporting catalogue and Internet channels are very different from those supporting a store channel. The typical retail distribution centre supporting a store channel is designed to receive cartons from vendors and ship cartons to a limited number of stores. In contrast, distribution centres supporting nonstore channels are designed to receive cartons and ship individual orders to a large number of customers. Since completely different distribution centre designs are required for supporting the different channels, multichannel retailers either have different distribution centres for the channels or designate separate areas within a single centre devoted to the different channels.

When the dot-com boom started, a number of store-based retailers lacked the capability to efficiently fulfill individual orders placed through their electronic channels. Thus they initially outsourced the fulfillment function when they added an Internet channel. For example, Toys "R" Us turned to Amazon for help after a disastrous 1999 holiday season when many of its customers did not receive their orders on time, creating many unhappy customers on Christmas morning. Toys "R" Us entered into a ten-year agreement outsourcing the fulfillment of its orders. Even though Amazon's fulfillment capability is very efficient, over time Toys "R" Us acquired this capability and found that outsourcing its electronic channel was an impediment to creating a unified, multichannel offering. So Toys "R" Us terminated its outsourcing contract with Amazon.[17]

Drop-shipping

Drop-shipping, or *consumer direct fulfillment*, is a system in which retailers receive orders from customers and relay these orders to vendors and then the vendors ship the merchandise ordered directly to the customer. Drop-shipping has been used for years by companies that sell bulky products such as lumber, iron, and petroleum, as well as catalogue and mail-order companies.[18]

From the retailer's perspective, drop-shipping reduces the retailer's supply chain costs and investment because the vendor, rather than the retailer, assumes the costs and risks of supplying merchandise to customers. The vendor has to build and operate the distribution centres, hire and pay for employees to pick and pack individual orders, and manage inventory. Drop-shipping is particularly attractive for retailers that do not have distribution centres capable of fulfilling individual orders from customers. However, drop-shipping can lengthen delivery times and increase costs, particularly for customers that order multiple items from different vendors. In addition, retailers do not have control over an aspect of their offering that is of importance to their customer—how and when orders are delivered.

> **drop-shipping** A supply chain system in which retailers receive orders from customers and relay these orders to a vendor and then the vendor ships the merchandise ordered directly to the customer; also called *consumer direct fulfillment*.

> **DID YOU KNOW?**
> The cost of processing a return can be up to three times the cost of an outbound shipment of an item.[19]

Collaboration between Retailers and Vendors in Supply Chain Management LO 5

As we discussed previously, retailers' and vendors' objectives for supply chain management are to minimize investments in inventory and costs and still make sure that merchandise is available when and where customers want it. Retailing View 9.1 at the beginning of this chapter illustrated how fast-fashion specialty retailers, such as Zara and H&M, excel at coordinating their stores, designers, and production capability to achieve these objectives.

Benefits of Coordination

Supply chain efficiency dramatically improves when vendors and retailers share information and work together. By collaborating, vendors can plan their purchases of raw materials and their production processes to match the retailer's merchandise needs. Thus, vendors can make sure that the merchandise is available "just in time," when the retailer needs it, without having to stock excessive inventory in the vendor's warehouse or the retailer's distribution centres or stores.

> **DID YOU KNOW?**
> Subway realized savings of more than 1 million miles and reduced carbon output by 1663 metric tonnes by persuading a packaging supplier to move 1000 miles closer to its distribution centre.[20]

bullwhip effect The buildup of inventory in an uncoordinated channel.

When retailers and vendors do not coordinate their supply chain management activities, excess inventory builds up in the system, even if the retail sales rate for the merchandise is relatively constant. This buildup of inventory in an uncoordinated channel is called the **bullwhip effect**. The effect was first discovered by Procter & Gamble, which saw that its orders from retailers for Pampers disposable diapers were shaped like a bullwhip, with wide swings in quantity ordered, even though retail sales were relatively constant (see Exhibit 9–6). Its retailers were ordering, on average, more inventory than they really needed.[22]

Research has found that the bullwhip effect in an uncoordinated supply chain is caused by the following factors:

- **Delays in transmitting orders and receiving merchandise.** Even when retailers can forecast sales accurately, there are delays in getting orders to the vendor and receiving those orders from the vendor. In an uncoordinated supply chain, retailers might not know how fast they can get the merchandise, and thus they overorder to prevent stockouts.

- **Overreacting to shortages.** When retailers find it difficult to get the merchandise they want, they begin to play the shortage game. They order more than they need to prevent stockouts, hoping they will receive a larger partial shipment. So, on average, the vendor ships more than the retailer really needs.

- **Ordering in batches.** Rather than generating a number of small orders, retailers wait and place larger orders to reduce order processing and transportation costs and take advantage of quantity discounts.[23]

These factors cause the bullwhip effect even when sales are fairly constant. However, for many retailers, sales are not constant. They go up dramatically when retailers put merchandise on sale and during special gift-giving times of the year. These irregularities in sales heighten the bullwhip effect and the buildup of inventory in the supply chain. Retailing View 9.3 describes the historical forces motivating retailers and vendors to collaborate on supply chain management.

Vendors and retailers have found that by working together, they can reduce the level of inventory in the supply chain and the number of stockouts in the stores. Four approaches for coordinating supply chain activities, in order of the level of collaboration, are (1) using EDI; (2) exchanging information; (3) using vendor-managed inventory; and (4) employing collaborative planning, forecasting, and replenishment.[24]

Using EDI

The use of EDI to transmit purchase order information reduces the time it takes for retailers to place orders and for vendors to acknowledge the receipt of orders and communicate delivery information about those orders. In addition, EDI facilitates the implementation of other collaborative approaches discussed in the following sections. However, the use of EDI without other collaborative approaches only addresses one factor discussed previously—the delay in transmitting and receiving orders—that causes the buildup of inventory in the supply chain.

Sharing Information

One of the major factors causing excessive inventory in the supply chain is the inability of vendors to know what the actual level of retail sales are. For instance, suppose a consumer packaged goods vendor offered discounts to retailers several times a year, hoping that the price reduction would be passed on to customers.[25] Instead, however, the retailers purchased extra inventory and kept the extra discounts to increase their margins. Just looking at the orders it received, the vendor might think that demand for its products had increased significantly and therefore increase its production, causing an inventory buildup. To reduce this effect, vendors are using the retailer's sales records and giving discounts based on sales rather than orders placed.

Sharing sales data with vendors is an important first step in improving supply chain efficiency. With the sales data, vendors can improve their sales forecasts, improve

exhibit 9–6 Bullwhip Effect in Uncoordinated Supply Chain

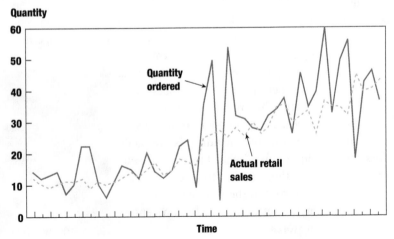

Quick Response and Efficient Consumer Response

Retailer–vendor collaboration in supply chain management grew out of activities undertaken by apparel manufacturers and retailers, called *quick response (QR)*, and by consumer packaged goods (CPG) manufacturers and supermarket retailers, called *efficient consumer response (ECR)*. In the mid-1980s, Milliken, a U.S. textile manufacturer facing severe price competition from imports, developed a strategy to compete on its speed to market rather than price. At the time, it took 66 weeks for the apparel industry to go from yarn at the manufacturer to clothing on a retail store fixture. Because no one in the supply chain knew what would be selling in a month, much less a year, the cost of that lengthy supply cycle was devastating. The apparel industry as a whole lost billions of dollars each year through price reductions on items customers didn't want and because they did not have enough of what they did want.

To address this supply chain inefficiency, Milliken joined with a children's apparel maker and large retail department store chain to compete through what it called "quick response." Quick response was modelled after the just-in-time (JIT) initiatives undertaken by Japanese automobile makers. The department store developed a sales forecast for a season. Milliken manufactured the fabric to meet the forecast but kept most of the fabric as "grey goods" that could be dyed different colours when orders for the specific colours came in. The apparel manufacturer cut and sewed a small initial assortment of garments and shipped them to the department store. The department store monitored the initial sales of colours and sizes and then transmitted this information to the

manufacturer and Milliken so that the remaining fabric could be dyed, cut, and sewed in the colours and sizes that consumers were buying.

Walmart and other discount store chains were the motivating force for collaboration between CPG manufacturers and supermarket retailers. Through the Food Marketing Institute, supermarkets, facing price competition from discount stores, commissioned Kurt Salmon Associates (KSA) to find out how they could compete more effectively. KSA found that the supermarkets had a significant cost disadvantage due to their inefficient supply chains. When CPG manufacturers held special trade promotions (discounting the wholesale price), supermarket chains would buy a six-month supply of the products, leaving them with $30 billion of excess inventory in their distribution centres. In 1993, the KSA report recommended a multipronged efficient consumer response approach, which involved collaboration between manufacturers and retailers to achieve efficient replenishment and promotions.*

Since these initiatives were launched, the grocery industry has made greater strides in improving its supply chain efficiencies than has the apparel industry because the manufacturing process for apparel is more complex and the number of SKUs is significantly larger.

*Kurt Salmon Associates, *Efficient Consumer Response: Enhancing Customer Value in the Grocery Industry* (Washington, DC: The Food Marketing Institute, 1993).

> **DID YOU KNOW?**
>
> Top-tier ECR adopters enjoy 6 percent better service levels, 5 percent higher on-shelf availability, and 10 days' lower finished-goods inventories than do low adopters or nonadopters of ECR practices.[26]

Sources: Sameer Kumar, "A Study of the Supermarket Industry and Its Growing Logistics Capabilities," *International Journal of Retail & Distribution Management* 36, no. 3 (2008), pp. 192–211; T. C. E Cheng and T. M. Choi, "Innovative Quick Response Programs in Logistics and Supply Chain Management," in *International Handbooks on Information Systems*, eds. Edwin Cheng and Tsan-Ming Choi (New York: Springer, 2010).

production efficiency, and reduce the need for excessive backup inventory. But additional levels of collaboration are needed to use this information effectively. The sales data reflect historical data, not what the retailer's plans are for the future. For example, the retailer might decide to delete a vendor's SKU from its assortment—a decision that clearly affects future sales. The two approaches discussed in the next sections introduce a forward-looking collaborative perspective.

Vendor-Managed Inventory

Vendor-managed inventory (VMI) is an approach for improving supply chain efficiency in which the vendor is responsible for maintaining the retailer's inventory levels. The vendor determines a reorder point—a level of inventory at which more merchandise is ordered. The retailer

vendor-managed inventory (VMI) An approach for improving supply chain efficiency in which the vendor is responsible for maintaining the retailer's inventory levels in each of its stores.

consignment When the vendor owns the merchandise until it is sold by the retailer, at which time the retailer pays for the merchandise.

collaborative planning, forecasting, and replenishment (CPFR) A collaborative inventory management system in which a retailer shares information with vendors. CPFR software uses data to construct a computer-generated replenishment forecast that is shared by the retailer and vendor before it's executed.

quick response (QR) delivery system System designed to reduce the lead time for receiving merchandise, thereby lowering inventory investment, improving customer service levels, and reducing distribution expenses; also known as a *just-in-time inventory management system*.

DID YOU KNOW?

Improvements in vendor-managed inventory can result in the elimination of between 20 and 30 percent of the previously required supply chain inventory.[27]

shares sales and inventory data with the vendor via EDI. When inventory drops to the order point, the vendor generates the order and delivers the merchandise.

In ideal conditions, the vendor replenishes inventories in quantities that meet the retailer's immediate demand and reduce stockouts with minimal inventory. In addition to better matching retail demand to supply, VMI can reduce the vendor's and the retailer's costs. Vendor salespeople no longer need to spend time generating orders on items that are already in the stores, and their role shifts to selling new items and maintaining relationships. Retail buyers and planners no longer need to monitor inventory levels and place orders.

For example, TAL Apparel Ltd., a Hong Kong shirt maker, produces garments for labels such as J.Crew, Calvin Klein, Banana Republic, and JCPenney. It supplies one in seven dress shirts sold in the United States and manages JCPenney's men's dress shirt inventory. TAL collects POS data for JCPenney's shirts directly from stores in North America and then runs the numbers through a computer model it designed. Next, TAL decides how many shirts to make and in what styles, colours, and sizes. It sends the shirts directly to each JCPenney store, bypassing the retailer's distribution centres and merchandise managers. Because TAL manages the entire process, from design to the ordering of yarn, it can bring a new style from the testing stage to full retail rollout in four months, much faster than Penney could on its own. The system, in effect, lets consumers, not merchandise managers, choose the styles.[28]

The use of VMI is not a new approach. Frito-Lay and other snack food, candy, and beverage vendors have used direct store delivery to manage the inventory of their products on supermarket VMI and shelves for a long time. However, technological advances have increased the sophistication of VMI. The sharing of POS transaction data, for instance, allows vendors to sell merchandise on consignment; the vendor owns the merchandise until it is sold by the retailer, at which time the retailer

pays for the merchandise. Consignment selling provides an incentive for the vendor to pick SKUs and inventory levels that will minimize inventory and generate sales. Because the vendor is bearing the financial cost of owning the inventory, retailers are more willing to allow the vendor to be responsible for determining the inventory plan and appropriate assortment for each store.

Although it is a more advanced level of collaboration than simply using EDI and sharing information, VMI has its limitations. While the vendor coordinates the supply chain for its specific products, it does not know what other actions the retailer is taking that might affect the sales of its products in the future. For example, Pepsi might not know that a supermarket will be having a big promotion in three weeks for a new beverage introduced by Coca-Cola. Without this knowledge, Pepsi would ship too much merchandise to the supermarket.

Collaborative Planning, Forecasting, and Replenishment

Collaborative planning, forecasting, and replenishment (CPFR) is the sharing of forecasts and related business information and collaborative planning between retailers and vendors to improve supply chain efficiency and product replenishment.[29] Although retailers share sales and inventory data when using a VMI approach, the vendor remains responsible for managing the inventory. In contrast, CPFR is a more advanced form of retailer–vendor collaboration that involves sharing proprietary information such as business strategies, promotion plans, new product developments and introductions, production schedules, and lead-time information. Retailing View 9.4 illustrates how West Marine uses CPFR to improve its supply chain efficiency.

Quick Response Delivery Systems

There are only two groups of retail businesses today: the quick and the dead.[30]

A quick response (QR) delivery system is an inventory management system designed to reduce the retailer's lead time for receiving merchandise, thereby lowering inventory investment, improving customer service levels, and reducing logistics expenses. QR is the integrating link between the information and the merchandise flows depicted in Exhibit 9–2.

Many of the concepts that comprise QR systems have been previously discussed in this chapter. In this section, however, we describe how they all work together. The origins of the present QR systems were derived from just-in-time (JIT) initiatives undertaken by manufacturers

West Marine Uses CPFR to Build a Competitive Advantage

West Marine's founder and chairman, Randy Repass, channelled his passion for boating into a business that revolutionized the way people shop for boating supplies. Forty years ago, when Randy started selling nylon rope out of his garage, boat supply stores were dark, disorganized places staffed by a couple of salty but indifferent clerks who preferred swapping sea stories with one another to helping customers find what they came in to buy. Randy's vision was to provide a one-stop shopping experience with great customer service for boaters. Today, West Marine has more than 400 stores across the United States and Canada and sells supplies through catalogue and Internet channels. The company offers more than 50 000 products, ranging from the rope that started it all to the latest in marine electronics.

The boating market is highly seasonal; more than 50 percent of sales occur between April and October. Whereas the holiday season and Christmas are the peak seasons for most retailers, West Marine's peak sales occur during the week before the 4th of July. In addition, boat supply retailers are very promotional, and this introduces more variation and uncertainty into sales forecasts. West Marine found that these wide variations in demand resulted in lost sales due to inefficiencies in its supply chain.

To address this issue, West Marine and its key suppliers implemented collaboration, planning, forecasting, and replenishment (CPFR) programs. The first step West Marine took was to meet with key suppliers to develop a better forecasting system. Now, every night, West Marine collects SKU-level sales and inventory information for each of its stores, and every day it generates a 52-week forecast for demand by store at the SKU level. The forecast factors in all marketing and promotional events. The forecast is shared with the suppliers so that they can order parts and schedule production.

West Marine has made CPFR an integral part of its merchandising and planning operations. Each West Marine category manager (CM) partners with a merchandise planner (MP). The CM is responsible for the vendor strategies and marketing relationships; the MP is responsible for directing the supply chain relationship. West Marine MPs and CMs conduct quarterly supply chain planning meetings with each CPFR supplier. These meetings involve teams from both companies and include the key marketing, forecasting, production planning, distribution, and transportation players. In addition, the planners from both sides engage in a monthly collaborative meeting that reviews results, manages current initiatives, and identifies and resolves any supply issues on the basis of the order forecast. Team members beyond the primary planners frequently attend and contribute to these monthly meetings as well.

West Marine uses CPFR to engage in collaborative planning and supply chain management with its vendors.

Sources: www.westmarine.com (accessed June 14, 2010); T. Schoenherr and V. M. R. Tummala, "Best Practices for the Implementation of Supply Chain Management Initiatives," *International Journal of Logistics Systems and Management* 4, no. 4 (2008), pp. 391–410.

and adapted for retailing. QR is part of the efficient consumer response (ECR) initiatives undertaken by packaged goods manufacturers and food and drugstore retailers.[33] EDI facilitates the exchange of data between retailer and vendors.

Originally, quick response delivery systems seemed better suited to basic items—such as underwear, paper towels, or toothpaste—than to high fashion. By its nature, however, fashion dictates being able to adjust quickly to the changing seasons as well as to new colours and styles. Thus, quick response is as important in managing fashion inventories as in managing basic-item inventories. Fashion retailers need to determine what's selling (so it can be reordered quickly) and what isn't selling (so it can be marked down).

To illustrate a QR system, consider how the system works at Zara, which we discussed in Retailing View 9.1 earlier in this chapter.[34] Zara, located in Galicia, Spain, is now the third-largest clothing retailer in the world, with profits growing at 30 percent per year. It operates over 500 stores in 31 countries, including nine Canadian stores—in Toronto, Montreal, Quebec City, Calgary, and Vancouver.

Benefits of a QR System The benefits of a QR system are reduced lead time, increased product availability, lower inventory investment, and reduced logistics expenses.

Reduces Lead Time By eliminating the need for paper transactions using the mail, overnight deliveries, or even fax, EDI in the QR system reduces lead time. Lead time is the amount of time between the recognition that an order needs to be placed and its arrival in the store, ready for sale. Since the vendor's computer acquires the data electronically, no manual data entry is required on the recipient's end. As a result, lead time is reduced even more, and vendor recording errors are eliminated. Thus, use of EDI in the QR system can cut lead time by a week or more. Shorter lead times further reduce the need for inventory because the shorter the lead time, the easier it is to forecast demand; therefore, the retailer needs less inventory.

Increases Product Availability and Lowers Inventory Investment In general, as a retailer's ability to satisfy customer demand by being in stock increases, so does its inventory investment. Yet with QR, the ability to satisfy demand can actually increase while inventory decreases! Since the retailer can make purchase commitments or produce merchandise closer to the time of sale, its inventory investment is reduced. Stores need less inventory because they're getting less merchandise on each order, but they receive shipments more often. Inventory is further reduced because the retailer isn't forecasting sales so far into the future. For instance, fashion retailers that don't use QR make purchase commitments as much as six months in advance and receive merchandise far in advance of actual sales. QR systems align deliveries more closely with sales.

The ability to satisfy customer demand by being in stock also increases in QR systems as a result of the more frequent shipments.

Reduces Logistics Expenses QR systems also have the potential to significantly reduce logistics expenses. Many retailers receive merchandise in their distribution centres, store it, consolidate shipments from multiple vendors, attach price labels and theft prevention devices, and then reship the merchandise to stores. Retailers have two options for reducing these logistics expenses using QR systems. They can either use a cross-docking warehouse system or they can negotiate a direct store delivery system. Cross-docking eliminates storage and some handling costs. Direct store delivery eliminates all distribution centre costs and transportation costs from the distibution centre to stores. If the merchandise is floor-ready, there's no need to devote expensive retail space to receiving and processing merchandise in the store, and sales associates can devote all of their attention to their customers.

Costs of a QR System Although retailers achieve great benefits from a QR system, it's not without costs. The logistics function has become much more complicated with more frequent deliveries. With greater order frequency come smaller orders, which are more expensive to transport. The greater order frequency also makes deliveries and transportation more difficult to coordinate.

QR systems also require a strong commitment by the retailer and its vendors to cooperate, share data, and develop systems such as EDI and CPFR. Successful QR systems not only require financial support from top management but also a psychological commitment to become partners with their vendors. Large retailers often apply their power to get their vendors to absorb many of these expensive logistics costs.

Radio Frequency Identification

Radio frequency identification (RFID) is a technology that allows an object or person to be identified at a distance by means of radio waves. The RFID devices or tags are attached to containers, shipping cartons, or even behind labels on individual items. They then transmit data about the object in which they are embedded. The RFID technology has two advantages over bar codes. First, the devices can hold more data and update the data stored. For instance, the device can keep track of where an item has been in the supply chain and even where it is stored in a distribution centre. Second, the data on the devices can be acquired in harsh environments without a visual line of sight—an environment in which bar-code labels won't work. Thus, RFID enables the accurate, real-time tracking of every single product, from manufacturer to checkout in the store. It eliminates the manual point-and-read operations needed to get data from UPC bar codes. Thus, RFID can significantly decrease warehouse, distribution, and inventory costs; increase margins; and provide better in-stock positions.

Several retailers are already taking advantage of this new technology. Walmart has requested that its top suppliers put RFID tags on all pallets, cases, cartons, and high-margin items.[37] Metro (Germany's largest retailer), Target, Best Buy, and Albertson's are also experimenting with RFID programs.[38] To meet these demands, vendors have been forced to make significant investments to acquire the necessary technology and equipment. Retailing View 9.5 describes how American Apparel innovated use of RFID on individual items instead of cartons or pallets, which are the typical current application in retailing.

Types of RFID Tags

There are three types of RFID tags: active, semi-passive, and passive tags. Active and semi-passive RFID tags use internal batteries to power their circuitry. An active tag also uses its battery to broadcast radio waves to a reader, whereas a semi-passive tag relies on the reader to supply its power for broadcasting. Because these tags involve more hardware than passive RFID tags, they are more expensive.

Active and semi-passive tags are mostly used for costly items that require tracking from about 100 feet or more. When tags must be read from even farther away, additional batteries can increase a tag's range to over 300 feet.

Passive RFID tags can be read from up to 20 feet away, and they have lower production costs, ranging from 7 to 20 cents each. The RFID industry is aiming to get the cost of a passive RFID tag down to 5 cents each once more retailers adopt them. These tags can be applied to less expensive merchandise such as cosmetics and some clothes. These tags are manufactured to be disposable, along with the disposable consumer goods on which they are placed.

Data about an item or carton can be encoded into an RFID chip and then can be accessed remotely to determine the presence of the item and where it should be.

radio frequency identification (RFID) A technology that allows an object or person to be identified at a distance by means of radio waves.

DID YOU KNOW?

Who returns merchandise? Women and affluent customers are more likely to return items than men and university students.[35]

DID YOU KNOW?

RFID has been ranked the 10th most innovative technology of the past 25 years by CNN.[36]

Benefits of RFID

Some of the benefits of RFID include the following:

- **Reduced warehouse and distribution labour costs.** Warehouse and distribution costs typically represent 2 to 4 percent of operating expenses for retailers. Replacing point-and-read, labour-intensive operations with sensors that track pallets, cases, cartons, and individual products anywhere in the facility can significantly reduce labour costs by as much as 30 percent.

- **Reduced point-of-sale labour costs.** Using RFID at the product level can help retailers reduce the labour costs needed for checking shelf inventory. In addition, RFID-enabled products will improve self-scan checkouts and increase the use of self-scans, thus shortening checkout times and reducing employee fraud.

- **Inventory savings.** RFID reduces inventory errors, ensuring that the inventory recorded is actually available. By tracking pieces more exactly, companies have more accurate information about what was sold and what inventory is actually needed.

- **Elimination of counterfeit merchandise.** Using RFID on individual items can help eliminate counterfeit merchandise.[41] For example, California planned for pharmaceutical manufacturers to utilize RFID technology starting in January 2009 for its mass serialization and e-pedigree requirements; however, the deal has now been delayed and is scheduled to go into effect in a phased manner between 2015 and 2017. A drug pedigree is a statement of origin that identifies each prior sale, purchase, or trade of a drug, including the date of the transactions and the names and addresses of all parties to them.[42] The primary purpose of an e-pedigree is to protect consumers from contaminated medicine or counterfeit drugs. As the product moves down the supply chain, each company is required to carry forward all previous e-pedigree information. In this way, the final point of sale has the complete lineage of every unit. Such a system would require fairly significant changes to the company's data interchange. The use of RFID forms the basis of such a secured supply chain system. Oregon and New York, as well as France, Japan, and Spain, are all making moves toward similar legislation.

- **Reduced theft.** With RFID, products can be tracked through the supply chain to pinpoint where a product is at all times; this helps reduce theft in transportation, at distribution centres, or in stores. RFID has already been successfully deployed in stores, particularly on costly items prone to theft, such as Gillette Mach 3 razor blades.

- **Reduced out-of-stock conditions.** Because RFID facilitates accurate product tracking, forecasts are more accurate and thus stockouts decrease. Using RFID, store managers can be automatically notified when specific SKUs are not on the shelves and need to be stocked, as noted in Retailing View 9.5.[43]

Impediments to the Adoption of RFID

A major obstacle to the widespread adoption of RFID has been the high costs, which make the present return on investment low. The cost of RFID tags is 15 cents per tag.[44] However, with demand increasing and tag production costs declining, the tags are expected to reach only 5 cents per tag, and they may be reusable in some applications.

Another reason RFID has not been adopted by more retailers is that it generates more data than can be efficiently processed; therefore, retailers find it difficult to justify the implementation costs. Most retailers are not capable of transmitting, storing, and processing the data that would be available about the location of pallets, cases, cartons, totes, and individual products in the supply chain.

Vendors are pushing back as well. Some claim that instead of saving labour, RFID tagging actually increases it: Bar codes are printed on cases at the factory, but because most manufacturers have yet to adopt RFID, those tags have to be put on by hand at the warehouse.

Finally, consumers, particularly in the United States, are wary that once the tags are on individual items, they could be used to track individual buyers—an obvious invasion of privacy.[45] The problem is less acute in the European Union, where retailers have educated consumers on RFID use and changed procedures to accommodate consumers' fears by developing tag-removal policies. Germany's Metro and England's Marks & Spencer are both using item-level RFID on a limited basis.

RFID at American Apparel

Known for its "Made in Downtown LA" motto, American Apparel is accustomed to turning heads. The Los Angeles–based company's RFID push began with a pilot program at one of the firm's New York stores. Every one of the roughly 40 000 items from basic T-shirts to shiny gold lamé hot shorts in the store was RFID-tagged.

The objective of American Apparel's RFID system is to provide improved inventory accuracy and better-stocked sales floors. American Apparel has an unusual approach to merchandising. It puts only one of everything on the floor to give the appearance of selling unique merchandise— customers can buy something no one else will be wearing. But that means that once an item is sold, that particular SKU is out of stock on the sales floor. To restock the store, employees would periodically take a list of items sold from the POS system and make trips to the stockroom, where they'd search for each item.

American Apparel saw quick benefits from the technology. As an item leaves the sales floor—because it has been sold, accidentally returned to the stockroom,

or stolen—its departure is displayed at stockroom workstations, enabling workers to quickly get the item restocked. Personnel can easily keep the sales floor fully stocked. The time required to do the weekly process of taking inventory of items in the store was reduced from 32 to 4 hours. This gives employees more time to assist customers directly and carry out other tasks.

American Apparel is experimenting with placing RFID tags on each item to ensure that all items are on display on store fixtures.

Sources: Claire Swedberg, "American Apparel Adds RFID to Two More Stores, Switches RFID Software," *RFID Journal*, January 12, 2010; Mary Catherine O'Connor, "American Apparel Makes a Bold Fashion Statement with RFID," *RFID Journal*, August 14, 2008.

SUMMARY

Supply chain management and information systems have become important tools for achieving a sustainable competitive advantage. Developing more efficient methods of distributing merchandise creates an opportunity to reduce costs and prices and ensure that the right merchandise is available when and where customers want it.

The systems used to control the flow of information to buyers and then on to vendors have become quite sophisticated. Retailers have developed data warehouses that provide them with intimate knowledge of who their customers are and what they like to buy. The data warehouses are being used to strengthen the relationships with their customers and improve the productivity of their marketing and inventory management efforts.

Most large retailers own and operate their own distribution centres. Some of the activities performed by the centre are managing inbound and outbound transportation, receiving and checking merchandise shipments, storing and cross-docking, and getting merchandise floor-ready.

In designing their supply chain management systems, retailers make decisions about what activities to outsource, when to use a push and pull system for replenishing stores, what merchandise to cross-dock, and whether to ship merchandise to stores through a distribution centre, use direct store delivery, or have products drop-shipped to customers.

Retailers and vendors are collaborating to improve supply chain efficiency. Electronic data interchange enables retailers to communicate electronically with their vendors. The Internet has accelerated the adoption of EDI. Other, more involving and effective collaborative approaches include information sharing, VMI, CPFR, and QR. These approaches represent the nexus of information systems and logistics management. They reduce lead time, increase product availability, lower inventory investments, and reduce overall logistics expenses.

Finally, RFID has the potential of further streamlining the supply chain. The small RFID devices are affixed to pallets, cartons, and individual items and can be used to track merchandise through the supply chain and store information, such as when an item was shipped to a distribution centre. Although still relatively expensive to be placed on all items, RFID technology can reduce labour, theft, and inventory costs.

KEY TERMS

advance shipping notice (ASN)

bullwhip effect

checking

collaborative planning, forecasting, and replenishment (CPFR)

consignment

cross-docked

direct store delivery (DSD)

dispatcher

distribution centre

drop-shipping

electronic data interchange (EDI)

floor-ready merchandise

freight forwarders

logistics

outsource

pick ticket.

public warehouses

pull supply chain

push supply chain

quick response (QR) delivery system

radio frequency identification (RFID)

receiving

reverse logistics

security policy

stockout

supply chain management

ticketing and marking

Universal Product Code (UPC)

vendor-managed inventory (VMI)

Get Out & Do It!

1. Interview the store manager working for a retailer. Write a report that describes and evaluates the retailer's information and supply chain systems. Use this chapter as a basis for developing a set of questions to ask the manager. Some of the questions might be these: Where is the store's distribution centre? Does the retailer use direct store delivery from vendors? How frequently are deliveries made to the store? Does the merchandise come in ready for sale? What is the store's percentage of stockouts? Does the retailer use a push or pull system? Does the store get involved in determining what merchandise is in the store and in what quantities? Does the retailer use VMI, EDI, CPFR, or RFID?

2. **INTERNET EXERCISE** Go to Barcoding Incorporated's website at **www.barcoding.com** and search for retail, warehouse management, and RFID. How is this company using technology to support retailers with information systems and supply chain management?

3. **INTERNET EXERCISE** Go to the website of *Stores Magazine* at **www.stores.org** and search for supply chain in the current issue. Summarize one of the recent articles, and explain how the key concept(s) described could make the shopping experience better for consumers and improve efficiency in the supply chain.

4. **INTERNET EXERCISE** Go to the website of Vendor Managed Inventory at **www.vendormanagedinventory.com/index.php** and answer the following questions: What is vendor-managed inventory? What are the benefits and limitations of a vendor-managed inventory approach?

DISCUSSION QUESTIONS AND PROBLEMS

1. Retail system acronyms include DSD, VMI, EDI, CPFR, and RFID. How are these terms related to one another?

2. Explain how an efficient supply chain system can increase a retailer's level of product availability and decrease its inventory investment.

3. This chapter presents some trends in logistics and information systems that benefit retailers. How do vendors benefit from these trends?

4. What type of merchandise is most likely to be cross-docked at retailers' distribution centres? Why is this often the case?

5. Why haven't more fashion retailers adopted an integrated supply chain system similar to Zara's?

6. Explain the differences between pull and push supply chains.

7. Consumers have five key reactions to stockouts: buy the item at another store, substitute a different brand, substitute the same brand, delay the purchase, or do not purchase the item. Consider your own purchasing behaviour, and describe how various categories of merchandise would result in different reactions to a stockout.

8. Abandoned purchases as a result of stockouts can mean millions of dollars a year in lost sales. How are retailers and manufacturers using technology to reduce stockouts and improve sales?

9. What is a Universal Product Code (UPC)? How does this code enable manufacturers, distributors, and retailers to track merchandise throughout the supply chain?

10. Reread Retailing View 9.2 about Netflix. How is this online retailer using inventory management and distribution centres to deliver the correct movies requested by customers?

Practise and learn online with Connect.

merchandise management

LEARNING OBJECTIVES

Lo1 Examine how the buying process is organized.

Lo2 Examine the types of merchandise management planning processes retailers use to manage merchandise categories.

Lo3 Discuss how retailers evaluate their buying performance.

Lo4 Explore how retailers forecast sales for merchandise classifications.

Lo5 Determine what trade-offs retailers must make to ensure that stores carry the appropriate type and amount of merchandise.

Lo6 Review how retailers plan their assortments.

Lo7 Explore merchandise budget plans and open-to-buy systems, and how they are prepared.

Lo8 Review how multistore retailers allocate merchandise to stores.

Lo9 Explore how retailers analyze the profitability of their merchandising decisions.

SPOTLIGHT ON RETAILING

Aldo Group Inc.: Canadian Global Success Story

Aldo is a household name in Canada that is synonymous with trendy shoes, but it is also "the most successful global retailer that Canada has ever built," according to Tim McGuire, a senior partner at consultancy McKinsey & Co., which has advised Aldo. Aldo Bensadoun, the son of a retailer who operated a small chain of shoe stores in France and Morocco and the grandson of a cobbler, completed his university studies at McGill University in Montreal. A degree in economics led him to a marketing research position, which found Bensadoun doing a project for a regional shoe chain. Eventually, the combination of past family history in the shoe business, knowledge of Canadian population trends, and smart business sense led him to open his own company.

The company had humble beginnings in 1972 in Montreal as a concession within Le Chateau clothing stores. He started his Aldo chain in 1980, rushing to find the next new fashion at an affordable cost—in effect, practising fast fashion before the industry coined the term. Today, Aldo is still a privately held company, operating over 1600 stores across all continents except Antarctica. The Canadian, American, Irish, and U.K. stores are corporate stores, while the other international stores are franchises. Currently, the Aldo Group has six banners, each catering to a distinct market segment: Aldo (the flagship brand, which represents approximately 1000 stores of the 1600), Aldo Accessories, Little Burgundy, Spring, Globo, and Locale. Further, the company boasts average sales per square foot of more than $1000 in Canada, which is more than twice that of other mall shoe chains.

Aldo primarily sells private-label, fashion-oriented shoes designed and made for the company banners; it also designs and produces exclusive footwear products that are sold under private and exclusive brand names for Kohl's, JCPenney, Hudson's Bay, and online retail giant Zappos.com. Analyzing population groups provides design inspiration; in fact, trends are often influenced by the environment, politics, and economics. The design team researches clothing designs and magazines to interpret the trends in footwear. Once it finds a workable idea, the Aldo Group requires a mere 5 to 12 weeks to get shoes to stores, compared with an industry average of 17 weeks.

Here in North America, the Aldo Group's rapidly increasing competition, such as Payless ShoeSource, Walmart, H&M, and Zara, is putting pressure on the company to find new avenues for growth and sharpening its fast-fashion (cheap-chic) strategy. Head office now receives hourly—rather than weekly—sales data, allowing it to make faster decisions about restocking top sellers and ditching losers. The speedy updates also shave the time it takes to get shoes on the shelf by as much as 30 percent.

Wanting to expand in North America without the huge spending required to open new stores, Mr. Bensadoun's solution was to wholesale products to other retailers. In 2011, he struck deals with Kohl's, JCPenney, Hudson's Bay, and Zappos.com to supply private-label and exclusive footwear and accessories. For instance, in hopes of attracting the 12- to 25-year-old demographic that is fashion obsessed and budget savvy, JCPenney launched a new 350- to 500-square-foot in-house shop that sells some 300 styles of women's and men's Aldo Call It Spring line. The in-house shop includes a line of Aldo handbags in addition to an Aldo shoe collection with the most expensive piece topping out at $59.99. Aldo revived the Pegabo line (discontinued Aldo brand and store) in a limited capacity, selling it exclusively through Hudson's Bay and its own banner, Locale.

Truly a success story, Aldo Bensadoun is one of Canada's richest retailers. Bensadoun continues to grow his fast-fashion shoe empire with quality and cutting-edge trends at affordable prices, season after season, in Canada and around the world. He believes that by always trying to change the Aldo recipe to fit into a playing field that is in constant evolution he can achieve annual sales of $3 billion by 2015, which would be double annual company sales from 2010.

Sources: Marina Strauss, "Aldo's Global Footprint," *The Globe and Mail*, September 3, 2010, http://www.theglobeandmail.com/report-on-business/small-business/sb-growth/going-global/aldos-global-footprint/article601117/?page=all (accessed September 27, 2012); "Aldo Culture," Aldo website, http://www.aldoshoes.com/ca-eng/culture (accessed September 27, 2012); Sarah St. Lifer, "JCPenney Launches 'Call It Spring' Collection with Aldo Shoes," *StyleList*, March 2, 2011, http://main.stylelist.com/2011/03/02/jcpenney-launches-call-it-spring-collection-with-aldo-shoes/ (accessed September 27, 2012); Danielle Jennings, "Pegabo Shoes," LoveToKnow Shoes, http://shoes.lovetoknow.com/Pegabo_Shoes (accessed September 27, 2012).

merchandise management The process by which a retailer attempts to offer the right quantity of the right merchandise in the right place at the right time while meeting the company's financial goal.

Merchandise management activities are undertaken primarily by buyers and their superiors, divisional merchandise managers (DMMs) and general merchandise managers (GMMs). Many people view these jobs as very exciting and glamorous. They think that buyers spend most of their time trying to identify the latest fashions and trends, attending designer shows replete with celebrities in Paris and Milan, and going to rock concerts and other glamorous events to see what the trendsetters are wearing. But in reality, the lives of retail buyers are more like those of Wall Street investment analysts than globe-trotting trend spotters.

Investment analysts manage a portfolio of stocks. They buy stocks in companies they think will increase in value and sell stocks in companies they believe do not have a promising future. They continuously monitor the performance of the stocks they own to see which are increasing in value and which are decreasing. Sometimes they make mistakes and invest in companies that do not perform well. So they sell their stock in these companies and lose money, but they use the money from the sold stocks to buy more attractive stocks. Other times, the stocks they buy increase dramatically in price, and they wish they had bought more shares.

Rather than managing a portfolio of stocks, retail buyers manage a portfolio of merchandise inventory. They buy merchandise they think will be popular with their customers. Like investment analysts, they use an information system to monitor the performance of their merchandise portfolio—to see what is selling and what is not. Retail buyers also make mistakes. When the merchandise they bought is not selling well, they get rid of it by putting it on sale so that they can use the money to buy better-selling merchandise. However, they also might take a chance and buy a lot of a new product and be rewarded when it sells well, while competitors, who were more conservative, don't have enough of the product.

Merchandise management is the process by which a retailer attempts to offer the right quantity of the right merchandise in the right place at the right time and meet the company's financial goals. Buyers need to be in touch with and anticipate what customers will want to buy, but this ability to sense market trends is just one skill needed to manage merchandise inventory effectively. Perhaps an even more important skill is the ability to analyze sales data continually and make appropriate adjustments in prices and inventory levels.

The first part of this chapter provides the background needed to understand the merchandise management process. In this introduction, we discuss how the process is organized, who makes the merchandise decisions, and how merchandise management performance is evaluated. The last part of the chapter examines the steps in the merchandise management process—forecasting sales, formulating an assortment plan, determining the appropriate inventory level, developing a merchandise management plan, allocating merchandise to stores, and monitoring performance. Other activities involved in merchandise management reviewed in subsequent chapters are buying merchandise (Chapter 11) and pricing (Chapter 12).

Merchandise Management Overview

This section provides an overview of the merchandise management process, including the organization of a retailer's merchandise management activities, the objectives and measures used to evaluate merchandise management performance, the differences in the process for managing fashion and seasonal merchandise versus basic merchandise, and the steps in the merchandise management process. In the following section, we review each of the steps in the merchandise management process.

The Buying Organization

Every retailer has its own system for grouping categories of merchandise, but the basic structure of the buying organization is similar for most retailers. Exhibit 10–1 illustrates this basic structure by depicting the organization of the merchandise division for a department store chain such as Holt Renfrew or Hudson's Bay. Exhibit 10–1 shows the organization of buyers in the merchandise division. A similar structure for planners parallels the structure for buyers.

Merchandise Group The highest classification level is the merchandise group. The organization chart shown in Exhibit 10–1 has four merchandise groups: (1) women's apparel; (2) men's, children's, and intimate apparel; (3) cosmetics, shoes, jewellery, and accessories; and (4) home and kitchen. Each of the four merchandise groups is managed by a general merchandise manager (GMM), who is often a senior vice president in the firm. Each of the GMMs is responsible for several departments. For example, the GMM for men's, children's, and intimate apparel makes decisions about how the merchandise

> **merchandise group** A group within an organization managed by the senior vice presidents of merchandise and responsible for several departments.

exhibit 10–1 Standard Merchandise Classification Scheme and Organizational Chart

How many SKUs are there in this picture?

department A segment of a store with merchandise that represents a group of classifications the consumer views as being complementary.

classification A group of items or SKUs for the same type of merchandise, such as pants (as opposed to jackets or suits), supplied by different vendors.

merchandise category An assortment of items (SKUs) the customer sees as reasonable substitutes for each other.

inventory is managed in five departments: men's dress apparel, men's sportswear, young men's apparel, children's apparel, and intimate apparel.

Department The second level in the merchandise classification scheme is the department. Departments are managed by divisional merchandise managers (DMMs). For example, the DMM highlighted in Exhibit 10–1 is in charge of children's apparel and manages the buyers responsible for six merchandise departments.

Classification The classification is the third level for categorizing merchandise and organizing merchandise management activities. Each divisional merchandise manager is responsible for a number of buyers or category managers. The children's apparel divisional merchandise manager in the exhibit is responsible for six buyers. Each buyer purchases a classification—a group of items or SKUs for the same type of merchandise (such as men's pants as opposed to men's jackets or suits) supplied by different vendors. A stock keeping unit (SKU) is the smallest unit available for keeping inventory control. In soft goods merchandise, for instance, an SKU usually means size, colour, and style. For example, a pair of girls' size 5, stonewashed blue, straight-legged Levis is one SKU. The exhibit highlights the one buyer responsible for girls' apparel sizes 4 to 6. In some cases, a buyer is responsible for several classifications.

Many retail organizations divide responsibility for buying merchandise between a buyer or category manager and a merchandise planner. Since the merchandise planning function is a relatively new concept, it's handled in various ways by different retailers. In some organizations, the category manager or buyer supervises the planners; in others, they're equal partners.

The planners' role is more analytical. They are responsible for buying the correct quantities of each item, allocating those items to stores, monitoring sales, and suggesting markdowns. In effect, they implement the assortment plan developed by the buyer. Together, the buyer and planner are the merchandising team. This team attempts to maximize the sales and profits of the entire classification, not just a particular category or brand.

Merchandise Category: The Planning Unit

The merchandise category is the basic unit of analysis for making merchandising management decisions. A merchandise category is an assortment of items that customers see as substitutes for one another. For example, a department store might offer a wide variety of girls' dresses sizes 4 to 6 in different colours, styles, and brand names. A mother buying a dress for her daughter might consider the entire set of dresses when making her purchase decision. Lowering the price on one dress may increase the sales of that dress but also decrease the sales of other dresses. Thus, the buyers' decisions about pricing and promoting specific SKUs in the category will affect the sales of other SKUs in the same category.

Some retailers may define categories in terms of brands. For example, Tommy Hilfiger might be one category and Polo/Ralph Lauren another category because the retailer feels that the brands are not substitutes for each other. A "Tommy" customer buys Tommy and not Ralph. Also, it is easier for one buyer to purchase merchandise and coordinate distribution and promotions for the merchandise offered by a national-brand vendor. Typically, a buyer manages several categories of merchandise.

Category Management While retailers, in general, manage merchandise at the category level, many supermarkets organize their merchandise management around brands or vendors. For instance, a supermarket chain might have three different buyers for breakfast cereals—one for Kellogg's, General Mills, and General Foods.[1] Managing merchandise within a category by brand can lead to inefficiencies because it fails to consider the interdependencies between SKUs in the category. For example, the three breakfast cereal buyers for a supermarket chain, one for each major brand, might each decide to stock a new product line of gluten-free breakfast cereals offered by Kellogg, General Mills, and General Foods. However, if the brand-organized buyers had taken a category-level perspective, they would have realized that the market for wheat-free cereals was limited and that the supermarket would generate more sales by stocking one brand of gluten-free cereals and using the space set aside for the other wheat-free cereal brands to stock a locally produced cereal that has a strong following among some customers. The category management approach to managing merchandise assigns one buyer or category manager to oversee all merchandising activities for the entire category. Category management can help ensure that the store's assortment includes the "best" combination of sizes and vendors—the one that will get the most profit from the allocated space.[2]

Category Captain Some retailers select a vendor to help them manage a particular category. The vendor, known as the category captain, works with the retailer to develop a better understanding of shopping behaviour, create assortments that satisfy consumer needs, and improve the profitability of the merchandise category.[3] Selecting vendors as category captains has its advantages for retailers. It makes merchandise management tasks easier and can increase profits. Vendors are often in a better position to manage a category than are retailers as they have superior information because of their focus on a specific category. In addition, they have acquired insights from managing the category for other retailers. A potential problem with establishing a vendor as a category captain is that the vendor could take advantage of its position. Suppose, for example, that Frito-Lay chose to maximize its own sales, rather than the retailer's sales, in managing the salty snack category. It could suggest an assortment plan that included most of its SKUs and exclude SKUs that are more profitable to the retailer, such as high-margin, private-label SKUs. Thus, retailers are becoming increasingly reluctant to turn over these important decisions to their vendors. They have found that working with their vendors and carefully evaluating their suggestions is a much more prudent approach.[4] There are also antitrust considerations. The vendor category captain could collude with the retailer to fix prices. It could also block other brands, particularly smaller ones, from access to shelf space.[5]

Stock Keeping Unit (SKU) A stock keeping unit (SKU) is the smallest unit available for inventory control. In soft-goods merchandise, for instance, an SKU usually means a particular size, colour, and style. For example, a pair of size 5, stonewashed, blue, straight-legged Levi jeans is an SKU.

Merchandise Management Process

Buyers forecast category sales, develop an assortment plan for merchandise in the category, and determine the amount of inventory needed to support the forecasted sales and assortment plan. Then, buyers develop a plan outlining the sales expected for each month, the inventory needed to support the sales, and the money that can be spent on replenishing sold merchandise and buying new merchandise. Along with developing the plan, the buyers or planners decide what type and how much merchandise should be allocated to each store. Having developed the plan, the buyer negotiates with vendors and buys the merchandise. Merchandise buying activities are reviewed in Chapter 11.

Finally, buyers continually monitor the sales of merchandise in the category and make adjustments. For example, if category sales are less than the forecast in the plan and the projected gross margin return on inventory investment (GMROI) for the category falls below the buyer's goal, the buyer may decide to dispose of some merchandise by putting it on sale and then use the money generated to buy merchandise with greater sales potential or to reduce the number of SKUs in the assortment to increase inventory turnover.

Although Exhibit 10–2 suggests that these decisions follow each other sequentially, in practice, some decisions may be made at the same time or in a different order. For example, a buyer might first decide on the amount of inventory to invest in the category, and this decision might determine the number of SKUs that can be offered in the category.

Retailers use two different types of merchandise management planning systems for managing (1) staple and (2) fashion merchandise categories.

Staple Merchandise Categories A staple merchandise category, also called a *basic merchandise category,* is a category that is in continuous demand over an extended time period. While consumer packaged-goods companies introduce many line extensions each year, the number of really new product introductions each year in these categories is limited. Some examples of staple merchandise categories include most categories sold in supermarkets, as well as white paint, copy paper, basic casual apparel such as T-shirts, and men's underwear.

Because sales of staple merchandise are fairly steady from week to week, it is relatively easy to forecast demand, and the consequences of making mistakes in forecasting are not great. For example, if a buyer overestimates the demand for canned soup and buys too much, the retailer will have excess inventory for a short period of time. Eventually, the canned soup will be sold without

category management The process of managing a retail business with the objective of maximizing the sales and profits of a category.

category captain A supplier that forms an alliance with a retailer to help gain consumer insight, satisfy consumer needs, and improve the performance and profit potential across the entire category.

stock keeping unit (SKU) The smallest unit available for keeping inventory control. In soft goods merchandise, an SKU usually means a size, colour, and style.

staple merchandise category A category of inventory that has continuous demand by customers over an extended period of time; also called *basic merchandise category.*

exhibit 10–2   Merchandise Planning Process

Merchandise Planning Process

- Forecast category sales
- Develop an assortment plan
- Determine appropriate level and product availability
- Develop a plan for managing inventory
- Allocate merchandise for stores
- Buy merchandise
- Monitor and evaluate performance and make adjustments

Forecasting the sales for fashion merchandise categories is much more challenging than doing so for staple categories. Buyers for fashion merchandise categories have much less flexibility in correcting forecasting errors. For example, if the laptop computer buyer for Best Buy buys too many units of a particular model, the excess inventory cannot be easily sold when a new upgraded model is introduced. Due to the short selling season for fashion merchandise, buyers often do not have a chance to reorder additional merchandise after an initial order is placed. So, if buyers initially order too little fashion merchandise, the retailer may not be able to satisfy the demand for the merchandise and will develop a reputation for not having the most popular merchandise in stock. Thus, an important objective of merchandise planning systems for fashion merchandise categories is to be as close to out of stock as possible at the same time that the SKUs become out of fashion.

Seasonal Merchandise Categories   A seasonal merchandise category consists of items whose sales fluctuate dramatically depending on the time of year. Some examples of seasonal merchandise are Halloween candy, Christmas ornaments, swimwear, and snow shovels. Both staple and fashion merchandise can be seasonal categories. For example, swimwear is a fashion merchandise category, and snow shovels are a staple merchandise category. Thus, seasonal merchandise has characteristics of both fashion and staple merchandise.

However, from a merchandise planning perspective, retailers buy seasonal merchandise in much the same way that they buy fashion merchandise. Retailers could store unsold snow shovels at the end of the winter season and sell them the next winter, but it is typically more profitable to sell the shovels at a steep discount near the end of the season rather than incur the cost of carrying this excess inventory until the beginning of the next season. Thus, plans for seasonal merchandise, like fashion merchandise, zero out merchandise at the end of the season.

These two different merchandise planning systems affect the nature of the approaches used to forecast and manage inventory.

Evaluating Merchandise Management Performance

Lo 3

As we discussed in Chapter 8, a good performance measure for evaluating a retail firm is return on assets (ROA). Return on assets is composed of two components: asset turnover and net profit margin percentage. But ROA is not a good measure for evaluating the performance of merchandise managers because they do not have control over all of the retailer's assets or all the expenses that the

continuous replenishment   A system of continuously monitoring merchandise sales and generating replacement orders, often automatically, when inventory levels drop below predetermined levels.

fashion merchandise category   Category of merchandise that typically lasts several seasons, and sales can vary dramatically from one season to the next.

seasonal merchandise category   Category of inventory whose sales fluctuate dramatically according to the time of the year.

having to resort to discounts or special marketing efforts. Because the demand for staple merchandise is predictable, merchandise planning systems for staple categories often involve continuous replenishment. These systems involve continuously monitoring merchandise sales and generating replacement orders, often automatically, when inventory levels drop below predetermined levels.

Fashion Merchandise Categories   A fashion merchandise category is in demand only for a relatively short period of time. New products are continually introduced into these categories, making the existing products obsolete. In some cases, the basic product does not change, but the colours and styles change to reflect what is "hot" that season. Some examples of fashion merchandise categories are athletic shoes, mobile phones, and women's apparel. Retailing View 10.1 describes how Mango creates and manages its fashion merchandise assortments.

retailer incurs. Merchandise managers have control only over the merchandise they buy (the retailer's merchandise inventory assets), the price at which the merchandise is sold, and the cost of the merchandise. Thus, buyers generally have control over the gross margin but not operating expenses, such as store operations, human resources, real estate, and logistics and information systems.

GMROI A financial ratio that assesses a buyer's contribution to ROA is gross margin return on inventory investment (GMROI). GMROI (typically pronounced "jim-roy") measures how many gross margin dollars are earned on every dollar of inventory investment made by the buyer. GMROI combines gross margin percentage and the sales-to-stock ratio, which is related to inventory turnover.

gross margin return on investment (GMROI) A financial ratio that assesses a buyer's contribution to return on assets: gross margin dollars divided by average (cost) inventory.

$$\text{GMROI} = \text{Gross margin} \times \text{Sales-to-stock ratio}$$

$$= \frac{\text{Gross margin}}{\text{Net sales}} \times \frac{\text{Net sales}}{\text{Average inventory at cost}}$$

$$= \frac{\text{Gross margin}}{\text{Average inventory at cost}}$$

The difference between the stock-to-sales ratio and inventory turnover is the numerator of the equation. When you are calculating the sales-to-stock ratio, the numerator is net sales. When you are calculating inventory turnover, the numerator is the cost of goods sold. To convert the sales-to-stock ratio to inventory turnover, simply multiply the sales-to-stock ratio by (1 − gross margin percentage).

Thus, if the sales-to-stock ratio is 9.0 and the gross margin percentage is .40, the inventory turnover for the category is 5.4:

$$\text{Inventory turnover} = 1 - \text{Gross margin percentage} \times \text{Sales-to-stock ratio}$$

$$5.4 = 1 - 0.4 \times 9.0$$

Buyers have control over both components of GMROI. The gross margin component is affected by the prices they set and the prices they negotiate with vendors when buying merchandise. The sales-to-stock ratio is affected by the popularity of the merchandise they buy. If they buy merchandise that customers want, it sells quickly and the sales-to-stock ratio is high. For example, Exhibit 10–3 shows the GMROI percentages for selected departments in discount stores. Jewellery, apparel, and housewares have the highest gross margin percentages. Their sales-to-stock ratios range from 8.75 (food) to 3.24 (jewellery). We might expect food to have the highest sales-to-stock ratio because it is perishable. It is either sold quickly or spoils. However, jewellery has a relatively low sales-to-stock ratio because the jewellery department needs to be stocked with many different items to satisfy customers who want to consider many different items before making a purchase decision.

Measuring Sales-to-Stock Ratio

Retailers normally express sales-to-stock ratios (and inventory turnover) on an annual basis rather than for part of a year. If the sales-to-stock ratio for a three-month season equals 2.3, the annual sales-to-stock ratio will be four times that number (9.2). Thus, to convert a sales-to-stock ratio based on part of a year to an annual figure, multiply it by the number of such time periods in the year.

The most accurate way to measure average inventory is to measure the inventory level at the end of each day and divide the sum by 365. Most retailers can use their information systems to get accurate average inventory estimates by averaging the inventory in stores and distribution centres at the end of each day. Another method is to take the end-of-month (EOM) inventories for several months and divide by the number of months, as shown in the example below:

DID YOU KNOW?

Even toilet paper has seasonal influences. Fancy toilet paper sells better during the holiday season between Thanksgiving and New Year's, since people have guests in their homes.

Month	End-of-Month at Retail Prices
January	$22 000
February	$33 000
March	$38 000
Total inventory	$93 000
Average inventory	$31 000

Managing Inventory Turnover

Increasing inventory turnover can increase sales volume, improve sales associates' morale, and provide more resources to take advantage of new buying opportunities.

exhibit 10–3 GMROI for Selected Departments in Discount Stores

Department	Gross Margin %	Sales-to-Stock Ratio	GMROI
Apparel	37	6.35	235
Housewares	35	4.63	162
Food	20	8.75	175
Jewellery	38	3.24	123
Furniture	31	4.09	90
Health and beauty supplies	22	5.14	113
Consumer electronics	21	5.05	106

Higher inventory turnover increases sales because new merchandise is continually available to customers. New merchandise attracts customers to visit the store more frequently because they know they will be seeing different merchandise each time they visit the store. When inventory turnover is low, the merchandise begins to look shopworn—slightly damaged from being displayed and handled by customers for a long time. Increasing the amount of new merchandise also improves sales associates' morale. Salespeople are excited about and more motivated to sell the new merchandise, and thus sales increase, increasing inventory turnover even further. Finally, when inventory turnover increases, more money is available to buy new merchandise. Having money available to buy merchandise late in a fashion season can open up profit opportunities. For instance, buyers can take advantage of special prices offered by vendors that have too much inventory left over at the end of the season.

One approach for increasing turnover is to reduce the number of SKUs within a category. However, if customers can't find the size or colour they seek—or even worse, if they can't find the brand or product line at all—due to the reduced assortment, patronage and sales can decrease. Customers who are disappointed on a regular basis will shop elsewhere and possibly urge their friends to do the same.

Excessively high inventory turnover causes frequent stockouts.

Another approach for increasing inventory turnover is to buy merchandise more often and in smaller quantities, as this reduces average inventory without reducing sales. But buying smaller quantities decreases the gross margin because buyers can't take advantage of quantity discounts and transportation economies of scale. Buying merchandise frequently in small quantities can also increase operating expenses, since buyers spend more time placing orders and monitoring deliveries.

Thus, buyers need to strike a balance while determining the level of inventory turnover. Some approaches for improving inventory turnover can lower GMROI by lowering sales volume, increasing the cost of goods sold, and increasing operating expenses.

In the following sections, each of the steps in the merchandise management process described in Exhibit 10–2 is examined, except for the step for buying merchandise, which is the subject of Chapter 11.

Forecasting Sales Lo 4

As indicated in Exhibit 10–2, the first step in merchandise management planning is to develop a forecast for category sales. The methods and information used for forecasting staple and fashion merchandise categories are discussed in this section.

Category Life Cycles

When developing a sales forecast, a retailer must be able to predict how well product categories will sell over time. Product categories typically follow a predictable sales pattern—sales start off low, increase, plateau, and then ultimately decline. Yet the shape of that pattern varies considerably from category to category and will help buyers forecast sales. This section describes the most fundamental form of sales pattern: the category life cycle. Using the category life cycle as a basis, we'll examine some commonly found variations on it: fad, fashion, staple, and seasonal.

In the retail industry, forecast is the term used for forecasting short-term sales and other financial factors based on current business conditions. For example, a six-month merchandise plan is created six to nine months prior to the beginning of the season. As the season begins and business starts to occur, planners will forecast sales, markdowns, etc. for the current month and perhaps the following two months as well. This process measures the actual results against the original plan and helps the merchandise teams manage and assess their original plan objectives. In summary, the term often used is *plan* or *budget*.

The category life cycle describes a merchandise category's sales pattern over time. The category life cycle (Exhibit 10–4) is divided into four stages: introduction, growth, maturity, and decline. Knowing where a category, or specific item within a category, is in its life cycle is important in developing a sales forecast and merchandising strategy.

When personal digital assistants (PDAs) were first introduced in 1996, the target market was businesspeople who were high-tech aficionados, people who wanted to be first in adopting an innovation and were willing to pay for the convenience of having a very small computer.[6] PDAs were very expensive compared to paper address and appointment books, and they weren't available at all stores that normally sell office supplies or computers. PDAs were next marketed to doctors, stockbrokers, and business executives, who use them for access to medical databases, stock markets, and e-mail. As categories reach the growth and maturity stages, they usually appeal to broader, mass-market customers who patronize discount stores and category specialists.

Knowing where a category is in its life cycle is useful for predicting sales. However, the shape of the life cycle can be affected by the activities undertaken by retailers and vendors. For instance, a vendor might set a low introductory price for a new product to increase the adoption rate of the product, or set a high price to increase profits even though sales might not grow as quickly. Care must be taken, however, that use of the category life cycle as a predictive tool does not adversely affect sales. If a product is classified as being in decline, it's likely that retailers will stock less variety and limit promotions. Naturally, sales will go down. Thus, the decline classification may actually become a self-fulfilling prophecy. Many products have been successfully maintained at the maturity stage because their buyers have maintained innovative strategies that are consistent with a mature product. For instance, Kellogg's Corn Flakes has been the best-selling ready-to-eat cereal over many decades because it has innovative advertising and competitive pricing.

Variations on the Category Life Cycle Most categories follow the basic form of the category life cycle: sales increase, peak, and then decline. Variations on the category life cycle—fad, fashion, staple, and seasonal—are shown in Exhibit 10–5. The distinguishing characteristics between them are whether the category lasts for many seasons, whether a specific style sells for many seasons, and whether sales vary dramatically from one season to the next. Life cycle trends can impact many different categories. For example, consider the popular colours for kitchen appliances, cars, and paint for home items such as bathroom fixtures that have now become jewellery for the home. A fad is a merchandise category that generates a lot of sales for a relatively short time—often less than a season. Examples are Pogs, Furbys, Pokémon, butterfly hair clips, and some licensed characters such as Star Wars action figures. More mainstream examples are certain computer games, new electronic equipment, and some apparel, such as cropped and flared jeans. Fads are primarily aimed at children and teens.

Fads are often illogical and unpredictable. The art of managing a fad comes in recognizing the fad in its earliest stages and immediately locking up distribution rights for merchandise to stores nationwide before the competition does. Marketing fads is one of the riskiest ventures in retailing because even if the company properly identifies a fad, it must still have the sixth sense to recognize the peak so that it can bail out before it's stuck with a warehouse full of merchandise.

Unlike a fad, a fashion is a category of merchandise that typically lasts

exhibit 10–4 The Category Product Life Cycle

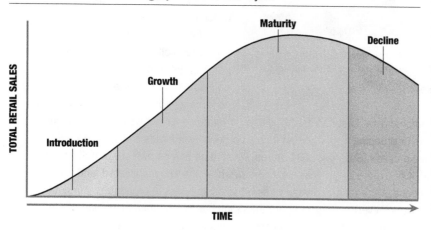

exhibit 10–5 Variations in Category Life Cycles

	FAD	FASHION	STAPLE
Sales over many seasons	No	Yes	Yes
Sales of a specific style over many seasons	No	No	Yes
Sales vary dramatically from one season to the next	No	Yes	No
Illustration (Sales against Time)			

several seasons, and sales can vary dramatically from one season to the next. A fashion is similar to a fad in that a specific style or SKU sells for one season or less. A fashion's lifespan depends on the type of category and the target market. For instance, double-breasted suits for men or certain colours are fashions with a life that may last several years. On the other hand, fashions such as see-through track shoes may last only a season or two. Retailing View 10.1 describes how Mango creates and manages fashion merchandise.

Fast Fashion at Mango

"We know how to improvise," says David Egea, Mango's merchandising director and a top executive. "To react and have what people want, we have to break some rules." Mango/MNG Holding SL, with over 850 stores in 81 countries, including the United States and Canada, typifies the new retail trend of "fast fashion," pioneered by Spain's Zara and Sweden's H&M. These chains fill their racks with a steady stream of new, gotta-have-it merchandise. The company's retail strategy combines stylistic and technological resources built on flexibility and speed, from design sketch to the store shelf.

Mango is famous for an eclectic mix of body-hugging styles. A black pinstriped jacket sells for $60 and a tight black minidress for $40. The retailer maintains tight controls over the design and manufacturing of its private-label merchandise. Last-minute changes, like substituting a fabric or dropping a hemline, are a built-in part of the creative process. So long as the company has fabric in stock, it can move a design from sketchpad to store in four weeks.

Mango's merchandise planning cycle begins every three months when designers meet to discuss important new trends for each of its main collections, which contain five or six mini-collections. So, shops receive a near-constant stream of new merchandise, ranging from clingy short dresses to work wear and sparkly evening gowns. New items are sent to its stores once a week, roughly six times as often as the typical North American clothing chain.

To get ideas for each collection, designers attend the traditional fashion shows and trade fairs. But they also stay close to the customer. They take photos of

Mango stocks high-fashion, trendy merchandise to attract its target shoppers.

stylish young women and note what people are wearing on the streets and in nightclubs. "To see what everyone's going to do for next season is very easy," says Egea. "But that doesn't mean this is the thing that is going to catch on." Hoping to stay au courant, design teams meet each week to adjust to ever-changing trends. Mango commissioned Penelope Cruz and her sister Monica to design a 25-piece collection to compete with the other fast-fashion companies that have used celebrities as designers. Top Shop released its Kate Moss collection, and H&M came out with a Madonna collection.

When collection designs are set, Mango's product management and distribution team assigns them personality traits, denoting SKUs as trendy, dressy, or suitable for hot weather. Depending on an item's personality, it heads to one of Mango's 731 stores, which also has its own set of traits, such as the climate, where the shop is located, and whether large or small sizes sell best. A proprietary computer program then matches compatible shops and styles.

Orders are sent to a distribution centre where clothes are scanned and dropped into one of 466 store-specific slots. Then they're boxed and shipped to shops, where managers can adjust store layouts daily on the basis of input from regional supervisors and headquarters.

Mango stores display only a limited merchandise assortment. On each rack, only one size per item is hung. This policy encourages a sense of urgency by playing on customers' worst fear: Maybe your size is going to run out.

Sources: www.mangoshop.com (accessed September 18, 2007); Beth Wilson, "Mango's Fast-Fashion Approach To Expansion," *WWD*, December 7, 2006, p. 23; and Sally Raikes, "Cruz Control," *Scotland on Sunday*, September 16, 2007 (accessed September 18, 2007).

Some questions that help buyers distinguish between fads and more enduring fashions are as follows:

- **Is it compatible with a change in consumer lifestyles?** Innovations that are consistent with lifestyles will endure. For example, certain jeans are an enduring fashion because they are comfortable to wear and can be worn on multiple occasions. Leather pants, on the other hand, can be hot and heavy, and are typically worn in the evening. They are a fad.

- **Does the innovation provide real benefits?** The switch to poultry and fish from beef is not a fad because it provides real benefits to a health-conscious society.

- **Is the innovation compatible with other changes in the marketplace?** For example, shorter skirts that resulted in a greater emphasis on women's hosiery are declining due to the growing emphasis on casual apparel.

- **Who adopted the trend?** If it is not adopted by large, growing segments such as working mothers, Baby Boomers, Generation Y, or the elderly, it is not likely to endure. Alternatively, if it is being adopted by teenagers, who are known to be fickle in their tastes, it is likely to fade quickly.

Items within the staple merchandise, also called basic merchandise, category are in continuous demand over an extended period of time. Even certain brands of basic merchandise, however, ultimately go into decline. Most merchandise in grocery stores, as well as housewares, hosiery, and women's intimate apparel are considered to be staple merchandise. Changing technology resulted in the decline of CD sales with the growth in demand for downloadable music. Retailing View 10.2 questions whether jeans are a fad, a fashion, or a staple.

10.2 | RETAILING VIEW

Are Jeans a Fad, a Fashion, or a Staple?

The answer to the question whether jeans are a fad, a fashion, or a staple, all depends on what style and market segment you are considering. For example, skinny jeans hit the market during the first decade of this millennium. After a decade of boot-cut pants, the skinny look was a major silhouette change. Designers and retailers attempted to change women's looks to upside-down triangle silhouettes, characterized by larger tops and narrower bottoms. At the same time, clothes steadily are becoming less flashy, with details like darts, stitching, and pleats instead of sequins, embroidery, and holes.

It doesn't take a fashion guru to realize that skinny jeans wouldn't look good on all women. But those retailers that could accurately predict the fashion lifecycle of these jeans profited handsomely.

A jeans fad like skinny jeans is more likely to succeed for retailers that cater to younger women, such as Urban Outfitters, Abercrombie & Fitch, and Bebe.

Retailers that target older women, such as Chico's, Talbots, and Ann Taylor, approached this silhouette more cautiously.

Although not as trendy as skinny jeans, boot-cut jeans have been a fashionable cut for several years. What's the difference between the relatively long-term success of the boot-cut fashion and the short-lived skinny jean? First and foremost, the boot-cut is a complementary silhouette for most bodies. As a result, it appeals to many large market segments.

Some jeans are considered staples from a merchandise management perspective. Levi's 501 jeans, for instance, was introduced in 1873 and remains popular all over the world. Wrangler, Lee, L.L. Bean, Lands' End, and private labels from JCPenney and other retailers are purchased by people of all ages and walks of life for work and play.

Can you predict the fashion cycle for high-waisted jeans?

Sources: Helen Tither, "Flares: Bigger, Better, Beautiful," *Manchester Evening News,* September 10, 2007 (accessed January 15, 2008); and Chelsea Emery, "Fashion Shift May Help Teen Retailers, Hurt Others," *The Washington Post,* June 11, 2006 (accessed January 15, 2008).

Seasonal merchandise is inventory whose sales fluctuate dramatically according to the time of the year. Both fashion and staple merchandise usually have seasonal influences. For instance, wool sweaters sell in fall and winter, whereas staples such as lawn mowers and garden tools are popular in spring and summer. Retailers carefully plan their purchases and deliveries to coincide with seasonal demand. Armed with information about where an item or a category is in its life cycle, retailers develop their sales forecast.

Forecasting Staple Merchandise

Use of Historical Sales   The sales of staple merchandise are relatively constant from year to year. Thus, forecasts are typically based on extrapolating historical sales. Because there are substantial sales data available, sophisticated statistical techniques can be used to forecast future sales for each SKU. However, these statistical forecasts are based on the assumption that the factors affecting item sales in the past will be the same and have the same effect in the future. Thus, even though sales for staple merchandise categories are relatively predictable, controllable and uncontrollable factors can have a significant impact on them.

Adjustments for Controllable Factors   Controllable factors include openings and closings of stores, the price set for the merchandise in the category, special promotions for the category, the pricing and promotion of complementary categories, and the placement of the merchandise categories in the stores. Some factors beyond the retailer's control are the weather, general economic conditions, special promotions or new product introductions by vendors, the availability of products, pricing, and promotional activities by competitors. Thus, buyers need to adjust the forecast on the basis of statistical projections to reflect the effects of these controllable and uncontrollable factors. Retailing View 10.3 illustrates how retailers use long-range weather forecasts to improve their forecasts.

Exhibit 10–6 illustrates the analysis of past unit sales data for a 30-cm, cast-iron, Lodge frying pan at a national home store chain to forecast sales for 2013. Exhibit 10–6a contains the sales data by quarter for the past eight years. The annual sales data are plotted in Exhibit 10–6b, and the quarterly sales data are plotted in Exhibit 10–6c. The annual sales pattern reveals a slight annual growth in sales of 3.3 percent; however, sales actually decreased in 2011 and then jumped 6 percent in 2012.

10.3 | RETAILING VIEW

Weather's Effect on Retail Sales

Retailers know that when hurricane season comes, they need to be ready with bottled water, batteries, flashlights, plywood, and generators. However, more subtle weather conditions, like a warmer-than-normal holiday season, can have a significant impact on retail sales.

To incorporate these weather effects in their forecasts, many retailers subscribe to long-range weather forecasting services. Merchandise managers use the information provided by these services to make decisions about the timing of merchandise deliveries, promotions, and price discounts. For example, if warmer weather is forecast this year than last for the preholiday season, full-line general merchandise retailers will plan to sell more electronics than winter apparel. Supermarkets that stock meat and other barbecue items in anticipation of sunshine are often left with unsold food if the weather is rainy and cold instead.

The first cold snap in the fall stimulates the sale of winter apparel.

Sources: Julia Werdiger, "Tesco, British Grocer, Uses Weather to Predict Sales," *New York Times*, September 2, 2009; "Forecasting Retail Successes: Walmart Turns to Weather Info to Plan Inventory," *DSN Retailing Today*, October 2006, pp. 13–14; Pia Sarkar, "Retailers Use Weather to Forecast Their Sales," *San Francisco Chronicle*, December 4, 2006.

exhibit 10–6a   Unit Sales by Quarter

Year	Quarter	Sales by Quarter	Annual Sales	Annual Sales Growth Rate	% Annual Sales by Quarter
2005	1	21074	93408		23%
	2	24123			26
	3	16066			17
	4	32145			34
2006	1	20728	90387	−3.2%	23
	2	23656			26
	3	15867			18
	4	30135			33
2007	1	21076	97984	8.4	22
	2	25259			26
	3	18585			19
	4	33064			34
2008	1	20617	99931	2.0	21
	2	26084			26
	3	18308			18
	4	34921			35
2009	1	21464	106192	6.3	20
	2	27568			26
	3	18996			18
	4	38163			36
2010	1	24401	114394	7.7	21
	2	28057			25
	3	21092			18
	4	40843			36
2011	1	23859	110562	−3.3	22
	2	27441			25
	3	19537			18
	4	39726			36
2012	1	24588	118963	7.6	21
	2	30788			26
	3	19869			17
	4	43718			37

exhibit 10–6b   Plot of Sales by Year

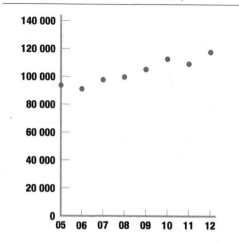

exhibit 10–6c   Plot of Sales by Quarter

The estimated quarterly sales would be

First-quarter sales = 123 245 × 0.21 = 25 881
Second-quarter sales = 123 245 × 0.26 = 32 044
Third-quarter sales = 123 245 × 0.18 = 22 184
Fourth-quarter sales = 123 245 × 0.35 = 43 136

The graph of quarterly sales shows a seasonal pattern, with sales greatest during the fourth quarter and lowest during the third quarter. The average percentage of annual sales for each quarter is 21 percent for the first quarter, 26 percent for the second quarter, 18 percent in the third quarter, and 35 percent in the fourth quarter. Even though people use frying pans throughout the year, there is a tendency to give them as holiday gifts, and people tend to cook more on the stove when the weather gets cold.

On the basis of these past unit sales data, the buyer could simply project the sales data and estimate the annual unit sales for the frying pans for 2009 as

2013 annual sales = 1.036 (3.6 percent growth)
     × 118 963 (2012 annual sales)
     = 123 245

However, these projections are based on the assumption that the factors affecting 30-cm, cast-iron, Lodge frying pan sales in 2009 will be the same and have the same effect as they have had for the past eight years. Even though sales for staple merchandise categories such as cookware are relatively predictable, controllable and uncontrollable factors can have a significant impact on them.

Forecasting Fashion Merchandise Categories

Forecasting sales for fashion merchandise is challenging because buyers typically need to place orders and commit to buying specific quantities between three and six months before the merchandise will be delivered and made available for sales. In addition, for fashion items, there often is no opportunity to increase or decrease the quantity ordered before the selling season has ended. Suppliers of popular merchandise usually have orders for more merchandise than they can produce and excess inventory of unpopular items. Finally, forecasting fashion merchandise sales is particularly difficult because some or all of the items in the category are new and different from units offered in previous seasons or years. Some sources of information that retailers use to develop forecasts for fashion merchandise categories are (1) previous sales data, (2) market research, (3) fashion and trend services, and (4) vendors.

Previous Sales Data Although items in fashion merchandise categories might be new each season, many items in a fashion category are often similar to items sold in previous years. Thus, accurate forecasts might be generated by simply projecting past sales data. For example, football video games might change from season to season with new games and editions, but while the SKUs are different each season, the total number of football video games sold each year might be relatively constant and predictable. Women's fashion dresses might change from season to season with new colours, styles, and fabrics. Whereas the SKUs are different each season, the total number of fashion dresses sold each year might be relatively constant and very predictable. Exhibit 10–7 shows Levi's sales by season over a ten-year period. Sales have been increasing by about 25 percent per season for

several years. Exhibit 10–7 illustrates a strong seasonality pattern. Typically, 40 percent of the annual sales occur in fall, 30 percent in winter, and 15 percent each in spring and summer. In the eighth year, the fall season was unusually strong due to early cold weather, whereas spring sales were particularly weak because of a temporary turndown in the local economy.

For fashion merchandise, where styles change from year to year, sales figures older than three years probably aren't very useful. When forecasting sales, retailers must identify real trends (either up or down) and try to isolate a real change in demand from random occurrences. Thus, the unusually high and low sales in the eighth year should be ignored when trying to forecast sales for the current season.

More Information About 10.1 shows a simple method of forecasting sales using the data from Exhibit 10–7.

Market Research Buyers for fashion merchandise categories undertake a variety of market research activities to help them forecast sales. These activities range from informal, qualitative research about trends affecting the category to more formal experiments and surveys.

To find out what customers are going to want in the future, buyers immerse themselves in their customers' world. For example, buyers look for information about trends by going to Internet chat rooms and blogs, attending soccer games and rock concerts, and visiting hot spots around town, such as restaurants and nightclubs, to find out what people are talking about and see what they're wearing. Buyers are information junkies and read voraciously. What movies are hits at the box office, and what are the stars wearing? Who is going to see them? What books and albums are on the Top Ten lists? What magazines are consumers purchasing? Are there themes that keep popping up?

Social media sites are important sources of information for buyers. Buyers learn a lot about their customers' likes, dislikes, and preferences by monitoring their past purchases and by monitoring their interactions with social network sites such as Facebook. Customers appear keen to submit their opinions about their friends' purchases, interests, polls, and blogs.

Retailers also use traditional forms of marketing research such as depth interviews and focus groups.

exhibit 10–7   Sales for Levi's Jeans at Trendsetters Department Store

Note: The peaks show the fall sales, typically 40 percent of annual sales; the horizontal lines typify 15 percent of annual sales each in spring and summer; and the dots (the winter sales) are typically 30 percent of annual sales. These data are for illustrative purposes only. They do, however, represent typical growth patterns for a category such as jeans.

The depth interview is an unstructured personal interview in which the interviewer uses extensive probing to get individual respondents to talk in detail about a subject. For example, one grocery store chain goes through the personal cheques received each day to identify customers to interview. Representatives from the supermarket chain call these customers and interview them to find out what they like and don't like about the merchandise in the store.

A more informal method of interviewing customers is to require that buyers spend some time on the selling floor waiting on customers. Buying offices for Target and Walmart are in Mississauga, Ontario, yet their stores are located throughout Canada. It has become increasingly hard for buyers in large chains to be attuned to local customer demand. Frequent store visits help resolve the situation. Some retailers require that their buyers spend a specified period of time, like one day a week, in a store.

A focus group is a small group of respondents interviewed by a moderator using a loosely structured format. Participants are encouraged to express their views and comment on the views of others in the group. To keep abreast of the teen market, for instance, some stores have teen boards consisting of opinion leaders who meet to discuss merchandising and other store issues. Abercrombie & Fitch brings in groups of teenagers and has them rate and trade off their preferences for different items.

depth interview
An unstructured personal interview in which the interviewer uses extensive probing to get individual respondents to talk in detail about a subject.

focus group A marketing research technique in which a small group of respondents is interviewed by a moderator using a loosely structured format.

10.1 | MORE INFORMATION ABOUT...

Forecasting Sales for Levi's Jeans

The procedure for forecasting sales by season is accomplished in two steps. First, the retailer determines a sales forecast for the entire year. Then it considers seasonal sales patterns for each season.

The accompanying exhibit summarizes sales by season for Levi's jeans for years 6 through 9 from Exhibit 10–7. For instance, during the fall season of year 6, the store sold $152 587 in jeans, which represents 41.9 percent of the total sales for year 6 ($152 587 ÷ $364 247 = 41.9 percent). The last column indicates the percentages of the increases for the previous three years: 30.1, 48.5, and 5 percent. The 30.1 percent increase from year 6 to year 7 was calculated as follows: ($364 247 − $476 835) ÷ $364 247. Unfortunately, the data don't show a consistent pattern due to unusually high sales in year 8. The buyer should probably discount the impact of year 8 sales on the forecast and examine sales increases from earlier years as well as more qualitative factors. The average sales increase over the previous nine years has been 25 percent, general economic indicators in the area are strong, and top management sees an opportunity to grow this classification, so the buyer estimates the sales increase for year 10 to be 30 percent. Thus, the sales forecast for year 10 is [($745 056 × 0.3) + $745 056] or $968 573.

The second step is to apply the seasonal sales pattern to the annual sales forecast to determine sales for each season. The percentage of annual sales occurring in each season has been fairly stable except in year 8. Thus, the buyer decides to apply the same percentages as those in years 7 and 9. To forecast sales for each season, the buyer multiplies the annual sales by each of the seasonal sales percentages. For instance, fall sales for year 10 should equal ($968 573 × 0.4) or $387 429.

Year	SEASON				Total	Percentage Increase
	Fall	Winter	Spring	Summer		
6	$ 152 587 41.9%	$ 114 440 31.4%	$ 57 220 15.7%	$ 40 000 11.0%	$ 364 247 100%	
7	190 734 40.0%	143 051 30.0%	71 525 15.0%	71 525 15.0%	476 835 100%	30.1%
8	400 000 56.5%	178 813 25.3%	40 000 5.6%	89 406 12.6%	708 219 100%	48.5%
9	298 023 40.5%	223 517 30.0%	111 758 15.0%	111 758 15.0%	745 056 100%	5.0%
6–9 (total)	1 041 344 45.4%	659 821 28.2%	280 503 12.2%	312 689 13.6%	2 294 357 100%	
10 (forecast)	387 429	290 572	145 286	145 286	968 573	

Asda, a full-line U.K. supercentre owned by Walmart, regularly surveys its customers to forecast the sales of new products. It e-mails images and descriptions of new products to its group of 18 000 customers, which it has termed its "Pulse of the Nation" group. The group is asked to respond, positively or negatively, and indicate whether they think the new products should be carried in the stores.[7]

Finally, many retailers have a program for conducting merchandise experiments. For example, Claire's, an international specialty accessory retail chain targeting teens, continually runs experiments to determine whether new merchandise concepts will produce adequate sales. It introduces the new merchandise into a representative sample of stores and sees what sales are generated for the items. Multichannel retailers often run similar experiments by offering new items on their websites before making a decision to stock them in their stores.

Fashion and Trend Services   There are many services that buyers, particularly buyers of apparel categories, can subscribe to that forecast the latest fashions, colours, and styles. For example, Doneger Creative Services offers a range of services related to trend and colour forecasting and analysis for apparel, accessories, and lifestyle markets in the women's, men's, and youth merchandise categories through its print publications, online content, and live presentations. Its colour forecast service provides colour direction for each season using dyed-to-specification colour standards plus suggested colour combinations and applications for specific categories. Its online clipboard reports present actionable information and style news from the runways to the streets.

Vendors   Vendors have proprietary information about their marketing plans, such as new product launches and special promotions that can have a significant impact on retail sales for their products and the entire merchandise category. In addition, vendors tend to be very knowledgeable about market trends for merchandise categories because they typically specialize in fewer merchandise categories than do retailers. Thus, information from vendors about their plans and market research about merchandise categories is very useful to buyers as they develop category sales forecasts.

Sales Forecasting for Services Retailers

Due to the perishable nature of services, services retailers face an even more extreme problem than fashion retailers. Their offering perishes at the end of the day, not at the end of the season. If there are empty seats when a plane takes off or a rock concert ends, the revenue that might have been generated from these seats is lost forever. However, if more people are interested in dining at a restaurant than there are tables available, a revenue opportunity also is lost. So services retailers have devised approaches for managing demand for their offering so that it meets but does not exceed capacity.

Some services retailers attempt to match supply and demand by taking reservations or making appointments. Physicians often overbook their appointments so that many patients have to wait. They do this so that they will always fill their capacity and not have unproductive, non-revenue-generating time. Restaurants take reservations so that customers will not have to wait for a table. In addition, the reservations indicate the staffing levels needed for the meal. Another approach is selling advance tickets for a service.[8]

Store-Level Forecasting

As retailers respond to increased competition, oversaturated markets, and shoppers who want more of everything for less, it is becoming increasingly important for retailers to become more efficient and quickly tailor merchandise offerings to meet the needs and desires of smaller and smaller market segments.[9] To do this requires the merchandise planner to predict sales at the store SKU (stock keeping unit) level (colours, sizes, etc.). The forecasting method described in the previous sections was performed by buyers at more aggregate levels, such as a region or a distribution centre servicing many stores, and it was done by category, not by SKU. The problem with forecasting at more aggregate levels is that store-level variability gets averaged or summed out of the data. This, for example, happens when one store sells more single-serving-sized food products and a different store sells more family-sized products. Combining results from the two stores results in demand data that report evenly distributed sales.

Although sophisticated systems infrastructure and computational power enable the move to store-level forecasting, traditional approaches are not designed to address the complexity and operational issues related to store-level data in a timely manner. To predict store-level demand, forecasting systems need to be able to measure simultaneously the impacts of many factors on unit sales. These factors include promotion, price, placement of merchandise in the store, substitution, competition, location, and others. These factors are described in Exhibit 10–8.

Setting Objectives for the Merchandise Plan

LO 5

Retailers cannot hope to be financially successful unless they preplan the financial implications of their merchandising

exhibit 10-8 Factors Impacting Sales Forecasts, Merchandise Plans, Budgets

Price The amount of unit sales of an item obviously depends on the price at which it is offered. Generally, with a few exceptions, raising the price causes unit sales to decrease, and vice versa. The question is, by how much? The answer can be found by determining the item's elasticity—the percentage change in unit sales resulting from a given percentage change in price. Thus, items that have a high elasticity are price-sensitive, and items with a low elasticity are insensitive to price.

Promotion The degree and type of promotion are also critical in determining the unit sales of an item. Promotional techniques include weekly circulars, store signage, end-caps and other special product displays, and manufacturer coupons and rebates.

Store Location There can be large variations in demand depending on store location. Snow shovels obviously have a much higher demand in Northern Ontario than in Vancouver. Even in the same metropolitan area, the same item could have a different demand depending on whether the store is in a downtown location or a suburban or rural location. Customer demographics also play a role. For example, the buying patterns in a store adjacent to a retirement community will be different from those in a store located in a residential neighbourhood with many young families.

Product Placement The amount of shelf space afforded an item, as well as its location on the shelf, can have a large impact on sales. A diagram that shows how and where specific products should be placed on the shelves, called a planogram, is created to help maximize sales.

Seasonality Some categories, most notably apparel, are highly seasonal in nature. In the extreme case, all of the sales of a particular merchandise category will occur during a single season. Seasonality also refers to increased sales associated with Christmas, Thanksgiving, Mother's Day, and others.

Other Factors There are many other factors that impact sales, usually to a lesser degree, but sometimes significantly. Among these are:

- *Product life cycle*—knowledge of whether product demand is growing, stable, or in decline, is important.
- *Product availability*—the degree to which the merchandise is, or is not, on the shelves ready for sale impacts sales.
- *Competitor price and promotional activity*—these also affect a retailer's sales.
- *Business cycles*—sales may be higher at the beginning of the month due to payroll cycles; also, sales are higher on weekends than on weekdays.
- *Weather*—late or early arrival of hot or cold weather can have a significant impact on sales of seasonal items.
- *Unusual events*—a new highway, an unexpected or severe storm, and other natural disasters can have a large local impact.
- *Cannibalization*—for example, decreasing the price of Apple Jacks would increase sales, but perhaps to the detriment of the sales of Froot Loops.
- *Complementary products*—putting hot dogs on sale will also cause an increase in sales of hot dog buns.

Source: Adapted from KhiMetrics.

---

activities. Financial plans start at the top of the retail organization and are broken down into categories, while buyers and merchandise planners develop their own plans and negotiate up the organization. Top management looks at the overall merchandising strategy. They set the merchandising direction for the company by:

- Defining the target market
- Establishing performance goals
- Deciding, on the basis of general trends in the marketplace, which merchandise classifications deserve more or less emphasis

Buyers and merchandise planners, on the other hand, take a more micro approach. They study their categories' past performance, look at trends in the market, and try to project the assortments for their merchandise categories for the coming seasons.

The planning process is similar for smaller retailers. Although there aren't as many layers of management involved in planning and negotiations, they still start with the firm's overall financial goals and break them down into categories.

The resulting merchandise plan is a financial buying blueprint for each category. It considers the firm's financial objectives along with sales projections and merchandise flows. The merchandise plan tells the buyer and planner how much money to spend on a particular category of merchandise in each month so that the sales forecast and other financial objectives are met. Once the merchandise plan is set, the buyers and planners develop the assortment plan. The buyers work with vendors choosing merchandise, negotiating prices, and developing promotions. The merchandise planners break down the overall financial plan into how many of each item to purchase and how they should be allocated to stores.

As you can imagine, there's a great deal of negotiating at each step. Merchandise managers and buyers compete with each other over the size of their merchandise budgets.

DID YOU KNOW?

Loblaw's President's Choice and no name control brands are the number one and number two packaged-goods brands by sales in Canada, respectively. Further, the Joe Fresh brand is the third-highest volume unit brand in Canada.[10]

Developing an Assortment Plan

Lo

variety The number of different merchandise categories within a store or department; also called *breadth*.

depth The amount of a particular item of merchandise that a retailer will stock, reflecting attributes such as brand, size, or colour.

All retailers face the fundamental strategic question of what type of retail format to maintain to achieve a sustainable competitive advantage. A critical component of this decision is determining what merchandise assortment will be carried. Merchandise decisions are constrained by the amount of money available to invest in inventory and the amount of space available in the store. Based on the financial objectives that have been set at the top and have trickled through the retail organization, decisions regarding variety, assortment, and product availability must be made. After forecasting sales for the category, the next step in the merchandise management planning process is to develop an assortment plan. An assortment plan is a list of SKUs that a retailer will offer in a merchandise category. The assortment plan thus reflects the breadth and depth that the retailer plans to offer in a merchandise category. After forecasting sales for the category, the next step in the merchandise management planning process is to develop an assortment plan (see Exhibit 10–2).

Category Breadth and Depth

The variety of a retailer's merchandise (also called *breadth*) is the number of different merchandising categories within a store or department and the retailer's depth of merchandise is defined as the number of SKUs within a category.

Services retailers also make assortment decisions. For example, some health clubs offer a large variety of activities and equipment from exercise machines to swimming, wellness programs, and New Age lectures. Others, like World Gym, don't offer much variety but have deep assortments of body-building equipment and programs. Some hospitals, such as big municipal hospitals found in most urban areas, offer a large variety of medical services, whereas others specialize in services such as trauma or prenatal care. For services retailers, the level of product availability is a sales forecasting issue.

Assortment planning involves decisions concerning the amount of merchandise choice that is available to the customer. Overstocking merchandise results in lower turnover and reduced profits; understocking may mean lost sales and unhappy customers who will take their business elsewhere. The ideal situation is the right merchandise, in the right quantity, at the right price, and at the right time.

Breadth of stock refers to the number of SKUs, which could be the variety of brands, sizes, or colours available to the customer.

- Broad assortment will include numerous choices.

- Narrow assortment will provide the customer with only a few choices.

Depth of merchandise, or the amount of a particular item that a retailer will stock, includes the attributes of brand, size, or colour; for example, how many styles of a specific brand of bicycle.

- Deep assortments refers to a large quantity of a single item.

- Shallow assortment consists of only a few of a single item.

Examples follow:

Broad and shallow assortment planning is typical of the fashion retailer Club Monaco, which will stock a broad assortment of styles to satisfy the style-conscious consumer but does not carry depth in any particular item. The fashion customer is more selective about style, size, and colour, and will change with the newest trends.

Narrow and deep assortment planning is an assortment typical of the mass merchandisers, such as Walmart and Target. The assortment mix has only a few choices in a particular category, but it is stocked in considerable depth so as to be seldom out of stock within that product group. There may be, for example, three brands.

Square assortment planning is a moderate assortment strategy that is adopted by traditional department stores. In order to provide customers with a greater product selection than the mass merchandisers, Hudson's Bay and Sears will adapt a square assortment plan. This assortment strategy is planned to have limited depth within the categories to avoid having an overstock situation that could result in markdowns and a loss of revenue at the end of the season.

In the context of merchandise planning, the concepts of breadth and depth are applied to a merchandise category rather than a retail firm. At the category level, variety reflects the number of different types of merchandise, and assortment is the number of SKUs per type. For example, the assortment plan for girls' jeans in Exhibit 10–9 includes ten types of varieties (traditional or boot-cut, regular denim or stonewashed, and three price points reflecting different brands). For each type, there are 81 SKUs (3 colours × 9 sizes × 3 lengths). Thus, this retailer plans to offer 810 SKUs in girls' jeans.

Determining Breadth and Depth

The process of determining the breadth and depth for a category is called editing the assortment. When editing the assortment for a category like jeans, the buyer considers the following factors: the firm's retail strategy, the effect of assortments on GMROI, the complementarities between categories, the effects of assortments on buying behaviour, and the physical characteristics of the store.

Retail Strategy The number of SKUs offered in a merchandise category is a strategic decision. For example, Costco focuses on customers who are looking for a few SKUs in a category (see Retailing View 10.4). In contrast, Best Buy focuses on consumers interested in comparing many alternatives in specific consumer electronic categories and thus offers more SKUs in each category.

The breadth and depth of the assortment in a merchandise category can affect the retailer's brand image.[12] Retailers might increase the assortment in categories that are closely associated with their image. For example, Costco typically has few SKUs per category, but it has a broad and deep assortment of wines in its U.S. stores because its offering in this category reinforces its image of offering quality products with good value.

Assortments and GMROI In developing the assortment plan, buyers need to be sensitive to the trade-off of increasing sales by offering greater breadth and depth but, at the same time, potentially reducing inventory turnover and GMROI because of the increased inventory investment. Increasing assortment breadth and depth also can decrease gross margin. For example, the more

exhibit 10–9 Assortment Plan for Girls' Jeans

Styles	Traditional	Traditional	Traditional	Traditional	Traditional	Traditional
Price levels	$20	$20	$35	$35	$45	$45
Fabric composition	Regular denim	Stonewashed	Regular denim	Stonewashed	Regular denim	Stonewashed
Colours	Light blue	Light blue	Light blue	Light blue	Light blue	Light blue
	Indigo	Indigo	Indigo	Indigo	Indigo	Indigo
	Black	Black	Black	Black	Black	Black
Styles	**Boot-Cut**	**Boot-Cut**	**Boot-Cut**	**Boot-Cut**		
Price levels	$25	$25	$45	$45		
Fabric composition	Regular denim	Stonewashed	Regular denim	Stonewashed		
Colours	Light blue	Light blue	Light blue	Light blue		
	Indigo	Indigo	Indigo	Indigo		
	Black	Black	Black	Black		

breaking sizes
Stocking out of a specific size or colour SKU.

SKUs offered, the greater the chance of breaking sizes—that is, stocking out of a specific size or colour SKU. If a stockout occurs for a popular SKU in a fashion merchandise category and the buyer cannot reorder during the season, the buyer will typically discount the entire merchandise type, thus reducing gross margin. The buyer's objective is to remove the merchandise type from the assortment altogether so that customers will not be disappointed when they do not find the size and colour they want.

Complementary Merchandise When buyers develop assortment plans, they need to consider the degree to which categories in a department complement each other.[14] For instance, DVD players may have a low GMROI, suggesting that the buyer carry a limited assortment. But customers who buy a DVD player might also buy complementary products and services such as accessories, cables, and warranties that have a high GMROI. Thus, the buyer may decide to carry more DVD-player SKUs to increase the more profitable accessory sales.

10.4 RETAILING VIEW

Costco Goes for Variety, or Does It?

The Costco experience is often described as a treasure hunt. Products can include everything from blue jeans, air conditioners, and computer games one day to books, children's toys, and diamond rings the next, plus a huge selection of food products. Costco keeps customers on their toes by offering a wide variety of merchandise that changes from day to day. This is the place where individual and business customers pay $55 to $110 per year for a membership to buy 24 rolls of toilet paper or none at all. This is where laundry detergent and Italian olive oil come in extra-large sizes and where a 1000-piece lot of Ralph Lauren golf jackets, selling at 75 percent below retail, will vanish in an afternoon. In Costco's 4-acre stores, you can also visit the meat counter with its onsite butchers, order a cake from the bakery, or pick up a prescription and talk to the resident pharmacist to receive health advice.

All of these disparate categories provide an illusion of expansive variety. A Walmart Supercentre carries as many as 125 000 items; a grocery store will stock approximately 40 000. Not so at Costco, where you will find just 3800 to 4000 carefully chosen products. This makes it easier for the company to manage inventory and to monitor prices obsessively. Three-quarters of the merchandise is basic stock, such as canned tuna and paper towels; the other items are discretionary, often with high-end brands such as Godiva chocolates and Waterford crystal. The stores' periphery offers a variety of services, including film development, an optical centre, a pharmacy, and a tire shop.

Costco's successful strategy is planned so that a pallet of product must bring in a specific amount of cash or it is out; it is about volume per item, operating with a margin of about 8 percent, and how to increase the volume per item. Traditional category management does not apply to Costco; for example, because Costco sells computer printers does not mean that it will sell printer paper. Unusual product juxtapositions, such as face creams next to crackers, are all part of a selling formula that homes in on the middle-class tastes for cross-shopping and impulse purchases.

The typical Costco customer is 35 to 55 years old and earns on average $100 000 in family income, about double the income of most Canadians. Costco's Canadian customers number about 3.5 million households, with up to 35 percent of its business in grocery. There are 60 Canadian Costco stores, whose average size is 165 000 square feet, with sales figures averaging about $118 million per store.

Growth continues internationally with 504 stores worldwide that have outpaced the sales of Sam's Club (which has 579 stores, and none in Canada). Internationally, Costco has extremely low operating expenses, pegged at 8.74 percent of sales, and an enviable shrink that is almost nonexistent. It is extreme attention to detail that has made Costco a retail success story.

Sources: Julia Drake, "Welcome to the Big Time: Big Stores, Big Products, Big Savings, Big Profits: They're All Part of the Costco Experience," *Canadian Grocer*, May 2001; and Ann Zimmerman, "Costco Goes for Variety, or Does It?" *Retailing*, McGraw-Hill Ryerson.

Effects of Assortment Size on Buying Behaviour

Offering large assortments provides a number of benefits to customers. First, increasing the number of SKUs that customers can consider increases the chance they will find the product that best satisfies their needs. Second, large assortments are valued by customers because they provide a more informative and stimulating shopping experience due to the complexity associated with numerous products and the novelty associated with unique items. Third, large assortments are particularly appealing to customers who seek variety—those who want to try new things.

However, offering a large assortment can make the purchase decision more complex and time-consuming.[15] Research has shown that customers actually buy more if there are modest reductions of redundant items in assortments, such as reductions in the number of different ketchup bottle sizes or low-share brands carried by a supermarket.[16]

Walmart, like many retailers, has initiated an SKU rationalization program—a program that increases inventory turnover by reducing the number of SKUs. The initiative was spurred by an industry study showing that shoppers thought Target had a larger assortment than Walmart. However, Walmart found just the opposite during its comparative shopping studies. Walmart thinks that the shoppers' perceptions of Target's assortment were influenced by Target's merchandise presentation rather than the number of SKUs it carries. So Walmart clarified its offering so that categories weren't diluted and fuzzy. Even with SKUs cut by 10 to 50 percent, Walmart has been able to achieve higher sales.[17] Other factors affecting how customers perceive assortments are discussed in Chapter 6.

model stock plan A summary of the desired inventory levels of each SKU stocked in a store for a merchandise category.

Physical Characteristics of the Store Buyers need to consider how much space to devote to a category. More space is needed to display categories with large assortments. In addition, a lot of space is needed to display individual items in some categories, and this limits the number of SKUs that can be offered in stores. For example, furniture takes up a lot of space, and thus furniture retailers typically display one model of a chair or sofa and then have photographs and cloth swatches or a virtual room on a computer to show how the furniture would look with different upholstery.

Multichannel retailers address the space limitations in stores by offering a greater assortment through their Internet and catalogue channels than they do in stores. For example, Staples offers more types of laptop computers and printers on its Internet site than it stocks in its stores. If customers do not find the computer or printer they want in the store, sales associates direct them to the company's Internet site and can even order the merchandise for them from a POS terminal.

Setting Inventory and Product Availability Levels

Lo 7

After developing the assortment plan, the third step in the merchandise planning process is to determine the model stock plan for the category.

Model Stock Plan

The model stock plan, illustrated in Exhibit 10–10, is the number of each SKU in the assortment plan that the buyer wants to have available for purchase in each store. For example, the model stock plan in Exhibit 10–10 includes nine units of size 1, short, which represent 2 percent of the 429 total units for girls' traditional $20 denim jeans in light blue. Note that there are more units for more popular sizes.

Retailers typically have model stock plans for the different store sizes in a chain. For example, retailers typically classify their stores as A, B, and C stores on the basis of their sales volume. The basic assortment in a category is stocked

The Chippery in Vancouver rates high on depth and low on breadth. It is the place to get fresh potato (or beet or yam) chips, a selection of gourmet dips, and fruit smoothies. That is it!

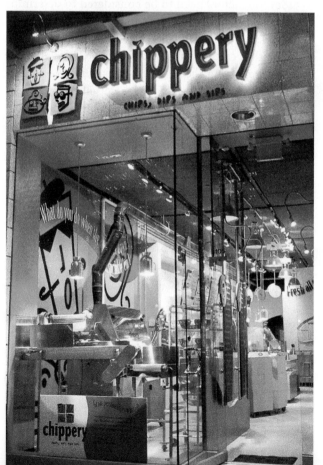

exhibit 10–10   Model Stock Plans

LENGTH		SIZE								
		1	2	4	5	6	8	10	12	14
Short	%	2	4	7	6	8	5	7	4	2
	units	9	17	30	26	34	21	30	17	9
Medium	%	2	4	7	6	8	5	7	4	2
	units	9	17	30	26	34	21	30	17	9
Long	%	0	2	2	2	3	2	2	1	0
	units	0	9	9	9	12	9	9	4	0
	Total 100%									
	429 units									

backup stock
The inventory used to guard against going out of stock when demand exceeds forecasts or merchandise is delayed; also called *safety stock* or *buffer stock*.

product availability
A measurement of the percentage of demand for a particular SKU that is satisfied.

service level   A measure used in inventory management to define the level of support or level of product availability; the number of items sold divided by the number of items demanded. Service level should not be confused with customer service. Also called *level of support*.

exhibit 10–11   Relationship between Inventory Investment and Product Availability

in C stores. For the larger stores, because more space is available, the number of SKUs increases. The larger A and B stores may have more brands, colours, styles, and sizes.

Product Availability

The number of units of backup stock, also called *buffer* or *safety stock,* in the model stock plan determines product availability. Product availability is defined as the percentage of the demand for a particular SKU that is satisfied. For instance, if 100 people go into a PetSmart store to purchase a small, Great Choice, portable kennel, but only 90 people can make the purchase before the kennel stock is depleted, the product availability for that SKU is 90 percent. Product availability is also referred to as the service level, or *level of support.*

The model stock plan needs more backup stock if the retailer wants to increase product availability, that is, increase the probability that customers will find the

product they want when they visit the retailer's store. Choosing an appropriate amount of backup stock is critical to successful assortment planning. If the backup stock is too low, the retailer will lose sales and possibly customers too when they find that the products they want are not available from the retailer. If the level is too high, scarce financial resources will be wasted on needless inventory rather than being more profitably invested in increasing variety or assortment.

Exhibit 10–11 shows the trade-off between inventory investment and product availability. Although the actual inventory investment varies in different situations, the general relationship shows that extremely high level of product availability results in a prohibitively high inventory investment.

Several factors need to be considered to determine the appropriate level of backup stock and thus the product availability for each SKU. Retailers often classify merchandise categories or individual SKUs as A, B, or C items, reflecting the product availability the retailer wants to offer. The A items are best-sellers bought by many customers. For example, white paint is an A item for Lowe's, and copy paper is an A item for Staples. A retailer rarely wants to risk A-item stockouts because running out of these very popular SKUs would diminish the retailer's image and customer loyalty. On the

Banana Republic tries to be the one-stop shop for its target market. It carries a large variety of merchandise categories.

other hand, lower product availability is acceptable for C items, which are purchased by a small number of customers and are not readily available from other retailers. Some other factors considered in determining backup stock levels and product availability are the fluctuations in demand, the lead time for delivery from the vendor, the fluctuations in vendor lead time, and the frequency of store deliveries. These factors are discussed in the next section.

The trade-off among variety, assortment, and product availability is a crucial issue in determining a retailer's merchandising strategy. Buyers have a limited budget for the inventory investments they can make in a category. Thus, they are forced to sacrifice breadth of merchandise if they opt to increase depth, or they must reduce both depth and breadth to increase product availability.

Establishing a Control System for Managing Inventory

The first three steps in the merchandise planning process—forecasting SKU and category sales, determining the assortment plan, and establishing product availability (see Exhibit 10–2) quantify the buyer's sales expectations and service level. The fourth step in the merchandise management process is to establish a control system for how the orders, deliveries, inventory levels, and merchandise sales will evolve over time. The objective of this control system is to manage the flow of merchandise into the stores so that the amount of inventory in a category is minimized but the merchandise will still be available when customers want to buy it. The differences between the control systems for staple and fashion merchandise are discussed in the following sections. Retailing View 10.5 describes how some retailers are utilizing server-based merchandise management systems.

Control System for Managing Inventory of Staple Merchandise

SKUs in a staple merchandise category are sold month after month, year after year. Lowe's sales of purple paint this month will be about the same as they were during the same month a year ago. If the sales of purple paint are below forecast this month, the excess inventory of purple paint can be sold during the following month. Thus, an automated continuous replenishment control system is used to manage the flow of staple merchandise SKUs and categories. The continuous replenishment system monitors the inventory level of each SKU in a store and automatically triggers a reorder of an SKU when the inventory falls below a predetermined level.

When planning the amount of inventory to order for a staple merchandise category such as paint, Lowe's buyers must consider current inventory, customer demand, lead time for replenishment, and backup stock needed to avoid stockouts in the department.

Flow of Staple Merchandise

Exhibit 10–12 illustrates the merchandise flow in a staple merchandise management system. At the beginning of week 1, the retailer had 150 units of the SKU in inventory and the buyer or merchandise planner placed an order for 96 additional units. During the next two weeks, customers purchased 130 units, and the inventory level decreased to 20 units. At the end of week 2, the 96-unit order from the vendor arrived, and the inventory level jumped up to 116 units. The continuous replenishment system placed another order with the vendor that will arrive in two weeks, before customer sales decrease the inventory level to zero and the retailer stocks out.

> **cycle stock** The inventory that goes up and down due to the replenishment process; also called base stock.

Inventory for which the level goes up and down due to the replenishment process is called cycle stock, or *base stock*. The retailer hopes to reduce the cycle-stock inventory to keep its inventory investment low. One approach for reducing the cycle stock is to reorder smaller quantities more frequently. But more frequent, smaller orders and shipments increase administrative and transportation costs.

exhibit 10–12 Merchandise Flow of a Staple SKU

Retailers Utilize State-of-the-Art Merchandise Management Systems

SAS has developed an integrated system to maximize retailers' profitability using several modules. These and similar systems are discussed in this and subsequent chapters. SAS's system provides a merchandise planning and forecasting module that forecasts sales and provides buyers with suggestions about how much of a particular category to buy. It also helps planners determine assortments, plan space in stores, and allocate merchandise to stores. Its revenue optimization module helps buyers determine optimal initial prices on the basis of costs, regional demand patterns, and competitive price information. This module also helps buyers determine optimal prices for promotions and markdowns.

The Children's Place has been an SAS customer since 2005. It uses the software to optimize regular and clearance pricing strategies, promotion decisions, and preseason planning. The system also allows its buyers to make adjustments throughout the selling season and review actual performance with respect to planned performance.

The Aldo Group has experienced greater margins and overall profitability as a result of using Oracle's retail merchandising application, which competes with SAS's systems. This type of application allows the retailer to recognize underperforming merchandise categories and make changes faster to increase inventory turnover. As a result, customers can have the best selection of merchandise available. "Oracle Retail Markdown Optimization allows our buyers to maintain focus on the positive aspects of the assortment. They have confidence in the system and the process to help manage in-season inventory and make the right decisions for the business, and that in turn frees time to look ahead to new seasons," says Lucia Cimaglia, general manager supply chain for the Aldo Group.

Sources: "ALDO Group Implements Oracle® Retail Solution to Optimize In-Season Inventory Management," Oracle press release, April 25, 2011, http://www.oracle.com/us/corporate/press/365790 (accessed February 24, 2013); www.sas.com/industry/retail/merchandise/ (accessed October 24, 2007); and "The Children's Place Retail Stores Inc. Chooses SAS for Advanced Merchandise Planning at Disney Store North America," SAS press release, March 7, 2007.

Because sales of the SKU and receipts of orders from the vendor cannot be predicted with perfect accuracy, the retailer has to carry backup stock, as a cushion, so that it doesn't stock out before the next order arrives. Backup stock is shown in yellow in Exhibit 10–12. Backup stock is the level of inventory needed to ensure merchandise is available in light of these uncertainties.

Determining the Level of Backup Stock Several factors determine the level of backup stock needed for an SKU. First, the level depends on the product availability the retailer wants to provide. As discussed previously, more backup stock is needed when the retailer wants to reduce the chances of a stockout and increase the availability of the SKU. Thus, if Lowe's views white paint as an A item and rarely wants to stock out of it, a higher level of backup stock is needed. However, if melon paint is a C item and 75 percent product availability is acceptable, the level of backup stock can be lowered.

Second, the greater the fluctuation in demand, the more backup stock is needed. Suppose a Lowe's store sells an average of 30 gallons of purple paint in two weeks. Yet in some weeks, sales are 50 gallons, and in other weeks, they are only 10 gallons. When sales are less than average, the store ends up carrying a little more merchandise than it needs. But when sales are much more than average, there must be more backup stock to ensure that the store does not stock out. Note in Exhibit 10–12 that during week 4, sales were greater than average, so the retailer had to dip into its backup stock to avoid a stockout.

Third, the amount of backup stock needed is affected by the lead time from the vendor. Lead time is the amount of time between the recognition that an order needs to be placed and the point at which the merchandise arrives in the store and is ready for sale. If it took two months to receive a shipment of purple paint, the possibility of running out of stock is greater than it would be if the lead time was only two weeks. The shorter lead times inherent in collaborative supply chain management systems like CPFR (described in Chapter 9) result in a lower level of backup stock required to maintain the same level of product availability.

Fourth, fluctuations in lead time also affect the amount of backup stock needed. If Lowe's knows that the lead time for purple paint is always two weeks, plus or minus one day, it can more accurately plan its inventory levels. But if the lead time is one day on one shipment and then ten days on the next shipment, the stores must carry additional backup stock to cover this uncertainty in lead time. Many retailers using collaborative supply chain management systems require that their vendors deliver merchandise within a very narrow window—sometimes two or three hours—to reduce the fluctuations in lead time and thus the amount of required backup stock.

Fifth, the vendor's fill rate also affects the retailer's backup stock requirements. For example, Lowe's can more easily plan its inventory requirements if the vendor normally ships every item that is ordered. If, however, the vendor ships only 75 percent of the ordered items, Lowe's must maintain more backup stock to be certain that the paint availability for its customers isn't adversely affected. The percentage of complete orders received from a vendor is called the fill rate.

Automated Continuous Replenishment Once the buyer sets the desired product availability and determines the variation in demand and the vendor's lead time and fill rate, the continuous replenishment systems for staple SKUs can operate automatically. The retailer's information system determines the inventory level at each point in time, the perpetual inventory, by comparing the sales made through the POS terminals with the shipments received by the store. When the perpetual inventory level falls below the predetermined level, the system sends an EDI reorder to the retailer's distribution centre and the vendor. When the reordered merchandise arrives at the store, the level of inventory is adjusted up.

However, it is difficult to achieve fully automated continuous replenishment of staple merchandise because of errors in determining the actual inventory. For example, the retailer's information system might indicate that ten Gillette Fusion razors are in the store when, in fact, ten razors were stolen by a shoplifter and there are actually zero razors in the store. Since there are no razors in the store, there are no sales and the automated continuous replenishment system will never reorder razors for the store. Such inaccuracies also can arise when an incorrect number of units is inputted into the information system about a shipment from the distribution centre to the store. To address these problems, store employees need to periodically check the inventory recorded in the system with the actual inventory in the store.

Inventory Management Report
The inventory management report provides information about the inventory management for a staple category. The report indicates the decision variables set by the buyer, such as product availability, the backup stock needed to provide the product availability, the order points and quantities plus performance measures such as planned and actual inventory turnover, the current sales rate or velocity, sales forecasts, inventory availability, and the amount on order. Exhibit 10–13 is an inventory management report for Rubbermaid bath mats.

The first five columns of Exhibit 10–13 contain the descriptions of each item, how many items are on hand and on order, and sales for the past 4 and 12 weeks. The first-row SKU is a Rubbermaid bath mat in avocado green. There are 30 units on hand and 60 on order. Thus, the quantity available of this SKU is 90. Sales for the past 4 and 12 weeks were 72 and 215 units, respectively.

Sales forecasts for the next 4 and 8 weeks are determined by the system using a statistical model that considers the trends in past sales and the seasonal pattern for the SKU. However, in this case, the buyer made an adjustment in the forecast for the next 4 weeks to reflect an upcoming special promotion on avocado, blue, and gold bath mats.

The product availability is a decision variable input by

lead time The amount of time between recognition that an order needs to be placed and the point at which the merchandise arrives in the store and is ready for sale.

fill rate The percentage of an order that is shipped by the vendor.

perpetual inventory An accounting procedure whose objectives are to maintain a perpetual or book inventory in retail dollar amounts and to maintain records that make it possible to determine the cost value of the inventory at any time without taking a physical inventory; also known as *book inventory system* or *retail inventory method (RIM)*.

Staple merchandise management systems are used for items like this rubber bath mat.

exhibit 10–13   Inventory Management Report for Rubbermaid SKUs

	Quantity On Hand	Quantity On Order	Sales Last 4 Wks	Sales Last 12 Wks	Forecast Next 4 Wks	Forecast Next 8 Wks	Product Availability	Backup Stock	Turnover Planned	Turnover Actual	Order Point	Order Quantity
RM- Bath												
RM Bath Mat - Avocado	30	60	72	215	152	229	99	18	12	11	132	42
RM Bath Mat - Blue	36	36	56	130	115	173	95	12	9	10	98	26
RM Bath Mat - Gold	41	72	117	325	243	355	99	35	12	13	217	104
RM Bath Mat - Pink	10	12	15	41	13	25	90	3	7	7	13	0

order point The amount of inventory below which the quantity available shouldn't go or the item will be out of stock before the next order arrives.

merchandise budget plan A plan used by buyers to determine how much money to spend in each month on a particular fashion merchandise category, given the firm's sales forecast, inventory turnover, and profit goals.

DID YOU KNOW?

More than 40 percent of retailers do not have a well-defined process for adjusting the four parameters of their inventory control system: product availability, order points, safety stock levels, and lead times.[18]

the buyer. For the avocado bath mat SKU, the buyer wants 99 out of every 100 customers to find it in stock. But the buyer is less concerned about stocking out of pink bath mats and thus sets its product availability at 90 percent. The system then calculates the necessary backup stock for the avocado bath mat based on a predetermined formula—18 units. This number is determined by the system based on the specified product availability, the variability in demand, the vendor delivery lead-time, and the variability in the lead-time.

The planned inventory turnover for the SKU, 12 times, is a decision variable also set by the buyer on the basis of the retailer's overall financial goals; it drives the inventory management system. For this SKU, the system determined that the actual turnover, based on the cost of goods sold and average inventory, is 11.

Order Point The order point is the amount of inventory below which the quantity available shouldn't go or the item will be out of stock before the next order arrives. This number tells the buyer that when the inventory level drops to this point, additional merchandise should be ordered. For this SKU, the buyer needs to place an order if the quantity in inventory falls to 132 or fewer units to produce the desired product availability.

Order Quantity When inventory reaches the order point, the buyer, or the system, needs to order enough units to ensure product availability before the next order arrives. Using the avocado bath mats in Exhibit 10–13 as an example, the order quantity is 42 units.

Control System for Managing Inventory of Fashion Merchandise

The control system for a fashion merchandise category is called a merchandise budget plan. The merchandise budget plan (Exhibit 10–14) specifies the planned inventory investment in dollars in a fashion merchandise category on the basis of how much merchandise will be ordered, delivered, and sold each month during the selling season. It is a financial plan that specifies how many dollars will be spent each month to support sales and achieve the desired GMROI objectives. The merchandise budget plan also considers the effects on GMROI from the active intervention of the buyer to make adjustments if the actual sales differ from planned sales.

The merchandise budget plan determines how much merchandise in dollars should be delivered in each month to achieve the GMROI goal for the period. The amount of merchandise that needs to be delivered during each month is based on the sales forecast, the planned discounts to employees and customers, and the level of inventory needed to support the sales. Most retailers use commercially available software packages to develop merchandise budget plans.

Exhibit 10–15 shows a six-month merchandise budget plan for men's casual slacks at a national specialty store chain. For a category like this, the buyer probably completes the plan in the fall for the following spring and summer. The buyer needs to plan how much merchandise should be delivered in each month to achieve the financial goals for the period. The "Monthly Additions to Stock" tells the buyer how much merchandise in retail dollars he or she needs to have, on average, at the beginning of each month for the retailer's financial goals to be met.

Data that can assist in making inventory decisions are available at www.bizstats.com in the form of industry benchmarks and at www.statscan.ca, which has retail and wholesale statistics.

Actual sales might differ from the sales forecasted in the merchandise budget plan. Even with this uncertainty though, the plan is used to coordinate the supply and demand for merchandise and ensure that the financial

exhibit 10–14 Sample Six-Month Merchandise Plan for a Menswear Retailer

SIX-MONTH MERCHANDISE PLAN				Spring / Fall	Feb. / Aug.	Mar. / Sept.	Apr. / Oct.	May / Nov.	June / Dec.	July / Jan.	Total
DEPARTMENT _Men's Furnishings_			Sales	Last Year	$ 26 000	$ 39 000	$ 39 000	$ 65 000	$ 52 000	$ 39 000	$ 260 000
DEPARTMENT NO. _327_				Plan							
FROM _August 1_ 20___				Actual							
TO _January 31_ 20___											
Department Control Data			Retail EOM	Last Year	103 000	103 000	129 000	116 000	103 000	104 000	
	L.Y.	T.Y.		Plan							
% Initial Markup	41.3			Actual							
% Reductions	9.0	11.0	Reductions	Last Year	3 510	3 510	2 340	2 340	3 510	8 190	23 400
% Maintained Markup	36.0			Plan							
% Alteration Expense	3.0	3.0		Actual							
% Cash Discount	1.0	1.0									
% Gross Margin	34.0		Retail BOM	Last Year	90 000	103 000	103 000	129 000	116 000	103 000	
% Operating Expense	31.0	32.0		Plan							
% Net Profit	3.0	3.0		Actual							
Season Turnover	2.5	2.5									
Control Period	4.5	4.5									
Planning and Authorization			Retail Purchases	Last Year	42 510	42 510	67 340	54 340	42 510	46 190	295 400
Buyer _J.J. Tranell_				Plan							
Merchandise Controller _A.P. Edwards_				Actual							
Date Prepared _6/15_			Cost Purchases	Last Year	24 953	24 953	39 529	31 888	24 953	27 114	173 390
				Plan							
Date Authorized _6/30_				Actual							

goals are realized. In addition, the plan coordinates the activities of buyers for different merchandise categories so that there is not too much merchandise in some categories and not enough in others. From a global perspective, the merchandise variety could become unbalanced and be less appealing to customers.

Take a close look at line 8, "Monthly Additions to Stock," in Exhibit 10–15. In the next few pages, we will systematically work through Exhibit 10–15 on our way to this last line. "Monthly Additions to Stock" tells the buyer how much money to spend in each month, given the category's sales forecast, GMROI, inventory turnover, and monthly fluctuations in sales. As such, the merchandise budget plan coordinates purchases to coincide with the category's financial goals.

Even relatively small stores now use advanced computer technologies like this one to plan merchandise budgets. Following are some equations that we will use in our examination of the merchandise budget plan. Note that BOM stands for "beginning of month" and EOM stands for "end of month."

Sales for month = Planned sales for season × Sales percentage allocation per month

BOM = Planned sales for month × Stock-to-sales ratio

Markdown = Planned sales for month × Reduction allocation percentage per month

Purchases = Sales + EOM (next month's BOM) + Markdown − BOM

Retail purchases = Retail BOM − Reductions + Retail EOM + Sales

In the remaining portion of this section, we will examine each line in the merchandise budget plan. The merchandise planning system illustrated here was developed by Marketmax.

Monthly Sales Percentage Distribution to Season (Line 1)

Line 1 of the plan projects what percentage of the total sales is expected to be sold in each month. Thus, in Exhibit 10–15,

shrinkage An inventory reduction that is caused by shoplifting by employees or customers, by merchandise being misplaced or damaged, or by poor bookkeeping.

21 percent of the six-month sales are expected to occur in April.

The starting point for determining the percentage distribution of sales by month is historical records. The percentage of total sales that occurs in a particular month doesn't vary appreciably from year to year. Even so, it's helpful to examine each month's percentage over a few years to check for any significant changes. For instance, the buyer realizes that the autumn selling season for men's casual slacks continues to be pushed further back into summer. Over time, this general shift toward earlier purchasing will affect the percentage distribution of sales by month. The distribution may also vary due to changes made by the buyer or the competitors' marketing strategies. The buyer must include special sales that did not occur in the past, for instance, in the percentage distribution of sales by month in the same way that they're built into the overall sales forecast.

Monthly Sales (Line 2)

Monthly sales equal the forecast total sales for the six-month period (first column = $130 000) multiplied by each sales percentage by month (line 1). In Exhibit 10–15, monthly sales for April = $130 000 × 21% = $27 300.

Monthly Reductions Percentage Distribution to Season (Line 3)

To have enough merchandise every month to support the monthly sales forecast, the buyer must consider factors that reduce the inventory level. Although sales are the primary reduction, the value of the inventory is also reduced by

In the seven days before Christmas, retailers have marked peaks in their sales that can amount to as much of 40 percent of their December sales figures.

markdowns, shrinkage, and discounts to employees. The merchandise budget planning process builds these additional reductions into the planned purchases. Otherwise, the retailer would always be understocked. Note that in Exhibit 10–15, 40 percent of the season's total reductions occur in April as a result of end-of-season sales.

Markdowns can be forecast fairly accurately from historical records. Of course, changes in markdown strategies—or changes in the environment, such as competition or general economic activity—must be taken into consideration when forecasting markdowns.

Discounts to employees are like markdowns, except that they're given to employees rather than to customers. Cost of the employee discount is tied fairly closely to the sales level and number of employees. Thus, its percentage of sales and dollar amount can be forecast fairly accurately from historical records.

Shrinkage is an inventory reduction that is caused by shoplifting by employees or customers, by merchandise being misplaced or damaged, or by poor bookkeeping. The buyer measures shrinkage by taking the difference between:

- The inventory's recorded value based on merchandise bought and received
- The physical inventory in stores and distribution

exhibit 10–15 Six-Month Merchandise Budget Plan for Men's Casual Slacks

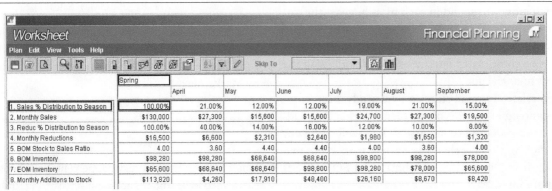

	Spring	April	May	June	July	August	September
1. Sales % Distribution to Season	100.00%	21.00%	12.00%	12.00%	19.00%	21.00%	15.00%
2. Monthly Sales	$130,000	$27,300	$15,600	$15,600	$24,700	$27,300	$19,500
3. Reduc % Distribution to Season	100.00%	40.00%	14.00%	16.00%	12.00%	10.00%	8.00%
4. Monthly Reductions	$16,500	$6,600	$2,310	$2,640	$1,980	$1,650	$1,320
5. BOM Stock to Sales Ratio	4.00	3.60	4.40	4.40	4.00	3.60	4.00
6. BOM Inventory	$98,280	$98,280	$68,640	$68,640	$98,800	$98,280	$78,000
7. EOM Inventory	$65,600	$68,640	$68,640	$98,800	$98,280	$78,000	$65,600
8. Monthly Additions to Stock	$113,820	$4,260	$17,910	$48,400	$26,160	$8,670	$8,420

		Spring			Summer		
	Six-month data	April	May	June	July	August	September
1. Sales % Distribution to Season	100.00%	21.00%	12.00%	12.00%	19.00%	21.00%	15.00%

		Spring			Summer		
Sales % Distrubution	Six-month data	April	May	June	July	August	September
2. Monthly Sales	$130 000	$27 300	$15 600	$15 600	$24 700	$27 300	$19 500

		Spring			Summer		
Reduction	Six-month data	April	May	June	July	August	September
3. % Distribution to Season	100.00%	40.00%	14.00%	16.00%	12.00%	10.00%	8.00%

(Physical inventories are typically taken semi-annually.) Shrinkage varies by department and season. Typically, shrinkage also varies directly with sales. So, if sales of men's casual slacks rise 10 percent, then the buyer can expect a 10 percent increase in shrinkage.

Monthly Reductions (Line 4)

The buyer calculates the monthly reductions in the same way as the monthly sales. The total reductions are multiplied by each percentage in line 3. In Exhibit 10–15, April reductions = $16 500 × 40% = $6600.

BOM (Beginning-of-Month) Stock-to-Sales Ratio (Line 5)

The stock-to-sales ratio specifies the amount of inventory that should be on hand at the beginning of the month to support the sales forecast and maintain the inventory turnover objectives. Thus, a stock-to-sales ratio of 2 means that we plan to have twice as much inventory on hand at the beginning of the month as we plan to sell for that month.

$$\text{Stock-to-sales} = \frac{\text{BOM}}{\text{Sales}}$$

The stock-to-sales ratio is equivalent to the amount of inventory on hand at the beginning of the month to support sales forecast and maintain the inventory objective for the category. A stock-to-sales ratio of 2 means two months of inventory, or approximately 60 days, is on hand at the beginning of the month. A stock-to-sales ratio of 1/2 represents a half month's supply of merchandise, or approximately 15 days. Many retailers express this relationship as weeks of inventory. Weeks of inventory is the months of supply times four weeks. So a stock-to-sales ratio and months of supply of 2 is equivalent to eight weeks of supply.

As you will see in the next few paragraphs, there is a direct relationship between GMROI, the sales-to-stock ratio, inventory turnover, and the stock-to-sales ratio. Importantly, if inventory turnover is six times per year, on average

you have a two-month supply of inventory, or an eight-week supply, and a BOM stock-to-sales ratio of 2. Likewise, a 24-inventory turn represents only a half-month's supply (2 weeks), or 15-day supply, that is, a BOM stock-to-sales ratio of 1/2.

The stock-to-sales ratios are calculated in four steps.

Step 1: Calculate Sales-to-Stock Ratio

GMROI is equal to the gross margin percentage times the sales-to-stock ratio. The sales-to-stock ratio is conceptually similar to inventory turnover except the denominator in the sales-to-stock ratio is expressed in retail sales dollars, whereas the denominator in inventory turnover is the cost of goods sold (sales at cost). The buyer's target GMROI for the category is 123 percent, and the buyer feels the category will produce a gross margin of 45 percent. Thus,

$$\text{GMROI} = \text{Gross margin \%} \times \text{Sales-to-stock ratio}$$
$$\text{Sales-to-stock ratio} = \text{GMROI} + \text{Gross margin percent}$$
$$= 123 \div 45 = 2.73$$

Because this illustration of a merchandise budget plan is for a six-month period rather than a year, the sales-to-stock ratio is based on six months rather than annual sales. So for this six-month period, sales must be 2.73 times the inventory at cost to meet the targeted GMROI.

Step 2: Convert the Sales-to-Stock Ratio to Inventory Turnover

Calculate inventory turnover as follows:

$$\text{Inventory turnover} = \text{Sales-to-stock ratio} \times \text{Gross margin percent}$$
$$= 2.73 \times (100 - 45)$$
$$1.50 = 2.73 \times 0.55$$

This adjustment is necessary because the sales-to-stock ratio defines sales at retail and inventory at cost, whereas inventory turnover defines both sales and inventory at cost. Like the sales-to-stock ratio, this inventory turnover is based on a six-month period.

stock-to-sales ratio Specifies the amount of inventory that should be on hand at the beginning of the month to support the sales forecast and maintain the inventory turnover objective.

inventory Goods or merchandise available for resale.

weeks of inventory The number of months of supply times four weeks.

Step 3: Calculate Average Stock-to-Sales Ratio

The average stock-to-sales ratio is:

$$\text{Average stock-to-sales ratio} = 6 \text{ months / Inventory turnover}$$
$$= 6 / 1.5$$
$$= 4$$

If preparing a 12-month plan, the buyer divides 12 by the annual inventory turnover. Since the merchandise budget plan in Exhibit 10–15 is based on retail dollars, it's easiest to think of the numerator as BOM retail inventory and the denominator as sales for that month. Thus, to achieve a six-month inventory turnover of 1.5, on average, the buyer must plan to have a BOM inventory that equals four times the amount of sales for a given month, which is equivalent to four months, or 16 weeks, of supply.

One needs to be careful when thinking about the average stock-to-sales ratio, which can be easily confused with the sales-to-stock ratio. These ratios are not the inverse of each other. Sales are the same in both ratios, but stock in the sales-to-stock ratio is the average inventory at cost over all days in the period, whereas stock in the stock-to-sales ratio is the average BOM inventory at retail. Also, the BOM stock-to-sales ratio is an average for all months. Adjustments are made to this average in line 5 to account for seasonal variation in sales.

Step 4: Calculate Monthly Stock-to-Sales Ratios

The monthly stock-to-sales ratios in line 5 must average the stock-to-sales ratio calculated previously to achieve the planned inventory turnover. Generally, monthly stock-to-sales ratios vary in the opposite direction of sales. That is, in months when sales are larger, stock-to-sales ratios are smaller, and vice versa.

To make this adjustment, the buyer needs to consider the seasonal pattern for men's casual slacks in determining the monthly stock-to-sales ratios. In the ideal situation, men's casual slacks would arrive in the store the same day and in the same quantity that customers demand them. Unfortunately, the real-life retailing world isn't this simple. Note in Exhibit 10–15 (line 8) that men's casual slacks for the spring season start arriving slowly in April ($4260 for the month), yet demand lags behind these arrivals until the weather starts getting warmer. Monthly sales then jump from 12 percent of annual sales in May and June to 19 percent in July (line 1). But the stock-to-sales ratio (line 5) decreased from 4.4 in May and June to 4.0 in July. Thus, in months when sales increase (e.g., July), the BOM inventory also increases (line 6) but at a slower rate, which causes the stock-to-sales ratios to decrease. Likewise, in months when sales decrease dramatically, such as in May (line 1), inventory also decreases (line 6), again at a slower rate, causing the stock-to-sales ratios to increase (line 5).

When creating a merchandise budget plan for a category such as men's casual slacks with a sales history, the buyer also examines previous years' stock-to-sales ratios. To judge how adequate these past ratios were, the buyer determines if inventory levels were exceedingly high or low in any months. Then the buyer makes minor corrections to adjust for a previous imbalance in inventory levels, as well as for changes in the current environment. For instance, assume the buyer is planning a promotion for Victoria Day. Since this promotion has never been done before, the stock-to-sales ratio for that May should be adjusted downward to allow for the expected increase in sales. Note that monthly stock-to-sales ratios don't change by the same percentage as the percentage distribution of sales by month is changing. In months when sales increase, stock-to-sales ratios decrease but at a slower rate. Because there is no exact method of making these adjustments, the buyer must make some subjective judgments.

BOM Stock (Line 6)

The amount of inventory planned for the beginning of the month (BOM) equals

$$\text{BOM inventory} = \text{Monthly sales (line 2)} \times \text{BOM stock-to-sales ratio (line 5)}$$

When doing this multiplication, sales drops out of the equation, leaving BOM stock. In Exhibit 10–15,

$$\text{BOM stock for April} = (\$27\,300) \times (3.6)$$
$$= \text{BOM inventory } \$98\,280$$

EOM (End of Month) Stock (Line 7)

The BOM stock from the current month is the same as the EOM (end-of-month) stock in the previous month. So to derive line 7, the buyer simply moves the BOM stock in line 6 down one box and to the left.

		Spring			Summer		
	Six-month data	April	May	June	July	August	September
3. Reduc. % Distribution to Season	100.00%	40.00%	14.00%	16.00%	12.00%	10.00%	8.00%
4. Monthly Reductions	$16 500	$6600	$2310	$2640	$1980	$1650	$1320

		Spring			Summer		
	Six-month data	April	May	June	July	August	September
5. BOM Stock to Sales Ratio	4.00	3.60	4.40	4.40	4.00	3.60	4.00

In Exhibit 10–15, the EOM stock for April is the same as the BOM stock for May, $68 640. We must forecast ending inventory for the last month in the plan.

Monthly Additions to Stock (Line 8)

The monthly additions to stock is the amount to be ordered for delivery in each month, given turnover and sales objectives.

Additions to stock = Sales (line 2) + Reductions (line 4)
+ EOM inventory (line 7)
− BOM inventory (line 6)

In Exhibit 10-15,

Additions to stock for April = $27 300 + 6600 + 68 640
− 98 280 = $4260

This formula isn't particularly enlightening, so consider the following explanation. At the beginning of the month, the inventory level equals BOM stock. During the month, merchandise is sold and various reductions, such as markdowns, occur. So BOM stock minus monthly sales minus reductions equals EOM stock if nothing is purchased. But something must be purchased to get back up to the forecast EOM stock. The difference between EOM stock if nothing is purchased (BOM stock − Sales − Reductions) and the forecast EOM stock is the additions to stock.

Evaluating the Merchandise Budget Plan

Inventory turnover, GMROI, and the sales forecast are used for both planning and control. Buyers negotiate GMROI, inventory turnover, and sales forecast goals with their superiors, the GMMs and DMMs. Then merchandise budgets are developed to meet these goals. Well before the season, buyers purchase the amount of merchandise specified in the last line of the merchandise budget plan to be delivered in those specific months—the monthly additions to stock.

After the selling season, the buyer must determine how the category actually performed compared with the plan. If the actual GMROI, turnover, and forecast are greater than those in the plan, performance is better than expected. However, performance evaluations should not be based solely on any one of these measures. Several additional questions should be answered to evaluate the buyer's performance: Why did the performance exceed or fall short of the plan? Was the deviation from the plan due to something under the buyer's control? (For instance, was too much merchandise purchased?) Did the buyer react quickly to changes in demand by either purchasing more or having a sale? Was the deviation instead due to some external factor, such as a change in competitive level or economic activity? Every attempt should be made to discover answers to these questions. Later in this chapter, several additional tools used to evaluate merchandise performance will be examined.

Open-to-Buy System

The open-to-buy system starts after the merchandise is purchased using the merchandise budget plan or staple merchandise system. That is, these systems provide the buyer with a plan for purchasing merchandise. The open-to-buy system is one that keeps track of merchandise flows while they're occurring. Specifically, open-to-buy systems record how much is spent each month, and therefore how much is left to spend.

Even if everything in the buyer's merchandise budget goes according to plan, without careful attention to the recordkeeping performed in the open-to-buy system, the buyer might buy too much or too little. In order for the merchandise budget plan to be successful (i.e., meet the sales, inventory turnover, and GMROI goals for a category), the buyer attempts to buy merchandise in quantities and with delivery dates such that the actual EOM stock for a month will be the same as the projected or forecasted EOM stock. For example, at the end of September, which is the end of the spring/summer season, the buyer would like to be completely out of spring/summer men's casual slacks, so there will be room for the fall collection. Thus, the buyer would want both the projected EOM stock and the actual EOM stock to equal zero.

			Spring			Summer	
	Six-month data	April	May	June	July	August	September
6. BOM Inventory	$98 280	$98 280	$68 640	$68 640	$98 800	$98 280	$78 000

			Spring			Summer	
	Six-month data	April	May	June	July	August	September
7. EOM Inventory	$65 600	$68 640	$68 640	$98 800	$98 280	$78 000	$65 600

			Spring			Summer	
	Six-month data	April	May	June	July	August	September
8. Monthly Additions to Stock	$113 820	$4260	$17 910	$48,400	$26 160	$8670	$8420

Calculating Open-to-Buy for the Current Period

Buyers develop plans indicating how much inventory for the merchandise category will be available at the end of the month. However, these plans might be inaccurate. Shipments might not arrive on time, sales might be greater than expected, and/or reductions (price discounts due to sales) might be less than expected. The open-to-buy is the difference between the projected EOM inventory and the planned EOM inventory. Thus, open-to-buy for a month is:

> Open-to-buy = Actual EOM planned inventory
> − Projected EOM inventory

The EOM planned inventory is taken from the merchandise budget plan, and the EOM projected inventory is calculated as follows:

Projected EOM inventory = Actual BOM inventory

+ Monthly additions actual (received new merchandise)

+ On order (merchandise to be delivered)

− Sales plan (merchandise sold)

− Monthly reductions plan

Thus, the projected EOM inventory will be less than the planned EOM inventory if sales or reductions are greater than the merchandise budget plan or less merchandise is delivered than planned.

Exhibit 10–16 presents the six-month open-to-buy for the same category of men's casual slacks discussed in the fashion merchandise planning section of this chapter. Consider May as the current month. The BOM stock (inventory) actual level is 59 500, but there is no EOM actual inventory yet because the month hasn't finished. When calculating the open-to-buy for the current month,

the projected EOM stock plan comes into play. Think of the projected EOM stock plan as a new and improved estimate of the planned EOM stock from the merchandise budget plan. This new and improved version takes information into account that wasn't available when the merchandise budget plan was made. The formula for projected EOM inventory for the category is:

Projected EOM inventory	=	Actual BOM inventory	$ 59 500
		+ Monthly additions actual	+ 7 000
		+ On order	+ 18 000
		− Sales plan	− 15 600
		− Monthly reductions plan	− 2 310
		=	$ 66 590

The open-to-buy for the current month is:

> Open-to-buy plan = EOM planned inventory
> − Projected EOM inventory
> $2050 = $68 640 − $66 590

Therefore, the buyer has $2050 left to spend in May to reach the planned EOM stock of $68 640. This is a relatively small amount, so we can conclude that the buyer's plan is right on target. But if the open-to-buy for May were $20 000, the buyer could then go back into the market and look for some great buys. If one of the vendors had too much stock of men's casual slacks, the buyer might be able to use the $20 000 to pick up some bargains that could be passed on to customers.

If, however, the open-to-buy was a negative $20 000, the buyer would have overspent the budget. Therefore, the buyer would have to cut back on spending in future months so that the total purchases would be within the merchandise budget. Alternatively, if the buyer believed that the overspending was justified because of changes in

exhibit 10–16 Six-Month Open-to-Buy

Loc - 10	Spring					
Merch - Aged Soft ...	April	May	June	July	August	September
EOM Stock Plan	$68,640	$68,640	$98,800	$98,280	$78,000	$65,800
EOM Actuals	$69,950					
BOM Stock Plan	$98,280	$68,640	$68,640	$98,800	$98,280	$78,000
BOM Stock Actual	$95,000	$59,500				
Monthly Additions Plan	$4,260	$17,910	$48,400	$26,180	$8,670	$6,420
Monthly Additions Actuals	$3,500	$7,000				
OnOrder	$45,000	$18,000	$48,400			
Sales Plan	$27,300	$15,800	$15,800	$24,700	$27,300	$19,500
Sales Actuals	$26,900					
Monthly Reductions Plan	$6,600	$2,310	$2,640	$1,980	$1,650	$1,320
Monthly Reductions Actuals	$1,650					
Projected EOM Stock Plan	$59,500	$66,590	$98,750	$70,070	$41,120	$20,300
Projected BOM Stock Plan	$24,570	$59,500	$66,500	$98,750	$70,070	$41,120
OTB	$0.00	$2,050	$2,050	$28,210	$36,880	$45,300

Where would higher-priced, low-sugar, organic, whole-wheat breakfast cereals do best—one dominated by the geodemographic segment "Urban & Urbane" (left) or "Foundation of the Nation" (right)?

the marketplace, a negotiation could take place between the buyer and the DMM, GMM, merchandise manager or planning director, etc. to negotiate open-to-buy (OTB).

Lo 8 Allocating Merchandise to Stores

After developing a plan for managing merchandise inventory in a category, the next step in the merchandise management process is to allocate the merchandise purchased and received to the retailer's stores. Research has found that these allocation decisions have a much bigger impact on profitability than does the decision about the quantity of merchandise to purchase.[20] In other words, buying too little or too much merchandise has less impact on category profit than making mistakes in allocating the right amount and type of merchandise to stores. Thus, many retailers have created positions called either "allocators" or "planners" to specialize in making store allocation decisions. Allocating merchandise to stores involves three decisions: (1) how much merchandise to allocate to each store, (2) what type of merchandise to allocate, and (3) when to allocate the merchandise to different stores.

Amount of Merchandise Allocated

Retail chains typically classify each of their stores on the basis of annual sales. Thus, A stores would have the largest sales volume and typically receive the most inventory, while C stores would have the lowest sales volume and receive the least inventory for a category. In addition to the store's sales level, when making allocation decisions for a category, allocators consider the physical characteristics of the merchandise and the depth of assortment and level of product availability that the firm wants to portray for the specific store.

Type of Merchandise Allocated

The process of allocating merchandise to stores that was just described is useful for fashion merchandise and new staple items. As merchandise sells, it must be replenished, either by the vendor or through distribution centres. Retailers use either a pull or a push distribution strategy to replenish merchandise. With a **pull distribution strategy**, orders for merchandise

> **pull distribution strategy** Strategy in which orders for merchandise are generated at the store level on the basis of demand data captured by point-of-sale terminals.

exhibit 10–17 Allocation Based on Sales Volume Breakdown by Store of Traditional $35 Denim Jeans

(1) Type of Store	(2) Number of Stores	(3) Percentage Of Total Sales, Each Store	(4) Sales per Store (total sales × col. 3)	(5) Store Type (col. 2 × col. 4)	(6) Unit Sales Per Store (col. 4/$35)
A	4	10.0%	$15 000	$60 000	429
B	3	6.7	10 000	30 000	286
C	8	5.0	7500	60 000	214

Total sales $150 000

exhibit 10–18   Example of Canadian Mosaics

Urban & Urbane	Foundation of the Nation
Hip and happening describe these 20 -34 years old single and common-law people living in charming older apartments in the city. University and graduate degrees in visual and cultural arts, communications, life sciences, and technology are the catalysts for launching their careers in health, finance, and technical occupations. Being in metropolitan areas, they are high users of transit and commuting. Although incomes are well below average they do not have children yet so household expenditures are low and they can spend time and money on themselves. They are moving up, moving on, and motivated!	West coast and Prairie cities are the home to this group of older people who rent an apartment or condominium and live alone. They are over 65 and likely collecting some type of retirement or government pension with incomes coming in below $40 000. As they have already accumulated most material goods, their spending is low, especially on computer technology, however they are interested in keeping healthy, spending on medical supplies, prescribed medicines and pharmaceuticals, and they contribute to public health plans. Reading newspapers keeps them informed and entertained but they may take a chance on a lottery ticket just for fun! They are generous and give to charities in Canada and, as they live in urban communities, they walk or take a short taxi ride to amenities.

push distribution strategy Strategy in which merchandise is allocated to stores based on historical demand, the inventory position at the distribution centre, as well as the stores' needs.

are generated at the store level on the basis of demand data captured by point-of-sale terminals. With a **push distribution strategy**, merchandise is allocated to the stores on the basis of historical demand, the inventory position at the distribution centre, and the needs of the stores. A pull strategy is used by more sophisticated retailers because it's more responsive to customer demand. In addition to classifying stores on the basis of their size and sales volume, retailers classify stores according to the characteristics of the stores' trading area. The profiles of trading areas are used in making store location decisions. Store trade area geodemographics are also used to develop merchandise assortments for specific stores. Consider the allocation decision of a national supermarket for its ready-to-eat cereal assortment. Some stores are located in areas dominated by segments called "Urban & Urbane," and other areas are dominated by the "Foundation of the Nation," as described in Exhibit 10–18.

The ready-to-eat breakfast cereal buyer would certainly want to offer different assortments for stores in these two areas. Stores with a high proportion of older retirees in their trading areas would have better results with an assortment of lower-priced, well-known brands and less expensive private-label cereals. Stores in areas dominated by the Urban & Urbane geodemographic segment would do better with an assortment with higher-priced brands that are low in sugar, are organic, and contain whole wheat. President's Choice private-label brands would be favoured by an upwardly mobile market segment.

Even the sales of different apparel sizes can vary dramatically from store to store in the same chain. Exhibit 10–19 illustrates this point. Some stores sell

exhibit 10–19   Apparel Size Differences for Store X and the Chain Average

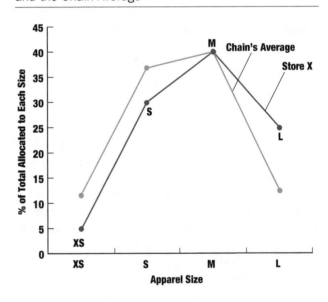

significantly more large sizes and fewer small sizes than is average for the chain. If the buyer allocated the same size distribution of merchandise to all stores in the chain, Store X would stock out of large sizes, have an oversupply of small sizes, or be out of some sizes sooner than other stores in the chain.

Timing of Merchandise Allocation

In addition to the need to allocate different inventory levels and types of merchandise across stores, differences in the timing of category purchases across stores need to be considered. To increase inventory turnover in the category, buyers need to recognize these regional differences and arrange for merchandise to be shipped to the appropriate regions when customers are ready to buy.

Retailers are considering the "paycheque cycle" when making merchandise allocation and promotion decisions, particularly in difficult economic times. Cash-strapped consumers are showing a tendency to make their largest purchases when they get their paycheques at the beginning of the month and to cut back on purchases as that money runs out toward the end of the month. Therefore, some supermarket chains devote more shelf space and promote larger-package sizes at the beginning of the month and small sizes at the end of the month.[21]

The issues involved in allocating merchandise inventory to stores, as just described, are particularly important for both fashion merchandise and new staple items. If merchandise sells and evolves into staple merchandise, it gets replenished over time, either by the vendor or through distribution centres.

Analyzing Merchandise Management Performance

The next step in the merchandise planning process (see Exhibit 10–2) is to analyze the performance of the process and make adjustments, such as ordering more or less merchandise, lowering prices to increase sales, allocating different assortments to specific stores, or changing the assortment and model stock plans. Three types of analyses related to the monitoring and adjustment step are (1) sell-through analysis, (2) ABC analysis of assortments, and (3) multiattribute analysis of vendors. The first analysis provides an ongoing evaluation of the merchandise management plan compared with actual sales. The remaining two analyses offer approaches for evaluating and altering the assortment plan using the specific SKUs in the plan and the vendors that provide the merchandise to support the plan.

Sell-Through Analysis Evaluating Merchandise Plan

A sell-through analysis compares actual and planned sales to determine whether more merchandise is needed to satisfy demand or whether price reductions (markdowns) are required. Exhibit 10–20 shows a sell-through analysis for blouses for the first two weeks of the season.

These blouses are high-fashion items that experience significant uncertainty in sales. Thus, after two weeks in the stores, the buyer reviews sales and determines if adjustments are needed. The need to make adjustments depends on a variety of factors, including experience with the merchandise in the past, plans for featuring the merchandise in advertising, and the availability of markdown money from vendors (funds that a vendor gives a retailer to cover lost gross margin dollars that result from markdowns).

In this case, the white blouses are selling significantly less well than planned. Examine the week 1 columns for the first SKU, the small white blouse. Planned sales were 20 units. The actual sales were 15 units. Therefore, the actual-to-plan percentage was −25 percent [(15−20)20 = −25 percent]. This means that actual sales were 25 percent less than the planned sales. In fact, the actual-to-plan percentage is negative for all of the white blouses and positive for all of the blue blouses.

Therefore, the buyer makes an early price reduction to ensure that the merchandise isn't left unsold at the end of the season. The decision regarding the blue blouses isn't as clear. The small blue blouses are selling slightly ahead of the plan, and the medium blue blouses are also selling well, but the large blue blouses start selling ahead of plan only in the second week. In this case, the buyer

sell-through analysis A comparison of actual and planned sales to determine whether early markdowns are required or whether more merchandise is needed to satisfy demand.

markdown money Funds provided by a vendor to a retailer to cover decreased gross margin from markdowns and other merchandising issues.

exhibit 10–20 Example of a Sell-Through Analysis for Blouses

Stock Number	Description		WEEK 1 Actual-to-Plan			WEEK 2 Actual-to-Plan		
			Plan	Actual	Percentage	Plan	Actual	Percentage
1011	Small	White silk V-neck	20	15	−25%	20	10	−50%
1011	Medium	White silk V-neck	30	25	−16.6	30	20	−33
1011	Large	White silk V-neck	20	16	−20	20	16	−20
1012	Small	Blue silk V-neck	25	26	4	25	27	8
1012	Medium	Blue silk V-neck	35	45	29	35	40	14
1012	Large	Blue silk V-neck	25	25	0	25	30	20

exhibit 10–21 *ABC* Analysis for Dress Shirts

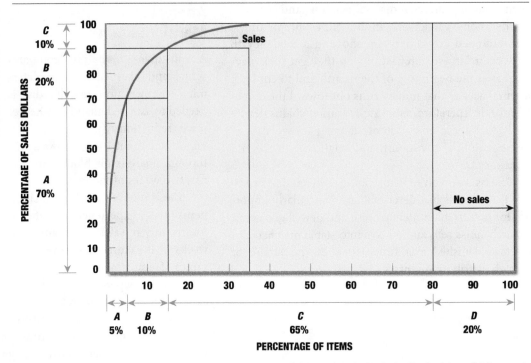

Source: Reprinted with permission of the The Free Press, a Division of Simon & Schuster, from the *Distribution Handbook*, James F. Robeson and Robert G. House, eds. Copyright © by the Free Press.

decides to wait another week or two before taking any action. If actual sales stay significantly ahead of planned sales, a reorder might be appropriate.

Evaluating the Assortment Plan and Vendors

ABC Analysis   An ABC analysis identifies the performance of individual SKUs in the assortment plan. It is used to determine which SKUs should be in the plan and how much backup stock and resulting product availability are provided for each SKU in the plan. In an ABC analysis, the SKUs in a merchandise category are rank-ordered by several performance measures, such as sales, gross margin, inventory turnover, and GMROI. Typically, this rank order reveals the general 80-20 principle; namely, approximately 80 percent of a retailer's sales or profits come from 20 percent of the products. This principle suggests that retailers should concentrate on the products that provide the biggest returns.

After rank-ordering the SKUs, the next step is to classify the items. On the basis of the classification, the buyer

Which of these shirts is an A item? B item?

determines whether to maintain the items in the assortment plan and, if so, what level of product availability to offer. For example, a men's dress shirt buyer might identify the A, B, C, and D SKUs by rank-ordering them by sales volume. The A items account for only 5 percent of the SKUs in the category but represent 70 percent of sales. The buyer decides that these SKUs should never be out of stock and thus plans to maintain more backup stock for A items, such as keeping more sizes of long- and short-sleeved white and blue dress shirts than of the B and C items.

The B items represent 10 percent of the SKUs and 20 percent of sales. These items include some of the other better-selling colours and patterned shirts and contribute to the retailer's image of having fashionable merchandise. Occasionally, the retailer will run out of some SKUs in the B category because it does not carry the same amount of backup stock for B items as it does for A items.

The C items account for 65 percent of SKUs but contribute to only 10 percent of sales. The planner may plan to carry some C items only in very small or very large sizes of the most basic shirts, with special orders used to satisfy customer demand.

exhibit 10–22 Multiattribute Analysis Method for Evaluating Vendors

Issues (1)	Importance Evaluation of Issues (I) (2)	PERFORMANCE EVALUATIONS OF INDIVIDUAL BRANDS ACROSS ISSUES			
		Brand A (P_a) (3)	Brand B (P_b) (4)	Brand C (P_c) (5)	Brand D (P_d) (6)
Vendor reputation	9	5	9	4	8
Service	8	6	6	4	6
Meets deliver dates	6	5	7	4	4
Merchandise quality	5	5	4	6	5
Markup opportunity	5	5	4	4	5
Country of origin	6	5	3	3	8
Product fashionability	7	6	6	3	8
Selling history	3	5	5	5	5
Promotional assistance	4	5	3	4	7
Overall evaluation a $\sum_{i=1}^{n} I_j \times P_{ij}$		280	298	212	341

$\sum_{i=1}^{n}$ = Sum of the expression.

I_i = Importance weight assigned to the ith dimension.

P_{ij} = Performance evaluation for jth brand alternative on the ith issue.

1 = Not important
10 = Very important

Finally, the buyer discovers that the remaining 20 percent of the SKUs, D items, have virtually no sales until they are marked down. Not only are these items excess merchandise and an unproductive investment, but they also distract from the rest of the inventory and clutter the store shelves. The buyer decides to eliminate most of these items from the assortment plan.

Multiattribute Analysis Method for Evaluating Vendors The multiattribute analysis method for evaluating vendors uses a weighted-average score for each vendor. The score is based on the importance of various issues and the vendor's performance on those issues. This method is similar to the multiattribute approach that can be used to understand how customers evaluate stores and merchandise, as we discussed in Chapter 3. Retailing View 10.6 describes Home Depot's system for vendor evaluation.

To better understand the multiattribute analysis method of evaluating vendors, either current or proposed, consider the example in Exhibit 10–22 for vendors of men's casual slacks.

A buyer can evaluate vendors using the following five steps:

1. Develop a list of issues to consider in the evaluation (column 1).[22]

2. In conjunction with the GMM, determine the importance weights for each issue in column 1 on a 1-to-10 scale (column 2), where 1 equals not important and 10 equals very important. For instance, the buyer and the merchandise manager believe that vendor reputation should receive a 9 because it's very important to the retailer's image. Merchandise quality receives a 5 because it's moderately important. Finally, a vendor's selling history is less important, so it could be rated 3.

multiattribute analysis method A method for evaluating vendors that uses a weighted average score for each vendor, which is based on the importance of various issues and the vendor's performance on those issues.

3. Make judgments about each individual brand's performance on each issue (remaining columns). Note that some brands have high ratings on some issues but not on others.

4. Develop an overall score by multiplying the importance of each issue by the performance of each brand or its vendor. For instance, vendor reputation importance (9) multiplied by the performance rating for brand A (5) is 45. Promotional assistance importance (4) multiplied by the performance rating (7) for vendor D is 28. This type of analysis illustrates an important point: It doesn't pay to perform well on issues that retailers don't believe are very important. Although vendor D performed well on promotional assistance, the buyer didn't rate this issue highly in importance, so the resulting score was still low.

5. To determine a vendor's overall rating, add the products for each brand for all issues. In Exhibit 10–22, brand D has the highest overall rating (341), so D is the preferred vendor.

Home Depot Takes Vendor Evaluations Seriously

Home Depot's vendor evaluation program focuses on three categories of excellence. The first, behavioural, helps it protect the reputation of its brand while instilling social and environmental responsibility into its vendor relationships. The second, manufacturing, is designed to improve product quality, cost, and innovation. The third, the supply chain category, is intended to reduce overall costs through process integration and standardization.

Home Depot has high expectations in terms of product quality, innovation, availability, on-time delivery, safety in production and shipping, compliance with laws and codes of conduct, and sensitivity to brand reputation. Its system measures service and ensures compliance specifically through the Vendor Center website.

Home Depot's vendor analysis scorecard gives everyone a quick view of how the vendor is doing. Green is good, but red isn't.

It features continuously updated information about how to do business with Home Depot, including the corporate performance policy, updates, news, information on events and training, and scorecards. Included in the laundry list of expectations is Home Depot's Social and Environmental Responsibility (SER) program, which addresses a wide range of issues related to vendors' proper treatment of their workers and the environment, including age requirements, wages, working conditions, emergency planning, health and safety, and prohibitions against forced labour, fraud, and discrimination. The program combines regular audits of vendor factories with extensive education to help vendors understand the retailer's expectations.

Home Depot posts online vendor scorecards, providing graphical representations of their performance levels. Each participating vendor is rated on criteria such as compliance with shipping-platform standards and import on-time delivery. The vendors and Home Depot can observe trends over 13-month periods. Green, yellow, and red "lights" for each category let vendors know how they have been rated at a glance.

Although Home Depot's compliance program focuses on education instead of punishment, vendors pay a price if they fail to meet the company's strict requirements. Fines for noncompliance with its shipping standards amount to $10 000 for the first violation and $25 000 each time thereafter.

Sources: "Retail Supply Chains: 'Back End' or Business Value?" www.Cognos.com, November 29, 2006; Robert J. Bowman, "Home Depot Turns Its Attention to Vendor Performance Management," SupplyChainBrain.com, June 2006.

SUMMARY

This chapter provides an overview of the merchandise management planning process. Merchandise is broken down into categories for planning purposes. Buyers and planners manage these categories, often with the help of their major vendors.

The key performance measures used to assess merchandise management are GMROI and its components, sales-to-stock ratio, inventory turnover, and gross margin. High inventory turnover is important for a retailer's financial success. But if the retailer attempts to push inventory turnover to its limit, stockouts and increased costs may result.

The steps in the merchandise management process are (1) forecasting category sales, (2) developing an assortment plan, (3) determining appropriate inventory levels and product availability, (4) developing a plan for managing inventory, (5) allocating merchandise to stores, and (6) monitoring and evaluating performance and making adjustments.

Buying systems for staple merchandise are very different from those for fashion merchandise. Because staple merchandise is sold month after month and the sales levels are predictable, an automated continuous replenishment system is often used to manage staple merchandise categories.

The sales forecast and inventory turnover work together to drive the merchandise budget plan for fashion merchandise. The sales forecast is broken down by month, based on historical seasonality patterns. It's necessary to purchase more in months when sales are forecast to be higher than average. Planned inventory turnover is converted to stock-to-sales ratios and used in the merchandise budget plan to determine the inventory level necessary to support sales.

Monthly stock-to-sales ratios are then adjusted to reflect seasonal sales patterns. The end product of the merchandise budget planning process is the dollar amount of merchandise a buyer should purchase each month for a category if the sales forecast and inventory turnover goals are to be met.

The open-to-buy system begins where the merchandise budget plan and staple goods inventory management systems leave off. It tracks how much merchandise is purchased for delivery in each month. Using an open-to-buy system, buyers know exactly how much money they've spent compared to how much they plan to spend.

Once the merchandise is purchased, merchandise buyers in multistore chains must allocate the merchandise to stores. The buyers must not only look at the differences in sales potential among stores but also consider the differences in the characteristics of the customer base.

The performance of buyers, vendors, and individual SKUs must be determined. Three different approaches can evaluate merchandise performance. The sell-through analysis is more useful for examining the performance of individual SKUs in the merchandise plan. The buyer compares actual with planned sales to determine whether more merchandise needs to be ordered or whether the merchandise should be put on sale. In an ABC analysis, merchandise is rank-ordered from highest to lowest. The merchandising team uses this information to set inventory management policies. For example, the most productive SKUs should carry sufficient backup stock to never be out of stock. Finally, the multi-attribute method is most useful for evaluating vendors' performance.

KEY TERMS

ABC analysis
backup stock
breaking sizes
category captain
category life cycle
category management
classification
continuous replenishment
cycle stock
department
depth
depth interview
fashion merchandise category
fill rate

focus group
forecast
gross margin return on investment (GMROI)
inventory
lead time
markdown money
merchandise budget plan
merchandise category
merchandise group
merchandise management
model stock plan
multiattribute analysis method
open-to-buy

order point
perpetual inventory
product availability
pull distribution strategy
push distribution strategy
seasonal merchandise category
sell-through analysis
service level
shrinkage
staple merchandise category
stock keeping unit (SKU)
stock-to-sales ratio
variety
weeks of inventory

Get Out & Do It!

1. **CONNECT EXERCISE** The merchandise budget plan determines how much merchandise should be purchased in each month of a fashion buying season (in dollars), given the sales and reduction forecast, inventory turnover goals, and the seasonal monthly fluctuations in sales. Access Student Resources in Connect and click on Merchandise Budget Plan in the additional resources for this chapter. The merchandise budget plan generally covers one fashion season for one merchandise category. This application presents both a one-month and a six-month example. In addition, practice calculations are presented for the one-month example, so have your calculator ready. Finally, in the calculation section, you have access to an Excel-based six-month merchandise budget plan that can be used for doing Case 20 in the text.

2. **CONNECT EXERCISE** The Vendor Evaluation Model utilizes the multiattribute analysis method for evaluating vendors, as described in the chapter. Access your Student Resources in Connect and click on Vendor Evaluation Model in the additional resources for this chapter. There are two spreadsheets. Open the first spreadsheet, vendor evaluation 1.xls. This spreadsheet is the same as Exhibit 10–22. If you were selling Brand A to the retailer, which numbers would change? Change the numbers in the matrix and see the effect on the overall evaluation. Go to the second spreadsheet, labelled evaluation 2.xls. This spreadsheet can be used to evaluate brands or merchandise you might stock in your store. Assume you own a bicycle shop. List the brands you might consider stocking and the issues you would consider in selecting brands to stock. Fill in the importance of the issues (10 = very important, 1 = not very important) and the evaluation of each brand on each characteristic (10 = excellent, 1 = poor). Determine which is the best brand for your store.

3. **INTERNET EXERCISE** Go to the home page of the following three retail trade publications: *WWD* at **www.wwd.com**, *Chain Store Age* at **www.chainstoreage.com**, and *Retailing Today* at **www.retailingtoday.com**. Find an article in each that focuses on managing merchandise. How can these articles assist retailers with merchandise planning decisions?

4. **INTERNET EXERCISE** Go to **www.sas.com/resources/brochure/sas-merchandise-intelligence-overview.pdf**. How does the SAS Merchandise Intelligence product provide retailers with information to support merchandise planning, forecasting, and measurement?

5. **GO SHOPPING** Visit a big-box office supply store and then a discount store to shop for school supplies. Contrast the breadth and depth offered at each. What are the advantages and disadvantages of breadth versus depth for each retailer? What are the advantages and disadvantages from the consumer's perspective?

DISCUSSION QUESTIONS AND PROBLEMS

1. Inventory shrinkage can be a problem for many retailers. How does the merchandise budget planning process account for inventory shrinkage?

2. Using the following information, calculate additions to stock:

Sales:	$24 000
EOM stock:	$90 000
BOM stock:	$80 000

3. Using the following information, calculate the average beginning-of-month stock-to-sales ratio for a six-month merchandise budget plan:

GMROI:	150%
Gross margin:	40%

4. Today is July 19. The buyer is attempting to assess his current open-to-buy given the following information:

Actual BOM stock:	$50 000
Monthly additions actual:	25 000
Merchandise on order to be delivered:	10 000
Planned monthly sales:	30 000
Planned reductions:	5 000
Planned EOM stock:	65 000

   What is the open-to-buy on July 19? What does this number mean to you?

5. Now it is July 31 and we need to calculate the open-to-buy for August given the following information:

Planned monthly sales:	$20 000
Monthly additions actual:	40 000
Planned markdowns:	5 000
Projected BOM stock:	50 000
Projected EOM stock:	30 000

Calculate open-to-buy and explain what the number means to you.

6. Typically, August school supplies sales are relatively low. In September, sales increase tremendously. How does the September stock-to-sales ratio differ from the August ratio?

7. Using the 80-20 principle, how can a retailer make certain that there's enough inventory of fast-selling merchandise and a minimal amount of slow-selling merchandise?

8. What is the order point and how many units should be reordered if a food retailer has an item with a seven-day lead time, ten-day review time, and daily demand of eight units? Say 65 units are on hand and the retailer must maintain a backup stock of 20 units to maintain a 95 percent service level.

9. A buyer at a sporting goods store in Vancouver receives a shipment of 400 ski parkas on October 1 and expects to sell out by January 31. On November 1, the buyer still has 375 parkas left. What issues should the buyer consider in evaluating the selling season's progress?

10. If you have a stock-to-sales ratio of 2, how many months of supply do you have? How many weeks of supply?

11. How and why would you expect variety and assortment to differ between a traditional bricks-and-mortar store and its Internet counterpart?

12. Simply speaking, increasing inventory turnover is an important goal for a retail manager. What are the consequences of turnover that's too slow? Too fast?

13. Assume you are the grocery buyer for canned fruits and vegetables at a five-store supermarket chain. Del Monte has told you and your boss that it would be responsible for making all inventory decisions for those merchandise categories. Del Monte will now determine how much to order and when shipments should be made. It promises a 10 percent increase in gross margin dollars in the coming year. Would you take Del Monte up on its offer? Justify your answer.

14. A buyer at Old Navy has received a number of customer complaints that he has been out of stock on some sizes of men's T-shirts. The buyer subsequently decides to increase this category's product availability from 80 percent to 90 percent. What will be the impact on backup stock and inventory turnover? Would your answer be the same if the product category were men's fleece sweatshirts?

15. Variety, assortment, and product availability are the cornerstones of the merchandise planning process. Provide examples of retailers that have done an outstanding job of positioning their stores on the basis of one or more of these issues.

16. The fine jewellery department in a department store has the same GMROI as the small appliances department, even though characteristics of the merchandise are quite different. Explain this situation.

17. A buyer is trying to decide from which vendor to buy a certain item. The item can be purchased as either a manufacturer brand or private-label brand. Using the following information, determine which vendor the buyer should use.

PERFORMANCE EVALUATIONS OF BRANDS			
Issues	**Importance Weight**	**Manufacturer Brand**	**Private-Label Brand**
Vendor reputation	8	5	5
Service	7	6	7
Meets delivery dates	9	7	5
Perceived merchandise quality	7	8	4
Markup opportunity	6	4	8
Demand-generating ability	5	7	5
Promotional assistance	3	6	8

buying strategies

LEARNING OBJECTIVES

Lo 1 Determine what branding options are available to retailers.

Lo 2 Explore the issues retailers should consider when sourcing internationally.

Lo 3 Examine how retailers prepare for and conduct negotiations with their vendors.

Lo 4 Investigate why retailers are building strategic relationships with their vendors.

SPOTLIGHT ON RETAILING

Partnering for Positive Impact

There's a shift taking place in the relationships and strategic partnerships that businesses in just about every sector are forming. The smaller, more interconnected and competitive the world gets, the more businesses are forming deeper, more genuine, and mutually beneficial partnerships based on shared values and goals. And few sectors are as well positioned to both drive this shift and benefit from it than the retail sector because relationships have always been at the core of its expertise and triumphs over marketplace adversity and challenges.

"Over the years, good retailers have made a huge effort to build relationships with staff and suppliers, but even more so with the community," says Paul McElhone, executive director of the University of Alberta's School of Retailing. "It's a big part of their success and it's more important than ever. Today's consumers are frustrated by companies that take and take from the community but don't give back. They're now supporting that with their wallets by supporting companies they feel are doing great work in the communities."

A CSR shift. Not that long ago, however, corporate social responsibility (CSR)—doing great work in the community—typically consisted of a retailer giving donations and/or volunteer hours to charitable causes. It was a philanthropic act that felt right but often seemed primarily a one-way street of giving. In the case of smaller retailers, frequently it didn't even have the added marketing benefit of being perceived as one of the good guys because many, such as Longo Brothers Fruit Markets Inc. (Longo's), simply didn't toot their own horn.

"Our founders, the Longo family, have always supported charities and community events since they founded the store in 1956," says Rob Koss, Longos' VP of marketing. "But they have been very humble about it."

In these days of public awareness and interest in social and environmental issues, retailers can no longer be humble. As consumers increasingly align themselves with retailers whose values they share, retailers have to let consumers know about what they stand for and show them that they walk the talk. In this, the non-profit sector has much to offer, especially when it comes to organizations that have developed a strong brand. Habitat for Humanity Canada, whose brand researchers have been put in the same league of strength as Starbucks, knows that its brand helps to strengthen the brand of its corporate partners, even ones with an already strong brand, such as Home Depot Canada. Longo's, which last year formed a strategic partnership with GE Appliances and Evergreen to sponsor the not-for-profit's Evergreen Brick Works community environmental centre, is also aware of the benefits of a partnership with a strong non-profit brand.

"Evergreen is respected and recognized, so it also helps the business brand," says Koss. "We do a lot of great things in the community and working with Evergreen is a nice way to advertise that we do help out without it being crass advertising."

For the greater good. Forming relationships and partnerships that allow retailers to communicate with consumers with informative and helpful interaction, versus blatant advertising, is part of the shift that's going on, as the culture of social media spreads into the offline world, according to RedFlagDeals.com's founder, Derek Szeto. "We do encourage business large and small to come in and answer questions and help our users, but we have to be careful with them coming in with a hard sell

because that might have a negative effect and wouldn't serve the retailer well. We're trying to do an education piece on how we can all help each other."

Aware of the influence and strength of their own brands, some non-profits are developing a new type of relationship with retailers: one of supplier. A recent example of this is Mothers Against Drunk Driving, which last December launched a new line of non-alcoholic beverages called MADD Virgin Drinks, to raise funds for the organization, educate on the need for designated drivers, and provide a non-alcoholic option for them. Not only do the retailers selling it benefit from the good CSR associated with the MADD brand, but they "also make a profit off the product," says Andrew Murie, MADD Canada's CEO. "It's a business type of donation rather than a charitable product. We benefit, our marketing partner benefits, and so does the retailer, and the customer has the satisfaction of knowing it's a win-win for everyone."

Identifying need and potential. The relationships that retailers such as Longo's and Home Depot are forming, however, are far more complex than simply about the power of brand. In the case of Longo's, the retailer joined forces with appliance manufacturer GE and top Toronto chefs to host demonstration-style cooking classes at its downtown Toronto store—with plans to expand the series to other stores across the GTA.

"It really comes down to the power of together. On the surface, it may seem strange for us to align with an appliance manufacturer, but when you peel it back, we have similar values, so it really makes sense," says Koss.

The partnership was born when GE's Philippe Meyersohn met Anthony Longo at a trade show. "We started talking and realized our organizations share similar values, including buying local and supporting local farmers. It's that commitment to our values that's resulted in it being so successful."

In order to remain competitive, says Koss, "I think we have to look at different ways. You have to understand your target demographics to make sure they align with a potential partner. For us the customer experience is first and foremost. We will never compromise our customer experience. So when we look at a partnership, we look at whether it will benefit the consumer."

Similarly, when it comes to Home Depot's support for Habitat ReStores, which sell gently used and new building materials to raise funds for Habitat's programs, the mutual benefits are multifold. Home Depot donates the majority of its return product to the ReStores. "We don't have a great way of tracking it but we estimate it represents $4.5 million to us," says Rob Voisin, director, ReStore Services. "We attribute a huge part of our success to our partnership with Home Depot. We can take problem product off their hand, whether it's returned product, or incorrectly ordered product, or discontinued product, so Home Depot doesn't have to have them shipped somewhere, including a landfill."

Home Depot has leveraged its partnership with Habitat to also help its own suppliers. "We have a few vendors who had established partnerships separately with Habitat and a couple of years ago they asked if they could use Home Depot stores as a hub to allow Habitat affiliates to come in and take some of that material. Now they're able to leverage their product donation through our stores and save money by using the existing structure."

Pushing the agenda. In other cases, retailers are forming strategic partnerships to push forward causes that affect the environment and society as well as their industry. David Smith, Sobeys' VP of retail strategy and sustainability, embarked on a leadership role back in 2008 to push sustainable seafood forward. It's a journey that has led the chain to initiate discussions and collaboration with a large network of players—from fishermen to NGOs, government, suppliers, and consumers. "This isn't consumer-driven, so it's up to us as retailers to lead the way," says Smith.

From Sobeys' perspective, the movement toward sustainable seafood has been slow, and as a result, it's a niche market. "The mainstream consumer is not really prepared to make a sacrifice for it," says Smith. "So you have to think of sustainability as a value-add. The issue needs a mainstream adoption. We have over 50 sustainable certified products, but also we're involved as a catalyst for change in the supply chain."

To that end, Sobeys held a national supplier summit with 150 of its suppliers to educate them on the issues of sustainable seafood and has also worked with partners on a website called ThisFish.info, which allows consumers to trace the journey of the fish they've purchased through the supply chain right to the fisherman who caught it.

Ultimately, Sobeys' leadership and partnerships for sustainable seafood, similar to the efforts being made by other retailers across the country, are about embracing the new strategic business mindset, which is all about collaboration that combines pragmatism and good business sense with shared values that can help create a sustainable and better future for earth, mankind—and retailer.

Source: Alexandra Lopez Pacheco, "Partnering for Positive Impact," *Canadian Retailer*, Spring 2012, Volume 22, Issue 2, pp. 40–41.

The preceding chapter outlined the merchandise management process and the steps in the process that buyers go through to determine what and how much merchandise to buy. After creating an assortment plan for the category, forecasting sales, and developing a plan outlining the flow of merchandise (how much merchandise needs to be ordered and when it needs to be delivered), the next step in the merchandise management process is to acquire the merchandise. The process for acquiring merchandise differs for well-known national brands and private-label brands that are available exclusively from the retailer. Thus, the first strategic decision that needs to be made is to determine the type of brands to buy for the category.

When buying merchandise, buyers meet with vendors at wholesale marketing or in their offices and negotiate many issues such as prices, delivery dates, payment terms, and financial support for advertising and markdowns. The buying process for private-label merchandise is often more complex. Some retailers have their own design and sourcing departments that work with buyers to specify the merchandise designs and then negotiate with manufacturers to produce the merchandise. Because merchandise is often manufactured outside of Canada, these retailers need to deal with the complexities of international business transactions. In other cases, buyers might negotiate with national-brand vendors or manufacturers to buy merchandise designed by the supplier exclusivity for the retailer.

Although buyers meet and negotiate with national-brand vendors and private-label manufacturers each season concerning new merchandise, there is a trend toward developing long-term strategic relationships with key suppliers. These partnerships enable the collaboration needed to develop the efficient supply chains discussed in Chapter 9, as well as joint merchandise and marketing programs.

Branding Strategies

Retailers and their buyers face a strategic decision about the mix of national brands and private-label brands sold exclusively by retailers. They can buy manufacturer brands such as Levi's, Kellogg's, or Black & Decker. Or they can develop their own private labels such as Old Navy jeans, President's Choice cookies from Loblaws, or Craftsman tools from Sears. Some use a mix of the two. In this section, we examine the relative advantages of these branding decisions, which are summarized in Exhibit 11–1.

Manufacturer Brands

A **manufacturer brand**, also known as a *national brand*, is a product designed, produced, and marketed by a vendor and sold to many different retailers. The manufacturer is responsible for developing the merchandise and establishing an image for the brand. In some cases, the manufacturer will use an umbrella or family-branding strategy in which its name appears as part of the brand name for a specific product, such as Kellogg's Corn Flakes. However, some manufacturers, such as Philip Morris—owner of Kraft Foods, Miller Brewing Company, as well as Philip Morris (tobacco products)—don't associate their name with the brand.

Some retailers organize some of their categories around their most important national brands. For instance, buyers in department stores are responsible for brands, such as Clinique or Estée Lauder, rather than for products, such as lipstick and fragrances. Clothing is also often organized by manufacturer brand (e.g., Polo/Ralph Lauren, Levi's, Liz Claiborne, or DKNY). These brands often have their own boutique within stores. Managing a category by national brand, rather than a more traditional classification scheme, is useful so that merchandise can be purchased in a coordinated manner around a central theme.

Buying from vendors of manufacturer brands can help store image, traffic flow, and selling/promotional expenses. Retailers buy from vendors of manufacturer brands because they have a customer following—people go into the store and ask for them by name. Loyal customers of manufacturer brands generally know what to expect from the products and feel comfortable with them, as with Samsonite luggage.

manufacturer brand A line of products designed, produced, and marketed by a vendor; also called a *national brand*.

DID YOU KNOW?

Health and beauty (74 percent), pet care (47 percent), breakfast cereal (63 percent), and laundry detergent (69 percent) are the categories where brand names far outpace rival private labels as the preferred choice for consumers.[1]

exhibit 11–1 Relative Advantages of Manufacturer versus Private Brands

Impact on Store	Type of Vendor	
	Manufacturer Brands	**Private-Label Brands**
Store loyalty	?	+
Store image	+	+
Traffic flow	+	+
Selling and promotional expenses	+	−
Restrictions	−	+
Differential advantages	−	+
Margins	?	?

+ advantage to the retailer, − disadvantage to the retailer, ? depends on circumstances.

licensed brand
Brand for which the licensor (owner of a well-known name) enters into a contractual arrangement with a licensee (a retailer or a third party). The licensee either manufactures or contracts with a manufacturer to produce the licensed product and pays a royalty to the licensor.

private-label brands Products developed and marketed by a retailer and available for sale only from that retailer; also called *store brands*.

DID YOU KNOW?

The number of shoppers who think brand-name packaging is more attractive than private-label packaging decreased 14 percent in the past year.[2]

Manufacturers devote considerable resources to creating demand for their products. As a result, relatively less money is required by the retailer for selling and promotional expenses for manufacturer brands. For instance, Guess? Inc., manufacturer of jeans and other casual clothing, attempts to communicate a constant and focused message to the consumer by coordinating advertising with in-store promotions and displays.

Manufacturer brands typically have lower realized gross margins than private-label brands. These lower gross margins are due to the manufacturer assuming the cost of promoting the brand and increased competition among retailers selling these brands. Typically, many retailers offer the same manufacturer brands in a market, so customers compare prices for these brands across stores. Retailers often offer significant discounts on some manufacturer brands to attract customers to their stores.

Stocking national brands may increase or decrease store loyalty. If the manufacturer brand is available through a limited number of retail outlets (e.g., Lancôme cosmetics or Diesel jeans), customers loyal to the manufacturer brand will also become loyal to the stores selling the brand. If, on the other hand, manufacturer brands are readily available from many retailers in a market, customer loyalty may decrease because the retailer can't differentiate itself from the competition.

Another problem with manufacturer brands is that they can limit a retailer's flexibility. Vendors of strong brands can dictate how their products are displayed, advertised, and priced. Jockey, for instance, tells retailers exactly when and how its products (such as underwear) should be advertised.

Licensed Brands A special type of manufacturer brand is a licensed brand, in which the owner of a well-known brand name (licensor) enters into a contract with a licensee to develop, produce, and sell the branded merchandise. The licensee may be either the retailer that contracts with a manufacturer to produce the licensed product or a third party that contracts to have the merchandise produced and then sells it to the retailer. Fashion designers often license their name to sunglass and perfume companies.

Licensed brands' market share has grown increasingly large in recent years. Owners of trade names not typically associated with manufacturing have also gotten into the licensing business. For instance, the manufacturer of the sweatshirt or baseball cap emblazoned with your university or college's logo pays your school a licensing fee. If it didn't, it would be infringing on the university or college's logo (a trademark) and therefore would be involved in counterfeiting.

Private-Label Brands

Private-label brands, also called *store brands*, are products developed by a retailer and available for sale only from that retailer. Victoria's Secret and The Gap are among the top 20 private-label brands. Exhibit 11–2 gives examples of more private-label brands. Retailers typically develop specifications for the merchandise and then contract with manufacturers who are often located in countries with developing economies to produce the products. But the retailer, not the manufacturer, is responsible for promoting the brand.

The size of retail firms has increased through consolidation, and private labels have assumed a new level of significance by establishing distinctive identities among retailers. Some retailers, such as The Gap and Club Monaco, sell their own labels exclusively as an integral element of their distinctiveness. Other retailers, such as Hudson's Bay and Sears, successfully mix manufacturer brands with their own retailer brands to project their unique image statement.

exhibit 11–2 Examples of Private-Label Brands

Industry	Store	Brand
Grocery stores	Metro	Irresistibles, Selection
	Loblaws	President's Choice, no name, Joe Fresh, Exact
	Sobeys	Compliments, Gourmet Minute
Mass merchandisers	Walmart	Great Value, Equate, Our Finest
	Target	Threshold, Market Pantry, Mossimo, Sutton & Dodge, Boots & Barkley
Department stores	Hudson's Bay	1670, Lord & Taylor, Hudson's Bay Signature Collection, Black Brown 1826, Gluckstein Home
	Sears	Kenmore, Craftsman, Martha Stewart
Specialty stores	Canadian Tire	Mastercraft
	Holt Renfrew	Holts, Miss Renfrew, hr2
	Home Depot	Husky, Ryobi, BEHR

Private-branded products now account for an average of 25 percent of the purchases in North America and roughly 45 percent in Europe.[3] Private-label dollar volume in supermarkets, drug chains, and mass merchandisers is increasing twice as fast as national brands. Retailing View 11.1 describes Asda's private-label strategy.

Private labels have always added value to retailers, and Hudson's Bay, Shoppers Drug Mart, and Loblaws are clearly leading the way. Hudson's Bay claims 60 percent of its apparel assortment is private brand, and this trend is expected to grow. Holt Renfrew, a retailer that earns most of its profit from carrying powerful, high-fashion brand names, has 25 percent of its apparel inventory in private brands with desirable price points.

Consumer attitudes are driving the trend. Consumers are replacing more expensive brands with private brands from retailers. The trend seems to be about price rather than designer label: Eighty percent of the jeans sold in Canada are under $39.

Offering private labels provides a number of benefits to retailers, as Exhibit 11–1 shows.

- The exclusivity of strong private labels boosts store loyalty. For instance, the MotoMaster line of auto parts and accessories in Canadian Tire won't be found at other stores.

- Private labels enhance store image if the brands are of high quality and fashionable.

- Successful private-label brands can draw customers to the store. They can be a good deal—10 to 18 percent less expensive than national brands in Canada and as much as 25 percent cheaper in Europe.[4]

- Retailers that purchase private-label brands don't have the same restrictions on display, promotion, or price that often encumber their strategy with manufacturer brands. Retailers purchasing private brands also have more control over manufacturing, quality control, and distribution of the merchandise.

- Gross margin opportunities may be greater with private-label brands.

But there are drawbacks to using private-label brands. Although gross margins may be higher for private-label brands than for manufacturer brands, there are other expenses that aren't readily apparent. Retailers must make significant investments to design merchandise, create customer awareness, and develop a favourable image for their private-label brands. When private-label manufacturers are located outside Canada, the complications become even more significant. Sales associates may need additional training to help them sell private-label brands against better-known brands. If the private-label merchandise doesn't sell, the retailer can't return the merchandise to the manufacturer. These problems are most severe for high-fashion merchandise.

Private-Label Options[5] Retail branding strategies have run the gamut from closely imitating manufacturer-brand packaging and products to distinct brand images, from low product quality and prices to premium positioning, and from nonexistent promotion and merchandising to intense activity. We group private brands into four broad categories: generic, premium, parallel, and exclusive.

Generic branding targets a price-sensitive segment by offering a no-frills product at a discount price. Known as *generic* or *house brands*, such unbranded, unadvertised merchandise is found mainly in drug, grocery, and discount stores. These products are used typically for commodities like milk or eggs in grocery stores and underwear in discount stores. Once the mainstay of private-label brands, the sales of generics have been declining. These products are labelled with the name of the commodity and thus actually have no brand name distinguishing them.

Premium branding offers the consumer a private label at a comparable manufacturer-brand quality, usually with modest price savings. Examples of premium labels include Loblaw's President's Choice, Tesco's Finest (U.K.), Marks & Spencer's St. Michael (U.K.), Woolworth Select (Australia), Pick and Pay's Choice (South Africa), and Albert Heijn's AH Select (Netherlands).[6] The premium brand attempts to match or exceed the product quality standard of the prototypical manufacturer brand in its category. There is no intention to duplicate the packaging or to trade off the brand equity of a particular manufacturer brand. However, consumers frequently perceive the retailer premium labels as competing manufacturer brands.

Retailer premium brands, with the appearance of comparability, compete directly with manufacturer national brands. To succeed, the retailer must commit the resources in market research, product development, quality control, and promotion in its market area commensurate with its manufacturer-brand competitors. Consequently, development of a premium branding program precludes many retailers that have few resources from diverting to this strategy. President's Choice, Loblaw's premium private label, competes on quality, not on price. Kellogg's has two scoops of raisins in its cereal, but

generic branding
A branding strategy that targets a price-sensitive segment by offering a no-frills product at a discount price.

premium branding
A branding strategy that offers the consumer a private label at a comparable manufacturer-brand quality, usually with a modest price savings.

DID YOU KNOW?

Private labels are big business in Europe: At Aldi and Lidl's, private brands account for 94 percent of their merchandise; at Tesco, 50 percent; at Walmart, 39 percent; and at Carrefour, 34 percent.[7]

U.K.'s Asda Loves Private Labels

The British supermarket retailer Asda, owned by Walmart, has a private-label portfolio that accounts for 45 percent of its grocery and 50 percent of its nonfood sales. Asda has extended its own label into such categories as healthy eating, organics, and food for kids and now is placing more emphasis on developing premium-priced private labels.

Asda offers six private-label brands in the food, health and beauty, and household categories. In addition, it has its successful George private-label clothing brand and a selection of Asda-branded financial services, including home, motor, and life insurance. Some of its brands include:

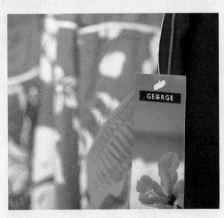

Asda, a U.K. chain owned by Walmart, developed George, a private-label apparel and footwear brand. Although very successful in the U.K, it has not been as successful in Walmart stores in the U.S. and Canada.

- Smart Price—Economy-value, no-frills food and general merchandise essentials.

- Best-in-Market—Everyday food and general merchandise items at low prices.

- Good for you!—Foods with lower fat content than standard Asda brand alternatives.

- Organic—Best-value organic "everyday" products.

- Onn—Mid-level eclectic brand with stylized designs.

- Extra Special—Asda's premium private-label food brand.

- More for Kids—Healthier, fun products for kids across the food and health and beauty categories.

The Extra Special premium private-label brand has grown from 40 SKUs in 2000 to more than 750 across categories that include confectionery, soft drinks, snacks, trifles, specialty breads, prepared meat and fish meals, and a wide range of cheeses and sliced meats. The criteria for an Extra Special branded product include better taste and the finest ingredients compared with standard alternatives or national premium equivalents, but affordable at a 10 to 15 percent lower price than competitors' premium private-label equivalents.

Asda's private-label clothing and footwear brand, George, is the fourth-largest apparel brand in the United Kingdom. Created by George Davies, the former owner of a successful chain of British apparel stores, George merchandise comprises sleek but inexpensive clothing, accessories, and undergarments for women and men. Walmart is importing George merchandise and selling it as part of its effort to upgrade its apparel offering. But George merchandise has not been as successful in the United States and Canada.

Sources: www.asda.co.uk (accessed October 16, 2007); "Odin Drives ASDA 'Extra Special' Range onto Shelves," *The Retail Bulletin*, August 30, 2007; Bill Condie, "Asda Plans to Spruce Up Tired George Label as Growth Slows Down," *Knight Ridder Tribune Business News*, September 14, 2007.

President's Choice cereal has four and is still cheaper. The Decadent chocolate chip cookie under the President's Choice label has 39 percent chocolate chips by weight, compared with 19 percent in Chips Ahoy! In addition, it uses real butter instead of hydrogenated coconut oil and quality chocolate instead of artificial chips. The resulting product is Canada's market leader in chocolate chip cookies, despite being sold only in 20 percent of the market held by Loblaw.[8]

The development of super-premium and luxury private-label ranges are becoming part of retailers multi-tier pricing strategies as they attract the attention of consumers seeking luxury at an affordable price. Loblaw Companies, marketer of the first and oldest Canadian premium private-label range under the President's Choice brand, was the first to announce its new and fairly extensive Black Label super-premium line. This new line is positioned as gourmet yet still affordable indulgences and luxuries and includes a range of product categories such as confectionery, cheese, pasta, and cookies.

In summer 2011, Walmart Canada test-marketed and launched its own black-label line of private-label food and beverages, which it named Our Finest. Its new premium-positioned private-label range features close to 200 SKUs.

Other retailers that have been developing and promoting new private-label brands in the super-premium and luxury brand segments include Shoppers Drug Mart (Life Premium Gourmet) and Jean Coutu (Desir Lait line of boxed chocolates). This strategy has helped increase overall customer traffic and spending in stores in the face of an increasingly competitive grocery retailing landscape.

Parallel branding represents private labels that closely imitate the packaging and product attributes of leading manufacturer brands but with a clearly articulated "invitation to compare" in its merchandising approach and on its product label. This invitation to compare on the product label was the basis for a recent legal action. Like copycat branding, parallel branding seeks to benefit from the brand equity of the manufacturer brand by closely imitating the national brand's packaging and product qualities. However, the invitation to compare leaves little doubt that different manufacturers produce the two products. Consequently, the imitative packaging does not constitute a trademark infringement. Nevertheless, patent considerations can be an issue if appropriate discretion is not used.

Parallel branding is a leveraging strategy used to bolster a retailer's private-brand sales. The closer two products are in form, logo, labelling, and packaging, the more they are perceived as substitutes. Parallel brands attempt to produce a product and packaging so similar to the manufacturer brand that the only noticeable difference between the two is price. This promotes the view that the parallel brand provides better value for the consumer. Manufacturer brands produce store traffic, and the parallel brand leverages this traffic into parallel brand sales through similar packaging and aggressive store signage, displays, and shelf location. For instance, Shoppers Drug Mart's Life brand products are placed next to the manufacturer's brands and often look like them.

An exclusive co-brand is developed by a national brand vendor, often in conjunction with a retailer, and is sold exclusively by the retailer. The simplest form of an exclusive co-brand is when a national brand manufacturer assigns different model numbers and has different exterior features for the same basic product sold by different retailers. For example, LG appliances sold at Home Depot might have different model numbers than LG appliances with similar features available at The Brick. These exclusive models make it difficult for consumers to compare prices for virtually the same appliance sold by different retailers. Since, the retailers are less likely to compete on prices when selling these exclusive co-brands, their margins for the products reach higher, and they are motivated to devote more resources toward selling the exclusive co-brands than they would for similar national brands.[9]

A more sophisticated form of exclusive co-branding is when a manufacturer develops an exclusive product or product category for a retailer. For example, Canadian manufacturer Gracious Living Group sells Eon Decking exclusively at The Home Depot Canada. Eon is a complete alternative decking system composed of plastic, dramatically reducing the need for wood. As the only 100% plastic product with a wood grain finish at The Home Depot, Eon is positioned as a premium product in their lumber and building materials assortment.[10] Levi's has also developed the Signature brand jeans for sale at Walmart. And Hudson's Bay's exclusive brands, as discussed in Retailing View 11.2, are not available from its competitors.

> **parallel branding**
> A branding strategy that represents a private label that closely imitates the trade dress (packaging) and product attributes of leading manufacturer brands but with a clearly articulated "invitation to compare" in its merchandising approach and on its product label.

> **exclusive co-brand**
> A brand developed by a national brand vendor, often in conjunction with a retailer, and sold exclusively by the retailer.

A Brand or a Store?

The distinction between a store and a brand has become blurred in recent years. Some large retailers have developed strong private-label merchandise. Other retailers, such as Roots, have such a strong brand name that the average consumer cannot make a distinction between store and brand. Roots, the Canadian casual clothing retailer, has capitalized on its strong name recognition by widening the variety of merchandise offered at its stores. It now sells a range of products, including home decorating items. Manufacturers are trying to emulate the success of retailers such as Zara, whose name has become a brand in its own right.

A natural extension of the retailer's brand strategy is to exploit strong retail name recognition by selling its products through channels other than its own stores. Starbucks made one of the most aggressive moves by a retailer to broaden its customer base. The coffee shop retailer that brought North America the "decaf latte" has teamed up with PepsiCo to market Frappuccino, a coffee-and-milk blend sold through traditional grocery channels. Starbucks is also engaged in a joint venture with Dreyer's Grand Ice Cream to distribute Starbucks coffee-flavoured ice cream and has entered into a long-term licensing agreement with Kraft Foods, Inc., to accelerate the growth of the Starbucks brand in the grocery channel.

On the other side of the distribution spectrum, several firms that have traditionally been exclusively manufacturers have become retailers. Examples are Apple, Guess?, Calvin Klein, Ralph Lauren, Levi's, Harley-Davidson, Sony, and Nike. Why have these manufacturers chosen to become retailers?

Only at Hudson's Bay

Hudson's Bay Company (HBC), which was incorporated in 1670 by a British royal charter under King Charles II, is Canada's leading department store. HBC offers well-edited assortments of national, private, and exclusive popular fashion, beauty, home, and accessory designers and brands. HBC operates 92 stores in 8 provinces across Canada, as well as its website, www.thebay.com. HBC's portfolio also includes Lord & Taylor, a department store with 48 full-line store locations in the United States, and Home Outfitters, Canada's largest home specialty superstore with 69 locations.

While Hudson's Bay (or The Bay) carries many high-profile brands such as Coach, the retailer is building a strong portfolio of private in-house and exclusive brands at its Bay and Lord & Taylor chains. The company recently released plans to trim to five—from twenty-five—private-label brands by end of 2013. In fall 2013, the company introduced a new private brand called 1670 for contemporary men's and women's apparel at "moderate price-points." It will expand its Lord & Taylor line in 2014 beyond cashmere fashions to a wide assortment of goods. The other labels include the Hudson's Bay Signature Collection, Gluckstein Home, and Black Brown 1826. These private-label brands complement the company's current offering of national brands and "fill some gaps" in the overall assortment in terms of faster response time to shifting trends and the flow and timing of merchandise shipments.

The push on its own private-label brands also gives the company more latitude in setting prices without having to match competitors' discounts, and it scales back on middlemen, which in turn helps to generate higher margins and keeps customers from going to its vendors' rival stores. "As you watch the proliferation of vendors opening their own stores, you're seeing the reverse proliferation of retailers doing their own product," said Marc Metrick, HBC's chief marketing officer. "That's all about controlling your own destiny. It's profitable and it's a key differentiator." HBC has set a five-year goal for private-label sales to reach 15 percent of its overall $3.9 billion in annual revenue (excluding the sold-off Zellers chain), up from 9 percent, according to its securities filings.

On March 26, 2013, HBC announced that it had acquired exclusive rights to the Kleinfeld Bridal brand in Canada. Kleinfeld is the largest luxury bridal retailer in the world and the luxury bridal salon featured on the reality show *Say Yes to the Dress* on the TLC cable network. Ronald Rothstein, co-owner of Kleinfeld, said it was attracted to Hudson's Bay because of its strong wedding registry business, its track record in selling luxury designer lines at The Room, and the savvy of Bonnie Brooks (president of Hudson's Bay) and Richard Baker (chief executive officer of Hudson's Bay).

According to Brooks, "Bringing Kleinfeld to Canada further supports [the] overall product differentiation strategy for Hudson's Bay, which is to deliver new, relevant, and exclusive brands and concepts to the marketplace. This incredible partnership will further [HBC's] position as Canada's headquarters and leading destination for gift registry, and now for designer bridal wear." In early 2014, Hudson's Bay will open a 20 000-square-foot Kleinfeld flagship salon on the seventh floor of its Toronto Queen Street store, with future locations in the downtown Vancouver and Montreal stores. Kleinfeld reportedly generates an estimated $1000 of sales per square foot per year, which could mean an additional $20 million per year for the Queen Street flagship store.

Sources: Marina Strauss, "Hudson's Bay says 'yes' to Kleinfeld's dresses," *The Globe and Mail*, March 26, 2013 (accessed May 3, 2013); "Hudson's Bay Company to Eliminate Most Private Label Brands," Retail-Insider.com, December 13, 2012, http://www.retail-insider.com/2012/12/hudsons-bay-company-to-eliminate-most.html (accessed May 3, 2013); Marina Strauss, "HBC putting its own stripe on merchandise with private labels," *The Globe and Mail*, December 10, 2012 (accessed May 1, 2013); "Hudson's Bay Says 'Yes' to Kleinfeld," CNW, news release, March 26, 2013, http://www.newswire.ca/en/story/1135757/hudson-s-bay-says-yes-to-kleinfeld# (accessed May 5, 2013); http://www.thebay.com; http://www.kleinfeldbridal.com.

- First, by becoming retailers they have total control over the way their merchandise is presented to the public. They can price, promote, and merchandise their line with a unified strategy. They don't have to worry about retailers cherry-picking certain items or discounting the price, for instance.

- Second, they can use these stores to test new merchandise and merchandising concepts. Based on these tests' results, they can better advise other retailers what to buy and how to merchandise their stores.

- Third, these manufacturers/retailers use their stores to showcase their merchandise to the public as well.

- Finally, although these stores often compete with stores that carry the same merchandise, some would argue that having a stronger retail presence creates a name recognition and synergy between the manufacturer and retailer that benefits both parties.

Lo 2

International Sourcing Decisions

A decision that's closely associated with branding decisions is to determine where the merchandise is made. Retailers involved in private branding are faced with many challenges related to international sourcing decisions. Retailers buying manufacturer brands usually aren't responsible for determining where the merchandise is made, but a product's country of origin is often used as a signal of quality. Certain items are strongly associated with specific countries, and products from those countries, such as gold jewellery from Italy or cars from Japan, often benefit from those linkages.

In this section, we'll first examine the cost implications of international sourcing decisions. Initially, it often looks like retailers can get merchandise from foreign suppliers more cheaply than from domestic sources. Unfortunately, there are lots of hidden costs, including managerial issues, associated with sourcing globally that make this decision more complicated. We then examine the trend toward sourcing closer to home or actually reversing the trend toward international sourcing by buying "made in Canada." This section concludes by exploring ethical issues associated with retailers who buy from vendors engaged in human rights and child-labour violations.

Costs Associated with Global Sourcing Decisions

A direct reason for sourcing globally rather than domestically is to save money. Retailers must examine several cost issues when making these decisions. The cost issues discussed in this section are country-of-origin effects, foreign currency fluctuations, tariffs, free trade zones, inventory carrying costs, and transportation costs.

Country-of-Origin Effects The next time you're buying a shirt made in Western Europe (e.g., Italy, France, or Germany), notice that it's probably more expensive than a comparable shirt made in a developing country such as Hungary, Ecuador, or Cambodia. These Western European countries have a reputation for high fashion and quality. Unfortunately for the Canadian consumer, however, the amount of goods and services that can be purchased from those countries is significantly less than the amount of merchandise that can be purchased from developing countries for the same amount of money. When making international sourcing decisions, therefore, retailers must weigh the savings associated with buying from developing countries with the image associated with buying merchandise from a country that has a reputation for fashion and quality.

Other countries might have a technological advantage in the production of certain types of merchandise and can therefore provide their products to the world market at a relatively low price. For example, Japan has always been a leader in the development of consumer electronics. Although these products often enter the market at a high price, the price soon drops as Japanese manufacturers learn to produce the merchandise more efficiently.

Foreign Currency Fluctuations An important consideration when making global sourcing decisions is fluctuations in the currency of the exporting firm. Unless currencies are closely linked, for example, between Canada and the United States, changes in the exchange rate will increase or reduce the cost of the merchandise.

Suppose, for instance, that Hudson's Bay was purchasing watches from Swatch in Switzerland for $100 000, which would be equivalent to 150 000 Swiss francs (SFr) if the exchange rate were 1.5 SFr for each dollar. If the dollar fell to, say, 1.1 SFr before the firm had to pay for the watches, it would end up paying $136 364 (or 150,000 SFr ÷ 1.1). The euro has all but eliminated this problem among the participating European countries.

Tariffs A tariff, also known as a *duty*, is a tax placed by a government on imports.[11] Import tariffs have been used to shield domestic manufacturers from foreign competition and to raise money for the government. In general, since tariffs raise the cost of imported merchandise, retailers have always had a strong incentive to reduce them. The General Agreement on Tariffs and Trade (GATT), the North American Free Trade Agreement (NAFTA), and foreign trade zones all reduce tariffs.

World Trade Organization The World Trade Organization (WTO) replaced GATT in 1996. With 144 member-countries, the WTO has become the global watchdog for free trade. As a result of the WTO and its predecessor GATT, worldwide tariffs have been reduced from 40 percent in 1947 to an estimated 4 percent in 2000.[12] The WTO will continue to push for tariff reductions on

tariff A tax placed by a government upon imports; also called *duty*.

manufactured goods as well as for liberalization of trade in agriculture and services.

North American Free Trade Agreement

The ratification of NAFTA on January 1, 1994, created a tariff-free market with 364 million consumers. NAFTA members are currently Canada, the United States, and Mexico. NAFTA is expected to strengthen North America's position when negotiating with the European Union.

Canadian retailers gain from NAFTA for two reasons. First, Mexican labour is relatively low-cost and abundant. Thus, retailers can either search for low-cost suppliers in Mexico or begin manufacturing merchandise there themselves. Maquiladoras—plants in Mexico that make goods and parts or process food for export—are plentiful, have lower costs than their Canadian counterparts, and are located throughout Mexico, particularly in border towns such as Nogales and Tijuana. Second, with the growing importance of quick response inventory systems, the time it takes to get merchandise into stores becomes ever more critical. Transit times are shorter and managerial control problems are reduced when sourcing from Mexico, compared to the Far East or Europe.

Free Trade Zones Retailers involved in foreign sourcing of merchandise can lower import tariffs by using free trade zones. A free trade zone is a special area within a country that can be used for warehousing, packaging, inspection, labelling, exhibition, assembly, fabrication, or transshipment of imports without being subject to that country's tariffs.

To illustrate how a free trade zone can benefit retailers, consider how German cars are imported to a foreign trade zone in Guatemala for distribution throughout Central America. The duty for passenger vehicles is 100 percent of the landed cost of the vehicle. The duty for commercial vehicles, however, is only 10 percent. The German manufacturer imported commercial vans with no seats or carpeting, and with panels instead of windows. After paying the 10 percent import duty, it converted the vans to passenger station wagons in the free trade zone in Guatemala and sold them throughout Latin America.

Inventory Carrying Cost The cost of carrying inventory is likely to be higher when purchasing from suppliers outside Canada than from domestic suppliers.

$$\begin{matrix} \text{Cost of} \\ \text{carrying} \\ \text{inventory} \end{matrix} = \begin{matrix} \text{Average} \\ \text{inventory} \\ \text{value} \\ \text{(at cost)} \end{matrix} \times \begin{matrix} \text{Opportunity} \\ \text{cost of capital} \end{matrix}$$

The opportunity cost of capital is the rate available on the next best use of the capital invested in the project at hand. It would include the cost of borrowing money for a similar investment, plus insurance and taxes.

Transportation Costs In general, the farther merchandise has to travel, the higher the transportation cost will be for any particular mode of transportation. For instance, the cost of shipping a container of merchandise by ship from China to Vancouver is significantly higher than the cost from Panama to Vancouver. Quick delivery via air express will increase end costs significantly.

Managerial Issues Associated with Global Sourcing Decisions

In the previous section, we examined the specific costs associated with global sourcing decisions. In most cases, retailers can obtain hard cost information that will help them make their global sourcing decisions. The managerial issues discussed in this section—quality control and developing strategic partnerships—are not as easily evaluated.

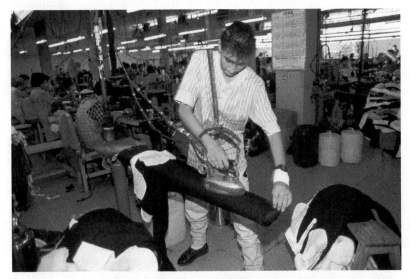

Maquiladoras are manufacturing plants in Mexico that make goods and parts or process food for export. They are very popular because their costs are lower than those of their Canadian and U.S. counterparts.

Quality Control When sourcing globally, it's harder to maintain and measure quality standards than when sourcing domestically. Typically, these problems are more pronounced in countries that are far away and underdeveloped. For instance, it's easier to address a quality problem if it occurs on a shipment of dresses from Costa Rica to Canada than if the dresses were shipped from Jakarta because Costa Rica is much closer than Indonesia.

There are both direct and indirect ramifications for retailers if merchandise is delayed because it has to be remade due to poor quality. Suppose Hudson's Bay is having pants made in Haiti. Before the pants leave the factory, Hudson's Bay representatives find that the workmanship is so poor that the pants need to be remade. This delay reverberates throughout the system. Hudson's Bay could have extra backup stock to carry it through until the pants can be remade, but more likely, however, it won't have advance warning of the problem, so the stores will be out of stock.

A more serious problem occurs if the pants are delivered to the stores without the problem having been detected. This could happen if the defect is subtle, such as inaccurate sizing. Customers can become irritated and question merchandise quality. Also, markdowns ensue because inventories become unbalanced and shopworn.

Building Strategic Partnerships The importance of building strategic partnerships is examined later in this chapter. It is typically harder to build these alliances when sourcing globally, particularly when the suppliers are far away and in underdeveloped countries. Communications are more difficult. There is often a language barrier, and there are almost always cultural differences. Business practices—everything from terms of payment to the issues of trade practices such as commercial bribery—are different in a global setting. The most important element in building a strategic alliance—maintaining the supplier's trust—is more arduous in an international environment.

Source Close to Home or Buy "Made in Canada"?

Some retailers are shifting suppliers from Asia and Europe to nearby Central American and Caribbean countries, or they're seeking products made in Canada. There are four reasons for this shift:

- First, it may be more profitable for the reasons detailed above.
- Second, quick response delivery systems and sourcing globally are inherently incompatible. Yet both are important and growing trends in retailing. Quick response systems are based on short and consistent lead times. Vendors provide frequent deliveries with smaller quantities. There's no room for defective merchandise. For a quick response system to work properly, there needs to be a strong alliance between vendor and retailer that is based on trust and a sharing of information through electronic data interchange (EDI) or radio frequency identification data (RFID) and collaborative planning, forecasting, and replenishment (CPFR). In the preceding section, we argued that each of these activities is more difficult to perform globally than domestically. Further, the level of difficulty increases with distance and the vendor's sophistication. Catalogue and Internet retailer Coldwater Creek (www.coldwatercreek.com), for instance, sources about 75 percent of its merchandise from North America, so it can purchase relatively small orders and receive quick delivery.[14]

- Third, some of their customers prefer products that are made in Canada. Retailers are simply reacting to their customers' quality perceptions.
- Fourth, it's easier to police potential violations of human rights and child labour. Hudson's Bay, Ralph Lauren, The Gap, Nordstrom, J. Crew, The Limited, and others have had to publicly deflect allegations about human rights, child labour, or other abuses involving factories and countries where their goods are made.[15]

Long the target of anti-globalization movements, Gap Inc. released a report in the spring of 2004 outlining its monitoring and enforcement of labour standards among its global suppliers. The report details by region the compliance efforts at the hundreds of factories in its supply chain. Walmart has notified its global suppliers that it will immediately drop them if they subcontract their work to factories that haven't been authorized by the retailer. The stricter measure comes from increasing calls for better safety oversight following the factory collapse and deadly fire in 2012 at Bangladesh factories that supplied clothing to Walmart and other retailers. Walmart has moved to have employees stationed in countries where it subcontracts to ensure compliance, rather than relying on third-party agents as it has in the past. Further, Walmart intends to list the factories that are not authorized to manufacture goods for Walmart on its website. "We want the right accountability and ownership to be in the hands of the suppliers," says Rajan Kamalanathan, vice president of ethical sourcing at Walmart.[16]

> **DID YOU KNOW?**
>
> The United States is Canada's third-largest supplier of apparel, after China and Bangladesh. Asian suppliers of low-cost apparel constitute the strongest foreign competition for U.S. apparel exporters to Canada.[17]

In response to the anti-sweatshop movement, high-profile companies like Reebok, Nike, and Liz Claiborne Inc. are publishing reports about audits undertaken in their factories.

Canadian consumers must understand that they are going to have to balance their desire for low prices with their concern for social responsibility before Third World sweatshop conditions improve dramatically. Unfortunately, there has been very little effort from the majority of Canadian retailers to improve Third World labour conditions.[19]

Connecting with Vendors

Now that we've examined the different branding decisions available to retailers and the issues surrounding global sourcing, we will concentrate on how and where retailers connect with their vendors. Retailers "go to market" to see the variety of available merchandise and to buy. A market, from the retail buyer's perspective, is a concentration of vendors within a specific geographic location, perhaps even under one roof or over the Internet. These markets may be Internet exchanges, permanent wholesale market centres, or temporary trade fairs. Retailers may also buy on their own turf, either in stores or at corporate headquarters. Finally, buyers can use resident buying offices that prearrange opportunities for buyers to visit vendors in major market centres in North America and abroad. Buyers of fashion apparel and accessory categories typically make major buying decisions five or six times a year, six months before the beginning of a season.

Buyers of staple merchandise replenish the merchandise on a continuous basis. A listing of over 3000 trade shows and market weeks for the fashion industry can be viewed at infomat (www.infomat.com).

Wholesale Market Centres

For many types of merchandise, retailers can do much of their buying in established market centres. Wholesale market centres have permanent vendor sales offices retailers can visit throughout the year. Probably the world's most significant wholesale market centre for many merchandise categories is in New York City. The Fashion Centre, also known as the Garment District, is located from Fifth to Ninth Avenues and from 35th to 41st Streets. An estimated 22 000 apparel buyers visit every year for five market weeks and 65 annual related trade shows. The Garment District has 5100 showrooms and 4500 factories.[20] The Garment District in Toronto is located in the Spadina Avenue and Queen Street West area.

The United States also has a number of regional wholesale market centres. The Dallas Market Centre, the world's largest, is a 7 million square-foot complex of six buildings.[21] Over 26 000 manufacturers and importers display their international products in its 2200 permanent showrooms and 460 000 square feet of temporary spaces. Some regional centres have developed into national markets for specific merchandise categories (for example, the Miami Merchandise Mart for swimwear).

Trade Shows

Many wholesale market centres host trade shows, also known as *merchandise shows* or *market weeks*. Permanent tenants of the wholesale market centres and vendors leasing temporary space participate. Here retailers place orders and get a concentrated view of what's available in the marketplace.

Although the high profile prêt-à-porter (ready to wear) is most obvious in New York, London, Milan, and Paris, Toronto is also quickly becoming an established fashion centre. One of the most anticipated events on Toronto's fashion calendar, the New Labels show, gives new designers the chance to showcase their innovations during the annual Fashion Week events.[22]

Another annual Toronto event is the Canadian Gift and Tableware Association's CGTA Gift Show. It offers attendees a unique, one-stop-shop experience featuring an expansive selection of quality gift products with over 1000 exhibitors displayed in 1 million square feet of space.[23]

Support Services for the Buying Process

Two services available to buyers that can help them more effectively acquire merchandise are resident buying offices and Internet exchanges.

Resident Buying Offices

Resident buying offices are organizations located in major buying centres that provide services to help retailers buy merchandise.

To illustrate how buying offices operate, consider how David Smith, owner of a Canadian prestige menswear store, utilizes his resident buying offices when he goes to market in Milan. Smith meets with market representative Alain Bordat of the Doneger Group, a buying office. Bordat, an English-speaking Italian, knows Smith's store and his upscale customers, so in advance of Smith's visit he sets up appointments with Italian vendors he believes would fit the Canadian store's image.

When Smith is in Italy, Bordat accompanies him to the appointments and acts as translator, negotiator, and accountant. Bordat informs Smith of the cost of importing the merchandise into Canada, taking into account duty, freight, insurance, processing costs, and so forth.

Once the orders are placed, Bordat writes the contracts and follows up on delivery and quality control. The Doneger Group also acts as a home base for buyers like Smith, providing office space and services, travel advisers, and emergency aid. Bordat and his association continue to keep Smith abreast of what's happening on the Italian fashion scene through reports and constant communication. Without the help of a resident buying office, it would be difficult, if not impossible, for Smith to penetrate the Italian wholesale market.

Internet Exchanges

Retail exchanges are providers of Internet-based solutions and services for retailers. The software and services offered by exchanges help retailers, manufacturers, and their trading partners reduce costs and improve efficiency by streamlining and automating sourcing and supply chain processes. They provide an opportunity for vendors and retailers to interact electronically rather than meeting face-to-face in a physical market. Retail exchanges can increase the efficiency of the buying process by offering software to support several of the systems discussed in previous chapters, such as reverse auctions; supply chain management; and collaborative planning, forecasting, and replenishment.

Two major retail exchanges, WorldWide Retail Exchange (WWRE) (http://wwre.globalsources.com) and GlobalNetXchange (GNX) (www.gnx.com), were launched in 2000 as non-profit organizations owned and supported by groups of large retailers. The objective of these exchanges was to promote collaboration between retailers and vendors. They planned to provide a single, central hub that connected trading partners. Retailers would have unlimited access to their vendors' production data, and vendors would have instant access to retailers' sales projections.

The original vision of GNX and WWRE had a number of flaws. First, the exchanges underestimated the technological complexity of building such an exchange. Although some companies such as Walmart and Liz Claiborne had built effective private exchanges, they were designed to connect one trading partner to many, not many to many, as GNX and WWRE envisioned. Second, the cost of the software to provide some services, such as reverse auctions, dropped in price to the point that individual retailers could afford to administer their own reverse auctions. Third, the retail industry is extremely competitive, and retailers are reluctant to share information, preferring instead to keep their data and plans secret.[24]

In 2005, the two exchanges merged. The combined entity includes about 50 food, drug, and apparel retailers, including Carrefour SA, Sears Holdings Corp., Walgreen Co., Kroger Co., and Federated Department Stores Inc. Executives of the newly merged exchanges continue

trade shows
Temporary concentrations of vendors that provide retailers opportunities to place orders and view what is available in the marketplace; also known as a *merchandise show* or *market week*.

retail exchanges
Electronic marketplaces operated by organizations that facilitate the buying and selling of merchandise using the Internet.

to hope that by creating a bigger and more sophisticated marketplace, retailers will be better equipped to face off against Walmart. The combined exchange will facilitate transactions for a retail group with about $1 trillion in combined annual sales.[26]

Using Internet Exchanges to Facilitate Buying

Retailers are exploring many strategies that provide consumers with the tools they need to purchase merchandise and services from them. Retailers also use the Internet for doing research for buying merchandise or services.

One of the most innovative and potentially useful developments stemming from retailers' growing level of sophistication with the Internet is retail exchanges. Retail exchanges are electronic marketplaces operated by organizations that facilitate the buying and selling of merchandise using the Internet. They provide an opportunity for vendors and retailers to interact electronically rather than meet face to face in a physical market. Retail exchanges can increase the efficiency of the buying process by integrating systems such as EDI with the ability to view merchandise and negotiate prices online. Although exchanges will never replace going to markets and interacting with vendors, they now make it possible for buyers to access any type of merchandise information with a mouse click.

Functions of Exchanges Retail exchanges are still evolving. As such, we still do not know which functions or activities will become the most valuable to retailers. Some of the more prominent exchange functions are directory, selection, pricing, collaboration, and content.

Directory No longer do buyers have to wander trade shows or showrooms. Retail exchanges enable them to search for merchandise by vendor or type of product electronically.

Selection Buyers can then narrow the search to a particular vendor. Much of what used to be accomplished in the vendor's showroom can now be done online. Buyers can view individual SKUs. With technology improving

all the time, they can be increasingly confident in the online catalogue's picture quality and colour. To help determine order quantities, buyers can obtain sales history from prior seasons for specific SKUs or for complementary products. Rather than travelling to Paris or Milan, buyers can replay runway fashion shows and obtain 360-degree views of merchandise from the comfort of their offices.

Pricing Retail exchanges utilize several pricing methods. In fact, the same exchange may use more than one pricing method depending on the situation. Merchandise can be offered at a fixed price where everyone pays the same amount. Or, the price of merchandise can be negotiated; in this case, the exchange acts as a broker between vendors and retailers. Finally, merchandise can be auctioned.

In traditional auctions like those conducted by eBay, there is one seller and many buyers. An auction conducted by retailer buyers is called a reverse auction because there is one buyer and many potential sellers. In reverse auctions, retail buyers provide a specification for what they want to a group of potential vendors. The competing vendors then bid down the price at which they are willing to sell until the buyer accepts a bid.[27] However, the retailer is not required to place an order with the lowest bidder. The retailer can choose to place the order at the price of the vendor who the retailer feels will provide the merchandise in a timely manner at the specified quality.

Reverse auctions have not been very popular with vendors. Few want to be anonymous contestants in bidding wars where price alone, not service or quality, is the sole basis for winning the business. Strategic relationships are also difficult to nurture when the primary interactions with vendors are through electronic auctions.[28]

The most common application for reverse auctions is to buy products and services used in retail operations rather than merchandise for resale. For example, a number of retailers worked together to develop a specification for POS terminal paper tape and then pooled their buying power to run a reverse auction and find a low-cost supplier that would meet all of their needs. Other operating materials that are frequently bought on reverse auctions are store carpeting, fixtures, and supplies. Reverse auctions can also be used by retailers to procure private-label merchandise, commodities, and seasonal merchandise such as lawn furniture.

Collaboration Collaboration with vendors on every phase of the production and distribution process may become the most important benefit of retail exchanges. EDI, quick response inventory systems, and CPFR are integral components of retail exchanges.

The fashion world, where a short time period from idea conception to store shelf is a key success factor, stands to benefit significantly from retail exchanges. Although retailers have always provided design input to their vendors, it is the speed and clarity with which collaboration is facilitated with exchanges that is important. Suppose a buyer spots a potentially hot item on the street or in a movie. She snaps a digital picture and sends it simultaneously to a designer in Hong Kong and a fabric supplier in Thailand. The designer works out the specifications for the item, while the supplier sends both parties electronic versions of the fabric. All three parties collaborate on fine-tuning the design and product specifications. Not only does this collaborative effort shorten the lead time to market, but it minimizes the potential for errors.

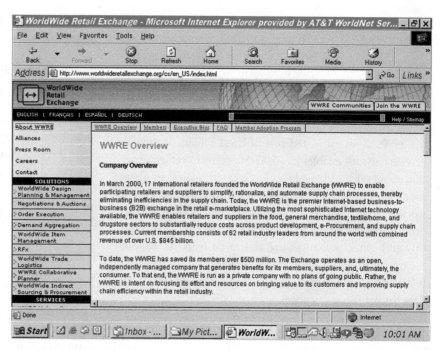

WorldWide Retail Exchange is a consortium exchange owned by retailers and used to facilitate the purchase of goods and services.

Collaboration with other retailers for sourcing merchandise also has potential, but it may be difficult to achieve. Competing retailers aren't used to talking to each other. In fact, antitrust legislation may prohibit them from so doing.

Content   Exchanges can even be an excellent source of general information. Many provide the latest industry news, trends, and fashions.

Types of Exchanges   There are three basic types of exchanges: consortium, private, and independent. These types of exchanges are defined in terms of who owns and operates the exchange.

Consortium Exchanges   A consortium exchange is a retail exchange that is owned by several firms within one industry. A firm must be a member of the consortium to participate in the exchange. The three consortium exchanges are Transora, the WorldWide Retail Exchange, and GlobalNetXchange.

- Transora is a consortium of 50 leading food, beverage, and consumer products companies, including Heinz, Gillette, Coca-Cola, Kraft Foods, Procter & Gamble, Sara Lee, Unilever, NV, and the Grocery Manufacturers of America (the leading trade organization in the grocery industry).

- The WorldWide Retail Exchange is a consortium composed of 61 retailers (not manufacturers), including Ahold (the Netherlands), Albertson's, Best Buy, The Boots Company (U.K.), CVS, The Gap, JCPenney, Target, and Safeway.

- GlobalNetXchange is also a consortium composed of retailers. They include Carrefour (France), Kroger, Metro AG (Germany), J. Sainsbury Plc (U.K), Coles Myer (Australia), Pinault-Printemps-Redoute SA (Europe), and Sears.

consortium exchange   A retail exchange that is owned by several firms within one industry.

private exchanges   Exchanges that are operated for the exclusive use of a single firm.

The potential advantage of these exchanges is that retailers can pool their buying power to get better prices and the fixed cost of developing the software and administering the exchange is shared across member-firms. However, coordinating the activities of different firms, and in some cases competing firms, has been difficult. There are often conflicting agendas among the founding members. Although not all members are in competition with one another, some are, making communication and goal setting complicated.[29] Also, since these exchanges are in competition with one another, companies are hesitant to back one for fear that it might be the wrong one. Finally, several major players have opted out of these consortia: Walmart, Costco, Home Depot, Aldi, Office Depot, and Staples, just to name a few.

Private Exchanges   Private exchanges are exchanges that are operated for the exclusive use of a single firm. Although currently relatively small in number, they represent large players such as Walmart and Dell Computer. These larger companies have the size and scale to develop and operate their own exchanges. For example, Walmart moved its existing information system, Retail Link, to the Internet.[30] Retail Link was built during the 1990s at an estimated cost of US$1 billion. Walmart's private network enables its 10 000 suppliers to get information about sales and inventory levels in every store. Its plans are to use its private exchange to consolidate purchasing worldwide, create global collaboration with its vendors, and bring suppliers online to compete for contracts. Although this and other exchanges are clearly designed to benefit the operator/owner, the vendors benefit from the strategic relationship and immediate access to sales and inventory data for planning purposes, such as CPFR.

Independent Exchanges An independent exchange is a retail exchange owned by a third party that provides the electronic platform to perform the exchange functions. For example, a retailer is interested in running a reverse auction for an air-conditioning system. It contacts an independent exchange such as FreeMarkets. In the previous weeks, the retailer's purchasing agent and prospective suppliers prepare for the auction with the help of FreeMarkets. Now, the purchasing agent and the 12 suppliers log on to a FreeMarkets secure private network, and the bidding begins. Within minutes, the purchasing agent has saved thousands of dollars from its historic spending level. New bids come in every couple of minutes, driving the unit price lower and lower. In the ensuing hours, more than 250 interactive bids are received, saving the retailer more than US$400 000—a 16 percent savings below its historic spending level of US$2.5 million.[31]

Negotiating with Vendors

Negotiations are as basic to human nature as eating or sleeping. A negotiation takes place any time two parties confer with each other to settle some matter. Negotiations take place between parents and their children about issues such as allowances. People negotiate with their friends about what to do on the weekend.

Business negotiations occur daily. People negotiate for higher salaries, better offices, and bigger budgets. Negotiations are crucial in buyers' discussions with vendors.

No one should go into a negotiation without intensive planning. We first provide guidelines for planning negotiations with vendors. Then we discuss some tips for conducting the negotiation face to face.

Guidelines for Planning Negotiations with Vendors

As a vehicle for describing how a buyer should prepare for and conduct a negotiation with a vendor, consider the hypothetical situation in which a men's designer shirt buyer at Sears is preparing to meet with the salesman from Tommy Hilfiger in the office in New York. The Sears buyer is ready to buy Tommy Hilfiger's spring line, but has some merchandising problems yet to be resolved from last season. Let's go over seven general guidelines for planning a negotiation session and for conducting a face-to-face negotiation session.

KNOWLEDGE IS POWER! The more the buyer knows about the vendor, the better his/her negotiating strategy will be.

Consider History Buyers need a sense of what has occurred between the retailer and vendor in the past. Sears and Tommy Hilfiger have had a long, profitable relationship; a sense of trust and mutual respect has been established. An established vendor may be more likely to take care of old problems and accept new demands if a long-term, profitable relationship already exists.

Assess Where Things Are Today Although Tommy Hilfiger shirts have been profitable for Sears in the past, three patterns sold poorly last season. Some vendors believe that once they've sold merchandise to the retailer, their responsibility ends. This is a short-term perspective, however. If the merchandise doesn't sell, a good vendor, like Tommy Hilfiger, will arrange to share the risk of loss. The Sears buyer will ask to return some merchandise or provide markdown money—funds a vendor gives a retailer to cover lost gross margin dollars due to markdowns and other merchandising issues—usually in the form of a credit to the Sears account.

Set Goals Besides taking care of last season's leftover merchandise, the Sears buyer has set goals in six areas for the upcoming meeting: additional markup opportunities, terms of purchase, transportation, delivery and exclusivity, communications, and advertising allowances.

Additional Markup Opportunities Vendors may have excess stock (manufacturers' overruns) due to order cancellations, returned merchandise from retailers, or simply an overly optimistic sales forecast. To move this merchandise, vendors offer it to retailers at lower-than-normal prices. Retailers can then make a higher-than-normal gross margin or pass the savings on to the customer. Since Sears is noted as a popular menswear store, it probably isn't interested in any excess inventory that Tommy Hilfiger has to offer. Off-price retailers such as Winners or Internet retailer Bluefly.com specialize in purchasing manufacturers' overruns (see Retailing View 11.4). Another opportunity for additional markups is with private-label merchandise as previously discussed.

Terms of Purchase   It's advantageous for buyers to negotiate for a long time period in which to pay for merchandise. Long terms of payment improve the firm's cash flow position, lower its liabilities (accounts payable), and can cut its interest expense if it's borrowing money from financial institutions to pay for its inventory. According to the *Competition Act*, however, a vendor can't offer different terms of purchase or prices to different retailers unless the difference can be cost-justified. But buyers would be remiss if they didn't ask for the best terms of purchase available.

Transportation   Transportation costs can be substantial, though this doesn't pose a big problem with the Tommy Hilfiger shirts due to their high unit cost and small size. Nonetheless, the question of who pays for shipping merchandise from vendor to retailer can be a significant negotiating point.

Delivery and Exclusivity   In retailing in general, and in fashion in particular, timely delivery is essential. Being the only retailer in a market to carry certain products helps a retailer hold a fashion lead and achieve a differential advantage. The buyer for Sears wants to be certain that shipment of the new spring line arrives as early in the season as possible, and that some shirt patterns won't be sold to competing retailers.

Communications   Vendors and their representatives are excellent sources of market information. They generally know what is and isn't selling. Providing good, timely information about the market is an indispensable and inexpensive marketing research tool, so the Sears buyer plans to spend at least part of the meeting talking about market trends to the Hilfiger sales representative.

Advertising Allowances   Retailers have the choice of advertising any product in the store. They can sometimes share the cost of advertising through a cooperative arrangement with vendors known as co-op advertising—a program undertaken by a vendor in which the vendor agrees to pay all or part of a pricing promotion. By giving retailers advertising money based on a percentage of purchases, vendors can better represent their product to consumers. Under the *Competition Act,* vendors are allowed to give advertising allowances on an equal basis—the same percentage to everyone—usually based on a percentage of the invoice cost. As a fashion retailer, Sears advertises heavily and would like Tommy Hilfiger to support a number of catalogues with a generous ad allowance.

Know the Vendor's Goals and Constraints   Negotiation can't succeed in the long run unless both parties believe they've won. By understanding what's important to Tommy Hilfiger, the Sears buyer can plan for a successful negotiating session. Generally, vendors are interested in providing a continuous relationship, testing new items, facilitating good communications, and providing a showcase to feature their merchandise.

A Continuous Relationship   Vendors want to make a long-term investment in their retailers. For seasonal merchandise such as men's designer shirts, they have to plan their production in advance, so it's important to Tommy Hilfiger that certain key retailers such as Sears continue their support. The buyer plans to spend some time at the beginning of the meeting reviewing their mutually profitable past and assuring the Tommy Hilfiger sales rep that Sears hopes to continue their relationship.

Testing New Items   There's no better way to test how well a new product will sell than to put it in a store. Retailers are often cautious with new items due to the risk of markdowns and the opportunity cost of not purchasing other, more successful merchandise. Yet vendors need their retailers to provide sales feedback for new items. Sears has always been receptive to some of Tommy Hilfiger's more avant-garde styles. If these styles do well in certain Sears stores, they'll likely succeed in similar stores around the country.

Communication   Just as Tommy Hilfiger can provide market information, Sears can share sales information. Also, the Sears buyer travels the world market and on one buying trip to England, found an attractive scarf, bought the scarf, and gave it to Tommy Hilfiger, who had it copied for a shirt. It was a big success!

Showcase   In certain urban centres—notably Toronto, New York, London, Milan, and Paris—vendors use large stores to showcase their merchandise. For instance, many North American buyers go to market in New York. Most stop at the major retailers to see what's new, what's selling, and how it's displayed.

A good understanding of the legal, managerial, and financial issues that constrain a vendor will facilitate a productive negotiating session. For instance, the Sears buyer should recognize from past experience that Tommy Hilfiger normally doesn't allow merchandise to be returned, but does provide markdown money. If the Hilfiger rep initially says that giving markdown money is against company policy, the Sears buyer will have strong objective ammunition for her position.

Plan to Have at Least As Many Negotiators As the Vendor There's power in numbers. Even if the vendor is more powerful, aggressive, or important in the marketplace, the retailer will have a psychological advantage at the negotiating table if the vendor is outnumbered. At the very least, the negotiating teams should be of equal number. The Sears buyer plans to invite a merchandise manager into the discussion if the Tommy Hilfiger rep comes with a sales manager.

Choose a Good Place to Negotiate The Sears buyer may have an advantage in the upcoming meeting since it will be in the Sears office. The buyer will have everything at her fingertips, such as information plus secretarial and supervisory assistance. From a psychological perspective, people generally feel more comfortable and confident in familiar surroundings. On the other hand, if the negotiation were to be in Hilfiger's office, Sears would be able to learn a lot about the Hilfiger company. In the end, the preferable location for a negotiation is a personal choice.

Be Aware of Real Deadlines To illustrate the importance of deadlines, consider when labour strikes are settled. An agreement is often reached one minute before everyone walks out. There's always pressure to settle a negotiation at the last minute. The Sears buyer recognizes that the Tommy Hilfiger sales rep must go back to the office with an order in hand since there is a quota to meet by the end of the month. The Sears buyer must get markdown money or permission to return the unsold shirts by the end of the week or there will not be sufficient open-to-buy to cover the orders the buyer wishes to place. Recognizing these deadlines will help Sears come to a decisive closure in the upcoming negotiation.

Establishing and Maintaining Strategic Relationships with Vendors

LO4

Maintaining strong vendor relationships is an important method of developing a sustainable competitive advantage. In previous chapters, we discussed some of the ways partnering relations can improve information, exchange,

planning, and the management of supply chains. For example, electronic data interchange could not be accomplished without the vendor and retailer making a commitment to work together and have a trusting relationship. In the same way, category management using category captains and CPFR (collaborative planning, forecasting, and replenishment) would be impossible without partnering relationships. In this section, we examine how retailers can develop strategic relationships and the characteristics of a successful long-term relationship.

Defining Strategic Relationships

Relationships between retailers and vendors are often based on arguing over splitting up a profit pie.[32] This is basically a win–lose relationship because when one party gets a larger portion of the pie, the other party gets a smaller portion. Both parties are interested exclusively in their own profits and are unconcerned about the other party's welfare. These relationships are common when the products are commodities and have no major impact on the retailers' performance. Thus, there is no benefit to the retailer to entering into a strategic relationship.

A strategic relationship, also called a *partnering relationship*, exists when a retailer and vendor are committed to maintaining the relationship over the long term and investing in opportunities that are mutually beneficial to the parties. In these relationships, it's important for the partners to put their money where their mouth is. They've taken risks to expand the pie—to give the relationship a strategic advantage over other companies.

Thus, a strategic relationship is a win–win relationship. Both parties benefit because the size of the pie has increased—both the retailer and vendor increase their sales and profits. Strategic relationships are created explicitly to uncover and exploit joint opportunities. Members in strategic relationships depend on and trust each other heavily; they share goals and agree on how to accomplish those goals; and they're willing to take risks, share confidential information, and make significant investments for the sake of the relationship.

A strategic relationship is like a marriage. When businesses enter strategic relationships, they're wedded to their partners for better or worse. For example, the U.K.'s Marks & Spencer had jointly developed a kitchen product with a vendor.[33] Four months after the product's introduction, the manufacturer realized that it had miscalculated the product's cost and, as a result, had underpriced the product and was losing money on the deal. It was a big hit at Marks & Spencer because it was underpriced. Marks & Spencer decided not to raise the price because the product was already listed in its catalogue. Instead, it helped the vendor re-engineer the product at a lower cost, cut its own gross margin, and gave that money to the manufacturer. It took a profit hit to maintain the relationship.

Maintaining Strategic Relationships

The four foundations of successful strategic relationships are mutual trust, open communication, common goals, and credible commitments.

Mutual Trust The glue in strategic relationships is trust. Trust is a belief that a partner is honest (reliable, stands by its word, sincere, fulfills obligations) and is benevolent (concerned about the other party's welfare).[34] When vendors and buyers trust each other, they're more willing to share relevant ideas, clarify goals and problems, and communicate efficiently. Information shared between the parties becomes increasingly comprehensive, accurate, and timely. There's less need for the vendor and buyer to constantly monitor and check up on each other's actions because each believes the other won't take advantage, given the opportunity.[35]

Strategic relationships and trust are often developed initially between the leaders of organizations. For example, when Walmart started to work with Procter & Gamble to coordinate its buying activities, Sam Walton got together with P&G's vice-president of sales on a canoeing trip. They discussed the mutual benefits of cooperating and the potential risks associated with altering their normal business practices. In the end, they must have concluded that the potential long-term gains were worth the additional risks and short-term setbacks that would probably occur as they developed the new systems.

Open Communication In order to share information, develop sales forecasts together, and coordinate deliveries, Walmart and P&G have to have open and honest communication. This may sound easy in principle, but most businesses don't like to share information with their business partners. They believe it is none of the other's concern. But open, honest communication is a key to developing successful relationships. Buyers and vendors in a relationship need to understand what's driving each other's business, their roles in the relationship, each firm's strategies, and any problems that arise over the course of the relationship.

Common Goals Vendors and buyers must have common goals for a successful relationship to develop. Shared goals give both members of the relationship incentive to pool their strengths and abilities and to exploit potential opportunities between them. There's also assurance that the other partner won't do anything to hinder goal achievement within the relationship.

For example, Walmart and P&G recognized that it was in their common interest to remain business partners—they needed each other—and to do so, both had to be allowed to make profitable transactions. Walmart can't demand prices so low that P&G can't make money, and P&G must be flexible enough to accommodate the needs of its biggest customer. With a common goal, both firms have incentive to cooperate because they know that by doing so, each can boost sales.

Common goals also help to sustain the relationship when expected benefit flows aren't realized. If one P&G shipment fails to reach a Walmart store on time due to an unfortunate event such as misrouting by a trucking firm, Walmart won't suddenly call off the whole arrangement. Instead, Walmart is likely to view the incident as a simple mistake and will remain in the relationship; this is because Walmart and P&G are committed to the same goals in the long run.

Credible Commitments Successful relationships develop because both parties make credible commitments to the relationship. Credible commitments are tangible investments in the relationship. They go beyond just making the hollow statement "I want to be a partner." Credible commitments involve spending money to improve the supplier's products or services provided to the customer.[36] For example, one of the strengths of the Walmart/P&G partnership is the obvious and significant investments both parties have made in EDI systems, CPFR forecasting systems, and material handling equipment.

Building Partnering Relationships

Although not all retailer–vendor relationships should or do become strategic partnerships, the development of strategic partnerships tends to go through a series of phases characterized by increasing levels of commitment:

- **Awareness.** No transactions have taken place. This phase might begin with the buyer seeing some interesting merchandise at a retail market or in an ad in a trade magazine. Reputation and image of the vendor

trust A belief that a partner is honest (reliable, stands by its word, sincere, fulfills obligations) and is benevolent (concerned about the other party's welfare).

DID YOU KNOW?

The population of Bentonville, Arkansas, the corporate headquarters for Walmart, is 17 000, with 7000 of these people working for Walmart. Another 7000 people representing vendors call on Walmart every month. More than 100 companies that are suppliers to Walmart have opened offices in Bentonville, including Hewlett-Packard, Clorox, Nabisco, and Procter & Gamble.[37]

DID YOU KNOW?

Walmart Canada has partnered with New York–based Mint-X Corp to introduce Great Value Mint-X Raccoon Repellent Garbage Bags.[38]

can play an important role in determining if the buyer moves to the next stage.

- **Exploration.** The buyer and vendor begin to explore the potential benefits and costs. At this point, the buyer may make a small purchase and try to test the demand for the merchandise in several stores. In addition, the buyer will get information about how easy it is to work with the vendor.

- **Expansion.** The buyer has collected enough information about the vendor to consider developing a longer-term relationship. The buyer and the vendor determine that there is a potential for a win–win relationship. They begin to work on joint promotional programs, and the amount of merchandise sold increases.

- **Commitment.** Both parties continue to find the relationship mutually beneficial, and it moves to the commitment stage and becomes a strategic relationship. The buyer and vendor make significant investments in the relationship and develop a long-term perspective toward it.

It is difficult for retailer–vendor relationships to be as committed as some supplier–manufacturer relationships. Manufacturers can enter into monogamous (sole source) relationships with other manufacturers. However, an important function of retailers is to provide an assortment of merchandise for their customers. Thus, they must always deal with multiple, sometimes competing suppliers. Regardless of which partner-building phase a retailer is in with a supplier, it is constantly involved in the give-and-take process of negotiations.

Legal and Ethical Issues for Buying Merchandise*

Given the many negotiations and interactions between retail buyers and vendors, ethical and legal issues are bound to arise. In this section, we'll view ethical and legal issues from both retailers' and vendors' perspectives (see, for example, Retailing View 11.3 for a discussion of socially responsible buying). The most fundamental question is whether a retailer and vendor have a binding contract for a particular transaction. If they do, the next question is how to resolve disputes under that contract. In addition, retailers should not take advantage of their position of power in the marketing channel. In this regard, we'll examine chargebacks, commercial bribery, slotting allowances, buybacks, and category management.

To protect their customers' interests and their own reputation, retailers must be cognizant of whether the merchandise is counterfeit or from the diverted market (the grey market). Vendors aren't likely to become legally entangled with their retailers so long as they sell to whoever wants to buy, sell whatever they want, and sell at the same price to all. But since most vendors don't want to be this free with their merchandise, we'll look at exclusive territories, exclusive dealing agreements, tying contracts, and refusals to deal.

Contract Disputes

Contract formation in the retail context is usually straightforward. The retailer places an order with a vendor that in most cases the vendor accepts. This creates a binding mutual obligation for the vendor to deliver the promised goods in exchange for the retailer agreeing to pay the specified price. Disputes arise when one party does not perform or when the parties disagree about details of the transaction such as the precise specifications of the goods.

Most retailers and vendors are more interested in continuing sales relationships than expensive litigation over legal rights. For this reason, many disputes are simply settled by negotiation and agreement between the two parties. It is common to include alternative dispute resolution provisions in contracts. Such provisions can include methods of settling the dispute that the parties agree upon, such as mediation, arbitration, or med-arb. Mediation involves selecting a neutral mediator to assist the parties in reaching a mutually agreeable settlement. Arbitration involves the appointment of an arbitrator who considers the arguments of both sides and then makes a decision that is usually agreed upon in advance as binding. Med-arb involves an initial attempt at mediation followed by binding arbitration if the mediation is unsuccessful. Overworked courts routinely enforce alternative dispute resolution contract provisions in the United States.

* This section was developed with the assistance of Professor Ross Petty, Babson College.

Retailers Buy Socially Responsible Products

Corporate social responsibility describes the voluntary actions taken by a company to address the ethical, social, and environmental impacts of its business operations. Retailers act socially responsible in many ways, from giving to charity, to donating time, to participating in philanthropic community activities. Recently, however, retailers have been increasing their efforts to buy merchandise in a socially responsible way.

Loblaw Companies chains, including Zehrs, Loblaws, Fortinos, Valu-Mart, Real Canadian Superstore, and Your Independent Grocer stores, led the growing movement in 2007 toward buying local and satisfying consumer demand when it came to sourcing its food with its "Ontario Grown-Picked at its Peak" program. Approximately 40 percent of produce in Loblaw stores is locally sourced during July and August. The produce program has had a positive impact on local economies and has helped to revive and support Ontario's family farms. In 2011, the Loblaw group introduced a new "Ontario corn-fed beef" label to identify local meat. The multi-year deal with the Ontario Cattle Feeders' Association saw beef from 500 Ontario cattle farms hitting the shelves, up from roughly 240 Ontario cattle farmers who were previously dealing with the company. Organic waste collected from select corporate stores in Ontario are sent to biogas facilities to generate renewable energy, while eight Quebec stores send their organic waste to local farms to be converted into compost material. Loblaw also has a goal to reduce non-recyclable packaging in its own private-label brand products by 50 percent by year-end 2013. Also, since 2007, the company has reduced the number of shopping bags from its stores by 2.5 billion, and reported a 73 percent reduction in shopping-bag use nationwide in 2010.

Some retailers are getting involved in fair trade, a socially responsible movement that ensures that producers receive fair prices for their products. The coffee retailers Starbucks and Timothy's offer some, but not all, blends that use fair-trade coffee. Walmart is investing heavily in fair-trade coffee, partially in response to a new corporate philosophy that goes beyond "everyday low prices" to "doing well by doing good." Bono, the U2 lead singer and an activist, is selling his high-priced fair-trade apparel line, Edun, to stores such as Holt Renfrew and Nordstrom. An independent study conducted in 2011 found that "Canadians express strong (and increasing) expectations of companies to act responsibly in poor countries. Nine in ten Canadians (91 percent) now expect companies to pay farmers/workers fairly, more than in previous years." There is also a strong consensus among consumers (71 percent) that third-party certification, such as that provided by the fair-trade system, is the best way to verify a product's claims.

Rona's wood products procurement policy gives preference to suppliers that offer sustainably sourced lumber. Since the end of 2010, all of the softwood lumber sold by Rona has been from certified forests. Further, Rona has created an online eco-responsible renovation guide that identifies for its customers a range of building materials, products, and processes, as well as an environmental life-cycle analysis.

Home Depot is encouraging its suppliers to apply to include their products in its Eco Options marketing campaign. Some products are obviously attractive to green customers, such as organic gardening products and high-efficiency light bulbs. But a number of less obvious products are also good for the environment. Electric chainsaws are green, because they are not gas-powered, and bug zappers reduce the use of poisonous sprays. Home Depot also has introduced some new environmentally sensitive products into its assortment, including solar-powered landscape lighting, biodegradable peat pots, and paints that discharge fewer pollutants. Home Depot encourages its vendors to use recyclable plastic or cardboard packaging. It estimates that a 5 per-cent reduction in packaging will prevent 667 000 metric tonnes of carbon dioxide from entering the atmosphere while also resulting in $3.4 billion in cost savings.

McDonald's Eco-Filter global packaging scorecard takes environmental considerations into account in its packaging choices. The Eco-Filter uses criteria such as packaging-weight reduction and use of recycled materials into its evaluation. Working with the World Wildlife Fund, McDonald's "Sustainable Land Management Commitment" requires suppliers to source raw materials, such as beef and palm oil, from certified sustainable sources. McDonald's Europe has helped persuade agribusiness giants to stop buying soybeans from newly deforested tracts in protected regions in the Amazon.

H&M (Hennes & Mauritz AB) has a goal of sourcing 100 percent of cotton from sustainable sources by 2020, which is considered to be an ambitious goal in the apparel sector. To reach this goal, H&M is actively involved in the Better Cotton Initiative (BCI). The BCI is a multi-stakeholder initiative that develops and promotes good farm practices, allowing more cotton to be grown while reducing water and chemical use and protecting both working conditions and biodiversity. In 2009, H&M began to investigate water-conscious denim production. Trials showed that process optimization could deliver water savings of up to 30 percent. In 2010, they produced denim following the approach on a greater scale and achieved water savings of approximately 50 million litres relative to previous production methods. In 2012, these techniques reduced water usage by an estimated 450 million litres compared to conventional production processes. By the end of 2011, H&M phased out 12 types of clothing hangers, replacing them with multi-function hangers to reduce waste—85 percent of its non-reusable hangers have been recycled.

A first-of-its-kind sales floor LED lighting retrofit to all of the overhead sales floor lighting was completed at the Brampton North Walmart Supercentre in Ontario. Completed by Canadian EcoLight LED Systems Corp., the retrofit involved changing close to 6000 lamps from traditional 25-watt fluorescent high efficiency lamps to 18-watt LED lights, reducing energy usage for store lighting by 28 percent. It is estimated that this small change could save approximately 283 000 kilowatt hours (kWh) per year, which will result in a savings of up to $26 000 per year.

These initiatives and many others suggest a complicated business model. Are socially responsible activities good for business? Some are more expensive than traditional products and initiatives. In the end, should retailers force more socially responsible products on their customers, or should they wait for customers to ask for them?

Sources: Jantzi-Sustainalytics, "Top 50 socially responsible corporations," *Maclean's*, June 9, 2011, www2.macleans.ca/2011/06/09/better-business (accessed December 9, 2013); "Loblaw Loves Local!" CNW, news release, July 28, 2007, www.newswire.ca/en/story/124827/loblaw-loves-local (accessed December 9, 2013); Josh Rubin, "Loblaws beefs up local content," *Toronto Star*, May 25, 2011, www.thestar.com/business/2011/05/25/loblaws_beefs_up_local_content.html (accessed December 9, 2013); "Shopping Choices Can Make a Positive Difference to Farmers and Workers in Developing Countries: Global Poll," GlobeScan, October 11, 2011, http://www.globescan.com/commentary-andanalysis/press-releases/press-releases-2011.html (accessed December 9, 2013); "Cotton," H&M website, n.d., http://about.hm.com/AboutSection/en/About/Sustainability/Commitments/Use-Resources-Responsibly/Raw-Materials/Cotton.html (accessed December 9, 2013); "Walmart Canada – LED Sales Floor Retrofit," ShareGreen.ca, January 15, 2013, www.sharegreen.ca/case-study/walmart-canada-led-sales-floor-retrofit (accessed December 9, 2013).

Chargebacks

chargeback A practice used by retailers in which they deduct money from the amount they owe a vendor.

commercial bribery A vendor's offer of money or gifts to a retailer's employee for the purpose of influencing purchasing decisions.

A chargeback is a practice used by retailers in which they deduct money from the amount they owe a vendor. There are two reasons for a chargeback. The first occurs when the retailer deducts money from an invoice because merchandise isn't selling. The second reason is vendor mistakes such as shoddy labelling, lost billings, wrong-size boxes or hangers, missing items, and late shipments. Although often legitimate contract disputes, chargebacks are frequently viewed as being unjustified by vendors. Retailers can use chargebacks as a profit centre. For instance, one senior executive at a large department store chain was told to collect US$50 million in chargebacks.[39] What makes chargebacks especially difficult for vendors is that once the money is deducted from an invoice, and the invoice is "paid," it is difficult to get the missing amount back, and negotiations or threats of litigation often appear to fall on deaf ears.

Commercial Bribery

Commercial bribery occurs in retailing when a vendor or its agent offers to privately give or pay a retail buyer "something of value" to influence purchasing decisions. Say a sweater manufacturer takes a department store buyer to lunch at a private club and then proposes a ski weekend in Banff. The buyer enjoys the lunch but graciously turns down the ski trip. These gifts could be construed as bribes or kickbacks, which are illegal unless the buyer's manager is informed of them (and is also not receiving private payments or gifts). In fact, the government doesn't allow money paid for bribes to be deducted as a business expense. From an ethical perspective, there's a fine line between the social courtesy of a free lunch and an elaborate free vacation.

To avoid these problems, many companies forbid employees from accepting any gifts from vendors. They want their buyers to decide on purchases based solely on what is best for the retailer. One major U.S. discount store chain specifically forbids the taking of "bribes, commissions, kickbacks, payments, loans, gratuities, or other solicitations, including any item of value from suppliers to the company." But many companies have no policy against receiving gifts, and some unethical employees accept and even solicit gifts, even if their company has a policy against it. A good rule of thumb is to accept only limited entertainment or token gifts, such as flowers or a bottle of wine, for Christmas, birthdays, or other occasions. When the gift or favour is perceived to be large enough to influence a buyer's purchasing behaviour, it's considered to be commercial bribery and therefore is illegal.

Slotting Allowances

A slotting allowance, also called a *slotting fee* when viewed from the vendor's perspective, is a fee paid by a vendor for space in a retail store.[40] They differ from commercial bribes in that they are made to the retailer itself rather than to an individual buyer. This is considered to be a legal form of competition among vendors for shelf space in Canada.

Here's an example. When Kraft or any other consumer package goods manufacturer wants to introduce a new product, it often pays a slotting allowance to grocery and discount store chains for the space (slot) on the shelf. The fee varies depending on the nature of the product and the relative power of the retailer. Products whose brand names command relatively low customer loyalty pay the highest slotting allowances. Likewise, large grocery chains can demand higher slotting allowances than small, independent stores. Industry reports estimate the total amount spent on slotting fees in the United States to be around US$16 billion per year.[41] The per-item store costs are estimated to be $3000 to $40 000.[42] At that rate, it may cost US$1 million or more to get national distribution of a new product!

Slotting fees are not only present in the food industry. They are becoming prevalent in other retail venues, such as those that sell over-the-counter drugs, apparel, magazines, and computer software. In the music industry, for instance, retailers regularly charge vendors for the right to display and sell their merchandise.

Some retailers argue that slotting allowances are a reasonable method for ensuring that their valuable space is used efficiently. Such fees cover their costs of adding a new SKU to their computerized system of inventory, knowing that most new products fail and the SKU must later also be removed.

As part of a program to develop strategic relationships, some manufacturers avoid slotting allowances by working closely with retail stores and sharing the financial risk of new products. For instance, Walmart reportedly refuses to charge slotting allowances, preferring instead to have vendors participate in its centralized purchasing system.[43]

Concerns with slotting allowances arise when a dominant firm uses them to exclude rivals. If a dominant vendor pays large slotting fees that rivals cannot match, then the fees may have the effect of limiting competition among vendors. This may be particularly true when the vendor pays to obtain the best retail display space or to limit the space available to rivals.[44] Similarly, retail competition may be injured when large retailers extract much larger slotting allowances than those available to smaller retailers, giving the large firms a cost advantage.[45]

Buybacks

Similar to slotting allowances, the buyback, also known as a *stocklift* or *lift-out*, is a strategy vendors and retailers use to get products into retail stores. Specifically, a buyback can occur under two scenarios. The first and most ethically troubling is when a retailer allows a vendor to create space for its goods by "buying back" a competitor's inventory and removing it from a retailer's system. In the second case, the retailer forces a vendor to buy back slow-moving merchandise.

Consider the following buyback scenario. At a national home improvement store chain, thousands of garden gloves manufactured by the store's main source of supply vanished almost overnight. The empty shelves were restocked with gloves made by another glove manufacturer. The second manufacturer purchased all of the original gloves in stock so it could fill the shelves with its own product. The purchased gloves were probably dumped into a sprawling underground pipeline for resale by faraway, perhaps foreign, retailers. There are about a half-dozen companies that provide buyback-type liquidation services.

Are buybacks illegal? Technically, a company with market power may violate laws if it stocklifts from a competitor so often as to shut it out of a market. But such cases brought under the *Competition Act* are difficult to prove.

Counterfeit Merchandise

Counterfeit merchandise includes goods made and sold without the permission of the owner of a trademark, a copyright, or a patented invention that is legally protected in the country where it is marketed. Trademarks, copyrights, and patents are all under the general umbrella of intellectual property. Intellectual property is intangible

---

slotting allowance Fee paid by a vendor for space in a retail-store; also called a *slotting fee*.

buyback A strategy vendors and retailers use to get products into retail stores, either when a retailer allows a vendor to create space for goods by "buying back" a competitor's inventory and removing it from a retailer's system, or when the retailer forces a vendor to buy back slow-moving merchandise; also called *stocklift* or *lift-out*.

counterfeit merchandise Goods that are made and sold without permission of the owner of a trademark, a copyright, or a patented invention that is legally protected in the country where it is marketed.

intellectual property Property that is intangible and is created by intellectual (mental) effort as opposed to physical effort.

DID YOU KNOW?

The RCMP conducted more than 400 investigations into counterfeit goods each year across the country, while Canadian industry estimates the knockoffs cost it as much as $30 billion annually.[46]

DID YOU KNOW?

Grey markets are significant as they now exceed $10 billion per year in North America and affect almost every major trademarked product. Grey markets are growing at more than 22 percent annually.[47]

and is created by intellectual (mental) effort as opposed to physical effort. A trademark is any mark, word, picture, device, or nonfunctional design associated with certain merchandise (for instance, the crown on a Rolex watch and the GE on General Electric products). A copyright protects original work of authors, painters, sculptors, musicians, and others who produce works of artistic or intellectual merit. The copyright protects only the physical expression of the effort, not the idea. This book is copyrighted, so these sentences cannot be used by anyone without the consent of the copyright owners. However, anyone can take the ideas in this book and express them in different words. The owner of a patent controls the right to make, sell, and use a product for a period of 20 years or a design for 14 years.

The nature of counterfeiting has changed over the past decade. Although manufacturers of high-visibility, strong-brand-name consumer goods are still tormented by counterfeiters, there's now a thriving business in counterfeit high-tech products such as software, CDs, and CD-ROMs. For instance, some experts believe that the software publishing and distribution industries lose almost US$12 billion a year.[48] Why is this type of merchandise so attractive to counterfeiters? It has a high unit value, is relatively easy to duplicate and transport, and has high consumer demand. For instance, suppose *Retailing Management* were available on a CD-ROM. It could be easily duplicated as a CD or reprinted as a book for a few dollars in a foreign country. Neither the publishers nor the authors would receive any money. In fact, it's likely that they wouldn't even know about the copyright infringement.

Retailers and their vendors have four avenues to pursue to protect themselves against the ravages of counterfeiting and intellectual property rights violations: product registration, legislative action, bilateral and multilateral negotiations, and measures taken by companies.[49]

First, the product must be trademarked, copyrighted, or patented in the countries in which it's sold. Unfortunately,

registration in Canada provides no protection in another country, although treaties and other international agreements allow for prompt and easy registration in other countries based on initial registration in Canada.

The second method of protection is through legislative action. Several laws protect businesses against counterfeiting. Counterfeiting is a criminal rather than a civil offence.

Third, the Canadian government is engaged in bilateral and multilateral negotiations and education to limit counterfeiting. For instance, the WTO has rules on intellectual property protection.

Finally, companies are aggressively taking steps to protect themselves. The International Anti-Counterfeiting Coalition is a group of 375 firms that lobbies for strong legal sanctions worldwide. Individual companies are also taking an aggressive stance against counterfeiting.

Grey-Market and Diverted Merchandise

A grey-market good is merchandise that possesses a valid North American registered trademark and is made by a foreign manufacturer but is imported into North America without permission of the trademark owner. Grey-market merchandise is not counterfeit. This merchandise often is the same quality and may actually be identical to merchandise brought into the country through normal channels.

Selling grey-market merchandise may be legal in the United States. Recently, the Supreme Court ruled that American manufacturers cannot stop discount stores from buying North American products overseas and selling them domestically at reduced prices if the foreign manufacturer and domestic trademark owner fall under a common corporate umbrella.[50] Interestingly, the European Court of Justice decided to allow grey-market imports only from one member-state to another but not from outside the European Union.[51]

Without realizing it, we see grey-market goods in the marketplace all the time. Some manufacturers of cars, jewellery, perfume, liquor, watches, cameras, crystal ware, ski equipment, tractors, baby powder, and batteries are all involved in grey marketing in the United States.

Here's an example of how the grey market for watches might work in the United States. To help create a prestigious image, to offset an unfavourable exchange rate, and to pad profit margins, Swiss watch manufacturers often charge a higher wholesale price in the United States than in Europe and other countries. A Swiss watchmaker such as Patek Philippe may sell 1000 watches to a retailer in Italy, whose price is about 30 percent less than an authorized retailer in the United States. The Italian retailer sells several of the more expensive watches that are slow sellers to a grey-market (unauthorized) retailer

Where Did T.J. Maxx Get Its Coach Handbags?

The national brands that off-price retailers like T.J. Maxx, Marshalls, Winners, Ross, and Loehmann's sell at lower prices than their department and specialty store competition come from a variety of sources. Sometimes the merchandise comes directly from manufacturers like Coach, the luxury leather goods maker, because the item was last year's model, it didn't sell well at retail and was returned by its luxury retail customer, or Coach overestimated demand and therefore had excess inventory leftover. Coach in particular sells less than 1 percent of its bags to off-price stores. Although luxury manufacturers prefer not to have their merchandise sold in off-price stores, having these off-price stores provides· an excellent opportunity to rid the luxury manufacturers of excess inventory.

Another source of Coach bags for off-price retailers may be luxury retailers. These retailers may have bought too many bags or specific styles that did not sell and need to dispose of them at the end of a season. One alternative is for the retailers to mark down the price and put the handbags on sale. But sales on luxury products like Coach bags might damage the retailer's image. Also, Coach may not want their bags sold at a discount at luxury stores. So, the retailer

might sell the excess inventory to off-price retailers like T.J. Maxx. This diverting of merchandise to an unauthorized retailer is creating a grey market for the Coach bags. If Coach discovers that one of its luxury retailers is diverting its newer merchandise to off-price retailers, it might refuse to sell to the retailer in the future.

Luxury brands' vendors hope that their products don't end up in off-price outlets, but they definitely fight to make sure that counterfeit products are not sold anywhere. While it is relatively harmless for grey-market luxury, branded products to end up in an off-price store, it is quite harmful to the luxury brands if a counterfeit bag is sold in a Walmart store.

Since the sale of counterfeit goods is illegal. Luxury brand vendors are taking steps to ensure that national retailers will not partake in their sale. Coach recently sued Target for selling counterfeit Coach bags in its stores. Similarly, the luxury conglomerate, LVMH, sued Walmart Stores for selling fake Fendi bags in its stores. In both of these cases, the vendors are very concerned that the image of their products will be damaged by having counterfeit merchandise sold in a discount store. Although it has not been confirmed as to whether these products were authentic or not, the publicity surrounding these lawsuits raise the question in consumers' minds as to whether luxury brands sold in discount stores such as Walmart and Target are real.

Off-price stores like T.J. Maxx regularly sell grey-market, but not counterfeit, merchandise.

in the United States. Both the Italian and U.S. retailers can make a profit, and the watches can still be sold to a U.S. customer significantly below the manufacturer's suggested retail price (MSRP).

Diverted merchandise is similar to grey-market merchandise except there need not be distribution across international boundaries. Suppose, for instance, fragrance manufacturer Givenchy grants an exclusive territory to all Hudson's Bay stores. A discount store in Toronto purchases Givenchy products from a wholesale distributor in Las Vegas and sells it for 20 percent below the suggested retail price. The merchandise is diverted from its legitimate channel of distribution, and the wholesaler in this case would be referred to as a diverter.

Some discount store operators argue that customers benefit from the lack of restriction on grey-market and diverted goods because it lowers prices. Competition with retailers selling grey-market and diverted merchandise forces authorized dealers to cut their prices.

Traditional retailers, on the other hand, claim grey-market and diverted merchandise has a negative impact on the public. They believe that important after-sale service will be unavailable through retailers of grey-market or diverted goods, because they do not have adequate training or access to appropriate replacement parts. They also think that a less expensive grey-market or diverted product may hurt the trademark's image. Importantly, the grey-market product may be an out-of-date model or not work properly in a different country. For example, Philip Morris makes cartons of Marlboro cigarettes in the United States earmarked for foreign markets where prices are lower. These cigarettes often carry warning labels that are different from the required U.S. Surgeon General's message. Further, the packages and formulation may be different as well.[52]

Vendors wishing to avoid the grey-market problem have several remedies. First, they can require all of their retail and wholesale customers to sign a contract stipulating that they will not engage in grey marketing. If a retailer is found in violation of the agreement, the vendor will refuse to deal with it in the future. Another strategy is to produce different versions of products for different markets. For instance, a camera manufacturer could sell the same camera in the United States and the European Union but with different names and warranties. This strategy would not prevent the European product from being sold in the United States. But distinctive packaging, design, instructions, and other features may discourage its sale.

Exclusive Territories

As noted in the diverted goods example above, vendors often grant exclusive geographic territory to retailers so that no other retailer in the territory can sell a particular brand. These territorial arrangements can benefit vendors by assuring them that "quality" retailers represent their products. In cases of limited supply, providing an exclusive territory to one retailer helps ensure that enough inventory can be carried to make a good presentation and offer the customer an adequate selection. For instance, by granting exclusive territories, the luxury Ferrari Automobile Company gives its dealers a monopoly for its products—a strong incentive to push Ferrari products. The dealers know there will be no competing retailers to cut prices, so their profit margins are protected. The retailer with an exclusive territory has the incentive to carry more inventory; use extra advertising, personal selling, and sales promotions; provide special displays and display areas; and develop special services for customers. The courts have tended to hold exclusive territories legal unless they restrict competition. Competition is restricted when other retailers have no access to similar products. For example, having exclusive Ferrari dealers wouldn't be a restraint of trade since other luxury cars are readily available to the public. On the other hand, if

De Beers, the South African diamond cartel, granted exclusive territories to certain jewellery retailers, this would probably be seen as a restraint of trade because diamonds wouldn't be readily available through other sources and the De Beers dealers would not compete directly against each other because of their exclusive territories.

Exclusive Dealing Agreements

An exclusive dealing agreement occurs when a manufacturer or wholesaler restricts a retailer to carrying only its products and nothing from competing vendors. Again, the effect on competition determines these contracts' legality. For instance, suppose a retailer signs an agreement with Lee to sell only its jeans. There's no real harm done to competition because other manufacturers have many alternative retail outlets, and Lee's market share isn't large enough to approach monopolistic levels.

Tying Contracts

A tying contract exists when a vendor and a retailer enter into an agreement that requires the retailer to take a product it doesn't necessarily desire (the *tied product*) to ensure that it can buy a product it does desire (the *tying product*). Tying contracts are illegal if they may substantially lessen competition or tend to create a monopoly, but the complaining party has the burden of proof. For example, a postcard jobber sued a postcard manufacturer for requiring that it purchase as many "local view" postcards as it did licensed Disney character postcards. The postcard manufacturer was the sole source for licensed Disney character postcards. The court dismissed the tying case because the jobber failed to prove a substantial lessening of competition.[53]

Refusal to Deal

The practice of refusing to deal (buy from or sell to) can be viewed from both suppliers' and retailers' perspectives.

Generally, both suppliers and retailers have the right to deal or refuse to deal with anyone they choose. But there are exceptions to this general rule when there's evidence of anti-competitive conduct by one or more firms wielding market power.

A manufacturer may refuse to sell to a particular retailer, but it can't do so for the sole purpose of benefiting a competing retailer. For example, Mattel decided not to offer certain popular Barbie packages to wholesale clubs. This action in itself would have been legal. However, it was determined that Mattel agreed to do so as part of a conspiracy among ten toy manufacturers orchestrated by Toys "R" Us to prevent wholesale clubs from underselling the same toy packages that Toys "R" Us sells. The refusal to deal then became an illegal group boycott. After the U.S. Federal Trade Commission enjoined this conspiracy, the ten toy manufacturers agreed to settle private antitrust lawsuits by distributing money to states for children's charities and distributing toys directly to children's charities such as Toys for Tots.[54]

In summary, any time two parties interact, there's a potential for ethical and legal problems. Buyers face issues such as how much to charge a vendor for shelf space in their stores or whether they should accept a gift or favour from a vendor with no strings attached. An eye toward fairness and the desire to maintain a strong relationship should dictate behaviour in these areas. Retailers must also be concerned with the origin of their merchandise. Specifically, is it counterfeit or grey-market merchandise? Vendors encounter a different set of issues. In general, vendors need not worry about legal problems when selling to retailers so long as they sell whatever the retailers want, to whoever wants to buy, at the same price to all. But when vendors start making restrictions and exceptions, there may be legal violations.

exclusive dealing agreement Restriction a manufacturer or wholesaler places on a retailer to carry only its products and no competing vendors' products.

tying contract An agreement between a vendor and a retailer requiring the retailer to take a product it does not necessarily desire (the tied product) to ensure that it can buy a product it does desire (the tying product).

SUMMARY

Retail buying involves various issues, including determining a retailer's branding strategy, sourcing objectives, and vendor relationship strategies. The reality is that the bigger the retailer, the more buying clout it wields in dealing with suppliers. Long-term vendor relationships are created to establish a win–win situation that will develop a sustainable competitive advantage for both parties involved. To survive, retailers must be able to count on a predictable supply of merchandise at competitive prices and with sufficient promotional support.

Retailers can purchase either manufacturers' brands or private-label brands. Each type has its own relative advantages. Choosing brands and a branding strategy is an integral component of a firm's merchandise and assortment planning process.

A large percentage of the merchandise we buy is manufactured outside of Canada. The decision to buy from domestic manufacturers or source internationally is a complicated one. The cost, managerial, and ethical issues surrounding global sourcing decisions were discussed. Buyers and their merchandise managers have several opportunities to meet with vendors, view new merchandise, and place orders. They can utilize Internet exchanges or visit their vendors at wholesale market centres such as Toronto, New York, Paris, or Milan. Virtually every merchandise category has at least one annual trade show at which retailers and vendors meet. Buyers often meet with vendors on their own turf—in the retail store or corporate offices. Finally, meetings with vendors are facilitated by resident buying offices. Market representatives of these resident buying offices facilitate merchandising purchases in foreign markets.

Retailers should prepare for and conduct negotiations with vendors. Successful vendor relationships depend on planning for and being adept at negotiations.

Retailers that can successfully team up with their vendors can achieve a sustainable competitive advantage. There needs to be more than just a promise to buy and sell on a regular basis. Strategic relationships require trust, shared goals, strong communications, and a financial commitment.

With thousands of annual transactions taking place between retailers and their vendors, there's plenty of room for ethical and legal problems. The issues of charging vendors for shelf space or taking bribes was discussed. There are also problems associated with counterfeit and grey-market merchandise and issues that vendors face when selling to retailers, such as exclusive territories and tying contracts. Care should be taken when making restrictions on which retailers they will sell to, what merchandise, how much, and at what price.

Retailers face a plethora of discount/payment date combinations. A working knowledge of these terms of purchase is essential for any person involved in merchandising. More important, the most advantageous application of the terms can make a significant impact on corporate profits.

KEY TERMS

alternative dispute resolution
arbitration
buyback
chargeback
commercial bribery
consortium exchange
copyright
counterfeit merchandise
diverted merchandise
exclusive co-brand
exclusive dealing agreement
free trade zone

generic branding
grey-market good
independent exchange
intellectual property
licensed brand
manufacturer brand
maquiladoras
market
med-arb
mediation
opportunity cost of capital
parallel branding

premium branding
private exchanges
private-label brands
retail exchanges
reverse auction
slotting allowance
strategic relationship
tariff
trade shows
trademark
trust
tying contract

1. **GO SHOPPING** Go to your favourite department or discount store. Perform an audit of national and private brands. Interview a manager to determine whether the percentage of private brands has increased or decreased over the last five years. Ask the manager to comment on the store's philosophy toward national versus private brands. On the basis of what you see and hear, assess its branding strategy.

2. **INTERNET EXERCISE** Go to the WorldWide Retail Exchange (**http://wwre.globalsources.com**). The WorldWide Retail Exchange and Global Sources have formed a strategic alliance. What is the WorldWide Retail Exchange? What is the exchange designed to do? What value does membership to the exchange provide for retailers? For suppliers?

3. **GO SHOPPING** See if you can find some counterfeit, grey-market, or diverted merchandise. Compare it with the real thing.

DISCUSSION QUESTIONS AND PROBLEMS

1. Do retailers take advantage of their power positions by charging slotting fees, buybacks, and chargebacks?

2. Assume you have been hired to consult with The Gap on sourcing decisions for sportswear. What issues would you consider when deciding whether you should buy from Mexico or China, or find a source in Canada?

3. How would the decision to source outside Canada affect a retailer's need to carry backup stock?

4. Does your favourite clothing store have a strong private-brand strategy? Should it?

5. When setting goals for a negotiation session with a vendor, what issues should a buyer consider?

6. What do you think will be the future of retail exchanges?

7. What factors should a buyer consider when deciding with which vendors to develop a close relationship?

retail pricing

LEARNING OBJECTIVES

Lo 1 Explore the factors retailers consider when pricing merchandise.

Lo 2 Examine the various pricing strategies retailers can use to influence consumer purchases.

Lo 3 Look at how the Internet is changing the way retailers price their merchandise.

SPOTLIGHT ON RETAILING

Pricing without Borders

Retailers across the country are facing massive challenges with respect to the price disparity between American and Canadian retail goods. Consumers aren't often aware of the reasons for this disparity, and more often than not believe that Canadian retailers are gouging them at the till.

"Canadian retailers are innovative and dedicated to bringing consumers the best product at the lowest price, but unfortunately they're operating on an uneven playing field that's tilted to favour American retailers," asserts Karen Pound, vice president of federal government relations for the Retail Council of Canada.

The retail sector is the largest industry in Canada, directly contributing $74.2 billion to the nation's gross domestic product in 2009. In addition, it plays a key role in bridging production and consumption, and affects other industries through the pioneering of innovative practices. In short, it's the foundation upon which the economy rests.

And yet, federal policies have conspired to put Canadian retailers at a disadvantage by ensuring that prices for consumer goods are consistently higher than they are south of the border.

According to Statistics Canada, in 2009, profit margins in the retail sector were just above 3.4 percent, compared to the profit margins in the U.S., which average 3.5 percent. As such, it becomes clear that retailers play a very small part in determining final prices of the goods they sell and that there are significant external factors at play that contribute to the often vast differences in pricing of Canadian products versus identical products sold in the U.S. These factors propel more people who live close to the border to dip into the U.S. to save the difference.

The steady flow of Canadians heading to the U.S. to shop is bound to turn into a flood in the wake of the federal government's decision to quadruple the exemption limit for goods being brought in from the U.S. Since June 2012, returning travellers who have been outside of Canada for more than 24 hours but less than 48 hours have been able to bring back $200 worth of tax-exempt goods. That's up from $50. For those out of Canada for 48 hours or more, the exemption is also quadrupled, from $200 to $800.

Given that the vast majority of Canadians live within an hour's drive of the border, this issue affects not just border communities, but the national economy as an entirety.

"The real bottom line here is that there are areas where governments can take action to help retailers compete but they're not doing it. We want the government to help level the playing field, instead of doing things to tip the balance in favour of our neighbours to the south," says Karen Pound.

Governments and consumers need to understand the particular pressures on retailers who operate businesses on the border. During a recent session before the Senate, the Retail Council of Canada outlined the four significant factors faced by Canadian retailers that contribute to differences in retail pricing between Canada and the U.S.:

- Import duties on finished goods
- Supply management affecting prices of food products such as dairy and poultry
- Vendor pricing in Canada
- Regulatory harmonization

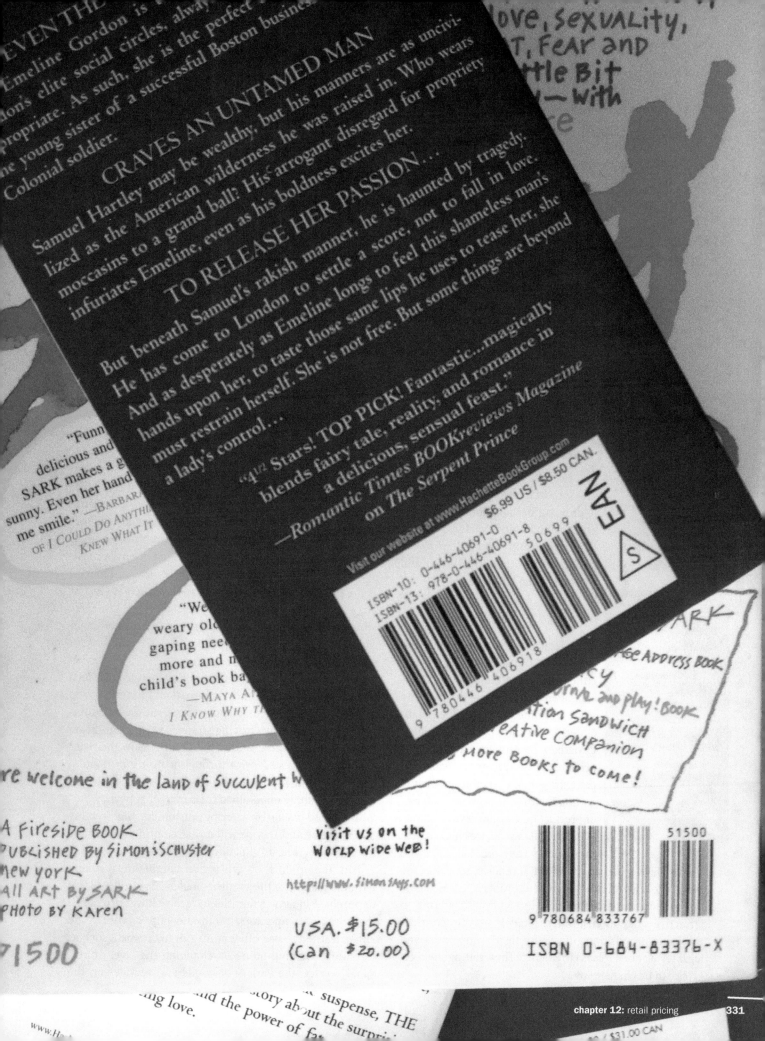

EVEN THE...
Emeline Gordon is...
...on's elite social circles, alway...
...propriate. As such, she is the perfect...
...ne young sister of a successful Boston busine...
Colonial soldier.

CRAVES AN UNTAMED MAN
Samuel Hartley may be wealthy, but his manners are as uncivi-
lized as the American wilderness he was raised in. Who wears
moccasins to a grand ball? His arrogant disregard for propriety
infuriates Emeline, even as his boldness excites her.

TO RELEASE HER PASSION...
But beneath Samuel's rakish manner, he is haunted by tragedy.
He has come to London to settle a score, not to fall in love.
And as desperately as Emeline longs to feel this shameless man's
hands upon her, to taste those same lips he uses to tease her, she
must restrain herself. She is not free. But some things are beyond
a lady's control...

"4½ Stars! TOP PICK! Fantastic...magically
blends fairy tale, reality, and romance in
a delicious, sensual feast."
—*Romantic Times BOOKreviews Magazine*
on *The Serpent Prince*

Visit our website at www.HachetteBookGroup.com

$6.99 US / $8.50 CAN.

EAN

ISBN-10: 0-446-40691-0
ISBN-13: 978-0-446-40691-8

50699

9 780446 406918

"Funn...
delicious and...
SARK makes a g...
sunny. Even her hand...
me smile." —BARBARA...
OF I COULD DO ANYTHI...
KNEW WHAT IT...

"We...
weary old...
gaping nee...
more and m...
child's book ba...
—MAYA A...
I KNOW WHY T...

...re welcome in the land of succulent w...

A FIRESIDE BOOK
PUBLISHED BY SIMON & SCHUSTER
NEW YORK
ALL ART BY SARK
PHOTO BY KAREN

71500

Visit us on the
WORLD WIDE WEB!

http://www.simonsays.com

USA. $15.00
(Can $20.00)

...SARK
...GE ADDRESS BOOK
...cy
...nal and play! Book
...tion sandwich
...eative companion
...more books to come!

51500

9 780684 833767

ISBN 0-684-83376-X

...suspense, THE
...story about the surpris...
...and the power of f...
...ng love.

Country pricing. It would be easy to assume that suppliers provide their goods at a single international or North American price, providing for a level playing field for retailers on both sides of the border. Unfortunately, the reality is far different. Many multinational vendors and suppliers who sell to Canadian retailers do so by way of contracts that are negotiated specifically for the Canadian market.

"Volume comes into play here. The United States is a giant compared to Canada, and as a result, U.S. retailers can get volume discounts more easily than Canadian retailers can," says Jamie Caswell, owner of Caswell's, a Niagara Falls clothing store. "I'm the second generation to operate the store; my son will be the third. In 53 years of business, we've never seen more challenging times because of the price disparity between our products and those sold across the river."

Caswell feels frustrated and hamstrung. Like most Canadian retailers, he works hard to provide his customers with the largest variety of products at the best available prices, but he's at the mercy of the suppliers who demand certain prices for their products. "I can't cut prices too much because the cost of doing business—rent, hydro, and so forth—remains the same," he says.

Country pricing is one of the largest contributors to the difference in pricing between Canada and the United States. The reality is that suppliers will charge Canadian retailers 50 percent more to buy their products than they charge retailers in the United States for identical products.

While the federal government may not have a direct role to play in the realm of country pricing, it is important that it does not perpetuate the ongoing misinformation to the Canadian public regarding the reasons for price differences. Suggesting that Canadian retailers are to blame for the difference in pricing is not only misleading, but it also acts to undermine the important relationships between Canadian retailers and their customers.

Source: Excerpt from Andrew Hind, "Pricing Without Borders," *Canadian Retailer*, summer 2012, volume 22, Issue 3, p. 41.

---

value Relationship of what a customer gets (goods/services) to what he or she has to pay for it.

The importance of pricing decisions is growing because today's customers demand good value. **Value** is the relationship between what the customer gets (goods/services) and what he or she has to pay for it.

$$\text{Value} = \frac{\text{Perceived benefits}}{\text{Price}}$$

Thus, retailers can increase value and stimulate more sales (exchanges) by either increasing the perceived benefits offered or reducing the price. To some customers, good value means always getting a low price. Increasingly, Canadian consumers have become price-sensitive. Others are willing to pay extra as long as they believe they're getting their money's worth in terms of product quality or service.

If retailers set prices higher than the benefits they provide, sales and profits will decrease. In contrast, if retailers set prices too low, their sales might increase but profits might decrease due to the lower profit margin. In addition to offering an attractive value to customers, retailers need to consider the value proposition offered by their competitors and legal restrictions related to pricing. Thus, setting the right price can be challenging.

Retailers have responded to their customers' needs with retail formats that emphasize low prices as a means of creating a differential advantage. National discount store chains that offer everyday low prices, such as Walmart, dominate many markets in many product categories. A close competitor in the price-oriented market is the membership-only warehouse club, such as Costco. Another retail format is the off-price retailer (e.g., Winners), which purchases closeout and end-of-season merchandise at lower-than-normal prices and passes the savings on to the customer.

Some of the more mature retailing institutions, such as department stores and supermarkets, have come to grips with these forms of price competition by adopting a more aggressive pricing strategy, with a significant amount of their merchandise being sold below the manufacturer's suggested price through a strong promotion orientation. Finally, many retailers, such as Harry Rosen, have successfully maintained their market appeal by providing good value by offering customers high-quality merchandise and service without attempting to offer the lowest prices (see also Retailing View 12.1).

In the middle of this price competition among national giants are the smaller retailers. Typically unable to purchase in large quantities to receive lower prices like their larger competitors, mom-and-pop retailers have either learned to use other strategies to compete such as extending opening hours or, changing the level of personal service, the variety of goods and services or, the company image, or they have gone out of business. For instance, to compete with Walmart's low prices, small retailers have developed niche strategies by providing a broader assortment of merchandise within a given product category and better service.

Pricing decisions are also being affected by the development of electronic channels. Consumers can easily compare the prices for branded products sold by different retailers. The Internet also makes it easier for consumers to compare product attributes in addition to price.

The Internet has facilitated the use of an auction pricing mechanism. People have used auctions to facilitate trade for centuries. As eBay has demonstrated, no longer do auction participants have to be located at the same place.

Getting the right product onto store shelves at the right time and at the right price is the basic formula for success in retailing. Increased competition has made it more important than ever to get that formula right.

Cost cutting issues might include the following:

- Buying merchandise offshore to maintain higher profit potential due to higher Canadian dollar
- Cutting packaging costs by including three languages—English, French, Spanish—to serve all North American markets
- Retailers and suppliers partnering to maintain competitive prices
- Using price optimization software technology to sell as much inventory as possible at the highest possible price

Although technology can help move products off store shelves quickly, the art of retailing lies in predicting demand patterns.

12.1 | **RETAILING VIEW**

Luxury More Than Higher Prices

Ron White, president of The Foot Shoppe, which operates five shops located in tonier parts of the Greater Toronto Area, agrees.

"We're dealing with a world in which someone will buy a Gucci fanny pack for their 16-year-old," he says.

"(But) as a luxury retailer, you have to try to look to exclusivity in brands without the flash. Many luxury consumers we see don't want the Gucci or Louis Vuitton labels. They're more into understated elegance. They're the ones who will wear an $1100 T-shirt under a blazer that you never see."

Fred Singer, president of the Edmonton-based Henry Singer Fashion Group, adds that catering to diversified luxury tastes is a matter of understanding the best of all worlds.

"We deal with people who want very high-end, exclusive product with no labels, and others who won't buy a product unless it has the label they want. We have those who buy designer jeans for the fit and fabric, others for the brand. Everyone's perception is different. Some want to buy a product for what it is, others for what it says."

As far as balancing it all, he says, it starts with having the right product offerings, for the right customers and getting exclusivity where possible.

"More than anything else, it's about relationship development and being knowledgeable about your products. That's what all luxury customers really want—good products with good service and a sense of security that you know what you are talking about," he says.

Larry Rosen, president and CEO of Harry Rosen, one of the nation's better-known chains of high-end menswear stores, notes that the luxury shopper of today is not only savvier about products and fashion trends, there is also a growing number of younger consumers who appreciate the value of a cashmere sweater.

"They won't buy as many things, but they will certainly buy better-quality items," he says. "They're better informed. They're seeking the labels that represent luxury and trust. They're looking for the same from us retailers."

In response to that, he says a major investment for Harry Rosen is staff education and training. "Even when I'm shopping myself, I love to talk to someone who is really educated about what they are selling. That's certainly what our customers want. That's the value they are looking for."

Source: Excerpt from "Spotlight on Luxury Retailing: Redefining the Luxury Experience," *Canadian Retailer*, November/December 2007, pp. 44–45, www.retailcouncil.org/cdnretailer.

Approaches for Setting Prices

Lo1

cost-oriented method A method for determining the retail price by adding a fixed percentage to the cost of the merchandise; also known as *cost-plus pricing*.

keystone method A method of setting retail prices in which retailers simply double the cost of the merchandise to obtain the original retail selling price.

demand-oriented method A method of setting prices based on what the customers would expect or be willing to pay.

competition-oriented method A pricing method in which a retailer uses competitors' prices, rather than demand or cost considerations, as guides.

Retailers want to set prices to maximize long-term profits. To do this, they need to consider the following:

- Cost, of the merchandise and services
- Demand, the price sensitivity of consumers
- Competition, because customers shop around and compare prices
- Legal considerations

The following sections examine three approaches for setting retail prices—cost-oriented, demand-oriented, and competition-oriented—and describe how retailers determine how much they need to sell to break even.

Under the cost-oriented method, the retail price is determined by adding a fixed percentage to the cost of the merchandise. For instance, a family-owned women's specialty store might use the keystone method of setting prices, in which it simply doubles the cost of the merchandise to obtain the original retail selling price. If a dress costs $50, the original selling price is $100. With the demand-oriented method, prices are based on what customers expect or are willing to pay. In this case, the retailer may have found a particularly good value at $50 but believes that the profit-maximizing price is $115. The retailer is aware of the price sensitivity of the consumers. With the competition-oriented method, prices are based on competitors' prices.

Which method is best? The answer is, all three! The cost-oriented method's strength is that it is quick, mechanical, and relatively simple to use. Retailers use it because they are making thousands of pricing decisions each week and cannot take the time to thoroughly analyze and determine the best price for each product.

As indicated by economic theory, the demand-oriented method's strength is that it allows retailers to determine which price will give them the greatest profit. But demand-oriented pricing is hard to implement, especially in a retailing environment with thousands of SKUs that require individual pricing decisions.

The competition-oriented method should be considered because it is always important to keep in mind what the competition is doing—after all, the customer does.

The degree to which a retailer sets the market price or follows the market leader is, however, a complicated issue.

Retailers need to consider costs, demand, and competition in setting prices. The cost-oriented method would be the starting point for setting a price. The competition-oriented method provides an outside check on the marketplace. The demand-oriented method is then used for fine-tuning the strategy. Retailers would start with a price based on costs and their profit goals, consider competition, and then perform tests to determine if it's the most profitable price.

Service retailers face challenges that aren't as important to merchandise retailers.

The Cost-Oriented Method of Setting Retail Prices

This section explains how retail prices are set on the basis of merchandise cost. Unfortunately, the process isn't always as simple as doubling the cost, which we described earlier. For instance, the retail price at which the product is originally sold may not be the same as the final retail selling price due to markdowns. So retailers have devised methods of keeping track of changes in the retail price so that they can achieve their overall financial goals.

Recall that the retailer's financial goals are set by top management in terms of a target return on assets. In the strategic profit model, return on assets is calculated as net profit margin multiplied by asset turnover. Pricing goals are determined primarily from net profit margin.

For pricing decisions, the key component of net profit margin is gross profit margin percentage (Gross margin ÷ Net sales). Retailers set initial prices high enough so that after markdowns and other adjustments (known as reductions) are made, they'll end up with a gross margin consistent with their overall profit goals (see Exhibit 12–1).

exhibit 12-1 Considerations in Setting Retail Prices

Markup Defined   Markup is an important and fundamental concept that is used in retail operations. As a form of cost-oriented pricing, it is a widely used pricing technique. Most retailers either use the MSRP (manufacturer's suggested retail price) or set prices by marking up the item's cost to yield a profitable gross margin. Then these cost-based prices are adjusted on the basis of insights about customer price sensitivity and competitive pricing.

When setting prices based on merchandise cost, retailers start with the following equation:

$$\text{Retail price} = \text{Cost of merchandise} + \text{Markup}$$

The markup is the amount added to the cost price in order to establish the retail price or the difference between the retail price and the cost of an item. Thus, if a sporting-goods retailer buys a tennis racquet for $75 and sets the retail price at $125, the markup is $50. Markup often serves as a guide for the retailer when pricing merchandise and in providing the forecasted operating profit. The appropriate markup is determined to cover all of the retailer's operating expenses (labour costs, rent, utilities, advertising, etc.) needed to sell the merchandise and produce a profit for the retailer. Markup can be expressed as a dollar figure or as a percent. Retailers find working with ratios to be more meaningful as it allows for comparisons within or among classifications and departments, among stores within an ownership group, and among stores using a centralized buying office. For example, HBC might compare markup ratios in small electrics of Hudson's Bay with those of Home Outfitters.

Markup can be calculated as a percent of either the retail price or the cost price but is typically calculated using the retail price. The calculation based on the retail price is more commonly used because retail expenses, markdowns, and profit are figured as dollars or percents of net sales, selling prices and discounts quoted to retailers by manufacturers are from retail list prices, and retail price data is more readily available than cost data. It is important to note that markup and expense data cannot be compared if they are not based on the same figures; both must be based either on cost or on retail figures. If a retailer buys a recliner chair for $200 and sells it for $600, the extra $400 covers operating costs and profit. The markup at retail is 66.7 percent or 200 percent at cost.

Calculating Markup Percent   The difference is in the denominator when calculating markup as either a percentage at retail or at cost. The markup percentage is the markup as a percentage of the retail price unless otherwise stated:

$$\text{Markup percentage (at retail)} = \frac{\text{Retail selling price} - \text{Merchandise cost}}{\text{Retail selling price}}$$

Thus, the markup percentage for the tennis racquet is:

$$\text{Markup percentage} = \frac{\$125 - \$75}{\$125} = 40\%$$

The retail price based on the cost and markup percentage is:

$$\text{Retail price} = \text{Merchandise cost} + \text{Markup}$$

$$\text{Retail price} = \text{Merchandise cost} + \text{Retail price} \times \text{Markup percentage}$$

$$\text{Retail price} = \frac{\text{Cost of merchandise}}{1 - \text{Markup percentage (as a fraction)}}$$

Thus, if a buyer for an office supply category specialist purchases calculators at $14 and needs a 30 percent markup to meet the financial goals for the category, the retail price needs to be:

$$\text{Retail price} = \frac{\text{Cost}}{1 - \text{Markup percent}} = \frac{\$14.00}{1 - 0.30} = 20$$

To calculate markup percentage at cost:

$$\text{Markup percentage (at cost)} = \frac{\text{Retail selling price} - \text{Merchandise cost}}{\text{Merchandise cost}}$$

When calculating markup, markup on retail is always less than 100 percent while markup on cost may exceed 100 percent. As markup goes up, the gap between the retail and cost percentages grows. Consider our furniture retailer in the previous example who buys a recliner chair for $200 and considers selling it for $300, $400, $500, or $600. The $300 price generates a markup at retail of 33.3 percent and 50 percent at cost, the $400 price a 50 percent markup at retail and 100 percent at cost, the $500 price a 60-percent markup at retail and 150 percent at cost, and the $600 price a markup of 66.7 percent at retail and 200 percent at cost.

A retail buyer can work with markup in three different ways: calculating markup percent when cost and retail are known, calculating retail when cost and markup percent are known, and calculating cost when retail and markup percent are known.

Markup % = $ Markup ÷ $ Retail

$ Retail = $ Cost ÷ Cost %

$ Cost = $ Retail × Cost %

When calculating markup percent when cost and retail are known, a buyer must determine if the markup achieved is sufficient to reach the department's planned goal. To find markup percent, find the markup dollars by subtracting $ cost from $ retail and then divide by retail dollars. A retailer's markup percentage can also be determined by taking into consideration planned retail operating expenses, profit, and net sales.

markup   The increase in the retail price of an item after the initial markup percentage has been applied but before the item is placed on the selling floor.

markup percentage   The markup as a percent of retail price.

Complete the Concept Check to help develop skill in learning the principles presented.

1. Calculate the markup percent on a ladies Guess watch that costs $45 and retails for $110.

2. The ladies accessory buyer at Hudson's Bay has sourced some hand-painted silk scarves for $240.00 a dozen at cost. (a) What is the retail price if a 50 percent markup is expected? (b) What is the retail price if a markup of 70 percent is expected?

3. Samantha buys a safari dress from the specialty store Cassis for $210.00. Determine the markup percent on the dress if it cost the store $80.00.

4. What is the cost price on the queen-size Serta mattress set that Kelly just purchased at Sleep Country for $2400 and provided the store with a 58 percent markup?

5. The paint department at Rona received a shipment for a paint promotion that cost $8.00 for each litre can of white primer and would retail for $24.99 each. Find (a) the markup percent and (b) the cost percent for a litre of white primer.

6. Find the markup percent on the following order of Tommy Hilfiger sportswear for Hudson's Bay store 138.

	$Cost	$Retail
14 capri pants	$26.25 each	$75.00 each
14 safari shorts	$15.75 each	$45.00 each
25 halter tops	$7.00 each	$20.00 each
40 V-neck T-shirts	$15.25 each	$35.00 each

7. The buyer for toddler boys at Old Navy needs to buy a group of T-shirts for an upcoming top sale. She sources 50 dozen striped T-shirts at $42/dozen, 12 dozen collared tees at $60/dozen, and 40 dozen scoop-neck tees at $45/dozen. If she plans on retailing them all at a sale price of $8.00 each, what markup percent will she realize on the merchandise?

8. The men's buyer at Old Navy needs to buy three different styles of shorts for an upcoming promotion. He buys 200 units of style 1032 for $12 each, 200 units of style 1034 for $16 each, and 200 units of style 1036 for $20 each. Much like the toddler buyer above, he would like to sell the shorts all at the same advertised price point. What unit retail price point will he be able to charge if he desires a 58 percent markup?

initial markup
The retail selling price initially placed on the merchandise less the cost of goods sold.

What is the markup percent on a sweater that costs $52 and retails for $115?

$$\text{Markup \%} = \$ \text{Markup} \div \$ \text{Retail}$$
$$= \$63 \div \$115$$
$$= 54.78\%$$

What is the planned markup for a sporting goods store that estimates its yearly operating expenses to be $65 000. The desired profit is $55 000 per year, including the owner's salary. Net sales are forecasted to be $300 000.

$$\text{Markup \%} = \frac{\text{Planned operating expenses} + \text{Planned profit}}{\text{Planned net sales}}$$
$$= \frac{\$65\ 000 + \$55\ 000}{\$300\ 000}$$
$$= 42\%$$

When calculating retail price when cost and markup percent are known, a buyer must evaluate the retail prices placed on the merchandise and take into account both the cost price and the markup percent needed. Buyers also need to evaluate the retail price to determine if consumers would be willing to buy the merchandise at that price. If the cost price and the markup percentage is known, it is necessary to find the cost percentage or cost complement before the retail price can be calculated. Complement of markup percent is 100 percent less markup percent on retail.

Calculate the retail price on a snowboard that costs $380 and has a markup of 56 percent.

$$\$ \text{Retail} = \$ \text{Cost} \div \text{Cost \%}$$
$$= \$380 \div 44\%$$
$$= \$864$$

Determine the cost of a men's dress shirt that retails for $78.00 and has a 55 percent markup.

$$\$ \text{Cost} = \$ \text{Retail} \times \text{Cost \%}$$
$$= \$78 \times 45\%$$
$$= \$35.10$$

Determining Initial Markup Initial markup can be calculated with percents or with specific dollar amounts. The same equation to calculate initial markup can be used when working with percents or dollar amounts since net sales always equals 100 percent. As all other percents are based on net sales, initial markup is the difference between the merchandise cost (COGS) and the original retail price placed on the goods, expressed as a percentage or dollar amount of retail value. Therefore, a loss can occur for a retailer if the initial markup placed on the goods (item or group of items) does not cover expenses and reductions. Retail reductions are things that reduce the retail value of goods, such as markdowns, employee discounts, special customer discounts, and inventory shrinkage.

There are other factors, such as workroom/alteration costs and cash discounts, that can affect the initial markup of merchandise. Workroom/alteration costs can increase the retail value of goods by adding additional value to the finished product (such as alterations to a suit or the cost of putting a table together). Cash discounts on the other hand represent a reduction in the cost of the goods (such as given to the store by the vendor for paying invoices early).

Initial markup

$$= \frac{\text{Expenses} + \text{Profit} + \text{Reductions} + \text{Alterations} - \text{Cash}}{\text{Net sales} + \text{Reductions}}$$

Determine the necessary initial markup percent for a retailer that has these planned figures.

Net sales	$200 000
Expenses	60 000
Reductions	15 000
Alteration costs	500
Cash discounts	250
Profit	7550

Initial markup

$$= \frac{\text{Expenses} + \text{Profit} + \text{Reductions} + \text{Alterations} - \text{Cash discounts}}{\text{Net sales} + \text{Reductions}}$$

$$= \frac{60\,000 + 7550 + 15\,000 + 500 - 250}{200\,000 + 15\,000}$$

$$= \frac{82\,800}{215\,000}$$

$$= 38.5\%$$

Determine the necessary initial markup percent for the following retailer. Calculate initial markup using $ and % values.

Net sales	$220 000
Expenses	30%
Markdowns	3.2
Employee discounts	5.3
Shortages	1.0
Alteration costs	.5
Cash discounts	.25
Profit	$16 500

Initial markup

$$= \frac{\text{Expenses} + \text{Profit} + \text{Reductions} + \text{Alterations} - \text{Cash discounts}}{\text{Net sales} + \text{Reductions}}$$

$$\% = \frac{30 + 7.5 + 9.5 + .5 - .25}{100 + 9.5} = 43.15\%$$

$$\$ = \frac{\$66\,000 + \$16\,500 + \$20\,900 + 1100 - 550}{\$220\,000 + \$20\,900} = 43.15\%$$

(Note that the same answer is obtained using both $ and % values.)

Determining Maintained Markup

Maintained markup is the actual sales realized for the merchandise when it is sold by the retailer minus its costs and is reported as a percent. Gross cost of goods sold does not reflect deductions for cash discounts and workroom costs. Gross cost of goods sold includes the following items from the income statement: opening inventory, gross purchases, less returns from vendor, net purchases, freight forward, and total merchandise handled. This differs from total cost of goods sold, which also includes cash discounts earned, net cost of merchandise sold, and net alteration/workroom costs. Maintained markup can be difficult to predict because it is based on the actual prices received rather than on planned sales. As a result, it is often calculated whenever the operating statement is prepared. Rather than calculating maintained markup on an individual purchase or a few items, retailers calculate it on the activity of an entire classification, department, or store for a given period or quarter.

Maintained markup $ = Net sales − Gross cost of goods sold
Maintained markup % = Maintained markup $ ÷ Net sales $

Determining the Initial Markup from Maintained Markup and Gross Margin

Initial markup is always greater than maintained markup so long as there are any reductions. Also, as discussed above, initial markup is expressed either in dollars or as a percentage of retail price. This is because retailers using the retail inventory method (RIM) of inventory accounting think of their inventory in "retail" rather than "cost" terms. Also, expressing initial markup as a percentage of retail price closely resembles the other accounting conventions of expressing net profit, gross margin, and maintained markup as percentages of net sales, which are, of course, at retail. Retailers recognize maintained markup as the more meaningful ratio when comparing initial markup to maintained markup because it is a more accurate reflection of actual movement of merchandise. Retailers cannot determine maintained markup, in advance as they do with initial markup although they do try to maintain the amount of profit (markup) on a particular classification, department, or store.

Maintained markup and gross margin are both percentages that are calculated on net sales figures rather than on original retail prices. The difference in the calculation lies in the COGS number. Maintained markup is the difference between net sales and gross cost of goods sold while gross margin is the difference between net sales and the total cost of goods sold. In other words, gross margin takes into consideration cash discounts and alteration/workroom costs into the calculation. If a retailer does not have any cash discounts or, workroom or alteration costs for the specified period, gross margin and maintained markup are the same. Thus, the only difference between the two terms is the workroom costs (such as alterations to a suit or the cost of putting a table together) and cash discounts (given to the store by the vendor for paying invoices early). Why do retailers make this distinction between maintained markup and gross margin? In many retail organizations, these workroom costs aren't controlled by the person who makes the pricing decision. For instance, the furniture buyer doesn't have control over costs associated with assembling a dining room table. In the same way, a buyer typically has no control over whether the accounting department takes the cash discounts offered to the company from its vendors for paying invoices early. But remember that, conceptually, maintained markup and gross margin are similar. Moores Clothiers has done an excellent job by collecting fees for alterations, a cost recovery.

The performance measure usually used to evaluate pricing decisions is gross margin. Exhibit 12–2 summarizes its components. We used the traditional accounting definition of gross margin:

Gross margin \$ = Net sales − Total cost of goods sold
Gross margin % = Gross margin \$ ÷ Net sales

Remember that gross margin is a financial term that expresses the difference between net sales (the price that the customer pays for merchandise) and the cost of the merchandise (the cost that the retailer paid for the merchandise). The gross margin return on investment (GMROI) is the financial ratio of gross margin dollars divided by the average cost of stock on hand.

The term *maintained markup* is very descriptive. It's the amount of profit (markup) a retailer plans to maintain on a particular category of merchandise. For example, in Exhibit 12–2, planned maintained markup is \$62 000 on sales of \$120 000, or 51.67 percent (\$62 000 ÷ \$120 000). In other words, to meet its profit goals, this retailer must obtain a 51.67 percent maintained markup.

A retailer's life would be relatively simple if the amount of markup it wanted to maintain (maintained markup) were the same as the initial markup.

exhibit 12–2 Sample Income Statement Showing Gross Margin

Net sales	\$120 000
− Cost of goods sold	58 000
= Maintained markup	62 000
− Alteration costs + Cash discounts	3 000
= Gross margin	\$ 59 000

Initial markup
= Retail selling price initially placed on the merchandise minus total cost of goods sold (COGS)

whereas,

Maintained markup
= The actual sales that you get for the merchandise minus gross cost of goods sold (COGS)

Why is there a difference? A number of reductions to the value of retail inventory occur between the time the merchandise is originally priced (initial markup) and the time it's sold (maintained markup). Reductions include markdowns, discounts to employees and customers, and inventory shrinkage (due to shoplifting, breakage, or loss). Initial markup must be high enough so that after reductions are taken out, the maintained markup is left. Thus, there is a difference between the initial and the maintained markup.

The difference between the initial and maintained markup is illustrated in Exhibit 12–3. The item illustrated costs \$0.60, and the initial price for the item is \$1.00, so the initial markup cost is \$0.40, and the initial markup percentage is 40 percent. However, the average actual sale price for the item is \$0.90. The reductions are \$0.10, so the maintained markup is \$0.30, and the maintained markup percentage is 33 percent (0.30/0.90).

The relationship between initial markup and maintained markup is

Initial markup = Maintained markup (as a % of net sales)
+ Reductions (as a % of net sales)/100%
+ Reductions (as a % of net sales)

Thus, if the buyer setting the price for the item shown in Exhibit 12–3 planned on reductions of 10 percent of actual sales and wanted a maintained markup of 33 percent, the initial markup should be:

Initial markup percentage = 33% + (\$0.10/\$0.90)
= 11.111%/100% + 11.111%
= 40%

and the initial retail price should be

Initial retail price = Cost/1 − Initial markup percentage
= \$0.60/1 − 0.40 = \$1.00

The Demand-Oriented Method of Setting Retail Prices

Demand-oriented pricing should be used in conjunction with the cost-oriented method to determine retail prices. Using this method, retailers not only consider their profit structure but also pay close attention to the effect that price changes have on sales. For instance, if customers are extremely price-sensitive, then a price cut can increase demand so much that profits actually increase. Alternatively, if customers are insensitive to price, raising

Complete the Concept Check to help develop skill in learning the principles presented.

1. A specialty store had the following planned figures. What is the initial markup?

Net sales	$124 000
Profit	$4 000
Expenses	$60 000
Employee discounts	$240
Markdowns	$3 200
Shortages	$1550

2. A specialty store had the following planned figures. What is the initial markup?

Net sales	
Profit	3.6%
Expenses	41%
Employee discounts	7.2%
Markdowns	4.8%
Shortages	1.0%

3. Calculate the initial markup using the following figures.

Net sales	$180 000
Expenses	38%
Employee discounts	8.3%
Markdowns	4%
Shortages	1%
Alterations	$124
Cash discounts	$280
Profit	12%

4. Calculate the maintained markup percent, using the following operating results for a specialty retailer.

Net sales		$375 000
Cost of goods sold	$35 000	
Gross purchases	$185 000	
Less, returns to vendor	−6 500	
Net purchases	$178 500	
Freight inward	+3 500	
Total merchandise handled	$182 000	
Closing inventory	−52 000	
Gross cost of merchandise sold	$130 000	
Cash discounts earned	−6 800	
Net cost of merchandise sold	$123 200	
Net alteration/ workroom costs	+2 500	
Total cost of merchandise sold		−125 700
Gross margin		$249 300

5. Calculate maintained markup and gross margin percent from the following operating results.

Net sales	$1 200 500
Cash discounts	$12 200
Alteration costs	$3 100
Gross cost of merchandise sold	$605 500

exhibit 12–3 Difference between Initial Markup and Maintained Markup

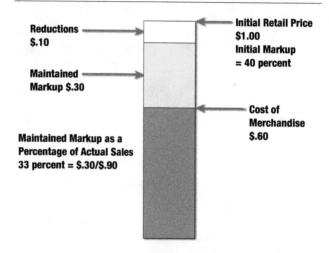

the price also can boost profits, since sales likely won't decrease. Demand-oriented pricing seeks to determine the price that customers are willing to pay and that will maximize profits.

To illustrate how an initial retail price is set using the demand-oriented method, we will use a hypothetical situation of Aritzia's new ribbed sleeveless T-shirt for women. Assume that the fixed cost of developing the product is $300 000 and the variable cost is $5 each. One benefit of private-label merchandise is the flexibility of being able to set any retail price. Aritzia decides to test the T-shirt in four markets at different prices. Exhibit 12–4 shows the pricing test's results. It's clear (from column 5) that a unit price of $10 is by far the most profitable ($450 000).

Although determining the optimal price based on a demand analysis is simple for one product, most retailers carry so many products that these tests become a very expensive proposition. Also, a retailer must have multiple outlets to be able to manipulate prices in this manner.

A more sophisticated method of determining the most profitable price is a *pricing experiment*. In a pricing experiment, a retailer actually changes the price in a systematic manner to observe changes in purchases or purchase intentions. Exhibit 12–5 shows an example of a simple experiment—a classic before/after experiment with control group design. Two stores are similar in size and customer characteristics. Their weekly sales for a compact microwave oven are almost identical (10 and 12 units per week), and the ovens are selling at the same price, $100. The price at the first store is changed to $80, but the second store's price is left at $100. Thus, the second store is used as a control to make sure that any change in sales is due to the price change rather than to some outside force such as competition or weather. Now sales at the first store jump to 21 units per week, while sales at the control store hit 13 units. Barring any circumstances

exhibit 12-4   Results of Pricing Test

Market	(1) Unit Price	(2) Market Demand at Price (in units)	(3) Total Revenue (col. 1 × col. 2)	(4) Total Cost of Units Sold ($300 000 fixed cost + $5 variable cost)	(5) Total Profits (col. 3 − col. 4)
1	$ 8	200 000	$1 600 000	$1 300 000	$300 000
2	10	150 000	1 500 000	1 050 000	450 000
3	12	100 000	1 200 000	800 000	400 000
4	14	50 000	700 000	550 000	150 000

exhibit 12-5   A Pricing Experiment

	Before	After
Store 1	10 units @ $100 Gross margin = $500	21 units @ $80 Gross margin = $630
Store 2 (Control)	12 units @ $100 Gross margin = $600	13 units @ $100 Gross margin = $650

unknown to the retailer, the change in sales is due to the price cut. And, by the way, the $100 price is more profitable than the $80 price in the second store! Since product cost is $50, the $100 retail price provides a $650 gross margin [($100 − $50) × 13 units], whereas the $80 price provides a $630 gross margin [($80 − $50) × 21 units].

In the past, these pricing experiments weren't regularly applied because of the time and expense of administering them. But now any retailer with point-of-sale terminals can run large-scale experiments. Retailers can utilize the data warehouses derived from their loyalty programs in conjunction with sales and price data to run experiments. These records cover what customers have purchased, prices paid, and conditions of sale (such as coupon usage and price specials). Demographic information on customers makes it possible to correlate price sensitivity with customer profiles.

Retailers and their vendors can also buy from private firms. For one of its many products, InfoScan, the company purchases information from individual supermarket chains on price and promotion activity that has been scanned through their POS terminals; it then aggregates data by region, chain, or market area.

The Competition-Oriented Method of Setting Retail Prices

As the name implies, when retailers use competition-oriented pricing, they set their prices on the basis of their competition rather than cost or demand considerations. Retailers can price either above, below, or at parity with the competition. The chosen strategy must be consistent with the retailer's overall strategy and its relative market position. Consider, for instance, Walmart and Birks as

we did previously. Walmart's overall strategy is to be the low-cost retailer for the merchandise it sells. It tries to price products it sells below competition. Birks, on the other hand, offers significant benefits to its customers including high quality, unique merchandise, impeccable service, and elegant locations. Those little blue boxes stamped with the Birks logo symbolize quality service and jewellery. Due to the unique nature of Birks' offering, it is able to set prices higher than its competitors'.

Market leaders cannot, however, ignore their small competitors. Suppose that a sporting goods store in North Bay, Ontario, consistently underprices Walmart on fishing gear. Walmart will adjust its prices to meet or even beat the competitor in that market.

What should small competitors do to compete with market leaders? A jewellery store could price at parity or below Birks. Additionally, it could strive for competitive advantages in assortment or service. A more difficult question is how a casual wear store can compete against Walmart's prices. It cannot compete head to head with Walmart on every item. To do so would probably put it out of business because it cannot achieve the buying quantities of scale of Walmart. Instead, it should pick items that are very visible to customers and generate margin on items that customers cannot readily compare. If Walmart is advertising jeans at $19.99, then the casual wear store should either carry other brands of jeans or bite the bullet and price with or below Walmart.

Collecting and Using Competitive Price Data[2]

Retailers work to provide a consistent shopping experience, and part of that requires consistency between a retailer's market strategy and its pricing position within a market. Most large retailers routinely collect competitive price data from competitors to see if they need to adjust their prices to remain competitive.

Competitive price data are typically collected using store personnel, third-party providers, and vendor representatives (whose interests often bias the data). Costing between $0.15 and $2.00 per price point to collect, competitive price comparisons are typically still performed using pen and paper and sometimes without the consent of the competitor. Because the costs associated with collecting and then managing the data are significant, retailers need to be very strategic when structuring competitive price projects.

How Retailers Reduce Price Competition
Retailers have two fundamental strategies available to them for reducing price competition:

- First, they can adopt an EDLP strategy. Conditioning customers to expect a fair and relatively low price on a typical market basket of merchandise enables a retailer to charge slightly higher prices on some individual items.

- Second, they can utilize some of the branding strategies described previously. For instance, they can develop lines of premium private-label merchandise. Since the competition doesn't have such merchandise, it is difficult for the customer to comparison shop.

Profit Impact of Setting a Retail Price: The Use of Break-Even Analysis

Now that we've examined how retailers set prices on the bases of the cost-, demand-, and competition-oriented methods, let's look at how retailers determine the volume of sales necessary for them to make a profit. A useful analytical tool is break-even analysis, which analyzes the relationship between total revenue and total cost to determine how much merchandise needs to be sold to achieve a break-even (zero) profit. For example, a retailer might want to know:

- Break-even volume and dollars for a new product, product line, or department
- Break-even sales change needed to cover a price change
- Break-even sales to cover a target profit
- Change in profit based on change in sales volume

Let's look more closely at the first two: the break-even volume of a new private-label product and the break-even sales change needed to cover a price change.

Calculating Break-Even for a New Product
Suppose PetSmart is considering the introduction of a new private-label, dry dog food targeting owners of older dogs. The cost of developing this dog food is $700 000, including salaries for the design team and testing the product. Because these costs don't change with the quantity of product that is produced and sold, they're known as fixed costs. PetSmart plans to sell the dog food for $12 a bag—the unit price. The variable cost is the retailer's expenses that vary directly with the quantity of product produced and

sold. Variable costs often include direct labour and materials used in producing the product. PetSmart will be purchasing the product from a private-label manufacturer. Thus, the only variable cost is the dog food's cost, $5, from the private-label supplier. The break-even point (BEP) quantity is the quantity at which total revenue equals total cost, and then profit occurs for additional sales.

$$\text{Break-even quantity} = \frac{\text{Fixed cost}}{\text{Actual unit sales price} - \text{Unit variable cost}}$$

$$= \frac{\$700\,000}{\$12 - \$5} = 100\,000 \text{ bags}$$

Thus, PetSmart needs to sell 100 000 bags of dog food to break even, or make zero profit, and for every additional bag sold, it will make $7 profit.

Now assume that PetSmart wants to make $100 000 profit from the new product line. The break-even quantity now becomes:

$$\text{Break-even quantity} = \frac{\text{Fixed cost}}{\text{Actual unit sales price} - \text{Unit variable cost}}$$

$$= \frac{\$700\,000 + \$100\,000}{\$12 - \$5} = 114\,286 \text{ bags}$$

Calculating Break-Even Sales
A closely related issue to the calculation of a break-even point is determining how much unit sales would have to increase to make a profit from a price cut or how much sales would have to decline to make a price increase unprofitable.[3] Continuing with the PetSmart example, assume the break-even quantity is 114 286 units based on the $700 000 fixed cost, the $100 000 profit, a selling price of $12, and a cost of $5. Now PetSmart is considering lowering the price of a bag of dog food to $10. How many units must it sell to break even if it lowers its selling price by 16.67 percent to $10? Using the formula,

$$\text{Break-even quantity} = \frac{\text{Fixed cost}}{\text{Actual unit sales price} - \text{Unit variable cost}}$$

$$= \frac{\$700\,000 + \$100\,000}{\$12 - \$5} = 160\,000 \text{ bags}$$

So if PetSmart decreases its price by 16.67 percent from $12 to $10, unit sales must increase by 40 percent: $(160\,000 - 114\,286) \div 111\,286$.

For another example of break-even sales, let's use the T-shirts from Aritzia and assume the break-even quantity is 57 143 units (based on the $300 000 fixed cost, the $100 000 profit, a selling price of $12, and a cost of $5). How many T-shirts must Aritzia sell to break even if it

break-even analysis A technique that evaluates the relationship between total revenue and total cost to determine profitability at various sales levels.

fixed costs Costs that are stable and don't change with the quantity of product that's produced and sold.

variable cost A cost that varies with the level of sales and that can be applied directly to the decision in question.

break-even point (BEP) The quantity at which total revenue equals total cost and beyond which profit occurs.

lowers its selling price by 16.6 percent to $10? Using the formula:

$$\text{\% break-even sales change} = \frac{-\% \text{ price change}}{\%CM + \% \text{ price change}} \times 100$$

where %CM stands for percentage contribution margin. Contribution margin is gross margin less any expense that can be directly assigned to the merchandise. In this example, since there are no variable costs besides the cost of the shirt, the contribution margin is the same as the gross margin. Also, don't forget the minus sign in the formula's numerator.

Contribution margin (CM) = Selling price − Variable costs
CM = $12 − $5 = $7
%CM = (CM ÷ Selling price) × 100
%CM = ($7 ÷ $12) × 100 = 58.33%

Substituting the %CM into the formula, we can calculate the break-even sales change:

$$\text{\% break-even sales change} = \frac{-(-16.6)}{58.33 + (-16.6)} \times 100 = 39.78\%$$

$$\text{Unit break-even sales change} = 39.78\% \times 57\,143 \text{ units} = 22\,731 \text{ units}$$

Thus, if Aritzia reduces its price to $10, it must sell an additional 22 731 units to break even. It should come as no surprise that when we add the break-even quantity at $12 to the break-even sales change to $10, we get 79 874 units (57 143 + 22 731)—almost the same break-even point of 80 000 units that we obtained using the first formula. (The difference is due to rounding.) The same formula can be used to determine the sales change necessary to break even with a price increase.

Price Adjustments

In Canada, retailers are relatively free to promote adjustments to the initial retail price with the hope of generating sales. In this section, we will examine markdowns, coupons, rebates, price bundling, multiple-unit pricing, variable pricing, and some special Internet pricing issues. Retailing View 12.2 describes how some retailers are trying to raise their gross margin percentage by avoiding markdowns.

Markdowns

Markdowns are price reductions from the initial retail price. Markdowns are initiated because the lower price induces price-sensitive customers to buy more merchandise.

Reasons for Taking Markdowns Retailers' decision to take markdowns can be classified as either clearance (to dispose of merchandise) or promotional (to generate sales).

Clearance Markdowns When merchandise is slow-moving, obsolete, at the end of its selling season, or priced higher than competitors' goods, it generally gets marked down for clearance purposes. This merchandise can become an eyesore and impair the store's image. Further, even if the merchandise can be sold in the following season, it may become shopworn or out of style. Also, the cost of carrying inventory is significant. If a buyer has to carry $10 000 of unwanted inventory at cost for a year with an annual inventory carrying cost of 35 percent, the cost would be $3 500 (or $10 000 × 0.35)—not a trivial amount!

Fashion retailers tend to order more merchandise than they forecast selling because they are more concerned about selling out of a popular item before the end of the season than about over-ordering and having to mark down excess merchandise. Stocking out of popular merchandise can have a detrimental effect on a fashion retailer's image, whereas discounting merchandise at the end of the season merely reduces maintained markup.

Markdowns are part of the cost of doing business, and thus retailers plan for markdowns. They set an initial markup high enough so that after markdowns and other reductions are considered, the planned maintained markup will be achieved. Thus, a retailer's objective shouldn't necessarily be to minimize markdowns. If markdowns are too low, the retailer is probably pricing the merchandise too low, not purchasing enough merchandise, or not taking enough risks with the merchandise being purchased.

Promotional Markdowns Using a high/low pricing strategy described earlier in this chapter, retailers employ markdowns to promote merchandise to increase sales. A buyer may decide to mark down some merchandise to make room for something new. An additional benefit is that the markdown sale generates cash flow to pay for new merchandise. Markdowns are also taken to increase customers' traffic flow. Retailers plan promotions in which they take markdowns for holidays, for special events, and as part of their overall promotional program. In fact, small portable appliances (such as toasters) are called *traffic appliances* because they're often in a *leader pricing* program and sold at reduced prices to generate in-store traffic. Retailers hope that customers will purchase other products at regular prices while they're in the store. Another opportunity created by markdowns is to increase the sale of complementary products. For example, a supermarket's markdown on hot dog buns may be offset by increased demand for hot dogs, mustard, and relish—all sold at regular prices.

Get Them While They're Hot

For years, retailers have lured customers into stores with sales and markdowns. Shoppers know when items will go on sale and often wait for bargains. Although this policy helps retailers sell more merchandise, it also decreases their gross margins. Frequent sales also may signal to customers that there might be something wrong with the merchandise or that it isn't good quality. Frequent sales can also damage a retailer's overall image. So retailers have devised tactics to reverse this cycle and encourage more customers to pay full price.

One method of reducing markdowns is to better control the quantities bought. By adopting a just-in-time inventory policy, in which small amounts of merchandise arrive just in time to be sold, customers perceive a scarcity and purchase at full price. Even if there are adequate quantities of merchandise available in the stockroom or in a distribution centre, displaying just a few items on the sales floor sends a signal to the customer to "buy them now, while they last!" If retailers simply change their displays frequently, customers will perceive that the merchandise is new and available in limited quantities.

Some retailers, such as Walmart, advertise everyday low prices, which implies that their products are already at low prices and therefore will not be further discounted. Even Hudson's Bay, long known for its

everyday sales, is promoting "Every Day Value," or "Bay Value" items on many of its racks. Costco doesn't need to advertise its low prices. Loyal customers return time after time to look for low-priced treasures.

A handful of retailers, like Coach, Lululemon, Apple, have taken a dramatically different approach. They focus on quality and image and therefore simply don't have sales! Customers accept this full-price message. It is an enviable position, to which most retailers can only aspire.

These tactics for preventing bargain hunting increase gross margins as well as inventory turnovers. When more products are sold at full price, gross margins naturally increase. As retailers trim their inventories to give a feeling of "buy now or be sorry," sales also will increase, and inventory will decrease, thus resulting in greater inventory turnover.

Sources: Allison Kaplan, "Rough Weather Behind Them, Retailers Are Starting to Trim Their Sales," *St. Paul Pioneer Press*, January 26, 2007 (accessed January 25, 2008); Jayne O'Donnell, "Retailers Try to Train Shoppers to Buy Now," *USA TODAY*, September 25, 2006 (accessed January 25, 2008); Linda Whitaker, *Managing Markdowns: Why Prevention Is Better than the Optimization Cure* (Carlsbad, CA: Quantum Retail Technology, 2007), (accessed January 25, 2008); Kris Hudson, "Turning Shopping Trips into Treasure Hunts," *The Wall Street Journal*, August 27, 2007, p. B1; and Timothy Taylor, "The final stretch," *Report on Business*, December 2011, pp. 27–31.

Optimizing Markdown Decisions Retailers have traditionally created a set of arbitrary rules for taking markdowns.[5] One retailer, for instance, flags markdown candidates when their weekly sell-through percentages fall below a certain value. Another retailer cuts prices on the basis of how long the merchandise has been in the store—marking products down by 20 percent after eight weeks, then by 30 percent after 12 weeks, and finally by 50 percent after 16 weeks.

Such a rules-based approach, however, is limited in several ways:

- First, it assumes that all the items within a category exhibit the same, consistent behaviour. So it treats a cashmere sweater the same way it treats a wool sweater.

- Second, a rules-based approach follows a fixed schedule; it's not sophisticated enough to determine how shifts in sales trends or other factors such as promotions or holidays will affect demand.

- Third, this approach fails to take gross margin into consideration; its only goal is to clear inventory.

Instead of relying on rules developed from averages, a retailer can benefit significantly from **merchandising optimization software**, a set of algorithms that monitors merchandise sales, promotions, competitors' actions,

merchandising optimization software
Set of algorithms (computer programs) that monitors merchandise sales, promotions, competitors' actions, and other factors to determine the optimal (most profitable) price and timing for merchandising activities, especially markdowns.

and other factors to determine the optimal (most profitable) price and timing for merchandising activities, especially markdowns. This software is currently being used by a growing number of major retailers and is commercially available from a number of specialty firms such as SAP.

The optimization software works by constantly refining its pricing forecasts on the basis of actual sales throughout the season. For example, the software recognizes that in early November, a winter item's sales are better than expected, so it delays taking a markdown that had been planned. Each week, as fresh sales data become available, it readjusts the forecasts to include the latest information. It computes literally thousands of scenarios for each item—a process that is too complicated and time-consuming for retailers to do on their own. It then evaluates the outcomes based on expected profits and other factors and selects the action that produces the best results.

Making good markdown decisions isn't all about relying on sophisticated computer software. Retailers must also work closely with their vendor partners to coordinate deliveries and help share the financial burden of taking markdowns.

Reducing the Amount of Markdowns by Working with Vendors

Retailers can reduce the amount of markdowns by working closely with their vendors to time deliveries with demand. Merchandise that arrives before it is needed takes up valuable selling space and can get shopworn or damaged. On the other hand, when merchandise arrives too late, retailers may have trouble selling it without extensive markdowns. Quick response inventory systems reduce the lead time for receiving merchandise so that retailers can more closely monitor changes in trends and customer demand, thus reducing markdowns.

Vendors have a vested interest in retailers' success. Vendors that are knowledgeable about the market and competition can help with stock selections. Of course, a retailer must also trust its own taste and intuition; otherwise, its store will have the same merchandise as all other stores. Retail buyers can often obtain markdown money—funds a vendor gives the retailer to cover lost gross margin dollars that result from markdowns and other merchandising issues. For instance, assume a retailer has $1000 worth of ties at retail that are given a 25 percent markdown. Thus, when the ties are sold, the retailer receives only $750. But if the vendor provides $250 in markdown money, the maintained markup is unaffected. In this way, the vendor helps share the risk. According to the *Competition Act*, markdown money

should be provided to all retailers on a proportionally equal basis, typically as a percentage of purchases. (Markdown money falls under the umbrella of potentially illegal price discrimination discussed in Appendix 12A, available on Connect.)

Determining Markdown Percent Markdowns are expressed as a percent of net sales and cannot be calculated until the merchandise is sold. To determine markdown percent, the dollar markdown must first be found by subtracting the new, reduced price from the previous price and then the net sales is divided into the dollar markdown number. Net sales equals the original retail price minus markdowns.

Markdown $ = Previous price − New, reduced price

Markdown % = Markdown $ ÷ Net sales $

A sporting goods retailer received six Burton snowboards that retailed for $800. All six snowboards were reduced to $580 for a weekend "Winter Wonderland Sale." What was the markdown percent on this snowboard?

$$\begin{aligned} \text{Markdown \$} &= \text{Previous price} - \text{New, reduced price} \\ &= 6 \times (\$800 - \$580) \\ &= 6 \times \$220 \\ &= \$1320 \end{aligned}$$

Sales from this snowboard = 6 × $580 = $3480

$$\begin{aligned} \text{Markdown \%} &= \text{Markdown \$} \div \text{Net sales} \\ &= \$1320 \div \$3480 \\ &= 37.93\% \end{aligned}$$

If December markdowns for the women's accessory department totalled $24 360 and net sales for the same month were $98 245, what was the markdown percent?

$$\begin{aligned} \text{Markdown \%} &= \text{Markdown \$ in December} \\ &\quad \div \text{Net sales for December} \\ &= \$24\,360 \div \$98\,245 \\ &= 24.8\% \end{aligned}$$

Calculate net sales for the produce department if markdowns for boxed strawberries were 59.6 percent of net sales and the markdown dollar amount was $37.25.

$$\begin{aligned} \text{Net sales} &= \text{Markdown \$} \div \text{Markdown \%} \\ &= \$37.25 \div 59.6\% \\ &= \$62.50 \end{aligned}$$

Liquidating Markdown Merchandise No matter what markdown strategy a retailer uses, some merchandise may still remain unsold. A retailer can use one of five strategies to liquidate this merchandise:

- "Job-out," sell the remaining merchandise to another retailer
- Consolidate the unsold merchandise
- Place the remaining merchandise on an Internet auction site such as eBay, or have a special clearance location on the retailer's website
- Give the merchandise to charity
- Carry the merchandise over to the next season

Selling the remaining marked-down merchandise to another retailer has been very popular among retailers. For instance, Winners purchases end-of-season merchandise from other retailers and sells it at deep discounts. This strategy enables the retailer to have a relatively short markdown period, provides space for new merchandise, and at the same time eliminates the often unappealing sale atmosphere. The problem with this strategy is that the retailer can recoup only a small percentage of the merchandise's cost—often a mere 10 percent.

Marked-down merchandise can be consolidated in a number of ways. First, the consolidation can be made into one or a few of the retailer's regular locations. Second, marked-down merchandise can be consolidated into another retail chain or an outlet store under the same ownership. Holt Renfrew (Last Call) uses this strategy. Finally, marked-down merchandise can be shipped to a distribution centre or a rented space such as a convention centre for final sale. This practice encourages a successful yet relatively short markdown period. Consolidation sales can be complex and expensive due to the extra transportation and recordkeeping involved.

| 12.3 | CONCEPT CHECK |

Complete the Concept Check to help develop skill in learning the principles presented.

1. During the month of May, the markdowns for shoes at Aldo totalled $18 600. Shoe sales for the month were $122 480. What was the markdown percent for May?

2. Children's Place six-month merchandise plan for the Guildford Town Centre, Surrey store indicated planned sales of $680 500 and planned markdowns of 30.6 percent. Find the planned markdown dollars.

3. Old Navy sold 200 pairs of men's shorts for $36 during their Victoria Day weekend sale. The shorts went back to their regular price of $45 after the weekend. What was the markdown percent?

The Internet is expected to be increasingly useful for liquidating marked-down merchandise. For example, an electronics store is partnering with eBay to sell goods it has received from trade-ins.

Giving clearance merchandise to charities is an increasingly popular practice. Charitable giving is always a good corporate practice. It is a way of giving back to the community and has strong public relations benefits. Also, the cost value of the merchandise can be deducted from income.

The final liquidation strategy—to carry merchandise over to the next season—is used with high-priced nonfashion merchandise, such as furniture. Generally, however, it's not worth carrying over merchandise because of excessive inventory carrying costs. Retailers need to be well aware of consumers' propensity to check out "value" on the Internet—for example, www.selloffvacations.com and www.autotrader.com.

first-degree price discrimination Charging customers different prices based on their willingness to pay.

second-degree price discrimination Charging different prices to different people on the basis of the nature of the offering.

coupons Documents that entitle the holder to a reduced price or some number of cents off the actual price of a product or service.

Markdowns and Price Discrimination Ideally, retailers would like to have the opportunity to charge customers as much as they would be willing to pay. This practice is called first-degree price discrimination. For instance, if a wealthy customer wants to buy something, the retailer charges more. If a price-sensitive customer comes in, the retailer charges less. Although this practice is legal and is widely used in some retail sectors, such as by automobile and antiques dealers (see Appendix 12A, available on Connect), it is impractical in a retail store with 20 000 SKUs and prices that are displayed for everyone to see. Recently, however, customers are initiating first-degree price discrimination by haggling.

Consider price discrimination versus market segmentation. For example, service retailers (kitchen companies, painting contractors, landscape companies) often spend time "sizing up" or qualifying the prospect and determining the scope of work, including expanding the request, before submitting a proposal.

Markdowns and the other widely used retail adjustment practices described in the next section are known as second-degree price discrimination—charging different prices to different people on the basis of their willingness to do something. For example, early-bird specials at a restaurant offer lower-priced meals before 6 PM.

Coupons

Coupons offer a discount on the price of specific items when they're purchased. Coupons are considered to be a second-degree price discrimination because they provide an incentive for price-sensitive customers to purchase more merchandise. Coupons are issued by manufacturers and retailers in newspapers, on products, on the shelf, at the cash register, over the Internet, and through the mail. Coupons are used because they are thought to induce customers to try products for the first time, convert those first-time users to regular users, encourage large purchases, increase usage, and protect market share against competition.

The evidence on couponing's overall profitability is mixed, depending on the product category. Since coupons have the seemingly positive effect of encouraging larger purchases than without coupons, the coupon promotion may be stealing sales from a future period without any net increase in sales. For instance, if a grocery store runs a coupon promotion on sugar, households may buy a large quantity of sugar and stockpile it for future use. Thus, unless the coupon is used mostly by new buyers, the net impact on sales will be negligible, and there will be a negative impact on profits because of the amount of the redeemed coupons and the cost of coupon redemption procedures. Unfortunately, it's very hard to isolate a market for new users without allowing current users to take advantage of the coupon promotion. If, on the other hand, the coupon is for a DVD or other product whose demand is not controlled by the degree of everyday usage, it might increase overall consumption (see Retailing View 12.4).

Rebates

A rebate is a portion of the purchase price returned to the buyer. Generally, the customer sends a proof of purchase to the manufacturer or a rebate clearinghouse that processes rebates for the manufacturer, and the customer is sent a rebate cheque. Rebates are most useful when the dollar amount is relatively large. Otherwise, it's not worth the customer's time and postage to redeem the rebate. For instance, rebates are often offered on cars, major and portable appliances, computers, and electronic products.

From the retailer's perspective, rebates are more advantageous than coupons since they increase demand in the same way coupons do, but the retailer has no handling costs.

Manufacturers like rebates because many consumers never bother to redeem them, allowing manufacturers to offer, in effect, phantom discounts.[7] Many advertisements prominently proclaim low prices, noting the requirement to send in for rebates in microscopic letters. Consumers are drawn to the store and purchase the product, but only 5 to 10 percent claim the rebate. As a result, consumer advocates hate rebates.

Manufacturers also like rebates because they let them offer price cuts to consumers directly. With a traditional price cut, retailers can keep the price on the shelf the same and pocket the difference. Rebates can also be rolled out and shut off quickly. That allows manufacturers to fine-tune inventories or respond quickly to competitors without actually cutting prices. Finally, because buyers are required to fill out forms with names, addresses, and other data, rebates become a great way to build a customer data warehouse. Retailers must comply with the Canadian privacy laws in effect when collecting customer information.

Price Bundling

Price bundling is the practice of offering two or more different products or services for sale at one price. For instance, McDonald's offers a value-meal bundle of a sandwich, french fries, and a soft drink at a discount compared with buying the items individually. Price bundling increases both unit and dollar sales by increasing the amount of merchandise bought during a store visit. The practice is an example of second-degree price discrimination because it offers more price-sensitive customers a lower-priced alternative.

Multiple-Unit Pricing

Multiple-unit pricing (or quality discounts) is similar to price bundling in that the lower total merchandise price increases sales, but the products or services are similar rather than different.[8] For example, a grocery store may sell three litres of fruit drink for $2.39 when the price per unit is 99 cents—a savings of 58 cents. Like price bundling, this strategy is used to increase sales volume. Depending on the type of product, however, customers may stockpile for use at a later time. Multiple-unit pricing is an example of second-degree price discrimination because customers who buy and consume more of a product are presumably more price-sensitive and thus attracted by the lower prices if they buy more units.

Variable Pricing[9]

Variable pricing means charging different prices in different stores to different demographic segments, a practice referred to as third-degree price discrimination. For example, movie theatres have lower ticket prices for seniors and students. Both groups are price-sensitive. Barnes & Noble.com discounted prices on the Internet compared to its bricks-and-mortar stores in order to compete with Amazon.com. Although this may be necessary in the short run because of these highly competitive, commodity-type products, it could cause ill will among customers who become accustomed to shopping in multiple channels.

Zone pricing refers to the practice of charging different prices in different stores, markets, or regions to address different competitive situations. For instance, food retailers may have up to four or five pricing zones in a single city. They'll have one zone if they're next to a Walmart and another zone if they're next to a less price-competitive regional chain. Prices can vary as much as 10 percent depending on the competition and the economic health of the neighbourhood.[10]

Variable pricing is easier in the food and drug retail sectors than for other stores because many do not item price—put a price tag on each item. It is easy to have different prices in various stores because it is so easy to change them—just scan the bar code on the shelf tag, change the price in the store's price database, and replace the shelf tag with a new label.

Variable pricing also doesn't conflict with their promotional strategy because many newspapers print different editions or can use different freestanding inserts (FSI), which are ads printed at the retailer's expense and distributed as an insert in the newspaper. Even if the newspaper doesn't use zones, a store might carry 40 000 SKUs, advertise 1000, and still have 39 000 left for variable pricing.

There are problems associated with variable pricing in traditional stores. First, as for multichannel retailers, if customers shop in more than one price zone, they will tend to be confused and annoyed. Also, third-degree price discrimination based on income and age is considered to be an unethical practice by many.

Pricing Strategies

In today's retail market, two opposing pricing strategies prevail: everyday low pricing and high/low pricing.[11] We will describe these two strategies and the conditions under which each is used.

Everyday Low Pricing

Many retailers have adopted an everyday low pricing (EDLP) strategy. This strategy emphasizes continuity of retail prices at a level somewhere between the regular nonsale price and the deep-discount sale price of the retailer's competitors. The term everyday low pricing is therefore somewhat of a misnomer. Low doesn't necessarily mean lowest. Although retailers using EDLP strive for low prices, they aren't always the lowest price in the market. At any given time, a sale price at a competing store or a special purchase at a warehouse club store may be the lowest price. A more accurate description of this strategy is therefore everyday same prices because the prices don't have significant fluctuations.

Several of the biggest Canadian retailers—Canadian Tire, Walmart, and Staples Business Depot—have adopted EDLP. In supermarket retailing, Loblaws, including Fortinos and Zehrs, is positioned as an EDLP store.[12] Although these retailers embrace EDLP as their strategy, they do occasionally have sales. They are just not as frequent as their high/low competitors.

Since it is difficult to always have the lowest prices, some retailers have adopted a low-price guarantee policy in which they guarantee that they will have the lowest possible price for a product or a group of products. The guarantee usually promises to match or better any lower price found in the local market. The promise normally includes a provision to refund the difference between the seller's offer price and the lower price.

High/Low Pricing

In a high/low pricing strategy, retailers offer prices that are sometimes above their competition's EDLP, but they use advertising to promote frequent sales. The sales undertaken by retailers using high/low strategies have become more intense in recent years. In the past, fashion retailers would mark down merchandise at the end of a season; grocery and drugstores would have sales only when their vendors offered them special prices or when they were overstocked. Today, many retailers respond to increased competition and a more price-conscious customer by promoting more frequent sales.

DID YOU KNOW?

Consumers' biggest complaint when shopping is that prices are too high.[13]

Which store is using a high/low pricing strategy, and which is using everyday low pricing?

more satisfied customers, higher sales, and fewer rain checks. (A rain check is given to customers when merchandise is out of stock; it is a written promise to sell customers merchandise at the sale price when the merchandise arrives.) In addition, a more predictable customer demand pattern enables the retailer to improve inventory turnover by reducing the average inventory needed for special promotions and backup stock.

High/low pricing strategy advantages:

- **Increase profit through price discrimination.** A high/low strategy allows retailers to charge higher prices to customers who are not price-sensitive and lower prices to price-sensitive customers. When fashion merchandise first hits the store, it's offered at its highest price. Fashion leaders, those who are less sensitive to price, and hard-to-fit customers often buy as soon as the merchandise is available. As the season progresses and markdowns are taken, more price-sensitive customers enter the market and pay a lower price for the same merchandise. Finally, hard-core bargain hunters enter the market for the end-of-season deep-discount sales at the end of each season—25 percent off merchandise that has already been marked down 33 to 50 percent.

- **Sales create excitement.** A "get them while they last" atmosphere often occurs during a sale. Sales draw crowds, and crowds create excitement. Some retailers augment low prices and advertising with special in-store activities such as product demonstrations, giveaways, and celebrity appearances.

- **Sales move merchandise.** All merchandise will eventually sell—the question is, at what price? Frequent sales enable retailers to move the merchandise, even though profits erode. The reasons retailers put certain merchandise on sale are discussed later in this chapter.

- **Emphasis is on quality.** A high initial price sends a signal to customers that the merchandise is high quality. When merchandise goes on sale, customers still use the original, or reference, price to gauge quality.

Pricing Services

Additional challenges arise when pricing services due to (1) the need to match supply and demand and (2) the difficulties customers have in determining service quality.[14]

Matching Supply and Demand

Services are intangible and thus cannot be inventoried. When retailers are selling products, if the products don't sell one day, they can be stored and sold the next day.

Deciding Which Strategy Is Best

rain check When sale merchandise is out of stock, a written promise to customers to sell them that merchandise at the sale price when it arrives.

EDLP approach advantages:

- **Reduced price wars.** Many customers are skeptical about initial retail prices. They have become conditioned to buying only on sale—the main characteristic of a high/low pricing strategy. A successful EDLP strategy enables retailers to withdraw from highly competitive price wars with competitors. Once customers realize that prices are fair, they'll buy more each time and buy more frequently.

- **Reduced advertising.** The stable prices caused by EDLP limit the need for weekly sale advertising used in the high/low strategy. Instead, retailers can focus on more image-oriented messages. In addition, EDLP retailers do not have to incur the labour costs of changing price tags and signs and putting up sales signs.

- **Reduced stockouts and improved inventory management.** An EDLP strategy reduces the large variations in demand caused by frequent sales with large markdowns. As a result, retailers can manage their inventory with more certainty. Fewer stockouts mean

However, when a plane departs with empty seats or a play is performed without a full house, the potential revenue from this unused capacity is lost forever. In addition, most services have limited capacity. For example, restaurants are limited in the number of customers that can be seated. Due to capacity constraints, services retailers might encounter situations in which they cannot realize as many sales as they could make.

To maximize sales and profits, many services retailers engage in yield management.[15] Yield management is the practice of adjusting prices up or down in response to demand to control the sales generated. Airlines are masters at yield management. Using sophisticated computer programs, they monitor the reservations and ticket sales for each flight and adjust prices according to capacity utilization. Prices are lowered on flights when sales are below forecasts and there is significant excess capacity. As ticket sales approach capacity, prices are increased.

Other services retailers use less sophisticated approaches to match supply and demand. For example, more people want to go to a restaurant for dinner or see a movie at 7:00 PM than at 5:00 PM. Restaurants and movie theatres thus might not be able to satisfy the demand for their services at 7:00 PM but have excess capacity at 5:00 PM. Thus, restaurants and movie theatres often price their services lower for customers who use them at 5:00 PM compared with 7:00 PM in an effort to shift demand from 7:00 PM to 5:00 PM.

Theatres use a variety of strategies to try to ensure that the seats are sold and sold at prices equivalent to what customers are willing to pay. Targeted direct mail coupons are often used when the play opens, and two-for-one tickets are introduced about halfway through the run. In some cities, like Toronto and Stratford, theatres partner with half-price ticket brokers, which sell unsold tickets for 50 percent off the ticket price, but only for performances that same day.

Priceline.com offers a unique pricing scheme for booking airline flights, hotel rooms, and rental cars that helps service providers match supply and demand and captures some profit through price discrimination. Customers can visit its website and specify the price they are prepared to pay and the acceptable range of times, days, and/or quality for a particular leisure travel service. For example, a customer can indicate she wants to fly from Montreal to Vancouver, anytime between 6:00 AM and 10:00 PM on September 14 or stay in any four-star hotel in Maui from January 15 to January 20. Thus, the service for which the customer is paying is opaque; the customer does not know the specific nature of the service that will be offered. Then, Priceline.com (www.priceline.com) accesses databases of participating suppliers to determine whether it can fulfill the customer's offer and whether it

wants to accept the price designated by the consumer. Consumers agree to hold their offers open for a specified period of time (generally, not longer than a minute) to determine whether they can or want to accept the offer. Once fulfilled, offers generally cannot be cancelled, making such purchases nonrefundable.

> **yield management**
> The practice of adjusting prices up or down in response to demand to control sales generated.

The service that Priceline.com offers benefits both buyers and sellers. Price-sensitive buyers save money, and sellers generate incremental revenue by selling their services at below retail prices but without disrupting their existing retail pricing structures.[16] Retailing View 12.3 provides another example of how the Internet has enabled price-sensitive buyers to save money.

Determining Service Quality

Due to the intangibility of services, it is often difficult for customers to assess service quality, especially when other information is not available.[17] Thus, if consumers are unfamiliar with a service or service provider, they may use price to make quality judgments. For example, most consumers have limited information about lawyers and the quality of legal advice they offer. They may therefore base their assessment of the quality of legal services offered on the fees they charge. They may also use other nondiagnostic cues to assess quality such as the size and decor of the lawyer's office.

Another factor that increases the dependence on price as a quality indicator is the risk associated with a service purchase. In high-risk situations, many of which involve credence services such as medical treatment or legal consulting, the customer will look to price as a surrogate for quality.

Because customers depend on price as a cue of quality and because price creates expectations of quality, service prices must be determined carefully. In addition to being chosen to manage capacity, prices must be set to convey the appropriate quality signal. Pricing too low can lead to inaccurate inferences about the quality of the service. Pricing too high can set expectations that may be difficult to match in service delivery.

Using Price to Stimulate Retail Sales

LO 2

In this section, we examine three techniques used by retailers to increase sales. Each of these techniques— leader pricing, price lining, and odd pricing—makes the processing of price information easier for consumers and therefore facilitates sales.

Haggling for a Better Price

While out shopping a few weeks ago, Regina Ranonis was trying to decide between trendy low-heeled boots or a more conservative style. Then the sales associate spoke up: If she would spring for both pairs, he would knock $270 off the total price.

Does this sound like the local flea market? It wasn't. A number of retailers are hoping to reel in sales by allowing haggling, or some form of it. The practice isn't entirely new—and it remains officially denied by most companies—but good consumers say they're getting deals everywhere, from Home Depot to Best Buy. Big-name stores such as Saks and Macy's say savvy shoppers who can cite competitors' prices may also find some wiggle room.

The Internet has given a real boost to haggling for bargains. Fashion sites such as RetailMeNot.com list promotional codes that can be used online at checkout. Because many retailers honour a lower price on the same item found at a competitor's store or Internet site, savvy customers use search engines to find the best deal.

Some retailers offer special prices to their best customers, either while in the store or through an e-mail alert. At Neiman Marcus, for instance, customers are regularly invited to "midday dash" sales that last for two hours. Customers receive an e-mail about the sale earlier the same day. They can purchase at 50 percent off by clicking on a link in the e-mail message.

If you think you can't haggle for a better price at national chain stores, think again.

Customers in most countries, except the United States, Canada, Australia, and parts of England, are expected to haggle. Chinese consumers even have taken haggling to a new level—group haggling! The practice, called *tuangou*, or team purchase, begins in Internet chat rooms, where consumers devise plans to buy items like appliances, food, or even cars in bulk. Next, they show up together at the stores and demand discounts.

Many of the biggest U.S. retailers, from The Gap to Pottery Barn, say they're sticking to firm no-haggling policies. Many retailers use cash registers that won't accept unauthorized discount prices without managerial approval. Some even have video cameras not only to watch shoppers but also to make sure the employees aren't cutting sweetheart deals for their friends.

Some of the best negotiating territory is at franchises, where owners have the flexibility to operate more like mom-and-pop shops. But even at major department stores and small chains, a growing number of managers are now authorized to lower a price to meet the competition or throw in free alterations or delivery. Many stores take pains to insist that haggling is off-limits, even as customers and sales associates say it goes on all the time. The policy is, "Try not to come down in price too much, but don't let the business walk out."

Sources: Susan Reda, "Do You Haggle?" Stores, June 2009, p. 6; Marianne Rohrlich, "Adventures in Haggling the Retailers' View," *New York Times*, January 29, 2009, p. D7; Jeanine Poggi and Lily-Hayes Kaufman, "How to Find Secret Shopping Savings," *Forbes*, April 7, 2009; Stephanie Rosenbloom, "High-End Retailers Offering More Discounts," *New York Times*, August 1, 2009; Matt Richtel, "Even at Megastores, Hagglers Find No Price Is Set in Stone," *New York Times*, March 23, 2009, p. A1.

Leader Pricing

leader pricing
A pricing strategy in which certain items are priced lower than normal to increase the traffic flow of customers or to increase the sale of complementary products.

In leader pricing, certain items are priced lower than normal to increase customers' traffic flow or to boost sales of complementary products. Reasons for using leader pricing are similar to those for coupons. The difference is that with leader pricing, merchandise has a low price to begin with, so customers, retailers, and vendors don't have to handle coupons.

Some retailers call these products *loss leaders*. In a strict sense, loss leaders are sold below cost. But a product doesn't have to be sold below cost for the retailer to be using a leader-pricing strategy.

Walmart, Amazon, and Target are using leader pricing to sell top-selling books. Prices for the books are nearly

70 percent below cover prices.[18] Since publishers charge 50 percent of a hardcover book's cover price, these mega-retailers are losing money on these sales. The purpose of this leader-pricing structure is to attract customers to the company's online site, where they may then order additional items. The danger is that independent booksellers or eBay merchants would purchase multiple copies for resale. To prevent independent bookstores from buying the best-sellers for resale, Walmart, Amazon, and Target have set purchasing limits on these books.

The best items for leader pricing are frequently purchased products such as white bread, milk, and eggs, or well-known brand names such as Coke used as loss leaders. Customers take note of ads for these products because they're purchased weekly. The retailer hopes consumers will also purchase their weekly groceries while buying loss leaders.

One problem with leader pricing is that it might attract shoppers referred to as cherry pickers, who go from one store to another, buying only items that are on special. These shoppers are clearly unprofitable for retailers.[19]

Price Lining

In price lining, retailers offer a limited number of predetermined price points within a classification. For instance, a tire store may offer tires only at $49.99, $69.99, and $89.99. Both customers and retailers can benefit from such a strategy for several reasons:

- Confusion that often arises from multiple price choices is essentially eliminated. The customer can choose the tire with either the low, medium, or high price. (There need not be three price lines; the strategy can use more or fewer than three.)

- From the retailer's perspective, the merchandising task is simplified. That is, all products within a certain price line are merchandised together. Further, the firm's buyers can select their purchases within the predetermined price lines.

Many retailers set prices to end in 9s because they believe customers will perceive the prices as lower than they actually are.

- Price lining can also give buyers greater flexibility. If a strict formula is used to establish the initial retail price (initial markup), there could be numerous price points. But with a price-lining strategy, some merchandise may be bought below or above the expected cost for a price line. Of course, price lining can also limit retail buyers' flexibility. They may be forced to pass up potentially profitable merchandise because it doesn't fit into a price line.

- Although many manufacturers and retailers are simplifying their product offerings to save distribution and inventory costs and to make the choice simpler for consumers, price lining can be used to get customers to "trade up" to a more expensive model. Research indicates a tendency for people to choose the product in the middle of a price line. So, for example, if a camera store starts carrying a "super deluxe" model, customers will be more likely to purchase the model that was previously the most expensive. Retailers must decide whether it's more profitable to sell more expensive merchandise or save money by paring down their stock selection.[20]

Odd Pricing

Odd pricing refers to the practice of using a price that ends in an odd number, typically a nine.[21] Odd pricing has a long history in retailing. In the nineteenth and early twentieth centuries, odd pricing was used to reduce losses due to employee theft. Because merchandise had an odd price, salespeople typically had to go to the cash register to give the customer change and record the sale. This reduced salespeople's chances to take money for an item from a customer, keep the money, and never record the sale. Odd pricing was also used to keep track of how many times an item had been marked down. After an initial price of $20, the first markdown would be $17.99, the second markdown $15.98, and so on.

Although results of empirical studies in this area are mixed,[22] many retailers believe that odd pricing can increase profits. Assume that shoppers in a grocery store don't notice the last digit of a price, so the retailer is free to round a price up to the nearest nine. So, if the price would normally be $2.90, the retailers would round up to $2.99. This tactic would increase sales by three percent, more than most grocery stores' entire profit margin, with no increase in costs (increase in sales: $2.99 − $2.90 = $0.090 or $0.090 ÷ $2.99 = 3% of sales).

price lining A pricing policy in which a retailer offers a limited number of predetermined price points within a classification.

odd pricing The practice of ending prices with an odd number (such as 69 cents) or just under a round number (such as $98 instead of $100).

DID YOU KNOW?

Each extra syllable in a price reduces the chances of its being recalled by 20 percent.[23]

For products that are believed to be sensitive to price, many retailers will round the price down to the nearest nine to create a positive price image. If, for example, the price would normally be $3.09, many retailers will lower the price to $2.99. This practice is so prevalent that when planning new-product introductions, many manufacturers plan their cost to retailers such that the retail price will be rounded to a nine or a ninety-nine. Some of the more sophisticated price optimization systems (discussed earlier in this chapter) are capable of taking these factors into account, using ending numbers to optimize profits and price image.

LO8 The Internet, Mobile Devices, and Price Competition

The growth of the electronic channel has changed the way consumers get and use information to make purchasing decisions based on price. Traditionally, price competition between store-based retailers offering the same merchandise was reduced by geography because consumers typically shop at the stores and malls closest to where they live and work. However, using the Internet, consumers can search for merchandise across the globe at a low cost.

Internet sites such as Shopzilla, RedLaser, TheFind, ShopStyle, and PriceGrabber.com allow customers to compare prices across a range of retailers.[25]

Searching for the lowest prices is facilitated by shopping bots. **Search engines** or *shopping bots* are computer programs that search for and provide a list of all Internet sites selling a product category or price of specific brands offered. To limit price comparisons, electronic retailers initially made it hard for customers to go from one Internet site to another. The electronic retailers used different interfaces so that customers needed to learn how to search through the offerings at each new site they visited. In addition, some Internet retailers electronically prevented shopping bots from accessing their sites, collecting information about the products sold at the site, or using these collected data to compare the prices offered at different electronic retailing sites.[26] Although these strategies made it more difficult to compare prices, they also made it more difficult to attract customers to websites.

Although consumers shopping electronically can collect price information with little effort, they can get a lot of other information about the quality and performance of products at a low cost. For instance, an Internet site that offers custom-made Oriental rugs can clearly show real differences in patterns and materials used in construction.

Retailers using an electronic channel can reduce the emphasis on price by providing better services and information. Because of these services, customers might be willing to pay higher prices for the merchandise. For example, Amazon.com provides a customer with the table of contents and synopsis of a book, as well as reviews and comments by the author, or authors, and people who

Using shopping bots such as Bottomdollar.com, consumers can easily collect and compare prices for branded merchandise sold through an electronic retail channel.

Group Buying Sites

Group buying sites such as WagJag, Groupon, LivingSocial, Google Offers, and Dealfind have surged in popularity. Many buying sites negotiate steep discounts on retail, services, and cultural events to subscribers in a generally free daily e-mail, which are activated when a certain number of people agree to buy. Consumer trust in the wisdom of crowds may be the reason why consumers eagerly participate in group buying now, when a number of group buying sites failed ten years ago. Potential purchasers are, most often, asked for credit card details, which will be charged only when a required number of purchasers register for the deal.

There are two basic types of group buying vendors: those who primarily target offers to a local audience and those who focus on national offers. Groupon and WagJag, for example, primarily serve local markets with their listings targeted at the city and sometimes the neighbourhood level. If they run national deals, they are usually local deals run in multiple markets. For instance, The Gap participated in a Groupon promotion during the summer of 2010 that generated over $10 million in sales in one day.

Most group buying sites work on a revenue-sharing model where they take some percentage of the discounted price of every offer sold. The revenue share is negotiated between the buying site and the vendor. It could look like this:

Retail price	$100
Discount (%)	40%
Discount ($)	$40
Offer price (customer pays)	$60
Revenue share (%)	35%
Revenue share ($) (group buying site gets this amount)	$21
Retailer share	$39

There are three fundamental variables to any offer: product, what is being sold; discount, how much is the discount; and quantity, how many are sold or can be sold. Ideally, an offer is one that is profitable after the discount and revenue share, attracts potential buyers, doesn't diminish the brand, and appeals to the type of customer who is likely to become a repeat customer.

For many retailers, the offer could take one of several different forms:

- **Excess inventory.** Group buying sites offer a channel beyond many retailers' physical or virtual presence when they have excess inventory to unload quickly.

- **Dollars for credits.** This common deal offer is where a customer pays, for example, $5 to use toward any good or service for 50 percent of $10.

- **Discounts on specific goods or service.** This is a more targeted discount on a specific good or service— for example, $20 for a pedicure, regularly $40.

- **Significant discount or loss leader.** Some retailers may offer a product near or below cost with the hopes of upselling customers to more expensive or continued purchases—for example, cosmetic clinics that discount the first Botox treatment as a way to acquire new customers for regular treatments.

Group buying websites make local marketing at scale accessible to retailers. But they don't make them instantly profitable or ultimately worthwhile. Retailers need to be smart about their offers, thoughtful about the customer experience, and rigorous in their measurement.

Sources: Alyshah Hasham, "Groupon and other group buying sites such as WagJag and LivingSocial benefit from consumer 'herd mentality': study," *Toronto Star*, February 23, 2012, http://www.thestar.com/printarticle/1135326 (accessed October 6, 2012); "The other contenders in the group buying clone wars," CNBC, December 6, 2010, http://www.cnbc.com/id/40495538/The_Other_Contenders_in_the_Group_Buying_Clone_Wars (accessed October 6, 2012); Alex Cohen, "The Ultimate Guide to Group Buying Sites," SIM Partners, September 19, 2012, http://searchenginewatch.com/article/2206458/The-Ultimate-Guide-to-Group-Buying-Sites (accessed October 6, 2012).

have read the book. When the customer finds an interesting book, Amazon's system is programmed to suggest other books by the same author or the same genre. Finally, customers can tell Amazon about their favourite authors and subjects and then receive e-mails about new books that might be of interest. The classic response to the question, What are the three most important things in retailing? used to be "location, location, location." In the world of electronic retailing, the answer is "information, information, information."[27]

SUMMARY

Canadian consumers are becoming increasingly price-sensitive; they put pressure on retailers to offer pricing strategies such as everyday low prices. Retailers must remember that value is the relationship between what the customer gets and what he or she has to pay. Price competition among retailers is a growing trend, often resulting in escalating lower prices ending in a price war in which there are few winners. Successful retailers will make pricing decisions to match their retail strategy objectives, and acknowledge store image, merchandise mix, and customer service offerings. Using the Internet, consumers can now search for merchandise across the globe. The number of stores that a consumer can visit to compare prices is no longer limited by physical distance.

In this chapter, we've answered several questions. First, what fundamental pricing strategies are retailers adopting? Retailers lie on a continuum from using pure everyday low pricing to pure high/low strategies, where prices start high but decrease with frequent sales. However, most EDLP retailers must resort to occasional sales, and most high/low pricers are attempting to create an image of providing customers good value.

Second, how do retailers set retail prices? There are three primary approaches for establishing prices: the cost-, demand-, and competition-oriented methods. Each method has its merits, but a mix of methods is best. In making pricing decisions, retailers also use break-even analyses to determine the volume of sales necessary for them to make a profit.

Third, since the initial retail price isn't necessarily the price at which the merchandise is finally sold, how do retailers adjust the initial retail price and how do these adjustments affect profits? Retailers have several tactics available, including markdowns, coupons, rebates, bundling, multiple-unit pricing, variable pricing, and special Internet pricing.

Finally, how do retailers use price to stimulate sales without resorting to price discrimination? Three strategies are prevalent: price lining, leader pricing, and odd pricing.

Additional challenges arise when pricing services, due to the need to match supply and demand and the difficulties customers have in determining service quality. Retailers use yield management techniques to match supply and demand for services.

Legal issues that impact pricing decisions come from two sides. Those that affect the buying of merchandise include price discrimination and vertical price-fixing. The legal pricing issues that affect consumers are horizontal price-fixing, predatory pricing, comparative price advertising, bait-and-switch, and scanned versus posted prices. These issues are considered in Appendix 12A, available on Connect.

KEY TERMS

- break-even analysis
- break-even point (BEP)
- competition-oriented method
- contribution margin
- cost-oriented method
- coupons
- demand-oriented method
- everyday low pricing (EDLP)
- first-degree price discrimination
- fixed costs
- high/low pricing
- initial markup
- item price
- keystone method
- leader pricing
- low-price guarantee policy
- maintained markup
- markdown money
- markdowns
- markup
- markup percentage
- merchandising optimization software
- multiple-unit pricing
- odd pricing
- price bundling
- price lining
- rain check
- rebate
- reductions
- search engines
- second-degree price discrimination
- value
- variable cost
- variable pricing
- yield management
- zone pricing

Get Out & Do It!

1. **INTERNET EXERCISE** Price bundling is very common in the travel and vacation industry. Go to the website for Sandals (**www.sandals.com**) and see what you can get—all for one price.

2. **GO SHOPPING** Go to a retailer who retails through bricks and clicks and examine the cost of items in the store and on the website. Do you find the same merchandise for sale in the store and online? Describe any differences observed.

3. **GO SHOPPING** Go to two different types of stores and try to bargain your way down from the tagged price. Explain your experience. Was there any difference in your success rate as a result of type of store or type of merchandise? Did you have better luck when you spoke to a manager?

4. **GO SHOPPING** Go to five different types of stores and ask the manager of each how he or she determines when to take markdowns and how much the markdown

should be. What rule-based approaches are they using? Are any using merchandising optimization software?

5. Go to your favourite food store and your local Walmart to find the prices for the market basket of goods below.

What was the total cost of the market basket at each store? How did the prices compare? Did Walmart live up to its slogan of "Always lower prices"?

Competitive Pricing: Grocery Store vs. Walmart						
Item	Size	Brand	Grocery	Walmart	Price Difference	Percent Savings
Grocery						
Ground coffee	369 g can	Tim Hortons				
Raisin Bran	675 g box	Kellogg's				
Pet Supplies						
Puppy Chow	1.6 kg bag	Purina				
Cleaning						
Liquid laundry detergent	1.47 l bottle	Tide				
Dryer sheets	80 count	Bounce				
Liquid dish detergent	591 ml bottle	Palmolive				
Health and Beauty						
Shampoo	355 ml bottle	Dove				
Toothpaste	170 ml tube	Colgate Total				

Total Cost of the Market Basket of Goods

DISCUSSION QUESTIONS AND PROBLEMS

1. How does merchandising optimization software help buyers make better markdown decisions?

2. Simple examination of markdowns could lead us to believe that they should be taken only when a retailer wants to get rid of merchandise that's not selling. What other reasons could a retailer have to take markdowns?

3. Do you know any retailers that have violated any of the legal issues discussed in Appendix 12A, available on Connect? Explain your answer.

4. Which of the pricing strategies discussed in this chapter are used by your favourite retailer? Do you think they're used effectively? Can you suggest a more effective strategy?

5. What is the difference in the pricing strategies of ebay. com, priceline.com, and staples.com? Which firm do you think will be the strongest in ten years? Why?

To answer Questions 6–10, go to Connect.

6. A department's maintained markup is 38 percent, reductions are $560, and net sales are $28 000. What's the initial markup percentage?

7. Maintained markup is 39 percent, net sales are $52 000, alterations are $1700, shrinkage is $500, markdowns are $5000, employee discounts are $2000, and cash discounts are 2 percent. What are gross margin in dollars and initial markup as a percentage? Explain why initial markup is greater than maintained markup.

8. Cost of a product is $150, markup is 50 percent, and markdown is 30 percent. What's the final selling price?

9. Manny Perez bought a tie for $9 and priced it to sell for $15. What was his markup on the tie?

10. Answer the following:
    a) The Gap is planning a new line of leather jean jackets for fall. It plans to retail the jackets for $100. It is having the jackets produced in the Dominican Republic. Although The Gap does not own the factory, its product development and design costs are $400 000. The total cost of the jacket, including transportation to the stores, is $45. For this line to be successful, The Gap needs to make $900 000 profit. What is its break-even point in units and dollars?
    b) The buyer has just found out that Club Monaco, one of The Gap's major competitors, is bringing out a similar jacket that will retail for $90. If The Gap wishes to match Club Monaco's price, how many units will it have to sell?

11. The manager of a sporting goods department planned to purchase $8400 worth of merchandise at cost. This merchandise was to retail at $14 000. At Supplier A he purchased $4340 at cost, with a retail value of $7000. At Supplier B he purchased $3720 at cost, with a retail value of $6300. What markup percentage must the buyer take on purchases from a third supplier, C, to meet the overall markup objective?

 Practise and learn online with Connect.

human resource management and staff training issues

LEARNING OBJECTIVES

LO1 Review how retailers build a sustainable competitive advantage by developing and managing their human resources.

LO2 Explore how organizational structure identifies the activities and tasks that need to be performed by employees and how these tasks determine the lines of authority and responsibilities in a retail firm.

LO3 Review various ways in which store managers compensate, motivate, train, evaluate, recruit, and select their employees.

LO4 Discuss the trends in human resource management that are impacting retailers today.

LO5 Understand the importance of shrinkage and the relationship between employee theft and customer and store visitor theft.

SPOTLIGHT ON RETAILING

Developing and Retaining Talent to Improve Operations and Save Costs

Constrained economic conditions have highlighted the need for Canadian retailers to offer increasingly innovative modes of learning for their employees, as well as increase knowledge and engagement, while positively affecting the bottom line. Because low talent retention produces a substantial drain on corporate resources, human resources leaders need to know which practices work and what they should focus on to retain and motivate their workforce. Talent retention is critically important for all retail organizations for two main reasons: Turnover is expensive, and top performers drive business performance.

Shoppers Drug Mart is one of the most recognized and trusted names in Canadian retailing, with over 1200 Shoppers Drug Mart and Pharmaprix stores in each province and three territories. Built on a foundation of professional expertise and personal service, Shoppers Drug Mart has been meeting Canadians' health care needs for 50-plus years.

What was once a small pharmacy in Toronto has become an indelible part of the lives of Canadians, young and old. Yet despite its growth, the company has never forgotten its origins. Shoppers Drug Mart has always remained true to the belief that the personal satisfaction of each and every customer is at the root of its success—and it can be ensured only by the commitment of people who realize that success is built one customer at a time. That performance culture is based on the retailer's CORE values: **Care**—improving the health and well-being of Canadians; **Ownership**—approaching every day with personal accountability and commitment; **Respect**—acting with integrity, respect, and openness every day; and **Excellence**—leading together through innovation and superior performance.

The culture of Shoppers Drug Mart is reflected in how it comes together to accomplish a common set of goals. In 2012, Shoppers Drug Mart was recognized with three prestigious awards that celebrate its employer programs and culture. In October, the company was named one of Canada's Top 100 Employers in recognition of its innovative employee programs in training and skills development, community involvement, and work environment. The retailer was also named the winner of the Retail Council of Canada's Excellence in Retailing Talent Development Award 2012, and it was designated one of Canada's Passion Capitalists in 2012. This award celebrates organizations that have achieved long-term success as a result of *passion capital*, a culture that possesses the energy, intensity, and sustainability to consistently generate superior results.

Engagement and recognition. Shoppers Drug Mart maintains that its continued success depends on an ability to attract and retain talented people and engage them in achieving the retailer's business goals, recognizing how important it is that employees understand the company's purpose and how employees impact the company's success. Engagement stems from keeping employees informed of progress, soliciting their feedback, and continuing to strengthen the communications vehicles to allow

this flow of information. Shoppers Drug Mart associate-owners hold regular face-to-face meetings with their employees. Central office leaders conduct quarterly meetings with their teams to discuss company performance, successes, and new initiatives.

The company values employees' views and ideas and encourages their feedback through an annual engagement survey for central and regional office and store employees. Employees' responses reflect the impact of employee programs and help to identify opportunities for improvement and track the company's progress. In 2012, 89 percent of central office employees and 94 percent of store employees responded to questions about the workplace, including such topics as recognition, career development, and community investment. This was the highest level of participation in the four-year history of the survey. Engagement scores increased overall, with improvement in many areas, including support for health and well-being, role in the community, and other factors. Higher levels of engagement positively impact the success of Shoppers Drug Mart in a number of ways, including increased retention.

Recognition is an important part of the corporate culture. Shoppers Drug Mart has several peer-nominated recognition programs. These programs are highly valued by associate-owners and employees as opportunities to further strengthen engagement and recognize excellence.

Leadership and development. Shoppers Drug Mart encourages continuous learning to assist employees in achieving their career development goals and to ensure that the company has the talent required to support growth and promote from within. Store and central office employees have access to a wide range of on-demand e-learning opportunities via the learning management portal Shoppers Drug Mart University (SDMU).

Shoppers Drug Mart introduced SDMU in a phased approach that started in 2010, says Mary Kalkanis, director of learning and development. The program is available to Shoppers employees across Canada and provides a unique mix of online, hands-on, and mentor-based learning structured into four areas: retail, pharmacy, corporate, and leadership.

For instance, to support the leadership development of store employees, Shoppers Drug Mart University offers several programs, including LEAD (Leadership Excellence and Development), from which 530 future associate-owners, store managers, and cosmetics managers graduated in 2012; and Building Your Business: The First 90 Days, a blended learning program comprised of e-learning, on-the-job training, and collaboration with a network of business resources, which was completed by 44 new associate-owners in 2012.

"Really, the business need driving it was to increase speed to productivity for our store employees as well as developing our corporate employees here in the office," Kalkanis said. The other objective, she said Kalkanis, was to make fewer outside hires and instead promote talent from within.

Up-and-coming employees would take leadership foundations, a two-day instructor-led program, followed by situational leadership, supplemented by an array of e-learning programs, including video-based talks by industry leaders, which can be taken by industry leaders, from the office, from their home, from the store, or from a mobile phone.

"We believe that learning is not just what you learn in a classroom, but learning is a continuous cycle," says Kalkanis. "We try to offer innovative learning programs for our employees so that it aligns with our brand. We're integrating convenience in easy, tangible ways for our employees."

SDMU was an instant success on several different levels. Kalkanis said that 68 percent of employees took courses in the first year, compared to an industry average of 20 percent for learning and development courses. "There was an appetite for it," she says. "And we took every opportunity to educate our store employees and corporate employees about its benefits and value."

Educate your employees and save costs. Kalkanis says that while the initial setup cost Shoppers around $500 000, she estimates that the annual cost savings are about $250 000 a year, mostly from administration and printing costs that are no longer needed from previous paper-based learning systems.

There are also intangible benefits. Employee engagement has increased by 10 percent since the company implemented SDMU, six percentage points at the end of 2011 alone, says Kalkanis, adding that the company is seeing the results through more internal promotions and increased productivity. Further, the programs have improved retention figures, trained employees into specialized positions, and boosted employee morale, which has in turn, improved customer service. More than 75 percent of graduates are placed in stores in a leadership role within three months of completing the program.

Sources: "Talent Retention: Six Technology-Enabled Best Practices," Oracle Corporation, June 2012; *Annual Report 2012*, Shoppers Drug Mart, http://corporate.shoppersdrugmart.ca/en-ca/investor-relations (accessed November 10, 2013); *Social Responsibility Report 2012*, Shoppers Drug Mart, http://corporate.shoppersdrugmart.ca/en-ca/social-responsibility/employee-relations (accessed November 10, 2013); and Eve Lazarus, "Developing Talent to Improve Operations and Save Costs," *Canadian Retailer*, Store 2012, Volume 22, Issue 4, pp. 72–73.

This chapter focuses on the organization and management of employees—the retailer's human resources. Howard Schultz, chairman and chief global strategist of Starbucks, emphasizes that "the relationship that we have with our people and the culture of our company is our most sustainable competitive advantage."[1]

Store managers, due to their daily contact with customers, have the best knowledge of customer needs and competitive activity. From this unique vantage point, store managers play an important role in formulating and executing retail strategies. Buyers can develop exciting merchandise assortments and procure them at low cost, but the retailer only realizes the benefits of the buyers' efforts when the merchandise is sold. Good merchandise doesn't sell itself. Store managers must make sure that the merchandise is presented effectively and offer services that stimulate and facilitate customer buying decisions.

Retailers achieve their financial objectives by effectively managing their five critical assets:

- Employees
- Locations
- Merchandise inventory
- Stores
- Customers

Human resource management is particularly important in retailing because employees play a major role in performing critical business functions. Retailing and other service businesses remain labour-intensive. Retailers rely on people to perform the basic retailing activities such as buying, displaying merchandise, and providing service to customers.

The activities undertaken to implement the retailer's human resource strategy, including recruiting, selecting, training, supervising, evaluating, and compensating sales associates, are typically undertaken by store management.

Store Management Responsibilities

Store managers are responsible for increasing the productivity of three of the retailer's principal assets: the firm's investments in its employees, its inventory, and its real estate. Most of this chapter is devoted to increasing labour productivity—namely, the sales generated by each store employee—by effectively managing them through recruiting and selecting good employees, training them to be more effective, and motivating them to perform at high levels (see Retailing View 13.1).

In addition to increasing labour productivity, store managers affect their stores' profits by controlling costs. The major costs are compensation and benefits for employees. Store managers are responsible for controlling these costs by efficiently scheduling labour. But store managers are also responsible for costs associated with operating and maintaining their buildings. Retailers are engaging in innovative cost-cutting initiatives that are also friendly to the environment. Another important retail cost-controlling activity is reducing inventory shrinkage resulting from shoplifting and employee theft.

Exhibit 13–1 outlines the steps in the employee management process that affect store employees' productivity: (1) recruiting and selecting effective people, (2) improving their skills through socialization and training, (3) motivating them to perform at higher levels, (4) evaluating them, and finally, (5) compensating and rewarding them.[2] Store managers also need to develop employees who can assume more responsibility and be promoted to higher-level management positions. By developing subordinates, managers help both their firms and themselves. The firm benefits from having more effective managers, and the manager benefits because the firm has a qualified replacement when the manager is promoted (see Exhibit 13–2).

exhibit 13–1   Steps in the Process of Managing Store Employees

1. Recruit and select employees
2. Socialize and train new employees
3. Motivate and manage employees to achieve store performance goals
4. Evaluate employee performance and provide feedback
5. Compensate and reward employees

management A strategic approach of an organization to achieve its objectives by developing policies and plans for allocating resources.

leadership The process by which a person attempts to influence another to accomplish some goal or goals.

coaching The activity of supporting people to achieve their goals by goal setting, training, advising, encouraging, and rewarding their successes.

average sale per transaction (AST) A measure that evaluates productivity by looking at the number of transactions processed per store or department and the average dollar sale per transaction.

It is important to clarify the term management as opposed to leadership or coaching. Management refers to the strategic approach of an organization to achieve its objectives by developing policies and plans and allocating resources. Human resource management then links the people with the strategic goals of the company. The term leadership refers to the ability of an individual to influence, motivate, and enable others to contribute toward the effectiveness and success of the organization. A good leader will act as a guide and lead by positive example. Coaching is the activity of supporting people so that they can achieve their goals, with goal setting, training, advising, encouraging, and rewarding their successes. Both John Stanton from Running Room and Chip Wilson from Lululemon have utilized leadership and coaching activities in their very successful retail strategies. They both actively lead and coach staff and customers to achieve their fitness, professional, and personal goals as well as meet the strategic goals of the company.

Lo 1

Gaining Competitive Advantage through Human Resource Management

Human resource management can be the basis of a sustainable competitive advantage for three reasons:

- First, labour costs account for a significant percentage of a retailer's total expenses. Thus, the effective management of employees can produce a cost advantage.

- Second, the experience that most customers have with a retailer is determined by the activities of employees who select merchandise, provide information and assistance, and stock displays and shelves.

- Third, these potential advantages, such as exceptional service, are difficult for competitors to duplicate.

Objectives of Human Resource Management

The strategic objective of human resource management is to align the capabilities and behaviours of employees with the short-term and long-term goals of the retail firm.[3] The productivity of human resource management can be measured in a number of ways, including average sale per transaction, sales per employee hour, sales per full-time equivalent, selling cost percent, and employee turnover.

Average sale per transaction (AST) is a measure that evaluates productivity by looking at the number of transactions processed per store or department and the average dollar sale per transaction.[4] A sale transaction can include several items rung up at the till at one time or one item. Since dollar amount of sales does not tell the whole story, this measure relates total gross sales to the number of transactions processed. When this dollar amount increases, the store is doing a better job of selling merchandise to the customer. In order to calculate average sale per transaction, divide the gross sales by the number of transactions.[5]

For example, if on Saturday gross sales of the shoe department were $36 800 and there were 225 transactions, the average sale per transaction would be:

$$\text{Average sale per transaction} = \text{Gross sales} \div \text{Number of transactions}$$
$$= \$36\ 800 \div 225$$
$$= \$163.56$$

A performance measure that is often used for performance review is the sales per employee hour or average sales per labour hour measure. This performance measure looks at the sales for a period to the number of hours

exhibit 13–2 Responsibilities of Store Managers

MANAGING STORE EMPLOYEES
Recruiting and selecting
Socializing and training
Motivating
Evaluating and providing constructive feedback
Rewarding and compensating

CONTROLLING COSTS
Increasing labour productivity
Reducing maintenance and energy costs
Reducing inventory losses

MANAGING MERCHANDISE
Displaying merchandise and maintaining visual standards
Working with buyers
Suggesting new merchandise
Buying merchandise
Planning and managing special events
Marking down merchandise

PROVIDING CUSTOMER SERVICE

employee(s) have worked during that period and can be calculated per shift, week, month, quarter, or year for a single employee or for more. Sales per employee hour is calculated by dividing net sales by the total number of hours worked by the employee or employees during the specified time frame.[6]

For example, if Sally worked 30 hours during the past week and her net sales for the week were $3480, her sales per employee hour for the week would be:

$$\text{Sales per employee hour} = \text{Net sales} \div \text{Number of employee work hours}$$
$$= \$3480 \div 30$$
$$= \$116.00$$

During the same week in the shoe department that Sally worked in, the net sales equalled $152 461. During that same week, employees worked 1275 hours, the sales per employee hour for the week for the department would be:

$$\text{Sales per employee hour} = \text{Net sales} \div \text{Number of employee work hours}$$
$$= \$152\,461 \div 1275$$
$$= \$119.67$$

In this example, Sally is underperforming relative to the rest of the department in terms of her sales per employee hour productivity number as she sold $3.58 less than the total employee average per hour for every hour that she worked that week.

Another common measure of productivity that retailers use is sales per full-time employee. As retail employs a large number of part-time workers, a method is needed to make sense of the many ways in which salary costs can accumulate. One method is to convert hours worked into a full-time equivalent, or FTE. A full-time employee as defined by Statistics Canada is a worker who is employed on a year-round basis and who works 35 to 40 hours per week. (Industry standard for a full-time work week is 40 hours per week or 2080 hours per year.) Having a standard way to measure is very important when making internal comparisons between departments or externally to other companies. Employment figures from Statistics Canada are expressed as FTEs, making this method especially useful when benchmarking. Sales per full-time employee equivalent is therefore the relationship between net sales for a specified period of time and the number of full-time equivalent employees who worked during that specified period of time.[7]

For example, a coffee shop in the mall had weekly sales of $43 296. Six part-time employees worked a total of 320 hours and two full-time employees worked 37.5 hours each. Calculate the sales per full-time equivalent.

$$\text{Sales per full time equivalent}$$
$$= \text{Net sales} \div \frac{\text{Number of}}{\text{full-time equivalents}}$$
$$= \$43\,296 \div 10.53$$
$$= \$4111.68$$

To determine the number of full-time equivalents (10.53) divide the number of part-time hours worked (320) by the number of hours that the retailer considers a full-time work-week (37.5) and then add the number of full-time employees (2).

Selling cost is the relationship between sales productivity and wages and can be calculated for an individual salesperson, a department, and the entire store.[8] This productivity measure is useful when scheduling salespersons on the selling floor to ensure profitability.

For example, if a department manager wanted to calculate the selling cost percentage for a salesperson who made $10 per hour and worked 20 hours last week when net sales were $4320, he would calculate:

$$\text{Selling cost \%}$$
$$= \text{Gross wages} \div \text{Net sales}$$
$$= \$200 \div \$4320$$
$$= 4.63\%$$

While employee productivity is directly related to the retailer's short-term profits, employee attitudes such as job satisfaction and commitment have important effects on customer satisfaction and subsequent long-term performance of the retailer. In addition to employee survey measures of these attitudes, a behavioural measure of these attitudes is employee turnover. Employee turnover is a ratio comparison of the number

sales per employee hour A common measure of productivity that retailers use by dividing net sales by the total number of hours worked by the employee or employees during the specified time frame.

sales per full-time employee A method used by retailers to calculate the many ways in which salary costs can accumulate.

full-time equivalent (FTE) The relationship between net sales for a specified period of time and the number of full-time equivalent employees who worked during that specified period of time.

selling cost The relationship between sales productivity and wages; can be calculated for an individual salesperson, a department, and the entire store.

employee productivity Output generated by employee activities. One measure of employee productivity is the retailer's sales or profit divided by its employee costs.

employee turnover The number of employees occupying a set of positions during a period (usually a year) divided by the number of positions.

DID YOU KNOW?

Labour costs typically are over 25 percent of sales and 50 percent of operating costs in service-oriented department and specialty stores.[9]

of employees a company must replace in a given time period to the average number of total employees. When a retailer must replace a worker, the retailer incurs direct and indirect expenses such as the cost of advertising to find a replacement, human resources costs, lost productivity, and new hire training. Many factors play a role in employee turnover rate and can stem both from employees and from the employer. Such factors as wages, benefits, family days, sick days, and job performance reviews are being used by retailers to reduce their employee turnover.

A failure to consider both long- and short-term objectives can result in mismanagement of human resources and a downward performance spiral, as shown in Exhibit 13–3. Often, when retailers' sales and profits decline due to increased competition, they respond by decreasing labour costs. They reduce the number of sales associates in stores, hire more part-timers, and spend less on training. Although these actions may increase short-term productivity and profits, they have an adverse effect on long-term performance because employee morale and customer service decrease.[13]

Managing both employee and customer expectations is not an easy task, but is necessary for success. Researchers have been able to demonstrate that happy, satisfied employees, working in the best interests of the company, have a positive influence on a retailer's overall performance.

The Human Resource Triad

Retailers such as Canadian Tire believe that human resources are too important to be left solely to the HR department.[14] The full potential of a retailer's human resources is realized when three elements of the human resource triad work together—HR professionals, store managers, and employees.

HR professionals, typically working out of the corporate office, have specialized knowledge of HR practices and labour laws. They are responsible for establishing HR policies that reinforce the retailer's strategy and provide the tools and training used by line managers and employees to implement the policies. The line managers, who primarily work in the stores, are responsible for bringing the policies to life through their daily management of employees working for them (see Retailing View 13.2). The employees also share in the management of human resources. They can play an active role in providing feedback on the policies, managing their own careers, defining their job function, and evaluating the performance of their managers and co-workers.

Special HR Conditions Facing Retailers

Human resource management in retailing is very challenging due to the following conditions:

- Need to use part-time employees
- Emphasis on expense control
- Changing demographics of the workforce

Retailers operating in international markets face additional challenges because of differences in work values, economic systems, and labour laws.

Part-Time Employees Most retailers are open long hours and weekends to respond to the needs of family shoppers and working people. In addition, peak shopping periods occur during lunch hours, at night, on weekends, and during sales promotions. To deal with these peak periods and long hours, retailers have to complement their one or two shifts of full-time (35 to 40 hours per week) store employees with part-time workers. Retailers use computerized scheduling systems that are designed to boost service and trim costs by matching staff size to customer

Recruiting Top Talent for Your Small Business

The recession and evolving demographics have forever changed the way that retailers recruit talent. Slowed profitability in North America and increased competition in both urban and suburban markets have resulted in the development of increasingly complex recruitment and retention initiatives by some retailers. But the impact of these influences has been felt by retailers of all sizes, presenting challenges with respect to recruitment of talented, service-oriented employees. In years past, prospective employees joined the retail industry to gain disposable income or experience. Now, candidates are looking not only for a job in the industry but also a career.

These trends have posed a challenge to small retailers that, despite their lack of resources, must compete directly with larger retail chains (to say nothing of other sectors) for the best and brightest talent. To meet this challenge, independent retailers across the country are using innovative HR approaches and best practices to successfully recruit top-end talent and chart a course for continued success.

From customer to associate. Heather Wolsey, owner of Seasons Gift Shop in St. Albert, Alberta, has never in her 12 years in business had any trouble finding employees, despite the fierce competition for labour taking place in Canada. The recipe for her success is a relatively simple one: Hire from amongst regular customers, stir in a great working atmosphere, add a dash of "targeted recruitment" (a pleasant term for poaching), and allow them to settle into a thriving business.

"I always hire my customers," Wolsey explains. "You already know their personality, they're familiar with your business, and you know they are passionate about the store and what it carries. A salesperson has to love what they sell, after all. That's the benefit of a small store in a small city: You build a relationship with customers."

She also instinctively knows that in order to attract the best talent in Canada today, retailers must enhance their value proposition by increasing their reputation as "the place to work" in the communities in which they operate. To that end, Wolsey ensures that the store is an extremely positive workplace. "Customers pick up on that," she asserts, "which makes Seasons Gift Shop a much-sought-after place to be employed.

"I want all my staff to have well-rounded lives, so I'm very flexible in accommodating my staff with scheduling requests. And I provide a number of perks, such as a bonus at Christmas, membership to a gym in the same strip mall, and, best of all, trips to trade shows in Vegas and other spots," she says, explaining her success in attracting and retaining salespeople.

Source: Andrew Hind, "Recruiting Top Talent for Your Small Business," *Canadian Retailer*, spring 2013, Volume 23, Issue 2, pp. 32–33.

exhibit 13–3 Downward Performance Spiral

traffic, hour by hour. These systems can factor the effects of store promotions, sporting events, graduations, and even the weather to determine the right staffing for different hours and days. To minimize costs, the systems suggest that retailers complement their full-time store employees with part-time employees. Further, they are usually offered no health or retirement benefits and little job security.

Expense Control Retailers often operate on thin margins and must control expenses. Thus, they are cautious about paying high wages to hourly employees who perform low-skill jobs. To control costs, retailers often hire people with little or no experience to work as sales associates, bank tellers,

Did You Know That You Can Reduce Staff Turnover and Increase Performance by Hiring the Right People?

It all begins, and sometimes ends, with your staff—a friendly greeting, knowledgeable advice, efficient service, and an appreciative smile. Your success in achieving better staff performance begins with your ability to hire properly. So how do you hire properly? Let's look at some quick tips that will help you select the right staff.

Reduce your staff turnover first! The first step in a strategic approach to recruiting is to slow down your turnover rates. Here's how you do it:

- Start figuring out why employees are leaving. Conduct exit interviews. You can't fix the problem if you don't know what it is.

- Spend more time coaching and talking with each member of your team. In the process, you'll improve your relationship, meaning they'll stay with you longer.

- Make them successful. People typically don't quit when they're winning. Give them the training they need to succeed.

- Do a comprehensive job of on-boarding new employees. Give them everything they need to feel comfortable and to be successful in the first month of employment.

Get out of your store and find your next employees. If you wait for candidates to show up on your doorstep, you'll wait a long time. Go visit the other stores in your shopping area and get the word out that you're looking for great staff. Networking will get you great results when you invest time in doing it.

Look for candidates like your top performers. Figure out what similarities exist between your best performers, including education, previous job experience, and even personality types. Then, look to hire candidates that match that profile. It doesn't guarantee they'll be successful, but it certainly improves your odds.

Conduct a minimum of two interviews. You can't accurately predict a candidate's success after spending just 20 minutes with them. Also, what message are you sending to the candidate if they get the job after a 15- to 20-minute interview? How important do you think they'll believe the job is? Make them earn it.

Standardize your interviews. All candidates must go through the same process and be asked the same questions. You can't compare candidates accurately unless you ask them the same questions. Figure out what the best questions to ask are and stick to them. No shortcuts!

Use assessments. Eliminate as much subjectivity as possible in the interview by having the candidate complete objective assessments that could include sales and service aptitude assessments, personality profiles, integrity assessments, and leadership profiles.

Check references. Take the time to call previous employers to gather as much supporting evidence as possible about the candidate you're about to hire. Would they hire them again? What responsibilities did they have? Were they successful in meeting those responsibilities? The best indicator of future performance is past performance.

Source: Retail Council of Canada and Graff Retail Group, "Did You Know That You Can Reduce Staff Turnover and Increase Performance by Hiring the Right People?" *Canadian Retailer*, spring 2013, p. 48.

and waiters. High turnover, absenteeism, and poor performance often result from the use of inexperienced, low-wage employees.

Overtime banked hours in Canada are 1.5 hours for each hour worked. This has become an issue in the contractor field where the government is auditing various companies and determining that too many employees are putting only one hour in the bank for each hour of overtime worked. This has led to large payouts by employers when this practice has been going on for many years. This practice can become a financial liability for businesses.

The lack of experience and motivation among many retail employees is particularly troublesome because these employees are often in direct contact with customers. Unlike manufacturing workers on an assembly line, the lowest-paid retail employees work in areas that are highly visible to customers. Poor appearance, manners, and attitudes can have a negative effect on sales and customer loyalty.

Employee Demographics As the retail consumer landscape continues to evolve and change, diverse communities are becoming a more important part of the total buying power. Research has indicated that having an employee population that reflects the consumer population can forge lasting connections, improve service outcomes, and potentially enhance financial performance. Recent research by Deloitte Touche Tohmatsu Limited[15] indicates that retailers have a huge opportunity to leverage a diverse workforce because of the following:

- Diverse employees provide access to better consumer insights as they understand the cultural nuances firsthand.

- A workforce that reflects key characteristics of shoppers motivates improved loyalty as those consumers feel more comfortable doing business with people who understand them and mirror their "community."

- The employee base is further strengthened by development of a pipeline of the best recruits.

Lo 2 Designing the Organization Structure for a Retail Firm

The organization structure identifies the activities to be performed by specific employees and determines the lines of authority and responsibility in the firm. The first step in developing an organization structure is to determine the tasks that must be performed. Exhibit 13–4 shows tasks typically performed in a retail firm. These tasks are divided into four major categories:

- Strategic management
- Administrative management (operations)
- Merchandise management
- Store management

To illustrate the connection between the tasks performed and the organization structure, the tasks are colour-coded. Orange is used to represent the strategic tasks, gold for the merchandise management, green for the store management, and blue for the administrative management tasks.

The strategic market and finance decisions are undertaken primarily by senior management: the CEO, COO, vice-presidents, and the board of directors representing shareholders in publicly held firms. Administrative tasks are performed by corporate staff employees who have specialized skills in human resource management, finance, accounting, real estate, distribution, and management information systems (MIS). People in these administrative functions develop plans, procedures, and information to assist operating managers in implementing the retailer's strategy.

In retail firms, the primary operating or line managers are involved in merchandise management and store management. These operating managers implement the strategic plans with the assistance of administrative personnel. They make the day-to-day decisions that directly affect the retailer's performance.

Organization Design Considerations

Once the tasks have been identified, the retailer groups them into jobs to be assigned to specific individuals and determines the reporting relationships.[16]

Specialization Rather than performing all the tasks shown in Exhibit 13–4, individual employees are typically responsible for only one or two tasks. Specialization, focusing employees on a limited set of activities, enables employees to develop expertise and increase productivity. For example, a real estate manager can concentrate on becoming expert at selecting retail sites, while a benefit manager can focus on becoming expert in developing creative and cost-effective employee benefits. Through specialization, employees work only on tasks for which they were trained and have unique skills.

But employees may become bored if they're assigned a narrow set of tasks, such as putting price tags on merchandise all day long, every day. Also, extreme specialization may increase labour costs. For example, salespeople often don't have many customers when the store first opens, mid-afternoon, or at closing. Rather than hiring a specialist for stocking shelves and arranging merchandise, many retailers have salespeople perform these tasks during slow selling periods.

Responsibility and Authority Productivity increases when employees have the proper amount of authority to effectively undertake the responsibilities assigned to them. For example, buyers who are responsible for the profitability of a merchandise category need to have the authority to make decisions that will enable them to fulfill this responsibility. They should have the authority to select and price merchandise for their category and determine how the merchandise is displayed and promoted.

Sometimes the benefits of matching responsibility and authority conflict with benefits of specialization.

> **organization structure** A plan that identifies the activities to be performed by specific employees and determines the lines of authority and responsibility in the firm.

> **specialization** The organizational structure in which employees are typically responsible for only one or two tasks rather than performing all tasks. This enables employees to develop expertise and increase productivity.

> **DID YOU KNOW?**
> Retail provides one out of every eight Canadian jobs.[17]

exhibit 13–4   Tasks Performed in a Retail Firm

STRATEGIC MANAGEMENT
- Develop a retail strategy
- Identify the target market
- Determine the retail format
- Design organizational structure
- Select locations
- Scan the retail enivornment
- Strategize brand development and repositioning
- Plan for succession (a major priority for senior management)

MERCHANDISE MANAGEMENT
- Buy merchandise
  - Locate vendors
  - Evaluate vendors
  - Negotiate with vendors
  - Place orders
- Control merchandise inventory
  - Develop merchandise budget plans
  - Allocate merchandise to stores
  - Review open-to-buy and stock position
- Price merchandise
  - Set initial prices
  - Adjust prices

STORE MANAGEMENT
- Recruit, hire, train store personnel
- Plan work schedules
- Evaluate performance of store personnel
- Maintain store facilities
- Locate and display merchandise
- Sell merchandise to customers
- Repair and alter merchandise
- Provide services such as gift wrapping and delivery
- Handle customer complaints
- Take physical inventory
- Prevent inventory shrinkage

ADMINISTRATIVE MANAGEMENT (OPERATIONS)
- Promote the firm, its merchandise, and services
  - Plan communication programs
  - Develop communication budget
  - Select media
  - Plan special promotions
  - Design special displays
  - Manage public relations
- Manage human resources
  - Develop policies for managing store personnel
  - Recruit, hire, train managers
  - Plan career paths
  - Keep employee records
- Distribute merchandise
  - Locate warehouses
  - Receive merchandise
  - Mark and label merchandise
  - Store merchandise
  - Ship merchandise to stores
  - Return merchandise to vendors
- Establish financial control
  - Provide timely information on financial performance
  - Forecast sales, cash flow, profits
  - Raise capital from investors
  - Bill customers
  - Provide credit

For example, buyers rarely have authority over how their merchandise is sold in the stores or through the Internet. Other employees, such as store managers who specialize in management of salespeople or designers who specialize in constructing websites, have this authority.

Reporting Relationships   After assigning tasks to employees, the final step in designing the organization structure is determining the reporting relationships. Productivity can decrease when too many or too few employees report to a supervisor. The effectiveness of supervisors decreases when they have too many employees reporting to them. On the other hand, if managers are supervising very few employees, the number of managers increases and costs go up. The appropriate number of subordinates ranges from four to 12, depending on the nature of their tasks, skills, and location.

Matching Organization Structure to Retail Strategy   The design of the organization structure needs to match the firm's retail strategy. For example, category specialists and warehouse clubs such as Future Shop and Costco target price-sensitive customers and thus are very concerned about building a competitive advantage based on low cost. They minimize the number of employees by having decisions made by a few people at corporate headquarters. These centralized organization structures are very effective when there are limited regional or local differences in customer needs.

On the other hand, high-fashion clothing customers often aren't very price-sensitive, but can be extremely demanding, and consumer preferences vary across the country. Retailers targeting these segments tend to have more managers and decision making at the local store level. By having more decisions made at the local store level, human resource costs are higher, but sales also increase since merchandise and services are tailored to meet the needs of local markets.

Retail Organization Structures and Design Issues

Retail organization structures differ according to the type of retailer and the size of the firm. For example, a retailer with a single store will have an organization structure quite different from a national chain. See expanded discussion in Appendix 13A (available on Connect) on the organization of a single-store retailer and a regional department store.

Two important issues in the design of a retail organization are:

- The degree to which decision making is centralized or decentralized
- Approaches used to coordinate merchandise and store management

In the context of a department store chain, the first issue translates into whether the decisions concerning activities such as merchandise management, information and distributions systems, and human resource management are made by the regional department stores or the corporate headquarters. The second issue arises because retailers divide the merchandise and store management activities into different organizations within the firm. Thus, they need to develop ways for coordinating these interdependent activities.

Centralization versus Decentralization

Centralization occurs when authority for retailing decisions is delegated to corporate managers rather than to geographically dispersed regional, district, and store managers; decentralization occurs when authority for retail decisions is assigned to lower levels in the organization.

Retailers reduce costs when decision making is centralized in corporate management:

- First, overhead falls because fewer managers are required to make the merchandise, human resource, marketing, and financial decisions. Centralized retail organizations can similarly reduce personnel in administrative functions such as marketing and human resources.

- Second, by coordinating buying across geographically dispersed stores, the company achieves lower prices from suppliers. The retailer can negotiate better purchasing terms by placing one large order rather than a number of smaller orders.

- Third, centralization provides an opportunity to have the best people make decisions for the entire corporation. For example, in a centralized organization, people with the greatest expertise in areas such as MIS, buying, store design, and visual merchandise can have all stores benefit from their skills.

- Finally, centralization increases efficiency. Standard operating policies are used for store and personnel management; these policies limit the decisions made by store managers. For example, corporate merchandisers do considerable research to determine the best method for presenting merchandise. They provide detailed guides for displaying merchandise to each store manager so that all stores look the same throughout the country. Because they offer the same core merchandise in all stores, centralized retailers can achieve economies of scale by advertising through national media rather than more costly local media.[18]

Decentralization also has strengths:

- Although centralization has advantages in reducing costs, the disadvantage of centralization is that it makes it more difficult for a retailer to adapt to local market conditions.

- In addition to problems with tailoring merchandise to local needs, the centralized retailer also may have difficulty responding to local competition and labour markets. Since pricing is established centrally, individual stores may not be able to respond quickly to competition in their market. Finally, centralized personnel policies can make it hard for local managers to pay competitive wages in their area or to hire appropriate types of salespeople.

However, centralized retailers are relying more on their information systems to react to local market conditions. By looking at buying patterns across a large number of stores, the centralized buyer might uncover opportunities that local managers would not see.

Large retailers are using their information systems to make more and more merchandise and operations decisions at corporate headquarters. For example, the corporate staff at Holt Renfrew is taking responsibility for operational activities such as distribution, information systems, private-brand merchandise, and human resource management policies. However, each Holt Renfrew store division is still responsible for the management of merchandise.

Coordinating Merchandise and Store Management

Small independent retailers have little difficulty coordinating their stores' buying and selling activities. Owner–managers typically buy the merchandise and work with their salespeople to sell it. Being in close contact with customers, the owner–managers know what their customers want.

On the other hand, large retail firms organize the buying and selling functions into separate divisions. Buyers specialize in buying merchandise and have limited contact with the store management responsible for selling it. Although this specialization increases buyers' skills and expertise, it makes it harder for them to understand customers' needs. Below, we discuss four approaches large retailers use to coordinate buying and selling.

Improving Appreciation for Store Environment
Fashion-oriented retailers use several methods to increase buyers' contact with customers and to improve informal communication between buyers and store personnel who sell the merchandise they buy. Management trainees, who eventually become buyers, are required by most retailers to work in the stores before they enter the buying office. During this six- to ten-month training period, prospective buyers gain appreciation for the activities

centralization The degree to which authority for making retail decisions is delegated to corporate managers rather than to geographically dispersed regional, district, and store management.

decentralization When authority for retail decisions is made at lower levels in the organization.

DID YOU KNOW?

The median number of stores in Canada per district manager is 11.[19]

extrinsic rewards
Rewards (such as money, promotion, and recognition) given to employees by their manager or the firm.

intrinsic rewards
Nonmonetary, intangible rewards employees get from doing their jobs.

performed in the stores, the problems salespeople and department managers encounter, and the needs of customers.

Making Store Visits Another approach to increasing customer contact and communication is to have buyers visit the stores and work with the departments they buy for. At Walmart, all managers (not just the buyers) are required to visit stores frequently and practise the company philosophy of CBWA (coaching by wandering around). This face-to-face communication provides managers with a richer view of store and customer needs than they can get from impersonal sales reports from the company's management information system. Spending time in the stores improves buyers' understanding of customer needs, but this system is costly because it reduces the time the buyer has to review sales patterns, plan promotions, manage inventory, and locate new sources of merchandise.

Assigning Employees to Coordinating Roles
Some retailers have people in the merchandise division (the planners who work with buyers) and the stores (the managers of sales and merchandise who work for the store managers) who are responsible for coordinating buying and selling activities. Many national retail chains have regional and even district staff personnel to coordinate buying and selling activities.

Involving Store Management in Buying Decisions
Another way to improve coordination between buying and selling activities is to increase store employees' involvement in the buying process. This process would be more typical of smaller retail chains in which a decentralized buying process would assist the retailer in offering the newest trend for a specific target market. In some cases, the involvement of staff will not only provide a retail opportunity but also has the potential to build staff loyalty.

Besides developing an organization structure, human resource management undertakes a number of activities to improve employee performance, build commitment in employees, and reduce turnover. In the following two sections of this chapter, we examine these human resource management activities.

Compensating and Motivating Retail Employees

A critical task of human resource management is to motivate employees to work toward achieving the firm's goals and implementing its strategy. The task is often difficult because employees' goals may differ from those of the firm. For example, a sales associate might find it more personally rewarding to creatively arrange a display than to help a customer. Retailers generally use three methods to motivate their employees' activities: policies and supervision, incentives, and organizational culture.

Store employees receive two types of rewards from their work: extrinsic and intrinsic. Extrinsic rewards are rewards provided by either the employee's manager or the firm, such as compensation, promotion, and recognition. Intrinsic rewards are rewards employees get personally from doing their job well. For example, salespeople often like to sell because they think it's challenging and fun. Of course, they want to be paid, but they also find it rewarding to help customers and make sales.[20]

Policies and Supervision

Perhaps the most fundamental method of coordination is to:

- Prepare written policies that indicate what tasks employees are responsible for
- Have supervisors/managers enforce these policies

For example, retailers may set policies on when and how merchandise can be returned by customers. If employees use the written policies to make these decisions, their actions will be consistent with the retailer's strategy.

But strict reliance on written policies can reduce employee motivation. Employees might have little opportunity to use their own initiative to improve performance of their areas of responsibility. As a result, they eventually might find their jobs uninteresting.

Relying on rules as a method of coordination leads to a lot of red tape. Situations will arise that aren't covered by a rule. Then employees will need to talk to a supervisor before they can deal with the situation.

Incentives

The second method of motivating and coordinating employees uses incentives to motivate them to perform activities consistent with the retailer's objectives. For example, buyers will be motivated to focus on the firm's profits if they receive a bonus based on the profitability of the merchandise they buy.

Some of the criteria that managers and employees could be measured on include customer satisfaction, average order dollar amount, market share, sales growth, top-of-mind awareness in a market, promotion from within, employee development, ideas and suggestions from staff that are implemented, and revenue per square foot. It should be remembered that there can be a negative impact with a straight commission program with respect to the credibility of a manager or sales associate's worth to the company. For example, the financial industry will now need to disclose how much they are going to be paid by a fund if the customer purchases that fund.

Types of Incentive Compensation Two types of incentives are commissions and bonuses:

- A commission is compensation based on a fixed formula, such as 2 percent of sales. For example, many retail salespeople's compensation is based on a fixed percentage of the merchandise they sell.

- A bonus is additional compensation awarded periodically based on an evaluation of the employee's performance. For example, store managers often receive bonuses at the end of the year based on their store's performance relative to its budgeted sales and profits.

Besides incentives based on individual performance, retail managers often receive additional income based on their firm's performance. These *profit-sharing* arrangements can be offered as a cash bonus based on the firm's profits or as a grant of stock options that link additional income to performance of the firm's stock.

A number of retailers such as Walmart and Home Depot use *stock incentives* to motivate and reward all employees, including sales associates. Employees are encouraged to buy shares in their companies at discounted prices through payroll deduction plans. These stock incentives align employees' interests with those of the company and can be very rewarding when the company does well. However, if growth in the company's stock price declines, employee morale declines too, corporate culture is threatened, and demands for higher wages and more benefits develop.[21]

An incentive compensation plan rewards employees on the basis of their productivity. Many retailers now use incentives to motivate greater sales productivity by their employees. With some incentive plans, a salesperson's income is based entirely on commission—called a straight commission. For example, a salesperson might be paid a commission based on a percentage of sales made minus the merchandise returned.

Incentive plans may include a fixed salary plus a commission on total sales or a commission on sales over quota. For example, a salesperson might receive a salary of $200 per week plus a commission of 2 percent on all sales over a quota of $50 per hour.

Incentive compensation plans are a powerful motivator for salespeople to sell merchandise, but they have a number of disadvantages. For example, it's hard to get salespeople who are compensated totally by commission to perform nonselling activities. Also, salespeople will concentrate on the more expensive, fast-moving merchandise and neglect other merchandise. Sales incentives can also discourage salespeople from providing services to customers. Finally, salespeople compensated primarily by incentives don't develop loyalty to their employer. The employer doesn't guarantee them an income, so they feel no obligation to the firm.

Under a straight commission plan, salespeople's incomes can fluctuate from week to week, depending on their sales. Because retail sales are seasonal, salespeople might earn most of their income during the Christmas season but much less during the summer months. To provide a steadier income for salespeople who are paid by high-incentive plans, some retailers offer a drawing account. With a drawing account, salespeople receive a weekly cheque based on their estimated annual income, and commissions earned are credited against the weekly payments. If the draw exceeds the earned commissions, the salespeople return the excess money they've been paid, and their weekly draw is reduced. If the commissions earned exceed the draw, salespeople are paid the difference.

Quotas are often used with compensation plans. A quota is a target level used to motivate and evaluate performance. Examples include sales per hour for salespeople or maintained margin and inventory turnover for buyers. For department store salespeople, selling quotas vary across departments due to differences in sales productivity levels.

A quota–bonus plan provides sales associates with a bonus when their performance exceeds their quota. A quota–bonus plan's effectiveness depends on setting reasonable, fair quotas, which can be difficult. Usually, quotas are set at the same level for everyone in a department, but salespeople in the same department may have different abilities or face different selling

commission Compensation based on a fixed formula, such as percentage of sales.

bonus Additional compensation awarded periodically, based on a subjective evaluation of the employee's performance.

incentive compensation plan A compensation plan that rewards employees on the basis of their productivity.

straight commission A form of salesperson's compensation in which the amount paid is based on a percentage of sales made minus merchandise returned.

drawing account A method of sales compensation in which salespeople receive a weekly cheque based on their estimated annual income.

quota Target level used to motivate and evaluate performance.

quota–bonus plan Compensation plan that has a performance goal or objective established to evaluate employee performance, such as sales per hour for salespeople and maintained margin and turnover for buyers.

DID YOU KNOW?

Seventy-three percent of consumers attribute their best customer service experience to store employees. Conversely, 81 percent of consumers attribute their worst customer service experience to employees.[22]

environments. Newly hired salespeople might have a harder time achieving a quota than more experienced salespeople. Thus, a quota based on average productivity may be too high to motivate the new salesperson and too low to effectively motivate the experienced salesperson. Quotas should be developed for each salesperson on the basis of his or her experience and the nature of the store area in which he or she works.[24]

Group Incentives To encourage employees in a department or store to work together, some retailers provide additional incentives based on the performance of the department or store as a whole. For example, salespeople might be paid a commission based on their individual sales and then receive additional compensation according to the amount of sales over plan, or quota, generated by all salespeople in the store. The group incentive encourages salespeople to work together in their nonselling activities and handling customers so that the department sales target will be achieved.[25]

Setting the Commission Percentage Assume that a specialty store manager wants to hire experienced salespeople. To get the type of person she wants, she feels she must pay $12 per hour. Her selling costs are budgeted at 8 percent of sales. With compensation of $12 per hour, salespeople need to sell $150 worth of merchandise per hour ($12 divided by 8 percent) for the store to keep within its sales cost budget. The manager believes the best compensation would be one-third salary and two-thirds commission, so she decides to offer a compensation plan of $4 per hour salary (33 percent of $12) and a 5.33 percent commission on sales. If salespeople sell $150 worth of merchandise per hour, they'll earn $12 per hour ($4 per hour in salary plus $150 multiplied by 5.33 percent, which equals $8 per hour in commission).

$$\text{Commission \$} = \text{Net sales} \times \text{Commission \%}$$

In addition to competitive salary, vacation, and tuition reimbursement as a retailer's key retention strategies, keeping your best requires attention to each employee as an individual. Retailers will need to be creative to keep their best employees eager to advance to become future company leaders.

Organizational Culture

The final method for motivating and coordinating employees is to develop a strong organizational culture.

An **organizational culture** is the set of values, traditions, and customs in a firm that guides employee behaviour. These guidelines aren't written in a set of policies and procedures; they are traditions passed along by experienced employees to new employees.[26]

Many retail firms have strong organizational cultures that give employees a sense of what they ought to do on their jobs and how they should behave to be consistent with the firm's strategy (see Retail Roundtable 13.3). For example, Harry Rosen's strong organizational culture emphasizes customer service, while Walmart's organizational culture focuses on reducing costs so that the firm can provide low prices to its customers.

An organizational culture often has a much stronger effect on employees' actions than rewards offered in compensation plans, directions provided by supervisors, or written company policies.

Harry Rosen emphasizes the strength of organizational culture in the policy manual given to new employees. The manual has one rule: Use your best judgment to do anything you can to provide service to our customers. Lack of written rules doesn't mean that Harry Rosen employees have no guidelines or restrictions on their behaviour. Its organizational culture guides employees' behaviour. New salespeople learn from other employees that they should always wear clothes sold at Harry Rosen, that they should park their cars at the outskirts of the parking lot so that customers can park in more convenient locations, and that they should offer to meet busy executives at their offices with new menswear trend items.

Developing and Maintaining a Culture Organizational cultures are developed and maintained through stories and symbols.[27] See http://stservicemovie.com for the story of Johnny, the grocery store bagger.

Disney strengthens its organizational culture through the labels it uses for its employees and by steeping employees in the culture during the selection process. Management and employees view themselves as part of a team whose job is to produce a very large show. Applicants are trying out for a role in the cast rather than being hired for a job. For hourly jobs, the casting director (the person in charge of recruiting) interviews applicants to determine if they can adapt to the company's strong organizational culture. Do they understand and accept the fact that Disney has strict grooming requirements (no facial hair for men, little makeup for women)? Is the applicant willing to work on holidays? After the initial screening, the remaining applicants are judged on how well they might fit in with the show. Current employees participate in the entire process—they assess the applicant's behaviours and attitudes while also providing first-hand information on their role in the "production."

Job Analysis

The job analysis identifies essential activities and is used to determine the qualifications of potential employees. For example, retail salespeople's responsibilities vary from company to company and from department to department within a store (see Exhibit 13–5).

Managers can obtain the information needed for a job analysis by observing employees presently doing the job and by determining the characteristics of exceptional performers. Exhibit 13–5 lists some questions that managers should consider in a job analysis for sales associates. Information collected in the job analysis is then used to prepare a job description.

Job Description

A job description includes activities the employee needs to perform and the performance expectations expressed in quantitative terms. The job description is a guideline for recruiting, selecting, training, and eventually evaluating employees.

Locating Prospective Employees

Staffing stores is becoming a critical problem because changing demographics are reducing the size of the labour pool.[28] Here are some suggestions being used by retailers to recruit employees in this tight labour market, in addition to placing ads in local newspapers and posting job openings on websites such as Monster.ca:

- Look beyond the retail industry.
- Use your employees as talent scouts.
- Provide incentives for employee referrals.
- Recruit from minority communities, immigrants, and seniors.
- Use the Internet to locate prospective employees. Today you cannot survive in business without computer skills. Employees comfortable with basic computer applications such as Word, Excel, and PowerPoint are not going to be challenged by point-of-purchase sales systems.
- Recruit from LinkedIn and other social networking sites.

Social Recruiting

It is not sufficient to just post job vacancies on online job boards such as Monster.ca or Workopolis. Job boards such as these should continue to be part of the recruiting mix a retailer uses, but the potential for LinkedIn and other social networking sites to play major roles in retail recruiting strategies is continuing to grow. Millions of potential employees profile themselves on these sites each year. Social recruiting isn't really new anymore. A social network such as LinkedIn combines job listings, candidate search, trusted referral options, and the power of networks for retail employers all in one place. In fact, 97.3 percent of recruiters polled by Bullhorn for the North American Staffing and Recruiting Trends Report used LinkedIn for recruiting in 2012.[29] According to the report, newer social networks also gained traction, with 19.1 percent of staffing professionals leveraging Google Plus in 2012 and 3.6 percent using Pinterest. The same study shows a decrease in the use of Facebook (51.3 percent in 2012 and 60.2 percent in 2011) and Twitter (48.8 percent used Twitter in 2012 compared to 51.5 percent in 2011). In contrast, more respondents used LinkedIn in 2012 than in 2011.

Screening Applicants to Interview

The screening process matches applicants' qualifications with the job description. Many retailers use automated

job analysis
Identifying essential activities and determining the qualifications employees need to perform them effectively.

job description
A description of the activities the employee needs to perform and the firm's performance expectations.

DID YOU KNOW?

According to a 2011 survey of recruiters who used social media to screen candidates, 69 percent said that they had screened out certain candidates for posting inappropriate photos, negative comments about a former employer, or discriminatory comments. This same survey revealed that Facebook and Twitter are the two most commonly used platforms for screening potential candidates during a hiring process.[30]

exhibit 13–5   Questions for Undertaking a Job Analysis

- How many salespeople will be working in the department at the same time?
- Do the salespeople have to work together in dealing with customers?
- How many customers will the salesperson have to work with at one time?
- Will the salesperson be selling on an open floor or working behind the counter?
- How much and what type of product knowledge does the salesperson need?
- Does the salesperson need to sell the merchandise or just ring up the orders and provide information?
- Is the salesperson required to make appointments with customers and develop a loyal customer base?
- Does the salesperson have the authority to negotiate price or terms of the sale?
- Does the salesperson need to demonstrate the merchandise?
- Will the salesperson be expected to make add-on sales?
- Is the appearance important? How should an effective salesperson look?
- Will the salesperson be required to perform merchandising activities such as stocking shelves and setting up displays?
- To whom will the salesperson report?
- Under what compensation plan will the salesperson be working?

Corporate Culture

It comes down to clarity. If we're clear about what we're doing and what our business objectives are, and we keep that communication open and we keep people involved, it becomes easier to be that purveyor of corporate culture. Many of our best ideas are coming from the field. Who knows better what the customer wants, what's working and what's not than that person who's dealing every day with a customer?

Tina Shane, vice-president, retail and customer experience, western Canada, Chapters

The strategic plan really helps to develop the corporate culture. It needs to be communicated to all employees, even the part-timers.

Rafik Louli, regional director, central regional office #3, LCBO

The store manager is the lynchpin of a retail operation. How do you make sure the store manager is equipped to be purveyor of the corporate culture at the store level?

As the company, you have to clearly define what that expectation is for your customer service and your corporate culture. Next is training. Most retailers are at a new company every six months due to attrition, so that corporate culture training and expression of ongoing expectations needs to be constant. Most people want to know what the expectations of them are so that when they go home at night they've got a sense of contribution and success.

Ron Hornbaker, interim CEO, Golf Town

It starts with the recruitment process. The Body Shop brand and the brand values are always a part of the hiring process. When you seek out those who already believe in the values that your organization stands for, the transition to become what we call a brand ambassador is really a natural one. Our rule here is to make sure we keep managers at every level engaged and informed in the evolution of the brand so that they always feel like they are a part of that process.

Carmela Aita, director, human resources, The Body Shop

Most of our store managers are brought up through the organization, so the culture and the understanding of how to represent Future Shop is handed down from generation to generation, through our managers, through our district managers, and through all of the things that we do.

Mike Hickey, general manager, Future Shop, Calgary

Source: Robert Price, "Recruiting, Retaining and Empowering Store Managers," *Canadian Retailer,* winter 2012, pp. 36–39.

Internet sites such as workopolis.com can be useful recruiting tools and ensure that job applicants are computer-literate.

prescreening programs as a low-cost method of identifying qualified candidates. Applicants either interact with a web-enabled store kiosk or call a toll-free telephone number, and a computer program asks some basic questions that the applicants answer using the keyboard or telephone buttons.

The questions are tailored to the retailer's specific needs and environment. For example, a mall-based chain selling music-themed merchandise asks, "Would you work in an environment where loud alternative music is played?" The response time for answering the questions is monitored and follow-up questions are asked when the answers are unusually slow. When applicants pass this automated prescreen, additional information is collected using application forms, reference checks, and tests.[31]

Application Forms

A job application form contains information about the applicant's employment history, previous compensation, reasons for leaving previous employment, education and training, and references. This information enables the manager to determine whether the applicant meets the minimum qualifications and also provides information for interviewing the applicant.[32]

References

A good way to verify the information given on an application form is to contact the applicant's references. Contacting references is also helpful for collecting additional information from people who've worked with the applicant. In addition, store managers should check with former supervisors not listed as references. Due to potential legal problems, however, many companies have a policy of not commenting on past employees.[33]

Store managers generally expect to hear favourable comments from an applicant's references or even from previous supervisors who may not have thought highly of the applicant. One approach for reducing the positive bias is to ask the reference to rank the applicant relative to others in the same position. For example, the manager might ask, "How would you rate Pat's customer service skill in relation to other retail sales associates you have worked with?" Another approach is to use a positively toned scale ranging from "somewhat effective" to "extremely effective."

The Internet has become an excellent source of information on prospective employees. A quick look at someone's Facebook entry can often reveal more about the person than a face-to-face interview. A Google search can also be useful for finding out information that may not appear on the job application or emerge through contacts with references.

Testing

Intelligence, ability, personality, and interest tests can provide insights about potential employees. For example, intelligence tests yield data about the applicant's innate abilities and can be used to match applicants with job openings and to develop training programs. However, tests must be scientifically and legally valid. They can be used only when the scores have been shown to be related to job performance. It is illegal to use tests assessing factors that are not job-related or that discriminate against specific groups.

Some retailers use tests to assess applicants' honesty and ethics. Paper-and-pencil honesty tests include questions to find out if an applicant has ever thought about stealing and if he believes other people steal ("What percentage of people take more than $1 from their employer?").[36] The use of lie detectors in testing employees is prohibited.

Realistic Job Preview

Turnover is reduced when the applicants understand both the attractive and unattractive aspects of the job. Many retailers want their new hires to have previous retail experience. They have found that experience, even if the previous job was significantly different than the new opportunity, gives the applicant an appreciation for what a life in retailing is all

DID YOU KNOW?

A total of 35 percent of respondents to a 2012 survey said that LinkedIn was their social media platform of choice for job searching.[40]

about. For example, PetSmart, a pet supply category specialist, has each applicant view a ten-minute video that begins with the advantages of being a company employee and then shows scenes of employees dealing with irate customers and cleaning up animal droppings. This type of job preview typically screens out 15 percent of the applicants who would most likely quit within three months if they were hired.[37]

Selecting Applicants

After screening applications, the selection process typically involves a personal interview. Since the interview is usually the critical factor in the hiring decision, the store manager needs to be well prepared and to have complete control over the interview. (See Retailing View 13.4 for a discussion of family interviews.)

Preparation for the Interview   The objective of the interview is to gather relevant information, not simply to ask a lot of questions. The most widely used interview technique, called the *behavioural interview*, asks candidates how they handled actual situations they have encountered in the past, situations requiring skills outlined in the job description. For example, applicants applying for a job requiring them to handle customer complaints would be asked to describe a situation in which they were confronted by someone who was angry with something they had done. Candidates are asked to describe the situation, what they did, and the outcomes of their actions. These situations also can be used to interview references for the applicants.[38]

An effective approach to interviewing involves some planning by the managers but also allows some flexibility in selecting questions. Managers should develop objectives for what they want to learn about the candidate. Each topic area covered in the interview starts with a broad question, such as "Tell me about your last job," designed to elicit a lengthy response. The broad opening question is followed by a sequence of more specific questions, such as "What did you learn from that job?" or "How many subordinates did you have?" Finally, managers must be careful to avoid asking questions that are discriminatory.[39]

Managing the Interview   Exhibit 13–6 shows questions the manager might ask. Here are some suggestions for questioning the applicant during the interview:

- Encourage long responses by asking questions such as "What do you know about our company?" rather than "How familiar are you with our company?"
- Avoid asking questions that have multiple parts.
- Avoid asking leading questions such as "Are you prepared to provide good customer service?"
- Be an active listener. Evaluate the information that is being presented and sort out the important comments from the unimportant ones. Some techniques for active listening are repeating or rephrasing information, summarizing the conversation, and tolerating silences.[41]
- Observe the applicant's behaviour in the interview—attitude, appropriate dress, eagerness to learn. Some managers interview candidates while giving them a tour through the store.

When the manager sees a display that's out of order, he might say, "While we're talking, would you help me straighten this out?" Some candidates will stand back; others will jump right in and help out. (*Hint:* You want to hire candidates from the second group.)

Legal Considerations in Selecting and Hiring Store Employees

Heightened social awareness and government regulations emphasize the need to avoid discrimination in hiring. Discrimination is specifically prohibited in the following human resource decisions: recruitment, hiring, discharge, layoff, discipline, promotion, compensation, and access to training.

Discrimination arises when a member of a protected class (women, minorities, etc.) is treated differently than nonmembers of that class (disparate treatment) or when an apparently neutral rule has an unjustified discriminatory effect (disparate impact). An example of disparate treatment occurs when a qualified woman does not receive a promotion given to a less qualified man. Disparate impact occurs when a retailer requires high school graduation for all its employees, thereby excluding a larger proportion of disadvantaged minorities, when at least some of the jobs (e.g., custodian) could be performed just as well by people who did not graduate from high school. In such cases, the retailer is required to prove the imposed qualification

More Parents Joining Kids on Job Interviews

Mom and Dad were there for your first day of school, so why not the first job interview? A survey conducted on behalf of RSM Richter, an accounting and business advisory firm, found that one in five Canadians believe parents should be allowed to attend job interviews with their children. Half the respondents thought that parents should play an important role in their children's career by supporting them, helping them make the right decisions, and offering advice.

"Any company that actively recruits should regularly track the attitudes and expectations of potential employees—especially those just entering the workforce—to ensure recruiting strategies match expectations," said Lisa Fusina, human resources manager, RSM Richter Toronto/Calgary. "It is understandable that parents want to help their children make the right career decisions in all aspects of their life, including their career."

While parents attending a job interview with children may be a rarity, more than half of respondents said parents should have the opportunity to review their children's employment contracts, and 47 percent agreed that parents should have a significant role in the career choices of their children.

Source: "More Parents Joining Kids on Job Interviews," *retailHR, Retail Human Resources Newsletter*, November/December 2008, p. 2.

exhibit 13–6 Interviewing Questions

EDUCATION

What were your most favourite and least favourite subjects in university? Why?

What types of extracurricular activities did you participate in? Why did you select those activities?

If you had the opportunity to attend school all over again, what if anything, would you do differently? Why?

How did you spend the summers during university?

Did you have any part-time jobs? Which of your part-time jobs did you find most interesting? What did you find most difficult about working and attending college or university at the same time? What advice would you give to someone who wanted to work and attend university at the same time?

What accomplishments were you most proud of?

PREVIOUS EXPERIENCE

What's your description of the ideal manager? Subordinate? Co-worker?

What did you like most/least about your last job?

What kind of people do you find it difficult/easy to work with? Why?

What has been your greatest accomplishment during your career to date?

Describe a situation at your last job involving pressure. How did you handle it?

What were some duties on your last job that you found difficult?

Of all the jobs you've had, which did you find the most/least rewarding?

What is the most frustrating situation you've encountered in your career?

Why do you want to leave your present job?

What would you do if ...?

How would you handle ...?

What would you like to avoid in future jobs?

What do you consider your greatest strength/weakness?

What are your responsibilities in your present job?

Tell me about the people you hired on your last job. How did they work out? What about the people you fired?

What risks did you take in your last job and what were the results of those risks?

Where do you see yourself in three years?

What kind of reference will your previous employer give?

What do you do when you have trouble solving a problem?

QUESTIONS THAT ARE DISCRIMINATORY AND CANNOT BE ASKED

Do you have plans for having children/a family? What are your marriage plans? What does your husband/wife do? What happens if your husband/wife gets transferred or needs to relocate? Who will take care of your children while you're at work? (Asked of men) How would you feel about working for a woman?

How old are you? What is your date of birth? How would you feel working for a person younger than you? Where were you born? Where were your parents born?

Do you have any handicaps? As a handicapped person, what help are you going to need to do your work? How severe is your handicap?

What's your religion? What church do you attend? Do you hold religious beliefs that would prevent you from working on certain days of the week?

Do you feel that your race/colour will be a problem in your performing the job? Are you of _____ heritage/race?

is actually needed to be able to perform the job.

Finally, legislation opens up job opportunities for the disabled by requiring employees to provide accommodating work environments. A disability is defined as any physical or mental impairment that substantially limits one or more of an individual's major life activities or any condition that is regarded as being such an impairment. Although merely being HIV positive does not limit any life activities, it may be perceived as doing so and is therefore protected as a disability. Similarly, extreme obesity may be either actually limiting or perceived as such and also is protected as long as the obese person can perform the duties of the job. (See Retailing View 13.5 for a discussion of recent retail requirements dictated by changes to the *Accessibility for Ontarians with Disabilities Act*.)

Building Employee Commitment

An important challenge in retailing is to reduce turnover.[42] High turnover reduces sales and increases costs. Sales are lost because inexperienced employees lack the skills and knowledge about company policies and merchandise to interact effectively with customers. Costs increase due to the need to continually recruit and train new employees.

To reduce turnover, retailers need to build an atmosphere of mutual commitment in their firms. When a retailer demonstrates its commitment, employees respond by developing loyalty to the company. Employees improve their skills and work hard for the company when they feel the company is committed to them over the long run, through thick and thin. Some approaches that retailers take to build mutual commitment are as follows:

- Developing employee skills through selection and training
- Empowering employees
- Creating a partnering relationship with employees[43]

Research indicates that engaging in these human resource management practices increases the firm's financial performance.[44]

Developing Skills

Two activities that retailers undertake to develop knowledge, skills, and abilities in their human resources are selection and training. Retailers that build a competitive advantage through their human resources are very selective in hiring people and make significant investment in training.

Selective Hiring The first step in building a committed workforce is recruiting the right people. Singapore Airlines, one of Asia's most admired companies, is consistently ranked among the top airlines in terms of service quality. Since its flight attendants are the critical point of contact with its customers, senior management is personally involved in their selection. Only 10 percent of the applicants make the initial screen; only 2 percent are hired.[45]

The job requirements and firm strategy dictate the type of people hired. Simply seeking the best and the brightest often is not the best approach. For example, at a category killer in outdoor gear, the motto is "You live what you sell." Outdoor enthusiasts are hired as sales associates so that they can help customers and serve as a resource for the buying staff. Chapters wants avid readers in its workforce.[46]

Socialization and Training After hiring employees, the next step in developing effective employees is introducing them to the firm and its policies. Retailers want the people they hire to become involved, committed contributors to the firm's successful performance. On the other hand, newly hired employees want to learn about their job responsibilities and the company they've decided to join. Socialization is the set of steps taken to transform new employees into effective, committed members of the firm. Socialization goes beyond simply orienting new employees to the firm. A principal objective of socialization is to develop a long-term relationship with new employees to increase productivity and reduce turnover costs (see Retail Roundtable 13.6).[47]

A key factor in socializing new employees is to create a training and work environment that articulates the retailer's culture and strategy. Training is particularly important in retailing because more than 60 percent of retail employees have direct contact with customers. They are responsible for helping customers satisfy their needs and resolve their problems. Two keys to success for a retailer are how it treats its employees and its emphasis on training.

Investing in developing employee skills tells employees that the firm considers them important. In response to the difficulty in finding qualified service workers, Marriott has made a considerable investment in recruiting and training entry-level workers. The training goes beyond the basics of doing the job to include grooming habits and basic business etiquette such as calling when you can't come to work.

Starbucks creates strong commitment in its employees through an organizational culture based on standards for coffee preparation and a supportive, empowering attitude

Ensuring Accessibility in Ontario's Retail Environment

The first day of 2013 was the deadline for store operators to comply with revised regulations of the *Accessibility for Ontarians with Disabilities Act* (AODA), which dealt not with ramps or the size of doorways, but rather with the way that consumers with mental and physical challenges should be treated by staff. That the changes demanded of retailers have more to do with employee behaviour than structural changes makes the adjustment less costly, though perhaps no less tricky, to pull off.

Thus, it's understandable that Ontario retailers are cautious in their appraisal of AODA customer service regulations and their potential impact. Where some see a headache-inducing bureaucratic hoop to jump through, others see an opportunity to improve overall customer service while targeting a specific—and growing— consumer segment.

The government of Ontario would certainly like retailers to see the AODA customer service standards in the more positive light, arguing that the changes required make as much sense in financial terms as they do morally. The act's literature makes the claim that people with disabilities will account for 40 percent of all income earned in the province within 20 years time, and refers to a Martin Prosperity Institute study that suggests that the AODA could spur a $9.6 billion increase in Ontario retail revenue.

According to the act, all retailers have to do to cash in on this supposed windfall is make a few additions to their customer service routine, such as making sure to accommodate service animals, providing written services for customers with hearing deficits, and speaking slowly and clearly to persons with developmental challenges. To comply, businesses with fewer than 20 employees are required to create an enhanced customer service plan and train staff on how to serve consumers with disabilities. Retailers with 20 or more employees must take the added steps of making paper copies of their customer service plans available to those who ask to see it and filing a compliance report to the Ontario government.

John Milloy, Ontario's minister of community and social services, has referred to AODA compliance as "easy to do" in press documents. Certainly, most of the customer service directives—such as simply asking a person in a wheelchair how they might be best served— seem based in common sense. And the government has supplied sample customer service plan templates, training videos, and guides to help facilitate the process.

Shoppers Drug Mart, for example, has bought into the idea of AODA customer service standards as good business strategy.

"Given that Canada has an aging population, it is expected that more and more people will be living with some form of disability, be it loss of hearing or mobility, and it is important that we ready ourselves to serve that growing demographic," says Tammy Smitham, director of communications and corporate affairs for Shoppers Drug Mart. Shoppers Drug Mart has posted its accessibility standards and accessible customer service practice on its website and, according to Smitham, complied with all other aspects of the legislation.

Dave Waye, human resources and compliance officer for Curry's Art Store, says his company has also managed to comply with AODA regulations without much difficulty. Furthermore, he says the process of doing so represented an opportunity to reaffirm the importance of customer service in general.

"In the broad sense, I don't think we see (the AODA standards) as a negative for the business, and in some ways you could even say it's a positive. It makes your staff more aware that customer service is number one," says Waye.

When it comes specifically to dealing with customers with disabilities, Waye says the AODA-mandated training may actually instill a greater confidence among employees.

"You know, we're in retail. Some of our staff are young. Some of them are high school students or first-year university students," he says. "They're part-timers and it's possible they've never come across someone with a disability.

"I don't think anyone would ever do something intentionally to offend, but they might do something just out of ignorance."

Waye believes this kind of accidental offence is less likely now that his staff have absorbed practical lessons on how to address different disabilities. But he stops short of saying that Curry's is looking to leverage its service of Ontarians with disabilities in its marketing initiatives.

"I wouldn't say that I view it that way, and that wasn't the way I presented it to the staff either," says Waye. "If this incents us to improve our levels of customer service, I guess it could well be a competitive advantage if others aren't doing the same. But I just think it's the right thing to do, and if it ends up being an advantage for us, too, that's great."

Private-sector retailers appear to be taking a wait-and-see approach to the AODA customer service requirements and any knock-on business effects. For the Liquor Control Board of Ontario (LCBO), however, the AODA is old hat. As a government organization, the LCBO was mandated to comply with the regulations two years ago.

Chris Layton, media relations co-ordinator for the LCBO, says the corporation's experience has been positive and that other retailers should look at the law as a boon to business.

"I think as a retailer you have to look at the regulations in something like the *Accessibility for Ontarians with Disabilities Act* as something that can help you create a more customer-friendly environment," says Layton. "We have not found compliance to be a challenge, but rather a way to better satisfy customers. And obviously having more satisfied customers has a positive effect on business."

Implementing AODA customer service standards does not appear to have been difficult for Ontario retailers and demographic trends to indicate that customers with disabilities represent a large and growing market. Whether this translates into increased revenue for retailers depends on many factors, including the degree to which employees effectively adhere to their training. For this reason, even those retailers who see potential opportunity couch their hopes in caution.

The AODA may bring with it great benefits, but for now it's just something that has to be done.

AODA Customer Service Standards

What retailers have to do to comply depends on their size. Retailers with fewer than 20 employees must create, implement, and train staff in a plan that does the following:

- Takes into account different communication requirements (Braille for the vision-impaired, for example) of people with disabilities
- Allows and creates space for devices such as wheelchairs and walkers, and service animals such as seeing-eye dogs
- Welcomes support persons for people with disabilities
- Informs customers when accessible services—for example, a ramp that is temporarily out of use—are unavailable
- Invites feedback from customers with disabilities

Retailers are also advised to take stock of their stores and make simple changes, such as putting items within reach of people in wheelchairs and making changes

to return policies out of consideration for the fact that some disabilities make it impossible to use fitting rooms. Retailers should also develop a system for responding to feedback.

Retailers with more than 20 employees must follow the same steps, but must also put their policies on paper and make them available to customers.

BETTER SERVICE, MORE REVENUE?

The government of Ontario has put forth the case that adopting AODA customer service regulations will result in increased revenue for retailers. Here are some key numbers from a Martin Prosperity Institute study assessing the economic impact of the AODA:

- Fifteen percent of Ontarians identified as persons with a disability in 2006, up from 14 percent in 2001. However, more than 31 percent of respondents in a Canadian Community Health Survey said that they had some difficulty with hearing, climbing stairs, or other challenges, so the number may be higher.

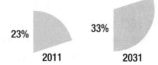

23% 2011   **33%** 2031

- Disability rates increase with age, and in Ontario, the percentage of the population over 55 is expected to increase from 23 percent to 33 percent by 2031.

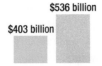

$403 billion $536 billion

- The income controlled by Ontarians with, or at risk of, disability will rise 33 percent to $536 billion by 2031.

- By 2031, 40 percent of all income in the province will be controlled by persons with disabilities or over the age of 55.

40%

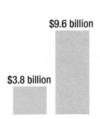

$3.8 billion $9.6 billion

- AODA implementation could spur an increase of $3.8 billion to $9.6 billion in retail sales in Ontario in the next five years alone.

Source: Matthew Semansky, "Ensuring Accessibility in Ontario's Retail Environment," *Canadian Retailer,* winter 2012, Volume 22, Issue 1, pp. 46–47.

toward employees. Recently Starbucks has created a partnership with Kids and Company, an organization that provides child care at a number of facilities in Ontario, Quebec, and Alberta. For a small annual membership fee paid by the company, Starbucks partners can have access to spots for their children. The company had a number of partners off on maternity leave who were unable to return to work because they couldn't find affordable child care. According to Sara Presutto, director of partner resources for Starbucks, the idea of keeping HR costs down isn't always a matter of deciding where to make the biggest cuts. As with the child care for its partners, it cuts recruiting and training costs by bringing back loyal partners who understand the corporate culture and the expectations of the job.[48]

Orientation Programs

Orientation programs are critical in overcoming entry shock and socializing new employees.[49] Orientation programs can last from a few hours to several weeks. The orientation and training program for new salespeople might be limited to several hours, during which the new salesperson learns the retailer's policies and procedures and how to use the POS terminal. On the other hand, the orientation program for management trainees might take several weeks.

Effective orientation programs need to avoid information overload and one-way communication. When new hires are confronted with a stack of forms and company policies, they get the impression the company is very bureaucratic. Large quantities of information are hard to absorb in a short period of time. New employees learn information best when it's parcelled out in small doses.

Store managers need to foster two-way communication when orienting new employees. Rather than just presenting information about their firm, managers need to give newly hired employees a chance to have their questions and concerns addressed.

In this structured training program, newly hired Moores salespeople learn about merchandise they will be selling.

The orientation program is just one element in the overall training program. It needs to be accompanied by a systematic follow-up to ensure that any problems and concerns arising after the initial period are considered.

Structured Program

During the structured program, new employees are taught the basic skills and knowledge they'll need to do their job. For example, salespeople learn what the company policies are, how to use the point-of-sale terminal, and how to perform basic selling skills; stockroom employees learn procedures for receiving merchandise. This initial training might include lectures, audio-visual presentations, manuals, and correspondence distributed to the new employees.

The initial structured program should be relatively short so that new employees don't feel they are simply back in school. Effective training programs bring new recruits up to speed as quickly as possible and then get them involved in doing the job for which they've been hired.

On-the-Job Training

The next training phase emphasizes on-the-job training. New employees are assigned a job, given responsibilities, and coached by their supervisor. The best way to learn is to practise what is being taught. New employees learn by doing activities, making mistakes, and then learning how not to make those mistakes again. Information learned through classroom lectures tends to be forgotten quickly unless it's used soon after the lecture.[50]

Employee Evaluation

Most retailers evaluate employees annually or semi-annually. Feedback from evaluations is the most effective method for improving employee skills. Thus, evaluations should be done more frequently when managers are developing inexperienced employees' skills. Managers should supplement these formal evaluations with frequent informal ones. Evaluations are only meaningful if employees know what they're required to do, what level of performance is expected, and how they'll be evaluated. Exhibit 13–7 shows a specialty store's criteria for evaluating sales associates.

An employee's overall evaluation is based on subjective evaluations made by the store manager and assistant managers. It often places equal weight on individual sales/customer relations activities and activities associated with overall store performance. By emphasizing overall store operations and performance, assessment criteria can motivate sales associates to work together as a team.

Analyzing Successes and Failures

Every new employee makes mistakes. Store managers should provide an atmosphere in which salespeople try out different approaches to providing customer service and selling merchandise. Store managers must recognize that some

Retention

We do an employee attitude survey every two years where they tell us what they're feeling, both from an attitude point of view and a satisfaction and engagement point of view. We don't only ask. We then have committees who identify areas of opportunities and work towards improving those deficiencies that are noted.

Rafik Louli, regional director, central regional office #3, LCBO

I think in retail, too much of the time the torch isn't passed along properly, the experiences aren't passed along, and that engagement and that empowerment isn't handed down to people often enough to give them that sense of belonging. I think that's one thing Future Shop does very well in retail. If someone comes up with a suggestion and presents it and the company goes with it, we make sure we celebrate it across all levels of the organization so that people know about it.

Mike Hickey, general manager, Future Shop, Calgary

From where you sit, why is retention so difficult for retailers? What is it that retailers, on the whole, aren't getting? What's missing from the current equation?

When we talk about retention, it comes down to engagement and development. Often the focus is on the front end of recruitment but for some, the longer term component of retention becomes a lesser priority. At The Body Shop, we identify succession plans and career paths for all associates to keep them engaged.

Carmela Aita, director, human resources, The Body Shop

Fundamentally, if an employee connects with the organization that they're working for and if they connect with what they're doing within the organization, then retention becomes less of an issue because the employee is already committed. For me, I've been promoted and I've moved from one coast to another and I've been recognized, and we do this all the time. Let's recognize people and provide feedback and make sure they know they have a future with us and that they are contributing to the company. That creates retention. Who doesn't want to feel valued? Who doesn't want to have a say?

Tina Shane, vice-president, retail and customer experience, western Canada, Chapters

What causes the issue of low retention is the fact that if people don't see a clear career path they tend to become frustrated and disillusioned. For a lot of retailers, they look at career paths as being defined, and unless somebody dies above me I have no chance of getting to that level. What retailers can do is change that thought process. Once that basic need for survival is met, the next thing people want to be is taught. If you take out that barrier to learning, you're going to keep people.

Ron Hornbaker, interim CEO, Golf Town

Source: Robert Price, "Recruiting, Retaining and Empowering Store Managers," *Canadian Retailer*, winter 2012, pp. 36–39.

exhibit 13-7   Factors Used to Evaluate Associates at a Specialty Store

50%
SALES/CUSTOMER RELATIONS

1. Greeting. Approaches customers within 1 to 2 minute with a smile and friendly manner. Uses open-ended questions.

2. Product knowledge. Demonstrates knowledge of product, fit, shrinkage, and price and can relay this information to the customer.

3. Suggests additional merchandise. Approaches customers at fitting room and cash/wrap areas.

4. Asks customers to buy and reinforces decisions. Lets customers know they've made a wise choice and thanks them.

25%
OPERATIONS

1. Store appearance. Demonstrates an eye for detail (colour and finesse) in the areas of display, coordination of merchandise on tables, floor fixtures, and wall faceouts. Takes initiative in maintaining store presentation standards.

2. Loss prevention. Actively follows all loss prevention procedures.

3. Merchandise control and handling. Consistently achieves established requirements in price change activity, shipment processing, and inventory control.

4. Cash/wrap procedures. Accurately and efficiently follows all register policies and cash/wrap procedures.

25%
COMPLIANCE

1. Dress code and appearance. Complies with dress code. Appears neat and well groomed. Projects current fashionable image.

2. Flexibility. Able to switch from one assignment to another, open to schedule adjustments. Shows initiative, awareness of store priorities and needs.

3. Working relations. Cooperates with other employees, willingly accepts direction and guidance from management. Communicates to management.

of these new approaches are going to fail, and when they do, managers shouldn't criticize the individual salesperson. Instead, they should talk about the situation, analyze why the approach didn't work, and discuss how the salesperson could avoid the problem in the future.

Empowering Employees

Empowerment is the process of managers sharing power and decision-making authority with employees (see Retailing View 13.7). When employees have the authority to make decisions, they are more confident in their abilities, have greater opportunity to provide service to customers, and are more committed to the firm's success.

The first step in empowering employees is to review employee activities that require a manager's approval.

Each store in the Whole Foods chain is a profit centre, with the store employees organized in ten self-managed teams. The teams are responsible and accountable for the store's performance. For example, the store manager recommends new hires. It takes a two-thirds vote of the team to actually hire the candidate. The team members pool their ideas and come up with creative solutions to problems. Empowerment of retail employees transfers authority and responsibility for making decisions to lower levels in the organization. These employees are close to the retailer's customers and in a good position to know what it takes to satisfy customers. For empowerment to work, managers must have an attitude of respect and trust, not control and distrust.[51]

Employee Feedback Survey

One of the primary benefits of an employee survey is to provide an opportunity for employees to give feedback to the retail organization. A well-designed employee survey can provide significant benefits in improving retention and organizational communication. In addition, if employees think that their personal needs and ideas are valued, this can build trust and commitment between managers and associates.

Employee feedback enables the retailer to identify gaps between organizational goals and actual policies. It helps align the retailer's goals and employee satisfaction by making employees participants in the process of business improvement and success.

All questionnaires must be anonymous and take no more than 30 minutes to complete. For larger retailers electronic or web-based questionnaires are the most efficient and cost-effective format. When designing a questionnaire, maintain consistency of question format, and use unbiased check boxes as an effective way to control responses. Open-ended responses allow employees to share their thoughts on issues. Retailers must act on the collected results of any survey. Never let data go unused. The value of employee feedback cannot be overstated.

empowerment
The process of managers sharing power and decision-making authority with employees.

promotion from within A staffing policy that involves hiring new employees only for positions at the lowest level in the job hierarchy and then promoting employees for openings at higher levels in the hierarchy.

flextime A job scheduling system that enables employees to choose the times they work.

job sharing When two or more employees voluntarily are responsible for a job that was previously held by one person.

managing diversity A set of human resource management programs designed to realize the benefits of a diverse workforce.

Developing Partnering Relationships with Employees

Four human resource management activities that build commitment through developing partnering relationships with employees are as follows:

- Reducing status differences
- Promoting from within
- Enabling employees to balance their careers and families
- Enabling employees to pursue outside interests such as athletics and community activities

Retailers such as Royal Bank Financial Group and Home Depot not only support Canada's Olympic athletes through financial contributions but also provide them with employment that recognizes their demanding training schedules.

Reducing Status Differences Many retailers attempt to reduce status differences between employees. With limited status differences, employees feel that they play an important role in the firm's achieving its goals and that their contributions are valued.

Status differences can be reduced symbolically through the use of language and cut substantively by lowering wage differentials and increasing communications between managers at different levels in the company. For example, hourly workers at Walmart are referred to as associates and managers are called partners, a practice that Sam Walton adopted when he started Walmart.

Whole Foods has a policy of limiting executive compensation to less than eight times the compensation of the average full-time salaried employee.

All Home Depot senior executives spend time in the stores, wearing the orange apron, talking with customers and employees. This "management by walking around" makes employees feel that their inputs are valued by the company and reinforces the customer service culture.

Promotion from within Promotion from within is a staffing policy that involves hiring new employees only for positions at the lowest level in the job hierarchy and then promoting employees for openings at higher levels in the hierarchy. Home Depot, Costco, and Walmart have had promotion-from-within policies.

Promotion-from-within policies establish a sense of fairness. When employees do an outstanding job and then outsiders are brought in over them, employees feel that the company doesn't care about them. Promotion-from-within policies also commit the retailer to developing its employees.[52]

Balancing Careers and Families The increasing number of two-income and single-parent families makes it difficult for employees to effectively do their jobs and manage their households. Retailers build employee commitment by offering services such as job sharing, child care, and employee assistance programs to help their employees manage these problems.

Flextime is a job scheduling system that enables employees to choose the times they work. With job sharing, two employees voluntarily are responsible for a job that was previously held by one person. Both programs let employees accommodate their work schedules to other demands in their life such as being home when children return from school.[53]

Many retailers offer child care assistance. Sears' corporate headquarters has a 20 000 square-foot daycare centre. At Eddie Bauer, a catalogue retailer in Seattle, the corporate headquarters cafeteria stays open late and prepares takeout meals for time-pressed employees. Some companies will even arrange for a person to be at an employee's home waiting for the cable guy to come or to pick up and drop off dry cleaning.[54]

Trends in Retail Human Resource Management

LO 4

In this final section, we discuss three trends in human resource management:

- The increasing importance of having a diverse workforce
- The growth in legal restrictions on HR practices
- The use of technology to increase employee productivity

Managing Diversity

Managing diversity is a human resource management activity designed to realize the benefits of a diverse workforce. Today, diversity means more than differences in skin colour, nationality, and gender.

Minority groups now embrace their differences and want employers to accept them for who they are. The appropriate metaphor is a salad bowl. Each ingredient in the salad is distinctive, preserving its own identity, but the mixture of ingredients improves the combined taste of the individual elements.[55] Diversity and equity in the workplace always make good business sense. Consider the Canadian population, comprising more than

FISH! Empowers Employees

FISH! is a management philosophy developed by ChartHouse and inspired by the Pike Place Fish Market in Seattle. The selling atmosphere at Pike Place is unusual. Employees, known as fishmongers, throw fish over the counter to co-workers for wrapping. The fishmongers also invite customers to get in on the action and try to catch fish. What could be a dull store is transformed into a place where customers and employees are smiling, laughing, and connecting with one another, while keeping an eye out for flying fish.

Amy's Ice Cream (a 13-store chain of premium ice cream shops in Austin, San Antonio, and Houston, Texas) has similarly transformed what could be a boring transaction into a fun experience. Visit an Amy's store, and you'll see employees performing in a manner you won't forget. They juggle with their serving spades, toss scoops of ice cream to one another behind the counter, and break-dance on the freezer top. If there's a line out the door, they might pass out samples or offer free ice cream to any customer who'll sing or dance or recite a poem or mimic a barnyard animal or win a 60-second cone-eating contest.

The four FISH! principles are:

1. Choose your attitude—look for the worst and you'll find it; choose to look for the best and you'll find opportunities heretofore unimagined;

2. Be there—being fully present for one another and diving into every task with your whole heart;

By giving employees the freedom to have fun at work, Pike Place Fish Markets employees reduce the delivery gap and improve customer service.

3. Make their day—small kindnesses turn even routine encounters into special memories;

4. Play—serious tasks are made fun through spontaneity and creativity.

By empowering employees to implement the FISH! principles the best way they can, companies facilitate great customer service. For example, "choose your attitude" can empower employees to effect change from within themselves. Positive attitudes spread to other employees and onto customers. Empowering employees to "play" on the job makes the working and buying atmosphere fun, and happy customers buy more.

Sources: www.charthouse.com (accessed November 12, 2007); www.amysicecream.com (accessed November 11, 2007); Laura Gee, "Some Companies Work to Put Fun in the Office," www.dailypress.com, October 23, 2007; Tanya Rutledge, "Amy Miller, Sweet Success," *Austin Business Journal*, December 24, 2004, p. 16; Marcia Hicks, "Revitalizing Your Call Center Via FISH! Philosophy," *Direct Marketing Magazine*, December 1, 2003; and Stephen C. Lundin, Harry Paul, and John Christensen, *Fish! A Remarkable Way to Boost Morale and Improve Results* (New York: Hyperion, 2000).

---

200 ethnic groups with multiple ties around the world. Businesses that embrace diversity are well positioned to be more competitive in world markets.[56]

Some legal restrictions promote diversity in the workplace by preventing retailers from practising discrimination based on non–performance-related employee characteristics. But retailers now recognize that promoting employee diversity can improve financial performance. By encouraging diversity in their workforce, retailers can better understand and respond to the needs of their customers and deal with the shrinking labour market.

Retail customers' racial and ethnic backgrounds are increasingly diverse. To compete in this changing marketplace, retailers need management staffs that match the diversity of their target markets. For example, 85 percent of the men's clothing sold in department stores is bought by women, and over 50 percent of Home Depot's sales are made to women. To better understand customer needs, department store and home improvement retailers feel that they must have women in senior management positions—people who really understand their female customers' needs.

The fundamental principle of managing diversity is the recognition that employees have different needs and require different approaches to accommodating those needs. Managing diversity goes beyond meeting equal employment opportunity laws. It means accepting and valuing differences. Some programs that retailers use to manage diversity involve offering diversity training, providing support groups and mentoring, and managing career development and promotions.[57]

Diversity Training Diversity training typically consists of two components: developing cultural awareness and building competencies. The cultural awareness component teaches people about how their own culture differs from the culture of other employees and how stereotypes they hold influence the way they treat people, often in subtle ways they might not realize. Then role-playing is used to help employees develop better interpersonal skills, including showing respect and treating people as equals.

Support Groups and Mentoring A mentoring program assigns assign higher-level managers to help lower-level managers learn the firm's values and meet other senior executives.[58]

Career Development and Promotions Although laws provide entry-level opportunities for women and minority groups, these employees often encounter a glass ceiling as they move through the corporation. A glass ceiling is an invisible barrier that makes it difficult for minorities and women to be promoted beyond a certain level.

Similarly, women in the supermarket business have traditionally been assigned to peripheral departments such as bakery and deli, while men were assigned to the critical departments in the store: meat and grocery. Even in the supermarket chain corporate office, women traditionally have been in staff-support areas such as human resource management, finance, and accounting, while men are more involved in store operations and buying. To make sure that more women have an opportunity to break through the glass ceiling in the supermarket industry, firms are placing them in positions critical to the firm's success.[60]

Legal and Regulatory Issues in Human Resource Management

In Canada, all employers and all employees must comply with the *Employment Standards Act,* which identifies standards based on provincial legislation. Historically, collective agreements helped shape employment standards that today apply to about two-thirds of Canadian workers who are not involved in a unionized work environment. Each of Canada's ten provinces and three territories developed its own employment standards legislation, all based on a common set of issues. The *Employment Standards Act* is a law that establishes minimum entitlements pertaining to such issues as wages; paid holidays and vacations; leave for maternity, parental care, and adoption; bereavement leave; termination notice; overtime pay; and limits on the maximum number of hours of work permitted per day or week.[62] Managing in this complex regulatory environment requires expertise in labour laws and skills in helping other managers comply with these laws. The major legal and regulatory issues involving the management of retail employees are as follows:

- Equal employment opportunity
- Compensation
- Labour relations
- Employee safety and health
- Sexual harassment
- Employee privacy

Equal Employment Opportunity Canadian employment equity legislation is not about favouring anybody—women, persons with disabilities, Aboriginal persons, or visible minorities. The law is about identifying and eliminating employment barriers. It is also about instituting positive policies and practices and making reasonable accommodations to ensure that persons in the designated groups achieve a degree of workforce representation that reflects their representation in Canadian society.[63] Illegal discrimination is the actions of a company or its managers that result in members of a protected class being treated unfairly and differently than others. A protected class is all of the individuals who share a common characteristic defined by the law. Companies cannot treat employees differently simply based on their race, colour, religion, sex, national origin, age, or disability status. There is a very limited set of circumstances under which employees can be treated differently. For example, it is illegal for a restaurant to hire only young, attractive servers because that is what its customers prefer. Such discrimination must be absolutely necessary, not simply preferred.

In addition, it is illegal to engage in a practice that disproportionately excludes a protected group even

Nuts and Bolts of Store Management

I don't like the buzzwords. But empowerment is key—the freedom to make a decision. Store managers need to know that if they make a decision, they aren't going to get chastised for making the decision. In fact, I want them to make a decision. If it gets to me, it's too late. They should have taken care of the customer long before it gets to me. As long as they feel free to make a decision, and you've clearly defined what your expectations for those decisions are, more often than not they're going to make the right one.

Ron Hornbaker, interim CEO, Golf Town

They need to be provided with a very clear set of expectations and support on how to achieve those expectations. They also need a comprehensive training program on everything from understanding their role in the business, understanding how to analyze results, enhancing their product knowledge, and to understand and be able to execute the desired customer experience that we're looking to provide as an organization.

Carmela Aita, director, human resources, The Body Shop

And if we talk about the nuts and bolts of store management. What do store managers need most from the organization to do their job well?

Every employee needs clear goals, short-term and long-term. That comes from our business plans—we have five-year business plans and annual business plans, clearly communicated, not only to store managers, but to every employee in the organization.

Rafik Louli, regional director, central regional office #3, LCBO

Store managers need three things. One is support from the organization to know they have the autonomy to make choices and make decisions that may not help the customer in the short-term, but will help them in the long-term. Second, they need the opportunity to learn and grow within an organization because nobody wants to become stale or stagnant. Third, you have to have the mindset that the customer needs to always come first. And, within your organization's structure your associates have to come first before everything.

Mike Hickey, general manager, Future Shop, Calgary

There needs to be that open-door policy so that if the store manager knows what you want but isn't clear about how to get there or what tools they might need to make it easier, they feel comfortable and understand that upper management will be ready and available to help at any time. That open communication needs to be extended out to others within the organization as well—that can help immensely.

Tina Shane, vice-president, retail and customer experience, western Canada, Chapters

Source: Robert Price, "Recruiting, Retaining and Empowering Store Managers," *Canadian Retailer*, winter 2012, pp. 36–39.

distributive justice
Exists when outcomes received are viewed as fair with respect to outcomes received by others.

procedural justice
An employee's perception of fairness (how he or she is treated) that is based on the process used to determine the outcome.

DID YOU KNOW?

An Ipsos-Reid poll reveals that 55 percent of Canadians have consciously decided to buy a product or service from one retailer rather than another because they felt the company was a good corporate citizen.[61]

though it might seem to be nondiscriminatory. For example, suppose that a retailer uses scores on a test to make hiring decisions. If a protected group systematically performs worse on the test, the retailer is illegally discriminating even if there was no intention to discriminate.

Compensation Laws relating to compensation define the 40-hour workweek, the pay rate for working overtime, and the minimum wage, and they protect employee investments in their pensions. In addition, they require that firms provide the same pay for men and women who are doing equal work of equal value.

Labour Relations Labour relations laws describe the process by which unions can be formed and the ways in which companies must deal with the unions. They precisely indicate how negotiations with unions must take place and what the parties can and cannot do.

Employee Safety and Health The basic premise of these laws is that the employer is obligated to provide each employee with an environment that is free from hazards that are likely to cause death or serious injury. According to Kerri O'Neill, a disability and wellness consultant at Staples Canada, health and safety is a concern for everybody. Retailers who are able to "work health and safety into daily aspects of the job and make it part of the culture instead of something they have to do," can "look at trends, be proactive and support a better trend." Examples of ways that managers can encourage a healthier lifestyle among workers by sponsoring gym memberships, offering employee discounts on health-related items, hosting in-store seminars with health experts, and paying in part or full for smoking cessation programs.[64]

Sexual Harassment Sexual harassment includes unwelcome sexual advances, requests for sexual favours, and other verbal and physical conduct. Harassment isn't confined to requests for sexual favours in exchange for job considerations such as a raise or promotion. Simply creating a hostile work environment can be considered sexual harassment. For example, actions that are considered sexual harassment include lewd comments, joking, and graffiti, as well as showing obscene photographs, staring at a co-worker in a sexual manner, alleging that

an employee got rewards by engaging in sexual acts, and commenting on an employee's moral reputation.

Customers can engage in sexual harassment as well as supervisors and co-workers. For example, female pharmacists find that some male customers demand lengthy discussions when they buy condoms. Pharmacists have difficulty dealing with these situations because they want to keep the person as a customer and also protect themselves from abuse.

Employee Privacy Employees' privacy protection is very limited. For example, employers can monitor e-mail and telephone communications, and search an employee's work space and handbag. However, employers cannot discriminate among employees when undertaking these activities unless they have a strong suspicion that employees are acting inappropriately.

Developing Policies The human resource department is responsible for developing programs and policies to make sure that managers and employees are aware of these restrictions and know how to deal with potential violations. These legal and regulatory requirements are basically designed to treat people fairly. Employees want to be treated fairly and companies want to be perceived as treating their employees fairly. The perception of fairness encourages people to join a company and leads to trust and commitment of employees to a firm. When employees believe they are not being treated fairly, they can either complain, stay and accept the situation, stay but engage in negative behaviour, quit, or complain to an external authority and even sue the employer.

Perceptions of fairness are based on two factors:

- *Distributive justice*, which arises when outcomes received are viewed as fair with respect to outcomes received by others. However, the perception of distributive justice can differ across cultures. For example, in the individualistic culture of Canada, merit-based pay is perceived as fair, whereas in collectivist cultures such as China and Japan, equal pay is viewed as fair.

- *Procedural justice*, which is based on fairness of the process used to determine the outcome. Canadian workers consider formal processes as fair whereas group decisions are considered fairer in collectivist cultures.[65]

Store Security Management

LO 5

An important issue facing store management is reducing inventory losses due to employee theft, shoplifting, mistakes, inaccurate records, and vendor errors.

Examples of employee mistakes are failing to ring up an item when it's sold and miscounting merchandise when it's received or during physical inventories. Inventory shrinkage due to vendor mistakes arises when vendor shipments contain less than the amount indicated on the packing slip.

According to the PwC's *Canadian Retail Security Survey 2012*, the 33.4 percent of internal theft further emphasizes the need for retailers to invest in strong internal policies and procedures as the criminal activity appears to be gaining momentum from within the core of retailers' operations. See Case 21, "Creating Loss Prevention Programs That Fit the Culture," for Lululemon's unique asset protection program.

In developing a loss prevention program, retailers confront a trade-off between providing shopping convenience and a pleasant work environment on the one hand and preventing losses due to shoplifting and employee theft on the other. The key to an effective loss prevention program is determining the most effective way to protect merchandise while preserving an open, attractive store atmosphere and a feeling among employees that they are trusted. Loss prevention requires coordination among store management, visual merchandising, and store design.

Shrinkage Incidents	2012	2008
Internal theft	33.4%	19.0%
External theft	43.0%	65.0%
Paperwork errors	19.9%	16.0%
Vendor fraud	3.7%	no data

Source: PWC Canada and Retail Council of Canada, *Securing the Bottom Line: Canadian Retail Security Survey, 2012*, p. 8, www.pwc.com/ca/retailsecuritysurvey (accessed December 20, 2013).

Merchandise Categories

Given the diverse group of respondents in the *Canadian Retail Security Survey 2012*, 25 different merchandise categories were identified that contribute most to shrinkage. The top three categories identified (in order) were alcohol, ladies apparel, and cosmetics and fragrances. Each of the categories is a high-volume and high-value category that appeals to criminal activity, both internal and external in nature (see Exhibit 13–8).

Calculating Shrinkage

Shrinkage is the difference between the recorded value of inventory (at retail prices) based on merchandise bought and received and the value of the actual inventory (at retail prices) in stores and distribution centres, divided by retail sales during the period. For example, if accounting records indicate inventory should be $1 500 000,

the actual count of the inventory reveals $1 236 000, and sales were $4 225 000, the shrinkage is 6.2 percent.

Shrinkage

= (Book inventory − Actual inventory) ÷ Net sales

= ($1 500 000 − $1 236 000) ÷ $4 225 000

= 6.2%

Reducing shrinkage is an important store management issue. Retailers' annual loss from shrinkage averages about 1.6 percent of sales.[68] Every dollar of inventory shrinkage translates into a dollar of lost profit.

Although more than 70 percent of shoplifting is performed by amateurs, professional shoplifters now account for an estimated $15 to $30 billion in losses annually, representing almost 25 percent of reported shoplifting cases. These gangs of professional thieves concentrate in over-the-counter medications, infant formula, health and beauty aids, electronics, and specialty clothing. This stolen merchandise is often sold by shoplifters on Internet auction sites.

With identity theft and payment fraud on the rise due to bogus purchases appearing on credit card statements or missing funds from bank accounts via credit card fraud, retailers increasingly see chargebacks

shrinkage An inventory reduction that is caused by shoplifting by employees or customers, by merchandise being misplaced or damaged, or by poor bookkeeping.

DID YOU KNOW?

The Ontario Service Safety Alliance reports that, over just eight years, Ontario employers paid more than $3.3 billion in direct costs because of musculoskeletal disorders, a common type of injury among retail workers.[66]

DID YOU KNOW?

It costs a retailer $20 to $30 to process a paper HR form, but processing the form over an intranet only costs $0.05 to $0.10.[67]

exhibit 13–8 The Top Merchandise Categories That Contribute Most to Shrinkage

Alcohol	Garden
Women's apparel	Gloves
Cosmetics and fragrance	Intimate apparel
Health and beauty	Jewellery
Denim	Ladies' accessories
Food/confectionary	Lighters
Men's apparel	Lumber
Footwear	Pens
Handbags	Power tools
Kids and baby	Sporting goods
Pharmacy/blades	Sunglasses
Bath and shower	Wallets
Electronics/DVDs	

Source: PWC Canada and Retail Council of Canada, *Securing the Bottom Line: Canadian Retail Security Survey*, 2012, p. 7, www.pwc.com/ca/retailsecuritysurvey (accessed December 20, 2013).

at the point-of-sale as a necessity of doing business. The generous returns policy instituted by many retailers has attracted criminals seeking a low-risk, high-reward way to make money.

On January 1, 2004, the *Personal Information and Protection of Electronic Documents Act* (PIPEDA) took effect in Canada. This privacy legislation outlined the responsibilities of Canadian businesses to the customers they serve.

The top three risks that companies face related to privacy damage are the following:

- Damage to reputation of the business
- Loss of customers
- Litigation costs

Canadian retailers need to launch employee training programs and develop privacy statements for display in the store and on their websites. Transparency is critical to the success of retail privacy policy guidelines.

For additional information, visit the office of the Privacy Commissioner of Canada at www.privcom.gc.ca.

Detecting and Preventing Shoplifting

Losses due to shoplifting can be reduced by store design, merchandise policies, special security measures, personnel policies, and prosecution of shoplifters.[69]

Store Design The following store design issues are used to reduce inventory shrinkage:

- Do not place expensive or small merchandise near entrance.
- Keep the height of fixtures low and arranged with no "blind spots" so that the store maintains open sight lines to store entrances and dressing rooms so employees can see customers in the store and watch for shoplifters while providing better service.
- Use mirrors. Strategically placed one-way observation mirrors and hanging mirrors can help store employees observe customers.
- Because cash wraps are always staffed, they should be near areas that theft is likely to occur. Cash wraps are the places in a store where customers can buy their purchases and have them "wrapped"—placed in a bag.

- Alternate clothing hanger directions. Professional shoplifters can steal a tremendous amount of clothing by grabbing it off the rack. If the hangers are alternated, it is difficult for thieves to steal a lot at once.

Merchandise Policies The following merchandise policies are utilized to reduce inventory shrinkage:

- Require a receipt for all returns, because many shoplifters steal with the intent of returning the merchandise for a cash refund.
- Lock up small, expensive items. Expensive apparel items can be chained. While locking merchandise in a cabinet or chaining expensive apparel decreases shrinkage, it may decrease sales by making it more difficult for customers to look at merchandise of interest.

Security Measures Store employees can be the retailer's most effective tool against shoplifting. They should be trained to be aware, visible, and alert to potential shoplifting situations. Exhibit 13–9 outlines rules for spotting shoplifters. Perhaps the best deterrent to shoplifting is an alert employee who is very visible. Exhibit 13–10 describes retailers' use of security measures. Another approach to deterring shoplifting is to embed dye capsules in the merchandise. If the capsules aren't removed properly by a store employee, they break and damage the merchandise.

By placing convex mirrors at key locations, employees can observe a wide area of the store. Closed-circuit TV cameras can be monitored from a central location, but purchasing the equipment and hiring people to monitor the system can be expensive. Some retailers install nonoperating equipment that looks like a TV camera to provide a psychological deterrent to shoplifters.

Although these security measures reduce shoplifting, they can also make the shopping experience more unpleasant for honest customers. The atmosphere of a fashionable department store is diminished when guards, mirrors, and TV cameras are highly visible. Customers may find it hard to try on clothing secured with a lock-and-chain or an electronic tag. They can also be uncomfortable trying on clothing if they think they're secretly being watched via a surveillance monitor. Thus, when evaluating security measures, retailers need to balance the benefits of reducing shoplifting with the potential losses in sales.

Electronic article surveillance is a promising approach to reducing shrinkage with little effect on shopping behaviour. In an **electronic article surveillance (EAS) system**, special tags are placed on merchandise. When the merchandise is purchased, the tags are deactivated by the POS scanner. If a shoplifter tries to steal the

exhibit 13–9   Spotting Shoplifters

DON'T ASSUME THAT ALL SHOPLIFTERS ARE POORLY DRESSED

To avoid detection, professional shoplifters dress in the same manner as customers patronizing the store. Over 90 percent of all amateur shoplifters arrested have either the cash, cheques, or credit to purchase the merchandise they stole.

SPOT LOITERERS

Amateur shoplifters frequently loiter in areas as they build up the nerve to steal something. Professionals also spend time waiting for the right opportunity, but less conspicuously than amateurs.

LOOK FOR GROUPS

Teenagers planning to shoplift often travel in groups. Some members of the group divert employees' attention while others take the merchandise. Professional shoplifters often work in pairs. One person takes the merchandise and passes it to a partner in the store's restroom, phone booths, or restaurant.

LOOK FOR PEOPLE WITH LOOSE CLOTHING

Shoplifters frequently hide stolen merchandise under loose-fitting clothing or in large shopping bags. People wearing a winter coat in the summer or a raincoat on a sunny day may be potential shoplifters.

WATCH THE EYES, HANDS, AND BODY

Professional shoplifters avoid looking at merchandise and concentrate on searching for store employees who might observe their activities. Shoplifters' movements might be unusual as they try to conceal merchandise.

merchandise, the active tags are sensed when the shoplifter passes a detection device at the store exit and an alarm is triggered.[70]

EAS tags do not affect shopping behaviour because customers do not realize they're on the merchandise. Due to the effectiveness of tags in reducing shoplifting, retailers can increase sales by displaying theft-prone, expensive merchandise openly rather than behind a counter or in a locked enclosure.

Some large national retailers insist that vendors install EAS tags during the manufacturing process because the vendors can install the tags at a lower cost than the retailers. In addition, retail-installed tags can be removed more easily by shoplifters. Vendors are reluctant to get involved with installing EAS tags because industry standards have not been adopted. Without these standards, a vendor would have to develop unique tags and merchandise for each retailer.[71]

Personnel Policies   The following personnel policies may help deter shoplifting:

- Use of mystery and honesty shoppers—people posing as real shoppers—to watch for employee and customer theft.

- Have store employees monitor fitting rooms. Fitting rooms provide a good environment for stealing.

- Store employees should be trained to be aware, visible, and alert to potential shoplifting situations.

- Provide excellent customer service. If employees know the customers and offer assistance, shoplifters will be deterred.

DID YOU KNOW?

A dishonest employee typically takes over $1000 worth of goods and cash, whereas the average customer shoplifter takes $128 in merchandise.[72]

---

exhibit 13–10   Activities used to manage loss prevention efforts 2008 and 2012

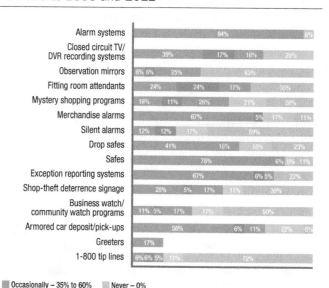

Legend: Always – 95% of the time · Frequently – 60% to 95% · Occasionally – 35% to 60% · Infrequently – less than 35% · Never – 0%

Source: "Securing the bottom line: Canadian retail security survey 2012," www.pwc.com/ca/retailsecuritysurvey. p.13

Holt Renfrew Uses Fingerprint Biometrics

Biometrics such as fingerprint recognition can be used for controlled access to POS systems, for manager approvals, and for transaction overrides. Holt Renfrew employees sign in with their fingertips, using biometrics scanning. Holt Renfrew is currently one of the only Canadian retailers using biometrics to track employee activities as part of their workforce management strategy. The concept eliminates problems of misplaced pass cards, shared passwords, and payroll discrepancies because fingerprint recognition is tied into the store's time and attendance system.

Biometrics such as fingerprint recognition can be used for controlled access to POS systems, for manager approvals, and for transaction overrides. This could also pave the way for consumer applications such as biometric payment at the POS.

Source: NCR Corporation NCRRealPOS™ 70 point-of-sale work station with integrated fingerprint reader.

Prosecution Many retailers have a policy of prosecuting all shoplifters. They feel a strictly enforced prosecution policy deters shoplifters. Some retailers also sue shoplifters in civil proceedings for restitution of the stolen merchandise and the time spent in the prosecution.

Reducing Employee Theft The most effective approach to reducing employee theft and shoplifting is to create a trusting, supportive work environment. When employees feel they're respected members of a team, they identify their goals with the retailer's goals. Stealing from their employer becomes equivalent to stealing from themselves or their family, and they go out of their way to prevent others from stealing from the "family." Thus, retailers with a highly committed workforce and low turnover typically have low inventory shrinkage. Additional approaches to reducing employee theft are carefully screening employees, creating an atmosphere that encourages honesty and integrity, using security personnel, and establishing security policies and control systems (see Retailing View 13.9).

Screening Prospective Employees As mentioned previously, many retailers use paper-and-pencil honesty tests and make extensive reference checks to screen out potential employee theft problems.

Using Security Personnel In addition to uniformed guards, retailers use undercover shoppers to discourage and detect employee theft. These undercover security people pose as shoppers. They make sure salespeople ring up transactions accurately.

Establishing Security Policies and Control Systems To control employee theft, retailers need to adopt policies relating to certain activities that may facilitate theft. Some of the most prevalent policies are:

- Randomly search containers such as trash bins where stolen merchandise can be stored
- Require store employees to enter and leave the store through designated entrances
- Assign salespeople to specific POS terminals and require all transactions to be handled through those terminals

Retailers use EAS tags to reduce shoplifting. The tags (left) contain a device that is part of the price tag. If the tags are not deactivated when the merchandise is purchased, the stolen merchandise will be detected when the shopper passes through the sensor gates (right) at the store exit.

- Restrict employee purchases to working hours
- Provide customer receipts for all transactions
- Have all refunds, returns, and discounts cosigned by a department or store manager
- Change locks periodically and issue keys to authorized personnel only
- Have a locker room where all employee handbags, purses, packages, and coats must be checked

13.10 | RETAIL ROUNDTABLE

Recruitment

It comes down to how you bring them into the organization. Realizing that a lot of talent will be leaving our organization, about four years ago we made it a priority to set up a succession plan. We developed what's called the Onboarding Program, a week-long residential program, and a mentor program to keep new hires on track and successful.

Rafik Louli, regional director, central regional office #3, LCBO

When I interview people for a retail manager position, more often than not they're coming from another retailer. Maybe the challenge is to articulate the advantages of being in retail and delivering that message at the university level. It's also important to recognize that we work within a really dynamic and exciting industry—retailers can attract people from other industries who have similar skill-sets and competencies.

Ron Hornbaker, interim CEO, Golf Town

The recruitment of top talent continues to be a priority within the retail industry. What can retailers, individually or as an industry, do to attract more people to retail?

Use employee networks. We use referrals from associates. Referrals who come into the store do better because they already know someone in the company. They can ask friends questions that maybe they can't ask during the interview: How's the leadership team? Does the company actually care about you?

Mike Hickey, general manager, Future Shop, Calgary

At The Body Shop, we work to highlight career paths and options within our organization to potential candidates that come on board so they understand what their potential path can look like. We as employers should be able to highlight career paths for those up-and-coming students and grads looking at retail as a career.

Carmela Aita, director, human resources, The Body Shop

From my perspective, retail is always about recruiting, and you have to always be ahead of the curve. How we do that is by spending a lot of time looking at overall compensation. So not just looking at wages or salary but other things we offer like benefits and recognition. The other piece is fit. If you start from the point of connecting with the right fit to the right offer, you start a few steps ahead of where you want to take people over the long-term.

Tina Shane, vice-president, retail and customer experience, western Canada, Chapters

Source: Robert Price, "Recruiting, Retaining and Empowering Store Managers," *Canadian Retailer*, winter 2012, pp. 36–39.

SUMMARY

Human resource management plays a vital role in supporting a retailing strategy. The organization structure defines supervisory relationships and employees' responsibilities. The four primary groups of tasks performed by retailers are strategic decisions by the corporate officers, administrative tasks by the corporate staff, merchandise management by the buying organization, and store management.

In developing an organization structure, retailers must make trade-offs between the cost savings gained through centralized decision making and the benefits of tailoring the merchandise offering to local markets—benefits that arise when decisions are made in a decentralized manner.

Two critical human resource management issues are the development of a committed workforce and the effective management of a diverse workforce. Building a committed workforce is critical in retailing because high turnover has a major impact on profitability. A key factor in reducing turnover is developing an atmosphere of mutual commitment.

Effective store management can have a significant impact on a retail firm's financial performance. Store managers increase profits by increasing labour productivity, decreasing costs through labour deployment decisions, and reducing inventory loss by developing a dedicated workforce.

A well-crafted, well-executed employee feedback survey can provide significant benefits to improve employee satisfaction and retention, as well as organizational communications that ultimately improve the retailer's success.

Increasing store employees' productivity is challenging because of the difficulties in recruiting, selecting, and motivating store employees. Employees typically have a range of skills and seek a spectrum of rewards. Effective store managers need to motivate their employees to work hard and to develop skills so that they improve their productivity. Store managers must establish realistic goals for employees that are consistent with the store's goals.

Store managers also must control inventory losses due to employee theft, shoplifting, and clerical errors. Managers use a wide variety of methods in developing loss prevention programs, including security devices, employee screening during the selection process, and building employee loyalty to increase attention to shoplifting.

The human resource department is also responsible for making sure that its firm complies with the laws and regulations that prevent discriminatory practices against employees and ensure that they have a safe work environment.

KEY TERMS

average sale per transaction (AST)
bonus
centralization
coaching
commission
decentralization
disability
discrimination
disparate impact
disparate treatment
distributive justice

drawing account
electronic article surveillance (EAS) system
employee productivity
employee turnover
empowerment
extrinsic rewards
flextime
full-time equivalent (FTE)
glass ceiling
illegal discrimination
incentive compensation plan

intrinsic rewards
job analysis
job application form
job description
job sharing
leadership
management
managing diversity
mentoring program
organization structure
organizational culture
procedural justice

promotion from within
quota
quota–bonus plan
sales per employee hour
sales per full-time employee
selling cost
shrinkage
socialization
specialization
straight commission

Get Out & Do It!

1. **GO SHOPPING** Go to a store and meet with the person responsible for personnel scheduling.
   - How far in advance is the schedule made?
   - How are breaks and lunch periods planned?
   - How are overtime hours determined?
   - What is the total number of budgeted employee hours for each department based on?
   - How is flexibility introduced into the schedule?
   - How are special requests for days off handled?
   - How are peak periods planned for?
   - What happens when an employee calls in sick at the last minute?

2. **GO SHOPPING** Go to a store and talk to the person responsible for human resource management to find out how salespeople are compensated and evaluated for job performance.
   - What are the criteria for evaluation?
   - How often are they evaluated?
   - How much importance does the store attach to a buyer's or manager's merchandising skill versus his or her ability to work with people?
   - For an associate, what action is taken if the person does not meet sales goals? Can goals be adjusted? Can associates be moved to another area or type of function?

- Do salespeople have quotas? If they do, how are they set?
- Can sales associates make a commission? If yes, how does the commission system work? What are the advantages and disadvantages of the system?
- If there is no commission system, are any incentive programs offered? Give an example of a specific program or project used by the store to boost employee morale and productivity.

3. **GO SHOPPING** Go to a store, observe the security measures in the store, and talk with the manager about the store's loss prevention program.
- Are there surveillance cameras? Where are they located?
- What is the store's policy against shoplifters?
- What are the procedures for approaching a suspected shoplifter?
- How are shoplifters handled?
- How are sales associates and executives involved in the security programs?

- Is employee theft a problem? Elaborate.
- How is employee theft prevented in the store?
- How is shrinkage prevented in the store?
- How is customer service related to loss prevention in the store?

4. **INTERNET EXERCISE** Go to **www.hrreporter.com**.

Canadian HR Reporter is an online guide to human resources management. Each issue provides real-world solutions to HR situations. Find and summarize the conclusions of articles addressing the HR challenges that retailers are facing, such as the management of a diverse workforce, international expansion, and the use of technology to increase productivity.

5. **INTERNET EXERCISE** Go to a national chain retailer's website and find its employment application form for sales associate. Assess the form for experience, education, and references.

DISCUSSION QUESTIONS AND PROBLEMS

1. Describe the similarities and differences in the organization of small and large retail companies. Why do these similarities and differences exist?

2. How can national retailers such as Best Buy and LaSenza, which both use a centralized buying system, make sure that their buyers are aware of the local differences in consumer needs?

3. What are the positive and negative aspects of employee turnover? How can a retailer reduce the turnover in its sales associates?

4. To motivate employees, several major department stores are experimenting with incentive compensation plans. Frequently, compensation plans with a lot of incentives don't promote good customer service. How can retailers motivate employees to sell merchandise aggressively and at the same time not jeopardize customer service?

5. Three approaches to motivating and coordinating employee activities are policies and supervision, incentives, and organization culture. What are the advantages and disadvantages of each?

6. Why should retailers be concerned about the needs of their employees? What can retailers do to satisfy the needs of employees?

7. How do on-the-job training and classroom training differ? What are the benefits and limitations of each approach?

8. Give examples of a situation in which a manager of a McDonald's fast-food restaurant must utilize different leadership styles.

9. Job descriptions should be in writing so employees clearly understand what's expected of them. But what are the dangers of relying too heavily on written job descriptions?

10. What's the difference between extrinsic rewards and intrinsic rewards? What are the effects of these rewards on the behaviour of retail employees? Under what conditions would you recommend that a retailer emphasize intrinsic rewards over extrinsic rewards?

11. Many large department stores are changing their salespeople's reward system from a traditional salary to a commission-based system. What problems can incentive compensation systems cause? How can department managers avoid these problems?

12. When evaluating retail employees, some stores use a quantitative approach that relies on checklists and numerical scores. Other stores use a more qualitative approach that requires less time checking and adding and more time discussing strengths and weaknesses in written form. Which is the better evaluation approach? Why?

13. What are the different methods for compensating employees? Discuss which methods you think would be best for compensating a sales associate, store manager, and buyer.

14. In addition to competitve salary, vacation, and tuition reimbursement as a retailer's key retention strategies, in what other ways can a retailer optimize employee satisfaction?

15. Discuss how retailers can reduce shrinkage from shoplifting and employee theft.

Practise and learn online with Connect.

building customer loyalty: customer relationship management and service strategies

LEARNING OBJECTIVES

Lo1   Define customer relationship management.

Lo2   Examine how retailers determine who their best customers are.

Lo3   Explore how retailers can build customer loyalty and increase their share of wallet.

Lo4   Discuss how customer service can build a competitive advantage.

Lo5   Determine the types of activities a retailer undertakes to provide high-quality customer service.

Lo6   Review how retailers can recover from a service failure.

SPOTLIGHT ON RETAILING

Loyalty Programs: Big Information Business

Customer loyalty management has become a pivotal component of a retailers' strategy to maximize a customer's lifetime value. In order to achieve sustainable business growth, retailers have realized that it is imperative to make shopping experiences enjoyable, with customer benefits and communications targeted so that customers want to return. Loyalty programs are often part and parcel of a comprehensive customer loyalty management strategy. A loyalty program is a structured and long-term marketing effort that provides incentives to repeat customers who demonstrate loyal buying behaviour.

The transactional part of a loyalty program—make a purchase, pick up points—is not what loyalty is about. Retailers want loyalty from their customers, but a lot of businesses have confused loyalty programs with points-based initiatives. The retailer gives the reward points in exchange for information. For example, it is the ability of the business to learn their customers' needs and wants and to tailor not just their merchandise to them but also the retail experience.

Sophisticated databases compile information to assist retailers to refine their merchandising mix and marketing strategy to gain bigger market share. Information is power, and thanks to the data amassed from loyalty programs, inquiring marketers know what music we listen to, what restaurants we prefer, and what brand names gain our loyalty. This valuable information allows the retailer to tailor its marketing programs to specific customer segments and to concentrate on profitable customers who will generate the most revenue. Retaining a current customer is far less costly than finding a new one. It is estimated that it costs ten times more for a company to attract a new customer. Only 12 to 15 percent of customers are loyal to a single retailer, according to the Center for Retail Management at Northwestern University. But that set of shoppers generates between 55 and 70 percent of company sales.

While retail loyalty programs have many purposes, the greatest value that is created for retailers is the ability to convert a faceless footfall into an identifiable customer and to measure and understand their individual behaviours. According to crmtrends.com, the basic benefits that form the basis of all loyalty program initiatives are the following:

- **Shift.** Acquire new customers.

- **Lift.** Increase the spending of existing customers.

- **Retention.** Improve the natural churn rate of customers.
- **Profit mix.** Shift spending to higher-margin products.

Hence, a winning loyalty program should enable customer acquisition, provide understanding of customer behaviour, increase customer spending, and enhance business profitability and customer service across various channels used by customers to interact with retailers, such as the store, web, mobile, kiosk, and paper.

Canadian consumers are quite familiar with loyalty programs as Canada is among the most mature and developed loyalty markets in the world. There are 120 million loyalty program memberships in Canada, with 90 percent of Canadians belonging to at least one loyalty program (compared to 74 percent in the United States and, for global comparison, 42 percent in India). However, unlike the United States, Canadian loyalty memberships are showing a slight (1 percent) decline since 2011. The loyalty industry in Canada is facing challenges that occur or that are similar to those in every mature marketplace. A plethora of options has made Canadian consumers even more selective about which programs they join and actually use. Canadian savvy combined with a crowded market means that retail loyalty programs must deliver much more relevance to attract and engage the Canadian consumer.

As the loyalty market has matured and grown, so too have the ways to earn rewards and the kinds of rewards that can be redeemed. In the past, Canadians based their purchasing decisions on value, price, and convenience. Today, consumers have shifted to some extent, away from a desire for possessions to a desire for experiences. Overall, consumers are looking for the meaningful, which includes value, engagement, and relevance.

At Aeroplan, for instance, more than 90 percent of members collect miles for travel, says David Klein, vice-president, marketing and innovation. But to further serve its customers, in 2012, Aeroplan launched a digital media store where members can turn miles into media downloads, a loyalty industry first in Canada.

In February 2013, the Air Miles for Social Change program added to its list of ways to earn rewards by partnering with the federal government and 15 YMCAs across Canada. The partnership enables families to earn Air Miles reward miles in ways that encourage physical activity, such as registering their children for day camps, using participating fitness facilities, or buying YMCA memberships.

Other recent trends that inject an element of fun and engagement for members of loyalty programs involve the use of social media and gamification. Gamification is the application of game thinking and game mechanics—including points, badges, or similar incentives—in nongame contexts in order to affect behaviour. Companies of all kinds are finding ways to put the structures and rules of games to work in business; consider Air Canada's frequent flyer status levels, Shoppers Drug Mart Optimum points, and Canadian Tire money.

Loblaw is integrating smartphone technology and sophisticated data collection and processing into its new PC Plus digital loyalty program. PC Plus offers a number of innovations, both for Loblaw and for its customers, such as cutting back on the cost and waste of paper flyers and offering customized deals that better match up with shoppers' actual buying habits. Loading offers to their PC Plus cards on their mobile devices allows members to earn points when they buy the qualifying items at participating Loblaw stores. Members also get bonus offers, flyer offers, and in-store offers to enjoy. The more offers they take advantage of, the more points they can earn: 1000 points is equivalent to $1. Once they accumulate 20 000 points, they can redeem $20 off of their grocery bill. It's a prime example of mobile, social gamification working today for a major Canadian company.

Air Miles has recently been using gamification to kick start its location-based (mobile) loyalty partnerships with merchants. Its main challenge was getting members to "check-in" (visit) the retail operations of its partners with their Air Miles app active on their mobile devices. By creating a contest among members to see who would visit the most partner locations, they leveraged gamification to get members engaged and help them understand the new programs.

The challenge for all loyalty programs is that people want to simplify their lives, to discard things that aren't absolutely essential. If a loyalty program does not maintain sufficient engagement with increasingly discerning customers and becomes only an extra card in the wallet, or an extra app on a mobile device, it will be dispensed.

Sources: Barbara Farfan, "Customer Loyalty Program," About.com, http://retailindustry.about.com/od/glossary/g/customerloyalty.htm (accessed July 2, 2013); Jeff Berry, "Lonely at the Top: The 2013 COLLOQUY Loyalty Census: Growth and Trends in Canadian Loyalty Program Action," COLLOQUY/a Loyalty One research group, July 2013; PostMedia News, "Canadians find value in loyalty programs," *Vancouver Sun*, April 11, 2013; "Harper Government partners with Air Miles Reward Program and YMCAs in Canada to Promote Healthy Living," www.phac-aspc.gc.ca/media/nr-rp/2013/2013_0220-eng.php (accessed July 3, 2013); "New YMCA Partnership with Air Miles and the Government of Canada," news release, www.ymca.ca/en/what's-new/new-ymca-partnership-with-air-miles-and-the-government-of-canada.aspx (accessed July 3, 2013); and Mark Hayes, "How to Use Gamification to Increase Sales," Shopify, May 30, 2013, www.shopify.com/blog/7988857-how-to-use-gamification-to-increase-sales#ixzz2ZVPCS1SL (accessed July 3, 2013).

Business press and companies are talking a lot about the importance of managing customer relationships. Companies are spending billions of dollars on computer systems to help them collect and analyze data about their customers. Putting customers at the centre of the business equation pays off in retail profits. Companies around the world are focusing on new and innovative ways to serve their customers.

Customer service is the activities and programs developed by retailers to make the shopping experience for their customers special. Customers base their evaluations of store service on their perceptions. Although these perceptions are affected by the actual service provided, service (due to its intangibility) is often hard to evaluate accurately. Five customer service characteristics that customers use to evaluate service quality are reliability, assurance, tangibility, empathy, and responsiveness.[1] Some cues that customers use to assess these service characteristics are the following:

- **Reliability.** Accuracy of billing, meeting promised delivery dates
- **Assurance (trust).** Guarantees and warranties, return policy
- **Tangibility.** Appearance of store, salespeople
- **Empathy.** Personalized service, receipts of notes and e-mails, recognition by name
- **Responsiveness.** Returning calls and e-mails, giving prompt service.

Employees can play an important role in customer perceptions of service quality.[2] Customer evaluations of service quality are often based on the manner in which store employees provide the service, not just the outcome. Consider the following situation: A customer goes to a store to return an electric toothbrush that isn't working properly. In one case, company policy requires the employee to ask the customer for a receipt, check to see if the receipt shows the toothbrush was bought at the store, examine the toothbrush to see if it really doesn't work properly, ask a manager if a refund can be provided, complete some paperwork, and finally give the customer the amount paid for the toothbrush in cash. In a second case, the store employee simply asks the customer how much he paid and gives him a cash refund. The two cases have the same outcome: The customer gets a cash refund. But the customer might be dissatisfied in the first case because the employee appeared not to trust the customer and took so much time providing the refund. In most situations, employees have a great effect on the process of providing services and, thus, on the customer's eventual satisfaction with the services.

Customer relationship management (CRM) is a business philosophy and set of strategies, programs, and systems that focus on identifying and building loyalty with a retailer's most valued customers. CRM is based on the philosophy that retailers can increase their profitability by building relationships with their better customers. By effectively managing merchandise inventory and adding services, stores provide extra value that supports the objective of building customer loyalty to increase their share of wallet. The goal of CRM is to develop a base of loyal customers who patronize the retailer frequently. In the following sections of this chapter, we discuss in more depth the objective of CRM programs and the elements in the CRM process.

customer relationship management (CRM) A business philosophy and set of strategies, programs, and systems that focuses on identifying and building loyalty with a retailer's most valued customers.

share of wallet The percentage of total purchases made by a customer in a store.

The CRM Process

Traditionally, retailers have focused their attention on encouraging customers to visit their stores, look through their catalogues, and visit their websites. To accomplish this objective, they have traditionally used mass media advertising and price promotions, treating all their customers the same. Now retailers are beginning to concentrate on providing more value to their best customers, using targeted promotions and services to increase their share of wallet—the percentage of the customers' purchases made from the retailer—with these customers. This change in perspective is supported by research indicating that it costs over six times more to sell products and services to new customers than to existing customers and that small increases in customer retention can lead to dramatic increases in profits.[3]

What Is Loyalty?

Customer loyalty, the objective of CRM, is more than having customers make repeat visits to a retailer and being satisfied with their experiences and the merchandise they purchased. Customer loyalty to a retailer means that customers are committed to purchasing merchandise and services from the retailer and will resist the activities of competitors attempting to attract their patronage. They have a bond with the retailer, and the bond is based on more than a positive feeling about the retailer.[4]

Loyal customers have an emotional connection with the retailer. Their reasons for continuing to patronize a retailer go beyond the convenience of the retailer's store or the low prices and specific brands offered by the retailer. They feel such goodwill toward the retailer that they will encourage their friends and family to buy from it.

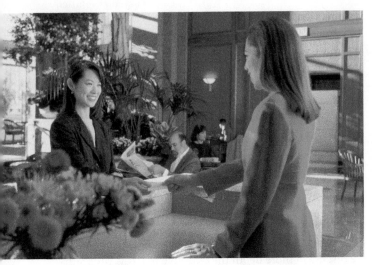

When guests check into five-star hotels like the Ritz-Carlton, they are greeted by name. Their preferences are known based on past visits. Everything possible is done to meet their needs and wants.

small, independent restaurants build loyalty by functioning as neighbourhood cafés, where waiters and waitresses recognize customers by name and know their preferences.

Harry Rosen sales associates will take new menswear collections to the offices of their busy loyal customers and provide personalized services for their styling and tailoring needs. Providing such memorable experiences is an important avenue for building customer loyalty.[6]

Overview of the CRM Process

Exhibit 14–2 illustrates that CRM is an iterative process that turns customer data into customer loyalty through four activities:

- Collecting customer data
- Analyzing the customer data and identifying target customers
- Developing CRM programs
- Implementing CRM programs

The process begins with the collection and analysis of data about a retailer's customers and the identification of target customers. The analysis translates the customer information into activities that offer value to the targeted customers. Then these activities are executed through communication programs undertaken by the marketing department and customer service programs implemented by customer contact employees, typically sales associates. Each of the four activities in the CRM process (Exhibit 14–2) is discussed in the following sections.

Collecting Customer Data

The first step in the CRM process is constructing a customer database. This database, referred to as a *customer data warehouse*, contains all of the data the firms have collected about its customers and is the foundation for subsequent CRM activities.

customer database
The coordinated and periodic copying of data from various sources, both inside and outside the enterprise, into an environment ready for analytical and informational processing. It contains all of the data the firm has collected about its customers and is the foundation for subsequent CRM activities; also called *customer data warehouse*.

Programs that encourage repeat buying by simply offering price discounts can be easily copied by competitors. In addition, these types of price promotion programs encourage customers to be always looking for the best deal rather than developing a relationship with one retailer. However, when a retailer develops an emotional connection with a customer, it is difficult for a competitor to attract the customer.[5]

All the elements of the retail mix contribute to the development of customer loyalty (Exhibit 14–1) and repeat-purchase behaviour. Customer loyalty can be enhanced by creating an appealing brand image and providing convenient locations, attractive merchandise at compelling prices, and an engaging shopping experience. However, personal attention is one of the most effective methods for developing loyalty. For example, many

exhibit 14–1 Loyalty Census Snapshot: Canada, 2008–2012

Industry Sector	2008 Memberships	2010 Memberships	Growth '08–'10	2012 Memberships	Growth '10–'12	Growth '08–'12
Coalition AIR MILES Aeroplan	9 500 000	10 000 000	5.26%	10 200 000	2%	7.37%
	4 000 000	4 000 000	0%	4 600 000	15%	15%
Financial Services	25 897 000	31 040 000	19.86%	31 910 000	2.80%	23.22%
Retail	57 850 000	57 340 000	−.88%	55 320 000	−3.52%	−4.37%
Travel, Gaming, Entertainment, Dining, Other	18 974 000	18 330 000	−3.39%	17 939 983	−2.13%	−5.45%
Total	116 221 000	120 710 000	3.86%	119 969 983	−.61%	3.23%

Source: Jeff Berry, "Lonely at the Top: The 2013 COLLOQUY Loyalty Census: Growth and Trends in Canadian Loyalty Program Activity," July 2013, p. 5, www.colloquy.com/files/2013-COLLOQUY-Canada-Census-Talk-white-paper.pdf (accessed December 20, 2013).

exhibit 14-2 The CRM Process Cycle

Customer Database

Ideally, the database should contain the following information:

- **Transactions.** A complete history of the purchases made by the customer, including the purchase date, the price paid, the SKUs purchased, and whether the merchandise was purchased in response to a special promotion or marketing activity.

Customers' sales information is recorded at POS terminals, stored in data warehouses, and used in CRM systems.

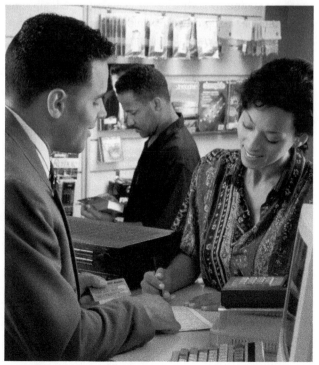

- **Customer contacts.** A record of the interactions that the customer has had with the retailer, including visits to the retailer's website, inquiries made through in-store kiosks, and telephone calls made to the retailer's call centre, plus information about contacts initiated by the retailer, such as catalogues and direct mail sent to the customer.

- **Customer preferences.** What the customer likes, such as favourite colours, brands, fabrics, and flavours as well as apparel sizes.

- **Descriptive information.** Demographic and psychographic data describing the customer that can be used in developing market segments.

- **Responses to marketing activities.** The analysis of the transaction and contact data provides information about the customer's responsiveness to marketing activities.

Different members of a household might have interactions with a retailer. Thus, to get a complete view of the customer, retailers need to be able to combine the individual customer data from each member of a household. For example, without these household-level data, a supermarket retailer might underestimate the importance of a household with several people who shop at the store.

The analysis of the customer database can provide important insights for planning merchandise assortment. For example, a supermarket chain sells over 300 types of cheese. Feta cheese ranked 295th in sales, which suggested it should not have a favourable position in the cheese department and might even be a candidate for elimination from the assortment. However, further analysis uncovered that feta cheese ranked 25th in sales for the supermarket's best customers.[7]

With today's technology, even small, independent retailers can create and use a customer database. For example, Gary Mead, a 34-year-old entrepreneur, uses his customer database to take on the giants: Domino's, Little Caesar's, and Pizza Hut. With a $2500 computer system, he keeps track of the purchase history of customers patronizing his restaurant. If customers don't order for 60 days, the system spits out a postcard with a discount to lure them back. Other promotions encourage customers to try all of the dishes offered by suggesting pasta dishes to pizza lovers. The database has 8500 customers in a town of 11 000; business has been increasing 25 to 30 percent each year.[8]

Loblaw unveiled a new loyalty program in May 2013 aimed at smartphone users. The PC Plus app lets customers collect points that can be redeemed for money off

frequent shopper program A reward and communication program used by a retailer to encourage continued purchases from the retailer's best customers.

loyalty program A program set up to reward customers with incentives such as discounts on purchases, free food, gifts, or even cruises or trips in return for their repeated business.

private-label credit card A credit card that has the store's name on it and is issued by the retailer.

their grocery bill, create shopping lists, browse flyers and link recipes to shopping lists on the go, and receive personalized offers based on products that the system determines each customer wants, based on past purchase history. For shoppers who do not have a smartphone, the program is also available in card form. Both the card and the app are free. Loblaw spent two-and-a-half years developing PC Plus, which incorporates points from the supermarket chains long-standing PC Financial credit card rewards program.[10] Retailing View 14.1 describes a British grocer's take on a similar customer-centric reward strategy.

Identifying Information

Constructing this database is relatively easy for catalogue and Internet shoppers and customers who use the retailer's credit card when buying merchandise in stores. Customers buying merchandise through nonstore channels must provide their contact information (their name and address) so that the purchases can be sent to them. Since some retailers issue their own credit cards, they can collect the contact information for billing when customers apply for the card. In these cases, the identification of the customer is linked to the transaction.

However, identifying most customers who are making in-store transactions is more difficult because they often pay for the merchandise with a debit card, cash, or a third-party credit card such as Visa and MasterCard. Common approaches that store-based retailers use to overcome this problem are:

- Asking customers for the identifying information
- Offering loyalty card programs
- Offering co-branded credit cards (Scotia Scene Visa, Walmart MasterCard, RBC Shoppers Optimum MasterCard)

Asking for Identifying Information   Some retailers such as The Source, Nine West, and the Container Store have their sales associates ask customers for identifying information such as their phone number, name, postal code, and/or when they ring up a sale.[11] This information

Frequent shopper cards are becoming so common that consumers cannot carry all of the cards in their wallets; key tags are an easy alternative.

is then used to create the transaction database for the customer. However, this approach has two limitations. First, some customers may be reluctant to provide the information and feel that the sales associates are violating their privacy. Second, sales associates might forget to ask for the information or decide not to spend the time getting and recording it during a busy period.

Offering a Frequent Shopper Card   A frequent shopper program, also called a loyalty program, is a program that identifies and provides rewards for customers who patronize a retailer. Some retailers issue customers a frequent shopper card, whereas others use a private-label credit card—a credit card that has the store's name on it—or a co-branded third-party credit card. In these cases, customer information is automatically captured when the card is scanned at the point of sale terminal. When customers enroll in one of these programs, they provide some descriptive information about themselves or their household and are issued a card with an identifying number. The customers then are offered an incentive to show the card when they make purchases from the retailer. Research has shown that customers generally prefer to get something extra—a reward—for their purchases, rather than lower prices.[12] Canadian consumers are more patient than their American counterparts. They're more willing to accumulate points and miles that yield free travel, in-store merchandise, or free reward catalogue redemptions. For example, a supermarket might offer frequent shoppers a point for every dollar spent in the store. The points can be redeemed for items in a gift catalogue or for free groceries. From the retailer's perspective, frequent shopper programs offer two benefits:

- Customers provide demographic and other information when they sign up for the program and then are motivated to identify themselves at each transaction.
- Customers are motivated by the rewards offered to increase the number of visits to the retailer and the amount purchased on each visit.

The major problems with using frequent shopper cards for identification are that the card is often squeezed out of the customer's wallet by other cards, the customer might forget to bring it to the store when shopping, or the customer might decide not to show it if he or she is in a hurry. Thus, retailers are recognizing that the optimal solution for interacting with today's customers will require a multichannel mix, including traditional media, direct mail,

Tesco Uses Data Collected from Its Frequent-Shopper Program

Tesco, the largest supermarket chain in the United Kingdom and the third largest in the world, has been very effective at analyzing and exploiting the data it collects through its Clubcard frequent-shopper program. To encourage customers to enroll in the program, Tesco gives them points for every pound they spend in its stores, on its website, and at its gas stations. Customers who spend 25 pounds a week for 10 weeks get double points. The points are redeemed by reducing the shopping bill when customers check out.

In addition, customers can get more benefits by joining one of Tesco's clubs. For example, members of the Baby and Toddler Club get expert advice and exclusive

Tesco uses retail analytics to alter its merchandise selection in stores, develop new products, and target specific customer groups.

offers to help them through the stages of parenting from pregnancy to childhood (tesco.com/babyclub). Members get discount coupons on baby essentials, a permit allowing them to park nearer to the store, and a free Pampers Hamper filled with baby items and special treats for the mother.

Analysis of the sales transactions identified six customer segments such as the "Finer Foods" segment, which includes affluent, time-strapped shoppers who buy upscale products, and the "Traditional" segment, shoppers who are homemakers and have time to cook meals. Unique marketing programs are developed for each of the segments.

Tesco frequently sends personalized coupon packages to Clubcard members. Some coupons are for products the customer normally buys, and others are for products that the retailer believes the customer would like to try. More than 1 million unique sets of coupons

are distributed for each promotion. Between 15 and 20 percent of the coupons are redeemed, compared with the industry average redemption rate of 1 to 2 percent.

Based on an analysis of the data, Tesco introduced "World Foods," which features Asian herbs and other ethnic food, into stores located in Indian and Pakistani neighbourhoods. However, when Tesco looked at the locations from which the customers travelled to buy the unique merchandise in these stores, it found that more than 25 percent of customers were coming from other neighbourhoods. This discovery led Tesco to add an assortment of World Foods to other stores.

Tesco also introduced a premium private-label brand, Tesco Finest, that includes duck pâté and premium wines and cheeses because it discovered, through retail analytics, that its affluent customers were not buying wine, cheese, fruit, and other higher-priced–higher-margin items from Tesco.

Sources: Yan Ma, Jianxun Ding, and Wenxia Hong, "Delivering Customer Value Based on Service Process: The Example of Tesco.Com," *International Business Research 3*, no. 2 (2010), pp. 131–135; Andrew Smith and Leigh Sparks, "Reward Redemption Behaviour in Retail Loyalty Schemes," *British Journal of Management 20*, no. 2 (2008), pp. 204–218; www.Tesco.com (accessed July 1, 2010).

SMS, voice, e-mail, and apps.[13] Mobile for instance, can serve as a replacement for the traditional loyalty card or key fob, offering a new way to load, accrue, and redeem rewards (see Retailing View 14.2).

Founded in 1992, Air Miles, Canada's premier coalition loyalty program, induces consumers to shop and collect air miles as a reward for loyalty to the retailer. Miles

can be earned with purchases made at more than 120 stores as well as 100 more online retailers. The Air Miles' databases compile information about customers and their shopping habits to assist retailers in tailoring merchandise and marketing strategies. According to Kelly Hlavinka of Colloquy Consulting, a loyalty consulting practice, Air Miles accounts for a 70 percent penetration level among the nation's households. No such national coalition exists in the United States.[15]

Frequent flyer programs such as Air Miles and Aeroplan are much more than simple loyalty programs. Both Aeroplan and Air Miles are coalition programs because they have

commercial partners. Aeroplan, for example, has more than 70 commercial partners in financial, retail, and travel sectors and makes money from the sale of its Aeroplan Miles to those commercial partners. Every time an Aeroplan member flies on Air Canada (partner), or uses a TD Aeroplan Visa (partner), or fills up a car with gas at an Imperial Oil (Esso) gas station (partner), the customer "earns"

14.2 | RETAILING VIEW

Retailers Increase Focus on Mobile Applications to Enhance Customer Loyalty, Reveals IDC Retail Insights

As the retail industry begins to recover from economic instability, customer loyalty applications and CRM innovations become the key drivers of retailers' go-to-market strategies. In a recent report, IDC Retail Insights discussed why and how retailers are accessing their CRM technology and loyalty schemes to deliver an immersive shopping experience.

The study draws upon extensive IDC Retail Insights resources, including previous research and interviews with vendors and retail end users. A related IDC consumer survey on CRM and loyalty found that the top three customer expectations from loyalty programs include transparent management of loyalty programs, access to special services and personalized promotions, and access to a wider range of products matching personal preferences. These findings confirm retailers' attention toward integrating their current CRM with the latest technology innovations to enhance the overall customer experience and increase business benefits generated by loyalty.

Innovation is the basis of this retail transition from traditional reward schemes to an omni-channel loyalty transparency. In order to address consumers' expectations and add value to the "earn points to redeem" schemes, it is imperative to look at loyalty management within its wider ecosystem. The report highlights that retailers must identify the right approach to implement innovative loyalty schemes.

For instance, multi-retailer loyalty schemes have become a successful example of partnership among several retailers. Key findings of this study show that:

- Loyalty is moving beyond points and discounts to become an integral part of a more encompassing

customer experience that will support same-shopper sales and gain of market share to increase or recover competitive advantage.

- Omni-channel retailers use insights to identify and understand a core group of their most-valued customers. From there, they can predict what might motivate changes in shopping behaviour that will make them even more loyal.

- Mobile loyalty applications represent an element of innovation that meets customer's demand for real-time, profile-relevant, and location-based information. Along with existing mobile loyalty card apps, allowing customers to be recognized, receive more personalized offers, and earn points, "first mover" retailers are taking into consideration the current opportunities represented by near-field communication (NFC) technology, which enables contactless payments through mobile devices.

"The mobile targeted retailing and rewarding approach is most likely what customers expect from a leading customer-centric retailer," says Ivano Ortis, international head of IDC Retail Insights. "We believe that the ability to create and foster loyalty, enhanced by the delivery of new services, is the key issue for retailers to obtain repeated and long-term customer engagements. With better insight into demand dynamics and customer behaviour provided by loyalty applications, retailers can measure the real increase in customer retention, providing an opportunity to drive repeated, larger, and more profitable customer transactions. Retailers must choose the loyalty management applications that deliver higher flexibility, scalability, and responsiveness to optimize the customer experience."

Source: "Retailers Increase Focus on Mobile Applications to Enhance Customer Loyalty, reveals IDC Retail Insights," International Data Group, August 1, 2011,

Aeroplan reward miles and the Aeroplan's commercial partners buy miles from Aeroplan. The partners are paying for the benefits of belonging and Aeroplan makes money on the spread between what it sells its points for and what it costs the program to buy the relevant reward. It also makes money by managing the rewards program for Air Canada. It further benefits from what is known in the industry as breakage, which is the estimated 17 percent of Aeroplan miles that will never be redeemed.[16]

Privacy and CRM Programs

Although detailed information about individual customers helps retailers provide more benefits to their better customers, consumers are concerned about retailers violating their privacy when they collect this information.

Privacy Concerns The degree to which consumers feel their privacy has been violated depends on:

- Their control over their personal information when engaging in marketplace transactions. Do they feel they can decide on the amount and type of information collected by the retailer?

- Their knowledge of the collection and use of personal information. Do they know what information is being collected and how the retailer will be using it? Will the retailer be sharing the information with other parties?[17]

These concerns are particularly acute for customers using an electronic channel because many of them do not realize the extensive amount of information that can be collected without their knowledge. In addition to collecting transaction data, electronic retailers can collect information by placing cookies on visitor's hard drives.

Cookies are text files that identify visitors when they return to a website. Due to the data in the cookies, customers do not have to identify themselves and use passwords every time they visit a site. However, the cookies also collect information about other sites the person has visited and what pages they have downloaded.[18]

Protecting Customer Privacy Canada's privacy law went into effect on January 1, 2004. The federal privacy legislation changed the way companies do business and how marketers collect, use, or disclose customer information in the course of a commercial activity within Canada. In order to be compliant with the legislation, organizations must appoint a privacy officer and implement detailed procedures to protect personal information. The *Privacy Act* is all about relationships with customers and employees and is based on ten principles for the protection of personal information. The Canadian Marketing Association outlines the basic principles:

1. *Accountability*—An organization will be responsible for ensuring that personal information in its possession, including information that has been transferred to a third party for processing, is secure and that the third party is compliant with the law.

2. *Identifying purposes*—How you plan to use customer data must be identified at the time of, or prior to, collection of the individual's information. If you want to use information already collected for a new purpose, you will have to identify the new purpose to your customer and obtain new consent.

3. *Consent*—You must have consent for the collection, use, or disclosure of personal data.

4. *Limiting collection*—If you make marketing lists available to third parties, you will have an obligation to ensure that you have obtained consent from consumers prior to passing their personal information on to third parties. You will also need to keep records of having received that consent.

5. *Limiting use, disclosure, and retention*—If you are using customer data as part of your marketing activities, you can retain this information as long as the individual is an active customer, or for the length of the marketing campaign.

6. *Accuracy*—Marketers are obligated to keep personal information on consumers as accurate and up-to-date as possible.

cookies Computer text files that identify visitors when they return to a website, so that customers do not have to identify themselves or use passwords every time they visit the site. Cookies also collect information about other sites the person has visited and what pages have been downloaded.

Sears provides a detailed description of its privacy policy on its website.

data mining
Technique used to identify patterns in data found in data warehouses, typically patterns that the analyst is unaware of prior to searching through the data.

market basket analysis Specific type of data analysis that focuses on the composition of the basket (or bundle) of products purchased by a household during a single shopping occasion.

DID YOU KNOW?

More than 50 percent of retailers with over US$500 million in annual sales are using data mining tools.[19]

7. *Safeguard security*—All those who are involved in the transfer, rental, sale, or exchange of mailing lists are responsible for protecting the data and taking appropriate measures to ensure against unauthorized access.

8. *Openness*—Organizations should undertake to develop privacy policies, train staff on the company's privacy practices, and make information available to the public concerning their privacy policy.

9. *Individual access*—Marketers will need to make customers' personal information available upon their request.

10. *Challenging compliance*—Marketers will be required to establish formal inquiry and complaint-handling procedures and make this known to consumers who enquire.

The Canadian Standards Association has developed an electronic resource, "The Privacy Code: A Matter of Privacy—Understanding and Applying the New Canadian Privacy Law," for any organization that needs assistance in making a smooth transition toward privacy law compliance.[20]

In summary, there is growing consensus that personal information must be fairly collected; the collection must be purposeful; and the data should be relevant, maintained as accurate, essential to the business, subject to the rights of the owning individual, kept reasonably secure, and transferred only with the permission of the consumer. To address these concerns, many retailers that collect customer information have privacy policies. They must clearly state what information is collected from each visitor and how it will be used, give consumers a choice as to whether they give information, and allow them to view and correct any personal information held by an online retail site. Retailers using an electronic channel must also ensure that consumer information is held securely and is not passed on to other companies without the permission of the customer.[21]

Analyzing Customer Data and Identifying Target Customers

The next step in the CRM process is analyzing the customer database and converting the data into information that will help retailers develop programs for building customer loyalty. Data mining is one approach commonly used to develop this information. Data mining is a technique used to identify patterns in data, typically patterns that the analyst is unaware of prior to searching through the data. For example, an electronic retailer discovered that customers who had bought mp3 players typically commuted to work by train. Using this information, the retailer experienced a 43 percent increase in mp3 sales when it redirected most of its communication budget from daytime television commercials to newspapers and billboards along the train tracks.[22]

Market basket analysis is a specific type of data analysis that focuses on the composition of the basket, or bundle, of products purchased during a single shopping occasion. This analysis is often useful for management in suggesting where to place merchandise in a store. For example, based on market basket analyses, Fortinos changed the traditional location of several items:

- Since bananas are the most common item in grocery carts, Fortinos Supercentres sell bananas next to the corn flakes as well as in the produce section.
- Kleenex tissues are in the paper-goods aisle and also mixed in with cold medicine.
- Measuring spoons are in housewares and also hanging next to baking supplies such as flour and Crisco shortening.
- Flashlights are in the hardware aisle and also with a seasonal display of Halloween costumes.

Identifying Market Segments

Traditionally, customer data analysis has focused on identifying market segments—groups of customers who have similar needs, purchase similar merchandise, and respond in a similar manner to marketing activities. For example, when Eddie Bauer analyzed its customer database, it discovered two types of shoppers. One group it calls "professional shoppers"—people who love fashion and value good customer service. The other group it calls "too busy to shop people"—people who want the shopping experience over as quickly as possible. The professional shoppers tended to use the alteration service, call the customer service desk, and seek out the same salesperson when they made purchases in the stores. On the other hand, the people too busy to shop typically shop from the catalogue and website. Eddie Bauer uses this information to develop unique advertising programs targeting each of these segments.

Eddie Bauer also discovered that morning shoppers are more price-sensitive and like to buy products on sale more than evening shoppers. Evening shoppers tended to be in the professional shopper segment. Using this information, Eddie Bauer installed electronic window posters in some test stores that allowed different images to be displayed at different times of the day. In the morning, the displays featured lower-priced merchandise and items on sale; in the evening, the more expensive and fashionable merchandise was displayed.[23]

Home Depot realized that 70 to 80 percent of its kitchen renovation department was coming from 20 to 30 percent of the department's customers.[24] It speculated that these heavy spenders might spend even more if it organized the department around meeting their needs. It knew that heavy-spenders want lots of choices and information. So it added more assortment, better-trained associates, a computer-aided design system, and suites of innovative kitchen layouts arranged so that customers could readily sense what their kitchen would look like after a renovation. The results—higher sales and profit per square foot than traditional departments designed to satisfy all customers.

Identifying Best Customers

Using information in the customer database, retailers can develop a score or number indicating how valuable the customers are to the firm. This score can then be used to determine which customers to target.

Lifetime Value   A commonly used measure to score each customer is called lifetime customer value. Lifetime customer value (LTV) is the expected contribution from the customer to the retailer's profits over his or her entire relationship with the retailer.

LTV is estimated by using past behaviours to forecast future purchases, gross margin from these purchases, and costs associated with servicing the customers. Some of the costs associated with a customer are the cost of advertising and promotions used to acquire the customer and the cost of processing merchandise that the customer has returned. Thus, a customer who purchases $200 on groceries from a supermarket every other month would have a lower LTV for the supermarket than a customer who buys $30 on each visit and shops at the store three times a week. Similarly, a customer who buys apparel only when it's on sale in a department store would have a lower LTV than a customer who typically pays full price and buys the same amount of merchandise.

These assessments of LTV are based on the assumption that the customer's future purchase behaviours will be the same as they have been in the past. Sophisticated statistical methods are typically used to estimate the future contributions from past purchases. For example, these methods might consider how recently purchases have been made. The expected LTV of a customer who purchased $600 on one visit six months ago is less than the LTV of a customer who has been purchasing $100 of merchandise every month for the last six months.

Customer Pyramid   Most retailers realize that their customers differ in terms of their profitability or LTV. In particular, they know that a relatively small number of customers account for the majority of their profits. This realization is often called the 80–20 rule—80 percent of the sales or profits come from 20 percent of the customers. Thus, retailers could group their customers into two groups based on the LTV scores. One group would be the 20 percent of the customers with the highest LTV scores, and the other group would be the rest. However, this two-segment scheme, "best" and "rest," does not consider important differences among the 80 percent of the customers in the "rest" segment.[25]

A commonly used segmentation scheme divides customers into four segments, illustrated in Exhibit 14–3. This scheme allows retailers to develop more appropriate

lifetime customer value (LTV)   The expected contribution from the customer to the retailer's profits over his or her entire relationship with the retailer.

80–20 rule   A general management principle stating that 80 percent of the sales or profits come from 20 percent of the customers.

DID YOU KNOW?

Although 50 percent of retail executives say their company collects data about individual customers, only 41 percent can identify their best customers.[26]

exhibit 14–3   The Customer Pyramid

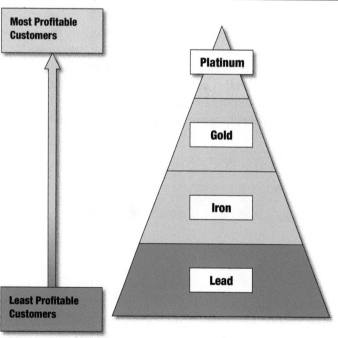

Source: Valerie Zeithaml, Roland Rust, and Katherine Lemon, "The Customer Pyramid: Creating and Serving Profitable Customers," *California Management Review* 43 (Summer 2001), p. 125. Reprinted by permission.

decile analysis A method of identifying customers in a CRM program that breaks customers into ten deciles based on their LTV (lifetime customer value). When using decile analysis, the top 10 percent of the customers would be the most-valued group.

RFM (recency, frequency, monetary) analysis Often used by catalogue retailers and direct marketers, a scheme for segmenting customers based on how recently they have made a purchase, how frequently they make purchases, and how much they have bought.

strategies for each of the segments. Each of the four segments is described below.

- **Platinum segment.** This segment is composed of the retailer's customers with the top 25 percent of LTVs. Typically, these are the most loyal customers who are not overly concerned about merchandise price and place more value on customer service.

- **Gold segment.** The next 25 percent of the customers in terms of their LTV make up the gold segment. These customers have a lower LTV than platinum customers because they are more price-sensitive. Even though they buy a significant amount of merchandise from the retailer, they are not as loyal as platinum customers and probably patronize some of the retailer's competitors.

- **Iron segment.** Customers in this third tier probably do not deserve much special attention from the retailer due to their modest LTV.

- **Lead segment.** Customers in the lowest segment can cost the company money. They often demand a lot of attention but do not buy much from the retailer. For example, real estate agents often encounter people who want to spend their weekends looking at houses but are really not interested in buying one.

The segmentation scheme described above differs from the segments of passengers in airline frequent flyer programs because it is based on LTV rather than miles flown. Thus, it recognizes that some customers who fly a lot of miles might be taking low-cost flights, whereas other customers, although flying the same number of miles,

might be much more profitable because they fly first class and don't seek discount fares.

Another common segment scheme, called decile analysis, breaks customers into ten deciles according to their LTV rather than the quartiles illustrated above. When using decile analysis, the 10 percent of the customers with the highest LTV would be in the top.

RFM Analysis RFM (recency, frequency, monetary) analysis, often used by catalogue retailers and direct marketers, is a scheme for segmenting customers according to how recently they have made a purchase, how frequently they make purchases, and how much they have bought. Exhibit 14–4 is an example of an RFM analysis done by a catalogue apparel retailer that mails a catalogue each month to its customers.

The catalogue retailer divides its customers into 32 groups or segments based on how many orders the customer has placed during the last year, how much merchandise the customer has purchased, and the last time the customer placed an order. Each segment is represented by one cell in Exhibit 14–4. For example, the customers in the upper-left cell have made one or two purchases in the last year, made a purchase within the last two months, and purchased less than $50 of merchandise.

Catalogue retailers often use this type of analysis to determine which customer groups should be sent catalogues. For each of the RFM groups, they will determine the percentage of customers in the group who made a purchase from the last catalogue sent to them. For example, 5 percent of the customers in the upper-left corner of Exhibit 14–4 placed an order from the last catalogue sent to them. With information about the response rate of each cell and the average gross margin from orders placed by customers in the cell, the catalogue retailer can calculate the expected profit from sending catalogues to the customers in each cell. For example, if the average gross margin from orders placed by customers in the

exhibit 14–4 RFM Analysis for a Catalogue Retailer

Frequency	Monetary	RECENCY			
		0–2 months	3–4 months	5–6 months	Over 6 months
1–2	<$50	0.050*	0.035	0.010	0.001
1–2	Over $50	0.050	0.036	0.011	0.001
3–4	<$50	0.080	0.050	0.015	0.006
3–4	Over $150	0.090	0.050	0.017	0.008
5–6	<$300	0.100	0.060	0.025	0.010
5–6	Over $300	0.120	0.080	0.027	0.012
Over 6	<$450	0.150	0.100	0.035	0.180
Over 6	Over $450	0.160	0.110	0.040	0.020

*Percentage of customers in the cell who made a purchase from the last catalogue mailed to them.

upper-left cell is $20 and the cost of sending a catalogue to customers in the cell is $0.75, the company would make $0.25 per customer from each catalogue mailed to the customers in the cell.

$20.00 contribution $\times$ 0.05 response
= $1.00 expected contribution − $0.75 cost
= $0.25 per customer

RFM analysis is basically a method of estimating the LTV of a customer using recency, frequency, and monetary value of past purchases. Exhibit 14–5 illustrates how RFM can be used for developing customer target strategies.

Customers who have made infrequent, small purchases recently are considered to be first-time customers. The objective of CRM programs directed toward this segment of customers is to convert them into early repeat customers and eventually high-value customers. CRM programs directed toward customers in the high-value segment (high frequency, recency, and monetary value) attempt to maintain loyalty, increase retention, and gain a greater share of wallet by selling more merchandise to them. On the other hand, customers who have not purchased recently either have low lifetime value and are not worth pursuing or are committed to another retailer and may be difficult to recapture. CRM programs designed to realize these objectives are discussed in the following section.

Lo3 Developing CRM Programs

Having segmented customers according to their future profit potential, the next step in the CRM process (see Exhibit 14–2) is to develop programs for the different customer segments. In the following sections, we discuss programs retailers use for:

- Retaining their best customers

- Converting good customers into high-LTV customers
- Getting rid of unprofitable customers

Customer Retention

Four approaches that retailers use to retain their best customers are:

- Frequent shopper programs
- Special customer services
- Personalization
- Community

Frequent Shopper Programs As mentioned previously, frequent shopper programs are used both to build a customer database by identifying customers with transactions and to encourage repeat purchase behaviour and retailer loyalty.[27] Retailers provide incentives to encourage customers to enroll in the program and use the card. These incentives are either discounts on purchases made from the retailer or points for every dollar of merchandise purchased. The points are then redeemable for special rewards. Some recommendations concerning the nature of the rewards offered are outlined in Exhibit 14–6.

Canadian Tire money is Canada's oldest loyalty program. The new Canadian Tire Advantage loyalty card and key fob, which was rolled out in early 2012, offers customers 1 percent back, or one point per dollar, on the value of purchases, and those using the new card in conjunction with the company's proprietary credit card, the Options MasterCard, accrue three points for every dollar spent. The rate for the iconic Canadian Tire paper money is 0.4 percent. Rob Shields, senior vice-president of marketing, claims that the company would not be phasing out the paper-based program, "It is highly emotional [and]

exhibit 14–5 RFM Target Strategies

Frequency	Monetary	RECENCY			
		0–2 months	3–4 months	5–6 months	Over 6 months
1–2	<$50	First-time customers		Low-value customers	
1–2	Over $50				
3–4	<$50	Early repeat customers		Defectors	
3–4	Over $150				
5–6	<$300	High-value customers		Core defectors	
5–6	Over $300				
Over 6	<$450				
Over 6	Over $450				

Source: Reprinted by permission of Harvard Business School Press. Adapted from Robert Blattberg, Gary Getz, and Jacquelyn Thomas, *Customer Equity: Building and Managing Relationships as Valuable Assets* (Boston: Harvard Business School Press, 2001), p. 18. Copyright © 2001 by the Harvard Business School Publishing Corporation; all rights reserved.

has terrific brand presence and brand link and the tangible nature some people just love." He noted that while many customers are still attached to using the "money" coupons, they want more convenient options and to collect rewards through different platforms. The new program "really complements the credit card more than the paper base," he said. "From a customer standpoint, the value creation for them is very good."[29]

A more complex loyalty program was required to better position the growing company against existing competitors and the arrival of new competitors such as Target in 2013. The new card program provides Canadian Tire much-needed data that other companies, such as Hudson's Bay, Petro-Canada, and Shoppers Drug Mart, have been mining for years.

Before the launch of the new program in 2012, Canadian Tire knew only about its credit card customers; everybody else was anonymous to them. "Loyalty programs are the most ubiquitous way that a retailer can actually start to understand who their customers are, how different they are, and [to] segment them," says Shields. "As a universal loyalty program across all tenders, we are [now] going to be capturing upwards of 70 percent of our transactions on a known customer basis."[30]

While a decade ago, Canadian Tire money was the most-loved loyalty program in Canada, the *Major Markets Retail Survey* from KubasPrimedia in 2011 found that Air Miles is the top loyalty program in Canada, with 79 percent of survey respondents enrolled in it. Canadian Tire was tied for second place with HBC Rewards, at 56 percent, followed by Shoppers Optimum at 54 percent and Aeroplan at 44 percent.[31]

Shoppers Drug Mart's Optimum loyalty card program has approximately 10 million active card holders and rewards shoppers with 10 points for every dollar spent. Shoppers Optimum also offers a credit card backed by the Royal Bank of Canada. The marketing information derived from the cards' data banks allows Shoppers Drug Mart to recognize the significant differences among Canadian regions and cater to customers' unique circumstances and buying habits in each area and as unique individuals. Loblaw announced in July 2013 it had reached a deal to buy Shoppers Drug Mart in a stock-and-cash deal valued at $12.4 billion. The deal brings together the country's largest grocer with Canada's largest pharmacy chain.[32]

Loblaw would not say how many customers it has in its points program, but said that when it launched its new PC Plus points program in 2013, it had a target of reaching about 15 million customers, which will be helped by the large base of Optimum members. Of particular value to Loblaw would be the customer database of Optimum customers in Quebec, where Shoppers runs its Pharmaprix stores and Loblaw has a smaller presence.[33]

Four factors limit the effectiveness of frequent shopping programs:

- First, they can be expensive. For example, a 1 percent price discount can cost large retailers over $100 million

exhibit 14–6   Recommendations for Frequent Shopper Reward Programs

Tiered   Rewards should be tiered according to the volume of purchase to motivate customers to increase the level of their purchases. These tiers can be based on individual transactions or cumulative transactions. For example, HBC Points Card and Shoppers Optimum Program reward customers with cumulative points based on dollars spent. Customers generally accept the idea that people who spend more should receive greater rewards.

Offer Choices   Not all customers value the same rewards. Thus, the most effective frequent shopper programs offer customers choices. For example, Coles Myer, a leading Australian retailer, originally offered customers air miles but shifted to a menu of rewards when it discovered that many customers did not value air miles. Tesco, a U.K. supermarket chain, lets customers cash in points for special discounts on entertainment, vacation packages, or sporting events. Sainsbury, a competitor, allows customers to use their points for vouchers that can be used to make purchases at a variety of retail partners such as British Gas.

Nonmonetary incentives are very attractive to some customers. For example, Holt Renfrew offers loyal customers the opportunity to attend by invitation only special shopping events, a Sotheby auction, or an underwater expedition to see the *Titanic*.

Some retailers link their frequent shopper programs to charitable causes. For example, Target donates 1 percent of all purchases charged to Target's Guest Card to a program that benefits local schools. Although these altruistic rewards can be an effective part of a frequent shopper program, such incentives probably should not be the focal point of the program. Research indicates that the most effective incentives benefit the recipient directly, not indirectly, as is the case with charitable contributions.

Reward All Transactions   To ensure the collection of all customer transaction data and encourage repeat purchases, programs need to reward all purchases, not just purchases of selected merchandise.

Transparency and Simplicity   Customers need to be able to quickly and easily understand when they will receive rewards, what the rewards are, how much they have earned, and how they can redeem the points they have accumulated. The ground rules need to be clearly stated. There should be no surprises or confusion.

Sources: Frank Badillo, *Customer Relationship Management* (Columbus, OH: Retail Forward, 2001); and Stephan Butscher, *Customer Clubs and Loyalty Programmes* (Aldershot, Hampshire: Ashgate Publishing, Limited, 2002).

a year. In addition, for a large retailer, the launch and maintenance investment (store training, marketing, fulfillment support, and information technology and systems costs) can be as high as $30 million. Annual maintenance costs can reach $5 million to $10 million when marketing, program support, offer fulfillment, customer service, and IT infrastructure costs are figured in. Then there are the marketing support costs needed to maintain awareness of the program.[34]

- Second, it is difficult to make corrections in programs when problems arise. Programs become part of the customer's shopping experience. Customers must be informed about even the smallest changes in programs. They react negatively to any perceived "take away" once a program is in place, even if they are not actively involved in it. The more successful the program, the greater the customer reaction to changes made by the retailer, and these negative reactions reduce customer trust and loyalty to the retailer.

- Third, it is not clear that these programs increase customer spending behaviour and loyalty toward the retailer.[35] For example, 48 percent of the customers enrolled in frequent shopper programs with supermarkets indicated they had spent more with the retailer than they would have if the program were not offered, but only 18 percent of customers enrolled in programs with apparel retailers indicated that the program increased spending.[36]

- Finally, and perhaps most important, is the difficulty of gaining a competitive advantage based on frequent shopper programs. Since the programs are so visible, they can be easily duplicated by competitors. For example, Tesco and Safeway, two large supermarket chains in the U.K., got into a loyalty card war. They played a game of "can you top this," which benefited their customers but reduced their profits until Safeway closed down its program.[37]

To avoid this problem, retailers are offering benefits to their best customers that are more personalized, based on their unique knowledge of the customer, and thus less visible to competitors. (See also Retailing View 14.3 for discussion of a health-driven loyalty partnership.)

Special Customer Services Retailers provide unusually high-quality customer service to build and maintain the loyalty of platinum customers. For example, the top-tier customers get calls from service reps several times a year for "a friendly chat" and get an annual call to wish them happy holidays. Due to these special services, the retention rates for top customers have increased 50 percent.

Sometimes these special services are very subtle. For example, at the retailer's website, only top-tier customers get the option to click on an icon that connects them to a live service agent for a phone conversation. Other customers never see this icon. When service reps bring up a customer's account, coloured squares flash on their computer screens. Green means the caller is a profitable customer and should be granted waivers and other special treatment. Reds are unprofitable customers who get no special treatment.[38]

1-to-1 retailing
Developing retail programs for small groups or individual customers.

Personalization An important limitation of CRM strategies developed for market segments, such as a platinum segment in the customer pyramid (Exhibit 14–3) or early repeat customers in the RFM analysis (Exhibit 14–4), is that each segment is composed of a large number of customers who are not identical. Thus, any strategy will be most appealing to only the typical customer in the segment, and not as appealing to the majority of customers in the segment. For example, customers in the platinum segment with the highest LTVs might include a 25-year-old single woman who has quite different needs than the 49-year-old working mother with two children.

With the availability of customer-level data and analysis tools, retailers can now economically offer unique benefits and target messages to individual customers. They now have the ability to develop programs for small groups of customers and even specific individuals. For example, a Harry Rosen salesperson can search the company's customer database, identify customers who have bought Hugo Boss suits in the past, and send them an e-mail informing them of the shipment of new suits that just arrived in the store. Developing retail programs for small groups or individual customers is referred to as **1-to-1 retailing**.

Many small, local retailers have always practised 1-to-1 retailing. They know each of their customers, greet them by name when they walk in the store, and then recommend merchandise they know the customers will like. These local storeowners do not need customer databases and data mining tools. They have the information in their heads. But most large retail chains and their employees do not have this intimate knowledge of their customers. Thus, the CRM process enables larger retailers to efficiently develop relationships similar to those that many small local retailers have.

The Internet channel provides an opportunity for retailers to automate the practice of 1-to-1 retailing. When registered customers log on to Amazon.com, the first page they see is personalized for them. Their name is displayed in a greeting, and products are displayed based on an analysis of their past purchase behaviour. For example, if a customer has bought mystery novels from Amazon.com in the past, the latest books from mystery book authors they have bought are presented.

Amazon.com provides personalized recommendations based on past purchases.

develop a sense of community among customers. The Internet channel offers an opportunity for customers to exchange information using bulletin boards and to develop more personal relationships with each other and the retailer. By participating in such a community, customers become reluctant to leave the "family" of other people patronizing the retailer.

For example, in addition to offering merchandise for sale, a sporting goods retailer could provide an opportunity for organizers of local sporting events to post information about these events on its website. The volunteers organizing youth soccer and baseball leagues and tennis and golf tournaments could provide information about meetings and game dates, times, and places. Then the retailer could collect information about the participants in local leagues and offer discounts to encourage the teams to buy their uniforms and equipment and facilitate their transactions.

cross-selling When sales associates in one department attempt to sell complementary merchandise from other departments to their customers.

These personalized rewards or benefits that customers receive are based on unique information possessed by the retailer and its sales associates. This information in the retailer's customer database cannot be accessed or used by competitors. Thus, it provides an opportunity to develop a sustainable competitive advantage.

The effective use of this information creates the positive feedback cycle in the CRM process. Increasing repeat purchases with a retailer increases the amount of data collected from the customer, which enables the retailer to provide more personalized benefits that in turn increase the customer's purchases from the retailer.

Retailing View 14.1 (earlier in this chapter) examined how U.K.-based Tesco uses the information collected through its Clubcard program to target promotions and tailor assortments in its stores to preferences of customers in the store's trading area. Mobile can also effectively connect members to on-the-go information, such as updated program information, program news, points accumulation, and reward announcements. Two examples of popular and successful loyalty programs that are multi-faceted and have efficiently blended multiple channels in one communication are Starbucks and Cineplex-Scene.

Community A fourth approach to building customer retention and loyalty is to

Converting Good Customers into Best Customers

In the context of the customer pyramid (Exhibit 14–3), increasing the sales made to good customers is referred to as *customer alchemy*—converting iron and gold customers into platinum customers.[39] Customer alchemy involves offering and selling more products and services to existing customers and increasing the retailer's share of wallet with these customers. For example, Tesco, the U.K. supermarket chain, added a second tier to its frequent shopper program to increase share of wallet.

The first tier has a traditional design to gather customer data. The second tier, targeted at its better customers, is more innovative. Customers earn a "key" when they spend US$38 or more in a single transaction. Fifty keys make the customer a "keyholder," 100 keys a "premium keyholder." When customers achieve these higher levels, they get discounts on popular entertainment events, theatre tickets, sporting events, and hotel vacations. The key program seeks to convert iron and gold customers into platinum customers. In the four years since starting the key program, Tesco has raised its market share from 13 percent to more than 17 percent.

The retailer's customer database reveals opportunities for cross-selling and add-on selling. Cross-selling is selling a complementary product or service in a specific

Air Miles for Social Change—Rewards Motivate Canadians to be Healthy

Today's not-for-profit organizations are becoming more creative in their approaches to foster change and deliver against their mission. And Air Miles for Social Change has proven that pairing change-driving initiatives with a rewards program can lead to unprecedented success. Canada's Heart and Stroke Foundation (HSF) is a case in point.

Background. According to the Heart and Stroke Foundation, *nine out of ten Canadians have a risk factor for heart disease and stroke*, and the incidence of these conditions is increasing at an alarming rate. To help combat these statistics, HSF partnered with Air Miles for Social Change, rewarding Canadians with Air Miles reward miles for participating in the following initiatives:

- Healthy Living mobile app
- Blood Pressure Action Plan
- E-tools such as risk assessment, online support, donations
- Heart Smart family e-newsletter
- Heart and Stroke Foundation lottery prize

Organizational challenges. HSF is one of the largest charities in Canada and has achieved significant results in advocacy, research, and education. HSF wanted to increase that impact by driving education and behaviour change with the Canadian population directly.

While many Canadians know they should reduce their risks for heart disease and stroke, only a small segment does so in a committed way. Only a third of Canadians eat five or more servings of vegetables and fruits a day, and 50 percent are physically inactive. Almost one-third of Canadian children are overweight or obese. As a result, 250 000 potential years of life are lost to these diseases.

Organizational objectives. To address the issue of consumer motivation, HSF clearly defined its goals for each initiative.

Mobile app objectives:

- Drive app downloads to build an installed user base.
- Empower Canadians with information and support to reduce risk of heart disease and stroke.

Blood Pressure Action Plan objectives:

- Equip Canadians aged 50 and over with tools to help them achieve and manage a healthy blood pressure.

E-tools objectives:

- Increase completions of the HSF "My Risk Assessment" and sign-ups for the HSF "My eSupport."
- Attract donations to HSF.

Heart Smart e-newsletter objectives:

- Drive online sign-ups.
- Provide practical, inspiring heart-healthy info, tips, and recipes for Canadian parents.

Heart and Stroke Foundation lottery objectives:

- Add more choice to prize options.

The engagement. Air Miles for Social Change was called on to help HSF achieve all of these objectives by incentivizing the population through tangible rewards. Air Miles for Social Change is a division of the Air Miles Reward Program, Canada's leading coalition loyalty program, which boasts more than two-thirds of Canadian households as members. Coalition loyalty programs reward members with miles for shopping at a variety of merchants. The miles can be redeemed for travel, merchandise, or cash discounts at the point of sale.

Air Miles for Social Change designed an incentive-based offering specific to each of the foundation's initiatives.

- **Mobile app.** In 2012, users could earn 25 reward miles by downloading the app and completing setup.
- **Blood Pressure Action Plan.** In 2012, participants earned 20 reward miles for signing up.
- **E-tools.** In 2011, participants earned 10 reward miles for completing the HSF risk assessment and registering for the My Health eSupport tool. Donors earned 5 to 30 reward miles, based on donation levels.
- **Heart Smart e-newsletter.** In 2012, 20 reward miles were offered at sign-up.
- **Heart and Stroke Lottery.** In 2012, early-bird ticket purchasers were given the chance to win either $30 000 cash or 200 000 reward miles. Plus, 40 000 prize winners could choose to win a 325 Air Miles reward miles bonus card. Almost 9 percent of all prize winners chose Air Miles reward miles as their prize, surpassing the goal of 7 percent.

Proven solutions. The results for each initiative's program exceeded all expectations, including:

- Mobile apps experienced over 9000 successful completions and downloads in a four-week period. The number of downloads after the launch of the first e-mail was 13 times higher than before.
- Over 14 000 people signed up for the Blood Pressure Action Plan in the month of November, nearly all of which were Air Miles collectors. This initiative exceeded the campaign goal by 281 percent.
- In the first four-and-a-half days, the partnership drove more e-tool risk assessment completions than HSF marketing had achieved in the preceding two-and-a-half years. An e-tool donation offer also drove a significant number of new, high-value donors to HSF.
- The Heart Smart e-newsletter had more than 31 000 sign-ups in four months, exceeding expectations.

Conclusions. The following conclusions were drawn as a result of the initiative:

- New marketing tools, such as a popular reward program targeting loyal members, can extend the power of an organization's existing communications initiatives.
- As a proven motivator for behavioural change, offering the right rewards can incentivize people to try a new activity, even if it requires effort or commitment.
- By offering the right reward via the right channels, an organization can also educate and attract new cash donors and new participants in fundraising efforts.

Going forward, Air Miles for Social Change and the Heart and Stroke Foundation are continuing to grow the partnership, evolving from test-and-learn tactical programs toward long-term sustainable behaviour change solutions. And when it comes to health, sustainable change is the best reward of all.

Source: Angela Simo Brown, "Rewards Motivate Canadians to Be Healthy," LoyaltyOne, http://www.loyalty.com/research-insights/case-studies/rewards-motivate-canadians-to-be-healthy (accessed December 20, 2013).

---

transaction, such as selling a customer a printer when he or she has decided to buy a computer. For example, a supermarket chain has a frequent shopper program, called the Gold Card program, for its best customers. When Gold Card member Debra Onsager enters the store, she "swipes" her card at a kiosk, and a high-speed printer provides a personalized shopping list with up to 25 deals. The deals offered are based on Debra's purchase history. If Debra's history shows she frequently purchases corn chips but does not buy dip, she'll get a deal on bean dip printed on her shopping list to encourage her to try a new product. If she passes up the deal this time in the market, the next time the value of the bean dip coupon will be automatically increased.

Add-on selling is selling additional new products and services to existing customers, such as a supermarket chain that explored the opportunity to offer dry cleaning services in its supermarkets. To determine the stores and customers that would find this new service appealing, it looked through its customer database for households with two-income professionals, 25 to 35 years old, who

sought one-stop shopping, as indicated by purchases of cosmetics, hosiery, and prepared meals.[40] Oprah Winfrey builds add-on sales for her offerings through a strong emotional bond with her target market.

Predictive analytics can help create cross-sell and up-sell opportunities at the point of sale. For example, Loblaw's new PC Plus program can make recommendations to members not only on their individualized purchase behaviour, but also on what other users with similar tastes have purchased and presumably enjoyed. The program will even create a grocery list and send recipes to the member's smartphone based on current promotions for that specific member. Harry Rosen associates use mobile CRM to provide real-time personalized service in-store and to update clients on new clothing items and events that match their specific interests.

In addition to these real-time recommendations, retailers can integrate other technologies into their loyalty programs, such as near-field communications or intelligent SoLoMo applications, as well as allow customers to use their smartphones to pay for purchases or redeem coupons.

Near-field communications (NFC) is a set of standards for smartphones and similar devices to establish radio communication with each other by touching them together or bringing them into close proximity, usually no more than a few inches. Present and anticipated applications include contactless transactions, data exchange, and simplified setup of more complex communications such as Wi-Fi.[41]

SoLoMo (social, local, and mobile) is the convergence of collaborative, location-based, and on-the-go technologies. SoLoMo applications allow advertisers to push notifications to potential customers who are geographically nearby. Examples of SoLoMo apps include Foursquare, AroundMe, and Yelp. Many of these services incorporate some aspects of gamification to encourage member retention.

Gamification is the application of game theory concepts and techniques to nongame activities. Generally speaking, the overarching goal of gamification is to engage participants with an activity they find fun in order to influence their behaviour. In marketing, a gamification initiative might address the cognitive and emotional aspects of game theory as well as the social ones by including a system of rules for participants to explore through active experimentation and discovery, awarding points or badges for levels of participation, displaying leaderboard scores to encourage competition, and offering prizes so that participants have a chance to win something of value.[42]

Dealing with Unprofitable Customers

In many cases, the bottom tier of customers actually have negative LTV. Retailers actually lose money on every sale they make to these customers. For example, catalogue retailers have customers who repeatedly buy three or four items and return all but one of them. The cost of processing two or three returned items is much greater than the profits coming from the one item that the customer kept. The process of no longer selling to these unprofitable customers can be referred to as "getting the lead out," in terms of the customer pyramid.[43] (See also Retailing View 14.4.)

Two approaches for getting the lead out are offering less costly approaches for satisfying the needs of lead customers, and charging the customers for the services they are abusing.

Implementing CRM Programs

Increasing sales and profits from the CRM programs is a challenge. For example, according to a study, 52 percent of the retailers surveyed indicated that they were engaged in some type of data mining, but 76 percent of those retailers undertaking data mining indicated that the activity had made no contribution to the bottom line.[44]

This experience of retailers emphasizes that effective CRM requires more than appointing a manager of CRM, installing a computer system to manage and analyze a customer database, and making speeches about the importance of customers. The effective implementation of CRM programs requires the close coordination of activities by different functions in a retailer's organization. The MIS department needs to collect, analyze, and make the relevant information readily accessible to employees implementing the programs—the front-line service providers and sales associates and the marketers responsible for communicating with customers through impersonal channels (mass advertising, direct mail, and e-mail). Store operations and human resource management need to hire, train, and motivate the employees who will be using the information to deliver personalized services.

Most retailers are product-centric, not customer-centric. Typically, there is no area of a retail firm organized by customer type—responsible for delivering products and services to types of customers. Perhaps in the future, retailers will have market managers to perform this coordinating function.

Customer Service

Customer service is the set of activities and programs undertaken by retailers to make the shopping experience more rewarding for their customers. These activities increase the value customers receive from the merchandise and services they purchase. All employees of a retail firm and all elements of the retailing mix provide services that increase the value of merchandise. For example, employees in the distribution centre contribute to customer service by making sure that the merchandise is in stock. The employees responsible for store design contribute by increasing the customer's convenience in getting to the store and finding merchandise and making shopping an enjoyable experience.

Exhibit 14–7 lists some of the services provided by retailers and/or shopping centres. Most of these services encourage customers to choose a specific retailer to buy products and services. Services, such as alterations and the assembly of merchandise, actually change merchandise to fit the needs of a specific customer. Some of these services are derived from the retailer's store design or website or from policies established by the retailer. However, this part of the chapter focuses on some of the most important personalized services provided by sales associates interacting directly with customers.

In the next section, we discuss retailers' opportunities to develop strategic advantage through customer service. Then we examine how retailers can take advantage of this opportunity by providing high-quality service.

SoLoMo (social, local, and mobile) The convergence of collaborative, location-based, and on-the-go technologies.

gamification The application of game theory concepts and techniques to non-game activities.

customer service The set of retail activities that increase the value customers receive when they shop and purchase merchandise.

LO 4

DID YOU KNOW?

The word *service* is from the Latin term *servus*, meaning "slave."[45]

Getting the Lead Out

One source of unprofitable customers is the practice of fraudulent returns, which costs retailers more than $15 billion each year. Some examples of these costly returns include people who buy a large-screen television for their Super Bowl party and then return it after the game or an expensive dress for a special occasion, returned after they wear it once. Professional returners even use the Internet to make money on fraudulent returns. Some people steal merchandise from a store, return it for credit slips, and then turn the credit slips into cash by selling them at a discount on eBay or other online auction sites.

Retailers like The Limited and Best Buy are fighting back against such high-tech fraud with high-tech defences. Limited Express's return policy says consumers have up to 60 days to return items. However, the company's return policy also notes that it uses an industrywide service operated by Return Exchange to authorize returns and that "under certain circumstances we reserve the right to deny returns." Return Exchange, based in Irvine, California, analyzes Limited Express's customer database and identifies customers who have an unusually high propensity for returning merchandise. When these customers return merchandise, the POS terminal generates a slip of paper that says "RETURN DECLINED," and the sales associate tells the customer to call the toll-free number at the bottom for more information.

Best Buy is undertaking a strategy to focus on gold and platinum customers and get rid of lead customers. To lure high spenders, it is providing more effective customer service. To discourage undesirable customers, it is reducing promotions that tend to draw them into the store and removing them from direct marketing lists.

The trickiest challenge may be to deter bad customers without turning off good ones.

Best Buy's campaign against undesirable customers pits it against dozens of websites such as FatWallet.com, SlickDeals.net, and TechBargains.com that trade electronic coupons and tips from former clerks and insiders, hoping to gain extra advantages against the stores. At SlickDeals.net, whose subscribers boast about techniques for gaining hefty discounts, a visitor recently bragged about his practice of shopping at Best Buy only when he thinks he can buy at below the retailer's cost.

Best Buy cannot bar undesirable customers from its stores, but it is taking steps to put a stop to their most damaging practices. It's enforcing a restocking fee of 15 percent of the purchase price on returned merchandise. To discourage customers who return items with the intention of repurchasing them at a "returned merchandise" discount, it is experimenting with reselling returned merchandise over the Internet, so the goods don't reappear in the store where they were originally purchased. Best Buy also cut ties to FatWallet.com, an online "affiliate" that had collected referral fees for delivering customers to Best Buy's website.

Rejecting customers is a delicate business. Filene's Basement was criticized on television and in newspapers for asking two Massachusetts customers not to shop at its stores because of their frequent returns and complaints. Best Buy's CEO apologized in writing to students at a Washington, D.C., school after employees at one store barred a group of black students while admitting a group of white students.

Sources: Jennifer Davis, "Retailers Use Technology to Thwart Would-Be Thieves," *San Diego Tribune*, June 13, 2007; www.fashion era.com/Trends_2006/2006_spring_fashion_trends_returns_consumer_fraud.htm (accessed September 20, 2007); and www.oracle.com/applications/retail/mom/retail-returns-management.html (accessed September 20, 2007).

Strategic Advantage through Customer Service

Good service keeps customers returning to a retailer and generates positive word-of-mouth communication, which attracts new customers.[46]

Providing high-quality service is difficult for retailers. Automated manufacturing makes the quality of most merchandise consistent from item to item. But the quality of retail service can vary dramatically from store to store and from salesperson to salesperson within a store. It's hard for retailers to control the performance of employees who provide the service. A sales associate may provide good service to one customer and poor service to the next customer.

In addition, most services provided by retailers are intangible—customers can't see or touch them. Clothing

exhibit 14–7   Services Offered by Retailers

Acceptance of credit cards	Display of merchandise	Presentations on how to use merchandise
Alterations of merchandise	Dressing rooms	Provisions for customers with special needs (wheelchairs, translators)
Assembly of merchandise	Extended store hours	Repair services
ATM terminals	Facilities for shoppers with special needs (physically challenged)	Rest rooms
Bridal registry	Gift wrapping	Return privileges
Cheque cashing	Layaway plans	Rooms for checking coats and packages
Child care facilities	Parking	Shopping carts
Credit	Personal assistance in selecting merchandise	Signage to locate and identify merchandise
Delivery to home or work	Personal shoppers	Special orders
Demonstrations of merchandise	Play areas for children	Warranties

standardization approach An approach used by retailers to provide customer service by using a set of rules and procedures so that all customers consistently receive the same service.

DID YOU KNOW?

Nearly one out of four shoppers who have a bad service experience will tell their friends about their experience and urge them not to shop there and/or will stop shopping at the store.[51]

can be held and examined, but the assistance provided by a sales associate or an electronic agent can't. Intangibility makes it hard to provide and maintain high-quality service because retailers can't count, measure, or check service before it's delivered to customers.

The challenge of providing consistent high-quality service provides an opportunity for a retailer to develop a sustainable competitive advantage. For example, Holt Renfrew devotes much time and effort to developing an organizational culture that stimulates and supports excellent customer service. Competing department stores would like to offer the same level of service but find it hard to match Holt Renfrew's performance.[47]

Customer Service Strategies

Customization and standardization are two approaches retailers use to develop a sustainable customer service advantage. Successful implementation of the customized approach relies on the performance of sales associates or the degree to which customer interactions can be customized using an electronic channel. The standardization approach relies more on policy, procedures, and store and website design and layout.[48]

Customization Approach   The customization approach encourages service providers to tailor the service to meet each customer's personal needs.[49] For example, sales associates in specialty stores help individual customers locate appropriate apparel and accessories.

Harry Rosen Does Customer Service   Excellence in customer service is nothing new to Harry Rosen Inc. Known for delivering unprecedented levels of personalized customer service to its customers, the company's sales

today account for nearly 40 percent of the high-end menswear market in Canada. Building on existing wireless technology, the retailer worked with Hewlett-Packard (HP) partner Technology Solutions International (TSI) to implement a wireless, Microsoft Windows–based solution on HP handheld devices. The retailer equipped all sales associates with the ability to access customer data and product preference information while on the sales floor, and gave managers insight into real-time sales data, so they could deliver consistent, excellent customer service to every customer entering the store—whether or not they had an appointment. The "mini CRM" system gives every Harry Rosen associate a complete 360-degree view of their customer. "Using the HP iPAQ hw6955 makes it easier for me to instantly know what type of merchandise my customers want—even if they don't know themselves!" says Harry Rosen sales associate Raymond Moseley. "Being able to access customer information directly from the sales floor eliminates the need for me to disengage from the sales process and leave my customer's side in order to look up information."[50]

The customized approach typically results in most customers' receiving superior service. But the service might be inconsistent because service delivery depends on the judgment and capabilities of the service providers. Some service providers are better than others, and even the best service providers can have a bad day. In addition, providing the customized service is costly since it requires more well-trained service providers or complex computer software.

Standardization Approach   The standardization approach is based on establishing a set of rules and procedures and being sure that they are implemented consistently.

By strict enforcement of these procedures, inconsistencies in the service are minimized. Through standardization, customers receive the same food and service at McDonald's restaurants across the globe. The food may not be exactly what customers want, but it's consistent and served in a timely manner at a low cost.

Store or website design and layout also play an important role in the standardization approach. In many situations, customers don't need the services employees provide. They know what they want to buy, and their objective is to find it in the store and buy it quickly. In these situations, retailers offer good service by providing a layout and signs that enable customers to locate merchandise easily, by having relevant information in displays, and by minimizing the time required to make a purchase.[53]

Retailing View 14.5 shows how IKEA uses a standardized, self-service approach with some unique elements.

Cost of Customer Service As indicated previously, providing high-quality service, particularly customized service, can be very costly. For over 100 years, the Savoy Hotel in London maintained a special place in the hearts of the world's elite. Maids switched off vacuum cleaners when greeting guests entering the hallway in the morning. Each floor had its own waiter on duty from 7 AM to 3 PM. Guests could get cotton sheets instead of the standard Irish linen sheets if they wished. Preferred fruits were added to the complimentary fruit bowl in each room.

14.5 | RETAILING VIEW

Customer Service at IKEA

IKEA is a global furniture retailer based in Sweden. Its concept of service differs from that of the traditional furniture store. The typical furniture store has a showroom displaying some of the merchandise sold in the store. Complementing the inventory are books of fabric swatches, veneers, and alternative styles customers can order. Salespeople assist customers in going through the books. When the customer makes a selection, an order is placed with the factory, and the furniture is delivered to the customer's home in six to eight weeks. This system maximizes customization, but the costs are high.

In contrast, IKEA uses a self-service model based on extensive in-store displays. At information desks in the store, shoppers can pick up a map of the store, plus a pencil, order form, clipboard, and tape measure. After studying the catalogue and displays, customers proceed to a self-service storage area and locate their selections using codes copied from the sales tags. Every product available is displayed in over 70 room-like settings throughout the 19 000 square-foot warehouse store. Thus, customers don't need a decorator to help them picture how the furniture will go together. Adjacent to the display room is a warehouse with ready-to-assemble furniture in boxes that customers can pick up when they leave the store.

IKEA effectively uses a self-service method to provide customer service through signage and information in displays and on the merchandise.

Although IKEA uses a "customers do it themselves" approach, it does offer some services that traditional furniture stores do not, such as in-store child-care centres and information about the quality of the furniture. Toddlers can be left in a supervised ballroom filled with 50 000 brightly coloured plastic balls. There are changing rooms in each store, complete with bottle warmers and disposable diaper dispensers. Displays cover the quality of products in terms of design features and materials, with demonstrations of testing procedures.

Sources: John Kelly, "A Good Place by Design," *Washington Post*, December 23, 2004, p. C.13; Mike Duff, "Late-Blooming IKEA U.S. Wears 20 Well," *DSN Retailing Today*, September 6, 2004, pp. 6–9.

Rooms were personally furnished for customers who regularly had extended stays at the hotel. At times, the hotel staff moved the customers' furniture, including personal pictures, from storage into their rooms when they arrived.

But this high level of personal attention is very costly to provide. The Savoy employed about three people for each of its 200 rooms, about double the average for a hotel. These services resulted in annual losses, and the hotel was eventually sold to a corporation that eliminated some of the services.

In many cases, however, good customer service can actually reduce costs and increase profits. A study by Andersen Consulting estimates that it costs 5 to 15 times more to acquire a new customer than to generate repeat business from present customers, and a 5 percent increase in customer retention can increase profits by 25 to 40 percent.[54] Thus, it costs a business much less to keep its existing customers satisfied and sell more merchandise to them than it does to sell to people who aren't buying from the business now.

Returns Rethink

Some people are admittedly shopaholics, which, when mixed with an indecisive nature, is disastrous for many retailers. These are the people who buy something one week, often wearing or using it, and expect to return it the next. These shoppers believe that anything is—and should be—returnable. Some customers may take advantage of a liberal return policy believing that the retailer wants the customer to be happy at any cost.

Harry Rosen has always upheld a policy of unconditional satisfaction for customers. They will even take back a well-worn, two-year-old suit if the customer becomes unhappy with it. The rationale: It's a way to bond with the customer and reinforce the relationship in a positive way. But many stores are taking a harder stance toward returns. The Gap now gives customers with a receipt two weeks to claim a full cash refund or exchange. New technology enabling customers to buy and burn their own copies caused HMV Canada to terminate its "no questions asked" policy, which used to include cash back for open CDs. The Retail Council of Canada concludes that a tougher position on returns can improve a retailer's profit by as much as 2 percent.[55]

Retailers need to consider the costs and benefits of service policies. For example, many retailers are reconsidering their "no questions asked" return policy. Home Depot's policy was to take back all merchandise and give cash back. Now, if customers don't have a receipt, they can get only a store credit. If they have a receipt, they can get cash back. With some consumer electronics products, customers must pay a 15 percent restocking charge for returned merchandise. Retailers are seeing too many big-screen TVs coming back the day after the Super Bowl and too many prom dresses coming back the day after prom night.[56]

The easy return policy is an important selling feature for the department stores. Customers will put up with a lack of other services, but the return policy is an established expectation and changing this liberal policy is difficult. Hudson's Bay allows a 30-day period for a cash refund with a receipt, after which a store credit is considered. The eagerness to please is also apparent at Sleep Country Canada, which offers a "comfort guarantee" that allows customers to return mattresses within 60 days. Despite many problems with returned merchandise, retailers strive to ensure many happy returns—for both sides of a sale. Remember that it is more cost-effective to keep a customer than to find a new one.

> **DID YOU KNOW?**
>
> About 6 percent of all merchandise purchased in stores is returned.[58]

> **DID YOU KNOW?**
>
> Among the retailers surveyed, only 30 percent responded to online customer service requests within 6 hours; 18 percent took 6 to 24 hours; 18 percent responded in one to three days; and 34 percent took longer than three days or did not answer the inquiry.[59]

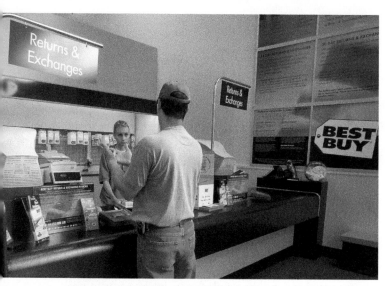

Future Shop and Best Buy have tightened their return policies to help dissuade the least profitable customers who abuse return privileges.

Customer Evaluation of Service Quality

LO 5

When customers evaluate retail service, they compare their perceptions of the service they receive with their expectations. Customers are satisfied when the perceived service meets or exceeds their expectations. They're dissatisfied when they feel the service falls below their expectations.[57]

service gap The difference between customers' expectations and perceptions of customer service, assessed in order to improve customers' satisfaction with their service.

knowledge gap The difference between customer expectations and the retailer's perception of customer expectations. This factor is one of four factors identified by the gaps model for improving service quality.

Role of Expectations

Customer expectations are based on a customer's knowledge and experiences.[60] For example, customers do not expect to get an immediate response to a letter or even a telephone call, but they expect to get a response to an e-mail the next time they turn on their computer.

Technology is dramatically changing the ways in which customers and firms interact. Customers now can interact with companies through automated voice response systems and place orders and check on delivery through the Internet. But customers still expect dependable outcomes, easy access, responsive systems, flexibility, apologies, and compensation when things go wrong. In other words, they still want good service. Now they just expect this level of service even when people are not involved.[61]

Expectations vary depending on the type of store. Customers expect a supermarket to provide convenient parking, to be open from early morning to late evening, to have a wide variety of fresh and packaged food that can be located easily, to display products, and to offer fast checkout. They don't expect the supermarket to have store employees stationed in the aisle to offer information about groceries or how to prepare meals. On the other hand, when these same customers shop in a specialty store, they do expect the store to have knowledgeable salespeople who can provide information and assistance.

Since expectations aren't the same for all types of retailers, a customer may be satisfied with low levels of actual service in one store and dissatisfied with high service levels in another store. For example, customers have low service expectations for self-service retailers such as discount stores and supermarkets. Walmart provides an unusual service for a discount store: An employee stands at the entrance to each store, greeting customers and answering questions. Because this service is unexpected in a discount store, customers evaluate Walmart's service positively, even though the actual level of service is far below that provided by a typical specialty store.

Department stores have many more salespeople available to answer questions and provide information than Walmart does. But customer service expectations are also higher for department stores. If department store customers can't locate a salesperson quickly when they have questions or want to make a purchase, they're dissatisfied.

When retailers provide unexpected services, they build a high level of customer satisfaction, referred to as *customer delight*.[62] Some examples of unexpected positive service experiences are:

- A restaurant sends customers who have had too much alcohol to drink home in a taxi and then delivers their cars in the morning.
- A men's store sews numbered tags on each garment so that the customer will know what goes together.
- A gift store keeps track of important customer dates and suggests appropriate gifts.

Customer service expectations vary around the world. Although Germany's manufacturing capability is world renowned, its poor customer service is also well known. People wait years to have telephone service installed. Many restaurants do not accept credit cards, and customers who walk into stores near closing time often receive rude stares. Customers typically have to bag merchandise they buy themselves. Because Germans are unaccustomed to good service, they don't demand it. But as retailing becomes global and new foreign competitors enter, German retailers are becoming more concerned.

On the other hand, the Japanese expect excellent customer service. In Canada, it's said that "the customer is always right." In Japan, the equivalent expression is *okyakusama ha kamisama desu*, "the customer is God." When a customer comes back to a store to return merchandise, he or she is dealt with even more cordially than when the original purchase was made. Customer satisfaction isn't negotiable. The customer is never wrong! Even if the customer misused the product, retailers feel they were responsible for not telling the customer how to use it properly. The first person in the store who hears about the problem must take full responsibility for dealing with the customer, even if the problem involved another department.

The Gaps Model for Improving Retail Service Quality

The gaps model (Exhibit 14–8 on the previous page) indicates what retailers need to do to provide high-quality customer service.[63] When customers' expectations are greater than their perceptions of the delivered service, customers are dissatisfied and feel the quality of the retailer's service is poor. Thus, retailers need to reduce the service gap (the difference between customers' expectations and perceptions of customer service) to improve customers' satisfaction with their service.

Four factors affect the service gap:

1. **Knowledge gap:** The difference between customer expectations and the retailer's perception of customer expectations.

2. **Standards gap:** The difference between the retailer's perceptions of customers' expectations and the customer service standards it sets.

3. **Delivery gap:** The difference between the retailer's service standards and the actual service provided to customers.

4. **Communication gap:** The difference between the actual service provided to customers and the service promised in the retailer's promotion program.

These four gaps add up to the service gap. The retailer's objective is to reduce the service gap by reducing each of the four gaps. Thus, the key to improving service quality is to:

- Understand the level of service customers expect
- Set standards for providing customer service
- Implement programs for delivering service that meets the standards
- Undertake communication programs to accurately inform customers about the service offered by the retailer

The following sections describe these gaps and methods for reducing them.

Knowing What Customers Want: The Knowledge Gap

The most critical step in providing good service is to know what the customer wants. Retailers often lack accurate information about what customers need and expect. This lack of information can result in poor decisions. For example, a supermarket might hire extra people to make sure the shelves are stocked so that customers will always find what they want, but it may fail to realize that customers are most concerned about waiting at the checkout line. From the customer's perspective, the supermarket's service would improve if the extra employees were used to open more checkout lines rather than to stock shelves.

standards gap
The difference between the retailer's perceptions of customers' expectations and the customer service standards it sets. This factor is one of four factors identified by the gaps model for improving service quality.

delivery gap The difference between the retailer's service standards and the actual service provided to customers. This factor is one of the four factors identified by the gaps model for improving service quality.

communication gap The difference between the actual service provided to customers and the service promised in the retailer's promotion program. This factor is one of the four factors identified by the gaps model for improving service quality.

exhibit 14–8 Gaps Model for Improving Retail Service Quality

The first step in providing good customer service is understanding customer expectations. This sales associate is conducting a survey to assess customer expectations.

Retailers can reduce the knowledge gap and develop a better understanding of customer expectations by undertaking customer research, increasing interactions between retail managers and customers, and improving communication between managers and employees who provide customer service.

Researching Customer Expectations and Perceptions

Market research can be used to better understand customers' expectations and the quality of service provided by a retailer. Methods for obtaining this information range from comprehensive surveys to simply asking some customers about the store's service.

Gauging Satisfaction with Individual Transactions

Another method for doing customer research is to survey customers immediately after a retail transaction has occurred. For example, Sears employees who deliver and assemble furniture in homes ask customers to complete a short survey describing how helpful, friendly, and professional the employees were. Airlines periodically ask passengers during a flight to evaluate the ticket-buying process, flight attendants, in-flight service, and gate agents.

Customer research on individual transactions provides up-to-date information about customers' expectations and perceptions. The research also indicates the retailer's interest in providing good service. Since the responses can be linked to a specific encounter, the research provides a method for rewarding employees who provide good service and correcting those who exhibit poor performance.

Focus Groups Rather than surveying many customers, retailers can use focus groups of eight to 12 customers to gain insights into expectations and perceptions. For example, store managers might meet three times a year for one-and-a-half to two hours with a select group of customers who are asked to provide information in a focus group about their experiences in the stores and to offer suggestions for improving service. The participants are rewarded with food and merchandise or money for their time and effort.

To reduce the knowledge gap, some managers may select customers who've made large and small purchases; they call these customers and ask them what they liked and didn't like about the store. With small purchasers, they probe to find out why the customers didn't buy more. Could they find everything they wanted? Did they get the assistance they expected from store employees?

Some retailers have consumer advisory boards composed of a cross-section of their preferred customers. Members of the board complete questionnaires three to four times a year on subjects such as holiday shopping problems, in-store signage, and service quality. In exchange for their input, members receive gift certificates. Restaurants and retailers often ask for comments regarding service.

Interacting with Customers Owner–managers of small retail firms typically have daily contact with their customers and thus have accurate firsthand information about them. In large retail firms, managers often learn about customers through reports, so they miss the rich information provided by direct contact with customers.

Stanley Marcus, founder of Neiman Marcus department stores, felt managers can become addicted to numbers and neglect the merchandise and customers. He used suspenders as an example of how buyers can make poor decisions by only looking at the numbers. Originally, suspenders came in two sizes: short and long. By analyzing the numbers, buyers realized they could increase turnover by stocking one-size-only suspenders. The numbers looked good, but the store had a lot of dissatisfied customers. With only one size, short men's pants fell down, and the fit was uncomfortable for tall men. "It comes back to the fact that the day is still only 24 hours long, and if you're a retailer, you've still got to spend some of those 24 hours with your customers and your products. You can't allow the computer to crowd them out as crucial sources of information."[66]

Customer Complaints Complaints allow retailers to interact with their customers and acquire detailed information about their service and merchandise. Handling complaints is an inexpensive means of isolating and correcting service problems.[67]

Although customer complaints can provide useful information, retailers can't rely solely on this source of market information. Typically, dissatisfied customers don't complain. To provide better information on customer service, retailers need to encourage complaints and make it easy for customers to provide feedback about their problems. For example, some retailers set up a complaint desk in a convenient location where customers can get their problems heard and solved quickly.

Feedback from Store Employees Salespeople and other employees in regular contact with customers often have a good understanding of customer service expectations and problems. This information will improve service quality only if the employees are encouraged to communicate their experiences to high-level managers who can act on it.

Some retailers regularly survey their employees, asking questions such as:

- What is the biggest problem you face in delivering high-quality service to your customers?
- If you could make one change in the company to improve customer service, what would it be?

Using Customer Research

Collecting information about customer expectations and perceptions isn't enough. The service gap is reduced only when retailers use this information to improve service. For example, store managers should review the suggestions and comments made by customers daily, summarize the information, and distribute it to store employees and managers.

Feedback on service performance needs to be provided to employees in a timely manner. Reporting the July service performance in December makes it hard for employees to reflect on the reason for the reported performance.

Finally, feedback must be prominently presented so that service providers are aware of their performance.

Setting Service Standards: The Standards Gap

After retailers gather information about customer service expectations and perceptions, the next step is to use this information to set standards and develop systems for delivering high-quality service. Service standards should be based on customers' perceptions rather than internal operations. For example, a supermarket chain might set an operations standard of a warehouse delivery every day to each store. But frequent warehouse deliveries may not result in more merchandise on the shelves or improve customers' impressions of shopping convenience.

To close the standards gap, retailers need to:

- Commit their firms to providing high-quality service
- Develop innovative solutions to service problems
- Define the role of service providers
- Set service goals
- Measure service

Commitment to Service Quality

Service excellence occurs only when top management provides leadership and demonstrates commitment. Top management must be willing to accept the temporary difficulties and even the increased costs associated with improving service quality. This commitment needs to be demonstrated to the employees charged with providing the service. For example, an L.L. Bean poster prominently displays the following inscription for employees who process customer orders:

> What is a customer? A customer is the most important person in this office … in person or by mail. A customer is not dependent on us … we are dependent on her. A customer is not an interruption in our work … she is the purpose of it. We are not doing her a favor by serving her … she is doing us a favor by giving us an opportunity to do so. A customer is not someone to argue or match wits with.[68]

Top management's commitment sets service quality standards, but store managers are the key to achieving those standards. Store managers must see that their efforts to provide service quality are noticed and rewarded. Providing incentives based on service quality makes service an important personal goal. Rather than basing bonuses only on store sales and profit, part of store managers' bonuses should be determined by the level of service provided. For example, some retailers use results of customer satisfaction studies to determine bonuses.

Developing Solutions to Service Problems

Frequently, retailers don't set high service standards because they feel service improvements are either too costly or not achievable with available employees. This reflects an unwillingness to think creatively and to explore new approaches for improving service.

Innovative Approaches Finding ways to overcome service problems can improve customer satisfaction and, in some cases, reduce costs. For example, when customers complained about the long wait to check out, many hotels felt they couldn't do anything about the problem. Marriott, however, thought of a creative approach to address this service problem. It invented Express Checkout, a system in which a bill is left under the customer's door the morning before checkout and, if the bill is accurate, the customer can check out by simply using the TV remote or calling the front desk to have the bill charged automatically to his or her credit card. See Retailing View 14.6 for a discussion of emerging mobile payment technology.

Using Technology   Many retailers are installing kiosks with broadband Internet access in the stores. In addition to offering customers the opportunity to order merchandise not available in the store, kiosks can provide routine customer service, freeing employees to deal with more demanding customer requests and problems. For example, customers can use kiosks to locate merchandise in the store and to indicate whether specific products, brands, and sizes are available in the store. Kiosks can also be used to automate existing store services such as gift registry management, rain checks, and credit applications, and preorder service for bakeries and delicatessens.

Customers can use a kiosk to find out more information about products and how they are used. For example, a Home Depot customer can go to a kiosk to find out how to install a garbage disposal and to get a list of all of the tools and parts that are needed for the installation. A Best Buy customer can use a kiosk to provide side-by-side comparisons of two Blu-ray players and to find more detailed information than is available from the shelf tag or from a sales associate. The customer can also access evaluations of the models as reported by *Consumer Reports*. The information provided by the kiosk could be tailored to specific customers by accessing the retailer's customer database. For example, a customer who is considering a new set of speakers might not remember the preamplifier purchased previously from Best Buy. This customer might not know whether the speakers are compatible with the preamplifier or what cables are needed to connect the new speakers. These concerns could be addressed by accessing the retailer's customer database through the kiosk.

Kiosks can also be used to provide customized solutions. For example, a customer, perhaps with the assistance of a salesperson, wants to design a home entertainment system. A kiosk could allow the customer to see what the system would look like after setup. Music store customers could use a kiosk to review and select

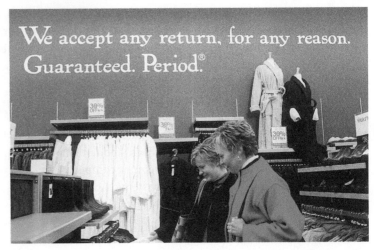

Lands' End emphasizes its commitment to high-quality service by providing an unconditional guarantee and setting high standards for employees.

tracks and make a custom compact disc. Finally, customers could use a kiosk to see how different colours of cosmetics would look on them without having to apply the cosmetics. These types of applications could complement the efforts of salespeople and improve the service they can offer to customers.[69]

Defining the Role of Service Providers

Managers can tell service providers that they need to provide excellent service, but not clearly indicate what excellent service means. Without a clear definition of the retailer's expectations, service providers are directionless.

The Ritz-Carlton Hotel Company has its "Gold Standards" printed on a wallet-size card carried by all employees. The card contains the hotel's motto ("We Are Ladies and Gentlemen Serving Ladies and Gentlemen"), the three steps for high-quality service (warm and sincere greeting, anticipation and compliance with guests' needs, and fond farewell), and 20 basic rules for Ritz-Carlton employees, including:

- Any employee who receives a complaint "owns" the complaint.
- Instant guest gratification will be ensured by all. React quickly to correct problems immediately.
- "Smile. We are on stage." Always maintain positive eye contact.
- Escort guests rather than giving directions to another area of the hotel.[70]

Setting Service Goals

To deliver consistent, high-quality service, retailers need to establish goals or standards to guide employees. Retailers often develop service goals based on their beliefs about

Adoption Problems Plague Digital Wallets

With published reports stating that 1 billion smartphones have already been sold worldwide, retailers are eyeing digital wallets as a way to complete mobile transactions. But first, retailers must overcome security, awareness, and integration issues.

Unlike traditional m-commerce, when a purchaser enters credit card information either through a mobile app or via a mobile site, digital wallets make use of technologies such as near-field communications (NFC). A mobile phone designed to work with NFC radio frequencies can enable a "contactless" payment in-store. Using this technology, MasterCard's PayPass, for example, enables a "tap-and-go" transaction at the point of sale (POS) through contactless readers. Similar to PayPass, Google has its own digital wallet, Google Wallet, which lets consumers virtually store their credit and debit account information in one place.

While still in its infancy, the market for digital wallets could reach $90 billion by 2017, up from $12.8 billion in 2012, representing a compound annual growth rate of 48 percent, according to Forrester Research. However, before benefiting from this emerging market, merchants must overcome significant hurdles, according to Denee Carrington, a Forrester analyst and author of the report *U.S. Mobile Payments Forecast*.

For starters, merchants must abide by the standards imposed by the U.S. Europay, MasterCard, Visa (EMV) smartcard payment system. This is an internationally accepted standard that enables chip cards, POS terminals, and automated teller machines to securely authenticate credit and debit card transactions. The benefits are even greater since EMV payments also incorporate personal identification numbers to ensure that a mobile payment transaction was completed by the person who owns the mobile device.

Already, 22 countries, including many in Europe, as well as Mexico, Brazil, and Japan, have accepted EMV technology, according to the Smart Card Alliance. The United States, however, lags behind. One of the main reasons, according to MasterCard Advisors, could be the convenience factor. U.S. merchants have gotten used to the current electronic payment infrastructure that has been in place for 30 years because it does "meet basic payment needs and maintains fraud at acceptable levels."

But because EMV paves the way for mobile transactions through chip-based technology, it will become an immediate priority for retailers in the years to come. Those merchants that fail to upgrade over the next couple of years could find themselves footing a majority of the bill, as opposed to the payment processor, should a fraudulent credit card transaction occur.

While merchants are not yet switching out their POS platforms to solely accommodate digital wallets, it would be a logical accompaniment to an EMV migration, as some analysts point out. "As long as they're doing a technology refresh, [merchants that] haven't upgraded to EMV...could incorporate capabilities like near-field communications, contactless readers, and rich graphical displays that would allow consumers to choose from a variety of payment instruments," observes Aaron McPherson, director of IDC's Financial Insights' Payments and Security Practice.

Retailers will also have to raise consumer awareness of digital wallets. While consumers might have heard of PayPal, Google Wallet, ISIS, V.me by Visa, and MasterCard PayPass Wallet, they don't necessarily know what each of the payment technologies accomplishes, according to *Digital Wallet Road Map 2013*, a mobile payment report by comScore. The study indicates that only 12 percent of consumers have used digital wallets other than PayPal. Of the 72 percent of respondents who were aware of PayPal's digital wallet, only 48 percent had used it.

"When we looked at future intent and presented people with a list of items that would increase their likelihood to use a digital wallet, security was number one and cost savings was next on the list," explains Andrea Jacobs, leader of comScore's Payments Practice. If a retailer provided a coupon or reward for local savings, 35 percent of people said it would increase their likelihood to use a digital wallet.

But as McPherson maintains, "hooking it all together on the back end and actually making the [rewards] offers will be a much trickier proposition because it's not so much a technology issue as it is a business and complexity issue." Rewards and loyalty will have a significant bearing on the payment methods that consumers choose. For instance, if a customer links a Citi Rewards card to a Google Wallet, and Citi offers rewards for usage, the vendors have to figure out if the rewards credits will appear in Google Wallet or in Citi's mobile app, McPherson says.

Source: Kelly Liyakasa, "Adoption Problems Plague Digital Wallets," *CRM Magazine*, April 2013, http://www.destinationcrm.com/Articles/Columns-Departments/Insight/Adoption-Problems-Plague-Digital-Wallets-88274.aspx (accessed July 8, 2013).

mystery shopper
Professional shopper who "shops" a store to assess the service provided by store employees.

the proper operation of the business rather than the customers' needs and expectations. For example, a retailer might set a goal that all monthly bills are to be mailed five days before the end of the month. This goal reduces the retailer's accounts receivable but offers no benefit to customers. Research undertaken by American Express showed customer evaluations of its service were based on perceptions of timeliness, accuracy, and responsiveness. Management then established goals (such as responding to all questions about bills within 24 hours) related to these customer-based criteria.

Employees are motivated to achieve service goals when the goals are specific, measurable, and participatory in the sense that they participated in setting them. Vague goals—such as "Approach customers when they enter the selling area" or "Respond to e-mails as soon as possible"—don't fully specify what employees should do, nor do such goals offer an opportunity to assess employee performance. Better goals would be "All customers should be approached by a salesperson within 30 seconds after entering a selling area" or "All e-mails should be responded to within three hours." These goals are both specific and measurable.

Employee participation in setting service standards leads to better understanding and greater acceptance of the goals. Store employees resent and resist goals arbitrarily imposed on them by management.

Measuring Service Performance

Retailers need to continuously assess service quality to ensure that goals will be achieved.[71] Many retailers do periodic customer surveys to assess service quality. Retailers also use mystery shoppers to assess their service quality. A mystery shopper is a professional shopper who "shops" a store to assess the service provided by store employees and the presentation of merchandise in the store. Some retailers use their own employees as mystery shoppers, but most contract with a firm to provide the assessment. Information typically reported by the mystery shoppers includes:

- How long before a sales associate greeted you?
- Did the sales associate act as if he or she wanted your business?
- Was the sales associate knowledgeable about the merchandise?

Retailers typically inform salespeople that they have "been shopped" and provide feedback from the mystery shopper's report. Some retailers offer rewards to sales associates who receive high marks and schedule follow-up visits to sales associates who get low evaluations.[72]

Meeting and Exceeding Services Standards: The Delivery Gap

To reduce the delivery gap and provide service that exceeds standards, retailers must give service providers the necessary knowledge and skills, provide instrumental and emotional support, improve internal communications and reduce conflicts, and empower employees to act in the customers' and firm's best interests.[73] Chat rooms offered through an electronic channel enable customers to help the retailer to provide services to others.

Giving Information and Training

Store employees need to know about the merchandise they offer as well as their customers' needs. With this information, employees can answer customers' questions and suggest products. This also instills confidence and a sense of competence, which are needed to overcome service problems.

In addition, store employees need training in interpersonal skills. Dealing with customers is hard—particularly when they're upset or angry. All store employees, even those who work for retailers that provide excellent service, will encounter dissatisfied customers. Through training, employees can learn to provide better service and to cope with the stress caused by disgruntled customers.

Mystery shoppers are professional shoppers who "shop" at a store to determine the service provided by store employees and the presentation of merchandise in the store.

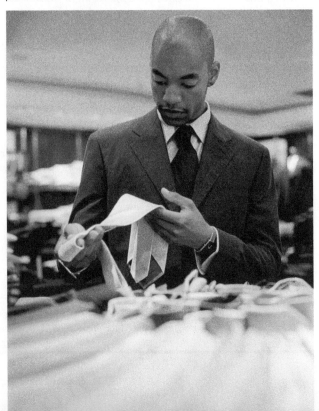

Specific retail employees (salespeople and customer service representatives) are typically designated to interact with and provide service to customers. However, all retail employees should be prepared to deal with customers. For example, Walt Disney World provides four days of training for its maintenance workers, even though people can learn how to pick up trash and sweep streets in much less time. Disney has found that its customers are more likely to direct questions to maintenance people than to the clean-cut assistants wearing Ask Me, I'm in Guest Relations buttons. Thus, Disney trains maintenance people to confidently handle the myriad of questions they'll be asked rather than responding, "Sorry, I don't know. Ask her."[74]

Toys "R" Us assesses customer satisfaction with checkout service by counting the number of abandoned shopping carts with merchandise left in the store because customers became impatient with the time required to make a purchase. After the firm noticed an alarming increase in abandoned carts, it developed a unique program to reduce customers' time in line waiting to pay. Cashiers' motions while ringing up and bagging merchandise were studied. Based on this research, a training program was developed to show cashiers how to use their right hand to record purchases on the POS terminal and their left hand to push merchandise along the counter. Counters were redesigned to have a slot lined with shopping bags in the middle of the counter. As the cashier pushes the merchandise along the counter, it drops into a bag. After the customer pays for the merchandise, the cashier simply lifts the bag from the slot and hands it to the customer, and a new bag pops into place.

Providing Instrumental and Emotional Support

Service providers need to have the instrumental support (the appropriate systems and equipment) to deliver the service desired by customers. For example, a hotel chain installed a computer system to speed up the checkout process. A study of the new system's effectiveness revealed that checkout time was not reduced because clerks had to wait to use the one stapler available to staple the customer's credit card and hotel bill receipts.

In addition to instrumental support, service providers need emotional support from their co-workers and supervisors. Emotional support involves demonstrating a concern for the well-being of others. Dealing with customer problems and maintaining a smile in difficult situations are psychologically demanding. Service providers need to be in a supportive, understanding atmosphere to deal with these demands effectively.[75]

Improving Internal Communications and Providing Support

When providing customer service, store employees must often manage the conflict between customers' needs and the retail firms' needs.[76] For example, many retailers have a no-questions-asked return policy. Under such a policy, the retailer will provide a refund at the customer's request even if the merchandise wasn't purchased at the store or was clearly used improperly. When Hudson's Bay inaugurated this policy, some employees refused to provide refunds on merchandise that had been worn or damaged by the customer. They were loyal Bay employees and didn't want customers to take advantage of their firm.

Retailers can reduce such conflicts by having clear guidelines and policies concerning service and by explaining the rationale for these policies. Once Bay employees recognized that the goodwill created by the no-questions-asked policy generated more sales than the losses due to customers' abusing the policy, they implemented the policy enthusiastically.

Conflicts can also arise when retailers set goals inconsistent with the other behaviours expected from store employees. For example, if salespeople are expected to provide customer service, they should be evaluated on the service they provide, not just on the sales they make.

Finally, conflicts can also arise between different areas of the firm. An auto dealer with an excellent customer service reputation devotes considerable effort to reducing conflict by improving communication among its employees. The dealership holds a town hall meeting in which employees feel free to bring up service problems. For example, the receptionist discussed her frustration when she couldn't locate a sales rep for whom a customer had called. The customer finally said, "Well, I'll just take my business elsewhere." She used this example to emphasize that sales reps should tell her when they slip out to run an errand. Now no one forgets that the front desk is the nerve centre of the dealership.

Empowering Store Employees

Empowerment means allowing employees at the firm's lowest level to make important decisions concerning how service is provided to customers. When the employees

instrumental support Support for retail service providers such as appropriate systems and equipment to deliver the service desired by customers.

emotional support Supporting retail service providers with the understanding and positive regard to enable them to deal with the emotional stress created by disgruntled customers.

DID YOU KNOW?

Two-thirds of the customers who put merchandise into an electronic shopping cart at a website do not complete the transaction.[77]

responsible for providing service are authorized to make important decisions, service quality improves.[79]

Nordstrom department stores provides an overall objective—satisfy customer needs—and then encourages employees to do whatever's necessary to carry out the objective. For example, a Nordstrom department manager bought 12 dozen pairs of hosiery from a competitor in the mall when her stock was depleted because the new shipment was delayed. Even though Nordstrom lost money on this hosiery, management applauded her actions to make sure customers found hosiery when they came to the store looking for it. Empowering service providers with only a rule such as "Use your best judgment" can cause chaos. At Nordstrom, department managers avoid abuses by coaching and training salespeople. They help salespeople understand what "Use your best judgment" means.

However, empowering service providers can be difficult. Some employees prefer to have the appropriate behaviours clearly defined for them. They don't want to spend the time learning how to make decisions or to assume the risks of making mistakes.

In some cases, the benefits of empowering service providers may not justify the costs. For example, if a retailer uses a standardized service delivery approach like McDonald's, the cost of hiring, training, and supporting empowerment may not lead to consistent and superior service delivery. Also, studies have found that empowerment is not embraced by employees in different cultures. For example, employees in Latin America expect their managers to possess all the information needed to make good business decisions. The role of employees is not to make business decisions; their job is to carry out the decisions of managers.[80]

Providing Incentives

As we discussed, many retailers use incentives, such as paying commissions on sales, to motivate employees. But retailers have found that commissions on sales can decrease customer service and job satisfaction. Incentives can motivate high-pressure selling, which leads to customer dissatisfaction. However, incentives can also be used effectively to improve customer service. For example, in one retail chain, managers distributed notes to store employees when they solved a customer's problem. The notes could be converted into a cash bonus. This program was particularly effective because the reward was provided at about the same time the appropriate behaviour occurred.

Communicating the Service Promise: The Communication Gap

A fourth factor leading to a customer service gap is a difference between the service promised by the retailer and the service actually delivered. Overstating the service offered raises customer expectations. Then if the retailer doesn't follow through, expectations exceed perceived service, and customers are dissatisfied. For example, if a store advertises that a customer will always be greeted by a friendly, smiling sales associate, customers may be disappointed if this doesn't occur. Raising expectations too high might bring in more customers initially, but it can also create dissatisfaction and reduce repeat business. The communication gap can be reduced by making realistic commitments and by managing customer expectations.

Realistic Commitments

Advertising programs are typically developed by the marketing department, while the store operations division delivers the service. Poor communication between these areas can result in a mismatch between an ad campaign's promises and the service the store can actually offer. This problem is illustrated by Holiday Inn's "No Surprises" ad campaign. Market research indicated hotel customers wanted greater reliability in lodging, so Holiday Inn's agency developed a campaign promising no unpleasant surprises. Even though hotel managers didn't feel they could meet the claims promised in the ads, top management accepted the campaign. The campaign raised customer expectations to an unrealistic level and gave customers who did confront an unpleasant surprise an additional reason to be angry. The campaign was discontinued soon after it started.

Managing Customer Expectations

How can a retailer communicate realistic service expectations without losing business to a competitor that makes inflated service claims? American Airlines' "Why Does It Seem Every Airline Flight Is Late?" ad campaign is an example of a communication program that addresses this issue. In print ads, American recognized its customers' frustration and explained some uncontrollable factors causing the problem: overcrowded airports, scheduling problems, and intense price competition. Then the ads described how American was improving the situation.

Information presented at the point of sale can be used to manage expectations. For example, theme parks and restaurants indicate the waiting time for an attraction or a table. Electronic retailers tell their customers if merchandise is in stock and when they can expect to receive it. Providing accurate information can increase customer satisfaction even when customers must wait longer than desired.[81]

Sometimes service problems are caused by customers. Customers may use an invalid credit card to pay for merchandise, may not take time to try on a suit and have it altered properly, or may use a product incorrectly because they failed to read the instructions. Communication programs can inform customers about their role and responsibility in getting good service and can give tips on how to get better service, such as the best times of the day to shop and the retailer's policies and procedures for handling problems.

Lo 6 Service Recovery

As we said, delivery of customer service is inherently inconsistent, so service failures are bound to arise. Rather than dwelling on negative aspects of customer problems, retailers should focus on the positive opportunities they generate. Service problems and complaints are an excellent source of information about the retailer's offering (its merchandise and service). Armed with this information, retailers can make changes to increase customer satisfaction.

Service problems also enable a retailer to demonstrate its commitment to providing high-quality customer service. By encouraging complaints and handling problems, a retailer has an opportunity to strengthen its relationship with its customers. Effective service recovery efforts significantly increase customer satisfaction, purchase intentions, and positive word of mouth. However, postrecovery satisfaction is less than that satisfaction prior to the service failure.[82]

Most retailers have standard policies for handling problems. If a correctable problem is identified, such as defective merchandise, many retailers will make restitution on the spot and apologize for inconveniencing the customer. The retailer will offer either replacement merchandise, a credit toward future purchases, or a cash refund.

In many cases, the cause of the problem may be hard to identify (did the salesperson really insult the customer?), uncorrectable (the store had to close due to bad weather), or a result of the customer's unusual expectations (the customer didn't like his haircut). In this case, service recovery might be more difficult. The steps in effective service recovery are:

- Listen to the customer
- Provide a fair solution
- Resolve the problem quickly[83]

Listening to Customers

distributive fairness Exists when outcomes received are viewed as fair with respect to outcomes received by others.

Customers can become very emotional over their real or imaginary problems with a retailer. Often this emotional reaction can be reduced by simply giving customers a chance to get their complaints off their chests.

Store employees should allow customers to air their complaints without interruption. Interruptions can further irritate customers who may already be emotionally upset. It's very hard to reason with or satisfy an angry customer.

Customers want a sympathetic response to their complaints. Thus, store employees need to make it clear they're happy that the problem has been brought to their attention. Satisfactory solutions rarely arise when store employees have an antagonistic attitude or assume that the customer is trying to cheat the store.

In 2004, Hudson's Bay launched an online survey for customers at its 99 Bay stores as well as its 300 Zellers and 45 Home Outfitters stores. The customer's receipt invited the shopper to go online and fill out a questionnaire, thus earning a chance to win 1 million HBC reward points (equivalent to $100). Feedback from the customer can pinpoint problems in specific departments, not enough sale items, or unfriendly service.

For many years, retailers have used mystery shoppers to provide feedback on customer services, but times have changed and customers are eager to log on and discuss their shopping experience. The advantage is that these are real customers who are in the store shopping and are not on the store's payroll. Customer service scores for the stores have improved since online feedback was initiated.[84]

Providing a Fair Solution

When confronted with a complaint, store employees need to focus on how they can get the customer back, not simply how they can solve the problem. Favourable impressions arise when customers feel they've been dealt with fairly. When evaluating the resolution of their problems, customers compare how they were treated in relation to others with similar problems or how they were treated in similar situations by other retail service providers. This comparison is based on observation of other customers with problems or on information about complaint handling learned from reading books and talking with others. Customers' evaluations of complaints' resolutions are based on distributive fairness and procedural fairness.[85]

Distributive Fairness   Distributive fairness is a customer's perception of the benefits received compared to their costs (inconvenience or loss). Customers want to

procedural fairness
The perceived fairness of the process used to resolve customer complaints.

get what they paid for. The customer's needs can affect the perceived correspondence between benefits and costs. For example, one customer might be satisfied with a rain check for a food processor that was advertised at a discounted price but was sold out. This customer feels the low price for the food processor offsets the inconvenience of returning to the store. But another customer may need the food processor immediately. A rain check won't be adequate compensation for him. To satisfy this customer, the salesperson must locate a store that has the food processor and have it delivered to the customer's house.

Customers typically prefer tangible rather than intangible resolutions to their complaints. Customers may want to let off steam, but they also want to feel the retailer was responsive to their complaint. A low-cost reward, a free soft drink, or a discount communicates more concern to the customer than a verbal apology.

If providing tangible restitution isn't possible, the next best alternative is to let customers see that their complaints will have an effect in the future. This can be done by making a note, in front of the customer, to a manager about the problem or writing to the customer about actions taken to prevent similar problems in the future.

Procedural Fairness   Procedural fairness is the perceived fairness of the process used to resolve complaints. Customers consider three questions when evaluating procedural fairness:

- Did the employee collect information about the situation?
- Was this information used to resolve the complaint?
- Did the customer have some influence over the outcome?

Resolving Problems Quickly

Customers are more satisfied when the first person they contact can resolve a problem. When customers are referred to several different employees, they waste a lot of time repeating their story. Also, the chance of conflicting responses by store employees increases.

Customers should be told clearly and precisely what they need to do to resolve a problem. When American Express cardholders ask to have an unused airline ticket removed from their bill, they're told immediately that they must return the ticket to the airline or travel agency before a credit can be issued. Fast service often depends on providing clear instructions.

SUMMARY

Customer relationship management is a business philosophy and set of strategies, programs, and systems that focus on identifying and building loyalty with a retailer's most valued customers. Loyal customers are committed to patronizing a retailer and are not prone to switching to a competitor. In addition to building loyalty, CRM programs are also designed to increase the share of wallet from the retailer's best customers.

CRM is an iterative process that turns customer data into customer loyalty through four activities:
- Collecting customer data
- Analyzing the customer data and identifying target customers
- Developing CRM programs
- Implementing CRM programs

The first step of the process is to collect and store data about customers. One of the challenges in collecting customer data is identifying the customer with each transaction and contact. Retailers use a variety of approaches to overcome this challenge.

The second step is analyzing the data to identify the most profitable customers. Two approaches used to rank customers according to their profitability are calculating the customer's lifetime value and categorizing customers on the basis of characteristics of their buying behaviour—recency, frequency, and monetary value.

Using this information about customers, retailers can develop programs to build loyalty in their best customers, increase their share of wallet with better customers (converting gold customers into platinum customers), and deal with unprofitable customers (getting the lead out).

Four approaches that retailers use to build loyalty and retain their best customers are:
- Launching frequent shopper programs
- Offering special customer service
- Personalizing the services they provide
- Building a sense of community

Retailers increase share of wallet through cross-selling and add-on selling. Unprofitable customers are dealt with by developing lower-cost approaches for servicing these customers. Effectively implementing CRM programs is difficult because it requires coordinating a number of different areas in a retailer's organization.

Due to the inherent intangibility and inconsistency of service, providing high-quality customer service is challenging. However, customer service also provides an opportunity for retailers to develop a strategic advantage. Retailers use two basic approaches to providing customer service: customization and standardization approaches. The customized approach relies primarily on sales associates. The standardized approach places more emphasis on developing appropriate rules and procedures and the store design.

Customers evaluate customer service by comparing their perceptions of the service delivered with their expectations. Thus, to improve service, retailers need to close the gaps between the service delivered and the customer's expectations. These gaps are reduced by knowing what customers expect, setting standards to provide the expected service, providing support so that store employees can meet the standards, and realistically communicating the service they offer to customers. Knowledge of service gaps can be determined by conducting focus groups.

Due to inherent inconsistency, service failures are bound to arise. These lapses in service provide an opportunity for retailers to build even stronger relationships with their customers.

KEY TERMS

add-on selling

communication gap

cookies

cross-selling

customer database

customer relationship management (CRM)

customer service

data mining

decile analysis

delivery gap

distributive fairness

80–20 rule

emotional support

frequent shopper program

gamification

instrumental support

knowledge gap

lifetime customer value (LTV)

loyalty program

market basket analysis

mystery shopper

near-field communications (NFC)

1-to-1 retailing

private-label credit card

procedural fairness

RFM (recency, frequency, monetary) analysis

service gap

share of wallet

SoLoMo (social, local, and mobile)

standardization approach

standards gap

Get Out & Do It!

1. GO SHOPPING Look in your wallet:
   a) What loyalty cards do you have?
   b) Why do you have these specific cards?
   c) Rate each card on a scale: 1 (poor) to 10 (fantastic).

2. INTERNET EXERCISE Contact the Canadian Marketing Association (CMA), a leading authority on privacy issues, at **www.the-cma.org**. What are the major issues confronting retailers? What seminars are being offered to assist retailers in understanding Canada's privacy legislation?

3. INTERNET EXERCISE Go to some of the retail sites that you frequent and compare their privacy policies. Which policies make you less concerned about violations of your privacy? Why? Which policies, or lack thereof, raise your concern? Why?

4. SHOPPING Are you a participant in a frequent shopper program? Why are you a member? Look at the Shoppers Optimum card program.
   a) How does a membership benefit the consumer?

   b) Would this membership card be of value to you personally? Explain why or why not.

5. INTERNET EXERCISE Visit **www.airmilesshops.ca**—the Air Miles virtual shopping mall. What are the shopping options and special promotions for Air Miles collectors? How does the website encourage you to participate and sign up for Air Miles? What information does it request from you?

6. GO SHOPPING Go to a local store and be a customer: Ask for assistance and suggestions regarding a potential purchase. Write a report describing your shopping experience, and make suggestions for improving the store's customer service.

7. GO SHOPPING Go to a discount store such as Walmart, a department store, and a specialty store to buy a pair of jeans. Compare and contrast the customer service you receive in the stores. Which store made it easiest to find the pair of jeans you would be interested in buying? Why?

1. What is CRM?

2. Why do retailers want to determine the lifetime value of their customers?

3. Why do customers have privacy concerns about frequent shopper programs that supermarkets have, and what can supermarkets do to minimize these concerns?

4. What are examples of opportunities for add-on selling that might be pursued by (a) travel agents, (b) jewellery stores, and (c) dry cleaners?

5. How would you suggest that a dry cleaner build greater loyalty and retention with its best customers?

6. Which of the following types of retailers do you think would benefit most from instituting CRM: (a) supermarkets, (b) banks, (c) automobile dealers, or (d) consumer electronic retailers? Why?

7. Develop a CRM program for a local store that sells apparel with your college or university's logo. What type of information would you collect about your customers, and how would you use this information to increase the sales and profits of the store?

8. How can a real estate agent deal with people who are just looking and not ready to buy? What are the agent's potential benefits and risks in undertaking these actions?

9. What are the different approaches retailers can use to identify customers with their transactions? What are the advantages and disadvantages of each approach?

10. A CRM program focuses on building relationships with a retailer's better customers. Some customers who do not receive the same benefits as the retailer's best customers may be upset because they are treated differently. What can retailers do to minimize this negative reaction?

11. For each of these services, give an example of a retailer for which providing the service is critical to its success. Then give an example of a retailer for which providing the service is not critical: (a) personal shoppers, (b) home delivery, (c) money-back guarantees, (d) credit.

12. Holt Renfrew and McDonald's are noted for their high-quality customer service. But their approaches to providing this quality service are different. Describe this difference. Why have the retailers elected to use these different approaches?

13. Is customer service more important for store-based retailers or electronic retailers? Explain.

14. Providing customer service can be very expensive for retailers. When are the costs of providing high-quality services justified? What types of retailers find it financially advantageous to provide high-quality customer service? What retailers can't justify providing high-quality service?

15. Gaps analysis provides a systematic method of examining a customer service program's effectiveness. Top management has told an information systems manager that customers are complaining about the long wait to pay for merchandise at the checkout station. How can the systems manager use gaps analysis to analyze this problem and suggest approaches to reducing this time?

16. How could an effective customer service strategy cut a retailer's costs?

17. Employees play a critical role in customer perceptions of quality service. If you were hiring salespeople, what characteristics would you look for to assess their ability to provide good customer service?

18. a) What is a focus group?
    b) Design ten open-ended questions to use in a customer focus group to determine a retailer's customer service gaps and make improvements.

Practise and learn online with Connect.

appealing to the customer: retail communication mix

LEARNING OBJECTIVES

LO1 Explore how retailers can build brand equity for their stores and their private-label merchandise.

LO2 Examine the individual elements of a retail communication strategy and how each element contributes to a successful communication campaign.

LO3 Review the strengths and weaknesses of different methods for communicating with customers.

LO4 Examine the steps involved in developing a communication program.

LO5 Review how retailers establish a communication budget.

SPOTLIGHT ON RETAILING

Hudson's Bay Adds a Bit of Shazam to Its Radio Ads

Hudson's Bay recently used the popular audio-scanning mobile app Shazam to drive listeners to the retailer's website in a new national radio campaign.

In the month before Christmas 2012, Bonnie Brooks, president and CEO of the retail chain (and its long-serving radio spokesperson), promoted the store's one-day Bay Day sales with 30-second radio commercials—a different ad running each day for each sale. Listeners who had the Shazam mobile app active when the spots aired were taken to that particular item on the store's mobile website. The app, produced by Pirate Radio in Toronto, recognizes special codes embedded into each radio spot.

After casual conversations with the Shazam team in Canada, it became clear that the special codes can "be embedded in really any audio file," said Patrick Dickinson, senior vice-president of marketing at the retailer.

The campaign ran until Christmas Eve with Hudson's Bay promoting the Shazam tie-in with daily newspaper ads across the country.

According to Dickinson, the app was a way for the retailer to connect with younger shoppers. "Because we are attracting a younger audience, we have younger merchandise in the store, we have contemporary brands now, and this is a great way to get to that consumer, get to that type of audience and connect with them," said Dickinson.

"It seemed like the one-day sales, where we have a different ad going out every single day, would be a great example of how to make this work, so we gave it a shot," he added.

At the end of the campaign, Shazam provided the retailer with a report on "how many people are tagging it [and] how many unique people are utilizing the service by individual spot," said Dickinson. "We put that data together with our own data—how many unique visitors we get to the web and what our conversion rates are—and it gives us a leg up in terms of evaluating this as a new media and to determine how best to proceed," he said.

Source: Kristin Laird, "The Bay adds a bit of Shazam to its radio ads," *Marketing*, November 26, 2012, http://www.marketingmag.ca/news/marketer-news/the-bay-adds-a-bit-of-shazam-to-its-radio-ads-66804 (accessed January 10, 2014).

A critical step in the retail management decision-making process is developing and implementing a communication program to:

- Build appealing brand images
- Attract customers to stores and Internet sites
- Encourage customers to buy merchandise

brand A distinguishing name or symbol (such as a logo, design, symbol, or trademark) that identifies the products or services offered by a seller and differentiates those products and services from the offerings of competitors.

private-label brands Products developed and marketed by a retailer and available for sale only by that retailer; also called *store brands*.

brand energy The concept that links the idea that a brand creates value through meaningful experiences rather than a focus on generating profits.

The communication program informs customers about the retailer as well as the merchandise and services it offers and plays a role in developing repeat visits and customer loyalty.

Communication programs can have both long-term and short-term effects on a retailer's business. From a *long-term perspective,* communication programs can be used to create and maintain a strong, differentiated image of the retailer and its store brands. This image develops customer loyalty and creates a strategic advantage. Thus, brand-image–building communication programs complement the objective of a retailer's CRM (customer relationship management) program.

On the other hand, retailers frequently use communication programs to realize the *short-term objective* of increasing sales during a specified time period. For example, retailers often have sales during which some or all merchandise is priced at a discount for a short time, for example, at the end of a season. Grocery stores usually place weekly ads with coupons that can be used to save money on purchases made during the week.

Retail advertising can be used to achieve long-term objectives such as building a brand image, or short-term sales. The Payless ShoeSource ad (above) generates short-term sales through a special promotion.

Using Communication Programs to Develop Brands and Build Customer Loyalty

A **brand** is the symbolic embodiment of all the information connected to the product and/or retailer and serves to create associations and expectations around it. A brand often includes a logo, fonts, colour schemes, symbols, and sound, which may be developed to represent implicit values, ideas, and even personality. In a retailing context, the name of the retailer is a brand that indicates to consumers the type of merchandise and services offered by the retailer. Some retailers develop **private-label brands** or store brands that are exclusively sold through their channels. In some cases this private-label merchandise bears the retailer's name, such as Shoppers Drug Mart aspirin. In other cases, special brand names are used, such as Hudson's Bay's Baycrest, Shoppers Drug Mart's Life, and Canadian Tire's Mastercraft. A retailer develops a brand by associating an image with the product and services that is branded into the consciousness of consumers. A brand is therefore one of the most valuable elements in a retailer's advertising strategy. One goal in brand recognition is the identification of a brand without the name of the company present. It is therefore important that a brand be protected legally by patent or copyright. The well-known brand of Apple is recognized for innovation in technology and has created immense success in the branding of iPod and iTunes.

Brand energy is the concept that links the idea that the brand creates value through meaningful experiences rather than a focus on merely generating profits. The energy that flows throughout the business develops a consistent way of thinking, feeling, and behaving toward the retailer and its products and services in all employees; an example is Mountain Equipment Co-op, where customers become members for a nominal fee and embrace its environmental philosophy.

Attitude branding is the choice to represent a feeling that is not necessarily connected with the product or retailer—for example, Nike: "Just Do It"; The Body Shop: "Trade Not Aid"; Dove: "Real Beauty." A great brand adds a sense of purpose to the experience. See, for example, Retailing View 15.2.

Value of Brand Image

Brands provide value to both customers and retailers. Brands convey information to consumers about the nature of the shopping experience—the retailer's mix—they will encounter when patronizing a retailer. They also affect the customers' confidence in decisions made to buy merchandise from a retailer. Finally, brands can enhance the customers' satisfaction with the merchandise and services they buy. Consumers feel different when wearing jewellery bought from Birks than from La Claire or lingerie from La Senza than from Target.

The value that brand image offers retailers is referred to as brand equity. Strong brand names can affect the customer's decision-making process, motivate repeat visits and purchases, and build loyalty. In addition, strong brand names enable retailers to charge higher prices and lower their marketing costs.

Customer loyalty to brands arises from heightened awareness of the brand and the emotional ties toward it. For example, some brands such as Canadian Tire are so well known by consumers that they are typically in a consumer's consideration set (see Retailing View 15.1). In addition, customers identify and have strong emotional relationships with some brands. For example, Winners has an image of offering fashionable merchandise at bargain prices. Going to Winners is a cool experience, and everybody now considers it cool to save money. High brand awareness and strong emotional connnections reduce the incentive of customers to switch to competing retailers.

A strong brand image enables retailers to increase their margins. When retailers have high customer loyalty, they can engage in premium pricing and reduce their reliance on price promotions to attract customers. Brands with weaker images are forced to offer low prices and frequent sales to maintain their market share.

Finally, retailers with strong brand names can leverage their brand to successfully introduce new retail concepts with only a limited amount of marketing effort. For example, The Gap has efficiently extended its brand to GapKids and BabyGap, and Roots extended its brand name to Roots Kids. Toys "R" Us extended its brand name to Kids "R" Us and Babies "R" Us.

A strong brand name creates a strategic advantage that is very difficult for competitors to duplicate. Many of the most brilliant marketers can be found in Canada, and many others around the world look to Canadian companies for best practices. For example, Canadian Tire has always stayed true to its core customers but, recognizing changing times, took an innovative approach to meeting the demands of the modern bride and groom. The launch of electronic "Celebration Stations" at 345 locations across Canada created an online bridal and gift registry that has a selection of 42 000 products from barbecues to kayaks.[1]

Building Brand Equity

The activities that a retailer needs to undertake to build brand equity for its firm or its private-label merchandise are as follows:

- Create a high level of brand awareness.
- Develop favourable associations with the brand name.
- Consistently reinforce the image of the brand.

attitude branding
The choice of a symbol that represents a feeling that is not necessarily connected with the product or retailer.

brand equity   The value that brand image offers retailers.

DID YOU KNOW?

Canadian Tire "money" was introduced in 1958 at Canadian Tire gas bars and started being promoted in the stores in 1961 as a customer loyalty initiative.

Winners uses advertising to build its image of offering fashionable merchandise at low prices.

Bienvenue au Québec: How Outsiders Become Local Quebec Retailers

There's a little known fact about how Tim Hortons adapted to the Quebec market. The chain was first called Tim Horton's (notice the apostrophe). The apostrophe was later lost to Quebec's language law, which stipulates that unless a business name is simply a personal name, it must be translated into French. Tim Horton's would have become *Les beignes de Tim Horton*. Rather than producing separate signage and marketing materials for the Quebec market, Tim Horton's became Tim Hortons from coast to coast. While it changed its name to maximize efficiencies instead of adopting a distinctly Quebecois identity and chose to offer essentially the same menu mix within the same restaurant environment, Tim Hortons has definitely struck a chord with Quebecers.

Headspace Marketing Inc., a Toronto-based marketing-communications consultancy helping clients build their brands in Quebec, asked 1000 Quebec men and women to rate how well or poorly 12 retail brands had adapted to their needs and expectations.[2] Of the 12 brands surveyed, three stand out as having best adapted to Quebecers' needs and wants.

Tim Hortons leads the pack with a 98 percent score. Canadian Tire follows with a score of 97 percent. With its green maple leaf logo, the "driving, playing, fixing, and living" store first opened in Quebec in 1939.

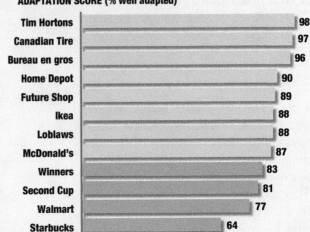

ADAPTATION SCORE (% well adapted)

Retailer	Score
Tim Hortons	98
Canadian Tire	97
Bureau en gros	96
Home Depot	90
Future Shop	89
Ikea	88
Loblaws	88
McDonald's	87
Winners	83
Second Cup	81
Walmart	77
Starbucks	64

Proudly Canadian, the retailer doesn't appear to have done things differently in Quebec. The merchandise mix, the unique products, and the Canadian Tire money featuring the well-known Scotsman Sandy McTire appear as popular in Rivière-du-Loup as in Kamloops.

Staples Business Depot in Quebec is the destination for office supplies. But don't expect to find a Staples sign on the building or anything about a depot. *Bureau en gros*, which loosely translated means "wholesale office supplies," is one of the top three brands among those tested that Quebecers felt best adapted to their needs.

---

brand awareness
The ability of a potential customer to recognize or recall that a particular brand name belongs to a retailer or product/service.

aided recall When consumers indicate they know the brand when the name is presented to them.

top-of-mind awareness The highest level of brand awareness; arises when consumers mention a brand name first when they are asked about a type of retailer, a merchandise category, or a type of service.

Brand Awareness Brand awareness is the ability of a potential customer to recognize or recall that the brand name is a type of retailer or product/service. Thus, brand awareness is the strength of the link between the brand name and type of merchandise or service in the minds of customers. There is a range of awareness from aided recall to top-of-mind awareness. Aided recall occurs when consumers indicate they know the brand when the name is presented to them. Top-of-mind awareness, the highest level of awareness, arises when consumers mention a brand name first when they are asked about the type of retailer, a merchandise category, or a type of service. For example, Best Buy has top-of-mind awareness if a consumer responds "Best Buy" when asked about retailers that sell consumer electronics. High top-of-mind awareness means that a retailer typically will be in the consideration set when customers decide to shop for a type of product or service.

Retailers build top-of-mind awareness by having memorable names; by repeatedly exposing their name to customers through advertising, locations, and sponsorships; and by using memorable symbols. Some brand names are easy to remember. For example, the name Home Depot, because "Home" is in its brand name, is memorable and closely associated with

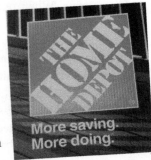

The name certainly has much to do with it but the offer is no different. Mind you, Quebecers are often pleasantly surprised to be consistently asked at the checkout if they found everything they were looking for.

Home Depot, Future Shop, IKEA, Loblaws, and McDonald's all get scores in the high eighties.

While many Quebecers call Loblaws "*Lobolah*," its President's Choice products and made-in-Quebec advertising seem to be resonating well with a market that loves a new twist on Habitant pea soup as much as unpasteurized cheese.

In many towns in Quebec, McDonald's restaurants are as visible as the now mostly empty churches and, perhaps because of the *poutine* on the menu, its community involvement, or its support of Alexandre Despaties—*un p'tit gars d'ici*—the quick-service restaurant chain gets good marks from Quebecers.

IKEA, concentrated in Montreal, also gets good marks from Quebecers who obviously have no problem making the trip to the Swedish store.

Winners, with an 83 percent score, has apparently done well in Quebec with its off-pricing strategy. The formula is the same and for a while the advertising featured a local spokesperson, Geneviève Brouillette. Everyone loves a bargain and Quebecers are no different. And unlike shoppers in the rest of Canada who are more likely to find shopping is a chore, Quebecers love it.

The giant Walmart gets a 77 percent score. Quebecers might like its everyday low prices and enjoy watching a TV spot featuring a young couple from Chicoutimi who bought all their Christmas decorations at the local Walmart; they seem to be less impressed by the corporation's labour relations.

So what can we learn from this? There don't appear to be universal rules. In some cases, having a French name, adapting the offering to Quebecers' tastes, or speaking their language through made-in-Quebec advertising might help increase a retailer's relevance and familiarity among shoppers in Quebec. One should keep in mind, however, that the basics of retailing (fair pricing, quality products, clean and accessible stores, well-stocked shelves, and outstanding service) make the difference in Quebec as everywhere else. Other surveys have also consistently highlighted the importance Quebecers attach to customer service. For example, when asked what the retailers who have deployed self-checkout should do with the staff being reallocated, 72 percent of Quebecers said "having easily accessible personnel in aisle, at a greeter station, or at a customer service desk to help locate product, answer questions, etc." Only 58 percent of Ontarians said so.[3]

Quebecers will handsomely reward those retailers who cater to their needs in a manner that recognizes them as people and shoppers. Knowing whether to adopt, adapt, or create for Quebec is the key to success.

Source: Headspace Marketing Inc., www.headspacemarketing.com/pdfs/knowledge_retailbrands.pdf.

home improvements, as is Canadian Tire with the automotive reference and the fact that this is a Canadian company.

Tim Hortons has high awareness because of the large number of stores it has. Customers walk and drive by the stores all the time. The sheer number of stores provides substantial exposure to its brand. Most Canadians are well aware of the popular "roll up the rim to win" promotion.

Symbols involve visual images that typically are more easily recalled than words or phrases and thus are useful for building brand awareness. For example, the images of Colonel Sanders and the golden

By using this symbol, Lululemon builds awareness for its offerings and makes it easier for customers to recall its name and image.

arches enhance the ability of customers to recall the names KFC and McDonald's.

Many Canadian retailers are finding that sponsorships are a cost-effective means of increasing their exposure as well as helping the communities that they serve. Take a Hike—an outdoor sporting goods store in Thunder Bay, Ontario—is passionate about sponsorships and participates in local festivals and outdoor activity workshops for the community. Its Socks for Shelter House program donates one pair of socks (retail value, $16) for every four pairs sold; suppliers also get involved and contribute to the worthy cause.[4]

Associations Building awareness is the first step in developing brand equity, but the value of the brand is largely based on the associations that customers make with the brand name. A brand association is anything linked to or connected with the brand name in a consumer's memory. For example, some of the associations that consumers might have with McDonald's are golden arches, fast food, clean stores, hamburgers, french fries, Big Mac, and Ronald McDonald. In the case of McDonald's, these links are so strong that when a consumer thinks of fast food, hamburgers, or french fries, they also think of McDonald's. These strong associations influence consumer buying behaviour. For example, when consumers think about camping, Mountain Equipment Co-op might immediately come to mind, stimulating a visit to a Mountain Equipment Co-op store or its website.

Some common associations that retailers develop with their brand name are as follows:

- **Merchandise category.** The most common association is to link the retailer to a category of merchandise. For example, Staples Business Depot would like to have consumers associate its name with office supplies. Then, when a need for office supplies arises, consumers immediately think of Staples Business Depot.
- **Price/quality.** Some retailers, such as Holt Renfrew, want to be associated with offering high prices and unique, high fashion merchandise. Other retailers, such as Walmart, want associations with offering low prices and good value.
- **Specific attribute or benefit.** A retailer can link its stores to attributes such as convenience (7-Eleven) or service (Harry Rosen).
- **Lifestyle or activity.** Some retailers associate their name with a specific lifestyle or activity. For example, The Nature Company, a retailer offering books and equipment to study nature, is linked to a lifestyle of interacting with the environment. Future Shop is associated with computers, software, and small office equipment.

The brand image is a set of associations that are usually organized around some meaningful themes. Thus, the associations that a consumer might have with McDonald's might be organized into groups such as kids, service, and type of food. Mountain Equipment Co-op nurtures its brand image of selling high-quality, functional products and providing helpful service for outdoor activity.

Consistent Reinforcement The retailer's brand image is developed and maintained through the retailer's communication program as well as other elements of the communication mix, such as merchandise assortment and pricing, the design of its stores and website, and the customer service it offers. To develop a strong set of associations and a clearly defined brand image, retailers need to be consistent, presenting the same message to customers over time and across all of the elements of the retail mix.

Rather than creating unique communication programs for sales associates, retailers need to develop an integrated marketing communication program—a program that integrates all of the communication elements to deliver a comprehensive, consistent message. Without this coordination, the communication methods might work at cross-purposes. For example, the retailer's TV advertising campaign might attempt to build an image of exceptional customer service, but the firm's sales promotions might all emphasize low prices. If communication methods aren't used consistently, customers may become confused about the retailer's image and therefore not patronize the store.

A unique example is Abercrombie & Fitch (A&F), which uses an integrated marketing communication program to reinforce its brand image associated with fun-loving, independent, and uninhibited teenagers and young adults. To stay on top of its target market's taste and find ideas for new merchandise, A&F sends employees to college and university campuses each month to chat with students about what they play, wear, listen to, and read.

The stores have comfortable armchairs, designed to be gathering places for its customers. They are staffed by high-energy "brand reps"; selling skills not required. The brand reps just need to fit the company's brand image, wear its apparel, and have fun inside the store.

A&F's main promotional tool has been its controversial "magalogue," a quarterly magazine–catalogue crammed with product information, sexual imagery, and provocative articles. A magalogue is a combination magazine and catalogue. Large blow-ups of enticing photographs from the magalogue appear in store displays.[6]

Toys "R" Us is using a similar approach to target teenagers. It has created RZone boutiques within its stores, which offer video games. The visual merchandising in the boutiques is designed to appeal to teenagers. To build its image of the RZone brand with teenagers, Toys "R" Us launched *RZone Magazine*. The glossy magazine has cutting-edge graphics and content desired by teen pop-culture junkies who listen to hybrid rap and rock music

Abercrombie & Fitch

CASUAL LUXURY

Abercrombie & Fitch uses webcasts as part of an integrated marketing communication program to reinforce its image associated with fun-loving, independent teenagers and young adults.

and watched MTV's *Total Request*. It reinforces the image and visual merchandising in the boutiques that associate the RZone brand with what is hot in the worlds of entertainment, sports, and gaming.[7]

Extending the Brand Name

Retailers can leverage their brand names to support their growth strategies. For example, IKEA used its strong brand image to successfully enter the Canadian home furnishing retail market; Laura introduced a Laura II collection for women wearing plus-sizes and Laura Petites for small sizes; and the Pottery Barn launched its Pottery Barn Kids catalogue to target children. In other cases, retailers have pursued growth opportunities using a new and unrelated brand name. For example, The Gap used the brand name Old Navy for its value concept, and HBC named its new home store concept Home Outfitters.

There are pluses and minuses to extending a brand name to a new concept. An important benefit of extending the brand name is that minimal communication expenses are needed to create awareness and a brand image for the new concept. Customers will quickly transfer the original brand's awareness and associations to the new concept. However, in some cases, the retailer might not want to have the original brand's associations connected with the new concept. For example, Abercrombie & Fitch decided to invest in building new and different brand images for Gilly Hicks and Hollister Co. rather than branding them with a similar name.

| 15.2 | RETAILING VIEW |

Reitmans Struts Its Stuff

Offering reasonably priced clothing designed for a mainstream target, Reitmans was in need of a makeover. Years of targeting a broad audience had created a perception of blandness, but even the most practical woman still wants to look fashionable.

But how to define "fashion"? The Reitmans consumer is aware of current trends and wants to look good, but in clothes that fit her life. This insight sparked a campaign that had been running for five years under the tagline "Designed for real life."

In 2008–09, the campaign took an even more tongue-in-cheek shot at high fashion. With the tagline "Reitmans one, haute couture zero," the campaign featured a pair of fashion experts demonstrating how runway trends fare in the real world compared to Reitmans' fashions.

TV highlighted the dangers of sporting runway couture in real life, while online banners and out-of-home advertising zeroed in on the key items promoted each season. The website gave more information and mix-and-match ideas. In stores, lines from the campaign were used in point-of-purchase displays.

The campaign created a unique personality and attitude for Reitmans in a largely undifferentiated category, and the brand has experienced substantial growth since the launch. "Designed for real life" has evolved into a mantra across all aspects of the business. "A brilliant, simple, and funny way to demonstrate the product and brand benefit," says Suzanne Sauvage, EVP/chief strategy officer at Nurun.

Source: Carey Toane, "Agency of the Year 2000, TAXI Ranks High." *Strategy* magazine, November 2009, p. 37. © Brunico Communications Ltd. Reprinted with permission.

direct marketing
A form of nonstore retailing in which customers are exposed to merchandise through print or electronic media; they then can purchase the merchandise by telephone, mail, or over the Internet.

These issues also arise as a retailer expands internationally. Associations with the retailer's brands that are valued in one country may not be valued in another. For example, French consumers prefer to shop at supermarkets that offer good service and high-quality grocery products, whereas German shoppers prefer supermarkets that offer low prices and good value. Thus, a French supermarket retailer with a brand image of quality and service might not be able to leverage its image if it decides to enter the German market.[8]

Retailers communicate using a mix of methods, such as advertising, sales promotion, publicity, e-mail, blogs, and social media such as Twitter, Facebook, Pinterest, and YouTube. In large retail firms, the communication mix elements examined are managed by the firm's marketing or advertising department and the buying organization. The other elements, such as store atmosphere and salespeople, are managed by store personnel and the head office. The following sections of this chapter examine the methods that retailers use to communicate with their customers and how they plan and implement their communication programs to build brand equity as well as short-term sales.

Methods of Communicating with Customers

LO 2

For any communication campaign to succeed, the firm must deliver the right message to the right audience through the right media, with the ultimate goal of profiting from long-term customer relationships rather than just short-term transactions. Reaching the right audience is becoming more difficult, however; as the media environment grows, it becomes more complicated and fragmented.[9]

No single type of media is necessarily better than another. The goal of a retail communication strategy is to use media so that the sum exceeds the total of individual media types. However, advances in technology have led to a variety of new, along with traditional, media options for consumers, all of which vie for consumers' attention. Print media have also grown and become more specialized. This proliferation of media has led many retailers to shift their promotional dollars from advertising to direct marketing, use of Internet sites, and other forms of promotion in search of the best way to deliver messages to their target audiences.

We now examine the individual elements of a retail communication strategy and the way each contributes to a successful communication campaign (see Exhibit 15–1). The elements can be viewed on two axes: passive and interactive (from a consumer's perspective), and offline and online. Note that as the retailers' repertoire of communication elements has expanded, so too have the ways in which retailers can communicate with their customers; so, for instance, direct marketing appears in three of the four boxes. Firms have also expanded their use of traditional media (e.g., advertising, public relations, and sales promotions) from pure offline to a combination of offline and online.

Direct Marketing

Direct marketing is measureable, trackable, database-building marketing that communicates directly with target customers to generate a response or transaction. Direct marketing contains a variety of traditional and new forms of marketing communication initiatives and is represented in three of the four quadrants in Exhibit 15–1. Traditional direct marketing includes mail and catalogues sent through the mail; today, it also includes Internet-enabled methods such as e-mail and mobile marketing.

The increased use of customer databases has enabled retailers to identify and track consumers over time and across purchase situations, and this has contributed to the growth of direct marketing. Retailers have been able to build these databases, thanks to consumers' increased use of credit and debit cards, store-specific credit and loyalty cards, online shopping, contesting, and social media groups, all of which require the buyer to give the seller personal information that becomes part of its database. Because firms understand customers' purchases better

exhibit 15–1 Elements in an IMC Strategy

INTERACTIVE

ONLINE		OFFLINE
• Direct marketing (e.g., mobile marketing) • Online marketing (e.g., website, blogs, social media)	• Personal selling • Sales promotions (e.g., contests, sweepstakes, special events, in-store demonstrations, pop-up stores)	
• Direct marketing (e.g., e-mail) • Banner ads (traditional) • YouTube commercials/ads	• Advertising • Sales promotions (e.g., coupons) • Public relations • Direct marketing (e.g., mail, circulars, catalogues, magalogues)	

PASSIVE

Source: Dhruv Grewal and Michael Levy, *Marketing*, 3rd ed. (New York: McGraw-Hill/Irwin, 2012).

when they possess such information, they can more easily focus their direct marketing efforts (call to action) appropriately. A **call to action** is the portion of the marketing or sales message that prompts potential consumers to perform a desired action within the desired time frame. Call-to-action phrases often use action verbs such as sign up, click here, register today, call now, or buy now. For example, American Eagle recently sent out this call to action via e-mail to its AERewards customers: "Limited Time Only! The heat is on … take an additional 50 percent off AE clearance."

Direct marketing retailers try to carefully target their customers so that they will be more receptive to their messages. Shoppers Drug Mart's Optimum card, for example, has a digital deals program that sends weekly e-mail deals and online printable coupons for items that Optimum cardholders have purchased previously, as well as identifies items that are in the current circular that match previous purchasing behaviour. "Generic marketing messages just don't resonate as much as we'd like them to," said David Harrington, the retailer's vice-president of business analytics and Optimum. "Customers demand much more of us. We have already got [them] as an engaged cardholder—it is kind of our obligation to send [targeted messaging] back to [them]."[10] These different forms of direct marketing demonstrate how this communication method can vary on both the interactivity and online/offline dimensions of Exhibit 15–1.

Direct Mail

Direct mail includes any brochure, catalogue, advertisement, or other printed marketing material delivered directly to the consumer through the mail or by a private delivery company.[11] Retailers have communicated with their customers through the mail for as long as the mail has existed. The direct mail piece can go to all customers, to a subset of customers according to their previous purchases, or even on a personalized basis to individual customers.

Retailers frequently use data collected at point-of-sale (POS) terminals to target their direct mail promotions. For example, Hudson's Bay keeps a database of all purchases made by its credit card and loyalty card customers. With information about each customer's purchases, the retailer can then target direct mail about a new perfume to customers with a history of purchasing such merchandise. Further, many retailers encourage their salespeople to maintain preferred customer lists and use them to mail out personalized invitations or notes.

Retailers also can purchase a wide variety of lists that help them target consumers with specific demographic profiles, interests, and lifestyles. For example, a home furnishings store could buy a list of subscribers to *Architectural Digest* in its trading area and then mail a catalogue or specific information about home furnishings to those upscale consumers. Canada Post offers direct mail business solutions for businesses that do not have access to internal lists or consumer data.

Although relatively expensive on a per-customer basis (because of printing, mail costs, and a relatively low response rate), direct mail is still extensively used by many retailers because people respond favourably to personal messages.

E-mail

E-mail is a direct marketing communication vehicle that involves sending messages over the Internet. E-mail, like other forms of electronic communications (e.g., websites, m-commerce), can be personalized to the specific consumer and thus is similar to communication delivered by salespeople. However, when the same message is delivered electronically to all recipients, electronic communications more closely resemble advertising. Retailers use e-mail to inform customers of new merchandise and special promotions, confirm the receipt of an order, and indicate when an order has been shipped.

E-mail marketing can reduce the time and effort involved in structuring a direct-to-consumer campaign versus using common offline direct marketing communication (print postal mailings or telesales) techniques. E-mail allows for real-time messaging and personalized messages to consumers. Retailers can send unique birthday or anniversary messages to customers or send individual deals to customers based on their buying habits (e.g., PC Plus program from Loblaw). Because e-mail takes less time to create and send than more traditional marketing mediums, communication with consumers can happen more frequently. Finally, e-mail marketing has an exponentially greater ability to track sales and user engagement. Retailers are able to track how many people opened an e-mail, how many customers clicked a link in an e-mail, which specific link within the e-mail was clicked, and whether the e-mail even made it to the customer's inbox.

Mobile Marketing

Mobile marketing, also called *m-commerce* or *mobile commerce*, is marketing through wireless handheld devices, such as cellular telephones, and involves completing a transaction via cellphone.[12]

call to action The portion of the marketing or sales message that prompts potential consumers to perform a desired action within the desired time frame.

direct mail Any brochure, catalogue, advertisement, or other printed marketing material delivered directly to the consumer through the mail or by a private delivery company.

e-mail A paid personal communication vehicle that involves sending messages over the Internet.

mobile marketing Communicating with and selling to customers through wireless handheld devices, such as cellular telephones; also called *m-commerce* or *mobile commerce*.

Smartphones have become far more than tools for placing calls; they offer a kind of mobile computer with the ability to obtain sports scores, weather, music, videos, and text messages, as well as to purchase merchandise. Smartphone usage has increased significantly, from 33 percent of Canadian cellphone users in March 2011 to 48 percent in March 2012.[13] Ninety-nine percent of the Canadian population has access to wireless services. A recent Nielsen survey found that more and more people are connecting to the Internet (whether through a computer or mobile phone) and for longer amounts of time. Time spent on PCs and smartphones was up 21 percent from July 2011 to July 2012, with app time more than doubling during this time period as more smartphone owners entered the market and the number of available apps multiplied.[14] Retailers' success with mobile marketing rests on integrating marketing communications with fun and useful apps that are consistent with consumer attitudes toward mobile devices (see Exhibit 15–2). In response, firms are steadily improving customers' potential experience with their mobile interfaces by creating applications for consumers. McDonald's Pick-n-Play used a mobile web URL to allow consumers to control a game

The RedLaser shopping comparison app for the iPhone takes a picture of a product's barcode and then lists the prices for that item at various retailers.

Foursquare encourages consumers to buy at participating retailers by offering discounts and special offers.

of Pong on an interactive billboard to win coupons. Retailing View 15.3 describes another innovative use of mobile marketing.

The RedLaser shopping comparison application takes a picture of a product's barcode and lists the prices for that item at various local retailers. Google Shopper has the same capability for Android. NearbyNow and Amazon's mobile applications allow users to buy products and complete their transactions though their cellphones.

Foursquare and WeReward target mobile phone users and send them marketing messages on the basis of GPS technology. Started by a video game aficionado, Foursquare awards points to consumers who try local retailers, enabling them to unlock "badges" and earn titles, such as "Mayor" of a particular venue.[15] The badges and titles entitle the recipient to discounts or special offers. For example, Starbucks Mayors can unlock their offers to get a $1 discount on a Frappuccino.[16] The application is based on GPS locations, so users can recommend nearby retailers to friends in the area. Furthermore, the application's data analytics capabilities allow retailers to track the impact of mobile marketing campaigns.

Tim Hortons' *Chill to Win* contest was an online contest with two ways to play for a chance to win prizes. On the game cup

exhibit 15–2   Interest in Mobile Advertising

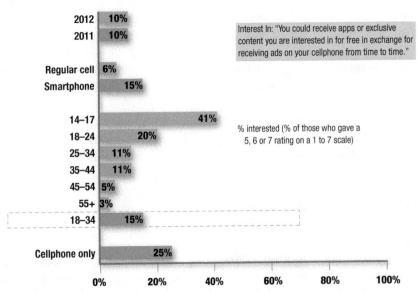

Interest In: "You could receive apps or exclusive content you are interested in for free in exchange for receiving ads on your cellphone from time to time."

% interested (% of those who gave a 5, 6 or 7 rating on a 1 to 7 scale)

- One in ten mobile phone owners (10%) would be interested in receiving apps or exclusive content in exchange for receiving ads on their device.

- Once again, interest decreases with age. Interest is highest among mobile owners between 14 and 17 years old (41%) and lingers at roughly 3% among those at least 55 years old.

- Interest is also higher among smartphone owners (15%), and residents of Ontario (12%) and the Atlantic provinces (14%).

- Interest is moderate at best among respondents 18 to 34 years old (15%).

Source: Quorus Consulting Group, *2012 Cell Phone Consumer Attitudes Study*, April 23, 2012, p. 26, http://cwta.ca/wordpress/wp-content/uploads/2011/08/CWTA-2012ConsumerAttitudes.pdf (accessed June 1, 2013).

Sportsgirl

Sportsgirl is an Australian multichannel fashion retailer that has utilized QR codes in its most recent digital strategy, creatively dubbed "Window Shop." Customers can make immediate purchases via their mobile devices (smartphone or tablet) by scanning the QR code on the Sportsgirl products that are displayed on the storefront's window. Sportsgirl updates the window weekly to feature the latest styles, creating a 24/7 shopping experience. All orders made via the QR codes are rewarded with a gift that is sent with the purchased product. According to the retailier, the aim of the Window Shop program is to bring Sportsgirl's superflagship-store product to all areas, providing greater choice for customers nationwide.

Source: Samantha Youl, "Sportsgirl Introduces Innovative QR Code Feature," *PowerRetail*, February 22, 2012, http://www.powerretail.com.au/multichannel/sportsgirl-qr-code-feature/#ixzz2VRqSmBJh (accessed June 1, 2013).

was a label, which contained an alphanumeric code (PIN code). This PIN code could be played at the Peel 'n' Play online game at www.chilltowin.com or on the customer's mobile device (smartphone or tablet) at m.chilltowin.com.

The foundation of mobile marketing is short codes, which were introduced in Canada in July 2003.[17] Short codes allow consumers to interact with retailers via text messaging. Instead of sending text messages to the regular ten-digit phone number, cellphone users send it to a short code, a five- or six-digit number or word/brand name. A short code becomes a *common short code (CSC)* when the same code is activated across multiple mobile phone networks, which greatly extends its reach to many more mobile phone customers.[18] Retailers can lease dedicated short codes for a period of three, six, or twelve months. Cost varies for *random short codes* (completely random in selection) and *selected short codes* (specifically requested codes). For example, Victoria's Secret uses a selected short code, text "start" to ANGEL (26435) and expect exclusive discounts via text message from the retailer. Canadian Tire uses a random short code for its Jumpstart mobile donation campaign: "Help Canadian Tire Jumpstart give kids a sporting chance! Donate by mobile phone today by simply texting the word JUMP to short-code 45678 and a $5 dollar donation will be on its way to the kids and added to your phone bill." Exhibit 15–3 graphs the increased usage of short code texting.

QR (quick response) codes are a specialized version of a two-dimensional (2D) barcode.[19] QR codes are intended to be scanned by the camera on a mobile phone, providing a fast and easy way to transfer information.[20] There are several different types of 2D barcodes, but the two most used by retailers are the QR code format and Microsoft Tag format. The Microsoft Tag works only with readers provided by Microsoft, and although it is currently free to create, there is no guarantee that it will always be free. QR codes have no licensing restrictions—so they will always be free—and are supported by a variety of readers.[21]

Retailers use QR codes in a variety of ways: product information, app-based user perks, discounts, sweepstakes, incentives, endorsement of the retail brand, check-in, instructions, sharing via social media, price comparison, and direct online shopping. Some QR codes

short code
A five- or six-digit number or word used for messaging.

QR code

Microsoft Tag

exhibit 15-3   Use of Short Code Texting

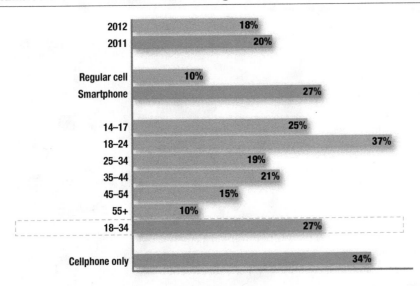

- Similar to 2011, one in five mobile phone users (18%) have sent or received a text message from an organization in the past.
- Just over one-quarter of mobile phone users (27%) between 18 and 34 have used short code texting this way in the past.
- Mobile users more likely to have used short code texting in the past are.
  - Smartphone owners (27%)
  - Cellphone only households (34%)
  - Those between 18 and 24 years old (37%)

% who have sent or received a text message from an organization

	Gender		Region					
	Male	**Female**	**BC**	**AB**	**MB/SK**	**ON**	**QC**	**ATL**
Have sent or received a text message from an organization	19%	17%	17%	19%	14%	16%	21%	22%

Source: Quorus Consulting Group, *2012 Cell Phone Consumer Attitudes Study*, April 23, 2012, p. 51, http://cwta.ca/wordpress/wp-content/uploads/2011/08/CWTA-2012ConsumerAttitudes.pdf (accessed June 1, 2013).

showrooming
Visiting a bricks-and-mortar store to research a product before purchasing it through electronic means after browsing online for the best price.

are even linked to store inventories and can tell you the quantity, size, and colour currently in stock of the product scanned.[22]

Customers can use the QR reader on their smartphones to get detailed information about the product they are considering. They can read consumer reviews, compare features with similar products, and in some cases, even e-mail details to a friend who might be giving advice.[23] Many stores have designed their own smartphone apps. While signs could just publicize the apps, the QR codes make it quick and easy to acquire the app. In many cases, these apps go beyond just providing product information and include styling advice, loyalty programs, social media, or check-in incentives and location-based discounts.[24]

Incentivizing consumers to interact with the brand using a mobile phone by offering discounts, special offers, and opportunities to win prizes or gifts with purchase with a QR code not only promotes reciprocity but also enables the transaction to occur in one step. (See Exhibit 15–4 for survey data about using smartphones to make purchases.) Stores use QR codes to connect to social media by sharing, as well as by checking in on sites such as Foursquare and Facebook. A check-in explicitly

endorses a product or retail brand to those connected to a user's profile. QR codes are also showing up in-store on shelf-talkers and price tags. QR codes provide the opportunity to add much more technical data than can fit on a retail package or tag. Best Buy uses QR codes to link the user to a specific mobile-optimized page for the product, while Sephora uses QR codes to offer demonstrations and instructions for cosmetics. Videos of this nature can also engage the consumer if a salesperson is not available for immediate assistance.[25]

According to a recent ClickIQ survey of 900 shoppers, half of all people who purchase products online first go to a bricks-and-mortar store to do their research.[26] Known as **showrooming**, this buzzword refers to the growing number of customers who browse the wares of traditional bricks-and-mortar retailers; feel, touch, and smell the merchandise; and then take out their smartphones and price around until they find the product they want for the lowest price—usually from an online retailer such as Amazon that doesn't have anywhere near the same overhead.[27] This trend makes it critical for retailers to provide an integrated shopping experience across multiple touchpoints through the path to purchase in order to maintain customers' loyalty to the brand and its products and services. Retailers can harness QR code technology to add value for consumers

exhibit 15–4   Interest in Mobile Payments

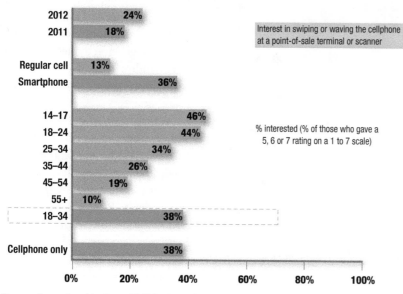

Interest in swiping or waving the cellphone at a point-of-sale terminal or scanner

2012	24%
2011	18%
Regular cell	13%
Smartphone	36%
14–17	46%
18–24	44%
25–34	34%
35–44	26%
45–54	19%
55+	10%
18–34	38%
Cellphone only	38%

% interested (% of those who gave a 5, 6 or 7 rating on a 1 to 7 scale)

- Almost one in four (24%) cellphone users are interested in the idea of swiping or waving their cellphone at a point-of-sale terminal or scanner. Interest in mobile payments increased significantly from 18% in 2011 to 24% in 2012.
- Nearly 4 in 10 respondents between 18 and 34 years old (38%) are interested in swiping or waving their phone for a purchase, a significant increase from 2011 (27%).
- Those more likely to be interested include:
  – Cellphone only households (38%)
  – Smartphone users (36%)
  – Men (29%)
  – Residents in BC and in Atlantic Canada (30%)
  – The younger respondents are, the more likely they are to be interested in this idea.

Source: Quorus Consulting Group, *2012 Cell Phone Consumer Attitudes Study*, April 23, 2012, p. 30, http://cwta.ca/wordpress/wp-content/uploads/2011/08/CWTA-2012ConsumerAttitudes.pdf (accessed June 1, 2013).

and harness showrooming to impact their revenue, as in the following examples:[28]

- **Cross-sell.** A consumer can scan a QR code for a TV, and instantly receive a promotion for a free HDMI cable with the purchase of the TV in-store.

- **Bundling.** If consumers scan multiple QR codes during a single in-store visit, they could receive an offer for a gift card if a specific set of products or dollar amount is purchased in the store during that store visit.

- **Behavioural.** A consumer that has scanned a QR code for a particular product type on a previous visit could trigger an alert if they scan a product in that product group during a subsequent visit. The alert could inform the customer that a brand within that product group is on sale.

- **Location/time specific.** Location data could be passed on if available to show exclusive deals only available at a specific store location, or content could be changed based on the time of day or weather.

- **Endless aisle.** Scanning a QR code for a jacket could provide a list of alternative sizes and colours that aren't stocked in that store. The consumer could then be offered the option of ordering the version she wants with just a few clicks on her smartphone or tablet and have it delivered to the store or her home.

In June 2013, Walmart Canada introduced mobile stores inside 50 bus shelters in the city of Toronto. Customers can use their mobile devices to scan posters with QR codes at these choice bus shelters to buy select items, including Pantene shampoo, Pampers diapers, and Tide detergent. The campaign was scheduled to run for four weeks and, according to Simon Rodrique, vice president of e-commerce for Walmart Canada, "allow[ed] [Walmart] to help Torontonians shop for essentials on the go, anywhere, at any time."[29]

Mobile shopping via smartphone is still in its infancy but is gaining traction with consumers. It is set to grow by around 40 percent year over year until around 2016.[30] Some larger retailers utilizing mobile in their communication strategies have reported significant rises in market share of mobile commerce transactions starting around the latter half of 2012. Add to that fact that people are spending more and more time on mobile apps (approximately 70 percent of smartphone users have downloaded apps to their phones[31]), and that there will be an estimated 10 billion mobile, Internet-enabled devices being used around the world by 2016,[32] and it is no surprise that retailers are embracing this as a method of communication (see Exhibit 15–5).

exhibit 15–5   Smartphone Shopping Adoption by Store Category

Smartphone Shopping Adoption by Store Category		Frequency of Use by Store	Mobile Influence Factor (2012)	Projected Influence Factor (2016)
Electronic/Appliances	49%	60.9%	8.3%	29.4%–33.7%
GM/Department/Warehouse	46%	52.5%	6.7%	23.8%–27.2%
Clothing/Footware	38%	56.2%	5.9%	21.1%–24.1%
Food/Beverage	35%	58.2%	5.7%	18.7%–23.0%
Books and Music	33%	57.1%	5.2%	17.3%–21.3%
Home Improvement/Garden	31%	53.5%	4.6%	15.2%–18.7%
Sporting Goods, Toys, Hobby	30%	56.7%	4.7%	15.6%–19.2%
Health/Personal Care/Drug	27%	58.4%	4.4%	14.5%–17.8%
Furniture/Home Furnishing	24%	58.7%	3.9%	12.9%–15.9%
Misc Including Office Supplies	22%	51.1%	3.1%	10.3%–12.7%
Convenience/Gas Station	19%	56.0%	3.0%	8.5%–11.2%
Weighted Average			**5.1%**	**17.2%–20.6%**

Note: The base for "Smartphone Shopping Adoption by Store Category" is survey respondents that own a smartphone and have ever used it to shop, either before they go to a store or in the store. The "Mobile Influence Factor" applies to all store sales in that category.

Source: Deloitte Development, *The Dawn of Mobile Influence: Discovering the value of mobile in retail*, 2012, p. 5, www.deloitte.com/assets/Dcom-UnitedStates/Local%20Assets/Documents/RetailDistribution/us_retail_Mobile-Influence-Factor_062712.pdf (accessed January 13, 2014).

blog   A public website where users post informal journals of their thoughts, comments, and philosophies; also called *weblog*.

social media   Media content distributed through social interactions; major online facilitators of social media include YouTube, Facebook, and Twitter.

Online Marketing

Websites   Retailers are increasing their emphasis on communicating with customers through their websites. Retailers use their websites to build their brand images; to inform customers of store locations, special events, and the availability of merchandise in local stores; and to sell merchandise and services.

In addition, some retailers provide services that help garner customer loyalty and indirectly increase sales. Office Depot's website, for example, has a business resource centre that provides advice and product knowledge, as well as a list of links to other businesses. By providing this information, Office Depot reinforces its image as the essential source of products, services, and information for small business.

Other retailers devote areas of their websites to community building. These sites offer an opportunity for customers with similar interests to learn about products and services that support their hobbies and to share information with others. Visitors to these websites can also post questions seeking information and/or comments about issues, products, and services. For example, Mountain Equipment Co-op (MEC), an outdoor apparel and equipment retailer, offers planning resources for hiking trips, bike tours, paddling, adventure travel, and other trips. By doing so, MEC creates a community of customers who engage in activities using the merchandise that MEC sells. The community thus reinforces MEC's brand image.

Many retailers also encourage customers to post reviews of products they have bought or used, and they even have visitors to their websites rate the quality of the reviews. Research has shown that these online product reviews increase customer loyalty and provide a competitive advantage for sites that offer them.

Blogs   A blog (also called *weblog*) contains periodic posts on a common web page. A well-received blog can communicate trends, announce special events, and create word-of-mouth, which is communication between people about a retailer.[33] Blogs connect customers by forming a community, allow the company to respond directly to customers' comments, and facilitate long-term relationships between customers and the company. By their very nature, blogs are supposed to be transparent and contain authors' honest observations, which can help customers determine their trust and loyalty levels. Nowadays, blogs are becoming more interactive as the communication between bloggers and customers has increased.

Many retailers utilize blogs as part of their communication strategy. A top-ranked retailer blog is Omnivoracious, Amazon's blog, which is, naturally, all about books. Dell, Apple, Sears, Best Buy, Lululemon, and QVC also have highly rated blogs.[34] Scan the QR code (right) to visit Lululemon's blog (http://blog.lululemon.com).

Social Media   Social media is media content distributed through social interactions. Social media leverage requires a good communication strategy coupled with appropriate content to reach out to the correct target audience and achieve the goals set out. Social media is not advertising; although it sounds simple and easy, social media is not easy and requires time and effort to make it useful. Content for social media platforms has to be engaging for online users or they will not be interested. Additionally, it has to come across as unbiased and focus on bringing out the best of the product and/or service rather than emphasizing the brand or retailer.[35]

Four major online facilitators of social media for retailers are YouTube, Facebook, Pinterest, and Twitter. As another online vehicle for word-of-mouth communication, online social media enable consumers to review, communicate about, and aggregate information about products, prices, and promotions. This type of social media also allows users to interact among themselves (e.g., form a community). Such online communities enable users to provide other like-minded consumers and retailers with their thoughts and evaluations about a retailer's products or services. A major benefit of social media is to have your customers share with their contacts, as 90 percent of consumers trust peer recommendations with only 10 percent trusting advertising.[36]

Retailers are using social media to engage their customers in a proactive dialogue. When a retailer provides content in social media, people often begin sharing and commenting on it. The retailer then must monitor the feedback and respond if necessary—especially if the commentary is negative. When a retailer finds an unhappy customer, it should recognize the event as a prime customer experience opportunity, engage the consumer, and attempt to remedy the situation. By proactively engaging with its customers, a retailer can build stronger relationships. Furthermore, retailers can help cultivate their images through social media that depict them in a certain way, adding a human element that otherwise might not exist.

The social networking site Shopstyle.com features clothing and accessories from hundreds of Internet stores. Shoppers can browse different looks that feature items across several retailers, put together outfits on their own, and then share and discuss with friends.

Not all social media have positive results though.[37] Social media eliminate boundaries, often exposing companies to customers' true (and sometimes mean) thoughts and behaviours. Consider the situation in which Kevin Smith, the popular director of films such as *Clerks* and *Dogma* and the actor who played Silent Bob in several of his movies, was removed from a Southwest Airlines flight because his large size required him to purchase two seats. Smith immediately tweeted about the situation to his more than 1.6 million Twitter followers. Then

Home Depot fosters its identity with instructional do-it-yourself videos on YouTube.

when he got onto another flight, he followed up with a picture of himself, proclaiming "Southwest Air! Look how fat I am on your plane! Quick! Throw me off!" Southwest quickly responded on its blog (scan the QR code in the opposite column), citing its

longstanding rules and concern for other passengers. But other responses have been equally split in support of the airline and Smith.[38]

YouTube   On this video-sharing social media platform, users upload, share, and view videos. This medium gives retailers a chance to express themselves in a different way than they have before. A retailer like television home shopping network HSN can broadcast its own channel, that is, a YouTube portal that contains content relevant only to the company's own products.[39] YouTube also provides an effective medium for hosting contests and posting instructional videos. Home Depot attracts more than 4400 viewers per day with an array of videos detailing new products available in stores, as well as instructional-do-it-yourself videos, such as "How to Tips for Mowing Your Lawn" and "How to Repair a Toilet."[40] These videos (scan the QR code [right] to visit Home Depot's YouTube portal) maintain the core identity of the Home Depot brand while also adding value for consumers, who learn useful ways to improve their homes.

Facebook   This social media platform with more than a billion active users gives companies a forum to interact with fans (see Exhibit 15–6). Retailers have access to the same features that regular users do, including a "wall" where they can post company updates, photos, and videos or participate in a discussion board.

An excellent example of a fan page is that of the discount clothing retailer Forever 21.[41] When a fan clicks to indicate that he or she "likes" a certain post, the message gets relayed into a news feed, so every friend of that user

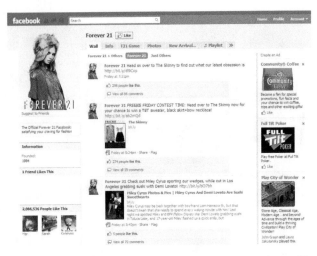

Retailers like Forever 21 are utilizing Facebook to communicate with its customers and create a sense of community.

sees what he or she likes, creating a huge multiplier effect.[42] Accordingly, marketers must consistently update and maintain their fan pages to exploit them as the tremendous assets they can be.

Twitter This microblogging site, in which users are limited to 140-character messages, is also a platform to facilitate communication using social media. Twitter provides another option for retailers and their customers to communicate using social media. Twitter has more than 228 million monthly active users (see Exhibit 15–7).

Twitter is actively used by both small and large retailers. Small retailers with limited marketing budgets love the immediate response they can induce by sending a promotional message. A local bakery tweets, "Two new scones: Lemon Blueberry and Chorizo Cheddar!" and gets responses from 400 Twitter followers—a huge captive audience for a local entity. Large retailers that have enough funds to mass-market through national campaigns use Twitter as a way to stay in personal touch with their customers. For instance, Best Buy (@BestBuy) tweets in-store deals to its followers: "Save $1000 on this LG washer + dryer pair: http://bbyurl.us/tgg Limited time only, in store only! via @BestBuy_deals." Walmart Canada offers many Twitter options to its customers, such as updates on food recipes and entertaining, as well as news from metropolitan areas and individual stores. For instance, Marc Angelo Foods (@MarcAngeloFoods) tweets "Are you shopping at the @walmartcanada location in Cambridge? Store 3152 is giving out free samples of our Marc Angelo products!" Retailing View 15.4 has an example of one retailer's effective use of Twitter.

Pinterest Pinterest is an online pinboard-style image-sharing website that is entirely driven by visuals. Users can share images found online, or they can directly upload images onto Pinterest. Using the Pin It button, users can share directly in their browser from any web page and can also share their pins on Twitter and Facebook. Research shows that 80 percent of all pins are re-pins, which means only 20 percent are original pins.[43] Globally, the site is most popular with women. In 2012, it was reported that 83 percent of the global users were women,[44] and in February 2013, Reuters and ComScore stated that Pinterest had 48.7 million users.[45] The average time spent on the site by users is 98 minutes per month (see Exhibit 15–8).

---

exhibit 15–6 Facebook

Total number of Facebook users: 1.26 billion

Total number of Facebook monthly active users: 1.19 billion

Total number of Facebook daily active users: 728 million

Percentage of millennials (15- to 34-year-olds) that use Facebook: 66%

Number of times daily that the Facebook Like or Share buttons are viewed: 22 billion

Eighty percent of social media users prefer to connect with brands through Facebook.

Country with most active Facebook users: Canada

More than half of all Canadians log onto Facebook at least once per month.

More than half of all Canadians log onto Facebook at least once per month.

On average, 61 percent of global users check Facebook at least once a day. In the U.S. 70 percent of them do; in Canada, it's 74 percent.

Pages with the most Canadian Likes: eminem, Tim Hortons, Family Guy, YouTube, and The Simpsons

Top brands by Likes: Tim Hortons, Subway, Skittles, Target Canada, and iTunes

A whopping 77 percent of B2C companies and 43 percent of B2B companies acquired customers from Facebook.

Seventy-four percent of marketers believe Facebook is important for their lead generation.

Sources: Jennifer Wadsworth, "Canadians are the most active Facebook users in the world," InsideFacebook.com, August 23, 2013, www.insidefacebook.com/2013/08/23/canadians-still-the-most-active-facebook-users-in-the-world; Ray C. He, "Introducing new Like and Share buttons," Facebook Developer blog, November 6, 2013, https://developers.facebook.com/blog/post/2013/11/06/introducing-new-like-and-share-buttons; Brian Honigman, "100 Fascinating Social Media Statistics and Figures From 2012," *The Huffington Post,* November 29, 2012, www.huffingtonpost.com/brian-honigman/100-fascinating-social-me_b_2185281.html?; Michael Stelzner, 2013 *Social Media Marketing Industry Report,* Social Media Examiner blog, May 21, 2013, www.socialmediaexaminer.com/social-media-marketing-industry-report-2013; Craig Smith, "By the Numbers: 64 Amazing Facebook User Statistics," Digital Marketing Ramblings blog, December 28, 2013, http://expandedramblings.com/index.php/by-the-numbers-17-amazing-facebook-stats/#.UtQ-6NK1yM4; Jeff Bullas, "46 Amazing Social Media Facts in 2013," October 25, 2013, www.jeffbullas.com/2013/10/25/46-amazing-social-media-facts-in-2013/#IAcpwvTuqjwz8bAc.99 (all accessed January 13, 2014).

exhibit 15–7 Twitter

There are over 500 million total Twitter users.

There are over 288 million active monthly Twitter users.

On average, over 400 million tweets are sent per day.

Fifty-six percent of customer tweets to companies are being ignored.

Thirty-two percent of all Internet users are using Twitter.

The most followed brand on Twitter is YouTube, with 19 million followers.

Eleven accounts are created every second on Twitter.

Sixty percent of Twitter users are using the social network via mobile.

Thirty-four percent of marketers have generated leads using Twitter.

Twitter's fastest growing age demographic is 55- to 64-year-olds with active users at 79 percent.

Twenty-nine percent of under 35s use Twitter and 17 percent plan to start.

The average millennial (15- to 34-year-olds) uses 2.5 social networks, with Facebook (66 percent), Twitter (29 percent), and Google+ (28 percent) the most popular.

Sources: Jeff Bullas, "46 Amazing Social Media Facts in 2013," October 25, 2013, www.jeffbullas.com/2013/10/25/46-amazing-social-media-facts-in-2013/ #IAcpwvTuqjwz8bAc.99; "Twitter 2012," Sirona Consulting blog, http://blog.sironaconsulting.com/.a/6a00d8341c761a53ef016767bafa2c970b-pi; Shea Bennett, "Why First Class Customer Service Is the Key to Social Media Success," AllTwitter blog, May 24, 2012, http://www.mediabistro.com/alltwitter/social-key-customer-service_b23050; Matt McGee, "Social Network Demographics: Pew Study Shows Who Uses Facebook, Twitter, Pinterest & Others," MarketingLand.com, September 14, 2012, http://marketingland.com/ social-network-demographics-pew-study-shows-who-uses-facebook-twitter-pinterest-others-21594; Holly Richmond, "The Growth of Mobile Marketing and Tagging," Microsoft Tag, March 21, 2011, http://tag.microsoft.com/community/blog/t/the_growth_of_mobile_marketing_and_tagging.aspx; "Infographic: Social Media Statistics for 2012," DigitalBuzz blog, January 3, 2012, www.digitalbuzzblog.com/social-media-statistics-stats-2012-infographic/ (all accessed January 13, 2014).

This social media site offers retailers and their brands an effective visual communication platform. Jewellery and accessories website Boticca.com, which was co-founded by former eBay and private equity executives, compared 50 000 shoppers referred from Pinterest to 50 000 shoppers referred from Facebook and said the Pinterest users spent way more money—$185 versus $85—but less time browsing the site.[46] While both Pinterest and Facebook are social media sites consumers visit to connect with people who have similar styles and interests, Pinterest is more often a destination for shopping inspiration, tracking, and product discovery. Forty-three percent of Pinterest members agree that they use Pinterest to "associate with retailers or brands with which

---

15.4 | **RETAILING VIEW**

KFC: The Power of a Single Tweet

With 2.5 million college scholarships awarded every year in the U.S., KFC knew it had to cook up something innovative to stir buzz around the brand's 75-scholarship Colonel's Scholars program. That's why KFC and Weber-Shandwick decided to do away with the tired old college scholarship essay and award a $20 000 scholarship based solely on a single tweet. Students had just 140 characters (including the hashtag #KFCScholar) to convince KFC execs why they deserved a scholarship.

Announced via a *USA Today* story, the scholarship tweet campaign generated more than 1000 media placements and tens of millions of media impressions, including two AP wire stories and multiple stories on CNN Headline News, MSNBC, The Weather Channel, and NBC national news. The program also captivated the online world, generating more than 9 million social media impressions as a result of tweets during the brief entry period. In all, more than 2800 applicants tweeted for their chance at $20 000, and the KFC Twitter handle saw a 20 percent jump in followers in just two weeks.

One of those followers was 17-year-old Amanda Russell, whose tweet, "Hey Colonel! Your scholarship's the secret ingredient missing from my recipe for success! Got the grades, drive, just need cash!" scored her the $20 000 college scholarship.

Source: Leyl Master Black, "5 Smart Social Campaigns to Learn From," Mashable.com, March 8, 2011, http://mashable.com/2011/03/08/ social-pr-campaigns/ (accessed January 14, 2014).

exhibit 15–8   Pinterest

Pinterest's three most popular pins: Hasselback Garlic Cheesy Bread Recipe, Rainbow Fruit Kabobs Photo, and Lovely Framing Compositions.

Percentage of shares by content: fashion, 10%; parenting, 16%; food, 18%

People share with Pinterest three times more often on mobile than on a computer.

Ninety-seven percent of the fans of Pinterest's Facebook page are women.

Over 80 percent of pins are re-pins.

Eighty percent of Pinterest users are women (66 percent in Canada), while 50 percent of all Pinterest users have children (38 percent in Canada).

Thirty-five percent of Canadian Pinterest users have a household income of over $100 000 per year.

Canada is the second-largest country of Pinterest users, following the United States.

Pinterest referrals spend 70 percent more money than visitors referred from non-social channels.

The average Pinterest user spends 98 minutes per month on the site, compared to 2.5 hours on Tumblr and 7 hours on Facebook.

Sixty-nine percent of online consumers who visit Pinterest have found an item they've bought or wanted to buy, compared with 40 percent of Facebook users.

The most popular age group on Pinterest is 25- to 34-year-olds.

Forty-three percent of people prefer Pinterest to associate with retailers or brands; 24 percent chose Facebook.

Nine percent of people have participated in contests or promotions via Pinterest.

iPads are the Pinterest user's device of choice.

Pinterest

Sources: Bob Gilbreath, "New Data Insights on Pinterest's Potential," MarketingLand.com, August 16, 2013, http://marketingland.com/new-data-insights-on-pinterests-potential-52323; "Infographic: All About How People Share on Pinterest," MarketingLand.com, October 25, 2013, http://marketingland.com/infographic-how-people-share-on-pinterest-63052; "How popular is pinterest.com?" Alexa.com, n.d., http://www.alexa.com/siteinfo/pinterest.com#demographics; "Pinterest Demographics," Cahoots blog, March 21, 2013, http://cahootsblog.com/2013/03/21/pinterest-demographics/; "Facts Tagged with Pinterest," FactBrowser.com, n.d., http://www.factbrowser.com/tags/pinterest/; Catharine Smith, "Pinterest's 15 Most Popular Pins of All Time," The Huffington Post, April 17, 2012, http://www.huffingtonpost.com/2012/04/17/pinterest-most-popular-pins_n_1431564.html; "Infographic: How Users Interact on Pinterest," Wishpond blog, n.d., http://blog.wishpond.com/post/44155339712/infographic-how-users-interact-on-pinterest; Brian Honigman, "100 Fascinating Social Media Statistics and Figures From 2012," The Huffington Post, November 29, 2012, www.huffingtonpost.com/brian-honigman/100-fascinating-social-me_b_2185281.html? (all accessed January 13, 2014).

sales promotions
Paid, impersonal communication activities that offer extra value and incentives to customers to visit a store or purchase merchandise during a specific period of time.

[they] identify." A greater percentage (55 percent) of Pinterest users have engaged with retailers and brands via Pinterest, compared to the percentage of Facebook users that engage retailers or brands on Facebook (48 percent). But how customers engage differs for each of the two social media platforms. Pinterest users are more likely to be "creators"—adding and sharing retailer/brand-related content—while Facebook users are more likely to be "participators"—interacting with promotional activities developed by retailers and brands.[47]

When Sephora, the beauty products retailer, revamped its website in April 2012, it was one of the first retailers to integrate the Pin It button throughout the site. Sephora coordinated the introduction of Pin It buttons with its "Paint the Town Sweepstakes" campaign. The company invited consumers to pin their beauty shopping lists. Pinners participating in the campaign were encouraged to re-pin the post on Sephora Sweepstakes Pinterest logo board in order to win one of ten Sephora by OPI Tinsel Town Collector's sets. With only 12 original pins, Sephora Sweepstakes pinboard gained nearly 100 000 followers and 8415 users re-pinned the post.[48] Within a few short months, Pinterest became a top ten referring site for Sephora.com. Sephora's head of digital, Julie Bornstein, told *VentureBeat* in an interview that Pinterest members spent 15 times more on the company's products than Facebook fans.[49] Sephora uses its "Trending Now" board on Pinterest to showcase its newest products. Hashtags tie new products to a specific campaign, and all products lead back to its e-commerce site. Further, Sephora invites participation by asking fans/followers to upload their own tagged photos, which then exposes the product collection to new audiences.

Sales Promotions

Sales promotions are special incentives or excitement-building programs that encourage consumers to purchase a particular product or service; they are typically used in conjunction with other advertising or personal selling programs. Like personal selling and telemarketing, sales promotions are a form of offline/interactive communications (Exhibit 15–1). Many sales promotions, such as free samples or point-of-purchase (POP) displays, attempt to build short-term sales; others, such as loyalty programs, contests, and sweepstakes, have become integral components of retailers' long-term customer relationship management (CRM) programs, which they use to build customer loyalty. The tools used in sales promotions, along with their advantages and disadvantages, are presented in Exhibit 15–9 and discussed below.

exhibit 15-9 Types of Sales Promotions

Promotion	Advantages	Disadvantages
Coupons	• Stimulate demand • Allow for direct tracing of sales	• Have low redemption rates • Have high cost
Rebates	• Stimulate demand • Increase value perception	• Are easily copied by competitors • May just advance future sales
Premiums (price or award)	• Build goodwill • Increase perception of value	• Consumers buy for premium, not product • Have to be carefully managed
Samples	• Encourage trial • Offer direct involvement	• Have high cost to the firm
POP displays	• Provide high visibility • Encourage brand trial	• Can be difficult to get a good location in the store • Can be costly to the firm
Special events	• Generate excitement and traffic	• Can be costly • Can distract customers from purchasing during the event
Pop-up stores	• Generate customer interest • Open up new markets and market segments	• Have high cost • Must hire store personnel • May take sales away from other company-owned stores

Coupons Coupons offer a discount on the price of specific items when they're purchased. Coupons are issued by manufacturers and retailers in newspapers, on products, on the shelf, at the cash register, over the Internet, and through the mail. Retailers use coupons because they are thought to induce customers to try products for the first time, convert first-time users to regular users, encourage large purchases, increase usage, and protect market share against competition. Some retailers have linked coupons directly to their loyalty programs. Drugstore giant Shoppers Drug Mart, for instance, tracks its customers' purchases from its Optimum loyalty card and gives them coupons that are tailored just for them.

Coupon promotions, like all temporary promotions, may be stealing sales from a future period without any net increase in sales. For instance, if a supermarket runs a coupon promotion on sugar, households may buy a large quantity of sugar and stockpile it for future use. Thus, unless the coupon is used mostly by new buyers, the net impact on sale is negligible, and there will be a negative impact on profits due to the amount of redeemed coupons and cost of the coupon redemption procedures.

Christine (aka Coupon Christine) is passionate about couponing and saving money. With sold-out workshops across her hometown of London, Ontario, and a growing couponing Facebook group, she's helping others become passionate about saving money using coupons.

Coupons may annoy, alienate, and confuse consumers and therefore do little to increase store loyalty.

Some stores, such as Loblaw retailers, are making coupons more effective by customizing coupon content to alter customers' purchasing habits. For instance, if a customer typically spends a small amount during each shopping trip, the customer will receive coupons that encourage larger purchases, such as "buy one, get one free." If another customer spends a lot each time she shops but shops sporadically, that customer will get coupons that expire relatively quickly. Unique coupons will also encourage customers to try new brands within categories that they normally purchase, or products that complement their usual purchases, such as shampoo to customers that purchase hair colour.[50]

Shopping bot sites, such as MyCoupons.com, provide customers with a large selection of coupons by bringing all the coupons available throughout the Internet onto one website. For instance, a customer might go to Target and find a KitchenAid mixer for $199.99. A cellphone scan of the bar code through ShopSavvy.com might find the same item at Walmart, which is a kilometre away, for $179.99. Then the customer might visit MyCoupons.com and see that Walmart is offering a $20 coupon, thus saving the customer $40 in a matter of minutes. Scan the QR code below to check out Checkout 51, which combines coupon-style savings with mobile technology to allow shoppers to accumulate savings and request money back.

A new breed of coupon, printed from the Internet or sent to or accessed via mobile phones, is packed with information about the customer who uses it. While the coupons look standard, their bar codes can be loaded with

coupons Documents, electronic or hard copy, that entitle the holder to a reduced price or X cents off the actual price of a product or service.

rebates Money returned to the buyer in the form of cash based on a portion of the purchasing price.

premium A type of sales promotion whereby an item is offered free of charge or at a bargain price to reward some type of behaviour, such as buying, sampling, or testing.

samples A small amount or size of a product given to potential customers as an inducement to purchase.

point-of-purchase (POP) An area where the customer waits at checkout.

special event Sales promotion program comprising a number of sales promotion techniques built around a seasonal, cultural, sporting, musical, or other event.

pop-up stores Stores in temporary locations that focus on new products or a limited group of products.

a startling amount of data, including identification about the customer, Internet address, Facebook page information, and even the search terms the customer used to find the coupon in the first place. For instance, if a customer comes into a store with a coupon for T-shirts, the information on the coupon could reveal whether the customer was searching for "underwear" or "muscle shirts."

Rebates

Rebates provide another form of discounts for consumers off the final selling price. In this case, however, the manufacturer, instead of the retailer, issues the refund as a portion of the purchase price returned to the buyer in the form of cash. Retailers generally welcome rebates from vendors because they generate sales in the same way that coupons do but the retailers incur no handling costs.

Many products, such as consumer electronics, offer rebates that may lower the price of the item significantly. Some vendors enjoy the added exposure of appearing on consumer websites, such as PriceGrabber.com and Nextag.com, that sort products by price and then link the customer to the retailer's website. Vendors offer such generous rebates because the likelihood that consumers will actually apply for the rebate is low. Other firms, such as Staples and Apple, have simplified the rebate redemption process with "Easy Rebates" (scan the QR code [left]) and Apple.com/promo.[51]

Premiums

A **premium** offers an item for free or at a bargain price to reward some type of behaviour, such as buying, sampling, or testing. Such rewards build goodwill among consumers, who often perceive high value in them. Premiums can be distributed in a variety of ways: They can be included in the product packaging, such as the toys inside cereal boxes; placed visibly on the package, such as a coupon for free milk on a box of Cheerios; handed out in the store; or delivered in the mail, such as the free-perfume offers Victoria's Secret mails to customers.

Samples

Samples offer potential customers the opportunity to try a product or service before they make a buying decision. Distributing samples is one of the most costly sales promotion tools but also one of the most effective. Quick-service restaurants and grocery stores frequently utilize sampling. For instance, Loblaw, Sobeys, Metro, and Walmart all provide samples of products to customers. Costco uses so many samples that customers can have an entire meal.

Point-of-Purchase (POP) Displays

Point-of-purchase (POP) is a merchandise display that is located at the point of purchase, such as the checkout counter in a supermarket. Retailers have long recognized that the most valuable real estate in the store is at the POP. Customers see products like a magazine or a candy bar while they are waiting to pay for their items and impulsively purchase them. In the Internet version of point-of-purchase display, shoppers are stimulated by special merchandise, price reductions, or complementary products that Internet retailers feature on the checkout screen.

Special Events

A **special event** is a sales promotion program comprising a number of sales promotion techniques built around a seasonal, cultural, sporting, musical, or some other special event.[52] Special events can generate excitement and traffic to the store. Apparel and department stores do trunk shows, made-to-measure events, and fashion shows. Sporting goods stores do demonstration of equipment, while grocery stores might have cooking classes. Bookstores do readings and book signings. Car dealerships can have rallies or shows of new or vintage models. Even if the sales registered during the event aren't significant, the long-term effect can be quite beneficial.

Pop-Up Stores

An extreme type of sales promotion is a pop-up store. **Pop-up stores** are temporary storefronts that exist for only a limited time and generally focus on a new product or limited group of products offered by a retailer. They are also used by some retailers during the holiday season to increase exposure and convenience shopping for their customers without having to invest in a long-term lease.

Gucci, the Italian leather retailer and manufacturer, has opened pop-up stores named Gucci-Icon Temporary in New York's SoHo, Miami Beach, Tokyo, London, Berlin, Paris, and Hong Kong. The stores featured limited-edition sneakers retailing for $500 to $600, with classic Gucci design elements and some special features like a silver or gold dog tag.[53]

Although most sales promotions are effective at generating short-term interest among customers, they aren't very useful for building long-term loyalty. Customers who participate in a promotion might learn more about a store and return to it, but typically customers attracted by sales promotions are interested in the promoted merchandise, not the retailer. Unfortunately, when a specific promotion is effective for a retailer, competing retailers learn about it quickly and offer the same promotion, which prevents the innovating retailer from gaining any long-term advantage.

Personal Selling

Personal selling is a communication process in which sales associates help customers satisfy their needs through face-to-face exchanges of information. It is a form of offline/interactive communication (Exhibit 15–1). The cost of communicating directly with a potential customer is quite high compared with other forms of promotion, but it is simply the best and most efficient way to sell certain products and services. Customers can buy many products and services without the help of a salesperson, but salespeople simplify the buying process by providing information and services that save customers time and effort. In many cases, sales representatives add significant value, which makes the added expense of employing them worthwhile.

Advertising

Advertising entails the placement of announcements and persuasive messages purchased by retailers and other organizations that seek to inform and/or persuade members of a particular target market or audience about their products, services, organizations, or ideas.[54] Retailers are the largest group of national advertisers, spending almost $16 billion annually. McDonald's and Target are among the ten largest advertisers in the United States, each spending more than $1 billion a year.[55] Walmart dropped out of the list of top ten advertisers in 2011, spending 28.8 percent less than it did the previous year. In the U.S., the ten largest retail advertisers represent 23.9 percent of the share of U.S. sales and include Macy's, Target, Sears, Walmart, Home Depot, JCPenney, Best Buy, Lowe's, Kohl's, and Gap Inc.[56] Mass advertising can entice consumers into a conversation with retailers, although it does not necessarily require much action by consumers, which places it on the passive end of the spectrum. Traditionally, advertising has been passive and offline (e.g., ads on TV, in magazines, and in newspapers; Exhibit 15–1). However, recently there has been a growth in online advertising. This section reviews advertising's traditional media and examines a method of lowering the retailer's advertising cost through cooperative advertising with vendors.

Newspapers Retailing and newspaper advertising grew up together over the past century. But the growth in retail newspaper advertising has slowed recently as retailers have begun using other media. Still, 57 percent of newspapers' advertising dollars are generated by retailers.[57] In addition to displaying ads with their editorial content, newspapers distribute **freestanding inserts**. A freestanding insert (FSI), also called a *preprint*, is an advertisement printed at the retailer's expense and distributed as an insert in the newspaper. However, there are so many FSIs in some newspapers that readers can become overwhelmed. As a result, some retailers have reduced the number of FSIs they use because of the clutter and because young readers, who may be their primary target markets, don't regularly read newspapers.

Because newspapers are distributed in well-defined local market areas, they're effective at targeting specific retail markets. Newspapers also offer a quick response. There's only a short time between the deadline for receiving the advertisement and the time that the advertisement will appear. Thus, newspapers are useful for delivering messages on short notice.

Newspapers, like magazines, effectively convey a lot of detailed information. Readers can go through an advertisement at their own pace and refer to part of the advertisement when they want. But newspaper ads aren't effective for showing merchandise, particularly when it's important to illustrate colours, because of the poor reproduction quality.

The life of a newspaper advertisement is short because the newspaper is usually discarded after it has been read. In contrast, magazine advertising has a longer life because consumers tend to save magazines and read them several times during a week or month.

Finally, the cost of developing newspaper ads is relatively low. However, the cost of delivering the message may be high if the newspaper's circulation is broader than the retailer's target market, requiring the retailer to pay for exposure that won't generate sales. In a recent study conducted by the Newspaper Association of America (NAA) on how America shops and spends, findings clearly demonstrate the power of newspapers and news websites and the influence this media has on consumer purchasing and planning behaviours. Here are some of the insights and highlights from that study:[58]

- Six in ten consumers used newspapers in the past week to plan shopping and purchasing decisions.

- Eight in ten consumers took action on a newspaper insert (in the last 30 days), including comparison shopping, sharing with others, and taking it to purchase.

- Sixty-four percent of consumers use coupons from a newspaper versus 53 percent from direct mail.

personal selling
A communication process in which salespeople help customers satisfy their needs through face-to-face exchanges of information.

advertising Paid communications delivered to customers through nonpersonal mass media such as newspapers, television, radio, direct mail, and the Internet.

freestanding insert (FSI) An advertisement printed at the retailer's expense and distributed as an insert in the newspaper; also called a *preprint*.

Reflecting a shift in marketing dollars away from mass advertising, several major retailers (including Walmart and the LCBO) are publishing glossy magazines, providing advice on health, fashion, food, drink, and lifestyle, as a way to keep their best customers coming back.

- Newspaper website visitors are (compared to overall adults) 40 percent more likely to have purchased something online or in-store in the past 30 days, 62 percent more likely to go online for coupons, 79 percent more likely to use a mobile phone in a store to comparison shop, and 80 percent more likely to use a shopping app on a mobile device.

Magazines Advertising in national magazines is mostly done by national retailers such as Target and The Gap. With the growth of local magazines, regional editions of national magazines, and specialized magazines, local retailers can take advantage of this medium. Retailers tend to use this medium for image advertising because the reproduction quality is high. Due to the lead time—the time between submitting the advertisement and publication—a major disadvantage of magazine advertising is that the timing is difficult to coordinate with special events and sales.

In April 2013, Walmart Canada and Rogers Media Inc. launched the country's newest magazine, *Walmart Live Better*, a multi-platform lifestyle brand. Top Canadian editors and contributors, including *Walmart Live Better's* editor-in-chief, Sandra Martin, provide readers the latest trends and tips in food, home, beauty, and fashion. The magazine is available for free at Walmart Canada Supercentres in English Canada, and is also available in digital formats for online, mobile, and iPad users. With a press run of 1 million copies per issue, it automatically becomes Canada's largest circulation magazine, according to Rogers.[60]

Produced by the Custom Content division within Rogers Media, the print edition of *Walmart Live Better* will be published six times a year, while the website will be updated regularly with exclusive, added-value content. In addition to print and digital, readers can engage with the Walmart brand through social media properties such as Walmart's Facebook page, the Live Better Pinterest page, or Twitter.[61]

Television Television commercials can be placed on a national network or a local station. A local television commercial is called a spot. Retailers typically use TV for image advertising, to take advantage of the high production quality and the opportunity to communicate through both visual images and sound. Television ads can also demonstrate product usage. For example, TV is an excellent medium for car, furniture, and consumer electronics dealers.

In addition to its high production costs, broadcast time for national TV advertising is expensive. Spots have relatively small audiences, but they may be economical for local retailers. To offset the high production costs, many vendors provide modular commercials, in which the retailer can insert its name or a "tag" after information about the vendor's merchandise.

The average North American over the age of 2 spends more than 34 hours a week watching live television, says a recent Nielsen report, plus another three to six hours watching taped programs.[62]

Radio Many retailers use radio advertising because messages can be targeted to a specific segment of the market.[63] Some radio stations' audiences are highly loyal to their announcers. When these announcers promote a retailer, listeners are impressed. The cost of developing and broadcasting radio commercials is relatively low.

One disadvantage of radio advertising, however, is that listeners generally treat the radio broadcast as background, which limits the attention they give the message. Consumers must get the information from a radio commercial when it's broadcast, so they can't refer to the advertisement for information they didn't hear or remember. As we discuss in the Spotlight on Retailing vignette at the beginning of this chapter, Hudson's Bay tried to change that by using the popular audio-scanning mobile app Shazam to drive listeners to the retailer's website as the app recognizes special codes embedded into each radio spot.[64]

Co-op Programs Co-op advertising (or *cooperative advertising*) is a promotional program undertaken by a vendor and a retailer working together. The vendor pays for part of the retailer's advertising but dictates some conditions. For example, Macy's paid for 25 percent ($371 million) of its 2011 $1.5 billion total gross ad costs through cooperative advertising allowances from suppliers. The retailer gets co-op ad money from more than 1000 vendors.[65] In addition to lowering costs, co-op advertising enables a retailer to associate its name and well-known national brands and use attractive artwork created by national brands. Mattel's biggest customer is Walmart (19 percent of 2011 global sales), followed by Toys "R" Us (11 percent) and Target (8 percent). The toy marketer (Barbie, Fisher-Price) spent 11 percent of 2011 sales on ads and promotion.[66]

Co-op advertising has some drawbacks though. First, vendors want the ads to feature their products, whereas retailers are more interested in featuring their store's name, location, and assortment of merchandise and services offered. This conflict in goals can reduce the effectiveness of co-op advertising from the retailer's perspective. Second, ads developed by the vendor often are used by several competing retailers and may list the names and locations of all retailers offering their brands. Thus, co-op ads tend to blur distinctions between retailers. Third, restrictions that the vendor places on the ads may further reduce their effectiveness for the retailer. For example, the vendor may restrict advertising to a period of time when the vendor's sales are depressed, but the retailer might not normally be advertising during that time frame.

Outdoor Billboards

Billboards and other forms of outdoor advertising are effective vehicles for creating awareness and providing a very limited amount of information to a narrow audience. Thus, outdoor advertising has limited usefulness in providing information about sales. Outdoor advertising is typically used to remind customers about the retailer or to inform people in cars of nearby retail outlets.[67] La Senza used sexy images on billboards in the Toronto area to promote Christmas sales of lingerie.

Public Relations

Public relations (PR) involves managing communications and relationships to achieve various objectives, such as building and maintaining a positive image of the retailer, handling or heading off unfavourable stories or events, and maintaining positive relationships with the media. In many cases, public relations activities support other promotional efforts by generating "free" media attention and general goodwill. The practice of PR is no longer dominated by one-way communication that seeks to simply transfer content from the retailer to the consumer. Retailers are getting creative with their PR strategies in light of the opportunities social media offers them. Many retailers are now using social media platforms such as Twitter, Facebook, blogs, Pinterest and others to promote, inform, and give feedback to engage in two-way conversations with their customers.

Clothes retailer Kenneth Cole, in a bid to encourage sales, started a provocative campaign on its own site asking customers to make a stand on controversial topics such as war, gay marriage, and guns. In the same fashion, the campaign encouraged customers to buy clothes based on what they think they look good in among what they wear. From a public relations perspective, it can be said that the retailer is brave to align such deep, serious societal issues with the current trends and choice of clothes people choose to wear; the opposite can also be said, that the retailer is insensitive and repulsive to even push out a campaign like this. What made matters worse was a tweet during the Egypt riots that jokingly said that the uproar in Cairo was due to the new spring collection that Kenneth Cole was pushing out, essentially encouraging people to buy more clothes while people are dying in Egypt.[68]

For years, Walmart did little to promote itself as a positive social force, believing its low prices would speak for themselves. But it increasingly has been subjected to public criticism from labour unions and environmentalists, so Walmart hired its first public relations firm. The public relations firm set up a war room to respond quickly to attacks or adverse news. Internet blogs and grassroots initiatives were developed to stimulate popular support for Walmart. The firm also looked for proactive opportunities to demonstrate Walmart's social consciousness. For example, after the devastating earthquake in Haiti, Walmart contributed more than $1.5 million in direct financial support as well as in-kind contributions, such as prepackaged food kits, blankets, and face masks. In addition, through various in-store and online fundraising campaigns, Walmart associates and customers globally have contributed more than $3 million for the relief effort.[69]

Walmart Canada donated and raised an average of $485 000 every week of 2011 as the corporate sponsor for four national charity partners (Children's Miracle Network, Breakfast Clubs of Canada, Canadian Red Cross, and Evergreen) and in support of more than 1000 other community-directed charity grants, surpassing $160 million dollars since 1994.[70]

Retailers also benefit when celebrities wear their fashions. For instance, when photos were posted on the Internet of First Lady Michelle Obama wearing a J.Crew cream-coloured cardigan and "dazzling dots" skirt on a visit to a cancer centre in London, the retailer's website sold out almost immediately.[71] The placement of designer apparel at media events like the Oscars benefits the retailer, the designer, and the celebrity. And nothing happens by accident. Public relations people on both sides help orchestrate the events to get the maximum benefit for both parties.

Another very popular PR tool is event sponsorship. Event sponsorship occurs when corporations support various activities (financially or otherwise), usually in the

public relations (PR) A retail communication tool for managing communications and relationships to achieve various objectives, such as building and maintaining a positive image of the retailer, handling or heading off unfavourable stories or events, and maintaining positive relationships with the media.

	Charity/Event	2011 Total Contribution
Children's Health, Education and Safety	Children's Miracle Network	$8 827 318.01
	Breakfast Clubs of Canada	$3 094 670.57
	RCMP Foundation	$445 000.00
	Scholarship/Education Programs	$192 500.00
Disaster Relief	Canadian Red Cross	$3 265 557.50
Community Greening and Environmental Education	Evergreen	$550 000.00
Additional Support	Local Matching Grants	$3 761 349.98
	Juno Beach Centre	$827 675.17
	Other initiatives	$3 703 804.20
	Total	**$25 348 875.52**

2011 Total Contributions	
Raised through fundraising	$15 million
Donated by Walmart Canada	$10 million
Total	**$25 million**

Source: Based on information from "2011 Review: National and Community Partnerships: Walmart Canada Corporate Social Responsibility Report," July 2012, http://walmartcsr.ca/index.php/en/community/community-involvement/2011-review-national-and-community-partnerships- (accessed January 14, 2014).

cultural or sports and entertainment sectors. Some retailers sponsor sporting events such as the Kia Toronto Football Academy, while others buy naming rights to a sporting venue, such as the Air Canada Centre, which is home to the Toronto Maple Leafs hockey club, the Toronto Raptors basketball club, and the Toronto Rock lacrosse team.

When retailers and vendors use product placement, they pay to have their product included in nontraditional situations, such as in a scene in a movie or television program. For instance, Liz and Jack of *30 Rock* discuss whether McDonald's McFlurry is the best dessert in the world. On CBS's *The Big Bang Theory*, Sheldon says that he "needs access to the Cheesecake Factory walk-in freezer." In *The Biggest Loser*, the contestants have to run from one Subway restaurant to the next.

Strengths and Weaknesses of Communication Methods

Lo 9

Communication methods differ in terms of control, flexibility, credibility, and cost (Exhibit 15–10).

Control

Retailers have more control when using paid versus unpaid communication methods. When using advertising, sales promotions, online marketing, direct marketing, and store atmosphere, retailers determine the message's content, and for advertising, direct marketing, and sales promotions, they control the time of its delivery. Since each salesperson can deliver different messages, retailers have less control over personal selling than other paid communication methods. Retailers have little control over the content or timing of publicity and word-of-mouth communications. Since unpaid communications are designed and delivered by people not employed by the retailer, they can communicate unfavourable as well as favourable information. For example, news coverage of food poisoning at a restaurant or discrimination at a hotel can result in significant declines in sales.

Flexibility

Personal selling is the most flexible communication method, because salespeople can talk with each customer, discover their specific needs, and develop unique presentations for them. Direct mail and online marketing are also very flexible because they can be personalized to specific customer interests. Other communication methods are less flexible. For example, traditional ads tend to deliver the same message to all customers.

Credibility

Because publicity and word of mouth are communicated by independent sources, their information is usually more credible than the information in paid communication sources. For example, customers see their friends and family as highly credible sources of information. Customers tend to doubt claims made by salespeople and in ads since they know retailers are trying to promote their merchandise.

Cost

Publicity and word of mouth are classified as unpaid communication methods, but retailers do incur costs to stimulate them. Paid impersonal communications often are economical. For example, a full-page ad in the *Toronto Star* costs about two cents per person to deliver the message in the ad. In contrast, personal selling, because of its flexibility, is more effective than advertising, but it is more costly. A ten-minute presentation by a retail salesperson paid $12 per hour costs the retailer $2—100 times more than exposing a customer to a newspaper, radio, or TV ad. Although maintaining a website on a server is relatively inexpensive, it is costly to design, to continuously update the site, and to promote the site to attract visitors. Direct marketing exhibit 15–10   Media Capability

Media	Targeting	Timeliness	Information Presentation Capacity	Life	Cost
Newspapers	Good	Good	Modest	Short	Modest
Magazines	Modest	Poor	Modest	Modest	High
Direct Mail	Excellent	Modest	High	Short	Modest
Television	Modest	Modest	High	Short	Modest
Radio	Modest	Good	Low	Short	Low
Internet					
Banner	Excellent	Excellent	Low	Modest	High
Website	Excellent	Excellent	High	Long	Modest
E-mail	Excellent	Excellent	Modest	Short	Low
Social Media					
Blog	Excellent	Excellent	High	Long	Low
Twitter	Excellent	Excellent	Low	Short	Modest
Facebook	Excellent	Excellent	High	Short	Modest
Pinterest	Excellent	Excellent	High	Short	Low
Outdoor Billboards	Modest	Poor	Very Low	Long	Modest
Shopping Guides	Modest	Modest	Low	Modest	Low
Yellow Pages	Modest	Poor	Low	Long	Low

communication can be sent to customers for about $2 per person reached, but the people reached are more targeted and therefore the spend could be more cost-effective than other communication methods.

Due to the differences just described, communication methods differ in their effectiveness in performing communication tasks and their effectiveness in different stages of the customer's decision making process. Typically, mass media advertising is most effective at building awareness. Online, direct, and newspaper advertising are effective for conveying information about a retailer's offerings and prices. Personal selling and sales promotion are most effective at persuading customers to purchase merchandise. Mass media and magazine advertising, publicity, online (websites, social media), and store atmosphere are most cost-effective at building the retailer's brand image and encouraging repeat purchases and store loyalty.

Planning the Retail Communication Process

Lo 4

Almost every retail business needs to promote itself in some way, reaching out to customers and potential customers. Exhibit 15–11 illustrates the four steps in developing and implementing a retail communication program: setting objectives, determining a budget, allocating the budget, and implementing and evaluating the mix.

Setting Objectives

Retailers establish objectives for communication programs to provide the following:

- Direction for people implementing the program
- A basis for evaluating its effectiveness

exhibit 15–11   Steps in Developing a Retail Communication Program

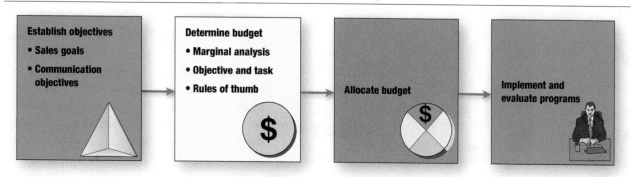

communication objectives Specific goals for a communication program related to the effects of the communication program on the customer's decision-making process.

Some communication programs have a long-term objective, such as creating or altering a retailer's brand image. Other communication programs focus on improving short-term performance, such as increasing store traffic on weekends.

Communication Objectives   While retailers' overall objective is to generate long- and short-term sales and profits, they often use communication objectives rather than sales objectives to plan and evaluate their communication programs. Communication objectives are specific goals related to the retail communication mix's effect on the customer's decision-making process.

Exhibit 15–12 shows hypothetical information about customers in the target market for a Zehrs grocery store. This information illustrates goals related to stages in the consumer decision-making process. Note that 95 percent of the customers are aware of the store (the first stage in the decision-making process) and 85 percent know the type of merchandise it sells. But only 45 percent of the customers in the target market have a favourable attitude toward the store, 32 percent intend to visit the store during the next few weeks, 25 percent actually visit the store during the next two weeks, and 18 percent regularly shop at the store.

In this hypothetical example, most people know about the store and its offerings. The major problem confronting the supermarket is the big drop between knowledge and favourable attitude. Thus, the store should develop a communication program with the objective of increasing the percentage of customers with a favourable attitude toward it.

To effectively implement and evaluate a communication program, objectives must be clearly stated in quantitative terms. The target audience for the communication mix needs to be defined along with the degree of change expected and the time period over which the change will be realized.

For example, a communication objective for the grocery store's program might be to increase—from 45 percent to 55 percent within three months—the percentage of customers within a ten-kilometre radius of the store who have a favourable attitude toward the store. This objective is clear and measurable. It indicates the task the program should address. The people who implement the program know what they're supposed to accomplish.

The communication objectives and approaches used by vendors and retailers differ, and these differences can lead to conflicts. Some of these points of conflict are as follows:

- **Long-term versus short-term goals.** Most communication done by vendors (manufacturers) is directed toward building a long-term image of their products. On the other hand, most retailer communication is typically used to announce promotions and special sales that generate short-term revenues.

- **Product versus location.** When vendors advertise their branded products, they don't care where the customer buys them. On the other hand, retailers don't care what brands customers buy as long as they buy them in their store.

  - **Geographic coverage.** Since people tend to shop at stores near their homes or workplaces, most retailers use local newspapers, TV, and radio to target their communication. On the other hand, most vendors sell their brands nationally and thus tend to use national TV and magazines.

  - **Breadth of merchandise offered.** Typically, vendors have a relatively small number of products to advertise. They can devote a lot of attention to developing consistent communication programs for each brand they make. Retailers offer a much broader set of products and often focus on building short-term sales.

Even though vendors and retailers have different goals, they frequently work together to develop mutually beneficial outcomes. An example is a coordinated program between Shoppers Drug Mart and Coppertone. The program offered a two-dollar-off coupon to the customer with the purchase of Coppertone sun care products. The addition of shelf-talker signs on shelves creates

exhibit 15–12   Communication Objectives and Stages in Consumers' Decision-Making Process at the Supermarket

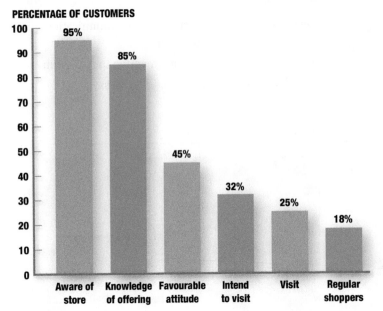

PERCENTAGE OF CUSTOMERS

Aware of store: 95%
Knowledge of offering: 85%
Favourable attitude: 45%
Intend to visit: 32%
Visit: 25%
Regular shoppers: 18%

awareness by providing information about the promotion and encouraging customer participation. The co-marketing promotion benefits both Shoppers Drug Mart and Coppertone by building sun care customers' loyalty.

Consumer Rights   In designing any consumer communication package, one of the objectives is to acknowledge and comply with consumer rights requirements. No retailer wants bad publicity as a result of consumer advocacy groups' negative press. Advances in consumerism have come in the form of federal and provincial legislation designed to protect the consumer and establish standards for manufacturers and retailers. The Consumers' Association of Canada (www.consumer.ca) seeks to uphold the following consumer rights:

- **The right to choice.** Consumers must have a choice of products offered by a variety of manufacturers and retailers. In fact, competition usually provides the benefit of lower prices to the consumer (*Competition Act*).

- **The right to be informed.** Consumers must have access to complete information about a product before buying it. For example, consider the importance of fabric content and care labelling, food ingredients and nutritional content (which are of extreme importance to people with food allergies), and information that will describe the potential dangers of using a product. Detailed information can be an asset in the case of lawsuits (*Packaging and Labelling Act, Textile Labelling Act, Weights and Measures Act*).

- **The right to safety.** The product must be safe for its intended use. This means that the product must be accompanied by instructions for its proper use and carry a guarantee of product quality and reliability as tested by the manufacturer. Federal agencies will take action to force businesses to recall defective products and issue public warnings (*Food and Drug Act, Hazardous Products Act*).

- **The right to be heard.** Someone will listen to consumers' complaints and take appropriate action to solve the problems. Many retailers have added customer service centres in the store to address customer concerns, and maintain a toll-free telephone number and/or a website so that customers can contact a service representative for immediate assistance.[72]

Developing the Promotional Message

Most retail promotional messages have a short life and are designed to have an immediate impact. This immediacy calls for a copywriting style that grabs the reader's attention. Exhibit 15–13 outlines specific suggestions for developing local newspaper ads.

Factors in Selecting Media   To convey their message with the most impact to the most consumers in the target market at the lowest cost, retailers need to evaluate media in terms of coverage, reach, cost, and impact of the advertising messages delivered through the medium.

Coverage   Coverage refers to the number of potential customers in the retailer's target market that could be

coverage The theoretical number of potential customers in the retailer's target market that could be exposed to an ad in a given medium.

exhibit 15–13   Suggestions for Developing Local Ads

1. Have a dominant headline	The first question a consumer asks is, What's in it for me? Thus, retailers need to feature the principal benefit being offered in the headline along with a reason why the consumer should act immediately. The benefit can be expanded on in a subhead.
2. Use a dominant element	Ads should include a large picture or headline. Typically, photographs of real people attract more attention than drawings. Action photographs are effective in getting readers' attention.
3. Stick to a simple layout	The ad's layout should lead the reader's eye through the message from the headline to the illustration and then to the explanatory copy, price, and retailer's name and location. Complex elements, decorative borders, and many different typefaces distract the reader's attention from the retailer's message.
4. Provide a specific, complete presentation	Ad readers are looking for information that will help them decide whether to visit the store. The ad must contain all of the information pertinent to this decision, including the type of merchandise, brands, prices, sizes, and colours. Consumers are unlikely to make a special trip to the store on the basis of vague information. Broadcast ads, particularly radio ads, tend to be very creative but often leave the consumer thinking, Gee, that was a clever ad, but what was it advertising?
5. Use easily recognizable, distinct visuals	Consumers see countless ads each day. Thus, to get the consumers' attention, retailers must make their ads distinct from those of the competition. Ads with distinctive art, layout, design elements, or typeface generate higher readership.
6. Give the store's name and address	The store's name and location are the two most important aspects of a retail ad. If consumers don't know where to go to buy the advertised merchandise, the retailer won't make a sale. The retailer's name and location must be prominently displayed in print ads and repeated several times in broadcast ads.

reach The actual number of customers in the target market exposed to an advertising medium.

cumulative reach The cumulative number of potential customers that would see an ad that runs several times.

cost per thousand (CPM) A measure that is often used to compare media. CPM is calculated by dividing an ad's cost by its reach.

impact An ad's effect on the audience.

Lowe's sponsorship for a NASCAR racing team generates publicity and builds brand awareness. However, this publicity could be unfavourable if its NASCAR team engaged in unsanctioned activities.

exposed to an ad in a given medium. For example, assume that the size of the target market is 100 000 customers. The local newspaper is distributed to 60 percent of the customers in the target market, 90 percent of the potential customers have a TV set that picks up the local station's signal, and 5 percent of the potential customers drive past a billboard. Thus, the coverage for newspaper advertising would be 60 000; for TV advertising, 90 000; and for the specific billboard, 5000.

Reach In contrast to coverage, reach is the actual number of customers in the target market exposed to an advertising medium. If, on any given day, 60 percent of the potential customers who receive the newspaper actually read it, then the newspaper's reach would be 36 000 (or 60 percent of 60 000). Retailers often run an ad several times, in which case they calculate the cumulative reach for the sequence of ads. For example, if 60 percent of the potential customers receiving a newspaper read it each day, 93.6 percent (or 1 minus the probability of not reading the paper three times in a row [0.40 × 0.40 × 0.40]) of the potential customers will read the newspaper at least one day over the three-day period in which the ad appears in the paper. Thus, the cumulative reach for running a newspaper ad for three days is 56 160 (or 93.6 percent × 60 000), which almost equals the newspaper's coverage.

When evaluating Internet advertising opportunities, the measure used to assess reach is the number of unique visitors—the number of different people who access the web page on which the ad is located.

Cost The cost per thousand (CPM) measure is often used to compare media. Typically, CPM is calculated by dividing an ad's cost by its reach. Another approach for determining CPM is to divide the cost of several ads in a campaign by their cumulative reach. If, for instance, in the previous example, one newspaper ad costs $500 and three ads cost $1300, the CPM using simple reach is $13.89, or $500/(36 000/1000). Using cumulative reach, the CPM is $23.15, or $1300/(56 160/1000). Note that the CPM might be higher using cumulative reach rather than simple reach, but the overall reach is also higher, and many potential customers will see the ad two or three times.

CPM is a good method for comparing similar-size ads in similar media, such as full-page ads in the *National Post* and the *Barrie Examiner*. But CPM can be misleading when comparing the cost-effectiveness of ads in different types of media, such as newspaper and TV. A TV ad may have a lower CPM than a newspaper ad, but the newspaper ad may be much more effective at achieving the ad's communication objectives, such as giving information about a sale.

Impact Impact is an ad's effect on the audience. Due to their unique characteristics, different media are particularly effective at accomplishing different communication tasks. Exhibit 15–14 shows the effectiveness of various media for different communication tasks. TV is particularly effective at getting an audience's attention, demonstrating merchandise, changing attitudes, and announcing events. Magazines are particularly appropriate for emphasizing the quality and prestige of a store and its offering and for providing detailed information to support quality claims. Newspapers are useful for providing price

exhibit 15–14 Effectiveness of Media by Communication Objective

Communication Task	Newspapers	Magazine	Direct Mail	TV	Radio	Websites	E-Mail	Outdoor	Social
Getting attention	Low	Medium	Medium	Medium	Low	Low	High	Medium	Medium
Identifying name	Medium	High	Low	Low	Low	Low	Medium	High	High
Announcing events	High	Low	High	High	Medium	Low	High	Low	High
Demonstrating merchandise	Low	Medium	High	High	Low	Highest	Low	Low	Medium
Providing information	Low	High	High	Low	Low	Highest	Medium	Lowest	High
Changing attitudes	High	Medium	High	High	Medium	High	Low	Low	High
Building brand image	Low	Medium	High	High	Low	High	Low	Low	High

information and announcing events. Websites are particularly effective for demonstrating merchandise and providing information. Outdoor advertising is most effective at promoting a retailer's name and location.

Determining Promotional Frequency and Timing

The frequency and timing of promotions determine how often and when customers will see the retailer's message.

Frequency   Frequency is how many times the potential customer is exposed to a promotional message. Frequency for Internet advertising is typically assessed by measuring the number of times a web page with the message is downloaded during a visit to the site.

The appropriate frequency depends on the message's objective. Typically, several exposures to a promotional message are required to influence a customer's buying behaviour. Thus, campaigns directed toward changing purchase behaviour rather than creating awareness emphasize frequency over reach. Ads announcing a sale are often seen and remembered after one exposure. Thus, sale ad campaigns emphasize reach over frequency.

Timing   Typically, a promotional message should appear on, or slightly precede, the days consumers are most likely to purchase merchandise. For example, if most consumers buy groceries Thursday through Sunday, then supermarkets should advertise on Thursday and Friday. Similarly, consumers often go shopping after they receive their paycheques at the middle and the end of the month. Thus, advertising should be concentrated at these times.

Lo 5   Setting the Communication Budget

The second step in developing a retail communication program is determining a budget (see Exhibit 15–11). The economically correct method for setting the communication budget is marginal analysis. Even though retailers usually don't have enough information to perform a complete marginal analysis, the method shows how managers should approach budget-setting programs.

The marginal analysis method for setting a communication budget is the approach retailers should use when making all of their resource allocation decisions, including the number of locations in a geographic area, the staffing of stores, and the floor and shelf space devoted to merchandise categories.

Marginal Analysis Method   Marginal analysis is based on the economic principle that firms should increase communication expenditures so long as each

E-mail communications are very cost-effective in targeting messages to specific customers.

additional dollar spent generates more than a dollar of additional contribution. The marginal analysis method is used to determine how much should be spent on the retailer's communication program.[74]

In Exhibit 15–15, column 1 indicates 21 different communication expense levels. The retailer estimates store sales (column 2), gross margin (column 3), and other expenses (columns 4 and 5). Then the retailer calculates the contribution excluding expenses on communications (column 6) and the profit when the communication expenses are considered (column 7). To estimate the sales generated by different levels of communications, the retailer can rely on judgment and experience, or might analyze past data to determine the relationship between communication expenses and sales. Historical data also provide information about the gross margin and other expenses as a percentage of sales.

Notice that at low levels of communication expenses, an additional $5000 in communication expenses generates more than a $5000 incremental contribution. For example, increasing the communication expense from $15 000 to $20 000 increases contribution by $10 800 (or $48 400 − $37 600). When the communication expense reaches $65 000, further increases of $5000 generate less than $5000 in additional contributions. For example, increasing the budget from $65 000 to $70 000 generates only an additional $4050 in contribution ($125 350 − $121 300).

In this example, the retailer determines that the maximum profit would be generated with a communication expense budget of $65 000. But he/she notices that expense levels between $55 000 and $70 000 all result in about the same level of profit. Thus, the retailer makes a conservative decision and establishes a $55 000 budget for communication expenses.

frequency   The number of times a potential customer is exposed to a promotional message.

marginal analysis   A method of analysis used in setting a promotional budget or allocating retail space, based on the economic principle that firms should increase expenditures as long as each additional dollar spent generates more than a dollar of additional contribution.

exhibit 15–15 Marginal Analysis for Setting a Retailer's Communication Budget

Level	Communication Expenses (1)	Sales (2)	Gross Margin Realized (3)	Rental Expense (4)	Personnel Expense (5)	Contribution Before Communication Expenses (6) = (3) − (4) − (5)	Profit After Communication Expenses (7) = (6) − (1)	
1	$0	$240 000	$96 000	$44 000	$52 200	$ (200)	$ (200)	
2	5 000	280 000	112 000	48 000	53 400	10 600	5 600	
3	10 000	330 000	132 000	53 000	54 900	24 100	14 100	
4	15 000	380 000	152 000	58 000	56 400	37 600	22 600	
5	20 000	420 000	168 000	62 000	57 600	48 400	28 400	
6	25 000	460 000	184 000	66 000	58 800	59 200	34 200	
7	30 000	500 000	200 000	70 000	60 000	70 000	40 000	Last year
8	35 000	540 000	216 000	74 000	61 200	80 800	45 800	
9	40 000	570 000	228 000	77 000	62 100	88 900	48 900	
10	45 000	600 000	240 000	80 000	63 000	97 000	52 000	
11	50 000	625 000	250 000	82 500	63 750	103 750	53 750	
12	55 000	650 000	260 000	85 000	64 500	110 500	55 500	
13	60 000	670 000	268 000	87 000	65 100	115 900	55 900	
14	65 000	690 000	276 000	89 000	65 700	121 300	56 300	Best profit
15	70 000	705 000	282 000	90 500	66 150	125 350	55 350	
16	75 000	715 000	286 000	91 500	66 450	128 050	53 050	
17	80 000	725 000	290 000	92 500	66 750	130 750	50 750	
18	85 000	735 000	294 000	93 500	67 050	133 450	48 450	
19	90 000	745 000	298 000	94 500	67 350	136 150	46 150	
20	95 000	750 000	300 000	95 000	67 500	137 500	42 500	
21	100 000	750 000	300 000	95 000	67 500	137 500	37 500	

objective-and-task method A method for setting a promotion budget in which the retailer first establishes a set of communication objectives and then determines the necessary tasks and their costs.

In most cases, it's very hard to do a marginal analysis because often retail managers don't know the relationship between communication expenses and sales. Note that the numbers in Exhibit 15–15 are simply the retailer's estimates; they may not be accurate.

Sometimes retailers do experiments to get a better idea of the relationship between communication expenses and sales. Say, for example, a catalogue retailer selects several geographic areas in Canada with the same sales potential. The retailer then distributes 100 000 catalogues in the first area, 200 000 in the second area, and 300 000 in the third area. Using the sales and costs for each distribution level, it could go through an analysis like the one in Exhibit 15–15 to determine the most profitable distribution level.

Other methods that retailers use to set communication budgets are the objective-and-task method and rules of thumb, such as the affordable, percentage-of-sales, and competitive parity methods. These methods are less sophisticated than marginal analysis but easier to use.

Objective-and-Task Method The objective-and-task method determines the budget required to undertake specific tasks for accomplishing communication objectives. To use this method, the retailer first establishes a set of communication objectives. Then the necessary tasks and their costs are determined. The sum total of all costs incurred to undertake the tasks is the communication budget.

Exhibit 15–16 illustrates how the retailer uses the objective-and-task method to complement the marginal analysis. The retailer establishes three objectives:

- To increase the awareness of the store
- To create a greater preference for his/her store among customers in the target market
- To promote the sale of merchandise remaining at the end of each season

The total communication budget the retailer requires to achieve these objectives is $55 300.

Besides defining the objectives and tasks, the retailer must also recheck the financial implications of the communication mix by projecting the income statement for next year using the communication budget (see Exhibit 15–17). This income statement includes an increase of $25 300 in communication expenses over last year. Upon

Objective: Increase from 25 percent to 50 percent over the next 12 months the percentage of target market living or working within 10 kilometres of our store who know of our store's location and product.	
Task: 480, 30–second radio spots during peak commuting hours (7:00 to 8:00 AM and 5:00 to 6:00 PM).	$12 300
Task: Sign with store name near entrance to mall.	4 500
Task: Display ad in the Yellow Pages.	500
Objective: Increase from 5 percent to 15 percent in 12 months the percentage of target market who indicate that our store is their preferred store to shop in.	
Task: Develop TV campaign to improve image and run 50, 30–second commercials.	$24 000
Task: Hold four information seminars followed by a wine-and-cheese social.	8 000
Objective: Selling merchandise remaining at end of season.	
Task: Special event.	$6 000
Total budget	$55 300

exhibit 15–17   Financial Implications of Increasing the Communication Budget

	Last Year	Next Year
Sales	$500 000	$650 000
Gross margin (realized)	200 000	260 000
Rental, maintenance, etc.	70 000	85 000
Personnel	60 000	64 500
Communications	30 000	55 300
Profit	$ 40 000	$ 55 200

examination, the retailer feels that this increase in the communication budget will boost annual sales from $500 000 to $650 000. Based on the retailer's projections, the increase in communication expenses will raise store profits. The results of the marginal analysis and the objective-and-task methods suggest a communication budget between $55 000 and $65 000.

Rule-of-Thumb Methods   In the previous two methods, the communication budget is set by estimating communication activities' effects on the firm's future sales or communication objectives. The rule-of-thumb method discussed in this section use an alternative logic.

Affordable Method   When using the affordable budgeting method, retailers first forecast their sales and expenses excluding communication expenses during the budgeting period. The difference between the forecast sales and expenses plus desired profit is then budgeted for the communication mix expenses. In other words, the affordable method sets the communication budget by determining what money is available after operating costs and profits are budgeted.

The major problem with the affordable method is that it assumes that the communication expenses don't stimulate sales and profit. Communication expenses are just a cost of business, like the cost of merchandise. When retailers use the affordable method, they typically cut "unnecessary" communication expenses if sales fall below the forecast rather than increase communication expenses to increase sales.

Percentage-of-Sales Method   The percentage-of-sales method sets the communication budget as a fixed percentage of forecast sales. Retailers use this method to determine the communication budget by forecasting sales during the budget period and using a predetermined percentage to set the budget. The percentage may be the retailer's historical percentage or the average percentage used by similar retailers.

The problem with the percentage-of-sales method is that it assumes the same percentage used in the past, or by competitors, is still appropriate for the retailer. Consider a retailer that hasn't opened new stores in the past but plans to open many new stores in the current year. It must create customer awareness for these new stores, so the communication budget should be much larger in the current year than in the past.

Using the same percentage as competitors also may be inappropriate. For example, a retailer might have better locations than its competitors. Due to these locations, customers may already have a high awareness of the retailer's stores. Thus, the retailer may not need to spend as much on communications as competitors with poorer locations spend.

rule-of-thumb method   A type of approach for setting a promotion budget that uses past sales and communication activity to determine the present communications budget.

affordable budgeting method   A budgeting method in which a retailer first sets a budget for every element of the retail mix except promotion and then allocates the leftover funds to a promotional budget.

percentage-of-sales method   A method for setting a promotion budget based on a fixed percentage of forecast sales.

competitive parity method An approach for setting a promotion budget so that the retailer's share of promotion expenses is equal to its market share.

high-assay principle A method of allocating a communication budget that uses the principles of marginal analysis. The retailer should allocate the budget to areas that will yield the greatest return.

DID YOU KNOW?

Supermarkets spend 1.1 percent of annual sales revenue on advertising, department store retailers spend 3.7 percent of sales, and women's apparel specialty retailers spend 4.7 percent of sales.[76]

One advantage of both the percentage-of-sales method and the affordable method for determining a communication budget is that the retailer won't spend beyond its means. Since the level of spending is determined by sales, the budget will go up only when sales go up and the retailer generates more sales to pay for the additional communication expenses. When times are good, these methods work well because they allow the retailer to communicate more aggressively with customers. But when sales fall, communication expenses are cut, which may accelerate the sales decline.

Competitive Parity Method

Under the competitive parity method, the communication budget is set so that the retailer's share of communication expenses equals its share of the market. For example, consider a sporting goods store in a small town. To use the competitive parity method, the owner–manager would first estimate the total amount spent on communications by all of the sporting goods retailers in town. Then the owner–manager would estimate his or her store's market share for sporting goods and multiply that market share percentage by the sporting goods stores' total advertising expenses to set its budget. Assume that the owner–manager's estimate of advertising for sporting goods by all stores was $5000 and the estimate of his or her store's market share was 45 percent. On the basis of these estimates, the owner–manager would set the store's communication budget at $2250 to maintain competitive parity.

Like the other rule-of-thumb methods, the competitive parity method doesn't allow retailers to exploit the unique opportunities or problems they confront in a market. If all competitors used this method to set communication budgets, their market shares would stay about the same over time (assuming that the retailers developed equally effective campaigns).

Allocating the Promotional Budget

After determining the size of the communication budget, the third step in the communication planning process is allocating the budget (see Exhibit 15–11). In this step, the retailer decides how much of its budget to allocate to specific communication elements, merchandise categories, geographic regions, or long- and short-term objectives. For example, a department store must decide how much of its communication budget to spend in each area where it has stores. Sears decides how much to allocate to appliances, hardware, and apparel. The sporting goods store owner–manager must decide how much of the store's $2250 communication budget to spend on promoting the store's image versus generating sales during the year and how much to spend on advertising and special promotions.

Research indicates that allocation decisions are more important than the decision on the amount spent on communications.[77] In other words, retailers often can realize the same objectives by reducing the size of the communication budget but allocating the budget more effectively.

An easy way to make such allocation decisions is just to spend about the same in each geographic region or for each merchandise category. But this allocation rule probably won't maximize profits because it ignores the possibility that communication programs might be more effective for some merchandise categories or for some regions than for others. Another approach is to use rules of thumb such as basing allocations on the sales level or contribution for the merchandise category.

Allocation decisions, like budget-setting decisions, should use the principles of marginal analysis. The retailer should allocate the budget to areas that will yield the greatest return. This approach for allocating a budget is sometimes referred to as the high-assay principle. Consider a miner who can spend his time digging on two claims. The value of the gold on one claim is assayed at $20 000 per tonne, whereas the assay value on the other claim is $10 000 per tonne. Should the miner spend two-thirds of his time at the first mine and one-third of his time at the other mine? Of course not! The miner should spend all of his time mining the first claim until the assay value of the ore mined drops to $10 000 a tonne, at which time he can divide his time equally between the claims.

Similarly, a retailer may find that its customers have a high awareness and very favourable attitude toward its women's clothing but may not know much about the store's men's clothing. In this situation, a dollar spent on advertising men's clothing might generate more sales than a dollar spent on women's clothing even though the sales of women's clothing are greater than the sales of men's clothing.

Planning, Implementing, and Evaluating Communication Programs— Three Illustrations

The final stage in developing a retail communication program is implementation and evaluation (see Exhibit 15–11).

In this final section of the chapter, we illustrate the planning and evaluation process for three communication programs—an advertising campaign by a small specialty retailer, a sales promotion opportunity confronting a supermarket chain, and a communication program emphasizing direct marketing undertaken by a large retail chain.

Advertising Campaign

South Gate West is one of several specialty import home-furnishings stores competing for upscale shoppers. The store has the appearance of both a fine antiques store and a traditional home-furnishing shop, but most of its merchandise is new Asian imports.[78]

The owner realized that his communication budget was considerably less than the budget of the local Pier 1 store. (Pier 1 is a large international import home-furnishings chain.) He decided to concentrate his limited budget on a specific segment and use highly distinctive copy and art in his advertising. His target market was experienced, sophisticated consumers of housewares and home decorative items. His experience indicated the importance of personal selling for more seasoned shoppers because they make large purchases and seek considerable information before making a decision. Thus, the retailer spent part of his communication budget on training his sales associates.

The advertising program that the retailer developed emphasized his store's distinctive image. He used the newspaper as his major vehicle. Competitive ads contained line drawings of furniture with prices. His ads emphasized the imagery associated with Asian furniture by featuring off-the-beaten-path scenes of Asian countries with unusual art objects. This theme was also reflected in the store's atmosphere.

To evaluate his communication program, the retailer needed to compare the results of his program with the objectives he developed during the first part of the planning process. To measure his campaign's effectiveness, he conducted an inexpensive tracking study. Telephone interviews were performed periodically with a representative sample of furniture customers in his store's trading area. Communication objectives were assessed using the following questions:

Communication Objective	Question
Awareness	What stores sell East Asian furniture?
Knowledge	Which stores would you rate outstanding on the following characteristics?
Attitude	On your next shopping trip for East Asian furniture, which store would you visit first?
Visit	Which of the following stores have you been to?

This end-aisle display of Fab is part of a special Colgate-Palmolive promotion in which the supermarket chain participated.

Here are the survey results for one year:

	Before Campaign	Six Months After	One Year After
Awareness (percentage mentioning store)	38%	46%	52%
Knowledge (percentage giving outstanding rating for sales assistance)	9	17	24
Attitude (percentage first choice)	13	15	19
Visit (percentage visited store)	8	15	19

The results show a steady increase in awareness, knowledge of the store, and choice of the store as a primary source of East Asian furniture. This research provides evidence that the advertising was conveying the intended message to the target audience.

Sales Promotion Opportunity

Many sales promotion opportunities undertaken by retailers are initiated by vendors. For example, Colgate-Palmolive might offer the following special promotion to Loblaws: During a one-week period, Loblaws can order Fab laundry detergent in the 2-kg size at 15 cents below the standard wholesale price. However, if Loblaws elects to buy Fab at the discounted price, the grocery chain must feature the 2-kg container of Fab in its Thursday newspaper ad at $1.59 (20 cents off the typical retail price). In addition, Loblaws must have an end-aisle display of Fab.

Before Loblaws decides whether to accept such a trade promotion and then promote Fab to its customers, it needs to assess the promotion's impact on its profitability. Such a promotion may be effective for the vendor but not for the retailer.

To evaluate a trade promotion, the retailer considers the following:

- The realized margin from the promotion
- The cost of the additional inventory carried due to buying more than the normal amount

- The potential increase in sales from the promoted merchandise

- The potential loss suffered when customers switch to the promoted merchandise from more profitable private-label brands

- The additional sales made to customers attracted to the store by the promotion.[79]

When Fab's price is reduced to $1.59, Loblaws will sell more Fab than it normally would. But Loblaws' margin on the Fab will be less because the required retail discount of 20 cents isn't offset by the wholesale discount of 15 cents. In addition, Loblaws might suffer losses because the promotion encourages customers to buy Fab, which has a lower margin than Loblaws' private-label detergent that customers might have bought. In fact, customers may stockpile Fab, buying several boxes, which will reduce sales of Loblaws' private-label detergent for some time after the special promotion ends. On the other hand, the promotion may attract customers who don't normally shop at Loblaws but who will visit to buy Fab at the discounted price. These customers might buy additional merchandise, providing a sales gain to the store that it wouldn't have realized if it hadn't promoted Fab.

Special Promotion Using a CRM/Campaign Management Tool A national retailer with 580 store locations used its CRM/campaign management system to plan, design, evaluate, and implement a special Canada Day promotion.[80] The diagram of the system is shown in Exhibit 15–18. The retailer has a customer database with purchase information complemented with additional customer information acquired through external sources.

After an initial planning meeting, the retailer decided to use direct mail, mobile marketing, and e-mail communication channels with supporting in-store promotions and existing advertising. Customers would need to bring in a coupon to take advantage of the special promotion. The goal of the campaign was to generate a 10 percent increase in sales during the Canada Day period.

Using the campaign management tool in the system, the retailer examined a number of what-if scenarios enabling the team to chart out all of the tasks, costs, and related deadlines to determine projected ROI. Initially, they wanted to target customers who had visited the stores and made a purchase within the last nine months. During the target market segmentation evaluation process, they determined that the counts were too low and increased the target criterion to customer purchases within the last 12 months. Using this criterion, the communication program would be directed to 2.6 million customers. A review of past holiday promotion programs suggested a response rate of 2.5 percent.

Based on the 2.5 percent response rate for 2.6 million customers, the number of people projected to visit the stores was 65 000. The special promotion was a $49 item, but the average sale once people were in the store was $99. On the basis of this information, the Canada Day event special promotion was targeted to generate gross sales between $3.1 million and $6.4 million.

The cost for the direct-mail piece was $0.65/piece and the e-mail piece was $0.03/e-mail. To mail and e-mail

exhibit 15–18 CRM/Campaign Management System

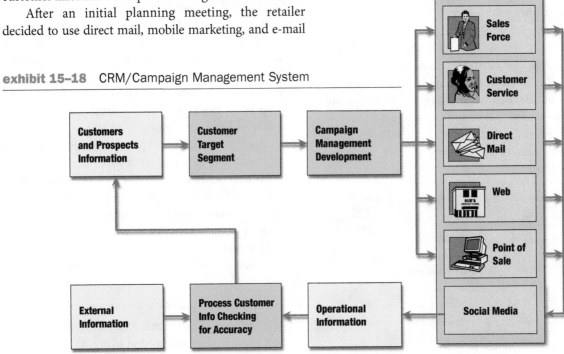

exhibit 15–19 Financial Analysis of Special Canada Day Promotion

Campaign Planning Financials				
Target Market Count			**Campaign Costs**	
Records in 12-month period	2.6 million		Direct mail ($0.65/piece)	$1 690 000
2.5% response rate			E-mail ($0.03/e-mail)	$78 000
Project response count	65 000		Total cost	$1 768 000
Gross Revenue			**Net Revenue (less product cost of 25%)**	
Special promotion $49/each	$3 185 000		$2 388 750	
Average sale $99/each	$6 435 000		$4 826 250	
		Campaign Profitability		
		Special promotion	$620 750	
		Average sale	$3 058 250	

2.6 million customers, the cost was $1 768 000. In determining the product costs on the special promotion item, a 75 percent markup was used. The campaign profitability margin was projected to be between $600 000 and $3.1 million. The financial analysis developed by the planning tool is shown in Exhibit 15–19.

Once the what-if analysis was completed and the campaign plan was built with all of the details and responsibilities of each department, it was set into action. The action plan includes all the required steps in the campaign process, along with the costs, responsibilities, and deadlines on the marketing production schedule. By putting the plan into production, all of the tasks are sent to the people responsible for completing them, so that deadlines and costs are tracked. Each department would receive a series of tasks specific to that department's deliverables:

- The creative department was assigned the responsibility of designing the direct mail piece with the coupon. It also designed the e-mail piece with a print coupon. Once the design process was completed and approved, the artwork was sent to the print vendor for printing and the marketing department for e-mail distribution.

- The database marketing department was responsible for sending the list of customers in the target market

analysis (the customers who had visited a store and made a purchase in the last 12 months) to the mail vendor. Each record in the customer database had a unique identifier so that the results of the campaign would be properly tracked and analyzed.

- The store promotions department had to make sure that the in-store promotional materials were consistent with the message in the campaign. Media services also had to verify consistency in all media with the campaign message.

During the entire campaign process, a management view of the financial information and campaign deliverables/deadline information was available. As the stores reported their customer sales, management's reports were automatically generated, and the response ROI was analyzed to determine if the marketing campaign was successful. The information from all of the customer touchpoints was collected, processed, and added to the customer database. The successful campaign was then templated for future use to save time in the planning phase for the next holiday campaign. The matrix solution allowed management to optimize resources and manage deadlines and deliverables, thus increasing productivity, efficiency, and ROI.

SUMMARY

In today's economy, where good news is often quickly matched by an equal portion of bad news, effectively competing and winning customers every day is vital to a retailer's success. The best retailers maintain their loyal customers and win new ones, pursuing larger market share by communicating through education, building brand awareness, and developing experiential involvement. Consumers today are both online and offline, and sometimes online while shopping offline. Online they are sharing, friend-validating, researching, learning, and developing a point of view. Offline there is touching, brand comparing, and brand associating.

The communication program can be designed to achieve a variety of objectives for the retailer. Objectives include building a brand image of the retailer in the customer's mind, increasing sales and store traffic, providing information about the retailer's location and offering, and announcing special activities. Retailers need to be where their customers are with both their messaging and their products and/or services.

Retailers communicate with customers through advertising, sales promotions, websites, store atmosphere, publicity, personal selling, e-mail, and word of mouth. These elements in the communication mix must be coordinated so that customers will have a clear, distinct image of the retailer and won't be confused by conflicting information.

Also, consumer rights requirements must be acknowledged and complied with.

Many retailers use rules of thumb to determine the size of the promotion budget. Marginal analysis (the most appropriate method for determining how much must be spent to accomplish the retailer's objectives) should be used to determine whether the level of spending maximizes the profits that could be generated by the communications mix.

The largest portion of a retailer's communication budget is typically spent on advertising and sales promotions. A wide array of media can be used for advertising. Each medium has its pros and cons. Newspaper advertising is effective for announcing sales, whereas TV ads are useful for developing an image. Sales promotions are typically used to achieve short-term objectives, such as increasing store traffic over a weekend. Most sales promotions are supported in part by promotions offered to the retailer by its vendors. Publicity and word of mouth are typically low-cost communications, but they are very difficult for retailers to control.

Direct marketing contains a variety of traditional and new forms of marketing communication initiatives, including Internet-enabled methods such as mobile marketing. The increased use of customer databases has enabled retailers to identify and track consumers over time and across purchase situations, contributing to more personalized promotional activity.

KEY TERMS

advertising
affordable budgeting method
aided recall
attitude branding
blog
brand
brand association
brand awareness
brand energy
brand equity
brand image
call to action
communication objectives
competitive parity method
co-op advertising
cost per thousand (CPM)

coupons
coverage
cumulative reach
direct mail
direct marketing
e-mail
freestanding insert (FSI)
frequency
high-assay principle
impact
integrated marketing communication program
magalogue
marginal analysis
mobile marketing
objective-and-task method

percentage-of-sales method
personal selling
point-of-purchase (POP)
pop-up stores
premium
private-label brands
public relations (PR)
reach
rebates
rule-of-thumb method
sales promotions
samples
short code
showrooming
special event
top-of-mind awareness

Get Out & Do It!

1. **INTERNET EXERCISE** Go to **www.youtube.com/user/ WestJet** and explain the success of WestJet ads in communicating to the customer.

2. **INTERNET EXERCISE** Go to **www.dove.ca/en/Social-Mission/Self-Esteem-Resources/default.aspx** and describe how Dove has connected to the female consumer through emotional messages with its Self-Esteem campaign.

3. **INTERNET EXERCISE** Review the trends at **www.trend-watching.com** for a future focus on advertising and consumer directions.

4. **GO SHOPPING** Go to a retail store and make a list of all of the specific elements and information in the store that communicate the store's image and the merchandise it is offering to customers.

5. **GO SHOPPING** Look though the freestanding inserts (FSIs) in your local newspaper. Evaluate the general use of FSIs, and select the FSIs that you think are most effective. Why are these FSIs more effective than the other ones?

6. **INTERNET EXERCISE** Visit the Consumers' Association of Canada at **www.consumer.ca**. Identify the nine consumer rights profiled on the site, and give a retail example of each.

7. **INTERNET EXERCISE** You can find more information about the use of radio as an advertising medium at the Radio Advertising Bureau site, **www.rab.com**. Based on this information, what types of retail messages can be delivered more effectively by radio compared to other media? How has the radio app Shazam potentially changed radio advertising opportunities for retailers?

8. **INTERNET EXERCISE** Read the *BusinessWeek* online article entitled, "How In-Store TVs Play to Shoppers," available at **www.businessweek.com/bwdaily/ dnflash/nov2004/nf20041122_9652.htm**. How are retailers using TV as an in-store communication tool? What are the key advantages of implementing in-store TV in the communications mix?

DISCUSSION QUESTIONS AND PROBLEMS

1. How do brands benefit consumers? Retailers?

2. How can advertising, personal selling, and promotion complement each other in an integrated marketing communications program?

3. As a means of communicating with customers, how does advertising differ from publicity?

4. Why is the newspaper the favourite medium used by retailers for advertising? What are the advantages and disadvantages of newspaper advertising? Why is the use of newspaper decreasing and use of direct mail increasing?

5. For which of the following growth opportunities do you think the retailer should use its brand name when pursuing the opportunity? Why?
   a) McDonald's starts a new chain of restaurants to sell seafood in a sit-down environment competing with Red Lobster.
   b) Sears starts a chain of stand-alone stores that sell just home appliances.
   c) Netflix starts a chain of stores selling consumer electronics.

6. What factors should be considered in dividing up the budget among a store's different merchandise areas? Which of the following should receive the highest advertising budget: fashionable women's clothing, men's underwear, women's hosiery, or kitchen appliances? Why?

7. Outline some elements in a communication program to achieve the following objectives:
   a) Increase store loyalty by 20 percent.
   b) Build awareness of the store by 10 percent.
   c) Develop an image as a low-price retailer.

   How would you determine whether the communication program met the objective?

8. Some retailers direct their advertising efforts toward reaching as wide an audience as possible. Others try to expose the audience to an advertisement as many times as possible. When should a retailer concentrate on reach? When should a retailer concentrate on frequency?

9. A retailer plans to open a new store near a university. It will specialize in merchandise such as T-shirts, sweatshirts, and accessories. Develop an integrated communication program for the retailer. What specific advertising media should the new store use to capture the university market?

10. Cooperative (co-op) advertising is a good way for a retailer to extend an ad budget. Why is it not always in a retailer's best interests to rely extensively on co-op advertising?

 Practise and learn online with Connect.

cases

Case	Title	Chapter
1	The Arrival of Target	1
2	Retailing in India—Impact of Hypermarkets	2
3	Sobeys Finds Its Fit with the Urban Crowd: Customer Behaviour	3
4	Attracting Generation Y to a Retail Career	3, 4, 13
5	Supplementing for Success in the Canadian Market	4
6	Abercrombie & Fitch and American Eagle Compete for 18- to 22-Year-Olds	5, 15
7	Vivah Jewellery: Location Strategy	5
8	Retail's Rural Frontier: Location Strategy	5
9	Stephanie's Boutique: Store Strategy	5
10	"Touch and Feel" at Sephora	6
11	Innovating the In-Store Experience	6
12	Building the Apple Store	6
13	A Grand New Look: Layout and Design	6
14	Mountain Equipment Co-op: Revitalizing a Brand	7
15	Tiffany & Co. and TJX: Comparing Financial Performance	8
16	The Chocolate Shop	8
17	Creating Loss Prevention Programs That Fit the Culture	9
18	Lindy's Bridal Shoppe: Assortments	10
19	Merchandise Strategy: Process for Success	10
20	McFadden's Department Store	10
21	Hughes: Developing a Buying Plan	11
22	Capital Sportswear: Buying	11
23	Shoppers Drug Mart: Pricing	12
24	How Much for a Good Smell? Pricing	12
25	Enterprise Rent-A-Car Focuses on Its People	13
26	HR Technology Is All about Connections	13
27	Preparing for Succession, Stitch by Stitch	13
28	Customer Service and Relationship Management at Nordstrom	14
29	Active Endeavors Analyzes Its Customer Database	14
30	Engaging with Customers through Social Media	14
31	Diamond in the Rough	14
32	Target Marketing with Google AdWords	15
33	Generating Advertising Revenue from a Digital Screen Network at Harrods of London	15

The night before Target opened its first store in Whitby, Ontario, during the retailer's second round of "soft" openings in Canada, a mid-March snowstorm blanketed the streets and left a cool wind in its wake.

But the bad weather didn't stop Keri Young from packing her 10-month-old son, Henry, to arrive in time for the 8 AM store opening.

"I'm pretty excited," she says. "I live nearby and drive by every day and I've been looking every day to see if it's open."

That kind of anticipation is something the U.S. chain is counting on as it opens 124 stores across Canada in [2013]—and it's the kind of anticipation its competition has been paying close attention to since Target announced plans to move north two years ago.

Depending on which expert you ask, Target's arrival in Canada is either a "catalytic event" for the retail industry in Canada or just another entry into a market already experiencing the benefits and challenges of an economy that is globalizing with an increasing number of new global retailers entering the country. Whatever the case, the country's retail landscape is shifting as big-name chains look north, and across the ocean, to a country with a stable economy, a strong dollar, and a retail market with lots of development potential.

Revolution?

Many experts point to the arrival of Walmart in Canada in the early 1990s as a significant turning point in Canadian retail. Walmart was a "breakthrough" with its efficiency and discount prices, says Jim Danahy, managing principal of retail consulting firm CustomerLAB.

But the time during which Walmart entered the Canadian market was vastly different than today. The arrival of Target comes at a time that signifies not just a turning point, but a near revolution within the industry. The emergence and growth of the omni-channel retail experience coupled with the continued proliferation of e-commerce activity in Canada is changing the way retailers operate their businesses. And where Walmart entered the market store by store, Target is arriving all at once, and it's arriving along with a wave of other global retailers, including H&M, Zara, J.Crew, Nordstrom, and more.

"This is not just an American phenomenon," he says. "It's about a global economic influence that's sending capital to a safe haven, with a stable economy and growth. It's also one that's understored by American and European standards."

But that's not to take away from Target's impact, Danahy adds. Target is spending $10 million per store on renovations—in a short span of time.

"This is a complete rebuild," he says. "The logistical exercise involved in this is something we've never seen at this level."

Jeff Doucette, principal at the consulting firm, Sales Is Not Simple, views Target's entry into Canadian retail as one of real influence. However, he disagrees about its potential to revolutionize the industry on its own.

"This is not the type of retail change we saw with Chapters Indigo that put immense pressure on small-town bookstores," he says. "Target won't impact pricing any more than Walmart and others already are. This is about new brands."

What both experts do agree on is that the Canadian landscape will not look the same a few years from now. Canada is a fertile ground for American and European retailers with little to no room for expansion at home. In the case of the U.S. retailers, a shared border and cultural similarities makes Canada an easy international move.

Then there's the money. Mall performance in Canada significantly outstrips mall performance south of the border. According to Colliers International 2012 spring report, Canadian malls were almost 50 percent more productive on a (US$) sales per square foot basis in 2011.

The turning point for Canadian retail came in the early part of last decade, according to Alex Arifuzzaman, a partner with InterStratics Consultants Inc. In 2001, sales per square foot were $320 in Canada and $360 in the U.S. Just over a decade later, Canada rings in at $603 per square foot with the U.S. trailing at $448 (all figures in U.S. dollars).

"The Canadian dollar has changed the economics and everything else dramatically," he says, adding that the geography of Canada is also making it an attractive market for foreign companies. While it may have one-tenth the population of the U.S., one-third of Canadians live within three major markets.

"They can get a very good presence by only investing in a few locations," Arifuzzaman says.

Several recent announcements underscore the desirability of the Canadian retail market. Spanish-owned Zara Homes has announced it will open a Canadian location at Toronto's Yorkdale Shopping Centre, even before it has moved into the U.S. Canada is also about to see major development of U.S. premium mall outlets. And then there is the long list of American retailers that have either announced plans to expand north or started sniffing for retail space, including Macy's, Bloomingdale's, JCPenney, Nordstrom, Kohl's, and more.

Customer Satisfaction

The person who matters most to all of these retailers is, of course, the customer. People like Keri Young in Whitby who travels south frequently both for wider selection and prices.

Arifuzzaman says the changes coming to retail in Canada will be good for consumers, for the most part. After all, competition drives down prices. And Target, like their competitors, will be required to maintain a sharp focus on its product offering and acute attention to customer service.

The challenge, he says, will be managing expectations. Canadians are used to flocking south for deep discounts, discounts they didn't find when Target opened its doors here in March.

"They'll be fine-tuning their pricing but they're not going to discount prices," he says, especially after its investment in real estate, people marketing, and everything else that's gone into their expansion efforts.

Doucette notes it would be difficult for U.S. retailers to offer the same prices on both sides of the border, even if the dollar is close to par.

Arifuzzaman agrees, "The question is how much do you want to compete? No one wants a price war."

Raising the Competitive Bar

There was a time when price was the game, according to Danahy, but not anymore. "It used to be that a new competitor would start a price war," he says. "Now they have to bring their 'A' game."

And that's exactly what Target is doing, according to John Torella, senior partner with J.C. Williams Group. He gives Target points for its bright, clean, easy-to-navigate, and well-signed stores but says it's the marketing side where the retailer really raises the bar. "They have great stuff on television. They have designer events. They have a website that's exciting, contemporary, and fresh. It's all very contemporary, new, now," he says.

Target is also omni-channel poised, tapping into multiple forms of media, from TV and flyers to pop-up stores and social media. It brings designer labels and strong Canadian associations, from the Toronto pop-up store featuring a line by Vancouver designer Jason Wu to its collaboration with Roots Canada. Target also attended Fashion Week in Montreal to get to know Quebec designers.

"I don't see any downsides. It's a win-win all around," says Torella, adding that Target will be joining a whole host of well-run, best-in-class Canadian companies that already raised the bar in this country, including brands such as Aritzia, Aldo, Lululemon, and others. He notes that these retailers do a great job of recruitment, offer a steady stream of new designs, provide customer service that is second to none, feature great store design, and show commitment to good management that is sustainable.

Despite the many Canadian companies that have already impacted the sector with their unique brands and offerings, Doucette believes that there are many other Canadian companies that have an opportunity to learn from the way Target operates.

"People underestimate how well Target is run," he says, adding many in the industry are "blown away" by the chain's back end and the way it gets product in store.

"It's about execution and service," Doucette says.

Paul Jacobson of Jacobson Consulting is less convinced that Target's entry into Canada will significantly alter the retail landscape.

"They'll aggressively sell their style just as many others have," he says. "Target will compete but so does everyone else. They're all always trying to improve their game."

Jacobson points to Statistics Canada data that show that retailers across the country have planned investments for 2013 in both construction and machinery/equipment. If nothing else, these data illustrate the fact that the industry is not asleep at the switch, but rather quite responsive to the changing industry and the challenges that these changes represent.

Jacobson also notes that demand will still exist for independent retailers. In fact, experts within the industry consider this to be a time of renaissance for the independent retailer, many of which are located in thriving urban and suburban neighbourhoods where residents are primarily young, professional, and seeking local shops offering specialized expertise and knowledge about a service or product.

Jacobson adds that it will take time to see the real impact of Target and other international retailers entering the country, but in the meantime it means two very important things for Canadians: investment and jobs.

The Job Market

When it comes to jobs, retail far outstrips manufacturing in Canada, and it's likely to remain so in this current climate, according to Jacobson. But will there be enough people to fill the jobs created by everything from mall construction to warehouse operations and management staff?

It will be a challenge, according to Rowan O'Grady, managing director, North America, at the recruiting firm Hays. He says it's possible to fill most frontline jobs. The challenge will be with skilled and managerial jobs.

"There are shortages everywhere," he says. "The expectation is that this will push up salaries."

Changes in the retail industry are also likely to impact on retail as a career in Canada, something many feel is long overdue here.

Paul McElhone, executive director of the School of Retailing at the University of Alberta, says Target offers a new opportunity for Canadians, especially business grads.

"American retailers build relationships by forming university partnerships. This allows them to get the best and brightest in the workforce," he says, adding that it offers a lesson that Canadian retailers can learn from, and is something that schools and the Retail Council of Canada have been championing for some time.

"With Target, 70 percent of their hires come through colleges and universities," he says. "They're looking for relationships with schools like ours."

But Brent Houlden, partner, national practice leader at Deloitte, warns Canada could lose out on some of the best jobs in retail: those in head office.

He says with Canadian chains, 10 to 12 percent of their profit goes to supporting their head office, but technology has made it easy for many U.S. retailers to run their stores from south of the border—and few people are trying to encourage them to leave there.

"What shocks U.S. retailers is how little government officials try to woo head offices and warehouses here," he says. "We don't understand the power of the head office. They're good jobs, and they're well-paying."

Real Estate Crunch

Despite all the benefits noted by experts in retail, one issue remains. Where will the retailers go?

Vacancy rates are below 5 percent in many urban centres, according to James Smerdon, vice-president, director of retail consulting, at Colliers International.

This is among the "most dynamic times" his industry has ever seen. For example, he says there's about $2.5 million in retail development to happen in metro Vancouver over the next five to seven years—a figure he says some have pegged closer to $7 million—and there is $10 million worth of retail projects approved or under development in Calgary.

The real pressure is in "A" grade centres in urban cores, and that's leading to some unintended consequences for their second cousins in more suburban areas. Swedish retailer H&M set up its first B.C. store in Coquitlam Centre rather than the downtown Pacific Centre simply because it wanted into the market, and there was no room in the city's marquee mall.

Cross-Border Conundrum

As seismic as all of these changes may be, some question the sustainability of this volume of retail.

"You've got all of these retailers coming in to feed on the Canadian market," Danahy says. "It's the same size pie, and they all have the same size forks."

There are also the issues of cross-border and online shopping to consider. Houlden says online shopping is behind much of the push for U.S. retailers coming to Canada, and it will influence the shape their stores take. For example, Nordstrom has been shipping to Canada for awhile now, and he says it's no fluke the retailer wants to set up shop in Yorkdale.

"They're picking that because that's where their customers live," he says.

This, he says, points to the fact that bricks-and-mortar retailing could very well be the strongest it's ever been in the country. It's also a reflection of the growth of e-commerce and online sales in Canada and begs the question: How are those in the industry planning to expand their online presence and marry it to their physical stores?

But will having ample access to these retailers take a bite out of cross-border shopping? Not likely, says Douglas Porter, chief economist and managing director, economic research at BMO.

"When you consider the average person who crosses the border, I doubt many are going exclusively for Target. Even at two or three stores, I'm still not convinced," he says. "By far and away, the draw is pricing. The reality is if the Canadian dollar was sitting at 80 cents—or even 90 cents—we wouldn't be having this conversation."

Resent results from Statistics Canada bear him out. In January [2013], the number of Canadians visiting the U.S. was up 5 percent from the year previous.

Just ask Keri Young, the Whitby mother who spent two hours on her first visit to the new Target in her neighbourhood, but still plans to head south at least once a year for a trip to the American version.

"Oh, there are still some items I like better down there," she says with a laugh.

Looking Ahead

The fickle nature of today's global economy makes it challenging to predict just what the Canadian retail scene will look like in five or ten years, though it is clear that Target is entering the Canadian market during a time of flux and change. The growth of e-commerce and the omni-channel retail experience, increasingly scares real estate opportunities heightened competition for skilled talent, the continued globalization of the Canadian market, as well as a host of other factors, will continue to shape and influence the industry. And as Target continues to become well and truly immersed within the Canadian market, the impact of its arrival will combine with these changes to present both challenges and opportunities for retailers across the country.

Discussion Questions

1. Target's arrival comes at a time that signifies not just a turning point, but a near revolution within the industry. Why do retail experts believe the country's retail landscape is shifting?

2. According to Alex Arifuzzaman, what was the turning point for Canadian retail?

3. Why does Arifuzzaman say the changes coming to retail will be good for consumers?

Source: Danielle Harder, "The Arrival of Target," *Canadian Retailer,* spring 2013, volume 23, issue 2, pp. 16–20.

CASE 2 Retailing in India—Impact of Hypermarkets

The history of India contains a wealth of change and alteration, and the modern era is no different as the country blossoms into a major player in the global economy. Sizable economic growth during the past decade, particularly in the retail sector, has changed the way consumers behave. Although the size of the current Indian retail sector is impressive, its potential really speaks to what retailing will mean in the future. The retail market in India was approximately $353 billion in 2010, and by 2014 it will reach $543 billion in total sales, of which modern retailing accounts for 27 percent.

International retailers are slowly making their way into India. India's government allows foreign companies to open only single-brand stores. Large retailers with more than one brand are required to engage in a joint venture with an Indian company. Walmart, Tesco, and Carrefour have opened hypermarkets in India, but doing so was not an easy process. Carrefour waited ten years to open its first store as a result of the restrictions. Hypermarkets—large retail outlets—combine the products found in a department store and supermarket, with the goal of turning shopping into an experience. The large store layouts and variety of merchandise force customers to spend more time in the stores, which in turn leads to more sales. The potential for hypermarkets in India sheds light on the country's changing retail landscape and the shopping habits of its consumers.

Before 2000, Indian consumers generally purchased many of their retail goods from local mom-and-pop stores called *kiranas,* which sold mainly provisions and groceries. Shopping at *kiranas* is easy and convenient, because the small stores serve specific neighbourhoods and establish personal relationships with their customers. The new infusion of hypermarkets threatens to rob local store owners of their customer base—approximately a 23 percent decrease in sales in one year.

There are over 300 hypermarkets and 6800 supermarkets in India. India has been experiencing 20 percent annual growth in retail markets. Hypermarket sales were expected to increase fivefold from 2009 to 2013, and supermarket sales were expected to increase 150 percent during the same period. Each new store opening may draw customers from 20 to 25 *kiranas* and fruit and vegetable stands, affecting over 100 000 vendors.

Most *kiranas* cannot compete with hypermarkets, because these larger retail outlets create more efficiency within the supply chain. Much local produce in India currently gets wasted, because the country lacks sufficient infrastructure. Even as it progresses through rapid development, India still lacks some amenities that Westerners take for granted, such as refrigeration in retail operations. If a large retailer wants to open a hypermarket in India, it will have to invest capital to ensure freshness throughout the supply chain and help reduce waste. The Indian government is expected to spend US$500 billion over the next few years to develop a world-class infrastructure, which should spur growth in the retail sector.

The lack of infrastructure underlies a related issue facing hypermarkets. Unlike in Western nations, India's rather poor roads and transportation systems do not allow retailers to locate on large plots of land on the outskirts of town, since fewer consumers can reach them. Therefore, hypermarkets must look for retail space in more urban areas, which provide little available real estate. Buying up space from existing stores means displacing local corner shops already inhabiting that space, and this may prompt protests from Indian consumers and store owners who value the Indian tradition that the *kiranas* represent. Yet larger retail outlets in India could have a dramatic impact on the economy, possibly creating millions of jobs in the next ten years. Although many Indians may not appreciate the notion of hypermarkets immediately, their presence is likely inevitable.

Much of the impetus for the emergence of hypermarkets in India also comes from changes among Indian consumers. The country's younger generations are exposed to a host of innovative products that were unknown to their parents. They are far more receptive to new products and ideas. In addition, this segment of the population reflects the shifting age demographics; more than half of India's current population is younger than 25 years of age. With such a large percentage of younger consumers, it seems inevitable that India's cultural tastes will evolve. The strong and abundant local *kiranas* have been a cultural mainstay, but they cannot efficiently offer Indians access to new and technologically advanced products. Because hypermarkets combine department stores and super-markets, they carry product lines that local vendors cannot. They sell brand-name products at affordable prices, thereby enabling Indians to purchase a wide assortment of goods that they otherwise could not have.

This shift, from local mom-and-pop stores to more organized retail outlets, is happening very quickly in India. It is embraced by many consumers despite the cultural and legal considerations associated with hypermarkets. Furthermore, because hypermarkets offer potential benefits for both the economy and the national infrastructure, local governments generally support the arrival of a hypermarket. The ultimate target market, however, is not the government but the consumers, and just as in any country at any time, the challenge lies in understanding what those consumers want and how to get it to them.

Discussion Questions

1. How might a hypermarket located in India appeal to consumers and orient them to shopping in larger stores?

2. Is the Indian government's willingness to spend $500 billion to improve the nation's infrastructure good news for international retailers? Why or why not?

3. Identify the main changes that mark Indian consumers. How can international retailers learn more about India's youthful demographic?

Sources: "Infra Red—India's Ambitious Development Plans Hinge on Attracting Private Capital," *The Economist,* July 8, 2010; "A Wholesale Invasion—a French Supermarket Chain Takes a Bet on India," *The Economist,* May 20, 2010; Armina Ligaya, "India Puts Squeeze on Hypermarkets," *National,* September 16, 2009; "India—Tier I & II Cities May Have 300 Hypermarkets by 2011," *RNCOS,* August 13, 2009; www.ibef.org/industry/retail.aspx (accessed July 15, 2010); "Coming to Market—Retailing in India," *The Economist,* April 15, 2006, p. 69; "Despite Growing Debt, the Indian Consumer Banks on Tomorrow," *India Knowledge@Wharton,* October 31, 2006; Ranjan Biswas, "India's Changing Consumers," *Chain Store Age,* May 2006; John Elliott, "Retail Revolution," *Fortune,* August 9, 2007, pp. 14–16; Amelia Gentleman, "Indians Protest Wal-Mart's Wholesale Entry," *New York Times,* August 10, 2007.

This case was written by Todd Nicolini, while an MBA student at Loyola College in Maryland, under the supervision of Professor Hope Corrigan, and Britt Hackmann, Babson College.

CASE 3 | **Sobeys Finds Its Fit with the Urban Crowd: Customer Behaviour**

Venture into Sobeys' latest Urban Fresh grocery store in downtown Toronto and your senses are set ablaze. Rows and rows of colourful, local, and organic produce and fragrant, fresh meals are set against a backdrop of contemporary design elements that give the space a high-end, gourmet shop feel.

"Our shoppers are foodies and they like to experiment with food, so we give them a lot to get excited about," says Mary Dalimonte, general manager, Fresh Service Format for Sobeys.

With a diverse selection of gourmet and grocery item staples, the 20 000 square-foot store, located at the bottom of a city centre condo, maximizes space with the use of vertical merchandizing and smaller-scale packaging. "This store caters to a four- to five-block radius of shoppers who won't be buying the ten-pound bag of potatoes," says Dalimonte. "They are condo dwellers—mostly singles or couples—who don't have a lot of space to store food." Even the grocery carts are smaller. "This is the ultimate urban grocery shopper cart with a place to put your purse and your coffee," she adds.

But a lack of space doesn't limit the variety of food offerings by any means. The Urban Fresh store features an extensive salad bar, a sushi section, a made-to-order pizza and pasta component, numerous prepared meals to go, as well as a café offering gourmet coffees with a selection of tables and chairs to enjoy them. "We want this to be our customers' place to come for a coffee on a Sunday, so we purposely put the chairs and tables facing the window. Even the benches outside face out to the street so our customers can people-watch—it's really meant to be a neighbourhood destination," says Dalimonte. The space also fits a substantial deli, butcher, and fish counter, complete with a fishmonger who offers samples and suggestions for dinner options. "Most people don't know what they're making tonight for dinner so we make it easy for them," she says.

While the supermarket giant opened the first of its smaller-scale "urban" grocery stores several years ago in Toronto, the model has evolved into what is now a chic, European-style food destination with a focus on freshness and style. This is made apparent from the blades of glass painted on the storefront windows and potted grass throughout the store to the hand-cut green wallpaper complete with tree motifs that expertly camouflage the condo's otherwise unsightly building structure. The floors are the original concrete, but they are buffed and tinted black to provide the urban feel.

The store's focal point, however, is a giant chandelier in a rotunda that will be incorporated into the new format Urban Fresh stores going forward. "The chandelier inspired the contemporary yet classic feel of the store. There really is a mix of traditional and contemporary going on here," says designer Charlane Codner, partner/

VP creative services for Fish Out of Water. A second rotunda with lights over the café creates another zone in the store, she adds.

Further exemplifying the classic feel are custom-made aisle ends made of painted medium density fibreboard, which resemble armoires that could easily pass for the ones found in someone's living space. Even the use of metro shelving to hold product throughout the store as opposed to traditional racks give the space a contemporary feel that the designers say really plays to the urban customer base.

"We also aimed to strike a balance between design and functionality," adds Codner. Case in point: the glass around the meat and seafood areas alleviates cool air flow from hitting the customer, but also features a visually enticing frosted vinyl layer imprinted with the wallpaper motif used throughout the rest of the store.

Even the signage throughout the space veers away from traditional grocery models by featuring a few super-size, vibrant graphics of food as opposed to lots of text. "It's subtle and sexy," says Codner. "It's food as romance. It has to speak for itself."

Lighting throughout the store is also used to emphasize the focus on food. Codner says high-intensity discharge lights throughout provide strong ambient light levels while metal halide lights give a punch in select areas.

Dalimonte says customer reaction to the store has been extremely positive. "We've been hearing really good things and those that come to visit that aren't from the area say they wish they had one of these stores near them," she says. "Customers like the ambience and really appreciate the attention to detail."

From a financial perspective, she says Sobeys is pleased with the performance of the Urban Fresh model so far. With 11 stores in Ontario and two in Alberta, she says "the sky's the limit" when it comes to future expansion. In fact, she says "Toronto residents will be very pleased at our next location."

Discussion Questions

1. Do you agree that stores in urban centres call for unique designs and product offerings? Why or why not?

2. Identify another retailer that has tailored its retail strategy and/or in-store design to meet the needs of the urban market.

Source: Rosalind Stefanac for the Retail Council of Canada, *Canadian Retailer,* January/February 2010, pp. 11–12.

CASE 4   Attracting Generation Y to a Retail Career

The Diva Brand

Diva is a specialty retail store focused on fast-fashion jewellery and accessories. The brand's origins are in Australia, but recent years have seen rapid international expansion, and the brand now has stores in America, Russia, and Europe. Diva is predominantly located in shopping centres, with some stores in high-street locations, and is always positioned in/around apparel fashion clusters. The stores are clean, simplistic, and brightly lit, reflecting their fast-moving, funky, and vibrant product range targeted at the youth market (predominantly, 15- to 25-year-old females). Diva's positioning sees it as the only fashion jewellery/hair accessory specialist retailer in Australia.

Due to Diva's recent expansion, staff numbers have grown significantly. However, Diva is confronted with the problem of attracting and retaining experienced and talented people, particularly from Generation Y. In an attempt to counteract this problem, Diva has implemented several internal talent policies to provide a point of difference and be an employer of choice, including:

- Training plans/workshops to fill skill gaps

- Career development program for top store managers
- Leadership development program for top regional managers
- Increased salary package offers for certain roles to attract talent/skill
- Global expansion, with new offers of career progression

Generational Differences in the Workforce

As a result of key demographic and lifestyle issues such as aging populations, declining fertility, delayed retirements, rising labour participation rates, and higher life expectancies, there is a demographic trough in the Asia Pacific workforce, in which there is soon to be smaller proportions of younger-aged members and larger cohorts of mature-aged workers. This is further compounded by a shrinking talent pool and the fact that retail is not perceived as a career of choice by the adult population, who have limited sight of career path opportunities "beyond the shop floor."

Although research acknowledges the pertinence of this issue in retailing today, it remains unclear how to effectively manage generational diversity in the workplace. This is not a new issue; however, wider age groups are culminating in less segregated work arrangements. In the past, older staff undertook senior managerial positions, while younger workers assumed front-desk or field positions. However, today it is common to see staff members from all age groups working together on projects, with senior employees managing across several generations or younger employees managing older generations. It is important to note that, if managed poorly, intergenerational impacts can cause conflict for employers and among employees, hampering workplace productivity and morale.

Retailers, as well as organizations from many other industries, therefore need to identify and adopt the best approaches in attracting and retaining staff across all retail functions, optimizing the experiences of mature-aged workers while capitalizing on the potential of young employees. This involves understanding each generation and its unique perspectives, communication styles, and working styles in order to provide tailored support. Each generation holds different perspectives of work, including the definition of an attractive working environment, leadership qualities, and preferred team-playing approaches, and has an individual information processing style. For example, Generation Y believes in having fluid work patterns and influencing job terms and conditions. Conversely, the Baby Boomer generation regards work as a primary security in life, while Generation X values a balance between work and life.

Generation Y

Born between 1981 and 2000, members of Generation Y were one of the key segments of focus in shop floor to boardroom given their sheer numbers and prospective employment in retail as recent or upcoming workforce entrants. While organizations have had time to understand Baby Boomers and Generation X-ers, determining the needs of Generation Y-ers has been challenging, especially given their vastly different values. This is particularly important given the significant career opportunities that exist for Generation Y in retailing. In better understanding the unique career motivations, perceptions, and aspirations of Generation Y, a number of focus groups were conducted with university students who were studying a business major and currently working in retail and high school students who were studying retail-related subjects and currently working in retail or interested in doing so. In terms of perceptions of working

in retail, research found that retail is simply not viewed as a career of choice by Generation Y. This is primarily due to the feeling that retail involves "just being a check-out chick," has limited or no career paths "beyond the shop floor" and is therefore a short-term employment solution, and has difficult conditions at times (e.g., long hours, repetitive tasks, low salaries). A related concern was that the retail industry is not generally perceived as prestigious in the eyes of the general public.

Despite such issues, there were a number of motivators (other than financial) for working in retail for Generation Y, such as improving one's social life and extending friendship circles, gaining work experience while studying, and following a particular passion (i.e., fashion). Generation Y-ers also reported a variety of career aspirations that were generally consistent with the courses or subjects they were studying. Despite the fact that few listed retail as their number-one career option, a strong desire was found for a career that could be facilitated by the retail industry, such as marketing, HR, or buying.

Focused on self-improvement, Generation Y-ers also expressed enjoyment in working for organizations that provide constant learning environments; they want to be involved in the organization's vision and mission, desire mobility and flexibility in the workplace, and seek instant gratification. Members of Generation Y also thrive on systematic feedback and value positive reinforcement at accelerated rates, as compared to previous generations. This is the primary reason that Generation Y questions starting at the bottom of the organizational ladder, having developed a strong desire for rapid career progression from years of high-level education.

Discussion Questions

1. How can Diva demystify what happens behind the scenes and make potential Generation Y employees aware of the opportunities available to them beyond the shop floor?

2. Diva has implemented a learning organizational culture in an attempt to attract and retain staff. Discuss the possible pros and cons of this strategy for Generation Y.

3. Give examples of how other organizations (perhaps even nonretailers) attract a Generation Y workforce. What could Diva learn from other organizations?

Source: This case was written by Sean Sands, Monash University, and Carla Ferraro, Monash University.

When award-winning U.S.-based specialty retailer The Vitamin Shoppe started exploring the possibility of expanding its operations into the Canadian market nearly two years ago, it already recognized the attractiveness of the robust retail industry in the country, particularly the health and wellness category. The supplement market is a $3 billion industry in Canada, which sees 70 percent of Canadian citizens taking supplements on a regular basis. The company also understood that there was clearly lots of room for another retailer of vitamins and health products to play. The questions they had, however, were far more philosophical in nature.

"We kicked off the official business effort internally about 18 months ago," explains Musab Balbale, The Vitamin Shoppe's director of business development. "There were two key questions that we asked initially. We first wanted to identify whether or not there was an opportunity for us to really create a compelling offering to the customer based on what our core values are—assortment, knowledge, and value. And the second was, do we have the organizational breadth internally to successfully execute against the opportunity?"

To answer its first question, the company, which branded itself as Vitapath for the Canadian market, didn't have to look any further than its product. It conducted a review of the competitive landscape in the country and identified a real opportunity to bring a unique offering to Canada.

"We view ourselves as a single destination in the market that serves the entire family," explains Balbale. "We carry not only vitamins and supplements focused on the health conscious consumer, but we also carry a strong line of sports supplements focused on the active consumer."

Whether the Vitapath customer is looking for gummy multivitamins for their kids, basic fish oils and supplements, or more obscure herbs for those people becoming more conscious about taking care of their health in specific ways, Balbale believes that the supplement retailer has it all. However, he points out that the product is only the beginning of the Vitapath experience.

"The level of assortment and breadth that we offer is unique to the market," he says. "That comes with a level of service and knowledge that engages the customer in conversation and imparts product value."

And because of this, Vitapath's store associates, called "health enthusiasts," are core to what the company is and what they do, which is serve customers.

"We want to wow our customers by impressing them by the level of engagement offered in our stores. We want that to be our differentiator."

To achieve this, the company knew that it needed to hire the right people—people who would believe in what the store stands for and become ambassadors for its products and values. It also knew that it could not stray from its objectives during the recruitment process.

"We hire on three filters—empathy, knowledge, and passion—and we never compromise on these core attributes when searching for talent," he says. "But we're particularly mindful of hiring people who want to serve customers and who are enthusiastic about good health and about nutritional education. We've found that if we hire with these criteria in mind, we get great people who are tremendous for our brand."

In its search for the right associates, the company talked to a lot of people and posted on job boards. But there was a very active aspect to its efforts, which included visiting nutritionist colleges and job fairs associated with nutritionist colleges to find talent. The company asked for recommendations from its suppliers and vendors in Canada, and also scoured LinkedIn to see if it could find interested people connected to the industry.

"In the end, we just talked to as many people as we possibly could," says Balbale. "And we're really pleased to say that we found the right people who fit our profile and who are enthusiastic about the opportunity."

The right people with the right attitude and knowledge level were hired to join the Canadian team; however, their journey was just beginning. Vitapath invited senior members of its store team, including the district manager and store managers, to spend three weeks in The Vitamin Shoppe's Buffalo stores close to the border to impart the softer cultural side of what the company is and what it aims to do. The team then entered into a sophisticated year-long training program that the company developed.

"We call it Vitapath University," explains Balbale. "It's an online training program that provides our health enthusiasts with the tools to become more knowledgeable and improve their customer service abilities."

The training combines online curriculum with in-store training exercises that focus on three things: 1) building category health knowledge, 2) building specific brand and product knowledge, and 3) focusing on developing empathetic customer engagement skills. Time is scheduled for each team member to train during store hours to complete three modules, each with three levels of learning within them, with a test at the end of each module and level.

The training program has been very well-received by the retailer's health enthusiasts as it prepares them to properly offer the service that Vitapath is building its brand on. And, what's more, the company has instituted a pay-for-knowledge program in which individuals receive an increase in pay for each level that they pass that's commensurate to the score with which they passed.

"Our store health enthusiasts really appreciate the program because it has real incentives for them to excel and grow and learn with the company," points out Balbale. "We think it provides the right feedback for all of the personal investment that our store health enthusiasts put into the company and serving our customers."

Aside from the customer and the health enthusiasts that serve them, the company also had to examine its internal breadth that Balbale speaks of to ensure that challenges related to expansion into Canada were met head on.

"This was our first expansion outside of the United States, and so we faced internally the challenges that any company does leaving its native market," explains Balbale. "We had to learn everything from managing multiple currencies, how to identify and comply with local regulations, whether it be financial or human resources related, finding local partners, our legal counsel, marketing partners, and folks that could build a construction for us and put our fixtures together in our stores."

The company tackled these challenges by making the expansion a company-wide effort. According to Balbale, Vitapath and its American parent The Vitamin Shoppe are both internally very operationally focused and have a pretty collaborative culture. The combination allowed them to tackle the challenges as they arose by making each of its business units responsible for delivering their respective solution in Canada.

"We worked really hard together to make sure that where those business units overlapped, we really understood the nuances and requirements so that we could deliver an exceptional experience for our Canadian customers."

What was most challenging for the company, however, was in developing operational processes that differ from those that they employ in the United States.

"In the United States we're a 582-store chain," says Balbale. "We have our own distribution centres, and we have all of the vendors ship to our distribution centres, which we then ship out to our stores. In Canada, because of our smaller scale with two initial stores, we chose to develop a direct-to-store delivery supply chain model."

The direct-to-store model involves product coming into the store that needs to be opened, counted, and audited, with all information communicated back to the vendor. Balbale admits that the process is not perfect, allowing too much room for error on both the store and vendor side, but that they are working through the challenges.

Another challenge faced by Vitapath in Canada, and another reason to implement the direct-to-store shipment of product, is in addressing challenges posed by Health Canada regulations, which differ significantly from those south of the border. In Canada, retailers offering supplements and other health food and vitamin products are required to sell only products that have been registered with Health Canada and that have received what's called a national products number. In addition to that, the full chain of control from manufacturing to delivery of product to the store needs to be licensed by Health Canada.

"In order to comply with Health Canada regulations, we're working primarily with Canadian brands and Canadian distributors—over 80 percent of our product is sourced locally."

This decision, however, was not only to simplify the sourcing strategy and to reduce the number of imports, but to ensure that Vitapath is a truly Canadian brand and Canadian distributor.

"It's a decision that we've come to be really proud of," says Balbale. "We'll continue to monitor our stores and will continue to listen to our customer. If there are gaps within our assortment that we can't fill from within Canada, we'll find brands and products in the U.S. to help strengthen that assortment. But we're really proud of the fact that Vitapath is a Canadian business. One that supports other Canadian businesses."

And the decision to partner primarily with Canadian manufacturers was also made easier due to the fact that the company already had great relationships with Canadian vendors from their work in the U.S.

"We've had some really great relationships with Canadian brands even before we entered the market. They actually helped us in understanding their view of the market and have been incredibly helpful to us in providing market insight and advice. And quite honestly, working so closely together has helped strengthen our relationship with them and it continues to provide already strong Canadian brands with opportunities in our stores in the United States. We really look to our suppliers and vendors as business partners and work together to make both of our businesses better."

Vitapath opened its first stores in Canada, both in the Greater Toronto Area, in January [2013]. And though it may be too early to tell exactly how the company's being received by its Canadian consumer, Balbale is extremely optimistic concerning the progress of the stores.

"We're here for the long run. We plan to open additional stores later in 2013 and 2014 and are looking at real estate actively. Vancouver certainly is an exciting market for us to go next. It has a particular focus on health and wellness which in some ways looks a lot like the West Coast in the United States. But right now we're focused on building out Toronto and building enough scale to support our brand and the infrastructure in Canada.

Discussion Questions

1. What is Vitapath's retail strategy? What is its target market and how does it try to develop an advantage over its competition?

2. Describe Vitapath's retail mix: product, price, promotion, people, place, process. How does its retail mix support its strategy?

3. What factors in the environment provided the opportunity for The Vitamin Shoppe to develop a new and potentially successful retail chain in Canada? What insight did Balbale have that perhaps other players in the health and wellness category did not?

4. What do you think the Vitapath brand could mean to consumers? How have the Vitapath management tried to affect the value of its brand name?

5. What do you believe will be the major challenges facing Vitapath as it goes forward? Is the brand advantage sustainable going forward? Can Vitapath defend its position against other health and wellness specialty retailers?

6. What other potential Canadian markets do you believe would support the growth of the brand? Why?

Source: Sean C. Tarry, "Supplementing for Success in the Canadian Market," *Canadian Retailer*, spring 2013, volume 23, issue 2, pp. 40–43.

CASE 6 Abercrombie & Fitch and American Eagle Compete for 18- to 22-Year-Olds

Jennifer Shaffer, a 19-year-old college student living in Cupertino, California, used to shop at Abercrombie & Fitch (A&F) once a month. She thought the prices were high, but the brand name and image appealed to her. As she says, "It's like I really had to have Abercrombie." Then an American Eagle (AE) store opened about 15 minutes from her home. "They look the same, and they're both really cute," she says. "But American Eagle's prices are a little cheaper."

Both A&F and AE are still growing into their present strategy of selling casual apparel to the teen, college, and university market. When A&F was established as an outdoor sporting goods retailer over 100 years ago, it sold the highest-quality hunting, fishing, and camping goods. It also outfitted some of the greatest explorations in the early part of the twentieth century, including Robert Perry's expedition to the North Pole and Theodore Roosevelt's trips to the Amazon and Africa.

Over time, its safari image became less attractive to consumers. The chain experienced a significant decline in sales and profits, and in 1977 it was forced to declare bankruptcy. The company, initially acquired by Oshman's Sporting Goods, did not experience a turnaround until The Limited Inc. acquired it in 1988. Initially, The Limited positioned A&F as a tailored clothing store for men. In 1995, The Limited repositioned A&F to target both men and women in the teen and college and university market, with an emphasis on casual American style and youth.

In 1999, The Limited (now Limited Brands) sold A&F. Now A&F operates 340 Abercrombie & Fitch stores, 205 Abercrombie kids stores, 507 Hollister Co. stores, and 16 Gilly Hicks (personal care products and intimate apparel) stores in the United States, as well as four Abercrombie & Fitch, eight Hollister Co., and two Abercrombie kids stores internationally. Furthermore, A&F offers its merchandise online.

American Eagle, although lacking the rich tradition of A&F, also was positioned as an outfitter when it started in 1977. Initially offering apparel only for men, AE shifted its focus to teens and college and university students in 1995. Its merchandise includes jeans, graphic T-shirts, accessories, outerwear, footwear, and swimwear. American Eagle operates more than 900 stores in the United States and Canada. The retailer also operates ae.com, which offers additional sizes and styles online. Under the aerie brand name, AE offers a collection of dorm wear and intimate apparel, available in 137 aerie stores, in AE stores, and at aerie.com.

Even though A&F and AE have evolved from their roots, their apparel still features an outdoor, rugged aspect. Both retail chains carry a similar assortment of polos, pants, T-shirts, shorts, jeans, outerwear, and sweaters. All the apparel and accessories at both chains appear under the stores' private-label brand. The Ivy League– and sportswear-inspired merchandise aims to fit the campus lifestyle of its target customer.

Abercrombie.com first drew Jennifer to an A&F store a couple of years ago. She recalls browsing the website with some girlfriends and looking at the muscular young men featured at the site. This young and sexy image is enhanced by store signage featuring scantily clad lacrosse players and young beachgoers.

Even though A&F devotes its advertising and marketing resources to reaching university-age consumers (18- to 22-years-old), many younger teenagers also patronize its stores. The company thus faces concerns that the image of its stores will suffer if they become a hangout for teenagers. The development of the Hollister chain, which targets 14- to 18-year-old students, represents one of its responses to preserve the A&F image while also catering to the growing teenage market.

Hollister stores are unique. The merchandise is 20 to 30 percent less expensive than A&F's merchandise, and the styling features brighter colours and larger logos. However, many teenagers fail to recognize the subtle differences. They contend that it is essentially the same merchandise except at lower prices.

Furthermore, Hollister stores are roughly 2000 square feet smaller than A&F stores, and the store design is completely distinct. Whereas A&F stores still convey outdoor ruggedness in their decor, Hollister stores present a California beach–inspired theme. The retailer wants customers to feel as though they are part of a beach party. This casual atmosphere provides young consumers with an enjoyable shopping experience, as the decor inspires and evokes memories of hot summer days at any time of the year.

Discussion Questions

1. What, if any, are the differences in A&F's and AE's retail strategies?

2. What are the brand images of A&F and AE? What words and phrases are associated with each retailer's brand name?

3. List other specialty apparel retailers that target the same customers as A&F and AE. How do these brands differentiate themselves in the competitive retail environment? Construct a product positioning map to illustrate each retailer's positioning.

4. Which retailer(s) has (have) the stronger competitive position?

Sources: www.abercrombie.com (accessed July 12, 2010); www.ae.com (accessed July 12, 2010); Abercrombie & Fitch Annual Report, 2009.

This case was written by Kristina Pacca of Loyola College of Maryland and Britt Hackmann of Babson College.

CASE 7   Vivah Jewellery: Location Strategy

In 1985, the first Vivah Jewellery store opened at Pickering Town Centre and heralded a new trend for Directions East—a wholesale distribution company that focused on gift items and art objects imported from the Far East. The company also carried jewellery items that were sold to select Canadian retailers and it wasn't long before jewellery, which represented 20 percent of the product lines, began to make up 80 percent of the sales. As a result, the decision was made to create a retail concept that would focus specifically on fashion jewellery and Vivah Jewellery was born.

The retail store was named after founder Zell Goodbaum's wife Vivah—an accomplished gold and silversmith with an artistic flair for jewellery design. The product lines reflected her preference for classic lines and simplicity, as well as a belief that fashion jewellery could be high quality and affordable. Vivah's love of handmade designs was embraced by retail customers who found that Vivah Jewellery offered a more affordable alternative to traditional jewellery stores such as Birks and Peoples and a step up from the fashion jewellery offerings of fashion retailers such as Suzy Shier and Reitmans. Major product lines include earrings, necklaces, bracelets, and rings—75 percent of which feature sterling silver and semi-precious stones.

The company cautiously began its retail concept with a kiosk location (approx. 200 square feet). The original kiosk location was extremely successful and more kiosk locations were added as the company began to slowly

expand—opening in locations that provided sufficient customer traffic to suit their small space needs. Today, the company has 29 retail locations in Ontario, six in British Columbia, and two in Alberta.

Kiosks are the venue of choice for most Vivah outlets but the company has a few traditional retail stores within shopping malls (referred to as in-line stores). The in-line stores are slightly larger than the kiosks (300 square feet on average) but small compared to most retail stores in malls. Surprisingly, kiosks may be small in size but the rental costs are not—kiosks, because of their central locations, can cost more than a traditional storefront location. Rental costs for kiosks and in-line mall locations vary depending on the mall's location and customer traffic.

Range of Monthly Rental Costs		
Ontario	**Low**	**High**
Kiosk	$3500	$5200
In-line store	$1700	$4500
B.C.		
Kiosk	$2500	$9900
In-line store	$2900	$6500

In addition to the monthly rental cost, malls often demand a percentage of monthly sales as well as a monthly contribution to the mall's marketing budget. Vivah focuses on small to medium-sized malls for the most part, as kiosk space rents in some of the larger malls are substantial. For example, Vivah had a kiosk location at the Toronto

Eaton Centre for several years and paid $12 000 a month in rent.

Vivah has also experimented with some non-traditional locations—a kiosk inside Credit Valley Hospital in Mississauga, a leased space inside Angie Strauss's Gallery in Niagara-on-the-Lake, and a retail store at the Fallsview Casino in Niagara Falls.

Due to the small physical size of the product lines (the average product takes up a half-inch of space) Vivah does not require a lot of space to carry a full product assortment. The average kiosk location is 200 square feet and carries 7000 to 8000 SKUs. Sales are fairly consistent through the year (with a spike during the Christmas season) as jewellery is often a special occasion purchase (Valentine's Day, Mother's Day, prom, graduation, weddings). On average, sales per square foot are $1500. Vivah offers a wide range of prices in its product lines, including one-of-a-kind designs that are sold at the higher end of the spectrum.

Price Range of Product Lines	
Earrings	$14.95–$149.95
Bracelets	$19.95–$499.95
Necklaces	$24.95–$999.99

Certain core product lines are carried at each Vivah location; however, store managers have the flexibility to adapt their product offerings to suit local market needs. The company continues to focus on sterling silver and semi-precious stones but has devoted more space to bridal jewellery product lines, which have proven to be an extremely successful addition to its retail offerings. The primary market for Vivah is women, 35 to 55 years of age, middle income, who appreciate jewellery but are not necessarily looking for cutting-edge or high-end items. The secondary market is the bride who is buying for herself as well as her wedding party.

The company spends a limited amount on advertising, relying on word of mouth, repeat customers, and the retail locations as the main form of promotion. To help reach the bridal market, the company advertises in *Wedding Bells* magazine and the magazine's website, and has access to the magazine's mailing and e-mail lists.

The Vivah management team is well aware that the retail industry is continually changing and that new retail concepts are being introduced all the time. Retail is extremely competitive and current downward economic trends are serious causes for concern for many small retailers. Management is interested in new formats that may provide growth opportunities for the company beyond the traditional mall environment. For example, Vivah management has considered acquiring retail space on cruise ships. The company has also been approached by some U.S. malls; however, at this point the retailer is wary of entering an even more competitive market where it has little experience and no brand awareness.

Vivah management has turned to your retail consulting firm to develop a retail strategy for the future.

Discussion Questions

1. In planning for the future, what kinds of information should Vivah seek out? Explain your answer.

2. What are Vivah's competitive advantages and disadvantages in comparison to other jewellery retailers? How can it reduce the disadvantages?

3. What other types of sites do you think Vivah should consider (besides those stated in the case)? Why?

Source: Courtesy of Terri Champion.

CASE 8 Retail's Rural Frontier: Location Strategy

Canada is an overwhelmingly urban nation, but the rural market remains significant: Figures from the 2006 Census show that the rural and small-town population counts have stayed relatively stable since 1981, at about six million. But looking beyond that figure, it's interesting to note that rural and small-town residents outnumber the 4.1 million Canadians who live in towns and cities with populations of between 10 000 and 99 999—and since 1981, the number of rural and small-town residents has actually *increased* in Ontario, British Columbia, Alberta, Manitoba, and Prince Edward Island. That trend is fuelled, in part, by the growing number of retirees and families leaving large cities in search of a less costly and quieter lifestyle.

New small-market formats are a response, in part, to rising expectations among rural consumers. Even if rural consumers don't shop on the Internet, many are using it to research their product choices, says Maureen Atkinson, a retail consultant with Toronto-based J.C. Williams Group. Urban families and retirees migrating to small communities are also bringing along their urban tastes, she adds. In some small communities, says Walmart Canada spokesperson Felicia Fefer, grassroots demand for more convenience and choice has motivated residents to ask for a Walmart store. That was the case in Labrador City, says store manager Corey Legge. "Customers have the same expectations here in an isolated community as they do in a city such as

St. John's," he said. "They expect to be able to get what they want: new items, seasonally correct items, price leadership, friendly and helpful associates, a clean and uncluttered store, and fast and efficient checkout and return service."

While expectations may be similar, rural consumers are markedly different from their urban cousins in other respects. According to research conducted by Bensimon Byrne, a Toronto-based ad agency, small-town Canadians still hold very traditional beliefs based on hard work, saving, community involvement, having a family, order and security, cooperation, and charitable giving. As consumers, residents of smaller communities are also more frugal. "Residents of small, mid-sized, and large communities share top concerns: the economy, health care, the environment, and ethics in government and politics," according to a recent report. "(But) residents of smaller communities value both tangible benefits (getting a good deal, getting the lowest possible price) and intangibles, such as brand comfort, nationalism, and community involvement, more than residents of large cities."

In more ways than one, "fitting in" is an important key to success in small communities. The North West Company typically enters a town through an acquisition or, in the case of some First Nations communities, through a partnership with a land development corporation. On occasion, the company has even submitted itself to a community referendum. Active community sponsorship and donation practices help increase community support. Nationally, The North West Company supports the Canadian Diabetes Association, but the company leaves a lot of discretion to its managers when it comes to charitable causes. In everyday dealings with customers, says Kennedy, a genuine sense of friendliness and helpfulness outweighs issues such as wait times.

Experienced rural retailers say companies must be sensitive to the impact their stores will have on the local economy. The North West Company often makes the case that its stores help keep money in the community by encouraging residents to shop locally, rather than travel to a regional centre. "We're not trying to dominate every local shopping category," adds Kennedy. "If three other locally owned retailers are going to go out of business because of you, that's not good."

In Parry Sound, Staples supported local revitalization efforts by locating its store downtown. The company also did all its hiring locally. "We found that very important in being accepted in the community," says John Castiglione, vice president of sales and operations. "One of the key elements is the importance of building relationships in small towns."

Finding qualified staff in smaller markets has never been a problem, says Canadian Tire's David Hicks, although building a part-time pool can be more challenging. As a result, the company's small-town stores usually have a higher proportion of full-time staff: about 60 percent compared with 40 percent in the typical urban store. Turnover also tends to be lower. Finding skilled workers is more of a challenge when it comes to maintenance and repairs. That's why Canadian Tire's new small-market format was developed with what Hicks calls a "capital lite" design. The stores feature easy-to-replace components and fixtures that help reduce building and maintenance costs. The design also allows Canadian Tire to enter and operate in lower volume markets in a more cost-effective manner.

Veterans of rural retailing warn that every small market is uniquely different, and companies must choose their communities and the appropriate merchandise mix with extreme care. One-industry resource towns with dramatic boom and bust cycles, for example, can present problems for the retailer that does not take the time to follow the global demand for that community's commodity. The fates of other smaller communities are not as precarious, however: In most of The North West Company's markets, says Kennedy, the population growth is 1.5 to 2.5 times the Canadian average. Some are regional centres serving wide areas, with a hospital, schools, perhaps a retirement home, and government offices. Other towns may have one or two strong manufacturing firms, or a healthy agriculture or tourism-based economy.

The product selection must be carefully tailored to each community. Hicks uses the example of motor oil: Canadian Tire dealers have learned through experience that many of their customers in small-town Ontario choose Quaker State, while the brand in rural Quebec is Pennzoil. "Any miss that you make in your assortment is exponentially more risky than in a larger store," says Hicks. "You have to do all your homework that much better."

Even more than with urban locations, the success of a small-market store depends on a strong manager. Effective rural retail managers are very entrepreneurial, community-oriented, and extremely astute in recognizing their positioning and the needs of their customers, says TruServ's president and CEO Bill Morrison. Retailers often give their small-market managers added flexibility in deciding what goes into their stores. At The North West Company, Kennedy says, managers are accountable for 70 to 80 percent of the product mix. That kind of independence is often associated with franchising, but the franchise model rarely works in rural and remote markets, he says, because few local investors can make the upfront investment. Many of the most successful rural managers are from the community and embrace the people and the lifestyle. "As a business, these communities are pretty good places to be," says Kennedy, "and they're good places to live." Achieving retail success makes them all the more enjoyable.

Discussion Questions

1. Identify a number of national chains already successfully operating in rural and small-town markets.

2. Why are larger retailers such as Staples Business Depot and Home Depot opening smaller stores and moving into rural Canada?

3. Explore some of the challenges retailing in a remote area might present.

Source: John Schofield, *Canadian Retailer,* March/April 2009, pp. 38–40.

CASE 9   `Stephanie's Boutique: Store Strategy`

Stephanie Wilson must decide where to open a ready-to-wear boutique she's been contemplating for several years. Now in her late 30s, she's been working in municipal government ever since leaving university, where she majored in fine arts. She's divorced with two children (ages five and eight) and wants her own business, at least partly to be able to spend more time with her children. She loves fashion, feels she has a flair for it, and has taken evening courses in fashion design and retail management.

Recently, she heard about a plan to rehabilitate an old arcade building in the downtown section of her city. This news crystallized her resolve to move now. She's considering three locations.

The Downtown Arcade

The city's central business district has been ailing for some time. The proposed arcade renovation is part of a master redevelopment plan, with a new department store and several office buildings already operating. Completion of the entire master plan is expected to take another six years.

Dating from 1912, the arcade building was once the centre of downtown trade, but it's been vacant for the past 15 years. The proposed renovation includes a three-level shopping facility, low-rate garage with validated parking, and a convention centre complex. Forty shops are planned for the first (ground) floor, 28 more on the second, and a series of restaurants on the third.

The location Stephanie is considering is 900 square feet and situated near the main ground floor entrance. Rent is $20.50 per square foot, for an annual total of $18 480. If sales exceed $225 000, rent will be calculated at 8 percent of sales. She'll have to sign a three-year lease.

Tenderloin Village

The gentrified urban area of the city where Stephanie lives is nicknamed Tenderloin Village because of its lurid past. Today, however, the neat, well-kept brownstones and comfortable neighbourhood make it feel like a yuppie enclave. Many residents have done the remodelling work themselves and take great pride in their neighbourhood.

About 20 small retailers are now in an area of the Village adjacent to the convention centre complex. Most of them are trendy, affordable restaurants. There are also three small women's clothing stores. The site available to Stephanie is on the Village's main street on the ground floor of an old house. Its space is also about 900 square feet. Rent is $15 000 annually with no coverage clause. The landlord knows Stephanie and will require a two-year lease.

Appletree Mall

This suburban mall has been open for eight years. A successful regional centre, it has three department stores and 100 smaller shops just off a major highway about ten kilometres from downtown. Of its nine women's clothing retailers, three are in a price category considerably higher than what Stephanie has in mind.

Appletree has captured the retail business in the city's southwest quadrant, though growth in that sector has slowed in the past year. Nevertheless, mall sales are still running 12 percent ahead of the previous year. Stephanie learned of plans to develop a second shopping centre east of town, which would be about the same size and character as Appletree Mall. But groundbreaking is still 18 months away, and no renting agent has begun to enlist tenants.

The store available to Stephanie in Appletree is two doors from the local department store chain's mall outlet. At 1200 square feet, it's slightly larger than the other two possibilities. But it's long and narrow—24 feet in front by 50 feet. Rent is $24 per square foot ($28 820 annually).

In addition, on sales that exceed $411 500, rent is 7 percent of sales. There's an additional charge of 1 percent of sales to cover common-area maintenance and mall promotions. The mall's five-year lease includes an escape clause if sales don't reach $411 500 after two years.

Discussion Questions

1. Give the pluses and minuses of each location.

2. What type of store would be most appropriate for each location?

3. If you were Stephanie, which location would you choose? Why?

Source: This case was prepared by Professor David Ehrlich, Marymount University.

CASE 10 "Touch and Feel" at Sephora

Sephora, a division of Moet Hennessy Louis Vuitton SA (LVMH), the world's largest luxury goods company, is an innovative retail concept from France that is changing the way cosmetics are sold. The store first arrived in the United States in mid-1998 with two store locations, in New York and Miami. Its flagship store, encompassing 21 000 square feet, opened in Rockefeller Center in New York City in October 1999. Now Sephora operates approximately 1000 stores in 14 countries worldwide, including 250 stand-alone stores in the United States and another 150 locations inside JCPenney department stores. In addition to its strong presence throughout the United States, it also runs stores in Canada, China, the Czech Republic, France, Greece, Italy, Luxembourg, the Middle East, Monaco, Netherlands, Poland, Portugal, Romania, Russia, Spain, and Turkey. The company continues to expand both in the United States and globally.

Most fashion-oriented cosmetics are still sold in department stores. The scent and cosmetics areas in these stores consist of counters devoted to products made by each manufacturer. Salespeople specializing in a specific line stand behind the counter and assist customers in selecting merchandise. Services include applying products to the customer's face and showing her how to use products and how the colours will look with her skin and hair colour, in addition to making suggestions. Although customers are not required to make a purchase in return for makeup lessons or full makeovers, many feel compelled to buy at least a lipstick or mascara in return for the services.

In contrast, Sephora uses an open-sell approach and offers customers over 200 brands of beauty products, including cosmetics, skin and hair care, and bath and body items and covering natural and organic products as well as gifts, personal care products, and shaving necessities for men. Brands cover new lines, best-sellers, classics, and an exclusive Sephora collection that accounts for about 10 percent of sales. The impressive store inventory totals over 13 000 different products—a collection that can be overwhelming for some shoppers. Customers can choose their own level of service, touching, feeling, and trying products on their own or soliciting advice from product consultants. Sephora takes great pride in training its employees about the history and use of the products in its stores, as well as in skills for customer interactions, to provide appropriate service to its shoppers.

Recently, cosmetic and skin care companies recognized that women need higher-than-expected levels of help navigating the dizzying array of beauty products and tools that regularly change in response to trends and celebrity endorsements. Previous estimates put the percentage of shoppers needing help at the makeup counter at about 20 percent, but recent research indicates the number may be over 50 percent. The economic downturn has also motivated women to replace a lipstick or gloss that works with the rest of their beauty arsenal rather than replacing their entire repertoire to reflect a new season or trend. These women need more assistance than they did in the past.

To meet the needs of these customers, Sephora provides all of its consultants with a four-day course that teaches them the science and uses of the products sold in stores. Consultants desirous of more education can enroll in advanced classes. Successful completion of these classes results in an "expert" pin for skin care, colour, and fragrance. Consultants wear their pins in stores so that customers know whom to go to for more information.

Classes are taught at Sephora University, the company's San Francisco–based training facility that opened in 2007. Using skills gained at the university, consultants answer customer questions, help women find the best solution to their skin care and beauty needs, and provide free, ten-minute in-store "express services" on a one-on-one basis to customers, covering specific topics such as matching foundation and skin type or transitioning makeup from day to night. Unlike department stores, where these learning sessions occur at the counter, Sephora express services occur in a salon-like setting on the store floor. Learning opportunities are directed to both consultants and managers so that all employees have the full range of knowledge they need to provide an optimal shopping experience for customers and the skills and insights necessary to run a successful and innovative cosmetic and skin care company.

This multichannel retailer also reaches customers through its highly interactive website (sephora.com). Shoppers using the website can search by hundreds of class and prestige brands, product category, editor's picks, hot new items, and Sephora favourites. Many retailers have been unsuccessful selling cosmetics online because customers cannot "touch and feel" products, because beauty products cannot be displayed properly in a two-dimensional format, or for reasons not yet understood. Yet Sephora has, once again, managed to set itself apart from competitors by making its website work while still yielding a profit. Some of the brands offered online are difficult to find in department stores, so the convenience of the Sephora site has tremendous appeal. For women who use a variety of brands, Sephora's one-stop shopping is also a significant asset. Women know they can find the brands they love at a reasonable price with no hassles.

Sephora also uses direct mail to market its products and services. Catalogues mailed several times each year include beauty tips and trends and showcase a variety of brands and products.

In October 2006, Sephora began expanding its reach even further by opening stores inside JCPenney stores. At about 1500 square feet, these stores within stores are smaller than their stand-alone counterparts and are the only beauty offering inside JCPenney. The assortment comprises nearly 50 brands; additional offerings include the Beauty Studio, with its ten-minute express services. In 2007, Sephora launched Beauty Insider, the company's loyalty program. Members accumulate points for purchases, and these points can be redeemed for perks such as free samples or limited-edition products.

Discussion Questions

1. Describe Sephora's target market.

2. Why would women prefer a choice between Sephora's combined self-service and service-oriented environment rather than the traditional model offered in department store cosmetic areas?

3. What training opportunities are available to Sephora employees? How does this training help set Sephora apart from its competitors?

4. How can a beauty retailer make multichannel retailing work? What makes Sephora's online site so successful?

5. What value do the Sephora stores within JCPenney offer to customers? To Sephora? To JCPenney?

Sources: www.sephora.com (accessed July 13, 2010); Susan Carpenter, "Brush Up at the Counter," *Los Angeles Times*, June 13, 2010; www.sephora.com/university/index.jhtml (accessed July 13, 2010); www.sephora.com/help/about_sephora.jhtml (accessed July 13, 2010).

This case was prepared by Barton Weitz, University of Florida, and Kate Woodworth.

| CASE 11 | Innovating the In-Store Experience |

Imagine riding an escalator in your favourite sports store on a Saturday morning. Suddenly, instead of the second-floor ski section destination you thought you were heading to, for a brief moment you are no longer on an escalator—or even in a sports store for that matter. Rather, you're riding a chairlift up a mountain and getting ready to mash some moguls in your mind. Sounds exciting, right?

This is just one of the many innovations and in-store surprises customers experience at Sport Chek's new Retail Lab store in midtown Toronto, which opened in January 2013. While the store is only 12 000 square feet, thanks to 140 digital screens and other technology, it feels much bigger.

"People call it multichannel, or omni-channel, but to the consumer it's just shopping," explains Michael Medline, president, FGL Sports. "You have to be consistent, but also exciting through all your channels. Our feeling is our stores can be very exciting for the consumer, which helps us compete with bricks-and-mortar and e-retailers as well. We wanted to take it to the next step."

A One-of-a-Kind Experience

In 2012, Sport Chek undertook a brand reformation captured by its new tagline, "Your Better Starts Here." The Yonge Street outlet in Toronto with its 140 digital screens, massive shoe wall with 500 different footwear styles, as well as a multitude of other in-store innovations, is a one-of-a-kind experience. It's also one that epitomizes Sport Chek's brand reinvention. And the company's "next step" in its evolution includes an ambitious strategic plan to grow the retail chain by 50 percent in terms of square footage over the next five years.

"We are not going to build ten lab stores, but we will take the learning from this test store and incorporate it into the flagship stores we are building and also retrofit it into many of our current stores as well," Medline adds.

It's this type of innovation that, in an ever-competitive, ever-changing shopping environment, is critical to a retailer's success. Despite technological advances and the rise of the online shopping channel, the in-store experience is still king; it's a key piece of a retailer's core business they can't afford to neglect.

Differentiating the Brand

When it comes to a brand's strength, it's also where retailers can really shine and truly separate themselves from their competitors to win the battle for customer loyalty. What is the added value you are giving them for choosing to shop at your store?

Joe Jackman, chief executive officer at Jackman Reinvention, partners with clients to help them build their brand and "become the most powerful version of themselves."

According to Jackman, there are two keys. The first is something he calls "core." This is a set of customer expectations of what they believe epitomizes a positive and productive service experience. The second is that unexpected part where there are opportunities to differentiate and build your brand. These two things need to work in tandem.

"The first is often overlooked and shouldn't be because it is foundational," Jackman explains. "I say that because you almost have to earn the permission to surprise and delight customers in unexpected ways by delivering what is first expected."

These customer expectations include all manner of touch points, including, but not limited to, the layout of the store, ease of navigation, access to the staff when they need them, displays that are not only easily accessed but also easy to understand, and a visual environment that is conducive to whatever the shopping occasions are.

"All of these things present opportunities to define the brand and take it to the next level, but the first job is to consistently deliver what the customer expects and that's the hardest part," Jackman adds.

Jackman points to Burberry's flagship store on Regent Street in London, England, which he had the opportunity to visit on a recent trip overseas, as one that epitomizes the ultimate in-store customer experience. What made it so special?

"They've created a stunning environment that celebrates not only their products but also their brand," he explains. "They've also integrated technology, but not in a superfluous way, which is one of the things that is happening now; technology for some equates to throwing a lot of screens in a store. But technology needs to be thoughtfully done and integrated.

"Burberry has done some amazing things to create a brand experience unlike any other," he adds. "The product looks amazing, and the staff are beyond good; they are brand ambassadors. That was my experience as someone who studies retail and as a customer."

Passionate People Drive the In-Store Experience

It's great to have the latest and greatest in technology, but all the digital screens and tablets alone do not equal a memorable in-store customer experience. You also need an all-star staff of passionate people who are knowledgeable and well-trained to emotionally connect with your

shoppers; the end-goal is for them to forge long-term relationships with each customer who enters your store.

"We couldn't do the things we are trying to do and will do if we didn't have great staff," comments Medline. "If you don't have the best products and the most knowledgeable and passionate staff, even with great technology, you are not going to succeed."

Medline believes his operations team is the best in the business, and it all starts from an extremely simple principle.

"We hire people who are passionate about sports," he says. "If you go to the Lab Store, you will see that. The people serving you will be unbelievably knowledgeable, not just about the product, but on how you can use the products."

Sport Chek's staff not only have the ability to recommend the right pair of shoes, but they will get to know more about why customers are making that purchase by asking the right questions, such as are they planning to run competitively or just to get in shape? At the Toronto Lab Store, customers can also participate in a comprehensive gait analysis on a special treadmill that will help staff determine the perfect shoe that is customized to their running style. Then, Sport Chek staff can enhance that in-store experience further by adding their experience.

"Our staff can talk to that customer about why they are running, where the best running trails are in town, or when the next 5K is," Medline says. "That is the future of the store experience. To compete, you have to have that value add. You have to be able to build in some ways; it's very old-fashioned in terms of that one-on-one interaction with the customer."

Professional Expert Advice

Golf Town also understands the important role its people play when it comes to enhancing the customers' in-store experience. Ron Hornbaker, EVP of Golf Town Operations Canada, reveals that the big-box golf retailer has added a lot of things in the past year to make its store more "experiental," such as the latest in swing analysis, club-fitting technology, and hiring more full-time Class A CPGA professionals to give in-store lessons.

"We have the best teaching equipment you can get," Hornbaker reveals. "We use a three-camera video system to record your swing. This video can be immediately downloaded and sent directly to your smartphone, complete with the pro's commentary."

Hornbaker says the best part is the cost, so there should be no excuse for golf enthusiasts to take a lesson or two at one of their stores. Lessons are $39.99 for a half-hour video lesson with one of their professionals, $99.99 for a series of three lessons, and $149.99 for a series of five.

Golf Town continues to lead the way with its try-before-you-buy philosophy by placing an emphasis on club fitting. All Golf Town stores are now equipped with "master fitters," with each store having a minimum of two—and some as many as three—of these certified staff.

"Since January [2013], we've spent more than a half a million dollars in this area by putting in new launch monitors in all our stores," he explains. "Most of the major golf manufacturers out there use the same software systems to fit pros and many PGA Tour players."

"If you go into a Golf Town store, part of what we pride ourselves in is that we want you to feel like you are on the course," Hornbaker adds. "We paint our ceilings blue, it's not cheap to do, but we do it because we want the customer to have that feeling of space and being outdoors. We also picked green carpeting on purpose."

Training for Knowledge

The other big innovation Golf Town launched last year to enhance its customers in-store experience is something called "Green Jacket Selling," its proprietary sales training program.

"This surrounds the question: 'What is it to be a Golf Town customer in one of our stores?'" Hornbaker explains. "If I'm a customer, how do I want someone to assist me with my golf purchase: Some of our research included hiring a mystery shopper to give us an objective look, and we designed our entire staff training program around that."

The Green Jacket Selling experience has an online learning and development system. Each sales associate is also assigned a mentor.

From virtual reality to tablets to passionate staff and mentorship programs that help store staff bring their products to life, the in-store customer experience continues to evolve and expand. Retailers that recognize the components that contribute to an exceptional one will reap the rewards. "The future of retailing is definitely exciting stores, but that has got to be based on great products and great staff," admits Michael Medline. "Sports lends itself to an exciting customer experience, and we are turning it up a notch."

Discussion Questions

1. What is the key piece of a retailer's core business they can't afford to neglect?

2. How can a brand's strength separate retailers from their competition and help them win the battle for customer loyalty?

3. How do passionate people drive the in-store experience?

Source: David McPherson, "Innovating the In-Store Experience," *Canadian Retailer,* spring 2013, volume 23, issue 2, pp. 22–25.

CASE 12 Building the Apple Store

Founded in 1976 by Steve Jobs and Steve Wozniak, Apple has become an innovative leader in the consumer electronics industry. In addition to offering traditional desktop and laptop computers, all of which feature Apple's OS X operating system, Apple essentially founded the digital music player when it introduced the iPod and online music store markets with iTunes; launched easy-to-use iPhones and iPads with increasingly more features; and introduced online movie/TV services through AppleTV and publishing and multimedia software.

Before Apple Retail Stores

During the early 1990s, Apple struggled as computer sales began shifting from specialized computer stores to mainstream retail stores. Big-box retailers such as Best Buy and Circuit City could offer a wider selection of computers at lower prices, although they lacked adequate customer service and support. These big-box retailers and specialized stores faced even more competition in the form of mail-order outlets, including CompuAdd, Gateway, and Dell.

Beginning in 1990, Dell shifted from selling its computers in warehouse and specialized computer stores to operating as an online direct mail-order company. Dell facilitated its online operations with an efficient online store that could handle high-volume sales. The online Dell store (dell.com) represented a new strategy for manufacturing: Computers were built as they were ordered. In turn, Dell could reduce inventory, because it no longer produced computers in mass quantities and then pushed inventory through the channel to resellers.

While establishing its online store, Apple needed to balance its direct orders with the sales initiated by its channel partners, mail-order resellers, independent dealers, and CompUSA, with which it initiated a "stores within stores" strategy to focus on Apple's products. Apple's partnership with CompUSA paid off. When the San Francisco CompUSA store was equipped with Macs, Apple's sales jumped from 15 to 35 percent of overall store sales.

Apple also put its own employees to work in various retail outlets to help inform and educate customers, as well as ensure its products were being displayed in working order. The company estimated it spent between $25 000 and $75 000 per month on this initiative. Apple executives soon realized they could not compete with PC brands by selling just laptops and desktops in big-box retail stores, because retailers could earn greater profits by selling lower-quality PC models. They had little to no incentive to sell Macs. Without its own retail store, Apple would always be at the mercy of the independent dealers and partners that operated with different strategic goals.

Designing the Apple Store

To compete with the PCs sold by big-box retailers, Apple needed to shift from selling its electronics through intermediaries to offering products directly through Apple Stores. This shift would not come easily. Steve Jobs, Apple's dynamic founder, first looked to bring in new executives. Mickey Drexler, former CEO of The Gap and now CEO of J.Crew, was hired in 1999 as part of Apple's board of directors.

Next, Jobs brought in Ron Johnson, who had been a merchandising executive with Target, to run Apple's retail division as vice president of retail operations.

Instead of launching stores from the start, Drexler suggested that Jobs rent a warehouse and build a prototype store, coined Apple Store Version 0.0. Apple executives then continuously redesigned the store until they achieved a layout that would entice shoppers to not only enter but also make purchases. The first store prototype was configured by product category, with hardware laid out according to the internal organization of the company rather than by how customers logically shop. Executives quickly decided to redesign the store to match customer interests better. Although the redesign cost Apple more than six months, the executives believed this time investment was necessary to achieve a successful store that could compete with well-established electronics retailers and remain consistent with the Apple brand. Its first store opened in Tyson's Corner, Virginia, in May 2001.

The Apple Store Layout

When considering a site for a retail store, Apple uses its customer base to forecast visitor volume and revenues. Most Apple Stores locate within existing shopping malls or lifestyle centres, where retail traffic is already present. There are two types of full-size stores, a street-facing building or an in-mall store. The stores range from 3600 to 20 000 square feet, although most fall in the 3000 to 6000 square-foot range. Storefronts are typically all glass with a backlit Apple logo, and the front display windows change occasionally to focus on the newest marketing campaign. Apple's internal team designs the window

displays, often using slot and cable systems to suspend design elements within the window. In some cases, the swinging entrance doors are in the middle, but in other stores, a logo wall appears in the middle with two doors located on either side. Store interiors feature only three materials: glass, stainless steel, and wood.

In addition to the retail floor, Apple Stores have backroom areas that sometimes include a public restroom, offices, and the inventory area. At some sites that lack sufficient space, inventory storage is located at a separate facility, always within walking distance. The store layout changes multiple times throughout the year. Apple executives organize planograms to coincide with the introduction of new products or heavily marketed merchandise. The layouts depend on the size of the store. A typical in-mall store locates merchandise in the front half of the store and customer service and support areas in the rear. Apple Stores carry fewer than 20 products, and every display piece is available for hands-on use so that customers can get an accurate feel for the available hardware and software.

On tables along the right wall, iPhones and iPods take up the front half of the store. Along the left wall, tables hold various models of general and high-end desktop and laptop computers. These displays give way to The Studio, a newer section hosted by experts who will answer application-oriented, creative questions. Two to three island tables in the front centre display software on Apple computers; additional island tables exhibit peripherals such as iPod docking stations and printers. A small children's area houses Apple computers running children's software. The Genius Bar takes up the back wall, with stools before a counter staffed with Apple experts for repairs and consultations. Larger stores also have a theatre area in the back, featuring a rear-projection screen with an audience area of either U-shaped wooden benches or full theatre seats in rows. This store layout is typical for a store located in a super-regional mall.

Apple Stores thus follow a free-form layout, which allows customers to browse the store according to their own interests. Signage hanging from the ceiling, for greater visibility, directs customers to specific areas within the store. Bright lighting draws attention to merchandise and creates a sense of excitement. Highlighted merchandise also helps draw customers strategically through the store. As customers browse the products, employees wearing Apple T-shirts and lanyards make themselves available to answer any questions.

Through its intensive development efforts, Apple has created a unique, customer service–oriented shopping experience. Customers can schedule face-to-face appointments at an Apple Store to test-drive products. One-to-one personal training sessions help customers become familiar with the array of Apple products. The company also offers free one-hour instructional or informational workshops every day for iPod, iPhone, and Mac owners. It also offers support for business customers by providing insight and advice about how to create a presentation from start to finish using Apple products.

Discussion Questions

1. Have you ever visited an Apple Store? If yes, did you make a purchase? Why or why not?

2. Why are Apple's store layout and atmosphere important?

3. Visit your local Apple Store. Does the layout of the store help to provide you with an excellent customer experience? Explain.

Sources: Philip Elmer-Dewitt, "Apple Ranks No. 4 in E-Retailing Survey," *Fortune*, May 5, 2010; www.apple.com/retail (accessed July 14, 2010); Daniel Eran, "Apple's Retail Challenge," 2006, www.roughlydrafted.com/RD/Q4.06/1DDD598A-7CE0-479EA6F9-912777CAB484.html (accessed July 14, 2010); www.ifoapplestore.com/the_stores.html (accessed July 14, 2010); Jerry Useem, "Apple: America's Best Retailer," *Fortune*, March 8, 2007.

This case was written by Brienne Curley, while an MBA student at Loyola College in Maryland, under the supervision of Hope Corrigan.

CASE 13 A Grand New Look: Layout and Design

Canada's oldest office supply company is proving that you're never too old to be hip.

Grand & Toy, the Canadian office-supply chain that first opened for business in 1882, has implemented an eye-catching, contemporary look to go with its new brand and service offerings.

Facing increasing competition from other office supply stores, Grand & Toy has rebranded itself over the past several years as the all-in-one service provider for emerging small business owners with several employees and complex business needs. Now, it has revamped three of its Vancouver retail locations with a new design that's literally showing customers the light.

Working with Toronto-based Shikatani Lacroix Design, Grand & Toy's newest stores are bright and airy, with lifestyle graphics and accents in orange and green that the designers say are meant to be aspirational. Each storefront features several tree-like merchandising systems comprised of LCD panels with looping video and signs emblazoned with words such as grow, inspire, and empower. "These panels are here to visually communicate the range of things offered at the store," says Shikatani president Jean-Pierre Lacroix. "We wanted customers to understand that this is going to be a different offering, from the store exterior right into the store."

Lacroix's team eliminated about 35 percent of the existing merchandise to be able to implement several new elements into the Vancouver stores. One key addition is the creation of floor-to-ceiling glass offices for the business solution advisors on hand to help customers plan their businesses. "These advisors really are the stars of the show," says Kevin Edwards, vice-president, marketing at Grand & Toy. "It's similar to having a personal banker assigned to your account when you go into your brand."

Another key element is the "creation area" at the back of the store that houses conventional services such as printing and photocopying, but also has a designer on staff to create business cards and PowerPoint templates. Customers can also go to the information hub at the centre of the store to see product demonstrations or access the product catalogue to order larger items (such as office furniture) not available in the store. "The goal really is to provide customers with the support and infrastructure so they can compete with larger corporations," says Lacroix, adding that both areas are rounded to allow customers more access points to service and information.

In spring 2009, Grand & Toy launched a website called GreenOffice, providing business owners a space to find and share resources to make their workplaces more eco-friendly. The premise is that even small businesses can implement green initiatives that are effective and affordable. In keeping with this theme, Lacroix says he and his team were very sensitive to the materials being used and tried to reuse as much as possible. All the display gondolas from the previous store, for example, were implemented into the new design, floors were kept as is, and all lighting was replaced with a more cost-effective option.

So far, the Vancouver stores are performing extremely well and customer reaction has been very favourable, says Edwards. "Customers are saying they didn't realize we were in all these businesses, so the design is really serving its purpose," he said.

In fact, he says the next step will be to retrofit existing stores with the new look in key small business areas. "We're learning as much as we can from the Vancouver stores so that we can really find out what makes sense to customers," he says. "The next focus is absolutely in Ontario and we're hoping to launch several of those in 2010."

Discussion Questions

1. Explain the importance of "atmospherics" as a tool in the retailer's merchandising mix.

2. Do you think that the way Grand & Toy has addressed the challenges it has faced and faces from Staples Business Depot is sufficient to ensure their ongoing success?

3. Discuss how store design and planning have been a critical part of Grand & Toy's new strategy execution.

Source: Rosalind Stefanac for the Retail Council of Canada, *Canadian Retailer*, September/October 2009.

CASE 14 Mountain Equipment Co-op: Revitalizing a Brand

Mountain Equipment Co-op (MEC) is a Canadian-owned and co-operatively run retailer that makes and sells outdoor recreation gear, clothing, and services to support its members in being active outdoors. As a co-op, MEC sells only to customers who hold a membership, which is technically a share that can be purchased by anyone. Over four decades, MEC has grown from the original six members to 3.9 million and to become a member costs $5, the same as it did in 1971. MEC sells more than 28 000 products at 17 stores across the country. In 2012, it reported sales of $302 million. The co-op exists to inspire and enable everyone to lead active outdoor lifestyles in a way that does the least harm and the most good—environmentally, socially, and economically.

Relative to some, MEC is a large retailer and brand but in reality it remains a relatively niche retailer in the larger sporting and leisure market. Technology is evolving rapidly, consumers are purchasing differently (online, mobile, and in-store), and the Canadian retail space is more competitive than ever. International retailers and new domestic competitors such as SAIL are opening across the country, coupled with the rise of e-commerce options such as Backcountry.com and Amazon. Supply chains are becoming more volatile and globally diverse. MEC itself has seen significant changes in their membership and recreation patterns, and an increase in urbanization. Today, 71 percent of its members live in urban centres.

In response to these changes, the co-op updated its five-year business sustainability strategy in 2012, with a focus on four pillars: product integrity, retail operations, member service, and community. The company expanded its product assortment, breaking it out into three categories (backcountry, active lifestyle, and lifestyle) to better serve its changing members in an authentic way. MEC invested in e-commerce to provide omni-channel access, and increased its outreach in stores to foster active communities through events, meet-ups, and clinics. Finally, it updated its social compliance strategy, which is dedicated to improving working conditions in factories that produce MEC-brand apparel and gear.

In summer 2013, David Labistour, MEC's CEO, wrote a blog post on the company's website to unveil the co-op's new brand identity and strategy. Entitled "Looking toward MEC's Future," he discussed how the co-op was evolving to include more urban activities and changing the iconic logo to remain vibrant and relevant to the 3.9 million members. Though MEC's largest change by far had already begun on the store shelves, the co-op's new mountain-free logo was the most polarizing transformation. According to MEC chief marketing officer Anne Donohoe, "In order to shake up perceptions and reach new audiences, something needed to shift. Keeping the mountains wasn't going to help [MEC] achieve [its] broader goals." The new marketing campaign includes the tagline, "We are all outsiders," which celebrates yoga alongside rock climbing, backcountry skiing, and dog-walking. The idea is to shift the iconic brand from something perceived as elitist and exclusive to "throwing open the doors of MEC to anyone who wants to get outside—whether to bike down a mountain or walk the dog."

Critics of both the new logo and MEC's new all-inclusive approach have been vocal on the company's social network. Tom Herbst, who served as CEO from 1974 to 1976 and again from 1978 to 1992, says the "mountain" in the name wasn't even there to begin with. "The original name it applied for was Outdoor Equipment Co-op," says Herbst. "It was intended to be a broad sort of thing, but was actually rejected by the B.C. Registry for being too broad!"

All of MEC's decisions and operations according to its charter are geared toward a member-centric mentality and are guided by its values: adventure, creativity, quality, integrity, leadership, co-operation, humanity, stewardship, and sustainability.

Discussion Questions

1. Has MEC stayed relevant, even as more competitors have entered the marketplace?

2. Has it adequately responded to the changes in the market? Is it meeting the needs of its members?

3. What are the International Co-operative Alliance principals and how has MEC put these values into practice? Go to http://www.ica.coop/en/what-co-op/co-operative-identity-values-principles and to http://www.mec.ca/AST/ContentPrimary/AboutMEC/AboutOurCoOp/MecCharter.jsp.

Sources: "What Matters and Why," MEC website, http://www.mec.ca/AST/ContentPrimary/AboutMEC/Sustainability/AccountabilityReport/Economics.jsp (accessed January 28, 2014); Linda Nguyen, "Mountain Equipment Co-op unveils new logo, name to appeal to urban customers," *Canadian Business,* June 18, 2013, http://www.canadianbusiness.com/business-news/mountain-equipment-co-op-unveils-new-logo-name-to-appeal-to-urban-customers/ (accessed January 28, 2014); "Looking toward MEC's future," MEC company blog, June 18, 2013, http://blog.mec.ca/?s=looking+toward+mec%27s+future (accessed January 28, 2014).

CASE 15 Tiffany & Co. and TJX: Comparing Financial Performance

The year 2012 marked the 175th anniversary of Charles Lewis Tiffany's opening of his store in downtown Manhattan in 1837. Tiffany & Co. is mostly known for its exquisite jewellery, but it also has additional luxury items in its product assortment. The Tiffany robin's egg "blue boxes" have become a ubiquitous status symbol, representing the company's brand quality and craftsmanship. Tiffany & Co. has a different strategy and marketing approach than other national retailers. Throughout its history, the company's mission has been to enrich the lives of its customers by creating enduring objects of extraordinary beauty that will be cherished for generations. Tiffany & Co. has accomplished this by crafting beautiful designs, using fine-quality materials and expert workmanship, and presenting those products to its customers at luxurious stores in high-end locations.

TJX Corporation, on the other hand, consists of a mix of stores under the names of TJ Maxx, HomeGoods, and Marshalls in the United States (with additional stores under different names in Canada and Europe). TJX strives to offer exceptional value through its four pillars of great fashion, brand, quality, and price. It works with a variety of national brands so that its merchandise assortments at these stores are ever-changing. It is willing to purchase less-than-full assortments of items, styles, sizes, and quantities from vendors and pass on the cost savings to its customers. So that it doesn't have to completely rely on merchandise from national-brand vendors for its assortment offerings, TJX offers some private-label merchandise, which is produced specifically for TJX only. TJX does not own any factories, but rather sources its private-label products with manufacturers. It keeps relatively low inventory levels, which has helped it produce relatively fast inventory turns while maintaining strong gross margins.

Discussion Questions

1. Calculate the following for both Tiffany and TJX using data from the abbreviated income statements and balance sheets in Exhibit 1.

   a. Gross margin percentage

   b. SG&A expense percentage

   c. Operating profit margin percentage

   d. Net profit margin (after taxes) percentage

   e. Inventory turnover

   f. Asset turnover

   g. Return on assets percentage

exhibit 1 2011 Financial Data for Tiffany and TJX (in thousands)

	Tiffany (Year Ending 1/31/2012)	TJX (Year Ending 1/28/2012)
	Income Statement	**Income Statement**
Net sales	$3 642 937	$23 191 455
Less: Cost of goods sold	$1 491 783	$16 854 249
Gross margin	$2 151 154	$6 337 206
Less: SG&A expenses	$1 442 728	$3 890 144
Operating profit margin	$708 426	$2 447 062
Less: Interest expense	$48 578	$35 648
Other income	$5 099	$0
Net income before taxes	$664 951	$2 411 414
Less: Taxes	$255 761	$915 324
Net income after taxes	$439 190	$1 496 090
	Balance Sheet	**Balance Sheet**
Cash	$433 954	$1 507 112
Accounts receivable	$184 085	$204 304
Inventory	$2 073 212	$2 950 523
Other current assets	$198 424	$470 693
Total current assets	$2 889 675	$5 132 632
Fixed assets	$767 174	$2 706 377
Long-term assets	$502 143	$442 596
Current liabilities	$626 677	$3 063 423
Long-term liabilities	$186 802	$2 008 892
Stockholders' equity	$2 348 905	$3 209 290

2. Compare and contrast the calculated financial figures for Tiffany and TJX. Analyze and discuss why the percentages and ratios differ for the two retailers.

3. Analyze which retailer has the better overall financial performance.

4. Why is ROA a good measure of a retailers' financial performance?

Sources: Tiffany & Co. Annual Report, 2012; TJX Corporation, Annual Report, 2012.

This case was prepared by Nancy J. Murray, University of Wisconsin–Stout, and Michael Levy, Babson College.

| CASE 16 | The Chocolate Shop |

The Chocolate Shop (CS) is a specialty chocolate shop that retails delicious chocolate morsels. It is owned by Susie and has been in business for three years. At the beginning of January 2013, the shop moved its location to a small, quaint building in St. Jacob's that it shares with two other boutiques of complementary items. It does not produce any chocolate but instead buys from a local supplier.

Sales

CS sells to retail customers; recently, the shop has expanded into producing small gift baskets to sell to local businesses (B2B) for customer appreciation gifts. This B2B has grown to 30 percent of the shop's 2013 sales, and CS offers these clients net 30 days. The other 70 percent of the 2013 business was from retail. Only 30 percent of retail pays cash and the other 70 percent pays by credit card, which costs CS 3 percent of these sales. This will continue in 2014. Susie puts her credit card fees with other expenses (miscellaneous) when comparing to the SME reports.

This year (2013), the shop's sales were projected to be $425 000 with the following seasonality patterns for the two segments of the business:

2013	Retail	B2B
January	3%	1%
February	21%	5%
March	16%	2%
April	9%	5%
May	2%	1%
June	4%	0%
July	4%	0%
August	4%	0%
September	2%	2%
October (est.)	12%	4%
November (est.)	8%	20%
December (est.)	15%	60%
Total	**100%**	**100%**

Susie is projecting that 2014 retail sales will rise by 2 percent as bus tours are expected to increase as the economy picks up. The B2B sales portion is projected to rise 5 percent as she continues to expand her sales through networking. Giving out samples at the October Chamber After Five was a great promotional tool for her this year. She believes the seasonality breakdown for the two segments will remain constant.

In 2015, Susie is projecting the same increases in the yearly sales again (2 percent for retail and 5 percent in B2B over 2014 sales).

Cost of Sales (Direct Costs)

Susie has developed a wonderful working relationship with her one supplier, Ascot Chocolates, which makes a full range of chocolate products. Turnaround is quick. She places orders, receives them, and pays COD one month in advance of the sales. She calculates that her cost of sales for her chocolate is 60 percent. She gets her packaging and wrapping material for 2 percent of her total revenue as she uses it (same month as sale). Again, she pays COD. That's all she considers to be direct expenses.

Advertising

Susie uses various methods of advertising but does find word of mouth is most reliable for her B2B segment. She does hire a window painter/decorator to merchandise her front window displays in January, March, May, September, and November. Each time it costs $200. Those same months, she prints brochures at a cost of $300 each time. In addition, she donates samples to the Chamber of Commerce and gift packages to various charities to a total of $1800 per year. She figures that occurs evenly throughout the year. She does have a static website basically showing her location and product list. It was set up last year, and she estimates she will spend $300 in April 2014 to update it slightly. In July 2014, she intends to get a vehicle wrap done. It will cost her $2000, and she will write this off as an advertising expense.

There is an advertising fund for St. Jacob's stores that gives them additional mentions and ads in community advertising. She pays $4000 a year for her share. It is paid in March each year.

Memberships (Professional Fees)

Susie does belong to the local Chamber of Commerce and some of its subcommittees and spends $360 per year payable in July each year. Plus, she finds her $600 membership in the Boutique Retail Association of Canada, payable in September each year, well worth the cost.

Professional Fees

Susie's total lawyer and accountant fees for the year are about $3200. She pays this in equal payments in January, April, July, and October.

Salaries for Employees

Susie works in the business during busy times but she is also the main sales and delivery person to the business accounts. She also does the purchasing, and the bookkeeping for the business. It is usually 60+ hours per week. She is single with no dependents. She withdraws $1250 per month and has set up no benefits for herself.

Her long-time friend and one full-time employee earns $15 per hour and works 160 hours per month. In addition, Susie has payroll expenses and some benefits she pays to her, adding up to an additional 25 percent per month.

She hires part-time worker(s) January to April and October to December. She pays them an average of $11 per hour, and they work assigned shifts amounting to another 120 hours per month. Their payroll expenses are an additional 18 percent of the wages.

Lease and Location Expenses

In January 2013, Susie opened the new location with a five-year lease. When she moved in, she made a deal with the landlord to make leasehold improvements. Her share was $6000 in leasehold improvements that she is depreciating over the entire length of the lease.

Her rent is $30 per square foot for her 1200 square feet of retail space. In addition, she pays an additional $2 per square foot (on her 1200) for common area maintenance (CAM). CAM covers a common lunchroom, washrooms, two parking spots, signage, and all interior and exterior maintenance. Her only location costs are minor maintenance and cleaning costs of approximately $250 per month.

Delivery Expenses

Susie has decided to bring her van into the business as of January 2014. It is an older white cargo van valued at $13 000. She estimates it will have a salvage value of $1000 in four years. There will be no cash transaction. She is going to put all vehicle maintenance and operating costs in a delivery account. She figures that will amount to $300 per month plus an extra $250 in December as that is her busy month for deliveries to businesses.

Other Monthly Expenses

Other monthly cash expenses for 2014 are estimated to be as follows:

Bank charges	$40
Utilities	$150
Telephone/Internet	$250
Insurance (content)	$100
Other/miscellaneous	$3000

Financing Arrangements

Susie has a good working relationship with her local bank. She has a secured line of credit against her house with a $100 000 limit on it. She pays 3.5 percent interest on it anytime she uses it. For this forecasting, she assumes she pays the full month's interest on the borrowed amount from the previous month. She also assumes she pays back everything in the next month and again borrows anything she needs. She realizes this is slightly overestimating the interest but finds it is the best way to track the interest and be conservative.

However, her house is for sale, meaning she will lose her secured line of credit, probably sometime in the summer of 2014. She may have cash reserves, or it might be tied up in legalities. She isn't planning to buy another house in the near future. For now, she is going to continue with her forecasting but this is troubling.

Her family has promised her a loan of $30 000 on January 1, 2014, to help with inventory expenses for Valentine's Day. They are charging her only 2.5 percent on any remaining principal. She has agreed to pay them $5000 principal and the yearly interest amount each December starting December 2014.

Depreciation (or Amortization)

Susie uses straight line depreciation for all her long-term assets. Anything associated with the building will be depreciated over the term of the lease.

Her store fixtures, cash register, etc. had an original value of $24 000 when she moved in January 2013 and were to be depreciated over six years; 2014 is their third year of usage. In addition, her computer equipment that she bought in January 2013 is worth $2000, and it should be depreciated over two years as she does like to keep up to date. She had no other depreciable items.

Balance Sheet Details

As of December 31, 2013, the shop's balance sheet included the following items:

- Cash on hand: $4000 (she likes to always keep a minimum monthly balance of $4000)
- Inventory on hand: $15 000
- Accounts receivable: $52 222 (will collect all of it in January 2014)
- Line of credit payable: $20 922
- Ending owner's equity: $72 100

She realizes it is important to have robust spreadsheets to help her with analysis and planning. She is looking to you to create this financial model and also use them to make sound recommendations to improve her business.

Discussion Questions

1. Prepare the following:
   a. Financial notes sheet(s) for all inputs and financial explanations used
   b. Monthly cash flow forecast for the year of 2014
   c. Pro forma income statement for the year of 2014. It must compare the percentage of sales to the SME benchmarking for "confectionery and nut stores" for the whole industry of incorporated businesses in Canada in 2014.
   d. Pro forma balance sheet as at December 31, 2014, compared to the December 31, 2013, statement (on same sheet, side by side)

2. Susie is concerned with her cash flow management. Examine her current practices for collection of monies—what is it costing her and what would be some alternatives to consider. Then in your recommendations, state what you think she should do and back it up with the potential savings/cash flow Susie could expect.

3. Flowing from the analysis, prepare three justified recommendations for Susie to improve her business in 2014. (Justified means you have done the analysis and can now recommend specific actions backed up by estimates and figures.)

This case was written by Barbara Rice.

CASE 17 | Creating Loss Prevention Programs That Fit the Culture

Based upon yoga principles of healthy living and integrity, Lululemon's asset protection program is intended to leverage the inherent goodness in people.

"In most asset management protection programs, 90 percent of the message is usually directed at the 1 percent who would actually steal. That creates an adversarial relationship and doesn't speak to most people," explains Rich Groner, Lululemon's asset protection regional manager, east U.S. "At Lululemon, our asset protection program begins with the assumption that most people are smart and have integrity. That's an important distinction. People tend to respond well when treated this way."

Unlike at many retailers where asset protection involves creating additional rules and safeguards, Lululemon resisted the urge to control stores from head office or put more procedures in place. Instead, it decided to focus on encouraging "great behaviour."

"Rather than enforcing a set of controls that by definition assume people are inclined to be dishonest, we try to empower our associates to act in harmony with one another and our customers. This is accomplished through creating a culture with three core principles: gratitude, integrity, and *Asteya*, a yoga term for non-stealing," explains Groner.

Appealing to the Goodness

Fostering a sense of gratitude for what one has in life—whether it be a job, material possessions, or relationships—is important. It invigorates people and creates a happy workforce, and is the opposite of entitlement, the main cause of theft.

Integrity encourages self-control and honesty, which is far more effective in reducing shrinkage than any corporate system or procedure could ever be.

Asteya is a root principle of yoga and has been adopted by Lululemon. Yoga, after all, is not just stretching but also a mantra for a healthy way of living. *Asteya* speaks to what you restrain yourself from doing. It's not just about stealing material objects, but also what you can steal from people—respect, confidence, reputation, and so on.

"We spend 80 percent of our time speaking to associates about these principles as opposed to any other asset protection message," says Groner. "It's all about exploring the question, 'What does it mean to be a great person?' It's a unique training program designed specifically to fit the healthy living culture of our company."

Loss prevention means securing your investments and securing your future. Retailers approach this in many different ways, but one commonality is that their loss prevention programs are founded on the belief that a company's greatest assets are its associates.

Discussion Questions

1. How does Lululemon's asset management program differ from that of other retailers?

2. What is the main cause of internal theft?

3. What does the *Asteya* principle adopted by Lululemon have to do with internal theft?

Source: Excerpt from Andrew Hind, "Protecting assets, and the bottom line," *Canadian Retailer*, store 2012, volume 22, issue 4, p. 59.

CASE 18 Lindy's Bridal Shoppe: Assortments

Located in Lake City (population 80 000), Lindy's Bridal Shoppe, a small bridal store, sells bridal gowns, prom gowns, accessories, and silk flowers. It also rents men's formal wear and performs various alteration services. Lindy Armstrong, age 33, has owned the store since its founding in March 2000. She's married to a high school teacher and is the mother of three young children. A former nurse, she found the demands of hospital schedules left too little time for her young family. An energetic, active woman with many interests, she wanted to continue to work but also have time with her children.

The silk flowers market enabled Lindy to combine an in-home career with child-rearing. She started Lindy's Silk Flowers with $75 of flower inventory in Vernon, a small town of about 10 000 people ten kilometres from Lake City. Working out of her home, she depended on word-of-mouth communication among her customers, mainly brides, to bring in business. As Lindy's Silk Flowers prospered, a room was added onto the house to provide more space for the business. Lindy was still making all the flowers herself.

Her flower-making schedule kept her extremely busy. Long hours were the norm. Lindy was approached by a young photographer named Dan Morgan, who proposed establishing a one-stop bridal shop. In this new business, Dan would provide photography, Lindy would provide silk flowers, and another partner, Karen Ross (who had expertise in the bridal market), would provide gowns and accessories. The new store would be located in Vernon in a rented structure. Shortly before the store was to open, Dan and Karen decided not to become partners and Lindy became the sole owner. She knew nothing about the bridal business. Having no merchandise or equipment, Lindy was drawn to an ad announcing that a bridal store in a major city was going out of business.

She immediately called and arranged to meet the owner. Subsequently, she bought all his stock (mannequins, racks, and carpet) for $4000. The owner also gave her a crash course in the bridal business. From March 2000 to December 2009, Lindy owned and operated a bridal gown and silk flowers store named Lindy's Bridal Shoppe in Vernon. The location was chosen primarily because it was close to her home. Although Vernon is a very small town, Lindy felt that location wasn't a critical factor in her store's success. She maintained that people would travel some distance to make a purchase as important as a bridal gown. Rent was $250 per month plus utilities. Parking was a problem.

During this period, Lindy's Bridal Shoppe grew. Bridal gowns and accessories as well as prom dresses sold well. As the time approached for Lindy to renew her lease, she wondered about the importance of location. A move to Lake City might be advisable. A much larger town than Vernon, Lake City is the site of a university. Lindy decided to move.

General Business Description

The majority of Lindy's Bridal Shoppe's current sales are made to individuals who order bridal gowns off the rack or from the catalogues of three major suppliers. At the time of the order, the customer pays a deposit, usually half of the purchase price. The balance is due in 30 days. Lindy would like payment in full at the time of ordering regardless of the delivery date. But payment is often delayed until delivery. Once ordered, a gown must be taken and the bill paid when delivered.

No tuxedos are carried in the store, so customers must order from catalogues. Fitting jackets and shoes are provided to help patrons size their purchases. Lindy's Bridal Shoppe rents its men's formal wear from suppliers. Payment from the customer is due on delivery. Certain times of the year see more formal events than others. Many school proms are held during late April and May, and June, July, and August are big months for weddings.

Since traditional dates for weddings are followed less and less closely, Lindy believes that the business is becoming less seasonal, though January and February are quite slow.

Promotion Practices

Lindy's Bridal Shoppe engages in various promotional activities but is constrained by her limited finances. The firm has no operating budget, which prevents any formal appropriation for advertising expenses. Newspaper ads constitute the primary promotional medium, though radio is occasionally used. Ads for prom dresses are run only during prom season. These ads usually feature a photograph of a local high school student in a Lindy's Bridal Shoppe gown plus a brief description of the student's activities.

Other promotional activities include bridal shows at a local mall. Lindy feels these have been very successful, though they're a lot of work. A recent prom show in a local high school used students as models. This proved to be an excellent way to stimulate sales. Lindy hopes to go into several other area high schools during the next prom season, though this will demand much planning.

Personnel

Lindy, the sole owner and also the manager of the firm, finds it hard to maintain a capable workforce. As a small company, Lindy's Bridal Shoppe can't offer premium salaries for its few positions. There's one full-time salesperson. The part-time staff includes a salesperson, alterations person, bookkeeper, and custodian. Lindy handles all the paperwork. Her responsibilities include paying bills, ordering merchandise and supplies, hiring and firing personnel, fitting customers, and selling various items. She makes all the major decisions that directly affect the firm's operations. She also makes all the silk flowers herself. It's time-consuming, but she isn't satisfied with how anyone else makes them.

Merchandise Offerings

Lindy's Bridal Shoppe's major product lines are new wedding, prom, and party gowns. No used gowns are sold. Discontinued styles or gowns that have been on the rack for a year are sold at reduced prices, primarily because discoloration is a major problem. Gowns tend to yellow after hanging on the racks for a year. A wide variety of accessories are provided. Lindy believes it's important that her customers not have to go anywhere else for them. These accessories include shoes, veils, headpieces, jewellery, and foundations. Slips may be rented instead of purchased. One room of Lindy's Bridal Shoppe is used only to prepare silk flowers.

Service Offerings

Lindy's Bridal Shoppe's major service offering is fitting and alteration. Most gowns must be altered, for which there's a nominal charge. Lindy feels that personal attention and personal service set her apart from her competitors. Emphasizing customer satisfaction, she works hard to please each customer. This isn't always easy. Customers can be picky, and it takes time to deal with unhappy people.

Location

Lindy's Bridal Shoppe is located at the end of Lake City's main through street. Initially, Lindy didn't think location was important to her bridal store's success, but she's changed her mind. Whereas business was good in Vernon, it's booming in Lake City. Vehicular traffic is high, and there's adequate, if not excess, parking. Lindy's Bridal Shoppe has a 12-year lease. Rent ($1800 per month) includes heat and water, but Lindy's Bridal Shoppe must pay for interior decoration. The physical facility is generally attractive, with open and inviting interior display areas. But some areas both inside and outside the store have an unfinished look.

Some storage areas require doors or screens to enhance the interior's appearance. The fitting room ceilings are unfinished, and the carpeting inside the front door may be unsafe. One other interior problem is insufficient space. There seems to be inadequate space for supporting activities such as flower preparation, customer fittings, and merchandise storage, which gives the store a cluttered look.

Several external problems exist. The signs are ineffective, and there's a strong glare on the front windows. This detracts from the effectiveness of the overall appearance and interior window displays. The parking lot needs minor maintenance. Parking lines should be painted and curbs must be repaired. Much should be done to add colour and atmosphere through basic landscaping.

Competition

Lindy's Bridal Shoppe is the only bridal shop in Lake City. Lindy believes she has four main competitors: Whitney's Bridal Shoppe is five kilometres from Lake City; Ender's Brides, a new shop with a good operation, is in Spartan City, 80 km away; Carole's is a large, established bridal shop in Smithtown, 110 km distant; and Gowns-n-Such is in Andersonville, 120 km away. A new store in Yorktown (25 km away) is selling used gowns and discontinued styles at reduced prices. Lindy watches this new- and used-gown store closely.

Some of her potential customers are buying wedding gowns from electronic retailers such as The Knot (www.theknot.com) and the Wedding Channel (www.weddingchannel.com). Although these electronic retailers are not making significant sales in her trading area now, Lindy is concerned that some of the services offered by these electronic retailers (such as gift registries, e-mail notices, wedding planning, and wedding picture displays) will attract her customers.

Financial Considerations

Basic financial information includes the following:

1. Markup: 50 percent
2. 2011 sales: $200 000 (estimated)
3. Average inventory: $70 000
4. Turnover: 3.0 (approximately)
5. Annual expenses are as follows:

Rent:	$19 200
Labour:	$24 000
Utilities:	$7000
Supplies:	$12 000
Equipment:	$4000
Miscellaneous:	$4000

6. Estimated total costs ($200 000 sales): $170 200
7. Implied profit including owner's salary: $29 800
8. Capital invested (equipment, $8000; inventory, $70 000): $78 000
9. ROI: $5800/$78 000 = 7.4 percent (assume owner salary of $24 000 per year)

The Future

Lindy Armstrong is uncertain about the future. She enjoys the business, but feels that she's working very hard and not making much money. During all the years of Lindy's Bridal Shoppe's operation, she hasn't taken a salary. She works 60 hours or more a week. Business is excellent and growing, but she's tired. She has even discussed selling the business and returning to nursing.

Discussion Questions

1. Could Lindy change the emphasis of her merchandise mix to increase her sales?
2. Which products should have more emphasis? Which should have less?
3. What personnel decisions must Lindy face to improve her business?
4. How could someone like Lindy Armstrong balance the demands of her family and her business?
5. If one of Lindy's competitors were to offer her $150 000 for her business, should she sell?

Source: This case was prepared by Linda F. Felicetti and Joseph P. Grunewald, Clarion University of Pennsylvania.

CASE 19 | Merchandise Strategy: Process for Success

Tom had just started his new job as vice president of merchandise. He knew that the categories he was now responsible for had been declining in performance for several years and he had been hired to turn those categories around. Tom recognized immediately that to accomplish this turnaround, he and his new team would need to develop a sound merchandise strategy. Tom called in his merchandising team, consisting of several groups, each representing a different category and composed of buyers, assistant buyers, and planners. He laid out a process to have each group gather valuable information on the categories for which it is responsible to be used in the creation of an overall merchandise strategy. Each group would gather information on customers, pricing, and products and evaluate

the information to identify growth areas for their category. But first Tom required each product category team group to develop a mission statement reflecting how the team would approach their business going forward.

Tom requested each category group, upon completion of their merchandise strategy, to prepare a brief presentation that expresses and supports their merchandise strategy as well as their recommendations regarding areas for future growth. The presentations would be reviewed by Tom, the general merchandise manager, and the president. Each merchandise strategy presentation would include details regarding the following material as they relate to the groups' product category and should be arranged in the following order.

Mission Statement

The mission statement is designed to include the guiding principles of the group and would include the following:

- **Need.** Why does the company need this product category?
- **Integration with corporate.** How does this category further the corporate mission?
- **Objectives.** What are the short- and long-term goals for this category?
- **Strategy.** What will the group do to achieve all the above?

Customer Profile

The customer profile identifies the target consumer to drive merchandise decisions for the product category and would include the following:

- **Customer demographics** (e.g., age, sex, race, income)
- **Customer spending and shopping habits** (e.g., regular price vs. sale price, weekend vs. weekday)
- **Customer product fashion dimension** (e.g., fashion vs. basic)
- **Customer quality preference dimension** (e.g., low quality vs. high quality)
- **Customer value dimension** (e.g., low importance vs. high importance)
- **Key volume price point triggers by product category** (e.g., polo shirt @ $19.99)

Product Guidelines

The product guidelines define characteristics that best suit the target consumer for the product category and would be based on the following information:

- **Style.** Look, feel, colour, shape, fashion direction (forward or laggard)
- **Sourcing.** Domestic, international, branded, private label, co-brand, designer
- **Quality.** Standards, material use, workmanship
- **Price.** Opening price points, mid-range price points, and high-end price points
- **Assortment.** Breadth versus depth of product assortment in the category

Pricing Strategy

The pricing strategy defines the price range of key product lines in the category in relation to the competition and helps define product sourcing and product hierarchy decisions. Pricing strategy should also reduce intra-company competition. Pricing strategy addresses internal and external competition and includes the following:

- **Assortment.** Product pricing by category to address internal competition
- **Competition.** Product pricing by category to address external competition

Recommended Growth Strategy

Opportunities for future growth are determined by the group and should be fully supported by the information the group compiled. The growth strategy includes the following:

- **Category and sub-category development**
- **New or expanded assortments**
- **Reduced or eliminated products, categories, or sub-categories**

Student Instructions

Each group should begin by selecting a retailer. The group should profile the retailer, its place in the industry, its position on merchandise assortments, and its positioning against its competition. Information at the corporate level that can be gathered that relates to the merchandise strategy (e.g., mission statement) should be included in the presentation. Bearing in mind the retailer selected, each team should select a product category or sub-category to be the focus of the merchandise strategy. For example:

- **Retailer.** Hudson's Bay
- **Product category.** Men's sportswear
- **Product sub-category.** Men's woven sport shirts

This selection scheme can be developed for any type of retailer. The goal is to select a category that is big enough but not so large as to require multiple strategies. (For example, menswear would require multiple strategies.) It may be best to review your selection with your instructor. Throughout the merchandise strategy process, you may need to use public industry data to fill in for information you will not be able to gather from the retailer directly. This may include store trips and online searches.

It is recommended that an initial meeting be held by the group to develop the mission statement. The mission statement sets the direction of the group in the process of gathering the appropriate information and analyzing the product, customer, pricing, and areas of growth.

When all the information is gathered, each group should again meet to develop the recommended growth strategy based on the mission statement and the data assembled from all group members. Next, each group should develop a brief PowerPoint-style presentation detailing their findings regarding mission statement, customer profile, product guidelines, pricing strategy, and recommended growth strategy. Each presentation should be structured in this order and address, at a minimum, each of the points outlined for each topic. Group members can use the notes section for each slide to detail the information they gathered, how it was obtained, and how they came to their conclusions. If information is obtained from published materials, proper citation should be given.

Discussion Questions

1. Which of the main components of a merchandise strategy are most valuable? Why?

2. Why is a mission statement so important to a merchandise strategy?

3. Does every merchant team have a merchandise strategy? Why or why not?

Source: This case was written by Robert P. Jones, University of Tennessee, and Michael Levy, Babson College.

CASE 20 McFadden's Department Store: Merchandise Systems

In this hypothetical case, McFadden's Department Store in Canada has been a profitable family-owned business since its beginning in 1910. Last year's sales volume was $180 million. More recently, however, many of its departments have been losing ground to national stores moving into the area. To complicate this problem, a recession equalling a 6.5 percent drop in sales in the coming year is predicted.

Department 121 is one of the more profitable departments in the store, maintaining a gross margin of 55 percent. Its basic merchandise is young men's clothing. Last year's sales reached $2 780 750 for the July–December season.

The highest sales period is the back-to-school period in August, when autumn fashions are supported by strong promotional advertising. Reductions (including markdowns, discounts to employees, and shrinkage) typically run 20 percent of sales. The percentage of reductions is spread throughout the season as follows:

July	August	September	October	November	December
10	20	15	10	10	35

By month, the percentages of annual sales for Department 121 within this six-month period had been distributed as follows:

	July	August	September	October	November	December
2011	3.6	10.1	9.2	6.4	4.8	9.1
2012	3.5	10.3	9.6	6.8	5.3	8.8
2013	3.5	10.5	9.6	6.2	5.5	8.2
2014	3.0	10.3	9.8	6.6	5.5	8.0

A pre-Christmas sale has been planned in an attempt to counterbalance the slackened sales period following the first of the year. The buyer has decided to bring in some new merchandise for the sale to go along with the remaining fall fashion merchandise. The buyer expects that this will increase December's percentage of annual sales to 30 percent above what it would be without the sale. Top management has emphasized that the department achieve a gross margin return on investment (GMROI) of 250 percent.

Forecasted ending stock level in December is $758 000. Additional information is available on the historical stock-to-sales ratio for this type of department. This information is taken from a similar department in another store that happens to have a lower average stock-to-sales ratio.

July	August	September	October	November	December
3.0	1.9	2.1	2.4	2.5	2.2

Discussion Question

1. Your task is to prepare a merchandise budget plan for McFadden's Department Store, Department 121 (young men's clothing). Calculate the following:

   a. Initial markup

   b. Monthly planned sales dollars

   c. Monthly planned reduction dollars

   d. BOM stock (inventory) figures by month

   e. Monthly planned purchases at retail

   f. Monthly planned purchases at cost

Source: This case was prepared by Michael Levy, Babson College, and Harold Koenig, Oregon State University.

exhibit 1 Last Year's Fall/Winter Sales Results for Oriental Rugs

Sales Volume Markup	$120 000 51.5%				
	Size	Percentage of Sales	Fabrication	Percentage of Sales	
	3′ × 5′	20%	Silk	15%	
	4′ × 6′	40	Cotton	25	
	6′ × 9′	15	Wool	60	
	8′ × 10′	10			
	9′ × 12′	15			

In this hypothetical case, a well-established, medium-sized Canadian department store, Hughes reflects consumers' needs by featuring popular names in fashion for the individual consumer, family, and home. It tries to offer a distinctive, wide assortment of quality merchandise with personalized customer service. The many customer services include personal shoppers; credit with in-house charge, MasterCard, and Visa; and an interior design studio. Hughes' pricing policy permits it to draw customers from several income brackets. Moderate-income consumers seeking value and fashion-predictable soft goods are target customers, as are upscale customers with a special interest in fashion.

The department store is implementing new marketing strategies to prepare for continuing growth and expansion. Hughes' merchandising philosophy is to attract the discerning middle-market customer who comprises 70 percent of the population as well as sophisticated fashion-conscious consumers who expect to buy high-quality, brand-name merchandise at competitive prices.

One portion of Hughes' buying staff is responsible for the Oriental rug department within home furnishings. The open-to-buy figure for this classification within the home furnishings division will be based on last year's sales history (Exhibit 1).

It has been projected that a 15 percent increase over last year's sales volume can be attained due to oriental rugs' continued popularity. This year's open-to-buy for fall/winter will be $66 200. The buying staff will be making its purchases for fall/winter in Amritsar, India, a city known for top-quality carpets. Ghuman Export Private, Ltd., of Amritsar, Punjab, India, is the manufacturer the buyers will contact.

Exhibit 2 shows information about Ghuman to use in the decision-making process.

exhibit 2 Ghuman's Wholesale Price List

Size	Fabrication		
	Silk	Wool	Cotton
3′ × 5′	$ 400	$ 250	—
4′ × 6′	700	500	$200
6′ × 9′	850	700	275
8′ × 10′	1200	1000	350
9′ × 12′	1400	1300	500

Colours: Background colours available are navy, burgundy, black, and cream.

Quantities required for purchase: No minimum orders required.

Payment plan: Payment can be made in Canadian dollars or Indian rupees. Letter of credit needs to be established prior to market trip.

Delivery: Air freight—10 to 14 days, delivery time; cost is usually 25 percent of total order.

Ocean freight: 39 days plus inland time is necessary; cost is usually 8–10 percent of total order.

Customer loyalty: Loyalty to customers is exceptional. Damaged shipments can be returned. Ghuman's philosophy is to help the retailers obtain a profit on their product lines.

Discussion Question

1. Work up a buying plan to use when buying from Ghuman. Decide how to distribute the allotted open-to-buy dollars among the available sizes, colours, and fabrications. Since it's an overseas manufacturer, consider additional costs such as duty and shipping, which also need to be covered by the allocated open-to-buy dollars.

Source: This case was prepared by Professor Ann Fairhurst, Indiana University.

"We need to have vendors who can take this burden off of us," said Ken Joynes, Capital Sportswear inventory manager. "We have had a sales increase of 20 percent over the last two years and my people can't keep up with it anymore."

In this hypothetical case, Keith Wilson, general manager of Capital Sportswear, reviewed the colourful chart showing the sales trend and replied, "I never thought I would have to complain about a sales increase, but it is obvious that the sales are well beyond our control. Something has to be done and that is why we are meeting today."

Capital Sportswear was founded by George Wilson in 1963 in a major metropolitan area. For years, Capital Sportswear has been successful in the sportswear market. In 2000, George Wilson retired, and his son, Keith Wilson, was appointed general manager. From the beginning, Keith Wilson has been a real go-getter. Recently completing his MBA, he has wasted no time in locating new markets for Capital Sportswear. He immediately contacted major universities and colleges and gained four-year exclusive contracts for apparel purchases made by the sports teams of their athletic departments.

Soon after, Capital's sportswear became popular among students. This growing demand for the company's products motivated Wilson to open two more retail stores. During the fall of 2013, sales had increased beyond expectations. Although the company achieved a successful reputation in the marketplace, sales growth has generated major problems.

In the beginning, operations were fairly smooth and the company's inventory control department updated most of its procedures. Joynes emphasized the crucial role of routinization in the overall inventory maintenance process to keep up with the increasing turnover. The sales increase was 20 percent, as opposed to the 12 percent that had been forecasted for 2014. It was this increase that initiated a series of problems in the inventory control department. To temporarily alleviate the backlog, Wilson authorized Joynes to lease an additional warehouse (see the replenishment level for July 2013 in Exhibit 1). It was decided that a maximum of 16 percent of the total inventory carrying costs was going to be dedicated to the off-premise inventory.

Worrying about not being able to meet demand on time, Joynes met with suppliers and asked them to provide more timely delivery schedules to Capital Sportswear. When he stated that the company was not going to tolerate any reasons for future delays, two major suppliers expressed their concerns about his lack of flexibility and requested price concessions. They simply indicated that Joynes's demand had to be supported by providing cash or reducing quantity discounts. Joynes ignored these comments and indicated how serious he really was by stating that Capital Sportswear could always find new suppliers.

By the end of a long discussion, arguments were beyond the manageable point and the two large suppliers decided to quit dealing with the company. After the meeting, Joynes received a memo from Wilson. Wilson was very concerned about the potential reactions of the rest of the vendors. He stated in his memo that since Capital Sportswear was continuously growing, it was expected to present a more supportive attitude to its suppliers. He expressed his belief that the company needed a cohesive atmosphere with the rest of the channel members, especially with its vendors.

During the next six months, Joynes had limited success in locating one or more large suppliers that would be able to deliver the products to Capital Sportswear on a timely basis. Faced with growing demand from the surrounding colleges and universities, he had to accumulate excess stock to avoid possible shortages. At the end of the six-month period, a memo from the accounting department of the company indicated the financial significance of the problem. In his memo, accounting manager Roger Boles simply addressed the high costs of inventory

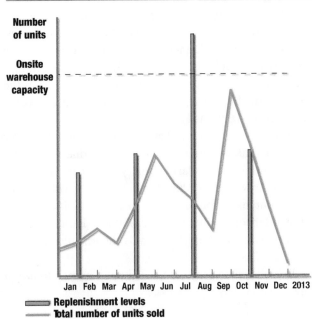

exhibit 1 Sales for Capital Sportswear in 2013

exhibit 2 Comparative Statement of Profit and Loss for Years Ended December 31

	2014(forecast)	2013	2012
Net sales	$165 000	$120 000	$100 000
Cost of sales			
Beginning inventory	7000	6000	4000
Purchases(net)	140 000	92 000	62 000
	147 000	98 000	66 000
Ending inventory	9000	7000	6000
	138 000	91 000	61 000
Gross profit	27 000	29 000	39 000
Expenses			
Stock maintenance	7500	5250	750
Rent	2500	1250	250
Insurance	4500	3500	1500
Interest	4500	2500	1000
Selling	3500	2500	2000
Promotion	7500	5500	4000
Supplies	2750	1500	250
Miscellaneous	2250	1500	250
	35 000	23 500	10 000
Net profit from operations	(8000)	5500	29 000
Other income			
Dividends	925	750	450
Interest	825	600	350
Miscellaneous	650	400	200
	2400	1750	1000
Net profit before taxes	(5600)	7250	130 000
Provision for income taxes	1008	1305	8100
Net profit after taxes	(4592)	5945	21 900

maintenance/security functions (for details, see Exhibit 2). He advised finding a substitute inventory policy to lower these cost figures.

Specifically, he stated that the rental cost for the additional warehouse had levelled off at 16 percent, well beyond the maximum. Keith Wilson immediately scheduled a meeting and asked the top managers to come up with the alternative plans to eliminate this problem. "I should have never let those suppliers quit," said Joynes. "It had a negative effect on our image, and now we all see the results."

"It's too late to worry about that," admonished Wilson. "Instead, we have to come up with a strategy to meet the demand effectively without increasing our costs to the detriment of profits. You realize that the university contracts will expire at the end of the year."

"That's the crucial fact," said Boles. "We simply cannot afford to stock up beyond the current level; it is just too expensive. It is well beyond the funds we have had even from the increased sales."

"In other words, the elimination of the excess inventory is necessary. Who are the vendors that we have at the moment?" asked Wilson.

"There are only three suppliers remaining after the last meeting," replied Joynes. "They are fairly small businesses, but we've been dealing with them for quite some time. They have been successful in keeping up with us, and the details of their operations are summarized in their report."

"It seems like we have a good selection here," said Wilson, after looking at the report in front of him. "If they mostly work with us, we should be able to influence the future direction of their operations. In other words, it should not be difficult to convince them that they need to upgrade their deliveries in such a way that we can eliminate our excess inventory."

"That would cut down the rental costs that we incur from the additional warehouse," said Boles.

"Obviously!" Wilson replied impatiently. "We will probably need to provide those vendors with a comprehensive support program. If we can convert the floor space of the warehouse from storage to sales, we will have additional funds in retail operations. We can invest a portion of these funds in supporting our vendors and improve our image by forming a cohesive network with them. Of course, there will be a limit to this support. After all, it will be expensive for us to make the transition, too. Therefore, I would like you to come up with an analysis for converting the existing system to a more efficient one. I would like to know what we can do and how we can do it. To be very honest, gentlemen, I do not want to increase the sales if we do not know how to handle that increase."

Discussion Questions

1. What is relationship management?

2. Explain how relationship management can benefit both retailer and supplier?

3. How might the use of a quick response system affect the financial performance of Capital Sportswear?

4. What problems would Wilson have implementing a quick response system with vendors?

Source: This case was prepared by S. Alton Erdem, University of Minnesota–Duluth.

Shoppers Drug Mart is a full-service retailer that offers shoppers the convenience of one-stop shopping at its drug/cosmetic/food combo stores. The chain features a variety of high-quality products at competitive prices but uses promotional pricing as well. Historically, Shoppers has enjoyed great success in its markets and had led the region for several years.

In this hypothetical case, one winter morning, Robert Ignacio, the director of strategic planning, had a more immediate concern. The wire services had reported that the Valumart grocery chain had announced plans for the construction of ten new food-and-drug combo centres throughout Shoppers' markets. After poring over current research and financial results, a decision had been made to examine category management as a defence against the encroachment of Valumart.

A decision was also made to pilot test category management in some categories before implementing a system-wide rollout. One of the categories chosen for the test was shampoo. Robert's immediate assignment was to review the product category and report back to management with an initial recommendation. Robert reviewed the events of the past few weeks and the information that he had obtained on the shampoo category. He had several third-party reports (Exhibits 1, 2, and 3) that provided background information about national trends in the shampoo category and trends in supermarkets. Another report (Exhibit 4) provided him with information on how Shoppers' shampoo sales compared to the rest of the market.

However, these reports did not provide Robert with information on how Shoppers stacked up against the competition in terms of its assortment and pricing. After some checking around, Robert found that he could order reports from third-party vendors that would provide him with an analysis of Shoppers and the competition on product mix and pricing. He had placed an urgent order for these analyses, which arrived via courier (Exhibits 5, 6, and 7).

Here are explanations of a few terms in the analyses:

- **UPC.** Supermarket terminology for SKU (stock-keeping unit)
- **UPCs handled.** Average number of UPCs stocked by food stores
- **UPC dollar velocity.** Revenue per UPC per store per week
- **HBA.** Health and beauty aids
- **Market.** All food stores
- **Remaining market.** All food stores excluding Shoppers

exhibit 1 Total Supermarket Dynamics: Shampoo—Aerosol, Liquid, Lotion, and Powder

52 Weeks	# Active UPCs	% New UPCs	# UPCs Handled	UPC Dollar Velocity
Category	1974	15%	235	$1.64
Brands	1714	16	229	1.65
Private label	241	12	5	1.33
Generic	19	—	1	1.00

exhibit 2 Shampoo Dollar Share

Trade Channel	12 Months Last Year	12 Months This Year
Food	51.7%	50.5%
Drug	25.6	25.0
Mass merchant	22.7	24.5

exhibit 3 Shampoo Growth

Trade Channel	Dollar Sales % Change Versus a Year Ago
Food	0.9%
Drug	4.2
Mass merchant	8.1

exhibit 4 Dollar Sales: Percent Change versus a Year Ago

	MARKET		SHOPPERS	
	13 Weeks	52 Weeks	13 Weeks	52 Weeks
Total dollar sales	+0.1	+1.2	−10.6	−4.5
HBA department	+1.5	+4.2	−8.5	−4.3
Shampoo category	−3.5	+0.7	−19.6	−9.7

exhibit 5 Competitive Price Comparison for Shampoo: Counts of Items Showing Differences from the Base Zone (Shoppers Drug Mart)

	Shoppers	Food #1	Mass Merch.	Chain Drug	Food #2
Competition is higher	0	87	0	101	0
Competition is same	103	0	0	0	59
Competition is lower	0	16	103	2	44
Competition does not carry	0	0	0	0	0

As Robert headed for the water cooler, feeling upbeat in the thought that he had a handle on the shampoo category, he ran into Hal Jeffreys, who was a long-time veteran of Shoppers and a vice-president of information systems. Knowing that Hal had at one time managed health and beauty aids at Shoppers, Robert mentioned his review of the shampoo category and the category management initiative. Hal said that for years he had a simple approach for category management: He would begin by generating a list of slow sellers in the category and then try to replace these slow sellers with new products or by increasing the shelf space for existing products. With the new information systems that Shoppers had installed in the past year, generating a slow seller list was very easy. To prove his point, Hal walked back with Robert to his office and, using his PC, generated a slow seller report for the shampoo category (Exhibit 8).

"See, technology has made this a real cinch," said Hal as he wondered whether the expense and effort of category management would produce net improvements over and above this very simple "knock off the slow seller" approach. "I'll try to come to your presentation tomorrow," said Hal as he left Robert's office.

As Hal left his office, Robert sank back into his chair with a knot in his stomach. He felt that he had jumped the gun in thinking that he had a handle on the shampoo category. Things seemed to be more complicated than they had appeared earlier in the day. Robert wondered whether the shampoo category seemed so difficult because it was the first attempt at category management. In any case, his

exhibit 6 Brand Importance Report for Shampoo: Shoppers Drug Mart versus Remaining Market for 13 Weeks

Description	Chain Sales	Chain Rank	Rem. Mkt. Rank	Rem. Mkt. Sales	Chain Mkt. Share	Chain Category Impt.	Rem. Mkt. Cat. Impt.
Clean & Soft	$108 826	1	1	$512 345	17.5%	14.5	13.0
1st Impressions	77 672	2	3	370 341	17.3	10.3	9.4
Mane Tame	64 446	3	4	244 160	20.9	8.6	6.2
Bargain Bubbles	56 864	4	2	433 300	11.6	7.6	11.0
Silky Style	43 198	5	6	147 773	22.6	5.8	3.7
Elegance	30 869	6	5	181 075	14.6	4.1	4.6

exhibit 7 Product Mix Summary Report: Shampoo Dollar Sales—13 Weeks

	Clean & Soft	1st Impressions	Mane Tame	Bargain Bubbles	Silky Style	Elegance	Private Label
Items carried							
Shoppers	25	25	15	21	13	5	7
Rem. mkt.	25	39	28	42	20	16	28
Sizes carried							
Shoppers	6	6	6	2	4	1	4
Rem. mkt.	7	10	11	3	5	4	6
Types carried							
Shoppers	6	7	6	19	4	5	6
Rem. mkt.	6	10	8	32	5	7	21

exhibit 8 Slow Seller Report: Shampoo for Shoppers Drug Mart, 13 Weeks versus a Year Ago

Item	Chain Sales	Chain Mkt. Shr.	Chain Subcat. Impt.	Rem. Mkt. Growth	Chain Growth	Chain Avg.% Stores Selling
Golden JJB Lq T 3 oz.	$3	9.9%	0.0	−51.2	−50.0	0%
1st Imprs. DF ND Lot. 11 oz.	10	0.7	0.0	−59.4	−99.4	0
Gentle GLD Lq. 11 oz.	11	100.0	0.0	−100.0	9.6	0
Golden AV Lq. T 3 oz.	12	22.4	0.0	13.2	−69.2	1
Suds PB Lq. 8 oz.	14	6	0.0	107.1	2.9	0
Silky Style X-B Lq. 18 oz.	14	1.6	0.0	−65.6	−99.5	0

immediate concern was to prepare for his presentation tomorrow. Since Hal Jeffreys would be in the audience, he knew that he would have to address the "knock out the slow sellers" perspective.

Discussion Questions

1. In this hypothetical case of Shoppers Drug Mart, what are the national sales trends in the shampoo category?

2. What are the differences in shampoo sales trends at Shoppers compared to the national trends?

3. What could be causing these differences?

4. Suggest a plan of action.

Source: Shoppers Drug Mart company website, www.shoppersdrugmart.ca (accessed online July 29, 2007).

This case was written by Professor Kirthi Kalyanam, Retail Management Institute, Santa Clara University. © Dr. Kirthi Kalyanam.

CASE 24 How Much for a Good Smell? Pricing

For the past two Christmas seasons, Courtney's, an upscale gift store, has carried a sweet-smelling potpourri in a plastic bag with an attractive ribbon. Heavily scented with cloves, the mixture gives a pleasant holiday aroma to any room, including the store.

Two years ago, the mixture cost $4.50 a bag. Courtney's (the only store in town that carried it) sold 300 pieces for $9.50. Courtney's supply ran out ten days before Christmas, and it was too late to get any more.

Last year, the manufacturer raised the price to $5.00, so Courtney's raised its retail price to $9.95. Even though the markup was lower than the previous year, the store owner felt there was "magic" in the $10 price. As before, the store had a complete sellout, this time five days before Christmas. Sales last year were 600 units.

This year, the wholesale price has gone up to $5.50, and store personnel are trying to determine the correct retail price. The owner once again wants to hold the price at $10 ($9.95), but the buyer disagrees: "It's my job to push for the highest possible markup wherever I can. This item is a sure seller, as we're still the only store around with it, and we had some unsatisfied demand last year. I think we should mark it at $12.50, which will improve the markup to 56 percent. Staying at $10 will penalize us unnecessarily, especially considering the markup would be even lower than last year. Even if we run into price resistance, we'll only have to sell 480 to maintain the same dollar volume."

The owner demurs, saying, "This scent is part of our store's ambiance. It acts as a draw to get people into the store, and its pleasant smell keeps them in a free-spending state of mind. I think we should keep the price at $9.95, despite the poorer markup. And if we can sell many more at this price, we'll realize the same dollar gross margin as last year. I think we should buy 1000. Furthermore, if people see us raising a familiar item's price 25 percent, they might wonder whether our other prices are fair."

Discussion Questions

1. What prices caused Courtney's new charges?

2. Which price would result in the highest profit?

3. What other factors should Courtney's consider?

4. What price would you charge, and how many units would you order?

Source: This case was written by Professor David Ehrlich, Marymount University.

CASE 25 Enterprise Rent-A-Car Focuses on Its People

Enterprise is the largest and most profitable car rental business (by sales [$15.4 billion], employees [74 000], and fleet [1.3 million vehicles]) worldwide. There are more than 8200 offices located conveniently where people live and work in the United States, Canada, the United Kingdom, Ireland, Germany, France, and Spain with additional franchised business partners worldwide. More than 6000 of these offices are in the U.S. alone, and there are currently more than 400 locations in Canada. This includes approximately 380 neighbourhood locations, all located within a short distance of the majority of Canadian homes, and more than

20 offices serving airports. Enterprise is a $750 million company in Canada, with more than 4300 Canadian employees and a fleet that exceeds 55 000 vehicles.

When Jack Taylor started Enterprise in 1957, he adopted a unique strategy. Most car rental firms targeted business- and leisure-travel customers who arrived at an airport and needed to rent a car for local transportation. Taylor decided to target a different segment—individuals whose own cars are being repaired, who are driving on vacation, or who for some other reason simply need an extra car for a few days. The traditional car rental companies have to charge relatively high daily rates because their locations in or near airports are expensive. Although the airport locations are convenient for customers travelling by air, they are inconvenient for people seeking a replacement car while theirs is in the shop or an extra car to drive for a few days. So Enterprise locates its rental offices in downtown and suburban areas, where much of its target market lives and works. The firm provides local pickup and delivery service at no cost in most areas.

Enterprise's human resource strategy is a key to its success. The company fosters a sense of ownership among its employees. For example, its management training program starts by defining a clear career path for each management trainee. Then it teaches employees how to build their own business. Their compensation is tied directly to the financial results of the local operation. Employees from the rental branch offices often advance to the highest levels of operating management.

The firm hires college and university graduates for its management trainee positions because it feels that these graduates demonstrate intelligence and motivation. Rather than recruiting the students with the highest marks, it focuses on hiring people who were athletes or actively involved in campus social activities. Enterprise wants people who were social directors or high-ranking officers of social organizations, such as student governments and campus clubs, because they typically have the good interpersonal skills needed to effectively deal with Enterprise's varied customers.

Jack Taylor's growth strategy was based on providing high-quality, personalized service so that customers would return to Enterprise when they needed to rent a car again. One of his often-quoted sayings summarizes his philosophy: "If you take care of your customers and employees the bottom line will take care of itself." But because operating managers were initially compensated on the basis of sales growth, not customer satisfaction, service quality declined.

The first step Enterprise took to improve customer service was to develop a customer satisfaction measure. The questionnaire, called the Enterprise Service Quality Index, was developed on the basis of input from the operating managers. Thus managers felt ownership of the measurement tool. As the index gained legitimacy, Enterprise made a big deal about it. It posted the scores for each location prominently in its monthly operating reports—right next to the net profit numbers that determined managers' pay.

The operating managers were able to track how they were doing and how all their peers were doing, because all of the locations were ranked. To increase the motivation of managers to improve the service at their location, Enterprise announced that managers could be promoted only if their customer satisfaction scores were above the company average. Then it demonstrated that it would abide by this policy by refusing to promote some star performers who had achieved good growth and profit numbers but had below-average satisfaction scores.

To provide a high level of service, new employees generally work long hours as they, like all Enterprise managers, are expected to jump in and help wash or vacuum cars when the agency gets backed up. But all this hard work can pay off. The firm does not hire outsiders for other than entry-level jobs—every position is filled by promoting someone already inside the company. Thus Enterprise employees know that if they work hard and do their best, they may very well succeed in moving up the corporate ladder and earn a significant income. The results of this strategy are impressive and they include many accolades and awards for Enterprise. They ranked in the top ten of *BusinessWeek*'s first-ever list of "Customer Service Champs" and they were ranked number five by *BusinessWeek* as one of the "50 Best Places to Launch a Career."

Discussion Questions

1. What are the pros and cons of Enterprise's human resource management strategy?

2. Would you want to work for Enterprise? Why or why not?

3. How does its human resource strategy complement the quality of customer service delivered by its representatives?

Source: This case was written by Barton Weitz, University of Florida, with Canadian revisions provided by Samantha Boucher, talent acquisition specialist human resources, and updates from Enterprise websites.

There are countless web-based resources coming to the fore that can help retailers of any size manage any or all HR functions, from recruiting, scheduling, and payroll, to workforce management and training. It's just a matter of how you apply them.

The Social Side of Recruitment and Retention

At IKEA Canada, Paul Clark, recruitment and succession manager in Burlington, Ontario, believes networking online is the way of the future. In fact, it has become a major part of his company's HR duties, including management recruiting. "The traditional way of posting jobs and advertising in newspapers is long gone," he says.

LinkedIn is a go-to resource for recruiting management and executive talent. That's a bonus for an organization that has 35 to 40 management positions in each location. "It lets you tap into a very specific talent pool and access and communicate with nonactive job seekers," Clark says.

The most talented people aren't necessarily looking for jobs, confirms Danielle Restivo, manager of corporate communications for LinkedIn Canada. That's why businesses would benefit from being more proactive. "'What retailers are looking for is the most efficient way to find the best talent, and this is a lot better than the 'post and pray' method."

Stephanie Corker, head of recruitment for Lululemon Athletica in Vancouver, says social networking at her operation may begin with recruitment, but it carries on once employees are on board. "Social media has helped us attract the right skill sets, and keep them."

The retailer leverages LinkedIn, Facebook, and Twitter to create a connected community. Each store's Facebook page, for example, is used for everything from product notification and local community news to sharing goals and showcasing employee achievements.

"People are excited to share their stories through Lululemon and hear what other employees are blogging about," Corker says. "Social media is also a great onboarding tool for new recruits."

Time and Money

Two of the most labour-intensive functions that keep managers on-site long after the doors close for business are scheduling and payroll. Whether running an operation with a few employees or a nationwide chain, online access to automated scheduling and payroll services is growing by leaps and bounds.

Anthony Rinella, CEO of Algrin Technologies Inc., a developer of SkedX, says communication is always a big challenge for retailers when it comes to scheduling. "Vacation days get lost, availability goes missing—it all leads to employee disengagement, bad customer service, and shortages on the floor."

With online scheduling services, employees know when they're working and managers know when they can work, notes Rinella. They can get to information through a computer or mobile device, and use text or e-mail to send out schedules and alerts electronically, post shifts to find replacements, or send notices to employees. "A retailer could easily reduce scheduling time from one to one-and-a-half hours to ten minutes a week for less than $5 per employee, per month," says Rinella.

Kerina Elliott, vice president, human resources, store operations and administration for M&M Meat Shops, has dispensed with her paper scheduling processes and is now using SkedX. "It used to take a few hours a month to arrange schedules and create all sorts of nuisance when it came to making changes with our old paper-based and call-in processes. Now it takes us half the time."

For payroll on a small scale, retailers are looking to features within mainstays such as QuickBooks to ease the time burden. "It's hard to stay on top of all the legislative changes, from TD1 forms and records of employment to amendments and T4s," says Brad Card, payroll senior product manager for Intuit Canada Ltd. "With an automated payroll system, regardless of how many employees you have, it literally takes two to three minutes to do your payroll."

"Once you get started, it's a very efficient way to do things, and it's much easier to keep information organized and in compliance with the government," agrees Maureen Burleson, president of The Montana Group, a provider of bookkeeping services to retailers and other businesses.

Subscribing to the Whole Nine Yards

On a grander scale, subscription-based online services are rapidly turning workforce management solutions into a viable option. "Regardless of whether you have 5, 50, or 500 employees, full workforce management is now affordable," says Bryan Gault, regional vice president for Payworks Canada. "You can use online services to track scheduling payroll, vacation information, training, work history, skill sets, and sick days—and to report on all that."

And the benefits to the retailer can be increased exponentially when working from a unified database through which all information can flow and populate other applications. "Whether you're looking at HR, time and attendance, or payroll, you only need to enter information once because it's the same database," Gault explains. "You don't have to re-create the wheel and duplicate entries. A retailer can even offer self-serve options for employees to view their information electronically."

Golf Town has been working with Payworks since 2009 to centralize workforce management functions for its 60 stores, says Susan Gilpin, director of HR. "Before, every store ran its own payroll. The biggest challenge was people moving between stores, because it meant processing it as a termination and new hire."

With an integrated workforce management approach, she says Golf Town can achieve the consistency it wants, knowing that information is accurate across the board, and that all the proper employment standards and practices are kept. "We took the administrative end away from managers, and that helps to keep them on the sales floor. That's a huge plus." She adds that in her world, web-based services have changed HR for administrators. "I came from an environment where a lot of resources were needed to run payroll. Now we can do it all with one analyst. And we've barely skimmed the surface of what the technology can do."

Accelerating the Learning Curve

The advent of sophisticated graphics and easy login access over high-speed networks has also changed the training picture dramatically, says Cara Danielson, associate vice president, learning & development, for Canadian Tire Corp. She reports it has managed to reduce 26 hours of learning to six for new Mark's Work Wearhouse employees by dispensing with manuals and binders in favour of an e-learning system. "It's also a lot more effective, so when our people hit the floor they're a lot more confident," she says.

The system can track "pretty much everything," Danielson adds. "Every module includes an assessment and a test, so we can upload progress, results, and test scores."

Mark's started out with 40 modules in 2009, and has grown the library to 376 modules that cover orientation, customer service, and product knowledge. Over time, Mark's has moved more and more into a graphic-rich gaming experience, from exercises in dressing a mannequin to navigating a virtual store online. "We're also introducing a social media aspect to share comments and learning experiences," Danielson says.

She reports that close to 85 percent of employees have completed e-learning training. "They love it, and we don't have any trouble getting them to take it." For Danielson, e-learning is a game-changer for getting more effective employees on the floor quicker. "Even before a new employee steps on the floor, they are ready to help customers. It creates an amazing learning environment."

Discussion Questions

1. What are the two most labour-intensive functions for human resource managers?

2. How have the following retail organizations used web-based resources to manage parts of their HR functions?

   a. Lululemon

   b. M & M Meat Shops

   c. Golf Town

   d. Canadian Tire Corp.

Source: Denise Deveau, "HR Technology Is All about Connections," *Canadian Retailer*, winter 2012, volume 22, issue 1, pp. 40–43.

CASE 27 Preparing for Succession, Stitch by Stitch

Before Jennifer Baird had even completed her studies at university, she had already started on the journey toward realizing her dream of becoming president of her family's business. Just eight years and a lot of hard work later, that dream has become a reality. At the ripe age of 30, Jennifer is now the president of Stitch It Clothing Alterations, the only national alterations company in North America with stores coast-to coast in Canada as well as a finger in the U.S. market. However, despite her youth, she explains that getting to this point is the result of a well-thought-out ten-year plan that her father Alain built. She also admits that if it had been up to her, the path to succession may have looked a little different.

When Jennifer eventually graduated from the halls of academia, she felt as though she was ready to take on the world. She had gained valuable experience working two different part-time retail jobs throughout her post-secondary years. She also believed that she already possessed an intimate knowledge of the industry and the business she was to one day run. With a business degree under her belt, to boot, she felt well and truly prepared to step into an office role at the company.

"Because I had already worked quite a bit in Stitch It stores during university, I thought that I had earned my stripes. I thought I could move right into head office," she explains. "Thank goodness my dad knew better. As soon as I graduated, he put me right back into the stores. He knew that I needed a deeper understanding of the basics of the business."

The First Stitch

Jennifer vividly remembers the beginning of her journey, "like it was yesterday," she quips, when she sat down with her father to create the ten-year succession plan that would result in an opportunity for her to run the family's national company. It was a plan that she recognized immediately as one that would clearly involve a lot of hard work focused on gaining the respect of Stitch It's 650 associates.

The plan started while Jennifer was in her second year of university at a time when the Baird family was given the opportunity to buy Stitch It back from the retail powerhouse that helped Alain grow the business in its early years. Alain, however, had no interest in buying the company back for himself. He was only interested in doing so if there were some succession planning involved. He asked Jennifer if it was something that she would consider.

"It was a big decision for me to make at the age of 21," she explains. "But I already possessed a passion for retail. And I already loved this company—I loved what it was about and how it was started. I didn't have to think about it too long. My immediate reaction was a resounding 'yes!'"

Hard Work and Understanding

Though her reaction may have been immediate, she was well aware that her rise to ascendancy within the company would not be. It was going to require a lot of hard work—hard work, at the insistence of her father, that involved working in every role and covering every aspect of the company, from office administrator to area supervisor. She even moved to Chicago where she was responsible for overseeing the opening of the company's six stores there.

"I've learned so much during this experience about production, training, hiring, and building a region. I've worked within an HR function, have worked customer service in our stores, have managed stores, and have led operations. I've pretty much worked within all of the facets of the business leading up to where I am today. Doing things this way has afforded me fantastic learning opportunities and prepared me for my role as president."

It's the skills that Baird has picked up while working in all of these capacities that she credits for her early successes. She also explains that the intimate knowledge of the company and all of its facets that she now possesses could never be learned in school or anywhere else.

"There is no substitute for learning your business from the ground up," she says. "The in-store experiences taught me so much about our business, including the fact that running a successful service business is not just about serving your external customer. It's about serving your internal customers as well. Our associates are the face of Stitch It; by working the front lines, I feel connected to both sets of our customers."

Baird goes on to explain her deep appreciation for her earlier experiences gained in the stores—experiences that help her today in her role as president.

"When I visit stores today, I know enough about the processes to test out new concepts and programs," she explains. "There have been many times when we come up with a great idea at head office but it just doesn't work when I get into a store. Unfortunately, this lesson is something that can go stale if you do not stay connected. I try to get into the stores as much as possible and hope to do even more of it as I get settled into my new role."

Openness and Communication

Beyond taking this step-by-step—or stitch-by-stitch—tactical approach to succession, which has given Baird the opportunity to learn all of the ins and outs of her family's business, she stresses open and honest communication as the other critical element to an effective succession plan.

"Communication is critical," she asserts. "I knew right away that it was going to be important for my father and me both to commit to keeping open and honest communication between us. That was the only way this was going to work. In family businesses, we often take communication for granted. It's easy to assume that family members will be on the same page, but that isn't always the case. Having structured conversations around the succession plan and how well it is going is crucial. We may be family, but we are not mind-readers."

The communication between Baird and her father continues to this day, allowing her to at all times be within reach of advice from the man who started the company and the benefits of this advice are not lost on Baird.

"My father and I have a meeting every single week where we talk about what's happening. We're in a transition period right now. I have taken over the president's role, but Alain is staying on full-time for two years to continue to mentor me. He makes sure that things are going well and allows me to make some mistakes while ensuring that 'both of his babies' are staying on the right course."

1. Why is succession planning becoming increasingly critical in retail?
2. How does Stitch It manage to meet the needs of its customers?

3. Where do you think the challenges and opportunities are for Stitch It?

Source: Sean C. Tarry, "Preparing for Succession, Stitch by Stitch," *Canadian Retailer*, winter 2013, volume 23, issue 1, pp. 12–16.

CASE 28 Customer Service and Relationship Management at Nordstrom

Nordstrom's unwavering customer-focused philosophy traces its roots to founder Johan Nordstrom's values. Johan Nordstrom believed in people and realized that consistently exceeding their expectations would lead to success and a good conscience. He built his organization around a customer-oriented philosophy. The organization focuses on people, and its policies and selections are designed to satisfy people. As simple as this philosophy sounds, few of Nordstrom's competitors have truly been able to grasp it.

A Focus on People

Nordstrom employees treat customers like royalty. Employees are instructed to do whatever is in the customer's best interest. Customer delight drives the values of the company. Customers are taken seriously and are at the heart of the business. Customers are even at the top of Nordstrom's so-called organization chart, which is an inverted pyramid. Moving down from the customers at the top of the inverted pyramid are the salespeople, department managers, and general managers. Finally, at the bottom is the board of directors. All lower levels work toward supporting the salespeople, who in turn work to serve the customers.

Employee incentives are tied to customer service. Salespeople are given personalized business cards to help them build relationships with customers. Uniquely, salespeople are not tied to their respective departments but to the customer. Salespeople can travel from department to department within the store to assist their customer, if that is needed. For example, a Nordstrom salesperson assisting a woman shopping for business apparel helps her shop for suits, blouses, shoes, hosiery, and accessories. The salesperson becomes the "personal shopper" of the customer to show her merchandise and provide fashion expertise. This approach is also conducive to building long-term relationships with customers, as over time the salesperson comes to understand each customer's fashion sense and personality.

The opportunity to sell across departments enables salespeople to maximize sales and commissions while providing superior customer service. As noted on a *60 Minutes* segment, "[Nordstrom's service is] not service like it used to be, but service that never was."

Despite the obsession with customer service at Nordstrom, ironically, the customer actually comes second. Nordstrom understands that customers will be treated well by its employees only if the employees themselves are treated well by the company. Nordstrom employees are treated almost like the extended Nordstrom family, and employee satisfaction is a closely watched business variable.

Nordstrom is known for promoting employees from within its ranks. The fundamental traits of a successful Nordstrom salesperson (e.g., commitment to excellence, customer service) are the same traits emphasized in successful Nordstrom executives.

Nordstrom hires people with a positive attitude, a sense of ownership, initiative, heroism, and the ability to handle high expectations. This sense of ownership is reflected in Nordstrom's low rate of shrinkage. Shrinkage, or loss due to theft and record-keeping errors, at Nordstrom is under 1.5 percent of sales, roughly half the industry average. The low shrinkage can be attributed in large part to the diligence of salespeople caring for the merchandise as if it were their own.

Employees at all levels are treated like businesspeople and empowered to make independent decisions. They are given the latitude to do whatever they believe is the right thing, with the customers' best interests at heart. All employees are given the tools and authority to do whatever is necessary to satisfy customers, and management almost always backs subordinates' decisions.

In summary, Nordstrom's product is its people. The loyal Nordstrom shopper goes to Nordstrom for the service received—not necessarily the products. Of course, Nordstrom does offer quality merchandise, but that is secondary for many customers.

Customer-Focused Policies

One of the most famous examples of Nordstrom's customer service occurred in 1975 when a Nordstrom salesperson gladly took back a set of used automobile tires and gave the customer a refund, even though Nordstrom had never sold tires! The customer had purchased the tires from a Northern Commercial Company store, whose retail space Nordstrom had since acquired. Not wanting the customer to leave the Nordstrom store unhappy, the salesperson refunded the price of the tires.

Nordstrom's policies focus on the concept of the *lifetime value of the customer*. Although little money is made on the first sale, when the lifetime value of a customer is calculated, the positive dollar amount of a loyal customer is staggering. The lifetime value of a customer is the sum of all sales and profits generated from that customer, directly or indirectly. To keep its customers for a lifetime, Nordstrom employees go to incredible lengths. In a Nordstrom store in Seattle, a customer wanted to buy a pair of brand-name slacks that had gone on sale. The store was out of her size, and the salesperson was unable to locate a pair at other Nordstrom stores. Knowing that the same slacks were available at a competitor nearby, the sales clerk went to the rival, purchased the slacks at full price using petty cash from her department, and sold the slacks to the customer at Nordstrom's sale price. Although this sale resulted in an immediate loss for the store, the investment in promoting the loyalty of the happy customer went a long way.

Nordstrom's employees try to never say no to the customer. Nordstrom has an unconditional return policy. If a customer is not completely satisfied, he or she can return the new and generally even heavily used merchandise at any time for a full refund. Ironically, this is not a company policy; rather, it is implemented at the discretion of the salesperson to maximize customer satisfaction. Nordstrom's advice to its employees is simply, "Use good judgment in all situations." Employees are given the freedom, support, and resources to make the best decisions to enhance customer satisfaction. The cost of Nordstrom's high service, such as its return policy, coupled with its competitive pricing would, on the surface, seem to cut into profit margins. This cost, however, is recouped through increased sales from repeat customers, limited markdowns, and, if necessary, the "squeezing" of suppliers.

Nordstrom's vendor relationships also focus on maximizing customer satisfaction. According to former CEO Bruce Nordstrom, "[Vendors] know that we are liberal with our customers. And if you're going to do business with us, then there should be a liberal influence on their return policies. If somebody has worn a shoe and it doesn't wear satisfactorily for them, and we think that person is being honest about it, then we will send it back." Nordstrom realizes some customers will abuse the unconditional return policy, but it refuses to impose that abuse back onto the vendors. Here again, the rule of "doing what is right" comes into play.

Nordstrom's merchandising and purchasing policies are also extremely customer-focused. A full selection of merchandise in a wide variety of sizes is seen as a measure of customer service. An average Nordstrom store carries roughly 150 000 pairs of shoes with a variety of sizes, widths, colours, and models. Typical shoe sizes for women range from 2½ to 14, in widths of A to EEE. Nordstrom is fanatical about stocking only high-quality merchandise. Once when the upper parts of some women's shoes were separating from the soles, *every* shoe from that delivery was shipped back to the manufacturer.

Discussion Questions

1. What steps does Nordstrom take to implement its strategy of providing outstanding customer service?

2. How do these activities enable Nordstrom to reduce the gaps between perceived service and customer expectations, as described in Chapter 14?

3. What are the pros and cons of Nordstrom's approach to developing a competitive advantage through customer service?

This case was written by Alicia Lueddemann, the Management Mind Group, and Sunil Erevelles, University of North Carolina, Charlotte.

CASE 29 Active Endeavors Analyzes Its Customer Database

Active Endeavors is an outdoor apparel and accessory retailer located in Iowa City, Iowa. The store is locally owned and has been in business for 13 years, and it has a reputation for high quality and product innovation. Its target market is high-income individuals with an interest in outdoor activities and travel.

Ken Stuart, the founder of the store, has felt pressure on profit margins and increased competition, especially due to the emergence of the Internet. He tries to remain on top of competition by offering new products and a wide and deep assortment, but he thinks there might be an opportunity to increase the store's market position by utilizing a transactional database of its customers. The store has the customers' transaction records, which include customer name and address, transaction date, products and quantity purchased, and purchase price.

exhibit 1 Customer Classification Based on Purchase History

Customer Group	Recency	Frequency	Monetary
1	Purchased within the last 3 months	Purchased 4 or more times	Purchased $337.63 or more
2	Purchased within the last 3 months	Purchased once	Purchased $18.90 or less
3	Purchased between the last 3 months and a year	Purchased 4 or more times	Purchased $338.63 or more
4	Purchased between the last 3 months and a year	Purchased once	Purchased $18.90 or less
5	Purchased more than a year ago	Purchased 4 or more times	Purchased $337.63 or more
6	Purchased more than a year ago	Purchased once	Purchased $18.90 or less

He is thinking of using the transactional database to design and target a direct mail campaign designed to increase traffic.

Ken analyzed the customers' past purchase behaviour using the RFM analysis and classified the customers into six groups (Exhibit 1). The cut-off figures for the classifications were unique to the store. He is now contemplating the customer profile and what to do with it.

Discussion Questions

1. Describe the type of customers in each group.

2. What would you recommend Active Endeavors do to get more business from each group?

This case was written by Edward Rhee, Stonehill College.

CASE 30 **Engaging with Customers through Social Media**

Leveraging social media to engage potential customers and better understand their preferences and needs can seem like a daunting task. Where should retailers start?

Retailers need to understand that the use of social media is not a fad that will disappear within the next six to twelve months. The number of users on social networking sites increases every day. There are approximately 1.25 billion users on Facebook and 500 million users of Twitter, for example.

Retailers need to choose the website that will benefit the specific needs of their business. Facebook is a great tool to help retailers become involved in conversations with customers about their own product or service. Twitter, on the other hand, represents one of the quickest and easiest ways to generate word of mouth among customers concerning sales, promotions, and new product releases.

Interacting with consumers on a day-to-day basis within an environment that encourages communication and sharing is vital to understanding consumer attitudes toward retailer brands and the company's reputation. Engaging with customers online allows retailers to extend their reach beyond their physical storefront. The promotional and marketing capabilities of social media offer retailers enormous opportunity to engage customers where they are and present them with real-time information regarding sales and services that can have an immediate effect on visits to the store. Whether their customer is located in a different town, city, province, or even country—leveraging social media will allow retailers to connect with that customer within seconds.

A website that best suits the specific needs of the business needs to be chosen, and retailers need to explore it to become comfortable with the tools. Getting staff involved and providing tutorials for those who may not be engaged in social media is also a good idea. The more the retailer and their staff know about the medium, the more effective tool it will be.

Management and staff need to understand the objectives behind using social media. A clear, concise description of the way the websites and their tools are to be used and how to communicate and connect within them is important. Uploading fresh and current content on a consistent basis will grab the attention and interest of customers and get them into the store. For example, Facebook allows retailers to upload video, audio, and images, which can be used to create really dynamic marketing content that will add great value to the online experience of the customer, increasing the effectiveness of the retailer's engagement with them.

Social media dismantles the old "retailer to customer" one-way interaction. Now, retailers can reach customers and engage with them in meaningful and live conversation, enabling them to become more proactive in their approach, giving them the opportunity to adjust their operations, products, or services to suit the needs and expectations of the customer. Online tools such as Google Alerts, Technorati, and Twitter Search are great ways to find out what customers are saying about them and the products and services they provide. Once they have listened and heard, they can respond to the attitudes of the consumer through improved pricing, product availability, or anything else that might help improve the shopping experience of their clientele.

Discussion Questions

1. Will social media become an essential part of the corporate marketing strategy for retailers?

2. What benefits can a retailer gain from using social media?

3. If you were assigned the task of improving the marketing efforts of a new Internet retailer, would you use social media? Why or why not? Does it depend on what the company is selling?

4. Have you ever followed a retailer on Twitter or belonged to a retailer's Facebook group? Was it a positive or negative experience? Did it affect your buying decision? In what ways?

Sources: Retail Council of Canada, *Canadian Retailer*, January/February 2010, p. 46; Jeff Bullas, "46 Amazing Social Media Facts in 2013," JeffBullas.com blog, October 25, 2013, http://www.jeffbullas.com/2013/10/25/46-amazing-social-media-facts-in-2013/#IAcpwvTuqjwz8bAc.99 (accessed January 28, 2014).

CASE 31 Diamond in the Rough

Ruth Diamond, president of Diamond Furriers, is concerned that sales in her store appeared to have flattened out. She is considering establishing a different method for compensating her salespeople. Diamond is located in an affluent suburb of Montreal. Ruth's father had founded the company 40 years earlier, and she had grown up working in the business. After his retirement in 1980, she moved the store into an upscale shopping mall not far from its previous location and sales boomed almost immediately, rising to just over $1 million in five years. However, once it reached that sales volume, it remained there for the next three years, making Ruth wonder whether her salespeople had sufficient incentive to sell more aggressively.

Diamond's staff is all women, ranging in age from 27 to 58 years. There are four full-timers and four part-timers (20 hours a week), all of whom have at least three years of experience in the store. All of them are paid at the same hourly rate ($15) with liberal benefits. Employee morale is excellent, and the entire staff displays strong personal loyalty to Diamond.

The store is open 78 hours a week, which means that there is nearly always a minimum staff of three on the floor, rising to six at peak periods. Diamond's merchandise consists exclusively of fur coats and jackets, ranging in price from $750 to more than $5000. The average unit sale is about $2000. Full-timers' annual sales average about $160 000, and the part-timers' are a little over half of that.

Diamond's concern about sales transcends her appreciation for her loyalty toward her employees. She asks them, for example, to maintain customer files and call their customers when new styles come in. Although some of them are more diligent about this than others, none of them appear to want to be especially aggressive about promoting sales.

She began to investigate commission systems and discussed them with some of her contacts in the trade. All suggested lowering the salespeople's base pay and installing either a fixed or a variable commission rate system.

One idea was to lower the base hourly rate from $15 to $12 and let them make up the difference through a 4 percent commission on all sales, to be paid monthly. Such an arrangement would allow them all to earn the same as they currently do.

However, she also realized that such a system would provide no incentive to sell the higher-priced furs, which she recognized might be a way to improve overall sales. So she also considered offering to pay 3 percent on items priced below $2000 and 5 percent on all those above.

Either of these systems would require considerable extra bookkeeping. Returns would have to be deducted from commissions. And she was also concerned that disputes might arise among her people from time to time over who had actually made the sale. So she conceived of a third alternative, which was to leave the hourly rates the same but pay a flat bonus of 4 percent of all sales over $1 million and then divide it among the salespeople on the basis of the proportion of hours each had actually worked. This "commission" would be paid annually, in the form of a Christmas bonus.

Discussion Questions

1. What are the advantages and disadvantages of the various alternatives Ruth Diamond is considering?

2. Do you have any other suggestions for improving the store's sales?

3. What would you recommend? Why?

This case was prepared by Professor David Ehrlich, Marymount University.

Australia's oldest retailer evolved from Appleton and Jones in 1835 to David Jones in 1838. Today, David Jones, or simply DJs, has dozens of department stores, predominantly in Australia's capital cities. Similar to many retailers, and despite having a mail-order business since the late 1800s, DJs suffered a few missteps with its online presence in the early 2000s. Now, however, the David Jones website, davidjones.com.au, is integral to DJs' daily operations.

Chris Taylor, a recent university graduate, manages DJs' online presence. Thanks to its successful website and changing media habits, David Jones is considering online advertising to drive targeted traffic to the website. Given the prominence of Google and sponsored search, Chris would like to test Google AdWords.

Starting late last century, search engines began to develop interactive advertising models based on user interests, such as keywords typed into a search engine. The concept, *sponsored search,* aligns online advertisements with search engine queries. In sponsored search—also known as paid search, keyword advertising, pay-per-click (PPC) advertising, and search advertising—advertisers pay for search engine traffic to their websites via link-based ads that search engines display in response to user queries. Thus, if a user searches Google using the keyword *retailers,* AdWords ads that mention retailing would appear. If the user clicks on an ad, the user then goes to a specific web page—the landing page—on the advertiser's website.

As the leading search engine, Google has driven developments in sponsored search beyond search engine results. In addition to placing advertisements on Google and affiliated search engine results, such as AOL.com and Ask.com, advertisers can place AdWords on other websites. Via its content network, Google dynamically matches ads to a web page's content and pays the website owner if a visitor clicks on the ad. Google's content network includes millions of websites in over 100 countries and 20 languages, such as the British travel site Lonely Planet and the French television channel M6. In the United States, for example, the *New York Times* earns revenue by placing AdWords on its web pages. Thus, advertisers can place AdWords on search engine results and on the millions of websites in Google's content network.

AdWords are simple text-based ads with four lines of copy predominantly in the right-hand column and at the top of Google search results. The first line, or headline, has a maximum of 25 characters. The next two lines and the final line with the website address have a maximum of 35 characters each. Two sample AdWords

advertisements for David Jones are shown in Exhibit 1. The copy is identical except for the first half of the third line, "Great holiday specials" versus "Expanded holiday hours." The ad on the left should interest value-conscious market segments, while the one on the right should attract consumers seeking after-hours shopping.

In addition to their simple and nonintrusive nature, AdWords' advantages over traditional advertising such as print or television include better segmentation and more direct targeting. Advertisers select the keywords and the geographic location of the person doing the search. For geographic segmentation, David Jones might want its ads to appear only for people in a key source market such as Sydney or Melbourne.

To target consumer interests, David Jones could use keywords such as *Christmas, holidays, shopping,* and *retailers.* But these keywords could be too expensive because they are so generic. Although generic terms may attract clicks on an AdWords advertisement, many of these clicks may be from random rather than targeted David Jones web shoppers. Unlike a cost-per-thousand model based on impressions, this contextual advertising based on keywords charges advertisers on a cost-per-click basis. Chris and her team want to pay for targeted clicks.

To minimize paying for unwanted clicks, online advertisers also include negative keywords such as *cheap* or *free.* Including the negative keyword *cheap* alongside the keywords *Christmas* and *shopping* means that no AdWords ads will show on search results for users keying in the three keywords *cheap, Christmas,* and *shopping.*

Furthermore, advertisers bid on the cost per click in a dynamic auction. When many advertisers bid on generic terms such as *Christmas* and *shopping,* this drives the cost up for these keywords. Thus clever advertisers bid on specific phrases such as *Christmas shopping* rather than on *Christmas* and *shopping.*

Chris and her team use four Google websites to understand and determine applicable content network websites, keywords, and estimated keyword costs:

- Google AdWords Glossary (https://adwords.google.com/support/bin/topic.py?topic=29)

exhibit 1 Sample AdWords

Christmas at David Jones	Christmas at David Jones
Convenient major city locations	Convenient major city locations
Great holiday specials; visit now	Expanded holiday hours; visit now
DavidJones.com.au	DavidJones.com.au

- Google Content Network (http://www.google.com/adwords/contentnetwork/)
- Google Keyword Tool (https://adwords.google.com/select/KeywordToolExternal)
- Google Traffic Estimator (https://adwords.google.com/select/TrafficEstimatorSandbox)

As AdWords accounts are easy to set up and manage, the testing possibilities are many. Major considerations that Chris and her team would like to test include:

- Appropriate keywords, keyword phrases, and negative keywords
- Geographic segmentation
- Advertising copy and appeals
- Keyword pricing
- Google's content network
- Aligning the landing page with the AdWords copy

The final point above—the landing page—leads to a key aspect of David Jones' online presence, its website. As davidjones.com.au illustrates, the website serves many target markets and offers many products. For example, online visitors may find information on store events, employment, publicly traded stock shares, and registration for e-mail alerts and bridal registries, as well as traditional department store products such as clothing. Effective AdWords align the advertising copy with the landing page. That is, the advertisement directs consumers to a relevant web page rather than to the David Jones home page at davidjones.com.au. The left-column ad in Exhibit 1, which focuses on holiday specials, would take visitors to a landing page with holiday specials. Similarly, the right-column ad in Table 1 would take visitors to a landing page featuring expanded holiday hours.

Discussion Questions

1. On the basis of your review of the David Jones website at davidjones.com.au, use examples to explain how different sections of the home page serve different audiences. What other audiences would you suggest David Jones serve via its website? Why?

2. On the basis of your review of the David Jones website, davidjones.com.au, design three separate AdWords advertisements.

This case was written by Jamie Murphy, Murdoch Business School; Meghan O'Farrell, Google; and Alex Gibelalde, Google.

CASE 33 Generating Advertising Revenue from a Digital Screen Network at Harrods of London

Retailers have slowly been implementing digital screen networks. In most instances, the messages are focused on branding and impacting the customer shopping experience. Very few networks, such as Walmart's SMART Network and, to a lesser extent, Target's Channel Red, have also been able to generate a stream of advertising revenue. In the department store category, Harrods is the only high-end luxury store to successfully sell advertising on its in-store digital signage network. Factors such as a solid and consistent customer base and the store's unique environment have contributed to the success of the signage.

It is difficult to imagine any retail environment as unique as Harrods. It is a key destination for millions of visitors who come to the United Kingdom every year (it is the U.K.'s third-largest tourist attraction). It houses the world's finest luxury brands across a million square feet of retail space. It has a history dating back to 1849 and can count the rich and famous from all corners of the globe as its customers. The brand is synonymous with luxury, the "finer things in life," and a range of merchandise unequaled under one roof. Average daily traffic is 45 000 customers (occasionally rising to 100 000 on special days). Many of them are high-net-worth individuals, including royalty from around the world, as well as celebrities and billionaires.

Advertisements on the network are sold to premium brands, such as Armani and Cartier. The medium is often sold as part of an integrated marketing campaign, which often includes other media such as posters, lift-wraps (signage on elevator doors), windows, and even pages in the Harrods magazine. Combined with other in-store media, screens are an integral part of the campaign, providing impact, awareness, and, often, directional signage leading customers to the "heart of the promotion"—the place where the product and the customer meet.

The specific location of each screen was carefully considered so that each customer would have a multi-screen sight line. In most cases, customers see more than one screen within their view. The same content appears simultaneously on each screen in the network, so the advertisers have high impact with their ads appearing several times at once.

In most cases, screens are positioned on the sides of escalators in the store. Unlike the case at many transport hubs, most customers in Harrods stand still on the moving steps. As they glide up to the next floor, they take in the view, which includes the digital screens. Each advertiser has a 15-second slot.

Harrods' digital screen network is managed all in-house. There is a dedicated ad sales team, operations team, and technical and creative team who are all committed Harrods employees who live and breathe the brand. These employees believe in and are included in how and what is being marketed. They sit in the building and pass by the media that they are selling and marketing 20 times a day. They also see with their own eyes the audience that they are selling to the advertisers. They see the clothes they are wearing, the limos that deliver them to the store, and the number of Harrods' famous green bags they are carrying. They can see the impact that the screens can have on a consumer purchasing decision, or even simply see customers watching content through their Dior sunglasses as they glide up an escalator.

Network staff also have relationships with the brands and the advertisers. They have a relationship which has been nurtured and developed so that they are working "alongside" a brand to find marketing solutions to drive brand sales and awareness, which in turn benefits not only the brand but also Harrods as a store.

The store is continuously changing, and as part of that development, additional digital screens are introduced as part of new departments and remodels. When Harrods first introduced its digital signage network, it realized that it had to do something special to integrate the screens into the environment. It didn't want screens hanging from ceilings above walkways that look tacky, amateur, and cheap. It invested heavily in each screen installation, with customized reinforced glass, polished steel bezels, additional cooling fans, and colour schemes that are consistent with the store's decor. This gave the screens a look of luxury. A lot of care, thought, and attention have been invested in each location to give the advertiser the optimum in presentation.

Harrods monitors the effectiveness of a campaign via sales data. It has some impressive results from advertisers who have enjoyed double-digit sales increases during and following a digital campaign in the store. You'd naturally be asking the question, "Well, why isn't everyone advertising on the screens?" The answer to this question involves many factors including, among other things, the following:

- The medium is new and many vendors are unfamiliar with its benefits.
- Vendors are not always sure about where the funding of digital screen ads should come from. That is, is it a marketing/advertising expenditure or an in-store promotional expenditure?
- There are creative challenges associated with messages. For instance, is the message capturing the attention of the customers? Does it have a call to action or an offer?

If there is one way to deter advertisers, then it's to have blank, malfunctioning screens. It seems obvious, but so many networks in retail lumber on with as many as 25 percent of the screens nonoperational. No wonder they find selling ads a struggle! Harrods has a zero-tolerance strategy within the operations team, resulting in the team's touring the store every morning before the store opens checking that all is as it should be. As well, it has invested heavily in preventive maintenance contracts, and has a backup stock of spare screens available, should a screen die and require replacement.

Digital networks can make money for a retailer. Harrods has realized both ad sales revenue and increased sales of advertised products. However, such results take significant investments in time, resources, and money. The future success for generating advertising sales is dependent on improvements in technical reliability of the hardware and software, combined with more investment in content and creativity. Interactivity via mobile/smartphones is clearly part of the future. Harrods is investing in the latest technology, implementing new and unique content that captures people's imagination, and working alongside brands that are prepared to invest to realize the benefits.

Discussion Questions

1. What are the reasons that Harrods has been successful at selling advertising on its digital signage network and other retailers have not? Why would consumer product manufacturers be interested in advertising on Harrods' network?

2. What are the pluses and minuses for a retailer offering a digital network in its stores?

This case was written by Steven Keith Platt, Platt Retail Institute, and Guy Cheston, director of advertising sales and sponsorship, Harrods.

glossary

1-to-1 retailing Developing retail programs for small groups or individual customers.

80–20 rule A general management principle stating that 80 percent of the sales or profits come from 20 percent of the customers.

ABC analysis An analysis that rank orders SKUs by a profitability measure to determine which items should never be out of stock, which should be allowed to be out of stock occasionally, and which should be deleted from the stock selection.

accessibility (1) The degree to which customers can easily get into and out of a shopping centre; (2) ability of the retailer to deliver the appropriate retail mix to the customers in the segment.

accounts payable The amount of money owed to vendors, primarily for merchandise inventory.

accounts receivable The amount of money due to the retailer from selling merchandise on credit.

accrued liabilities Liabilities that accumulate daily but are paid only at the end of a period.

actionability Means that the definition of a market segment must clearly indicate what the retailer should do to satisfy its needs.

adaptability A company's recognition of cultural differences and adaptation of its core strategy to the needs of local markets.

add-on selling Selling additional new products and services to existing customers, such as a bank encouraging a customer with a chequing account to also apply for a home improvement loan from the bank.

advance shipping notice (ASN) An electronic document received by a retailer's computer from a supplier in advance of a shipment.

advertising Paid communications delivered to customers through nonpersonal mass media such as newspapers, television, radio, direct mail, and the Internet.

affordable budgeting method A budgeting method in which a retailer first sets a budget for every element of the retail mix except promotion and then allocates the leftover funds to a promotional budget.

aided recall When consumers indicate they know the brand when the name is presented to them.

alternative dispute resolution A provision included in a contract between retailer and vendor to help avoid litigation in the case of a dispute. Can include methods of settling the dispute that the parties agree upon, such as mediation, arbitration, or med-arb.

amount and quality of parking facilities A store's having enough parking spaces, close enough to the building, that the store is ideally accessible to customers, but not so many open spaces that the store is viewed as being unpopular. A standard rule of thumb is 5.9 spaces per 1000 square feet of retail store space.

analogue approach A method of trade area analysis, also known as the *similar store* or *mapping approach,* that is divided into four steps: (1) describing the current trade areas through the technique of customer spotting; (2) plotting the customers on a map; (3) defining the primary, secondary, and tertiary area zones; and (4) matching the characteristics of stores in the trade areas with the potential new store to estimate its sales potential.

anchors Major retailers located in a shopping centre.

arbitration Used in the case of a dispute between retailer and vendor that involves the appointment of a neutral party–the arbitrator–who considers the arguments of both sides and then makes a decision that is usually agreed upon in advance as binding.

artificial barriers In site evaluations for accessibility, barriers such as railroad tracks, major highways, or parks.

assets Economic resources, such as inventory or store fixtures, owned or controlled by an enterprise as a result of past transactions or events.

asset turnover Net sales divided by total assets.

atmospherics The design of an environment via visual communications, lighting, colours, music, and scent to stimulate customers' perceptual and emotional responses and ultimately to affect their purchase behaviour.

attitude branding The choice of a symbol that represents a feeling that is not necessarily connected with the product or retailer.

average sale per transaction (AST) A measure that evaluates productivity by looking at the number of transactions processed per store or department and the average dollar sale per transaction.

backup stock The inventory used to guard against going out of stock when demand exceeds forecasts or merchandise is delayed; also called *safety stock* or *buffer stock.*

bargaining power of vendors A competitive factor that makes a market unattractive when a few vendors control the merchandise sold in it. In these situations, vendors have an opportunity to dictate prices and other terms, reducing retailer's profits.

barriers to entry Conditions in a retail market that make it difficult for firms to enter the market.

benefit segmentation A method of segmenting a retail market on the basis of similar benefits sought in merchandise or services.

big-box stores Large, limited-service retailers.

blog A public website where users post informal journals of their thoughts, comments, and philosophies; also called *weblog.*

bonus Additional compensation awarded periodically, based on a subjective evaluation of the employee's performance.

bootleg The sale of imitation goods where there is little or no attempt at hiding the fact that the product is counterfeit.

bottom-up planning When goals are set at the bottom of the organization and filter up through the operating levels.

brand A distinguishing name or symbol (such as a logo, design, symbol, or trademark) that identifies the products or services offered by a seller and differentiates those products and services from the offerings of competitors.

brand association Anything linked to or connected with the brand name in a consumer's memory.

brand awareness The ability of a potential customer to recognize or recall that a particular brand name belongs to a retailer or product/service.

brand energy The concept that links the idea that a brand creates value through meaningful experiences rather than a focus on generating profits.

brand equity The value that brand image offers retailers.

brand images Sets of associations consumers have about a brand that are usually organized around some meaningful themes.

brand loyalty Indicates customers like and consistently buy a specific brand in a product category. They are reluctant to switch to other brands if their favourite brand isn't available.

break-even analysis A technique that evaluates the relationship between total revenue and total cost to determine profitability at various sales levels.

break-even point (BEP) The quantity at which total revenue equals total cost and beyond which profit occurs.

breaking bulk A function performed by retailers or wholesalers in which they receive large quantities of merchandise.

breaking sizes Stocking out of a specific size or colour SKU.

bullwhip effect The buildup of inventory in an uncoordinated channel.

buyback A strategy vendors and retailers use to get products into retail stores, either when a retailer allows a vendor to create space for goods by "buying back" a competitor's inventory and removing it from a retailer's system, or when the retailer forces a vendor to buy back slow-moving merchandise; also called *stocklift* or *lift-out*.

buying process The stages customers go through to purchase merchandise or services.

buying situation segmentation A method of segmenting a retail market based on customer needs in a specific buying situation, such as a fill-in shopping trip versus a weekly shopping trip.

call to action The portion of the marketing or sales message that prompts potential consumers to perform a desired action within the desired time frame.

catalogue channel A nonstore retail format in which the retailer communicates directly with customers using catalogues sent through the mail.

category captain A supplier that forms an alliance with a retailer to help gain consumer insight, satisfy consumer needs, and improve the performance and profit potential across the entire category.

category life cycle A merchandise category's sales pattern over time.

category management The process of managing a retail business with the objective of maximizing the sales and profits of a category.

category signage Signage within a particular department or sector of the store, category signs are usually smaller than directional signs. Their purpose is to identify types of products offered; they are usually located near the goods to which they refer.

category specialist A discount retailer that offers a narrow but deep assortment of merchandise in a category and thus dominates the category from the customers' perspective. Also called *category killer*.

central business district (CBD) The traditional downtown business area of a city or town.

centralization The degree to which authority for making retail decisions is delegated to corporate managers rather than to geographically dispersed regional, district, and store management.

chargeback A practice used by retailers in which they deduct money from the amount they owe a vendor.

checking The process of going through goods upon receipt to make sure that they arrived undamaged and that the merchandise received matches the merchandise ordered.

checkout areas The places in a store where customers can purchase merchandise and have it "wrapped"—placed in a bag; also called *cash-wrap areas*.

classification A group of items or SKUs for the same type of merchandise, such as pants (as opposed to jackets or suits), supplied by different vendors.

closeout retailers Off-price retailers that sell a broad but inconsistent assortment of general merchandise as well as apparel and soft home goods, obtained through retail liquidations and bankruptcy proceedings.

coaching The activity of supporting people to achieve their goals by goal setting, training, advising, encouraging, and rewarding their successes.

collaborative planning, forecasting, and replenishment (CPFR) A collaborative inventory management system in which a retailer shares information with vendors. CPFR software uses data to construct a computer-generated replenishment forecast that is shared by the retailer and vendor before it's executed.

combination stores Retailers that sell both food and nonfood items.

commercial bribery A vendor's offer of money or gifts to a retailer's employee for the purpose of influencing purchasing decisions.

commission Compensation based on a fixed formula, such as percentage of sales.

communication gap The difference between the actual service provided to customers and the service promised in the retailer's promotion program. This factor is one of the four factors identified by the gaps model for improving service quality.

communication objectives Specific goals for a communication program related to the effects of the communication program on the customer's decision-making process.

comparable store sales growth The sales growth in stores that have been open for over one year; also called *same-store sales growth*.

competition-oriented method A pricing method in which a retailer uses competitors' prices, rather than demand or cost considerations, as guides.

competitive parity method An approach for setting a promotion budget so that the retailer's share of promotion expenses is equal to its market share.

competitive rivalry The frequency and intensity of reactions to actions undertaken by competitors.

composite segmentation A method of segmenting a retail market using multiple variables, including benefits sought, lifestyles, and demographics.

congestion The amount of crowding of either cars or people.

consideration set The set of alternatives the customer evaluates when making a merchandise selection.

consignment When the vendor owns the merchandise until it is sold by the retailer, at which time the retailer pays for the merchandise.

consortium exchange A retail exchange that is owned by several firms within one industry.

continuous replenishment A system of continuously monitoring merchandise sales and generating replacement orders, often automatically, when inventory levels drop below predetermined levels.

contribution margin Gross margin less any expense that can be directly assigned to the merchandise.

convenience stores Stores that provide a limited variety and assortment of merchandise at a convenient location with speedy checkout.

conventional supermarket A self-service food store that offers groceries, meat, and produce with limited sales of nonfood items, such as health and beauty aids and general merchandise.

cookies Computer text files that identify visitors when they return to a website so that customers do not have to identify themselves or use passwords every time they visit the site. Cookies also collect information about other sites the person has visited and what pages have been downloaded.

co-op advertising A program undertaken by a vendor in which the vendor agrees to pay all or part of a promotion for its products; also called *cooperative advertising*.

copyright A regulation that protects original works of authors, painters, sculptors, musicians, and others who produce works of artistic or intellectual merit.

corporate social responsibility (CSR) Voluntary actions taken by a company to address the ethical, social, and environmental impacts of its business operations and the concerns of its stakeholders.

cost of goods sold Amount on an income statement that represents the cost of purchasing raw materials and manufacturing finished products.

cost-oriented method A method for determining the retail price by adding a fixed percentage to the cost of the merchandise; also known as *cost-plus pricing*.

cost per thousand (CPM) A measure that is often used to compare media. CPM is calculated by dividing an ad's cost by its reach.

counterfeit merchandise Goods that are made and sold without permission of the owner of a trademark, a copyright, or a patented invention that is legally protected in the country where it is marketed.

coupons Documents, electronic or hard copy, that entitle the holder to a reduced price or X cents off the actual price of a product or service.

coverage The theoretical number of potential customers in the retailer's target market that could be exposed to an ad in a given medium.

cross-docked Items that are unloaded from the shippers' truck and within a few hours reloaded onto trucks going to stores. These items are prepackaged by the vendor for a specific store, such that the UPC labels on a carton indicate the store to which it is to be sent.

cross-sectional ratio analysis The analysis of a financial ratio of a company with the same ratio of different companies in the same industry.

cross-selling When sales associates in one department attempt to sell complementary merchandise from other departments to their customers.

cross-shopping A pattern of buying both premium and low-priced merchandise or patronizing expensive, status-oriented retailers and price-oriented retailers.

culture The meaning and values shared by most members of a society.

cumulative attraction The principle that a cluster of similar and complementary retailing activities will generally have greater drawing power than isolated stores that engage in the same retailing activities.

cumulative reach The cumulative number of potential customers that would see an ad that runs several times.

current assets Cash or any assets that can normally be converted into cash within one year.

current liabilities Debts that are expected to be paid in less than one year.

customer database The coordinated and periodic copying of data from various sources, both inside and outside the enterprise, into an environment ready for analytical and informational processing. It contains all of the data the firm has collected about its customers and is the foundation for subsequent CRM activities; also called *customer data warehouse*.

customer loyalty Customers' commitment to shopping at a store.

customer relationship management (CRM) A business philosophy and set of strategies, programs, and systems that focuses on identifying and building loyalty with a retailer's most valued customers.

customer returns The value of merchandise that customers return because it is damaged, it doesn't fit, and so forth.

customer service The set of retail activities that increase the value customers receive when they shop and purchase merchandise.

cycle stock The inventory that goes up and down due to the replenishment process; also called *base stock*.

data mining Technique used to identify patterns in data found in data warehouses, typically patterns that the analyst is unaware of prior to searching through the data.

data warehouse The coordinated and periodic copying of data from various sources, both inside and outside the enterprise, into an environment ready for analytical and informational processing. It contains all of the data the firm has collected about its customers and is the foundation for subsequent CRM activities.

decentralization When authority for retail decisions is made at lower levels in the organization.

decile analysis A method of identifying customers in a CRM program that breaks customers into ten deciles based on their LTV (lifetime customer value). When using decile analysis, the top 10 percent of the customers would be the most-valued group.

delivery gap The difference between the retailer's service standards and the actual service provided to customers. This factor is one of the four factors identified by the gaps model for improving service quality.

demalling The activity of revitalizing a mall by demolishing a mall's small shops, scrapping its common space and food courts, enlarging the sites once occupied by department stores, and adding more entrances to the parking lot.

demand-oriented method A method of setting prices based on what the customers would expect or be willing to pay.

demographic segmentation A method of segmenting a retail market that groups consumers on the basis of easily measured, objective characteristics such as age, sex, income, and education.

department A segment of a store with merchandise that represents a group of classifications the consumer views as being complementary.

department store A retailer that carries a wide variety and deep assortment, offers considerable customer services, and is organized into separate departments for displaying merchandise.

depth interview An unstructured personal interview in which the interviewer uses extensive probing to get individual respondents to talk in detail about a subject.

depth of merchandise The number of SKUs within a merchandise category; also called *assortment* and *depth of stock*.

depth The amount of a particular item of merchandise that a retailer will stock, reflecting attributes such as brand, size, or colour.

destination stores Retail stores in which the merchandise, selection, presentation, pricing, or other unique feature acts as a magnet for customers.

digital signage Signs whose visual content is delivered digitally through a centrally managed and controlled network and displayed on a television monitor or flat-panel screen.

direct investment The investment and ownership by a retail firm or a division or subsidiary that builds and operates stores in a foreign country.

direct mail Any brochure, catalogue, advertisement, or other printed marketing material delivered directly to the consumer through the mail or by a private delivery company.

direct marketing A form of nonstore retailing in which customers are exposed to merchandise through print or electronic media; they then can purchase the merchandise by telephone, mail, or over the Internet.

direct-response advertising Advertisements on TV and radio that describe products and provide an opportunity for customers to order them.

direct selling A retail format in which a salesperson, frequently an independent distributor, contacts a customer directly in a convenient location (either at a customer's home or at work), demonstrates merchandise benefits, takes an order, and delivers the merchandise to the customer.

direct store delivery (DSD) A method of delivering merchandise to stores in which vendors distribute merchandise directly to the stores rather than going through distribution centres.

disability Any physical or mental impairment that substantially limits one or more of an individual's major life activities or any condition that is regarded as being such an impairment.

discount store A general merchandise retailer that offers a wide variety of merchandise, limited service, and low prices; also called *mass merchandiser* and *full-line discount store.*

discrimination An illegal action of a company or its managers that results when a member of a protected class (women, minorities, etc.) is treated differently from nonmembers of that class (see *disparate treatment*) or when an apparently neutral rule has an unjustified discriminatory effect (see *disparate impact*).

disparate impact In the case of discrimination, when an apparently neutral rule has an unjustified discriminatory effect, such as when a retailer requires high school graduation for all its employees, thereby excluding a larger proportion of disdvantaged minorities, when at least some of the jobs (e.g., custodian) could be performed just as well by people who did not graduate from high school.

disparate treatment In the case of discrimination, when members of a protected class are treated differently than nonmembers of that class, such as when a qualified woman (protected class) does not receive a promotion given to a less qualified man.

dispatcher A person who coordinates deliveries from the vendor to the distribution centre or stores, or from the distribution centre to stores.

distribution centre A warehouse that receives merchandise from multiple vendors and distributes it to multiple stores.

distribution channel A set of firms that facilitate the movement of products from the point of production to the point of sale to the ultimate consumer.

distributive fairness Exists when outcomes received are viewed as fair with respect to outcomes received by others.

distributive justice Exists when outcomes received are viewed as fair with respect to outcomes received by others.

diversification opportunity A strategic investment opportunity that involves an entirely new retail format directed toward a market segment not presently being served.

diverted merchandise Merchandise that is diverted from its legitimate channel of distribution; similar to grey-market merchandise except there need not be distribution across international boundaries.

downtown location The central business district located in the traditional shopping area of smaller towns, or a secondary business district in a suburb or within a larger city, generally featuring lower occupancy costs, fewer people, fewer stores, smaller overall selection of goods or services, and fewer entertainment and recreational activities than more successful primary central business districts.

drawing account A method of sales compensation in which salespeople receive a weekly cheque based on their estimated annual income.

drop-shipping A supply chain system in which retailers receive orders from customers and relay these orders to a vendor and then the vendor ships the merchandise ordered directly to the customer; also called *consumer direct fulfillment.*

drugstore Specialty retail store that concentrates on pharmaceuticals and health and personal grooming merchandise.

electronic article surveillance (EAS) system A loss-prevention system in which special tags placed on merchandise in retail stores are deactivated when the merchandise is purchased. The tags are used to discourage shoplifting.

electronic data interchange (EDI) The computer-to-computer exchange of business documents from retailer to vendor and back.

electronic retailing A retail format in which the retailers communicate with customers and offer products and services for sale over the Internet. Also called *e-tailing, online retailing,* and *Internet retailing.*

e-mail A paid personal communication vehicle that involves sending messages over the Internet.

emotional support Supporting retail service providers with the understanding and positive regard to enable them to deal with the emotional stress created by disgruntled customers.

employee productivity Output generated by employee activities. One measure of employee productivity is the retailer's sales or profit divided by its employee costs.

employee turnover The number of employees occupying a set of positions during a period (usually a year) divided by the number of positions.

empowerment The process of managers sharing power and decision-making authority with employees.

end caps Display fixtures located at the end of an aisle.

ethics A system or code of conduct based on universal moral duties and obligations that indicate how one should behave.

everyday low pricing (EDLP) A pricing strategy that stresses continuity of retail prices at a level somewhere between the regular nonsale price and the deep-discount sale price of the retailer's competitors.

exclusive co-brand A brand developed by a national brand vendor, often in conjunction with a retailer, and sold exclusively by the retailer.

exclusive dealing agreement Restriction a manufacturer or wholesaler places on a retailer to carry only its products and no competing vendors' products.

exclusive geographic territory A policy in which only one retailer in a certain territory is allowed to sell a particular brand.

expenses Costs incurred in the normal course of doing business to generate revenues.

extended problem solving A buying process in which customers spend considerable time at each stage of the decision-making process because the decision is important and they have limited knowledge of alternatives.

external sources of information Information provided by the media and other people.

extrinsic rewards Rewards (such as money, promotion, and recognition) given to employees by their manager or the firm.

factory outlets Outlet stores owned by a manufacturer.

fair trade Purchasing practices that require producers to pay workers a living wage, well more than the prevailing minimum wage, and offer other benefits, such as on-site medical treatment.

fashion merchandise category Category of merchandise that typically lasts several seasons, and sales can vary dramatically from one season to the next.

fashion/specialty centre A shopping centre that is composed mainly of upscale apparel shops, boutiques, and gift shops carrying selected fashions or unique merchandise of high quality and price.

feature areas Areas designed to get the customer's attention that include end caps, promotional aisles or areas, freestanding fixtures and mannequins that introduce a soft goods department, windows, and point-of-sale areas.

fill rate The percentage of an order that is shipped by the vendor.

financial resources Enable companies to make strategic decisions, such as expansion into international markets, requiring significant and ongoing financial commitment, often at the expense of short-term profit.

first-degree price discrimination Charging customers different prices based on their willingness to pay.

fixed assets Assets that require more than a year to convert to cash.

fixed costs Costs that are stable and don't change with the quantity of product that's produced and sold.

flextime A job scheduling system that enables employees to choose the times they work.

floor-ready merchandise Merchandise received at the store ready to be sold, without the need for any additional preparation by retail employees.

focus group A marketing research technique in which a small group of respondents is interviewed by a moderator using a loosely structured format.

forecast To estimate or calculate in advance: predict the future.

four-way fixture A fixture with two cross-bars that sit perpendicular to each other on a pedestal. Also known as a *feature fixture*.

franchisee The owner of an individual store in a franchise agreement.

franchising A contractual agreement between a franchisor and a franchisee that allows the franchisee to operate a retail outlet using a name and format developed and supported by the franchisor.

franchisor The owner of a franchise in a franchise agreement.

free-form layout A store design, used primarily in small specialty stores or within the boutiques of large stores, that arranges fixtures and aisles asymmetrically. Also called *boutique layout*.

freestanding fixtures Fixtures and mannequins located on aisles that are designed primarily to get customers' attention and bring them into a department.

freestanding insert (FSI) An advertisement printed at the retailer's expense and distributed as an insert in the newspaper; also called a *preprint*.

freestanding site A retail location that is not connected to other retailers.

free trade zone A special area within a country that can be used for warehousing, packaging, inspection, labelling, exhibition, assembly, fabrication, or transshipment of imports without being subject to that country's tariffs.

freight forwarders Companies that purchase transport services. They then consolidate small shipments from a number of shippers into large shipments that move at a lower freight rate.

frequency The number of times a potential customer is exposed to a promotional message.

frequent shopper program A reward and communication program used by a retailer to encourage continued purchases from the retailer's best customers.

frontal presentation A method of displaying merchandise in which the retailer exposes as much of the product as possible to catch the customer's eye.

full-time equivalent (FTE) The relationship between net sales for a specified period of time and the number of full-time equivalent employees who worked during that specified period of time.

gamification The application of game theory concepts and techniques to non-game activities.

generic branding A branding strategy that targets a price-sensitive segment by offering a no-frills product at a discount price.

gentrification A process in which old buildings are torn down or are restored to create new offices, housing developments, and retailers.

geodemographic segmentation A market segmentation system that uses both geographic and demographic characteristics to classify consumers.

geographic information system (GIS) A computerized system that enables analysts to visualize information about their customers' demographics, buying behaviour, and other data in a map format.

geographic segmentation Segmentation of potential customers by where they live. A retail market can be segmented by countries, provinces, cities, and neighbourhoods.

glass ceiling A figurative barrier that makes it difficult for minorities and women to be promoted beyond a certain level.

global culture A company's embracing a multicultural perspective and developing an infrastructure that makes maximal use of local management.

globally sustainable competitive advantage One of the characteristics of retailers that have successfully exploited international growth opportunities.

global strategy Replicating a retailer's standard retail format and centralized management throughout the world in each new market.

gondola An island type of self-service counter with tiers of shelves, bins, or pegs.

grey-market good Merchandise that possesses a valid North American registered trademark and is made by a foreign manufacturer but is imported into North America without permission of the trademark owner.

grid layout A store design, typically used by grocery stores, in which merchandise is displayed on long gondolas in aisles with a repetitive pattern.

gross margin The difference between the price the customer pays for merchandise and the cost of the merchandise (the price the retailer paid the supplier of the merchandise). More specifically, gross margin = net sales − cost of goods sold (= maintained markup) − alteration cost + cash discounts; also called *gross profit*.

gross margin return on investment (GMROI) A financial ratio that assesses a buyer's contribution to return on assets: gross margin dollars divided by average (cost) inventory.

habitual decision making A purchase decision involving little or no conscious effort.

hedonic benefit Shopping for pleasure, entertainment, and/or to achieve an emotional or recreational experience.

hedonic needs Needs motivating consumers to go shopping for pleasure.

high-assay principle A method of allocating a communication budget that uses the principles of marginal analysis. The retailer should allocate the budget to areas that will yield the greatest return.

high/low pricing A strategy in which retailers offer prices that are sometimes above their competition's everyday low price, but they use advertising to promote frequent sales.

Huff gravity model A trade area analysis model used to determine the probability that a customer residing in a particular area will shop at a particular store or shopping centre.

hypermarkets Large combination food (60–70 percent) and general merchandise (30–40 percent) retailers.

idea-oriented presentation A method of presenting merchandise based on a specific idea or the image of the store.

identifiability Permits a retailer to determine a market segment's size and with whom the retailer should communicate when promoting its retail offering.

illegal discrimination The actions of a company or its managers that result in members of a protected class being treated unfairly and differently than others.

impact An ad's effect on the audience.

impulse products Products that are purchased by customers without prior plans. These products are almost always located near the front of the store, where they're seen by everyone and may actually draw people into the store.

incentive compensation plan A compensation plan that rewards employees on the basis of their productivity.

independent exchange A retail exchange owned by a third party that provides the electronic platform to perform the exchange functions.

infomercials TV programs, typically 30 minutes long, that mix entertainment with product demonstrations and solicit orders placed by telephone from consumers.

information search The stage in the buying process in which a customer seeks additional information to satisfy a need.

ingress/egress The means of entering/exiting the parking lot of a retail site.

initial markup The retail selling price initially placed on the merchandise less the cost of goods sold.

input measure A performance measure used to assess the amount of resources or money used by the retailer to achieve outputs.

in-store kiosks Spaces located within stores containing a computer connected to the store's central offices or to the Internet.

instrumental support Support for retail service providers such as appropriate systems and equipment to deliver the service desired by customers.

integrated marketing communication program The strategic integration of multiple communication methods to form a comprehensive, consistent message.

intellectual property Property that is intangible and is created by intellectual (mental) effort as opposed to physical effort.

interest The amount charged by a financial institution to borrow money.

interest income The income a retailer can generate through proprietary credit cards, bank deposits, bonds, treasury bills, fixed income investments, and other investments.

internal sources of information Information in a customer's memory such as names, images, and past experiences with different stores.

intertype competition Competition between retailers that sell similar merchandise using different formats, such as discount and department stores.

intratype competition Competition between retailers of the same type (e.g., Loblaws versus Sobeys).

intrinsic rewards Nonmonetary, intangible rewards employees get from doing their jobs.

inventory Goods or merchandise available for resale.

inventory turnover Net sales divided by average retail inventory; used to evaluate how effectively managers utilize their investment in inventory.

item price The practice of marking prices only on shelves or signs and not on individual items.

job analysis Identifying essential activities and determining the qualifications employees need to perform them effectively.

job application form A form a job applicant completes that contains information about the applicant's employment history, previous compensation, reasons for leaving previous employment, education and training, personal health, and references.

job description A description of the activities the employee needs to perform and the firm's performance expectations.

job sharing When two or more employees voluntarily are responsible for a job that was previously held by one person.

joint venture An entity formed when the entering retailer pools its resources with a local retailer to form a new company in which ownership, control, and profits are shared.

keystone method A method of setting retail prices in which retailers simply double the cost of the merchandise to obtain the original retail selling price.

kiosk A small selling space offering a limited merchandise assortment.

knockoff A copy of the latest styles displayed at designer fashion shows and sold in exclusive specialty stores. These copies are sold at lower prices through retailers targeting a broader market.

knowledge gap The difference between customer expectations and the retailer's perception of customer expectations. This factor is one of four factors identified by the gaps model for improving service quality.

leader pricing A pricing strategy in which certain items are priced lower than normal to increase the traffic flow of customers or to increase the sale of complementary products.

leadership The process by which a person attempts to influence another to accomplish some goal or goals.

lead time The amount of time between recognition that an order needs to be placed and the point at which the merchandise arrives in the store and is ready for sale.

leased department An area in a retail store leased or rented to an independent company. The leaseholder is typically responsible for all retail mix decisions involved in operating the department and pays the store a percentage of its sales as rent.

liabilities Obligations of a retail enterprise to pay cash or other economic resources in return for past, present, or future benefits.

licensed brand Brand for which the licensor (owner of a well-known name) enters into a contractual arrangement with a licensee (a retailer or a third party). The licensee either manufactures or contracts with a manufacturer to produce the licensed product and pays a royalty to the licensor.

lifestyle centre A shopping centre with an outdoor, traditional streetscape layout with sit-down restaurants and a conglomeration of specialty retailers.

lifestyle segmentation A method of segmenting a retail market based on consumers' lifestyles.

lifetime customer value (LTV) The expected contribution from the customer to the retailer's profits over his or her entire relationship with the retailer.

limited-assortment supermarkets Supermarkets offering a limited number of SKUs; also called *extreme-value food retailers*.

limited problem solving A purchase-decision process involving a moderate amount of effort and time. Customers engage in this type of buying process when they have some prior experience with the product or service and their risk is moderate.

locavore movement A movement whose adherents' primary source of food originates within a specified radius of where they live.

logistics Part of the supply chain process that plans, implements, and controls the efficient, effective flow and storage of goods, services, and related information from the point of origin to the point of consumption to meet customers' requirements.

long-term liabilities Debts that will be paid after one year.

low-price guarantee policy   A policy that guarantees that the retailer will have the lowest possible price for a product or group of products, and usually promises to match or better any lower price found in the local market.

loyalty program   A program set up to reward customers with incentives such as discounts on purchases, free food, gifts, or even cruises or trips in return for their repeated business.

macro-environment   The external environment that the retailer cannot control, including competition, economic stability of the trade area, the technology that will make retailing more efficient, the regulatory and ethical environment in which the business operates, and the social trends, including consumer behaviour and lifestyle and demographic trends.

magalogue   A combination magazine and catalogue.

maintained markup   The amount of markup the retailer wishes to maintain on a particular category of merchandise; net sales minus cost of goods sold.

mall   A shopping centre with a pedestrian focus where customers park in outlying areas and walk to the stores.

management   A strategic approach of an organization to achieve its objectives by developing policies and plans for allocating resources.

managing diversity   A set of human resource management programs designed to realize the benefits of a diverse workforce.

manufacturer brand   A line of products designed, produced, and marketed by a vendor; also called a *national brand*.

maquiladoras   Manufacturing plants in Mexico that make goods and parts or process food for export to North America.

marginal analysis   A method of analysis used in setting a promotional budget or allocating retail space, based on the economic principle that firms should increase expenditures as long as each additional dollar spent generates more than a dollar of additional contribution.

markdown money   Funds provided by a vendor to a retailer to cover decreased gross margin from markdowns and other merchandising issues.

markdowns   The price reductions in the initial retail price.

market   A group of vendors in a concentrated geographic location or even under one roof or over the Internet; also known as a *central market*.

market basket analysis   Specific type of data analysis that focuses on the composition of the basket (or bundle) of products purchased by a household during a single shopping occasion.

market expansion opportunity   A strategic investment opportunity that employs the existing retailing format in new market segments.

market penetration opportunity   An investment opportunity strategy that focuses on increasing sales to present customers using the present retailing format.

markup   The increase in the retail price of an item after the initial markup percentage has been applied but before the item is placed on the selling floor.

markup percentage   The markup as a percent of retail price.

m-commerce   The purchase of products and services through mobile devices.

med-arb   Used in the case of a dispute between retailer and vendor that involves an initial attempt at mediation followed by binding arbitration if the mediation is unsuccessful. See *mediation* and *arbitration*.

mediation   Used in the case of a dispute between retailer and vendor that involves selecting a neutral party—the mediator—to assist the parties in reaching a mutually agreeable settlement.

mentoring program   The assigning of higher-level managers to help lower-level managers learn the firm's values and meet other senior executives.

merchandise budget plan   A plan used by buyers to determine how much money to spend in each month on a particular fashion merchandise category, given the firm's sales forecast, inventory turnover, and profit goals.

merchandise category   An assortment of items (SKUs) the customer sees as reasonable substitutes for each other.

merchandise group   A group within an organization managed by the senior vice presidents of merchandise and responsible for several departments.

merchandise management   The process by which a retailer attempts to offer the right quantity of the right merchandise in the right place at the right time while meeting the company's financial goal.

merchandising optimization software   Set of algorithms (computer programs) that monitors merchandise sales, promotions, competitors' actions, and other factors to determine the optimal (most profitable) price and timing for merchandising activities, especially markdowns.

micro-environment   All of the things within the retailer's control, including the retail product that will be sold, the price for the product, the store location, the promotion and visual image of the store, the processes, and human resource management decisions.

mission statement   A broad description of the scope of activities a business plans to undertake.

mixed-use development (MXD)   Development that combines several uses in one complex—for example, shopping centre, office tower, hotel, residential complex, civic centre, and convention centre.

mobile marketing   Communicating with and selling to customers through wireless handheld devices, such as cellular telephones; also called *m-commerce* or *mobile commerce*.

model stock plan   A summary of the desired inventory levels of each SKU stocked in a store for a merchandise category.

multiattribute attitude model   A model of customer decision making based on the notion that customers see a retailer or a product as a collection of attributes or characteristics. The model can also be used for evaluating a retailer, product, or vendor. The model uses a weighted average score based on the importance of various issues and performance on those issues.

multichannel retailer   Retailer that sells merchandise or services through more than one channel.

multilevel system   A retail format in which people serve as master distributors, recruiting other people to become distributors in their network.

multinational strategy   A strategy that involves changing a retailer's products and image to reflect the international marketplace, using a decentralized format, learning about the country's culture, and changing the retail concept to adapt to cultural differences and cater to local market demands.

multiple-unit pricing   Practice of offering two or more similar products or services for sale at one price.

mystery shopper   Professional shopper who "shops" a store to assess the service provided by store employees.

natural barriers   Barriers, such as rivers or mountains, that affect accessibility to a site.

near-field communications (NFC)   A set of standards for smartphones and similar devices to establish radio communication with each other by touching them together or bringing them into close proximity, usually no more than a few inches.

net profit   A measure of the overall performance of a firm; revenues (sales) minus expenses and losses for the period.

net profit margin The profit (after tax) a firm makes divided by its net sales.

net sales The total number of dollars received by a retailer after all refunds have been paid to customers for returned merchandise.

North American Industry Classification System (NAICS) Classification of retail firms into a hierarchical set of six-digit codes based on the types of products and services they produce and sell.

notes payable Current liabilities representing principal and interest the retailer owes to financial institutions (banks) that are due and payable in less than a year.

objective-and-task method A method for setting a promotion budget in which the retailer first establishes a set of communication objectives and then determines the necessary tasks and their costs.

odd pricing The practice of ending prices with an odd number (such as 69 cents) or just under a round number (such as $98 instead of $100).

off-price retailer A retailer that offers an inconsistent assortment of brand-name, fashion-oriented soft goods at low prices.

omni-channel retailing Seamless integration between all channels so that shoppers can shop any way they want with the exact same results.

open-to-buy The plan that keeps track of how much is spent in each month, and how much is left to spend.

operating expenses Costs, other than the cost of merchandise, incurred in the normal course of doing business, such as salaries for sales associates and managers, advertising, utilities, office supplies, and rent.

opportunity cost of capital The rate available on the next-best use of the capital invested in the project at hand. The opportunity cost should be no lower than the rate at which a firm borrows funds, since one alternative is to pay back borrowed money. It can be higher, however, depending on the range of other opportunities available. Typically, the opportunity cost rises with investment risk.

order point The amount of inventory below which the quantity available shouldn't go or the item will be out of stock before the next order arrives.

organization structure A plan that identifies the activities to be performed by specific employees and determines the lines of authority and responsibility in the firm.

organizational culture A firm's set of values, traditions, and customs that guide employee behaviour.

outlet centres Typically feature stores owned by retail chains or manufacturers that sell excess and out-of-season merchandise at reduced prices.

outlet stores Off-price retailers owned by a manufacturer or a department or specialty store chain.

output measure Measure that assesses the results of retailers' investment decisions.

outsource Obtain a service from outside the company that had previously been done by the firm itself.

overstored trade area An area having so many stores selling a specific good or service that some stores will fail.

owners' equity The amount of assets belonging to the owners of the retail firm after all obligations (liabilities) have been met; also known as *net worth* and *shareholders' equity*.

parallel branding A branding strategy that represents a private label that closely imitates the trade dress (packaging) and product attributes of leading manufacturer brands but with a clearly articulated "invitation to compare" in its merchandising approach and on its product label.

party plan system Salespeople encourage people to act as hosts and invite friends or co-workers to a "party" at which the merchandise is demonstrated. The host or hostess receives a gift or commission for arranging the meeting.

percentage-of-sales method A method for setting a promotion budget based on a fixed percentage of forecast sales.

perpetual inventory An accounting procedure whose objectives are to maintain a perpetual or book inventory in retail dollar amounts and to maintain records that make it possible to determine the cost value of the inventory at any time without taking a physical inventory; also known as *book inventory system* or *retail inventory method (RIM)*.

personal selling A communication process in which salespeople help customers satisfy their needs through face-to-face exchanges of information.

pick ticket A document that tells the order filler how much of each item to get from the storage area.

planogram A diagram created from photographs, computer output, or artists' renderings that illustrates exactly where every SKU should be placed.

point-of-purchase (POP) An area where the customer waits at checkout.

point-of-sale (POS) areas Areas where the customer waits at checkout. This area can be the most valuable piece of real estate in the store, because the customer is almost held captive in that spot; also called *point-of-purchase (POP) areas*.

point-of-sale signage Signs placed near the merchandise they refer to so that customers know the price and other detailed information.

polygons Trade areas whose boundaries conform to streets and other map features rather than being concentric circles.

popping the merchandise Focusing spotlights on special feature areas and items.

pop-up stores Stores in temporary locations that focus on new products or a limited group of products.

positioning The design and implementation of a retail mix to create in the customer's mind an image of the retailer relative to its competitors; also called *brand building*.

post-purchase evaluation The evaluation of merchandise or services after the customer has purchased and consumed them.

power centre Shopping centre that is dominated by several large anchors, including discount stores, off-price stores, warehouse clubs, or category specialists.

power perimeter The area around the outside walls of a supermarket that have fresh-merchandise categories.

premium A type of sales promotion whereby an item is offered free of charge or at a bargain price to reward some type of behaviour, such as buying, sampling, or testing.

premium branding A branding strategy that offers the consumer a private label at a comparable manufacturer-brand quality, usually with a modest price savings.

price bundling The practice of offering two or more different products or services for sale at one price.

price lining A pricing policy in which a retailer offers a limited number of predetermined price points within a classification.

primary zone The geographic area from which the store or shopping centre derives 60 to 65 percent of its customers; also called *primary trade area*.

private exchanges Exchanges that are operated for the exclusive use of a single firm.

private-label brands Products developed and marketed by a retailer and available for sale only by that retailer; also called *store brands*.

private-label credit card A credit card that has the store's name on it and is issued by the retailer.

procedural fairness The perceived fairness of the process used to resolve customer complaints.

procedural justice An employee's perception of fairness (how he or she is treated) that is based on the process used to determine the outcome.

product availability A measurement of the percentage of demand for a particular SKU that is satisfied.

productivity measure The ratio of an output to an input determining how effectively a firm uses a resource.

promotional aisle or area Aisle or area of a store designed to get the customer's attention. An example might be a special "trim-the-tree" department that seems magically to appear right after Halloween every year for the Christmas holidays.

promotional allowances Payments made by vendors to retailers to compensate the latter for money spent in advertising a particular item.

promotional signage This signage describes special offers and may be displayed in windows to entice the customer into the store.

promotion from within A staffing policy that involves hiring new employees only for positions at the lowest level in the job hierarchy and then promoting employees for openings at higher levels in the hierarchy.

proprietary store credit card system A system in which credit cards have the store's name on them and the accounts receivable are administered by the retailer; also known as an *in-house credit system*.

psychographics Refers to how consumers live, how they spend their time and money, what activities they pursue, and their attitudes and opinions about the world they live in.

public relations (PR) A retail communication tool for managing communications and relationships to achieve various objectives, such as building and maintaining a positive image of the retailer, handling or heading off unfavourable stories or events, and maintaining positive relationships with the media.

public warehouses Warehouses that are owned and operated by a third party.

pull distribution strategy Strategy in which orders for merchandise are generated at the store level on the basis of demand data captured by point-of-sale terminals.

push distribution strategy Strategy in which merchandise is allocated to stores based on historical demand, the inventory position at the distribution centre, as well as the stores' needs.

pyramid scheme When a firm and its program are designed to sell merchandise and services to other distributors rather than to end users.

quick response (QR) delivery system A system designed to reduce the lead time for receiving merchandise, thereby lowering inventory investment, improving customer service levels, and reducing distribution expenses; also known as a *just-in-time inventory management system*.

quota Target level used to motivate and evaluate performance.

quota–bonus plan Compensation plan that has a performance goal or objective established to evaluate employee performance, such as sales per hour for salespeople and maintained margin and turnover for buyers.

racetrack layout A type of store layout that provides a major aisle to facilitate customer traffic that has access to the store's multiple entrances. Also known as a *loop*.

radio frequency identification (RFID) A technology that allows an object or person to be identified at a distance by means of radio waves.

rain check When sale merchandise is out of stock, a written promise to customers to sell them that merchandise at the sale price when it arrives.

reach The actual number of customers in the target market exposed to an advertising medium.

rebates Money returned to the buyer in the form of cash based on a portion of the purchasing price.

receiving The process of filling out paperwork to record the receipt of merchandise that arrives at a store or distribution centre.

reductions Markdowns; discounts to employees and customers; and inventory shrinkage due to shoplifting, breakage, or loss.

reference group One or more people whom a person uses as a basis of comparison for his or her beliefs, feelings, and behaviours.

region In retail location analysis, refers to a part of the country, a particular city, or a census metropolitan area (CMA).

regional centre Shopping mall that provides general merchandise (a large percentage of which is apparel) and services in full depth and variety.

regression analysis A statistical approach based on the assumption that factors that affect the sales of existing stores in a chain will have the same impact on stores located at new sites.

Reilly's law of retail gravitation A model used in trade area analysis to define the relative ability of two cities to attract customers from the area between them.

related diversification opportunity A diversification opportunity strategy in which the retailer's present offering and market share something in common with the market and format being considered.

retail chain A firm that consists of multiple retail units under common ownership and usually has some centralization of decision making in defining and implementing its strategy.

retailer A business that sells products and services to consumers for their personal or family use.

retailer loyalty Indicates that customers like and habitually visit the same retailer to purchase a type of merchandise.

retail exchanges Electronic marketplaces operated by organizations that facilitate the buying and selling of merchandise using the Internet.

retail format The retailers' type of retail mix (product, price [value], promotion [communication], place, people, and processes).

retail format development opportunity An investment opportunity strategy in which a retailer offers a new retail format—a format involving a different retail mix—to the same target market.

retailing A set of business activities that adds value to the products and services sold to consumers for their personal or family use.

retailing concept A management orientation that holds that the key task of a retailer is to determine the needs and wants of its target markets and to direct the firm toward satisfying those needs and wants more effectively and efficiently than competitors do.

retail market A group of consumers with similar needs (a market segment) and a group of retailers using a similar retail format to satisfy those consumer needs.

retail market segment A group of customers whose needs will be satisfied by the same retail offering because they have similar needs and go through similar buying processes.

retail strategy A statement that indicates (1) the target market toward which a retailer plans to commit its resources, (2) the nature of the retail offering that the retailer plans to use to satisfy the needs of the target market, and (3) the bases upon which the retailer will attempt to build a sustainable competitive advantage over competitors.

retained earnings The portion of owners' equity that has accumulated over time through profits but has not been paid out in dividends to owners.

return on assets (ROA) Net profit after taxes divided by total assets.

reverse auction   Auction conducted by retailer buyers. Known as a reverse auction because there is one buyer and many potential sellers. In reverse auctions, retail buyers provide a specification for what they want to a group of potential vendors. The competing vendors then bid down the price at which they are willing to sell until the buyer accepts a bid.

reverse logistics   The process of capturing value from and/or properly disposing of merchandise returned by customers and/or stores.

RFM (recency, frequency, monetary) analysis   Often used by catalogue retailers and direct marketers, a scheme for segmenting customers based on how recently they have made a purchase, how frequently they make purchases, and how much they have bought.

road condition   Includes the age, number of lanes, number of stoplights, congestion, and general state of repair of roads in a trade area.

road pattern   A consideration used in measuring the accessibility of a retail location via major arteries, highways, or roads.

rounder   A round fixture that sits on a pedestal. Smaller than the straight rack, it is designed to hold a maximum amount of merchandise. Also known as a *bulk fixture* or *capacity fixture*.

rule-of-thumb method   A type of approach for setting a promotion budget that uses past sales and communication activity to determine the present communications budget.

sales per employee hour   A common measure of productivity that retailers use by dividing net sales by the total number of hours worked by the employee or employees during the specified time frame.

sales per full-time employee   A method used by retailers to calculate the many ways in which salary costs can accumulate.

sales per linear foot   A measure of space productivity used when most merchandise is displayed on multiple shelves of long gondolas, such as in grocery stores.

sales per square foot   A measure of space productivity used by most retailers since rent and land purchases are assessed on a per-square-foot basis.

sales promotions   Paid, impersonal communication activities that offer extra value and incentives to customers to visit a store or purchase merchandise during a specific period of time.

samples   A small amount or size of a product given to potential customers as an inducement to purchase.

satisfaction   A post-consumption evaluation of the degree to which a store or product meets or exceeds customer expectations.

saturated trade area   A trade area that offers customers a good selection of goods and services, while allowing competing retailers to make good profits.

scale economies   Cost advantages due to the size of a retailer.

scrambled merchandising   The offering of merchandise not typically associated with the store type, such as clothing in a drugstore.

search engines   Computer programs that simply search for and provide a listing of all Internet sites selling a product category or brand with the price of the merchandise offered; also called *shopping bots*.

seasonal merchandise category   Category of inventory whose sales fluctuate dramatically according to the time of the year.

secondary zone   The geographic area of secondary importance in terms of customer sales, generating about 20 percent of a store's sales; also called *secondary trade area*.

second-degree price discrimination   Charging different prices to different people on the basis of the nature of the offering.

security policy   The set of rules that applies to activities in the computer and communications resources that belong to an organization.

selling cost   The relationship between sales productivity and wages; can be calculated for an individual salesperson, a department, and the entire store.

selling, general, and administrative expenses (SG&A)   Operating expenses, plus the depreciation and amortization of assets.

sell-through analysis   A comparison of actual and planned sales to determine whether early markdowns are required or whether more merchandise is needed to satisfy demand.

service gap   The difference between customers' expectations and perceptions of customer service, assessed in order to improve customers' satisfaction with their service.

service level   A measure used in inventory management to define the level of support or level of product availability; the number of items sold divided by the number of items demanded. Service level should not be confused with customer service. Also called *level of support*.

services retailer   Organization that offers consumers services rather than merchandise. Examples include banks, hospitals, health spas, doctors, legal clinics, entertainment firms, and universities.

shareholders' equity   The amount of assets belonging to the owners of the retail firm after all obligations (liabilities) have been met.

share of wallet   The percentage of total purchases made by a customer in a store.

shopping centre   A group of retail and other commercial establishments that is planned, developed, owned, and managed as a single property.

short code   A five- or six-digit number or word used for messaging.

showrooming   Visiting a bricks-and-mortar store to research a product before purchasing it through electronic means after browsing online for the best price.

shrinkage   An inventory reduction that is caused by shoplifting by employees or customers, by merchandise being misplaced or damaged, or by poor bookkeeping.

situation audit   An analysis of the opportunities and threats in the retail environment and the strengths and weaknesses of the retail business relative to its competitors.

skeletal statement   An analysis of the five key categories found in all operating statements.

SKU (stock keeping unit)   The smallest unit available for keeping inventory control. In soft goods merchandise, an SKU usually means size, colour, and style.

slotting allowance   Fee paid by a vendor for space in a retail store; also called a *slotting fee*.

socialization   The steps taken to transform new employees into effective, committed members of the firm.

social media   Media content distributed through social interactions; major online facilitators of social media include YouTube, Facebook, Pinterest, and Twitter.

SoLoMo (social, local, and mobile)   The convergence of collaborative, location-based, and on-the-go technologies.

special event   Sales promotion program comprising a number of sales promotion techniques built around a seasonal, cultural, sporting, musical, or other event.

specialization   The organizational structure in which employees are typically responsible for only one or two tasks rather than performing all tasks. This enables employees to develop expertise and increase productivity.

specialty store   Store concentrating on a limited number of complementary merchandise categories and providing a high level of service in an area typically under 8000 square feet.

standardization approach An approach used by retailers to provide customer service by using a set of rules and procedures so that all customers consistently receive the same service.

standards gap The difference between the retailer's perceptions of customers' expectations and the customer service standards it sets. This factor is one of four factors identified by the gaps model for improving service quality.

staple merchandise category A category of inventory that has continuous demand by customers over an extended period of time; also called *basic merchandise category*.

stock keeping unit (SKU) The smallest unit available for keeping inventory control. In soft goods merchandise, an SKU usually means a size, colour, and style.

stockout A situation occurring when an SKU that a customer wants is not available.

stock-to-sales ratio Specifies the amount of inventory that should be on hand at the beginning of the month to support the sales forecast and maintain the inventory turnover objective.

store advocates Customers who like a store so much that they actively share their positive experiences with friends and family.

straight commission A form of salesperson's compensation in which the amount paid is based on a percentage of sales made minus merchandise returned.

straight rack A type of fixture that consists of a long pipe suspended with supports going to the floor or attached to a wall.

strategic alliance Collaborative relationship between independent firms. For example, a foreign retailer might enter an international market through direct investment but develop an alliance with a local firm to perform logistical and warehousing activities.

strategic profit model (SPM) A tool used for planning a retailer's financial strategy based on both margin management (net profit margin), asset management (asset turnover), and financial leverage management (financial leverage ratio). Using the SPM, a retailer's objective is to achieve a target return on owners' equity.

strategic relationship Long-term relationship in which partners make significant investments to improve both parties' profitability; also called a *partnering relationship*.

strategic retail planning process The steps a retailer goes through to develop a strategic retail plan. It describes how retailers select target market segments, determine the appropriate retail format, and build sustainable competitive advantages.

strengths and weaknesses analysis A critical aspect of the situation audit in which a retailer determines its unique capabilities—its strengths and weaknesses relative to its competition.

strip centre A shopping centre that usually has parking directly in front of the stores and does not have enclosed walkways linking the stores.

subculture A distinctive group of people within a culture. Members of a subculture share some customs and norms with the overall society but also have some unique perspectives.

supercentres Large stores (160 000 to 200 000 square feet) combining a discount store with a supermarket.

superregional centre Shopping centre that is similar to a regional centre; but because of its larger size, it has more anchors and a deeper selection of merchandise, and it draws from a larger population base.

superstore A large supermarket between 35 000 and 45 000 square feet in size.

supply chain management The set of approaches and techniques firms employ to efficiently and effectively integrate their suppliers, manufacturers, warehouses, stores, and transportation intermediaries to efficiently have the right quantities at the right locations, and at the right time.

sustainable competitive advantage A distinct competency of a retailer relative to its competitors that can be maintained over a considerable time period.

SWOT analysis An analysis of strengths, weaknesses, opportunities, and threats, designed to assess both the micro- and macro-environments and their relation to the retailer.

symbiotic store A store that does not create its own traffic and whose trade area is determined by the dominant retailer in the shopping centre or retail area; also called a *parasite store*.

target market The market segment(s) toward which the retailer plans to focus its resources and retail mix.

tariff A tax placed by a government upon imports; also called *duty*.

television home shopping A retail format in which customers watch a TV program demonstrating merchandise and then place orders for the merchandise by phone; also called *teleshopping*.

tertiary zone The outermost ring of a trade area that includes customers who occasionally shop at the store or shopping centre; also called *tertiary trade area*.

ticketing and marking Procedures for making price labels and placing them on the merchandise.

time-series analysis A comparison of a variable to itself over time.

tonnage merchandising A display technique in which large quantities of merchandise are displayed together.

top-down planning One side of the process of developing an overall retail strategy where goals are set at the top of the organization and filter down through the operating levels.

top-of-mind awareness The highest level of brand awareness; arises when consumers mention a brand name first when they are asked about a type of retailer, a merchandise category, or a type of service.

trade area A geographic sector that contains potential customers for a particular retailer or shopping centre.

trademark Any mark, work, picture, or design associated with a particular line of merchandise or product.

trade shows Temporary concentrations of vendors that provide retailers opportunities to place orders and view what is available in the marketplace; also known as a *merchandise show* or *market week*.

traditional strip centre A shopping centre that is designed to provide convenience shopping for the day-to-day needs of consumers in their immediate neighbourhood.

traffic flow The balance between a substantial number of cars and not so many that congestion impedes access to the store.

trust A belief that a partner is honest (reliable, stands by its word, sincere, fulfills obligations) and is benevolent (concerned about the other party's welfare).

tying contract An agreement between a vendor and a retailer requiring the retailer to take a product it does not necessarily desire (the tied product) to ensure that it can buy a product it does desire (the tying product).

understored trade area An area that has too few stores selling a specific good or service to satisfy the needs of the population.

Universal Product Code (UPC) The black-and-white bar code found on most merchandise that is used to collect sales information at the point of sale using computer terminals that read the code. This information is transmitted computer to computer to buyers, distribution centres, and then to vendors, who in turn quickly ship replenishment merchandise.

unrelated diversification Diversification in which there is no commonality between the present business and the new business.

utilitarian benefit A motivation for shopping in which consumers accomplish a specific task, such as buying a suit for a job interview.

utilitarian needs Needs motivating consumers to go shopping to accomplish a specific task.

value Relationship of what a customer gets (goods/services) to what he or she has to pay for it.

value retailers General merchandise discount stores that are found in low-income urban or rural areas and are much smaller than traditional discount stores, less than 9000 square feet.

variable cost A cost that varies with the level of sales and that can be applied directly to the decision in question.

variable pricing Charging different prices in different stores, markets, or zones.

variety The number of different merchandise categories within a store or department; also called *breadth*.

vending machine retailing A nonstore format in which merchandise or services are stored in a machine and dispensed to customers when they deposit cash or use a credit card.

vendor-managed inventory (VMI) An approach for improving supply chain efficiency in which the vendor is responsible for maintaining the retailer's inventory levels in each of its stores.

vertical integration An example of diversification by retailers involving investments by retailers in wholesaling or manufacturing merchandise.

vertical merchandising A method whereby merchandise is organized to follow the eye's natural up-and-down movement.

visibility The customers' ability to see the store and enter the parking lot safely.

visual merchandising The presentation of a store and its merchandise in ways that will attract the attention of potential customers.

warehouse club A retailer that offers a limited assortment of food and general merchandise with little service and low prices to ultimate consumers and small businesses.

weeks of inventory The number of months of supply times four weeks.

wholesale-sponsored voluntary cooperative group An organization operated by a wholesaler offering a merchandising program to small, independent retailers on a voluntary basis.

yield management The practice of adjusting prices up or down in response to demand to control sales generated.

zone pricing Charging different prices for the same merchandise in different geographic locations to be competitive in local markets.

endnotes

Chapter 1

1. John Stanton, "You Can Do It," *CIBC Run: Training Guide,* 2003.
2. For a more detailed discussion of distribution channels, see Louis W. Stern, Adel I. El-Ansary, Erin Anderson, and Anne T. Coughlan, *Marketing Channels* (Englewood Cliffs, NJ: Prentice Hall, 2002).
3. Mike Farrell, "Back to School: Grading Your Marketing Initiatives," *Canadian Retailer,* store 2012, Volume 22, Issue 4, pp. 10–11.
4. www.bsr.org (accessed May 21, 2007).
5. "Corporate Social Responsibility Practices Present Opportunity for Canadian Retailers," *Canadian Retailer,* September/October 2009, www.retailcouncil.org/cdnretailer, p. 4.
6. Luciano Barin Cruz and Eugenio Avila Pedrozo, "Corporate Social Responsibility and Green Management: Relation between Headquarters and Subsidiary in Multinational Corporations," *Management Decision 47,* no. 7 (2009), pp. 1174–1199.
7. "Retail by the Numbers," *Canadian Retailer,* holiday 2012, Volume 22, Issue 6, p. 54.
8. John Torella, *Retail Trends in Canada, 2008,* http://carf.ca/seminars/art_instore_torella.shtml (accessed January 27, 2010).
9. Steve Ladurantaye, "Canada's retail market now matches U.S. per capita," *The Globe and Mail,* May 11, 2011.
10. Sherry Cooper, "Canadian Retailing: A Changing Picture," *BMO Capital Markets Economics,* 2011.
11. *Consumer Trends Update: Canada's Changing Retail Market,* Office of Consumer Affairs, Industry Canada, http://www.ic.gc.ca/eic/site/oca-bc.nsf/eng/ca02852.html, p. 4.
12. Ibid., p. 7.
13. Christopher Daniel and Tony Hernandez, *Canada's Leading Retailers—Latest Trends and Strategies,* 11th Edition (Toronto: Centre for the Study of Commercial Activity, 2011).
14. Ibid., Table 4, p. 13.
15. Ibid., Table 4, p. 13.
16. *Consumer Trends Update: Canada's Changing Retail Market,* p. 12.
17. J. Harrison, "Faces of Canadian Retail Changing: BMO," *Business in Vancouver,* May 24, 2011.
18. Ibid.
19. Marina Strauss, "Aldo's Global Footprint," *The Globe and Mail,* September 3, 2010; Marina Strauss, "Loblaw's Joe Fresh Hooks Up with JC Penney," *The Globe and Mail,* July 25, 2012; *Consumer Trends Update: Canada's Changing Retail Market,* p. 13.
20. *Global Powers of Retailing 2013 – Retail Beyond,* Deloitte, www.deloitte.com/consumer/business, p. G11.
21. Ibid., p. G20.
22. "Ingvar Kamprad," en.wikipedia.org/wiki/Ingvar_Kamprad (accessed May 25, 2007).
23. *Global Powers of Retailing 2013 – Retail Beyond,* Deloitte, pp. G9–G17.
24. Carolyn Green, "London Drugs: A Prescription for Success," *Canadian Retailer,* July/August, 2003; Alexandra Lopez-Pacheco, "For the greater good," *Canadian Retailer,* Store 2012, Volume 22, Issue 4, pp. 54–55.
25. Sarah Butler, "Would You Like a Bag with That, Madam?" *London Times,* October 7, 2006.

Chapter 2

1. Pierre Mercier, Rune Jacobsen, and Andy Veitch, "Ten Trends That Are Reshaping the Retail Industry," BCG Perspectives, August 9, 2012, https://www.bcgperspectives.com/content/articles/retail_digital_economy_retail_2020_competing_in_changing_industry/ (accessed October 13, 2012).
2. Kenric S. Tyghe and Sara Kohbodi, "Loblaw Companies Ltd.," Canada Research, Raymond James, January 16, 2012, http://www.raymondjames.ca/en_ca//equity_capital_markets/equity_research/sample_research/docs/Loblaw%20Companies%20Ltd.%20011612.pdf (accessed February 2, 2013).
3. Larry Greenberg, "Hudson's Bay Faces Challenges from Southern Rival," *The Wall Street Journal,* May 24, 1996, p. B4.
4. "Corporate Overview," Target Canada website, http://pressroom.target.ca/pr/tgt-en/corporate-overview.aspx (accessed September 8, 2012).
5. Carlta Vitzthum, "Just-in-Time Fashion-Spanish Retailer Zara Makes Low-Cost Lines in Weeks by Running Its Own Show," *The Wall Street Journal,* May 18, 2001, p. B1; and Benjamin Jones, "Madrid: Zara Pioneers Fashion on Demand," *Europe,* September 2001, pp. 43–44.
6. Marianne Wilson, "Disposable Chic at H&M," *Chain Store Age,* May 2000, pp. 64–66.
7. *Demystifying the online shopper: 10 myths of multi-channel retailing,* PwC, 2013, http://www.pwc.com/ca/en/retail-consumer/multi-channel-customer-survey-canadian-perspective.jhtml (accessed July 2013).
8. Hollie Shaw, "Landlord Rivalries at Root of Store Wars," *National Post,* July 16, 2003.
9. Denise Deveau, "Big Box Shrinkage in a Post-Internet World," *Canadian Retailer,* spring 2012, Vol. 22, Issue 2, pp. 46–47.
10. David P. Schulz, "Triversity Top 100 Retailers: The Nation's Biggest Retail Companies," www.stores.org, 2001.
11. "Calgary to Welcome Canada's First Nordstrom Store," CTV News, September 13, 2012, http://www.ctvnews.ca/business/calgary-to-welcome-canada-s-first-nordstrom-store-1.954303#ixzz26f0iUg6H (accessed July 2013).
12. Daniel Christopher, Joseph Aversa, and Tony Hernandez, *Canada's Leading Retailers: Latest Trends and Strategies,* 7th ed., Centre for the Study of Commercial Activity, Ryerson University, 2009-03, p. 13.
13. Tracie Rozhon, "Main Street's Latest Threat," *New York Times,* June 14, 1999, p. A25; "Annual Report of Categories," *Drug Store News,* May 17, 1999; and "Annual Report on Drug Chains," *Drug Store News,* April 26, 1999.
14. "Retail by the Numbers," *Canadian Retailer,* summer 2012, Vol. 22, Issue 3, p. 54.
15. "Shoppers Drug Mart shareholders OK Loblaw takeover," Canadian Press, September 12, 2013, http://www.cbc.ca/news/business/shoppers-drug-mart-shareholders-ok-loblaw-take-over-1.1699685 (accessed December 13, 2013).
16. Hollie Shaw, "Spending Spree Will Continue," *National Post,* January 6, 2003.
17. Leanne Delap, "Hard-Core Winners Addicts Tell All," *Globe and Mail,* February 28, 2004.
18. Marina Strauss, "Dollarama turns up heat on Walmart," *Globe and Mail,* September 15, 2011.
19. Debby Garbato Stankevich, "More Value to a Dollar: With Traditional Discounters Concentrating Market," *Retail Merchandiser,* October 2001, pp. 21–23.
20. Hollie Shaw, "Supermarket Offers Health Club," Canadian Press Newswire, November 8, 1999.
21. "Food Industry Glossary: Conventional Supermarket," Food Marketing Institute, http://www.fmi.org/research-resources/fmi-research-resources/food-industry-glossary/'c'-supermarket-terms (accessed September 27, 2013).
22. http://www.fmi.org/docs/facts_figs/grocerydept.pdf.
23. "Low-end grocery stores carve out niche," *The (Harrisburg, PA) Patriot-News,* October 13, 2004, http://www.tmcnet.com/usubmit/2007/10/13/3012485.htm (accessed September 27, 2013).
24. "About M&M," M&M Meat Shops website, http://www.mmmeatshops.com/en/aboutmm/index.asp?curURL=%2Fen%2Findex%2Easp (accessed September 27, 2013).

25. *Language of the Food Industry* (Washington, DC: Food Marketing Institute, 1998).

26. "Voting with your Trolly," *The Economist,* December 7, 2006.

27. Pete Russell, "No market share growth for private label in Canada," *Canadian Grocer,* March 21, 2011, http://www.canadiangrocer. com/uncategorized/no-market-share-growth-for-private-label-in-canada-5277 (accessed September 27, 2013).

28. Tyghe and Kohbodi, "Loblaw Companies Ltd.," p. 9.

29. Ibid., p. 10.

30. Ibid., p. 10.

31. "Markets in Motion," in "66th Annual Report of the Grocery Industry," *Progressive Grocer,* April 1999, p. 31.

32. Shaw, "Supermarket Offers Health Club."

33. *Language of the Food Industry.*

34. Personal communication, Bryan Gildenberg, M. Ventures, February 2002.

35. "About Us: History," Loblaw Companies Limited website, http://www.loblaw.ca/English/About-Us/history/default.aspx (accessed September 27, 2013).

36. Tyghe and Kohbodi, "Loblaw Companies Ltd.," p. 19.

37. Sandra J. Skrovan, "Industry Brief: Warehouse Clubs," PricewaterhouseCoopers, June 2001, p. 7.

38. *The Canadian Food Retail Sector: Opportunities for Swiss Companies,* "Top Canadian Food Retailers 2010," CIBC World Markets, Estimated 2010 Food Sales, p. 17, http://www.s-ge. com/en/filefield-private/files/2344/field_blog_public_files/1272 (accessed September 27, 2013).

39. George Strachan, Keith Wills, and Yukihiro Moroe, "Retail Surprises: A Look Back from 2005," Goldman Sachs, December 2000, pp. 9–10.

40. "Alimentation Couche-Tard Inc., Google Finance, http://www. google.com/finance?q=TSE%3AATD.B&fstype=ii&ei=EPdVUOi DK83LqQHhnwE, (accessed September 2, 2012).

41. "Our Company," Couche-Tard website, http://www.couche-tard. com/corporate/the-network.html (accessed September 2, 2012).

42. www.eatzis.com.

43. Peter O'Dowd, "The British Are Coming to Change Our Grocery Stores," ABC News Business Unit, April 19, 2007; Jennifer Halterman, "Tesco's U.S. Invasion Update" (Columbus, OH: Retail Forward, September 2006).

44. "A Supermarket Business Survey of Consumers Shows That the More Prepared Foods They Buy, the Bigger the Ring at the Checkout," *Supermarket Business,* July 15, 2001, pp. 37, 40+.

45. Personal communication, Jo Natale, Wegmans, February 2002.

46. *The Canadian Food Retail Sector: Opportunities for Swiss Companies,* p. 12.

47. Sean Silcoff, "What keeps online retail in Canada from clicking?" *The Globe and Mail,* May 12, 2012, http://www.theglobeandmail. com/report-on-business/what-keeps-online-retail-in-Canada-from-clicking/article4178807/?page=all (accessed February 9, 2012); and Hollie Shaw, "Canadian shoppers, bricks-and-mortar retailers finally embracing the Web," *Financial Post,* December 8, 2012, http://www.business.financialpost.com/2012/12/08/canada-embraces-online-retail-shopping/ (accessed February 9, 2012).

48. Thad Rueter, "E-retail spending to increase 62% by 2016," *Internet Retailer,* February 27, 2012, http://www.internetretailer. com/2012/02/27/e-tail-spending-increase-45-2016 (accessed September 27, 2013).

49. Silcoff, "What keeps online retail in Canada from clicking?"

50. Ibid.

51. Lindsay Shugerman, "Catalog merchandise marketing," Catalogs. com Info Library, http://www.catalogs.com/info/b2b/catalog-merchandise.html, data from U.S. Census Bureau (accessed October 19, 2009).

52. Eve Lazarus, "Loyalty: Beyond Points and Discounts," *Canadian Retailer,* spring 2012, Vol. 22, Issue 3, pp. 48–49.

53. Jens Hansegard, "IKEA's New Catalogs: Less Pine, More Pixels," *Wall Street Journal,* August 23, 2012, http://online.wsj. com/article/SB10000872396390444508504577595414031195148. html (accessed September 2, 2012).

54. Laurens Bianchi, "IKEA Adds Interactivity to Its Cataogues," ViralBlog, July 23, 2012, http://www.viralblog.com/mobile-and-apps/ikea-adds-interactivity-to-its-catalogues/ (accessed September 27, 2013).

55. Retail Council of Canada, *Retail Technology in Canada* report.

56. Jeffery Ball, "In Digital Era, Marketers Still Prefer a Paper Trail," *Wall Street Journal,* October 16, 2009.

57. Ibid.

58. Dirk Perrefort and Susan Silvers, "Inside the Mall, a Class of Cultures," *McClatchy-Tribune Business News,* January 7, 2010.

59. http://www.dsa.ca/content/industry/news.php.

60. Ibid.

61. http://dsa.org/pubs/numbers/.

62. www.dsa.org/pubs/numbers/calendar05factsheet.pdf (accessed June 7, 2007).

63. Ibid.

64. "T-commerce! On Sale Now for a Limited Time!" *Cable-world,* December 4–17, 2006; "Will Viewers Buy into Shopping Via TV Ads?" *NMA,* October 13, 2005.

65. "Smartphones," *State of the Media: Social Media Report 2012,* Nielsen. www.nielsen.com/US/en/reports/2012/state-of-the-media-social-media-report-2012.html.

66. "2001 State of the Vending Industry Report," *Automatic Merchandiser,* www.amonline.com/current/industryreports.shtml.

67. Ibid.

68. "Looking ahead: Innovation a must for Canadian vending operators," *Canadian Vending,* Spring 2012, http://www.canadianvending. com/content/view/2970/136/.

69. Dana Flavelle, "New Fit for Vending Machines," *Toronto Star,* January 15, 2010, (accessed July 26, 2013).

70. Mehgan Belanger, "Convenience to the Max," *Convenience Store News,* 42, no. 14, November 13, 2006, pp. 57–58.

71. "Japanese Retailing—Marketplace Is Alive and Kicking," *Retail Week,* April 27, 2001, p. 16.

72. Valarie Zeithaml, A. Parasuraman, and Leonard Berry, "Problems and Strategies in Services Marketing," *Journal of Marketing,* 49 (Spring 1985), pp. 33–46; and Stephen W. Brown and Mary Jo Bitner, "Services Marketing," *AMA Management Handbook,* 3rd ed. (New York: AMACOM Books, 1994).

73. This section is based on material in Lyda Hyde, "Multi-Channel Integration: The New Retail Battleground," PricewaterhouseCoopers, 2001; and Joseph Alba, John Lynch, Barton Weitz, Chris Janiszewski, Richard Lutz, Alan Sawyer, and Stacy Woods, "Interactive Home Shopping: Consumer, Retailer, and Manufacturers Incentives to Participate in Electronic Markets," *Journal of Marketing* 61 (July 1997), pp. 38–53.

74. David Moin, "Getting Personal," *Women's Wear Daily Internet Supplement,* May 2000, pp. 10–17.

75. Deloitte, "2011 Spring Consumer Pulse Survey," March 2011.

76. "40+ years in the making; the new "Shop MEC" iPhone app is now available," MEC website, news release, December 17, 2012, http://mediaroom.mec.ca/2012/12/40-years-in-the-making-the-new-shop-mec-iphone-app-is-now-available.

77. Rachel Ledford, "The Connected Customer," *E-Retailing Intelligence Update* (Columbus, OH: Retail Forward, November 2001), p. 6.

78. Reid Claxton, "Customer Safety: Direct Marketing's Undermarketed Advantage," *Journal of Direct Marketing* 9 (Winter 1995), pp. 67–78.

79. *Deloitte's Store 3.0 Survey: The Next Evolution,* Deloitte, September 2011, p. 7.

80. *Deloitte's 2012 Retail Study: The Rise of the Connected Consumer,* 2012 Edition, Deloitte, p. 17.

81. *Deloitte Digital: The Dawn of Mobile Influence, 2012,* Deloitte, p. 3.

82. Ibid., p. 4.

83. Google/IPSOS OTX MediaCT, "The Mobile Movement. Understanding Smartphone Users," April 2011.

84. *Deloitte Digital: The Dawn of Mobile Influence, 2012,* p. 5.

85. Ibid., p. 9.

86. Ibid.

87. Darren Hitchcock, "Five ways to embrace omni-channel retailing," Econsultancy.com, August 29, 2012 (accessed October 2, 2013).

88. Michael de Kare-Silver, "Multi-Channel vs. Omni-Channel," *Digital Prospects,* www.dekaresilver.com/downloads/multi-channel-vs-omni-channel.pdf (retrieved July 30, 2013).

89. Brian Kilcourse, "Gaming Google: The Growing Importance of Omni-channel," *Retail Systems Research,* March 1, 2011 (retrieved July 30, 2013).

90. Andrew Solmssen, "Omni-Channel Marketing: Your Next Challenge," *ClickZ,* August 17, 2012, http://www.cmo.com/content/cmo-com/home/articles/2012/8/17/omnichannel-marketing-your-next-challenge.fram.html (retrieved October 2, 2013).

91. Kenneth Clow, David Kurtz, John Ozment, and Beng Soo Ong, "The Antecedents of Consumer Expectations of Services: An Empirical Study across Four Industries," *Journal of Services Marketing* 11 (May–June 1997), pp. 230–248; and Ann Marie Thompson and Peter Kaminski, "Psychographic and Lifestyle Antecedents of Service Quality Expectations," *Journal of Services Marketing* 7 (1993), pp. 53–61.

92. Susan Stellin, "Online Customer Service Found Lacking," *New York Times,* January 3, 2002, p. C1.

93. Mary Jo Bitner, "Self-Service Technologies: What Do Customers Expect? In This High-Tech World, Customers Haven't Changed—They Still Want Good Service," *Marketing Management,* Spring 2001, pp. 10–15.

94. Timothy Keiningham and Terry Vavra, *The Customer Delight Principle* (Chicago: American Marketing Association, 2002).

95. A. Parsuraman and Valarie Zeithaml, "Understanding and Improving Service Quality: A Literature Review and Research Agenda," in B. Weitz and R. Wensley, eds., *Handbook of Marketing* (London: Sage, 2002).

96. Michael Harline and O. C. Ferrell, "The Management of Customer-Contact Service Employees: An Empirical Investigation," *Journal of Marketing* 60 (October 1996), pp. 52–70; and Lois Mohr and Mary Jo Bitner, "The Role of Employee Effort in Satisfaction with Service Transactions," *Journal of Business Research* 32 (March 1995), pp. 239–252).

97. Russ Martin, "Canadian Tire joins digital incubator to improve retail and online offering," *Marketing Magazine,* March 21, 2013, http://www.marketingmag.ca/news/marketer-news/canadian-tire-joins-digital-incubator-to-improve-retail-and-online-offering-74899.

98. "The Shopping Channel Celebrates 25 Years of Great Shopping with Big Birthday Celebration," news release, February 1, 2012, http://www.newswire.ca/en/story/914233/the-shopping-channel-celebrates-25-years-of-great-shopping-with-big-birthday-celebration.

99. Paul Lima, "Instant Gratification," *Profit,* April 2002, p. 56; Sandra Guy, "Stores Juggle Service with High-Tech Savvy," *Chicago Sun-Times,* July 1, 2002, p. B12; Julie Clark, "The Importance of Kiosks in Retail Has Grown," *Display and Design Ideas,* September 2001, p. 18; and Ken Clark, "Confused about Kiosks," *Chain Store Age,* November 1, 2000, p. 96.

100. http://retailindustry.about.com, April 4, 2001.

101. Bob Tedeschi, "Bricks-and-Mortar Merchants Struggling to Assess Web Sidelines," *New York Times,* September 3, 2001, p. C3.

102. "Organizing for Cross-Channel Retailing," white paper, J.C. Williams Group, Toronto, 2008; "Customer Centricity Drives Retail's Multichannel Imperative," white paper, IBM Global Business Services, Armonk, NY, 2008.

103. "The Next Evolution: Store 3.0: An executive perspective on retailer readiness for tomorrow's store," Deloitte, 2011, p. 2.

104. Google, "Our Mobile Planet: Canada," May 2012.

105. "Will Smarter Phones Make for Smarter Shoppers?" Deloitte, June 2011.

106. Sebastian Van Baal and Christian Dach, "Free Riding and Customer Retention across Retailers' Channels," *Journal of Interactive Marketing* 19 (Spring 2005), pp. 75–85.

107. Dun and Bradstreet Corporate Starts (New York: Dun and Bradstreet, 1998).

108. Jim Simmons and Shizue Kamikihara, "Commercial Activity in Canada," Centre for the Study of Commercial Activity, Ryerson University, Report 2009-02, p. 53.

109. Bill Quinn, *How Wal-Mart Is Destroying America (and the World): And What You Can Do About It* (Berkeley, CA: Ten Speed Press, 2000).

Chapter 3

1. For a detailed discussion of customer behaviour, see J. Paul Peter and Jerry C. Olson, *Consumer Behavior and Marketing Strategy,* 6th ed. (New York: McGraw-Hill, 2002); and Michael R. Solomon, *Consumer Behavior: Buying, Having, and Being,* 5th ed. (Upper Saddle River, NJ: Prentice Hall, 2002).

2. *Retailing 2015: New Frontiers,* PricewaterhouseCoopers and TNS Retail Forward, 2007, pp. 9–10, www.pwc.com/es_CL/cl/publicaciones/assets/retailing2015.pdf (accessed October 16, 2013).

3. Liz C. Wang, Julie Baker, Judy A. Wagner, and Kirk Wakefield, "Can a Retail Website be Social?" *Journal of Marketing* 71, no. 3 (2007), pp. 143–157; Gianluigi Guido, Mauro Capestro, and Alessandro M. Peluso, "Experimental Analysis of Consumer Stimulation and Motivational States in Shopping Experiences," *International Journal of Market Research* 49, no. 3 (2007), pp. 365–386.

4. Guido, Capestro, and Peluso, "Experimental Analysis"; Woonbong Na, Youngseok Son, and Roger Marshall, "Why Buy Second-Best? The Behavioral Dynamics of Market Leadership," *Journal of Product & Brand Management* 15, no. 1 (2007), pp. 16–22; Min-Young Lee, Kelly Green Atkins, Youn-Kyung Kim, and Soo-Hee Park, "Competitive Analyses Between Regional Malls and Big-Box Retailers: A Correspondence Analysis for Segmentation and Positioning," *Journal of Shopping Center Research,* April 2006, pp. 81–98.

5. Sylvie Morin, Laurette Dube, and Jean-Charles Chebat, "The Role of Pleasant Music in Servicescapes: A Test of the Dual Model of Environmental Perception," *Journal of Retailing* 83, no. 1 (2007), pp. 115–130; Nicole Bailey and Charles S. Areni, "When a Few Minutes Sound Like a Lifetime: Does Atmospheric Music Expand or Contract Perceived Time?" *Journal of Retailing* 82, no. 3 (2006), pp. 189–202; Michael A. Jones and Kristy E. Reynolds, "The Role of Retailer Interest on Shopping Behavior," *Journal of Retailing* 82, no. 2 (2006), pp. 115–126; Shu pei Tai, "Impact of Personal Orientation on Luxury-Brand Purchase Value," *International Journal of Marketing Research* 47, no. 4 (2005), pp. 429–454.

6. Jess W.J. Weltrereden, "Substitution or Complementarity? How the Internet Changed City Centre Shopping," *Journal of Retailing and Consumer Services* 14, no. 3 (2007), pp. 192–207; Shun Yin Lam, Albert Wai-Lap Chau, and Tsunhin John Wong, "Thumbnails as Online Product Displays: How Consumers Process Them," *Journal of Interactive Marketing* 21, no. 1 (2007), pp. 36–59.

7. Teresa Lindeman, "Retailers Try to Convince Customers to Stick Around," *Miami Herald,* April 26, 2007.

8. Melody Vargas, "Frequent Leisure Time Shoppers Spend More per Trip," *About Retailing,* July 11, 2006.

9. Brian T. Ratchford, Debabrata Talukdar, and Myung-Soo Lee, "The Impact of the Internet on Consumers' Use of Information Sources for Automobiles: A Re-Inquiry," *Journal of Consumer Research* 34, no. 1 (2007), pp. 111–119; Glenn J. Browne, Mitzi G. Pitts, and James C. Wetherbe, "Cognitive Shopping Rules for Terminating Information Search in Online Tasks," *MIS Quarterly* 31, no. 1 (2007), pp. 89–104; John Graham, "How to Profit from Customer Buying-Cycle Basics," *Printer and Publisher* 69, no. 2 (2006).

10. www.nearbynow.com (accessed June 27, 2007).

11. John P. Mello Jr., "Solo Hunters, Social Gatherers and the Online Marketplace," *E-Commerce Times,* May 25, 2007 (accessed December 24, 2007); Helene F. Jaillet, "Web Metrics: Measuring Patterns in Online Shopping," *Journal of Consumer Behavior* 2, no. 4 (2003), pp. 369–381.

12. Thomas Pack, "Kicking the Virtual Tires: Car Research on the Web," *Information Today,* January 2009, p. 44.

13. Bob Tedeschi, "Shopping Site Offers a Way to Raid a Celebrity's Closet," *The New York Times,* November 13, 2006 (accessed December 24, 2007); Steven Bellman, Eric J. Johnson, Gerald L. Lohse, and Naomi Mandel, "Designing Marketplaces of

the Artificial with Consumers in Mind: Four Approaches to Understanding Consumer Behavior in Electronic Environments," *Journal of Interactive Marketing* 20, no. 1 (2006), pp. 21–33.

14. Bob Tedeschi, "A Richer Trip to the Mall, Guided by Text Messages," *The New York Times*, March 5, 2007 (accessed December 24, 2007); Alice Z. Cuneo, "'Yard' Sale? Sprite Talks to Teens with Mobile Promotions," *Advertising Age* (Midwest region edition), June 11, 2007, p. 23.

15. Paul Dwyer, "Measuring the Value of Electronic Word of Mouth and its Impact in Consumer Communities," *Journal of Interactive Marketing* 21, no. 2 (2007), pp. 63–79; Pallavi Gogoi, "Retailers Take a Tip from MySpace," *BusinessWeek*, February 13, 2007.

16. Cecilie Rohwedder, "For a Delicate Sale, a Retailer Deploys 'Stocking Fellas,'" *The Wall Street Journal*, December 21, 2006, p. A1.

17. Manu De Ros, "The rise of omni-channel retail: definition and 5 tips," Selligent.com, http://www.selligent.com/en/blogs/tips-practices/the-rise-of-omni-channel-retail-definition-and-5-tips/ (accessed October 18, 2013).

18. Teresa F. Lindeman, "Macy's Sees Food as the Way to the Wallet," *Boston Globe*, May 14, 2007.

19. Chris T. Allen, Karen A. Machleit, Susan Schultz Kleine, and Arti Sahni Notani, "A Place for Emotion in Attitude Models," *Journal of Business Research* 58, no. 4 (2005), pp. 494–499; Armin Scholl, Laura Manthey, Roland Helm, and Michael Steiner, "Solving Multiattribute Design Problems with Analytic Hierarchy Process and Conjoint Analysis: An Empirical Comparison," *European Journal of Operational Research* 164, no. 3 (2005), pp. 760–777; Richard Lutz, "Changing Brands Attitudes through Modification of Cognitive Structure," *Journal of Consumer Research* 1, no. 1 (1975), pp. 125–136.

20. Dong-il Yoo and Hiroshi Ohta, "Optimal Pricing and Product Planning for New Multiattribute Products based on Conjoint Analysis," *International Journal of Production Economics* 38, no. 2, 3 (1995), pp. 245–253; Richard J. Lutz and James R. Bettman, "Multi-Attribute Models in Marketing: A Bicentennial Review," in *Consumer and Industrial Buying Behaviour*, eds. A.G. Woodside, J.N. Sheth, and P.D. Bennett (New York: Elsevier-North Holland, 1977), pp. 13–50; William L. Wilkie and Edgar D. Pessimier, "Issues in Marketing's Use of MultiAttribute Attitude Models," *Journal of Marketing Research*, November 1973, pp. 428–441.

21. Pat West, P. Brockett, and Linda Golden, "A Comparative Analysis of Neural Networks and Statistical Methods for Predicting Consumer Choice," *Marketing Science* 16, no. 4 (1997), pp. 370–391.

22. Peter R. Darke, Amitava Chattopadhyay, and Laurence Ashworth, "The Importance and Functional Significance of Affective Cues in Consumer Choice," *Journal of Consumer Research* 33, no. 3 (2006), pp. 322–328; David Bell, Tech-Hua Ho, and Christopher Tang, "Determining Where to Shop: Fixed and Variable Costs of Shopping," *Journal of Marketing Research* 35 (August 1998), pp. 352–370.

23. John G. Lynch and Gal Zauberman, "Construing Consumer Decision Making," *Journal of Consumer Psychology* 17, no. 2 (2007), pp. 107–112; Wayne D. Hoyer and Steven Brown, "Effects of Brand Awareness of Choice for a Common, Repeat-Purchase Product," *Journal of Consumer Research*, September 1990, pp. 141–149.

24. Pallavi Gogoi, "I Am Woman, Hear Me Shop," *BusinessWeek*, February 14, 2005, p. 23.

25. Peter N. Child, Suzanne Heywood, and Michael Kliger, "Do Retail Brands Travel?" *McKinsey Quarterly*, no. 1 (2002), pp. 25–34.

26. Andras Vag, "Simulating Changing Consumer Preferences: A Dynamic Conjoint Model," *Journal of Business Research* 60, no. 8 (2007), pp. 904–911; Richard J. Lutz, "Changing Brand Attitudes through Modification of Cognitive Structure," *Journal of Consumer Research* 1 (March 1975), pp. 49–59.

27. Jeanette Borzo, "From Lands' End to Fair Trade," *Business 2.0*, December 2006, p. 31.

28. Joan Voight, "Getting a Handle on Customer Reviews," *Adweek* 48, no. 26 (June 25–July 2, 2007), pp. 16–17; Nanda Kumar and Izak Benbasat, "The Influence of Recommendations and Consumer Reviews on Evaluations of Websites," *Information Systems*

Research 17, no. 4 (2006), pp. 425–441; Bob Tedeschi, "Help for the Merchant in Navigating a Sea of Shopper Opinions," *The New York Times*, September 4, 2006.

29. Ibid.

30. Claire Cain Miller, "Closing the Deal at the Virtual Checkout Counter," *The New York Times*, October 12, 2009.

31. NewAd Media.

32. "Beware of Dissatisfied Consumers: They Like to Blab," *Knowledge@Wharton*, March 8, 2006, based on "Retail Customer Dissatisfaction Study 2006," conducted by the Jay H. Baker Retailing Initiative at Wharton and The Verde Group (accessed December 24, 2007); "The Lowdown on Customer Loyalty Programs: Which Are the Most Effective and Why," *Knowledge@ Wharton*, September 6, 2006; Sandra Kennedy, "Keeping Customers Happy," *Chain Store Age*, February 2005, p. 24; Heiner Evanschitzky, Gopalkrishnan Iyer, Josef Hesse, and Dieter Ahlert, "E-Satisfaction: A Re-Examination," *Journal of Retailing* 80, no. 3 (2004), pp. 239–252; Emin Babakus, Carol Bienstock, and James Van Scotter, "Linking Perceived Quality and Customer Satisfaction to Store Traffic and Revenue Growth," *Decision Sciences* 35 (Fall 2004), pp. 713–738; Jarrad Dunning, Anthony Pecotich, and Aron O'Cass, "What Happens When Things Go Wrong? Retail Sales Explanations and Their Effects," *Psychology & Marketing*, July 2004, pp. 553–568; Richard Oliver, Roland Rust, and Sajeev Varki, "Customer Delight: Foundations, Findings, and Managerial Insights," *Journal of Retailing* 73 (Fall 1997), pp. 311–336; Chezy Ofir and Itamar Simonson, "The Effect of Stating Expectations on Customer Satisfaction and Shopping Experience," *Journal of Marketing Research* 44, no. 1 (2007), pp. 164–174.

33. Piyush Sharma, Bharadhwaj Sivakumaran, and Roger Marshall, "Impulse Buying and Variety Seeking: A Trait-Correlates Perspective," *Journal of Business Research* 63 (March 2010), pp. 276–283; David H. Silvera, Anne M. Lavack, and Fredric Kropp, "Impulse Buying: The Role of Affect, Social Influence, and Subjective Wellbeing," *Journal of Consumer Marketing* 25, no. 1 (2008), pp. 23–33; Ronan De Kervenoael, D. Selcen, O. Aykac, and Mark Palmer, "Online Social Capital: Understanding E-Impulse Buying in Practice," *Journal of Retailing and Consumer Services* 16 (July 2009), pp. 320–328.

34. "Let's Play Shopping," *Marketing Week*, November 22, 2001, pp. 45–47; Conway Lachman and John Lanasa, "Family Decision-Making Theory: An Overview and Assessment," *Psychology & Marketing* 10 (March–April 1993), pp. 81–94; and Robert Boutlier, "Pulling the Family Strings," *American Demographics*, August 1993, pp. 44–48.

35. Jean Darian, "Parent-Child Decision Making in Children's Clothing Stores," *International Journal of Retail & Distribution Management* 26 (October 1998), pp. 421–432; Kay Palanand and Robert Wilkes, "Adolescent-Parent Interaction in Family Decision Making," *Journal of Consumer Research* 24 (September 1997), pp. 159–171; Christy Fisher, "Kidding around Makes Sense," *Advertising Age*, June 27, 1994, pp. 34, 37; and Sharon Beatty and Salil Talpade, "Adolescent Influence in Family Decision Making: A Replication with Extension," *Journal of Consumer Research* 31 (September 1994), pp. 332–341.

36. "Bring the Family ... Bring the Kids," *Travel Agent Caribbean and Bahamas Supplement*, April 7, 1997.

37. Dianne Pogoda, "It's a Matter of Time: Stores Keep Traffic Moving, Cash Flowing," *Women's Wear Daily*, April 9, 1996, pp. 1, 8.

38. Susan Reda, "What Are Shoppers Saying About You?" *Stores*, February 2007.

39. Bruce Horovits, "Alpha Moms Leap to Top of Trendsetters," *USA Today*, March 27, 2007; Alexander Frenzel Baudisch, "Consumer Heterogeneity Evolving from Social Group Dynamics: Latent Class Analysis of German Footwear Consumption 1980-1991," *Journal of Business Research* 60, no. 8 (2007), pp. 836–847; Julie Juan Li and Chenting Su, "How Face Influences Consumption: A Comparative Study of American and Chinese Consumers," *International Journal of Market Research* 49, no. 2 (2007), pp. 237–256.

40. Susan Reda, "What Are Shoppers Saying about You?," *Stores*, February 2007.

41. Judy Waytiuk, "Discounter Diversity," *Marketing Magazine*, May 19, 2003; David Chow, "Reaching New Canadians," *Strategy Magazine*, September 22, 2003; Natalie Rivard, "Reaching Tween Girls in Quebec," *Strategy Magazine*, December 1, 2003.

42. Soyeon Shim and Mary Ann Eastwick, "The Hierarchical Influence of Personal Values on Mall Shopping Attitudes and Behaviors," *Journal of Retailing* 74 (Spring 1998), pp. 139–160.

43. Cyndee Miller, "Top Marketers Take a Bolder Approach in Targeting Gays," *Marketing News*, July 4, 1994, pp. 1–2.

44. Geng Cui, "The Different Faces of the Chinese Consumer," *China Business Review*, July 1997, pp. 34–42.

45. Robert Verdisco, "Gender-Specific Shopping," *Chain Store Age*, February 1999, pp. 26–28; Matthew Klein, "He Shops, She Shops," *American Demographics*, March 1998, pp. 34–40; and Suein Hwang, "From Choices to Checkout, the Genders Behave Very Differently in Supermarkets," *The Wall Street Journal*, March 22, 1994, pp. A1, A4.

46. Donna Myers, "Cater to Women Shoppers, Ask What They Want," *Casual Living*, August 2009.

47. *State of the Media: The Social Media Report*, Nielsen, December 4, 2012, p. 6, http://www.nielsen.com/us/en/insights/reports-downloads/2012/state-of-the-media-the-social-media-report-2012.pdf (accessed October 21, 2013).

48. "AOL Research Findings Determines Driving Forces behind Women's Online Content Consumption," BusinessWire, April 14, 2011, http://www.businesswire.com/news/home/20110414006018/en/AOL-Research-Findings-Determines-Driving-Forces-Women%E2%80%99s (accessed October 16, 2013); http://advertising.aol.com.

49. *Retailing 2015: New Frontiers*, PricewaterhouseCoopers and TNS Retail Forward, 2007, p. 3, www.pwc.com/es_CL/cl/publicaciones/assets/retailing2015.pdf (accessed October 16, 2013).

50. Ibid., p. 8.

51. Faith Popcorn, *Evolution* (New York: Hyperion Press, 2000); David Foot and Daniel Stoffman, *Boom Bust & Echo 2000* (Toronto: Macfarlane Walter & Ross, 1998); Oliver Bertin, "Harley-Davidson's Great Ride to the Top," *Globe and Mail*, July 4, 2003; Don Tapscott, Growing Up Digital (New York: McGraw-Hill, 1998); Brad Adgate, "Everything You'd Care to Know about Teens," *Horizon Media*, October 29, 2003.

52. Michael J. Weiss, *The Clustered World* (Boston: Little, Brown, 2000).

53. Sharon Jayson, "It's Cooler Than Ever to Be a Tween," *USA Today*, September 2, 2009.

54. http://www.tetrad.com/demographics/canada/environics/prizmc2.html.

55. GD Sourcing, "Research and Retrieval," *The Business Newsletter*, June 26, 2003, gdsourcing.com; Michael Adams, *Better Rich Than Happy* (Toronto: Penguin Books, 2000).

56. John Lorinc, "The Autonomous Rebel," *U of T Magazine*, Winter 2011, http://www.magazine.utoronto.ca/all-about-alumni/michael-adams-environics-stayin-alive-book/, accessed (October 16, 2013).

57. Deena M Amato-McCoy, "A Point of Differentiation," *Chain Store Age*, January 2007, pp. 26–27; Jeff Zabin, "The Importance of Being Analytical," *Brandweek*, July 24, 2006, p. 21; Mindy Fetterman, "Best Buy Gets in Touch with Its Feminine Side," *USA Today*, December 20, 2006.

Chapter 4

1. Roger Evered, "So What Is Strategy?" *Long Range Planning* 16 (Fall 1983), p. 120.

2. See David Aaker, *Strategic Market Management*, 6th ed. (New York: John Wiley, 2001); and A. Coskun Samli, *Strategic Marketing for Success in Retailing* (Westport, CT: Quorum Books, 1998).

3. Michael Porter, *On Competition* (Boston: Harvard Business School Press, 1998); and Michael Porter, "What Is Strategy?" *Harvard Business Review*, November–December 1996, pp. 61–78.

4. Bridget Finn and Gary Heavin, "How to Grow a Chain That's Already Everywhere," *Business 2.0*, March 2005, p. 52; Clarke Canfield, "No-Frills Fitness Club Takes Its Alternative Route to Small Towns," *Los Angeles Times*, November 26, 2004, p. C4.

5. www.mafazineluiza.com.br (accessed April 4, 2010); Guillermo D'Andrea, "Latin American Retail: Where Modernity Blends with Tradition," International Review of Retail, Distribution and Consumer *Research* 20 (February 2010), pp. 85–101; Rob Katz, "How Magazine Luiza Courts the Poor," *HBS Working Knowledge*, April 18, 2007.

6. Anthony Boardman and Aidan Vining, "Defining Your Business Using Product-Customer Matrices," *Long Range Planning* 29 (February 1996), pp. 38–48; and R.L. Rothschild, *How to Gain and Maintain Competitive Advantage in Business* (New York: McGraw-Hill, 1984).

7. Cynthia Montgomery, "Creating Corporate Advantage," *Harvard Business Review*, May-June 1998, pp. 71–80; Shelby Hunt and Robert Morgan, "The Comparative Advantage Theory of Competition," *Journal of Marketing* 59 (April 1995), pp. 1–15; Kathleen Conner and C.K. Prahalad, "A Resource-Based Theory of the Firm: Knowledge versus Opportunism," *Organizational Science* 7 (September-October 1996), pp. 477–501; David Collins and Cynthia Montgomery, "Competing on Resources: Strategy for the 1990s," *Harvard Business Review* 73 (July–August 1995), pp. 118–128; William Werther and Jeffrey Kerr, "The Shifting Sands of Competitive Advantage," *Business Horizons* 38 (May–June 1995), pp. 11–17; "10 Quick Wins to Turn Your Supply Chain into a Competitive Advantage," January 2002, http://retailindustry.about.com/ library/bl/bl_ksa0112.htm ?terms=competitive+advantage; and "Multi-Channel Integration: The New Retail Battleground," Retail Forward, Inc., March 2001, www.pwcris.com.

8. Jeffrey H. Dyer and Harbir Singh, "The Relational View: Cooperative Strategy and Sources of Interorganizational Competitive Advantage," *Academy of Management Review* 23 (October 1998), pp. 660–679; Robert M. Morgan and Shelby Hunt, "Relationship-Based Competitive Advantage: The Role of Relationship Marketing in Marketing Strategy," *Journal of Business Research* 46 (November 1999), pp. 281–290; Shelby D. Hunt and Robert M. Morgan, "The Comparative Advantage Theory of Competition," *Journal of Marketing* 59 (April 1995), pp. 1–15.

9. Gerrard Macintosh and Lawrence Lockshin, "Retail Relationships and Store Loyalty: A Multi-Level Perspective," *International Journal of Research in Marketing* 14 (1997), pp. 487–497.

10. Jo Marney, "Bringing Consumers Back for More," *Marketing Magazine*, September 10, 2001, p. 33; Kathleen Seiders and Douglas Tigert, "Impact of Market Entry and Competitive Structure on Store Switching/Store Loyalty," *International Review of Retail, Distribution and Consumer Research* 7, no. 3 (1997), pp. 234–256; and Niren Sirohi, Edward McLaughlin, and Dick Wittink, "A Model of Consumer Perceptions and Store Loyalty Intentions for a Supermarket Retailer," *Journal of Retailing* 74 (June 1998), pp. 223–247.

11. www.llbean.com (accessed April 12, 2010).

12. Richard Czerniawski and Michael Maloney, *Creating Brand Loyalty: The Management of Power Positioning and Really Great Advertising* (New York: AMACOM, 1999); S. Chandrasekhar, Vinod Sawhney, Rafique Malik, S. Ramesh Kumar, and Pranab Dutta, "The Case of Brand Positioning," *Business Today*, June 7, 1999, pp. 131–140; Bernard Schmitt, Alex Simonson, and Joshua Marcus, "Managing Corporate Image and Identity," *Long Range Planning* 28 (October 1995), pp. 82–92; Tim Ambler, "Category Management Is Best Deployed for Brand Positioning," *Marketing*, November 29, 2001, p. 18; and Harriet Marsh, "Why New Look Must Take Stock," *Marketing*, March 29, 2001, p. 17.

13. Amy Merrick, "Tired of Trendiness, Former Shoppers Leave Gap, Defect to Competitors," *The Wall Street Journal*, December 6, 2001, p. B1.

14. Mary Jo Bitner, "Self-Service Technologies: What Do Customers Expect?" *Marketing Management*, Spring 2001; Mary Jo Bitner,

Steven W. Brown, and Matthew L. Meuter, "Technology Infusion in Service Encounters," *Journal of the Academy of Marketing Science,* March 2000; Mary Jo Bitner and Valerie Zeithaml, *Services Marketing,* 2nd ed. (Burr Ridge, IL: McGraw-Hill/Irwin, 1999); Leonard Berry, "Relationship Marketing of Services Growing Interest: Emerging Perspectives," *Journal of the Academy of Marketing Science* 23 (Fall 1995), pp. 236–245; and Mary Jo Bitner, "Building Service Relationships: It's All about Promises," *Journal of the Academy of Marketing Science* 23 (Fall 1995), pp. 246–251.

15. Hollie Shaw, "Harry Rosen Dons New Look for Expansion: CEO's Pragmatic View," *Financial Post,* September 3, 2008; Shaun Proulx, "Harry Goes Lofty, Large and Luxe," *The Globe and Mail,* September 3, 2008; Denise Power, "Harry Rosen Embracing Technology," *Daily News Record,* February 12, 2007, p. 16.

16. S.A. Shaw and J. Gibbs, "Procurement Strategies of Small Retailers Faced with Uncertainty: An Analysis of Channel Choice and Behaviour," *International Review of Retail, Distribution and Consumer Research* 9, no. 1 (1999), pp. 61–75.

17. "Global Brands Face Up to International Retailing," *Marketing Week,* October 26, 2000, p. 32.

18. Richard Cuthbertson, Gerd Islei, Peter Franke, and Balkan Cetinkaya, "What Will the Best Supply Chains Look Like in the Future?" *European Retail Digest,* Summer 2006, pp. 7–15; "Competitive Advantage through Supply Chain Innovation," *Logistics & Transport Focus,* December 2004, pp. 56–59.

19. Werther and Kerr, "The Shifting Sands of Competitive Advantage."

20. Roger Kerin, Vijay Mahajan, and P. Rajan Varadarajan, *Contemporary Perspectives on Strategic Market Planning* (Boston: Allyn & Bacon, 1991), Ch. 6. See also Susan Mudambi, "A Topology of Strategic Choice in Retailing," *International Journal of Retail & Distribution Management,* 1994, pp. 22–25.

21. Erin White, "Abercrombie Seeks to Send Teeny-Boppers Packing," *The Wall Street Journal,* August 30, 2001, pp. B1, B4.

22. Sarah Ellison, "Carrefour Finds It Difficult to Build Single Global Brand," *The Wall Street Journal,* August 30, 2001, www.wsj.com.

23. www.tescocorporate.com/page.aspx?pointerid=3DB554FCAE344 BD88EEEEFA63D71B831 (accessed July 30, 2007).

24. Anita McGahan, "Sustaining Superior Profits: Customer and Supplier Relationships," *Harvard Business Online,* http://harvard-businessonline. hbsp.harvard.edu, March 1, 1999, pp. 1–7; and Randolph Beard, "Regulation, Vertical Integration and Sabotage," *Journal of Industrial Economics* 49, no. 3, (2001), pp. 319–333.

25. Digitalbuzzblog.com.

26. www.businessweek.com/magazine/content/05_46/b3959003.htm (accessed July 30, 2007).

27. Donald Lehman and Russell Winer, *Analysis for Marketing Planning,* 5th. ed. (Burr Ridge, IL: McGraw-Hill/Irwin, 2001).

28. Andrew Campbell, "Mission Statements," *Long Range Planning* 30 (December 1997), pp. 931–935.

29. Alfred Rappaport, *Creating Shareholder Value: The New Standard for Business Performance* (New York: Wiley, 1988); Robert C. Higgins and Roger A. Kerin, "Managing the Growth-Financial Policy Nexus in Retailing," *Journal of Retailing* 59, no. 3 (Fall 1983), pp. 19–47; and Roger Kerin, Vijay Mahajan, and P. Rajan Varadarajan, *Contemporary Perspectives on Strategic Market Planning* (Boston: Allyn & Bacon, 1991), Ch. 6.

30. See Linda Gatley and David Clutterbuck, "Superdrug Crafts a Mission Statement," *International Journal of Retail and Distribution Management* 26 (October–November 1998), pp. 10–11, for an interesting example of the process used by a U.K. drugstore chain to develop a mission statement.

31. David Aaker, *Strategic Market Management,* 6th ed. (New York: John Wiley, 2001).

32. Michael Porter, "Strategy and the Internet," *Harvard Business Review,* March 2001, pp. 63–78; and Michael Porter, *Competitive Strategy* (New York: Free Press, 1980).

33. "The Estée Lauder Companies Inc.," *Hoovers Online,* 2002, www. hoovers.com/premium/profile/8/0,2147,40148,00.html.

34. "L'Oréal SA," *Hoovers Online,* 2002, www.hoovers.com/premium/profile/2/0,2147,41772,00.html.

35. Terry Clark, P. Rajan Varadarajan, and William M. Pride, "Environmental Management: The Construct and Research Propositions," *Journal of Business Research* 29, no. 1 (January 1994), pp. 23–39; James Lang, Roger Calantone, and Donald Gudmundson, "Small Firm Information Seeking as a Response to Environmental Threats and Opportunities," *Journal of Small Business Management,* January 1997, pp. 11–29; and Masoud Yasai-Ardekani and Paul Nystrom, "Designs for Environmental Scanning Systems: Tests of a Contingency Theory," *Management Science* 42 (February 1996), pp. 187–204.

36. Bill Quinn, *How Wal-Mart Is Destroying America (and the World): And What You Can Do About It* (Berkeley, CA: Ten Speed Press, 2000).

37. Erin White, "Retail Brand Buys Brooks Brothers from Marks & Spencer for $225 Million," *The Wall Street Journal,* November 23, 2001; and Andrew Ross Sorkin, "Owner of Casual Corner Chain in Deal for Brooks Brothers," *New York Times,* November 23, 2001.

38. David Aaker, *Strategic Market Management,* 6th ed. (New York: John Wiley, 2001); G. Stalk, "Competing on Capabilities: The New Rules of Corporate Strategy," *Harvard Business Review,* March-April 1992, pp. 51–69; and Donna Cartwright, Paul Boughton, and Stephen Miller, "Competitive Intelligence Systems: Relationships to Strategic Orientation and Perceived Usefulness," *Journal of Managerial Issues* 7 (Winter 1995), pp. 420–434.

39. Blair Cameron, "The Recession Hangover: How Inflation Is Changing Canadian Retail," Joint Research from Loyalty One and the Retail Council of Canada, August 2011, p. 5, www.retail-council.org/training/research/industry/RecessionHangover.pdf (accessed October 21, 2013).

40. Brendan Soucie, "March 2012–Canadian eCommerce Monthly Trends Report," Demac Media, April 5, 2012, www.demacmedia. com/canadian-ecommerce-monthly-trends/canadian-ecommerce-statistics-series-march-2012/ (accessed October 21, 2013).

Chapter 5

1. Hiawatha Bray, "Microsoft Takes Page from Apple Retail Plan," *Boston Globe,* July 18, 2009.

2. Michael E. Porter, *Competitive Strategy: Techniques for Analyzing Industries and Competitors* (Simon & Schuster Trade, 1998).

3. Matt Woolsey, "World's Most Expensive Addresses," *Forbes,* July 17, 2008.

4. Robert W. Buckner, *Site Selection: New Advancements in Methods and Technology* (New York: Lebhar-Friedman Books, 1998), p. 18.

5. Karen A. Machleit, Sevgin A. Eroglu, and Susan Powell Mantel, "Perceived Retail Crowding and Shopping Satisfaction: What Modifies This Relationship?" *Journal of Consumer Psychology* 9, no. 1 (2000), p. 29.

6. Buckner, *Site Selection,* pp. 31–32.

7. Buckner, *Site Selection,* Ch. 15; and Christian Harder, *GIS Means Business* (Redlands, CA: Environmental Systems Research Institute, Inc., 1997).

8. Buckner, *Site Selection.*

9. Harder, *GIS Means Business.*

10. David L. Huff, "Defining and Estimating a Trade Area," *Journal of Marketing* 28 (1964), pp. 34-38; and David L. Huff and William Black, "The Huff Model in Retrospect," *Applied Geographic Studies* 1, no. 2 (1997), pp. 22–34.

11. Tammy Drezner and Zvi Dressner, "Validating the Gravity-Based Competitive Location Model Using Inferred Attractiveness," *Annals of Operations Research* 111 (March 2002), pp. 227–441.

12. William J. Reilly, "Method for the Study of Retail Relationships," *Research Monograph* no. 4, (Austin: University of Texas Press, 1929), University of Texas Bulletin No. 2944. See also MacKenzie S. Botttum, "Reilly's Law," *Appraisal Journal,* vol. 57, April 1989, pp. 166–172; and Michael D. D'Amico, Jon M. Hawes, and Dale M. Lewison, "Determining a Hospital's Trading Area: An Application of Reilly's Law," *Journal of Hospital Marketing,* vol. 8, no. 2, 1994, pp. 121–129.

13. Richard L. Nelson, *The Selection of Retail Locations* (New York: F.W. Dodge, 1959), p.149.

14. Conseil Quebecois du Commerce de Detail (CQCD). "Vive la différence!" *Canadian Retailer*, March/April, 2004.

15. Buckner, *Site Selection*, Ch. 15.

16. "Back to the Future," *New York Times Magazine*, April 6, 1997, pp. 48–49.

17. *The SCORE: Shopping Center Operations, Revenues, and Expenses* (New York: International Council of Shopping Centres, 2004).

18. Eddie Baeb, "A Mall Struggles to Defend Its Glitz," *Crain's Chicago Business* 23, no. 9 (February 29, 2000), p. 3; Elin Schoen Brockman, "As Malls Die, the Next Generation Re-Creates the Past," *New York Times*, August 8, 1999, p. 4; Kevin Kenyon, "Power Moves: New Formats Help Developers Rejuvenate Enclosed Centers," *Shopping Centers Today*, October 8, 1999; and Herb Greenberg, "Dead Mall Walking," *Fortune* 141, no. 9 (May 1, 2000), p. 304.

19. Kevin Kenyon, "Mall of America Turns Trash into Cash," *Shopping Centers Today*, www.icsc.org/srch/sctl. October 1997, pp. 5–6.

20. Debra Hazel, "Demalling for Dollars," *Shopping Centers Today*, January 2, 2001; and Suzette Hill, "To De-Mall or EMall? Shaping Web Shopping," *Apparel Industry Magazine* 61, no. 2 (February 2000), pp. 36–38.

21. Patricia Williams, "$355M Vaughan Mall Built on Themes: Innovative Design Reflects Canadian Culture," *Daily Commercial News and Construction Record*, Vol. 76: June 19, 2003; and Rebecca Sullivan, "Construction Begins on Vaughan Mills," Canada Newswire, Ottawa: June 16, 2003.

22. Julie Elliott, "Retail Gets a Breath of Fresh Air," *National Post*, November 3, 2003.

23. Edmund Mander, "Defining a Hot Concept Lifestyle Centers Elude Classification," *Shopping Centers Today*, August 2001, pp. 1, 44–45.

24. Lois Huff and Stephanie Shamroski, "Outlet Centers: The Search for Value," Retail Forward, Inc., May 2001.

25. Ray A. Smith, "Outlet Centers in the U.S. Turn Upmarket in Amenities," *The Asian Wall Street Journal*, June 8, 3002, p. 11.

26. "Simon Property Group and Calloway REIT Celebrate the Start of Construction on Toronto Premium Outlets® With Groundbreaking Ceremony on April 25," Simon Property Group, news release, April 10, 2012.

27. Jennifer Steinhauser, "It's a Mall ..., It's an Airport," *New York Times*, June 10, 1998, pp. C1, C4.

28. Connie Robbins Gentry, "The Rebirth of City Development," *Chain Store Age*, May 2000, pp. 83–90.

29. Nancy Kaffer, "Downtowns Become Boomertowns," *Metromode*, October 25, 2007.

30. Marina Strauss, "Baby, Come Back: Department Stores Woo the 'Sweet Spot' Shopper," *Globe and Mail*, October 16, 2009, www.theglobeandmail.com/life/style/baby-come-back-department-stores-woo-the-sweet-spot-shopper/article1326698/ (retrieved October 24, 2009).

Chapter 6

1. "Growing Pains," *Chain Store Age*, August 2005, p. 31A.

2. "Canada GDP Annual Growth Rate," *Trading Economics*, www.tradingeconomics.com/canada/gdp-growth-annual (accessed June 23, 2013).

3. Mitchell Mauk, "The Store as Story," *VM & SD*, October 2000, pp. 23, 25.

4. M. Joseph Sirgy, Dhruv Grewal, and Tamara Mangleburg, "Retail Environment, Self-Congruity, and Retail Patronage: An Integrative Model and a Research Agenda," *Journal of Business Research* 49, no. 2 (August 2000), pp. 127–138.

5. Kathleen Purvis, "It's Scary: Your Supermarket Shopping Is Done by Design," *Seattle Times*, June 19, 2002, based on research by Kevin Kelly.

6. Julia Werdigier, "To Woo Europeans, McDonald's Goes Upscale," *The New York Times*, August 25, 2007 (accessed December 28, 2007).

7. Linda Matchan, "The Sleek, Smooth Design of Apple's iPod Is Now Mirrored in the Architecture of Some of the Company's High-Profile Stores," *Boston Globe*, June 29, 2006.

8. Eileen Bridges and Renée Florsheim, "Hedonic and Utilitarian Shopping Goals: The Online Experience," *Journal of Business Research* 61 (April 2008), pp. 309–314; Ravindra Chitturi, Rajagopal Raghunathan, and Vijay Mahajan, "Delight by Design: The Role of Hedonic versus Utilitarian Benefits," *Journal of Marketing* 72 (May 2008), pp. 48–63; Andrew Smitha and Leigh Sparks "It's Nice to Get a Wee Treat If You've Had a Bad Week," *Journal of Business Research* 62 (May 2009), pp. 542–547.

9. Stacey Menzel Baker, Jonna Holland, and Carol Kaufman-Scarborough, "How Consumers with Disabilities Perceive 'Welcome' in Retail Servicescapes: A Critical Incident Study," *Journal of Services Marketing* 21, no. 3 (2007), pp. 160–173; Robert Pear, "Plan Seeks More Access for Disabled," *New York Times*, July 16, 2008, p. 11: Rosemary D. F. Bromley and David L. Matthew, "Reducing Consumer Disadvantage: Reassessing Access in the Retail Environment," *International Review of Retail, Distribution & Consumer Research* 17, no. 5 (2007), pp. 483–501; Marianne Wilson, "Accessible Fixtures," *Chain Store Age* 83, no. 2 (February 2007).

10. See, for example, *Disabled in Action of Metropolitan New York, Inc. et al. v. Duane Reade, Inc.*, U.S. District Court, Southern District of New York, Civil Action No. 01 Civ. 4692 (WHP), 2004; *Californians for Disability Rights v. Mervyn's*, Superior Court of California, No. 2002-051738 (RMS), 2003; *Shimozono, et al. v. May Department Stores Co. d/b/a Robinsons-May*, Federal Court, Central District of California, Case No. 00-04261 (WJR), 2001; *Access Now, et al., v. Burdines, Inc.*, Federal Court, Southern District of Florida, Case No. 99-3214 (CIV), 2000.

11. Michael Barbaro, "Department Stores Settle Disability Lawsuit," *Washington Post*, February 9, 2005, p. E02.

12. M. A. McColl and L. Jongbloed (eds.), "Disability and Social Policy in Canada" (2nd ed.), *Captus University Publications*, 2006, Concord, ON; Michael Prince, "Does Canada Need a National Disability Act?" *Public Lecture*, 2007; Michael J. Prince, *Absent Citizens: Disability Politics and Policy in Canada*, University of Toronto Press, Toronto, 2009.

13. Mary Ann McColl, Mike Schaub, Lauren Sampson, and Kevin Hong, "A Canadians With Disabilities Act?" *Canadian Disability Policy Alliance Secretariat*, Summer 2010.

14. http://www.aodacompliance.com (accessed June 2013).

15. http://www.osler.com/NewsResources/Details.aspx?id=3236 (accessed June 2013).

16. http://www.aodacompliance.com (accessed June 2013).

17. Claire Wilson, "The Harlem Revival Brings in the Shops," *The New York Times*, April 18, 2007 (accessed January 4, 2008).

18. Joseph Weishar, "Moving Targets." *Visual Merchandising and Store Design*, September 1990.

19. "International Interior Store Design Competition," *Visual Merchandising and Store Design*, February 1996, pp. 35–76.

20. Fiona Soltes, "It's the Message, Not the Medium," *Stores*, October 2007, p. 26; Michael Curran, "Now Playing: Interactive Retail Marketing 2.0," *Stores*, August 2007, p. 92; Katherine Field, "Digital Signage: A Powerful New Medium," *Chain Store Age*, May 2006, p. 204; Steven Keith Platt, Kingshuck Sinha, and Barton Weitz, *Implications for Retail Adoption of Digital Signage Systems* (Chicago, IL: Platt Retail Institute, 2004).

21. Raymond R. Burke, "Behavioral Effects of Digital Signage," *Journal of Advertising Research* 49 (June 2009), pp. 180–186.

22. "Five Easy Steps," *VM & SE*, June 2000, pp. 42–43.

23. Mindy Fetterman and Jayne O'Donnell, "Just Browsing at the Mall? That's What You Think," *USA Today*, September 1, 2006; Paco Underhill, *Why We Buy: The Science of Shopping* (New York: Simon and Schuster, 2000).

24. Lorrie Grant, "Department Stores Ring up Centralized Checkouts; Cost-Cutting, Success of Kohl's Help Drive Trend," www.plainvanillashell.com, *Retail and Development News*, June 6, 2002; and Eileen Smith, "Retail Giants Change Checkouts," www.courierpostonline.com, June 13, 2002.

25. Joseph Weishar, "The Business of the Wall," *Visual Merchandising and Store Design*, October 1985.

26. Sara Bauknecht, "Smart Mirror Matches Fashion Rather Than Reflect," *Pittsburgh Post-Gazette*, December 14, 2009.

27. Bo Begole, Takashi Matsumoto, Wei Zhang, Nicholas Yee, Juan Liu, and Maurice Chu, "Designed to Fit: Challenges of Interaction Design for Clothes Dressing Room Technologies," in *Human-Computer Interaction: Interacting in Various Application Domains* (Berlin/Heidelberg: Springer, 2009); Jeanine Poggi, "Dressing Rooms of the Future," *Forbes*, July 22, 2008.

28. The concept of atmospherics was introduced by Philip Kotler, "Atmosphere as a Marketing Tool," *Journal of Retailing* 49 (Winter 1973), pp. 48–64. The definition is adapted from Richard Yalch and Eric Spangenberg, "Effects of Store Music on Shopping Behaviour," *Journal of Service Marketing* 4, no. 1 (Winter 1990), pp. 31–39.

29. Pierre Chandon, J. Wesley Hutchinson, Eric T. Bradlow, and Scott H. Young, "Does In-Store Marketing Work? Effects of the Number and Position of Shelf Facings on Brand Attention and Evaluation at the Point of Purchase," *Journal of Marketing* 73 (November 2009), pp. 1–17.

30. Eric R. Spangenberg, David E. Sprott, Bianca Grohmann, and Daniel L. Tracy, "Gender-Congruent Ambient Scent Influences on Approach and Avoidance Behaviors in a Retail Store," *Journal of Business Research* 59, no. 12 (2006), pp. 1281–1287; Anna S. Mattila and Jochen Wirtz, "Congruency of Scent and Music as a Driver of In-Store Evaluations and Behavior," *Journal of Retailing* 77, no. 2 (Summer 2001), pp. 273–289.

31. "The Need for Speed," *WWD*, November 5, 1998, p. 2.

32. S. Silcoff, "One of the Few Labels to Succeed Internationally," *National Post*, April 24, 2004.

33. Brooks Barnes, "Disney's Retail Plan Is a Theme Park in Its Stores," *New York Times*, October 13, 2009.

34. www.charthouse.com (accessed July 1, 2010).

35. "Atmosphere as a Marketing Tool," *Journal of Retailing* 49 (Winter 1973), pp. 48–64. The definition is adapted from Richard Yalch and Eric Spangenberg, "Effects of Store Music on Shopping Behavior," *Journal of Service Marketing* 4, no. 1 (Winter 1990), pp. 31–39.

36. Anna S. Mattila and Jochen Wirtz, "Congruency of Scent and Music as a Driver of In-Store Evaluations and Behavior," *Journal of Retailing* 77, no. 2 (Summer 2001), pp. 273–289.

37. Teresa A. Summers and Paulette R. Hebert, "Shedding Some Light on Store Atmospherics; Influence of Illumination on Consumer Behavior," *Journal of Business Research* 54, no. 2 (November 2001), pp. 145–150.

38. Susan Franke, "Architects, Experts Say Proper Design Can Propel Shoppers into Stores," *Pittsburgh Business Times*, July 12, 2002.

39. For a review of this research, see Joseph A. Bellizzi and Robert E. Hite, "Environmental Color, Consumer Feelings, and Purchase Likelihood," *Psychology and Marketing* 9, no. 5 (September-October 1992), pp. 347–363.

40. J. Duncan Herrington and Louis Capella, "Effects of Music in Service Environments: A Field Study," *Journal of Services Marketing* 10, no. 2 (1996), pp. 26–41.

41. Richard F. Yalch and Eric R. Spangenberg, "The Effects of Music in a Retail Setting on Real and Perceived Shopping Times," *Journal of Business Research* 49, no. 2 (August 2000), pp. 139–148; Michael Hui, Laurette Dube, and Jean-Charles Chebat, "The Impact of Music on Consumers' Reactions to Waiting for Services," *Journal of Retailing* 73, no. 1, (1997), pp. 87–104; and Julie Baker, Dhruv Grewal, and Michael Levy, "An Experimental Approach to Making Retail Store Environmental Decisions," *Journal of Retailing* 68 (Winter 1992), pp. 445–460.

42. Maxine Wilkie, "Scent of a Market," *American Demographics*, August 1995, pp. 40–49.

43. Anna S. Mattila and Jochen Wirtz, "Congruency of Scent and Music as a Driver of In-Store Evaluations and Behavior," *Journal of Retailing* 77, no. 2 (Summer 2001), pp. 273–290.

44. Cathleen McCarthy, "Aromatic Merchandising: Leading Customers by the Nose," *Visual Merchandising and Store Design*, April 1992, pp. 85–87.

45. Velitchka Kalchteva and Barton Weitz, "How Exciting Should a Store Be?" *Journal of Marketing*, Winter 2006, pp. 34–62.

46. Ibid.

47. Jung-Hwan Kim, Minjeong Kim, and Jay Kandampully, "The Impact of Buying Environment Characteristics of Retail Websites," *Service Industries Journal* 27, no. 7 (2007), pp. 865–880; David Cunningham, Liz Thach, and Karen Thompson, "Innovative E-Commerce Site Design: A Conceptual Model to Match Consumer MBTI Dimensions to Website Design," *Journal of Internet Commerce* 6, no. 3 (2007), pp. 1–27.

48. James J. Cappel and Zhenyu Huang, "A Usability Analysis of Company Websites," *Journal of Computer Information Systems* 48, no. 1 (2007), pp. 117–123.

49. Benjamin P.C. Yen, "The Design and Evaluation of Accessibility on Web Navigation," *Decision Support Systems* 42, no. 4 (2007), pp. 219–235.

50. "Tips on Improving the Checkout Process," www.e-consultancy.com, August 17, 2007.

51. Ibid.

Chapter 7

1. "Corporate Overview," Target Canada website, http://pressroom.target.ca/corporate (accessed September 8, 2012); "Target says it's 'thrilled' by Canadian response to store openings," CTV News, March 28, 2013, http://www.ctvnews.ca/business/target-says-it-s-thrilled-by-canadian-response-to-store-openings-1.1215409 (accessed April 6, 2012).

2. Lawrence Stevenson, Joseph Shlesinger, and Michael Pearce, *Power Retail* (Whitby, ON: McGraw-Hill Ryerson, 1999); and Jonathan Reynolds and Christine Cuthbertson, *Retail Strategy: The View from the Bridge* (Amsterdam: Elsevier, 2004).

3. "2013 Global Powers of Retailing," *Stores*, January 2013, pp. G17–G21.

4. Frank Badillo, "Global Retail Outlook," *Retail Forward*, May 2009; *2009 Global Development Index* (New York: Kearney, 2009).

5. Han Ben-Shjabat, Mike Moriarty, and Deepa Bahgara, *Windows of Hope for Global Retailing* (Chicago: Kearney, 2009); Ken Schepy, "Retailing in India: Challenges and Opportunities," *Chain Store Age*, July 2008; Mehul Srivastava, "Big Retailers Still Struggle in India," *Business Week India*, October 16, 2009.

6. "China's Retail Revolution: An Interview with Walmart's Ed Chan," *BusinessWeek*, October 2009.

7. Brenda Sternquist, *International Retailing*, ABC Media Inc., 1998; "A Tiger, Falling behind a Dragon," *The Economist*, June 21, 2003; "Two Systems, One Grand Rivalry," *The Economist*, June 21, 2003.

8. Jane Barrett, "Designer Heralds Upturn as Retail Sales Rise 9%," *National Post*, April 14, 2004.

9. "Big in Beijing," *W Magazine*, September 2012, http://www.wmagazine.com/travel/2012/09/giorgio-armani-beijing-recommendations (accessed November 18, 2013).

10. Bernard Wysocki, Jr., "In Developing Nations, Many Youth Are Big Spenders," *The Wall Street Journal*, June 26, 1997, pp. A1, A11.

11. Elisabeth Rosenthal, "Buicks, Starbucks and Fried Chicken. Still China?" *New York Times*, February 25, 2002, http://www.nytimes.com/2002/02/25/international/asia/25CHIN.html?pagewanted=all (accessed November 18, 2013).

12. David Woodruff, "For French Retailers, a Weapon against Wal-Mart," *The Wall Street Journal*, September 27, 1999, pp. B1, B4; and David Woodruff, "Carrefour Is Mounting a Push into Japanese Markets," *The Wall Street Journal*, June 15, 1999, p. B7.

13. Geoff Wissman, "Critical Issues: The Top 100 Retailers Worldwide 2000," *Retail Forward, Inc.*, August 2001, p. 16.

14. Sarah Raper, "Gap's Tour de Force," *WWD*, July 1, 1999, p. 3.

15. Geoff Wissman, "Critical Issues: The Top 100 Retailers Worldwide 2000," *Retail Forward, Inc.*, August 2001, p. 16.

16. "Retailers Are Trying to Go Global," *The Economist Newspaper* (U.S. ed.), June 19, 1999, p. 1.

17. "The World Is Not Their Oyster," *Chain Store Age*, May, 2001, p. 60.

18. This section is adapted from "Winning Moves on a Global Chessboard: Wal-Mart and Costco in a Global Context," Goldman Sachs Investment Research, May 12, 2000.

19. Lisa Penaloza and Mary Gilly, "Marketer Acculturation: The Changer and the Changed," *Journal of Marketing* 63 (Summer 1999), pp. 84–95.

20. Sarah Ellison, "Carrefour Finds It Difficult to Build Single Global Brand," *The Wall Street Journal,* August 30, 2001.

21. Erik Gordon, "Taking the Plunge?" *Chain Store Age Supplement,* December 1997, pp. 14–23; and "Shopping the World," *The Economist Newspaper,* June 18, 1999, pp. 1–2.

22. "Handcuffs on High Street," *The Economist,* May 13, 2000, p. 62.

23. "East 57th Street Again Tops Retail List Highest Rents in the World," *New York Times,* December 9, 2001.

24. Christopher Daniel, Joseph Aversa, and Tony Hernandez, *Canada's Leading Retailers: Latest Trends and Strategies,* 7th ed., CSCA Centre for the Study of Commercial Activity, Ryerson University, 2009, p. 12.

25. "Handcuffs on High Street," *The Economist,* May 13, 2000, p. 62.

26. Ibid.

27. Jean-Pierre Jeannet and H. David Hennessey, *Global Marketing Strategies,* 5th ed., (Boston: Houghton Mifflin, 2000); and "What's the Best Way to Set up Shop?" *Chain Store Age Global Retailing Supplement,* December 1997, pp. 32–35.

28. Greg Silverman and David Wasserman, "Retailing in Latin America," *Global Retail Forward,* July 2001, p. 13; Stephanie Shamroski, "Retailing in Turkey," *Global Retail Forward,* January 2000, p. 6; Ira Kalish and Stephanie Shamroski, "Global Retail Intelligencer," *Global Retail Forward,* April 2001, p. 2; Philip Walker, "Retailing in India," *Global Retail Forward,* March 2000, p. 12; Lois Huff and Stephanie Shamroski, "Retailing in the United Kingdom," *Global Retail Forward,* December 2000, p. 17; and Marianne Wilson, "Thinking Big," *Chain Store Age,* July 1, 2001, p. 47.

29. "An Opening Door Policy," *Chain Store Age,* January 2000, pp. 62–63.

30. www.marksandspencer.com

31. Ted Fishman, "The Chinese Century," *New York Times Magazine,* July 4, 2004, p. 26.

32. David Barboza, "In Roaring China, Sweaters Are West of Sock City," *New York Times,* December 24, 2004, p. C2.

33. "Wal around the World," *The Economist,* December 8, 2001, p. 8; and "Pooled Assets," *Chain Store Age,* June 1, 2001, p. 50.

34. Rob Deloney, "McDonald's Banks on Franchising in China," *National Post,* September 9, 2003.

35. Alex Gillis, "Spanish Armada," *National Post,* October 1, 1999.

36. Erik Gordon, "Taking the Plunge?" *Chain Store Age Global Retailing Supplement,* Ernst & Young, December 1997, pp. 14–23.

37. "Chain Stores in India," *The Economist,* May 29, 2008.

38. Dana Flavelle, "Swedish Gap Poised to Enter the Canadian Clothing Market," *Toronto Star,* January 15, 2004.

39. Barbara Hogan Galvin, "Outlet Center Challenge," *Shopping Centers Today,* June 2001, pp. 25–28.

40. *Global Powers of Retailing 2013: Retail Beyond,* Deloitte, January 2013, http://www.deloitte.com/assets/Dcom-Australia/Local%20 Assets/Documents/Industries/Consumer%20business/Deloitte_ Global_Powers_of_Retail_2013.pdf (accessed November 18, 2013).

41. Ibid., p. G4.

42. Ibid., p. G13.

43. Ibid., p. G17.

44. Ben-Shjabat, Moriarty, and Bahgara, *Windows of Hope for Global Retailing.*

45. Jeet Heer and Steve Penfold, "McFelafels, McHuevos, McLuks," *National Post,* February 15, 2003.

46. Jacqueline Thorpe, "India the Jewel in Global Market," *National Post,* April 16, 2004.

47. Christopher Daniel, Joseph Aversa, and Tony Hernandez, *Canada's Leading Retailers: Latest Trends and Strategies,* 7th ed., CSCA Centre for the Study of Commercial Activity, 2009, p. 12.

48. Mitch Moxley, "Mountain Co-op Adding to City Locations," *National Post,* June 18, 2004.

Chapter 8

1. Patrick Dunne and Robert Lusch, *Retailing,* 5th ed. (Mason, OH: Southwest, 2000) pp. 39–40.

2. "Diversity at McDonald's: A Way of Life," *Nation's Restaurant News,* January, 2005, pp. 92–95.

3. 2007 annual report, Lululemon Athletica Inc., April 8, 2008, http://files. shareholder.com/downloads/LULU/0x0xS909567-08-415/1397187/ filing.pdf.

4. Stanley B. Block, Geoffrey A. Hirt, and Douglas J. Short, *Foundations of Financial Management,* 8th ed. (Whitby ON: McGraw-Hill Ryerson, 2009), pp. 23, 28.

5. http://cbdd.wsu.edu/kewlcontent/cdoutput/TOM505/page25. htm, Chapter 8: Analysis of Financial Statements.

6. Lawrence J. Gitman, *Principles of Managerial Finance,* 12th ed. (Upper Saddle River, NJ: Pearson Prentice Hall), p. 118.

7. 2011 annual report, Lululemon Athletica Inc., March 22, 2012, http://files.shareholder.com/downloads/LULU/2082031029x0x 587082/683BDA4A-C6DC-42DB-9217-6188143C9EA2/2011_ annual_report.pdf.

8. http://www.loblaw.ca/.

9. Nadine Bells. "From cars to books, Canadians pay more for everything," *Daily Brew,* June 2012, http://ca.news.yahoo.com/blogs/ dailybrew/cars-books-canadians-pay-more-everything-163054422. html.

10. Jane O'Donnel, "Retailers Want a Place in Your Wallet," *USA Today,* July 10, 2006.

11. Average retail inventory is estimated from the balance sheet inventory. Assume the end-of-year inventory on the balance sheet is average cost inventory: Average retail inventory = Average cost inventory/(1 − Gross margin percent (expressed as a decimal)).

12. To illustrate, suppose Net sales = $50,000 and Average inventory at retail = $10,000; Inventory turnover = $50,000 ‚ $10,000 = 5. To convert inventory turnover expressed at retail to turnover at cost, we multiply by the cost complement, which is the percentage of net sales represented by the cost of goods sold. If the gross margin is 40 percent, the cost complement is 60 percent (100% − 40%). By multiplying the numerator and denominator by 60 percent, the result is cost of goods sold divided by the average inventory at cost. Thus, inventory turnover is 5 whether it is calculated using retail or cost figures.

13. The rationale behind this equation is as follows: The sales-to-stock ratio is expressed with the numerator at retail and the denominator at cost. To get inventory turnover, both numerator and denominator must be at either retail or cost. 100% − Gross margin % is the percentage of net sales represented by the cost of goods sold (also known as the cost complement). By multiplying the sales-to-stock ratio by the cost complement we, in essence, convert the numerator (sales) to the cost of goods sold and therefore have numerator and denominator both expressed at cost.

14. James Surowiecki, "The Most Devastating Retailer in the World," *The New Yorker,* September 18, 2000, p. 74.

15. This section is adapted from William R. Davidson, Daniel J. Sweeney, and Ronald W. Stampfl, *Retailing Management,* 5th ed. (New York: John Wiley & Sons, 1984).

16. Terry Pristin, "Owning Your Retail Space Is Not Just for The Big Guys Anymore," *The New York Times,* March 29, 2006.

17. Although the use of asset turnover presented here is helpful for gaining appreciation of the performance ratio, capital budgeting or present value analyses are more appropriate for determining the long-term return of a fixed asset.

18. Bryan Gildenberg, Mventures, personal communication, February 2002.

19. All categories of shares, including preferred shares, paid-in capital, and treasury shares, are included with common shares for simplicity.

20. "A Strong and Useful Light," *Harvard Business Review* 80, no. 5 (May 2002), p. 12.; John D. Sterman and Nelson P. Repenning, "Nobody Ever Gets Credit for Fixing Problems That Never Happened: Creating and Sustaining Process Improvement," *Harvard Business Online,* July 1, 2001; Loren Gary, "The Right Kind of Failure," *Harvard Management,* update article, January 1, 2002; Gary Sutton, *The Six-Month Fix: Adventures in Rescuing Failing Companies* (New York: John Wiley & Sons, November 2001); and

Bernard Salanie, *The Microeconomics of Market Failures* (Boston: MIT Press, November 2000).

21. Daniel J. Sweeney, "Improving the Profitability of Retail Merchandising Decisions," *Journal of Marketing,* January 1973, pp. 60–68.

Chapter 9

1. David Simchi-Levi, Philip Karminsky, and Edith Simchi-Levi, *Designing and Managing the Supply Chain: Concepts, Strategies, and Case Studies,* 4th ed. (New York: McGraw-Hill/Irwin, 2010); Roberta S. Russell, *Operations Management: Creating Value along the Supply Chain,* 7th ed. (Hoboken, NJ: Wiley, 2010); Barbara Flynn, Michiya Morita, and Jose Machuca, *Managing Global Supply Chain Relationships: Operations, Strategies and Practices* (Hauppauge, NY: Nova Science, 2010); Faustino Taderera, *Logistics and Supply Chain Management: Warehousing, Distribution* (Saarbrücken, Germany: Lap Lambert Academic, 2010); Jayaraman Vaidyanathan, "Creating Competitive Advantages through New Value Creation: A Reverse Logistics Perspective," *Academy of Management Perspectives* 21, no. 2(2007), pp. 56–73.

2. Lee Holman and Greg Buzek, "What's the Deal with Out-of-Stocks?" *IHL Group,* December 2008.

3. Holman and Buzek, "What's the Deal with Out-of-Stocks?"

4. "Bharti Enterprises and Walmart Join Hands in Wholesale Cash-and-Carry to Serve Small Retailers, Manufacturers and Farmers," PR Newswire, August 6, 2007.

5. Jesper Aastrup and Herbert Kotzab, "Forty Years of Out-of-Stock Research—and Shelves Are Still Empty," *International Review of Retail, Distribution and Consumer Research,* February 20, 2010, pp. 147–164; Jesper Aastrup and Herbert Kotzab, "Analyzing Out-of-Stock in Independent Grocery Stores: An Empirical Study," *International Journal of Retail & Distribution Management* 37, no. 9 (2009), pp. 765–789; Mike Griswold, "Out of Stock," *Forbes,* December 14, 2006.

6. "Bar Codes Change the Way Retailers Stocked, Priced Products," *Boston Globe,* June 29, 2004, p. C1.

7. Kristine Miller, "Fashion's New Fast Lane," *Forbes,* September 12, 2006.

8. Constance Hays, "What Walmart Knows about Customers' Habits," *New York Times,* November 14, 2004, p. C1.

9. Council of Supply Chain Management Professionals, http://cscmp.org/ (accessed August 18, 2007).

10. Susan Elzey, "Location Part of Store Closing," *Knight Ridder Tribune Business News,* July 19, 2007; Dollar General Corporation, 10-K form, filed with the SEC on February 2, 2007; Amy Sung, "Dollar General Cites Progress with Store Receiving System," *Supermarket News,* October 10, 2005, p. 49.

11. www.businessdictionary.com/definition/freight-forwarder.html (accessed June 19, 2010).

12. Oliver E. Williamson, "Outsourcing: Transaction Cost Economics and Supply Chain Management," *Journal of Supply Chain Management* 44, no. 2, pp. 5–16; Salla Lutza and Thomas Ritter, "Outsourcing, Supply Chain Upgrading and Connectedness of a Firm's Competencies," *Industrial Marketing Management* 38 (May 2009), pp. 387–393; Erin Anderson and Barton Weitz, "Make or Buy Decisions: Vertical Integration and Marketing Productivity," *Sloan Management Review* 27 (Spring 1986), pp. 3–19.

13. Huaqin Zhang and Guojie Zhao, "Strategic Selection of Push-Pull Supply," *Modern Applied Science* 2, no. 1 (2008).

14. Andreas Otto, Franz Josef Schoppengerd, and Ramin Shariatmadari, *Direct Store Delivery: Concepts, Applications and Instruments* (New York: Springer, 2009).

15. Eric P. Jack, Thomas L. Powers, and Lauren Skinner, "Reverse Logistics Capabilities: Antecedents and Cost Savings," *International Journal of Physical Distribution & Logistics Management* 40, no. 3 (2010), pp. 228–246; S. Dowlatshahia, "A Cost-Benefit Analysis for the Design and Implementation of Reverse Logistics Systems: Case Studies Approach," *International Journal of Production Research* 48, no. 5 (January 2010), pp. 1361–1380; James Stock and J. P. Mulki, "Product Returns Processing: An Examination

of Practices of Manufacturers, Wholesalers/Distributors, and Retailers," *Journal of Business Logistics* 30, no. 1 (2009), pp. 33–63; Michael Bernon and John Cullen, "An Integrated Approach to Managing Reverse Logistics," *International Journal of Logistics: Research & Applications* 10, no. 1 (2007), pp. 41–56.

16. David Blanchard, "Supply Chains Also Work in Reverse," *Industry Weekly,* May 1, 2007 (accessed January 8, 2008).

17. Keith Regan, "Toys 'R' Us Wins Right to End Amazon Partnership," *E-Commerce Times,* March 3, 2006.

18. "Top 12 Drop-Shipping Best Practices," *Multichannel Merchant,* October 27, 2009; Karen E. Klein, "How Drop-Shipping Works for Retailers and Manufacturers," *BusinessWeek,* September 23, 2009; and Elliot Rabinovich, Manus Rungtusanatham, Timothy M. Laseter, "Physical Distribution Service Performance and Internet Retailer Margins: The Drop-Shipping Context," *Journal of Operations Management* 26 (November 2008), pp. 767–781.

19. Sherry Chiger, "Reverse Logistics: Every Department's Challenge," *Multichannel Merchant* 3, no. 6 (2007).

20. M. V. Greene, "Subway Taking a Fresh Approach to Greening Its Supply Chain," *Stores,* September 2009.

21. Mattias Holweg, Stephen Disney, Jan Holmstrom, and Johanna Smaros, "Supply Chain Collaboration: Making Sense of the Strategy Continuum," *European Management Journal* 23 (April 2005), pp. 170–181.

22. Huynh Trung Luong and Nguyen Huu Phien, "Measure of Bullwhip Effect in Supply Chains: The Case of High Order Autoregressive Demand Process," *European Journal of Operational Research* 183, no. 1 (2007), pp. 197–209; Hau Lee, V. Padmanabhan, and Seungjin Whang, "The Bullwhip Effect in Supply Chains," *Sloan Management Review,* Spring 1997, pp. 93–102.

23. Seung-Kuk, Paik, and Prabir K. Bachi, "Understanding the Causes of the Bullwhip Effect in a Supply Chain," *International Journal of Retail & Distribution Management* 35, no. 4 (2007), pp. 308–324.

24. www.ecrnet.org (accessed June 4, 2009).

25. V. G. Narayanan and Ananth Raman, "Aligning Incentives in Supply Chains," *Harvard Business Review,* November 2004, pp. 94–102.

26. Mohsen Attaran and Sharmin Attaran, "Collaborative Supply Chain Management: The Most Promising Practice for Building Efficient and Sustainable Supply Chains," *Business Process Management Journal* 13, no. 3 (2007), pp. 390–404.

27. www.i2.com/industries/consumer_industries/vmi/vendor_managed_inventory.cfm (accessed June 15, 2010).

28. Lisa Harrington, "The Consumer Products Supply Chain: Shopping for Solutions," http://inboundlogistics.com, August 2006; Jamie Swedberg, "Collaboration Can Speed Fashion Cycle," *Apparel Magazine,* June 2004, p. 33.

29. Chang, Tien-Hsiang, Hsin-Pin Fu, Wan-I Lee, Yichen Lin, and Hsu-Chih Hsueh, "A Study of an Augmented CPFR Model for the 3C Retail Industry," *Supply Chain Management* 12, no. 3 (2007), pp. 200–209; Attaran and Attaran, "Collaborative Supply Chain Management."

30. "Flow-Through DC Yields Savings for Fred Meyer," *Chain Store Age,* October 1995, pp. 64–66; quote by Mary Sammons, senior vice-president, Fred Meyer.

31. www.ic.gc.ca/eic/site/dsib-logi.nsf/eng/pj00462.html.

32. *Canadian Low Cost Country Sourcing Survey,* Supply Chain and Logistics Association, 2007.

33. Barbara E. Kahn and Leigh McAlister, *Grocery Revolution: The New Focus on the Consumer* (Reading, MA: Longman, Addison-Wesley, 1997).

34. James Surowiecki, "The Most Devastating Retailer in the World," *The New Yorker,* September 18, 2000, p. 74; and William Echikson, "The Mark of Zara," *BusinessWeek,* May 29, 2000, p. 98.

35. Ken Clark, "Coping with Returns," *Chain Store Age,* November 1, 2000, p. 124; based on focus group research by the Reverse Logistics Executive Council and the University of Nevada's Center for Logistics Management.

36. S. P. Singh, M. McCartney, J. Singh, and R. Clarke, "RFID Research and Testing for Packages for Apparel, Consumer Goods, and

Fresh Produce in the Retail Distribution Environment," *Packaging Technology and Science* 21 (2008), pp. 91–102.

37. Gary McWilliams, "Walmart's Radio-Tracked Inventory Hits Static," *Wall Street Journal*, February 15, 2007, p. B1.

38. Ibid.; Zeynep Ton, Vincent Dessain, and Monika Stachowiak-Joulain, "RFID at the Metro Group," *Harvard Business School Publications* (9-606-053), November 9, 2005.

39. B. C. Hardgrave, S. Langford, M. Waller, and R. Miller, "Measuring the Impact of RFID on Out of Stocks at WalMart," *MIS Quarterly Executive* 7, no. 4 (2008).

40. Rebecca Logan, "American Apparel Tries Item-Level Tagging On for Size," *Stores*, July 2008.

41. Rhonda Ascierto, "IBM Updates Web Sphere RFID with Drug ePedigree," *CBR*, August 9, 2007.

42. FDA 2006 Compliance Policy Guide for the Prescription Drug Marketing Act.

43. B. Hardgrave, Matthew Waller, and R. Miller, "Does RFID Reduce Out of Stocks? A Preliminary Analysis," Sam M. Walton College of Business, University of Arkansas, Information Technology Research Institute, November 2005, http://itri.uark.edu/research/display.asp?articles=ITRI-WP058-1105.

44. Michael Mecham, "RFID in Dollars and Sense," *Aviation Week & Space Technology*, June 15, 2009.

45. Lynn A. Fish and Wayne C. Forrest, "A Worldwise Look at RFID," *Supply Chain Management Review*, April 2007, pp. 48–55.

Chapter 10

1. Jesper Aastrup, David B. Grant, and Mogens Bjerr, "Value Creation and Category Management through Retailer-Supplier Relationships," *International Review of Retail, Distribution and Consumer Research*, December 2007, pp. 523–545.

2. Jonathan O'Brien, *Category Management in Purchasing: A Strategic Approach to Maximize Business Profitability* (London: Logan Page, 2009).

3. Dal-Young Chun and Jack M. Cadeau, "How Supplier Category Management Policy Influences Category Sales Performance," *Asia Pacific Journal of Marketing and Logistics* 22, no. 2 (2010), pp. 222–231; Arto Lindblom and Rami Olkkonenb, "An Analysis of Suppers' Roles in Category Management Collaboration," *Journal of Retailing and Consumer Services* 15 (January 2008), pp. 1–8.

4. Subir Bandyopadhyay, Anna Rominger, and Savitri Basaviaha, "Developing a Framework to Improve Retail Category Management through Category Captain Arrangements," *Journal of Retailing and Consumer Services* 16 (July 2009), pp. 315–319.

5. Joshua D. Wright, "Antitrust Analysis of Category Management: Conwood v United Tobacco," *Supreme Court Economic Review* 17, no. 1 (2009), pp. 27–35.

6. Walter S. Mossberg, "Palm's New Hand-Held Goes Mano a Mano with Blackberry," *Wall Street Journal*, January 31, 2002, p. B1.

7. Joel Warady, "Asda Takes the 'Pulse of the Nation,'" *Retail Wire*, July 16, 2009.

8. Jinhong Xie and Steven Shugan, "Advance Selling," in *Handbook of Pricing Research in Marketing*, ed. V. Rao (Northhampton, MA: Edward Elgar, 2009), pp. 451–477.

9. This section was developed with the assistance of KhiMetrics.

10. AC Nielsen Store view, 52 weeks ending December 19, 2009.

11. Lian Bratt and Ann Zimmerman, "Retailers Cut Back on Variety, Once the Spice of Marketing," *Wall Street Journal*, June 26, 2009.

12. Stephan Hamilton and Timothy Richards, "Product Differentiation, Store Differentiation, and Assortment Depth Management," *Management Science* 55 (August 2009), pp. 1368–1376.

13. Herb Sorensen, "How Supermarkets Manage the 'Long Tail' of In-Store Media?" *Retail Wire*, November 5, 2008.

14. Ram Bezawada, S. Balachander, P.K. Kannan, and Venkatesh Shankar, "Cross-Category Effects of Aisle and Display Placements: A Spatial Modeling Approach and Insights," *Journal of Marketing* 73 (May 2009), pp. 99–110.

15. Tammy Worth, "Too Many Choices Can Tax the Brain, Research Shows Having a Wealth of Options Can Lead to Poor Decision Making, Experts Say," *Los Angeles Times*, March 16, 2009.

16. Susan Broniarczyk, "Product Assortment," in *Handbook of Consumer Psychology*, eds. Curtis Haugtvedt, Paul Herr, and Frank Kardes (New York: Psychology Press, 2008), pp. 708–755.

17. Warren Thayer, "Changes in the Wind at Walmart," *RFF Retailer*, February 17, 2009.

18. "Inventory Management 2003: An Overview," *Chain Store Age*, December 2003, p. 3A.

19. *Securing the Bottom Line: Canadian Retail Security Survey 2012*, PwC, http://www.pwc.com/ca/en/retail-consumer/security-survey.jhtml (accessed November 29, 2013).

20. Murali Mantrala, P. Sinha, and A. Zoltners, "Impact of Resource Allocation Rules on Marketing Investment-Level Decisions and Profitability," *Journal of Marketing Research* 29, no. 2 (May 1992), pp. 162–175.

21. Anjali Cordeiro, "Consumer Goods Makers Heed 'Pay-check Cycle,'" *Wall Street Journal*, February 23, 2009.

22. These issues were taken from Janet Wagner, Richard Ettenson, and Jean Parrish, "Vendor Selection among Retail Buyers: An Analysis by Merchandise Division," *Journal of Retailing* 65, no. 1 (Spring 1989), pp. 58–79.

Chapter 11

1. "Private Label: Battles with brand names over quality and price," *Checkout*, The Integer Group and M/A/R/C Research (www.shopperculture.com), May 2012, p. 3.

2. "Private Label: Battles with brand names over quality and price," p. 2.

3. Robin Rusch, "Private Labels: Does Branding Matter?" Brandchannel.com, May 13, 2002; www.brandchannel.com/features-effect.asp?id=94 based on research by John Stanley of John Stanley Associates.

4. Rusch, "Private Labels: Does Branding Matter?"; and www.brandchannel.com/features-effect.asp?id=94.

5. Michael Harvey, "The Trade Dress Controversy: A Case of Strategic Cross-Brand Cannibalization," *Journal of Marketing Theory and Practice* 6, no. 2 (Spring 1998), pp. 1–15.

6. "Best Global Brands 2007," *BusinessWeek*, August 6, 2007.

7. www.privatelabelmag.com/issues/pl-nov-2009/globalanalysis.cfm (accessed January 13, 2010); Nirmalya Kumar and Jan-Benedict E.M. Steenkamp, *Private Label Strategy: How to Meet the Store Brand Challenge* (Boston: Harvard Business Press, 2007).

8. Kumar and Steenkamp, *Private Label Strategy*.

9. Mark Beren, Shantanu Dutta, and Steven Shugan, "Branded Variants: A Retail Perspective," *Journal of Marketing Research*, February 1996, pp. 9–20.

10. http://www.eonoutdoor.com/decking.php.

11. Export tariffs are used in some less developed countries to generate additional revenue. For instance, the Argentine government may impose an export tariff on wool that is exported. An export tariff actually lowers the competitive ability of domestic manufacturers, rather than protecting them, as is the case with import tariffs.

12. "Border Battles," *The Economist*, October 3, 1998, p. 6.

13. www.gbmabc.com/canada/en/retailapparelmarketincanada2010.pdf.

14. Personal communication, David Gunter, director of corporate communications, Coldwater Creek, July 2002.

15. Steven Greenhouse, "18 Major Retailers and Apparel Makers Are Accused of Using Sweatshops," *New York Times*, January 14, 1999, p. A9.

16. www.walmart.ca/wms/microsite/CorpVal/Annual%20Report/WM_CSR08_En4.pdf.

17. Anne D'Innocenzio, "Wal-Mart Warns Suppliers on Stricter Measures," Associated Press, January 22, 2013, http://bigstory.ap.org/article/wal-mart-warns-suppliers-stricter-measures (accessed December 9, 2013).

18. www.gbmabc.com/canada/en/retailapparelmarketincanada2010.pdf.

19. "Labor Forces Review," *Daily News*, April 26, 1998.

20. www.fashioncenter.com.

21. www.dallasmarketcenter.com.

22. Erin Silver, "Fashion Week in Toronto: A Day for the New Guys," *Toronto Fashion*, March 21, 2002.

23. "One-stop-shop!" CGTA Gift Show, 2002.

24. Dan Scheraga, "Collaboration Evolves," *Chain Store Age*, July 2005, p. 58.

25. Hollie Shaw, "Loblaw pledges to stay in Bangladesh, improve safety after building collapse," *Financial Post*, May 2, 2013, http://business.financialpost.com/2013/05/02/loblaw-pledges-to-stay-in-bangladesh-improve-safety-after-building-collapse.html (accessed May 3, 2013).

26. Janet Adamy, "Retail Exchanges Plan Merger to Vie with Wal-Mart," *Wall Street Journal*, April 26, 2005, p. B7.

27. Sandy Jap, "Online Reverse Auctions: Issues, Themes, and Prospects for the Future," *Journal of the Academy of Marketing Science* 30, no. 4 (Fall 2002); forthcoming M.L. Emiliani, "Business-to-Business Online Auctions: Key Issues for Purchasing Process Improvement," *Supply Chain Management: An International Journal* 5, no. 4 (2000), pp. 176–186.

28. Richard Wise and David Morrison, "Beyond the Exchange: The Future of B2B," *Harvard Business Review*, November–December 2000, pp. 86–96.

29. Tim Laseter, Brian Long, and Chris Capers, "B2B Benchmark: The State of Electronic Exchanges," *strategy+business*, 4th quarter, 2001, www.strategy-business.com/search/Archives.

30. Ibid.

31. Adapted from V. Kasturi Rangan, "FreeMarkets Online," Harvard Business School case #9-598-109, February 1999.

32. Barton Weitz and Sandy Jap, "Relationship Marketing and Distribution Channels," *Journal of the Academy of Marketing Sciences* 23 (Fall 1995), pp. 305–320; and F. Robert Dwyer, Paul Shurr, and Sejo Oh, "Developing Buyer-Seller Relationships," *Journal of Marketing* 51 (April 1987), pp. 11–27.

33. Nirmalya Kumar, "The Power of Trust in Manufacturer-Retailer Relationships," *Harvard Business Review*, November-December 1996, pp. 92–106.

34. Erin Anderson and Anne Coughlan, "Structure, Governance, and Relationship Management," in *Handbook of Marketing*, eds. B. Weitz and R. Wensley (London: Sage, 2002).

35. Erin Anderson and Barton Weitz, "The Use of Pledges to Build and Sustain Commitment in Distribution Channels," *Journal of Marketing Research* 29 (February 1992), pp. 18–34.

36. Ibid.

37. Jim Yardley, "Vendorville," *New York Times Magazine*, March 8, 1998, p. 62.

38. http://www.plstorebrands.com.

39. Thomas J. Ryan, "Financial Forum: Chargeback Debate Roars on as Practice Remains Fact of Life," *WWD*, June 1, 1998, pp. 14, 16.

40. Similar types of fees charged to vendors are display fees (paid for special merchandising and display of products) and pay-to-stay fees (paid to continue stocking and displaying a product).

41. Ramarao Desiraju, "New Product Introductions, Slotting Allowances, and Retailer Discretion," *Journal of Retailing* 77, no. 3 (Fall 2001), p. 335. Estimate taken from *Advertising Age*, March 13, 2000, p. 75.

42. Ibid.

43. Stephanie Thompson, "Wal-Mart Stomps to Top of Supermarket Heap," AdAge.com, April 29, 2002, www.adage.com/news.cms?newsid=34573.

44. *Conwood Company, LLP v United States Tobacco Co.*, 2002 Fed App/0171P (6th Cir. 2002).

45. Federal Trade Commission, "World's Largest Manufacturer of Spice and Seasoning Products Agrees to Settle Price Discrimination Charges," FTC press release, March 8, 2000.

46. www.cbc.ca/news/background/consumers/counterfeit.html.

47. Irvine Clarke III and Margaret Owens, "Trademark Rights in Gray Markets," *International Marketing Review* 17, no. 2/3 (2000), p. 272.

48. "Software Piracy," *The Economist*, June 27, 1998, p. 108.

49. This section draws from Michael R. Czinkota and Ilkka A. Ronkainen, *International Marketing*, 6th ed. (Cincinnati: South-Western, 2000).

50. *Kmart Corp. v. Cartier, Inc.*, 486 U.S. 281 (1988).

51. *Sebao Inc. v. GB Unic. SA*, 1999 E.T.M.R. 681.

52. Suein L. Hwant, "Tobacco: As Cigarette Prices Soar, a Gray Market Booms," *Wall Street Journal*, January 28, 1999, p. B1.

53. *Southern Card & Novelty v. Lawson Mardon Label*, 138 F.3d 869 (1998).

54. *In re Toys R Us Antitrust Litigation*, 191 F.R.D. 347 (E.D.N.Y. 2000).

Chapter 12

1. *2010 Accenture Holiday Luxury Shopping Survey*, quoted in Tom Jacobson, Ray Florio, and Tiago Salvador, "The Premium of Value: Pricing and Promoting Luxury to the New Consumer," Accenture, p. 4.

2. This section was developed with the assistance of KhiMetrics.

3. This section is based on Thomas T. Nagle and Reed K. Holden, *The Strategy and Tactics of Pricing: A Guide to Profitable Decision Making* (Prentice Hall, 2002).

4. Amy Merrick, "Priced to Move: Retailers Try to Get Leg Up on Markdowns with New Software," *Wall Street Journal*, August 7, 2001, p. A1.

5. D. Soman, "Does Holding on to a Product Result in Increased Consumption Rates?" *Advances in Consumer Research* 24 (1997), pp. 33–35; Brian Wansink, "Do We Use More When We Buy More? The Effects of Stockpiling on Product Consumption," *Advances in Consumer Research* 25 (1998), pp. 21–22; and Valerie S. Folkes, Ingrid M. Martin, and Kamal Gupta, "When to Say When: Effects of Supply on Usage," *Journal of Consumer Research* 20, no. 3, (December 1992), pp. 467–477.

6. "Levi Strauss Reacquires a Pair of Jeans, at Markup," *Wall Street Journal*, May 29, 2001, p. 13A.

7. William M. Bulkeley, "Rebates' Big Appeal: Many People Neglect to Redeem Them," *Wall Street Journal*, February 10, 1998, pp. B1–B2.

8. Carl Shapiro, Carol Shapiro, and Hal R. Varian, *Information Rules: A Strategic Guide to the Network Economy* (Harvard Business School Publishing, 1998).

9. This section was developed with the assistance of KhiMetrics.

10. Dan Scheraga, "One Price Doesn't Fit All," *Chain Store Age*, March 2001, pp. 104–105; taken from research by Mark Husson, who tracks the supermarket sector for Merrill Lynch.

11. Christopher S. Tang, David R. Bell, and Teck-Hua Ho, "Store Choice and Shopping Behavior: How Price Format Works," *California Management Review* 43, no. 2 (Winter 2001), pp. 56–74; and Alan Sawyer and Peter Dickson, "Everyday Low Prices vs. Sale Price," *Retailing Review* 1, no. 2 (1993), pp. 1–2, 8.

12. Christopher S. Tang, David R. Bell, and Teck-Hua Ho, "Store Choice and Shopping Behavior: How Price Format Works," *California Management Review* 43, no. 2 (Winter 2001).

13. "Survey Reveals Shoppers' Peeves," *Chain Store Age*, May 2000, p. 54.

14. Valarie A. Zeithaml and Mary Jo Bitner, *Service Marketing: Integrating Customer Focus across the Firm*, 4th ed. (New York: McGraw-Hill, 2005)

15. Arvind Sahay, "How to Reap Higher Profits With Dynamic Pricing," *MIT Sloan Management Review* 48, no. 4 (2007), pp. 53–60; Barry Berman, "Applying Yield Management Pricing to Your Service Business," *Business Horizons* 48 (March/April 2005), pp. 169–182; Ramao Desiraju and Steven Shugan, "Strategic Service Pricing and Yield Management," *Journal of Marketing* 63 (January 1999), pp. 44–56.

16. Priceline.com 10-K report, filed with the Securities and Exchange Commission, December 26, 2006.

17. Thomas T. Nagle and Reed K. Holden, *The Strategy and Tactics of Pricing*, 3rd ed. (Upper Saddle River, NJ: Pearson, 2002); Glenn Voss, A. Parasuraman, and Dhruv Grewal, "The Roles of Price, Performance and Expectations in Determining Satisfaction in Services Exchanges," *Journal of Marketing* 62, no. 4 (October 1998), pp. 46–61.

18. Jeffrey A. Trachtenberg and Miguel Bustillo, "Amid Price War, Three Retailers Begin Rationing Books," *Wall Street Journal*, October 30, 2009.

19. Leigh McAlister, Edward I. George, and Yung-Hsin Chien, "A Basket-Mix Model to Identify Cherry-Picked Brands," *Journal of Retailing* 85, no. 4 (2009), pp. 425–436.

20. Itamar Simonson, "Shoppers Easily Influenced Choices," *New York Times*, November 6, 1994, p. 311; based on research by Itamar Simonson and Amos Tversky, www.nytimes.com.

21. This section was developed with the assistance of KhiMetrics.

22. This discussion has been going on for at least 70 years; see Louis Bader and James De. Weinland, "Do Odd Prices Earn Money?" *Journal of Retailing* 8 (1932), pp. 102–104. For recent research in this area, see Karen Gedenk and Henrik Sattler, "The Impact of Price Thresholds on Profit Contribution—Should Retailers Set Nine-Ending Prices?" *Journal of Retailing* 75, no. 1 (1999), pp. 33–57; Robert M. Schindler and Patrick N. Kirby, "Patterns of Rightmost Digits Used in Advertised Prices: Implications for Nine-Ending Effects," *Journal of Consumer Research* 24 (September 1997), p. 192–201; and Mark Stiving and Russell S. Winer, "An Empirical Analysis of Price Endings with Scanner Data," *Journal of Consumer Research* 24 (June 1997), pp. 57–67.

23. Marc Vanhuele, Gilles Laurent, and Xavier Dreze, "Consumers; Immediate Memory for Prices," *Journal of Consumer Research* 33, no. 2 (2006), pp. 163–172.

24. https://play.google.com/store/apps/details?id=com.biggu.shopsavvy&hl=en.

25. Claire Cain Miller, "Mobile Phones Become Essential Tool for Holiday Shopping," *New York Times*, December 18, 2009; Geoffrey A. Fowler and Yukari Iwatani Kane, "Price Check: Finding Deals with a Phone: New Mobile Applications Use Bar-Code Scanners, GPS to Help Comparison-Shoppers" *Wall Street Journal*, December 16, 2009.

26. Rebecca Quick, "Web's Robot Shoppers Don't Roam Free," *Wall Street Journal*, September 3, 1998, pp. B1, B8.

27. Xing Pan, Brian Ratchford and Venkatesh Sankar, "Why Aren't the Prices for the Same Items the Same at Me.com and You.com? Drivers of Price Dispersion among E-Tailers," working paper, Robert H. Smith Business School, University of Maryland, 2001; Erik Brynjolfson and Michael Smith, "Frictionless Commerce? A Comparison of Internet and Conventional Retailer," *Management Science* 46, no. 4, April 2000), pp. 563–585.

Chapter 13

1. Susan Jackson and Randall Schuler, *Managing Human Resources through Strategic Relationships*, 8th ed. (Mason, OH: Southwestern, 2003), p. 5.

2. H. John Bernardin, *Human Resource Management: An Experiential Approach*, 4th ed. (Burr Ridge, IL: McGraw-Hill, 2006); Raymond Noe, John Hollenbeck, Barry Gerhart, and Patrick Wright, *Fundamentals of Human Resource Management*, 2nd ed. (Burr Ridge, IL: McGraw-Hill, 2006).

3. Michael Bergdal, "Our 'People' Culture Is a Major Competitive Asset," *Stores*, April 1999, pp. 114–115; Raphael Amit, "Human Resources Management Processes: A Value-Creating Source of Competitive Advantage," *European Management Journal*, April 1999, pp. 174–182; Tim Ambler, "Valuing Human Assets," *Business Strategy Review* 10 (Spring 1999), pp. 57–58; Tony Grundy, "How Are Corporate Strategy and Human Resources Strategy Linked?" *Journal of General Management* 23 (Spring 1998), pp. 49–73; and Gerard Farias, "High Performance Work Systems: What We Know and What We Need to Know," *Human Resource Planning* 21 (June 1998), pp. 50–55.

4. Shari Waters, "Measuring Retail Performance and Productivity: Tracking Retail Sales," http://retail.about.com.od/marketingsalespromotion/a/measuring_sales.htm.

5. Cynthia R. Easterling, Ellen L. Flottman, Marian H. Jernigan, amd Beth E.S. Wuest, *Merchandising Mathematics for Retailing*, 4th ed. (Upper Saddle River, New Jersey: Pearson), p. 78.

6. T.J. Schier, "Sales per Employee," http://ezinearticles.com/?sales-per-employee&id=312758.

7. Bradley James Bryant, "How to Calculate FTE Hours," eHow.com, www.ehow.com/how_5096086_calculate-fte-hours.html.

8. Easterling, Flottman, Jernigan, and Wuest, *Merchandising Mathematics for Retailing*, p. 76.

9. *Merchandising and Operations Costs Report* (New York: Fairchild Publications, 1999).

10. "Hay Group study finds employee turnover in retail industry is slowly increasing," news release, Hay Group, May 7, 2012, http://www.haygroup.com/ww/press/details.aspx?id=33790.

11. Anthony Rucci, Steven Kirn, and Richard T. Quinn, "The Employee-Customer-Profit Chain at Sears," *Harvard Business Review*, January-February 1998, pp. 82–97.

12. *Retailing: Mirror on America* (Washington, DC: National Retailer Federation, 2002).

13. Jeffrey Pfeffer, *The Human Equation* (Boston: Harvard Business School Press, 1998), pp. 26–28.

14. D. Roth, "My Job at the Container Store," *Fortune*, January 10, 2000, pp. 74–78.

15. Alison Kenney Paul, Thom McElroy and Tonie Leatherberry, "Diversity as an Engine of Innovation: Retal and Consumer Goods Companies Find Competitive Advantage in Diversity," *Deloitte Review* issue 8, 2011.

16. Michael Gold and Andrew Campbell, "Do You Have a Well-Designed Organization?" *Harvard Business Review*, March 2002, pp. 117–125; and Richard L. Daft, *Essentials of Organization Theory and Design*, 2nd ed. (Cincinnati: South-Western College Publishing, 2000).

17. "A Changing Retail Landscape: An Analysis of Emerging Human Resource Trends," November 2009. Presented in partnership Retail Council of Canada and Human Resources and Social Development Canada, p. 9.

18. Walter Loeb, "Unbundling or Centralize: What Is the Answer?" *Retailing Issues Letter* (College Station: Center for Retailing Studies, Texas A&M University, May 1992).

19. Dave Crisp, "Human Resources Keeps Evolving," *Canadian Retailer*, November/December 2003.

20. Carol Sansone and Judith M. Harackiewicz, *Intrinsic and Extrinsic Motivation: The Search for Optimal Motivation and Performance* (San Diego: Academic Press, 2000).

21. Patricia Sellers, "Can Home Depot Fix Its Sagging Stock?" *Fortune*, March 4, 1996, pp. 139–145; and Bob Ortega, "What Does Wal-Mart Do If Stock Drop Cuts into Workers' Morale?" *Wall Street Journal*, January 4, 1995, pp. A1, A5.

22. James Fitzsimmons and Mona Fitzsimmons, *Service Development: Creating Memorable Experiences* (Thousand Oaks, CA.: Sage Publications, 2000); and Suzanne Barry Osborn, "Is Your Customer Being SERVED?" *Chain Store Age*, November 1, 2000, p. 52.

23. Mitchell Brown, "The New Old," *Canadian Retailer*, March/April 2009, p. 36.

24. David Good and Charles Schwepker, "Sales Quotas: Critical Interpretations and Implications," *Review of Business* 22 (Spring-Summer 2001), pp. 32–37.

25. Todd Zenger and C. R. Marshall, "Determinants of Incentive Intensity in Group-Based Rewards," *Academy of Management Journal* 43 (April 2000), pp. 149–63.

26. Susan Jackson and Randall Schuler, *Managing Human Resources through Strategic Relationships*, 8th ed. (Mason, OH: Southwestern, 2003), p. 141.

27. Beverly Kaye and Betsy Jacobson, "True Tales and Tall Tales: The Power of Organizational Storytelling," *Training & Development* (March 1999), pp. 44–51; and Nancy L. Breuer, "The Power of Storytelling," *Workforce* (December 1998), pp. 36–42.

28. Aaron Bernstein, "Too Many Workers? Not for Long," *BusinessWeek*, May 20, 2002, p. 126.

29. *Two Steps Forward One Step Back: 2013 North American Staffing and Recruiting Trends Report*, Bullhorn, http://www.bullhorn.com/sites/default/files/na_trends_report_2013.pdf.

30. "Managing Your Online Image Across Social Networks," The Reppler Effect blog, September 27, 2011, http://blog.reppler.com/2011/09/27/managing-your-online-image-across-social-networks/; Joseph Walker, "Facebook to Launch Job

Board," *FINS Technology,* July 6, 2012, http://it-jobs.fins.com/Articles/SBB0001424052702304141204577510933875917766/Facebook-To-Launch-Job-Board.

31. Debby Stankevich, "Retailers Focus on Optimizing Technology," *Retailer Merchandiser,* March 2002, pp. 55–58; Ginger Koloszyc, "Tight Labor Market Spurs High-Tech Employment Screening," *Stores,* July 1998, pp. 77–81; and David Schulz, "Small Retailers Turn to Pre-Employment Screening Services," *Stores,* May 1998, pp. 72–74.

32. Sarah Fister, "Separating Hires from Liars," *Training,* July 1999, pp. 22–24.

33. Jane Bahls, "Available Upon Request," *HR Magazine,* January 1999, pp. S2–S7.

34. Paul Taylor, "Providing Structure to Interviews and Reference Checks," *Workforce, Workforce Tools Supplement,* May 1999, pp. S11–S55; and Allen Huffcutt and David Woehr, "Further Analysis of Employment Validity: A Quantitative Evaluation of Interviewer-Related Structuring Methods," *Journal of Organizational Behaviour* 20 (July 1999), pp. 549–556.

35. Richard C. Hollinger and Amanda Adams, *2006 National Retail Security Survey* (Gainesville: University of Florida, 2007), p. 16.

36. John Bernardin and Donna Cooke, "Validity of an Honesty Test in Predicting Theft among Convenience Store Employees," *Academy of Management Journal* 36 (October 1993), pp. 1097–1099.

37. Kal Lifson, "Turn Down Turnover to Turn Up Profits," *Chain Store Age,* November 1, 1996, pp. 64–66.

38. John Bible, "Discrimination in Job Applications and Interviews," *Supervision,* November 1998, pp. 9–12; Laura Williamson, James Campion, Mark Roehling, Stanley Malos, and Michael Campion, "Employment Interview on Trial: Linking Interview Structure with Litigation Outcomes," *Journal of Applied Psychology* 82 (December 1997; pp. 900–913; and Peter Burgess, "How Those 'Innermost Thoughts' Are Revealed," *Grocer,* March 9, 1996, pp. 60–62.

39. Lucette Comer and Tanya Drollinger, "Active Empathetic Listening and Selling Success: A Conceptual Framework," *Journal of Personal Selling and Sales Management* 9 (Winter 1999), pp. 15–29; and C. David Sheppard, Stephen Castleberry, and Rick Ridnour, "Linking Effective Listening with Sales Performance: An Exploratory Investigation," *Journal of Business and Industrial Marketing* 12 (1997), pp. 315–321.

40. Achievers, "Achievers and Experience Inc. Reveal Class of 2012 Study Results to Understand the Needs of the Future Workforce," news release, San Francisco and Boston, April 3, 2012.

41. John McKinnon, "Retailers Beware!" *Florida Trend,* June 1996, pp. 20–21.

42. This section is based on Chapter 3 in Jeffrey Pfeffer, *The Human Equation* (Boston: Harvard Business School Press, 1998).

43. Gary Dessler, "How to Earn Your Employees' Commitment," *Academy of Management Executive* 13 (May 1999), pp. 58–59; Deb McCusker, "Loyalty in the Eyes of Employers and Employees," *Workforce,* November 1998, pp. 23–28; and David L. Stum, "Five Ingredients for an Employee Retention Formula," *HR Focus,* September 1998, pp. S9–S11.

44. Shari Caudron, "How HR Drives Profits: Academic Research and Real-World Experience Show How HR Practices Affect the Bottom Line," *Workforce,* December 2001, pp. 26–30; and "HR's New Role: Creating Value," *HR Focus,* January 2000, pp. 1–4.

45. Ling Sing Chee, "Singapore Airlines: Strategic Human Resource Initiatives," in *International Human Resource Management: Think Globally and Act Locally,* ed. Derek Torrington (New York: Prentice Hall, 1994), pp. 314–330.

46. "State of the Industry Operational Management," *Chain Store Age,* August 1, 1998, p. 17A.

47. Daniel Cable and Charles Parson, "Socialization Tactics and Person-Organization Fit," *Personnel Psychology* 54 (Spring 2001), pp. 1–24; and Cheri Young and Craig Lundberg, "Creating a First Day on the Job," *Cornell Hotel and Restaurant Administration Journal,* December 1996, pp. 26–29.

48. "A Tall Order," *retailHR, Canadian Retailer,* March/April 2009, p. 25.

49. John Wanous and Arnon Rechers, "New Employee Orientation Program," *Human Resource Management Review* 10 (Winter 2000), pp. 435–452; and Charlotte Garvey, "The Whirland of a New Job," *HR Magazine* 46 (June 2001), pp. 110–116.

50. Bert Versloot, Jan Jong, and Jo Thijssen, "Organisational Context of Structured on-the-Job Training," *International Journal of Training and Development* 5 (March 2001), pp. 2–23.

51. Graham L. Bradley and Beverley A. Sparks, "Customer Reactions to Staff Empowerment: Mediators and Moderators," *Journal of Applied Social Psychology,* May 2000, pp. 991–1003; Martin Beirne, "Managing to Empower? A Healthy Review of Resources and Constraints," *European Management Journal,* April 1999, pp. 218–226; and Mohammed Rafiq, "A Customer-Oriented Framework for Empowering Service Employees," *Journal of Services Marketing* 12 (May–June 1998), pp. 379–397.

52. Shankar Ganesan and Barton Weitz, "The Impact of Staffing Policies on Retail Buyer Job Attitudes and Behaviors," *Journal of Retailing,* Spring 1996, pp. 231–245.

53. Janet Wiscombe, "Flex Appeal—Not Just for Moms," *Workforce,* March 2002, p. 18; Leslie Faught, "At Eddie Bauer You Can Work and Have a Life," *Workforce,* April 1997, pp. 83–88; and Davan Maharaj, "A Suitable Schedule: Flextime Gains as Employers Agree There's More to Life than Work," *Los Angeles Times,* July 10, 1998, p. D2.

54. Charles J. Hobson, Linda Delunas, and Dawn Kesic, "Compelling Evidence of the Need for Corporate Work/Life Balance Initiatives: Results from a National Survey of Stressful Life-Events," *Journal of Employment Counseling,* March 2001, pp. 38–42; and Jeffrey Hill, Alan J. Hawkins, Maria Ferris, and Michelle Weitzman, "Finding an Extra Day a Week: The Positive Influence of Perceived Job Flexibility on Work and Family Life Balance," *Family Relations,* January 2001, pp. 49–57.

55. R. Roosevelt Thomas, "From Affirmative Action to Diversity," *Harvard Business Review,* March–April 1990, pp. 107–117.

56. Michael Petrou, "Employment Equity Is about Hiring the Best," *Ottawa Citizen,* December 21, 2003.

57. Kathleen Iverson, "Managing for Effective Workforce Diversity," *Cornell Hotel & Restaurant Administration Quarterly,* April 2000, pp. 2–7; Parshotam Dass, "Strategies for Managing Human Resource Diversity: From Resistance to Learning," *Academy of Management Executive* 13 (May 1999), pp. 68–69; and Philip Rosenzweig, "Strategies for Managing Diversity," *Financial Times,* March 6, 1998, pp. 6–9.

58. Audrey J. Murrell, Faye J. Crosby, and Robin J. Ely, eds., *Mentoring Dilemmas: Developmental Relationships within Multicultural Organizations* (Mahwah, NJ: Erlbaum, 1999); Max Messmer, "Mentoring: Building Your Company's Intellectual Capital," *HR Focus,* September 1998, pp. S11–S13; and Erik Van Slyke, "Mentoring: A Results-Oriented Approach," *HR Focus,* February 1998, pp. 14–15.

59. "Helping the World One Employee at a Time," *Canadian Retailer,* November/December 2003.

60. Linda Wirth, *Breaking through the Glass Ceiling: Women in Management* (Washington DC: International Labour Office, 2001); Sheila Wellington, "Cracking the Ceiling," *Time,* December 7, 1998, p. 187; Alison Maitland, "Cracks Appear in Glass Ceiling," *Financial Times,* April 8, 1999, p. 22; and Tammy Reiss, "More Cracks in the Glass Ceiling," *Business Week,* August 10, 1998, p. 6.

61. "Helping the World One Employee at a Time," *Canadian Retailer,* November/December 2003.

62. Ontario Federation of Labour, Employment Standards Act, October 2000.

63. Gary Dessler, Nina Cole, Patricia Goodman, and Virginia Sutherland, *Fundamentals of Human Resources Management in Canada,* Toronto: Pearson, 2004.

64. Robert Price, "Feeling Groovy (… and How to Make Sure Your People Stay that Way)," *Retailer's Guide for Independent Retailers and Store Managers: Health & Safety,* 5, no. 3.

65. A. Colquitt, "On the Dimensionality of Organizational Justice: A Construct Validation of a Measure," *Journal of Applied Psychology* 86 (2001), pp. 386–400.

66. Price, "Feeling Groovy ...."
67. Mary Wagner, "Don't Call Us," *Internet Retailer,* June 2002, pp. 8–9.
68. www.retailcouncil.org/cdnretailer, *Canadian Retailer,* March/April 2009, p. 7.
69. Mike Delaney, "How to Beat Shoplifting," about.com, April 26, 2006, accessed January 25, 2008; Ronald Bond, "Preventing Retail Theft," www.entrepreneur.com, July 1, 2007, accessed January 25, 2008.
70. "Combating Shrink at the Source," *Chain Store Age,* December 2000, p. 152.
71. Ginger Koloszyc, "Supermarkets Find Growing Payoff in EAS Anti-Shoplifting Systems," *Stores,* February 1999, pp. 28–30; and "Sales Up, Shrink Down with Source Tagging," *Chain Store Age,* August 1998, p. 84.
72. Timothy Henderson, "Loss Prevention Software Aids in Retail Fight against Costly Employee Theft," *Stores,* March 2001, pp. 68–72.

Chapter 14

1. A. Parsuraman and Valarie Zeithaml, "Understanding and Improving Service Quality: A Literature Review and Research Agenda," in eds. B. Weitz and R. Wensley, *Handbook of Marketing* (London: Sage, 2002).
2. Michael Hartline and O.C. Ferrell, "The Management of Customer-Contact Service Employees: An Empirical Investigation," *Journal of Marketing* 60 (October 1996), pp. 52–70; and Lois Mohr and Mary Jo Bitner, "The Role of Employee Effort in Satisfaction with Service Transactions," *Journal of Business Research* 32 (March 1995), pp. 239–252.
3. Fredrick Reichfeld, *The Loyalty Effect* (Cambridge, MA: Harvard Business School Press, 1996).
4. See Stephanie Coyles and Timothy Gokey, "Customer Retention Is Not Enough," *McKinsey Quarterly* 2 (2002), pp. 3–14.
5. Anna S. Mattila, "Emotional Bonding and Restaurant Loyalty," *Cornell Hotel and Restaurant Administration Quarterly,* December 2001, pp. 73–80; and Susan Fournier, Susan Dobscha, and David Glen Mick, "Preventing the Premature Death of Relationship Marketing," *Harvard Business Review,* January–February 1998, pp. 42–50.
6. B. Joseph Pine and James Gilmore, *Experience Economy: Work Is Theatre and Every Business a Stage* (Boston: Harvard-Business Press, 1999).
7. Frank Badillo, *Retail Perspectives on Customer Relationship Management* (Columbus, OH: Retail Forward, February 2001), p. 33.
8. "Cooking Up a Deep-Dish Database," *BusinessWeek,* November 20, 1995, p. 160.
9. www.businesswire.com/cgi-bin/mmg.cgi?eid=5542833 (accessed May 10, 2010).
10. "Loblaw's loyalty program aims for the smartphone age," *Canadian Grocer,* May 6, 2013, www.canadiangrocer.com/top-stories/loblaw-launches-all-digital-loyalty-program-25407? (accessed July 8, 2013); Denise Brunsdon, "Loblaws' new 'PC Plus' loyalty program is really a game in disguise," *Canadian Business,* May 9, 2013, www.canadianbusiness.com/blogs-and-comment/loblaw-pc-plus-gamification (accessed July 8, 2013); Marina Strauss, "Loblaw targets a well-oiled loyalty program," *The Globe and Mail,* February 28, 2012, www.theglobeandmail.com/globe-investor/loblaw-targets-a-well-oiled-loyalty-program/article4171761 (accessed July 8, 2013).
11. Lorie Grant, "Why Do Cashiers Want Your Digits?" *USA Today,* April 23, 2002, p. B1.
12. www.cmbinfo.com/pdf/WSI_Nordstrom.pdf (accessed September 8, 2007).
13. Mark Friedman and Kelly Hlavinka, "Fully Charged: Delivering the Mobile Advantage Throughout the Customer Lifecycle," *PARTNERtalk LoyaltyOne/Colloquy,* January 2013, p. 4.
14. Doris Hajewski, "Small Grocer Keeps Pace by Marketing Loyalty," *Milwaukee Journal Sentinel,* May 1, 2002, p. B1.
15. www.businesswire.com/cgi-bin.cgi?eid=5542833 (accessed May 10, 2010).
16. www.cbc.ca/consumer/story/2009/08/06/f-reward-cards.html#ixzz0oOPFyDeU (accessed May 10, 2010).
17. George Milne, "Privacy and Ethical Issues in Database/Interactive Marketing and Public Policy: A Research Framework and Overview of the Special Issue," *Journal of Public Policy and Marketing* 19 (Spring 2000), pp. 1–7.
18. Dan Scheraga, "Courting the Customer," *Chain Store Age,* January 2000, p. 88; Ro Panepinto, "Preventative Customer Care," *Response,* October 1999, pp. 46–53; and Steve Larsen, "Personalization Without Privacy Won't Sell: Build Trust by Keeping Customers Informed," *Internet Retailer,* November 1999, p. 70.
19. "Data Mining/CRM: Search for an ROI," *Chain Store Age,* October 1, 2001, p. 24.
20. Jill Clayton, "Employers Brace for Privacy Law," *National Post,* December 15, 2003; Matthew McClearn, "Full Disclosure," *Canadian Business,* Vol. 76, November/December 2003; "New Privacy Law Takes Effect January 1, 2004," Canada NewsWire, Ottawa: December 1, 2003; and Amanda Maltby, "Adapting to Canada's New Privacy Rules," *Marketing Magazine,* November 3, 2003.
21. Christopher Robertson and Ravi Sarathy, "Digital Privacy: A Pragmatic Guide for Senior Managers Charged with Developing a Strategic Policy for Handling Privacy Issues," *Business Horizons* 45 (January-February 2002), pp. 2–6.
22. Jill Dyche, *The CRM Handbook* (Upper Saddle River, NJ: Addison-Wesley, 2002), pp. 134–135.
23. Frank Badillo, *Retail Perspectives on Customer Relationship Management* (Columbus, OH: Retail Forward, February 2001), p. 25.
24. George Stalk Jr., "In Praise of the Heavy Spender," *Globe and Mail,* May 21, 2007.
25. Valarie Zeithaml, Roland Rust, and Katherine Lemon, "The Customer Pyramid: Creating and Serving Profitable Customers," *California Management Review* 43 (Summer 2001), p. 124.
26. "Retailers Plan to Invest in CRM in 2002," CyberAtlas, January 23, 2002, www.cyberatlas.internet.com.
27. See Werner Reinartz and V. Kumar, "On the Profitability of Long-Life Customers in a Noncontractual Setting: An Empirical Investigation and Implications for Marketing," *Journal of Marketing* 64 (October 2000).
28. Ken Gofton, "Pinpointing Loyalty," *Marketing,* January 21, 1999, p. 65.
29. Hollie Shaw, "New Canadian Tire loyalty program may challenge iconic paper tender," *Financial Post,* February 15, 2012 (accessed July 2, 2013).
30. Ibid.
31. Ibid.
32. Linda Nguyen, "Loblaw and Shopper's say Optimum loyalty program to stay the same," Canadian Press, July 15, 2013.
33. Ibid.
34. James Cigliano, Margaret Georgladis, Darren Pleasance, and Susan Whalley, "The Price of Loyalty," *McKinsey Quarterly* 4 (2000), p. 73.
35. Graham Dowling and Mark Uncles, "Do Customer Loyalty Programs Really Work?" *Sloan Management Review* 38 (Summer 1997), pp. 71–82.
36. James Cigliano, Margaret Georgladis, Darren Pleasance, and Susan Whalley, "The Price of Loyalty," *McKinsey Quarterly* 4 (2000), p. 70.
37. "Loyalty: At What Cost?" *Marketing,* May 16, 2002, pp. 48–50.
38. "Why Service Stinks," *Business Week Online,* October 23, 2000.
39. Roland Rust, Valarie Zeithaml, and Katherine Lemon, *Driving Customer Equity* (New York: Free Press, 2002), Ch. 13.
40. Frank Badillo, *Retail Perspectives on Customer Relationship Management* (Columbus, OH: Retail Forward, February 2001), pp. 33–34.
41. http://en.wikipedia.org/wiki/Near_field_communication#cite_ref-WhatIsNFC_1-0.
42. http://searchcloudapplications.techtarget.com/definition/gamification.
43. Roland Rust, Valarie Zeithaml, and Katherine Lemon, *Driving Customer Equity* (New York: Free Press, 2002), Ch. 13.
44. "Retail IT 2001," *Chain Store Age,* October 1, 2001, p. 24.
45. Murray Raphael, "Tell Me What You Want and the Answer Is Yes," *Direct Marketing,* October 1996, p. 22.
46. Valarie Zeithaml, Leonard Berry, and A. Parasuraman, "The Behavioral Consequences of Service Quality," *Journal of Marketing* 60 (April 1996), pp. 31–46.

47. Robert Spector and Patrick McCarthy, *The Nordstrom Way: The Inside Story of America's #1 Customer Service Company,* 2nd ed. (New York: John Wiley, 2001).

48. G. Odekerken-Schroder, K. De Wulf, H. Kasper, M. Kleijnen, J. Hoekstra, and H. Commandeur, "The Impact of Quality on Store Loyalty: A Contingency Approach," *Total Quality Management* 12 (May 2001), pp. 307–322; and Benjamin Schneider and David Bowen, *Winning the Service Game* (Boston: Harvard Business School Press, 1995).

49. Banwari Mittal and Walfried Lassar, "The Role of Personalization in Service Encounters," *Journal of Retailing* 72 (Spring 1996), pp. 95–109.

50. http://www.hp.com/canada/portal/smb/success_stories/stories/harry_rosen.html (accessed July 10, 2013)

51. "Driving Customers Away," *Chain Store Age,* June 2001, p. 39.

52. "Retailers Join the War Effort," *Chain Store Age,* June 1994, p. 15.

53. Roger Bennett, "Queues, Customer Characteristics and Policies for Managing Waiting-Lines in Supermarkets," *International Journal of Retail and Distribution Management* 26 (February-March 1998), pp. 78–88; and Julie Baker and Michaelle Cameron, "The Effects of the Service Environment on Affect and Consumer Perceptions of Waiting Time: An Integrative Review and Research Propositions," *Journal of the Academy of Marketing Science* 24 (Fall 1996), pp. 338–349.

54. William Parsons, "Give the Lady What She Wants," *Chain Store Age,* November 1995, pp. 86–87.

55. Rebecca Eckler, "Sometimes ... You Have to Test Drive It," *National Post,* August 26, 2003; and Deirdre McMurdy, "Returns Rethink," *National Post,* December 21, 2002.

56. Martha McNeil Hamilton and Dina El Boghdady, "The Spirit of Giving Back; Shoppers Discover Stricter Policies for Returning Gifts," *Washington Post,* December 27, 2001, p. E01; and "Retailers Get Strict on Merchandise Returns," *St. Louis Post-Dispatch,* May 17, 2002, p. C1.

57. A. Parsuraman and Valarie Zeithaml, "Understanding and Improving Service Quality: A Literature Review and Research Agenda," in eds. B. Weitz and R. Wensley, *Handbook of Marketing* (London: Sage, 2002); and Praveen Kopalle and Donald Lehmann, "Strategic Management of Expectations: The Role of Disconfirmation Sensitivity and Perfectionism," *Journal of Marketing Research,* August 2001, pp. 386–401.

58. "Retailers Get Strict on Merchandise Returns," *St. Louis Post-Dispatch,* May 17, 2002, p. C1.

59. Susan Stellin, "Online Customer Service Found Lacking," *New York Times,* January 3, 2002, p. C1.

60. Kenneth Clow, David Kurtz, John Ozment, and Beng Soo Ong, "The Antecedents of Consumer Expectations of Services: An Empirical Study across Four Industries," *Journal of Services Marketing* 11 (May–June 1997), pp. 230–248; and Ann Marie Thompson and Peter Kaminski, "Psychographic and Lifestyle Antecedents of Service Quality Expectations," *Journal of Services Marketing* 7 (1993), pp. 53–61.

61. Mary Jo Bitner, "Self-Service Technologies: What Do Customers Expect? In This High-Tech World, Customers Haven't Changed—They Still Want Good Service," *Marketing Management,* Spring 2001, pp. 10–15.

62. Timothy Keiningham and Terry Vavra, *The Customer Delight Principle* (Chicago: American Marketing Association, 2002).

63. The following discussion of the gaps model and its implications is based on Deon Nel and Leyland Pitt, "Service Quality in a Retail Environment: Closing the Gaps," *Journal of General Management* 18 (Spring 1993), pp. 37–57; Valarie Zeithaml, A. Parasuraman, and Leonard Berry, *Delivering Quality Customer Service* (New York: Free Press, 1990); and Valarie Zeithaml, Leonard Berry, and A. Parasuraman, "Communication and Control Processes in the Delivery of Service Quality," *Journal of Marketing* 52 (April 1988), pp. 35–48.

64. http://retailindustry.about.com, April 4, 2001.

65. "Driving Customers Away," *Chain Store Age,* June 2001, p. 39.

66. "Merchant Prince: Stanley Marcus," *Inc.,* June 1987, pp. 41–44.

67. U. Chapman and George Argyros, "An Investigation into Whether Complaining Can Cause Increased Consumer Satisfaction," *Journal of Consumer Marketing* 17, 2000, pp. 9–19; Tibbett L. Speer, "They Complain Because They Care," *American Demographics,* May 1996, pp. 13–15; and Jagdip Singh and Robert Wilkes, "When Customers Complain: A Path Analysis of Key Antecedents of Customer Complaint Response Analysis," *Journal of the Academy of Marketing Science* 24 (Fall 1996), pp. 350–365.

68. www.llbean.com

69. Sandra Guy, "Stores Juggle Service with High-Tech Savvy," *Chicago Sun-Times,* July 1, 2002, p. B12; Julie Clark, "The Importance of Kiosks in Retail Has Grown," *Display and Design Ideas,* September 2001, p. 18; and Ken Clark, "Confused about Kiosks," *Chain Store Age,* November 1, 2000, p. 96.

70. Paul Hemp, "My Week as a Room-Service Waiter at the Ritz," *Harvard Business Review,* June 2002, pp. 50-62; and Len Berry, *On Great Customer Service* (New York: Free Press, 1995), pp. 73–74.

71. See Chuck Chakrapani, *How to Measure Service Quality and Customer Satisfaction: The Informal Field Guide for Tools and Techniques* (Chicago: American Marketing Association, 1998).

72. David Lipke, "Mystery Shoppers," *American Demographics,* December 2000, pp. 41–44; and "Mystery Shopping's Lightweight Reputation Undeserved," *International Journal of Retail and Distribution Management* 27 (February–March 1999), pp. 114–117; Rachel Miller, "Undercover Shoppers," *Marketing,* May 28, 1998, pp. 27–30; and Jennifer Steinhauer, "The Undercover Shoppers," *New York Times,* February 4, 1998, p. D1.

73. See Jim Poisant, *Creating and Sustaining a Superior Customer Service Organization: A Book about Taking Care of the People Who Take Care of the Customers* (Westport, CT: Quorum Books, 2002); "People-Focused HR Policies Seen as Vital to Customer Service Improvement," *Store,* January 2001, p. 60; Michael Brady and J. Joseph Cronin, "Customer Orientation: Effects on Customer Service Perceptions and Outcome Behaviors," *Journal of Service Research,* February 2001, pp. 241–251; and Michael Hartline, James Maxham III, and Daryl McKee, "Corridors of Influence in the Dissemination of Customer-Oriented Strategy to Customer Contact Service Employees," *Journal of Marketing* 64 (April 2000), pp. 25–41.

74. Disney Institute and Michael Eisner, *Be Our Guest: Perfecting the Art of Customer Service* (New York: Disney Editions, 2001).

75. Alicia Grandey and Analea Brauburger, "The Emotion Regulation behind the Customer Service Smile," in *Emotions in the Workplace: Understanding the Structure and Role of Emotions in Organizational Behavior,* eds. R. Lord, R. Klimoski, and R. Kanfer (San Francisco: Jossey-Bass, 2002); and Mara Adelman and Aaron Ahuvia, "Social Support in the Service Sector: The Antecedents, Processes, and Consequences of Social Support in an Introductory Service," *Journal of Business Research* 32 (March 1995), pp. 273–282.

76. Mark Johlke and Dale Duhan, "Supervisor Communication Practices and Service Employee Job Outcomes," *Journal of Service Research,* November 2000, pp. 154–165.

77. Moria Cotlier, "Adieu to Abandoned Carts," *Catalog Age,* October 2001, p. 39.

78. Alan Randolph, and Marshall Sashkin, "Can Organizational Empowerment Work in Multinational Settings?" *Academy of Management Executive* 16 (February 2002), pp. 102–116.

79. Conrad Lashley, *Empowerment: HR Strategies for Service Excellence* (Boston: Butterworth/Heinemann, 2001).

80. Alan Randolph, and Marshall Sashkin, "Can Organizational Empowerment Work in Multinational Settings?" *Academy of Management Executive* 16 (February 2002), pp. 102–116; and Graham Bradley and Beverly Sparks, "Customer Reactions to Staff Empowerment: Mediators and Moderators," *Group and Organization Management* 26 (March 2001), pp. 53–68.

81. Piyush Kumar, Manohar Kalawani, and Makbool Dada, "The Impact of Waiting Time Guarantees on Customers' Waiting Experiences," *Marketing Science* 16, no. 4 (1999), pp. 676–785.

82. James Maxham, "Service Recovery's Influence on Consumer Satisfaction, Positive Word-of-Mouth, and Purchase Intentions," *Journal of Business Research,* October 2001, pp. 11–24; and Michael McCollough, Leonard Berry, and Manjit Yadav, "An Empirical Investigation of Customer Satisfaction after Service Failure and Recovery," *Journal of Service Research,* November 2000, pp. 121–137.

83. "Correcting Store Blunders Seen as Key Customer Service Opportunity," *Stores,* January 2001, pp. 60–64; Stephen W. Brown, "Practicing Best-in-Class Service Recovery: Forward-Thinking Firms Leverage Service Recovery to Increase Loyalty and Profits," *Marketing Management,* Summer 2000, pp. 8–10; Stephen Tax, Stephen Brown, and Murali Chandrashekaran, "Customer Evaluations of Service Complaint Experience: Implications for Relationship Marketing," *Journal of Marketing* 62 (April 1998), pp. 60–76; Amy Smith and Ruth Bolton, "An Experimental Investigation of Customer Reactions to Service Failures and Recovery Encounters: Paradox or Peril?" *Journal of Services Research* 1 (August 1998), pp. 23–36; and Cynthia Webster and D.S. Sundaram, "Service Consumption Criticality in Failure Recovery," *Journal of Business Research* 41 (February 1998), pp. 153–159.

84. Marina Strauss, "Mining Customer Feedback, Firms Go Undercover and Online," *Globe and Mail,* May 13, 2004.

85. Ko de Ruyter and Martin Wetsel, "The Impact of Perceived Listening Behavior in Voice-to-Voice Service Encounters," *Journal of Service Research,* February 2000, pp. 276–284.

Chapter 15

1. Stephanie Gordon and Michael Szego, "A Road Map for Retail Marketers," *Marketing Magazine,* February 24, 2003.

2. Survey conducted by Headspace Marketing Inc. from August 17 to 21, 2005. For the survey, a representative randomly selected sample of 2000 adult Quebecers were interviewed by telephone. With a sample of this size, the results are considered accurate to within ±3.1 percentage points, 19 times out of 20, of what they would have been had the entire adult Quebec population been pulled. The data were weighted to ensure the sample's regional and age/sex composition reflects that of the actual Quebec population. This survey reviewed twelve retailer brands in Quebec. The results in no way reflect an exhaustive assessment of all retailer brands conducting business in Quebec. They serve to better understand the variables that influence Quebecers' perceptions of those retailers' ability to adapt to the needs and expectations of Quebec shoppers. Given that awareness levels have a significant impact on the results, they have been adjusted to eliminate the effect of brand awareness on brand evaluation. The rating scale therefore represents a brand's perceived ability to adapt based only on the rating of those respondents able to assess the brand.

3. Ipsos-Reid/NCR survey conducted from September 10 to September 13, 2004.

4. Denise Deveau, "Spreading the Good Word through Sponsorships," *Canadian Retailer,* March/April 2004.

5. http://www.comscore.com/

6. "The Return of SEX," May 13, 2002, p. 34; Amy Barrett, "To Reach the Unreachable Teen," *BusinessWeek,* September 18, 2000, p. 78; and Terilyn Henderson and Elizabeth Mihas, "Building Retail Brands," *McKinsey Quarterly,* Summer 2000, pp. 110–115.

7. Molly Prior, "TRU Launches RZone Magazine for Teen Pop-Culture Enthusiasts," *DSN Retailing Today,* July 8, 2002, p. 4.

8. Peter Childs, Suzanne Heywood, and Michael Kliger, "Do Retail Brands Travel?" *McKinsey Quarterly* 1 (2001), pp. 12–16.

9. Chris Barrows, "Unauthorized Verses," *Inventing the Future, Honoring the Past: Journal of Integrated Marketing Communications 2009,* pp. 27–30 (Evanston, IL: Northwestern University).

10. Hollie Shaw, "Loblaw debuts digital loyalty program amid Target, Walmart competition," *Financial Post,* May 6, 2013, http://business.financialpost.com/2013/05/06/loblaw-debuts-loyalty-smartphone-app-as-grocery-retail-war-heats-up (accessed January 13, 2014).

11. www.frederiksamuel.com/blog/ad-dictionary (accessed October 29, 2007).

12. Fareena Sulta and Andrew J. Rohm, "How to market to Generation (M)obile," *MIT Sloan Management Review,* Summer 2008.

13. Quorus Consulting Group, *2012 Cell Phone Consumer Attitudes Study,* April 23, 2012, http://cwta.ca/wordpress/wp-content/uploads/2011/08/CWTA-2012ConsumerAttitudes.pdf (accessed June 1, 2013).

14. The Nielsen Company, *State of the Media: The Social Media Report 2012,* December 4, 2012, www.nielsen.com/us/en/insights/reports-downloads/2012/state-of-the-media-the-social-media-report-2012.print.html (accessed May 6, 2013).

15. Shane Snow, "Inside Foursquare: Checking In Before the Party Started," *Wired* magazine, May 24, 2010, www.wired.com/business/2010/05/inside-foursquare-checking-in-before-the-party-started-part-i/all (accessed January 13, 2014).

16. Ludovic Pricat, "When Cliché Becomes Reality: Starbucks Coupons for Foursquare Mayors," www.gpsbusinessnews.com/When-Cliche-Becomes-Reality-Starbucks-Coupons-for-Foursquare-Mayors_a2265.html, May 26, 2010.

17. Canadian Wireless Telecommunications Association, "Mobile Marketing," www.txt.ca/english/business/marketing.php (accessed June 1, 2013).

18. Ibid.

19. "QR Code Essentials," Denso ADC, 2011, www.nacs.org/LinkClick.aspx?fileticket=D1FpVAvvJuo%3D&tabid=1426&mid=4802 (accessed June 3, 2013).

20. RetailGeek.com, "Best Buy Deploys QR Codes to Enhance Shopping Experience," September 15, 2010, http://retailgeek.com/best-buy-deploys-qr-codes-to-enhance-shopping-experience (accessed June 3, 2013).

21. Ibid.

22. "Retail QR Codes," Business Card QR Codes website, www.businesscardsqrcode.com/retail-qr.html (accessed June 3, 2013).

23. "Retailers Use of QR Codes," nellymoser website, www.nellymoser.com/action-codes/qr-codes-retail-stores/retailers-use-of-qr-codes (accessed June 3, 2013).

24. Ibid.

25. Ibid.

26. ScanLife, "The Showrooming Effect: How Retailers Can Use QR Codes to Create Opportunity," October 2012, p. 2, www.scanlife.com/blog/wp-content/uploads/2012/10/Showrooming-Whitepaper_ScanLife_FINAL.pdf (accessed January 13, 2014).

27. Eve Lazarus, "Unpacking Showrooming," *Canadian Retailer,* spring 2013, Volume 23, Issue 2, pp. 37–38.

28. Scanlife, "The Showrooming Effect," p. 4.

29. Jennifer Kwan, "Wal-Mart invades Toronto bus stops," Yahoo! Canada, June 7, 2013, http://ca.finance.yahoo.com/blogs/insight/wal-mart-invade-toronto-bus-stops-190600620.html (accessed June 13, 2013).

30. David Mercer, "The 3 best shopping carts for mobile e-Commerce (m-commerce)," SME Pals, September 19, 2012, http://wsm4b.com/mobile-ecommerce/3-best-shopping-carts-mobile-ecommerce-m-commerce (accessed June 3, 2013).

31. Quorus Consulting Group, *2012 Cell Phone Consumer Attitudes Study.*

32. David Mercer, "The 3 best shopping carts for mobile e-Commerce (m-commerce)."

33. Greet Van Hoye and Filip Lievens, "Social Influences on Organizational Attractiveness: Investigating If and When Word of Mouth Matters," *Journal of Applied Social Psychology* 37, no. 9 (2007), pp. 2024–2047; Robert East, Kathy Hammond, and Malcolm Wright, "The Relative Incidence of Positive and Negative Word of Mouth: A Multi-Category Study," *International Journal of Research in Marketing* 24, no.2 (2007), pp. 175–184; Tom Brown, Thomas Barry, Peter Dacin, and Richard Gunst, "Spreading the Word: Investigating Antecedents of Consumers' Positive Word-of-Mouth Intentions and Behaviours in a Retailing Context," *Journal of the Academy of Marketing Science* 33 (Spring 2005), pp. 123–139.

34. Erin Jo Richey, "15 Top Internet Retailers Who Blog," flatfrogblog.com, January 7, 2010.

35. EASTWEST Public Relations, "Social Media: A #PR Perspective," April 30, 2013, www.eastwestpr.com/2013/04/social-media-a-pr-perspective/#sthash.7W8ippXH.dpuf (accessed January 13, 2014).

36. The Nielsen Company, "Global Advertising Consumers Trust Real Friends and Virtual Strangers the Most," July 7, 2009, http://www.nielsen.com/us/en/newswire/2009/global-advertising-consumers-trust-real-friends-and-virtual-strangers-the-most.html (accessed May 6, 2013).

37. Chrysanthos Dellarocas, "Strategic Manipulation of Internet Opinion Forums: Implications for Consumers and Firms," *Management Science* 52 (October 2006), pp. 1577–1593; Liyun Jin, "Business Using Twitter, Facebook to Market Goods," *Pittsburgh Post-Gazette,* June 21, 2009.

38. Christi Day, "Not So Silent Bob," Nuts About Southwest blog, February 14, 2010, www.blogsouthwest.com/blog/not-so-silent-bob.

39. "Brand Channels," YouTube, www.gstatic.com/youtube/engagement/platform/autoplay/advertise/downloads/YouTube_BrandChannels.pdf (accessed April 2010).

40. Home Depot Branded Channel, www.youtube.com/user/homedepot?blend=2&ob=4#p/a (accessed June 2013).

41. Forever 21 Facebook Fan Page, www.facebook.com/#!/Forever21?ref=ts (accessed June 6, 2013).

42. Ibid.

43. Michalik, M. (2013, Feb 03). Pinterest statistics, interaction and engagement. Retrieved from http://www.viralblog.com/social-media/pinterest-statistics-users-interaction-and-engagement/.

44. "Pinterest: A Review of Social Media's Newest Sweetheart," Engauge blog, March 21, 2012, http://blog.engauge.com/2012/03/paper-pinterest-a-review-of-social-medias-newest-sweetheart/ (retrieved January 2, 2013).

45. "Start-up Pinterest wins new funding, $2.5 billion valuation," Reuters, February 20, 2013.

46. Laura Hazard Owen, "Pinterest vs. Facebook: Whose users spend more?" GigaOm blog, May 8, 2012 (accessed June 2, 2013).

47. "Pinterest vs. Facebook: Which Social Sharing Site Wins at Shopping Engagement?" bizrateinsights.com, October 15, 2012.

48. R. Lum, "7 Interesting Pinterest Marketing Campaigns," May 2, 2012, http://www.creativeguerrillamarketing.com/social-media-marketing/5-interesting-pinterest-marketing-campaigns/.

49. http://venturebeat.com/company/sephora/ and http://venturebeat.com/2013/02/27/sephora-our-pinterest-followers-spend-15x-more-than-our-facebook-followers/.

50. Sarah Mahoney, "Study: Coupons Make Consumers Blush," *Marketing Daily,* February 17, 2009; personal communication with Rob Price, VP of retail marketing, CVS, June 16, 2009.

51. www.stapleseasyrebates.com/img/staples/paperless/pages/Landing.html (accessed June 6, 2013).

52. www.marketingpower.com/_layouts/Dictionary.aspx?dLetter=S (accessed June 28, 2010).

53. www.freshnessmag.com/2009/08/06/gucci-sneakers-pop-up-shop-gucci-icon-temporary/ (accessed July 2, 2010).

54. American Marketing Association, *Dictionary of Marketing Terms* (Chicago: American Marketing Association, 2008).

55. "100 Leading National Advertisers," *Advertising Age,* Volume 83, Number 26, June 25, 2012, p. 21.

56. Ibid., p. 24.

57. Newspaper Association of America, *PEW Research Center's Project for Excellence in Journalism 2012 State of the News Media,* http://stateofthemedia.org/2012/newspapers-building-digital-revenues-proves-painfully-slow/newspapers-by-the-numbers/ (accessed June 4, 2013).

58. "2013 NAA Study: How America Shops and Spends," Omniture Site Catalyst, April 2013, EnquirerMedia.com, http://www.enquirermedia.com/images/NAA2013.pdf (accessed June 6, 2013).

59. "Top 100 Advertisers," *Advertising Age,* September 17, 1999, p. 16.

60. Linda Barnard, "Walmart Canada launches glossy magazine," *Toronto Star,* April 8, 2013, http://www.thestar.com/life/2013/04/08/walmart_canada_launches_glossy_magazine.html.

61. "Rogers Media and Walmart Canada Unveil Walmart Live Better Multiplatform Magazine," news release, CNW, April 8, 2013, http://www.newswire.ca/en/story/1142077/rogers-media-and-walmart-canada-unveil-walmart-live-better-multiplatform-magazine.

62. David Hinckley, "Americans spend 34 hours a week watching TV, according to Nielsen numbers," *New York Daily News,* September 19, 2012, http://www.nydailynews.com/entertainment/tv-movies/americans-spend-34-hours-week-watching-tv-nielsen-numbers-article-1.1162285.

63. "Maximizing the Potential of Audio Advertising," *Chain Store Age,* March 1995, p. B13.

64. Kristin Laird, "The Bay adds a bit of Shazam to its radio ads," *Marketing Magazine,* November 26, 2012, http://www.marketingmag.ca/news/marketer-news/the-bay-adds-a-bit-of-shazam-to-its-radio-ads-66804.

65. "100 Leading National Advertisers," p. 14.

66. Ibid., p. 18.

67. Cyndee Miller, "Outdoors Gets a Makeover," *Marketing News,* April 10, 1995, pp. 1–26; and Teresa Andreoli, "From Retailers to Consumers: Billboards Drive the Message Home," *Discount Store News,* September 19, 1994, p. 14.

68. EASTWEST Public Relations, "Social Media: A #PR Perspective."

69. www.walmartstores.com/haiti (accessed July 3, 2010).

70. "2011 Review: National and Community Partnerships: Walmart Canada Corporate Social Responsibility Report," July 2012, http://walmartcsr.ca/index.php/en/community/community-involvement/2011-review-national-and-community-partnerships-(accessed January 14, 2014).

71. Nicole Carter, "Michelle Obama J.Crew Outfits in London Prompt Shopping Frenzy Stateside," *New York Daily News,* April 3, 2009.

72. "Flow-Through DC Yields Savings for Fred Meyer," *Chain Store Age,* October 1995, pp. 64–66; quote by Mary Sammons, senior vice-president, Fred Meyer.

73. Gary Witkin, "Effective Use of Retail Marketing Database," *Direct Marketing,* December 1995, pp. 32–35.

74. Stephen Smith, Narendra Agrawal, and Shelby McIntyre, "A Discrete Optimization Model for Seasonal Merchandise Planning," *Journal of Retailing* 74 (Summer 1998), pp. 193–222; Scott Neslin and John Quilt, "Developing Models for Planning Retailer Sales Promotions: An Application to Automobile Dealerships," *Journal of Retailing* 63 (Winter 1987), pp. 333–364; and Arthur Allaway, J. Barry Mason, and Gene Brown, "An Optimal Decision Support Model for Department-Level Promotion Mix Planning," *Journal of Retailing* 63 (Fall 1987), pp. 216–241.

75. "2013 Mobile Future in Focus," comScore, February 22, 2013, www.comscore.com/Insights/Presentations_and_Whitepapers/2013/2013_Mobile_Future_in_Focus (accessed January 14, 2014).

76. George Belch and Michael Belch, *Advertising and Promotion,* 5th ed. (New York: McGraw-Hill, 2001), pp. 227–228.

77. Murali Mantralla, "Allocating Marketing Resources," in eds. Barton Weitz and Robin Wensely, *Handbook of Marketing* (London: Sage, 2002), pp. 409–435.

78. This example is adapted by William R. Swinyard, professor of business management, Brigham Young University, from the "Overseas Airlines Service" case.

79. Ronald Curhan and Robert Kopp, "Obtaining Retailer Support for Trade Deals: Key Success Factors," *Journal of Advertising Research* 27 (December 1987-January 1988), pp. 51–60.

80. This illustration was provided by Kathy Perry, senior vice-president, Matrix Technology Group, Inc., www.mxtg.net.

credits

Name Index

Company Index